Dreamweaver CS5

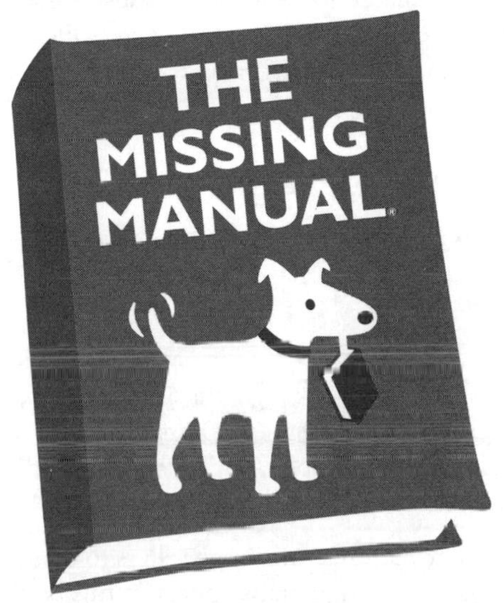

David Sawyer McFarland

POGUE PRESS™
O'REILLY®

Beijing · Cambridge · Farnham · Köln · Sebastopol · Taipei · Tokyo

Dreamweaver CS5: The Missing Manual

by David Sawyer McFarland

Printed in the United States of America.

Published by O'Reilly Media, Inc., 1005 Gravenstein Highway North, Sebastopol, CA 95472.

O'Reilly Media books may be purchased for educational, business, or sales promotional use. Online editions are also available for most titles: *safari.oreilly.com*. For more information, contact our corporate/institutional sales department: 800-998-9938 or *corporate@oreilly.com*.

Printing History:

June 2010: First Edition.

ISBN: 978-1-449-38181-3

[M]

Table of Contents

Part Two: Building a Better Web Page

Part Three: Bringing Your Pages to Life

Part Six: Dynamic Dreamweaver

The Missing Credits

About the Author

David Sawyer McFarland is president of Sawyer McFarland Media, Inc., a Web development and training company in Portland, Oregon. He's been building Web sites since 1995, when he designed his first website: an online magazine for communication professionals. He's served as the Webmaster at the University of California at Berkeley and the Berkeley Multimedia Research Center, and he has helped build, design, and program numerous websites for clients including Macworld.com, among others.

In addition to building websites, David is also a writer, trainer, and instructor. He's taught Web design at the UC Berkeley Graduate School of Journalism, the Center for Electronic Art, the Academy of Art College, and the Art Institute of Portland. He currently teaches in the Multimedia Program at Portland State University. He's written articles about Web design for Practical Web Design, Macworld magazine and CreativePro.com.

David is also the author of *CSS: The Missing Manual*, and *JavaScript: The Missing Manual*.He welcomes feedback about this book by email: *missing@sawmac.com*. (If you're seeking technical help, however, please refer to the sources listed in Appendix A.)

About the Creative Team

Peter McKie (editor) is an editor at Missing Manuals. He graduated with a master's degree from Boston University's School of Journalism and lives in New York City, where he researches the history of old houses and, every once in a while, sneaks into abandoned buildings. Email: *pmckie@gmail.com*.

Adam Zaremba (production editor) recently received his M.A. from the Editorial Institute at Boston University. He lives in Chestnut Hill, Mass., and does, in fact, like green eggs and ham.

Nancy Reinhardt (copy editor) is a freelance copy editor living in the Midwest who enjoys swimming, biking, and history. She is an avid reader and writer of romance novels and is currently shopping her first book. Email: *reinhardt8@comcast.net*.

Julie Hawks (indexer) is an indexer for the Missing Manual series. Her other life includes photography, tinkering with databases, and enjoying nature. Email: *juliehawks@gmail.com*.

Murray R. Summers (technical reviewer) is an Adobe Certified Web Site Developer, Dreamweaver Developer, and Community Professional, and has co-authored a book on Dreamweaver templates and contributed chapters to several books on Dreamweaver. His company, Great Web Sights, has been active in web development since 1998. Murray lives in rural Philadelphia with his wife Suzanne. His daughter, Carly, is currently attending Clemson University (go Tigers!).

John C. Bland II (technical reviewer) is the founder of Katapult Media, Inc., which focuses on software and web development using technologies like ColdFusion, Flash, PHP, Java, the .NET Platform, and Objective-C (iPhone OS, Mac OS X, and so on). He is a co-author of *ColdFusion Web Application Framework* and *Flex 4 in Action*. An Adobe Community Professional, John continues to contribute to the community that helped mold him into the developer he is today. John blogs regularly on his blog at *www.johncblandii.com*.

Acknowledgements

Many thanks to all those who helped with this book, including Deb Pang Davis, the design mastermind behind ChiaVet.com, and my technical editors, Murray Summers and John Bland, whose critiques have provided a comfortable safety net to protect me from any embarrassing gaffes. Thanks also to my students, who've helped me understand Dreamweaver better and always seem to come up with at least one question that I have no answer for.

Finally, thanks to Peter McKie, whose strong editing hand has helped make my writing more active and accurate; to my wife, Scholle, for being such a strong supporter of my writing and a wonderful partner in my life; my mom and Doug; Mary, David, Marisa, and Tessa; Phyllis and Les; my son, Graham, who has taught me that robots, spaceships, Star Wars, and Legos are much more important than writing books; and to my daughter, Kate, who would have been much happier if I wrote a book about Elmo, Big Bird, and Cookie Monster.

—Dave McFarland

Introduction

Websites continue to evolve, growing in scope and complexity every year, with new features popping up to make the Web look and work better. Even people building personal websites use various programming languages and server technologies to dish up content. Throughout its history, Dreamweaver has managed to keep pace with this changing landscape.

Dreamweaver CS5 is no exception: It's capable of doing more than any previous version. Whether you're creating database-enabled PHP pages, using Cascading Style Sheets (CSS) for cutting-edge design effects, dipping into the dynamic world of JavaScript and AJAX, or simply sticking to straightforward HTML pages, Dreamweaver has just about all the tools you need.

Any enterprising designer can create web pages, Cascading Style Sheets, and even JavaScript programs with a simple text editor. In fact, Dreamweaver CS5 provides a powerful text editor that lets you handcraft basic text files or complex database-driven pages. But why go to all that trouble when Dreamweaver's *visual* page-building approach, where you use friendly buttons, dialog boxes, and panels to create a web page, and let Dreamweaver tackle the hard chore of writing the underlying HTML code, makes creating beautiful and complex websites so much easier? Whether you're new to building web pages or a hard-core, hand-coding HTML jockey, Dreamweaver is a powerful tool that lets you build websites quickly and efficiently, without compromising the quality of your code.

What Dreamweaver Is All About

Dreamweaver is a complete website development and management program. It works with web technologies like HTML, XHTML, CSS, JavaScript, and PHP.

Dreamweaver's Cascading Style Sheet support lets you create fast-loading, easily modified page designs, while its unique "Spry" technology provides one-click access to complex, interactive layout options like drop-down menus.

Dreamweaver also includes plenty of tools for managing websites once you build them. You can check for broken links, use templates to streamline site-wide page changes, and reorganize your site in a flash with the program's site management tools.

Note: Get used to the acronym CSS, which you'll encounter frequently in this book. It stands for Cascading Style Sheets, a set of rules you develop to dictate the look of your pages. Dreamweaver CS5 includes advanced CSS creation, testing, and editing.

It's also a serious tool for creating *dynamic* (database-driven) websites. You can now turn your company's database of products into an easily updated online catalog—or turn that cherished recipe collection into an online culinary resource for an adoring public. You can even create web pages that let you update and delete database records, while keeping designated areas of your site secure from unauthorized visitors. Best of all, Dreamweaver CS5 does the programming for you.

But if you like to program PHP yourself, Dreamweaver CS5 adds new tools aimed at coders, including code hints to help you quickly add PHP functions to a page, and Live View so you can preview the results of dynamic pages right within Dreamweaver's document window.

If you've never used Dreamweaver but have already built one or more sites, you won't have to start over again to use Dreamweaver. It happily opens web pages and websites that were created in other programs without destroying any of your carefully handcrafted code.

Why Dreamweaver?

Other web design programs are on the market—dozens of them, in fact. But Dreamweaver is one of the leaders, thanks to key benefits like these:

- **Visual page-building**. If you've spent any time using a text editor to punch out the HTML code for your Web pages, you know the tedium involved in adding even a simple item like a photograph to a page. When your boss asks you to add her photo to the company home page, you launch your trusty text editor and type in something like this: *<img src="images/staff/bigcheese.jpg" width="100" height="150" alt="The Boss">*.

  Not only is this approach prone to typos, but it also separates you from what you want the page to *look* like.

  Dreamweaver, on the other hand, gives you a *visual* approach to building web pages, called Design view. When you work in Design view, if you put an image on your budding web page, Dreamweaver displays the picture on the page. As in a word processor, which displays documents onscreen just as they'll look when you print them out, Dreamweaver provides a very close approximation of what your page will look like in a web browser (and the Live View feature actually *does* display the page through a web browser—right inside Dreamweaver!).

- **Complex interactivity, simply**. You've probably seen web pages where an image (on a navigation bar, for example) lights up or changes appearance when you move your mouse over it. Dynamic effects like this—mouse rollovers, alert boxes, and navigational pop-up menus—usually require programming in JavaScript, a language browsers understand. While JavaScript can do amazing things, it requires time and practice to learn.

  Dreamweaver CS5 includes an easy-to-use and innovative JavaScript-based technology called *Spry*. With Spry, you can easily create interactive, drop-down menus (Chapter 5), add advanced layout elements like tabbed panels (Chapter 13), and add sophisticated form validation to prevent site visitors from submitting forms without the proper information (Chapter 12).

- **Solid code**. Every now and then, even in Dreamweaver, you may want to put aside the visual view and look at a page's underlying HTML. You may want to tweak the code that Dreamweaver produces, for example, or you may be a long-time HTML hand-coder and wonder how Dreamweaver codes.

  Adobe realizes that many professional web developers do a lot of work "in the trenches," typing HTML, CSS, and JavaScript code by hand. In Dreamweaver, you can edit its raw HTML to your heart's content. Switching back and forth between the visual mode—called Design view—and Code view is seamless and, best of all, nondestructive. Unlike many visual web page programs, where making a change in the visual design mode stomps all over the underlying HTML code, Dreamweaver respects hand-typed code and doesn't try to rewrite it (unless you ask it to).

  You can even use "Split view" to see your HTML code side-by-side with a representation of your final page, and you can switch between Code and Design view. In addition, Dreamweaver can open many other types of files commonly used on websites, such as external JavaScript files (.js files), so you don't have to switch to another program to work on them. Dreamweaver's CS5 "related files" toolbar lists all JavaScript, CSS, or server-side files used by the current document. For hand-coders, this feature means that editing a page's CSS or JavaScript is just a click away (instead of a time-draining File→Open ... hunt for that danged file). Chapter 11 has the full scoop on how Dreamweaver handles writing and editing code.

- **Site management tools.** Rarely will you build just a single web page. More often, you'll be creating and editing pages that work together to form part of a website. Or you may be building an entire website from scratch.

  Either way, Dreamweaver's site management tools make your job easier. From managing links, images, pages, and other media to working with a team of people and moving your site onto a web server, Dreamweaver automates many of the routine tasks every webmaster faces. Part 4 of this book looks at how Dreamweaver helps you build and maintain websites.

- **Database-driven Websites**. Data makes the world go round. Whether you're a human-resource records manager or a high school teacher, you probably keep track of a lot of information. Today, companies and individuals store reams of information in database systems like Microsoft Access or Oracle 10g. Dreamweaver CS5 can help you bring that information to life, from accessing it—such as the latest items in your company's product catalog—to updating and editing it online, without having to learn a lot of programming. Part 6 of this book offers a gentle introduction to building dynamic websites.

UP TO SPEED

Hand Coding vs. WYSIWYG Editors

Creating Web pages in a text editor was long considered the best way to build websites. The precise control over HTML available when you hand-write code was (and often still is) seen as the only way to assure quality web pages.

Hand-coding's reputation as the only way to go for pros is fueled by the behavior of many visual page-building programs that add unnecessary code to pages–code that affects how a page appears and how quickly it downloads over the Internet.

But hand-coding is time-consuming and error-prone. One typo can render a web page useless.

Fortunately, Dreamweaver brings solid code-writing to a visual environment. Since its earliest incarnation, Dreamweaver has prided itself on its ability to produce clean HTML and its tolerance for code created by other programs–including text editors. In fact, Dreamweaver includes a powerful built-in text-editing mode that lets you freely manipulate the HTML of a page–or any other code, including JavaScript, Visual Basic, XML, PHP, or ColdFusion Markup Language.

But the real story is that the code produced when you work in Design mode is as solid and well-written as hand-hewn code. Knowing this, you should feel free to take advantage of the increased productivity that Dreamweaver's visual-editing mode brings to your day-to-day work with its one-click objects, instant JavaScript, and simplified layout tools. Doing so won't compromise your code, and will certainly let you finish your next website in record time.

Honestly, no web design program is really WYSIWYG ("what you see is what you get"). Because every browser interprets the HTML language slightly differently, web design is more like WYSIRWYGOAGD: "what you see is roughly what you'll get, on a good day." That's why Dreamweaver's Live View and integration with Adobe Browserlab (a browser-testing service) can help you make sure your pages ***really*** look the way you want them to.

Finally, if you have experience hand-coding HTML and CSS, you'll be pleasantly surprised by Dreamweaver's powerful text-editing capabilities. In fact, even though Dreamweaver has a reputation as a *visual* Web page editor, it's also one of the best text-editing programs on the market. Many improvements made in Dreamweaver CS5 were designed specifically for people who spend time looking at raw HTML, CSS, JavaScript and PHP code.

- **Have it your way.** As if Dreamweaver didn't have enough going for it, the program's engineers have created a completely customizable product, or, as they call it, *extensible*. Anyone can add to or change Dreamweaver's menus, commands, objects, and windows.

Suppose, for example, that you hardly ever use any of the commands in the Edit menu. By editing one text file in the Dreamweaver Configuration folder, you can get rid of unwanted menu items—or even add commands of your own creation. This incredible flexibility lets you customize the program to fit the way you work, and even add features that Adobe's programmers never imagined. Best of all, the Adobe Exchange website includes hundreds of free and commercial extensions for Dreamweaver. See Chapter 22 for details.

- **CS5, Part of the Creative Suite.** Dreamweaver isn't alone—it's part of a much larger family of design tools that include Adobe Photoshop and Illustrator. Ultimately all these programs will work together seamlessly and share a common appearance. Dreamweaver CS5 sports the same interface as the rest of the Creative Suite, so if you're a long-time Photoshop or Illustrator user, you'll feel at home with the design. In addition, Adobe integrated Dreamweaver CS5 with Photoshop so you can use its "Smart Object" technology to keep your site's graphics in sync with any changes you make to an original Photoshop file.

What's New in Dreamweaver CS5

If you've never used Dreamweaver before, see Chapter 1 for the grand tour. If you're upgrading from Dreamweaver CS3 or some other version, you'll find that Dreamweaver CS5 offers a host of new features.

- **CSS improvements.** Each version of Dreamweaver provides more refined tools for creating, editing, and testing CSS. This version is no exception. Dreamweaver CS5 now lets you temporarily turn on and off the individual CSS properties for a style—this useful testing feature means you can quickly see the effect of a particular property on a style. In addition, the new CSS Inspect tool lets you hover over areas of a page and visually identify normally invisible style properties, such as padding and margins, as well as see which styles affect the HTML tag the mouse is hovering over. This feature is great for quickly identifying how CSS affects elements on a page—a useful task for fine-tuning your styles or trying to figure out why a particular element looks the way it does.

- **Simplified site setup.** Naturally, setting up a site in Dreamweaver is a critical task. In previous versions of the program, this process was called "defining a site" and it's necessary for making sure Dreamweaver correctly handles links, can upload files to a web server, and for taking advantage of the program's many site-management tools, such as Templates and Library items. Setting up a site is sometimes confusing for people new to Dreamweaver, so Dreamweaver CS5 simplifies the process by asking only for the information needed to get a particular task done—now, the program makes it clear that to get started with a site, you just need to provide two pieces of information. Only when you get to more advanced tasks, like uploading files to a web server, does the program ask for additional information, such as the address of your web server and the username and password you use to connect to and upload files to your site.

- **Enhanced CSS starter pages.** CSS-based layout is a challenge. It's not as intuitive as a page layout program such as InDesign, and it often involves knowing how different browsers react to CSS. Previous versions of Dreamweaver came with "CSS Starter Pages"—complete HTML and CSS files for the most common types of page layouts. However, the CSS for these pages was often confusing to those new (and even some not so new) to CSS. Dreamweaver CS5 introduces new Starter Pages that provide the same layout as those in earlier versions, but use much simpler CSS, meaning it's easier to understand how the pages work and how to modify them so they look the way you want them to.
- **Adobe BrowserLab integration.** Adobe's BrowserLab is a great service for testing your web pages in a wide variety of browsers. One of the challenges of web design is creating pages that look the same in Internet Explorer, Firefox, Safari, Opera, and Chrome. BrowserLab provides screenshots of your page in different browser so you can identify display problems—if you don't have access to both a Mac and Windows computer, running lots of different web browsers, this simple service can really speed up the testing of your web designs. Dreamweaver CS5 now puts a BrowserLab control panel directly inside the program, so using it is as easy as choosing File→Preview in Browser→Adobe BrowserLab.
- **PHP coding improvements.** Adobe put a lot of work into make Dreamweaver CS5 a great tool for PHP programmers. Support for PHP Code Hinting (meaning Dreamweaver can make writing PHP code faster by suggesting code as you type) as well as Site-Specific Code Hinting are great productivity boosts to serious PHP coders.
- **And more.** Dreamweaver CS5 features lots of other little tweaks and improvements under the hood, including fixed bugs that plagued early versions; a new spell-check library with a wider range of support for different languages; support for the file version control system Subversion 1.6 and lots of improvements to Dreamweaver's basic Subversion support; and Live View navigation so you can actually click through your site right within Dreamweaver to preview pages.

HTML, XHTML, CSS, and JavaScript 101

Underneath the hood of any web page—whether it's your uncle's "Check out this summer's fishin'" page or the front door of a billion-dollar online retailer—is nothing more than line after line of ordinary typed text. You embed simple commands, called *tags*, within this text. Web browsers know how to interpret these commands to properly display pages. When you create a page with these commands in them, the document becomes known as an HTML page (for Hypertext Markup Language), and HTML is still at the heart of most of the Web.

The HTML code that creates a web page can be as simple as this:

```
<!DOCTYPE HTML PUBLIC "-//W3C//DTD HTML 4.01 Transitional//EN" "http://www.
w3.org/TR/html4/loose.dtd">
<html>
<head>
<title>Hey, I am the title of this Web page.</title>
```

```
</head>
<body>
<p>Hey, I am some body text on this Web page.</p>
</body>
</html>
```

While it may not be exciting, this short bit of HTML code is all you need to make an actual web page.

Document Types

The first line of code above:

```
<!DOCTYPE HTML PUBLIC "-//W3C//DTD HTML 4.01 Transitional//EN" "http://www.
w3.org/TR/html4/loose.dtd">
```

is called the "doctype" and it simply identifies what flavor of HTML you used to write the page. There are two common doctypes—HTML 4.01 and XHTML 1.0—and each has two different styles: *strict* and *transitional*. Dreamweaver can create any of these types of HTML documents—you simply tell it which flavor you want when you create a new web page (see page 40) and Dreamweaver handles the rest.

But it's important that you always use a doctype, because without one, different browsers display CSS differently, and your pages will look different depending on your visitor's browser. Fortunately, you won't have to worry about this issue as long as you create your pages in Dreamweaver.

Of Tags and Properties

In the preceding example—and, indeed, in the HTML code of any web page you examine—you'll notice that most commands appear in *pairs* surrounding a block of text or other commands.

These bracketed commands, like the <p> command that denotes the beginning of a paragraph, constitute the "markup" part of HTML (hypertext *markup* language) and are called *tags*. Sandwiched between brackets, tags are simply instructions that tell a web browser how to display a page.

The starting tag of each pair tells the browser where the instruction begins, and the closing tag tells it where the instruction ends. A closing tag always includes a forward slash (/) after the first bracket symbol (<), so the closing tag for the paragraph command above is </p>.

Fortunately, Dreamweaver can generate all these tags *automatically*. You don't have to memorize or even type these commands (although many programmers still enjoy doing so for greater control). Behind the scenes, Dreamweaver's all-consuming mission is to convert your visual designs into underlying codes like these:

- The tag <html> appears once at the beginning of a web page and again (with an added closing slash) at the end. This tag tells a browser that the information contained in the document is written in HTML, as opposed to some other language. All the contents of the page, including any other tags, appear between these opening and closing <html> tags.

If you were to think of a web page as a tree, the <html> tag would be its trunk. Springing from the trunk are two branches that represent the two main parts of any web page: the head of the page and the body.

- The *head* of a web page, surrounded by <head> tags, contains the title of the page. It may also provide other, invisible information (such as search keywords) that browsers and web search engines use.

  In addition, you can include information the browser uses to format the page's HTML and to add interactivity. You can store CSS styles and JavaScript code in the head, for example, or you can embed links to external CSS and JavaScript files. In fact, Dreamweaver's Spry widgets (Chapter 13) achieve their interactive effects with the help of JavaScript code stored in separate files on a server and linked from a page's head.

  The *body* of a web page, identified by its beginning and ending <body> tags, contains all the information that appears inside a browser window—headlines, text, pictures, and so on. In Dreamweaver, the blank white portion of the document window represents the body area. It resembles the blank window of a word processing program.

Most of your work with Dreamweaver involves inserting and formatting text, pictures, and other objects in the body portion of a document. Many tags commonly used in web pages appear within the <body> tag. Here are a few:

- You can tell a Web browser where a paragraph of text begins with a <p> (opening paragraph tag), and where it ends with a </p> (closing paragraph tag).
- The <strong> tag emphasizes text. If you surround some text with it and its partner tag, </strong>, you get boldface type. The HTML snippet <strong>Warning!</strong> would tell a web browser to display the word "Warning!" in bold type on the screen.
- The <a> tag, or anchor tag, creates a link (hyperlink) in a web page. A link, of course, can lead anywhere on the Web. How do you tell the browser where the link should point? Simply give address instructions to the browser inside the <a> tags. For instance, you might type *<a href="http://www.missingmanuals.com/">Click here!</a>*.

  The browser knows that when your visitor clicks the words "Click here!" it should go to the Missing Manuals website. The *href* part of the tag is called, in Dreamweaver, a *property* (you may also hear the term *attribute*), and the URL (the Uniform Resource Locator, or web address) is the *value*. In this example, *http://www.missingmanuals.com* is the value of the *href* property.

Fortunately, Dreamweaver exempts you from having to type any of these codes and provides an easy-to-use window called the *Property inspector* for adding properties to your tags and other page elements. To create links the Dreamweaver way (read: the easy way), turn to Chapter 5.

Note: For a full-fledged introduction to HTML, check out *Creating a Web Site: The Missing Manual*. For a primer that's geared to readers who want to master CSS, pick up a copy of *CSS: The Missing Manual*. And if you want to add interactivity to your Web pages (beyond the cool, ready-to-use features offered by Dreamweaver) then you might be interested in *JavaScript: The Missing Manual*. End of advertisements: now back to your regularly scheduled book.

XHTML, Too

Like any technology, HTML has evolved over time. Although standard HTML has served its purpose well, it's always been a somewhat sloppy language. Among other things, it allows uppercase, lowercase, or mixed-case letters in tags (<body> and <BODY> are both correct, for example) and permits unclosed tags (so that you can use a single <p> tag without the closing </p> to create a paragraph). While this flexibility may make page-writing easier, it also makes life more difficult for web browsers, smart phones, and other technologies that must interact with data on the Web. Additionally, HTML doesn't work with one of the hottest Internet languages: XML, or Extensible Markup Language (see page 548 for a quick intro to XML).

To keep pace with the times, an improved version of HTML called XHTML was introduced back in 2000 and you'll find it used frequently on many sites (in fact, XHTML is just an "XML-ified" version of HTML). Dreamweaver CS5 can create and work with XHTML files as well as plain HTML. If you understand only HTML, don't worry—XHTML isn't a revolutionary new language that takes years to learn. It's basically HTML, but with somewhat stricter guidelines. For example, the HTML page code shown on page 6 would look like *this* in XHTML:

```
<!DOCTYPE html PUBLIC "-//W3C//DTD XHTML 1.0 Transitional//EN"
"http://www.w3.org/TR/xhtml1/DTD/xhtml1-transitional.dtd">
<html xmlns="http://www.w3.org/1999/xhtml">
<head>
<title>Hey, I am the title of this Web page.</title>
<meta http-equiv="Content-Type" content="text/html; charset=iso
8859-1" />
</head>
<body>
<p>Hey, I am some body text on this Web page.</p>
</body>
</html>
```

Notice that everything below the <head> is *nearly* the same as the HTML page. The doctype that begins the page, however, is different from what you saw earlier. It looks basically the same, but, in this case, it merely says that the page is using a particular brand of HTML, called XHTML, and more specifically a type of XHTML called Transitional 1.0. (Don't worry—Dreamweaver automatically writes all this code when you create a new XHTML page.)

As you can see, the real code used to make the page is much like HTML. To make an XHTML file comply with XML, however, you have to keep a few strict rules in mind:

- **Begin the page with a document-type declaration and a namespace.** That's the first few lines in the code above. They simply state what type of document the page is and point to files on the Web that contain definitions for this type of file. A doctype isn't actually required for regular HTML, but it is for XHTML. However, a document-type declaration (or DTD) is important for both HTML and XHTML since it affects how web browsers display a page—stick with any of the DTDs Dreamweaver writes and you'll be OK.
- **Tags and tag attributes must be lowercase.** Unlike in HTML, typing the tag <BODY> in an XHTML file is incorrect. It must be lowercase like this: <body>.
- **Quotation marks are required for tag attributes.** For example, a link written like this: *<a href=http://www.missingmanuals.com>* is valid in HTML, but doesn't work in XHTML. You have to enclose the value of the *href* property in quotation marks: *<a href="http://www.missingmanuals.com">*.
- **All tags (even empty ones) must be closed.** To create a paragraph in XHTML, for example, you must begin with <p> and end with </p>. However, some tags don't come in pairs. These tags, called *self-closing tags*, have no closing tag. The line break tag is one example. To indicate a self-closing tag, you must include a backslash at the end of the tag, like this: <br />.

If all this seems a bit confusing, don't worry. Dreamweaver automatically follows all these strict XHTML rules, so creating an XHTML page in Design view won't feel one bit different from creating an old-style HTML page. (For more information on creating an XHTML page in Dreamweaver, see page 40.) In fact, with just a couple of exceptions, it doesn't really matter which version of HTML or XHTML you use—pick one and let Dreamweaver take care of the rest.

Note: When W3C–the group responsible for coming up with many Internet technologies–introduced XHTML, the web development community heralded it as the next big thing, and an intermediate step in the transition to XML as the prime language of the Web. History has shown that that prediction was a bit grandiose. As it turns out, the complexity of moving to XML has kept browser manufacturers from following the XML path the W3C laid down. In fact, the W3C has closed down the XHTML working group in favor of a new version of HTML, called HTML 5–actually a move ***away*** from XML and back to plain HTML, albeit an enhanced version of HTML. Since all the browser manufacturers are behind HTML 5 (and some browsers are already adopting parts of it), it's a good bet that, down the line, HTML 5 will be the new big thing. So if your know-it-all co-worker says that you MUST use XHTML because it's the future, just say "What about HTML 5?" That should keep him quiet. To learn more about HTML 5, visit *www.w3.org/html/wg/html5/*.

Adding Style with Cascading Style Sheets

HTML used to be the only language you needed to know. You could build pages with colorful text and graphics and make words jump out using different sizes, fonts, and colors. But today, you can't add much visual sophistication to a site without CSS. CSS is a formatting language that lets you design pages with sophisticated layouts and enhanced text. (CSS can provide site-wide design consistency of headings and subheads, for example, create a unique-looking sidebar, and add a special graphics treatment for quotations, and so on.)

From now on, think of HTML as merely the scaffolding you use to organize a page. It helps identify and structure page elements. Tags like <h1>, <h2>, and <title> denote headlines and assign them relative importance: a *Heading 1* is more important than a *Heading 2*, for example (and can affect how a search engine like Google adds a page to its search listings). The <p> tag indicates a basic paragraph of information. Other tags provide further structural clues: for example, a <ul> tag identifies a bulleted list (to make a list of recipe ingredients more intelligible).

Cascading Style Sheets, on the other hand, add *design flair* to that highly structured HTML content, making it more beautiful and easier to read. Take a look at the CSS Zen Garden site, for example (*www.csszengarden.com*). Each of the striking, very different websites profiled there use the same underlying HTML. The only difference among them—and the sole reason they look so different in style and design—is that each uses a different style sheet. Essentially, a CSS style is just a rule that tells a browser how to display a particular element on a page—for example, to make an <h1> tag appear 36 pixels tall, in the Verdana font and the color orange.

But CSS is more powerful than that. You can use it to add borders, change margins, and even control the exact placement of an element on a page.

To be a successful web designer, you need to get to know Cascading Style Sheets. You'll learn more about this exciting technology throughout this book. In fact, it's so important for current web design that this edition of *Dreamweaver: The Missing Manual* includes a new chapter dedicated to troubleshooting CSS problems.

Add Interactivity with JavaScript

A normal web page—just regular HTML and CSS—isn't very responsive: about the only interaction visitor have with the page is clicking a link to load a new page. JavaScript is a programming language that lets you supercharge your HTML with animation, interactivity, and dynamic visual effects. It can also make a web page more useful, by supplying immediate feedback to visitors. For example, a JavaScript-powered shopping cart page can instantly display a total cost, with tax and shipping, the moment a visitor selects a product to buy; or JavaScript can produce an error message immediately after someone attempts to submit a web form that's missing information.

JavaScript's main selling point is its immediacy. It lets web pages respond instantly to your visitors' actions: clicking a link, filling out a form, or merely moving the mouse around the screen. JavaScript doesn't suffer from the frustrating delay associated with "server-side" programming languages like PHP, which rely on communication between a web browser and a web server—in other words, JavaScript doesn't rely on constantly loading and reloading pages. It lets you create pages that look like and respond with the immediacy of a desktop program.

If you've visited Google Maps (*http://maps.google.com*), you've seen JavaScript in action. Google Maps lets you view a map, zoom in to get a detailed view of streets, and zoom out to get a birds-eye view of how to get across town, the state, or the nation, all the while working from the same page. While there have been lots of map sites before Google, they always required reloading multiple web pages (a usually slow process) to get to the information you wanted.

The JavaScript programs you create can range from the really simple (such as popping up a new browser window with a web page in it) to full-blown "web applications," such as Google Docs (*http://docs.google.com*), which let you create presentations, edit documents, and build spreadsheets using your web browser—all as though the program were running directly on your computer.

JavaScript programming can be difficult, but Dreamweaver has plenty of tools that let you add sophisticated interactivity to your sites—from animations to drop-down navigation menus—with just a few clicks of your mouse.

The Very Basics

You'll find very little jargon or nerd terminology in this book. You will, however, encounter a few terms and concepts you'll encounter frequently in your computing life:

- **Clicking**. This book gives you three kinds of instructions that require you to use your computer's mouse or trackpad. To *click* means to point the arrow cursor at something on the screen and then—without moving the cursor—press and release the clicker button on the mouse (or laptop trackpad). To *double-click*, of course, means to click twice in rapid succession, again without moving the cursor. And to *drag* means to move the cursor while holding down the button.
- **Keyboard shortcuts**. Every time you take your hand off the keyboard to move the mouse, you lose time and potentially disrupt your creative flow. That's why many experienced computer fans use keystroke combinations instead of menu commands wherever possible. Ctrl+B (⌘-B for Mac folks), for example, is a keyboard shortcut for boldface type in Dreamweaver (and most other programs).

  When you see a shortcut like Ctrl+S (⌘-S), it's telling you to hold down the Ctrl or ⌘ key and, while holding it down, type the letter S, and then release both keys. (This command, by the way, saves changes to the current document.)
- **Choice is good**. Dreamweaver frequently gives you several ways to trigger a particular command—by selecting a menu command *or* by clicking a toolbar button *or* by pressing a key combination, for example. Some people prefer the speed of keyboard shortcuts; others like the satisfaction of a visual command available in menus or toolbars. This book lists all the alternatives; use whichever you find most convenient.

About This Book

Despite the many improvements in software over the years, one feature has grown consistently worse: documentation. Until version 4, Dreamweaver came with a printed manual. In MX 2004, all you get was a *Getting Started* booklet. Now all you get is a cardboard box with a DVD in it. To get any real information, you need to delve into the program's online help screens.

But even if you have no problem reading a help screen in one window as you work in another, something's still missing. At times, the terse electronic help screens assume you already understand the discussion at hand, and hurriedly skip over important topics that require an in-depth presentation. In addition, you don't always get an objective evaluation of the program's features. Engineers often add technically sophisticated features to a program because they *can*, not because you need them. You shouldn't have to waste your time learning tools that don't help you get your work done.

The purpose of this book, then, is to serve as the manual that should have been in the box. In this book's pages, you'll find step-by-step instructions for using every Dreamweaver feature, including those you may not even have quite understood, let alone mastered, such as Libraries, Layout view, Behaviors, and Dreamweaver's Spry tools. In addition, you'll find honest evaluations of each tool to help you determine which ones are useful to you, as well as how and when to use them.

Note: This book periodically recommends ***other*** books, covering topics that are too specialized or tangential for a manual on Dreamweaver. Careful readers may notice that not every one of these titles is published by Missing Manual parent, O'Reilly Media. While we're happy to mention other Missing Manuals and books in the O'Reilly family, if there's a great book out there that doesn't happen to be published by O'Reilly, we'll let you know about it.

Dreamweaver CS5: The Missing Manual is designed to accommodate readers at every technical level. The primary discussions are written for advanced-beginner or intermediate computer users. But if you're new to building web pages, special sidebar articles called "Up To Speed" provide the introductory information you need to understand the topic at hand. If you're a web veteran, on the other hand, keep your eye out for similar boxes called "Power Users' Clinic." They offer more technical tips, tricks, and shortcuts for the experienced computer fan.

About→These→Arrows

Throughout this book, and throughout the Missing Manual series, you'll find sentences like this one: "Open the System→Library→Fonts folder." That's shorthand for a much longer instruction that directs you to open three nested folders in sequence, like this: "On your hard drive, you'll find a folder called System. Click to open it. Inside the System folder window is a folder called Library; double-click it to open it. Inside *that* folder is yet another folder called Fonts. Double-click to open it, too."

Similarly, this kind of arrow shorthand helps to simplify the business of choosing commands in menus, as shown in Figure I-1.

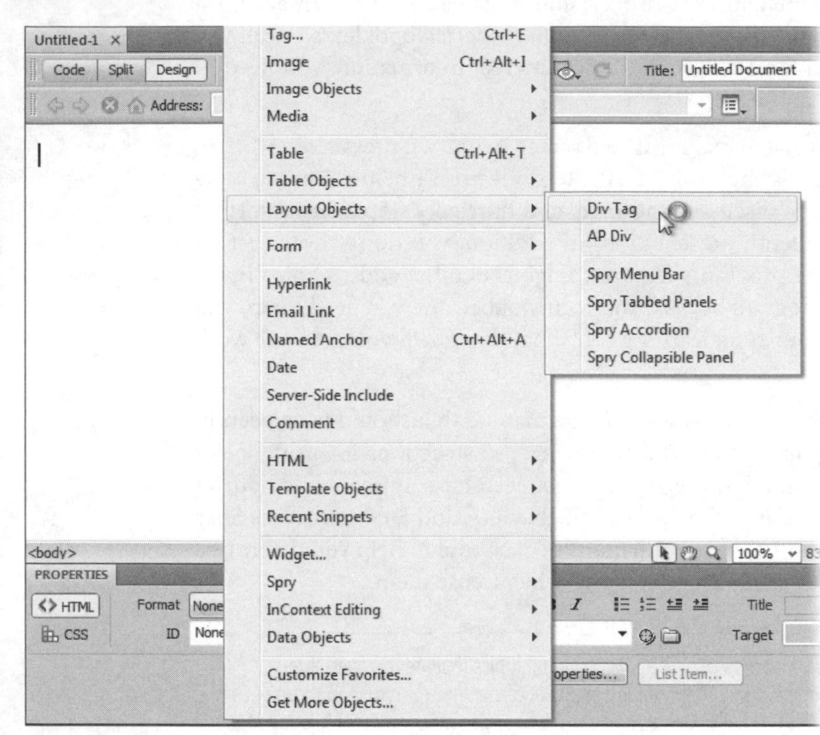

***Figure I-1:** When you read Choose Insert→Layout Objects→Div Tag in a Missing Manual, that means, "Click the Insert menu to open it. Then click Layout Objects in that menu and choose Div Tag in the resulting menu.*

Macintosh and Windows

Dreamweaver CS5 works almost precisely the same way on the Macintosh as it does in Windows. Every button in every dialog box is exactly the same; the software response to every command is identical. In this book, the illustrations have been given even-handed treatment, alternating between the various operating systems where Dreamweaver feels at home (Windows XP, Windows Vista, and Mac OS X).

One of the biggest differences between Mac and Windows software is the keystrokes, because the Ctrl key in Windows is the equivalent of the Macintosh ⌘ key. And the key labeled Alt on a PC (and on non-U.S. Macs) is the equivalent of the Option key on American Mac keyboards.

Whenever this book refers to a key combination, therefore, you'll see the Windows keystroke listed first (with + symbols, as is customary in Windows documentation); the Macintosh keystroke follows in parentheses (with - symbols, in time-honored Mac fashion). In other words, you might read, "The keyboard shortcut for saving a file is Ctrl+S (⌘-S)."

About the Outline

Dreamweaver CS5: The Missing Manual is divided into six parts, each containing several chapters:

- **Part One: Building a Web Page** explores Dreamweaver's interface and takes you through the basic steps of page-building. It explains how to add and format text, how to link from one page to another, how to spice up your designs with graphics, and introduces you to Cascading Style Sheets.
- **Part Two: Building a Better Web Page** takes you deeper into Dreamweaver and provides in-depth CSS coverage. In addition, you'll get step-by-step instructions for creating advanced page layouts, as well as advice on how to view and work with the underlying HTML code of a page.

Warning: Previous versions of this book contained a chapter on HTML frames–a method of displaying several web pages in a single browser window. This technique is going the way of the dodo bird. Since Dreamweaver CS5 is full of so many useful and exciting features and this book's already bursting at its seams (any more pages, and this book would have to come with a medical warning to those with bad backs), the frames chapter has been moved online. You can find it, free of charge, at *www.sawmac.com/missing/dw8/appc.pdf*.

- **Part Three: Bringing Your Pages to Life** helps you add interactivity to your site. From using forms to collect information from site visitors to adding interactive page widgets like tabbed interfaces with the Spry framework, this section guides you through adding animation, multimedia, and other interactive effects with ease.
- **Part Four: Building a Website** covers the big picture: managing the pages and files on your website, testing links and pages, and moving your site onto a web server connected to the Internet. And since you're not always working solo, this section covers features that let you work with a team of web developers.
- **Part Five: Dreamweaver CS5 Power** shows you how to take full advantage of such timesaving features as Libraries, Templates, and History panel automation. It also covers Dreamweaver's Extension Manager, a program that can add hundreds of new free and commercial features to the program.
- **Part Six: Dynamic Dreamweaver** presents a gentle introduction to the often confusing and complex world of database-driven websites. You'll learn what you need to know to build a dynamic site; how to connect Dreamweaver to a database; and how to use Dreamweaver to build pages that can display database information as well as how you add, edit, and delete database records. The last chapter of this section covers the powerful XSLT tools for converting XML files (including RSS feeds) into browser-ready web designs.

Living Examples

This book is designed to get your work onto the Web faster and more professionally; it's only natural, then, that half the value of this book also lies on the Web.

As you read the book's chapters, you'll encounter a number of *living examples*—step-by-step tutorials you can build yourself, using raw materials (like graphics and half-completed web pages) that you can download from either *www.sawmac.com/dwCS5/* or from this book's "Missing CD" page; to get to the latter, go to the Missing Manuals home page (*www.missingmanuals.com*), click the Missing CD link, scroll down to *Dreamweaver CS5: The Missing Manual*, and then click the link labeled "Missing CD."

You might not gain very much from simply reading these step-by-step lessons while relaxing in your porch hammock. But if you take the time to work through them at the computer, you'll discover that these tutorials give you unprecedented insight into the way professional designers build Web pages.

You'll also find, in this book's lessons, the URLs of the finished pages, so that you can compare your Dreamweaver work with the final result. In other words, you won't just see pictures of Dreamweaver's output in the pages of the book; you'll find the actual, working web pages on the Internet.

About MissingManuals.com

At *www.missingmanuals.com*, you'll find articles, tips, and updates to *Dreamweaver CS5: The Missing Manual*. In fact, we invite and encourage you to submit such corrections and updates. To keep the book as up-to-date and accurate as possible, each time we print more copies of this book, we'll make any confirmed corrections you've suggested. We'll also note such changes on the website, so that you can mark important corrections into your own copy of the book, if you like. (Click the book's name, and then click the Errata link, to see the changes.)

In the meantime, we'd love to hear your own suggestions for new books in the Missing Manual line. There's a place for that on the website, too, as well as a place to sign up for free email notification of new titles in the series. And while you're online, you can also register this book at *www.oreilly.com* (you can jump directly to the registration page by going here: *https://epoch.oreilly.com/register/default.orm*). Registering means we can send you updates about this book, and you'll be eligible for special offers like discounts on future editions.

Safari® Books Online

Safari® Books Online is an on-demand digital library that lets you easily search over 7,500 technology and creative reference books and videos to find the answers you need quickly.

With a subscription, you can read any page and watch any video from our library online. Read books on your cellphone and mobile devices. Access new titles before they're available for print, and get exclusive access to manuscripts in development and post feedback for the authors. Copy and paste code samples, organize your favorites, download chapters, bookmark key sections, create notes, print out pages, and benefit from tons of other timesaving features.

O'Reilly Media has uploaded this book to the Safari Books Online service. To have full digital access to this book and others on similar topics from O'Reilly and other publishers, sign up for free at *http://my.safaribooksonline.com*.

CHAPTER

1

Dreamweaver CS5 Guided Tour

Dreamweaver CS5 is a powerful program for designing and building websites. If you're brand-new to Dreamweaver, turn to page 1 to get a quick look at what this program can do and what's new in this latest version. This chapter provides a basic overview of the different windows, toolbars, and menus you'll use every time you build a web page. You'll also learn to set up the program so you can begin building web pages. And, because *doing* is often a better way to learn than just *reading*, you'll get a step-by-step tour of web page design—the Dreamweaver way—in the tutorial at the end of this chapter.

The Dreamweaver CS5 Interface

Dreamweaver CS5's interface shares the look and feel of other programs in the Adobe "Creative Suite," like Photoshop, Illustrator, and Flash. Out-of-the-box, Dreamweaver organizes its various windows as a unified whole (see Figure 1-1). That is, the edges of all the different windows touch; resizing one window affects the others around it. This type of interface is common on Windows computers, but Mac fans accustomed to independent floating windows might find this look strange. Give it a chance. As you'll soon see, this design has some benefits. (But, if you just can't stand this locked-in-place style, you can detach the various panels and then place them wherever you'd like on the screen; see page 31 for directions.)

Many of the program's individual windows assist with specific tasks, like building style sheets, and you'll read about them in the relevant chapters. But you'll frequently interact with four main groups of windows: the document window, the application bar, the Property inspector, and panel groups.

Note: The look of these windows depends on what kind of computer you're using (Windows or Macintosh) and what changes you make to the program's preference settings. Even so, the features and functions generally work the same way. In this book, where the program's operation differs dramatically in one operating system or the other, special boxes and illustrations (labeled "For Macs Only" or "For Windows Only") will let you know.

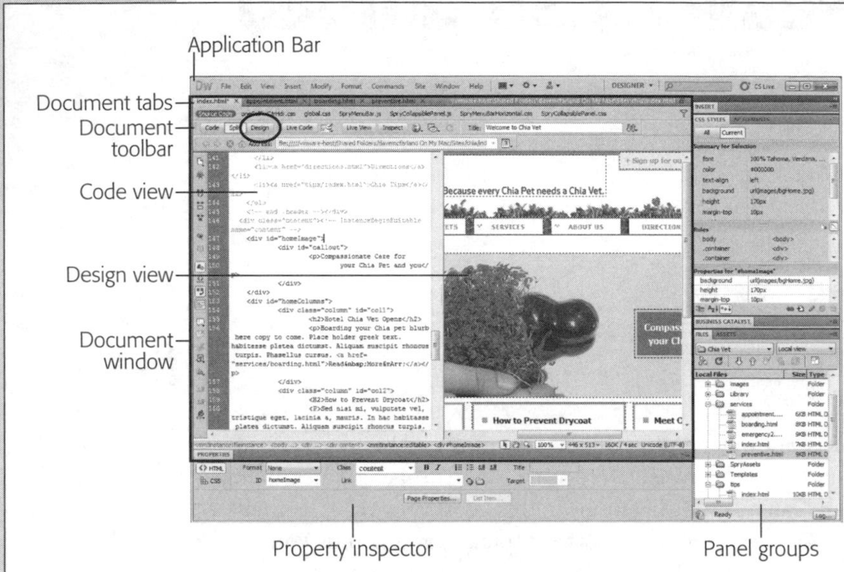

Figure 1-1: *Out-of-the-box, Dreamweaver documents appear in "Split view"—HTML code on the left and the web page design on the right. If you prefer to see how your page looks as you add and delete elements, click the Design button (circled) in the Document toolbar; that hides the HTML view and brings the page view full-screen. To switch among open documents, click a file's tab immediately above the Document toolbar.*

The Document Window

You build web pages in the *document window*. As in a word processor, simply click inside the document window, and then type to add text to a page. You'll work in this window as you build a page, and you'll open new document windows as you add pages to your site or edit existing ones.

Several other screen components provide useful information about your document. They may appear in different locations on Windows computers and on Macs (see Figures 1-1 and 1-2, respectively), but they work the same way. For example:

- **Title bar (Mac only).** The title bar displays the name of the file on which you're currently working. In addition, if the page is XHTML-compliant (see page 9), Dreamweaver indicates that in parentheses. For instance, in the example shown in Figure 1-2 the web page is written in XHTML, and saved as a file named *index.html*.
- **Document tabs.** When you have more than one web document open at a time, small tabs appear at the top of the document window—one for each open file. The name of the file appears in the tab; to switch to a file, just click its tab. In

Windows, the Document tab bar also displays where you saved the file you're working on (see Figure 1-1).

- **Related files bar.** The related files bar lists all CSS (cascading style sheets), JavaScript, and server-side programming pages (like PHP) the current web page uses. You'll learn more about external files, such as external style sheets (page 111), JavaScript files (page 452), and server side pages (Section 6), later in this book. But as a quick summary, it's common in current web design to have other files supply design and interactivity to a page of HTML. Web designers frequently work on these files, so the related files bar lets you quickly jump to and work on external style sheets, JavaScript, and other "helper" files.
- **Document toolbar.** The Document toolbar (see Figure 1-2) lets you change the title of a page, switch between Design and Code views, jump to Live view (to see how the page looks and works in a web browser), preview the page in different web browsers, and change the look of the document window. You'll read about its various buttons and menus in the relevant chapters of this book, but you'll want to be aware of the Code, Split, and Design buttons (circled in Figure 1-2). They let you see, respectively, just the raw HTML of the file you're working on; a split view showing that code in one half of the window and the visual, design view in the other half; and, finally, a button for showing just the design of the page. When you first install Dreamweaver, it displays your pages in split view, with both the raw HTML code and visual design side-by-side. In this book, we'll assume you're in Design view (the visual, "this is what your page will pretty much look like in a browser" view) most of the time. (To make the toolbar visible if it's not already, choose View→Toolbars→Document.)

Note: You may find two other toolbars, the Standard toolbar and Style Rendering toolbar, useful. The Standard toolbar is common on many Windows programs and includes buttons for frequent file and editing tasks like creating a new page, opening a page, saving one or all open documents, cutting, copying, pasting, and undoing and redoing actions. (Dreamweaver hides this toolbar until you summon it by choosing View→Toolbars→Standard.) The Style Rendering toolbar comes in handy when you work with CSS. You'll learn how to use it on page 322.

- **Browser navigation toolbar.** New in Dreamweaver CS5, this toolbar works with the program's Live View feature. When you click the Live View button in the Document toolbar, Dreamweaver displays your page in a web browser built right into the program. As a result, you can see what your page will look like in a browser (Dreamweaver uses WebKit—basically the Safari web browser—for this feature). You can ctrl-click (⌘-click) a link on the page and Dreamweaver will load that page. You'll find Live View especially useful with the server-side web pages discussed in Part Six of this book. You can hide this toolbar—a good idea since it takes up valuable screen space—by unchecking View→Toolbars→Browser Navigation. Turn it back on by selecting that menu option again.

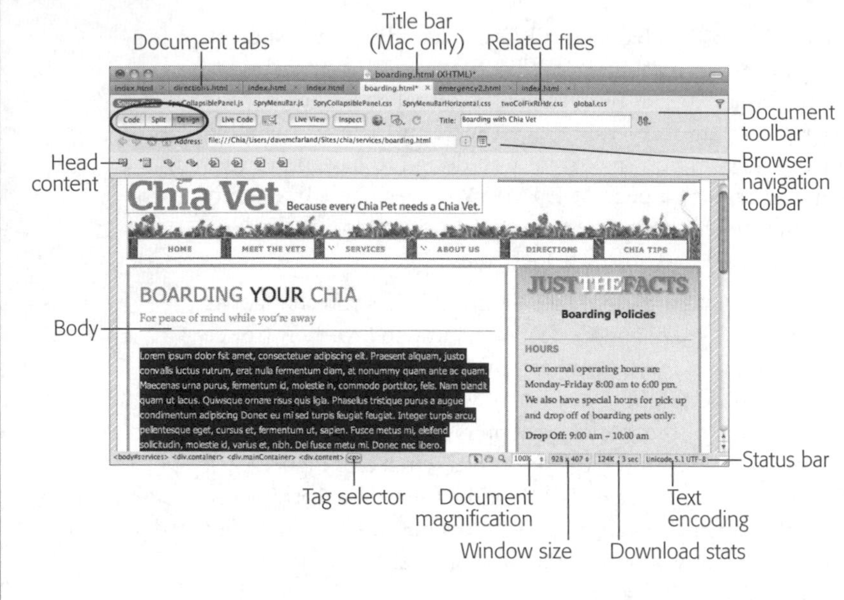

Figure 1-2: *A document window like this represents each web page; here's where you add text, graphics, and other objects as you build a page. The status bar at the bottom of the window provides some useful information. It shows you how quickly the page will download and the way the page encodes text—"encoding" refers to the characters the computer uses to represent text onscreen. Today's web pages use UTF-8, which lets you include lots of different characters—including letters from non-Latin based languages. On page 76, you'll see how UTF-8 lets you easily include fancy typographic characters—like that em-dash you just passed and real ellipses.*

- **Head content.** Most of what you put on a web page winds up in the body of the page, but some elements are specific to the region of the page called the *head* (see Figure 1-2). This is where you put things like the page's title, the *meta tags* (for example, a description of the page, or keywords used in the page) that provide information for some search engines and browsers, JavaScript programs, and links to CSS files (Chapter 4).

  None of this information actually appears on your page when it's "live" on the Internet, but you can have a look at it in Dreamweaver by choosing View→Head Content. You'll see a row of icons representing the different bits of information in the head.

The Tag selector (labeled in Figure 1-2) is extremely useful. It provides a sneak peek at the HTML that, behind the scenes, composes your web page. It indicates how Dreamweaver nests HTML tags in your document to create what you see on the page. In addition, the Tag selector lets you isolate, with a single mouse click, an HTML tag and all the information inside it. That means you can cleanly remove a page element or set its properties (see page 28), add behaviors (Chapter 14), or precisely control the application of styles (Chapter 4).

You'll make good use of the Tag selector in the tutorials to come. For experienced Dreamweaver fans, it's one of the program's most useful tools.

Tip: In Design view, clicking the <body> tag in the Tag selector is usually the same as pressing Ctrl+A (⌘-A) or choosing Edit→Select All: It selects everything in the document window. However, if you've clicked inside a table (Chapter 7), or inside a <div> tag (see page 331), choosing Edit→Select All selects only the contents of the table cell or <div> tag. In this case, you need to press Ctrl+A (⌘-A) several times to select everything on the page. After you do, you can press the Delete key to instantly get rid of everything in your document.

Careful, though: Pressing Ctrl+A (⌘-A) or choosing Edit→Select All in Code view selects all the code. Deleting *code* gives you an empty file—and an invalid web page.

The Insert Panel

Dreamweaver provides many different windows for working with the various technologies required to build and maintain a website. Dreamweaver calls most of its windows *panels*, and they sit in tidy groups on the right edge of your screen. The various panels and their uses will come up in relevant sections of this book, and you'll learn how to organize panels on page 31. But two panels are worth mentioning up front: the Insert panel and the Files panel.

If the document window is your canvas, the Insert panel holds your brushes and paints, as you can see in Figure 1-3. Although you can add text to a web page simply by typing in the document window, the Insert panel's click-to-add approach simplifies the process of adding elements like images, horizontal rules, forms, and multimedia elements. Want to put a picture on your web page? Just click the Images icon.

Note: Adding elements to your web page this way may feel like magic, but the Insert panel is really just a quick way to add code to a page, whether it's HTML, XHTML, JavaScript, or server-side code like PHP (see Part Six of this book). Clicking the Images icon, for instance, simply inserts the <img> tag into the underlying HTML of your page. Of course, Dreamweaver's visual approach hides that code and cheerfully displays a picture on the page.

GEM IN THE ROUGH

The Window Size Pop-Up Menu

Creating pages that look good on a panoply of monitor sizes set to a wide range of resolutions is one of the most difficult tasks facing web designers. After all, not everyone uses a 21-inch monitor or views websites with the browser window maximized to fill the whole screen. Nothing's more dispiriting than spending a solid week designing the coolest-looking web page, only to have your client call up and say that your design doesn't fit his 17-inch monitor (a painfully common story).

You could simulate browser windows of different sizes by dragging the resize handle at the lower-right corner of the document window. But Dreamweaver has a better tool for such experiments: the Window Size pop-up menu on the status bar at the bottom of your document window. Clicking the black arrow next to the window-size stats lets you choose a different setting for the document window, as shown here. Use this feature to test your page on different-size browser windows. The numbers indicate the width and height in pixels.

(Note to Windows folks: If you maximized your document window, this feature doesn't work. Choose Window→Cascade to "unlock" the document window from its space on the screen. Now you're free to resize the window and use the Window Size pop-up menu. Unfortunately, this eliminates the nifty document tabs that let you quickly switch among open documents—as pictured in Figure 1-1. To get them back, in the document window, just click the Maximize window button.)

The first pair of numbers indicates the amount of usable space in the document window; the numbers in parentheses indicate the resolution of the monitor. In other words, the fourth option shown here indicates that if someone has an 800 × 600 monitor and maximizes the browser window, she has 760 × 420 pixels of space to display a web page. (Even though a monitor's resolution is, say, 800 × 600, after you subtract the space required to display the browser's toolbar, location bar, status bar, and other "chrome," 760 × 420 pixels of page space is available.) Most computers support at least 1024 × 768, so choosing this option is a good way to see the minimum size screen of your site guests.

Keep in mind when you create your designs that if you have a 24-inch monitor, you have a lot more vertical space than someone with a 17-inch monitor. That means that if you put a large photo at the top of the page, you might easily see any text or other content that appears below the photo, but others may not see that content until they scroll down, moving that large picture out of the way.

In any case, note that the Window Size pop-up menu doesn't actually set the size of your web page or add any code to your page; web pages are usually fluid, and can grow or shrink to the size of each visitor's browser window. For techniques that let you exercise greater control over your page presentation, see Chapter 9.

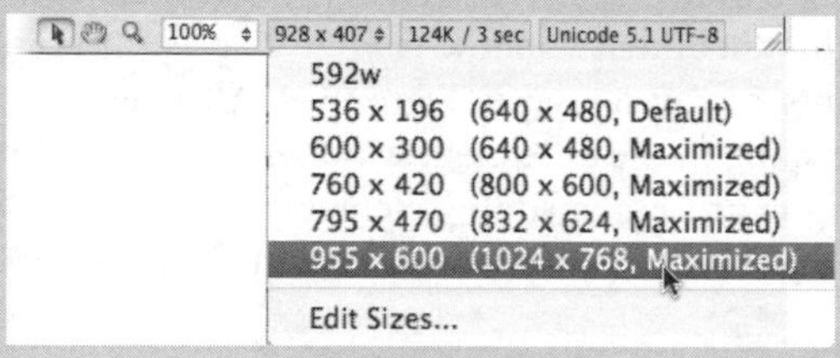

When you first start Dreamweaver, the Insert panel is open. If you ever close it by mistake, you can open it again by choosing Window→Insert or by pressing Ctrl+F2 (⌘-F2). On the other hand, if space is at a premium on your screen, you can close the Insert panel and use the Insert *menu* instead. The commands in the Insert menu duplicate all the objects available from the Insert panel. You can even turn the Insert panel into a toolbar above the document window, as described in Figure 1-3.

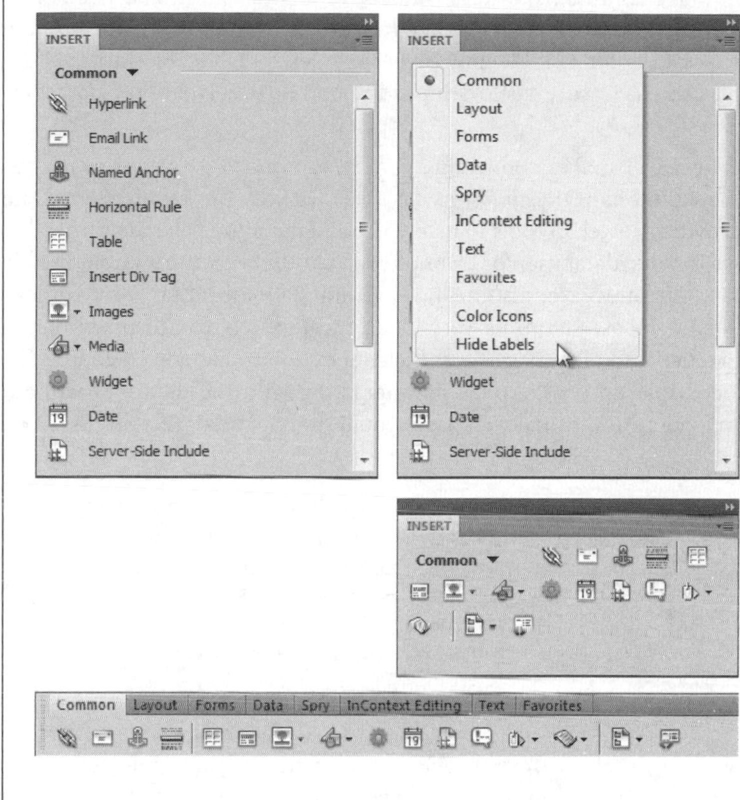

Figure 1-3: *The Insert panel has many faces and, depending on how large your monitor is, several space-saving techniques for displaying it. Normally, the Insert panel displays the objects under each drop-down menu category in a single list with an icon and a name—for example, the picture of an envelope and the label "Email link" (top left). Unfortunately, this tall list takes up a lot of screen real estate. You can display the Insert panel's buttons in a more compact way by hiding the labels. When you choose Hide Labels from the panel's category menu (top right image), Dreamweaver displays the icons side by side in rows, taking up a lot less space (middle right image). Finally, you can turn the Insert panel into an Insert bar that appears above the document window instead of grouped with the right-hand panels; this space-saving option is a favorite among many Dreamweaver users. To get the Insert toolbar, choose Classic from the Workspace switcher menu (see Figure 1-6).*

The Insert panel offers eight sets of objects, each available by selecting an option from the menu at the top of the panel (see Figure 1-3, top right) or by clicking one of the tabs on the Insert toolbar (bottom image in Figure 1-3):

- **Common objects.** In addition to images, tables, and email links—which you'll use frequently in everyday web design—this category of the Insert panel offers access to Dreamweaver's *template* features. Templates let you build basic web page designs that you can use over and over again on your site, speeding up page development and facilitating easy updates. See Chapter 20 for details.
- **Layout objects.** The objects in this category help you control the layout of a web page by organizing a page's contents using CSS or HTML tables. In addition, this panel includes Dreamweaver's Spry widgets that let you add sophisticated, interactive page elements, such as drop-down menus and animated, collapsible panels, so you can fit more information in less space on a page (see Chapter 13).

- **Form objects.** Want to get some input from visitors to your website? Use forms to let them make comments, order products, or answer questions. The Forms category lets you add form elements like radio buttons, pull-down menus, and text boxes (see Chapter 12). Dreamweaver includes sophisticated form validation so you can make sure visitors input the correct information *before* they submit the form.
- **Data.** Dreamweaver makes connecting your web pages to databases as easy as clicking a few buttons (OK, *almost* as easy; see Part Six for details). The Data category provides powerful tools to help you build dynamic pages: controls that add records to your database, for example, or that update information already in a database. Dreamweaver also includes several data tools that work without a complicated database setup. Its Spry dataset feature lets you display interactive data in a table, so visitors can sort the data by column and even change the information displayed on the page by interacting with the data—all without having to reload an additional web page (you'll find Spry datasets discussed on page 544).

Tip: If you're a long-time Dreamweaver user, you know that versions of the program before Dreamweaver CS4 displayed tool buttons in color; now it displays the buttons in the Insert panel as black-and-white–if you liked it better the old way, just right-click the Insert panel and then choose Color Icons. Better yet, you can move the Insert panel back to its old location above the document window by selecting Classic from the Workspace switcher menu (see Figure 1-6). This action not only brings back the old Insert *bar*, it also adds color to all the buttons.

- **Spry.** Spry is a technology from Adobe that lets you easily add interactive features to your site: from drop-down navigation menus to animated effects to complex displays of data. Basically, Spry is a simple way for web designers to insert complex JavaScript programming into websites. The Spry category of the Insert panel gathers together all of Dreamweaver's Spry features. You'll find the same buttons spread throughout the Insert panel; for example, the Spry tools related to form validation also appear in the Form objects category, while the Spry dataset buttons are also available from the Data category.
- **InContext Editing.** If you build websites that non-web-savvy folk will update, Adobe offers a commercial service called InContext Editing, which lets average people edit web pages using a simple web-based interface. Unfortunately, at the time of this writing, Adobe was in the process of closing down the InContext Editing program, and folding its features into another Adobe product called Business Catalyst. Business Catalyst is a web hosting service for web designers whose clients require sophisticated e-commerce capability, mail-list management, advanced web statistics, and automated tools to manage and update their websites. Dreamweaver CS5 includes a Business Catalyst panel that lets you download and install a Dreamweaver extension (see page 822 for more on

extensions) to help you manage sites created for Business Catalyst. According to Adobe, the InContext Editing tools in Dreamweaver will eventually work with Business Catalyst, but until then (and until you want to let Adobe host your websites) you're better off staying away from this category in the Insert panel.

- **Text objects.** To format type—make it bold or italic, for instance—turn to Dreamweaver's Text category. Most of the buttons here aren't technically objects; they don't insert new objects onto the page. Instead, they format text already present on the page. For the most part, the Property inspector offers the same formatting options and is a more common tool for formatting text.

Note: You might find it disorienting to use the options in the Text objects category. Some "text objects" create incomplete HTML and actually dump you into the raw HTML of a page, leaving the nice visual Design view behind. In general, the Property inspector and Text menu let you do everything in the Text objects tab—more quickly and more safely.

- **Favorites.** Perhaps the most useful category, Favorites can be anything you want it to be. That is, after you discover which objects you use the most (like the Image command, if you work with a lot of graphics), you can add them to this set of personal tools. You may find that once you populate this category, you'll never again need the other categories in the Insert panel. For instructions on adding objects to your Favorites tools, see the box on the opposite page.
- **ASP, PHP, ColdFusion.** If you're building database-driven web pages, you'll discover yet another category of objects. The exact name of the category depends on the server model you use (PHP, Microsoft's Active Server Pages, or Adobe's ColdFusion server, for example), but it always contains frequently used code snippets for the appropriate programming language. See Part Six for more on working with these technologies.

The Files Panel

The Files panel is another Dreamweaver element you'll turn to frequently (see Figure 1-4). It lists all the web files—web pages, graphics, Flash movies, and so on—that make up your website. It gives you a quick way to open pages you want to work on (in the panel, just double-click the file name). It also lets you switch between different sites you're building or maintaining, and provides some valuable tools for organizing your files. If the Files panel isn't open, summon it by choosing Window→Files or by pressing F8 (Shift-⌘-F on Macs).

To use the Files panel effectively, you need to create a local site for each website you work on—setting up a site is a specific Dreamweaver task, and one of the most important steps in using Dreamweaver correctly. You'll learn how to do this later in this chapter, starting on page 37.

FREQUENTLY ASKED QUESTION

Adding Favorite Objects to the Insert Panel

Help! I'm tired of wading through so many pull-down menus to find all my favorite Dreamweaver objects. How can I see all of my most-used objects in one place?

Dreamweaver includes a marvelous productivity tool: the Favorites category of the Insert Panel. It lets you collect your most-used objects in a single place, without any interference from the buttons for HTML tags and objects you never use. Maybe you use the Common category's Email Link object all the time, but never touch the Named Anchor object. This is the timesaving feature for you.

To add objects to the Favorites category, right-click (Control-click) anywhere on the Insert panel (or the Insert toolbar if you're using Dreamweaver's Classic view as described on page 35). From the shortcut menu, choose Customize Favorites to open the Customize Favorite Objects window. All the objects available in all the Insert categories appear in the left-hand list. Select an object and then click the >> button to add it to your Favorites. (You can view the objects for just one category by selecting the category from the "Available objects" menu.) Repeat with other objects, if you like.

To rearrange the order of the toolbar buttons, click one and then click the up or down arrow to move it in the panel. Depending on how you display the panel buttons (with or without labels, as described on page 34), buttons listed higher in the list appear either toward the top of the panel or toward the beginning of the rows of buttons. You can even use the Add Separator button to insert a thin gray line between buttons–to separate one group of similar objects (graphic-related objects, say) from another (such as form objects). Unfortunately, you can't group Favorite objects into submenus. Each item you add becomes a single button on the Insert bar.

To delete a button or separator from the list, select it and then click the trash icon. Click OK to close the window and create your new list of Favorite objects, which are now available under the Favorites category of the Insert panel.

After you create your Favorites tab, you can always add more objects (or delete ones you no longer need) by right-clicking (Control-clicking) the Insert bar and then, from the shortcut menu, choosing Customize Favorites.

The Property Inspector

After dropping in an image, table, or anything else from the Insert panel, you can use the Property inspector to fine-tune its appearance and attributes. Suppose, for example, that your boss has decided she wants her picture to link to her personal blog. After highlighting her picture in the document window, you can use the Property inspector to add the link.

The Property inspector (Figure 1-5) is a chameleon. It's aware of what you're working on in the document window—a table, an image, some text—and displays the appropriate set of properties (that is, options). You'll use the Property inspector extensively in Dreamweaver.

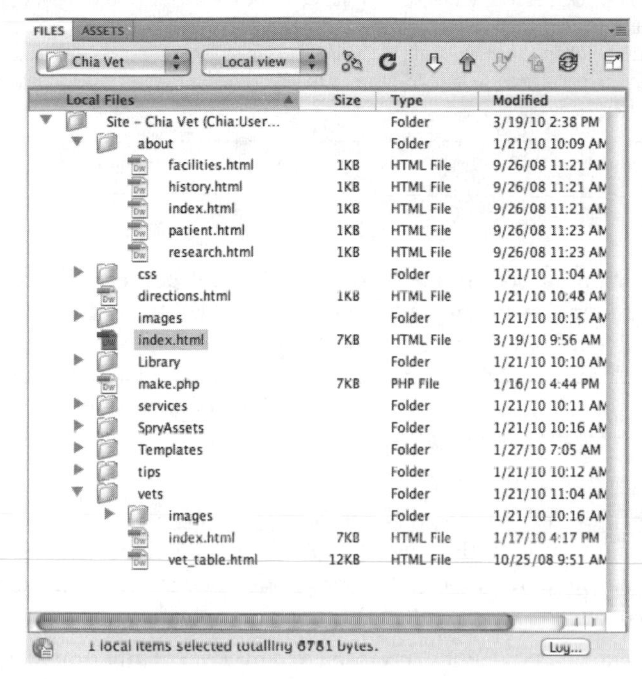

Figure 1-4:
The Files panel provides a bird's-eye view of your site's files. But it's more than just a simple list—it also lets you quickly open files, rename and rearrange them in the site, and more. You'll learn about the Files panel in detail in "Organizing Your Workspace" on page 31.

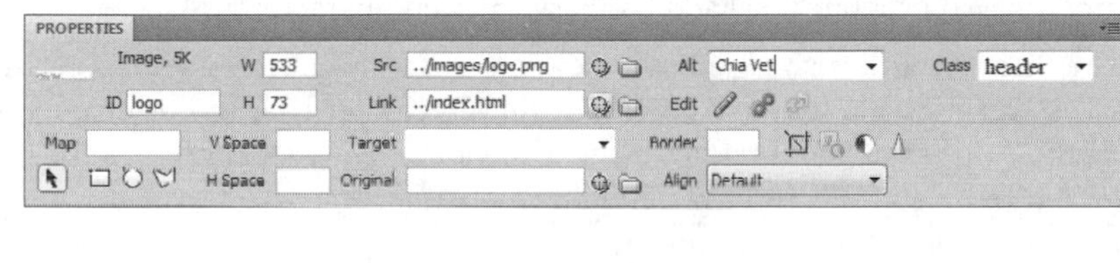

Figure 1-5:
If you don't see the Property inspector, you can open it by choosing Window→Properties or pressing Ctrl+F3 (⌘-F3).

For now, though, here are two essential tips to get you started:

- In the Property inspector, double-click any blank gray area to hide or show the bottom half of the inspector, where Dreamweaver displays a set of advanced options. (It's a good idea to leave the inspector fully expanded, since you may otherwise miss some useful options.)
- At its heart, the Property inspector simply displays the attributes of HTML tags. The *src* (source) attribute of the <img> (image) tag, for instance, tells a web browser where to find an image file.

  You can most easily make sure you're setting the properties of the correct object by clicking its tag in the Tag selector (see page 23).

Note: When you work with text, the Property inspector has two buttons–labeled HTML and CSS–that let you work with either the HTML properties related to text, or create CSS styles. You'll read more about this in Chapter 3, but here's a quick pointer: when you want to create paragraphs, headlines, bulleted lists, and bold or italic text, click the HTML button. When you want to change the appearance of text (its font, color, and size), use the CSS button–or, better yet, use the CSS Styles panel, described on page 113, to choose from a much wider range of formatting options.

The Application Bar

The Application bar's main purpose in life is to let you switch between different document views (for example, between Code and Design view), to configure the program's windows, and to give you a shortcut for getting help, defining sites, downloading extensions, and accessing Adobe's online services (such as BrowserLab and Acrobat.com). You can find all the options listed here in the program's main menus, too. Figure 1-6 shows its location in Windows (top) and on a Mac (bottom). Here's what it offers:

- The **Code/Design View** menu lets you switch between the visual Design view (a rough approximation of what the page will look like in a web browser) and the raw HTML. You can also see both the design and code at the same time. Ppage 415 has more on that option (called Split view).
- The **Extensions** menu gives you quick access to Dreamweaver's Extension Manager and the Adobe Exchange website. Extensions are add-on features (some are free and some cost money) that let you do more with Dreamweaver. You'll find extensions discussed on page 822. You can also use the menu to find "widgets," prepackaged programs that add JavaScript-driven interactivity to a page.
- The **Sites** menu lets you "define" a new site or "manage" the sites you already have. You'll learn a lot more about Dreamweaver sites later in this chapter, in "Setting Up a Site," but basically a site is the folder where you keep all the files for one particular site. If you're designing more than one website, you can define multiple sites within Dreamweaver.
- The **Workspace** switcher lets you reorganize the program's layout of windows. You can choose one of the workspaces supplied by Dreamweaver or, as discussed in "The Insert Panel" earlier, you can create your own layout to organize the ultimate workspace for your sites.
- The **Community Help** box is a search function. But unlike the "Help" box you find in most programs, this search field lets you search the entire Internet for useful information related to Dreamweaver. Type a search term in the box and then hit Enter (Return)—the Adobe Help program launches, loading a web page related to your search, and a list of links to other, related web pages. This help function is a bit better than just using Google—you never know what that'll turn up—since Adobe handpicks all the sites that turn up in a search. So you won't be getting "helpful" advice from the blogger down the street who just bought Dreamweaver and decided to post his thoughts.

- The **CS Live** menu provides access to online services from Adobe, such as useful web tools like Adobe BrowserLab, which lets you preview a web page in a variety of different browsers and operating systems. It's also a gateway to less useful (at least for web designers) tools such as Adobe Story (for collaborative screenplay writing) and Acrobat.com (can you say "cross-marketing vehicle" three times fast?) The actual contents of this menu are pulled off the web each time you use Dreamweaver, so the options you see will vary.

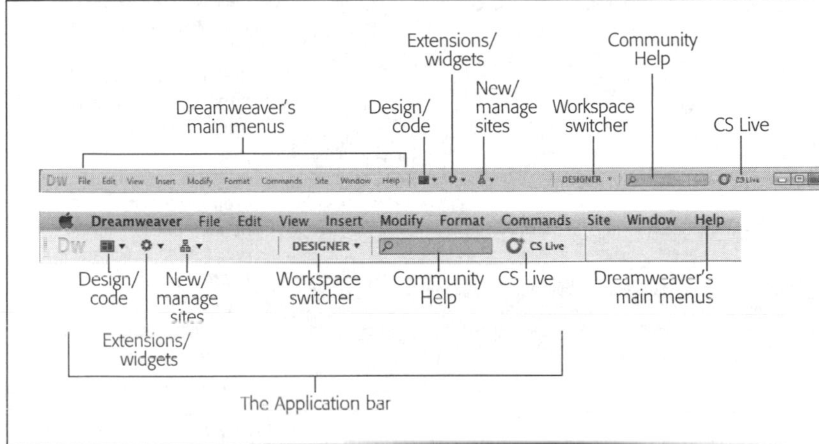

***Figure 1-6:** Dreamweaver's Application bar looks slightly different on Windows (top) and Macs (bottom).*

Organizing Your Workspace

Dreamweaver's basic user interface includes the document window, Application bar, Property inspector, and panel groups (see Figure 1-7). All these windows act like a unified whole; that is, if you resize one window, the other windows resize to fit the space. For example, you can drag the left edge of the panel groups (circled in Figure 1-7) and drag it to the left to make the panels wider, or to the right to make them thinner. The other windows that touch the panels (the document window and Property inspector) change their widths accordingly. This kind of joined-at-the-hip interface is common in Windows applications, but may feel a bit weird for Mac enthusiasts. (If you prefer the "floating palette" look and feel common to a lot of programs, you can set up Dreamweaver that way as well—see page 32.)

You can control the panel in many ways to help customize your workspace:

- You can open a particular panel from the Window menu. For example, to open the Files panel, choose Window→Files.
- If the panel is closed but its tab is visible (for example the CSS Styles tab in Figure 1-7), double-click the tab to open it. Double-click the tab again, and the panel (and any other panels grouped with it) closes.

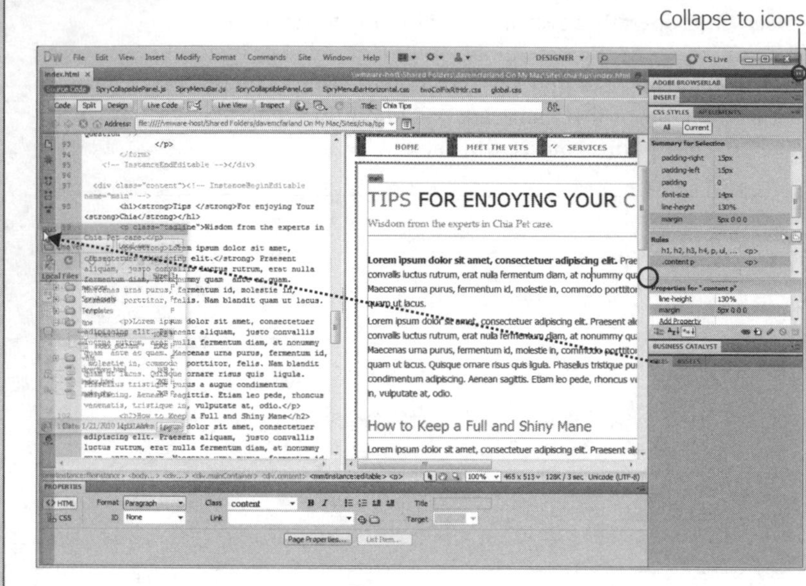

***Figure 1-7:** You can move individual panels to other parts of the screen—you're not limited to keeping all the panels on the right side. In this figure, grabbing the Files panel's tab lets you drag the panel to the left edge of the screen. A ghosted version of the panel appears as you drag it around. When you see a thick blue line on the screen's edge, drop the tab to create a panel that takes up the entire edge of the screen. In other words, in this figure, dropping the Files panel tab creates a full-height column on the left edge of the screen composed entirely of the Files panel—the document window and Properties inspector move to the right to make room.*

- Drag the line between an open panel and another panel to resize a panel. For example, if you want to make the Insert panel (pictured in Figure 1-7) taller, grab the thick border line between that panel and the panel group containing the CSS Styles and AP Elements tabs.
- To completely close a panel so that even its tab no longer appears, right-click (Control-click) the tab and then choose Close. (Choose Close Tab Group to hide the tab and any other tabs it's grouped with.) To get the panel back, you need to use the Window menu or use the panel's keyboard shortcut—for example, the F8 key (Shift-⌘-F on Macs) opens and closes the Files panel.
- If you want to hide all windows *except* for documents, choose Window→Hide Panels or press F4—a useful trick when you want to maximize the amount of screen space dedicated to showing the web page you're working on. To bring back all of Dreamweaver's administrative windows, press F4 again or choose Window→Show Panels.

Floating panels

As mentioned in Figure 1-7, you can drag a panel by its tab to another part of the screen. Dragging it to the edge of the screen docks the panel on that edge. However, if you drag a panel and drop it when it's not near a screen's edge, then it becomes a floating panel (see Figure 1-8). Floating panels are often nuisances, since they hide whatever's beneath them, so you often end up having to move them out of the way just to see what you're doing. However, they come in handy when you have two monitors. If that's the case, you can dedicate your main monitor to the document window and Property inspector (and maybe your most important panels), and then drag a bunch of floating panels onto your second screen.

To "unfloat" a floating panel, simply drag it to the edge of your screen (if you have more than one monitor, drag the panel to one of the edges of your *main* monitor). If you already have panels at that edge, drag the panel to either the bottom of the panels (to dock it at the bottom of the column of panels), between other panel groups (to insert that panel in its own group between other panels) or next to another panel's tab to group the panels together.

Tip: Drag a panel to either side of a docked column of panels to create a second column. In other words, you can create two, side-by-side, columns of panels.

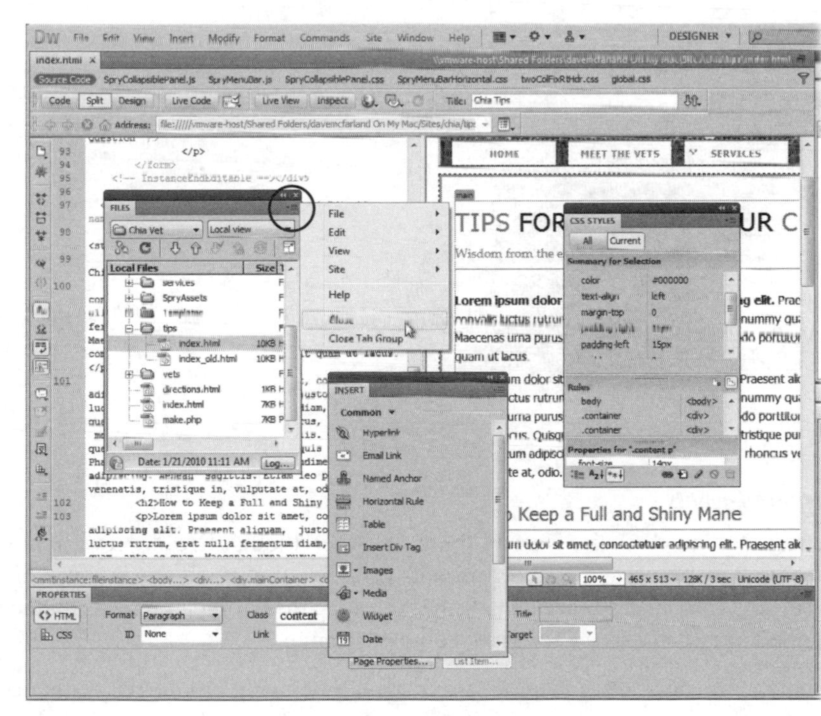

Figure 1-8: *Here, the Files, Insert, and CSS Styles panels are floating. Each panel has its own Context menu icon (circled on Files panel at left side of image). Clicking the button reveals a shortcut menu that lets you work with features specific to that panel. This menu also offers generic panel actions, such as closing the panel. If you find you've made a mess of your workspace and want to return to the way Dreamweaver normally lays out its panels, use the Workspace switcher discussed in "Workspace Layouts".*

Iconic panes

As if you didn't already have enough ways to organize your panels, Dreamweaver includes yet another way to display them. By clicking the "Collapse to Icons" button at the top right of a column of panels (see Figure 1-7) you can shrink the panels to a group of much smaller icons (see Figure 1-9). To reopen the controls for a particular panel you've just shrunk, just click the icon. For example, in Figure 1-9, clicking the CSS Styles icon opens the CSS Styles panel to the left. Once you finish working with the panel, and click elsewhere on the screen, the pop-up panel disappears. This so-called iconic view is particularly good if you have a small monitor and need to preserve as much screen real estate as possible.

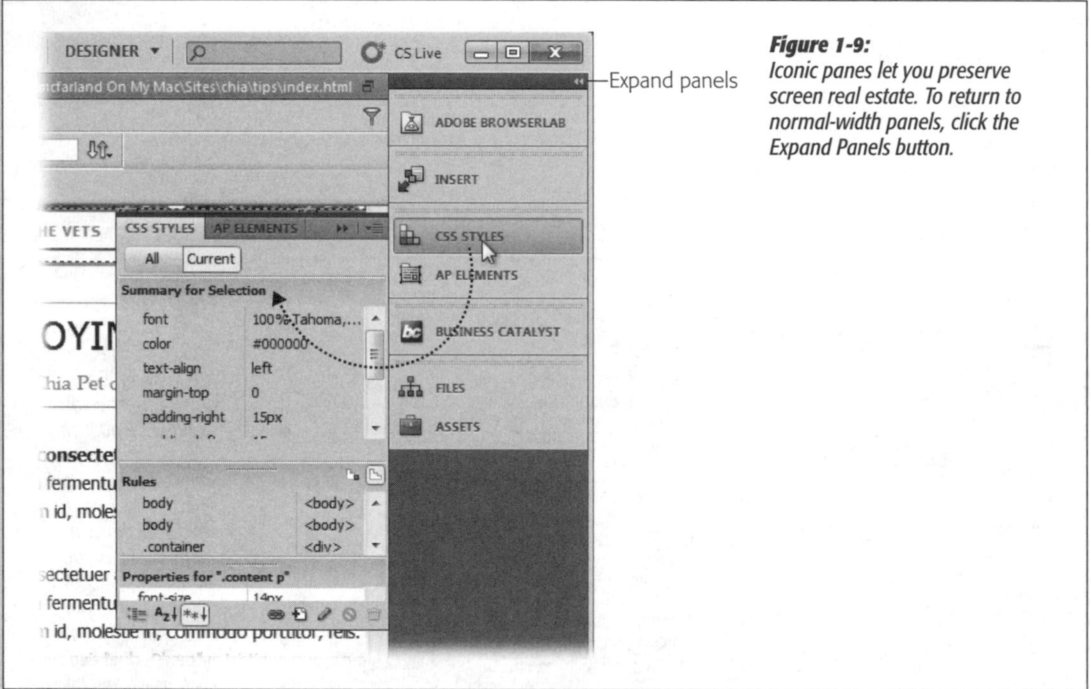

Figure 1-9: *Iconic panes let you preserve screen real estate. To return to normal-width panels, click the Expand Panels button.*

Workspace Layouts

Sometimes too much choice is a bad thing, and even though Dreamweaver's interface means you can pretty much organize its windows and panels any way you like, it also means you can easily accidentally click or drag the wrong thing and suddenly find panels strewn across the screen or completely gone.

Fortunately, Dreamweaver includes a wonderful, timesaving productivity enhancer that ensures you always have your windows organized the way you want, and you can quickly return to that setup if you accidentally move your panels. The Workspace Layouts feature lets you save the position and size of Dreamweaver's panels and windows as a custom "layout," which you can return to by simply selecting the layout's name from the Workspace Switcher menu in the Application bar (see Figure 1-6) or by choosing Window→Workspace Layout.

For example, when you work on a database-driven website, you may like to have the Application panel group and the Snippets panel open, but keep the CSS panel tucked away. When you work on design-heavy sites, on the other hand, you probably want the CSS panel open, but could care less about the Tag Inspector. You can create a different layout for each situation and then simply switch between them.

Note: Dreamweaver CS3 veterans should check out the "Classic" layout, which puts the Insert panel back up at the top of the screen. Even if you're new to Dreamweaver, the Classic layout is a great way to free up space in the already crowded grouping of panels on the right edge of the screen.

In addition, Dreamweaver comes preprogrammed with eight layouts designed to configure the interface to match the needs of designers, coders, application developers, and those who like to spread their windows and panels across two monitors. You should try each one (use the Workspace switcher menu in the Application bar [Figure 1-6]) to see which you like best. You can then tweak that layout by closing or opening other panels, rearranging panels, and so on, until you find the perfect layout for you. Then just save that layout (as described below) so you can call it up any time. Here are a few other tips when you're ready to lay down a custom layout:

- Open the panels you work with most frequently. For example, choose Window→Files to open the Files panel.
- Increase or decrease the height of a panel by dragging up or down the empty space to the right of a panel or panel-group name (see Figure 1-10).

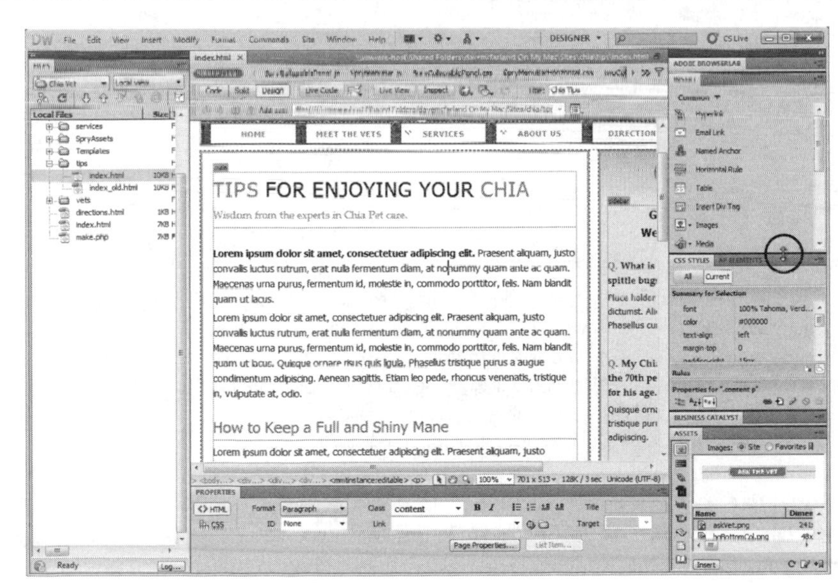

Figure 1-10: *Resizing a panel is as easy as dragging up or down (circled at bottom of Insert panel on right). If you're lucky enough to have a large monitor, it's often helpful to put the Files panel by itself on either the left or right side of the screen.*

- You can move a panel to another area of your screen by dragging its tabs as described in Figure 1-7. This trick is especially useful if you have a large monitor, since you can place one group of panels on the right edge of the monitor and another group either next to the first one or on the left side of the monitor. As described in "Floating panels" on page 32, you can also create floating panels. If you've got two monitors hooked up to your computer, you can spread the panels across both monitors.

To save your layout, select New Workspace from the "Workspace switcher" menu in the Application bar (see Figure 1-11) or, alternatively, choose Window→Workspace Layout→New Workspace. The Save Workspace dialog box appears; type in a name for the layout and then click OK. (If you type the same name as a layout you already saved, Dreamweaver lets you know and gives you the option to replace the old layout with the new one. You have to do this to update a layout you previously created.) Dreamweaver saves your new layout.

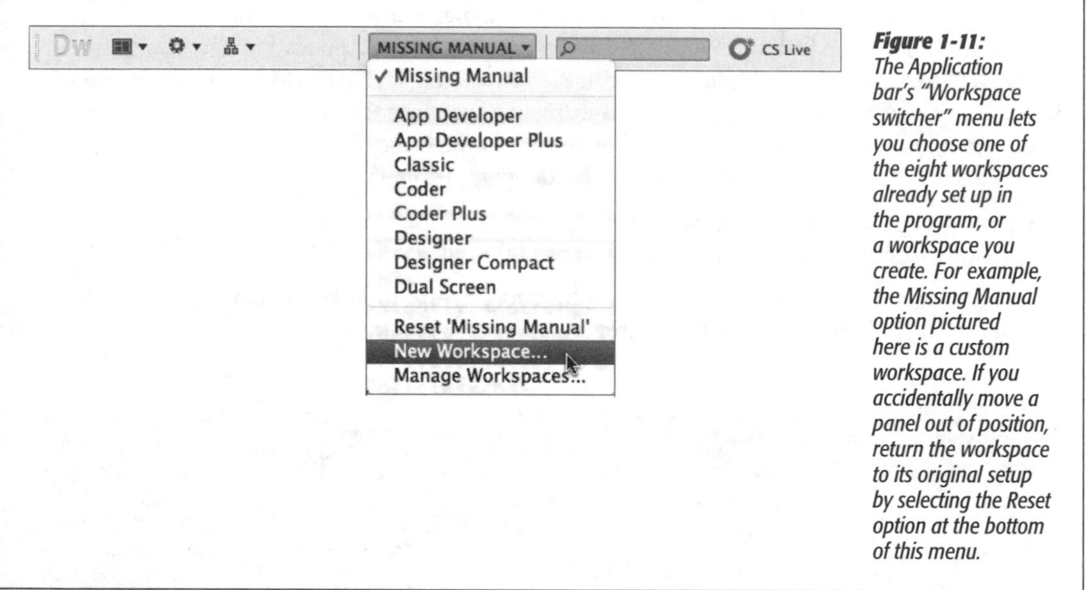

Figure 1-11: *The Application bar's "Workspace switcher" menu lets you choose one of the eight workspaces already set up in the program, or a workspace you create. For example, the Missing Manual option pictured here is a custom workspace. If you accidentally move a panel out of position, return the workspace to its original setup by selecting the Reset option at the bottom of this menu.*

Tip: The Workspace layout feature is also handy if you share your computer with other people. You can create your own Workspace Layout–use your own name when naming the layout–with all the panels and windows exactly where you like them. Then, when you go to use the computer and the bozo before you has rearranged the entire workspace, just select your layout from the Application bar or the Window→Workspace Layouts menu.

To switch to a layout you already saved, simply select your workspace from the Application bar (see Figure 1-11) or choose Window→Workspace Layout→*The Name of Your Layout*. After a brief pause, Dreamweaver switches to the selected layout.

Setting Up a Site

Whenever you build a new website or want to edit an existing one you created elsewhere, you have to introduce Dreamweaver to it—a process called *setting up a site.* This is *the* most important first step when you start using Dreamweaver, whether you plan to whip up a five-page website, build a thousand-page online store, or edit the site your sister built for you. At its most basic, defining a site lets Dreamweaver know where you store your web pages on your computer, and makes sure Dreamweaver correctly inserts images and adds links to the pages of your site. In addition, if you want to take advantage of Dreamweaver's many timesaving site management tools, such as the link checker (see page 671), Library items (Chapter 19), Templates (Chapter 20), and FTP tool for moving your web files to a web server (Chapter 18), you *have* to set up a site.

Note: Dreamweaver CS5 introduces a completely revamped site setup procedure. If you're a longtime Dreamweaver user, you'll find the "Site Definition Wizard" gone, and that basic site setup is easier. However, you'll also find some changes–such as setting up a connection to your web server or to a testing server–that are more confusing to use (when you're ready to upload files to your web server turn to Chapter 18).

There are a lot of ways to configure your site, depending on your needs. For example, if you're ready to move web pages to the Web, you need to tell Dreamweaver how to connect to your web server. But you only need to do a couple of things to get started using Dreamweaver effectively:

1. **Choose Site→New Site to open the Site Setup window (see Figure 1-12).**

   You only need to provide a couple of pieces of information.

2. **In the "Site name" field, type a name for your site.**

   The name you type here is solely for your own reference, to help you identify the site in Dreamweaver's Files panel; it won't appear on the Web.

3. **Click the folder icon to the right of the "Local site folder" field.**

   The Choose Root Folder window opens, where you choose a folder on your hard drive that will serve as your *local site's root folder*. This is a folder on your computer where you'll store all of your site's files—the HTML documents and graphics, CSS files, and other web files that make up your website.

Note: Another way to think of the local site folder: It's the folder on your computer in which you'll put your site's home page.

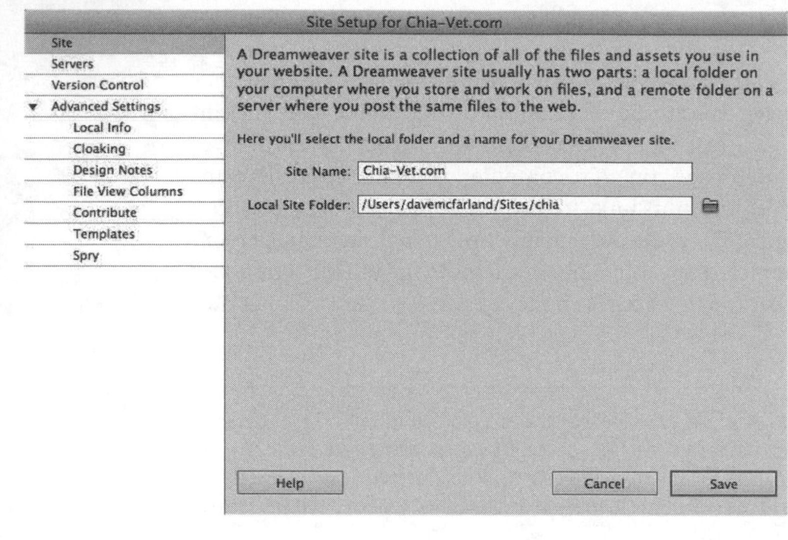

Figure 1-12: *The Site Setup window lets you tell Dreamweaver about your site–where you store your files, how to connect to your web server so you can upload files to the Internet, and so on. To get started, you only need to provide the two pieces of information in this window. You'll find the other categories discussed later in the book: the Servers category lets you connect to a web server to upload files to your website (Chapter 18) and point Dreamweaver to a "testing server" for complex, database-driven websites (Part Six); the Version Control category is for those using the (very complex) Subversion system (most people–the author of this book included– never use this option, but if you're curious, see the box on page 713 for more information). You'll find the Advanced settings discussed in step 5 below and elsewhere in this book.*

4. **Browse to and select a folder for your site's files.**

   Figure 1-13 demonstrates the process for Windows and Macs. If you're editing an existing site, select the folder that contains the site's files. If you're creating a new site, create a folder for that site using the New Folder button in this window.

5. **For a few additional options, select Advanced from the left-hand list of setup categories (see Figure 1-14).**

   This step is optional and you can happily skip it to begin building web pages. You'll find most of the categories in the Advanced Setting category discussed elsewhere in the book, but you may want to visit the options in the Local Info category:

- The **Default Images** folder field lets you select (or create) a folder inside your site folder that holds the images you'll use on your web pages. Choosing an images folder is useful only if you tend to add images from outside your site folder—for example, if you have images sitting on your desktop or in another folder on your hard drive. If that's the case, Dreamweaver automatically copies those files to the images folder you specify here. (Dreamweaver will still copy image files to your site without setting this option, but each time you add an image from outside your site folder, you have to tell Dreamweaver where to save the file. But, if you'll primarily use images saved somewhere in your site, skip this setting.)
- The **"Links relative to"** setting determines how your pages link to other files within your site: for example, how Dreamweaver writes links to other pages in your site, links to images in your site, and links to external files, like Cascading Style Sheet files, Flash movies, and so on. Unless you're an experienced web designer, stick with the normal, "Document" setting here—you can read about the difference between (and uses for) Document and Site Root relative links on page 159.
- **Type the web address for your site in the Web URL box:** for example *www.chiat-vet.com/*. If you don't yet have a web address, then you can leave this blank. In some cases, you may need to add some more information after the domain name. For example, the address for your website might look something like this: *www.somecollege.edu/~bob*. Or you might be responsible for maintaining just part of a larger site—sometimes called a "sub site." Regardless, just type the address you normally type into a web browser to visit your site. For example, *www.mybigcompany.com/marketing/*.

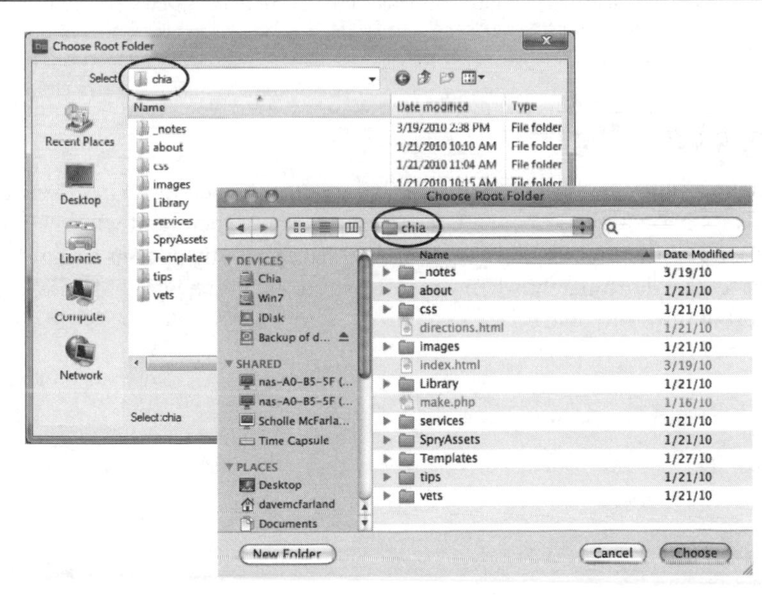

Figure 1-13:
The dialog box for selecting a folder in Windows (top) is pretty much the same as the one for Macs (bottom). You can verify which folder you're about to select by looking in the Select field for Windows (circled in top image) or in the path menu on a Mac (circled in bottom image).

- **Leave the Case-sensitive links checking box unchecked.** This is useful only when you have web pages and files on a Unix server that allows files with the same name but different letter cases: for example, HOME.html, home.html or HoMe.html. Since Macs and Windows machines don't let you do this, you'll probably never have a site that has files named like this.
- **Keep the Enable Cache box checked.** Dreamweaver creates a site cache for each site you set up. That's a small database that tracks pages, links, images, and other site components. The cache helps Dreamweaver's site management tools avoid breaking links, lets Dreamweaver warn you when you're about to delete important files, and lets you reorganize your site quickly. The only reason to uncheck this box is if you have a really large website (tens of thousands of pages and images) and you notice that Dreamweaver is really slow whenever you begin to work on the site, move a file, change a file's name, delete a file, or perform one of Dreamweaver's other "site management" tasks. In that case, you may see a box saying "updating the site cache" or "checking links" that stays open and prevents you from using Dreamweaver for a minute or more—basically your site is so big that Dreamweaver has to spend a lot of time keeping track of your files and links.

6. **Click the Save button to finish the site setup process.**

   Your site's files (if there are any yet) appear in the Files panel. Now you're ready to create web pages and take advantage of Dreamweaver's powerful site-building tools.

Note: Dreamweaver lets you set up *multiple* websites at a time, a handy feature if you're a web designer with several clients, or if your company builds and manages more than one site. To define an additional site, choose Site→New Site and then repeat the steps starting on page 37. You can then switch from one site to another using the Sites menu in the Files panel (see Figure 16-6, later).

Creating a Web Page

After you define a site, you'll want to start building pages. Just choose File→New or press Ctrl+N (⌘-N on a Mac) to open Dreamweaver's New Document window (see Figure 1-15). It's a little overwhelming at first. You have so many options it's hard to know where to start. Fortunately, when you just want to create a new HTML file, you can skip most of these options.

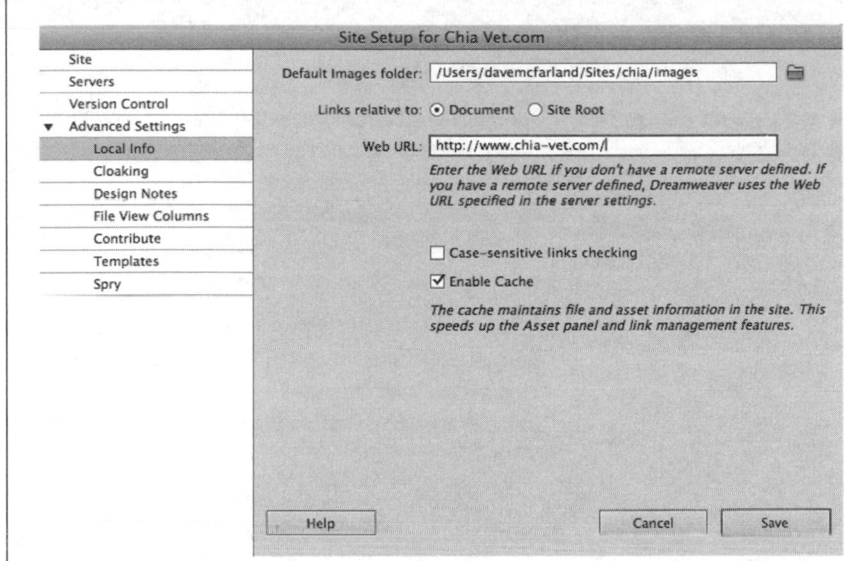

***Figure 1-14:** You can happily use Dreamweaver without ever visiting the Advanced Settings options listed in the left-hand column of the Site Setup window. The Local Info options are discussed above, and the other options are discussed elsewhere in this book: Cloaking on page 708, Design Notes on page 721, File View Columns on page 650, Contribute on page 750, Templates in Chapter 20, and Spry on page 188.*

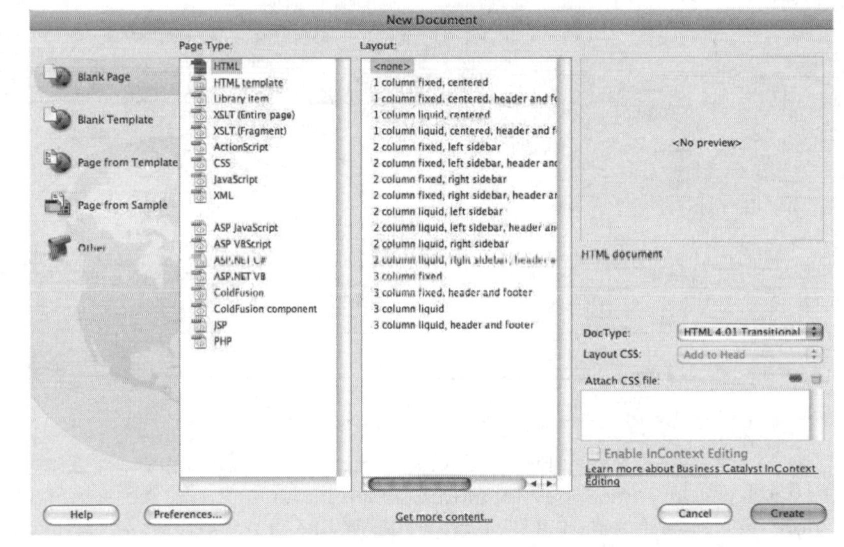

***Figure 1-15:** The New Document window lets you create nearly every type of web document under the sun. Dreamweaver CS5 includes a revamped set of prepackaged CSS layouts, using the latest web design techniques. You can learn more about these "CSS Layouts" in Chapter 9.*

UP TO SPEED

Terms Worth Knowing

During the tutorial in these pages–and, indeed, everywhere in Dreamweaver–you'll encounter a few terms frequently heard at web designer luncheons:

Root folder. The first rule of managing a website is that every piece of the site you're working on–web page (HTML) documents, graphics images, sound files, and so on–must sit in a single master folder on your hard drive. This folder is the *root* folder for your website, and because it's on your computer it's called the *local* root folder. Dreamweaver calls this your local site folder. The *root* (a.k.a site folder) is the master, outer, main folder–think of it as the edge of the known universe for that site: Nothing exists outside the root. Of course, to help organize your site's files, you can include any number of subfolders *within* that main folder.

When you finish creating your site, you'll move the files in that root folder onto a web server for the world to see. The folder you place your site files into on the server is called the *remote root folder*.

Local site. The usual routine for creating web pages goes like this: You create the page on your own computer–using a program like Dreamweaver–and then you upload it to a computer on the Internet called a web server, where your handiwork becomes available to the masses. So, it's very common for a website to exist in two places at once, one copy on your computer and the other on the server.

The copy on your own computer is called the *local site*, or the development site. Think of the local site as a sort of staging ground, where you build your site, test it, and modify it. Because the local site isn't on a web server, the public can't see it and you can freely edit and add to it without affecting the pages your visitors see (they're on the remote site, after all).

Remote site. When you add or update a file, you move it from your local site to the remote site. The *remote*, or live, site is a mirror image of the local site. Because you create the remote site by uploading your local site, it has the same folder structure as the local site, and contains the same files. Only polished, fully functional pages go online to the remote site; save the half-finished, typo-ridden drafts for your local site. Chapter 18 explains how to use Dreamweaver's FTP features to define and work with a remote site.

(If you're using Dreamweaver's database features, by the way, you'll encounter yet another term: a *testing server*. You'll find the lowdown on this kind of server, which you use to test database features, on page 833)

To create a basic HTML file for a web page:

1. **From the left-hand list of document categories, choose Blank Page.**

   The Blank Page category lets you create a new empty document—this might be a web page or something a bit more esoteric like an XML file (see page 548 for more on XML), an external JavaScript file, or one of the several server-driven pages, such as a PHP file (discussed in Part Six).

   Both the Blank Template and "Page from Template" categories relate to Dreamweaver's Template feature discussed in Chapter 20. The "Page from Sample" category lets you choose from several different files with already-created designs.

It's best to avoid these—they're old and left over from earlier versions of the program, aren't very attractive, and don't use the best techniques for building a web page. Dreamweaver CS5 does ship with some useful page layouts you can access from the Blank Page category. You'll learn about these in Chapter 10. The last category, Other, lets you create documents for different programming languages like ActionScript or Java—unless you're a Flash or Java programmer, you probably won't ever need these.

2. **From the Page Type list, choose HTML.**

   You can also create other types of documents, most of which you'll learn more about later in this book, such as PHP for database-driven sites (see Part Six of this book), XSLT files for processing XML (Chapter 27), templates (Chapter 20), library items (Chapter 19), or CSS files (Chapter 4).

3. **From the Layout list, choose "<none>".**

   "<none>" creates a blank document. The other choices ("1 column elastic, centered", "1 column elastic, centered, header and footer", and so on) are predesigned page layouts. These designs (not to be confused with the designs under the "Page from Sample" category) use CSS, which you'll learn much more about starting in Chapter 4. Because CSS-based layout can be tricky, Dreamweaver includes all the code you need to create many of the most common types of page designs. You'll learn more about this feature in Chapter 10.

4. **Select a document type from the DocType menu.**

   Selecting a document type identifies the type of HTML you'll use on the page you create. It affects how Dreamweaver writes the HTML code and how a web browser understands it. Fortunately, since Dreamweaver writes all the code for you, you don't need to worry about the subtle differences between the different document types.

   XHTML 1.0 Transitional is the normal setting in Dreamweaver, but HTML 4.01 Transitional, HTML 4.01 Strict, and XHTML 1.0 Strict are also fine choices. The transitional doc types let you use a few HTML tags and properties that have been phased out of the strict types. Most notably, transitional doc types can use the "target" property for links—a simple way to force links to open in a new browser window.

   If you don't really understand or care about doc types, just select HTML 4.01 Transitional. But make sure you avoid None (which can force browsers to display pages in what's called "quirks mode" and makes perfecting designs difficult) and XHTML 1.1 (which requires a special setting on your web server to work properly).

Note: If you don't want to deal with the New Document window every time you create a new page, choose Edit→Preferences in Windows or Dreamweaver→Preferences on a Mac. In the Preferences dialog box, click the New Document category and then turn off the "Show New Document Dialog on Control-N" checkbox.

While you're at it, you can specify the type of file Dreamweaver creates whenever you press Ctrl+N (⌘-N). For example, if you usually create plain HTML files, choose HTML. But if you usually create dynamic pages (like PHP pages), choose a different type of file–PHP, for example.

With these settings, pressing Ctrl+N (⌘-N) instantly creates a new blank document of your choosing. (Choosing File→New, however, still opens the New Document window.)

5. **Click Create.**

   Dreamweaver opens a new, blank web page ready for you to save and title (see Figure 1-16).

6. **Choose File→Save.**

   The Save As dialog box appears. You need to save the file somewhere inside the local root folder. You can save it inside any subfolder within the root folder as well.

7. **Type a name for the file and then click Save.**

   Make sure the name doesn't contain spaces or any characters except letters, numbers, hyphens, and underscores, and that it ends in either .html or .htm.

   Although most operating systems let you save files with long names, spaces, and characters like #, $, and &, some browsers and servers have trouble interpreting anything other than letters and numbers.

   Furthermore, web servers rely on file extensions like .htm, .html, .gif, and .jpg to know whether a file is a web page, graphic, or some other type of file. Dreamweaver for Windows automatically adds the extension to your saved document names. But on the Mac—which lets you save files without extensions—make sure the file ends in the suffix .html or .htm when you save it.

8. **At the top of the document window, click inside the Title box and then type a name for the page (see Figure 1-16).**

   Every new document Dreamweaver creates has the unflattering title Untitled Document. If you do a quick search on Google for "Untitled Document", you'll find (at the time of this writing) 27,500,000 results (obviously there are still some people who need to pick up a copy of this book). Dreamweaver probably created most of those pages. You should change this to a descriptive title indicating the main topic of the page, like "Contact Chia Vet," "About Chia Vet's Chia Pet Services," or "Technical Specifications for the Anodyne 3000 Indoor Lawn Mower." Not only is replacing "Untitled Document" more professional, but providing a descriptive title can improve a web page's ranking among search engines. In addition, the title appears on Google's, Yahoo's, and Bing's search listings.

The Dreamweaver Test Drive

Although reading a book is a good way to learn the ins and outs of a program, nothing beats sitting in front of your computer and taking a program through its paces. Many of this book's chapters, therefore, conclude with hands-on training: step-by-step tutorials that take you through the creation of a real, working, professionally designed website for the fictional company Chia Vet.

Figure 1-16: *A new blank web page. Always remember to title the page by clicking inside the Title box at the top of the document window (circled) and then entering a descriptive title.*

The rest of this chapter, for example, introduces Dreamweaver by taking you step by step through the process of building a web page. It shouldn't take more than an hour. When it's over, you'll have learned the basic steps of building any web page: creating and saving a new document, adding and formatting text, inserting graphics, adding links, and making the program work for you (the finished tutorial is pictured in Figure 1-33).

If you already use Dreamweaver and want to jump right into the details of the program, feel free to skip this tutorial. (And if you're the type who likes to read first and try second, read Chapters 2 through 5 and then return to this point to practice what you've just learned.)

Note: The tutorial in this chapter requires the example files from this book's website, *http://www.sawmac.com/dwcs5/*. Click the Download Tutorials link to download the files. The tutorial files are stored as ZIP files, a type of file that compresses a lot of different files into one, smaller file.

Windows folks should download the file and then double-click it to open the archive. Click the Extract All Files option and then follow the instructions of the Extraction Wizard to unzip the files and place them on your computer. Mac users, just double-click the file to decompress it.

After you download and decompress the files, you should have a MM_DWCS5 folder on your computer, containing all the tutorial files for this book.

Phase 1: Getting Dreamweaver in Shape

Before you get started working in Dreamweaver, you need to make sure the program's set up to work for you. In the following steps, you'll double-check some key Dreamweaver preference settings and organize your workspace using the Workspace Layout feature.

First, make sure your preferences are all set:

1. **If it isn't already open, start Dreamweaver.**

   Hey, you've got to start with the basics, right?

2. **Choose Edit→Preferences (Windows) or Dreamweaver→Preferences (Mac).**

   The Preferences dialog box opens, listing a dizzying array of categories and options (see Figure 1-17).

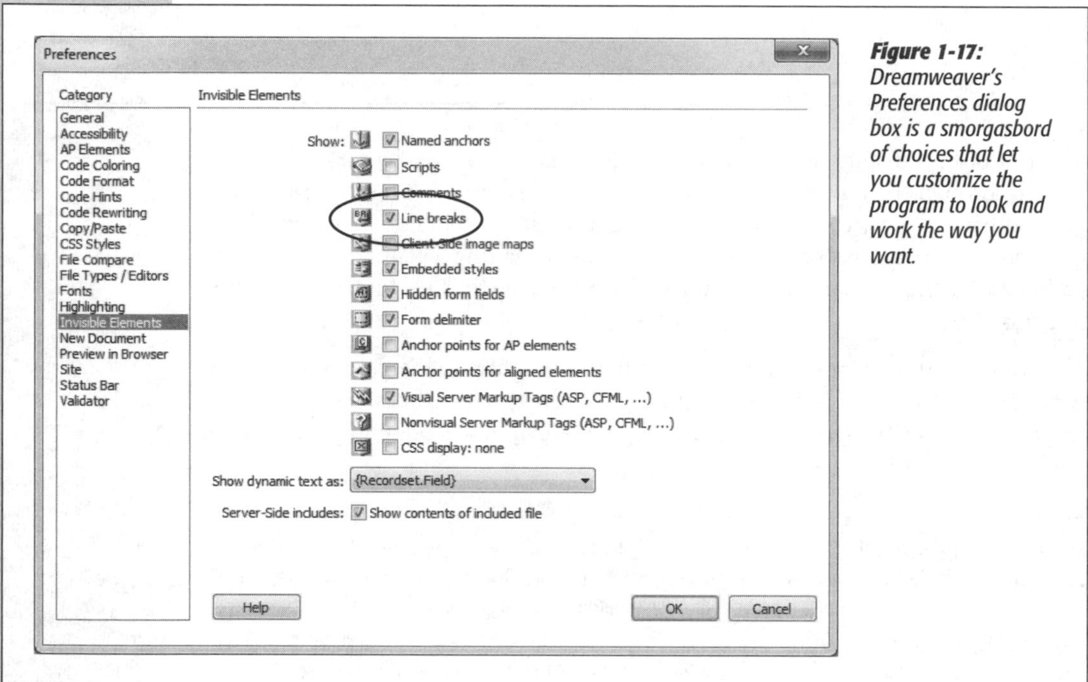

***Figure 1-17:** Dreamweaver's Preferences dialog box is a smorgasbord of choices that let you customize the program to look and work the way you want.*

3. **In the Preferences dialog box, select the Invisible Elements category and then turn on the fourth checkbox from the top, labeled Line Breaks (see Figure 1-17, circled).**

   Sometimes, when you paste text from other programs, like Microsoft Word or an email program, Dreamweaver displays separate paragraphs as one long, single paragraph broken up with invisible characters called *line breaks* (for you HTML-savvy readers, this is the <br> tag). Normally, you can't see the line break character in Dreamweaver's Design view. This setting makes the character visible—represented in the document window by a little gold shield—so you can easily select and remove it.

4. **Click OK.**

   The Preferences dialog box closes. You're ready to get your workspace in order. As noted at the beginning of this chapter, Dreamweaver offers many windows to help you build web pages. For this tutorial, though, you need only three: the Insert panel, the document window, and the Property inspector. But, for good measure (and to give you a bit of practice), you'll open another panel and rearrange the workspace a little. To get started, you'll make sure Dreamweaver is displaying the space-saving Classic workspace.

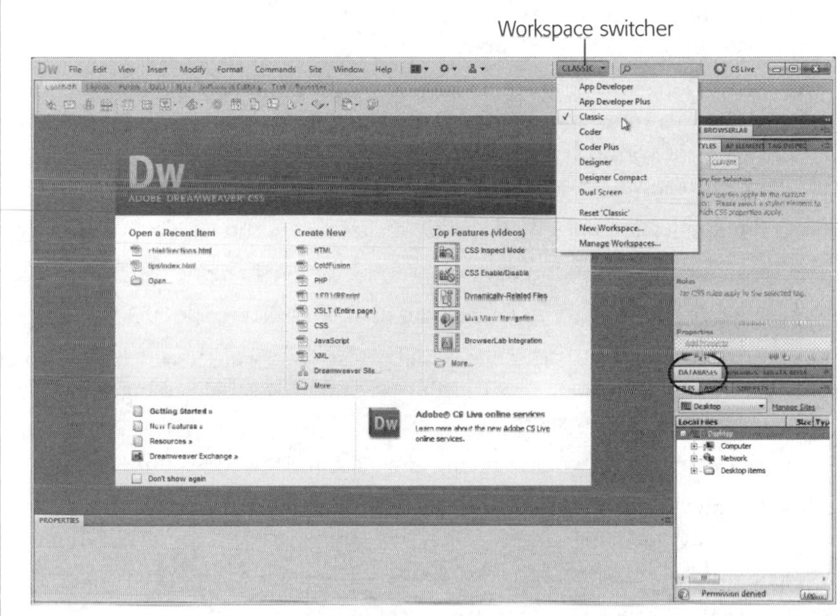

***Figure 1-18:** The Dreamweaver Welcome screen pictured in the middle of this figure lists recently opened files in the left column. Clicking one of the file names opens that file for editing. The middle column provides a quick way to create a new web page or define a new site. In addition, you can access introductory videos and other getting-started materials from this screen (right-hand panel). You see the Welcome screen only when you have no other web files open.*

5. **From the "Workspace switcher" on the Application bar, select Classic (see Figure 1-18), or go to Window→Workspace Layout from the main menu bar and then select "Classic" from the drop-down menu.**

   If you see Classic already selected, choose "Reset 'Classic'", which moves any panels that were resized, closed, or repositioned back to their original locations. The Classic workspace built into Dreamweaver puts the Property inspector at the bottom of the screen, turns the Insert Panel into an Insert Toolbar that appears either in the Application Toolbar or directly below it, opens the CSS styles and Files panels on the right edge, and displays two other groups of closed tabs.

You only need the Databases panel when you work with database-driven websites so, even though the panel is currently closed, there's no reason to keep its tab (and the tabs for the other database-related panels) around, so you'll close that group of tabs next.

6. **Right-click (Control-click) on the Databases tab (circled in Figure 1-18), and choose Close Tab Group from the pop-up menu.**

   The Databases panel and its three tabs disappear (you can always get it back by selecting Window→Databases.) The CSS Styles panel is very useful; it also is composed of three panes stacked one on top of the next, so giving it plenty of vertical room is a good idea.

7. **Drag the thick line that appears between the top of the Files panel and the bottom of the CSS Styles panel (circled in Figure 1-19) until the Files panel is about half the size of the CSS Styles panel.**

   Now the workspace looks great. It has the most common panels you'll be working with for this tutorial (and for much of your web page building). Since this arrangement of windows is so useful, you'll want to save this as a layout (ok, maybe you don't want to save this layout…just play along.)

8. **From the Application bar's Workspace switcher menu, choose New Workspace.**

   The Save Workspace window appears, waiting for you to name your new layout.

9. **Type Missing Manual (or any name you like), and then click OK.**

   You just created a new workspace layout. To see if it works, switch to another one of Dreamweaver's Workspace layouts, see how the screen changes, and then switch back to your new setup.

10. **From the Workspace switcher menu, choose App Developer Plus.**

    This step moves the panels around quite a bit, and even displays some panels in Dreamweaver's iconic mode (as described on page 34). This layout's a bit too complicated for our needs, so you'll switch back.

11. **From the Workspace switcher menu, choose Missing Manual (or whatever you named your custom space in step 9).**

    Voilà! Dreamweaver sets up everything the way you want it. You can create multiple layouts for different websites or different types of sites.

Phase 2: Creating a Website

As discussed on page 37, whenever you want to use Dreamweaver to create or edit a website, your first step is always to show Dreamweaver the location of the *site folder* (also called root folder)—the master folder for all your website's files. You do this by *setting up a site*, like so:

1. **Choose Site→New Site.**

   The Site Setup window appears. Dreamweaver CS5 has greatly simplified site setup, so you only need to provide two pieces of information to get started using Dreamweaver.

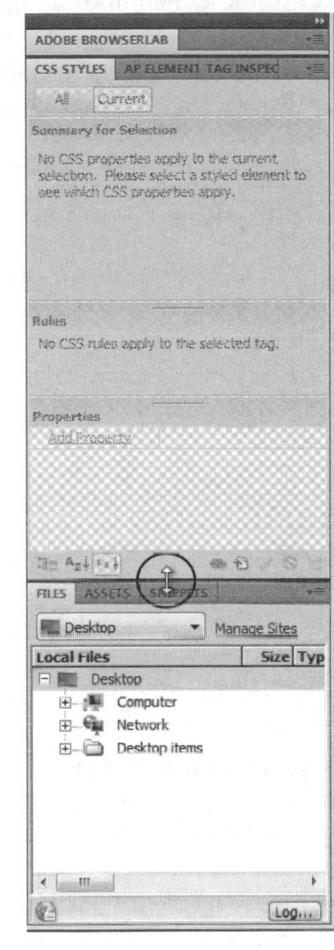

Figure 1-19:
Make a panel taller or shorter by dragging the thick line separating two panels (circled). The options in some panels, like the CSS Styles panel here, are dimmed if you don't have a web page open. You can also minimize a panel group by clicking its tab. For example, clicking the "Files" tab in this figure would hide the Files panel (the list of files), and expand the CSS Styles panel–a good technique if you need more space for a particular panel.

2. **Type *Tutorial 1* in the Site Name field.**

   The name you type here is solely for your own reference, so you can identify the site in Dreamweaver's Site menu. Dreamweaver also asks where you want to store the website's files. In this example, you'll use one of the folders you downloaded from this book's website (at other times, you'll choose or create a folder of your own).

3. **Click the folder icon next to the label "Local Site Folder".**

   The Choose Root Folder window opens, so that you can choose a folder on your hard drive to serve as your *local root folder*. (This is the folder on your computer where you'll store the HTML documents and graphics, CSS, and other web files that make up your website.)

4. **Browse to and select the Chapter01 folder located inside the MM_DWCS5 folder you downloaded earlier. Click the Select (Choose) button to set this folder as the local root folder.**

   This process is discussed in step 3 on page 37. Click the folder icon to the right of the "Local site folder" field. At this point, you've given Dreamweaver all the information it needs to successfully work with the tutorial files.

Note: You'll find finished versions of all of the tutorials from this book in the MM_DWCS4 folder. The finished version of this tutorial is located in the Chapter01_finished folder.

---

5. **Click the Save button to close the Site Setup window.**

   After you define a site, Dreamweaver creates a *site cache* for it (see page 40). Since there are hardly any files in the Chapter01 folder, you may not even notice this happening—it goes by in the blink of an eye.

Phase 3: Creating and Saving a Web Page

"Enough already! I want to build a web page," you're probably saying. You'll do just that in this phase of the tutorial:

1. **Choose File→New.**

   The New Document window opens (see Figure 1-15). Creating a blank web page involves a few clicks.

2. **From the left-hand list of document categories, select Blank Page; in the Page Type list, highlight HTML; and from the Layout list, choose <none>. From the DocType menu in the bottom right of the window, select "HTML 4.01 Transitional".**

   HTML (and XHTML as well) actually has two "flavors." The "Transitional" type keeps your pages compatible with older browsers, and gives you a wider range of HTML properties to work with. If you've grown up with regular HTML, it's perfectly fine to select "HTML 4.01 Transitional". (In fact, it's even OK to select "XHTML 1.0 Transitional", if you prefer.)

3. **Click Create.**

   Dreamweaver opens a new, blank HTML page. Even though the underlying code for an HTML page differs in slight ways depending on which document type you chose (HTML 4.01 Transitional, XHTML 1.0 Strict, and so on), you have nothing to worry about: Dreamweaver manages all that code so you don't have to.

   If you see a bunch of strange text in the window, you're looking at the underlying HTML; you're in either Code or Split view. At the top left of the document window, click the Design button to tell Dreamweaver to display the page in its visual layout mode.

4. **Choose File→Save.**

   The Save As dialog box opens.

   Always save your pages right away. This good habit prevents serious headaches if the power goes out as you finish that beautiful—but unsaved—creation.

5. **Save the page in the Chapter01 folder as "directions.html".**

   You could also save the page as *directions.htm*; both .html and .htm are valid extensions for HTML files.

   Make sure you save this page in the correct folder. In Phase 2 (page 48), you defined the Chapter01 folder as the root of the site—the folder that holds all the pages and files for the site. If you save the page in a different folder, Dreamweaver gets confused and its site management features don't work correctly.

Tip: When you save a file, you can quickly jump to the current site's root folder. In the Save As dialog box, click the Site Root button–that takes you right to the root folder. This little trick also works when you open or link to a file.

---

6. **If the document window toolbar isn't already open, choose View→Toolbars→Document to display it.**

   The toolbar at the top of the document window provides easy access to a variety of tasks you'll perform frequently, such as titling a page, previewing it in a web browser, and looking at the HTML source code.

7. **In the toolbar's Title field, select the text "Untitled Document", and then type Directions to Chia Vet Headquarters.**

   The Title field lets you set a page's title—the information that appears in the title bar of a web browser. The page title also shows up as the name of your page when someone searches the web using a search engine like Bing or Google. In addition, a clear and descriptive title that identifies the main point of the page can also help increase a page's ranking among the major search engines.

   Dreamweaver CS5 adds a Browser Navigation toolbar that appears directly below the Document toolbar (see Figure 1-2). It's intended to help web designers working on complex web applications like the WordPress blogging system or the Drupal content management system. However, it mostly just wastes vertical space. You'll hide it now.

8. **Choose View→Toolbars→Browser Navigation.**

   The toolbar disappears. Now you'll set some basic properties of the page.

9. **On the Property inspector (see Figure 1-26), click the Page Properties button, or choose Modify→Page Properties.**

   The Page Properties dialog box opens (see Figure 1-20), letting you define the basic attributes of each web page you create. Six categories of settings control attributes like text color, background color, link colors, and page margins.

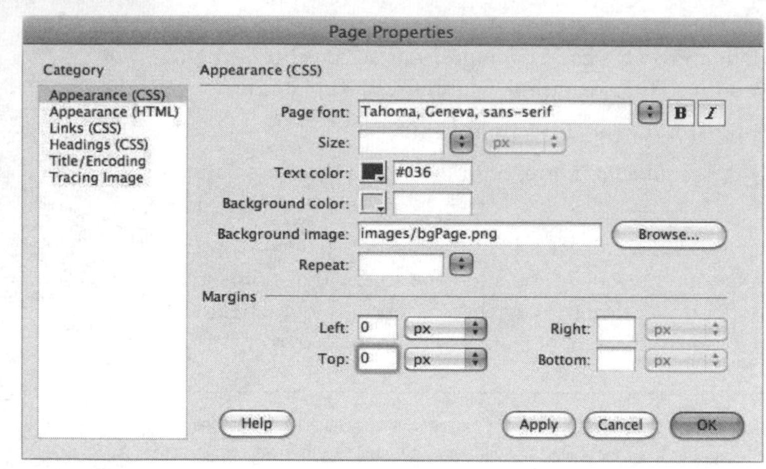

***Figure 1-20:** Dreamweaver clearly indicates which property settings use CSS and which rely on HTML. You should avoid the category labeled "Appearance (HTML)". The options in that category add old, out-of-date code to your web pages.*

10. **From the "Page font" menu, select "Tahoma, Geneva, sans-serif".**

    This sets a basic font (and two backup fonts, in case your visitor's machine lacks Tahoma) that Dreamweaver automatically uses for all the text on a page.

    As you'll see later in this tutorial, though, you can always specify a different font for selected text.

    Next, you'll set a basic text color for the page.

11. **Next to the "Text color" label, click the small gray box. From the pop-up color palette, choose a color (a dark color like a royal blue works well).**

    Unless you intervene, all web page text starts out black; the text on this page reflects the color you select here. In the next step, you'll add an image to the background of the page to liven it up.

Note: Alternatively, you could type a color, like *#333333*, into the box beside the palette square. That's *hexadecimal* notation, which is familiar to HTML coding gurus. Both the palette and the hexadecimal color-specifying field appear fairly often in Dreamweaver (see the box on page 56).

---

12. **To the right of the "Background image" field, click the Browse button.**

    The Select Image Source window appears (see Figure 1-21). Use it to navigate to and select a graphic.

13. **Click the Site Root button at the top of the window (bottom of the window on Macs). Open the folder named "images", select the file named *bgPage.png*, and then click the OK (Choose on a Mac) button.**

In Dreamweaver, you can also just double-click a file to select it *and* close the window you used to select the file. For example, you can accomplish both steps—selecting the *bgPage.png* file *and* clicking the OK button—by just double-clicking the file.

Note to Windows Users: Normally, Windows doesn't display a file's extension. So when you navigate to the images folder in step 13 above, you might see *bgPage* instead of *bgPage.png*. Since file extensions are an important way people (and web servers) identify the different types of files used on a website, you may want Windows to display extensions. Here's how: In Windows Explorer, navigate to and select the MM_DWCS5 folder (the folder containing this book's tutorials). Then, if you're using Windows XP, choose Tools→Folder Options. If you're on Vista or Windows 7, choose Organize→"Folder and search options". In the Folder Options window, select the View tab, and then turn off the "Hide extensions for known file types" checkbox. To apply this setting to these tutorial files, click OK; to apply it to all the files on your computer, click the "Apply to Folders" button, and then click OK.

---

14. **In the Left and Top margin boxes, type *0*.**

    This step removes the little bit of space web browsers insert between the contents of your web page and the top and left sides of the browser window. The size of this margin varies from browser to browser, so it's good to set this value yourself to make sure the page appears consistently across the different browsers.

    If you like, you can change this setting to make the browser add more space to the top and left side of the page. In fact, you can even add a little extra empty space on the *right* side of a page. (The right margin control is especially useful for languages that read from right to left, like Hebrew or Arabic.) Note, however, that the *bottom* margin has no effect on the page display.

15. **Click the Links category, and then add the following properties: in the Link color field, type *#EC6206*; in the "Visited links" field, type *#93BD00*; in the "Rollover links" field, type *#779A00*; and in the "Active links" color field, type *#CAE0EC* (see Figure 1-22).**

    These hexadecimal codes specify specific web page colors (see the box on page 56 for more about this notation).

    Links come in four varieties: regular, visited, active, and rollover. A *regular* link is a plain old link, unvisited, untouched. A *visited* link is one you've already clicked, as noted in a browser's History list. An *active* link is one you're currently clicking (you're pressing the mouse button when you're over the link). And finally, a *rollover* link indicates how the link looks when you mouse over it without clicking. You can choose different colors for each of these link states.

    While it may seem like overkill to have four different colors for links, the regular and visited link colors provide useful feedback to web visitors by telling them which links they've already followed and which remain to be checked out. For its part, the rollover link gives you instant feedback, changing color as soon as you move your cursor over it. The active link color isn't that useful for navigating a site since its color changes so briefly you probably won't even notice it.

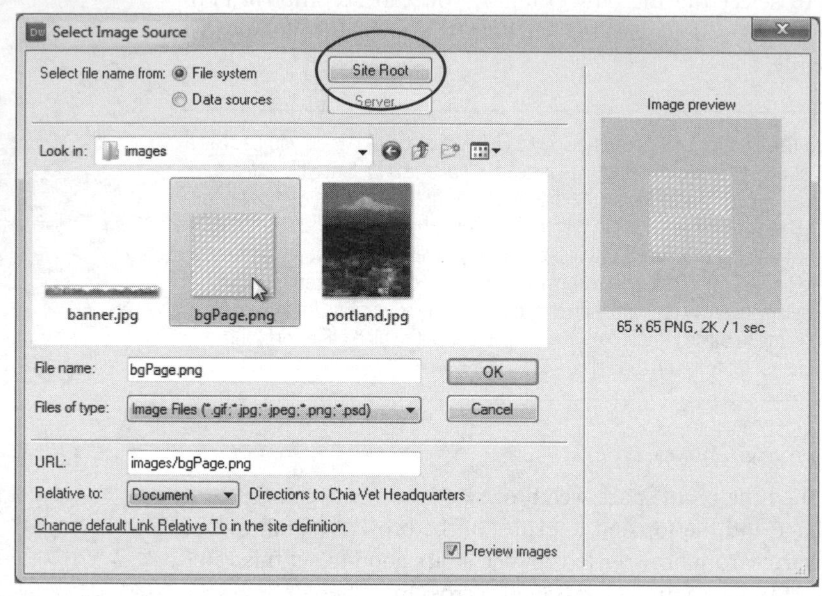

Figure 1-21: *Use the Select Image Source window to insert graphics on a web page. The Site Root button (circled) gives you a quick way to jump to the local site root—a nifty way to always know where you are when you search for a file. On the Mac, the Site Root button appears at the bottom-right of the window.*

Note: Although Dreamweaver uses the term *rollover* link, in the world of Cascading Style Sheets, this is called a *hover* link.

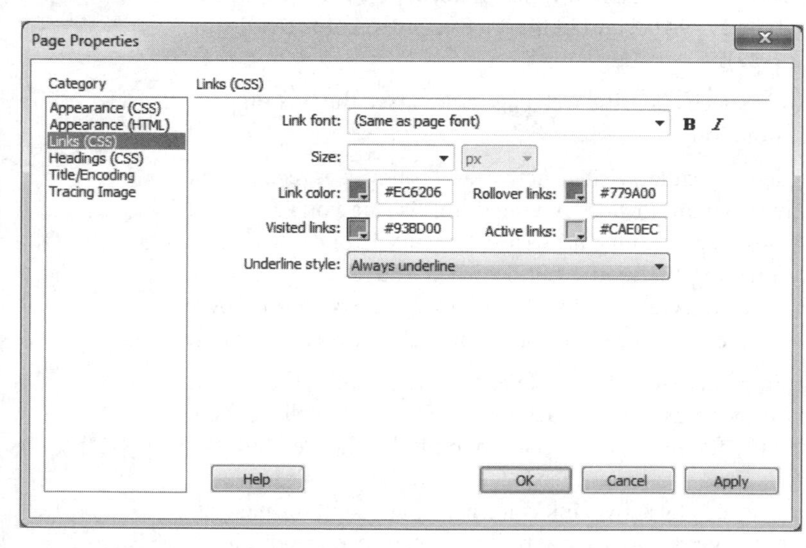

Figure 1-22: *You can set several different properties for links using the Links category of the Page Properties dialog box. You can choose a different font and size for links, as well as specify colors for four different link states. Finally, you can choose whether (or when) a browser underlines links. Most browsers automatically do, but you can override this behavior with the help of this dialog box and Cascading Style Sheets (see page 180).*

16. **Click OK to close the window and apply these changes to the page.**

    You return to your document window. You see an asterisk next to the file name at the top of the document window—Dreamweaver is telling you that you haven't saved a page you edited, a nice reminder to save your file frequently and prevent heartache if the program suddenly shuts down (see circled image in Figure 1-23).

***Figure 1-23:** An asterisk next to a file name (circled) means you've made changes to the file, but haven't yet saved it–quick, hit Ctrl+S (⌘-S on a Mac)!*

17. **Choose File→Save (or press Ctrl+S [⌘-S]).**

    Save your work frequently. (This isn't a web technique as much as a computer-always-crashes-when-you-least-expect-it technique.)

Phase 4: Adding Images and Text

Now you'll add the real meat of your web page: words and pictures.

1. **On the Insert bar's Common tab, from the Image menu, select Image (see Figure 1-24).**

   Alternatively, choose Insert→Image. Either way, the Select Image Source dialog box opens. (If you didn't choose the Classic view from the Workspace switcher—step 5 on page 47—then the Insert bar is really the Insert panel and it appears in the right-hand group of panels as pictured in Figure 1-3).

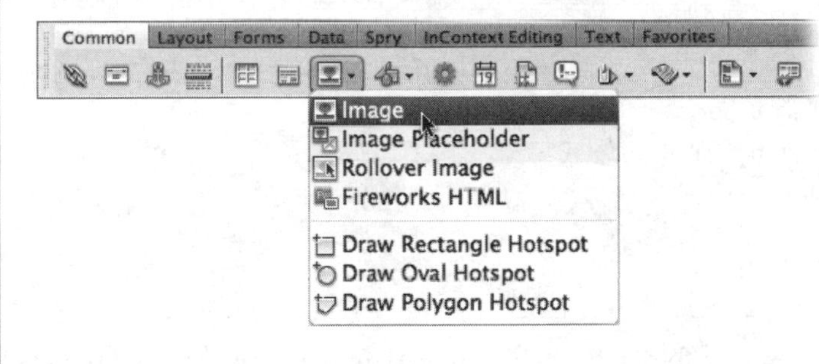

***Figure 1-24:** Some of the buttons on Dreamweaver's Insert bar do double duty as menus (the ones with the small, black, down-pointing arrows). Once you select an option from the menu (in this case, the Image object), it becomes the button's current setting. If you want to insert the same object again (in this case, an image), you don't need to use the menu again–just click the button.*

UP TO SPEED

Using Dreamweaver's Color Box

In the Property inspector, the Modify Page Properties window, and various other places throughout the program, Dreamweaver calls that innocent-looking gray box the *color box*. You can use it to choose a color for the selected web page element in any of three ways.

First, you can click one of the colors on the pop-up rainbow palette that appears when you click the color box.

Second, you can use the eyedropper cursor that appears when you click the color box. This cursor is "loaded," meaning you can click any spot on your screen—even outside the dialog box—to select a color, a trick that comes in handy when you want to use a color from an image elsewhere in your document (to have headline text match the color in an image, for example). You can even sample a color from another application (from any visible window, Dreamweaver or not): Just move the eyedropper over the color, and then click. (This click may take you out of Dreamweaver. Just return to Dreamweaver, and the color you sampled is listed in the color property box.)

Finally, you can click the Color Picker icon, shown here, to launch the Windows or Mac color-picker dialog box, which lets you choose from millions of colors.

If you decide you don't want to add color, or want to remove a color you already applied, click the Default Color button. Without a specific color setting, web browsers use default colors for the element in question. For instance, text on a web page is usually black unless you specify otherwise.

Next to the color box in any Dreamweaver dialog box is a blank text field. If you know your web colors, you can type their *hex* codes (the hexadecimal characters that represent a certain color; see below) into this box, which is sometimes faster and more precise than clicking the rainbow palette.

The Palette Options menu is of limited use. It lets you select a different set of (very limited) rainbow colors for your palette. The first two choices, for example, contain the outdated web-safe color palette—a limited collection of 216 colors that display accurately on any computer screen. The web-safe palette made sense back when graphics cards were expensive and dinosaurs ruled the earth. Today, however, most monitors can display millions of colors. Likewise, the Grayscale palette offers 256 somber shades of gray (you'll find them most useful for Ingmar Bergman tribute sites). To really exercise your color creativity, use your computer's color-picker, and select from the millions of colorful options available to computers today.

Hexadecimal notation is a way to represent web colors using a six-digit code, like this: #FE3400. (Hexadecimal notation is a system computers use for counting. In this system, you count like this: 0, 1, 2, 3, 4, 5, 6, 7, 8, 9, A, B, C, D, E, F. The # tells the computer that the following sequence is a series of hexadecimal numbers—in this case, three pairs of them.) The best way to learn a color's hex value is to choose the color you want by clicking on it in the palette and then looking at the code that Dreamweaver writes in the text box next to it. Hex colors comprise three pairs of numbers. For example, the number above, #FE3400, is really, FE, 34, and 00. Each pair represents a number for red, green, and blue color values, which, when combined, make up a color. You sometimes see only three numbers like this: #F00—that's shorthand used when both numbers in a pair are the same. For example, you can shorten #FF0011 to just #F01.

2. **Browse to the images folder in the Chapter01 folder, and then double-click the graphics file called banner.jpg.**

   The Image Tag Accessibility window appears. Fresh out of the box and onto your computer, Dreamweaver automatically turns on several accessibility preferences. They're designed to make your web pages more accessible to people who use alternative devices for viewing websites—for example, people with viewing disabilities who require special web browser software, such as a screen reader, which literally reads the contents of a web page out loud. Of course, images aren't words, so they can't be spoken. But you can identify an image by adding what's called an *alt* property. This is a text description of the graphic (an *alternative* to seeing the image) that's useful not only for screen-reading software, but for people who deliberately *turn off* pictures in their web browsers so web pages load faster. (Search engines also look at alt properties when they index a page, so an accurate alt description can help your site's search engine rankings.)

Note: If you don't see the Image Tag Accessibility window, press Ctrl+U (⌘-U) to open the Preferences panel, and then select the Accessibility category, turn on the Images checkbox, and then click OK.

---

3. **In the Alternate Text box, type *Chia Vet*. Click OK to add the image to the page.**

   The banner picture appears at the top of the page, as shown in Figure 1-27. A thin border appears around the image, indicating that you have it selected. Note that the Property inspector changes to reflect the properties of the selected item, the image in this case.

Note: You can also add or edit the *alt* text in the Property inspector (Figure 1-25).

---

4. **Deselect the image by clicking anywhere else in the document window, or by pressing the right arrow key.**

   Keep your keyboard's arrow keys in mind—they're a great way to deselect a page element *and* move your cursor into place to add text or more images.

5. **Press Enter to create a new paragraph. Type *Directions to Chia Vet Headquarters*.**

   Notice that the text is a dark color and uses the Tahoma (or, if you don't have Tahoma installed, the Geneva) font; you set these earlier, in the Page Properties dialog box. The Property inspector now displays text formatting options.

Note: The key called Enter on a Windows keyboard is named Return on most Macintosh keyboards. On the Mac, you can press either Return or Enter.

---

6. **In the Property inspector, click the HTML button, and then, from the Format menu, choose Heading 1 (see Figure 1-26).**

   The text you just typed becomes big and bold—the default style for Heading 1. This Format menu offers a number of different paragraph types. Right now, the text doesn't stand out enough, so you'll change its color next.

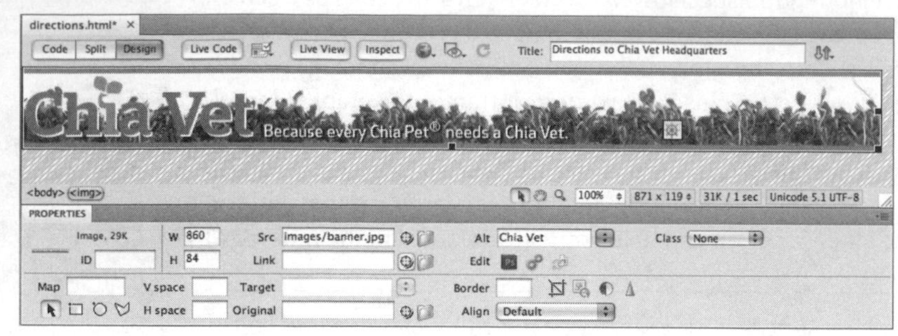

Figure 1-25: *When you select an image in the document window, the Property inspector reveals the image's dimensions. In the top-left corner of the inspector, a small thumbnail image appears, as does the word "Image" (to identify the type of element you selected) and the image's file size (in this case, 29 KB). You'll learn about other image properties in Chapter 6.*

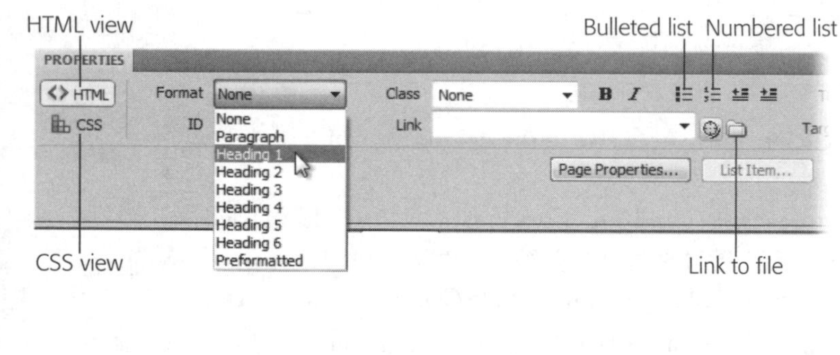

Figure 1-26: *The Property inspector includes two views: HTML and CSS. The HTML view, shown here, lets you control the HTML tags Dreamweaver applies to text: bulleted lists, paragraphs, links, and so on. The CSS view provides a simple interface for creating Cascading Style Sheets so you can format text to look great.*

7. **Select the text you just typed.**

   You can do so either by dragging carefully across the entire line or by triple-clicking anywhere inside the line. (Unlike the Format menu, which affects an entire *paragraph* at a time, many options in the Property inspector—like the one you'll use next—apply only to *selected* text.)

8. **In the Property inspector, click the CSS button to switch to CSS properties. From the "Targeted rule" menu, choose "New CSS Rule". In the color field in the Property inspector, replace the value that's listed with *#EC6206* (or select a color using the color box, if you prefer), and then hit Enter.**

The New CSS Rule window opens. This window (which you'll learn a lot more about in Chapter 4) lets you create new CSS styles. In this case, you'll create a type of style, called a tag style, which Dreamweaver will apply to any Heading 1 (or <h1> tag) on a page.

9. **From the top menu, select "Tag (redefines an HTML element)".**

   Notice that the field below that menu changes to display "h1". This is called a selector—and once you define its characteristics, it tells a web browser how to display any text that has an <h1> tag applied to it.

   Don't worry about any of the other settings in this window; you'll learn the details soon.

10. **Click OK.**

    Dreamweaver has just created a new CSS style. Now, wasn't that easy? Next you'll add more text.

11. **Click to the right of the heading text to deselect it. Press Enter to create a new paragraph below the headline.**

    Although you may type a headline now and again, you'll probably get most of your text from word processing documents or emails from your clients, boss, or coworkers. To get that text into Dreamweaver, you simply copy it from the document and paste it into your web page.

12. **In the Files panel, double-click the file directions.txt to open it.**

    This file is just plain text. No formatting, just words. To get it into your document, you'll copy and paste it.

13. **Click anywhere inside the text, and then choose Edit→Select All, followed by Edit→Copy. Click the directions.html tab to return to your web page and, finally, choose Edit→Paste.**

    You should see a few gold shields sprinkled among the text (circled in Figure 1-27). If you don't, make sure you complete step 3 on page 46. These shields represent line breaks—spots where text drops to the next line without creating a new paragraph. You'll often see these in pasted text. In this case, you need to remove them, and then create separate paragraphs.

14. **Click one of the gold shields, and then press Enter (Return). Repeat this for any other gold shields in the document window.**

    This deletes the line break in the document (it actually deletes the
 HTML tag) and creates two paragraphs out of one. At this point, the pasted text is just a series of paragraphs. To give it some structure, you'll add headings and two numbered lists.

15. **Click in the paragraph with the text line "Address". In the Property inspector, click the HTML button, and then choose Heading 2 from the Format menu.**

    This step changes the paragraph to a headline—making it bigger and bolder.

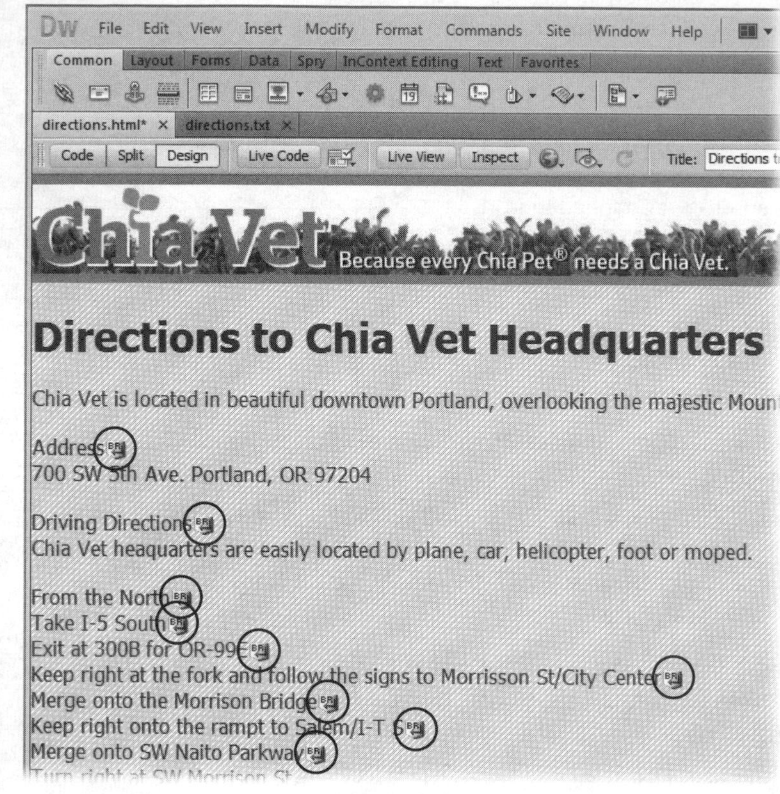

Figure 1-27: *Line breaks (circled) often crop up when you copy and paste text from other programs into Dreamweaver. Follow the steps on page 46 to make sure you can see the line breaks in Design view.*

16. **Repeat the last step for the lines of text "Driving Directions" and "For Geocachers" (near the end of the page).**

    You now have one heading 1 and three heading 2 headlines. To further structure the contents of this page, you'll add one last level of headlines.

17. **Click in the paragraph with the text line "From the North", and then choose Heading 3 in the Format menu. Repeat this step for the text "From the South".**

    To add a bit more style to this page, you'll format the heading 3 headlines next.

18. **Triple-click the headline "From the South" to select it. In the Property inspector, click the CSS button. In the field next to the color box, replace the color currently there with #779A00 and then hit Enter.**

    The New CSS Rule window appears again. Now you'll create a style for formatting <h3> tags.

19. **From the top menu, select "Tag (redefines an HTML element)".**

    You should see h3 in the middle field.

20. **Click OK.**

    Notice that the text changes to green. You'll see that the headline "From the North" is also green. The style you just created applies to all <h3> tags.

21. **Triple-click one of the green headlines. In the Property inspector, click the I (for Italic) button.**

    This action italicizes the text and updates the h3 style you created earlier—that's why the other Heading 3 headline is now italicized, too.

22. **Select the seven paragraphs under the "From the North" headline. For example, drag from the start of the first paragraph down to the end of the seventh paragraph.**

    You can also drag up starting from the end of the last paragraph. Either way, you've selected all seven paragraphs listing driving directions to Chia Vet headquarters.

23. **On the Property inspector, click the HTML button, and then click the Ordered List button (see Figure 1-26).**

    The paragraphs turn into a single, step-by-step, numbered list. You'll now do the same for the other set of directions.

24. **Repeat steps 22 and 23 for the six paragraphs below the "From the South" headline.**

    Now you see two numbered lists (called "ordered lists" in HTML-speak). Finally, you'll highlight the company name where it appears in the text.

25. **Near the top of the page, select "Chia Vet" at the beginning of the sentence that starts with "Chia Vet is located in".**

    You'll make the name bold.

26. **Make sure the HTML button is pressed in the Property inspector, and then click the B button.**

    The text changes appearance but the New CSS Rule window doesn't appear. Even though you find the B (for bold) button on both the HTML and CSS views of the Property inspector, they do different things. When you select the HTML B button, it inserts the HTML <strong> tag—used to "strongly" emphasize text. But when you press the CSS B button, it adds CSS code to make the text look bold. It's a subtle but important difference that you'll read about on page 106. In this case, you want to use the HTML <strong> tag to emphasize your company's name.

27. **Repeat step 26 for both the "Chia Vet" text that appears about halfway down the page and the text "*Chia-Vet.com*" at the very bottom of the page. Save the page.**

    You'll add a few more design touches remain to the page, but first you should see how the page looks in a real web browser.

FREQUENTLY ASKED QUESTION

The Mysterious Haunted Steering Wheel

When I select a paragraph, an image…heck, anything at all, in Design View, a weird icon appears. It looks like a ship's steering wheel. What is it and how do I get rid of it?

You click this steering-wheel icon to open the Code Navigator window. That window (described in detail on page 317) lists the CSS styles related to whatever page element you selected. It's useful for people who like to skip Dreamweaver's user-friendly CSS Styles panel to create and edit CSS, and who prefer to hand-edit their CSS code. If you're new to CSS, this isn't a useful tool and that goofy icon, which looks like something Ahab's ghost misplaced, gets in the way. To hide it, click the icon to open the Code Navigator and check the Disable box in the bottom-right of the Code Navigator window. If you ever want to turn it back on, choose View→Code Navigator to open the Code Navigator window and uncheck the Disable box.

Phase 5: Preview Your Work

Dreamweaver is as close as a web design program can get to a WYSIWYG application, meaning that for the most part, What You See (in the document window) Is What You Get (on the Web).

At least that's how it's supposed to work. But Dreamweaver may display *more* information than you'll see on the Web (including "invisible" objects and table borders) and may display *less* (it sometimes has trouble rendering complex designs).

Furthermore, much to the eternal woe of web designers, different browsers display pages differently. Pages you view in Internet Explorer don't always look the same in other browsers, like Firefox or Safari. In some cases, the differences may be subtle (for example, text may be slightly larger or smaller). In other cases, they can be dramatic: Some of the advanced page-layout techniques described in Chapter 10 can look *awful* in older browsers (you'll learn how to deal with many of these problems throughout this book).

Note: If you don't happen to have a Windows computer, a Mac, and every browser ever made, you can take advantage of Adobe's BrowserLab service, which takes screenshots of your page in a variety of browsers running on a variety of operating systems. You'll learn about BrowserLab on page 667.

If you're designing web pages for a company intranet and only have to worry about the one web browser your IT department puts on everyone's computer, you're lucky. Most people have to deal with the fact that their sites must withstand scrutiny from a wide range of browsers, so it's a good idea to preview your web pages using whatever browsers you expect your visitors to use. Fortunately, Dreamweaver lets you preview a web page using any browser you have installed on your computer.

One quick way to check a page in a web browser is to use Dreamweaver's built-in Live View feature, which lets you preview a page using a browser that's built into Dreamweaver.

1. **In the Document toolbar, click the Live View button (circled in Figure 1-28).**

   The Live View button highlights. The page doesn't look that different—for a simple page like this it won't, but Live View is great for testing JavaScript interactivity, like the kind provided by Dreamweaver's Spry tools, such as the Spry Menu Bar (page 184), and for previewing more complex CSS.

   There is one problem with the Live View feature: it uses WebKit (the main engine behind Apple's Safari browser and Google's Chrome browser). This isn't the most common web browser, so it's not how most visitors will view your site. You want to test your page designs in other browsers, too. Fortunately, Dreamweaver makes it easy to jump straight to any web browser installed on your computer.

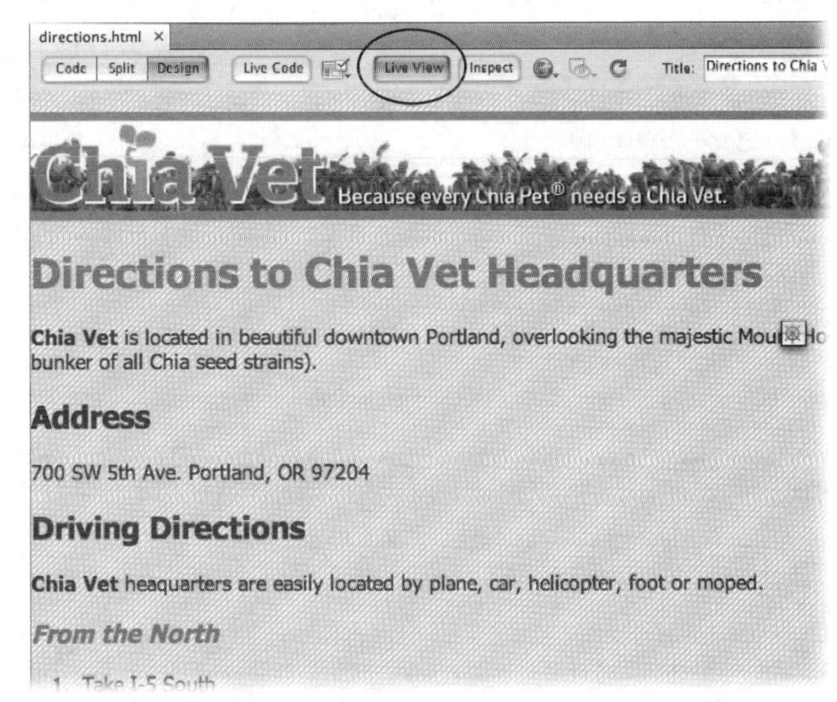

Figure 1-28: *The Live View feature lets you preview a page in a real web browser built into Dreamweaver.*

2. **Click the Live View button again to exit Live View.**

   This is an important and easily overlooked step. When you're in Live View, you can't edit a page. Since a page in Live View can look very much like it does in Design View, it's easy to try to work on the page while you're in Live View and say "Hey, what's going on? Dreamweaver isn't working any more!" So, always remember to exit Live View when it's time to work on your pages.

To preview your page in a web browser, you need to make sure Dreamweaver knows which browsers you have installed and where they are.

3. **Choose File→"Preview in Browser"→Edit Browser List.**

   The "Preview in Browser" preferences window opens (see Figure 1-29). When you install Dreamweaver, it detects browsers installed on your computer; a list of them appears in this window. If you installed a browser after you installed Dreamweaver, then it doesn't appear in this list, so you need to follow steps 2 and 3 next; otherwise, skip to step 4.

4. **Click the + button.**

   The Add Browser or Select Browser window opens.

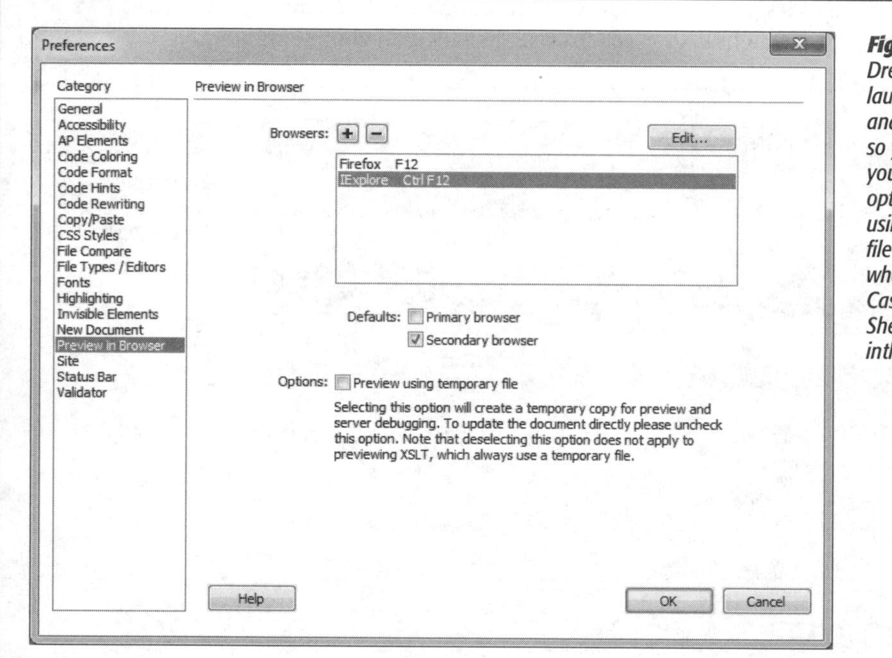

Figure 1-29: *Dreamweaver can launch a web browser and load a page in it so you can preview your design. One option—"Preview using temporary file"—comes in handy when you work with Cascading Style Sheets, as described in the Note on page 156.*

5. **Click the Browse button. Search your hard drive to find the browser you want to add to this list.**

   Dreamweaver inserts the browser's default name in the Name field of the Add Browser window. If you wish to change its name for display purposes within Dreamweaver, select it, and then type in a new name. (But don't do this *before* you select the browser, since Dreamweaver erases anything you typed as soon as you select a browser.)

6. **In the window's Browser list, select the browser you most commonly use. Turn on the Primary Browser box. Click OK.**

   You just designated this browser as your *primary* one when you work in Dreamweaver. You can now preview your pages in this browser with a simple keyboard shortcut: F12 (Option-F12 on a Mac).

   If you like, you can also choose a secondary browser, which you can launch by pressing the Ctrl+F12 (⌘-F12) key combination.

   Now you're ready to preview your document in your favorite web browser. Fortunately, Dreamweaver makes it easy.

7. **Press the F12 key (Option F12 on a Mac) or choose File→ "Preview in Browser" and, from the menu, select a browser.**

   The F12 key (Option-F12 on Mac) is the most important keyboard shortcut you'll learn. Macintosh fans: Unfortunately, Apple has assigned the F12 key to the Dashboard program, so it takes two keys to preview the page—Option and F12 together (however, you can change this by creating your own keyboard shortcuts, as described on page 817). This keyboard shortcut opens the web page in your primary browser, so you can preview your work.

   If you're using a Macintosh laptop, you may have to press Option-F12 and the function (fn) key in the lower-left corner of the keyboard.

   You can also use the "Preview in Browser" menu in the document window to preview a page (see Figure 1-30).

Note: If you use the Preview in Browser menu (see Figure 1-30) to select one of the browsers installed on your computer, you'll notice two other options: "Preview in Device Central" and "Preview in Adobe BrowserLab". The first option, Device Central, is a program that lets you preview web pages in mobile devices. Since the there are many different mobile devices using many different web browsers, mobile web design can be tricky, and Device Central isn't 100 percent accurate for all mobile devices. However, it's good for previewing Flash-based sites that target mobile devices. You'll learn about the Adobe BrowserLab option in depth on page 667.

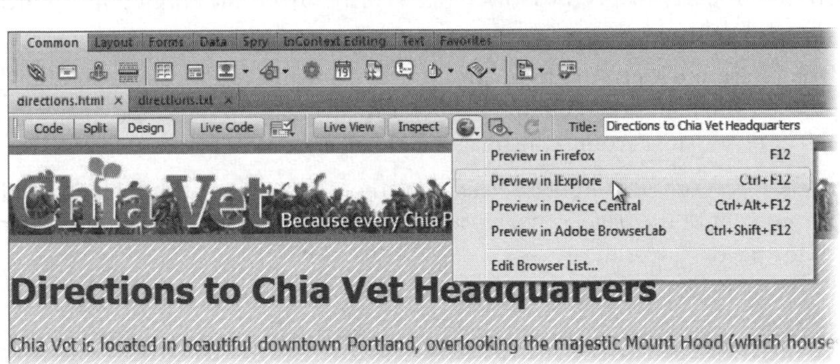

Figure 1-30: *The "Preview in Browser" menu in the document window is another way to preview a page. This menu has the added benefit of letting you select any browser on your computer, not just the ones you assigned keyboard shortcuts.*

8. **When you're done previewing the page, go back to Dreamweaver.**

   Do so using your favorite way to switch programs on your computer—by using the Windows taskbar, or the Dock in Mac OS X.

Phase 6: Finishing the Page

You've covered most of the steps you need to finish this web page. Now you just need to add a graphic, format the copyright notice, and provide a little more structure to the appearance of the page.

1. **In the "Address" headline, click just before the "A".**

   This step places the cursor at the beginning of the headline. You'll insert a graphic here.

2. **From the Common category on the Insert panel, click the Image button (see Figure 1-24).**

   You can also choose Insert→Image or use the keyboard shortcut Ctrl+Alt+I (⌘-Alt-I).

3. **Browse to the images folder in the Chapter01 folder, and double-click the graphics file called portland.jpg.**

   Again, the Image Tag Accessibility window appears. You need to provide a good description for this image.

Note to Windows Users: As noted above (page 53) Windows doesn't display a file's extension (unless you tell it to). So when you navigate to the *images* folder in step 3 above, you might see *portland* instead of *portland.jpg*.

---

4. **Type Portland skyline, and then press OK.**

   Look at the Property inspector. It displays properties specific to images. You'll learn more about these options in Chapter 6, but now you'll learn a quick way to make text wrap around an image.

5. **In the Property inspector's lower-right corner, from the Align pop-up menu, choose Right.**

   The image moves to the right edge of the page and text wraps around its left side. (If you chose the Left option, Dreamweaver would move the image to the left and wrap text around the image's right side.)

   Look for a copyright notice at the bottom of the page. It's not really related to the content of the page, so you'll add a line to visually separate it from the rest of the page.

Note: Although the left and right options for an image's align property are quick ways to force text to wrap around an image, they aren't valid options for the "strict" versions of HTML or XHTML (see page 7). CSS provides a more flexible technique–known as a *float*–to achieve this same effect. You'll learn about it on page 228.

6. **Scroll to the bottom of the page, click before the letter C in "Copyright 2009", and then choose Insert→HTML→Horizontal Rule.**

   A gray line appears above the copyright notice. The copyright appears a little big, so you'll format it next.

Tip: You can also add a line above a paragraph of text using the CSS *border* property. See page 230.

7. **Select all the text in the copyright paragraph.**

   You can either triple-click inside the paragraph or drag from the beginning of the paragraph to the end.

8. **Click the CSS button in the Property inspector, and then, from the Size menu, choose 12.**

   The New CSS Rule window opens again. This time you want to create a style that applies only to this one paragraph of text—not every paragraph—so you need to use what's called a class style.

9. **Leave the default setting, "Class (can apply to any HTML element)", for the Selector Type box, type .copyright in the selector field (circled in Figure 1-31), and then click OK.**

   Class names begin with a period—that's how browsers identify the CSS style as a class. Notice that the copyright notice text gets smaller.

   The legal department of Chia Vet headquarters has decided that every page on the site must link to an official corporate statement. You'll add a link for that next.

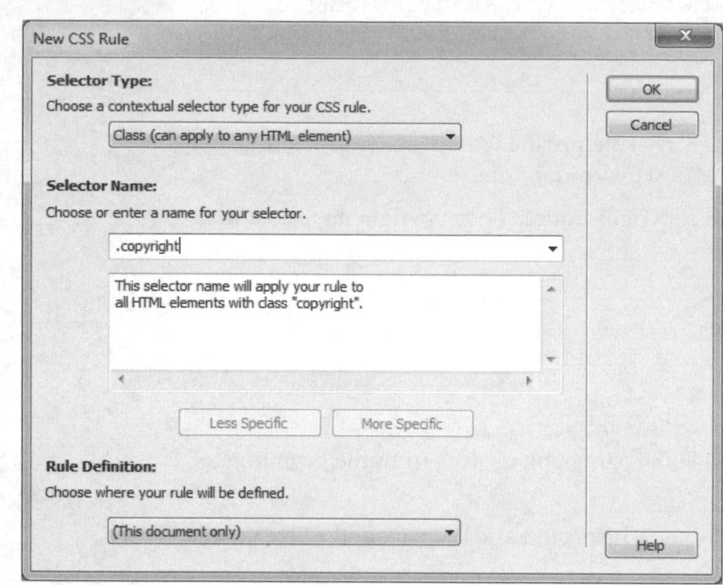

Figure 1-31: *The New CSS Rule window lets you create CSS styles. You can choose among many different types of styles. In this case, you're creating a class style named ".copyright". Class styles work a lot like styles in word processors–to use them, you select the text you want to format, and then apply the style.*

10. **At the bottom of the page, select the text "Read our full legal statement".**

    To create a link, you just need to tell Dreamweaver which page you want to link to. You can do this several ways. Using the Property inspector is the easiest.

11. **In the Property inspector, click the HTML button; click the folder icon that appears to the right of the link field (see Figure 1-26).**

    The Select File dialog box appears.

12. **Click the Site Root button (top of the dialog box in Windows; bottom of dialog box on a Mac), and double click the file named *legal.html*.**

    The Site Root button jumps you right to the folder containing your site. It's a convenient way to move quickly to your root folder. Double-clicking the file tells Dreamweaver to insert the HTML needed to create a link.

    If you preview the page in a web browser, it looks all right…well, not really. The text is kind of hard to read against the blue striped background, it's too wide if you expand your web browser on a large monitor, and the photo is hanging way out on the right-hand side of the browser. To fix these problems, you'll create a new layout element—a box to contain all the content on the page.

13. **Click anywhere inside the page, and then choose Edit→Select All or press Ctrl+A (⌘-A on a Mac).**

    You selected the entire contents of the page. You'll wrap all text and images in a <div> tag to create a kind of container for the page contents.

14. **Choose Insert→Layout Objects→Div Tag.**

    The Insert Div Tag window opens (see Figure 1-32). A <div> tag simply provides a way to organize content on a page by grouping HTML—think of it as a box containing other HTML tags. For example, to create a sidebar of navigation links, news headlines, and Google ads, you would wrap them all in a <div> tag. It's a very important tag for CSS-based layouts. You'll read more about the <div> tag on page 331.

    Next, you need to create a style that provides the instructions needed to format this new <div> tag. You've already used the Property inspector to create a style, but that works only for text. To format other tags, you need to create a style in another way.

15. **Click the New CSS Rule button at the bottom of the Insert Div Tag window.**

    The New CSS Rule window appears (a CSS style is technically called a "rule"). This window lets you specify the type of style you create, the style's name, and where Dreamweaver should store the style information. You'll learn all the ins and outs of this window in Chapter 4.

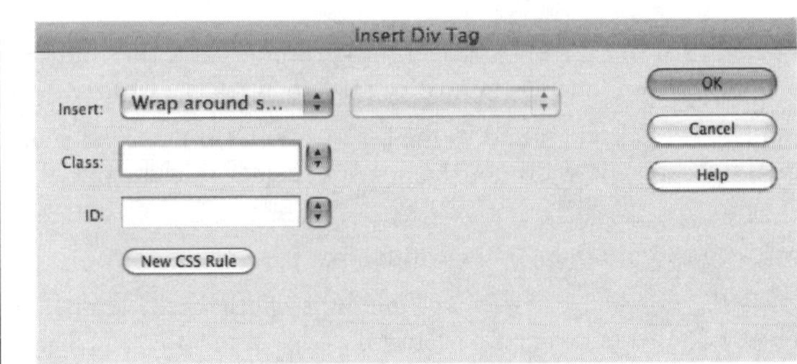

Figure 1-32: *The Insert Div Tag window provides an easy way to divide sections of a web page into groups of related HTML–like the elements that make up a banner, for example. You'll learn about all the different functions of this window on page 333.*

16. **From the top menu, choose ID, and then type #wrapper in the "Choose or enter a name" field. Make sure you have "This document only" selected in the bottom menu. Click OK,**

    The "CSS Rule definition" window appears (see Figure 1-33). (There's a lot going on in this box, but don't worry about the details at this point. You'll learn everything there is to know about creating styles later in this book. This part of the tutorial is intended to give you a taste of some of a web designer's daily page-building duties. So relax and follow along.)

    This window is the command center for defining the formatting properties, such as text color, font, and size, for a style. CSS has quite a few properties, which Dreamweaver divides into eight categories. First, you'll add a background color for this <div> element.

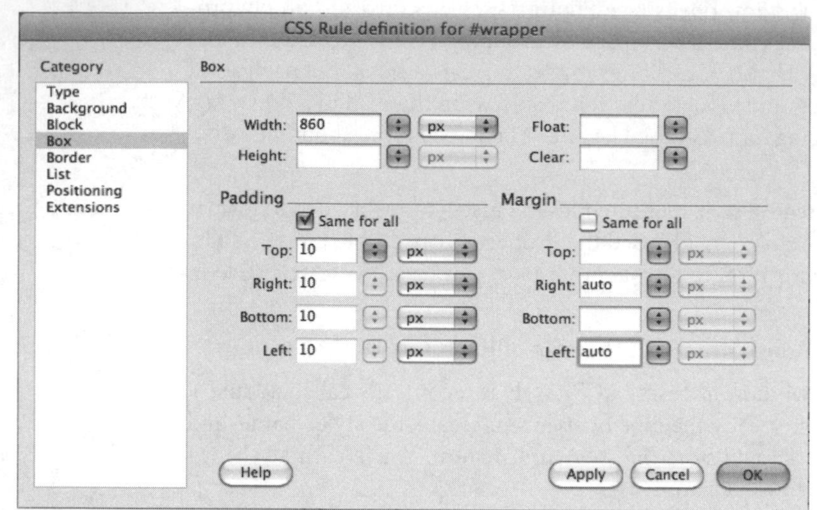

Figure 1-33: *The "CSS Rule definition" window lets you set over 60 CSS properties (divided into eight categories) that control the formatting of everything from text to images to entire web pages.*

17. **From the left-hand list of categories, select Background. Click the color box that appears to the right of "Background-color", and then select a white swatch.**

    This action adds a white background to the box, making sure the text stands out. Next you'll set a specific width for the box, and center it in the middle of the browser window.

18. **Click the Box category, and then, in the width box, type *860*.**

    This step makes the box 860 pixels wide—the same width as the banner. To make sure the text doesn't butt right up against the edge of the box, you'll add a little space (called *padding*) around the inside of this style.

19. **In the Top box under Padding, type *10* (make sure the "Same for all" checkbox is turned on).**

    This action adds 10 pixels of space inside the box, essentially pushing the text and the graphics away from the edges of the box.

20. **Under the Margin settings, uncheck the "Same for all" box, and then, from both the right and left margin menus, select "auto".**

    The auto property for the right and left margin is your way of telling a web browser to automatically supply a left and right margin—in this case, as you'll see in a moment, it has the effect of centering the <div> element in the middle of a browser window.

21. **The CSS Rule Definition window should now look like Figure 1-33. Click OK to complete the style.**

    The Insert Div Tag window reappears, and the name of the style you just created—"wrapper"—appears in a box labeled ID.

22. **In the Insert Div Tag window, click OK.**

    This inserts the new <div> tag and at the same time applies the style you just created. Now it's time to take a look at your handiwork.

23. **Choose File→Save. Press the F12 key (Option-F12 on a Mac) to preview your work in your browser (Figure 1-34).**

    Test the link to make sure it works. Resize your browser and watch how the page content centers itself in the middle of the window.

Congratulations! You've just built your first web page in Dreamweaver, complete with graphics, formatted text, and links. If you want to compare your work with the finished product, go to Chapter01_finished in the Tutorials folder and load the file *directions.html*.

Much of the work of building websites involves using the procedures covered in this tutorial—defining a site, adding links, formatting text, placing graphics, creating styles, and inserting divs. The next few chapters cover these basics in greater depth and introduce other important tools, tips, and techniques for using Dreamweaver to build great web pages.

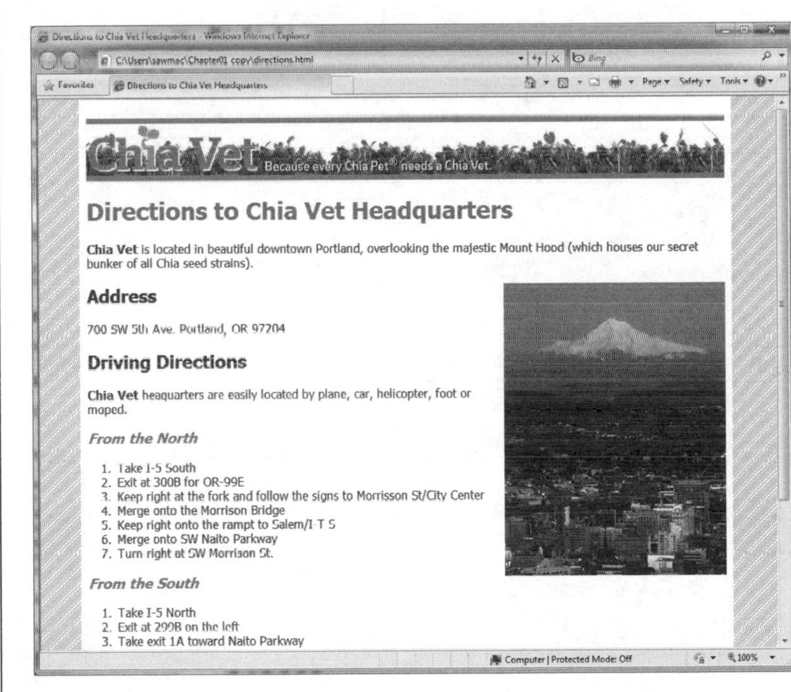

Figure 1-34: *The finished tutorial file should look like this.*

Tip: To get a full description of every Dreamweaver menu in a handy, printable PDF, go to this book's Missing CD page (*www.missingmanuals.com/cds*) and download Appendix B, "Menu by Menu Commands."

CHAPTER

2

Adding Text to Your Web Pages

Nowadays, streaming video, audio, and high-quality graphics are what draw most people to websites. After all, it's exciting to hear the latest song from your favorite band, see a preview of a yet-to-be released blockbuster, or tune in to YouTube to see the kid down the street embarrass himself in front of a billion Web viewers.

But the fact is, the Web is primarily woven with *words*. iPad reviews, Brad Pitt and Angelina Jolie gossip, and countless personal blogs about cats still drive people to the Web. As you build web pages and websites, you'll spend a lot of your time adding and formatting *text*. To get your message across effectively, you need to understand how Dreamweaver works with text.

This chapter covers the not-always-simple act of getting text *into* your Dreamweaver documents. In Chapter 3, you'll read about formatting this text so that it looks professionally designed.

Adding Text in Dreamweaver

In many ways, Dreamweaver works like a word processing program. When you create a new document, the blinking cursor appears at the top of the page, ready for you to begin typing. When you finish a paragraph, you press Enter or Return to start a new one. Text, as well as anything else you add to a web page, starts at the top of the page and works its way to the bottom. But you can't type in some kinds of characters, like a copyright symbol, from the keyboard, and other kinds, like a nonbreaking space, require special keyboard combinations. Here's how to access those special characters.

Adding Special Characters

Many useful special characters—such as copyright or trademark symbols—don't appear on your keyboard, making them difficult or impossible to type. Dreamweaver's Insert bar's Text tab lets you use a variety of symbols and international characters quickly by clicking an icon.

To open the Text tab:

1. **On the Insert panel, choose the Text category.**

   If you can't see the Insert panel, choose Window→Insert to open it, or use the keyboard shortcut Ctrl+F2 (⌘-F2).

   The panel shown in Figure 2-1 appears. Many of the options let you add common HTML tags like the <b> (bold) and <strong> (strong) tags, most of which you can apply more easily using the Property inspector or keyboard shortcuts, as discussed in the next chapter. This panel also features less frequently used tags like <abbr> (abbreviation) or <dl> (definition list). You can satisfy your curiosity about these tags by using Dreamweaver's HTML reference (see page 448), but their names give you an idea of when you might want to use them.

   The last option on the panel is actually a menu that offers a wide range of symbols and international characters. Unlike regular Western characters, such as *a* or *z*, Dreamweaver represents these special characters in HTML by a code name or number. For instance, Dreamweaver adds the trademark symbol (™) as *™* in a page's HTML (another way to write this symbol in HTML is like this: ™).

Tip: If you like card games or just want to add a heart to a web page without using a graphic, choose the Other Characters option from the Insert panel, as pictured in Figure 2-1, and type *♥* to get a heart character, *♦* for a diamond, *♠* for a spade, or *♣* for a club. (Don't forget the semicolon at the end of each–that's part of the code).

---

2. **From the menu at the end of the Insert panel, select the symbol you want to insert (see Figure 2-1).**

   Dreamweaver inserts the appropriate HTML code into your web page. (Alternatively, you can select the Other Characters option to bring up the wider-ranging Insert Other Character dialog box shown in Figure 2-1.)

Note: If you set the encoding of your page to anything other than Western European or Unicode (UTF-8) in the Page Properties window (by choosing Modify→Page Properties, and then clicking the Title/ Encoding category), you can reliably insert only line breaks and nonbreaking spaces. The other special characters available from the Character category of the Objects panel may not work (see the box on page 87 for more about how encoding works).

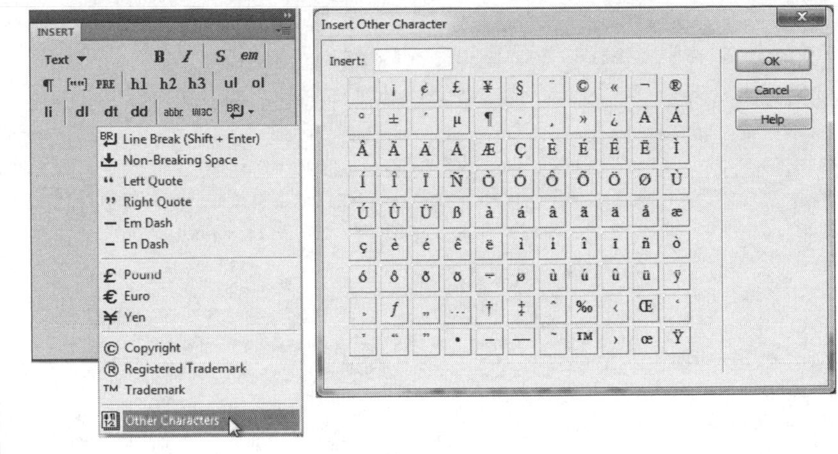

***Figure 2-1:** Selecting Other Characters from the Text panel (left) brings up the Insert Other Character dialog box (right). However, there are even more characters in the Western alphabet than this dialog box lists. You can find a table listing these characters and their associated entity names and numbers at* www.evolt.org/article/ala/17/21234/.

Line Breaks

Pressing Enter creates a new paragraph, exactly like in a word processor. Unfortunately, Web browsers add extra space above and below paragraphs—which is a real nuisance if you're trying to create several single-spaced lines of text, like this:

702 A Street
Boring, OR
97009 USA

Here, each part of the address is on its own line, but it's still just a single paragraph (and shares the overall formatting of that paragraph, as you'll learn in the next chapter).

Tip: If you want to *entirely* dispense with the space that browsers insert between paragraphs, don't use line breaks each time. Instead, use CSS to eliminate the top and bottom margins of the <p> tag, as described in the Tip on page 140.

To create this single-spaced effect, you need to insert a *line break* at the insertion point, using one of these techniques:

- Press Shift+Enter.
- On the Insert panel's Text category, from the Characters menu, select Line Break (the first menu option at top in Figure 2-1).
- Choose Insert→ HTML→ Special Characters→Line Break.

POWER USERS' CLINIC

Keyboard Shortcuts for Special Characters

Dreamweaver uses UTF-8 (also called Unicode) encoding when you create a new page (unless you specify otherwise). Without getting into the messy details, basically UTF-8 lets you include almost any type of character available to the languages of the world–it lets a Chinese speaker embed actual Chinese characters into a page, for example. When you use the Other Characters window (Figure 2-1), Dreamweaver inserts what's called an HTML entity–a code that replaces the real character: for example, the © symbol is represented by *©*. But UTF-8 lets you add the actual symbol to a page–the trick is knowing how to do that with the keyboard.

On the Mac, you have a handful of keyboard shortcuts for directly typing a special character like a curly quote mark onto a page. Here are a few of the most common: Option+; to get a true ellipsis (three periods in a row); Option+Shift+- for an em-dash (–); Option+] for opening single quote ('); Option+Shift+] for closing single quote ('); Option+[for opening double-quote ("); Option+Shift+[for closing double-quote ("); and Option+G for a copyright symbol(©). You can also use the Mac Character Palette to insert unusual symbols using Unicode (for information on the Mac character palette visit *www.apple.com/pro/techniques/glyphspalette*).

In Windows, you must press the Alt key, type the Unicode value using your keyboard's numeric keypad, and then release the Alt key. Note that you can't use the regular number keys for this–you must use the numeric keypad. For example, to add an ellipsis, hold down the Alt key, type *0133*, and then release the Alt key. Here are a few others: open single quote is Alt+0145; closing single quote is Alt+0146; opening double-quote is Alt+0147; and closing double-quote is Alt+0148. But, it's easier to just use the Windows character map to insert special symbols and characters. (Visit *http://tinyurl.com/5blqek* to learn how to use the Windows character map.)

Note: When you insert a line break in Dreamweaver, you may get no visual hint that it's even there; after all, a regular paragraph break and a line break both create a new line of text.

This scenario is especially likely if you copy text from programs other than Microsoft Word or Excel. Text from other programs–especially email programs–can be loaded with an infuriating number of line breaks. To add to the confusion, a line break may go unnoticed if it occurs at the end of a long line. Your only hope is to make line breaks visible.

To do so, choose Edit→Preferences (or Dreamweaver→Preferences on the Mac), or press Ctrl+U (⌘-U). Click the Invisible Elements category. Make sure the Line Breaks checkbox is turned on. Now you see each line break appear as a small gold shield. (If after doing this, you still don't see the line break character, choose View→Visual Aids, and make sure the Invisible Elements checkbox is turned on.)

You can select a line break by clicking the shield, and then delete it like any page element. Better yet, select the shield, and then hit Enter or Return, to eliminate the line break *and* create a new paragraph.

Another way to avoid pasting some hidden line breaks is the Paste Special command (see page 80).

Nonbreaking Spaces

Sometimes the way a sentence breaks over two lines in your text can distort what you're trying to say, as shown in Figure 2-2. In this case, a *nonbreaking space* can save the day. It looks just like a regular space, but it acts as glue that prevents the words on either side from being split apart at the end of a line. For example, adding a nonbreaking space between the words "Farmer" and "Says" in Figure 2-2 ensures that those words won't get split across a line break, and helps clarify the presentation and meaning of this headline.

To insert a nonbreaking space between two words, delete the regular space already between the words (for example, by clicking after the space and pressing the backspace key), and then do one of the following:

- Press Ctrl+Shift+Space bar (⌘-Shift-Space bar).
- On the Insert panel's Text category, from the Characters menu, select Non-Breaking Space (the second menu option in Figure 2-1, left).
- Choose Insert→HTML→Special Characters→Non-Breaking Space.

Hybrid potato is edible farmer says.
Hybrid potato is edible farmer says.

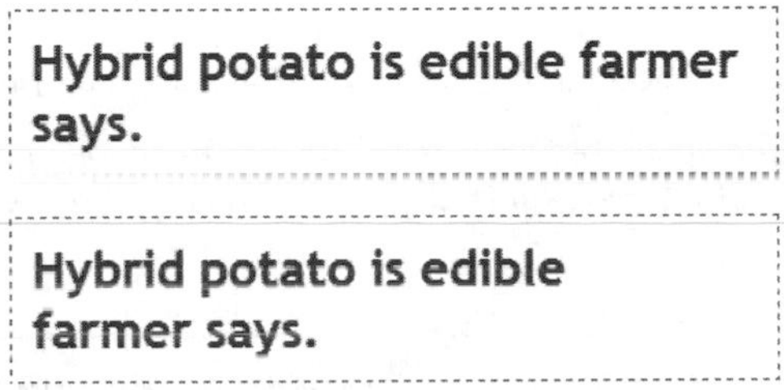

Figure 2-2:
Headlines sometimes split between lines leaving a single word alone on a line (top)–in typography this is known as a "widow." Adding a nonbreaking space (bottom) can prevent widows and clarify a headline's meaning.

Multiple Spaces

You may have noticed that if you type more than one space in a row, Dreamweaver ignores all but the first space. This isn't a glitch in the program; it's standard HTML. Web browsers ignore any spaces following the first one.

Therefore, a line like "Beware   of   llama," with several spaces between each word, would appear on a web page like this: "Beware of llama." Not only do Web browsers ignore multiple spaces, but they also ignore any spaces that aren't *between* words. So if you hit the space bar a couple of times to indent the first line of a paragraph, you're wasting your time. A Web browser doesn't display any of those spaces (Dreamweaver doesn't display those spaces either).

This feature makes good sense, because it prevents web pages from being littered with extraneous spaces that many people insert when writing HTML code. (Extra spaces in a page of HTML often make the code easier to read.)

There may be times, however, when you *want* to add more space between words. For example, consider the text navigation bar at the bottom of a web page, a common web page element that lists the different sections of a website. Visitors can click one of the section titles to jump directly to a different area of the site. For clarity, many designers like to add multiple spaces between the text links, like this:

News   Classifieds   Jobs

Or, you may want to add space at the beginning of the first line of a paragraph to create the kind of indent that's common to paragraphs in some books (but not this one). One simple way to add space is to insert multiple nonbreaking spaces as described in the previous section. A Web browser *will* display every nonbreaking space it encounters, so you can add multiple nonbreaking spaces between words, letters, or even at the beginning of paragraphs. This technique has a few downsides, though: You have to type a bunch of nonbreaking spaces, which takes work, and adds code to your web page, making it download a bit slower.

You can enlist Cascading Style Sheets (CSS) to add space as well. While you won't get in-depth detail on CSS until Chapter 4, here are a few CSS properties (formatting rules) to tuck in the back of your mind when you need to add space to your text:

- To indent the first line of a paragraph, use the *text indent* property (page 142).
- To add space between words in a paragraph, use the *word spacing* property (page 140).
- To increase or decrease the space between letters, use *letter spacing* (page 140).
- And, if you want to increase the space between text links as in the example above, you can add either left and right *margins* or *padding* to each link (page 341).

Note: If you often add multiple spaces, Dreamweaver offers a shortcut. Choose Edit→Preferences to open Dreamweaver's Preferences window (on a Mac, choose Dreamweaver→Preferences instead). Click the General category. Then, under "Editing options", turn on "Allow multiple consecutive spaces". Now, whenever you press the space bar more than once, Dreamweaver inserts *nonbreaking* spaces.

In fact, Dreamweaver is even smarter than that. It inserts a regular space if you press the space bar just once, a nonbreaking space followed by a regular space if you hit the space bar twice, and a nonbreaking space followed by a regular space followed by multiple nonbreaking spaces if you hit the space bar repeatedly. Since nonbreaking spaces act like glue that keeps words stuck together (see the previous section), the extra regular spaces let the lines break normally, if necessary.

Adding a Date to Your Page

The Insert panel's Common category offers an icon called Date (it looks like the page of a calendar). Clicking this icon or choosing Insert→Date opens the Insert Date dialog box (Figure 2-3), which lets you insert today's date, as your computer understands it, onto your web page in progress. You can also specify whether to include the day of the week and the current time.

Select the format you wish from the Date Format list. You have 13 different formats to choose from, such as March 7, 1974 or 3/7/74.

You may wonder why Dreamweaver includes an insert-date function anyway. How hard is it to type *Thursday, July 12*?

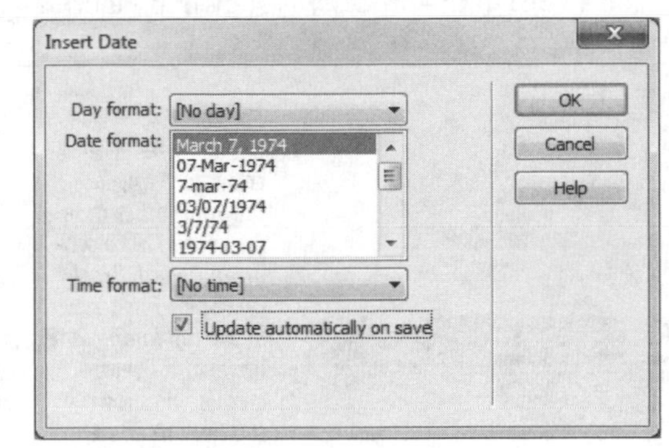

Figure 2-3:
When you insert a Date object (a placeholder for the actual date) onto a web page, you have several additional options: If you want to add the day of the week, choose the format you want from the "Day format" pop-up menu. You may also choose to add the current time in hours and minutes–in either military time (22:18) or regular time (10:18 PM)–from the "Time format" pop-up menu.

Actually, the real value of the Insert Date feature lies in the "Update automatically on save" checkbox. Choosing this option forces Dreamweaver to *update* the date each time you save the document.

You can use this feature to stamp a web page with a date that indicates when the contents were last updated. For example, you might type *This page was last revised on:* and then choose Insert→Date and select the "Update automatically on save" option. Now, each time you make a change to the page, Dreamweaver automatically changes the date to reflect when you saved the document. You never again have to worry about it.

Copying and Pasting Text

If you're building websites as part of a team or for clients, your writers are likely to send you their copy in the form of word processing documents. If the text comes in a Microsoft Word document or Excel spreadsheet, you're lucky. Dreamweaver includes commands for pasting text from these two types of files. If you're using Windows, you can even import those kinds of files directly into a web page using File→Import→Word/Excel Document (see page 84).

Simple Copy and Paste

For non-Microsoft-spawned text, you can, of course, still simply copy and paste, like generations of web designers before you.

Open the document in whatever program created it—WordPad, TextEdit, your email program, or whatever. Select the text you want (by dragging through it, for example), or choose Edit→Select All (Ctrl+A [⌘-A]) to highlight all text in the document. Then choose Edit→Copy, or press Ctrl+C (⌘-C), to copy it. Switch to Dreamweaver, click in the document window where you wish the text to go, and then choose Edit→Paste (Ctrl+V [⌘-V]).

This routine pastes the text into place. Unfortunately, you lose all text formatting (font type, size, color, bold, italic, and so on) in the process, as shown in Figure 2-4.

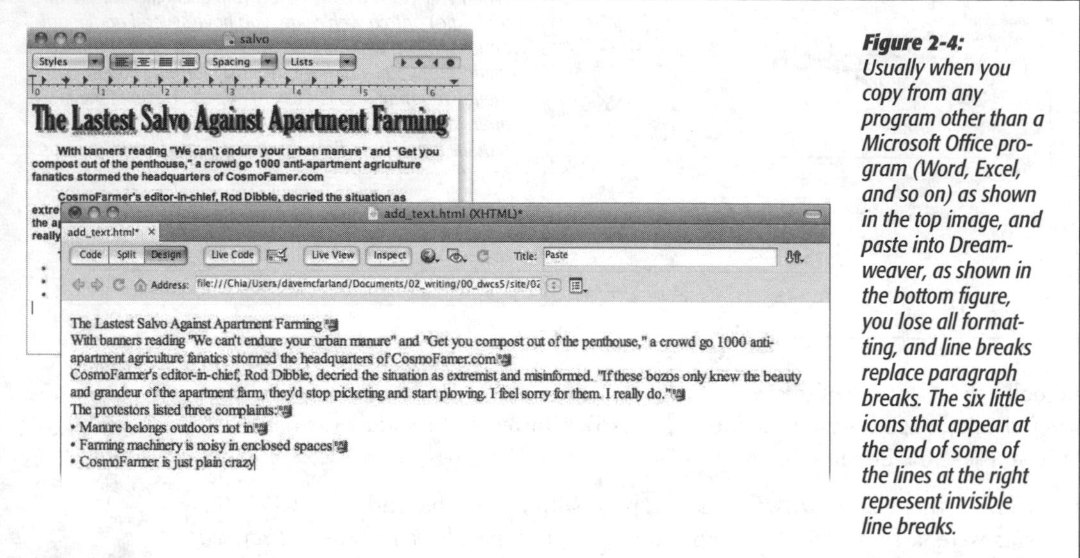

Figure 2-4: *Usually when you copy from any program other than a Microsoft Office program (Word, Excel, and so on) as shown in the top image, and paste into Dreamweaver, as shown in the bottom figure, you lose all formatting, and line breaks replace paragraph breaks. The six little icons that appear at the end of some of the lines at the right represent invisible line breaks.*

Furthermore, you may find the pasted paragraphs separated by line break characters, not standard carriage returns. Strangely enough, this means that when you paste in a series of paragraphs, Dreamweaver treats them as though they were one gargantuan paragraph. These line break characters can pose problems when you try to format what you *think* is a single paragraph. To identify these line breaks, see the Note on page 76.

Tip: If you *have* to copy and paste text from non-Microsoft programs, you do have one way to get paragraphs (and not just lines separated by the line break character) when you paste into Dreamweaver. Just make sure whoever's typing up the original documents inserts an empty paragraph between each paragraph of text. Pressing Enter (or Return) twice at the end of a paragraph does that. When you copy and paste, Dreamweaver removes the empty paragraphs *and* pastes the text as regular paragraphs.

Paste Special

Dreamweaver also includes a Paste Special command that supports four different paste methods, ranging from plain text to highly formatted HTML. In actual use, however, Dreamweaver supports only the first two for *all* pasting operations. The last two are available only when pasting from Microsoft Word or Excel.

- Text only. This option is the most basic of all. It pastes text without any formatting whatsoever. Dreamweaver even ignores paragraphs and line breaks, so you end up with essentially one long sentence. Though you won't want this effect often, it can come in handy when you copy a long paragraph of text from an email program that's added unnecessary line breaks at the end of each line of email text.
- Text with structure. Dreamweaver tries to preserve the structure of the text, including paragraphs, headers, bulleted lists, and so on. This option doesn't retain any formatting applied to text, such as boldface or italic. You'll use this option with most non-Microsoft Office copied text. In most cases, however, Dreamweaver ends up preserving only paragraphs, and misses bulleted lists and headers.
- Basic formatting. When pasting with Basic formatting, Dreamweaver includes the same elements as the "Text with structure" option, but also includes text formatting such as boldface, italic, and underlining. This is the method Dreamweaver uses when pasting Microsoft Word or Excel information, as described in the next section.
- Full formatting. This option includes everything offered by Basic formatting, but also attempts to paste CSS information that can control the font size and color, paragraph margins, and more. Full formatting is available only when you copy and paste from Word or Excel (see the next section).

Note to Windows Users: You can copy an entire page of HTML from Firefox or Internet Explorer, and then paste it into Dreamweaver. Click inside a web page, press Ctrl+A to select the entire page, and then press Ctrl+C to copy the HTML. Then switch to Dreamweaver, click inside an empty page, and press Ctrl+V to paste. Dreamweaver copies all the HTML, and, sometimes, even graphics. This text comes in with "full formatting," but note that no style sheets come along for the ride.

You can override Dreamweaver's default behavior and choose a different paste method with the Paste Special command. Choose Edit→Paste Special to open the Paste Special window (see Figure 2-5). Here, you can choose which of the four techniques you wish to use…sort of. You're limited to what Dreamweaver can paste. For non-Microsoft Office products, you can use only the first two options—the others are grayed out—whereas you can choose from any of the four with text copied from Word or Excel.

For text copied from most programs, it's best to use "Text with structure" and keep the "Retain line breaks" checkbox turned on. You still have to manually replace line breaks with paragraphs as described in the Note on page 76, but without the "Retain line breaks" option selected, Dreamweaver removes single hard returns, resulting in one long paragraph of text.

For Word or Excel information, there are a few options worth considering, as described next.

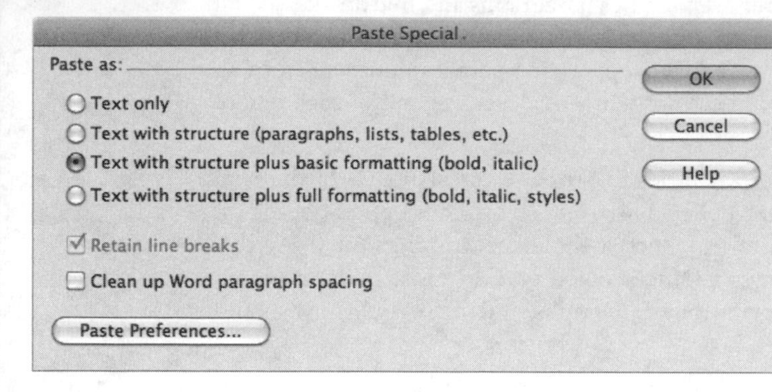

Figure 2-5: *The Paste Special command lets you paste text copied from other programs. If you want Dreamweaver to apply the same setting each time you use the Paste Special command, click the Paste Preferences button. This opens the Preferences window. Select whatever settings–Basic formatting, for example–that you want Dreamweaver to apply every time you use the Paste Special command.*

Pasting Text from Word: The Basic Method

While text from other applications doesn't retain much beyond paragraph formatting when pasted into Dreamweaver, Dreamweaver includes both basic and advanced ways to copy and paste Word text.

Frequently, you'll just want to preserve basic formatting, like bold or italic text, headlines, and bulleted lists. You won't need (and in most cases, won't want) more extravagant formatting, like different fonts, colors, or margin settings. After all, you're the Web designer, and you'll use your own design sense—and Dreamweaver's CSS-based formatting tools—to add beauty to basic text.

Pasting Word text works like any copy/paste action described in the previous section. Just select the text in Word, copy it, switch to Dreamweaver, and then choose Edit→Paste to drop it into a web page. You don't have to spend a lot of time reformatting the pasted text (see bottom-left image in Figure 2-6) since Dreamweaver preserves many basic formatting options:

- Any paragraphs formatted with Word's built-in Heading styles (Heading 1, Heading 2, and so on) get the HTML heading tags <h1> (or Heading 1), <h2>, <title>, and so on.
- Paragraphs remain paragraphs…most of the time. Actually, the way Dreamweaver pastes paragraphs depends on both how Word formatted the paragraphs to begin with and whether you turn on the Paste Special window's "Clean up Word paragraph spacing" setting (see Figure 2-5). If you do, paragraphs you paste from Word appear as one large paragraph, with line break characters at the end of each paragraph. Not the best way to get an HTML paragraph. To get Dreamweaver to paste each paragraph as a paragraph, choose Edit→Paste Special, turn off the "Clean up Word paragraph spacing" checkbox, and then click OK.

Note: If the Word document you're copying from has an empty line between each paragraph (in other words, an empty paragraph generated by pressing the Enter key twice after each paragraph), make sure you *do* have the "Clean up Word paragraph spacing" checkbox turned on. This precaution eliminates those empty paragraphs.

- Bold and italic text maintain their look in Dreamweaver (the actual HTML tags, however, can vary, as described on page 106).
- Basic alignment options (left, right, and center) remain intact. Justified text, on the other hand, gets pasted as left-aligned text. (You can compensate for this small oversight by using the justified alignment option on the Property inspector, described on page 87.)
- Numbered lists come through as numbered lists in Dreamweaver (see page 98) *if* you used Word's automatic numbered-list feature to create them.

Tip: Suppose you've copied some HTML code, maybe out of the Source view of an actual web page, or from a "How to Write HTML" website. You'll notice that when you paste it into Dreamweaver's Design view, all the HTML tags appear in the document window, complete with brackets (<>) and other assorted messiness. That's because to get HTML into a page (and make it work like HTML), you have to go into Code view and paste the HTML directly into the page's code. Code view is discussed in depth on page 87.

- If you use Word's built-in list-bulleting feature, you end up with a proper HTML bulleted list (see page 98). If you create your own bulleted list style in Word, make sure to select the "list" type when you create the style; otherwise, copying and pasting a custom bulleted list might just paste plain paragraphs of text, not a bulleted list.
- Graphics from Word documents get pasted as graphics. In fact, even if the original graphics aren't in a web-ready format (if they're BMP, TIFF, or PICT files, for example), Dreamweaver converts them to either the GIF or JPEG formats that web browsers understand. Dreamweaver even copies the files to your local site root *and* links them correctly to the page. (Chapter 6 covers images in depth.)

Note: Keep in mind a couple of caveats when you paste from Word. First, you can't copy and paste more than a couple hundred KB worth of text, so you have to transfer really long documents in pieces (or better yet, spread them out among multiple web pages). And second, the ability to keep basic HTML formatting in place when pasting works only with versions of Word later than Office 97 (for Windows) or Office 98 (for Mac).

Pasting Text with Word Formatting

If you simply must keep that three-inch-tall, crazy, cartoon-like orange font, you can turn to the Full Formatting option of the Paste Special command. After copying text from Word and returning to Dreamweaver, choose Edit→Paste Special or press Ctrl+Shift+V

(⌘-Shift-V). When the Paste Special window appears, choose the Full Formatting option, and then click OK. (If you want to make your Paste Special selection the default setting in Dreamweaver, click the Paste Preferences button to open the Preferences Window. Choose the setting you want—for example, "Text with full structure and formatting"—and then click OK to make that the Paste Special command's default.)

Dreamweaver pastes the text with as much formatting as possible, including margins, fonts, and text colors and sizes (see bottom-right image in Figure 2-6). Behind the scenes, Dreamweaver pastes the text *and* adds CSS code that attempts to approximate the look of the text in Word.

Note: Sometimes when you paste from Word (even using the standard Paste command) you end up with empty <a> tags in your HTML. They appear as gold shields in Dreamweaver's Design view (circled in Figure 2-6). The links might look something like this: <a name="OLE_LINK1" id="OLE_LINK1"></a>. Feel free to delete them–this is just some unnecessary crud that Word adds.

Unfortunately, all this extra code increases the document's file size and download time, and can interfere with future formatting changes. What's worse, most of your visitors won't even be able to *see* some of this formatting—such as when you use uncommon font. For these reasons, it's best to skip this feature, paste Word text using the regular Paste command, and then create your own styles to make the text look great (you'll learn about styles and CSS in Chapter 4).

Pasting Excel Spreadsheet Information

Dreamweaver also lets you paste information from Microsoft Excel. Options include a basic method—using the standard Ctrl+V (⌘-V) or Edit→Paste command—and a format-rich method, using the Full Formatting option of the Paste Special window: choose Edit→Paste Special (or press Ctrl+Shift+V [⌘-Shift-V]), choose Full Formatting from the Paste Special window, and then click OK. Both methods paste spreadsheet information as an HTML table composed of cells, rows, and columns. (See Chapter 7 for more on tables.)

But unlike pasting from Word, the basic Paste command from Excel preserves *no* formatting: It doesn't even hang on to bold and italic. The Full Formatting option, however, preserves advanced formatting like fonts, font sizes, text colors, and cell background colors.

Importing Word and Excel Documents (Windows)

Windows fans can also import material directly from a Word or Excel file into any Dreamweaver document. Just place the cursor where you wish to insert the text or spreadsheet, and then choose File→Import→Word Document (or Excel Document). An Open File dialog box appears; find and double-click the Word or Excel document you want to import.

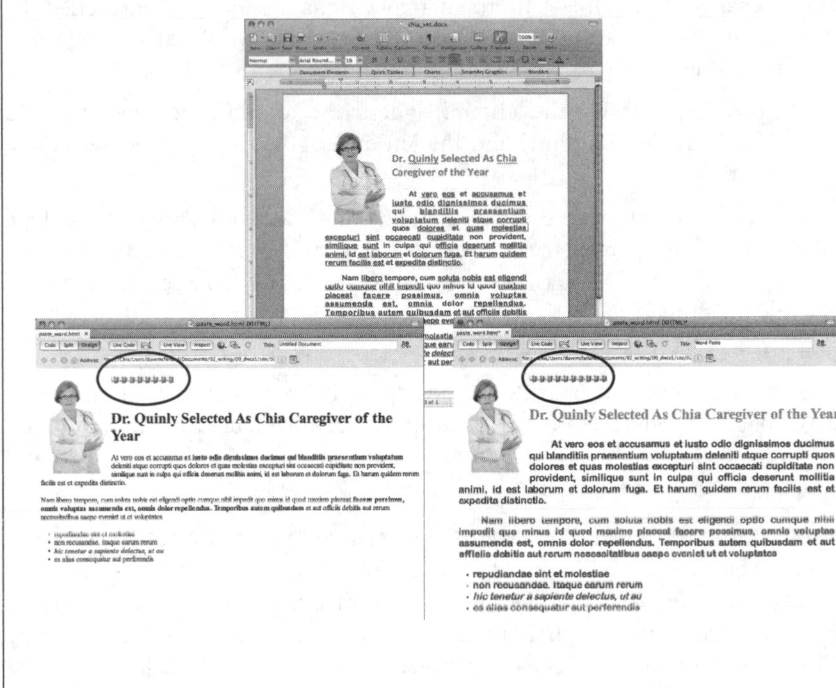

***Figure 2-6:** Dreamweaver lets you paste Word text (and graphics)–like the contents of the Word file (top)–into a web page while preserving basic formatting options like headlines, italic, paragraphs, and bold (bottom left). The Paste Special command lets you preserve more advanced formatting, such as fonts, colors, sizes, and margins (bottom right). But this special treatment comes at a price: Dreamweaver embeds the CSS code needed to get this fancy formatting into the HTML, making it very time-consuming to change.*

Dreamweaver captures the information just as if you'd used Edit→Paste. That is, for Word documents, Dreamweaver carries over basic formatting like bold, italic, headlines, and paragraphs, and imports and converts images. The importing process doesn't create style sheets or apply advanced formatting. For Excel documents, you get just an organized table of data—no formatting.

Selecting Text

After you get text into your Dreamweaver document, you'll undoubtedly need to edit it. You'll delete words and paragraphs, move sentences around, add words, and fix typos.

The first step in any of these procedures is learning how to select text, which works much as it does in word processors. You drag your cursor across text to highlight it, or just click where you wish the selection to begin, and then hold down the Shift key as you click at the end of the selection. You can also use shortcuts like these:

- To select a word, double-click it.
- To select a paragraph, triple-click anywhere in it.

- To select a line of text, move your cursor to the left of the line of text until the cursor changes from an I-beam to an arrow, signaling that you've reached the left-margin selection strip. Click once to highlight one line of text, or drag vertically in this selection strip to select multiple lines.
- While pressing Shift, use the left and right arrow keys to select one letter at a time. Use Ctrl+Shift (⌘-Shift) and the left and right arrow keys to select one *word* at a time.
- Ctrl+A (⌘-A) selects everything in the body of a page—text, graphics, and all. (Well, this isn't 100 percent true: If you use tables or <div> tags [page 331] to organize a page, then Ctrl+A may select just the text within a table cell or <div> tag; clicking the <body> tag in the Tag selector [page 23] is a more sure-fire method of selecting everything on a page.)

Once you selected text, you can cut, copy, or delete it. To move text to another part of the web page, or even to another Dreamweaver document, use the Cut, Copy, and Paste commands in the Edit menu. You can also move text around by dragging and dropping it, as shown in Figure 2-7.

Once copied, the text remains on your Clipboard and you can place it again and again (until you copy something else to the Clipboard, of course). When you cut (or copy) and paste *within* Dreamweaver, all the code affecting that text comes along for the ride. If you copy a paragraph that includes bold text, for example, then you copy the HTML tags both for creating a paragraph and for producing bold text.

Note: Not *all* formatting necessarily comes along for the ride. With Dreamweaver's support for Cascading Style Sheets, most of your text formatting includes some CSS formatting, and, unfortunately, cutting and pasting text from one document to another does *not* always copy the CSS code. So on some occasions, you may copy text from one document, paste it into another, and find that the formatting disappears. See the box on page 125 for details.

To delete any selection, press Delete or choose Edit→Clear.

Spell Checking

You spend a lot of time perfecting your web pages, making sure the images look great, the text is properly formatted, and everything aligns to make a beautiful visual presentation. But one step is often forgotten, especially given the hyper-speed development process of the Web—making sure your pages are free of typos.

Spelling mistakes give an unprofessional impression and imply a lack of attention to detail. Who wants to hire an "illustraightor" or "Web dezyner"? Dreamweaver's spell checking feature can help you.

POWER USERS' CLINIC

Decoding Encoding

In some cases, when you copy a symbol like © from Word and then paste it into Dreamweaver, you see *©* in the HTML. Other times you see the actual symbol (©). What you get in the HTML depends on the type of *encoding* Dreamweaver uses on your web page. Unless you work with languages other than English, encoding isn't much of an issue; you can work happily without ever worrying about how Dreamweaver encodes HTML for a web page. But if you commonly need to type characters that don't appear on the standard English keyboard, such as Chinese, Kanji, or simply the accented letters of French or Spanish, Dreamweaver's encoding method is helpful.

Computers don't think in terms of letters or any of the other symbols we humans normally use to communicate with each other. Computers think in terms of bits and bytes. They represent every letter or symbol displayed on a web page by a numeric code. The process of converting those symbols to computer-friendly code is called *encoding*. But since the world is filled with many different symbols–Latin, Chinese, Kanji, Arabic, Cyrillic, Hebrew, and so on–there are many different *encoding schemes* used to accommodate all the different alphabets of the world. Versions of Dreamweaver prior to CS3 used Western Latin encoding, which handles most of the characters in English and Western European languages. But it doesn't handle all symbols. That's why when you copy a © symbol from Word and paste it into a web page with Western Latin encoding, you end up with *©* in your HTML instead of the copyright symbol. *©* is called an *entity*, and Web browsers know that when they see that particular entity, they should display a true copyright symbol.

Dreamweaver uses a newer type of encoding when it creates a web page–Unicode. Unicode (which Dreamweaver refers to as *Unicode 4.0 (UTF-8)*, or *UTF-8* for short) accommodates many of the alphabets of the world, so you can mix Kanji with Cyrillic with English on a single page, and all of those alphabets display as they should in a browser. A page encoded with Unicode also produces slightly different HTML when you paste symbols from other programs. Instead of using entities in the page, like *”* for a curly right quotation mark, you see the actual character (") in the HTML. This quality generally makes HTML much easier to read. However, if you've previously built a site using a different encoding scheme, like *Japanese (Shift JIS)*–yes, that's the actual format name–you may want to stick to that method.

You probably won't ever need to change Dreamweaver's encoding scheme, but if you're updating a site and want to upgrade to the new Unicode encoding (maybe so you can type © instead of *©* in your HTML) just choose Modify®Page Properties, click the Title/Encoding category, and then select a method from the encoding menu. If you want to change the default encoding for all new documents (for example, if you absolutely must stick with the Shift JIS encoding to match the encoding method of other pages on your site) choose Edit®Preferences (Dreamweaver®Preferences on a Mac), click the New Document category, and then select an option from the Default Encoding menu. Note that if, later on, you switch back to Unicode 4.0 (UTF-8), make sure you select "C (Canonical Decomposition)" from the "Normalization" field, and leave the "Include Unicode Signature" checkbox *turned off* (otherwise the page may not display correctly in current browsers).

Finally, if you use the Insert Special Character menu ("Line Breaks"), then Dreamweaver always inserts an HTML entity (*®*, for example) instead of the actual symbol (™), even in a UTF-8 page. You can, however, type many of these symbols on your keyboard, as described in the Power Users' Clinic on page 76.

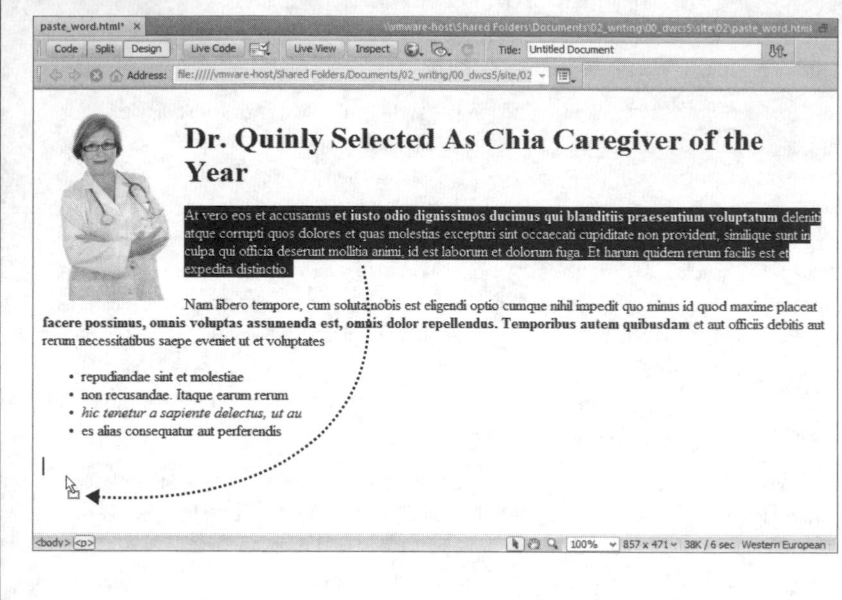

Figure 2-7: *You can move a blob of selected text simply by dragging it to another location in the document window. Point to a spot inside your highlighted selection, and the cursor changes from an I-beam to an arrow; you can now drag the selection. Let go of the mouse button to drop your selection at the spot indicated by the horizontal bar, as shown here. This technique works with graphics and other objects you've selected in the document window, too. You can even move a copy of the selection by pressing Ctrl (Option on a Mac) as you drag and drop.*

About Dictionaries

Before you start spell checking, make sure you have the right *dictionary* selected. Dreamweaver comes with 37 of them, ranging from Bulgarian to Turkish (including three variants for English, and four for German [huh?]). When it checks your spelling, the program compares the text in your document against the list of words in one of these dictionaries.

Note: Dreamweaver CS5 includes a new dictionary system. It supports many more languages and the dictionaries are more complete (they have more words in them) than previous versions.

To specify a dictionary, choose Edit→Preferences (Dreamweaver→Preferences in Mac OS X)—or press Ctrl+U (⌘-U)—to open the Preferences dialog box. Select the General category, and then, from the Spelling Dictionary pop-up menu at the bottom of the window, choose a language.

GEM IN THE ROUGH

Clean Up Word

From Word, you can save any document as a web page, essentially turning a Word document into HTML. This method's drawback is that Word produces hideous HTML code. One look at it, and you'd think that your cat fell asleep on the keyboard.

Here's what's happening: To let you reopen the document as a Word file when the time comes, Word injects reams of information that adds to the file size of the page. This is a particular problem with the latest versions of Word, which add loads of XML and Cascading Style Sheet information.

Fortunately, Dreamweaver's Clean Up Word HTML command can strip out most of that unnecessary code and produce leaner web pages. To use it, open the Word HTML file just as you would any other web page, by choosing File→Open. Once the file is open, choose Commands→Clean Up Word HTML.

The Clean Up Word HTML dialog box opens; Dreamweaver automatically detects whether the HTML was produced by Word 97/98 or a later version of Word, and then applies the appropriate rules for cleaning up the HTML.

Unfortunately, Dreamweaver doesn't always catch the junk thrown into the page by Word, so if you have the original Word document, you're better off just opening it, copying the contents, and pasting it into Dreamweaver. Then you can use Dreamweaver's tools for formatting the text so that it looks just the way you want it to, without any unnecessary code.

Performing the Check

Once you select a dictionary, open the web page whose spelling you wish to check. You can check as much or as little text as you like, as follows:

1. **Highlight the text (which can be even a single word).**

   If you want to check the *entire* document, make sure that nothing is selected in the document window. (One good way to do this is to click in the middle of a paragraph of text.) Like spell checkers in other programs, you must place the cursor at the beginning of the document to begin spell checking from the top of the page.

Note: Unfortunately, Dreamweaver doesn't offer a site wide spell-checking feature. You must check each page individually.

2. **Choose Text →Check Spelling (or press Shift+F7).**

   The Check Spelling dialog box opens (see Figure 2-8). If the selected word isn't in Dreamweaver's dictionary, then it appears in the top field of the box, along with a list of suggested alternative spellings.

   The first suggestion is listed in the "Change to" field.

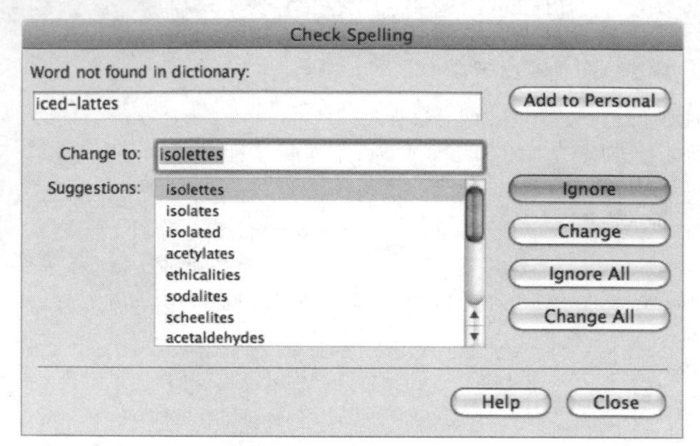

Figure 2-8:
Dreamweaver's spell-checking feature checks only words in the document window. It can't check the spelling of comments, <alt> tags, or any text that appears in the head of the document, with the exception of the page's title. Nor can you spell-check an entire website's worth of pages with a single command; you need to check each page individually.

3. **If the "Change to" field is correct, click Change.**

   If Dreamweaver has correctly flagged the word as misspelled but the correct spelling isn't in the "Change to" field, double-click the correct spelling in the list. If the correct spelling isn't in the list, type it into the "Change to" box yourself.

   Then click the Change button to correct this one instance, or click Change All to replace the misspelled word everywhere it appears in the document.

   Dreamweaver makes the change and moves on to the next questionable spelling.

4. **If the word is actually correctly spelled (but not in Dreamweaver's dictionary), click Ignore, Ignore All, or "Add to Personal".**

   If you want Dreamweaver to ignore this word *every* time it appears in the document, rather than just this instance of it, click Ignore All.

   On the other hand, you'll probably use some words that Dreamweaver doesn't have in its dictionaries. You may, for instance, use a client's name throughout your web pages. If that name isn't in Dreamweaver's dictionary, Dreamweaver consistently claims that it's a spelling error.

   To teach Dreamweaver the client's name so that the Check Spelling dialog box doesn't pop up, click "Add to Personal". Dreamweaver adds the word to your personal dictionary, which is a special dictionary file that Dreamweaver also consults when checking your spelling.

   After you click Ignore or Change, Dreamweaver moves on to the next word it doesn't recognize. Begin again from step 3. If you didn't begin the spell check at the beginning of the document, once Dreamweaver reaches the end of the document, it asks if you want to continue spell-checking from the beginning.

5. **To end spell-checking, click Close.**

CHAPTER

3

Text Formatting

Getting text onto a web page (Chapter 2) is a good start, but effective communication requires effective design. Large, bold headlines help readers scan a page's important topics. Colorful text focuses attention. Bulleted sentences crystallize and summarize ideas. Just as a monotonous, low-key voice puts a crowd to sleep, a vast desert of plain HTML text is sure to turn visitors away from the important message of your site. In fact, text formatting could be the key to making your *Widgets Online 2009 Sale-a-Thon* a resounding success instead of an unnoticed disaster. Figure 3-1 shows two model examples of good—and bad—text formatting.

Text formatting is actually a two-step process. First you apply the appropriate HTML tag to each chunk of text, and then you use Cascading Style Sheets (CSSes) to make that text look great. You add the HTML tags not so much to format the text (though they *can* do that, with the undesired side effect that different browsers can interpret the tags differently), but to *structure* the text into logical blocks. Once you identify those blocks, you can use Cascading Style Sheets to format them to your liking—and not just in the current page, but across your site. That's one of the big benefits of Cascading Style Sheets.

For example, you'd use the <h1> (Heading 1) tag to indicate the most important heading on a page, while you'd use the <ol> (ordered list) tag to list a series of numbered steps. This process of structuring your text with HTML not only does some rudimentary formatting (the resulting page has a large, boldfaced headline and a numbered list), it structures your text so that search engines and alternative browsing devices, like screen readers for the vision-impaired, can weight the relative importance of each block of text. It doesn't really matter to most people surfing the web with Internet Explorer or Firefox. That's where CSS comes in. You use CSS to fine-tune the visual appeal of text by changing fonts, applying color, adjusting font size and a lot more.

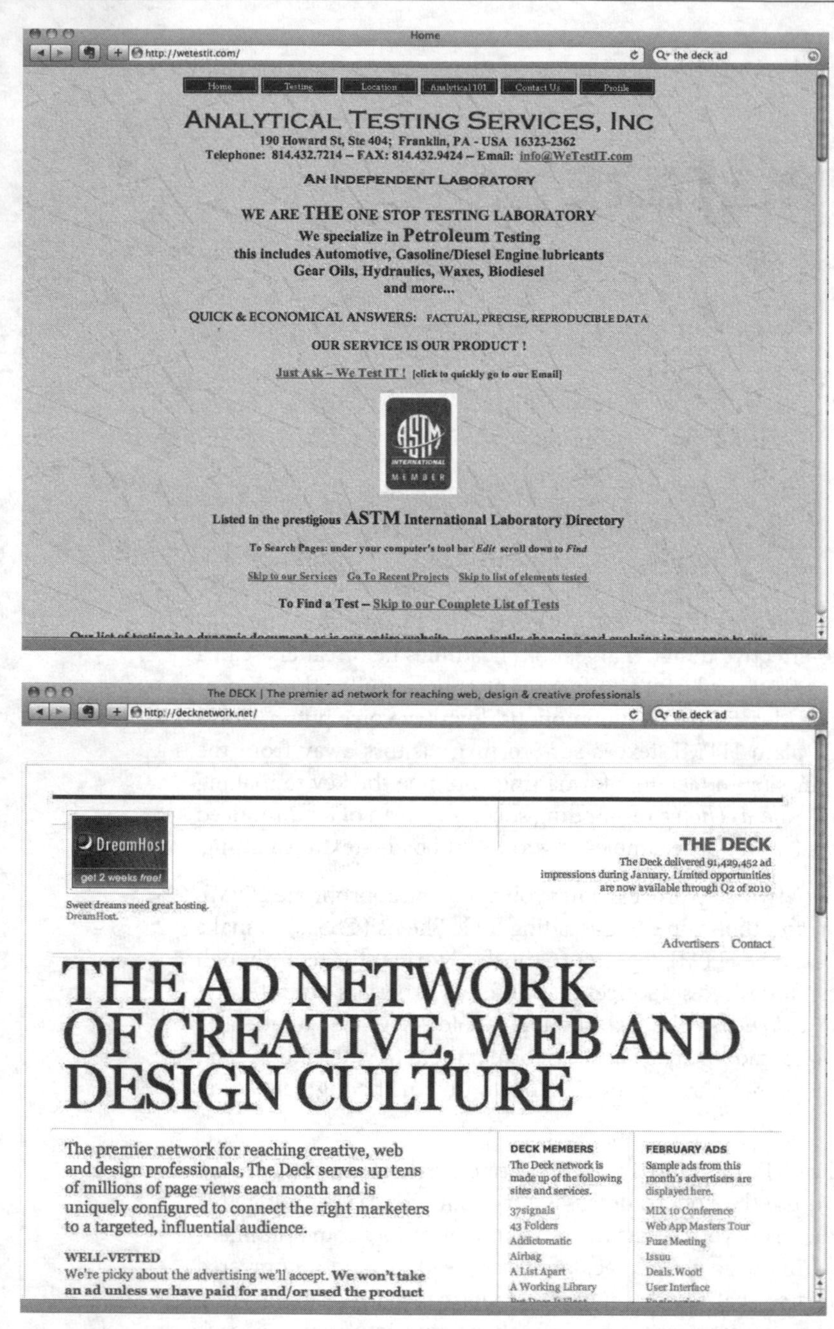

Figure 3-1:
Both these pages use different type fonts, colors, and sizes to display text, but the one at bottom uses large, bold type to immediately direct your attention to the site's purpose. Other areas of the page use different type size and color to indicate their relative importance. In the page at the top, by contrast, nothing really stands out. Even the site's name is so close in size to the other text on the page that it doesn't make much of a statement. The text shares similar font sizes and types throughout the page, making it difficult to focus your attention on any one area.

The fundamental difference between HTML and CSS is so important that Dreamweaver CS5 treats these two technologies separately by splitting the Property inspector into two tabbed areas, one for HTML and one for CSS. That way, you'll always know when you're applying which formatting code (see Figure 3-2). In this chapter, you'll learn to use HTML tags to structure text on a web page; in the next chapter, you'll create beautiful typography with CSS.

Paragraph Formatting

Just as you use paragraphs to help organize your thoughts into clear, well-structured, cohesive units when you write a paper or letter, you organize content on web pages into blocks of information with HTML tags (see page 6 for more about tags). The most basic block of information is a simple paragraph, which you identify in HTML with a paragraph tag, like this:

```
<p>Hello. This is one paragraph on this web page.</p>
```

A web browser considers everything between the opening <p> and closing </p> tags part of the same paragraph. You can apply many Dreamweaver formatting options—headlines, lists, indentations, and alignment, for example—only to an entire paragraph at a time, as opposed to individual words. In a word processor, you'd call this kind of formatting *paragraph* formatting; in web design, it's called *block-level* formatting. Either way, the idea is the same: The formatting you apply affects an entire paragraph (that is, a *block* of text, whether that block is just one sentence or several sentences) at a time. (You can apply *character-level* formatting, on the other hand, to individual words or even letters. Bold and italic formats fall into this category, as described later in this chapter.)

Paragraphs

If you create a new document in Dreamweaver and start typing right away, the text you type has no paragraph formatting at all, as indicated by the word None in the Format menu at the left side of the Property inspector (see Figure 3-2). (*None* isn't an HTML tag; it just means that you aren't using *any* of the paragraph tags this menu offers—<p>, <h1>, and so on.)

However, when you press Enter or Return, Dreamweaver transforms that text into a new paragraph, complete with opening and closing <p> tags, as shown earlier. Still, your newly born paragraph has no *design* applied to it. When your site visitors look at it, the font and size of your type are determined by their browser preference settings. For example, if a visitor sets his browser to display unformatted text as Vladimir Script, your page will look as though John Hancock wrote it.

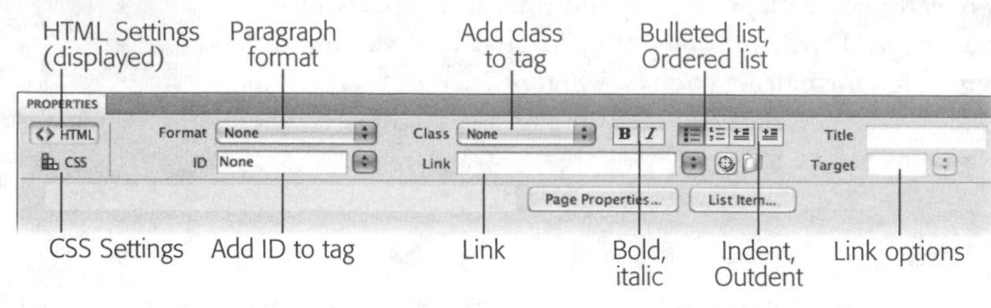

***Figure 3-2:** The HTML properties options include both paragraph- and character-level formatting options. The choices labeled here in bold apply to an entire paragraph. The other options represent inline, or character-level, formatting options; they apply only to the currently selected text.*

UP TO SPEED

Separating Structure from Presentation

HTML isn't about good looks or fancy design. Instead, the HTML tags you use to format text apply a *structure* to your page, providing valuable insight into how you organized the content. In fact, most visitors to your site won't ever see, and probably don't care, which HTML tags you use. But Google, Bing, and other search engines do care. They use your HTML tags to determine which text is the most important and understand what your page is really about.

Google, for example, puts a lot of stock in <h1> tags, seeing the text inside as defining "what this page is all about." That's why search engine experts recommend using only one <h1> tag per page, and suggest that you make the text very descriptive: <h1>My page</h1> isn't good, but <h1>The Ultimate Chia Pet Resource</h1> is.

In general, use HTML to structure your page as you would a report or term paper. For example, the Heading 1 (<h1>) tag indicates a headline of the highest level and, therefore, of greatest importance; the smaller Heading 2 (<h2>) tag represents a headline of slightly lesser importance: a subhead. You can see this kind of structure in this book. Each section begins with a headline ("Paragraph Formatting," on page 93, for example), and includes subheads that further divide the content into logical blocks of information.

Structure is more about organizing content than it is about making a page look pretty. Regardless of whether this book uses different colors and fonts in its headlines, the fundamental organization–chapter title, main headlines, subheads, bulleted lists, numbered instructions, and paragraphs of information–remain the same.

HTML is also important for devices that don't read or can't display CSS. For example, people with vision impairment often rely on screen readers (programs that literally read the text on a page out loud) to surf the Web. For screen readers, good HTML structure is the only way to understand a page–clear use of headlines, paragraphs, and other tags help a screen reader convey the structure of a page to its user.

You can add the Paragraph format to any block of text. Since a paragraph format affects all the text in the block, you don't need to select any text as a first step. Simply click anywhere inside the block of text, and then do one of the following:

- In the Property inspector (Figure 3-2), from the Format menu, choose Paragraph.
- Choose Format→Paragraph Format→Paragraph.
- Press Ctrl+Shift+P (⌘-Shift-P).

Note: Much to the chagrin of web designers, web browsers display a line's worth of blank space before and after many block-level elements, like headings and paragraphs. This visual gap is distracting, but unfortunately, you can't get rid of it with regular HTML. However, many of the formatting limitations of HTML, including this one, go away when you use CSS. See page 140 to fix this problem.

Headlines

Headlines announce information ("The Vote Is In!") and help organize content. Just as this book uses different levels of headings to introduce its topics—from chapter titles all the way down to subsections—the HTML heading tag comes in a variety of sizes, to indicate the content's importance. Headlines range in size from 1 (most important) to 6 (least important), as shown in Figure 3-3.

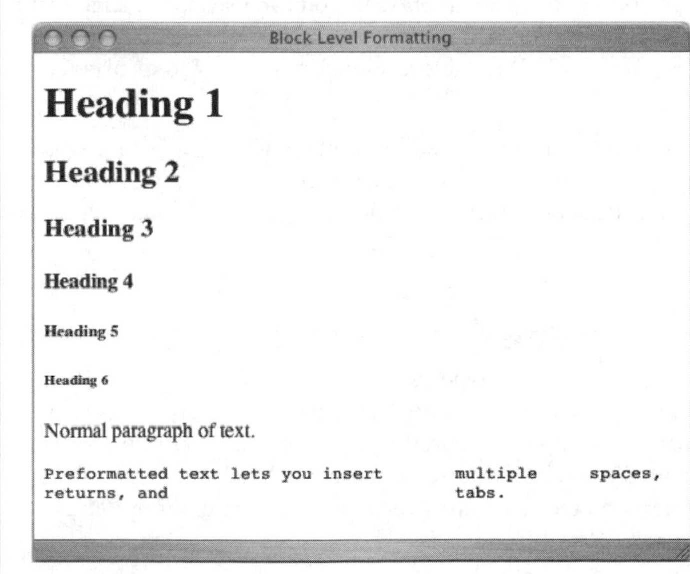

Figure 3-3: *You can apply any of eight basic paragraph formats to a block of text: Headings 1 through 6, Paragraph, and Preformatted. If you don't add any special modifications to the individual paragraph formats, then they vary in size, font, and boldness, as you can see here.*

To turn a paragraph into a headline, click anywhere inside the line, or block, of text and then do one of the following:

- From the Format menu in the Property inspector, select one of the heading levels (Heading 1 through Heading 6).
- Choose Format→Paragraph Format→Heading 1 (or Heading 2, Heading 3, and so on).
- Press Ctrl+1 (⌘-1), for the Heading 1 style, Ctrl+2 (⌘-2) for Heading 2, and so on.

Preformatted Text

Web browsers normally ignore extra spaces, tabs, and other blank-space characters in the underlying HTML when they display web pages. However, using the Preformatted paragraph format, you can override this behavior. Preformatted paragraphs display *every* text character in a paragraph, including tabs, multiple spaces, and line breaks, so you don't have to resort to multiple nonbreaking space characters (see page 76) to insert more than one space at a time.

The original idea behind the Preformatted format was to display tabular data—like the information in a spreadsheet—without the use of tables. That's why preformatted paragraphs show up in a *monospaced* font like Courier. In monospaced fonts, each letter of the alphabet, from *i* to *w*, has the same width and takes up the same amount of horizontal space on a page, making it easy to align letters in columns. That's also why, when you use this paragraph style, you can use tabs to align text in columns. (When you use any other paragraph format, web browsers ignore tabs.) These days, however, using an HTML table is a much better way to display data in columns; see Chapter 7.

Nonetheless, the Preformatted format can still be useful—when you want to display sample HTML or programming code, for example. You can add the Preformatted format to any block of text. Simply click inside the block, and take one of these two steps:

- In the Property inspector, choose Format→Preformatted.
- Choose Format→Paragraph Format→Preformatted Text.

Keep in mind that preformatted text appears exactly as you enter it. Unlike normal paragraph text, lines of preformatted text don't automatically wrap if they're wider than your visitor's display. That means that if you present your visitor with a really long line of preformatted text, she has to scroll horizontally to see all of it. To end a line of preformatted text and create another, you must press the Enter or Return key, thus creating a manual line break.

Paragraph Alignment

All text in a web page starts out aligned with the left edge of the page (or, in the case of tables, to the left edge of a table cell). But you may want to center text in the middle of the page—perhaps an elegantly centered title—or align it to the right side. You can even create nice straight margins on *both* sides of a paragraph, using the justification option.

Note: Although justified text looks elegant in a book, the limited resolution of computer monitors can make small type that's justified difficult to read.

The best way to align text is to create a CSS style and set the *text-align* property to left, right, center, or justified. In fact, Dreamweaver CS5 puts all alignment options for the Property inspector in the CSS view of the inspector—you'll learn how to use these settings on page 137.

However, it *is* possible to use HTML properties to align text. It's not the way most pros do it, but it can come in handy when you want to whip out a page quickly or you have to create HTML emails (which usually don't do so well with CSS).

To change a paragraph's alignment the HTML way, click inside a paragraph, and do one of the following:

- Choose Format→Align→Left, Center, Right, or Justify.
- Use one of the following keyboard shortcuts:
  Left: Ctrl+Alt+Shift+L (Shift-Option-⌘-L)
  Centered: Ctrl+Alt+Shift+C (Shift-Option-⌘-C)
  Right: Ctrl+Alt+Shift+R (Shift-Option-⌘-R)
  Justify: Ctrl+Alt+Shift+J (Shift-Option-⌘-J)

Note: You can remove an alignment by reapplying the *same* alignment. For instance, if you right-align a paragraph, choosing Format→Align→Right removes all alignment information and returns that paragraph to its original setting.

Indented Paragraphs

Dreamweaver's Property inspector includes a button that looks like the indent buttons on the formatting toolbars of word processors. However, that button doesn't really create an indent; it actually inserts the HTML blockquote tag (thought it actually has a different function when working with lists, as described on page 102). The blockquote tag is meant to set apart quoted material, such as an excerpt from a book or part of a famous speech. However, since HTML indents blockquotes from the left and right edges of the page, some novice web designers use the tag to indent text.

This method of indenting text isn't a good idea for a couple of reasons. First, the tag indents from *both* sides of a page, so it doesn't make sense for a regular paragraph of text. In addition, you don't have any control over how *much* space a visitor's browser adds to the margins of the paragraph. Most browsers insert about 40 pixels of blank space on the left and right sides of a blockquote.

As you'll see on page 341, CSS gives you precise control over indented elements using the *margin* or *padding* properties. However, if you *do* want to quote passages of text, you should use the blockquote tag. To do so, just click inside a paragraph or any block-level element (like a heading), and do one of the following:

- On the Property inspector, click the Blockquote button (see Figure 3-2, where it's labeled Indent).
- Choose Format→Indent.
- Press Ctrl+Alt+] (⌘-Option-]).

If you ever want to remove the block quote, you can use Dreamweaver to *outdent* it. (Yes, *outdent* is a real word—ever since Microsoft made it up.)

To remove a <blockquote> tag, click inside the paragraph, and then do one of the following:

- On the Property inspector, click the Outdent button (see Figure 3-2).
- Choose Format→Outdent.
- Press Ctrl+Alt+[(⌘-Option-[).

Creating and Formatting Lists

Lists organize the everyday information of our lives: to-do lists, grocery lists, least favorite celebrity lists, and so on. On web pages, lists are indispensable for presenting groups of items, such as links, company services, or a series of instructions.

HTML offers formatting options for three basic types of list (see Figure 3-4). The two most common are *bulleted* lists (called *unordered* lists in HTML-speak) and *numbered* lists (called *ordered* lists in HTML). The third and lesser-known list type, the *definition* list, comes in handy when you want to create glossaries or dictionary entries.

Bulleted and Numbered Lists

Bulleted and numbered lists share similar formatting. Dreamweaver automatically indents items in both types of list, and automatically precedes each list item by a character—a bullet, number, or letter, for example:

- Unordered, or bulleted, lists, like this one, are good for groups of items that don't necessarily follow any sequence. A web browser precedes each list item with a bullet.
- Ordered lists are useful when presenting items that follow a sequence, such as the numbered instructions in the following section. Instead of a bullet, a number or letter precedes each item in an ordered list. Dreamweaver suggests a number (1, 2, 3, and so on), but you can substitute Roman numerals, letters, and other variations.

You can create a list from scratch within Dreamweaver, or apply list formatting to text already on a page.

Creating a new bulleted or numbered list

When you make a new list in Dreamweaver, you start by choosing a list format, and then typing in the list items:

1. **In the document window, click the point at which you want to start a list.**

   See Chapter 2 for details on adding text to a web page.

2. **In the Property inspector, click the Ordered or Unordered List button to apply the list format (see Figure 3-2). (The Unordered option is also known as a Bulleted list.)**

   Alternatively, you can choose Format→List→Unordered List or Ordered List. Either way, the first bullet or number appears automatically in your document.

3. **Type in the first list item, and then press Enter or Return. Repeat until you've added all items in the list.**

   The text you type appears after the bullet or number (*Organic Compost*, for example, in the bulleted list in Figure 3-4). When you press Return, a new bullet or number appears, ready for your next item. (If you just want to move to the next line *without* creating a new bullet, then insert a line break by pressing Shift+Enter [Shift-Return].)

4. **When you finish the list, press Enter or Return twice.**

The double hard return ends the list and creates a new empty paragraph.

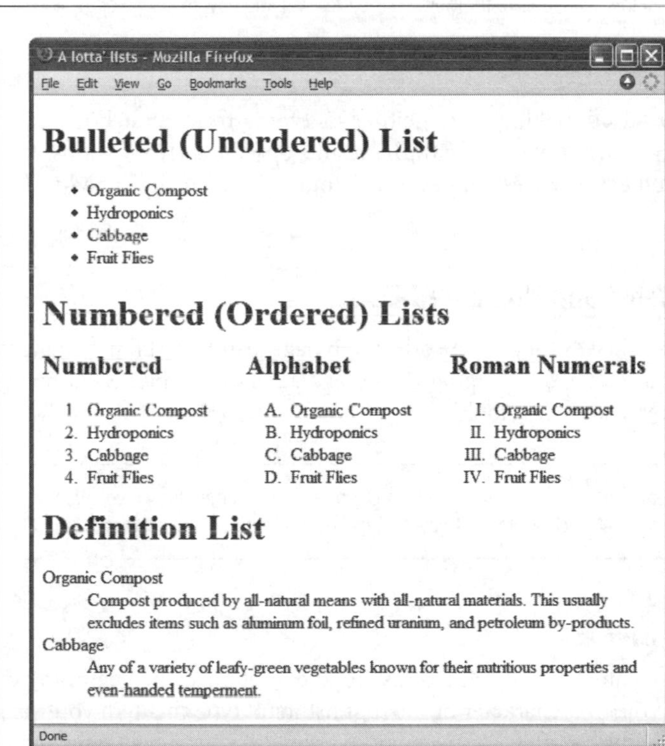

Figure 3-4: *HTML has several predefined list formats, including bulleted lists and definition lists, both of which let you organize information into orderly units. Once you tell Dreamweaver that you intend to create a bulleted or numbered list, it automatically adds the bullets or numbers for you.*

Formatting existing text as a list

You may have several paragraphs of text that you've already typed or pasted in from another program. You can easily change any such group of paragraphs into a list:

1. **Select the text you wish to turn into a list.**

   The easiest way to do that is to drag from the first list item straight down to the last item. Lists are block-level elements; each paragraph, whether it's a headline or regular paragraph, becomes one bulleted or numbered item in the list. In other words, you don't actually need to select all the text in either the first or last paragraph.

2. **Apply the list format.**

   Just as you created a list from scratch as described above, click either the Unordered or Ordered List button in the Property inspector, or choose from the Format→List submenu. The selected paragraphs instantly take on the list formatting, complete with bullets or automatic numbering.

Note: You may sometimes run into this problem: You select what looks like a handful of paragraphs and apply the list format, but only one bullet (or number) appears. This glitch arises when you've used the line break <br> tag to move text down a line in a paragraph. While it's true that using the <br> tag visually separates lines in a paragraph into separate blocks, the text is still part of single paragraph, which appears as only *one* bulleted or numbered item. The presence of multiple <br> tags can be a real problem when pasting text from other programs. See page 76 for more on the <br> tag and how to get rid of these pesky critters.

Whichever way you started making a list—either by typing from scratch or reformatting existing text—you're not stuck with the results of your early decisions. You can add onto lists, add extra spaces, and even renumber them, as described in the following section.

Reformatting Bulleted and Numbered Lists

HTML tags define lists, just as they define other web page features. Making changes to an existing list is a matter of changing those tags, using Dreamweaver's menu commands and Property inspector tools.

Note: Web browsers generally display list items stacked directly one on top of the other. If you want to add a little breathing room between each list item, use the CSS *margin* property, as described on page 341.

Adding new items to a list

Once you create a list, you can easily add items. To add an item at the beginning of a list, click in front of the first character of the first list item, type the item you wish to add, and then press Enter or Return. Dreamweaver makes your newly typed item the first entry in the list, adding a bullet or number accordingly (and renumbering the other list items, if necessary).

To add an item at the middle or end of a list, click at the end of the *previous* list item, and then press Enter or Return. The insertion point appears after a new bullet or number; type your list item on this new line.

Formatting bullets and numbers

Bulleted and numbered lists aren't limited to just the standard round, black bullet or the numbers 1, 2, and 3. You can choose from two bullet types and a handful of numbering schemes. Here's how to change these settings:

1. **Click once inside any list item.**

   Strangely enough, you can't change the properties of a list if you first select the entire list, an entire single list item, or several list items.

2. **Open the List Properties dialog box (Figure 3-5).**

   To do so, either click the List Item button in the bottom half of the Property inspector or choose Format→List→Properties. (If the list is inside a table cell, your only choice is to use the Format menu. In this situation, the List Item button doesn't appear in the Property inspector.)

List Properties
List type: Numbered List
Style: Roman Large (I,...
Start count: 2 (Number)
List item
New style: [Default]
Reset count to: (Number)
OK
Cancel
Help

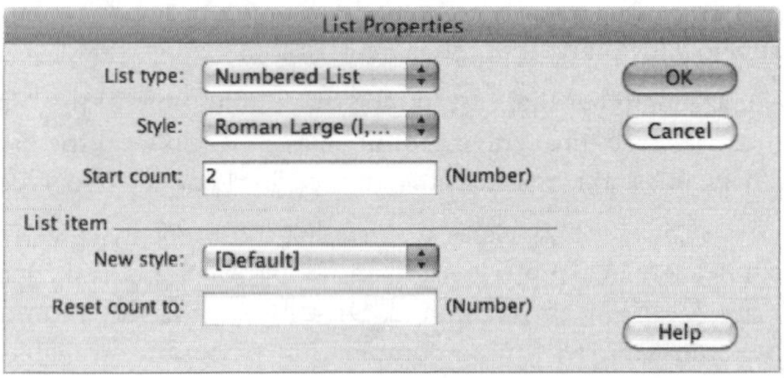

Figure 3-5. *The List Properties dialog box lets you set the type and style of a list. For example, if you select a numbered list, you can choose from five different styles: Number (1, 2, 3); Roman Small (i, ii, iii); Roman Large (I, II, III); Alphabet Small (a, b, c); and Alphabet Large (A, B, C). While the options in the top half of this window apply to an entire list (every item with the <ol> or <ul> tag), the options below the label "List Item" apply to just the single list item you clicked before opening the List Properties dialog box.*

3. **Skip the "List type" pop-up menu.**

   The List type menu lets you turn a numbered list into a bulleted list, or vice versa. But why bother? You can achieve the same thing by simply selecting a bulleted list and clicking the numbered list button in the Property inspector and vice versa. In addition, this menu has two other options—Directory List and Menu List—which insert obsolete HTML you should avoid.

4. **Choose a bullet or numbering style.**

   Bulleted lists can have three different styles: *default*, *bullet*, and *square*. In most browsers, the default style is the same as the bullet style (a simple, solid, black circle). As you might guess, the square style uses a solid black square for the bullet character.

Numbered lists, on the other hand, have a greater variety of style options. Dreamweaver starts you off with a simple numbering scheme (1, 2, 3, and so on), but you can choose from any of five styles for ordered lists, as explained in Figure 3-5.

Tip: You can achieve the same effect as step 4 above using CSS. Not only does CSS give you wider options—you can use a graphic you created as a bullet, for example—but you avoid inserting obsolete HTML.

---

5. **Set the starting number for the list.**

   You don't have to begin a numbered list at 1, A, or the Roman numeral I. You can start it at another number if you wish—a trick that can come in handy if, for example, you create a web page that explains how to rebuild a car's engine. As part of each step, say you want to include a photograph. You create a numbered list, type in the directions for step 1, hit Return, and then insert an image (as described in Chapter 5). You hit Return again, and then type in the text for step 2. Unfortunately, the photo, because it's technically an item in an ordered list, now has the number 2 next to it, and your real step 2 is listed as 3!

   If you remove the list formatting from the photo to get rid of the 2, then you create one list above it and another below it. Step 2, *below* the photo, now thinks it's the beginning of a new list—and starts over with the number 1! The solution is to make the list below the photo think it's a *new* list that begins with 2.

   To start a list at something other than 1, type the starting number in the "Start count" field (Figure 3-5). You must enter a number, even if you want the list to use letters. So, to begin a list at D instead of A, in the "Start count" field, type *4*.

   In fact, you can even change the style of a *single* list item. For instance, you could change the third item in a numeric list from a 3 to the letter C. (Of course, just because you *can* doesn't mean you should. Dreamweaver is very thorough in supporting the almost overwhelming combination of options available in HTML, but, unless you're building a Dadaist revival site, how often do you want a list that's numbered 1, 2, C, iv, 1?)

6. **Click OK to apply the changes.**

Note: Most of the settings in the List Properties dialog box produce invalid HTML for both strict versions of HTML and XHTML. If you use this dialog box, stick to XHTML transitional or HTML transitional documents (see page 7 for more on picking a document type).

Nested lists

Some complex outlines require multiple *levels* of lists. Legal documents, for instance, may list major clauses with capital letters (A, B, C, and so on) and use Roman numerals (i, ii, iii, and so on) for subclauses (see Figure 3-6).

You can easily create such nested lists in Dreamweaver using the Property inspector's indent button; Figure 3-6 shows the steps.

You can change the style of a nested list—for example, change the nested list in Figure 3-6, middle, into a bulleted list—by clicking the appropriate list type in the Property inspector. Changing the nested list's type doesn't affect the list type used for the un-nested (that is, the outer) list. In other words, changing the nested list in Figure 3-6, middle, from a numbered list to a bulleted list doesn't change the outer list to a bulleted list.

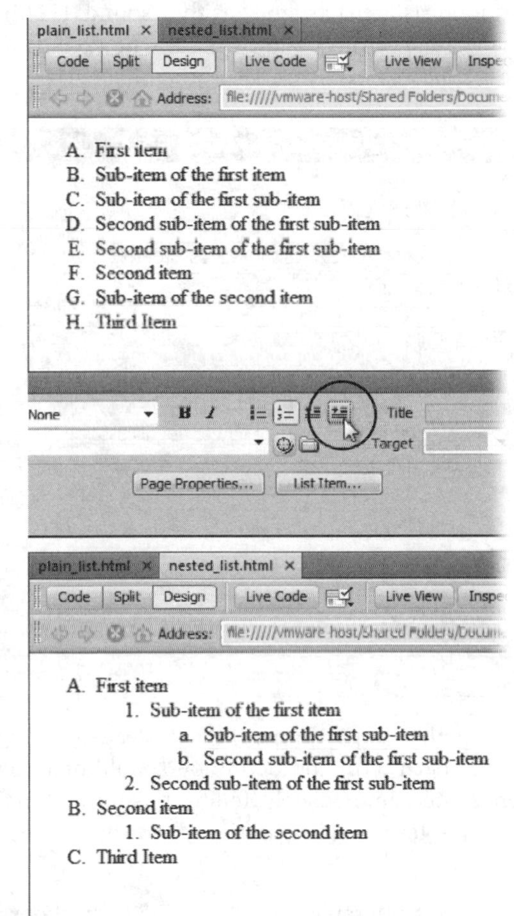

Figure 3-6:
Top: To create a nested list, start with a single list–in this case, a numbered list using capital letters instead of numbers.

Middle: Select a subtopic, and then click the Indent button (circled) or choose Format→Indent.

Bottom: The item becomes a nested list, indented from the main list and with its own numbering. Notice, too, that the major points have been renumbered–letter E from the top figure is the letter B in the bottom figure–to reflect the list's new order.

Tip: You can also create a nested list by hitting the Tab key to indent a list item to another level. Shift-Tab outdents the list item.

Definition Lists

You can use *definition lists* to create dictionary or glossary entries, or whenever you need to present a term and its definition. Each item in a definition list is composed of two parts: a word or term, and its definition.

Note: Behind the scenes, Dreamweaver creates an entire definition list using the <dl> tag. Each item in the list is then composed of two tags: <dt> for the definition term or word, and <dd> for the definition itself.

As you can see in Figure 3-4, definition lists aren't as fancy as they sound. HTML presents the first item in the list—the word or term—on its own line with no indent, and the second item—the definition—appears directly underneath, indented.

FREQUENTLY ASKED QUESTION

When Not to Approach the Insert Panel

I like the convenience of the Insert panel. Should I use its Text category to format text?

In a word, no. Unlike most of the other categories in the Insert panel, people use the Text category mainly when working in Code view (see Chapter 11) or to insert special characters, like the copyright symbol, as described on page 74. It contains many of the same formatting options as the Property inspector; the *h1, h2*, and *h3*, for instance, are the same as Headings 1, 2, and 3 in the Property inspector's Format pop-up menu.

However, using some of the options, such as *li*, can generate invalid HTML if you don't use it correctly. Furthermore, despite its usual tidiness, Dreamweaver doesn't clean up code produced this way.

In fact, some of these options, when used in Design view, actually split the document window in two, showing the HTML code on one side and Design view on the other. This arrangement is confusing if you're not accustomed to seeing–or just uninterested in–the raw HTML code. All major text-formatting options are available from the Property inspector and Format menu. If you stick to these two tools, you can safely avoid the Text category.

You can't create a definition list using the Property inspector. Instead, start by creating a list of definitions and terms: Each term and definition should be in its own paragraph, and the definition should immediately follow the term. Next, highlight the paragraphs that contain the terms and definitions, and then choose Format→List→Definition List.

To turn a definition list *back* to regular paragraphs, select it, and then choose Format→List→None or, in the Property inspector, click the Outdent button.

Removing and Deleting List Items

Dreamweaver lets you take items out of a list two ways: either by removing the list *formatting* from an item or items (and changing them back into normal paragraphs) or by deleting their text outright.

Removing list formatting

To remove list formatting from one or more list items (or an entire list), highlight the lines in question, and then choose Format→List→None (or, in the Property inspector, just click the Outdent button). You've just removed all list formatting; the text remains on the screen, now formatted as standard paragraphs. (For nested lists, you need to click the Outdent button once for each level of indent.)

If you reformat an item in the middle of a list using this technique, it becomes a regular paragraph, and Dreamweaver turns the items above and below it into separate lists.

Deleting list items

You can easily delete a list or list item with the Tag selector in the document window's status bar (see Figure 3-7). To delete an entire list, click anywhere inside the list, click its tag in the Tag selector—<ul> for a bulleted list or <ol> for a numbered list—and then press Delete. You can also, of course, drag through all the text in the list, and then press Delete.

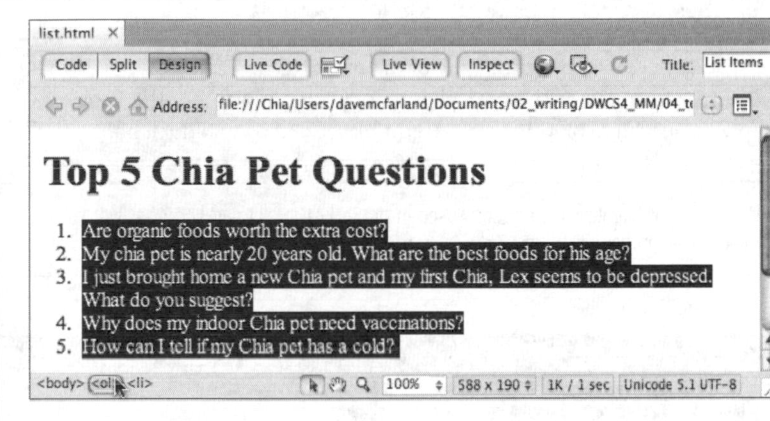

Figure 3-7: *The Tag selector (at the bottom left of the document window) is a great way to quickly and accurately select an HTML tag and its contents. Clicking the <ol> (ordered list) tag, for instance, selects the entire numbered list, as shown here. Clicking the <li> tag selects just one list item.*

To delete a single list item, click that item in the document window, click the <li> tag in the Tag selector, and then press Delete.

Tip: You can rearrange a list by dragging a list item to another position within the list. If it's an ordered list (1, 2, 3, and so on), Dreamweaver automatically renumbers the list. For example, if you select an item numbered 4 and drag it to the second position in the list, then Dreamweaver changes the item to 2, and renumbers all the items that follow.

However, selecting a list item can be tricky. If you simply drag to select the text, you don't actually select the list item itself, with all its formatting and numbering. To be sure that you select a list item *and* its formatting, in the document window's status bar, click the <li> tag in the Tag selector (see Figure 3-7). Now, when you drag the selection to a new position in the list, the number (or bullet) follows. You can also copy or cut the selected list item, and then paste it into another position in the list.

Text Styles

The simple formatting applied by a paragraph format isn't much to write home about, much less to advertise on a résumé. Browsers generally display a Heading 1, for instance, in black and bold using a large Times New Roman font. As mentioned in the "Headlines" section on page 95, this type of paragraph formatting is intended to provide structure, not good looks.

In the next chapter you'll learn how to make your web pages stand out using Cascading Style Sheets. With CSS you can apply different fonts, colors, and sizes to your text. However, you can also apply a handful of HTML tags to a selection of text. Dreamweaver refers to these as *styles*, but in reality they're intended to provide more information about the text—for example, if you have a "Learn HTML" web page, you can apply the *code* tag to programming code that you want to display in a unique format on the page.

As shown in Figure 3-8, HTML offers a host of different text styles, some of which fulfill obscure purposes. For instance, the Code and Variable styles are intended to format programming code, while the Sample style represents the output from a computer program—not exactly styles you'll need often in promoting, say, your *Cheeses of the World* mail-order company.

To use these styles, select the text (using any of the methods described on page 85), and then apply a format from the Format→Style menu. (You can also use the Property inspector to apply the <strong> or <em> tags to emphasize text by making it bold or italic.)

Note: Use italic with care. While italic is frequently used in printed material to add *emphasis* or when referencing a book title, it can be difficult to read on a computer screen, especially at small type sizes.

UP TO SPEED

When Bold and Italic Are Neither

You may be confused by the HTML code that Dreamweaver produces when making text bold or italic. Instead of using the <b> tag–the original HTML code for bold–Dreamweaver uses the <strong> tag. And instead of <i> for italic, clicking the Property inspector's I button gets you <em>, or the emphasis tag. That's because Adobe decided to follow industry practices rather than stick to an old tradition.

For most purposes, <strong> and <em> behave identically to <b> and <i>. The results look the same–bolded or italicized–in most browsers. However, when screen readers (software or equipment that reads web pages aloud for the benefit of the visually impaired) encounter these tags, the <strong> tag triggers a loud, strong voice. The <em> tag also brings an emphasis to the voice of screen readers, though with less strength than the <strong> tag.

Since most browsers simply treat the <strong> tag like the <b> tag, and the <em> tag like the <i> tag, you'll probably never notice the difference. However, if you prefer the simple <b> and <i> tags, choose Edit→Preferences. Select the General category, and then turn off the checkbox labeled "Use <strong> and <em> in place of <b> and <i>".

Unless you intend to include content whose meaning is supported by the tag (for example, you include some sample computer code on a page, so you format it with the Code style), you're better off avoiding such styles. But if you think one of them might come in handy, you can find more about these styles by consulting Dreamweaver's built-in HTML reference; see page 448. In particular, avoid the underline and strikethrough styles. Both have been deprecated (see page 94) in the HTML 4 standard, and may produce no effect in future browsers. (You can, however, turn to the text-formatting abilities of CSS to put lines through and under any text you like. See page 140 for more.)

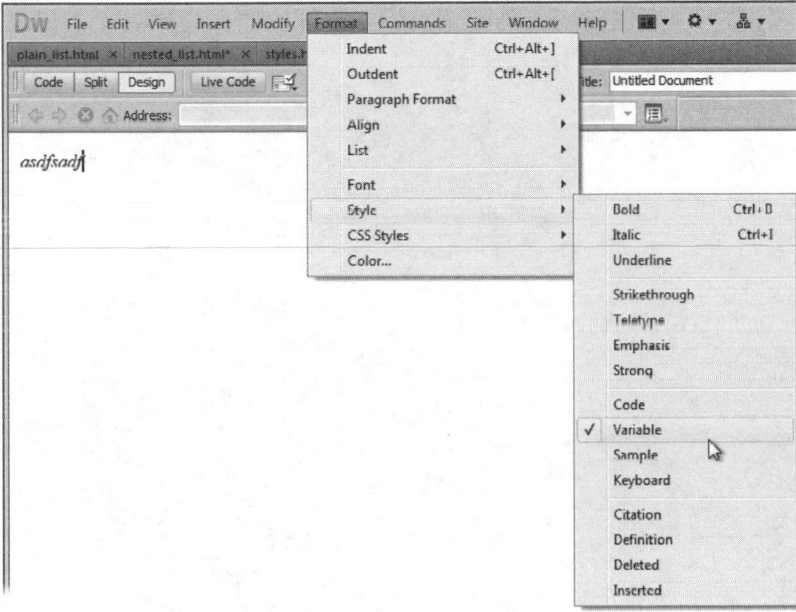

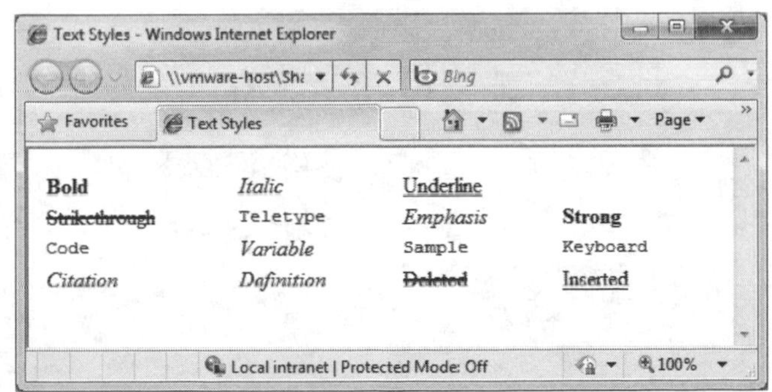

Figure 3-8:
Top: While the Property inspector lets you apply bold and italic styles to text, the Format→Style menu offers a larger selection of styles. Don't be confused by the term "styles," which, in this case, merely refers to different HTML tags. They're unrelated to CSS styles and are intended to identify very specific types of text, like citations from a book or magazine.

Bottom: As you can see, the many style options are usually displayed in bold, italic, the browser's monospaced font (usually Courier), or some combination of the three. But don't worry about how they look "out of the box"—as you'll learn in the next chapter, you can make any of those tags appear any way you wish by applying CSS.

CHAPTER

4

Introducing Cascading Style Sheets

What you see on a web page when you use garden-variety HTML tags like <h1>, <p>, and <ul>, pales in comparison to the text and styling on display in, say, a print magazine. If web designers had only HTML to make their sites look great, the Web would forever be the ugly duckling of the media world. HTML doesn't hold a candle to the typographic and layout control you get when you create a document in even the most basic word processing program.

Fortunately for web designers, you can change the ho-hum appearance of HTML using a technology called Cascading Style Sheets (CSS). CSS gives you the tools you need to make HTML look beautiful. If you think of HTML as the basic structure of a house (the foundation, walls, and rooms), then CSS is the house's interior decoration (the paint, carpeting, and the color, style, and placement of furniture). CSS gives you much greater control over the layout and design of your pages. Using it, you can add margins to paragraphs (just as in a word processor), colorful and stylish borders to images, and even dynamic rollover effects to text links. Best of all, Dreamweaver's streamlined approach lets you combine many of these design properties into powerful, centralized *style sheets* that let you control pages throughout your site.

CSS is a large topic. It's also the heart of today's cutting-edge web design. So instead of dedicating just a single chapter to it, this book provides instruction in the fine art of using CSS in nearly every chapter. In this chapter, you'll learn the basics of CSS and how to use Dreamweaver's powerful CSS tools. In the next few chapters you'll learn how CSS can improve the look of common web page elements like links, images, and tables. Once you're comfortable with the basics, you'll find in-depth information on CSS in Chapters 8 and 9. And in Chapter 10, you'll learn how to harness the power of CSS to fully control the layout of a web page.

Cascading Style Sheet Basics

If you've used styles in programs like Microsoft Word or Adobe InDesign, CSS will feel familiar. A *style* is simply a rule describing how a browser should format a particular piece of HTML. (A *style sheet* is a collection of these styles.)

You can create a single style, for example, that formats text with the font Arial, colored red, and with a left margin of 50 pixels. You can also create styles specifically for images; for instance, you can create a style that aligns an image along the right edge of a web page, surrounds the image with a colorful border, and adds a 50-pixel margin between the image and the surrounding text.

Once you create a style, you can apply it to text, images, or other elements on a page. For example, you could select a paragraph of text and apply a style to it to instantly change the text's size, color, and font. You can also create styles for specific *tags*, so that, for example, a browser displays all <h1> elements in your site, in the same style, no matter where they appear.

Why Use CSS?

In the past, HTML alone provided basic formatting options for text, images, tables, and other web page elements. But today, professional web designers use CSS to style their pages. In fact, the older HTML tags used to format text and other page elements have been phased out by the World Wide Web Consortium (W3C), the organization that defines Web standards, in favor of CSS. And following along with industry practice, Dreamweaver CS5 has made it impossible (unless you write the code yourself) to add obsolete HTML tags such as the <font> tag.

CSS has many benefits over HTML. With CSS, you can format paragraphs to resemble those that appear in a book or newspaper (with the first line indented and no space between each paragraph, for example), and control the leading (the space between lines of type in a paragraph). When you use CSS to add a background image to a page, you get to decide how (and whether) it tiles (repeats). HTML can't even begin to do any of these things.

Even better, CSS styles take up much less space than HTML's formatting options, such as the much-hated <font> tag. CSS usually shaves off a lot of kilobytes from text-heavy pages, while maintaining a high level of formatting control. As a result, your pages look great *and* load faster.

Style sheets also make it easier to update your site. You can collect all your styles into a single file linked to every site page. When it's time to change every <h2> tag to lime green, you edit a style in the style sheet file, and that change immediately ripples through your site, *wherever* that style is used. You can thus completely change the appearance of a site by simply editing a single style sheet.

POWER USERS' CLINIC

Getting to Know (and Love) CSS

Cascading Style Sheets are an exciting–and complex–addition to your web building toolkit, worthy of entire books and websites. For example:

- For an excellent tutorial on CSS, visit W3 Schools' CSS tutorials at *www.w3schools.com/css/*.
- If you want to get help *and* learn more about CSS, the CSS-Discuss mailing list (*www.css-discuss.org*) gives you access to a great community of CSS enthusiasts. Just be prepared for an overflowing inbox, and be aware of the etiquette spelled out on the list's home page.
- You'll also find a helpful collection of wisdom generated on the CSS-Discuss Wiki at *http://css-discuss.incutio.com*. This site provides insider tips, tricks, and resources for solving many common CSS problems.
- For the ultimate source of information, turn to the World Wide Web Consortium's website: *www.w3.org/Style/CSS*. The W3C is the body responsible for many of the standards that drive the Web–including HTML and CSS. (Beware: This site is the ultimate authority on the matter, and reads like a college physics textbook.)
- For a great list of CSS-related sites, visit the Information and Technology Systems and Services website at the University of Minnesota, Duluth: *www.d.umn.edu/itss/support/Training/Online/webdesign/css.html*.
- If you just love to curl up by the fireplace with a good computer book, try *CSS: The Missing Manual* by David McFarland (hey, that name rings a bell). It's written in the same style as this book, with in-depth coverage of CSS and step-by-step tutorials that guide you through every facet of this complicated technology.

CSS may sound like a cure-all for HTML's anemic formatting powers, but truth be told, it is a bit tricky to use. For example, CSS support varies from browser to browser, so you need to test your pages thoroughly on a variety of browsers. Even modern browsers–like Internet Explorer 8 for Windows, Firefox, Opera, and Safari–have their share of weird CSS behavior.

Fortunately, Dreamweaver CS5 is better than ever at displaying complex CSS-based designs, so you can develop your general design in Dreamweaver, and then use the preview feature to fine-tune your designs for different browsers. Or even better, use Adobe's BrowserLab service to generate screenshots of your page taken from a wide range of browsers on both Windows and Mac computers. You'll learn how to use this service on page 667.

Internal vs. External Style Sheets

Each new style you create gets added to a style sheet that you store either in the web page itself (in which case it's an *internal style sheet*), or in a separate file called an *external style sheet*.

Note: You may hear the term "embedded style sheet." It's the same thing as an internal style sheet.

Internal style sheets appear in the <head> portion of a web page, and contain styles that apply only to that page. An internal style sheet is a good choice when you have a very specific formatting task for a single page. For example, you might want to create a unique format the for text and table of a chart that appears only on a single page.

Tip: When you create a new page design, it's often easier to add styles to an internal style sheet. Once you're satisfied with the design, you can export the styles to an external style sheet–for use by all your site's pages–as described on page 306.

An external style sheet, on the other hand, contains only styles—no HTML—and you can link numerous pages to it. In fact, you can link every page on your site to this style sheet, giving your site a uniform, sitewide set of styles. For instance, you can put a headline style in an external style sheet, and link every page on the site to that sheet. Every headline on every page then shares the same look—instant design consistency! Even better, when the boss (or the interior decorator in you) calls up and asks you to change the color of the headlines, you need to edit only a single file—the external style sheet—to update hundreds or even thousands of web pages.

You can create both types of style sheet easily in Dreamweaver, and you aren't limited to choosing one or the other. A single web page can have both an external style sheet (for styles that apply to the whole site, including this page) and an internal style sheet (for page-specific formatting). You can even attach multiple external style sheets to a single page.

Types of Styles

Styles come in several flavors. The most common are *class, ID*, and *tag* styles.

A *class style* is one you create, name, and attach manually to selected text (in other words, text you select with your cursor) or to an HTML tag. Class styles work much like styles in word processing and page layout programs. If you want to display the name of your company in bold and red wherever it appears in a web page, you can create a class style named *company* that formats text in boldface and red letters. You would then select your company's name on the page, and apply this style.

An *ID* style lets you format a *unique* item on a page. Use ID styles to identify an object (or an area of a page) that appears only once—like a website's logo, copyright notice, main navigation bar, or a banner. Designers frequently use IDs when they create CSS-based layouts like those you'll learn about in Chapter 9. An ID style is similar to a class style in that you name the style and apply it manually. But you can apply a class to many different elements on a page, and you can apply an ID to only one tag or object per page. (It's okay to use multiple IDs on a single page, so long as each ID name is different.)

The other major type of CSS style is called a *tag style*, and it applies to an individual HTML tag globally, as opposed to individual pages or selections. Suppose you wanted to display every Heading 1 paragraph in the Arial font. Instead of creating a class style and applying it to every Heading 1 on the page, you could create a tag style for the <h1> tag. In effect, you redefine the tag so that a browser displays it in Arial.

The main benefit to redefining an HTML tag this way is that you don't have to apply the style by hand. Since the new style says that *all* <h1> tags must use Arial, a browser displays <h1> tags in Arial wherever it encounters them.

These HTML tag styles are the easiest way to format a page. For one thing, there's no need to select the tag manually and apply the style; wherever the tag appears, a browser automatically applies the style.

Nevertheless, sometimes only a class style will do, such as when you want to format just a few words in a paragraph. Simply redefining the <p> tag won't do the trick, since that would affect the entire paragraph (and every other paragraph on your site). Instead, you have to create a class style and apply it to just the words you wish to style. In addition, class styles are handy when you want to format just one instance of a tag differently from others. If you want to format the introductory paragraph on a page differently from all other paragraphs on the page, then you create a class style and apply it to that first paragraph. (Another solution is a slightly more complicated, but more flexible, type of style called a *descendent selector*—you'll read about those later, on page 298.)

Note: In addition to classes and tag styles, other types of styles provide added control for particular situations. You can read about these more advanced styles starting on page 297.

Creating Styles

Dreamweaver gives you several ways to create CSS styles. For text, you can use the Property inspector's CSS mode to apply a font, font size, font color, font weight, and alignment to selected text. To create styles for elements other than text (like images or tables), or to tap into the dozens of other CSS properties not listed in the Property inspector, use the CSS Styles panel (see Figure 4-1). To get a complete overview of the style creation process, you'll look at both methods—starting with the more versatile CSS Styles panel, and then moving onto the Property inspector.

Phase 1: Set Up the CSS Type

Dreamweaver gives you many ways to create a new style: On the CSS Styles panel, click the new style button (which Dreamweaver calls the New CSS Rule button; see Figure 4-1); right-click anywhere in the CSS Styles panel, and then, from the menu that appears, select New; or choose Format→CSS Styles→New. The New CSS Rule dialog box appears (Figure 4-2), where you begin creating your new style. (In the technical language of CSS, a style is actually called a *rule*, but for simplicity's sake this book uses the term *style*. After all, *Cascading Rule Sheets* doesn't have much of a ring to it.)

Here's a quick tour of your choices:

- **Selector Type.** From the Selector Type menu, choose the kind of style you want to create. *Class* creates a style that you manually apply to page elements, *ID* creates a style that you can use only once on the page, and *Tag* creates an HTML style that Dreamweaver automatically applies to each occurrence of the tag). See the previous section for a discussion of these three types.

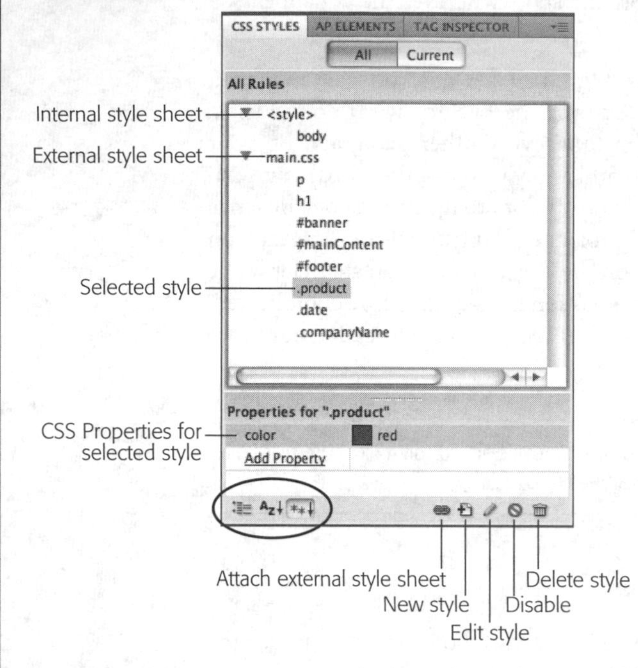

Figure 4-1:
With the "All" button selected, the CSS Styles panel lists the names of all the styles the current page uses, including those in both external and internal style sheets. Here, one external style sheet–main.css–contains five styles. The first two are tag styles (notice that the names match various HTML tags), while the next three are ID styles (note the # at the beginning of the name), and the last three are class styles (note the period before the name). You also see one tag style defined in an internal style sheet–the one listed below "<style>". Click the minus (_) icon (arrow on Mac) to the left of the style sheet to collapse the list of styles, hiding them from view. The "Properties" list in the bottom half of the panel lets you edit a style (see page 304); the three buttons at the bottom left of the panel (circled) control how Dreamweaver displays the Properties list.

You'll want to use the fourth type of style, *Compound*, to create more advanced style types, such as pseudo-classes, attribute selectors, and descendent selectors. You'll learn about these styles in various parts of the book; you can find a detailed discussion starting on page 297.

In addition, if you've selected something on a page (such as a paragraph, an image, or a headline), Dreamweaver highlights the Compound option and, in the Selector Name field, suggests what's called a *descendent selector*. You'll learn more about descendent selectors on page 298, but basically, they're a type of style that applies formatting to nested page elements, that is, to page elements within *other* HTML tags. For example, *"div p"* is a descendent selector that formats any paragraph (that's where the *p* comes) that appears within a <div> tag. So in cases where you want a descendent selector, choose Compound selector.

- **Selector Name.** If you selected Class or ID from the Selector Type menu, enter a name for the new style. According to the rules of CSS, you have to start class style names with a period—*.copyright*, for example—and ID style names with a # symbol—*#banner*, for example. Dreamweaver automatically adds the proper symbol if you forget.

  Another class or ID style name rule: A letter must follow the period or # symbol. After that, you can use any combination of letters and numbers, but avoid unusual characters and spaces. For example, *.logo, #main_content, #column2* all work fine. Dreamweaver lets you know if you use any invalid characters.

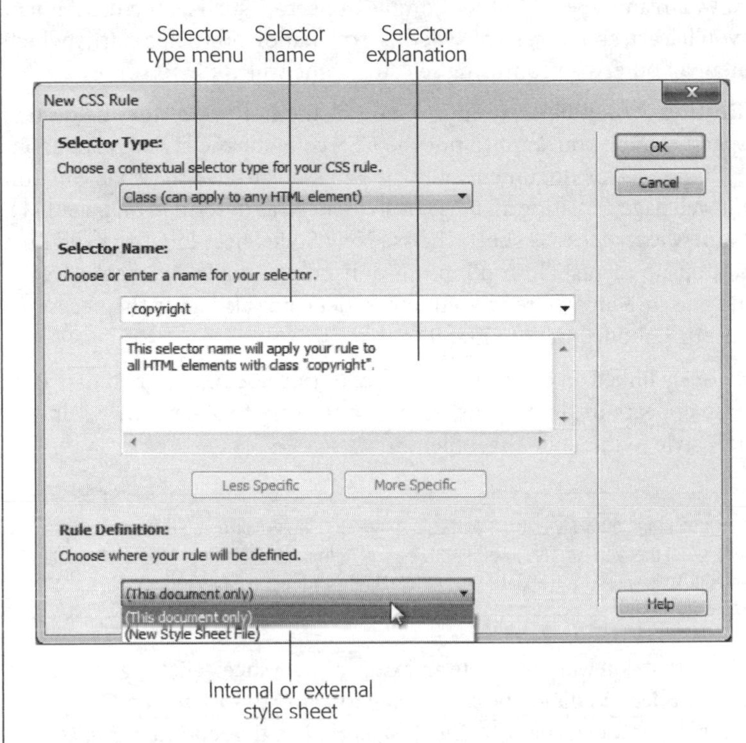

Figure 4-2: *In the New CSS Rule dialog box, you choose a type of style, give it a name, and decide whether to put the style in an internal or external style sheet. You use the two dimmed buttons, labeled Less Specific and More Specific, when you type a special type of CSS selector called a descendent selector (see page 298).*

If you chose the Tag style instead, choose the HTML tag you want to redefine from the Selector Type pop-up menu.

Note: If you're an HTML guru, you may find it faster to skip the Selector Name pop-up menu and just type the tag (minus the brackets) in the text box. For example, if you want to create a style for all unordered (bulleted) lists, type *ul*.

If you select the Compound option, Dreamweaver lets you type any valid CSS selector type in the Selector field (you'll learn about more selectors on page 297). You use this feature for some advanced CSS tricks, but you can also use it just to create a tag or class style.

Note that when you add a class, ID, tag, or other selector to the Selector Name field, Dreamweaver briefly explains to which HTML elements it will apply the selector. For example, Figure 4-1 displays the New CSS Rule dialog box in the process of creating a new class style named *.copyright*. The dialog box explains that Dreamweaver will apply this rule to all the HTML elements to which you assigned the *class* property *copyright* (in other words, to all the text and tags you applied the class copyright, as described on page 119). For simple styles like class and tag styles, this explanation is pretty much like "Uh, yeah. Tell me something I don't know, Dreamweaver." But for complex selectors such as the descendent selectors you'll learn about on page 298, this explanation box helps clarify which page element an otherwise confusing selector name will apply to.

- **Rule Definition.** The Rule Definition menu at the bottom of the dialog box lets you specify where you want to put the CSS code for the style you're about to create. Choose "This document only" if you want to use the style only on the current web page (creating an *internal* style sheet, as described on page 111). To create a new *external* style sheet, choose New Style Sheet File from the Rule Definition pop-up menu. This option not only creates a new external CSS file (which you can save anywhere in your site folder), but also adds the necessary code in the current document to link it to that file.

  If you previously linked an external style sheet to this document, then that style sheet's name appears in the pop-up menu, indicating that Dreamweaver will add the new style to this style sheet file.

Tip: If you create a bunch of internal styles on a particular page, and later realize you'd like to turn them into an external style sheet that you can use in other pages, you're in luck. Dreamweaver includes many tools for managing your style sheets. You'll learn how to use them starting on page 306.

If you indicate that you want to create an external style sheet, clicking OK brings up a Save Style Sheet As dialog box. Navigate to your site's folder, and then type in a name for the new external CSS file. Just as HTML files end in .html, so CSS files end in .css.

Note: If you'll be using this style sheet for all your site's pages, you may want to save it in your site's root folder, or in a folder specifically dedicated to style sheets, and give it a general name like *site_styles.css, main.css* or *global.css*. (You don't have to type the .css file name extension, by the way. In this case, Dreamweaver adds it.)

No matter what Selector Type option you select (Class, ID, Tag, or Compound), clicking OK brings you to the CSS Rule Definition window.

Phase 2: Defining the Style

The CSS Rule Definition window provides access to all the available formatting for styling text, graphics, tables, and other HTML tags (see Figure 4-3). You'll learn about each of the properties throughout this book.

When you finish defining a style, click OK at the bottom of the Rule Definition window. Dreamweaver adds the style to the specified style sheet, and displays it in the CSS Styles panel (Figure 4-1).

The real trick to defining a style is mastering all the properties available, such as borders, margins, and background colors, and *then* learning how to use them reliably in different browsers. You'll learn about different CSS properties starting on page 128.

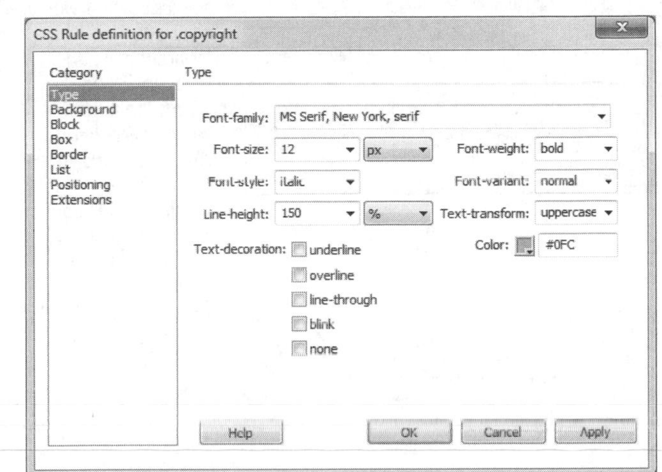

Figure 4-3:
For ultimate formatting control, Dreamweaver lets you set dozens of different Cascading Style Sheet properties from the CSS Rule Definition window. You'll learn about these options throughout this book. For example, you can find the Type properties shown here discussed on page 128.

Creating a Style with the Property Inspector

The Property inspector's CSS mode lets you quickly create (or modify) styles, such as choosing a font or a font size (see Figure 4-4), for text you select. In CSS mode, the Property inspector looks a lot like a formatting bar in a word processing program: dedicated buttons let you make text bold or italic, control alignment, and set font type, size, and color. All these controls use CSS properties to achieve their effects.

To use the CSS mode, select some text on the page. For example, drag your cursor to select a portion of text, double-click to select a word, or triple-click to select an entire paragraph or headline. Then, from the Property inspector, select an option—for example, choose a selection of fonts from the font menu. If you don't have a style currently applied to the selection, you see <New CSS Rule> in the Targeted Rule menu on the Property inspector (see Figure 4-4, top), and when you apply a format, Dreamweaver opens the New CSS Rule dialog box (Figure 4-1).

Now it's up to you to pick the type of style, name it, and decide where to store it; just follow the same steps you used to create a new style using the CSS Styles panel, as described on page 113. You're free to create a class, tag, ID, or other style. After you create the new style, you return to the Property inspector (you skip the Rule Definition window). The Property inspector then lists the new style name in the Targeted Rule menu and displays the formatting you selected (for example, the font you choose appears in the Font menu).

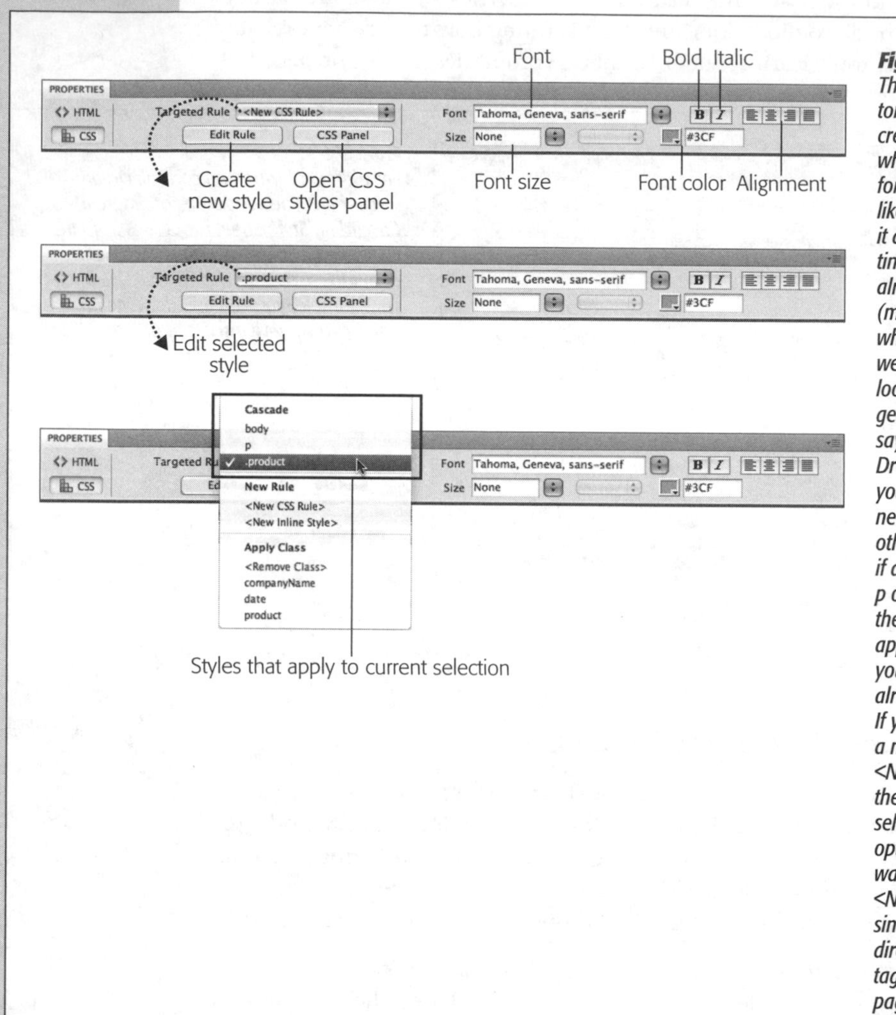

***Figure 4-4:** The Property inspector's CSS mode either creates a new style when you select a formatting option like font size (top) or it adds the formatting property to an already existing style (middle). You can tell which action Dreamweaver will take by looking at the Targeted Rule menu–if it says <New CSS Rule>, Dreamweaver lets you create a brand new class, tag, ID, or other style. However, if a style name (like p or .copyright in the middle image) appears in that menu, you're editing an already existing style. If you want to create a new style, select <New CSS Rule> from the menu before you select a formatting option. Normally you want to avoid the <New Inline Style>, since this adds CSS directly to an HTML tag, making the web page's file size larger and the file slower to load and harder to update. However, inline styles come in handy when you need to create HTML emails, since that's the most reliable way to add CSS to an email message.*

Let's look at a basic example. Suppose you wanted to format a copyright notice at the bottom of the page in a way that's different from other text on the page. You would first triple-click the copyright paragraph to select the text, and then choose whatever formatting options you want from the CSS mode of the Property inspector—for example, select 12 from the Size menu to create small, 12-pixel type.

At this point, Dreamweaver opens the New CSS Rule dialog box and, from the Selector Type menu, you select Class, and then, in the Selector Name field, type *.copyright*. You could then store the file in either an external or internal style sheet as described on page 116. When you close the New CSS Rule window, Dreamweaver applies a new class style named *copyright* to the paragraph and the Size box in the Property inspector displays "12" to denote the text's pixel size.

The Property inspector's CSS Mode behaves differently, however, if you already have a style applied to the selected text. In that case, the style appears in the Targeted Rule menu. For example, in Figure 4-3 (bottom), you already applied the class style *product* to the selected text, so you see ".product" listed in that menu. At this point, choosing another formatting option from the Property inspector—for instance, clicking the bold button, or selecting a font from the font menu—doesn't create a new style, it simply adds the new format to the existing style.

For example, say you create a .copyright class style with a font size of 12 pixels. If you select that copyright text again and then select a font color, Dreamweaver updates the .copyright class style—it adds the CSS color property to the style. Making additional formatting choices also updates the style.

Using Styles

Once you create styles, you can easily apply them. In fact, if you created HTML tag styles, you don't need to do anything to apply them: Their selectors (see the box on page 120) automatically dictate which tags they affect.

Applying a Class Style

You can apply class styles to any selection in the document window, whether it's a word, an image, or an entire paragraph. In fact, you can apply a class style to *any* individual HTML tag, such as a <p> (paragraph), <td> (table cell), or <body> tag. You can even select just a single word within a paragraph and apply a style to it.

Applying a class style to text

Start out by selecting some words. Then, from the Property inspector, select the style name—you can do this either in HTML mode, in which case you select the name from the class menu (Figure 4-5, top), or in CSS mode, where you use the Targeted Rule menu (Figure 4-5, bottom).

UP TO SPEED

Anatomy of a Style

When you style a page, Dreamweaver automatically handles the details of adding the proper CSS code to it, but if you're looking for a way to impress your neighbors, here's the behind-the-scenes scoop on how it works.

When you create an internal style sheet, Dreamweaver adds a pair of <style> tags to the head of the page. The opening <style> tag tells a web browser that the following information isn't HTML–it's CSS code. When the browser encounters the closing </style> tag, it knows the CSS style information has ended.

Within the <style> tag, you see one or more styles (reminder: in CSS-speak, styles are also called "rules"). An HTML tag style for the Heading 1 tag (<h1>), for example, might look like this:

```
h1 {
font-size: 24px;
color: #003399;
}
```

The first part–h1–is called a *selector* (in CSS-speak) and indicates what the style applies to. In this case, wherever the <h1> (Heading 1) tag appears in the web page's code, a browser applies this style.

The information between the braces–{}–states what formatting the browser should apply. The preceding code contains two formatting instructions for the <h1> tag. Each is called a *declaration* and is composed of a *property* and a *value*. For instance, *font-size: 24px* is one declaration, with a property of *font-size* and a value of *24px*. In other words, this rule tells a browser that it should make text inside an <h1> tag 24 pixels tall. The second declaration makes a browser display the text of all <h1> tags in the color #003399.

A class style looks just like an HTML tag, except that instead of a tag, the selector is a name you supplied, preceded by a dot, like this:

```
.company {
font-size: 24px;
color: #003399;
}
```

Styles stored in an external style sheet look exactly the same; the only difference is that external style sheets don't include the <style> tags and must not include any HTML code. In Dreamweaver you can easily get a look at the raw style information of an external style sheet: Near the top of the document window, in the list of related files, just click the CSS file's name (see Figure 1-2).

To style an entire paragraph, triple-click within the paragraph (or heading) to select it, and then use the Property inspector to select a style. When you style an entire paragraph, you're actually telling Dreamweaver to apply the style to the <p> tag. In that case, Dreamweaver adds a special *class* property to the page's code, like this: <p class="company"> (for a class style named *.company*).

Tip: You can also add a class to an entire paragraph or heading simply by clicking anywhere inside the paragraph, and then, from the Property inspector, choosing the class name–just make sure you don't select a piece of text, or Dreamweaver applies the style just to the selected text, not the entire paragraph.

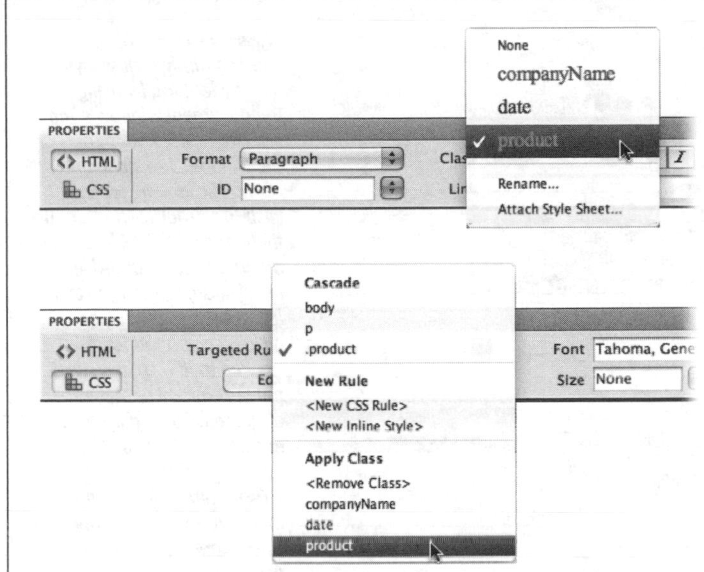

Figure 4-5:
The easiest way to apply a class style is through the Property inspector. For non-text elements like images or tables, a Class menu appears in the top right of the Property inspector. For text, you apply class styles by using either the Class menu if the Property inspector is in HTML mode (top) or the Targeted Rule Menu when it's in CSS mode (bottom). Dreamweaver uses only the bottom section of the Targeted Rule Menu (the stuff below "Apply Class") to add (or remove) a class from a text selection. The other items listed let you create new styles, or view the styles that apply to the selection.

On the other hand, if you apply a class to a selection that isn't a tag—like a single word that you double-click—Dreamweaver wraps the selection within a <span> tag like this: <span class="company">Chia Vet</span>. This tag, in other words, applies a style to a *span* of text that Dreamweaver can't identify by a single tag.

Applying a class style to objects

To apply a class style to an object (like an image or a table), start by selecting the object. As always, the Tag selector at the bottom of the document window is a great way to select a tag. Then, at the top right of the Property inspector, use the Class pop-up menu to select the style name.

Note: You can apply any class style to any element, although doing so doesn't always make sense. If you format a graphic with a style that specifies bold, red Courier type, it doesn't look any different.

Other class styling options

You can also apply a class style by selecting whatever element you wish to style, choosing Format→CSS Styles, and then, from the submenu, selecting the style. Or you can right-click (Control-click) the style's name in the CSS Styles panel, and then, from the pop-up menu, choose Apply. Finally, you can also apply a class from the document window's Tag selector, as shown in Figure 4-6.

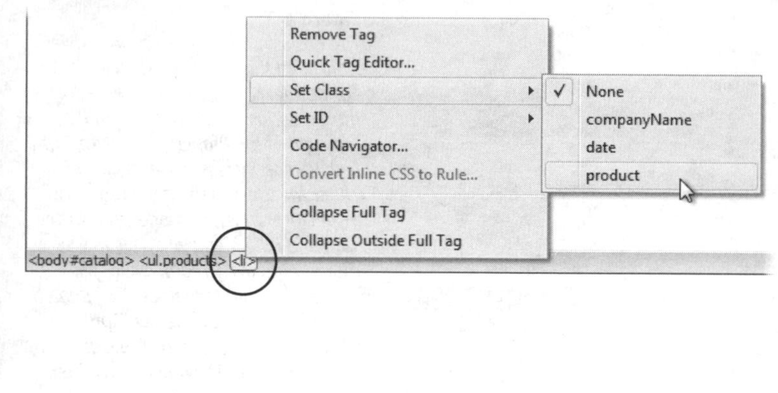

Figure 4-6: *You can apply a class style directly to a tag by using the document window's Tag selector at the bottom of the window. Just right-click (Control-click) the tag you wish to format (circled), and then, from the Set Class submenu, select a class style. In addition, the Tag selector lets you know if a tag has a class style or an ID style applied to it. If so, the style's name is added at the end of the tag. For example, in this figure, the body has an ID of catalog applied to it (<body#catalog>) and an unordered list has the class products applied to it (<body.products>).*

Removing a Class Style

To remove a class style from text on a web page, select the text, and then, from the Property inspector (see Figure 4-5), choose None from the Class menu (HTML mode) or <Remove Class> from the Targeted Rule menu (CSS mode). To remove a class style from another object (like an image), select the object, and then, from the Property inspector's Class menu, choose None. You can also choose Format→CSS Styles→None to remove a style from any selection (even non-text elements like images or tables).

Note: If you applied a class style to a selection of text, you don't have to select *all* the text to remove the style. Just click anywhere inside it, and then select None from the Property inspector's Class menu or <Remove Class> from the Targeted Rule menu. Dreamweaver is smart enough to realize that you want to remove the style applied to the text. (If you applied the style to a tag, then Dreamweaver removes the Class property. If you applied the style using the <span> tag, Dreamweaver removes the <span> tag.)

You can't, however, remove *tag* styles from HTML tags. For example, suppose you redefined the <h2> tag using the steps outlined on page 113. If your page has three Heading 2 (<h2>) paragraphs, and you want the third heading to have a different style from the other two, you can't simply "remove" the <h2> style from the third heading. You need to create a new *class* style with all the formatting options you want for that third heading, and then apply it directly to this particular <h2> tag. (By the magic of CSS, the class formatting options override any existing tag style options—see page 311 for more on this sleight of hand.)

Applying IDs to a Tag

To apply an ID to text, just select the text, and use the ID menu in the HTML mode of the Property inspector (see Figure 4-5, top). Since you can apply each ID name only once per page, the menu lists only unassigned IDs—IDs that exist in your style sheet but that you haven't applied to a tag on the page.

For non-text elements, select the element, and then, in the Property inspector, type the ID name into the ID field. (For some elements, the ID field is unlabeled, but you can always find it on the far left of the Property inspector.)

You can also use the Tag selector as outlined in Figure 4-6. Just use the Set ID menu in the contextual menu that appears when you right-click (Ctrl-click) the tag.

Tip: The Tag selector tells you whether you applied an ID to a tag by including the # symbol with the ID name. In Figure 4-6, for example, *body#catalog* indicates that the <body> tag has an ID named "catalog" applied to it.

Whenever you apply an ID to a tag, Dreamweaver adds a bit of HTML code to your page. For instance, an ID style named *#copyright* applied to a paragraph looks like this in the HTML: <p id="copyright"> (this is just like the "class" property that's added when you use class styles, as described on page 119).

To remove an ID from a text element, select the text, and then, from the Property inspector's ID menu, select None. For non-text elements, select the element, and then, in the Property inspector's ID field, delete the ID name.

Linking to an External Style Sheet

Whenever you create an external style sheet while adding a style to a web page, Dreamweaver automatically links it to the current document. To use its styles in a different web page, you must *attach* it to the page.

To do so, open the web page to which you want to add the style sheet. Then, on the CSS Styles panel, click the Attach External Style Sheet button (see Figure 4-1). (If the CSS Styles panel isn't open, choose Window→CSS Styles or press Shift-F11.)

Tip: You can also use the Property inspector to attach a style sheet. Just select "Attach Style Sheet" from the Class menu in HTML mode (see Figure 4-5, top).

The Attach External Style Sheet window appears (see Figure 4-7). Click Browse. In the Select Style Sheet File dialog box that appears, navigate to and double-click the CSS (.css) file you wish to attach to the document. If the style sheet you select is outside the current site—for example, it's in another one of your websites—Dreamweaver offers to copy the style sheet file into your site's root folder; click Yes.

The Attach External Style Sheet window provides two other options: how to attach the style sheet, and what type of "media" you want the styles to apply to. The "media" setting is optional and dictates when Dreamweaver applies the styles. For example, you can one set of styles for when you print a page and another set for when a browser displays it. You'll find in-depth information on media types and how to use them on page 322.

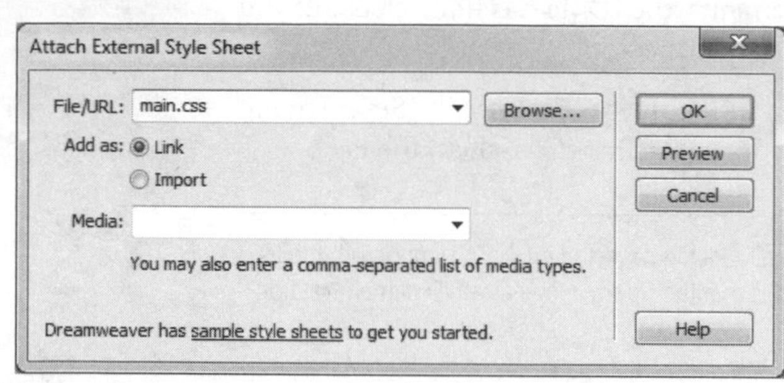

Figure 4-7:
Adding styles from an external style sheet is as simple as browsing for the file, and then clicking OK. Choosing a media type is optional.

When you attach an external style sheet, you can either "link" it or "import" it. These two choices are nearly identical; they're simply two different ways to attach an external style sheet to a web page. The method preferred by the pros, link, is also Dreamweaver's suggested choice. Save yourself an extra click, and just go with the link option.

Tip: You can preview the effect of the style sheet on your page by clicking the Preview button in the Attach External Style Sheet window.

After choosing your options, click OK, and Dreamweaver adds the necessary HTML to the head of the web page, and automatically formats any tags in the document according to the style sheet's tag styles. You see the formatting changes take place in the document window immediately after you attach the style sheet.

If the style sheet contains *class* styles, on the other hand, you don't see their formatting effects until you apply them to an element on the page, as described on page 119.

Manipulating Styles

As with anything in Dreamweaver, styles are easy enough to edit, delete, or duplicate; all you need is a map of the terrain.

Editing Styles

While building a website, you almost always continually refine your designs. That chartreuse color you assigned to the background of your pages may have looked great at 2 a.m., but it loses something in the light of day.

Fortunately, one of CSS's greatest selling points is how easy it is to update a website's formatting.

Note: Although this section focuses mainly on how to style your text, you also use CSS styles to add background colors, background images, borders, and to accurately position elements on a page. The next few chapters show you how to style links, images, tables, forms, and other page elements with CSS.

Dreamweaver provides many ways to edit styles:

- In the CSS Styles panel, select a style (Figure 4-2) and then click the Edit Style button to open the Rule Definition window (Figure 4-3; this is the same window you used to create the style). Make your changes, and then click OK to return to the document window. Dreamweaver reformats the page to reflect your changes .
- Double-clicking the name of a style in the CSS panel also opens the Rule Definition window. Actually, depending on a preference setting—or a setting someone else may have tweaked while using your computer—double-clicking a style in the CSS panel may display the—eeek!—raw CSS code in Code view. To change this behavior, open the Preferences window (Ctrl+U [⌘-U]), click the CSS Styles category, and then select the "Edit using CSS dialog" button.

FREQUENTLY ASKED QUESTION

When Formatting Disappears

Sometimes when I copy text from one web page and paste it into another page, all the formatting disappears. What's going on?

When you use Cascading Style Sheets, keep in mind that the actual style information is stored either in the <head> of a web page (for internal style sheets) or in a separate CSS file (an external style sheet). If a page includes an internal style sheet, when you copy text, graphics, or other page elements, Dreamweaver copies those elements and any class or ID style definitions that content uses. When you paste the HTML into another page, Dreamweaver writes the styles into the <head> of that page. This feature can save you some time, but it doesn't solve all your woes. It doesn't, for example, copy any *tag styles* you created, nor does it carry over most advanced styles (see page 297 for more on advanced styles). So if you copy and paste some text–say, an <h1> tag styled with an h1 tag style–the <h1> tag and its contents end up in the other page, but the style information doesn't.

In addition, if you copy and paste text from a page that uses an external style sheet, the styles themselves don't go along for the ride. So if you copy a paragraph that has a class style applied to it and paste it into another document, the code in the paragraph is pasted (<p class="company"> for instance), but the actual "company" style, with all its formatting properties, isn't.

The best solution is to use a common external style sheet for all the pages on your site. That way, when you copy and paste HTML, all the pages share the same styles and formatting. So in the preceding example, if you copy a paragraph that includes a class style–class="company"–into another page that shares the same style sheet, the paragraphs look the same on both pages. See pages 116 and 123 for more on how to create one of these uber sitewide external style sheets.

In the CSS Styles panel, right-click (Control-click) the name of a style, and then, from the shortcut menu, choose Edit, which also opens the Rule Definition window. Make your changes to the style and then click OK to return to the document window.

Tip: The properties pane in the CSS Styles panel offers yet another, faster way to edit a style. This advanced technique requires a bit of CSS savvy and is discussed on page 304.

Deleting a Style

At some point, you may find you created a style that you don't need after all. Maybe you redefined the HTML <code> tag and realized that you never use it. You don't need to keep it around, taking up precious space in the style sheet.

To delete a style, make sure you have the CSS Styles panel open (Window→CSS Styles), and the All button highlighted (see Figure 4-1). Click the name of the style you wish to delete, and then press your keyboard's Delete key (you can also click the Trash can icon at the bottom of the panel). You can remove all the styles in an internal style sheet (as well as the style sheet itself) by selecting the style sheet—indicated by "<style>" in the CSS Styles panel (see Figure 4-1)—and pressing Delete (or clicking the Trash can icon). If you "trash" an *external* style sheet, however, you merely unlink it from the current document without actually deleting the .css file.

Unfortunately, deleting a class style *doesn't* delete any references to the style in your site's pages. For example, if you created a style called *.company* and applied it throughout your site, and you then delete that style from the style sheet, Dreamweaver doesn't remove the <span> tags or class properties that refer to the style. Your pages are still littered with orphaned code like this—<span class="company">CosmoFarmer </span>—even though the text loses its styling. (See how to solve this problem using Dreamweaver's powerful "Find and Replace" tool on page 801.)

Renaming a Class Style

You can rename any style by selecting it in the CSS Styles panel, pausing a second, and then clicking the name again. This makes the name editable, at which point you can type a new name in its place. Of course, if you change a style named *p* to a style named *h1*, you've essentially removed the style for the <p> tag and added an <h1> style to the style sheet—in other words, all the paragraphs in your pages would lose their formatting, and all <h1> tags would suddenly change appearance. Alternatively, you could open the .css file in Code view and then edit the name. However, when it comes to class styles, just changing the name doesn't do much good if you've already applied the style throughout your site. The *old* class name still appears in the HTML everywhere you used it.

FREQUENTLY ASKED QUESTION

When Undo Won't Do

Sometimes when I edit a style—say, to change a font color—I can undo that change. But sometimes, I'm unable to undo changes I've made to a style. What gives?

You can undo only changes made to a document you're currently working on. Say you added an internal style sheet (see page 111) to a document. If you edit one of those styles, Dreamweaver lets you undo those changes. Because the styles in an internal style sheet are a part of the web page you're working on, choosing Edit→Undo undoes the last change you made.

However, if you're using an external style sheet, you're actually working on two *different* files at the same time—the web page you're building, and the style sheet file in which you add, delete, or edit styles. So if you're designing a web page and edit a style in the external style sheet, you're actually making a change to the style sheet file. In this case, choosing Edit→Undo undoes only the last change made to the *web page*. If you want to undo the change you made to the external style sheet, you need to use Dreamweaver's related files feature. The name of the external style sheet appears on the Related Files toolbar, which appears below the title of the web page file; click the file's name to move to its code, and then choose Edit→Undo. Click the Source Code button to return to your web page (you'll learn more about the Related Files toolbar on page 433).

What you really need to do is rename the class style, and *then* perform a find-and-replace operation to change the name wherever it appears in your site. Dreamweaver includes a handy tool to simplify this process.

To rename a class style:

1. **In the Property inspector, choose Rename in the Class menu (Figure 4-5).**

   The Rename Style window appears (Figure 4-8).

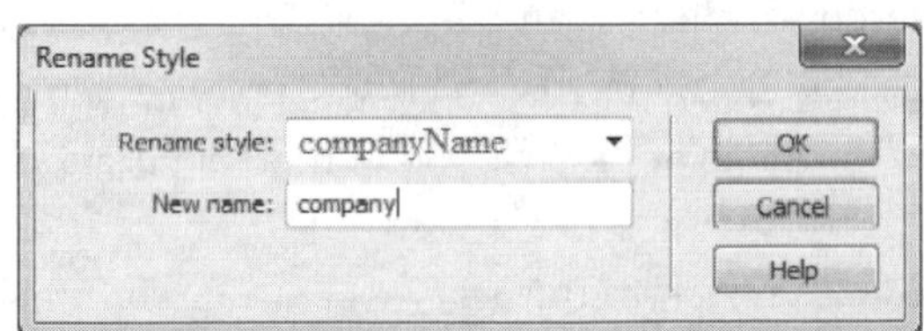

Figure 4-8: *The Rename Style tool is a fast and easy way to change the name of a class style even if you used the style hundreds of times throughout your site.*

2. **From the top menu, choose the name of the style you wish to rename.**

   This menu lists all the class styles in the page's stylesheets, both internal and external.

3. **In the "New name" box, type the new style name.**

   You must follow the same rules for naming class styles as described on page 114. But, just as when creating a new class, you don't need to precede the name with a period—Dreamweaver takes care of that.

4. **Click OK.**

   If the style whose name you're changing is an internal style, Dreamweaver makes the change. Your job is complete.

   If the style belongs to an external style sheet, however, Dreamweaver warns you that other pages on the site may also use this style. To successfully rename the style, you have to use Dreamweaver's "Find and Replace" tool to search the site and update all the pages that use the old style name. In that case, continue to step 5.

5. **If you get cold feet, click Cancel to call off the name change, or click Yes to open the "Find and Replace" window, where you should click Replace All.**

   One last warning appears, reminding you that you can't undo the find-and-replace.

Note: If you click No in the warning box that appears after step 4, Dreamweaver still renames the style in the external style sheet, but it doesn't update your pages.

---

6. **Click Yes.**

   Dreamweaver goes through each page of your site, dutifully updating the name of the style everywhere it appears.

Duplicating a Style

Dreamweaver makes it easy to duplicate a CSS style, which is handy when you've created, say, an HTML tag style, and then decide you'd rather make it a class style. Or you may want to use the formatting options from one style as a starting-off point for a new style. Either way, you start by duplicating an existing style.

You can do so two ways. The easiest is to open the CSS Styles panel (Window→CSS Styles), right-click (Control-click) the name of the style you want to duplicate, and then, from the shortcut menu, choose Duplicate.

The Duplicate CSS Rule window appears (Figure 4-9), where you can give the duplicated style a new name, reassign its Type setting, use the "Define in" menu to move it from an internal to an external style sheet, and so on.

When you click OK, Dreamweaver adds the duplicate style to the page or external style sheet. You can then edit the new style just as you would any other, as described on page 124.

Text Formatting with CSS

One of the best uses for Cascading Style Sheets is to convert the drab appearance of HTML text into lavishly designed prose. Or, if you like a somber, corporate style, CSS can help with that, too. Whatever your design inclination, you can improve the look of your web text using CSS.

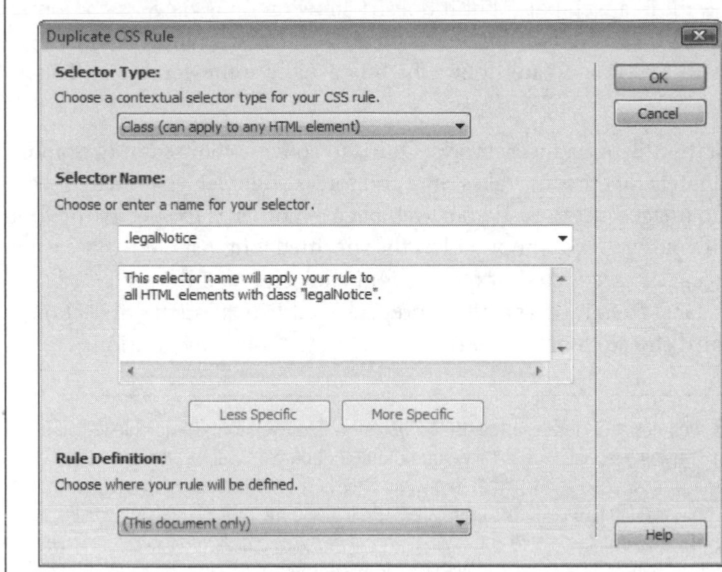

Figure 4-9: *The Duplicate CSS Rule dialog box looks and acts just like the New CSS Rule box (Figure 4-2). You can select a new style type, name it, and then add it to an external or internal style sheet. The only difference is that the duplicated style retains all the original style's CSS properties.*

You can define six text-related CSS properties using the CSS mode of the Property inspector (see Figure 4-4), or use the full-blown CSS Rule Definition window to deploy more than 64 CSS properties. The most commonly used properties for text are stored in the Type (Figure 4-14) and Block categories, while the List category offers several options for formatting bulleted and numbered lists.

Note: You can apply nearly every CSS property to text. For example, you can use the border property to underline text, and the margin property to remove space between paragraphs. You'll find those properties and others not listed in the Type or Block categories introduced later in this book (you don't want to blow your circuits too quickly). For now, you'll learn the most type-centric properties.

Choosing a Font

Formatting fonts for the Web is very much like using fonts in a word processor. Sadly, it carries some of the same drawbacks. For example, if you create a beautiful document in Microsoft Word, using fancy fonts you just bought from a small font company in Nome, Alaska, you're in for a rude surprise when you email the document to your boss. He won't see anything resembling the memo on *your* screen. That's because he doesn't own the same fonts. He'll see some default font on his computer—Times, perhaps. Fonts show up in a distributed document only if each recipient has the same fonts installed.

On the Web, you're in the same predicament. You're free, as a web designer, to specify *any* font you want in a web page, but it doesn't show up on a viewer's computer unless she's installed the same font on her system. If she hasn't, your visitor's web browser shows your text in a default font, which is usually some version of Times, Arial, or Courier.

You can deal with this dilemma several ways. One is to convert your text into graphic images—unfortunately that process takes time and forces your web visitors to download byte-hogging images just to read your web page. Another is to specify the font you'd *like* to use; if your viewer's computer has the specified font installed, that's what she'll see. You can specify secondary or tertiary font choices, too, if the preferred font isn't available. In fact, Dreamweaver offers prepackaged lists of such "first choice, second choice, third choice" fonts, as you'll find out in the following section.

Note: Recently, some web designers have started using what are called "web fonts"– downloadable fonts you can use on your site using special CSS. Basically, you put the font on your web server, and add CSS to your site that lets visitors download and use that font while they view your site. Astonishingly, it works in all major browsers (and even in IE 5 and up)! There are a few tricks to the process, including using a special IE-only font format. You can read more about web fonts at *http://webfonts.info/* and download ready-to-go, free web fonts (which include the required CSS to make them work) from *www.fontsquirrel.com/fontface*. Unfortunately, Dreamweaver CS5 doesn't provide any support for web fonts–you have to hand code the CSS for this–and Design view doesn't display the web fonts.

Applying font formatting

You can use either the Font menu in the Property inspector's CSS mode (Figure 4-3) or the CSS Rule Definition window's Font-family menu (Figure 4-12). In either case, you're actually either creating a new style as described on page 113 or updating an existing style.

You'll soon discover that Dreamweaver's font menus aren't quite what you're used to. When you apply a font to text, you have to choose from one of the prepackaged lists just described; a typical choice is something like "Arial, Helvetica, sans-serif". In other words, you can't just choose a single font, such as Helvetica.

If the first font isn't installed on your visitor's computer, the browser looks down the list until it finds a font that is. Different operating systems use different fonts, so these lists include one font that's common on Windows and another, similar-looking font that's common on the Mac. Arial, for instance, is found on all Windows machines, while Helvetica is a similar font for Macs.

That's it. You've just selected one of Dreamweaver's preinstalled fonts, and any text the CSS style formats will use the font you selected. If you'd like a greater degree of control over the fonts your page displays, read on.

UP TO SPEED

Knowing Your Font Types

You can find literally tens of thousands of different fonts to express your every thought: from bookish, staid, and classical typefaces to rounded, cartoonish squiggles.

Most fonts are divided into two categories: serif and sans-serif. Graphic designers often use serif fonts for long passages of text, as it's widely believed that serifs–small decorative strokes ("hands" and "feet") at the extremities of a letter's main outline–gently lead the eye from letter to letter, making the text easier to read. Examples of serif fonts are Times, Times New Roman, Georgia, and Minion, the font in the main body paragraphs of this book.

Designers often use sans-serif ("without serifs") fonts for headlines, thanks to their clean and simple appearance. Arial, Helvetica, Verdana, and Formata are all sans-serif fonts (you're reading Formata right now). Some people believe that you should use only sans-serif fonts on web pages because they think the delicate decorative strokes of serif fonts don't display well on the coarse resolution of a computer screen. This is an aesthetic judgment, so you should feel free to pick the fonts you think look best.

There are other classes of fonts as well, such as script fonts that resemble handwriting and display fonts that are usually bold, fun, and difficult to read at small font sizes. However, there's not much overlap between operating systems with these types of fonts, so you won't see them used frequently on web pages.

Creating custom font lists

Dreamweaver CS5 comes with 13 preset font lists, which incorporate fonts common to both Windows and Macs. But you can easily stray from the pack and create your own lists. If you proceed with the custom approach, make sure you know what fonts your visitors have—easily done if you're designing a corporate intranet and know what computers your company uses—and always specify one font that you *know* is installed. This way, while your page may not look exactly as you intended, it'll at least be readable.

Note: Technically, you can specify any number of fallback fonts in one of these lists, not just first, second, and third choices. Your list can range anywhere from just a single font to a long list arranged in order of preference.

Here's how you create a new "first choice, second choice, third choice" font list.

1. **Open the Edit Font List dialog box.**

   From the Property inspector's Font menu (visible only in CSS mode), choose Edit Font List, or choose Format→Font→Edit Font List. Either way, the Edit Font List dialog box appears (Figure 4-10).

   - Marker Felt Wide, Comic Sans MS, fantasy
   - Century Gothic, Gill Sans, Arial, sans-serif

- Franklin Gothic Medium, Arial Narrow, sans-serif
- Optima, Segoe UI, Arial, sans-serif

2. **Select a first-choice font from the "Available fonts" list, or type in the font name.**

   Dreamweaver lists all the fonts installed on your computer in the "Available fonts" menu. Simply click to select the font you wish to add.

   Alternatively, you can type a font's name into the box that appears directly below the list of available fonts—a handy trick if you want to include a font that isn't installed on your computer (a Windows font when you're working on a Mac, for example).

3. **Add the font you just highlighted to your new, custom font list by clicking the << button (or just double-clicking the font name).**

   Your first-choice font appears in the "Chosen fonts" list.

4. **Repeat steps 2 and 3 for each font you want to include in your custom list.**

   The order in which you add the fonts is the order in which they appear on the list. These become the "first choice, second choice, third choice" fonts.

   Unfortunately, there's no way to change the order of the fonts once you add them. So if you accidentally put the fonts in the wrong order, you must delete the list by clicking the minus (–) button (at the upper-left corner of the dialog box) and start over.

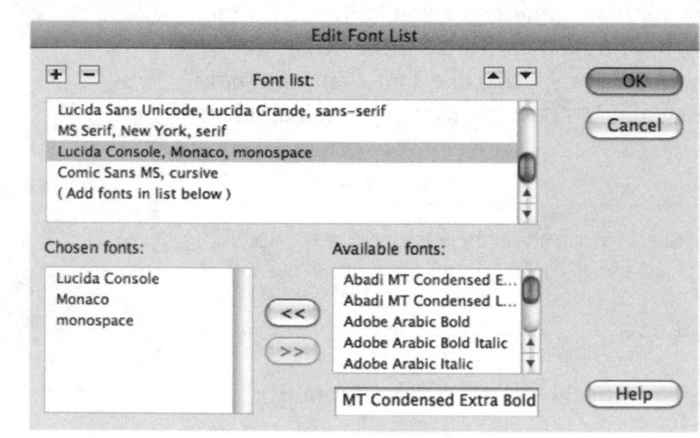

Figure 4-10: *In the Edit Font dialog box, you can not only create your own font lists, but you can edit, remove, or reorder the predefined lists. When you click a list in the "Font list" menu, the "first choice, second choice, third choice" fonts appear in the lower-left corner. To remove a font from that list, click the font name, and then click the >> button. To add a font to the list, select a font in the "Available fonts" menu, and then click the << button. Finally, to reorder the font lists as they appear in the Property inspector, the CSS Rule Definition window's Font menu, or Format→Font menu, and then click the arrow keys near the upper-right corner of the dialog box.*

POWER USERS' CLINIC

Font Convergence

While Windows PCs and Macs used to come with very different sets of preinstalled fonts, there's been some convergence in the past few years. These days, you can count on the average PC or Mac having the following fonts: Arial, Arial Black, Arial Narrow, Comic Sans MS, Courier, Courier New, Georgia, Times New Roman, Trebuchet MS, Verdana, and Webdings.

If your audience includes people running Unix or Linux, all bets are off. In that case, stick to these three fonts: Helvetica (make sure to also specify Arial for Windows owners), Times (Times New Roman for Windows), and Courier (Courier New for Windows).

You can find a concise comparison that lists fonts friendly to both Windows and Macs at *www.speaking-in-styles.com/web-typography/Web-Safe-Fonts/* and another useful list at *http://dustinbrewer.com/fonts-on-the-web-and-a-list-of-web-safe-fonts*. You can find a great article on the subject at *http://24ways.org/2007/increase-your-font-stacks-with-font-matrix*.

To jump-start your adventures, here are a few font combinations that work relatively well for both Windows and Mac visitors:

- Marker Felt Wide, Comic Sans MS, fantasy
- Century Gothic, Gill Sans, Arial, sans-serif
- Franklin Gothic Medium, Arial Narrow, sans-serif
- Optima, Segoe UI, Arial, sans-serif

5. **Add a generic font family.**

   This last step isn't strictly necessary, but it's a good idea. If your web page visitor is some kind of anti-font radical whose PC doesn't have *any* of the fonts you chose, his browser will substitute the generic font family you specify here.

   Generic fonts are listed at the bottom of the list of "Available fonts" and include "cursive", "fantasy", "monospace", "sans-serif", and "serif". On most systems, the monospaced font is Courier, the serif font is Times, and the sans-serif font is Arial or Helvetica. Select a generic font that's similar in appearance to the fonts in your list. For instance, choose "sans-serif" if your list consists of sans-serif fonts like Helvetica or Arial; choose "serif" if you specified fonts like Times or Georgia; or choose "monospace" for a font like Courier.

6. **Click OK.**

   Your new font package appears in the Property inspector's Font menu, ready to apply.

Changing the Font Size

Varying the sizes of fonts on a web page is one way to direct a viewer's attention. Large type screams "Read Me!"—excellent for attention-grabbing headlines—while small type fades into the background—perfect for necessary but unexciting legal mumbo-jumbo like copyright notices.

Unless you specifically define its size, text in a regular paragraph appears at the default size specified by your visitor's web browser: In most browsers today, that's 16 pixels. However, not only can people change that default size (much to the eternal frustration of web designers), but different operating systems have been known to display text at different sizes. Bottom line: You can't really assume that text will appear the same size on all your guests' monitors.

You can use either the Size menu in the Property inspector's CSS mode (Figure 4-11) or the CSS Rule Definition window's Font-size menu (Figure 4-12). In either case you're either creating a new style as described on page 113 or updating an existing style. The choices available from the Size menu break down into four groups:

- The *None* option removes any size information applied to the text. The text returns to its default size.

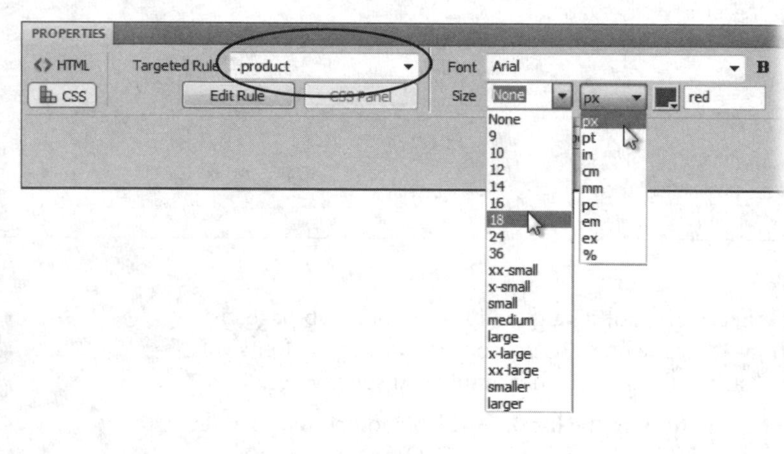

Figure 4-11: *You can set a dizzying array of font sizes using CSS. When you use the Property inspector's CSS mode to set the size of text, you either create a new style–in which case you see <New CSS Rule> listed in the Targeted Rule field (circled)–or you edit an already existing style, as shown here. In this case, the class style, .product, is listed, so picking a font size edits that CSS style.*

- The numeric choices—*9 through 36*—indicate how tall you wish to make the text, measured in pixels. Nine-pixel-tall text is nearly unreadable, while 36 pixels makes a bold statement. One benefit of pixel sizes is that text appears nearly the same across different browsers and different operating systems, overcoming the problems mentioned above.
- The options *xx-small* through *xx-large* indicate fixed sizes, replacing the sizes 1 through 7 used with the old HTML <font> tag. The *medium* size is usually the same as the default size.
- The last two choices—*smaller* and *larger*—are relative sizes, meaning that they shrink or enlarge the selected text based on the default size in your page. These choices come in handy when you define a base font size for the entire page using the Page Properties window (see Figure 1-20).

Suppose you set the default size of text on a page at 12 pixels. If you apply a "larger" size to a selection of text, then it gets bigger (the exact amount varies by web browser). If, later, you change the base size to 14 pixels (in Page Properties), all of that "larger" text will also increase proportionally.

To change the size of text, simply select it, and then, from the Property inspector, choose a new size (Figure 4-11), or edit the appropriate CSS style as described on page 124. If you applied a number (that is, a pixel value), you have an additional option: If you don't like any of the sizes listed, you can type in any number you wish. In fact, unlike HTML, browsers can handle humongous text—hundreds of pixels tall, if that's what you're into.

You're not limited to pixels, either. The Units pop-up menu (to the right of the Size menu, shown in Figure 4-11) lets you use as the unit of measure pixels, points, inches, centimeters, millimeters, picas, ems, percentages, or exes (an *ex* is the width of the letter X in the current font). Most of these measurement systems aren't intended for onscreen display. The most popular options are:

- *Pixels* are great for ensuring that text looks the same size across different browsers and operating systems. The downside, however, is that Internet Explorer 6 doesn't let web surfers adjust the pixel size. So people who can't see well, or whose monitors are set to very high resolutions, are stuck with your choice of pixel size. Make it too small, and they won't be able to read your text. (Fortunately, all other browsers don't have this problem.)

Note: This isn't entirely true. You *can* tweak Internet Explorer to allow resizing of pixel-sized text, but you have to change some of the default settings of the browser. That's something most people would never do.

- *Ems* are a relative measurement, meaning that the actual point size varies.

  One em is equal to the default font size. So suppose a web browser's default font size is 14 pixels tall. In that case, 1 em would mean 14 pixels tall, 2 ems would be twice that (28 pixels), and 1.5 ems would be 21 pixels.

  The advantage of ems is that they let web visitors using Internet Explorer 6 (a dwindling minority) control the size of onscreen text. If it's too small, they can increase the base font size. In Internet Explorer, you make this adjustment by choosing an option from the View→Text Size menu. Any text measured in ems then changes according to the web browser's new setting.

Note: You don't need to use ems to allow non-IE 6 browsers (in other words, the vast majority of the world) to resize text. In fact, all current browsers have a "Zoom" command that enlarges not only text but all other page elements (pictures, page layouts, and so on).

You can use pixels and ems together. You could, for instance, set the base font size of your page to 16 pixels, and then use ems for other parts of the page. For example, you could set headlines to 2 ems, making them 32 pixels tall. If you later thought the overall text size of the page was too small or too large, you could simply change the base font size for the page, and the headlines and all other text would resize proportionally.

Note: As you get more advanced with CSS, you'll probably run into some weird problems with em or percentage text sizes due to an advanced concept known as the *cascade*. The gruesome details begin on page 125.

- *Percentages* (%) are another relative size measurement. When applied to text size, they're functionally equivalent to ems—100% is the same as 1 em, 200% is 2 ems, and 75% is .75 ems. If you're more comfortable with the notion of percentages than the typography-inspired ems, use percentage values instead.

The other measurement options, like inches and millimeters, don't make as much sense as pixels, ems, and percentages because you can't consistently measure them on monitors. For example, Windows is set to 96 pixels to the inch, whereas Mac OS X is set to 72 pixels per inch—but people can change even these settings, so there's no reliable way to measure an "inch" on a computer screen. The upshot is that if you're not worried about IE 6's inability to resize text, you're safe using pixel values—they're easier to understand, more consistent across browsers, and work fine with the zoom feature of all currently shipping browsers.

Picking a Font Color

Most color formatting in Dreamweaver, whether for text or a table cell, makes use of its *color box*.

To set the color of text, use the CSS Color property. You can choose a color in the Property inspector's CSS mode, or assign a text color in the Text category of the CSS Rule Definition window (Figure 4-12). In both cases, you encounter Dreamweaver's color box as described on page 56. You can pick a color by clicking the color well and, from the pop-up color palette, selecting a color, or you can type in a *hexadecimal number* (see page 56) of the color you want. (Clearly, the latter is the option for hard-core HTML geeks. After all, surely you've memorized the hex number of that light shade of blue you always use—#6699FF, isn't it?)

Adding Bold and Italic

You can use the Property inspector to make text bold or italic. Depending on which mode the inspector is in—HTML or CSS—clicking the B or I button does different things. In HTML mode, the B button wraps selected text with the <strong> HTML tag, while the I button wraps text with the <em> (for emphasis) tag. However, in CSS mode, the B button sets the CSS *font-weight* property to bold, while the I button sets the CSS *font-style* property to italic. In other words, those two buttons either insert HTML tags or add CSS properties to a style.

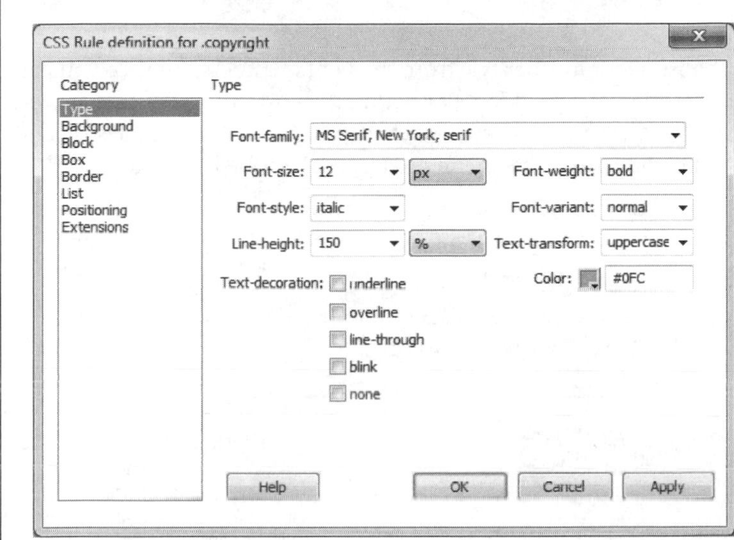

Figure 4-12: *While you can set some text formatting using the Property inspector, the CSS Rule Definition window's Type category offers additional formatting options. For example, you get the ability to control the space between lines of text, and an option to change the case of text–to make text upper- or lowercase.*

If you want to just change the appearance of text, use CSS mode, but if you actually want to emphasize some text because it's important for the sentence's meaning, use HTML mode. For example, if you want the word "Monday" to stand out on a page, use CSS. But for a sentence like "He *never* makes mistakes" the emphasis on "never" is important to understanding the sentence; in that case, use HTML mode. The people viewing your site might not notice the difference, but Google, other search engines, and screen reading software will.

Note: If you use the Property inspector's CSS mode, the B button only makes type bold or removes bold formatting you previously applied. In the case of headlines, which browsers automatically display as bold, clicking the B button has no effect. To remove the bold formatting from headlines, you have to use the CSS Style Definition window, and, from the font-weight menu, select *normal* (see Figure 4-12).

Aligning Text

The alignment buttons in the Property inspector's CSS mode (Figure 4-3) set the CSS text-align property to either *left, right, center*, or *justify*. These same options are available under the Block category of the CSS Rule Definition window (Figure 4-17).

CSS Type Properties in the Rule Definition Window

As its name implies, the Rule Definition window's Type category lets you set formatting options that affect text (see Figure 4-12). Several of these settings are the same as those available from the Property inspector in CSS mode and you learned about them in depth starting on page 128. To summarize, this category of CSS properties includes:

- **Font.** You choose a font for the style from the Font menu. As discussed on page 129, you choose from *groups* of fonts rather than the specific one you have your heart set on. Dreamweaver also lets you create your own "first-choice, second-choice…" font choices from this menu, exactly as described on page 131.
- **Size.** As described on page 133, you can choose from among many different systems for sizing text, but the most common are pixels, ems, and percentages.
- **Weight.** Weight refers to the thickness of the font. The Weight menu offers 13 choices. Normal and bold are the most common, and they work in all browsers that understand CSS. See Figure 4-13 for details.

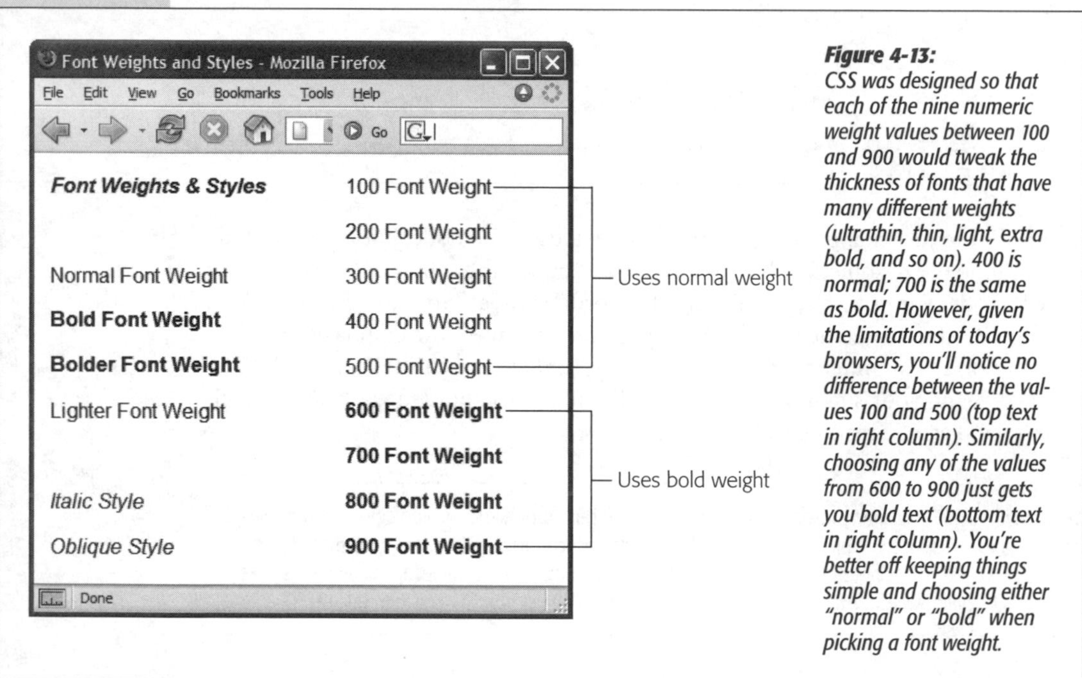

Figure 4-13: *CSS was designed so that each of the nine numeric weight values between 100 and 900 would tweak the thickness of fonts that have many different weights (ultrathin, thin, light, extra bold, and so on). 400 is normal; 700 is the same as bold. However, given the limitations of today's browsers, you'll notice no difference between the values 100 and 500 (top text in right column). Similarly, choosing any of the values from 600 to 900 just gets you bold text (bottom text in right column). You're better off keeping things simple and choosing either "normal" or "bold" when picking a font weight.*

- **Style.** In this peculiar instance, Style means italic, oblique, or normal text. Technically, italic is a custom-designed, emphatic version of a typeface, *like this*. Oblique, on the other hand, is just a computerized adaptation of a normal font, in which each letter is inclined a certain number of degrees to the right. In practical application, there's no visible difference between italic and oblique in web browsers.

- **Variant.** This pop-up menu simply lets you specify small-caps type, if you like—a slightly formal, fancy-looking type style much favored by attorneys' offices.
- **Line Height.** Line height, otherwise known as *leading* (pronounced "LED-ing"), refers to the space between lines of text in a paragraph (see Figure 4-14). To create more space between lines, set the line height greater than the font size. (If you type a number without a % sign, Dreamweaver assumes you're specifying a line height in pixels. You can change the units of measure using the pop-up menu to the right of the Line Height field.)

Tip: A good approach for line height is to type in a percentage measurement, such as *120%*, which is relative to the size of the text; so if your text were 10 pixels tall, the space from the base of one line of text to the next would be 12 pixels (120% of 10). Now, if you change the size of the text, the *relative* space between lines remains the same.

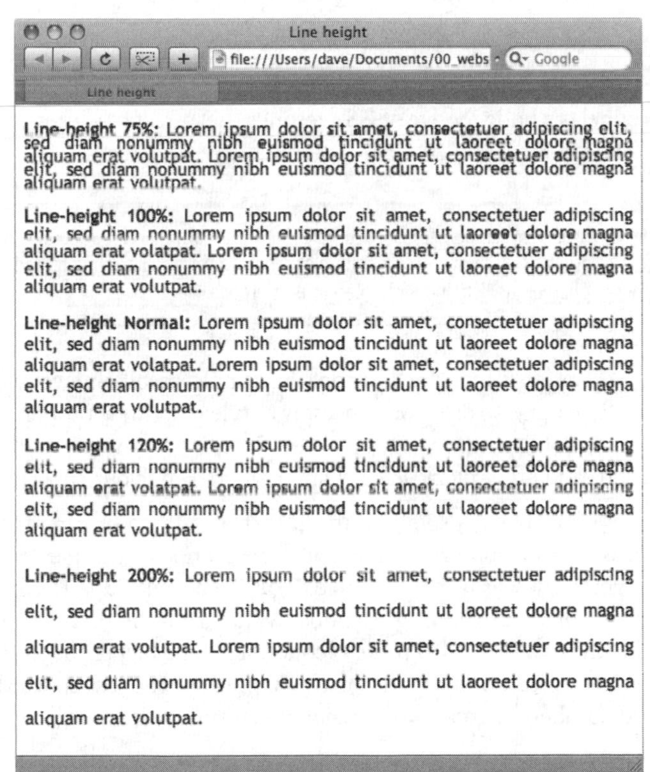

Figure 4-14:
Control the space between lines with the Line Height property in the CSS Rule Definition dialog box. In this example, each paragraph's text is set in 16-pixel Trebuchet MS. With CSS, you can make lines bump into each other by setting a low line-height value (top paragraph), or spread them far apart by using a larger value (bottom paragraph).

"Normal", the default setting (third paragraph in Figure 4-14), uses a line height that's slightly larger than the height of the text. You don't get access to the pop-up menu of measurement units (pixels, points, %, and so on) unless you type a number in this box.

- **Case.** From this menu, you can automatically capitalize text. To capitalize the first letter of each word, choose "capitalize". The "uppercase" option gives you all capital letters, while "lowercase" makes all the letters lowercase. The factory setting is "none", which has no effect on the text.
- **Decoration.** This strange assortment of five checkboxes lets you dress up your text, mostly in unattractive ways. "Underline", "overline", and "line-through" add horizontal lines below, above, or directly through the affected text, respectively. Turning on "blink" makes affected text blink on and off (but only in a few browsers); unless you want to appear on one of those "worst website of the week" lists, avoid it. You can apply any number of decorative types per style, except with "none", which, obviously, you can't choose along with any of the other options. The "none" setting is useful for hiding the underlines that normally appear below links.
- **Color.** Set the color of the style's text using Dreamweaver's color box, described on page 56.

Block Properties

The Block Properties panel is a hodgepodge of CSS settings that affect how browsers display letters and words (see Figure 4-15).

Tip: To completely remove the space between paragraphs, set the Top and Bottom margin for paragraphs to 0 in the CSS Rule Definition window's Box category. This setting also helps remove space before and after headlines. To indent paragraphs, set the Left and Right margin properties.

Despite this category's name, these properties don't just apply to block-level elements (paragraphs, headlines, and so on). You can apply a style with these properties to even a single word or two. (The one exception is the Text Align property, which applies only to paragraphs and other block-level elements.) Here are your choices:

- **Word spacing.** This property helps you clean up text by adding or removing space *between* words. The default value, "normal", leaves a normal, single space between words. If you want words in a sentence to be   spaced   apart   like this, then type a value of about 10 pixels. (Choose Value from the first pop-up menu and then the units you want from the second one.) The bigger the number, the larger the gap between words. You can also *remove* space between words by using a negative number—a great choice when you want to make your pages difficult to read.
- **Letter spacing.** This property works just like word spacing, but governs the space between *letters*. To add space l i k e t h i s, type a value of about 5 pixels. The result can make long passages hard to read, but a little space between letters can add a dramatic flair to short headlines and movie titles.

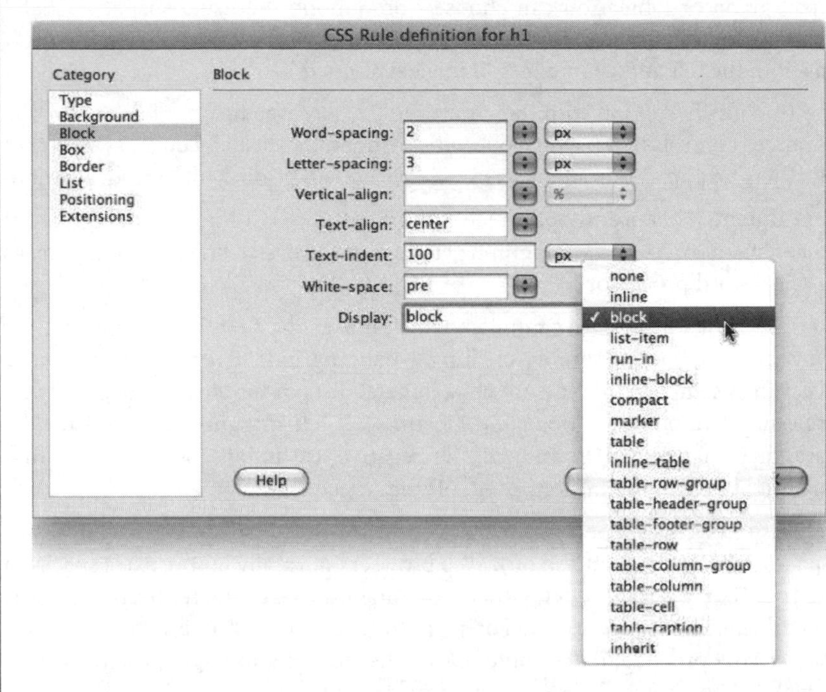

Figure 4-15: *The Block category is an eclectic mix of (mostly) text properties. However, you can use the Display property on images, tables, and any other selection or HTML tag. Although the list is long, most of these options, alas, don't work in all browsers.*

- **Vertical alignment.** With this property, you can change the vertical placement of an object—such as an image or text—relative to the items around it. For example, you could move text above or below surrounding text to format a trademark character, copyright symbol, or footnote reference using the options "super" and "sub". If you wanted to add the trademark symbol to, say, *Chia Pet™*, then you'd select the letters TM and set the vertical alignment to "super". In addition, for more accurate control, you can type a value (like 10%) to raise an object above its normal baseline, or a negative value (like –10% or –5 pixels) to move an object down.

  Vertical alignment also works with graphics, and designers often use the options Top, Bottom, and Middle with HTML table cells to position content within a cell.

Note: The "sub" and "super" alignment options don't change text size. If you want to create true subscript or superscript (for chemical symbols, trademark or copyright symbols, and so on), you should also use a smaller font size in the style; 75% works great.

- **Text align.** This property controls the alignment of a block-level element like a paragraph or table. You can choose from among the usual suspects—"left", "center", "right", or even "justify". (Like the text in this paragraph, justified text has both the left and right edges of the text aligned.)

  Use the "justify" option with care, however. Because web browsers don't have the advanced controls that page-layout software does, they usually do an awful job of justifying text on a computer screen. The results can be difficult to read, and ugly.

- **Text indent.** This useful option lets you indent the first line of a paragraph. If you enter 15 pixels, each paragraph gets an attractive first-line indent, exactly as in a real word processor.

  You can also use a *negative* number, which makes the first line extend past the *left* margin of the paragraph, creating a hanging indent (or *outdent*)—a nice effect for a sentence that introduces a bulleted lists or for glossary pages. If you use a negative number, it's a good idea to set a left-margin (page 341) for the paragraph that equals the value of the negative text indent, otherwise the first line might extend too far to the left, off the screen!

- **Whitespace.** This property controls how the browser displays extra white space (spaces, tabs, returns, and so on). Web browsers normally ignore extra spaces in the HTML of a page, reducing them to a single space character between words and other elements as described on page 76. The "pre" option functions just like the HTML <pre> tag: Extra white space (like tabs, multiple spaces, and hard returns) that you put *in the HTML code* appear in the document window (see page 125 for more on this option). The "nowrap" option prevents lines from breaking (and wrapping to the next line) when they reach the end of the browser window.

- **Display.** This property defines how a browser should display a particular element, like a paragraph or link. The range of choices for this property may overwhelm you—and you may be underwhelmed when you find out that browsers don't support most of these options.

  The only three options that work reliably across browsers are "none", "inline", and "block". The "block" option treats any item styled with this property as a block—separated from other content by space above and below it. Paragraphs and headings normally appear this way. But you can apply this value to a link (which normally appears inside a block-level element like a paragraph) to turn it into its own block. Usually, you have to click directly on the text or image inside a link to jump to the linked page. But when you set a link's display to "block", its entire width—even areas where no text appears—is clickable.

  The "inline" option treats the item as though it's part of the current block or paragraph, so that any item styled with this property (like a picture) flows together with other items around it, as if it were part of the same paragraph. People frequently use this property to take a bulleted list of links and turn it into a horizontal navigation bar. The Spry Menu bar, discussed on page 184, uses this technique to create a horizontal menu. For a good tutorial on this topic, visit *http://css.maxdesign.com.au/listutorial/horizontal_introduction.htm*.

The "none" option is the most fun: It turns off the display of an item. In other words, any text or item styled with this option doesn't appear on the page. You can use JavaScript programming to switch this property on and off, making items seem to appear and disappear. In fact, Dreamweaver's Change Property behavior gives you one simple way to do this (see page 616).

List Properties

To exercise greater control over bulleted and numbered lists, use the CSS options in the CSS Rule Definition window's List category (see Figure 4-16).

- **Type.** Select the type of bullet you want to use in front of a list item. Options include: "disc", "circle", "square", "decimal" (1., 2., 3.), "lower-roman" (i, ii, iii), "upper-roman" (I, II, III), "lower-alpha" (a, b, c), "upper-alpha" (A, B, C), and "none" (no bullet at all).

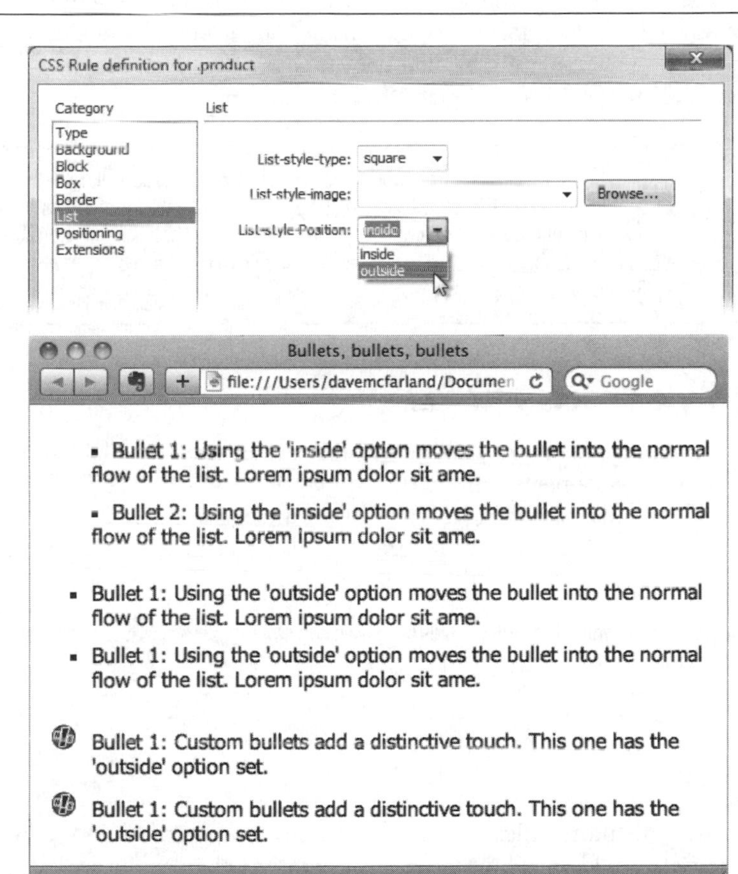

Figure 4-16:
Top: Take control of your bulleted and numbered lists using the CSS Rule Definition window's List category. With Cascading Style Sheets, you can even supply your own graphic bullets.

Bottom: A bullet-crazed web page, for illustration purposes. Parading down the screen, you can see "inside" bullets, "outside" bullets, and bullets made from graphics.

- **Bullet image.** For the ultimate control of your bullet icon, skip the boring options preprogrammed into a web browser (like disc, circle, square, or decimal) and supply your own. Click the Browse button, and then, from your site folder, select a graphics file. Make sure the graphic is appropriate bullet material—in other words, small.

Tip: The Background Image property, which you'll learn about on page 231, is a more versatile solution to adding bullet images to a list. Since you can accurately position a background image, you can easily tweak the placement of your bullets. Here's how to do it: Create a style for the <li> tag (or a class style that you apply to each <li> tag); make sure you set the List property type to "none" (this hides the bullet); set the background image to your graphical bullet; and play with the background position values (page 234). Playing with the padding values (page 341) helps position the text relative to the image.

- **Position.** This property controls where the bullet is placed relative to the list item's text. The "outside" option places the bullet outside the margin of the text, exactly the way bulleted lists normally look. "Inside", on the other hand, displays the bullet within the text margin, so that the left edge of the *bullet* aligns with the left margin; Figure 4-16 should make the effect clearer.

Note: If you want to adjust the amount of space web browsers normally use to indent lists, set the left padding property (see page 341) to 0, and set the left margin (see page 341) to the amount of indent you'd like. Sometimes you want no indent at all–for example, if you're creating a list of links that should look like buttons, not bulleted items–set both the left padding and left margin to 0 (while you're at it, set the bullet type to "none" as described above).

Cascading Style Sheets Tutorial

In this tutorial, you'll practice the basic techniques required to create and edit styles. Make sure you grasp the fundamentals covered in the following pages: You'll be building lots of style sheets in the other tutorials in this book using these same methods. For this tutorial, you'll create an external style sheet for formatting pages on the Chia Vet website.

Note: Before getting started, download the tutorial files from *www.sawmac.com/dwCS5/*. See the Note on page 45 for more details.

Setting Up

Once you download the tutorial files and opened Dreamweaver, you need to set up a site for this tutorial. You learned how to do this in the first chapter, but we'll step through the few basic steps as a quick recap—practice makes perfect!

1. **Choose Site→New Site.**

   The Site Setup window appears.

2. **For the Site Name, type *CSS Tutorial.***

   The only other step required to set up a site is to tell Dreamweaver where it can find the site's files.

3. **To the right of the "Local site folder" box, click the folder icon.**

   The Choose Root Folder window appears (see Figure 1-13). This is just a window onto your computer's file system; navigate to the proper folder just as you would when working with other programs.

4. **Navigate to and select the Chapter04 folder located in the MM_DWCS5 folder. Click the Select button (Choose on Macs) to select this folder, and then, in the Site Setup window, click OK to complete the process of defining a site.**

   You should see two files—*about.html* and *services.html*—in the Files panel. (If you don't see the Files panel, choose Window→Files to open it.)

Creating an External Style Sheet

In this example, you'll create a collection of styles for the Chia Vet website.

1. **In the files panel, double-click the file named *services.html.***

   The web page contains a listing of services Chia Vet offers. The page has a few headline tags and a bunch of paragraphs. The page's text is plain, boring-looking HTML, so you'll use CSS to spiff it up.

   To start, you'll create a style for the first headline.

Note: You can, of course, also open a file by choosing File→Open and navigating to the folder where the file you wish to open resides.

---

2. **Triple-click the headline "Chia Vet Services".**

   This selects the entire headline. You'll now use the Property inspector to select a font.

3. **Make sure you have the CSS button pressed in the Property inspector (see Figure 4-3), and then, from the Font menu, choose "Palatino Linotype, Book Antiqua, Palatino, serif".**

   Because the headline had no style applied it, Dreamweaver opens the New CSS Rule window (see Figure 4-17). You'll first pick the type of style you wish to create.

4. **From the Selector Type menu at the top of the window, select Tag.**

   This step lets you create a style for a particular HTML tag, in this case, the <h1> tag. In other words, you're going to create a formatting rule that automatically applies to every heading 1 paragraph.

5. **The Selector Name field should have "h1" listed, but if it doesn't, use the middle drop-down menu to select "h1".**

   Next you'll choose where to store the CSS code for this new style—in this case, in an external style sheet.

6. **From the bottom menu, choose New Style Sheet File, as pictured in Figure 4-17. Click OK.**

   The Save Style Sheet File As dialog box appears. You're about to create the file—an external style sheet—that stores the styles for this page.

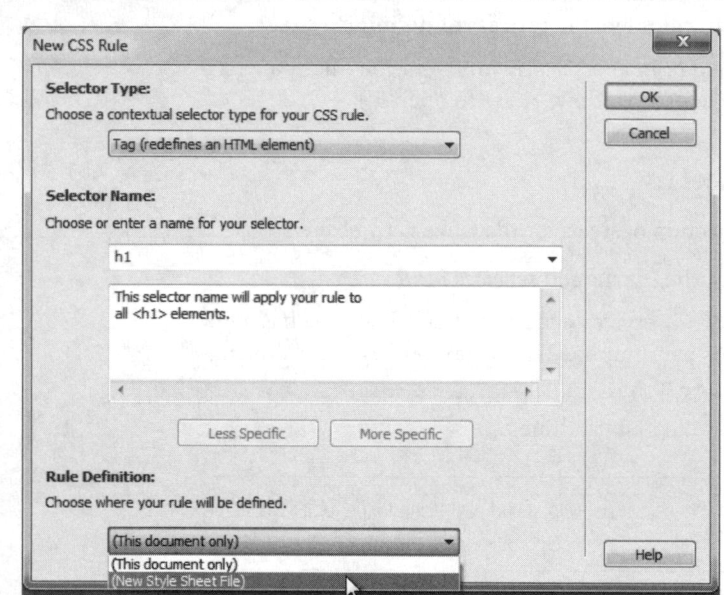

Figure 4-17:
The New CSS Rule window has changed a lot since the last version of Dreamweaver, but the three basic tasks it requires are the same: Pick the type of style you want to create; name the style; and pick where Dreamweaver should store the CSS code. Notice how the large text box explains what web page elements the style will apply to–in this case all <h1> tags.

7. **Click the Site Root button (top of the dialog box on Windows, bottom right on Macs).**

   The Site Root button is a handy shortcut. It automatically takes you to the local site folder for the site you're currently working on, saving you the effort of manually navigating there. (OK, in this example, you're already in the local site folder, but you should know about this button and what it does—it really does come in handy for getting you to the top level folder of the current site after you open files from other sites located elsewhere on your hard drive, or folders deeply nested inside the current site.)

8. **In the File Name box (the Save As field on the Mac), type *global.css*, and then click Save.**

   Cascading Style Sheet files always end in .css; that's how web servers and browsers can tell what kind of files they are.

Notice how the headline now uses the new font. You created a style and added an external style sheet to your site in just a couple steps. Now, you'll add some color.

9. **Make sure you still have the headline selected, and then, in the Property inspector's Color field, type *#779A00* (see Figure 4-18).**

   You can use the color box to select another color if you prefer.

   The New CSS Rule window doesn't appear this time, because now you're editing the h1 tag style you created previously. Time to change the size of the font.

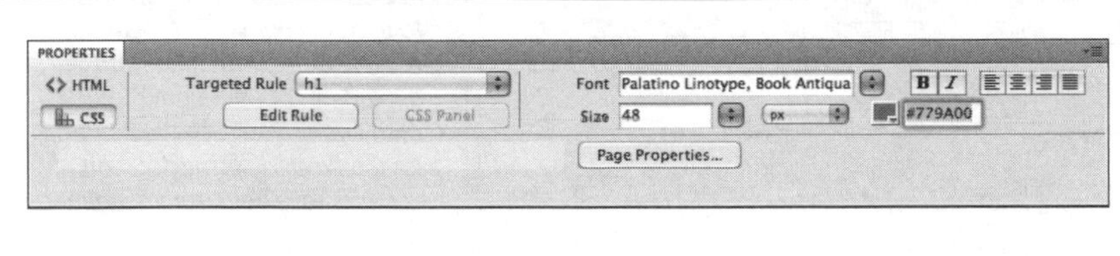

***Figure 4-18:** Choosing properties for an element that already has a style applied to it—like the h1 tag style here—updates that style.*

Note: If the New CSS Rule window appears again at either steps 9 or 10, something went wrong. Click the Cancel button. You must have accidentally selected some other text—maybe just part of the headline—before using the Property inspector. To get back on track, triple-click the top headline again, and then repeat step 9 or 10.

10. **In the Property inspector's Size box, type *48*.**

    The Property inspector should now look like Figure 4-18. You just set the font size to 48 pixels tall. You've pretty much reached the limit of what the Property inspector is capable of, but you've barely scratched the surface of Cascading Styles Sheets. In the next part of this tutorial, you'll learn how to edit a style and access the wide range of formatting options that CSS offers.

Editing a Style

1. **Make sure you have the CSS Styles panel open (Window→CSS Styles), and make sure you have the All button selected at the top of the panel.**

   This displays all the style sheets attached to this page (in this case, just *global.css*).

2. **If it isn't already, expand the list of styles in the *global.css* style sheet by clicking the + icon (arrow on the Mac) to the left of "global.css".**

   This lists all the styles you've added to the external style sheet—just the one h1 tag style at this point.

3. **In the list, double-click "h1".**

   This action opens the CSS Rule Definition window, where you can access a range of CSS properties (see Figure 4-19). First, you'll remove the bold formatting from the headline.

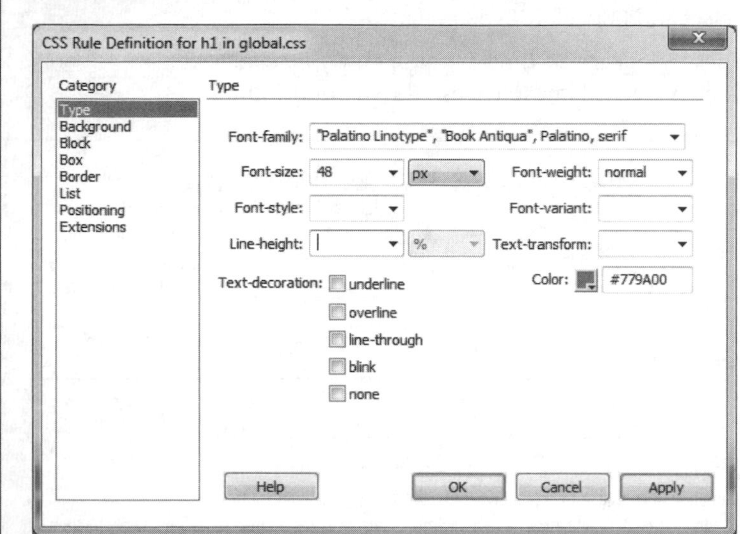

Figure 4-19: *The CSS Rule Definition window provides access to many more CSS properties than the Property inspector. In addition, you have to use the Font-weight menu to remove bold formatting from a heading tag–no matter how many times you click the B button on the Property inspector, you can't remove bold from headlines.*

4. **From the Font-Weight menu, choose "normal", and then click the Apply button.**

   You can preview the look of a tag style without closing the CSS Rule Definition window by clicking the Apply button—just drag the window out of the way of the headline.

   When formatting text, you can use many other non-text related CSS properties. For example, you can add border lines to any element on a page.

5. **In the category list, click Border.**

   The CSS Rule Definition window now displays all the properties that add a border around a style. You can control each border individually, or use the same line style for all four edges. In this case, you'll add lines to just the top and bottom of the headline.

6. **Click to turn off all three "Same for all" checkboxes. For the Top border, choose "solid" from the top Style menu, type *7* in the top Width box, and type *#F93* in the top Color box. For the Bottom border, choose "solid" from the Style menu, type *2* in the Width box, and type *#F93* in the color box.**

   The window should now look like Figure 4-20. As mentioned on page 56, #F93 is shorthand for #FF9933. If you click the Apply button now, you may notice that the top border is a little too close to the top of the headline. You can add a little breathing room using the CSS Padding property.

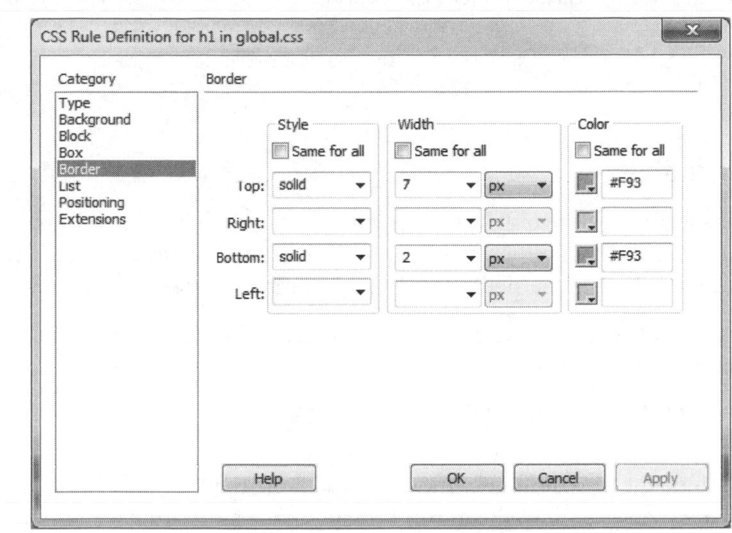

Figure 4-20: *Use the Border properties to add rules to any or all of the four edges of an object. You can emphasize a headline by underlining it, or give an image a stylish border around its edges.*

7. **In the Rule Definition window, click the Box category. Uncheck the "Same for all" box underneath Padding, and then, in the "Top padding" box, type 5.**

   Padding is the space between the edge of an element (where the border appears) and the stuff inside the element (like text). In this case, adding 5 pixels of top padding adds 5 pixels of space between the top border line and the headline's text. You'll learn more about padding on page 341.

8. **Click OK to close the window and complete editing the style.**

   Now you have a distinctive-looking headline. But you've just started building styles for this page.

9. **Choose File→Save All Related Files.**

   The Save All Related Files command can be a real lifesaver when you work with external style sheets. Even though you're looking at and working on a web page (*services.html* here), each time you add a style, Dreamweaver updates the external style sheet file (*global.css*). So most of the work you've done so far has gone into updating the *global.css* file. Unfortunately, the regular keyboard shortcut to save a file, Ctrl+S (⌘-S), saves only changes to the file you can see—in this case, the web page. Make sure you invoke the Save All Related Files command frequently, otherwise you could lose all the changes you made to an external style sheet if Dreamweaver or your computer crashes. (You can even set your own keyboard command for the Save All Related Files command. See page 817 for details.)

Tip: The File→Save All command is also useful. It saves every file you have open with unsaved changes. Feel free to use this command frequently even if you might want to undo some of those changes–Dreamweaver's smart enough to let you undo changes you made to a file even after you save those changes (but only if don't close the file in the meantime).

Adding Another Style

The Property inspector isn't the only way to create a style—in fact, since it offers a limited number of formatting options, it isn't even the best way to create a style. The CSS Styles panel provides a faster method with more comprehensive choices.

1. **At the bottom of the CSS Styles panel, click the New CSS Rule button (the + button pictured in Figure 4-1).**

   The New CSS Rule window appears. You'll create another tag style for the Heading 2 tag.

2. **From the top menu, choose Tag; in the Selector Name field, type *h2* (or select "h2" from the menu); and, in the bottom menu, make sure you have "global.css" selected. Click OK.**

   This action adds a new tag style to the *global.css* style sheet. You'll set a few text properties next.

3. **From the Font-family menu, choose "Palatino Linotype, Book Antiqua, Palatino, serif".**

   You'll use the same font as in Heading 1, but you'll change its size and color.

4. **In the Size box, type *24* and, in the Color box, type *#EC6206*.**

   This creates medium-sized, orange text. To make the headline stand out a bit, you'll make all the text uppercase. Fortunately, you don't have to hold down the caps-lock button and retype each headline to do so—there's a CSS property that can do it for you.

5. **From the Text-transform menu, choose "uppercase".**

   One problem with this design is the large gap between the subheads and the paragraphs following them. The Heading 2 paragraphs ("Preventative Care", for example) introduce the paragraph that follows. Removing the gap that appears between the heading and the following paragraph would visually tie the two together better. To make this change, you must first remove the margin below each headline.

6. **In the left-hand list of CSS categories, select Box. In the Margin area, turn off the "Same for all" checkbox; in the Bottom box, type *0*.**

   This should remove any space that appears below the Heading 2 tags.

7. **Click OK to close the Rule Definition window and finish editing the style.**

   The space between the headlines and the paragraphs hasn't changed a bit. What gives? Paragraphs and headlines have space both above *and* below. The space you're seeing is actually the *top* margin of the paragraph tag.

   Top and bottom margins have a peculiar feature: They don't add up like 1+1=2. In other words, a web browser doesn't add the bottom margin of Heading 2 to the top margin of the paragraph to calculate the total space between the two blocks of text. Instead, a web browser uses the margin with the *largest* value to determine the space between paragraphs (a lot of text layout programs, including word processors, share this behavior).

   For example, say the <h2> tag has a bottom margin of 12 pixels, while the paragraph following has a top margin of 10 pixels. The total space between the two isn't 22 pixels (10+12)—it's 12 pixels (the value of the larger margin). So, if you remove the bottom margin of the headline, the gap between the two blocks of text isn't gone—it's now 10 pixels, the top margin value for the paragraph. That's the situation here: you need to modify the paragraphs' top margin as well. You can do that by creating another style.

8. **In the CSS Styles Panel, click the New CSS Rule button.**

   The New CSS Rule window appears. You'll create a tag style to control how browsers will format paragraphs.

9. **From the top menu, choose Tag; in the Selector Name box, type *p*, and then, in the bottom menu, make sure you have "global.css" selected. Click OK to create the style.**

   Before getting to that pesky margin, first set some basic type options.

10. **From the Font-family menu, choose "Trebuchet MS, Arial, Helvetica, sans-serif", and then, in the Font-size box, type *14*.**

    CSS provides a lot of control over type, including the ability to adjust the leading, or space between, lines in a paragraph.

11. **In the Line-height box, type *150*, and then, from the pop-up menu to the right, choose %.**

    The line-height property controls the space between lines of text. In this case, you've set that space to 150%, which means that each line will be 150% (or 1.5 times) the size of the font. A setting of 150% adds more space than usual between each line of text in a paragraph—the result is more white space and a more luxurious feel.

    Now back to that margin problem.

12. **Click the Box category; in the Margin section, uncheck the "Same for all" box. Type *5* in the Top box, and *75* in the Left box.**

    The window should now look like Figure 4-21. The 5-pixel top margin adds just a small amount of space between the paragraph and the <h2> tag above it—completely removing all space between the two would make them seem crowded together. The 75-pixel left margin is just for fun. This margin indents the paragraphs from the left edge of the page by 75 pixels, creating a distinctive look that makes the Heading 2 paragraphs stand out even more.

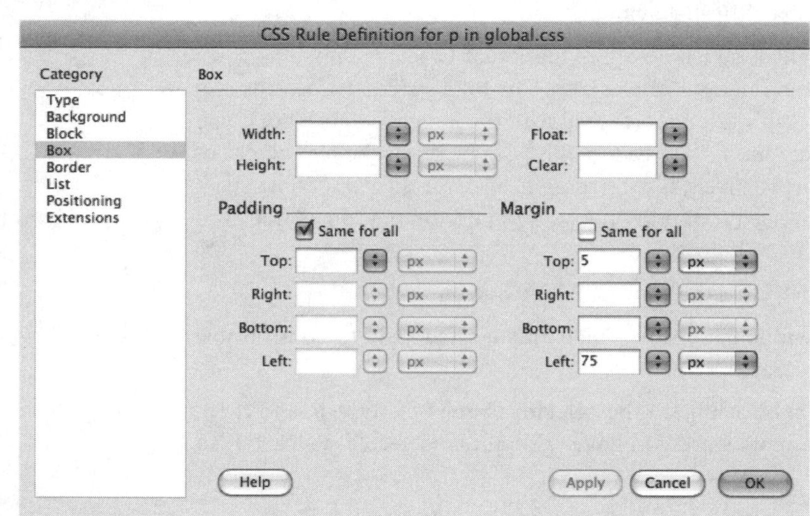

Figure 4-21: *To remove space that appears above a paragraph, a headline, or other block of text, set the top margin to 0. To completely remove the space that appears between paragraphs, set the bottom margin to 0 as well.*

13. **Click OK; choose File→Save All Related Files.**

    The page is nearly complete. Just one more style to create.

Creating a Class Style

Now you'll create a style to format the copyright notice at the bottom of the page. It's inside a regular paragraph (<p> tag), so it's getting all its formatting from the p tag style. Here's an instance where you'd like to style a single paragraph without affecting the other paragraphs on the page. A class style is perfect for this kind of specific styling task.

1. **On the CSS Styles panel, click the New CSS Rule button** (+).

    The New CSS Rule window opens. This time, you'll create a class style rather than an HTML tag style.

2. **From the top menu, select Class. In the Selector Name box, type *.copyright* (with a period before it).**

   Class styles always begin with a period—however, if you leave it out, Dreamweaver puts it in.

Note: Some beginners think that whenever you create a new style, you also need to create a new external Style Sheet. On the contrary, you can–and should–store more than one style in a single external style sheet. In fact, if you're creating a set of styles for an entire site, put them all in the same external style sheet.

---

3. **Make sure you have "global.css" selected in the bottom menu, and then click OK.**

   You're adding yet another style to the external style sheet you created at the beginning of this tutorial. The CSS Rule Definition window appears. You'll add a few new properties to make this style look different from the rest of the text on the page.

4. **In the Size box, type *12*; from the Font-weight menu, choose "bold"; and for the Color, type *#666666* or use the Color box to select a gray color.**

   The smaller text and lighter gray color make the copyright notice less prominent on the page; the bold setting makes it stand out from the other paragraphs. Finally, you'll add a line above the copyright to separate it from the page.

5. **In the category list, click Border.**

   The CSS Rule Definition window now displays all the properties used to put a border around a style. In this case, you'll add a line above the copyright notice.

6. **Click to turn off all three "Same for all" checkboxes. For the Top border, choose "dashed" from the Style menu, type *1* in the Width box, and type *#93BD00* in the color box.**

   You have several different styles of borderlines to choose from, including dashed (see page 230 for the different types of borders). Lastly, you'll add a little space between the border and the text.

7. **In the left-hand list of CSS categories, click the Box category. Uncheck the "Same for all" box in the Padding area, and then, type *5* in the Top box.**

   While margins control the space between elements (like the gap between paragraphs), *padding* controls the space between the content and the content's border. In other words, adding padding pushes a border further away from the text (or other content) you're styling.

   You'll change the copyright notice's margin settings as well.

8. **In the Margin area, uncheck the "Same for all" box, and then type *25* in the Top box and *0* in the Left box.**

   The window should look like Figure 4-22. The 25 pixels of top margin pushes the copyright notice away from the bottom of the paragraph of text above it. In addition, since Dreamweaver indents all the paragraphs 75 pixels from the left edge, you need to set the left margin of the copyright notice to 0. This essentially overrides the 75-pixel margin from the p tag style and lets the copyright notice hug the left edge of the page.

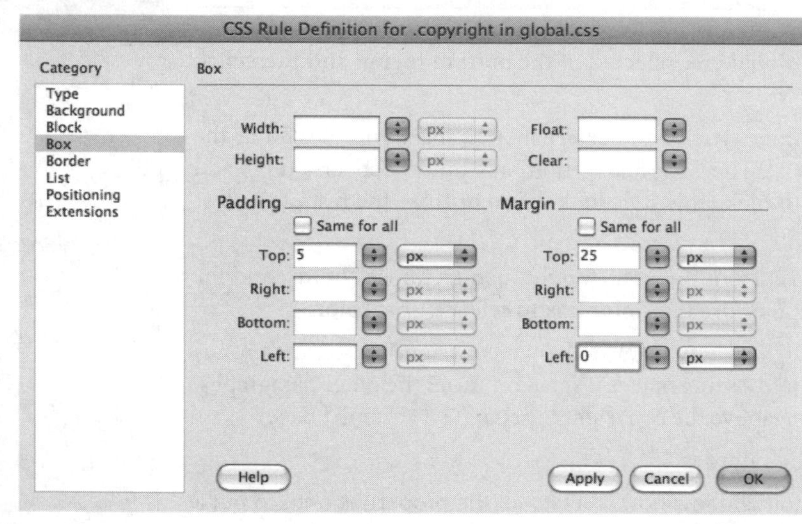

Figure 4-22: *The difference between padding and margin is subtle, but important. Both properties add space around content you're styling. And if you don't have a background color, image, or border, both properties pretty much act the same. However, when you do have a background color, image, or border, padding adds space between the content and the edge of the backgrounds and borders. Margins add space outside the border and background.*

9. **Click OK.**

   The Rule Definition window closes, but this time, nothing's changed in the document window. Unlike HTML tag styles, class styles don't show up anywhere until you apply them by hand.

10. **Scroll to the bottom of the page, and select the last paragraph with the copyright notice.**

    This action sets you up for applying the style. You can also just click anywhere inside the paragraph (without selecting any text) to apply a class style to it.

11. **In the Property inspector, click the HTML button, and then, from the Class menu, choose "copyright" (see Figure 4-23).**

    Boom—the copyright notice suddenly changes size, color, and grows a line above it. Magic. You may also notice that the copyright still uses the same font as the other paragraphs. In fact, it has "inherited" that font type from the p tag style—you'll learn about inheritance, an advanced CSS concept, on page 311.

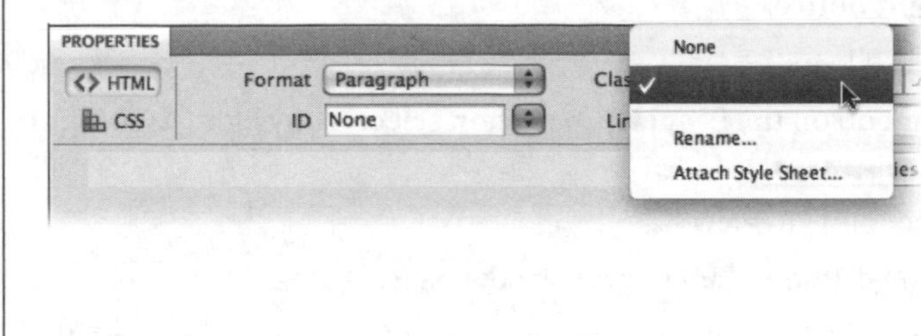

Figure 4-23: *The Class menu in the HTML mode of the Property inspector lists all class styles. It also displays the style name using the style's text formatting–in this case, bold, gray text. Notice that the menu lists only class styles; tag styles don't appear in this menu, since you don't apply them manually. You can also apply a class using the Property inspector's CSS Mode, as described on page 119.*

Attaching an External Style Sheet

Now that you've created these styles, you may wonder how you can use them on other pages—after all, that's the beauty of external style sheets. Once created, it's a simple process to add a style sheet to other pages in the site.

1. **Choose File→Save All Related Files; close the *services.html* page.**

   You'll open a new web page to attach the external style sheet to it.

2. **Choose File→Open. In the Files panel, double-click the file *about.html* to open it.**

   This file is another page for the Chia Vet website. It has no formatting yet, so you'll attach the external style sheet you just created.

3. **On the CSS Styles panel, click the Attach Style Sheet button (see Figure 4-1).**

   The Link External Style Sheet window appears.

4. **Click the Browse button.**

   The Select Style Sheet dialog box appears.

5. **Navigate to the Chapter04 folder (or click the Site Root button), and then double-click the *global.css* file.**

   Don't forget the Site Root button. It appears on every window in which you need to save, open, or select a file. It's a great shortcut to make sure you're working in the correct folder for your site.

   You can ignore the other settings in the Attach External Style Sheet window for now (they're described on page 123).

6. **Click OK to attach the style sheet to the page.**

   Dreamweaver instantly formats the headlines and main text of the story. Pretty cool—and very efficient. You need to apply the *.copyright* class style only to the last paragraph on the page.

7. **Scroll to the bottom of the page, and then click anywhere inside the paragraph with the copyright notice.**

   Next you'll add a style to the tag.

8. **From the Class menu on the Property inspector, select "copyright" (see Figure 4-23).**

   This page is done. Time to view it.

9. **Press F12 (Option-F12 on Mac) to preview the page.**

   Dreamweaver probably prompts you to save your files; go ahead and do that. The finished page should look something like Figure 4-24. If you'd like to compare your finished product to the completed version, you'll find those pages in the Chapter04_finished folder in the tutorials folder.

Note: You may need to hit your browser's refresh button to see the most recent changes you made to the style sheet. This is one problem you'll encounter when you design pages with external style sheets–web browsers often *cache* them (see page 689). Normally that's a good thing–it means visitors to your site have to wait only once for the file to download. But when you're in the midst of a design, frantically switching back and forth between Dreamweaver and a web browser preview, the browser might retrieve the older version of the external style sheet that it saved in its cache rather than the newly updated file on your computer. (The Safari browser is particularly aggressive at holding onto cached files, so if you preview in that browser, make sure to reload the page when you do.)

You can work around this problem: Open the Preferences window (Edit→Preferences [Dreamweaver→Preferences on Mac]); select the "Preview in Browser" category, and then turn on the "Preview using temporary file" box. Now, when you preview the page, Dreamweaver actually makes a temporary file on your computer that incorporates both the CSS and HTML of the page. This defeats a browser's cache so that now you're seeing the very latest changes. This setting has the added benefit of stopping Dreamweaver's annoying "You must save your file before previewing" dialog box each time you preview a page.

Figure 4-24: *CSS offers a lot of design tools to produce beautiful typography for your web pages. In addition, an external style sheet lets you quickly, easily, and consistently add style to hundreds of pages without much work.*

CHAPTER

5

Links

The humble hyperlink may not raise many eyebrows anymore, but the notion that you can navigate a whole sea of information, jumping from one island of content to another with a simple click, is a relatively recent and powerful invention. Interested in a particular band? Go to Google, type in the band's name, *click* to go to its website, *click* to go to the page that lists its upcoming gigs, *click* to go to the website for the club where the band is currently playing, and *click* to buy tickets.

Although embedding links is a basic task in building web pages, and even though Dreamweaver—for the most part—shields you from the complexities of doing so, they can be tricky to understand. The following section provides a brief overview of links, including some of the technical distinctions between the different types. The rest of the chapter helps turn you into a link-crafting maestro, with sections on formatting the appearance of your links and on creating a navigation menu.

Note: If you already understand links, or are just eager to start using Dreamweaver, jump to "Adding a Link" on page 165.

Understanding Links

Links are snippets of code that give web browsers directions to get from one page to another on the Web. What makes links powerful is that the distance covered by those directions doesn't matter. A link can lead to another page on the same site just as easily as it can lead to a page on a web server halfway around the globe.

Behind the scenes, a simple HTML tag called the anchor (<a>) tag makes each and every link work. Links come in three flavors: *absolute, document-relative*, and *root-relative*. See page 163 for some examples of each link type in practice.

Absolute Links

When people want to mail you a letter, they ask for your address. Suppose it's 123 Main St., Smithville, NY 12001, USA. No matter where in the country your friends are, if they write *123 Main St., Smithville, NY 12001, USA* on an envelope and mail it, their letters will get to you. That's because your address is unique—just like an absolute link.

Similarly, every web page has a unique address, called a *URL* (most people pronounce it "you are el"), or Uniform Resource Locator. If you open a web browser and type *http://www.sawmac.com/dwcs5/index.html* into the address bar, the home page for this book opens.

This URL is an *absolute link*—it's the complete, unique address for a single page. Absolute links always begin with *http://*, and they always lead to the same page, no matter where the link appears—an absolute link in a web page can call up another page within the same site or a page on another site entirely. You'll use absolute links any time you link to a web page *outside of your own site*—that's the *only* way a web browser can go from a page on your site to a page on another site. However, when you want to call up a page within your own site, there's another way to write the link (see "Document-Relative Links" below), that frees your pages from the constraints of absolute links, letting you easily put the pages you create anywhere on the Web—or even view them "offline," right on your desktop—a feat that's impossible with absolute links.

The bottom line: use absolute links when you want to link to a page on another website.

Document-Relative Links

Suppose you, the resident of 123 Main Street, drop in on a couple who just moved into a house directly across the street from you. After letting them know about all the great restaurants nearby, you tell them about a party you're having at your place.

When they ask you where you live, you could say, "I live at 123 Main St., Smithville, NY 12001, USA," but your neighbors would probably think you needed a little psychiatric help. Instead, you'd say something like, "Just walk across the street and there you are." Of course, you can't use these instructions as your mailing address, and they wouldn't make sense, either, for a neighbor who lived seven houses down. Those directions only help the neighbors across the street get from their house to yours.

When you want to create a link from one web page to another within the same website, you use a similar shorthand, called a *document-relative link*. In essence, a document-relative link—like the directions you give your neighbor—tells a browser where to find a page *relative* to the current page. If two pages are in the same folder, for instance, the path is as simple as "Go to that page over there." In this case, the link is simply the name of the file you wish to link to: *index.html*, for example. You can leave off all that *http://www.your_site.com/* business, because you're already on that site and within that directory.

Document-relative links can be finicky, however, because they're completely dependent on the location of the page containing the link. If you move that page to another part of your site—filing it in a different folder, for example—the link won't work (it's as though your neighbors moved across town—they couldn't walk across the street to get to your house any longer). That's why working with document-relative links has traditionally been one of the most troublesome chores for web designers, even though this kind of link is ideal for linking from one page to another in the same site.

Fortunately, Dreamweaver makes working with document-relative links so easy, you may forget what all the fuss is about. Whenever you save a page with a document-relative link in a different folder—a maneuver that would normally shatter all the links on the page—Dreamweaver quietly *rewrites* the links so they still work. Even better, using the program's site management tools, you can cavalierly reorganize your site without fear, moving files and folders without harming the delicate connections between your site's files. (You'll learn about Dreamweaver's site management features in depth in Part Four.)

Root-Relative Links

Root-relative links describe how to get from one page to another within the same site, just like document-relative links. However, in this case, the link describes the path relative to the site's *root folder*—the folder that contains the home page and other pages, folders, and files that make up your site. (For a detailed description of the root folder and structuring a website, see Chapter 16.)

Imagine you work in a big office building. You need to get to a co-worker's office in the same building for a meeting, so you call her for directions. She may not know the precise directions from your office to hers, but she can tell you how to get from the building's entrance to her office. Since you both know where the building's front door is, these directions work well. In fact, she can give the same directions to anyone else in the building, and since they all know where the entrance is, they'll be able to find her office, too. Think of the office building as your site, and its front door as the *root* of your site. Root-relative links always begins with a slash (/). This slash is a stand-in character for the root folder—the front door—of the site. The same root-relative link always leads to the same page, no matter where it is on your website.

If you use Dreamweaver for all your web page development, you probably won't need root-relative links, but they can come in handy. For example, suppose you're asked to create a new page for an existing website. Your client gives you text, some graphics, and a list of the other pages on the site that this page needs to link to. The problem is, your client doesn't know where on the site the new page needs to go, and his webmaster won't return your calls.

Fortunately, you can use root-relative links to solve this dilemma. Since these links work no matter where the page is on your site, you could complete the page and let the client put it where it belongs—and the links will still work.

There's one major drawback to using root-relative links: They don't work when you test them on your own computer. If you view a web page sitting on your computer's hard drive, clicking a root-relative link in a browser either doesn't work, or produces only a "File not found" error. Root-relative links work only when the pages with them are on a web server. That's because the technology behind web servers understand root-relative links, but your personal computer doesn't.

UP TO SPEED

Parts of a URL

Each chunk of a URL helps a web browser locate the proper web page. Take the following URL, for instance: *http://www.sawmac.com/dwcs5/index.html*.

- http://. This portion specifies the *protocol*, the communications technology a browser must use to interact with a web server. *HTTP* stands for *hypertext transfer protocol*; you use it when you want to see a web page, as opposed to protocols like *ftp* (where you transfer files to and from a server) and *mailto* (where you send email messages to mail servers).
- *www.sawmac.com*. This identifies the computer that's dishing out the website in question–that is, it's the address of the web *server*. The www part identifies a website within the *domain sawmac.com*. It's possible to have multiple websites in a single domain, such as *http://news.sawmac.com, http://secret.sawmac.com*, and so on.
- /dwcs5/. This is the name of a folder (also called a directory) on the web server.
- index.html. This is the name of the actual document or file the web browser will open–it's the file name of the web page itself. These are the HTML documents that Dreamweaver creates.

One solution to the root-relative links problem is to install a web server on your computer and put your site files inside it. This is the approach you take when building the dynamic sites discussed in Part Six of this book.

Note: There's one exception to the "root relative links don't preview correctly" dilemma. Dreamweaver provides two ways to preview a web page: *with* a temporary file or *without* one. The temporary-file option has a couple of advantages: You can preview a page without having to save it first, and you can preview–on your local computer–any root-relative links you created. To turn this feature on, open Preferences (Edit→Preferences or, on a Mac, Dreamweaver→Preferences), click the "Preview in Browser" category, and turn on the Preview Using Temporary File checkbox. Behind the scenes, Dreamweaver secretly rewrites root-relative links as *document relative* links whenever it creates a temporary file. If you see files in your site with weird names like TMP2zlc3mvs10.htm, those are the temporary files Dreamweaver creates. Feel free to delete them.

Unless you have a specific reason to use root-relative links (like your IT department says you have to), it's best to stick to document-relative links for your pages, but keep this discussion in mind. You'll see later that Dreamweaver's site management features use root-relative paths to track your site's files behind the scenes.

Note: You can run into trouble with root-relative links if the site you're working on is located within a folder inside the web server root folder. For example, say your buddy gives you space on his web server. He says you can put your site in a folder called *my_friend*, so your URL is *http://www.my_buddy.com/my_friend/*. In this case, your web pages don't sit at the root of the site—they're in a folder *inside* the root. So a root-relative link to your home page would be */my_friend/index.html*. Dreamweaver can handle a situation like this, but only if you provide the correct URL of your site—*http://www.my_buddy.com/my_friend*—when you set it up (see Figure 5-1).

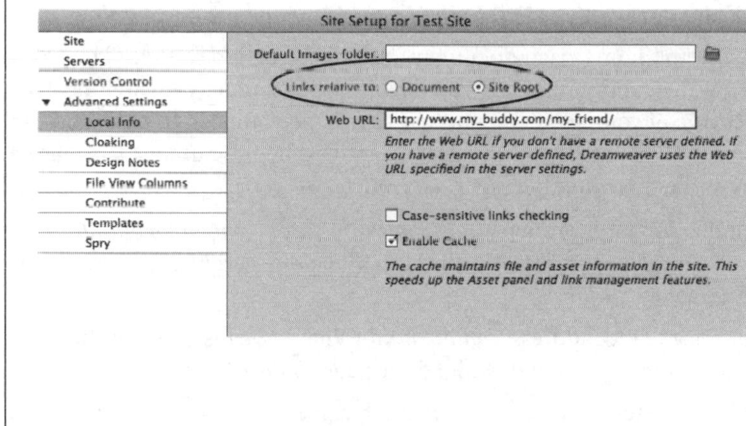

Figure 5-1:
When you set up a site in Dreamweaver, you can identify the URL of the site even if it's in a subfolder within the root folder—it's the site's actual address on the Internet. Expand the list of Advanced Settings options in the left of the window, click the Local Info category, and then type the full web address to your site in the web URL box. You can also tell Dreamweaver which type of link—document-relative or site root-relative—it should use when creating a link to another page on your site (circled). You can always return to this window if you want to change this option. Choose Site→Manage Sites, select your site, and then click Edit.

Link Types in Action

Figure 5-2 shows a website as it appears on a hard drive: folders filled with HTML documents and graphics. Here's a closer look at some links you might find on those pages, and how they might work.

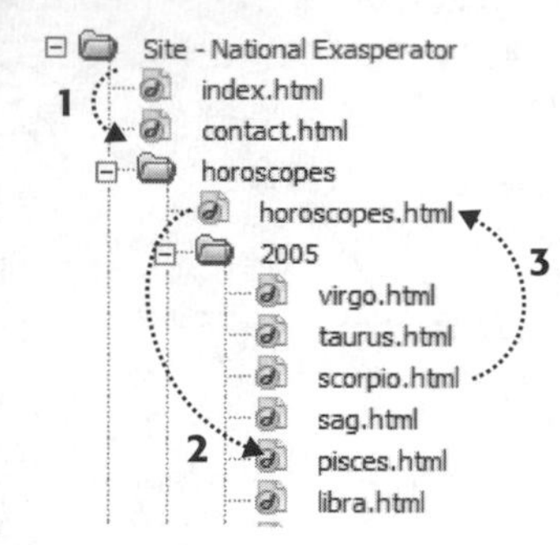

Figure 5-2:
Here are a few examples of links for a fictitious website located at http://www.nationalexasperator.com. The three lines show the connections between the original page (where each line starts) and the page it links to (where each arrow ends).

Link from the Home page (index.html) to the Contact Us page (contact.html)

Most websites call the home page document *index.html* or *index.htm*. (The exact name depends on the configuration of your web server. Contact your web host, or the person in charge of your server, to confirm the name you need to use.) You can link from this page to the *contact.html* page—identified by the number 1 in Figure 5-2—using any of the three link types:

- Absolute link address: *http://www.nationalexasperator.com/contact.html*. What it means: Go to the website at *http://www.nationalexasperator.com* and download the page *contact.html*.
- Document-relative link address: *contact.html*. What it means: Look in the same folder as the current page and download the page *contact.html*.
- Root-relative link address: */contact.html*. What it means: Go to the top-level folder of this site and download *contact.html*.

Tip: If you can write an absolute URL, you can easily write a root-relative URL. Simply strip off the *http://* and the web server name. In the example above, erasing the *http://www.nationalexasperator.com* in the absolute address leaves */contact.html*–the root-relative path.

Link from the Horoscopes page to the Pisces page

Now imagine you're building a web page that you want to link it to another page that's inside a subfolder of your site. Here's how you'd use each of the three link types to open a document nested in a subfolder (called "2005", in this case), as identified by the number 2 in Figure 5-2:

- Absolute link address: *http://www.nationalexasperator.com/horoscopes/2005/pisces.html*. What it means: Go to the website at *http://www.nationalexasperator.com*, look in the folder *horoscopes*, then look in the folder *2005*, and then download the page *pisces.html*.

- Document-relative link address: *2005/pisces.html*. What it means: From the current page, look in the folder *2005* and download the page *pisces.html*.
- Root-relative link address: */horoscopes/2005/pisces.html*. What it means: Go to the top-level folder of this site, look in the folder *horoscopes*, then look in the folder *2005*, and then download the page *pisces.html*.

Link from the Scorpio page to the Horoscopes page

Now suppose you're building a web page that's in a deeply nested folder, and you want it to link to a document that's outside of that folder, like the link labeled 3 in Figure 5-2:

- Absolute link address: *http://www.nationalexasperator.com/horoscopes/horoscopes.html*. What it means: Go to the website at *http://www.nationalexasperator.com*, look in the folder *horoscopes*, and download the page *horoscopes.html*.
- Document-relative link address: *../horoscopes.html*. What it means: Go up one level—outside of the current folder—and download the page *horoscopes.html*. In website addresses, a slash / represents a folder or directory. The two dots (..) mean, "Go up one level," into the folder that *contains* the current folder. So to link to a page that's up two levels—for example, to link from *scorpio.html* to the home page (*index.html*)—you would use ../ twice, like this: *../../index.html*.
- Root-relative link address: */horoscopes/horoscopes.html*. What it means: Go to the top-level folder of this site, look in the folder *horoscopes*, and download the page *horoscopes.html*.

Executive Summary

In short: Use absolute URLs to link to pages *outside* your site, use document-relative links to link to pages *within your site*, and, unless you know what you're doing (or your IT department tells you that you have to), avoid using root-relative links altogether.

Adding a Link

If all that talk of links gets you confused, don't worry. Links *are* confusing, and that's one of the best reasons to use Dreamweaver. If you can navigate to a document on your own computer or anywhere on the Web, you can create a link to it in Dreamweaver, even if you don't know the first thing about URLs and don't intend to learn the details of how to configure them.

Browsing for a File

To create a link from one page to another on your local website, use the Property inspector's "Browse for File" button (see Figure 5-3) or its keyboard shortcut, as described in the following steps.

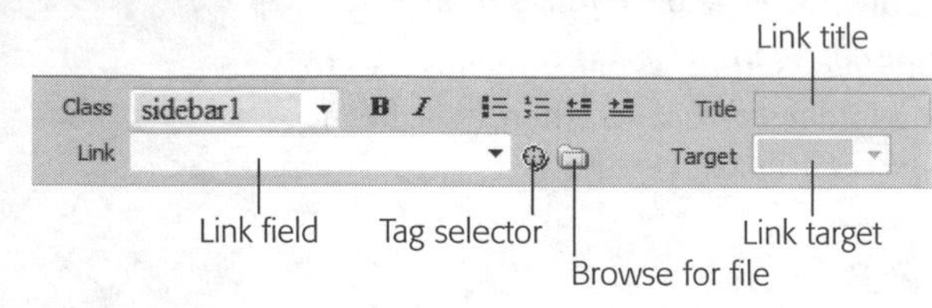

Figure 5-3:
The Property inspector provides three ways to add links to a web page: the Link field, the "Point to file" tool, and the "Browse for File" button.

To browse for a file in Dreamweaver, you use the same type of dialog box that you use to open or save a file, making "Browse for File" the easiest way to add a link. (To link to a page on *another* website, you need to type the web address into the Property inspector. Turn to page 169 for instructions.)

1. **In the document window, select the text or image you want to link from.**

   You can select a single word, a sentence, or an entire paragraph. When you add a link to text, the selected words appear in blue and underlined (depending on your visitors' web browser settings), like billions of links before them.

   In addition, you can turn a picture into a link—a great trick for adding attractive navigation buttons When you do, the image has a blue border around it, much like linked text has a blue underline (fortunately, with some simple CSS, you can get rid of that blue outline—see the tip on page 168).

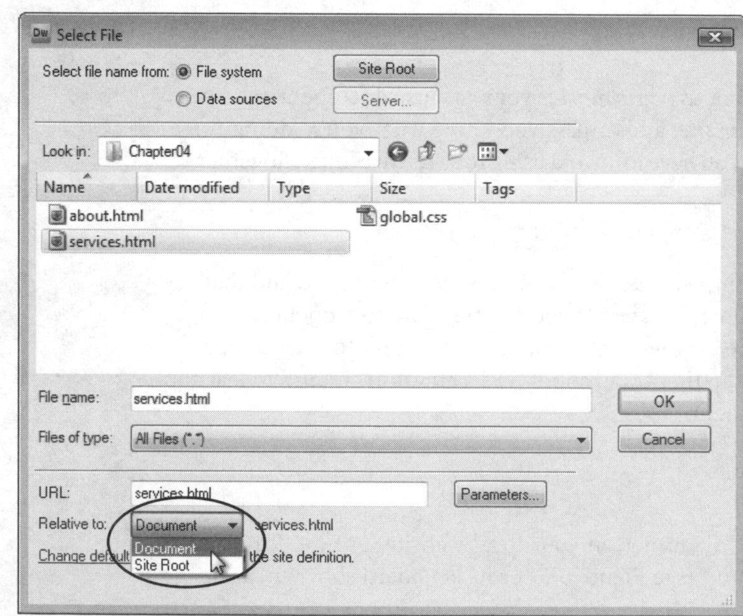

Figure 5-4:
In Windows, the Select File dialog box lets you browse your computer to select the target file for a link. When you set up your site, you can tell Dreamweaver whether to use document- or site root-relative links (see Figure 5-1.) However, if you ever find the need to temporarily switch to a different type of link (to root-relative, for example, if you set up your site to use document-relative), use the "Relative to" pop-up menu (circled). You probably won't ever need to do this, but Dreamweaver gives you the option.

2. **In the Property inspector, click the folder icon—that's the "Browse for File" button.**

   Or, choose Modify→Make Link, or press Ctrl+L (⌘-L). In any case, the Select File dialog box opens (see Figure 5-4 for Windows, Figure 5-5 for Mac).

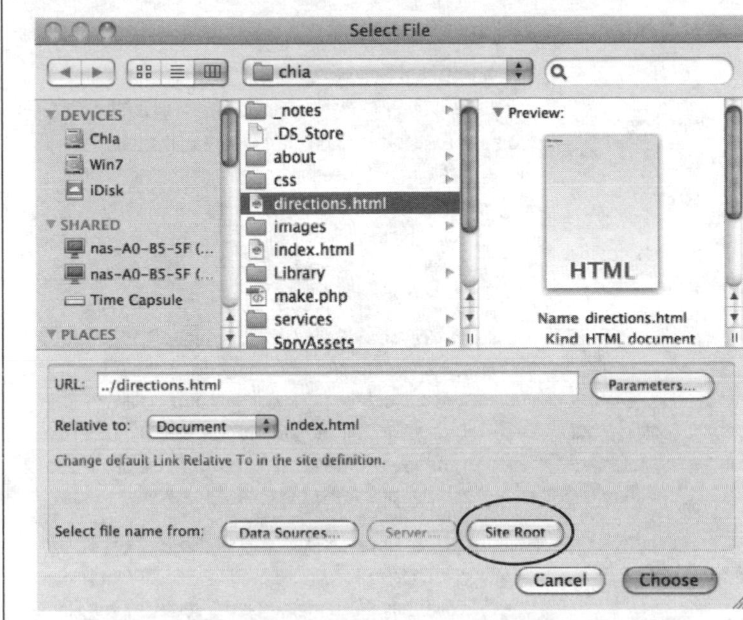

***Figure 5-5:** Every file in a website needs to be somewhere inside what's called a local root folder (see the box on page 42). This master folder holds everything on the site, including other folders with other files. Because it's so central to your web files, Dreamweaver includes a Site Root button (circled) to every window that requires selecting or saving a file. (This example shows what you see on a Mac; on Windows computers, the button's at the top of the window as shown in Figure 5-4.) Click this button and you jump straight to your site's root (so you know exactly where you are on your hard drive), making it easy to navigate to the file you need.*

3. **Navigate to and select the file you want the link to open.**

   The file should be a web page that's part of your site. In other words, it should be in the local root folder (see the box on page 42), or in a folder therein.

   Remember: To a website, the root folder is like the edges of the known universe—nothing exists outside of it. If you try to link to a file *outside* the root folder, Dreamweaver tells you 'it's a problem and offers to copy the file to the root folder. Accept the offer.

Tip: You can double-click the name of a file in the Select File dialog box and Dreamweaver selects the file *and* closes the Select File dialog box in one step…or is that two steps?

---

4. **Make sure you select the correct type of link—Document or Site Root—from the "Relative to" menu.**

   As noted earlier in this chapter, document-relative links are usually the best choice. Root-relative links (which is actually short for *Site Root-relative links*) don't work when you preview your site on your own computer. (They do, however, work once you move them to your web server.)

Note: You can skip step 4: Just set the type of link you want in the Site Setup window, and then forget about it. Dreamweaver always uses the link type you specified there. See Figure 5-1 for details.

FREQUENTLY ASKED QUESTION

The Mysterious Triple Slashes

Why do my links start with file:///?

Links that begin with *file:///* (*file:///C:/missingmanual/book_site/cosmo/subscribe.html*, for example) aren't valid links on the Web. Rather, they're temporary addresses that Dreamweaver creates as placeholders for links it will rewrite later. (A *file:///* path tells Dreamweaver to look for the file on your computer.) You'll spot these addresses when you add document-relative links to a page you haven't saved, or when you work with files outside of your site's local root folder.

Suppose you're working on a web page that contains your company's legal mumbo-jumbo, but you haven't yet saved it. After adding a document-relative link to your home page, you notice that the Property inspector's Link field begins with *file:///*. Since you haven't yet saved your legal page, Dreamweaver doesn't know its folder location and so it can't create a relative link telling a browser where to go to get the page. So it creates a temporary link, which helps it keep track of which page to link to. Once you save the page somewhere in your site, Dreamweaver rewrites the link in proper document-relative format, and the *file:///* disappears.

Likewise, Dreamweaver can't write a "legitimate" link (a link that will really work in a web browser) to a file outside the local root folder. Since it considers anything beyond the root folder outside the bounds of the site, Dreamweaver can't write a link to "nowhere." So, if you save a page *outside* the local root folder, Dreamweaver writes all document-relative links on that page as file paths beginning with *file:///*. (This problem can also crop up if you use Dreamweaver without first setting up a site–that's why that simple site setup process [described on page 37] is so important.)To avoid this invalid link problem, always save your web pages inside the local root folder or in a folder *inside* of the local root folder. To learn more about root folders and websites, see Chapter 16.

If you have set up a site and you *link to* a page–or add an image (Chapter 6)–stored outside the local root folder, Dreamweaver has the same problem. However, in this instance, Dreamweaver gives you the option of copying the out-of-bounds file to a location of your choosing within the root folder.

5. **Click OK (Windows) or Choose (Mac) to apply the link.**

   The text or image now links to another web page. If you haven't yet saved the other web page into your site, Dreamweaver doesn't know how to write the document-relative link. Instead, it displays a dialog box saying that it will assign a temporary path for the link until you save the page—see the box above.

After you apply a link, linked text appears underlined and colored (using the color defined by the Page Properties window, which is shown in Figure 1-20). Images have a blue borderline around them. Press F12 (Option-F12 on a Mac) to preview the page in your browser, where you can click the link.

Tip: To get rid of the ugly blue border around linked images, create a CSS style for the <img> tag (see page 113 if you're unsure about creating styles) and set its border style to "none" (see page 230). The tutorial at the end of this chapter has an example of this, on page 197.

Using the Point-to-File Tool

You can also create links by dragging from the Property inspector to the Files panel (shown in Figure 5-6). If your site involves a lot of links, learning to use the Point-to-File tool will save you time and energy.

To use this trick effectively, position your document window and Files window side by side, as shown in Figure 5-6.

1. **In the document window, select the text or image you want to turn into a link.**

   Make sure you have both the Property inspector and Files window open. To open the Property inspector, choose Window→Properties. To open the Files window, choose Window→Files. (Before using the Files window, you need to create a local site, as described on page 37.)

2. **Drag the Point-to-File icon from the Property inspector onto a web page in the Files window (see Figure 5-6).**

   Or you can Shift-drag the selected text or image in the document window to any web page in the Files panel, bypassing the Property inspector altogether.

Tip: You can also drag a file from the Files panel into the Link box (in the Property inspector) to link to it.

---

3. **After dragging over the correct web page, release the mouse button.**

   The selected text or image in your web page now links to the file you just pointed to.

Note: Bizarre Bug Alert: If you use two monitors as you build web pages, the Point-to-File icon might not work. If your main monitor (the one with the Start menu for Windows, or the one where a program's menu bar appears on Macs) is on the right, and the second monitor is on the left, then the Point-to-File icon *may not* work. Then again, it might! Strange, but true.

Typing (or Pasting) the URL or Path

If you need to link to another website, or you feel comfortable working with document-relative links, you can also simply type the URL or path to the page into the Property inspector. Note that this manual insertion technique and the hyperlink object tool discussed next are the *only* ways to add links to pages *outside* the current website.

1. **In the document window, select the text or image you want to make into a link.**

2. **In the Property inspector, type the URL or the path to the file into the Link field (see Figure 5-3).**

   If the link leads to another website, type an absolute URL—that is, a complete web address, starting with *http://*.

Tip: An easier approach is to copy a complete URL—including the *http://*—from the address bar in your browser window and paste it into the Link field.

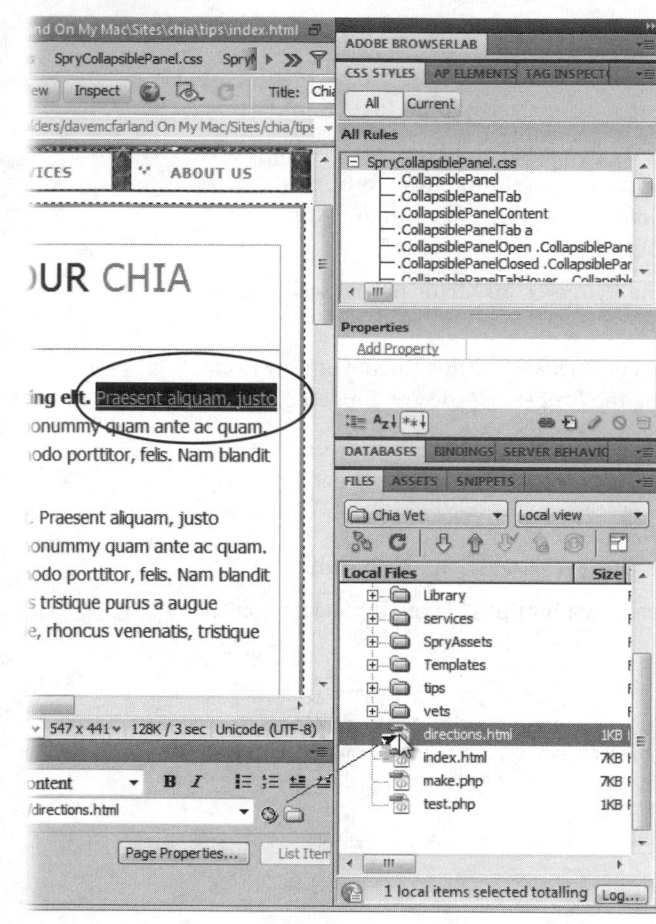

Figure 5-6:
In this figure, select some text (circled) in the document window that you want to turn into a link. To link to another page, drag from the Point-to-File icon (the bull's-eye icon in the Property inspector) to a web page in the Files panel (right). In this example, Dreamweaver creates a link to the web page called directions.html. You could also Shift-drag from the selected text to the page directions.html in the Files panel to create the same link.

To link to a page on your own site, type a document-relative link (see page 163 for some examples). Letting Dreamweaver write the correct path using the browsing or point-to-file techniques described above is a good way to avoid typos. But typing the path can come in handy when, say, you want to create a link to a page you haven't yet created, but you know where it'll go.

3. **Press Enter (Return) to apply the link.**

   While you don't necessarily have to hit Enter (Return)—sometimes you can just click elsewhere on the page and keep working—Dreamweaver has been known to forget the link and not apply it. This is true for most fields in the Property Inspector—so if you type information directly into the Property inspector (to create a link, add a title property, and so on) get into the habit of hitting the Enter (Return) key to make sure your change sticks.

Note: If you're adding an absolute link to a website without specifying a web page, add a final forward slash (/) to the end of the address. For example, to link to Yahoo, type *http://www.yahoo.com/*. The final slash tells the web server that you're requesting the default page (home page) at *Yahoo.com*.

Although leaving out the slash works, too (*http://www.yahoo.com*), the server has to do a little extra work to figure out which page to send back, resulting in a slight and unnecessary delay.

Also include the final slash when you provide a link to the default page inside a folder on a site, like this: *http://www.sawmac.com/dwcs5/*, saves the browser from first requesting a file named dwcs5, and then requesting the default page inside the folder dwcs5.

Using the Hyperlink Object

Dreamweaver provides yet another way to add a link. The Hyperlink object in the Common category of the Insert panel (Figure 5-7) lets you insert a link with many optional properties. Its only real benefit is that it lets you add text and a link in one step (instead of adding text to a page, selecting it, and *then* applying a link). Unfortunately, this tool only works with text (not graphics) and some of the optional properties don't work in all browsers.

Figure 5-7:
The Insert panel's Common category includes three link-related objects: the Hyperlink (to add links), the Email link (to add links for email addresses), and the Named anchor (to add links within a page). As discussed in Figure 1-3, the Insert panel can look like a toolbar (as pictured here), or as a panel grouped with the other panels on the right side of the screen.

If you're still interested, here's how it works. Start by clicking on the page where you wish to insert a link. Then:

1. **Choose Insert→Hyperlink or click the chain icon on the Insert bar.**

   The Hyperlink dialog box opens (see Figure 5-8). To apply a link to text already on the page, select the text first, and then choose Insert→Hyperlink.

2. **In the Text box, type the text you want to appear on the page.**

   Whatever you type here is what you'll see on the page, and what your audience will click to follow the link. If you previously selected some text on the page, it shows up in the Text box automatically.

3. **Click the folder icon and search for the page you want to link to.**

   Alternatively, you can type a URL in the Link box.

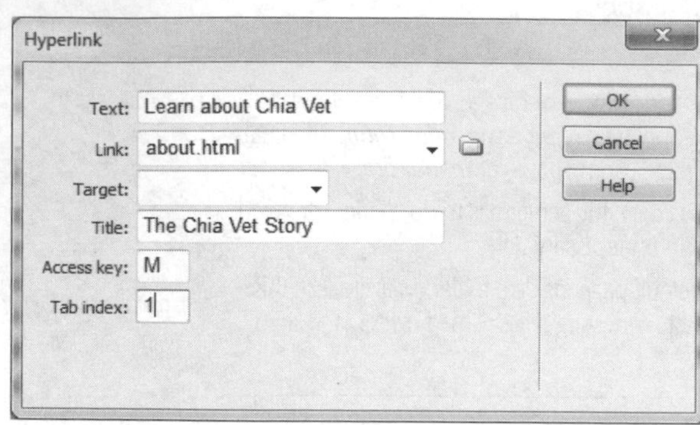

Figure 5-8:
You can apply everything, except the "Access key" and "Tab index" properties, shown in this dialog box to an image or existing text using the Property inspector. Also, keep in mind one somewhat special case: If you want to add an Access key and Tab index to an already existing link, you have a couple of options: go into Code view (as described in Chapter 11) and hand edit the HTML, or use the Tag inspector to access all the properties available to a particular link. (For details, see page 440.)

FREQUENTLY ASKED QUESTION

Targeting and Titling Links

What are the Title box and Target menu in the Property inspector for?

A link's *Title* property supplies additional information about a link, usually to clearly indicate where the link leads. For example, if you linked "Click here for more" to an article describing different types of termites, the link text alone doesn't clearly explain where this link goes–click for more of *what*, you might ask. In this case, you could add the title "A complete list of termite species" in the Property inspector (see Figure 5-3). The title property is optional, and if the link text already clearly explains where the link leads, don't bother setting the title property. In fact, you can avoid the title property altogether if you write text that explains where the link leads: "Click here for a complete list of termite species," for example.

However, in the case of linked images (such as a logo that also acts as a link back to a site's home page), adding a title is a very good idea. Search engines like the title property in this case, because it lets them know the purpose of the link; people who use screen readers (programs that help those with vision problems surf the Web) also benefit, since the title property can be read out loud and the visitor will know where the link goes. The title property has one other unique feature: web browsers display a pop-up tooltip window with the title's text when a guest moves her mouse over the link.

The *Target* menu has nothing to do with the accuracy of your links, nor with shooting ranges. It deals with how a browser displays the destination page when you click a link.

You can have the new page (a) replace the current page in the browser window (the way most links work); (b) open in a new browser window (choose the *_blank* option); or (c) appear in a different *frame* on the same page (for details about this increasingly obsolete technology, see the online-only chapter about frames, located at *www.sawmac.com/missing/dw8/appc.pdf*).

_blank is pretty much the only option used these days, but be careful if your pages use the "Strict" forms of HTML 4.01 and XHTML 1.0: the Target attribute isn't valid code for strict doctypes (see page 7).

4. **Set the target page for the link.**

   If you want the link to open in the same window—like most links—don't select anything. To make the page open in a new window, select the *_blank* option (see the box on page 172 for more on targeting a link).

   The last three options are more interesting.

5. **Type a title for the destination page.**

   This property is optional. As described in the box on page 172, most browsers display the title in a small tooltip window when a visitor moves his mouse over the link.

6. **Type a key in the "Access key" box.**

   An *access key* lets you trigger a link from your keyboard. Internet Explorer, Safari, and Firefox understand this property in conjunction with the Alt key (Control key for Firefox on a Mac and Control+Alt keys for Safari and Chrome on a Mac). For example, if you type *h* in the "Access key" box, then a visitor to your page can press Alt+H (Control-H) to mouselessly open that link. Of course, unless people who visit your site are psychic, it's a good idea to provide the access key next to the link itself, as in "Home Page (Alt+H)".

Note: Opera has a special method for using access keys with links: access-key mode. Press Shift+ESC while viewing a page in Opera to see all the access keys defined on the page.

---

7. **In the "Tab index" box, type a number for the tab order.**

   In most browsers, you can press the Tab key to step through the links on a page (and boxes on a form). This feature not only provides useful keyboard control of your browser, it also lets people who can't use a mouse due to disabilities cycle through the links.

   Normally when you press Tab, web browsers highlight links in the order in which they appear in the page's HTML. The Tab index, by contrast, lets *you* control the order in which links light up as visitors tab through them. For example, you can give your navigation buttons priority when someone presses Tab, even if they aren't the first links on the page.

   For the first link in the order, type *1* here. Number other links in the order you want the Tab key to follow. If you aren't concerned about the order of a particular link, leave this option blank or type in *0*. The web browser will highlight that link after the visitor has tabbed through all links that *do* have a Tab index.

EXTENSION ALERT

QuickLink Is Quick Work

Dreamweaver makes it easy to add innovative commands and tools–including those written by independent, non-Adobe programmers–to your copy of the program. You can read a lot more about these add-on programs, called *extensions*, in Chapter 22.

When you work with links, one extension that really comes in handy is QuickLink. Created by renowned Dreamweaver guru Tom Muck, this extension instantly turns text into either a *mailto* or an *absolute* URL. You can find QuickLink at *http://www.tom-muck.com/extensions/help/quicklink/*. Amazingly, even though this extension hasn't been updated since Dreamweaver MX 2004, it still works in CS5.

Once you install the extension, here's how it works: Suppose you insert your cursor somewhere on a web page in Dreamweaver and type the text, "You can download the free PDF viewer at *http://www.adobe.com*." To turn *http://www.adobe.com* into a real link, you can either select the text and then go to the Property inspector and type *http://www.adobe.com/*, or–with QuickLink–simply select the text and choose Commands→QuickLink. QuickLink writes the proper code in the Property inspector, including the initial (and mandatory) *http://*, even if those characters were missing from the original text. (Note that this extension has one small bug: After you install it, the QuickLink command will appear *twice* in the Commands menu. Either one works.)

QuickLink also converts email addresses to proper *mailto* links: Just select the email address (*missing@sawmac.com*, say), apply the QuickLink command, and watch as the extension automatically inserts the correct code (mailto: *missing@sawmac.com*) into your page.

For even faster action, create a keyboard shortcut for this command; Shift+Ctrl+L is a good one. (See page 817 for more on keyboard shortcuts.)

Adding an Email Link

If you want to invite your site visitors to email you, an *email link* is the perfect solution. When someone clicks an email link, her email program launches automatically, and a new message opens with your email address already in the To field. Your guest can then just type her message and send it off.

An email link looks like this: *mailto:info@chia-vet.com*. The first part (*mailto*) indicates the type of link, while the second part (*info@chia-vet.com*) specifies the email address.

Note: Email links work only if the person who clicks the link has an email program set up and running on his computer. If someone visits your site from a computer at the public library, for example, he might not be able to send email. If this drawback troubles you, you can solicit feedback using a *form* (as discussed in Chapter 12), which has neither the limitations nor the easy setup of an email link.

You can create an email link much the way you create any other Dreamweaver link: by selecting some text or an image and typing the *mailto* address, as shown above, into the Link field in the Property inspector. To simplify this process, Dreamweaver offers a quick way to insert an email link:

1. **Under the Insert panel's Common category, click the "Email link" icon, which looks like an envelope (see Figure 5-7).**

   Alternatively, choose Insert→Email link. Either way, if you've already typed the text (*Email me!*) on your web page, select it first. The Email Link dialog box opens (see Figure 5-9).

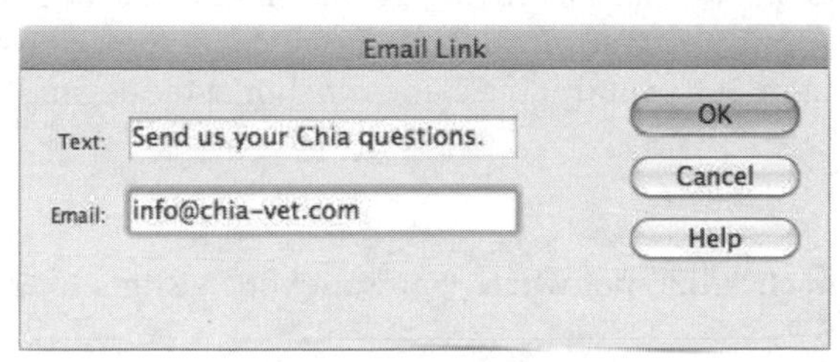

Figure 5-9: *The Email Link dialog box lets you specify the text that appears in the email link and in the email address. You can also select some text you've already added to the document and click the Email Link icon on the Objects panel. The text you select appears in the Text field in this dialog box.*

2. **In the Text field, type the text that you want to appear on the web page.**

   This text can indicate the link's purpose, like *Email the webmaster*. (If you select text in the document first, it automatically appears in the Email Link Text field.)

3. **Type an email address into the E-Mail field.**

   This is the address that appears in your visitors' email program when they click the link. (You don't have to type *mailto*:—Dreamweaver adds it automatically.)

4. **Click OK.**

   Dreamweaver adds the text to the page, complete with a *mailto* link.

Note: Some people don't add email links to their websites because they're afraid of spammers' automated programs that search the web and collect email addresses. There are some tricks to fool these "spambots," but spammers have figured most of them out. The fact is, spammers can attack even "Contact Us" web forms. If you're absolutely obsessed with never being spammed, then leave your email address off your site. However, many businesses rely on people contacting them for more information, and the harder you make it for a legitimate visitor to contact you, the fewer legitimate contacts you'll receive–after all, you wouldn't have much of a freelance design business if you never provided a way for someone to contact you. Your best bet is to let the spam come, but add a spam filter to your email program to separate the wheat from the chaff.

Linking Within a Web Page

Clicking a link usually loads a web page into the browser window. But what if you want to link not only to a web page, but to a specific *spot* on that page? See Figure 5-10 for an example. You can do so two ways: by using HTML's *named-anchor* property or by adding an ID to the target section. The named-anchor method has been around since the earliest days of the Web; it uses a special type of link designed to auto-scroll to a particular spot on a page. The ID technique, while newer, works with all current web browsers; here, you give the destination spot on the page a unique ID. You'll learn about both methods below.

Method 1: Creating a Named Anchor

Creating a named-anchor link is a two-step process: First you add and name an anchor to the page you want to link to, thus identifying the destination for the link; then you add a link that goes to that named anchor. For instance, in the Table of Contents example shown in Figure 5-10, you'd add a named anchor at the beginning of each chapter section.

To create a named anchor:

1. **In the document window, click the spot where you want your visitors to end up.**

   You want to add a named anchor here.

2. **Insert a named anchor.**

   You can do so using any of three methods: Choose Insert→Named Anchor; press Ctrl+Alt+A (⌘-Option-A); or, from the Insert bar, select the Common category and click the Named Anchor icon (see Figure 5-7).

3. **Type the name of the anchor in the Insert Named Anchor dialog box.**

   Give each anchor a unique name (something short and easy to remember). HTML doesn't allow spaces or punctuation marks, and if you include any, Dreamweaver displays an error message and strips out the offending characters.

4. **Click OK to insert the named anchor.**

   Dreamweaver displays a gold shield with an anchor in it. Click this icon to see the name of the anchor in the Property inspector. (If you don't see it, see the opposite page for details on hiding and showing anchors.)

The Named Anchor icon (the gold shield) is the key to removing or editing the anchor later: just click the icon and press Delete to get rid of it, or click it and change its name in the Property inspector. (Deleting the name in the Property inspector deletes the anchor from the page.)

Method 2: Adding an ID

Instead of adding a named anchor, you can assign an ID to the destination spot of a page. For example, if you want to link to a subhead way down on a page (for example a Heading 2, or <h2> tag), you can assign an ID to that heading. For text, you can add an ID by clicking anywhere inside a paragraph and, in the Property inspector's ID box, type the name you want to use. As with named anchors, you can't use spaces or punctuation marks.

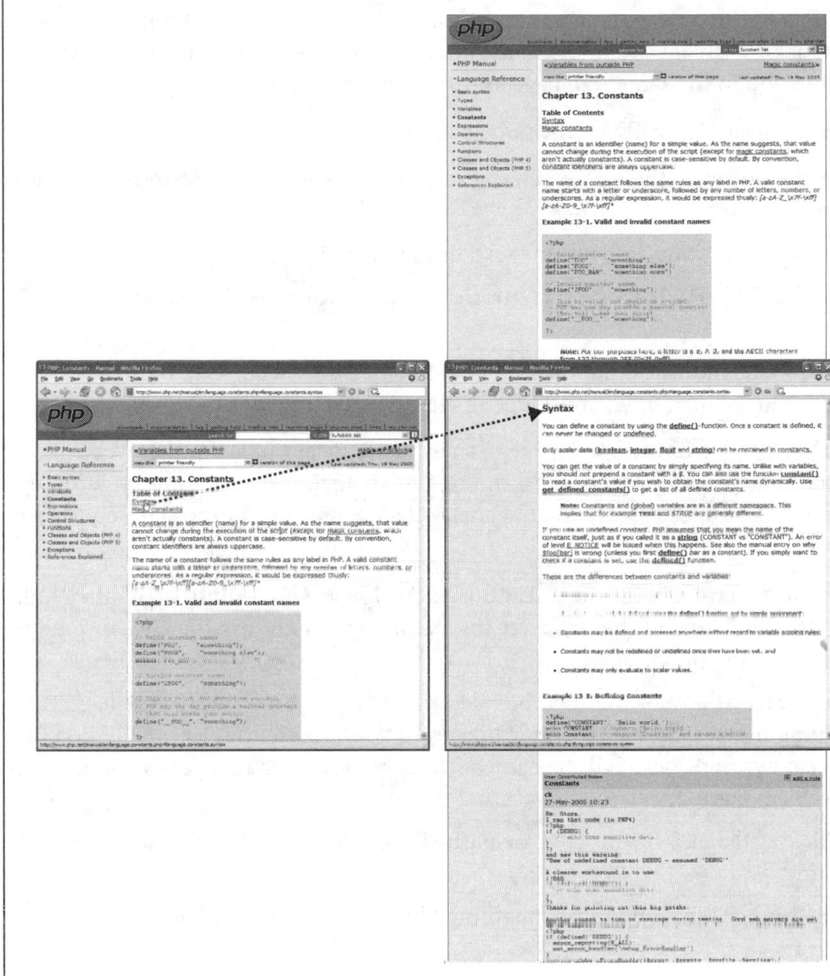

Figure 5-10: *To make it easy for visitors to navigate long web pages, you might list the contents for that page first, and use anchor links within each entry so that, when a visitor clicks a link (left) she jumps down to the appropriate section of the page (right).*

For non-text elements, like images or tables, select the tag (the Tag selector discussed on page 23 is the best way), and type the ID name in the ID box on the left side of the Property inspector.

One other note: You might use IDs in another context, to identify and style discrete sections of your page by adding an ID to a tag and then styling the page using CSS (see page 112 for more on ID styles). The good news is you can use that same ID name as the destination point in an ID link. However, you can add an ID name to a tag whether you style the tag or not. And, if you decide to style the tag later, you can use the same ID name in the style sheet.

Linking to an Anchor or ID

Creating a link to a named anchor or ID isn't all that different from linking to a web page. Once you create and name an anchor or add an ID name to a tag, you can link to it from within the same web page, or from a different page.

To link to an anchor or ID on the same page:

1. **In the document window, select the text or image you want to make into a link.**

   For example, drag across some text, or highlight a graphic.

2. **In the Property inspector's Link field, type #, followed by the anchor or ID name.**

   The # sign indicates that the link goes to a named anchor. So, to link to an anchor named *directions*, you'd type in *#directions*.

You can also link from one web page to a particular location on another web page in your site. The process is the same as linking to an anchor on the same page, except that you have to specify not only the anchor name, but the path to the web page as well:

1. **In the document window, select the text or image you want to turn into a link. In the Link field of the Property inspector, type or choose the URL or path of the page to link to.**

   You can use any of the methods described above: browsing, Point-to-File, or typing in the path name. Unfortunately, if you browse to select the linked file, Dreamweaver doesn't display any anchors or IDs on that page, so you need to perform one extra step.

2. **Click at the end of the URL or path. Type # followed by the anchor or ID's name.**

   The Link field should look something like this: *contact.html#directions*.

Viewing and Hiding Anchors

A named anchor isn't visible in a web browser; it appears in Dreamweaver as an anchor-on-a-gold-shield icon. Like other invisible elements—line breaks, for instance—you can hide named anchors in Dreamweaver by choosing View→Visual Aids→Invisible Elements, or choosing Visual Aids→Invisible Elements from the Visual Aids menu in the toolbar (see Figure 9-12). (If anchors still don't appear, visit the Preferences window, pictured in Figure 1-17, and in the Invisible Elements category, make sure you have the Anchor box turned on.)

Dreamweaver never displays ID names in document view, however, and there's no way to change that.

FREQUENTLY ASKED QUESTION

Anchors Away

When I click a link to an anchor or ID, the web browser is supposed to go to the page and display the anchor or the tag with the specified ID at the top of the browser window. But sometimes the linked-to spot appears in the middle of the browser. What's that about?

Web browsers can't scroll beyond the bottom of a web page, so if you have an anchor or ID near the bottom of a page, the browser can't pull the page all the way up to the anchor point. If one of your own web pages exhibits this problem, and it really bothers you, the fix is simple: create a style for the <body> tag and add *bottom padding* (page 341). This adds space between the bottom of the page and the last bit of content on the page, so browsers can scroll the page all the way to the anchor.

Modifying a Link

At some point, you may need to change or edit a link. Perhaps the URL you were linking to has changed, or you simply no longer need that link.

Changing a Link's Destination

As you'll read in Part Four, Dreamweaver provides some amazing tools for automatically updating links in your pages to keep your site in working order, even if you move files around. But even Dreamweaver isn't smart enough to know when a page on someone *else's* website has been moved or deleted. And you may decide you simply need to change a link so that it points to a different page on your own site. In both of these cases, you'll need to change the links by hand:

1. **Select the text link or picture link.**

   The existing link path appears in the Property inspector's Link field.

2. **Use any of the techniques described on page 165 to specify the link's new target.**

   For example, click the "Browse for File" button in the Property inspector and locate a different web page in your site, or type a complete URL to point to another page outside your site. The destination of the link changes to the new URL, path, or anchor.

Removing a Link

Sometimes, you want to stop a link from linking—when the web page you were pointing to no longer exists, for example. You want the text or image on your web page to stay the same, but you want to remove the disabled link. In that case, just select the link text or image and then use one of these tactics:

- Choose Modify→Remove Link, or press Ctrl+Shift+L (⌘-Shift-L).
- Delete the text in the Link field of the Property inspector and press the Enter or Return key.

The text or image remains on your web page, but it no longer links to anything. If it's a text link, the color changes from your site's link color to the normal text color for the page.

Of course, if you're feeling particularly destructive, you can delete the link's text or image itself, which simultaneously deletes the link.

Styling Links

You can control the basic look of links from the Links category of the Page Properties window (Figure 5-11). To open it, choose Modify→Page Properties→Links (CSS), press Ctrl+J (⌘-J)→Links (CSS), or click the Page Properties button in the Property inspector (this button appears only when you have either nothing on the page selected or you have text selected; it doesn't appear if you have an image selected, for example). Then click "Links (CSS)".

The top set of options—font, size, bold, italic—sets the basic formatting for every link on the page. The next group of options sets the color of the links under specific conditions. Web browsers keep track of how a visitor interacts with the links on a page: when he moves his mouse over a link, for example. Each link has four modes (called *states*): a plain, unvisited link is just called a *link*; a link that a visitor has already clicked (determined by the browser's pages-viewed history) is called a *visited* link; a link that a guest's mouse is currently over is technically called a *hover* state (but Dreamweaver refers to it as a *rollover* link); and a link in the process of being clicked (where a visitor has pushed but not released his mouse button) is known as an *active* link.

Each of these states provides useful feedback for your visitors, and you can style each one individually. In most web browsers, a plain link appears blue until you visit the page it links to—then that link turns purple. This helpful color-coding lets a visitor know whether to follow a link: "Hey, there's a page I haven't seen," or, "Been there, done that."

The rollover (or hover) link is particularly useful in telling visitors they can click the link, and it lends itself to a lot of creative potential. For example, you can completely change the look of a link when a visitor mouses over it; you can change its color, add a background image, or change its background color (page 231). (To get neat effects like this, you need to go beyond the Page Properties window and set styles for your links, as described in the next section.)

Finally, an *active* link is for that fleeting moment when a visitor clicks a link but has yet to release the mouse button. It happens so fast that it's usually not worth spending too much time formatting the active link state.

Note: Internet Explore applies the active link style to any link a visitor *tabs* to (some web surfers can't, or don't want to, use a mouse, and rely on the keyboard to navigate websites.) Firefox, Safari, Opera, and Chrome use yet another link state, called *focus*, to style links that someone reaches via the Tab key. See the note on page 182 for more on a link's focus state.

The Page Properties window (Figure 5-11) lets you change the color for each link state. In addition, the "Underline style" menu lets you control whether a browser underlines a link (the default); displays nothing beneath a link; displays an underline when a guest mouses over the link; or underlines a link but removes it when a visitor mouses over the link. Since web surfers are accustomed to thinking of underlined text as a big "CLICK ME" sign, think twice before removing underlines from links. Without some clear indication that the text is a link, visitors may never see (or click) the links on your page.

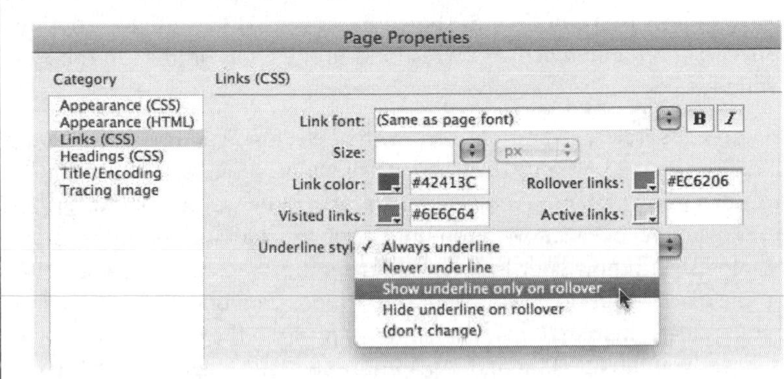

Figure 5-11:
The Page Properties' Links (CSS) window lets you set basic properties for the links on a web page, including their font, color, and size. This window is mainly a shortcut for creating CSS styles.

One problem with using the Page Properties window to set link properties is that those settings only apply to the current page. Fortunately, you don't need to set the Page Properties on every page of your site; you can move the styles you create in the Page Properties window to an external style sheet (see page 111 if you don't know what an external style sheet is). In fact, the Page Properties window actually creates CSS styles to format links; it's just that Dreamweaver creates those styles in the page itself using an internal style sheet. If you use the Page Properties window for one page, you can export those styles or even drag them into an external style sheet. (To learn how to do that, see page 306.) Alternatively, you can bypass the Page Properties window altogether and create CSS link styles from scratch—which you'll learn about in the next section.

CSS and Links

Using the CSS Styles panel to create styles for your links gives you access to many more formatting options besides font, color, and size. In fact, you can apply nearly every CSS property to links. For example, you can use all the text options discussed on page 128—font size, weight, variant, letter spacing, and so on—to format a link. In addition, you can add a border (page 230) and a background color (page 231) to a link to make it look like a button.

To format the look of all links, create a tag style (page 112) for the <a> tag (the tag used to create links) using the instructions on page 113. To create a different look for a particular link (if you want that "Buy Now!" link to be bigger and bolder than other links on a page, for example), create a class style (page 112) and apply it directly to that link.

To control how a link looks for different states (link, visited, hover, and active), you need to dip a little deeper into the CSS pool and use what's called a *pseudo-class*. As you've read, a selector is merely the part of a style that instructs a browser where to apply a style—*h1* is the selector for formatting every Heading 1 paragraph, for example. When you select Compound from the Selector Type menu at the top of New CSS Rule window, Dreamweaver lets you select one of four *pseudo-classes*, each of which refer to a different type of link, as shown in Figure 5-12. These four options (*a:link, a:visited, a:hover*, and *a:active*) correspond to the types of links in the Page Properties window.

To use a pseudo-class, select Compound from the Selector Type menu at the top of the New CSS Rule window, and then choose the appropriate selector from the Selector Name drop-down menu. For example, to format the way a link looks when a guest mouses over it, choose *a:hover*. You don't have to set all four pseudo-classes: If you're not interested in how your links look during the nanosecond that a visitor clicks it, skip the *a:active* option. If you want to set more than one of these pseudo-classes, you must create them in the order that they appear in the menu, or the styles may not display as you intended them. (A helpful mnemonic for remembering this rule is LoVe HAte—that is, *:link* comes before *:visited*, which comes before *:hover*, which comes before *:active*.)

Note: Safari, Firefox, and Chrome understand an additional pseudo-class related to links: *a:focus*. This selector applies when a visitor uses the Tab key to move from one link to another on a page. Each time she jumps to a new link, the browser highlights it and gives the link "focus." Of the different versions of Internet Explorer, only IE 8 understands the *a:focus* pseudo-class, but all versions of IE treat a:active as if it were a:focus.

To create a style that formats a link when a visitor tabs to it (instead of mouses over it), create what's called a group style. Here's how: When you create the "highlighted" style, choose Compound for the selector type. For the selector name, type in a:focus, a:active. This applies the "tabbed to" highlight style for all current browsers.

Using these styles, you can make your link text appear red and underscored before a visitor clicks the link, twice as large when he mouses over it, purple and boldfaced when he clicks it, and pale pink after he visits the linked site. (Granted, if you try this design, Martha Stewart may never hire you to design her site, but you get the point.)

Note that these link pseudo-classes have one drawback: setting them affects *all* the links on a page. In that respect, pseudo-classes are like tag styles.

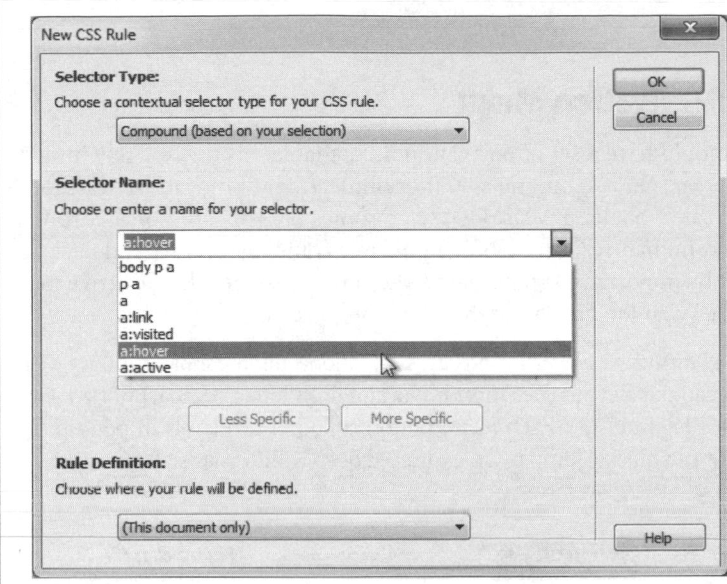

Figure 5-12: *The drop-down menu that appears when you select "Compound" as the selector type (from the top menu) lists the four link pseudo-classes. In addition, you may see one or more other names at the top of the list–for example, the "body p a," "p a," and "a" selector names you see in this menu. The Selector Name menu lists all the possible style names you can apply to what you have selected on the page. In this case, you put the cursor inside a link, which was inside a paragraph before you clicked the New CSS Rule button. As a result, Dreamweaver suggests creating a "body p a" style or a "p a" style. These styles are called descendent selectors–you'll learn about them on page 298.*

Tip: Dreamweaver CS5 lets you quickly preview link states in Design view. Choose View→Toolbars→Style Rendering to open the Style Rendering toolbar sandwiched between the Related Files toolbar (page 433) and the Document toolbar (page 21). Buttons labeled :l (for the link state), :v (for visited), :h (for hover), :a (for active) and f: (for focus) appear at the right side of the toolbar. Clicking any of them displays the CSS design for the selected state: for example, click the :h button to see all the links on a page as they'll appear when a mouse hovers over them. You'll learn more about the Style Rendering toolbar on page 322.

If you want to apply a style to only certain links on a page, here's what to do: create a new style (click the + button in the Styles panel, for example); choose Compound from the Selector Type menu in the New CSS Rule window (Figure 5-12); and then, in the Selector Name box, type a class name followed by a colon and the appropriate link state. For example, to change the look of a "Buy Now!" link only, you could create a style called *.buyNow:link*; to make that link look different when someone mouses over it, you'd name the link *.buyNow:hover*.

After naming the style (and saving it into an external style sheet), follow the steps on page 116 to create the look for that style (choose a font, select a color, and so on). After you create the style, simply apply the style class to the link (or links) you want to style using any of the techniques described on page 119. (In the example above, the class name is *buyNow*, and that's what you'll see listed in the Property inspector's Class menu

Note: Descendent selectors provide a more efficient—but more complex—way to format specific links differently from all the others on a page. You'll find this advanced CSS concept discussed on page 298.

Creating a Navigation Menu

Every website should have a set of navigation links that let visitors quickly jump to the site's main areas. On a shopping site, those links might point to the categories of products for sale—books, DVDs, CDs, electronics, and so on. For a corporate intranet, links to human resources, office policies, company events, and each department might be important. Whatever the site, a web designer should strive to get visitors where they want to go via the shortest route possible.

Dreamweaver CS5 includes a powerful and easy navigation-building tool—the Spry Menu Bar. With it, you can put all your site's most important links into a compact horizontal or vertical menu (see Figure 5-13). Each menu button supports two levels of pop-up submenus, so a visitor can quickly jump to a page buried deep within your site's structure.

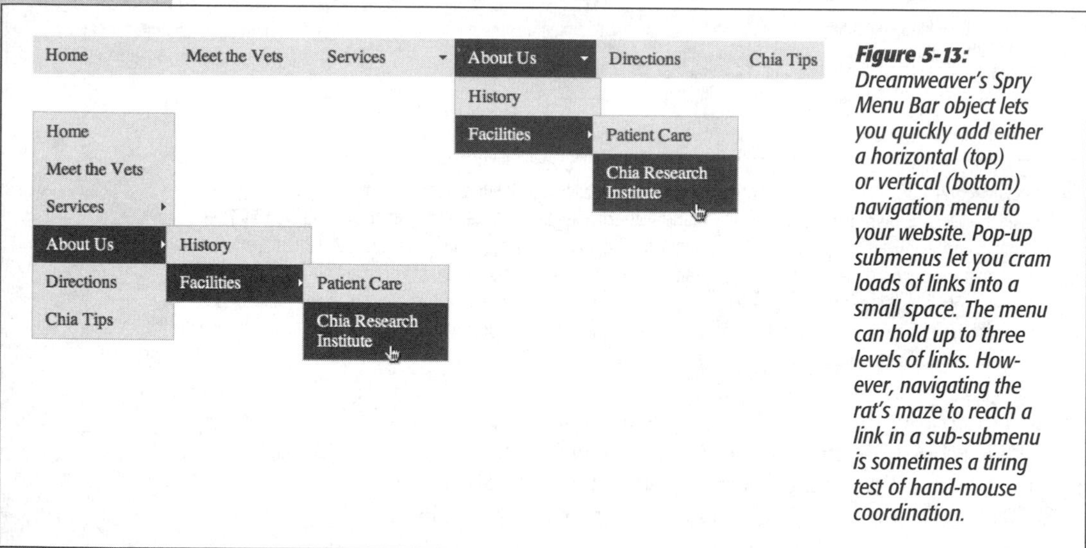

Figure 5-13: *Dreamweaver's Spry Menu Bar object lets you quickly add either a horizontal (top) or vertical (bottom) navigation menu to your website. Pop-up submenus let you cram loads of links into a small space. The menu can hold up to three levels of links. However, navigating the rat's maze to reach a link in a sub-submenu is sometimes a tiring test of hand-mouse coordination.*

The Spry Menu Bar is just one of the many "Spry" tools in Dreamweaver CS5. You'll learn a lot more about what Adobe calls the "Spry Framework" in Chapter 13, but in a nutshell, Spry is a collection of advanced JavaScript programs that let you add lots of dynamic effects to your web pages. (If you're familiar with the old Dreamweaver Behaviors, Spry is like those—on steroids.)

Adding a Menu

The first step in inserting a Spry menu is deciding where on the page to put it. A horizontal menu bar, with buttons sitting side by side, works well near the top of a page, either at the very top or below the area dedicated to a logo (often called a "banner"). A vertical menu bar, whose buttons are stacked one on top of the other, usually sits at the left edge of a page, below the banner area. To add a Spry menu:

1. **In the document window, click the spot where you want to insert the menu.**

   When you learn more about web page layout in Chapter 10, you'll discover that most elements on a page—like graphics, paragraphs, and menus—go inside <div> tags, which you use to define the beginning and end of that element. (If you've built sites in the past, you may have used HTML tables to lay out web pages. If you're still using tables, you'd insert the menu in a table cell.)

2. **Click the Insert Spry menu button on the Layout category of the Insert panel (Figure 5-14).**

   You'll also find this button on the Spry tab of the Insert Bar, or you can choose Insert→Spry→Spry Menu Bar. In any case, the Spry Menu Bar window appears asking whether you want a horizontal or vertical menu bar.

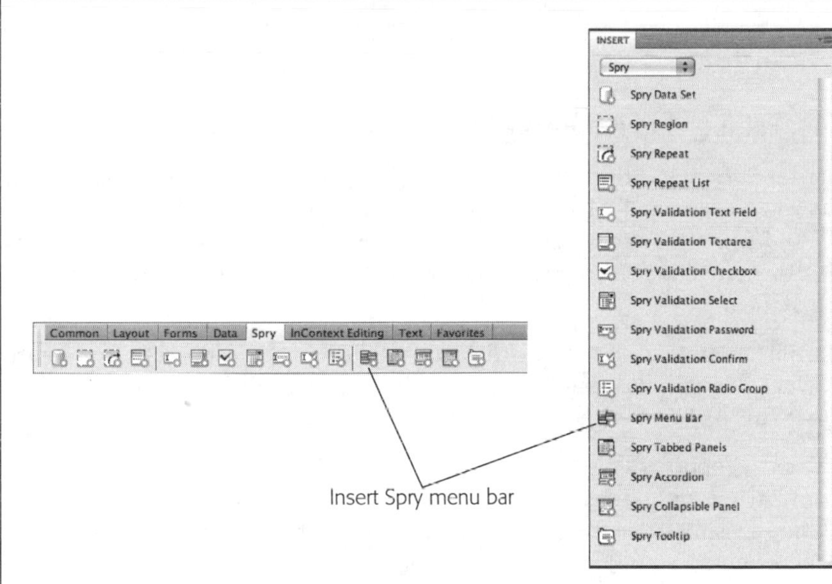

Figure 5-14:
The Insert Spry Menu button appears on the Insert panel. You can find it either under the Spry category or the Layout category. Here, you can see the Spry category of the Insert Panel in both Classic View (left) and the normal view (right). You'll find information on Classic View in the note on page 35.

3. **Depending on the type of menu you want, choose either the Horizontal or Vertical radio button and then click OK.**

   Dreamweaver inserts a "starter" menu containing a few links and pop-up menus (Figure 5-15). You can change and add links using the Property inspector, as described next.

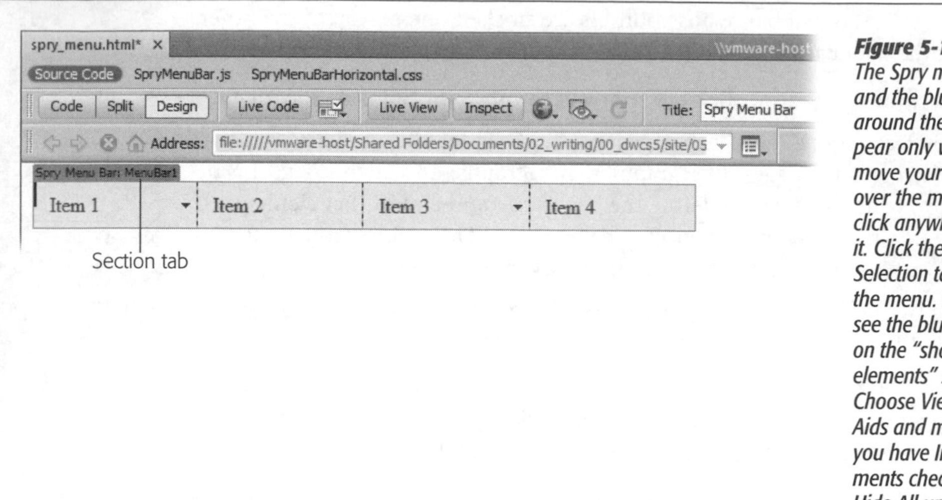

***Figure 5-15:** The Spry menu tab and the blue outline around the menu appear only when you move your mouse over the menu, or click anywhere inside it. Click the blue Selection tab to edit the menu. If you can't see the blue tab, turn on the "show invisible elements" setting: Choose View*Visual Aids and make sure you have Invisible Elements checked and Hide All unchecked.*

Adding, Editing, and Removing Links

The starter Spry menu that Dreamweaver inserts onto your page isn't very useful (unless you coincidentally have four sections on your site named Item 1, Item 2, Item 3, and Item 4). To make the menu your own you need to re-label the buttons and link them to pages on your site; you can also add more buttons and assign links to each of them.

To edit the Spry menu, select it by clicking the blue Spry Selection tab (see Figure 5-15). Once selected, the menu's labels and links appear in the Property inspector (Figure 5-16).

A Spry menu supports up to three levels of menus. Dreamweaver always displays the main navigation buttons; each can have its own pop-up menu, which only appears when a visitor mouses over the button. And each button on the *second* level of menus (the pop-up menu) can have its own pop-up menu. Dreamweaver represents each of these three menu levels with a column in the Property inspector (see Figure 5-16), and each column has its own set of widgets so you can add, delete, and move menu buttons.

Note: The Spry pop-up menu depends on JavaScript. While most people surfing the Web use browsers with JavaScript turned on, some either purposefully turn it off or use a browser that doesn't understand it. That means that someone visiting your site might *never* see the options in the pop-up menus. Because of this slightly irksome fact, always make sure that the buttons on the main navigation menu link to a page that, in turn, links to the pages listed in the pop-up menus. If you don't, some people won't be able to visit some pages on your site.

To edit one of the main navigation buttons on a Spry menu, select the button's label (for example, Item 1) in the left-hand column of the Property inspector; in the Text box, change the label to the text you want to appear on the nav button ("Home" or "About Us," for example). Then add a link using the "Browse for File" button or by typing the URL into the Link box (see page 165 for more on setting links). You can leave the Title and Target boxes empty (see the box on page 172 for descriptions of these properties).

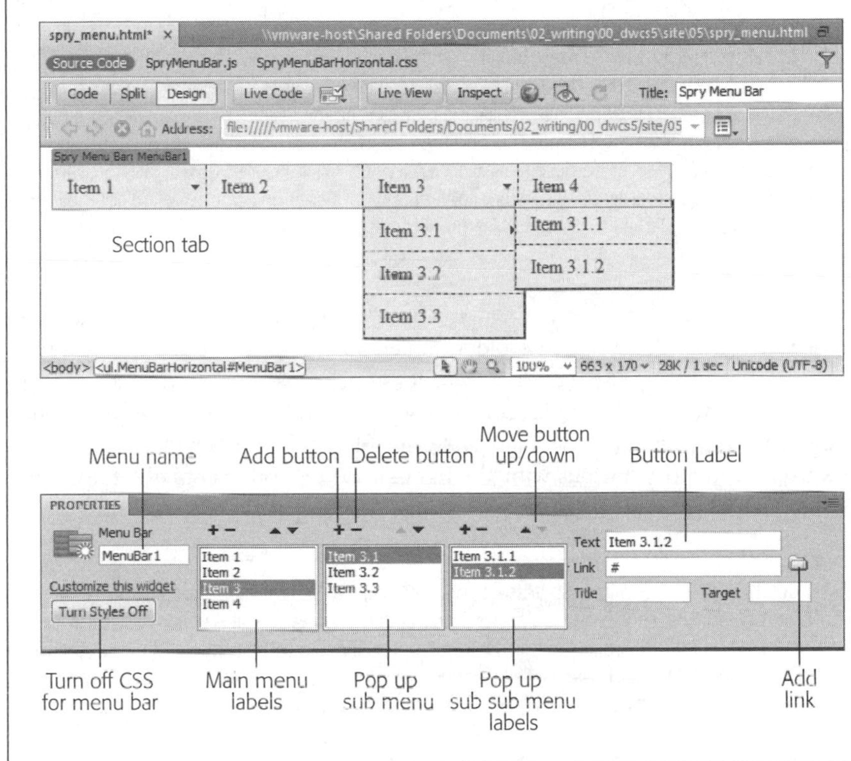

Figure 5-16: *Dreamweaver provides a generic name for each Spry menu it inserts—like MenuBar1. There's no harm in leaving that name (you'll never see it on the page), but feel free to change it to something more descriptive like mainNavigation. The only requirement is that you use only letters and numbers, and no spaces or punctuation (the naming rules are the same as for class styles, as described on page 114).*

To add a button to the main menu, click the + button above the left-hand column. Dreamweaver inserts a new "Untitled Item" in the list of links. Change the button's label in the text box, and then set a link using either method discussed in the previous paragraph.

To delete a button from the main nav bar, click its name in the left-hand column, and then click the – (minus) button at the top of the column. You can also rearrange the order of the buttons by selecting a name from the list and clicking the up or down arrow (on a horizontal menu bar the up arrow moves the button to the left, while the down arrow moves the button to the right).

You add, edit, and arrange submenus the same way: Select the Spry menu (click the blue menu tab [Figure 5-15]); and then, in the Property inspector, select the menu item to which you want to add a submenu. For example, in Figure 5-16, to add another button to the pop-up menu that appears when a visitor mouses over the "Item 3" button, select Item 3 from the left-hand column, and then click the + button in the *middle* column. Dreamweaver highlights the new button, and you can delete and rearrange buttons in the submenu using the minus and up and down arrow buttons at the top of that menu's column. To work with a sub-submenu (the third level of menus), first select an item from the left-hand column, and then click an item in the middle column.

Note: You can also edit a Spry menu's text and links in the document window. The main nav buttons are always visible, so you can click inside one to edit the text or change the link. To see a pop-up menu in the document window, select the Spry menu (click the blue tab); in the Property inspector, select a menu item in the first column that has a pop-up menu, and then select any button in the pop-up submenu list. That pop-up menu appears in the document window (as pictured in Figure 5-16). In fact, the pop-up menu won't *disappear* (potentially covering other content on your page) until you select one of the other main nav buttons from the left-hand column in the Property inspector.

When Dreamweaver inserts a Spry menu, it adds a bunch of files to your site. Dreamweaver places those files in a folder named SpryAssets in your site's local root folder (a message listing the names of the files appears as soon as you save a page after inserting a menu). These files control the look and functionality of the menu: Dreamweaver adds one CSS file, one JavaScript file, and some image files (for the arrows used to identify buttons with submenus). When you eventually move your pages to your web server, make sure you upload these ancillary files as well.

Tip: If you don't like the folder name "SpryAssets", or if you'd like to store these supporting files in a different folder on your site, choose Site→Manage Sites to open the Manage Sites window; select your site from the list; and then click the Edit button. Doing so opens the Site Setup window (the one you used when you first defined the site). Click Advanced Settings in the left side of the window to reveal a list of advanced options. Click the Spry category, and then click the Folder icon to locate another folder on the site. If you select a new folder after you inserted a Spry object into a page, just drag the files from the SpryAssets folder to the new folder in the Files panel (the one you just told Dreamweaver to use for all Spry files). (See page 648 for more information on moving files using the Files panel.) You can then safely delete the empty SpryAssets folder.

Changing the Look of the Navigation Menu

The "direct from the manufacturer" look of Spry menus leaves something to be desired. The battleship gray buttons and vibrant, "Hey, look at me, I'm purple!" rollovers aren't the most pleasing combination. Because Dreamweaver formats the menu with a collection of CSS styles, the power to improve the look of Spry menus is within your reach. Unfortunately, decoding Dreamweaver's tangle of CSS requires a guidebook. Basically, the process involves identifying the name of the CSS style responsible for the format you want to change, and then editing that style using the basic techniques you learned on page 124, or using one of the advanced methods discussed on page 304.

POWER USERS' CLINIC

Spry Menus Behind the Scenes

A Spry menu might look like a fancy navigation bar made up of colorful buttons and interactive pop-up menus, but under the hood it's just a simple bulleted list of links. Some pretty clever CSS creates the cool-looking buttons, and well-crafted JavaScript provides the dynamic behavior that makes the pop-up menus pop).

Since the HTML behind a menu is so simple, it can be easier to edit Spry menus if you remove the fancy CSS. To do this, select the Spry menu by clicking its blue tab (Figure 5-15) and then, in the Property inspector, click the Turn Styles Off button (Figure 5-16). Bam! You have an ugly bulleted list, just like the ones you learned about in Chapter 3. In fact, you can use the same techniques described on page 98 to add, edit, and delete bulleted items. The text you add to each bulleted item will appear on the navigation bar button: Select this text and add a link as described on page 165.

The primary set of bullets (the ones furthest to the left) represent the main navigation buttons. The pop-up menus are just nested lists, as described on page 102. Take this simple list:

```
* Home
* Our Services
    * Consultation
    * Garden Planning
        * Basic Apartment Plan
        * Deluxe Apartment Plan
* Contact Us
```

This would produce a navigation bar with three buttons, labeled "Home", "Our Services", and "Contact Us". Moving the mouse over the "Our Services" button opens a pop-up menu with two other buttons, labeled "Consultation" and "Garden Planning". In other words, the bullets labeled "Consultation" and "Garden Planning" are a nested list inside the bulleted item named "Our Services", while the two bullet items "Basic Apartment Plan" and "Deluxe Apartment Plan" are a nested list inside the "Garden Planning" bulleted item.

If you decide to take this quick-and-dirty approach to editing Spry menus, keep one thing in mind: Dreamweaver expects any bulleted item containing a nested list (a pop-up menu) to have a special CSS class applied to it: *MenuBarItemSubmenu*. In the example above, you'd need to apply this style to both the "Our Services" and "Garden Planning" list items. To do so, click inside the bulleted item (the one containing the nested list), and use the Class menu in the Property inspector's HTML mode to apply the *MenuBarItemSubmenu* style (turn to page 119 for a refresher on applying class styles).

Tip: You can preview the Spry menu bar—complete with interactive pop-up menus—by using Dreamweaver's Live View. Click the Live View button at the top of the document window or choose View→Live View. Now you can mouse over the menu and see its buttons highlight and submenus pop up. In other words, it's just like viewing the page in a web browser. To leave Live View, click the Live View button a second time, or choose View→Live View again.

For example, if you want to change the font that a menu uses, open the CSS Styles panel (Window→CSS Styles) and then click the All button to see all the styles available for a page. Dreamweaver stores the styles for menu bars in their own style sheets (*SpryMenuBarVertical.css* for vertical menu bars and *SpryMenuBarHorizontal.css* for horizontal menu bars). Expand the list of styles (click the + symbol to the left of the style sheet name in the CSS Styles panel), and then double-click *ul.MenuBarVertical a* (if you're working on a vertical menu) or *ul.MenuBarHorizontal a* (for a horizontal menu). This opens the Style Definition window for that style. You can then change the menu's font (see page 128).

Note: The strange style names used for Spry menus (*ul.MenuBarVertical a*, for example) are called *descendent selectors*. They're an advanced type of CSS selector used to pinpoint very specific elements in a page. You can read about them on page 298. But for now, here's the ultra-quick cheat sheet for descendent selectors: Read them from right to left. The element on the far right is the element that Dreamweaver will ultimately style. In this example, it's a link–the a represents the <a> tag used for the links in the navigation bar. The "ul.MenuBarVertical" part specifies an unordered list (ul) that has a class of *MenuBarVertical* applied to it. So running that selector through the universal translator produces this instruction: "Format every <a> tag that appears inside a bulleted list with the class MenuBarVertical like this…." In other words, only the links inside the Spry Menu Bar are affected by this style.

Spry menus offer two types of menu button: a regular menu item, and a submenu item (see Figure 5-17). A regular menu item is a button without a pop-up menu attached; a guest clicks the button and goes to a new page. A submenu button is any button that produces a pop-up menu when a visitor mouses over it. In addition, these two button types each have two looks: the button as it sits on the page, and the button as your guest mouses over it (its rollover look).

Formatting regular menu buttons

You can define the look of a regular menu button, and simultaneously set the basic look for all the menu bar buttons, by editing the *ul.MenuBarHorizontal a* style (for a horizontal menu) or *ul.MenuBarVertical a* style (for a vertical menu). Just double-click the style's name in the CSS Styles panel to edit it.

You can set any of the CSS text properties discussed on page 128, such as font, font size, and font color. All the buttons will share these settings (except font color, because it always changes when a visitor rolls her mouse over any button—if you want to use the same font color in that instance, you'll need to specify that color in the styles discussed in the next section).

In addition, this style controls the background color of both regular buttons and submenu buttons. To change the background color, edit the appropriate style (for example, *ul.MenuBarVertical a* for a vertical menu) and change the background color option found under the Background category of the Rule Definition window.

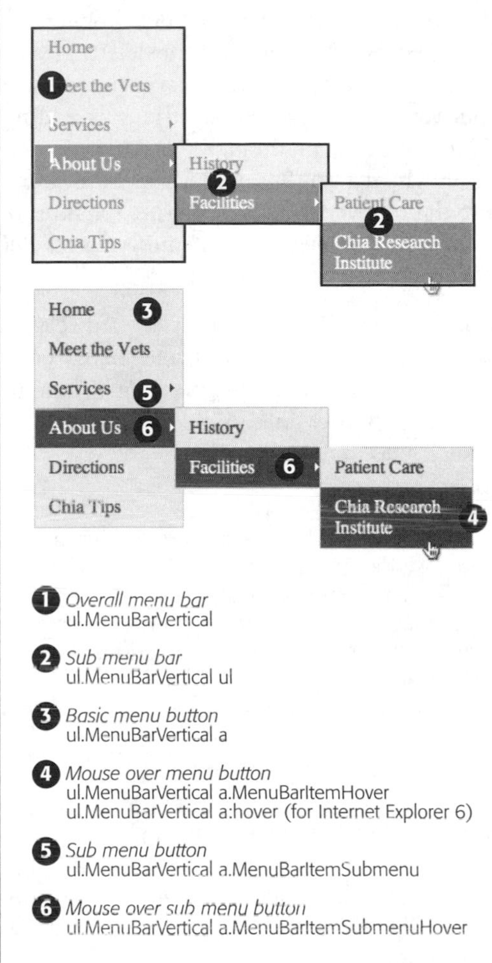

Figure 5-17:
It takes quite a few CSS styles to make Dreamweaver's Spry menu look good. Labeled here are the main styles for formatting the unordered lists that make up the overall menu, the pop-up menus (top), and the individual buttons (bottom). Sometimes you want to change the look of an entire menu and not just a single button. For example, you might want to add a border around all four edges of the main menu. In this case, edit the ul.MenuBarVertical style (or ul.MenuBarHorizontal for a horizontal menu). The ul.MenuBarVertical ul style or ul.MenuBarHorizontal ul style controls a pop-up menu's overall look and placement.

You can also add border lines to the buttons—for example, a line separating each button—by setting the border properties for this style (see page 230 for more on CSS borders). Set the *padding* (page 341) to control the space between the text on a button and the edge of the button. To make the text appear close to the edges of the button, decrease the padding; to place empty space around the text, increase the padding.

Note: If you add a horizontal menu bar, you may run into one particularly frustrating problem: That's when a column of your page, which should appear right below the menu bar, actually appears much further down the page, usually beneath another column, such as a sidebar. This problem only appears under unusual circumstances–when you use CSS-based layouts with the Float property and when one of the menu buttons is taller than the others (and even then you won't always see the problem). The dreaded "float drop" (no joke) causes this problem, and you'll find a solution on page 409.

Formatting rollover menu buttons

Visitors get instant feedback when they interact with a Spry menu. Moving the mouse over a menu button changes the color of the button and its text, letting visitors know "Hey, I'm a link, click me!" The rollover buttons Dreamweaver creates have a purple background and white text, but you can change those settings by editing either the *ul.MenuBarVertical a.MenuBarItemHover* or the *ul.MenuBarHorizontal a.MenuBarItemHover* style (depending on whether you inserted a vertical or horizontal menu). In addition, to make sure the rollovers work in Internet Explorer 6, you must edit either the style *ul.MenuBarVertical a:hover*, or *ul.MenuBarHorizontal a:hover*.

Locate a style in the CSS Styles panel, and double-click it to edit it. Dreamweaver-created styles only set text color and background color properties, but you're free to change any CSS property. For example, if you added border lines between buttons in the menu bar, you could alter the color of those border lines for the rollover button. Or you could make text appear bold when a guest hovers over it.

Note: The name of the style used for rollover menu buttons is actually a combination of three different selectors and is so long that its full name doesn't even fit in the CSS Styles panel: *"ul.MenuBarHorizontal a.MenuBarItemHover, ul.MenuBarHorizontal a.MenuBarItemSubmenuHover, ul.MenuBarHorizontal a.MenuBarSubmenuVisible"* (the name will be slightly different for a vertical menu). This peculiar style is called a *group selector*. It's an efficient way to apply similar formatting rules to multiple elements on a page (see page 303 for an explanation of group selectors).

Formatting submenu buttons

Submenu buttons (the buttons that produce a pop-up menu when a guest mouses over) look nearly identical to other menu buttons. In fact, the two styles mentioned above, which control a menu in its normal and rollover states, define the basic formatting for submenu buttons as well. The only visible difference is the small arrow that appears on the right edge of a submenu button (see Figure 5-17). It visually indicates the presence of a pop-up menu; it's a kind of "there's more this way" icon.

You can replace the graphics Dreamweaver uses for submenus: they're named SpryMenuBarDown.gif, SpryMenuBarDownHover.gif, SpryMenuBarRight.gif, and SpryMenuBarRightHover.gif. (You'll only find the two "down" arrow graphics in horizontal menus.) Create your own arrow graphics (in GIF format) with the same names and replace the original graphic files, which are located in the SpryAssets folder (unless you changed the name and location as described in the Tip on page 188). The graphics should be small enough to be visible in the menu buttons—the ones that Dreamweaver supplies are 4 × 7 pixels (right arrow) and 7 × 4 pixels (down arrow)—and you should include versions for both the normal and roll-over states of the submenu button.

Tip: You can *permanently* replace the arrow graphics Dreamweaver uses with your own graphics. First, go into the Dreamweaver configuration folder. In Windows, you'll find it at C:\Program Files\Adobe\Adobe Dreamweaver CS5\configuration\Shared\Spry\Widgets\MenuBar; on Macs you'll find these images in Applications→AdobeDreamweaverCS5→configuration→Shared→Spry→Widgets→MenuBar.Makesureyour graphic files have the exact same names as those Dreamweaver uses. (The CSS files used to provide the basic styles for the Spry Menu Bar are also in this folder, so you could even edit these if you wanted a different set of "starter styles" for your menus–just make sure to back up the original CSS files!)

If you want to further customize the submenu button appearance (for example, to change the font just for submenu buttons), edit either the *ul.MenuBarVertical a.MenuBarItemSubmenu* or *ul.MenuBarHorizontal a.MenuBarItemSubmenu* style. The *ul.MenuBarVertical a.MenuBarItemSubmenuHover* style controls the rollover state for submenu buttons in vertical menus; for horizontal menus, it's *ul.MenuBarHorizontal a.MenuBarItemSubmenuHover.*

Changing the width of menus and buttons

Spry menu buttons have preset widths. The main navigation menu buttons are each 8 ems wide, while the buttons on pop-up menus are 8.2 ems high (see page 133 for information on ems). If your navigation buttons have a lot of text on them, 8 ems may be too narrow to fit everything in. Or, 8 ems may be too much space if the menu text is small and made up of short words like "Home," "About," and "Contact." You can adjust the width of buttons and menus by opening the appropriate CSS Style (discussed next) and adjusting the style's *width* property. For example, double-click the style name in the CSS Styles panel, and then change the *width* property in either the Box or Positioning categories of the CSS Rule Definition window. (The CSS Properties Pane provides an even quicker method, as discussed in Figure 5-18.) Here are the settings you can edit:

- **Main menu width.** The *ul.MenuBarVertical* style sets the overall width of a menu. (Setting the width of a horizontal menu has no effect, since the width of a horizontal menu is determined by the number of buttons on the menu.) For a vertical menu bar, use the same width value for the menu as you do for the button width (discussed next).
- **Main menu button width.** The width of the buttons that appear on the main Spry menu are determined by the *ul.MenuBarVertical li* style or *ul.MenuBarHorizontal li* style. You may want the button to be just as wide as the text inside it—in other words, have buttons of different widths based on the amount of text in the button's label. For this effect, set the width of this style to *auto*. Variable width buttons look good for horizontal menus, but not for vertical menus, where the staggered right edges of the stacked column of buttons looks uneven and distracting.
- **Pop-up menu width.** Control the overall width of pop-up menus with the *ul.MenuBarVertical ul* or *ul.MenuBarHorizontal ul* style. The width you set for this style should match the width for the pop-up menu buttons, covered next.

- **Pop-up menu button width.** The *ul.MenuBarVertical ul li* and *ul.MenuBarHorizontal ul li* styles control the width of pop-up menu buttons on the vertical and horizontal menu, respectively. Dreamweaver's normal setting is 8.2 ems, but you can adjust this to create wider or narrower buttons.

Tip: If you want to add space between buttons in a horizontal menu bar, add some left or right margin to the *ul.MenuBarHorizontal li* style. You then have to set that same margin (left or right) for the *ul.MenuBarHorizontal ul li* style to 0.

Positioning pop-up menus

The pop-up menus on vertical menu bars overlap the button that opens them (see Figure 5-17). This stacking appearance gives the menu a 3-D look, as if the pop-up menu really were popping out of the page. However, you may want the pop-up menu to appear directly next to the menu button, or to overlap it even more dramatically.

To change the position of a pop-up menu, edit the *ul.MenuBarVertical ul* (or *ul.MenuBarHorizontal ul*) style (see Figure 5-18). The CSS *margin* property controls the placement of the menu. For a vertical menu, the pop-up menu has a –5% top margin; this places the top of the pop-up menu a little *above* the submenu button that triggers it. The left margin is set to 95%, which moves the pop-up menu to the far right of the submenu button. To make the pop-up menu appear directly to the right and aligned with the top of the submenu button, change the top margin to 0 and the left margin to 100%. To make the pop-up menu overlap even more, you could change –5% to –10% for the top margin, and 95% to 85% for the left margin.

A horizontal menu's pop-up menu appears directly below the submenu button that triggers it. Its margin setting is 0. If you wish to make that menu overlap the submenu button, change the top margin to –5% and the left margin to 5%.

Note: The look of sub-submenus for the horizontal menu bar is controlled by a style named *ul.MenuBarHorizontal ul ul*. There is no sub-submenu style for vertical menus, but you could create one named *ul.MenuBarVertical ul ul*.

Removing a Spry menu

To get rid of a Spry menu, select it (for example, click the blue tab shown in Figure 5-15), and then press the delete key. In addition to removing the HTML for the menu, Dreamweaver also—as long as there are no other Spry menus on the page—removes the menu's linked external style sheet and JavaScript file.

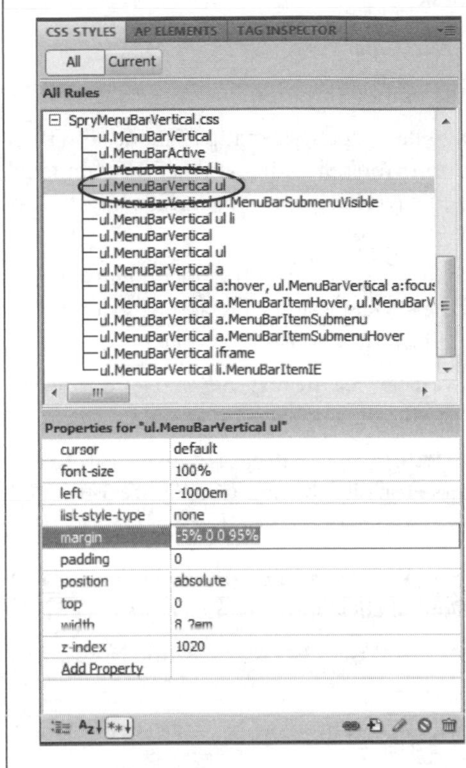

Figure 5-18:
Dreamweaver's CSS style sheet for Spry menus lists the pop-up menu style, ul.MenuBarVertical ul, in this case, twice. The first one listed (circled) controls the positioning of the pop-up menu. The second one controls the border around it (why two? Great question, for which nobody except Adobe has an answerÉand they're not telling.) Double-click the style to edit its properties using the Rule Definition window. For a really quick edit, like changing the position of a pop-up menu by adjusting its margin property, you can use the Properties pane of the CSS Styles panel (pictured in the bottom half of this image.) Just select the current value for the property and type in a new value. For example, in this image, clicking the "-5% 0 0 95%" value (which represent the top, right, bottom, and left margin values, respectively) to the right of the word "margin" lets you type in a new value: 0 0 0 100%, say. You'll find editing with the Properties Pane discussed on page 304.

Link Tutorial

In this tutorial, you'll put the lessons in this chapter to use. You'll learn how to link to other pages on your own site, link to another site on the Web, and use Dreamweaver's Spry Menu Bar to create a great-looking navigation bar—complete with fancy JavaScript-driven pop-up menus. The completed page will look like the one shown in Figure 5-28.

Note: You'll need to download files from *www.sawmac.com/dwcs5/* to complete this tutorial. See the Note on page 45 for more details.

Linking to Other Pages and Websites

Once you downloaded the tutorial files and open Dreamweaver, define a new site as described on page 37: Name the site *Site Navigation*, and then select the Chapter05 folder (inside the MM_DWCS5 folder). In a nutshell: Choose Site→New Site. In the Site Setup window, type *Site Navigation* into the Site Name field, click the folder icon next to the Local Site Folder field, navigate to and select the Chapter05 folder, and then click Choose or Select. Finally, click OK.

Once again, you'll be working on a page from *Chia-Vet.com*.

1. **In the files panel, double-click the file named *tips.html*.**

   You can also open the file by choosing File→Open, selecting its name, and then clicking the OK (Select on Macs) button. You're looking at a nearly completed web page with multiple columns but no navigation bar. (You'll learn how to create this kind of layout in Chapter 9.)

   If Dreamweaver opens the page in Split view, meaning the document window shows both the raw HTML code and the visual Design view, at the top left of the document window, click the Design button (or choose View→Design).

   In the upper-right corner of the page you can see the text "Sign up for our newsletter". You want that to link to a newsletter sign-up page on the site.

2. **Select the text "Sign up for our newsletter". In the Property inspector, to the right of the Link box, click the "Browse for File" button (see Figure 5-3).**

   The Select File window opens.

3. **Click the Site Root button (at the top on Windows, and bottom right on Macs) to go to the site's main or root folder. Double-click the file named newsletter.html.**

   The Select File window closes. That's it? Yup. You just created a link. Now, you'll learn an even faster way.

4. **In the top left of the page, click the logo image to select it. Make sure the Files panel is open (Window→Files).**

   On many websites, you'll find that the site's logo is actually a clickable link to the site's home page. That's not the case here, so you'll turn the large Chia Vet logo into a direct route to the home page.

5. **In the Property inspector, drag the small Point-to-File icon (see Figure 5-6) beside the Link box into the Files panel; move your mouse over the file index.html, and then release the mouse button.**

   Dreamweaver added the link to your page. (Unless you have a particular configuration of double monitors as explained in the note on page 169. In that case, use the technique in steps 3 and 4 to link to the *index.html* file.) You'll also notice that the logo image now has a big blue outline—you'll fix that soon.

   Note that if you wanted to link the selected text or image in the examples above to a page on another website, you couldn't use either of the methods outlined here. Instead, you'd need to type in an absolute URL, as you'll see in the next two steps.

6. **Scroll to the bottom of the page. In the footer you see small gray type that reads "A division of *CosmoFarmer.com*". Select the text "*CosmoFarmer.com*".**

   You want this text to link to this site's parent company.

7. **In the Property inspector, in the Link box, type *http://www.cosmofarmer.com/*, and then press Enter or Return.**

   Now the text links to the CosmoFarmer website. Unfortunately the blue links don't fit in with the Chia Vet color palette, and the logo still has a big blue outline around it. You'll remedy that in the next section.

Formatting Links

You can change the look of links using a little CSS. First, you'll remove the clunky blue border from the logo.

1. **Make sure the CSS Styles panel is open (Window→CSS Styles); at the bottom of the panel, click the + button.**

   The New CSS Rule window opens. (For a refresher on creating CSS styles, see page 113.)

2. **From the top menu, select Tag; in the Selector Name box, type img (or choose img from the menu); and, at the bottom of the window, select "global.css" from the "Rule Definition" menu. Click OK to create the style.**

   The CSS Rule Definition window opens. The blue line around the image is a border that a web browser applies to the link (it's the equivalent of the blue underline used for text links). To remove it, you just turn off borders for this style.

3. **In the left hand list of CSS categories, select Border; in the Top style menu, select "none".**

   Make sure you have the "Same for all" checkbox turned on (this removes the border from all four sides).

4. **Click OK.**

   The blue border around the image disappears. Now it's time to change the look of the links.

5. **Create a new tag style for the <a> tag.**

   You should be getting used to this routine by now, but here's a recap: At the bottom of the CSS Style panel, click the + button; from the top menu, choose Tag; in the Selector Name box, type *a* (or select *a* from the menu). Make sure the Rule Definition box says "global.css", and then click OK. The New CSS Rule Definition window appears.

6. **In the Type menu, type *#EC6206* for the Color property; from the font-weight menu, select Bold, and then click OK.**

   The newsletter sign-up link in the top right of the page loses its bright blue color in favor of the orange color used in the Chia Vet logo. You'll now change how the links look when a guest hovers over them.

7. **In the CSS Styles panel, click the + button; in the New CSS Rule window from the top menu, select Compound, and then, from the Selector Name pull-down menu, select a:hover. Click OK.**

   Again, the CSS Rule Definition window appears.

8. **From the CSS Rule Definition window's Type category, type *#779A00* in the Color field, and then, in the Decoration area, turn on the "none" checkbox (see Figure 5-19). Click OK to finish the style and return to the document window.**

   To see how this rollover style works, you'll use Dreamweaver's Live View.

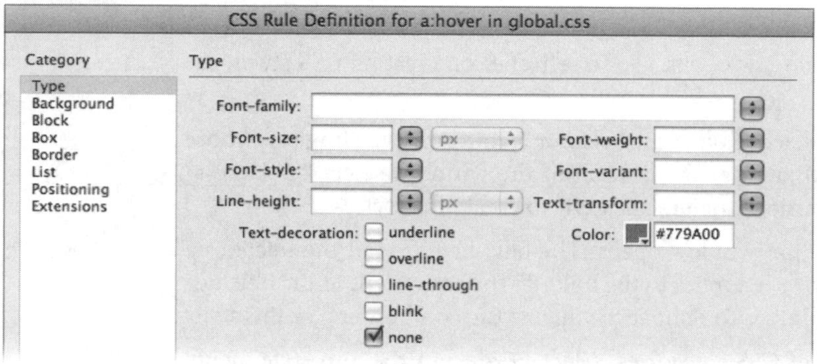

Figure 5-19: *To completely remove an underline from a link, set the CSS Text-decoration property to "none". You can create a look similar to an underline (but with a lot more design choices) by turning this underline off, and then using the CSS border property to create a dotted, dashed, or different color underline.*

9. **At the top of the Document window, click the Live View button (or choose View→Live View).**

   Live View lets you preview the look (and functionality) of a web page directly in Dreamweaver. Dreamweaver includes an embedded version of Apple's WebKit (pretty much the Safari web browser). With Live View you can interact with JavaScript as well as view CSS hover effects: Move your mouse over the "Sign up for our newsletter" link in the top right of the page, and you see the link change to green and the underline disappear. (Of course Safari isn't Internet Explorer or Firefox, so you still need to preview the page in those browsers to make sure it looks good. You'll hear more about Live View on page 578.)

10. **Click the Live View button (or choose View→Live View) a second time to leave Live View.**

    You can't edit a page in Live View, so you always need to click out of it when you're ready to work on your page again. Now you'll add a Spry menu bar.

Adding a Navigation Bar

One of Dreamweaver's most exciting tools is the Spry Menu Bar. This sophisticated combination of HTML, CSS, and JavaScript lets you easily create slick-looking navigation bars with rollover effects and drop-down menus. Since the Dreamweaver engineers have done all the complex programming for you, you just have to insert, modify, and format the menu to make it fit perfectly into your website design.

1. **Return to Dreamweaver and make sure you have the file tips.html open; click right below the Chia Vet logo inside the grassy background image (circled in Figure 5-20).**

   You'll insert a horizontal menu bar that spans most of the page's width. Placing it near the top of the page, as part of the banner, lets site visitors easily find and use it.

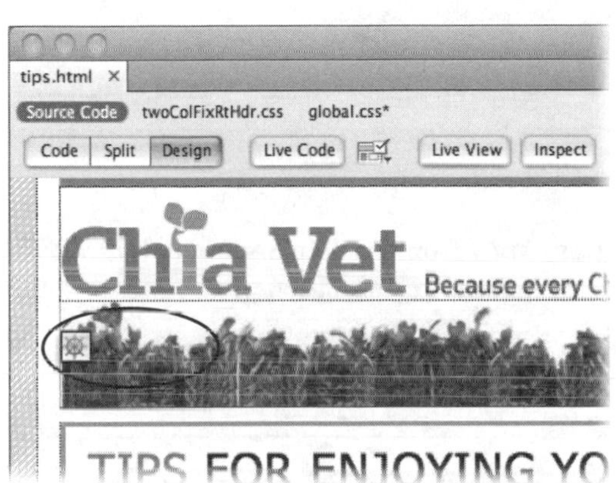

Figure 5-20: *What's that strange ship's steering wheel (inside the circled area), you ask? It's called the Code Navigator. You use it to navigate to the CSS code that formats the current selection–it's useful mostly to people of the "I love to edit raw CSS code" type. You'll learn about it on page 317. (You can make the steering wheel go away: click it to open the Code Navigator, and check the "Disable navigator" box. To bring the steering wheel back, aye captain, choose View→Code Navigator and uncheck that same box).*

2. **Choose Insert→Spry→Spry Menu Bar.**

   Alternatively, you could click the Spry Menu Bar button on the Layout tab of the Insert bar (Figure 5-14). Either way, the Spry Menu Bar window appears.

3. **Choose the Horizontal option, and then click OK.**

   A gray menu appears at the top of the page with four buttons: Item 1, Item 2, Item 3, and Item 4 (see Figure 5-21).

4. **Choose File→Save.**

   A window appears letting you know that Dreamweaver just added six new files to your site. Click OK to dismiss this window. Dreamweaver places these files inside a new folder named SpryAssets. You can see the folder listed in the Files panel, although you may need to press the "Refresh" button (the circle with an arrow tip) first.

   The next step is to change the button labels, add new buttons, and create links.

5. **In the document window, click the blue Spry Menu Bar tab, which appears just above the new menu (circled in Figure 5-21).**

   If you don't see that tab, move your mouse over the menu until it appears. If you still can't see the tab, see Figure 5-15 for a solution.

   The Property inspector changes to display the menu bar's properties.

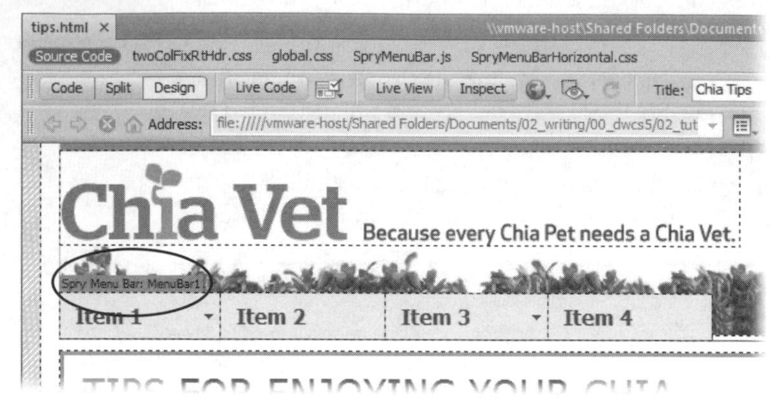

Figure 5-21: *The Spry Menu Bar starts life with four plain-looking buttons. Item 1 and Item 3 each have a down-pointing arrow icon, indicating that a pop-up menu will appear when visitors mouse over either of them.*

6. **In the Property inspector, select Item 1 from the left column of button labels; in the Text box, type Home (see Figure 5-22), and then press Enter or Return.**

   Notice in the document window that the first button now says "Home". Now you'll add a link.

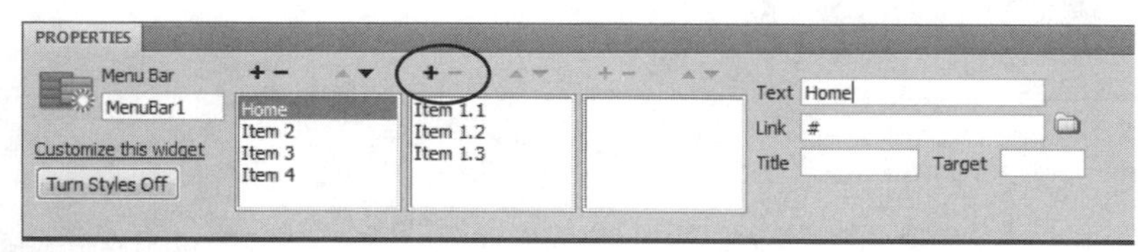

Figure 5-22: *Use the + and - buttons at the top of each column to add or remove buttons from a menu.*

7. **To the right of the Link box, click the "Browse for File" button (the folder icon).**

   This is the same process you followed earlier to add a link to one of the sidebar paragraphs.

8. **In the Select File window, click the Site Root button (top of window for Windows, bottom right on Macs); double-click the index.html file.**

   You've labeled your first button and created the first link on this menu bar. Unfortunately, Dreamweaver has added a pop-up menu to this button with three additional buttons. Since the Home button isn't really a "section" of the site with additional pages, you don't need that submenu.

9. **In the middle column in the Property inspector, select item 1.1 and press the – (minus) button at the top of that column (circled in Figure 5-22).**

   Dreamweaver removes the top button from the list. If you look in the document window, you'll see the pop-up menu. When you select an item inside one of the submenu columns in the Property inspector, Dreamweaver temporarily displays the pop-up menu. This is a great way to preview what the pop-up menu will look like in action.

Note: If the Property inspector no longer shows the properties for the Spry Menu Bar, just click the bar's blue tab in the document window.

10. **Repeat step 9 for Item 1.2 and Item 1.3.**

    After removing Item 1.3, notice that the down-pointing arrow on the Home button in the document window disappears. Because there's no longer a pop-up menu associated with this link, Dreamweaver removes the arrow graphic. Now you'll add another button.

11. **Repeat steps 6–8 for Item 2: Change its label to Meet the Vets, and then link to the meet_vets.html file located in the site root folder.**

    The button's text on the page changes. You'll also notice that it doesn't fit inside the button. That's OK for now; you'll change both the size of the text and the size of the buttons in a little bit. Next you'll edit another button and edit its pop-up menu.

12. **Repeat steps 6–8 for Item 3: Change its label to Services, and then link to the index.html file located inside the folder named services.**

    It's common to place web pages for a particular section of a site into a folder dedicated to that section; for example, here you have all the pages relating to Chia Vet services inside a folder named *services*. In addition, web designers store the main page for a section in its folder and name the page *index.html*. You'll see why on page 640. For this tutorial, just keep in mind that, although you'll link to an *index.html* page several times, each time you're linking to a *different* file inside a different folder.

    This button also has a pop-up menu, but instead of deleting it, you'll just change the pop-up menu button labels to match the Chia Vet site.

13. **In the middle column in the Property inspector, select Item 3.1; change its label to Preventative Care, and then link it to the preventative.html file inside the services folder.**

    This button has its own pop-up menu (a sub-submenu). But you don't need it here.

14. **From the far right column in the Property inspector, select and delete Item 3.1.1 and Item 3.1.2.**

    Use the same technique described in Step 9 (just select the item, and then click the - button at the top of its column).

15. **Repeat step 13 for Item 3.2 and Item 3.3: Label one Boarding and link it to boarding.html inside the services folder; label the other Emergency Services and link it to the emergency.html file in the services folder.**

    The menu's coming together. You just need to add a few more buttons and a couple of pop-up menus.

16. **Repeat steps 6–8 for Item 4: Change its label to About Us, and then link to the index.html file located inside the about folder.**

    This button requires a pop-up menu, but Dreamweaver hasn't supplied one. You'll have to create the buttons for it yourself.

17. **Make sure the Spry Menu bar is still selected (if not, click its blue tab) and that About Us is selected in the left column in the Property inspector; click the + button in the middle column to add a new button for a pop-up menu.**

    This adds a new pop-up menu and button. You just need to label and link it.

18. **In the Text field, type *History*, and add a link to the file history.html inside the about folder.**

    Now you'll add one more button to this pop-up menu.

19. **Click the + button in the middle column to add another button to the About Us pop-up menu. Label it *Facilities* and link to *facilities.html* in the about folder.**

    This button will have its own pop-up menu.

20. **Make sure Facilities is selected in the Property Inspector, and then, in the far right column, click the + button.**

    Dreamweaver adds "Untitled Item" to this column, creating another pop-up menu. Time to label and link.

21. **Repeat step 18: Use Patient Care for the label, and then link to the patient.html file inside the about folder.**

    By now you should be nearly an expert at adding, editing, and linking buttons and pop-up menus. Just a few more buttons to go.

22. **Repeat steps 20 and 21. Label the new button Chia Research Institute, and then link it to research.html in the about folder.**

    This adds one more button (thankfully the last one) to the sub-submenu. The Property inspector should now look like Figure 5-23. Now you have just two more buttons to add to the main navigation bar.

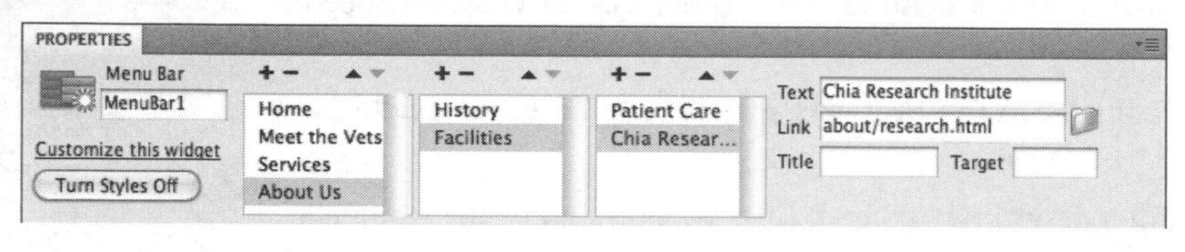

***Figure 5-23:** The highlighted items in the left and middle columns indicate which buttons a visitor would have to roll over in order to see the options in the far right-hand column.*

23. **Click the + button in the far-left column to add another button to the main navigation menu. Label it Directions, and link to directions.html in the main site folder (the root folder).**

    Just one more button on the main menu.

24. **Repeat step 23: Name the button Chia Tips and link to tips.html in the main site folder.**

    That's actually a link to the very page you're working on.

    You're done! Thankfully, once you craft a navigation bar, you can reuse it throughout your site, so you don't have to go through this laborious procedure for each page of your site. (Dreamweaver's Template feature can make the process even easier, as described in Chapter 20.)

    You can press the Live View button to test the menu bar without leaving Dreamweaver. Make sure to click the Live View button again when you're done taking the menu bar for a spin.

Styling the Menu Bar

The basic look of a Spry menu probably doesn't fit the design of your site, so learning to edit the CSS that Dreamweaver supplies is an important skill. In this part of the tutorial, you'll edit the look of the buttons and pop-up menus, and replace the premade arrow graphics with custom images.

1. **Let's start with the basic look of the buttons.**

   Make sure you have the CSS Styles panel open (Window→CSS Styles) with the All button at the top of that panel highlighted.

   When you inserted the menu bar, Dreamweaver attached an external style sheet named *SpryMenuBarHorizontal.css* to the page. This style sheet contains all the styles you need to modify the look of the menu.

2. **Click the + button (arrow icon) to the left of *SpryMenuBarHorizontal.css*.**

   The list expands to display all the styles for this style sheet. While you're at it, hide the list of styles in both the *global.css* style sheet and the *twoColFixRtHds.css* style sheet by clicking the – (minus) button to their left. (The oddly named *twoColFixRtHdr.css* file is part of Dreamweaver's built-in CSS layouts. You'll learn how to work with these layouts in Chapter 10.)

3. **In the CSS Styles panel, double-click the style ul.MenuBarHorizontal a (it's about half way down the list of styles).**

   The CSS Rule Definition window opens, displaying the current settings for this style. This particular style is called a descendent selector. You'll learn about that type of style on page 298, but in a nutshell, you read the style from right to left, with the rightmost element being the object of this style. In this case, the style will apply to an <a> tag (a link), but only when the link is inside an unordered list (*ul*) that has the class *MenuBarHorizontal* applied to it. In other words, this style applies to every link inside the Spry Menu Bar. You'll make some type changes first.

4. **From the Font-family menu, select "Tahoma, Geneva, sans-serif"; in the font-size menu, type *11*; from the font-weight menu, choose "bold"; from the text-transform menu, choose "uppercase"; and change the color to #779A00.**

   The window should look like Figure 5-24. Next, you'll change the background color of the buttons to plain white.

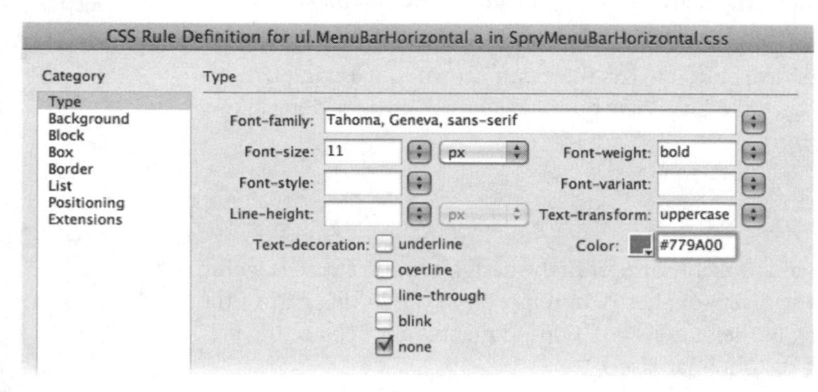

***Figure 5-24:** Changing the text properties for the "ul. MenuBarHorizontal a" style defines the basic styles for all the menu buttons; only the color property (for rollover states) is different among the links. Make sure you don't deselct the "none" option under Text-decoration, or a line appears underneath the text in each button.*

5. **Click the Background category, and select white for the background color.**

   You can also just type *#FFF* into the text field to the right of the color box. The text inside each button is aligned to the left edge; for a bit of variety (and more practice with Dreamweaver) you'll center align the text.

6. **Click the Block category, and select "center" in the text-align menu.**

   The buttons will look better with thick, distinctive borderlines drawn across the top of each button.

7. **Click the Border category; turn off all three "Same for all" checkboxes; for the top border, select "solid" from the Style menu, type *2* in the Width menu, and set the color to #EC6206.**

   Next, you'll give the text inside a little breathing room.

8. **Click the Box category; change the padding settings so that the Top and Bottom padding are both 5px and the Left and Right padding are 3px each.**

   The window should now look like Figure 5-25. You can quickly set these values by typing in *5px* (*3px* if you're setting the left and right padding), instead of typing 5 (or 3) in the first box, and then choosing px from the menu to the right.

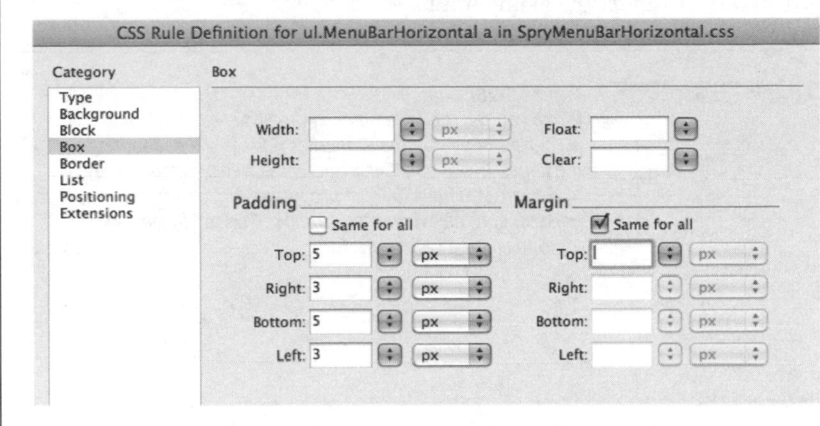

***Figure 5-25:** Adding padding to the navigation buttons adds white space inside the button, separating the text inside the button from the button's edges. This process makes for a larger clickable target and more prominent buttons.*

9. **Click OK to finish editing the style.**

   The text on the buttons looks pretty good, but to fill up the banner area the buttons could be a little wider and spaced apart a bit.

10. **In the CSS Styles Panel, select the ul.MenuBarHorizontal li style (circled in Figure 5-26).**

    Don't double-click the style name or that'll open the Style Definition window—you'll use a quicker method to edit this style. Here's another descendent selector style—it applies to every <li> tag (list item) inside the Spry Menu Bar. For a quick edit to an already defined property, in the CSS Styles panel, you can use the Properties pane (it's at the bottom of the CSS Styles window; you may have to extend it by hovering over it until your cursor changes to a double line, and then drag the border up). Notice that the style currently has a fixed width of "8em". You'll change that.

11. **Click "8em" to the right of "width" in the Properties pane, type *125* into the first box, and choose px from the second pull-down menu (or just type *125px* in the first box).**

    You can also *add* a CSS property using the Properties pane.

12. **At the bottom of the Properties Pane, click the Add Property link; either type margin-left in the box or click the menu button and select margin-left from the list of CSS properties; press the Tab key, and then type *15px*. Hit the Enter (or Return) key to make your edits take effect.**

    The CSS Properties pane should look like Figure 5-26. You just added 15 pixels of space to the left side of each list item—this effectively spreads out the buttons, adding a bit of space between each. The main navigation buttons are all 125 pixels wide, but if you save and preview the page now (or press the Live View button at the top of the document window), you see that the pop-up menus look a bit weird—there's a strange border that doesn't fit the buttons. In addition, the pop-up menu buttons are wider than the main navigation buttons, and they don't sit directly under the main buttons.

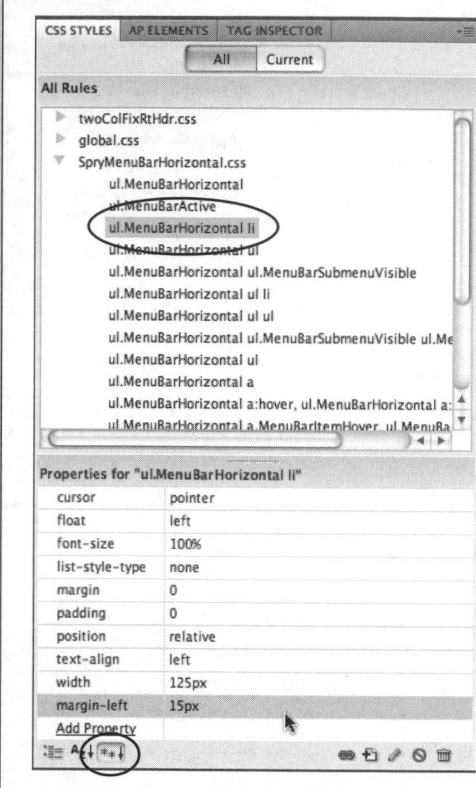

Figure 5-26:
When you select a style name in the Styles panel, all of its properties appear in the Properties pane in the bottom half of the panel. To see only the properties currently set for the style, make sure you have the "set properties" button (bottom circle) pressed. Click any value (for example, "125px" in the width field here) to edit the CSS property.

Top: When setting a measurement (like width or height) in the Properties pane, you don't have to type a value in the first field, and *then* use the measurements menu to select a value like px, em, or %. It's faster to type the measurement value *along with* the number—for example, type *125px*—and then hit Enter (or Return) to make the change stick.

---

13. **Repeat steps 10 and 11 for the ul.MenuBarHorizontal ul style (skip step 12 though—you don't change the left margin on this style).**

    You have two *ul.MenuBarHorizontal ul* styles; for this step, edit the first style (near the top of the list of styles). The second instance of this style adds a border around the pop-up menus, which doesn't look good, so you'll remove it.

14. **In the CSS Styles panel, select the second ul.MenuBarHorizontal ul (about half way down the list of styles), and click the Trash can icon (delete button) in the lower-right of the CSS Styles panel.**

    Alternatively, you can hit Delete to remove the style.

Finally, you'll position and resize the submenus so they line up underneath and match the main buttons. The submenus are indented because of the way nested lists work. A nested list is actually a bulleted list that's inside an item in another list—in other words, a nested list includes list items (the <li> tag) inside the <li> tag of the main list.

In this example, the main navigation buttons ("Home", "Meet the Vets", and so on) make up the main list, and a submenu (for example, the ones that appear under "Services") is a series of list items inside those main buttons. This means that in step 12, you added 15 pixels of left margin to every <li> item—so you indented the main navigation button 15 pixels, and then you indented every button on the submenu *another* 15 pixels. But you want that left margin on the main navigation buttons only, not in the submenus, too. So you need to edit the style that applies just to the submenu buttons.

15. **In the CSS Styles panel, select the style ul.MenuBarHorizontal ul li. Using the Properties pane, set the width to 125px, and add a margin-left property and set it to 0.**

    This style, another descendent selector, applies to list items (the <li> tag), but only to list items that appear inside a <ul> tag that is itself inside a <ul> tag with the class *MenuBarHorizontal* applied to it. In other words, this style affects only the list items inside a nested list. You can review steps 10 to 12 to see how to make these changes. In this case, you're setting the left margin to 0 in order to remove the indent you see on the submenus.

Submenus and Rollover Buttons

Overall, the menu bar is looking good and works well. There are just a few tweaks left. The rollover buttons don't look so great—electric purple just doesn't fit the look of Chia Vet. In addition, the sub-submenu (the one that appears when you mouse over the Facilities button under the About Us menu) appears too far to the right of the button that triggers it. You'll tackle that problem first.

1. **In the CSS Styles panel, double-click the style ul.MenuBarHorizontal ul ul.**

   This style is used to style a—take a deep breath—bulleted list that's inside a bulleted list that's inside a bulleted list with the class *MenuBarHorizontal* applied to it. Since, under the hood, the HTML for a Spry Menu Bar is just a bunch of nested lists (page 189), this style affects third-level unordered lists—or the sub-submenu of the navigation bar—in other words, the Patient Care and Chia Research Institute buttons here.

2. **In the CSS Rule Definition window, select the Box category. Change the top margin setting to 0, and the left margin setting to 125px.**

   Make sure you change the % setting to px, so that Dreamweaver positions the sub-submenu in a precise pixel location relative to the button that triggers it. In this case, Dreamweaver will position the sub-submenu directly to the right of the button.

3. **Click OK to close the CSS Rule Definition window and finish editing the style.**

   Now it's time to turn your attention to the appearance of the buttons when the mouse rolls over them. You actually need to edit several styles: one for regular buttons and two others for buttons that open pop-up menus.

4. **In the CSS Styles panel, select the style ul.MenuBarHorizontal a.MenuBar ItemHover (a little over half of the way down the list of styles).**

   You may need to expand the width of the Styles panel to see the full name of the styles: Drag the gray bar separating the document window and panel groups to the left. Actually, it's a much longer group of styles named "*ul.MenuBarHorizontal a.MenuBarItemHover, ul.MenuBarHorizontal a.MenuBarItemSubmenuHover, ul.MenuBarHorizontal a.MenuBarSubmenuVisible*", but you'll probably only be able to see the first part. Notice that, in the Properties pane, a background color and text color are set; you'll change these.

5. **In the Properties pane, click the color box to the right of "background-color", and then type *#CAE0EC*; click the #FFF value next to the color property, and then type *#333*.**

   The style you just changed won't affect Internet Explorer 6; there's another style you have to change to get the rollover effect in that browser.

6. **In the Styles panel, select ul.MenuBarHorizontal a:hover, and then repeat step 5.**

   Again, the actual style name is a bit longer and includes an additional selector: "*ul.MenuBarHorizontal a:hover, ul.MenuBarHorizontal a:focus*".

   For some strange reason, Internet Explorer 6 has its own style for the button rollovers, so whenever you update the rollover style used for the other browsers—*ul.MenuBarHorizontal a.MenuBarItemHover*—you also have to update this style to match.

   Now, you'll replace Dreamweaver's default arrow graphics with arrows custom made to match the Chia Vet site.

7. **Open the Files panel (Window→Files), and then expand the folder named NEW_NAV_IMAGES so you can see the four files inside that folder.**

   To expand the folder, click the + (arrow on a Mac) button. The four image files in this folder are named exactly the same as the ones Dreamweaver supplies. You can just drag these into the SpryAssets folder to replace the old ones.

8. **In the NEW_NAV_IMAGES folder, click one of the image files to select it; then hold down the control key (⌘ key) and click each of the remaining three files. Once selected, drag them into the SpryAssets folder (see Figure 5-27).**

   Dreamweaver lets you know that you're about to replace some existing files; that's what you want to do, so click the "Yes to All" button.

   You're almost there, but one bug crops up in Internet Explorer 6—the navigation bar has a huge space below it. This bug is one of the many you'll find in IE. The fix is pretty obscure, but it works.

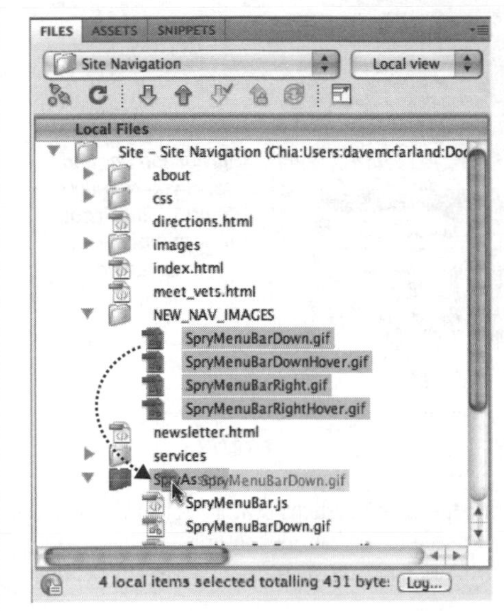

Figure 5-27:
The Files panel offers more than just a list of files in a website. It also lets your rearrange, rename, and create web page files. You'll learn how to get the most out of this useful tool on page 648.

9. **In the Styles panel, select ul.MenuBarHorizontal. At the bottom the Properties Pane, click the Add Property button; type *zoom*; press Tab, and then type *1*.**

   This adds an IE-only CSS style named *zoom* to the menu bar style. This property lets you zoom into page content, but with a setting of 1 it has absolutely no visual impact on the page in any browser. However, it's a way of knocking IE 6 upside the head so that it correctly displays the menu. The reason it works is a bit of a mystery—you can find out more about this technique at *http://haslayout.net/haslayout*, and *CSS: The Missing Manual* has an in-depth discussion of Internet Explorer bugs and the use of *zoom:1* to fix them.

   Fortunately, you won't always (and hopefully won't even usually) need to turn to this technique. However, if you do discover that IE 6 is displaying parts of a page completely differently from other browsers, including IE 7, slapping a *zoom:1* on the offending element's style sometimes works. Dreamweaver's Check Browser Compatibility tool can help, too (see page 398).

   Now, you can take the menu bar for a spin. However, you have one more step if you plan on previewing this page using either Internet Explorer 6 or 7 for Windows.

10. **Choose File→Save All Related Files; Press the F12 (Option-F12) key to preview the finished product.**

    Move your mouse over the buttons. It should look like Figure 5-28 (you may need to press your browser's Reload button to make it load the new graphics).

    You'll also find a completed version of this tutorial in the Chapter05_finished folder that accompanies the downloaded tutorial files.

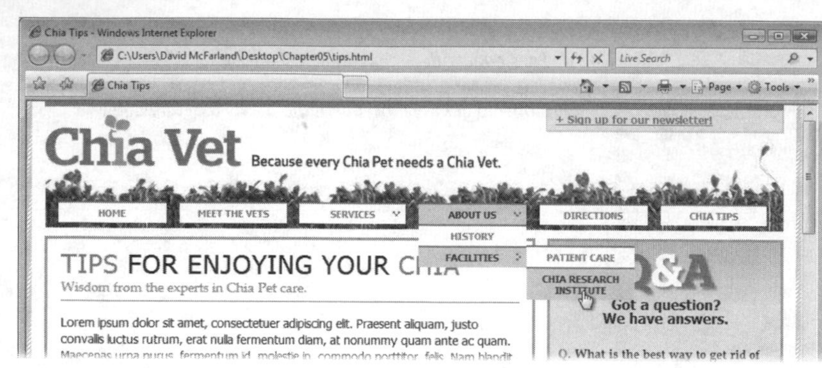

Figure 5-28: *Adding a Spry menu may take quite a few steps, but it delivers a high-quality dynamic navigation bar and saves you countless hours of JavaScript programming and browser testing.*

Note: When you preview an unsaved page, or a page that uses an external style sheet that's opened and unsaved, Dreamweaver pops up an annoying "save these files" window. You must click Yes to see the newest version of the page. If you're getting tired of this window, you can use the "Preview using temporary file" feature. It's described on page 156.

Tip: To get a full description of every Dreamweaver menu in a handy, printable PDF, go to this book's Missing CD page (*www.missingmanuals.com/cds*) and download Appendix B, "Menu by Menu Commands."

CHAPTER 6

Images

Nobody believes that a picture is worth a thousand words more than today's web designers, as evidenced by the highly visual nature of the Internet. In fact, it's not difficult to stumble onto a home page composed almost entirely of graphics, as you can see in Figure 6-1.

Even if you don't want to go that far, understanding how to use graphics on a web page effectively is invaluable. Whether you want to plop a simple photo onto your page, cover it with clickable "hotspots," or design an interactive set of buttons that light up when a cursor passes over them, Dreamweaver makes the job easy.

Adding Images

If you were writing out the HTML instructions for your web page by hand, you'd insert an image into a web page using the image tag: <img>. For example, the HTML snippet `<img src="images/george.jpg">` tells a browser to display a graphic file named *george.jpg*, which you can find in the *images* folder. (An image tag's primary property is called the *source* [src] property; it indicates the URL or path to the graphics file.)

Dreamweaver automatically does all the necessary coding for you when you insert a picture into your fledgling web page. Here are the steps:

1. **Save the web page that will include the image.**

   To insert an image, Dreamweaver has to know where to find it, which could be anywhere on your hard drive. As with links, saving the page before you proceed lets Dreamweaver correctly determine the path from the page you just saved to the image.

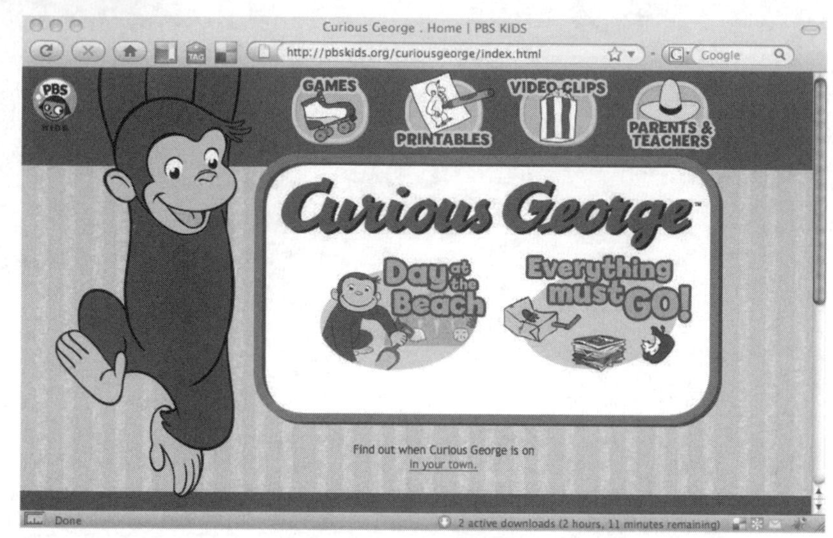

Figure 6-1: *Some websites rely almost exclusively on graphics for both looks and function. The home page for the Curious George website at* http://pbskids.org*, for instance, uses graphics not just for pictures of the main character, but also for the page's background and navigation buttons.*

2. **In the document window, click the place where you want to insert the image.**

   You can choose anywhere within a paragraph, a cell in a table (see Chapter 7), or a <div> tag (see page 333). To set a graphic apart from other text, press Enter (Return) first to create a blank line to give the image its own paragraph.

3. **Choose Insert→Image.**

   Alternatively, from the Insert panel's Common category, you can click the Image button (see Figure 6-2). Or, if you're a keyboard shortcut fan, press Ctrl+Alt+I (⌘-Option-I).

   In any case, the Select Image Source dialog box opens. This box is nearly identical to the Select File window that appears when you add a link to a page (see Figure 5-4). The only difference is the presence of a Preview Images checkbox—turn it on to see a thumbnail of the image you select in the Preview window.

4. **Browse to and then select the graphics file you wish to add to the page.**

   The file must be in one of the formats that work on the Web: GIF, JPEG, or PNG.

   Store the file somewhere in the local site folder (see page 42) or in one of its subfolders. If you don't, Dreamweaver can't add the correct path to your web page.

Note: The primary file format for Fireworks, Adobe's web-friendly image-editing program, is PNG (just as Photoshop's format is PSD). However, a native Fireworks file contains additional data the program uses to keep track of fonts, layers, and other information. That extra data significantly increases file size. So always make sure you use the Export command in Fireworks to properly compress the image into a GIF, JPEG, or PNG (without all the extra Fireworks info) file.

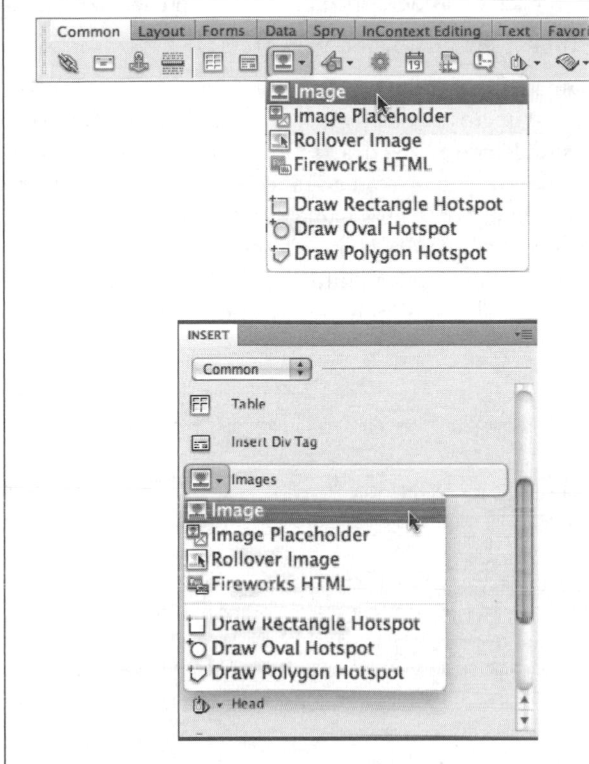

Figure 6-2:
The Image menu on the Insert panel's Common category provides tools that let you add graphics to your pages. If you're using Dreamweaver's "Classic" workspace (top) the Insert panel is actually a toolbar near the top of your screen. The "Designer" workspace (bottom) displays the Insert panel grouped with the other panels on the right edge of the screen. See page 31 for more on Dreamweaver workspaces.

That's why, if you select a graphic for insertion that's not already in your site folder, Dreamweaver offers to add a *copy* of it there. If you choose Yes, then a Copy File As dialog box opens so you can save the file in your local root folder, renaming it if you wish. If you choose No, then Dreamweaver uses a file-relative path (beginning with *file:///*) for the image's src property. But clicking No is a bad idea: While you can see the graphic as you work in Dreamweaver on your computer, the graphic doesn't appear once you move the document to the Web (see the box on page 62).

Tip: Dreamweaver lets you choose a Photoshop (PSD) file from the Select Image dialog box when you insert an image, but it doesn't actually insert the PSD file. It opens a second window where you can save the image as a GIF, JPEG, or PNG file with web-appropriate optimization settings. Ppage 216 has the full story on this feature.

5. **Click OK (Windows) or Choose (Mac).**

   You should see an Image Tag Accessibility Attributes window, which lets you assign an "alternate" text description of the image (for the benefit of those who can't see your images—those using screen reading software, for instance). If you don't see this window, somewhere along the line, you or someone else turned off this option—you can turn it back on as described in the box on page 226.

6. **Type a short text description of the image, and then press OK.**

   Dreamweaver inserts the image. The options in the Image Tag Accessibility Attributes window are described in greater detail on page 224 and the box on page 226, but in a nutshell, you should add a brief description for any image that adds meaning to a page. For example, if you insert a graphic of your company's logo, the alternative text should be your company's name. Optionally use the Accessibility Attributes window's second option—Long Description—to link to another page with detailed information about an information-heavy graphic, such as a chart or map. You'll almost always skip it, but for more details on how it works, see the box on page 226.

Tip: Dreamweaver also permits several drag-and-drop techniques so you can quickly add images to your pages.

Make sure you've set up a site as described on page 37. Then open the Files window (press F8). You can drag any graphics file from that window right into an open Dreamweaver document. You can also drag graphics in from the Assets panel, as described on page 658.

Dreamweaver even lets you drag a graphic from your desktop onto a web page. If you do this, Dreamweaver dutifully informs you that you must copy the file into your site folder (and provides a dialog box that lets you specify *which* folder), so that the image shows up properly on the Web. (You can even define a default images folder for a site, so that when you drag an image onto a page, Dreamweaver automatically copies it into the correct folder; see page 642.)

Dreamweaver even lets you drag Photoshop files into a Dreamweaver document.

Adding an Image Placeholder

You'll often find yourself working on a website without all the pieces of the puzzle. You may start building a page, even when your client has yet to give you all the text she wants there. Or you may find that a photograph hasn't been shot, but you want to get the page ready for it. Other times, you may be responsible for building web pages while another designer creates banners and navigation buttons.

To help out in these kinds of situations, Dreamweaver includes the Image Placeholder button. It lets you insert a placeholder—called an *FPO* (For Placement Only) image in publishing lingo—so you can stake out the space on a page for a graphic that isn't ready yet. This way, you can lay out the basic structure of a page without waiting for all its graphics.

To insert a placeholder, do one of the following:

- Choose Insert→Image Placeholder.
- On the Insert bar's Common category, select the Image Placeholder icon from the Image menu (see Figure 6-2).

In the window that appears (see Figure 6-3), type a width and height for the image, which determines how much space the placeholder reserves on the page. This should match the dimensions of the final image. The Name and "Alternate text" fields are optional. (If you fill them out, they appear in the Name and Alt boxes of the image's Property inspector, as discussed next.)

The Color box lets you specify a color for the placeholder—presumably to make the placeholder more colorful than the default gray color. Avoid this option: It inserts inline CSS code that Dreamweaver doesn't removed when you replace the placeholder with a real graphic, adding unnecessary code to the page. Worse, if the image you eventually use has any transparent areas, the color defined here shows through the graphic!

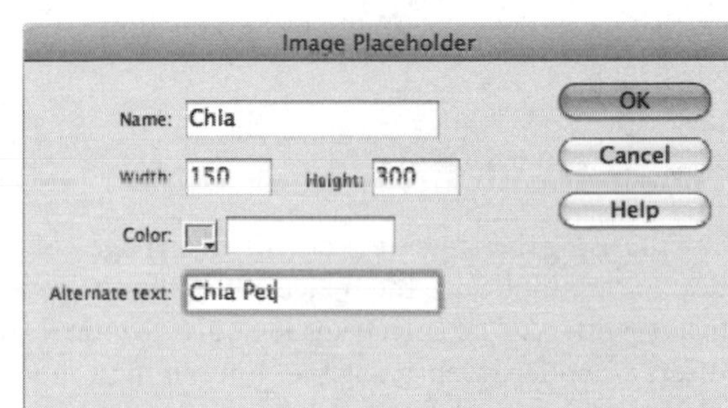

Figure 6-3:
The values you type for Name, Width, Height, and "Alternate text" appear in the Property inspector after you insert an image placeholder. The Color option just lets you choose a color for the placeholder (but don't do it or you'll add unnecessary code to your page, which Dreamweaver doesn't remove once you add a real graphic).

Warning: Dreamweaver takes the name you give a placeholder and uses it as an ID attribute to the <img> tag. Both JavaScript and CSS use IDs. If the name you provide for the image placeholder is the same as an ID name for a CSS style you created, you can run into some weird display problems. Bottom line: Unless you plan on using a CSS ID style to format the image or JavaScript to control the image, just leave the name field empty when you insert the placeholder.

Of course, using a placeholder doesn't do you any good if you don't eventually replace it with a real image. Once you've got the image that should finally appear on the page, on the web page, just double-click the placeholder. The Select Image Source window appears. Follow steps 4 through 5 on page 212 to insert the new image.

If you also own Fireworks, Adobe's web graphics companion program, the image placeholder gives you an added benefit. When you select an image placeholder in the document window, the Property inspector includes a button called Create. Click this button to launch Fireworks and open a new, blank graphics document set to the exact dimensions you specified earlier. You can then create your graphic in Fireworks. After you save the file, Fireworks exports it to whatever folder you specify, and then automatically inserts it into your document, replacing the placeholder image.

Inserting an Image from Photoshop

Since Adobe (the maker of Photoshop) bought Macromedia (the maker of Dreamweaver), it was only a matter of time before it brought these two powerful programs together. Dreamweaver streamlines the process of moving images back and forth between Photoshop and Dreamweaver. You can add a Photoshop document to a web page two ways: Insert a PSD file (Photoshop's native format), or copy an image from Photoshop, and then paste it into a Dreamweaver document.

The first method—inserting a PSD file—supports what Adobe calls *Smart Objects*, which lets Dreamweaver keep track of whether you update the original Photoshop file, and if so, gives you the option to update the compressed, web-ready version of the image. Nice. That's great news if you're the type who's constantly tweaking your artwork in Photoshop. The second method—copying and pasting from Photoshop—doesn't keep track of any changes to the original Photoshop file. Both methods are explained in the following pages.

Method 1: Using the Insert Image Object

You can insert a regular Photoshop file using the same steps described on page 211 for inserting GIF, JPEG, or PNG files. For example, use the Image button on the Insert panel (Figure 6-2), or choose Insert→Image. The Select Image Source window appears, just as it does when you insert a standard web-ready file. You can then choose a Photoshop document (a .psd file), and click the OK (Choose on Mac) button. Instead of just inserting the image, however, Dreamweaver opens an Image Preview window that lets you choose how to optimize the graphic (see Figure 6-4).

Tip: You can also insert a PSD file by dragging it directly from the desktop (or any folder) and dropping onto a Dreamweaver document. If you stored the PSD file somewhere inside your local root folder, you can also drag it from the Files panel and drop it onto the page.

Although Dreamweaver gives you lots of options, the decision-making process can be boiled down to three steps:

1. **From the Format menu (circled in Figure 6-4), choose the graphic format you want to use on your page.**

   You get to choose from three Web-friendly formats: GIF, JPEG, and PNG (see the box on page 217). In general, you'll want to choose PNG8 for images with solid colors and text, like logos; use JPEG for photos. And if you really want to have 256 levels of transparency (great for drop shadow effects, but—as noted on page 217—not so great for Internet Explorer 6), then choose PNG32.

Note: You can't import animated GIF images using the Image Preview window; instead, you need to export an animated GIF from the program in which you created it (like Fireworks or Photoshop).

UP TO SPEED

GIFs, JPEGs, and PNGs: The Graphics of the Web

Computer graphics come in hundreds of different file formats. The assorted acronyms can be mind-numbing: JPEG, GIF, TIFF, PICT, BMP, EPS, and so on.

Fortunately, the limited graphics formats the Web uses make things simpler. All of today's web browsers support three common graphics formats, each of which provides good *compression*; through clever computer manipulation, compression reduces a graphic's file size so it can travel more rapidly across the Internet. The format you choose depends on the image you wish to add to your page.

GIF (Graphics Interchange Format) files provide good compression for images with big areas of solid color: logos, text, simple banners, and so on. GIFs also offer single-color transparency, meaning you can make one color in the graphic disappear, permitting the background of a web page to show through part of the image. In addition, you can create limited animations with GIF files (like a flashing "Buy Me" button). (If you don't need to animate an image, the PNG8 format discussed below is a better choice than GIF.)

GIF images support a maximum of only 256 shades of color, generally making photos look posterized (in other words, not completely realistic). That radiant sunset photo you took with your digital camera won't look so good as a GIF file.

JPEG (Joint Photographic Experts Group) graphics, on the other hand, pick up where GIFs leave off. JPEG graphics support millions of colors, making them ideal for photos. Not only do JPEGs do a better job on photos, they compress multicolored images much better than GIFs, because the JPEG compression algorithm considers how the human eye perceives adjacent color values; when your graphics software saves a JPEG file, it runs a complex color analysis to lower the amount of data required to accurately represent the image. On the downside, JPEG compression makes any text you have in an image and large areas of solid color look blotchy, so it's not a good choice for logos or simple drawings.

Finally, the PNG (Portable Network Graphics) format includes the best features of GIFs and JPEGs, but you need to know which version of PNG to use for which situation. PNG8 is basically a replacement for GIFs. Like GIF, it supports 256 colors and basic one-color transparency. However, PNG8 usually compresses images to a slightly smaller file size than GIF, so PNG8 images download a tiny bit faster than the same image saved in the GIF format.

PNG24 and PNG32 offer the expanded color palette of JPEG images, without any loss of quality. This means that photos saved as PNG24 or PNG32 tend to be higher quality than JPEGs. But before you jump on the PNG bandwagon, JPEG images offer very good quality and a *much* smaller file size than either PNG24 or PNG32. In general, JPEG is a better choice for photos and other images that include lots of colors.

Finally, PNG32 offers one more feature that no other format does: 256 levels of transparency (also called *alpha transparency*), which means you can actually see the background of a web page through a drop shadow on a graphic, or even create a graphic with 50 percent opacity (meaning you can see through it) to create a ghostly translucent effect on a page. Unfortunately, Internet Explorer 6 for Windows doesn't support PNG32's 256 levels of transparency—instead of seeing through the transparent areas, IE6 replaces the transparent areas with a hideous blue background. (Several JavaScript-based techniques—see *http://labs.unitinteractive.com/unitpngfix.php*, for example—help IE 6 display PNG transparency correctly.) Fortunately, Internet Explorer 7 and 8 do support PNG transparency, as do Firefox, Safari, Chrome, and Opera.

2. **Set your image's optimization settings.**

   The exact optimization choices depend on the graphic format you selected in step 1 (see discussion below). Make your choices using the menus and buttons on the window's left-hand side.

   In the right half of the Image Preview dialog box, Dreamweaver shows you what the final, optimized graphic will look like; you can even compare different optimization settings (see Figure 6-4). The preview window also displays information about the final optimized graphic, such as its file type, the quality or kind of compression it uses, the number of colors it supports, the final size of the file, and how long the file will take to download over a 56K dial-up modem.

   Figure 6-4 shows what the image looks like when you save it as a JPEG (top preview image) and as a PNG8 file (bottom preview image). The JPEG version has a quality of 60 (see "JPEG optimization options" on page 219 for a discussion of this property), supports millions of colors, and is 18.79 kilobytes (K) in size. The PNG24 version, on the other hand, is 529.79 K! Given the comparable image quality, JPEG is the obvious choice.

3. **Click OK, and then name and save the file on your site.**

   Dreamweaver saves the new image file and places it into your page—at this point it's a GIF, JPEG, or PNG file. Dreamweaver adds a small icon in the upper-left corner of the image (see Figure 6-20) to indicate that the image is a *Smart Object* and retains a link to the original PSD file. What makes it "smart" is that Dreamweaver tracks any changes to the PSD file—if you decide to open Photoshop and add some cool effect to the image, Dreamweaver knows you changed the original. At this point you can update the image on your web page directly in Dreamweaver. Ppage 240 shows you how.

When you insert a Photoshop image this way, Dreamweaver, unfortunately, ignores images you made using Photoshop's "slice" tool. This handy tool lets web designers export just bits and pieces of a complete web page design in Photoshop—for example, you could design the look of a site's home page in Photoshop, show it to your client for feedback, then export just parts of the design as separate images files, like a logo in the upper-left corner of the document, individual navigation icons along the top, or a photo in the middle of the document.

So if you want to use an exported slice as a graphic on your web page, the import-from-Photoshop technique isn't the best; Dreamweaver tries to insert the entire image, not the individual slices you defined in Photoshop.

However, there's a workaround: As pictured in Figure 6-4, you can use the Image Preview box's crop tool to extract just one rectangular area from the image; Dreamweaver optimizes and imports only that part of the file. Best of all, Dreamweaver *remembers* the crop you set, so you can update the image and retain just the cropped portion when you update the image file.

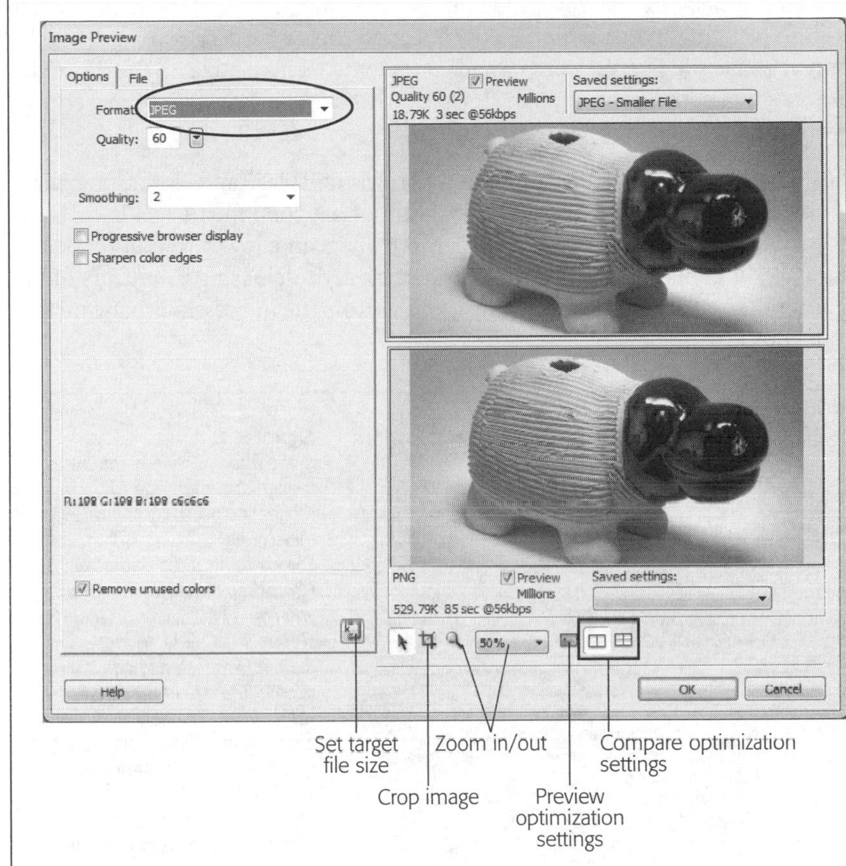

Figure 6-4: *Picking the proper optimization for an image is usually just a matter of trial and error, so you'll often want to see how an image looks and compresses as a JPEG and a PNG file before you decide which format to choose. You can compare different file types and optimization settings side by side by clicking either the "2-up" or "4-up" buttons at the bottom of the window (circled). Two-up lets you compare two optimization settings (pictured here), while four-up shows four previews. This is a great way to see which file format gives you the best-looking image at the smallest file size.*

Tip: For ultra-precise cropping control, click the Image Preview box's File button (Figure 6-5, top left); check the "Export area" box; and then enter precise pixel values the crop where it should start, and how wide and tall it should be.

Cropping an image this way has no effect on the original PSD file—it remains full size. You can even use different parts of the same image (have multiple Smart Objects, in other words). Just follow the Insert→Image routine each time. When you update the original Photoshop document, you can update every Smart Object based on that document.

JPEG optimization options

Dreamweaver doesn't give you many choices for optimizing JPEG images (see Figure 6-4). Basically, you can select a quality level that affects both how good the image looks and its size. The higher the quality, the larger the file; the worse the quality, the smaller the file. Dreamweaver's Quality setting runs from 1 (low quality/small file) to 100 (high quality/large file). Eighty is a good choice for very good quality and fairly manageable file size; 60 works when you want to keep file size on the slim side. The exact setting depends on what the image looks like, so preview different settings until you're satisfied both with how the image looks and the file size.

For most images, turning on the "Progressive browser display" and "Remove unused colors" checkboxes trims down the file size without harming the image. In fact, the "progressive" setting lets the browser display the image in a lower resolution before it finishes loading the entire graphic file, "progressively" increasing the quality of the image until the entire graphic loads. This gives visitors the impression that your site is loading quickly.

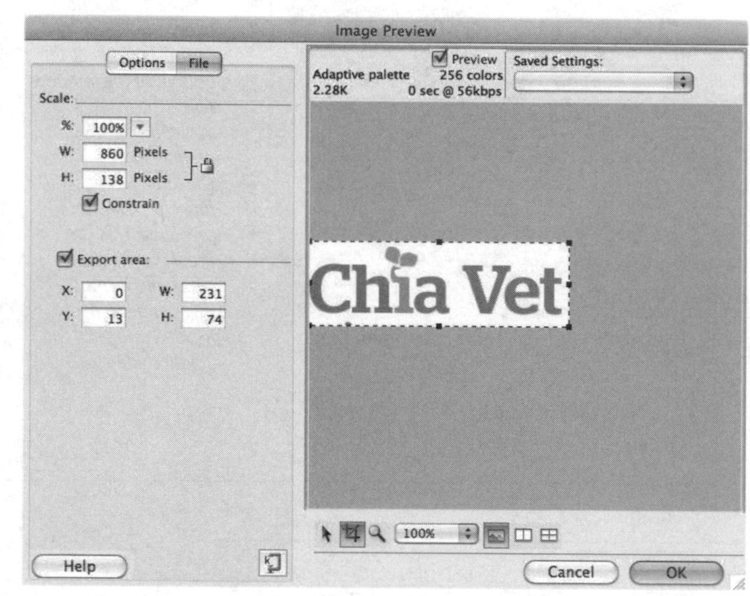

Figure 6-5:
In the Image Preview window, the options under the File tab let you precisely control the scale of your final image. For example, if the original Photoshop image is very large, you could type 25 in the Scale section's "%" field, to make the final, imported image 25 percent the size of the Photoshop image. This setting has no effect on the Photoshop document itself, just the final image. PARAGRAPH BREAK You can also import just a selected area of the image by turning on the "Export area" checkbox and then specifying the part of the image you want to export to your site. You can export different areas of the same image. Doing so lets you take a web page draft and insert separate bits of it, such as individual icons and a banner).

Smoothing an image using the pull-down menu gives you a smaller file size, but it makes the image look out of focus,. Turning on the "Sharpen color edges" checkbox can make the image look more in focus, but usually at a significantly higher file size. You might want to experiment with these options on different images, but you'll probably skip these two settings most of the time.

GIF and PNG8 optimization options

GIF and PNG8 files have identical optimization settings; in most cases, you get a smaller file size from a PNG8 file than from a GIF. The number of colors an image has—the size of its *palette*, in other words—contributes most to its file size. Fewer colors mean a smaller file size. Most of the settings available for GIF and PNG8 images control the number and type of colors you can use (see Figure 6-6).

For optimal compression settings with a GIF or PNG8 image, follow these two steps:

1. **From the Palette menu, select Adaptive.**

   Since both image types are limited to just 256 colors, this menu determines which colors your image will use. You have a lot of options here, but you can ignore all but Adaptive, which means that Dreamweaver picks the best 256 colors from the image itself. (The other options select colors from palettes that aren't necessarily contained inside the image. This ability used to be important when people had monitors that displayed only 256 colors—back when Duran Duran ruled the air waves; but today, these other palettes usually distort the look of the original image.)

Tip: To convert a color image into a black-and-white GIF or PNG8 file, choose Grayscale from the Palette menu.

---

2. **In the "Number of Colors" menu, select a value (Figure 6-6).**

   You can tell Dreamweaver to use from 2 to the maximum of 256 colors in the image. If the original Photoshop image started out with only 64 colors, choosing 256 doesn't add colors or quality to the image. However, you can often choose a *lower* number, eliminating colors from the graphic, and reducing the file size significantly without overly harming the image's final quality. Again, each image is different, so trial and error is the best way to balance the minimum number of colors you need with the quality you want.

The Loss option (available only for GIF images) also decreases file size at the cost of image quality. In general, increasing the "loss" setting makes an image look spotted and windswept, so, unless you're going for a special effect, use a low loss setting or none at all. The Dither option is intended to make up for lost colors—for example, when you choose "32" from the "Number of Colors" menu when an image is a vibrant sunset with millions of colors. Skip this setting: It makes images look blotchy and really increases a file's size. If you have an image with millions of colors, save it as a JPEG file, not a GIF or PNG8.

PNG optimization options

If you save a file in the PNG8 format, you have the same options as GIF images (see the previous section). If you choose PNG24 or PNG32, your choices are simple… well, actually, you don't have any choices. In the Image Preview window, just click OK, and then save the file. But as mentioned in the box on page 217, while PNG24 and

PNG32 can offer higher image quality than JPEGs, they usually produce significantly larger file sizes. However, PNG32 is the only format that lets you tap into 256 levels of transparency.

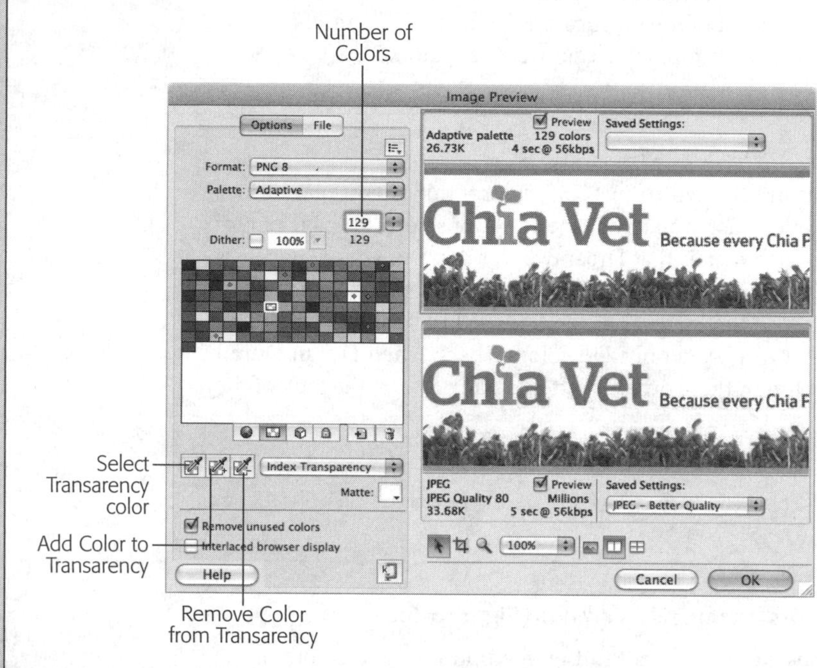

Figure 6-6: *The transparency tools for GIF and PNG8 images let you select one or more colors as "transparent"—that is, colors that disappear from the image, allowing the web page background to show through. From the Transparency menu, select Index Transparency; click the Select Transparency Color tool and then, within the preview image, click the color you wish to disappear (a white background, for example). To add additional colors, use the same process with the "Add Color to Transparency" tool.*

Method 2: Copying and Pasting from Photoshop

You can also copy a selection (a layer, an entire image, or a "slice" created with the web-oriented slicing tool) from Photoshop, and paste it into a Dreamweaver web page. When you do this, the Image Preview window appears—the same window you use when inserting a Photoshop document. Follow the same steps described on page 218 for optimizing and saving the pasted image. However, unlike a Photoshop image inserted using the Insert panel or the Insert menu, Dreamweaver doesn't consider a pasted image a Smart Object. It still keeps track of the *location* of the original PSD (useful for editing, as you'll see on page 243), but it doesn't notify you if someone updates the original PSD file.

Tip: To select all the layers in a Photoshop document, first select the entire image (Select→All), and then choose Edit→Copy Merged. This copies all the layers to the clipboard. If you want to copy just a portion of a layered image, use the Marquee tool to make a rectangular selection, and then choose Edit→Copy Merged.

Modifying an Image

After you insert a graphic, you can work on it in several ways: Attach a link to the image, align it on the page, or add a border and margin to it, to name a few. Dreamweaver also includes some basic tools that let you crop, resize, optimize, sharpen, and adjust contrast and brightness (see page 235).

As with most objects on a web page, you set image properties using the Property inspector (see Figure 6-7).

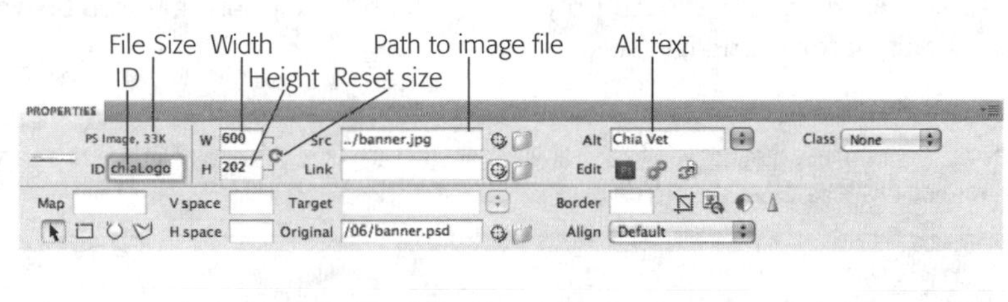

Figure 6-7: *The Property inspector shows the selected graphic's dimensions, source, alignment, border, and margins. To the left of the file size (33K), you see either Image (meaning a regular GIF, PNG, or JPEG file) or PS Image (meaning the image is coming from a Photoshop document).*

Adding an ID to an Image

In the Property inspector, just to the right of an image's thumbnail, you'll see a small field where you can type in an ID for that image (see Figure 6-7). Most of the time, you'll leave this field blank.

However, if you plan to add interactive effects to the image—like the rollover effect discussed on page 246—using Dreamweaver behaviors (see Chapter 14) or your own JavaScript programming, you'll need to add an ID. Whatever name you choose should use only letters and numbers—no spaces or other punctuation. Furthermore, since this adds an ID to the image (see page 112), the name must be unique on the page. Following this rule lets JavaScript "talk" to a specific image.

When you add an ID, Dreamweaver adds both a Name property and an ID property to the image tag. Most browsers still use the name tag, but the ID tag is JavaScript's standard way to identify an object on a page. (Cascading Style Sheets also use IDs, as described on page 112, so you could also use the ID you give the image to create a unique format for just that image—for example, to add a border.)

Note: JavaScript uses the image name or ID that you type in the Image Placeholder box for its own reference; no one actually sees this name in a web browser. In other words, this box isn't the place to give your graphic a text label that shows up when your reader has her browser graphics turned off. For that purpose, read on.

Adding a Text Description to an Image

Not everyone who visits your website gets to see those stunning photos of your summer vacation. Some people deliberately turn off graphics when they surf, enjoying the Web without the wait, since graphics-free pages appear almost instantly. Other people have vision impairments that prevent them from enjoying the web's visual aspects. They rely on special software that reads web page text aloud, including any labels you give your graphics.

To assist web surfers in both situations, make a habit of setting an image's Alt property. Short for *alternative text*, the Alt property is a text description that web browsers use as a stand-in for the image (see Figure 6-8).

Note: Dreamweaver normally reminds you to add an Alt property each time you add an image to a page, but you can turn off this setting. See the box on page 226 to make sure it's on.

To add a text description to an image, type it in in the Property inspector's Alt field. If you're naming navigation buttons, for example, you could use the text that appears on the button, such as *Home* or *Products*. For images that carry greater meaning—such as a photo of the product itself—you might use a more detailed description: "Photo of Sasquatch relaxing at his lodge in the Adirondacks."

Note: In some cases, a description is more of a distraction than a help. For example, you might insert an image of an intricate swirling line to act as a visual divider between two paragraphs. The image doesn't actually convey any meaningful information; it's just for decoration. In an instance like this, click the pop-up menu that appears in the Property inspector, to the right of the Alt field. This menu lets you choose one option: <empty>. Use the <empty> Alt property for images that don't add meaning to a page, like decorative elements. This trick helps your pages meet accessibility requirements without adding distracting and unnecessary descriptions.

Changing an Image's Size

A graphic's Width and Height properties do more than determine its screen size; they also help web browsers load the graphic quickly and efficiently. Since the HTML of a web page downloads before any graphics do, browsers display the text on a page first, and add the images as they arrive. If you don't include width and height attributes with an image, the browser doesn't know how much space on the page to reserve, so it has to redraw the page after it downloads each image. As a result, the pages appear to "stutter" with each redraw. This disconcerting behavior does little for your reputation as a cool, competent web designer.

Fortunately, you don't have to worry about specifying a picture's dimensions yourself: Whenever Dreamweaver inserts an image into a page, it automatically calculates its width and height, and enters those values into the Property inspector's W and H fields (see Figure 6-7).

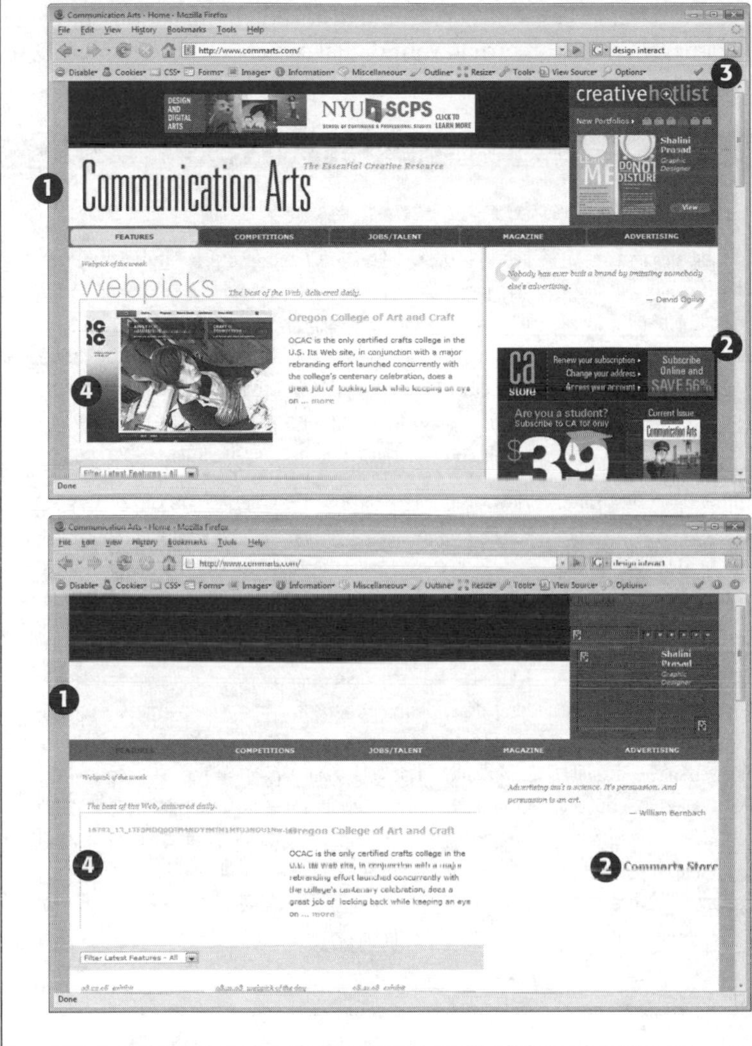

Figure 6-8: *The Alt property is an important aid for Web surfers who can't see the graphics on your page. Top: This page uses graphics for the site's logo (1), ads (2), sub-sections (3), and story highlights (4). Bottom: When you turn off your browser's graphics, the lack of Alt text makes the site inscrutable (1). Good Alt text–like the "Commarts Store" text (2) clearly describes the graphic's message. Bad Alt text is either misleading or uninformative. For example, the Alt text for the Creative Hot List image (3) is "CHL Logo", which is pretty meaningless. A better description would simply be the text already in the image: "Creative Hot List." And the bizarre Alt text "16793_13_LTE5MDQ0OTM4NDYtMTM1MTU3NDU1Nw" for the site's main story (4) won't help anyone, or even a computer, understand what that image is.*

You can, if you like, shrink a graphic by typing smaller values into the W and H fields, but doing so doesn't do anything to speed up the download time. You make the picture *appear* smaller, but a browser still has to download the entire file. To make your graphic smaller in both appearance and file size, you have to shrink it in an image-editing program like Fireworks or Photoshop, or use Dreamweaver's Resample Image tool, described on page 236. Not only do you get an image that's exactly the size you want, but the image usually looks better and you trim a few bytes off its file size (and maybe even save a second or two of download time).

On the other hand, setting width and height values that are *larger* than the dimensions of a graphic merely distorts the image by stretching it, creating an undesirable pixelated effect. If you want a larger image without distortion or pixilation, start with a larger original image. To do so, return to your digital camera or stock photo CD, or recreate the graphic at a larger size in Photoshop or Fireworks.

POWER USERS' CLINIC

Making Accessible Websites

Many people using the Web have disabilities that make reading, seeing, hearing, or using a mouse difficult. Visually impaired people, for example, may not benefit from images on the screen, even if they have software that reads a web page's text aloud.

Dreamweaver includes a number of features that make your websites more accessible. That's good news if you're building a site for the federal government or one of the many states that support Section 508 of the Workforce Investment Act. This law requires websites built for or funded by the government to offer equal or equivalent access to everyone. Throughout this book, you'll find tips for using Dreamweaver's accessibility features.

The Alt property described on page 224 is an important first step for assisting visually impaired web surfers. For complex images, such as a graph that plots changes in utility rates over time, you can supply a more detailed description on a separate web page. The *Longdesc* (long description) property of an image lets you specify a link to a page containing a text description of the image. Some web browsers understand this property, letting visually impaired visitors jump to the description page.

While you can't find the *Longdesc* property in the Property inspector, Dreamweaver displays a field for it in the Accessibility Options window every time you insert a graphic. If you don't see the window, turn it on by choosing Edit→Preferences (Dreamweaver→Preferences on the Mac) to open the Preferences window. Select the Accessibility category, and then turn on the Images checkbox.

Now, whenever you insert a graphic, you can quickly set the Alt text and specify an HTML page for the long description. (You can also use the Tag inspector described on page 441 to add a *Longdesc* property to a graphic you already inserted into a page.)

Note that you're *not required* by Section 508 to use the long description property for images. It's merely recommended if the image is particularly complex or includes information that you can't explain in the Alt property—for example, graphs or images that include a lot of text. You'll probably rarely, if ever, find yourself adding a long description for an image. For an overview of web accessibility and helpful tips on making accessible sites, visit *http://www.w3.org/WAI/gettingstarted/*.

Some Properties to Avoid

You'll notice that the Property inspector includes a few other properties (see Figure 6-7) that seem intriguing and possibly useful—Align, V Space, H Space, and Border. They affect how browsers position an image inside a block of text (or next to another image), and the size of its margins and borders. Steer clear of these properties. Not only are they Web-Design-Circa-1999, but they're on the way out and unsupported in the strict versions of HTML and XHTML. In addition, they offer anemic design control. For example, you can't easily dictate the color of the border around the image, or specify different margins for both the right *and* left or bottom *and* top edges of an image.

Fortunately, Cascading Style Sheets once again come to the rescue, as discussed next.

Note: If you're not obsessed with building a site that meets the strictest HTML/XHTML standards, the Align menu's left and right options are useful. They move an image to either the left or right side of a page (or table cell, or <div>) and force other content, like text, to wrap around it. You can achieve the same effect with the CSS Float property, as described below.

WORKAROUND WORKSHOP

Watch Those Resize Handles!

After you insert an image in the document window, a thin black border appears around it, indicating that it's selected. Three small black squares—the resize handles—appear on the right edge, bottom edge, and lower-right corner, as circled in the illustration.

Dragging these handles changes the graphic's width and height—or, rather, in the Property inspector, the Width and Height properties. Pressing Shift while dragging the corner handle keeps the proportions of the image the same. The graphic file itself remains unchanged.

However, dragging one of these handles to make the picture appear bigger is almost always unsuccessful, resulting in distortion and ugly pixilation.

You can far too easily accidentally grab and drag those pesky resize handles. In fact, sometimes you may resize a graphic and not even know it. Perhaps you accidentally dragged the left resize handle a few pixels, making the graphic wider, but not enough to notice.

Fortunately, the Property inspector lets you know when a graphic differs from its original size: It boldfaces the number in the W or H field to tell you that the Width or Height property now differs from the actual dimensions of the graphic.

Better yet, clicking the letter W or H in the Property inspector resets the Width or Height property to its original dimensions, undoing your little slip of the mouse. Clicking the "Reset size" icon (see Figure 6-7) resets both properties.

Controlling Images with CSS

Cascading Style Sheets aren't just for stylizing text. You can also use CSS's design power to add borders to an image, force text to wrap around an image, and even add images to the background of other elements. For example, the CSS *background-image* property lets you place an image in the background of a web page, or add a graphical background to a link, headline, or any HTML tag.

In general, you probably don't want to create a tag style (see page 112) for <img>. That type of style affects *every* image on a page (or on an entire site if you use a side-wide external style sheet). And while you may want a bright red, 10-pixel border around each thumbnail in a photo gallery, you probably don't want that border around the site's logo or the navigation buttons on that same page. You're more likely to create class styles that you manually apply to certain graphics. In the thumbnail example, create a class style with the proper border setting, and then apply that class to each gallery image (you can be even more efficient and use a *descendent selector* as described on page 298).

Wrapping Text Around an Image

When you add an image to a page, you might initially find yourself staring at a bunch of empty white space around the image (see Figure 6-9, top). Not only does this waste precious screen real estate, it's usually unattractive. Fortunately, you can wrap text around images using the CSS *float* property (see Figure 6-9, bottom).

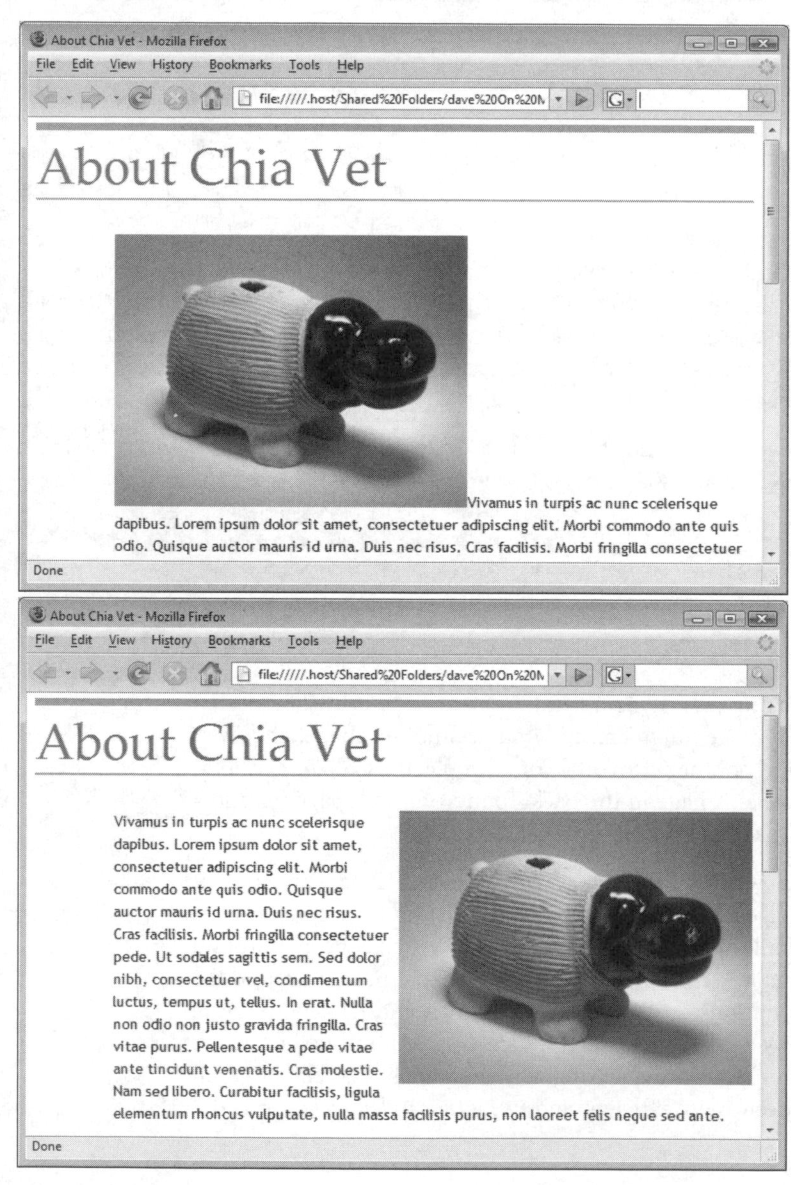

Figure 6-9:
Placing an image on the same line as text (top) creates unsightly open space, which you can put to better use. By floating an image to the right (bottom) or left, you force content that would otherwise sit beneath the image to wrap around it.

To do so, in the CSS Rule Definition window's Box category, set the *float* property (see Figure 6-10). You can float an element *left* or *right*. If you want an image to appear on the right side of a page and have text flow around its left and bottom edges, choose "right" from the Float menu. The Float property behaves just like the right and left alignment options for images (see the following Note).

Note: The Float property has many uses, from positioning images on the right or left side of a page to creating thumbnail photo galleries to laying out entire web pages. You'll learn about using it for layout in Chapter 10. For an excellent introduction and set of tutorials on the float property in general, visit *http://css.maxdesign.com.au/floatutorial/*. Book lovers should pick up *CSS: The Missing Manual* for in-depth discussion, tutorials, and practical tips on using floats.

One thing to keep in mind with floats: The floated element must appear *before* anything you want to wrap around it. Say you have a paragraph of text you'd like to wrap around a right-floated image. You need to insert the image before the text (a good spot is before the first letter in the wraparound paragraph). If you float an image to the right but place the image after the text, the image moves to the right, but the paragraph remains above the image.

You'll frequently use the Margin property with floats (see Figure 6-10). A margin is the outermost space surrounding an element. It lets you add space between one element and another. So for a right-floated image, it's usually a good idea to add a little *left*, *bottom*, and *top* margin. This creates a bit of breathing room between the image and anything that wraps around it; omitting a left margin on a right-floated image can cause text to butt right up against the image.

You can specify a margin using any of the measurement values—pixels, percentages, and so on—CSS supports.

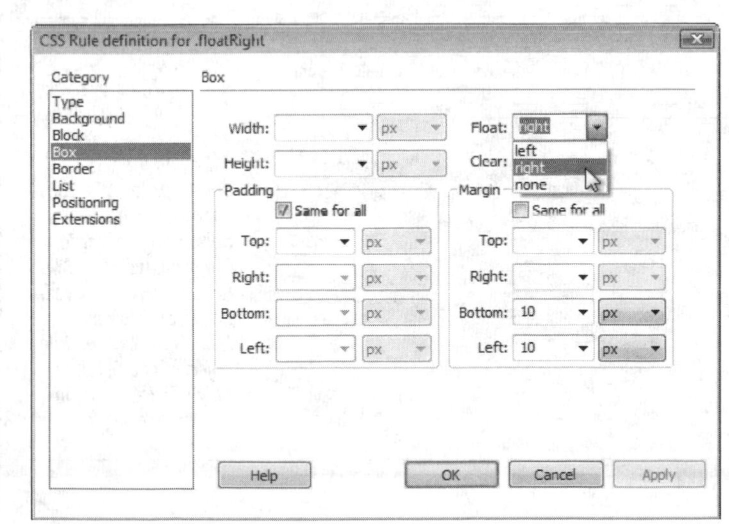

Figure 6-10: *The Box category contains some of the most-used CSS properties: the Float property to align images and other page elements to the left or right; the Margin property to add or remove space between elements (like adding space between the edge of a right-floated image and the text that wraps around the image); and the Padding property to add space between the content within an element and the edges of the element.*

Adding Borders

As you saw in the tutorial for Chapter 4, you can add a border to any element on a page—a paragraph, or even a single word. But borders can really add impact to a photo on a page, because they give the image a polished "frame-like" appearance; in addition, borders can help unify a page full of thumbnail images.

You control the border, logically enough, from the CSS Rule Definition window's Border category (see Figure 6-11). You can control each *side* of the border independently, with its own width and color settings by specifying the three main border properties:

- **Style.** This menu lets you specify the type of line a web browser draws for the border. It gives you more options than a frame shop: "none" (the default), "dotted", "dashed", "solid", "double", "groove", "ridge", "inset", and "outset" (see Figure 6-12). You can use a different style for each edge, or, from the top menu, select a style, and then turn on the "Same for all" box to apply a style to all four borders.

Note: You have to select a style from the pop-up menu to see the borders. If you leave this option blank or select "none", you don't see the borders even if you set its width and color.

- **Border Widths.** You can set border widths for each side of a styled object. Choose one of the preset widths—"thin", "medium", "thick", or "auto"—or choose "(value)" from the pop-up menu and type a value into the Width box, and then, from the pop-up menu to the right, select a unit of measurement. Again, you can choose from a range of units: pixels, percentage, inches, and so on (see page 133 for more on CSS units of measure). If you want to eliminate the border on one side, type *0* into the appropriate box (or, from the Style menu, choose "none").

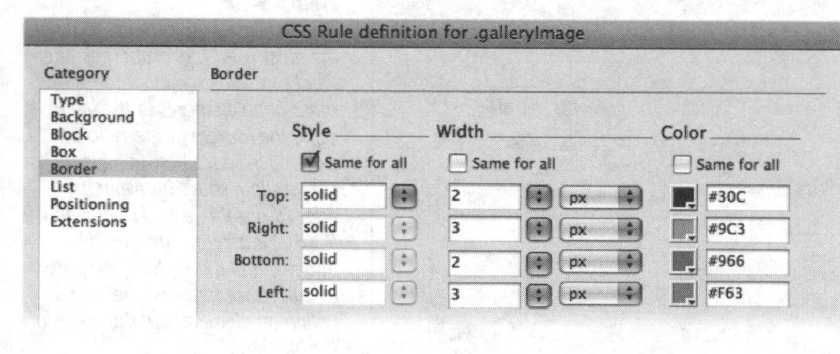

Figure 6-11: *Add colorful and stylish borders to paragraphs, images, tables, and links with the CSS Border properties. Turning on only the bottom border for a paragraph is a great way to add a horizontal rule between paragraphs. While HTML's Horizontal Rule object also does this, only CSS lets you control the rule's color.*

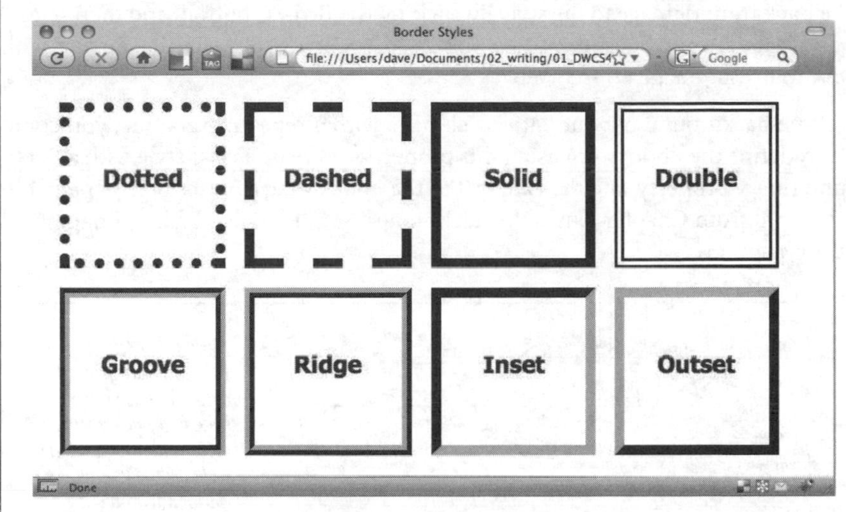

Figure 6-12: *CSS provides eight border styles. Some, like "double", "ridge", and "groove", look good only with a thick border (more than 1 pixel).*

- **Border Colors.** You can color each of the four borders individually using the ubiquitous Dreamweaver color box. If you don't assign any colors but do assign border *widths*, the borders match the color of the surrounding text.

If you use borders to "frame" an image, you can use the *padding* property to add space between the image and the border—this simulates the appearance of the cardboard mat used in professionally framed photographs. Padding is the gap that separates the style's content—such as a paragraph of text or an image—and its border.

You set the padding from the CSS Style Definition window's Box category (see Figure 6-10). If you put a 1-pixel border around an image and want to add 10 pixels of space between the image and the border, type *10* into the Top padding box, and then, from the pop-up menu, choose "pixels". Turn off the "Same for all" box if you wish to set the padding around each edge separately; then, type values into each of the other three boxes.

Background Images

Inserting an image into a page as described on page 211 isn't the only way you can add graphical beauty to a web page. CSS also lets you add an image to the background of any tag. You can put a graphic in the background of a page, enhance a headline with an icon, or add your own custom graphics to links (in fact, the arrow icons used for the Spry Menu Bar discussed in "Creating a Navigation Menu" are images applied to a link's background).

You control background images by setting the following properties in the CSS Rule Definition window's Background category (see Figure 6-13).

Background image

Add a background image to the style by clicking the Browse button, and then selecting an image from your site. You can also type in an absolute URL, starting with *http://*, to use an image off the Web.

To fill the background of your entire web page with a repeating graphic, you could either redefine the <body> tag using this property, or create a class style with a Background Image property, and then apply it to the <body> tag as described on page 119 (the tutorial from Chapter 1 uses this technique—see "Phase 4: Adding Images and Text" on page 55).

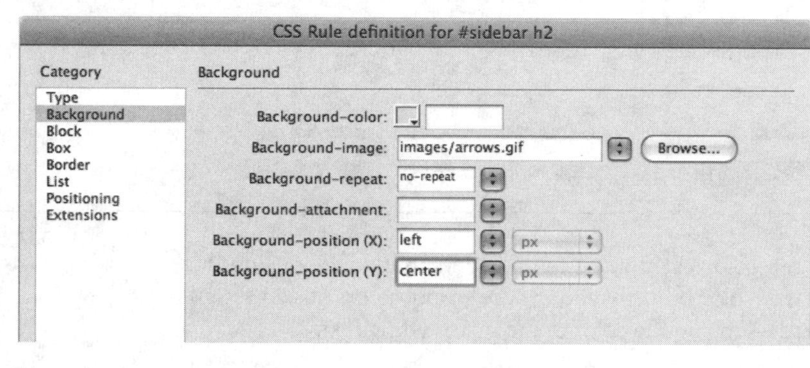

Figure 6-13: *The CSS Background category lets you specify a background color and image for a style. While you won't frequently apply a background color to an image (after all, the image would usually cover up anything behind it), it can come in handy when you use it with the padding property (see page 341) to create a customized "mat" color.*

You can even control how an image tiles (repeats) and where Dreamweaver puts it on the page (see the following sections). Furthermore, you can add background images to any *individual* element on your page: paragraphs, tables, layers, and so on.

Background images appear above any background color, so you can (and often will) combine the two. For example, you may want to position an interesting graphic on top of a colorful background image.

Note: One common byte-saving technique when you use navigation buttons on a site is to create an image that has all the characteristics of a button–burnished edges and so on–but without a label. You use this generic button as the background image for navigation links on a page. The links themselves include regular text–"Home", "About Us", and so on–but the background of each link makes them look like graphical buttons. This technique's main benefit is that you don't need to create separate graphics for each button.

Background repeat

When displaying the background for a web page, a browser usually *tiles* the background image. That is, it repeats the image over and over again, across and down. A small image of a carrot added to the background of a page appears as a field of carrots—one next to another, row after row. (Not all web designers use a background image for their pages; some leave the background white or set a color property, such as black for sites that use white text.)

But with CSS, you can control *how* the background image repeats. You can select from the following options:

- *repeat* tiles the image horizontally and vertically. This is how browsers normally display a background image.
- *repeat-x* and *repeat-y* display a horizontal and vertical band of images, respectively. If you want a single row of images at the top of a page, use the *repeat-x* option; it's a good way to add a graphical background to a banner. *repeat-y*, on the other hand, is great for a graphical sidebar that appears down the edge of a page.
- *no-repeat* displays the image only once (see the examples in Figure 6-14).

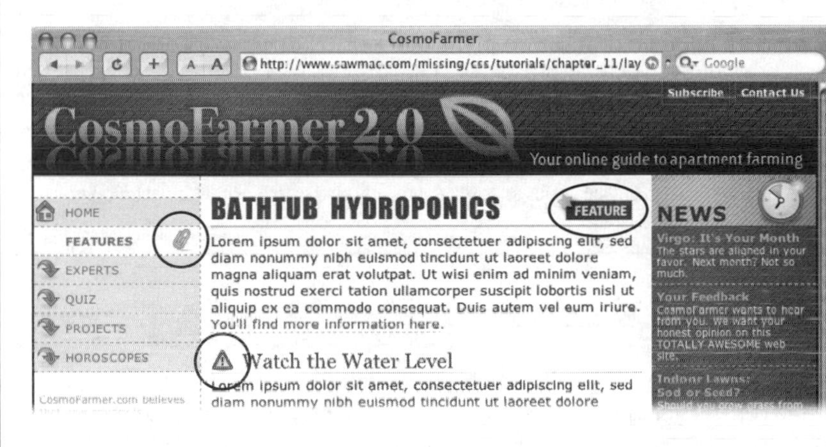

Figure 6-14: *Background images aren't just for the body of a web page. You can apply styles that include background images to any page element, including links, headlines, and paragraphs of text. The circled graphics in this image are just a few examples of background images, here displayed just once.*

Background attachment

By default, the background image on a page scrolls with the rest of the page, so that as you scroll down to read a long web page, the image scrolls along with the text.

But using CSS, you can lock the image in place by choosing "fixed" from the Attachment menu. Say you add your company's logo to the background of a page and set the Repeat property (described above) to "no-repeat". The logo now appears only once in the upper-left corner of the page. If you use the "fixed" option for this property, when a visitor scrolls the page, the logo remains fixed in the upper-left corner. (Choosing "scroll" from the Attachment menu means, of course, that the background image scrolls with the page—this is a default behavior, so you needn't choose this option.) Note that "fixed" really works out only when you apply an image to the body of a page—the image stays fixed when the rest of the content scrolls.

Horizontal and vertical position

Using these controls, you can specify a position for the affected text or other web page element. The Horizontal Position options are: "left", "center", and "right". You can also choose "(value)", type an exact number in the box, and then, from the menu to the right, select a unit of measure. Similarly, the Vertical Position options include "top", "center", and "bottom", or you can enter a specific value.

These positioning options refer to the position of the styled object. Suppose you create a class style that includes a background image with both the horizontal and vertical positions set to *center*. Then say you apply that class style to a paragraph. The background image would appear in the center of that *paragraph*, not in the center of the web page.

Likewise, if you set the horizontal position of an image to 10 pixels and the vertical position to 20 pixels, the image would start 10 pixels from the left edge of the paragraph and 20 pixels from the top edge.

And if you wanted to place an image in the exact center of a page, you'd choose "center" from both the Horizontal and Vertical Position menus, set the Repeat property to "no-repeat", and then apply the style to the page's <body> tag.

Note: You can even use percentage values to position a background image. For information on how that works, visit *http://tinyurl.com/yt7eqt*.

Editing Graphics

Nothing's ever perfect, especially when you're building a website. Corrections are par for the course—not just to a web page, but to the pictures on it, as well. Perhaps a picture is a tad too dark, or you'd like to crop out the rowdy coworker being escorted out by security from your company's holiday party.

In the hands of less capable software, you'd face a tedious set of steps each time you wanted to edit a graphic. You'd have to open Photoshop, Fireworks, or whatever graphics program you prefer; choose File→Open; navigate to your website folder; find the graphic that needs touching up (if you can even remember its name); and then open it to make your changes.

Dreamweaver includes tools that handle many basic graphics-editing tasks. For more complex work, like changing the text on a button from "Now Firing" to "Now Hiring", you do need to switch to a different program. But even here, Dreamweaver is considerate of your time; it lets you access your favorite graphics program with just a couple of clicks.

Dreamweaver's Built-In Editing Tools

Dreamweaver includes four tools for cropping, resizing, sharpening, and adjusting the brightness and contrast of images (see Figure 6-15). Suppose your boss emails you his portrait with instructions to put it on his "Meet the boss" page. Unfortunately, it's too big and too dark. Rather than launch a separate image-editing program, you can simply add the photo to the page, and then make the corrections within Dreamweaver.

But first, a warning: All of Dreamweaver's tools change the *original* GIF, PNG, or JPEG image in your site folder. If you shrink a graphic and later change your mind, you may be out of luck. It's a good idea, therefore, to back up your images before you use these tools. In addition, if you add a Photoshop document and create a Smart Object (page 216), the tools discussed next break the link with the Photoshop file. That means that, for Smart Objects, you're better off editing the original Photoshop document as discussed on page 240. The reason? That retains the relationship between the image on your web page and Photoshop; if you edit the graphic in Photoshop at some point, Dreamweaver notifies you, and you can update the image on your site.

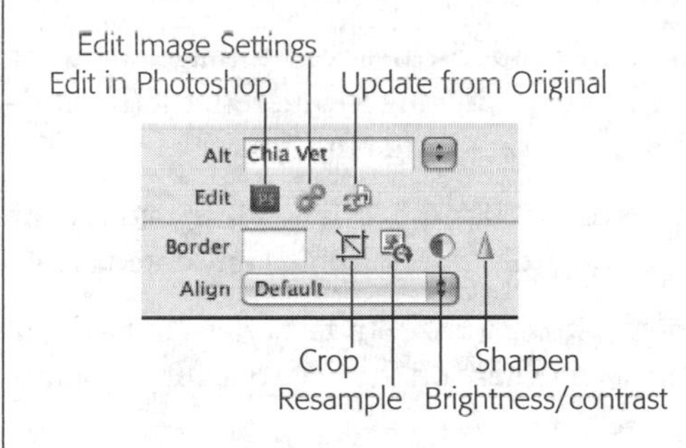

Figure 6-15: *The Property inspector includes tools for editing images directly inside Dreamweaver.*

Furthermore, remember that if you use that same file on other pages, your modifications appear on those pages, too. For instance, if you decide to shrink your company logo on one page, you may find the smaller logo on *every* page on your site! What's worse, the image's width and height settings don't change on the other pages, so the logo looks unnaturally pixelated on those pages. If you want to change a graphic on only one page, make a copy of it first, insert the *copy* in the page you wish to change, and then modify just that image file. That way, the rest of your site keeps the original graphic.

Of course, if you discover right away that you made a change you don't want, you can choose Edit→Undo or press Ctrl+Z (⌘-Z). Until you close the page, you can undo multiple image changes.

EASTER EGG HUNT

Meet the Geeks Behind Dreamweaver

Want to see pictures of the engineers behind Dreamweaver? OK, maybe you don't, but you *can*. Go to the Property inspector and select an image in the document window. On the left side of the Property inspector, Ctrl+double-click (or ⌘-double-click) the thumbnail of the graphic. A picture of one of Dreamweaver's programmers appears, along with his or her name. Ctrl (C) double-click the thumbnail repeatedly to cycle through the names and pictures of other members of the Dreamweaver team.

Cropping an image

Dreamweaver's Crop tool can remove extraneous or distracting parts of an image. You can use it to focus on a single person, or to get rid of those teenagers making faces in the corner.

To do so, select the graphic you want to crop, and then, on the Property inspector, click the Crop tool (see Figure 6-15). Alternatively, choose Modify→Image→Crop.

You'll see a rectangular box with eight handles appear inside the image; anything outside the box is cropped out. Move this box (by dragging it) and resize it (by dragging the handles) until you've got just what you want inside the box.

When you're done, double-click inside the box, or click the Property inspector's Crop tool again. Dreamweaver crops the image, discarding the graphic's unwanted areas.

To undo a crop you don't like, simply press Ctrl+Z (⌘-Z). In fact, you can back out before you've used the Crop tool at all; click anywhere on the page outside the image to make the cropping box go away.

Resampling an image

If a photo is just too big to fit on a web page, you could select the image and use one of the resize handles to alter its dimensions. Unfortunately, graphics you shrink this way give you the worst of both worlds: They look muddier than they were before, and they download slowly because you're still grabbing the larger image.

You can, however, use this resizing technique with Dreamweaver's Image Resample tool to resize the actual graphic. You'll end up with a trimmed-down file with its appearance intact.

To use the Resample tool, select an image and then resize it using the resize handles. (Shift-drag to prevent distortion.) When you're done, click the Resample button in the Property inspector (Figure 6-15). Dreamweaver resizes the image file.

You can even make an image *larger* than the original using this technique. The end result isn't perfect—even Dreamweaver can't create image information that was never there—but the program does its best to prevent the image from looking too pixelated. You don't want to enlarge images this way often, but in a pinch, it's a quick way to make a photo just a little bit larger.

Dreamweaver changes the actual graphic file, altering its width and height. If you change your mind about resampling the image, your only option is the old Undo command, Ctrl+Z (⌘-Z).

Brightness and contrast

If an image on a page is too light, dark, or washed out, you can use Dreamweaver's Brightness/Contrast dialog box to fix it.

First, select the picture, and then click the Brightness/Contrast icon in the Property inspector (Figure 6-15). In the Brightness/Contrast dialog box (Figure 6-16), move the Brightness slider to the right to lighten the image (great for underexposed interior shots), or to the left to darken the image. The Contrast control works in the same way: right to increase contrast (making dark colors darker and light colors lighter), left to decrease contrast (moving all colors toward gray).

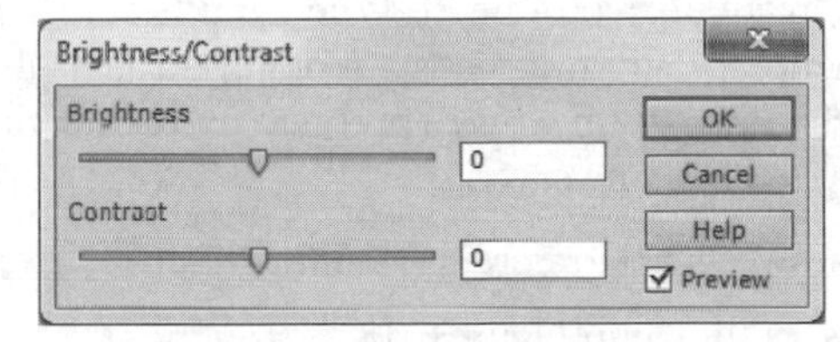

Figure 6-16:
If you've ever used image-editing software like Fireworks or Photoshop, this dialog box should look familiar. Make sure you have the Preview checkbox turned on so you can see your changes right in the document window before you click OK.

You'll often use the Brightness and Contrast sliders in conjunction. Brightening (lightening) an image also has a fading effect. By increasing the contrast at the same time, you restore some punch to a brightened image.

As with the other image-editing controls, if you're unhappy with the changes you made, choose Edit→Undo or press Ctrl+Z (⌘-Z) to return the image to its previous glory.

Sharpening images

Sometimes graphics, even those from some scanners and digital cameras, look a little fuzzy, especially if you resample the image (see previous page). Dreamweaver's Sharpen tool helps restore clarity and make such images "pop." It works like similar tools in graphics-editing programs: It increases the contrast between an image's pixels to create the illusion of sharper, more focused graphics. (Insert your own Sharper Image joke here.)

To use the tool, select a graphic, and then, on the Property inspector, click the Sharpen icon (Figure 6-15). The Sharpen window appears, as shown in Figure 6-17. Move the slider to the right to increase the amount of sharpening, or type a number in the box (10 is maximum sharpening; 0 is no change). You probably won't use the maximum setting unless you're going for a special effect, since it tends to highlight "noise" in the image, creating an unappealing halo effect around pixels. Once you select a level of sharpening you like, click OK.

If you're unhappy with the results, just press Ctrl+Z (⌘-Z), or choose Edit→ Undo.

Figure 6-17:
The Sharpen box can make fuzzy pictures "pop." Make sure you have the Preview checkbox turned on so you can see the effect on the image as you move the slider.

Setting Up an External Editor

When you double-click an image file in the Files panel, your favorite image-editing program launches and opens the file, ready for you to edit. When you first install Dreamweaver, it tries to figure out which program to use by looking through the software installed on your computer. But if you want to use a program other than the one Dreamweaver assigns, you need to tell Dreamweaver.

1. **Choose Edit→Preferences (Dreamweaver→Preferences on the Mac).**

   The Preferences dialog box opens, as shown in Figure 6-18.

2. **In the left pane, click File Types/Editors.**

   The Preferences box displays your preferred editing programs for different types of files. In the bottom half of the box, two columns appear: Extensions and Editors.

3. **From the Extensions list, select a graphic extension.**

   The box lists three types of graphic files: GIFs, JPEGs, and PNGs. You can choose a different editing program for each type of file if you like. You can add filename extensions for file types not shown by clicking the + button above the Extensions list.

4. **Click the + button above the Editors list.**

   The Select External Editor dialog box opens.

5. **On your hard drive, find the program you want to use to edit the selected type of graphics file.**

   It can be Photoshop, Photoshop Elements, Fireworks, or whatever.

6. **If you wish to make this program the primary program for editing this type of file, click Make Primary.**

   This *primary* editor is the one Dreamweaver opens when you choose to edit the graphic. (You can define other, less frequently used editors, as well. See the Tip at the end of this list.)

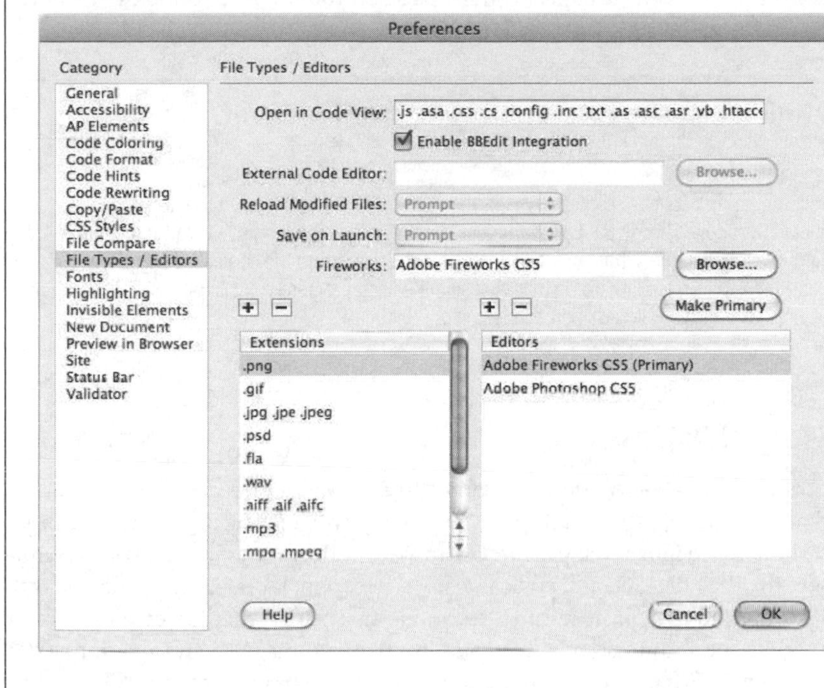

Figure 6-18: *You can tell Dreamweaver to use certain programs for editing different types of files, such as JPEG, GIF, or PNG files. If you have .fla (Flash files), .mp3 (music files), or other types of non-HTML files on your site, you can assign programs to those file types as well—double-clicking the file in the Files panel launches the associated editing program. The BBEdit integration box is just for Mac users, who might as well uncheck this box—you won't need this code editor since Dreamweaver has its own powerful text editor (see Chapter 11 for more on Dreamweaver's code-editing features).*

7. **Repeat steps 3–6 for each type of graphics file you work with.**

   Dreamweaver treats GIFs, JPEGs, and PNGs as separate file types, so you need to assign an editor to each. Of course, most people choose the same program for all three file types.

8. **Click OK to close the Preferences dialog box.**

   From now on, whenever you need to touch up a graphic on your web page, just select it, and then click Edit in the Property inspector (see Figure 6-7). Alternatively, in the Files panel, you can simply double-click the file, or Ctrl-double-click (⌘-double-click) the image on the page. In any case, your graphic now opens in the graphics program you set as your primary editor in step 6.

Note: If you insert a Photoshop image using either the Insert method (page 216) or the copy and paste method (page 222), clicking the Property inspector's Edit button launches Photoshop and opens the original PSD file—no matter what the image's file type.

Now you can edit the graphic and save changes to it. When you return to Dreamweaver, the modified image appears on the page. (If you're a Photoshop or Fireworks fan, you're in even better shape; read on.)

Tip: You aren't limited to just one external editor for each file type. For instance, if there's a Fireworks feature you need, even though Photoshop is your primary editor, you can still jump to Fireworks directly from Dreamweaver.

The trick is to right-click (Control-click) the image you want to edit, whether it's in the document window or the Site Files window. Choose the Edit With menu. If you added the other image editor to your preferences (Figure 6-18), then the submenu lists that editor. Otherwise, from the contextual menu, select Browse, and then, in the resulting dialog box, choose the editing program you want to use. That program opens, with the graphic you clicked open and ready for your edits.

Editing Smart Objects

Since Adobe makes the ubiquitous Photoshop as well as Dreamweaver, it makes sense that the two programs should work together. As you read on page 216, you can get a Photoshop image into a web page in Dreamweaver in two ways. First, you can simply insert the PSD file. Second, you can copy a selection, layer, slice, or entire image in Photoshop, and then paste it into Dreamweaver. The first method creates a Smart Object, while the second simply lets you optimize the image to create and insert a GIF, JPEG, or PNG file. In both cases, Dreamweaver keeps track of the PSD file, and gives you a way to return to and edit the original Photoshop image. However, the editing process is different for each method, as explained in the following pages.

Smart Objects really are a, well, smart idea. They let you preserve an original high-resolution Photoshop file as the main source of one or more web-ready graphics. Since producing web graphics often entails reducing a file's size, any edits you make to the image are best made to the highest quality version of that image. For example, if you want to change the font in your company's logo, don't edit the GIF or PNG file you used on a web page. Instead, edit the higher-quality PSD version of the logo in Photoshop. Smart Objects make this easy.

You can launch Photoshop, and then open the PSD file to work on it, or better yet, you can launch Photoshop directly from Dreamweaver—on the page, select the Smart Object, and then click the Property inspector's "Edit in Photoshop" button (see Figure 6-19). This opens the PSD file in Photoshop, where you can make the desired edits—modify the company logo, crop the image, use creative filters, and so on. When you're done, save and close the file.

Tip: You can also launch Photoshop to edit a Smart Object's original Photoshop document directly from the Files panel. Right-click (Control-click) the Smart Object–which is a GIF, PNG, or JPEG file in the Files panel–and then, from the contextual menu that appears, choose "Edit Original with Photoshop".

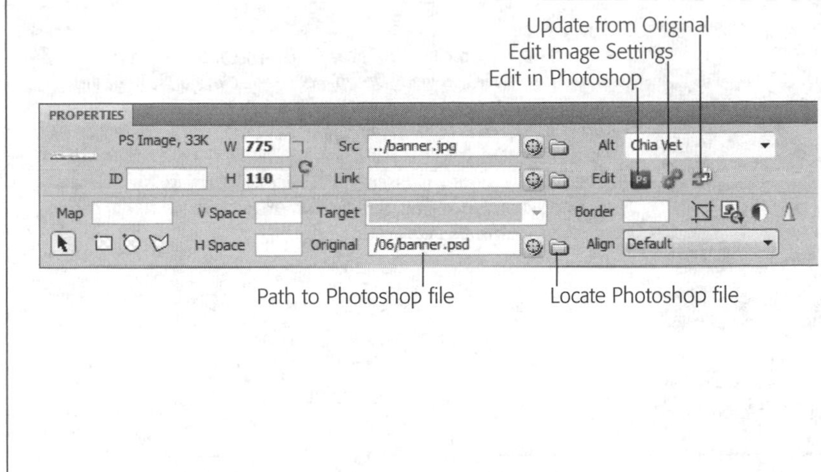

Figure 6-19: *When you use Smart Objects on a web page, the Property inspector includes an "Update from original" button, which lets you update an image whenever you change the image's original Photoshop source file. You can also revisit the original image settings–for example if you decide you want a PNG8 instead of a GIF image or if you want to change the compression settings–by clicking the Edit Image Settings button.*

Smart objects are "smart" because they keep track of any changes to the original PSD file. You can recognize a Smart Object by the recycling logo that appears in the upper-left of the image in Dreamweaver's Design view (see Figure 6-20). Immediately after you insert a Photoshop image, the two arrows in the icon are green, meaning that the image on the page is based on the latest version of the file (Figure 6-20, top). If you update the Photoshop document in Photoshop, the bottom arrow turns red (Figure 6-20, middle). This means someone modified the original Photoshop document. To sync the web page file with the original, select the image, and then click the Update From Original button in the Property inspector (see Figure 6-19). You can also right-click (Control-click) the image, and select Update From Original from the contextual menu.

When you update an image this way, Dreamweaver retains all the previous optimization settings—including the file format (JPEG, GIF, or PNG), cropping, resizing, and file name.

Smart Object warnings

Sometimes you see a warning symbol (a yellow triangle with an exclamation mark) as part of the Smart Object icon (see Figure 6-20, bottom). That means one of two things: either Dreamweaver can't locate the original PSD file, or you resized the inserted image in Dreamweaver—probably by dragging the resize handles as discussed on page 227.

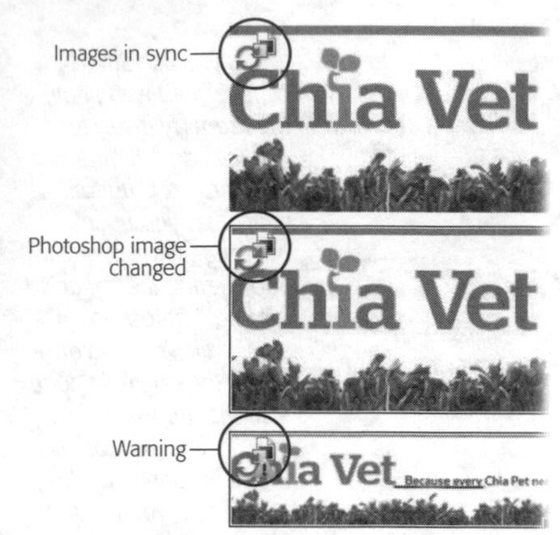

Figure 6-20:
A Smart Object is a GIF, PNG, or JPEG file you imported from Photoshop. In Design view, Dreamweaver displays an icon at the top-left of the image indicating that it's a Smart Object. If one of the arrows in the icon is red, the image doesn't match the Photoshop file. If the bottom arrow is red (middle), someone has changed the Photoshop file since you inserted it. Dreamweaver also displays a warning symbol (a yellow triangle with exclamation mark) in certain situations, described below.

If Dreamweaver loses track of a PSD file, simply select the Smart Object (you need to be in Design view), and then click the folder icon in the Property inspector (to the right of the Original box; see Figure 6-19). This opens the Select Original File window—just a basic "pick a file on your computer" dialog box. Navigate to the PSD file, and then select it. Unfortunately, once Dreamweaver loses track of the PSD file, it also loses all the optimization information, such as the file format, name of the web-ready file, and any cropping and optimization edits you made. You have to set all these options again, as described on page 218.

The second instance in which you can see the yellow warning symbol is when you resize an image in Dreamweaver. If you make the image on the page *smaller* than the original PSD file (for example, by dragging the resize handles, or by entering smaller width and height values in the Property inspector [see Figure 6-7]), click the Property inspector's "Update from Original" button (see Figure 6-19). Doing so re-exports the original image (using all your optimization settings) so that it matches the new size you set on the page. (This has no affect on the original PSD image; it always remains the same size and quality.)

However, if you resize the image on the page so that it's *larger* than the original PSD file, the yellow warning icon remains, no matter what. In this case, it indicates that the PSD file doesn't have enough pixels to make the image the size you want without affecting the image's quality. In other words, you can't make the images on your page larger than the Photoshop file they come from without getting a worse quality image.

Tip: If you resize a Smart Object on a page, you can return it to its original size (that is, the size of the image in the original Photoshop file). In Design view, right-click (Control-click) the Smart Object, and then, from the menu that appears, choose "Reset size to original". Unfortunately, you'll only find this option useful if you inserted the entire Photoshop image–if you cropped the image when you inserted it (see Figure 6-5) and then reset the image to its original size, Dreamweaver resizes the *cropped* image to the size of the original Photoshop document, distorting the web page image).

Editing Images Pasted from Photoshop

When you add an image from Photoshop using the copy-and-paste method (see page 222), Dreamweaver keeps track of the original Photoshop document. It lists the path to the original PSD file in the Property inspector (see Figure 6-19). Clicking the Property inspector's "Edit in Photoshop" button launches Photoshop and opens the original PSD file. At this point, you can make any edits you want to the image.

Unfortunately, Dreamweaver doesn't keep track of your *edits*. Getting an edited image back *into* Dreamweaver is a bit clunky. There's no "I'm done, export this image back to Dreamweaver" button; instead, you need to copy the revised image and paste it back into Dreamweaver. Copy the image (or portion of the image you wish to use) in Photoshop, and then return to Dreamweaver. Select the image you want to replace in Design view, and then choose Edit→Paste. Dreamweaver quickly replaces the old image with the new one. One nice thing: You don't have to revisit the Image Preview window (see Figure 6-4). Dreamweaver remembers your optimization settings—including the file name.

Tip: You may want to use different bits of one Photoshop document on a page. You might create a single-page mock-up that includes icons, photos, and graphical navigation buttons. Use the Photoshop Slice tool to identify each graphic element, and then use the Select Slice tool to select a slice. Choose Edit→Copy to copy just that slice.

Optimizing an Image

You can optimize an image—compress it so it downloads faster—by clicking the Optimize image button in the Property inspector. After clicking the button, the Image Preview window appears. This is the same window that appears when you import a Photoshop file (see Figure 6-4). Although the Optimize feature does leave you with a smaller image file, you should usually avoid it. That's because when you optimize a GIF, JPEG, or PNG image, you're compressing an already compressed file. Applying additional optimization degrades the image's quality.

In addition, you shouldn't convert a JPEG file into a GIF, or vice versa. The image almost always ends up looking worse. If you have a JPEG file that you think should be a GIF (see page 217 for some guidelines), or you simply want to see if you can shave a few more bytes from a file by optimizing it again, it's best to return to the original Photoshop, Fireworks, or Illustrator file, if available, and use that program's export or "Save for Web" feature to generate a new GIF, JPEG, or PNG file.

If you decide to ignore this warning (or you don't have the original image and really need to optimize the image further), follow the directions on page 219. Once you make your changes, click OK in the Preview Image window. Dreamweaver optimizes the image again. You can choose Edit→Undo to back out of the change.

Image Maps

As Chapter 5 makes clear, you can easily turn a graphic into a clickable link. You can also add *multiple* links to a single image.

Suppose your company has offices all over the country and you want to provide an easy way for visitors to locate the nearest one. One approach is to list all the state names and link them to separate pages for each state. But that's boring! Instead, you could use a map of the United States—a single image—and turn each state's outline into a hotspot linked to the appropriate page, listing all the offices in that state.

The array of invisible link buttons (called *hotspots*) responsible for this magic is called an *image map*. Image maps contain one or more hotspots, each leading somewhere else.

Here's how to create an image map:

1. **Select the graphic you wish to make into an image map.**

   The Property inspector displays that image's properties and, in the lower-left corner, the image map tools (see Figure 6-21, bottom). These tools appear in the lower half of the Property inspector, which you can see only if you have the Property inspector fully expanded, as described on page 28.

2. **In the Property inspector's Map field, type a name for the map.**

   The name should contain only letters and numbers, and can't begin with a number. If you don't give the map a name, Dreamweaver automatically assigns it the ingenious name *Map*. You don't really need to change the name; your visitors never see it, the browser uses it just to find it. If you create additional image maps, Dreamweaver calls them *Map2, Map3*, and so on.

3. **Select one of the image map tools.**

   Choose the rectangle, circle, or polygon tool, depending on the shape you have in mind for your hotspot. For instance, in the image in Figure 6-21, the polygon tool was used to draw each of the oddly shaped hots

---

Note: If you have the image accessibility preference setting turned on (page 226), then you get a window reminding you to add an Alt property to the hotspot you're about to draw. Each hotspot can have its own Alt description.

---

4. **Draw the hotspot.**

   To use the rectangle and circle tools, click directly on your picture; drag diagonally to form a rectangle or circle. To make a perfect square, press Shift while you drag the rectangle tool. (The circle tool always creates a perfect circle.)

   To draw an irregularly shaped hotspot using the polygon tool, click once to define one corner of the hotspot. Continue clicking until you define each corner of the hotspot. Dreamweaver automatically joins the corners to close the shape.

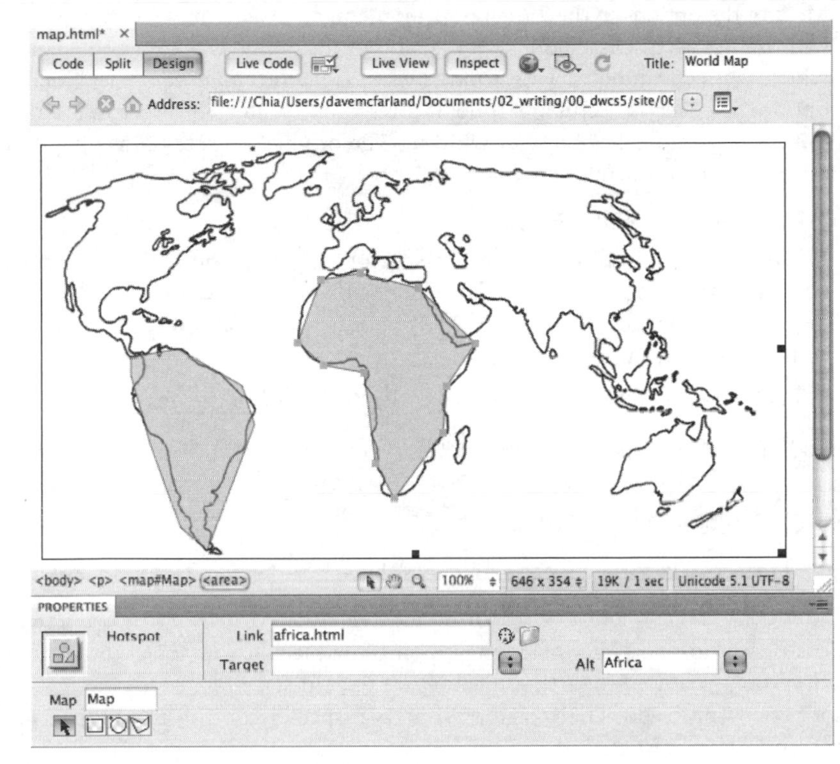

Figure 6-21: *Each link on an image map is called a hotspot. Shown here are hotspots around South America and Africa. When you select a hotspot, the Property inspector displays its Link, Target, and Alt properties. The lower half of the inspector displays the name of the map, as well as tools for selecting and drawing additional hotspots.*

Dreamweaver fills the inside of the hotspot with a light blue tint to make it easy to see (your visitors won't see the blue highlighting).

If you need to adjust the hotspot you just drew, click the arrow tool in the Property inspector. You can drag the light blue square handles to reshape or resize the hotspot, or drag inside it to move the whole thing. If you change your mind about the hotspot, press Delete to get rid of it.

Note: After you draw a hotspot, the drawing tool remains active so you can draw additional hotspots. To disengage it, click the arrow tool.

---

5. **Add a link to the hotspot.**

   After you draw a hotspot, that hotspot is selected; its properties appear in the Property inspector (see Figure 6-21). Use any of the techniques discussed on page 165 to link this hotspot to another web page or anchor.

6. **If necessary, set the Target property.**

   Most of the options in the Target pop-up menu are useful only when you work with frames, as discussed on page 172, and in the online chapter about frames, which you can find at *www.sawmac.com/missing/dw8/appc.pdf*. The "_blank" option, however, is useful any time: It forces your visitor's browser to load the linked page into a *new* browser window. The original page remains open, underneath the new window.

7. **Set the hotspot's Alt property.**

   By typing a label into the Property inspector's Alt box, you provide a written name for this portion of the graphic. As noted on page 224, *alt* tags are extremely important to people who surf the Web with graphics turned off, or who use text-to-speech reading software.

8. **Repeat steps 2–7 for each hotspot you wish to add to an image.**

   As you work, you can see the light blue hotspots filling in your image map.

Editing a Hotspot's Properties

As noted in step 4, you can change a hotspot's shape by dragging its tiny square handles. But you can also change its other properties—like which web page it links to.

To do so, click to select the image map. Using the black arrow tool—the hotspot selection tool— on the Property inspector's far left side (see Figure 6-21), click the hotspot you want to edit. Then use the Property inspector controls to edit the Link, Target, and Alt properties.

If you're having a fit of frustration, you can also press Delete or Backspace to delete the hotspot altogether.

Rollover Images

Rollover images are common interactive elements on the Web. People frequently use them for navigation buttons (see Figure 6-22), but you can use them anytime you wish to dramatically swap one image for another. Say you put a photo of a product you're selling on a web page. The photo links to a page that describes the product, and lets the visitor purchase it. To add emphasis to the image, you could add a rollover image so that when a visitor moves his mouse over the photo, *another* image—for example, the same image but with "Buy Now!" or "Learn more" printed across it—appears. You've almost certainly seen rollovers in action, where your mouse moves over a button on a web page and the image lights up, or glows, or turns into a frog.

Figure 6-22:
Rollover graphics appear frequently in navigation bars. Before your cursor touches a rollover button, like the Horoscopes link here (top), it just sits there blankly. But when your cursor arrives, the button changes appearance (bottom) to indicate that the graphic has a functional purpose–in this case, "I'm a link. Click me."

This simple change in appearance is a powerful way to inform visitors that the graphic is more than just a pretty picture—it's a button that actually does something. Rollovers usually announce that the image is a link. (Though you can use them for other creative effects, as described on page 607.)

Behind the scenes, you create a rollover by preparing *two different* graphics—a "before" version and an "after" version. One graphic appears when the web page first loads, and the other appears when your visitor mouses over the first. If the cursor then rolls away without clicking, the original image pops back into place.

You achieve this dynamic effect by using *JavaScript*, a programming language that lets you add interactivity to web pages. You saw JavaScript in action with the Spry Menu Bar (page 184). Aside from Spry objects, Dreamweaver includes many prewritten JavaScript programs, called *behaviors*, that let you add rollover images and other interactivity to your pages. (You can find more about behaviors in Chapter 14.)

To insert a rollover image, start by using a graphics program to prepare the "before" and "after" button images. Unless you're going for a bizarre distortion effect, both images should be exactly the same size. Store them somewhere in your website folder.

Then, in the document window, click the spot where you want to insert the rollover image. If you're building a navigation bar, you might place several images (the buttons) side by side.

Choose Insert→Image Objects→Rollover Image (or, on the Insert panel's Common category, click the Rollover Image button). Either way, the Insert Rollover Image dialog box appears (see Figure 6-23). Fill in the blanks like this:

- **Image name.** Type a name for the graphic. JavaScript requires *some* name for the rollover effect. If you leave this blank, Dreamweaver gives the image an unimaginative name—like Image2—when you insert a rollover. However, if you plan to later add additional interactive effects (Chapter 14), you may want to change it to something more descriptive, to make it easier to identify the graphic.

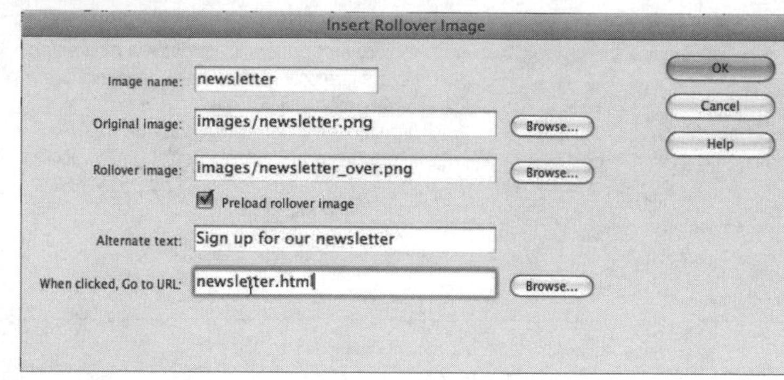

Figure 6-23: *This box lets you specify the name, link, and image files browsers should use for the rollover effect. "Preload rollover image" forces the browser to download the rollover image file along with the rest of the page, avoiding a delay when a guest mouses over the image for the first time.*

- **Original image.** When you click the top Browse button, a dialog box appears, prompting you to choose the graphic you want to use as the "before" button—the one that appears when the web page loads.
- **Rollover image.** When you click the second Browse button, Dreamweaver prompts you to choose the "after" graphic image—the one that appears when your visitor mouses over the first one.
- **Alternate text.** You can add a text description for a rollover button just as you can for any graphic, as described on page 224.
- **When clicked, go to URL.** Most web pages use rollover images as navigation elements that, when clicked, take the surfer to another page. In this box, you specify what happens when your visitor actually falls for the animated bait and *clicks* the rollover button. Click the Browse button to select a web page from your site (see page 165 if you're not sure how to set a link), or, if you wish to link to another website, type an absolute URL (see page 160) beginning with *http://*.

When you click OK, you return to your document window, where only the "before" button image appears. You can select and modify it just as you would any other image. In fact, it's just a regular image with a link and a Dreamweaver behavior attached.

You can see the rollover in action right from Dreamweaver. Click the Live View button near the top of the Document window—this turns on the embedded WebKit browser so you can actually see the JavaScript in action as it appears in a browser (or at least as it appears in Apple's Safari browser, which uses WebKit). When you're done, click the Live View button again to return to editing the page. To see how the rollover works in other browsers, press the F12 key (Option-F12 on a Mac) or use the File→"Preview in Browser" command.

You can achieve the same effect as the rollover behavior with a little more effort, using Dreamweaver's Swap Image behavior, discussed on page 607. In fact, this versatile behavior lets you create multiple, simultaneous image swaps where several images change at the same time.

Tutorial: Inserting and Formatting Graphics

In this tutorial, you'll learn how to insert a photo, add a rollover image, and apply CSS to improve the look of a web page. You'll also learn how to use background images to enhance the look of headlines.

Note: You'll need to download the tutorial files from *http://www.sawmac.com/dwCS5/* to complete this tutorial. See the note on page 45 for more details.

Setting Up

Once you download the tutorial files and open Dreamweaver, set up a new site as described on page 37. You should be pretty good at this routine by now, but here's a quick recap, as well as the introduction of another setting that's helpful when you work with images.

1. **Choose Site→New Site.**

   The Site Setup window appears.

2. **Click the Advanced button, and, for the Site Name, type *Images*. To the right of the "Local Site Folder" box, click the folder icon.**

   The Choose Local Root Folder window appears. This is just a window into your computer's file system; navigate to the proper folder just as you do when you work with other programs.

3. **Navigate to MM_DWCS5 folder, and then select Chapter06. Click the Select (Windows) or Choose (Mac) button to identify this folder as the local root folder.**

   The just completed steps are the only ones required to define the site; however, you'll find one other setting useful when working with images.

4. **Click the Advanced Settings option in the left-hand side of the window to reveal seven additional categories.**

   Most of the options here are related to Dreamweaver's site management tools, its Spry widgets, and the Contribute web editing program, but the options in the Local Info category are useful for links (see Figure 5-1) and inserting images.

5. **Select the Local Info category. To the right of the "Default Images folder" box, click the folder icon. Inside the Chapter06 folder, double-click the images folder. Click Select, and then, in the Site Setup window, click Save to complete the process of setting up the site.**

   By defining a default location for image files, certain operations, like dragging an image from the desktop or inserting a Photoshop image, go faster—Dreamweaver already knows where you want those images to go.

Adding an Image

Once again, you'll work on a page from the Chia Vet site.

1. **In the Files panel double-click the file named *about.html*.**

   If you need a refresher on the Files panel, see page 27 and Figure 1-4.

2. **Click directly after the letter "t" at the end of the "About Chia Vet" headline at the top of the page.**

   You'll add an image after the headline advertising the Chia Vet newsletter.

3. **Choose Insert→Image. Navigate to the *images* folder, and then double-click the file newsletter.png.**

   The Image Tag Accessibility Attributes window appears. (If it doesn't, that's OK, just fill out the Property inspector's Alt box with the text "Sign up for our newsletter", and skip the next step.)

4. **In the Alternate text box, type *Sign up for our newsletter*, and then click OK.**

   A small icon advertising the Chia Vet newsletter appears. A black outline and three black boxes (resize handles) indicate that the image is selected—if you don't see the boxes, click the image to select it.

   Next you'll link this image to the newsletter page.

5. **In the Property inspector, to the right of the Link box, click the folder icon. Click the Site Root button to make sure the Chapter06 (the local site) folder is selected and double-click the *newsletter.html* page.**

   If you need a recap on linking, check out page 165.

   You added a link to the graphic, which results in an ugly blue line around the image (you actually don't see this line until you deselect the image); in addition, the image is a bit too close to the headline. You can fix both problems with a little CSS.

6. **Make sure the CSS Styles panel is open (Window→CSS Styles); in the panel's bottom right, click the Create New Style button (the + button).**

   The New CSS Rule window appears. You'll create a class style to apply to the image, and store the CSS information in an already attached external style sheet.

7. **From the top menu, select Class; in the Selector Name box, type *.newsImage*; in the bottom menu, select *global.css*, and then click OK.**

   The CSS Rule Definition window appears. First, you'll get rid of the blue border.

8. **From the Rule Definition window, select the Border category, and then, from the Top style menu, choose "none".**

   This routine is the same as step 3 on page 197 . Next, you'll add a bit of space to the left of the image.

9. **Select the Box category. Under Margin, uncheck the "Same for all" box and then, in the Left margin box, type *50*. Click OK to complete the style.**

   Nothing happens, yet. You have to apply the class style.

10. **Click the image to select it. In the Property inspector, from the Class menu, choose *newsImage*.**

    The blue border disappears and the image moves 50 pixels to the right.

Inserting a Photoshop File

Dreamweaver makes it easy to insert and optimize files from Photoshop.

1. **Find the word *Vivamus* at the beginning of the first paragraph, and click just to the left of the letter *V*. Choose Insert→Image.**

   You can also use the Insert Image button in the Insert Panel's Common category (see Figure 6-2). Either way, the Select Image Source window appears. Now you'll select a PSD file.

2. **Click the Site Root button, and then double-click the *hippo.psd* file.**

   The Image Preview window appears. Dreamweaver suggests converting the PSD file to a JPEG image with a quality setting of 80%. Since this is a photo, JPEG is a good choice, but you can still squeeze a few precious bytes from the file by reducing the quality slightly.

3. **In the top left of the window, type *70* in the quality box.**

   The image is also a bit too big. You can make the web-ready version of the image smaller when you insert it (without affecting the original Photoshop file).

4. **In the top left of the window, click the File tab (circled in Figure 6-24). In the Scale percentage box, type *50*; click OK to optimize the image. Click the Save button to save the file as *hippo.jpg*.**

   Notice that when the Save Web Image window appears, Dreamweaver has the *images* folder selected—that's because of step 5 on page 249, where you specified the default images folder.

5. **In the Image Tag Accessibility Attributes window's Alternate Text box, type Chia Hippo, and then click OK.**

   A big photo appears on the page (see Figure 6-25). You'll notice the Smart Object logo in the top-left corner (circled in Figure 6-25), and three resize handles (black squares that appear on the bottom right corner, bottom edge, and right edge of the photo). The photo's still a bit large, but you can resize it in Dreamweaver.

6. **Hold down the Shift key, and drag the image's resize handle up and to the left until the image is about ¼ its original size.**

   If you don't see the resize handles, click the image to select it. The Shift key makes sure the image scales proportionally, which, in turn, ensures that you don't accidentally distort the image. The exact dimensions don't matter; just resize the image to a smaller size that you like.

   Now you see a yellow warning sign in the image's upper-left corner (see Figure 6-26). This means that the dimensions of the image no longer match the width and height specified in the HTML—by resizing the image, you change the HTML but not the actual image file. As mentioned in the box on page 227, this isn't a good idea—the image doesn't look as good and the file is larger than it needs to be (meaning it will download more slowly). Fortunately, because this is a Smart Object, you can easily recreate a JPEG file that matches the smaller dimensions you just specified while maintaining the image's original quality.

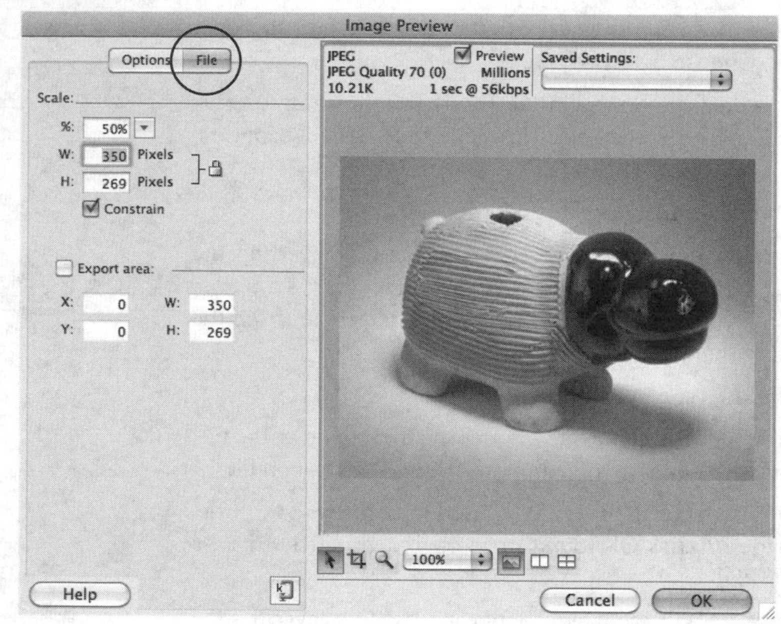

Figure 6-24: *When you import an image from Photoshop, you can generate a file that's much leaner, size-wise, than the original. The File tab of the Image Preview window lets you resize the imported image's physical dimensions, thereby creating a smaller file while leaving the original Photoshop file untouched. In addition, you can import a specific area of the image by checking the "Export area" box, and then specifying a width, height, and starting position for the portion of the image you wish to extract. Use the X box to specify how many pixels you want to exclude from the left edge of the image, and the Y box to specify the number of pixels to crop from the top. For example, if you type 100 in the X box and 50 in the Y, the exported image crops 100 pixels from the left side of the image, and 50 pixels from the top.*

7. **In the Property inspector, click the "Update from Original" button (circled in Figure 6-26).**

   Dreamweaver re-optimizes the image based on the Photoshop file. This means that, behind the scenes, Dreamweaver creates a new JPEG image—complete with all your original optimization settings (except, of course, the 50% size you set in step 4). Modifying an image using Smart Objects, aside from being very fast, is the best way to assure a high-quality web image.

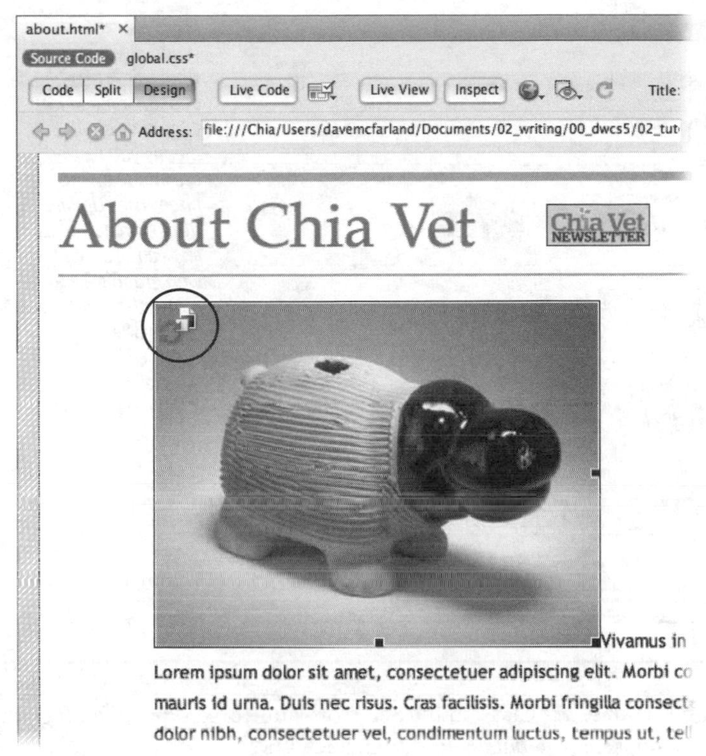

Figure 6-25: *An image positioned like this one is called an "inline" element in HTML—that means it sits right next to letters on a line of text. In other words, the image is sort of like a really, really tall letter. Unfortunately, that phenomenon usually leaves large areas of white space on the page.*

If you own Photoshop CS4 or CS5, launch it now (if you don't have Photoshop, just skip to the next paragraph); then, in the Chapter06 folder, open the *hippo.psd* file, and edit it—apply a filter, add some text, or whatever. Save the file, and then return to Dreamweaver. You'll see that a red "out-of-sync" arrow. Select the image, press the "Update from Original" button again, and Dreamweaver creates a new image from the edited PSD file. You'll now see the new, filter-enhanced, version of the image, without having to make a stop at the Image Preview window. Very cool.

You still have a few things to do with this image. For example, all the story's text appears below the image, leaving a large and unattractive white space to the image's right. To fix this, you'll create a style that moves the photo to the right side of the page and lets text wrap around it.

8. **In the CSS Styles panel, click the Create New Style button (the + button) in the panel's bottom right.**

   The New CSS Rule window appears. You'll create a class style to apply to the image, and store the CSS information into the already attached *global.css* style sheet.

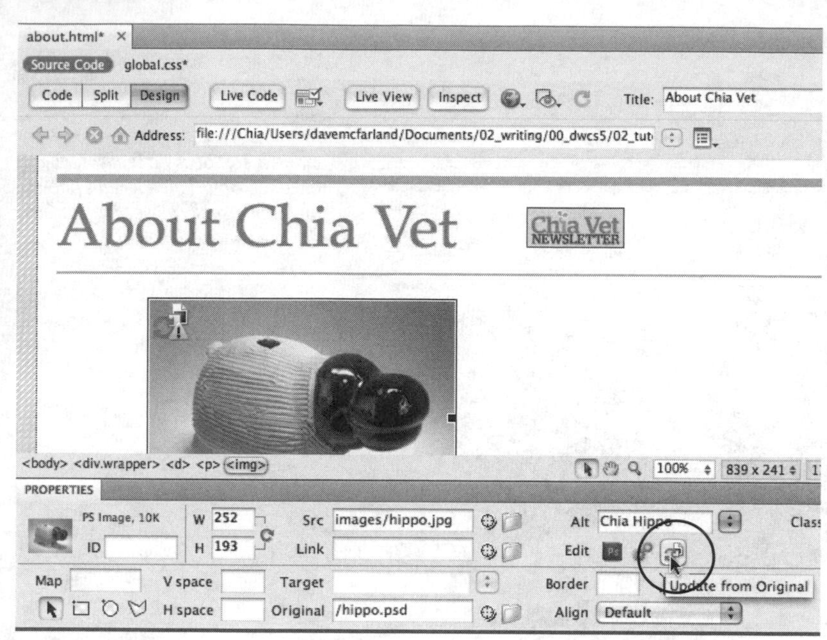

Figure 6-26: *When a warning icon (the yellow triangle) appears on a Smart Object, it usually means you resized the image on the page. The "Update from Original" button lets you recreate the web graphic file to match the dimensions you're after.*

From the top menu, select Class; in the Selector Name box, type *.photoRight*; in the bottom menu, select *global.css*, and then click OK.

Class names should be descriptive; in this case, photoRight is a good name to identify a style that aligns a photo to the right.

The CSS Rule Definition window appears. Time to add a decorative border.

9. **From the left-hand list of categories, Select Border; from the top Style menu, choose "solid"; in the Width box, type *2*; from the Color box, select "black" (or any color you like).**

   Leave all three "Same for all" checkboxes turned on to make sure a web browser draws the border around all four sides of the photo. Next, you'll add to the style to move the photo to the right and force the text to wrap around it.

10. **Click the Box category; from the Float menu, select "right"; uncheck the "Same for all" box for the Margin settings. In the Bottom margin box, type *10*; and in the Left margin box, type *15*. In the Top padding box, type *10*.**

    The window should look like Figure 6-27. Now it's time to finish and apply the style.

11. **Click OK to finish the style.**

    Because you just created a class style, its formatting power won't take affect until you apply it to the image.

12. **Select the photo on the page, and then, from the Property inspector's Class menu, choose *photoRight*.**

    The newly inserted image moves to the right, the text wraps around it, and a border appears (see Figure 6-28).

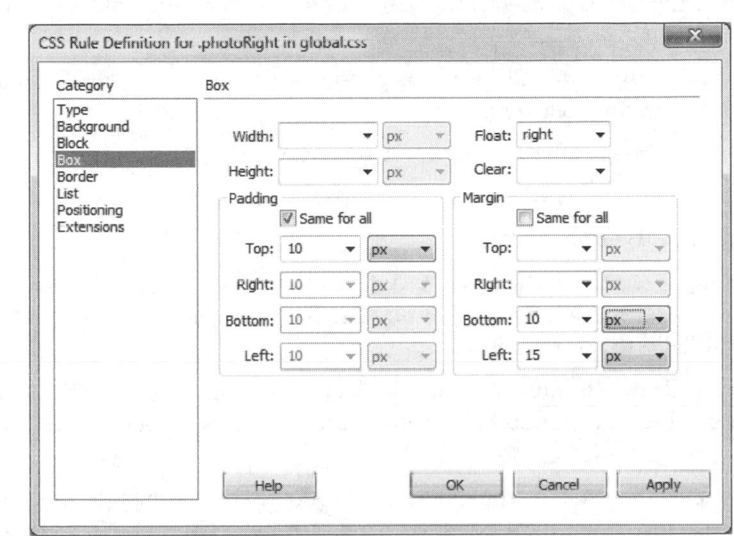

***Figure 6-27:** When you float an image to the right (or left), it's a good idea to add some margin to the side of the image around which text will wrap. This adds white space between the text and graphic, making the design feel less cramped and cluttered.*

***Figure 6-28:** A floated image, like the Chia Hippo here, adds a professional, magazine-like quality to a web page. Of course, it would probably look a lot more professional if it weren't a picture of a terra-cotta hippo.*

Inserting a Rollover Image

The Chia Vet Newsletter logo you added is intended to get visitors to sign up for the company's monthly newsletter. A rollover image would more effectively grab people's attention.

1. **At the top of the web page, select the Chia Vet newsletter icon. Hit Delete to remove the image.**

   Oh, your hard work is gone! Hey, it was good practice, and now you'll add a much more interesting rollover image.

2. **Choose Insert→Image Objects→Rollover Image.**

   The Insert Rollover Image window appears (see Figure 6-29).

3. **In the name box, type *newsletter*.**

   The name you give here won't appear anywhere on the page. It's just an internal name—a way for the JavaScript programming that triggers the image rollover to identify and "talk" to the graphic.

4. **Click the first Browse button, and then, in the images folder, double-click the *newsletter.png* file; click the second Browse button, and then double-click the *newsletter_over.png* file.**

   You just selected the two files you need for the rollover effect—the first appears when the page loads, and the second when a visitor moves her mouse over the image. For the rollover to work, you need to supply a link (and while you're at it, some alt text is a good idea, too).

5. **In the Alternate text box, type *Signup for our newsletter*; at the bottom of the window, click the Browse button; in the file selection window that appears, click the Site Root button, and then double-click the *newsletter.html* file.**

   The window should now look like Figure 6-29. Time to finish inserting the rollover image and apply the class style you created earlier.

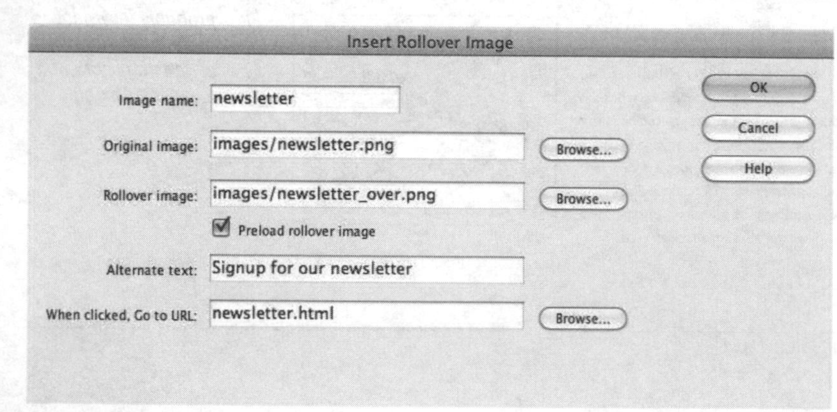

Figure 6-29: *In one window, you can set up everything you need to add dynamic rollover images to a page. Dreamweaver handles all the messy JavaScript programming that makes the whole thing work.*

6. **Click OK to insert the Rollover image. From the Property inspector's Class menu, choose "newsImage".**

   The image moves to the right about 50 pixels. Time to check out the rollover.

7. **At the top of the Document window, click the Live View button.**

   Move your mouse over the newsletter icon and see it change. Magic! When you're done having fun, click the Live View button again to return to editing the page.

Using Background Images

The HTML <img> tag isn't the only way to add an image to a web page. You can also use the CSS *background-image* property to give any HTML tag a graphical backdrop. You added a background image to the body of a web page in the first tutorial (page 52). In fact, this page already has a background image applied to it (the blue and white cross-hatched pattern). But you can add a background image to other HTML tags as well. Below, you'll add a background image to each of the second-level headings on the page.

1. **Make sure you have the CSS Styles panel open (Window→CSS Styles), with the All button at the top of the panel selected.**

   The All button lets you view all the styles attached to a page. In this case, you see one style sheet—*global.css*. You're going to edit an already existing style in that external style sheet file.

2. **If you can't see any styles listed under *global.css* in the Styles panel, click the + (flippy triangle on Mac) to the left of *global.css* to expand the list. Double-click the style named *h2*.**

   This tag style formats all Heading 2 headlines on the page. The CSS Rule Definition window opens.

3. **In the Rule Definition window, select the *Background* category; click the Browse button, navigate to the *images* folder, and then double-click the file *vet_logo.png*.**

   The image is a simple icon for the veterinary profession (of which Chia Vet is a member, of course). It should appear only once at the left side of the headline; because the normal behavior of a background image is to repeat indefinitely, you need to make sure the graphic appears only once.

4. **From the Background-repeat menu, choose "no-repeat".**

   Normally, a web browser puts a background image in the top-left corner of whatever the image is added to—for example, the top left corner of a web page or, in this case, the top left corner of the *h2* tag. For precise placement of the background image, you can specify both a horizontal and vertical position. You can use either pixels, percentages, or predefined placement options. Here, you want the image to appear on the far left, and centered vertically in the middle of the headline.

5. **Choose "left" from the "Background-position (X)" menu, and "center" from the "Background-position (Y)" menu.**

   The window should look like Figure 6-30.

6. **Click the Apply button to see the effect.**

   The Apply button lets you see how the style is shaping up. (If nothing happens when you press Apply, you may still be in Live View from step 7 on page 257, or one of the orange headlines isn't visible). That's OK, just read the following description of what the page should now look like. You'll see that the headline text overlaps the image. In addition, because the graphic is taller than the text, the top and bottom part of the image are clipped off. You can fix both these problems by adding a little padding.

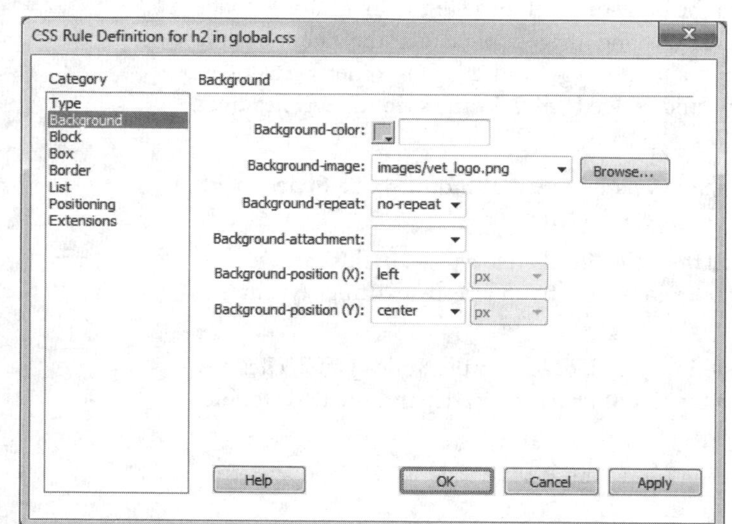

Figure 6-30: *Selecting "no-repeat" from the Repeat menu displays an image just once in the background instead of tiling it. The Horizontal and Vertical position options work well for single-image situations, since they let you accurately place that single image.*

7. **Click the Box category; under the Padding area, uncheck the "Same for All" box, type *10* in the Top box, type *0* in the right box, type *10* in the bottom box, and type *55* in the left box.**

   Padding is the space between the content inside a tag (like the text in the heading) and the outer edge of the tag (see Figure 9-11 for a visual of how this works). It lets you add space between a border and text; here, the padding makes room in the h2 header for the background image. (Padding settings don't affect background images.)

   Finally, you'll scoot the whole headline (including the background image) over just a little bit to the right.

8. **Type *20* in the left margin box, and then click OK to finish the style.**

   The margin property adds space around the edges of an element, and moves not just the text but also the borderline and background images as well.

9. **Hit F12 (Option-F12) to preview the page in a web browser.**

   Your finished design should look like Figure 6-31. You'll find a completed version of this tutorial in the Chapter06_finished folder that accompanies the downloaded tutorial files.

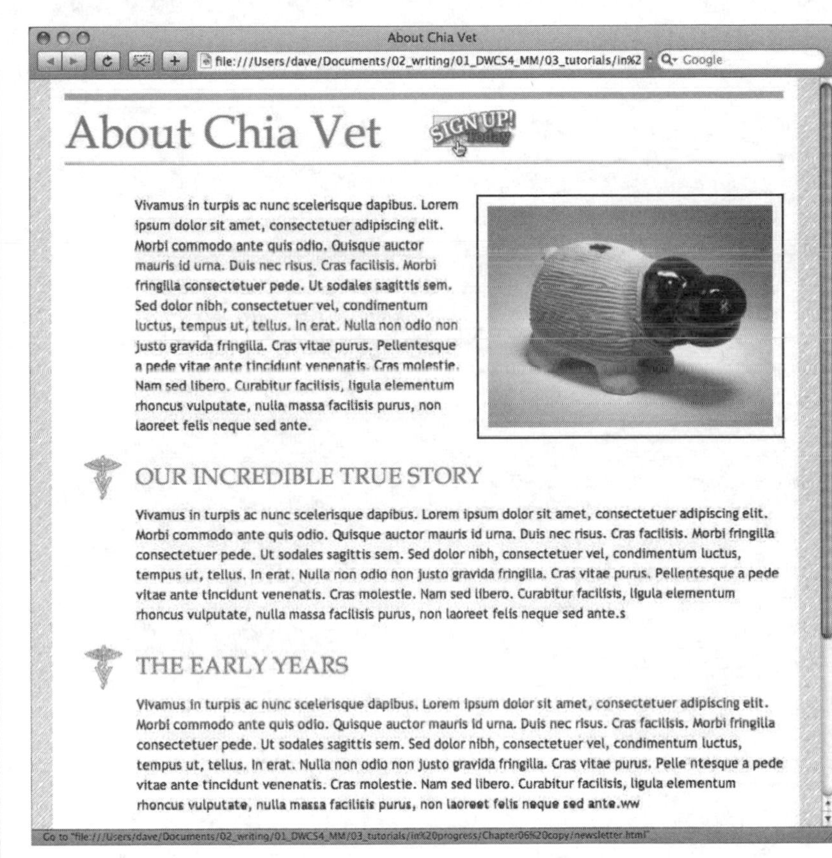

Figure 6-31: *Photos, icons, and other graphic elements add visual interest to any web page, while rollover images (the "Sign Up!" button at top) add interactivity and a sense of fun.*

CHAPTER

7

Tables

The HTML <table> tag has had a somewhat infamous existence in the world of web design. It was originally intended to present scientific data in a spreadsheet-like manner. But as the Web grew, graphic designers got into the web design game. They wanted to recreate the types of layouts seen in magazines, books, and newspapers (in other words, they wanted to make good-looking websites). The most reliable tool at the time was the <table> tag, which designers morphed into a way to create columns, sidebars, and, in general, precisely position elements on a page.

The wheel has turned again. Today, with nearly everyone on the planet using advanced browsers like Internet Explorer, Firefox, Safari, and Opera, web designers use a more facile page-styling technique—CSS-based layout. Table-based layout is an aging dinosaur that produces pages heavy with code (which means they download slower), are hard to update, and are hostile to alternative browsers such as screen readers, mobile phones, and text-only browsers.

This chapter shows you how to use tables for their intended purpose: displaying data and other information best presented in rows and columns (Figure 7-1). If you're a long-time web designer who still uses tables for page layout, you can use Dreamweaver and the instructions in this chapter to continue that technique. However, you're better off making the switch to CSS-based layout. Dreamweaver's advanced CSS tools and Dreamweaver CS5's new and improved CSS Layouts can make building these types of pages much simpler. You'll learn all about CSS layout in Chapter 10.

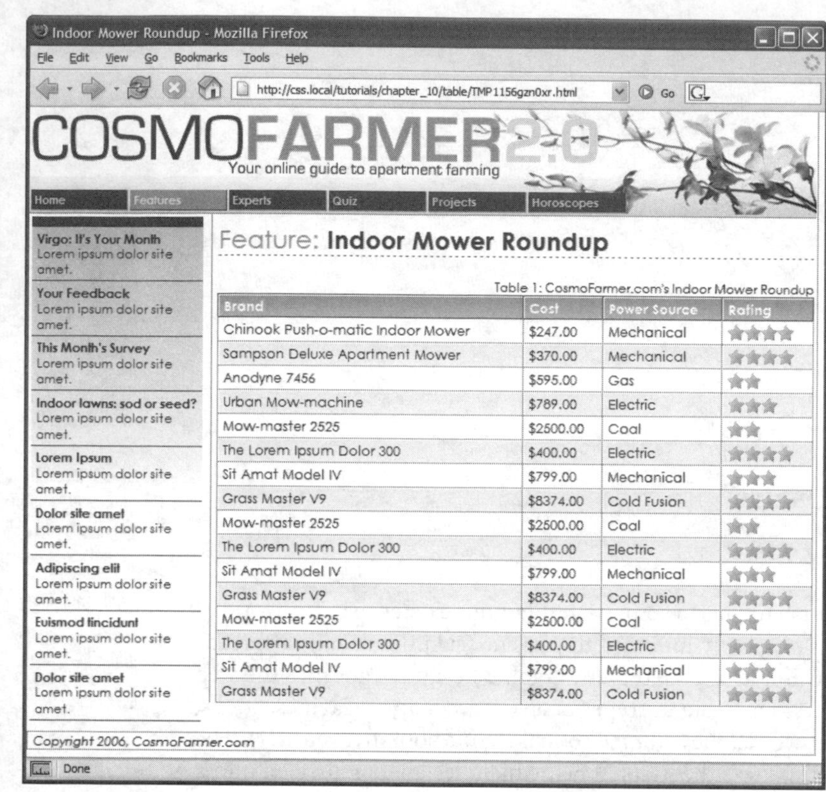

Figure 7-1: *You can do all your page layout and design with CSS, and use tables for their intended purpose—displaying rows and columns of information. The list of products in the center of this page is nestled inside a basic <table> tag, while the rest of the page is laid out using CSS.*

Table Basics

A table is a grid of rows and columns that intersect to form *cells*, as shown in Figure 7-2. If you've used a spreadsheet before, an HTML table should feel familiar.

A table row usually represents a collection of data for a single item. In Figure 7-1, for example, each row holds data for one brand of mower. A table column represents data of a particular type. The first column in Figure 7-1 contains the name of each mower, while the second column displays its cost. A table cell, then, holds one piece of data for a particular row, like the exact price of the Chinook Push-O-Matic Lawn Mower.

You create a table using three HTML tags. You set the boundaries of the table with the <table> tag. Then, within this structure, you create two types of cells, each with a different HTML tag.

You create a cell that contains data—$247.00, for instance—with the <td> or *table data* tag. Browsers align the text inside a <td> to the left edge of the cell.

A cell that identifies the type of information in a row or column is called a table header, and it uses a <th> or *table head* tag. Text inside a <th> tag appears centered and in boldface.

In Figure 7-1, all the cells in the table's top row are table headers, since they identify what type of data appears in the cells below: Brand, Cost, and so on.

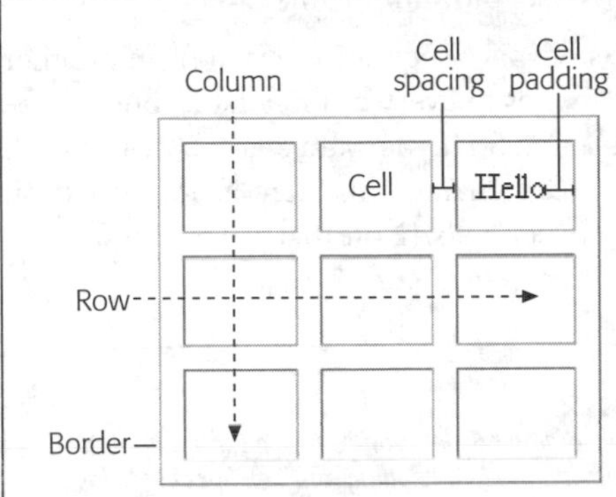

Figure 7-2: *Rows, columns, and cells make up a table. Cell spacing specifies how many pixels of space appear between cells. Cell padding, on the other hand, provides a space between the four sides of the cell and the cell's content.*

Inserting a Table

One of the main problems with HTML tables is that they require a lot of HTML code. Not only is this one reason why CSS is a better page layout method than HTML, it's also a good reason to use Dreamweaver to create a table. If you've ever hand-coded an HTML table, you know what a tangled mess of code it requires; one typo can sink your whole page. Fortunately, Dreamweaver makes creating HTML tables simple.

1. **In the document window, position your cursor where you want to insert a table.**

   You can add a table anywhere you can add a paragraph of text. You can even add a table inside *another* table, by clicking inside a table cell.

2. **Choose Insert ‣Table.**

   You can also click the Table button on the Insert panel. It appears under both the Common category and the Layout category. You can also press Ctrl+Alt+T (⌘-Option-T). Either way, the Table dialog box opens (see Figure 7-3).

3. **Using the Rows and Columns fields, specify how many rows and columns you want in your table.**

   Don't fret too much over your estimate, since you can always add or remove rows or columns later.

4. **Type the amount of cell padding, in pixels, you want for the table.**

   Cell padding is the margin inside the cell—the space from the edge of a cell to its contents (see Figure 7-2). Unfortunately, this property applies to *every* cell in a table (it also applies equally to all four sides of the cell). You can't specify cell padding for individual cells, nor can you pad cell margins uniquely in all four directions (you can't for example, specify10 pixels of space on the left side of the cell, but only 5 pixels at the top) unless you use the CSS *padding* property as described on page 341. People often either type 0 or leave this box empty, and then use the CSS *padding* property to control padding on individual table cells (via the <td> and <th> tags).

5. **Type the amount of cell spacing, in pixels, you want for the table.**

   Cell spacing specifies how many pixels of space separate one cell from another (see Figure 7-2). Again, this property applies to every cell in a table, but, unlike padding, there's no effective CSS equivalent. So if you want space between each cell, you should add a value here (you can change this later, as described on page 268). Type *0* to remove any space between cells. (Note that leaving these fields empty isn't the same as setting them to zero; see Figure 7-3.)

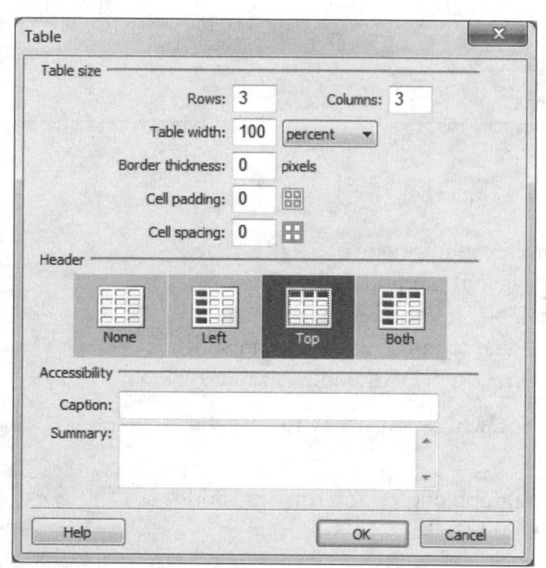

Figure 7-3:
The Table dialog box lets you control a table's appearance. Leaving the Cell Padding and Cell Spacing fields empty isn't the same as setting them to 0. If these properties are empty, most browsers insert 1 pixel of cell padding and 2 pixels of cell spacing. If you notice unwanted gaps between cells in a table, or between content in a table and the cell's edges, empty settings here are the likeliest culprit. To truly leave zero space, set Cell Padding and Cell Spacing to 0. (Dreamweaver remembers the settings you use. When you use the Insert Table dialog box again, it starts with the same settings you entered previously.)

6. **Using the "Table width" field, specify how wide you want the table to be (in units that you specify using the pop-up menu).**

   Tables can have either a specified, fixed minimum width, or they can take up a specified percentage of the space available on the page. To set a fixed width, choose Pixels as the unit of measure, and then, in the "Table width" field, type a pixel amount. Fixed-width tables remain the same size regardless of the browser window's size.

   Percentage-width tables grow or shrink relative to the space available. If you place a 100% wide table on a blank web page, the table stretches all the way across your visitor's browser window, no matter how wide or narrow he has it set. But the percentage isn't always based on the overall browser window width. If you place a table *inside* another object—either another table cell, or within a <div> tag—that has a set width, Dreamweaver calculates the percentage based on that object. Say you have a sidebar on a page, and the sidebar is 300 pixels wide; if you insert an 80% wide table inside the sidebar, then the table takes up 80 percent of 300 pixels, or 240 pixels.

Tip: Sometimes Internet Explorer 6 for Windows treats 100% as a little bigger than 100%. This confounding behavior can cause 100% wide tables in CSS layouts to not fit (usually forcing the table to jump down below most of the page design). Using a slightly smaller percentage, like 99% or 98%, usually fixes this glitch.

---

7. **In the "Border thickness" box, type a number, in pixels, for the border.**

   If you don't want a border, type *0*. Dreamweaver uses dotted lines in Design view to help you identify rows, columns, and cells whose border is 0. (The dotted lines won't appear on your finished page.) Again, CSS offers a much better way to add borders (see page 230).

8. **Using the buttons in the middle of the dialog box, select a Header option.**

   The Header property inserts the <th> tag to create the cells in the top row or left-hand column. <th> is a table header tag; it indicates that a cell is a *headline* for a column or row of data, which names the kind of content that appears in the cells below the column headline or to the right of the row headline. A table that displays a company's yearly sales figures, broken down by region, might have a top row of headers for each year ("2008," "2009," "2010"), while the left column would have table headers identifying each region ("Northwest," "West," "South," and so on).

   The only visible change you get with a <th> tag is that web browsers display the text in bold type and center-aligned. However, this option also makes the table more accessible by telling screen readers (used by the visually impaired) that the cell serves as a header for the information in the column. (You can always change the look of these cells using CSS; just create a style for the <th> tag, as described on page 113.)

9. **In the bottom section of the Table dialog box, add any Accessibility settings you wish to use.**

   In the Caption box, type information identifying the table; it appears, centered, above the table. Use the Summary box when you want to explain a particularly complex data table. This information doesn't show up in a browser window; it's intended to clarify the contents of a table to search engines and screen readers. Basic data tables (just simple rows and columns) don't need a summary; search engines and screen readers can understand them just fine. It's only when you create a complex table with merged cells (see page 279) and multiple levels of headers that you might want to fill out the summary box.

For more information on these options and to get a complete rundown on table accessibility, visit *www.w3.org/TR/WCAG10-HTML-TECHS/#tables*.

10. **Click OK to insert the table.**

    Once you add a table to a page, you can begin filling its cells. A cell works like a small document window; you can click inside it and add text, images, and links using the techniques you've already learned. You can even insert a table inside a cell (a common technique in the bad old days of table-based layout).

    To move the insertion point from one cell to the next, press Tab. When you reach the last cell in a row, the Tab key moves the insertion point to the first cell in the row below. And if the insertion point is in the last *cell* of the last row, pressing Tab creates a new row at the bottom of the table.

    Shift+Tab moves the cursor in the *opposite* direction—from the current cell to a cell to the left.

Selecting Parts of a Table

Tables and their cells have independent properties. For example, a table and a cell can have different alignment properties. But before you can change any of these properties, you must first *select* the tables, rows, columns, or cells you want to affect.

Selecting a Table

You can select a table in the document window a number of ways:

- Click the upper-left corner of the table, or anywhere on the bottom edge. (Be careful using the latter technique, however. It's easy to accidentally *drag* the border, adding a height property to the first table cell in the bottom row.)
- Click anywhere inside the table, and then select the <table> tag in the document window's status bar (see page 23 to learn about the Tag selector).
- Click anywhere inside the table, and then choose Modify→Table→Select Table.
- Right-click (Control-click) inside a table, and then, from the shortcut menu, choose Table→Select Table.
- If the insertion point is in any cell inside the table, pressing Ctrl+A (⌘-A) twice selects the table.

Once selected, a table appears with a thick black border and three tiny, square resize handles—at the right edge, bottom edge, and lower-right corner.

Selecting Rows or Columns

You can also select an entire row or column of cells by doing one of the following:

- Move your cursor to the left edge of a row or the top edge of a column. When it changes to a right- or down-pointing arrow, click, as explained in Figure 7-4.

- Click a cell at either end of a row, or the first or last cell of a column, and then drag across the cells in the row or column to select them.
- Click any cell in the row you wish to select, and then click the <tr> tag in the Tag selector (the <tr> tag is how HTML indicates a table row). This method doesn't work for columns.

When you select a cell, it has a dark border around it. When you select multiple cells, each has a dark border (see Figure 7-4).

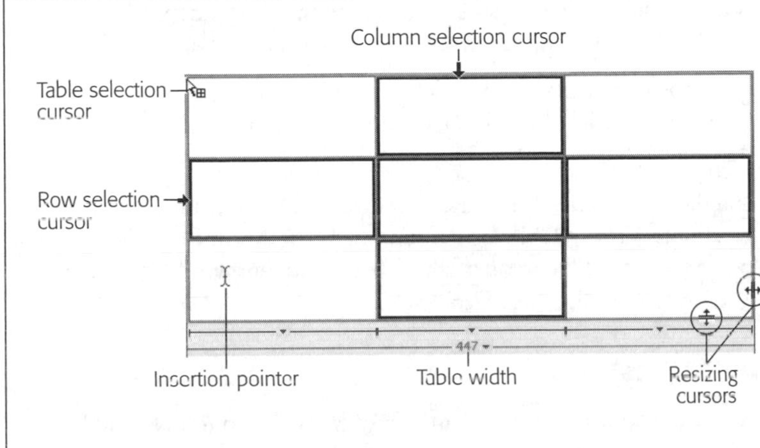

Figure 7-4: *When you work with tables, the cursor takes on many different roles. The Table selection cursor lets you select the entire table. When the cursor turns into an arrow (pointing either right or down), you can click to select a row or column of cells. The insertion-point cursor lets you click to insert content into a cell. When you pass the cursor over a resize handle, it becomes a resize icon, which you can drag to resize rows, columns, or the entire table.*

Selecting Cells

To select one or more cells:

- Drag over adjoining cells. A solid black border appears around a cell when you select it.
- To select several cells that aren't necessarily adjacent, Ctrl-click (⌘-click) them one at a time. (You can also Ctrl-click [⌘-click] an already selected cell to deselect it.)
- Click a cell, and then Shift-click another cell. Your two clicks form diagonally opposite corners of an imaginary rectangle; Dreamweaver highlights all cells within it.
- Use the Tag selector (see page 23) to select a cell. Click inside the cell you wish to select, and then click the <td> tag in the Tag selector. HTML identifies table cells with the <td>, or *table data,* tag.
- If the insertion point is inside the cell you want to select, press Ctrl+A (⌘-A).

Expanded Table Mode

If you remove all padding, cell spacing, and borders from a table, you may find it difficult to select tables and individual cells. This phenomenon is especially true if you nest tables within table cells (a common table-layout technique). To help you out, Dreamweaver offers an Expanded Table mode. Clicking the Expanded button on the Layout category of the Insert panel adds visible borders to every table and cell, and increases onscreen cell padding. (Choosing View→Table Mode→Expanded Tables does the same thing.) Expanded Table mode never changes the actual page code; it merely affects how the page looks in Design view. The guideline borders and extra spacing don't appear in a web browser.

If you simply use tables to display data, you'll probably never need Expanded Table mode, but if you have to edit old web pages built with complicated table layouts, Expanded mode is a big help.

To return to Standard view, click the Standard button on the Layout category of the Insert panel, or choose View→Table Mode→Standard Mode. You can also click the Exit link that appears in the blue toolbar above the document window (this toolbar appears only when you're in Expanded Table mode.)

Formatting Tables

When you first insert a table, you set the number of rows and columns, as well as the table's cell padding, cell spacing, width, and borders. You're not stuck, however, with the properties you first give the table; you can change any or all of these properties, and set a few additional ones, using the Property inspector.

When you select a table, the Property inspector changes to reflect that table's settings (see Figure 7-5). You can adjust the table by entering different values for width, rows, columns, and so on in the appropriate fields.

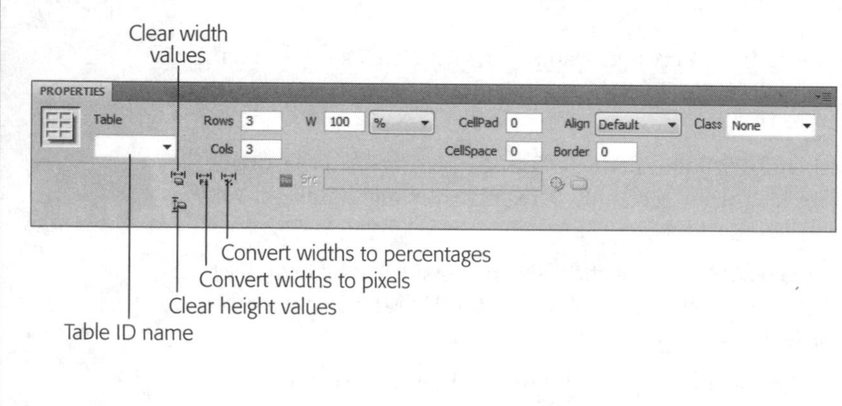

***Figure 7-5:** When you select a table, you can do everything in the Property inspector, from adjusting its basic structure to fine-tuning its appearance. Dreamweaver includes two menus–Table on the far left and Class on the far right–which let you apply a CSS ID selector or a class style (page 112) to a table.*

In addition, the Property inspector lets you set alignment options, and add colors or a background image, as described next.

Aligning Tables

In the normal flow of a web page, a table acts like a paragraph, header, or any other HTML block-level element. Browsers align it to the left of the page, with other elements placed either above or below it.

But you can make several useful changes to the way a table interacts with the text and other elements on a page. After selecting the table, use one of the three alignment options in the pop-up menu on the right of the Property inspector:

- The Left and Right options align the table with the left or right page margins. Anything you then add to the page—including paragraphs, images, or other tables—wraps around the right or left side of the table. You can also apply the CSS Float property to a table (just as with images) to achieve the same effect (see page 228).
- The Center option makes the table sit in the center of the page, interrupting the flow of the elements around it. Nothing wraps around the table.

Note: Some of the properties Dreamweaver lets you adjust to make tables look better aren't technically valid for some of the different HTML "document types" Dreamweaver creates. Dreamweaver can create HTML 4.01 Transitional, XHTML 1.0 Transitional, and several other types of HTML documents. In general, HTML 4.01 Transitional and XHTML 1.0 Transitional are commonly used document types–XHTML 1.0 Transitional is the "out of box" setting in Dreamweaver. However, the more "strict" types, like HTML 4.01 Strict and XHTML 1.0 Strict, don't support some table properties–the *align* property discussed above, is one of them.

This discrepancy is more a technicality than a design nuisance; most web browsers still display the alignment you select, even when you create HTML and XHTML Strict documents. The newer and recommended method is to use CSS properties to accomplish the same display goals; for example, using CSS to set the left and right margins of a table to "auto" centers the table on the page, while applying a CSS Left Float and Right Float property is the same as the Left and Right align options.

Clearing Height and Width Values

When creating complex table designs, it's easy to get yourself into a situation where width and height measurements conflict and produce unreliable results. For example, it's possible to set one cell to 300 pixels wide, and later set another cell *in the same column* to 400 pixels wide. Since a Web browser can't do both (how can one column be both 300 *and* 400 pixels wide?), you might not get the results you want.

In tables with many cells, these kinds of problems are tough to ferret out. That's when you'll find the following timesaving tools—located behind the obscure-looking buttons in the Property inspector's bottom half (see Figure 7-5)—handy. They let you delete the width and height measurements and start from scratch (see page 274).

- Clicking the Clear Height Values button removes the height properties of the table and each cell. Doing so doesn't set the heights to zero; it simply deletes the property altogether.
- Clicking the Clear Width Values button does the same thing with the width properties of a table and its cells (see page 274).

Two additional buttons let you convert pixel-based table widths to percentage measurements, and vice versa. In other words, if a table is 600 pixels wide and you click the "Convert Widths to Percentages" button, then Dreamweaver assigns percentages to the table and each cell whose width you specified using pixels.

These percentages depend on how much of the document window your table takes up when you click the button. If the document window is 1200 pixels wide, that 600-pixel-wide table changes to a 50 percent width. Because you'll rarely do this, don't waste your brain cells memorizing such tools.

Warning: Dreamweaver CS5 doesn't provide access to outdated table properties like *border color, background color*, and *background image* from the Property inspector. Instead, you should use the CSS equivalents: *border* (page 230), *background-image* (page 231), and *background-color* (page 231). You'll find examples of how to use CSS to add background images, colors, and borders to a table in the tutorial at the end of this chapter. In addition, you'll learn how to use the very valuable *border-collapse* property on page 293.

Resizing a Table

While you define the width of a table when you first insert it, you can always change the width later. To do so, select the table, and then take either of these steps:

- Type a value into the W (width) box on the Property inspector, and then choose a unit of measure, either pixels or percentages, from the pop-up menu.
- Drag one of the resize handles on the right edge. (Avoid the handle in the right corner of the table—this adds a *height* property to the first cell in the bottom row. If you do add a *height* property this way, you can easily remove it using the "Clear Height Values" button in the Property inspector—see Figure 7-5.)

In theory, you can also convert a table from a fixed unit of measurement, such as pixels, to the stretchy, percentage-style width setting—or vice versa—using the two "Convert Table Width" buttons at the bottom of the Property inspector (see Figure 7-5). What these buttons do depends on the size of the current document window in Dreamweaver. For example, suppose the document window is 700 pixels wide, and you inserted a table that's 100 percent wide. Clicking the "Convert Table Widths to Pixels" button sets the table's width to around 700 pixels (the exact value depends on the margins of the page). However, if your document window were 500 pixels wide, clicking the same button would produce a fixed-width table of around 500 pixels wide.

Note: The HTML <table> tag doesn't officially have a Height property. Dreamweaver, however, adds Height properties to table cells when you drag their top or bottom borders, but it won't add a height property to the table tag, which is a good thing, since it's invalid HTML. You could add it manually—<table height="500">—since most browsers understand the Height property and would obey your wishes. But since it's not standard code, there's no guarantee that newer browsers will support this maneuver.

You have several alternatives: First, you could decide not to worry about height. After all, it's difficult to control the height of a table precisely, especially if there's text in it. Since text sizes appear differently on different operating systems and browsers, the table may grow taller if your guest's text is larger, no matter where you set the height. Or you could use the CSS *height* property (page 360) to set a height for a table.

The "Convert Table Width to Percentages" buttons take the opposite tack. They set the width of a table and its cells to percentages based on the amount of the document window's width and height they cover at the moment. The bigger the current document window, the smaller the percentage.

Because the effects of these buttons depend on the document window's size, you'll find yourself rarely, if ever, using them.

Modifying Cell and Row Properties

Cells have their own properties, separate from the properties of the table itself. So do table *rows*—but not columns (see the box on page 273).

When you click inside a cell, the top half of the Property inspector displays the cell's text formatting properties; the bottom half shows the properties for the cell itself (see Figure 7-6).

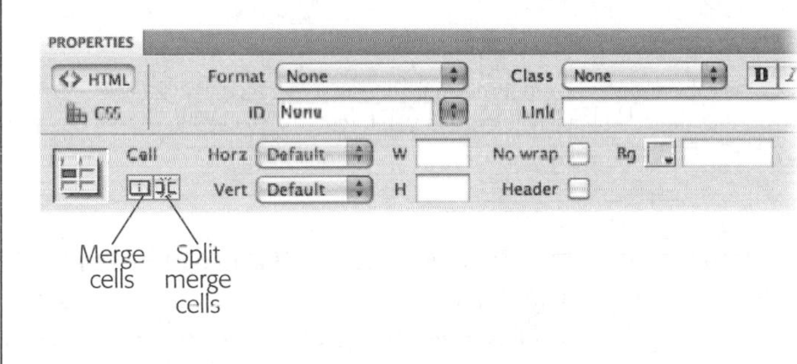

Figure 7-6: *The Property inspector displays the settings of a cell. If you select an entire row of cells, or select <tr> in the Tag selector, the background color property (listed as Bg on the Property inspector shown here) applies to the <tr> tag—to the whole row, in other words. But the Width, Height, No Wrap, or Header options affect the individual cells in the row only.*

Alignment Properties

At the outset, a cell's contents hug the left wall and float halfway between the top and bottom of the cell. After selecting a row, a cell, or several cells, you can change these alignments using the Property inspector. For example, the Horz (Horizontal) menu (see Figure 7-6) offers Left, Center, Right, and Default alignment options. (Default produces the same effect as Left without adding any extra HTML code.)

Note that these options are distinct from the *paragraph* alignment options discussed in Chapter 3. In fact, you can mix and match the two. Suppose you have a table cell containing four paragraphs. You want to center-align all but the last paragraph, which you want right-aligned. To do so, you could set the alignment of the *cell* to Center, and then select just the last paragraph and set its alignment to Right. The paragraph's alignment overrides the alignment applied by the cell.

You can set the vertical alignment property in the same manner. Select the cells, and then use one of the five options available in the Property inspector's Vert (Vertical) menu: Default (the same as Middle), Top, Middle, Bottom, or Baseline. The baseline option aligns the bottom of the first line of text in the cell to the baseline of text in all the other cells in the row—really only useful if the type in the different cells is different sizes and you're an extremely picky designer (which you might be, and that's OK.)

Note: The CSS *text-align* property (located in the Block category of the CSS Rule Definition window) provides the same effect as Horizontal cell alignment; the *vertical-align* property (in the Block category of the CSS Rule Definition window) is the CSS replacement for a cell's vertical alignment.

Table Header

The Table Header option lets you convert a <td> tag to a <th> tag, which is useful when you want to turn, say, the row at the top of a table into a header. It works just like the column or row header options available in the Table dialog box, described on page 265.

Note: You can also uncheck the Table Header box to turn a table header into a regular table cell. This is handy when you insert a table that shouldn't have headers, but you forgot to unselect the header option in the Table dialog box (see Figure 7-3).

You usually use this option for tables that include actual tabular data, like a spreadsheet, to indicate the meaning of the data that appears in the other cells in a row or column. For example, you may have a table containing data from different years; each cell in the top row could identify the year of the data in the cells below it.

While Dreamweaver lets you change a single cell into a header, you'll most likely apply this to the top row or left column of cells.

A Property to Forget

The No Wrap option is of such little value that you'll probably go your entire web career without using it.

But for the sake of thoroughness—and in case you actually find a use for it—here's a description. The No Wrap property prevents a web browser from wrapping a line of text within a cell onto multiple lines. The browser widens the cell instead, so that it accommodates the line without line breaks. The result is almost never useful or attractive. Furthermore, in some browsers, if you specify a width for the cell, the No Wrap option doesn't work at all!

POWER USERS' CLINIC

The Dawn of Columns

As far as the standard HTML language is concerned, there really isn't any such entity as a column. You create tables with the <table> tag, rows with the <tr> tag, and cells with the <td> tag—but there's no column tag. Dreamweaver calculates the columns based on the number of cells in a row. If there are seven rows in a table, each with four cells, the table has four columns. In other words, the number of cells in the rows determines the number of columns.

Two tags introduced in HTML 4—the <colgroup> and <col> tags—let you control various attributes of columns in a table. Unfortunately, Dreamweaver provides no easy way to add them. You can find out more about them, however, by checking out Dreamweaver's built-in HTML reference (see page 448).

Cell Decoration

Cells needn't be drab. As with tables, you can give individual cells background colors, or even background graphics. However, just as with tables, you should avoid the decorative table cell options available in the Property inspector. Instead, use CSS—the *background-color* property (page 231) to add a color to a cell, the *background-image* property (page 231) to add a graphic to the background of a cell, and the *border* property (page 230) to add color borders around cells.

FREQUENTLY ASKED QUESTION

Suddenly Jumbo Cells

When I added some text to a cell, it suddenly got much wider than the other cells in the row. What gives?

It isn't Dreamweaver's fault, it's how HTML works.

Web browsers (and Dreamweaver) display cells to match the content inside. For example, say you add a three-column table to a page. In the first cell of the first row, you type in two words, you leave the second cell empty, and add a 125-pixel wide image in the third cell of that row. Since the image is the biggest item, its cell is wider than the other two. The middle cell, with nothing in it, is given the least amount of space.

Usually, you don't want a web browser making these kinds of decisions. By specifying a width for a cell (page 274), you can force a browser to display a cell with the dimension you want. But keep in mind that there are exceptions to this rule; see "The contents take priority" on page 274.

Setting Cell Dimensions

Specifying the width or height of a particular cell is simple: Select one or more cells and then type a value in the Property inspector's W (width) or H (height) field. You can specify the value in either pixels or percentage. For instance, if you want a 50-pixel-wide cell, type in *50*. For a cell you want to take up 50 percent of the total table width, type in *50%*. Read the next section for details on the tricky business of controlling cell and table dimensions.

You can also resize a column or row of cells by dragging a cell border. As your cursor approaches the cell's border, it changes shape to indicate that you can begin dragging. Dreamweaver also provides an interactive display of cell widths (circled in Figure 7-7) when you use this method. This helpful feature lets you know the exact width of your cells at all times, so you can drag a cell to a precise width.

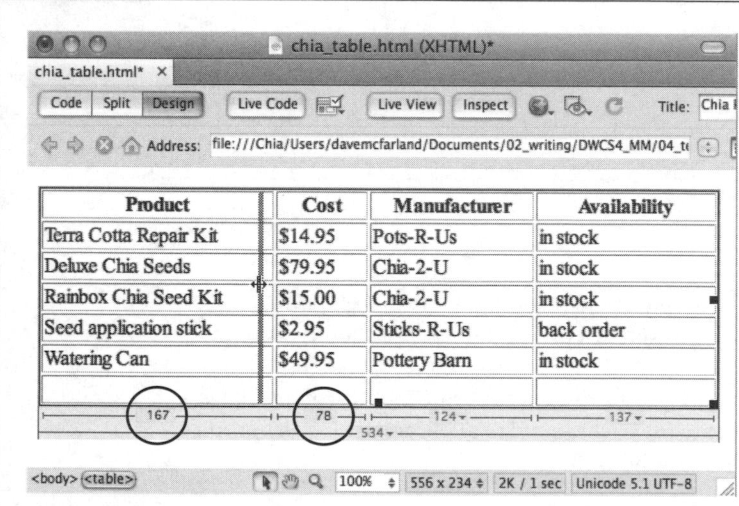

Figure 7-7: *As you drag the border between cells, Dreamweaver shows you the changing widths of the two adjacent cells in real time. The width values change to blue and update themselves as you move your mouse.*

Tips for Surviving Table-Making

Nothing is more confounding than trying to get your tables laid out exactly as you want them. Many beginning web designers throw their hands up in despair when working with tables, which often seem to have minds of their own. Here are a few problems that often confuse designers—and some ways that make working with them more straightforward.

The contents take priority

Say you create a 300-pixel-wide table and set each cell in the first row to 100 pixels wide. You insert a larger graphic into the first cell, and suddenly—kablooie! Even though you set each cell to 100 pixels wide, as shown in Figure 7-8, the column with the graphic is much wider than the other two.

That's because an individual cell can't be smaller than the largest piece of content inside it. In this case, although you told the cell to be 100 pixels wide, the image is 120 pixels wide, which forces the first column to grow (and the others to shrink) accordingly.

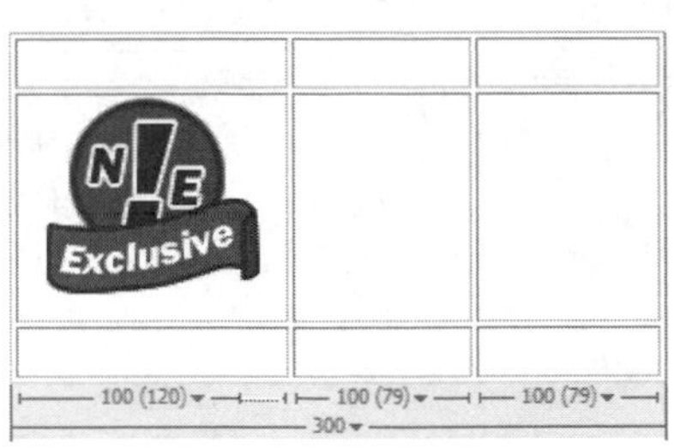

Figure 7-8:
Because a Web browser can't shrink the image or hide part of it, the cell has to grow to fit it. That first column of cells is now 120 pixels wide; the other two columns must shrink in order to keep the table 300 pixels wide. The numbers at the bottom of each cell indicate its width as set in the HTML–100–and the actual width as displayed in Dreamweaver in parentheses (120, 79, and 79).

There's no such thing as column width–only cell width

To set the width of a column of cells, you have to set the width of only *one* cell in that column. Say you have a table with three rows and three columns. You need to set only the width for the top row of cells; you can (and should) leave the cell widths for the remaining cells in the two bottom rows empty. In fact, that's what Dreamweaver does automatically—when you drag a vertical border between cells, Dreamweaver only modifies the Width property of the top cells.

This principle can save a lot of time and, because it reduces the amount of code on a web page, it makes your pages load (and therefore appear) faster. The same holds true for the height of a row. You need only to set the height of a single cell to define the height for its entire row. When you drag a horizontal border, Dreamweaver adds a height property to the first cell in the row above the border.

Do the math

Calculators are really useful when you build tables. Although you *could* create a 400-pixel-wide table with three 700-pixel-wide columns, the results you'd get on the screen could be unpredictable (after all, 700 + 700 + 700 does not equal 400).

As it turns out, web browsers' loyalty is to *table* width first, and then column widths. If the combined widths of your columns add up to the width of your table, you'll save yourself a lot of headaches.

Don't forget that you need to account for borders, cell padding, and cell spacing. For example, say you create a 500-pixel-wide table with two columns and 10 pixels of padding. If you want the first column 100 pixels wide, you'd set the width value to 80 pixels: 10 pixels of left padding + 80 pixels of cell space + 10 pixels of right padding = 100 pixels total width.

WORKAROUND WORKSHOP

Beware the Resize Handles

Dreamweaver provides several techniques for resizing tables and cells while in Design view. Unfortunately, the easiest method–dragging a cell or table border–is also the easiest to do by mistake. Because moving the cursor over any border turns it into the Resize tool, almost every Dreamweaver practitioner drags a border accidentally at least once, overwriting carefully calculated table and cell widths and heights.

In addition, if you grab either of the two bottom resize handles (they look like black squares) when you have a table selected, you'll set the table's height property. As mentioned in the box on page 271, it's actually invalid HTML to add a height attribute to the table tag.

On occasions like these, don't forget Dreamweaver's undo feature, Ctrl+Z (⌘-Z). And if all is lost, you can always clear the widths and heights of every cell in a table (using the Property inspector's buttons) and start over by typing in new cell dimensions (see Figure 7-5).

Adding and Removing Cells

Even after you insert a table into a web page, you can add and subtract rows and columns. The text or images in the columns move right or down to accommodate their new next-door neighbors.

Adding One Row or Column

To add a single row to the table, you can use any of these approaches:

- Click inside a cell. On the Insert panel's Layout category, click the Insert Row Above button (see Figure 7-9) to add a row above the current row. Click the Insert Row Below button to add a row below the current row.
- Click inside a cell. Choose Modify→Table→Insert Row, or press Ctrl+M (⌘-M), to insert a new row of cells above the current row. Alternatively, you can right-click (Control-click) a cell, and then, from the shortcut menu, choose Table→Insert Row.
- To add a new row at the end of a table, click inside the last cell in the table, and then press Tab.

The new rows inherit all the properties (except width) of the row you originally clicked.

To add a single *column* of cells:

- Click inside a cell. On the Insert bar's Layout tab, click the "Insert Column to the Left" button (see Figure 7-9) to add a column to the left of the current column. Click the "Insert Column to the Right" button to add a column to the right of the current column.
- Click inside a cell, and then choose Modify→Table→Insert Column.

- Click inside a cell, and then press Ctrl+Shift+A (⌘-Shift-A).
- Right-click (Control-click) a cell, and then, from the shortcut menu that appears, choose Table→Insert Column.

In each case, a new column appears to the left of the current column.

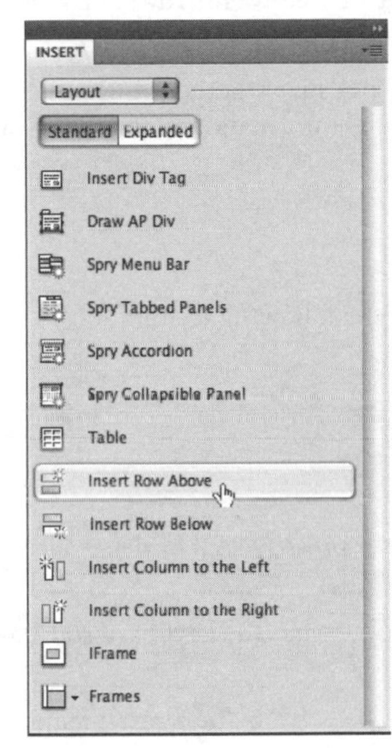

Figure 7-9:
Four buttons in the Layout category of the Insert panel make it easy to add columns and rows. They also make it easy to control where a new row or column goes—a feat not possible with a simple keyboard shortcut. On a side note, you'll find the IFrame button on the Insert panel less than helpful—it merely jumps to Code view and inserts the HTML <iframe> tag. You don't get a WYSIWYG display when you add iframes. (iframes let you embed an HTML page within another page. You can read up on this technology at http://www.cs.tut.fi/~jkorpela/html/iframe.html.*)*

Adding Multiple Rows or Columns

If you need to add a lot of cells to a table, you can use a special dialog box that lets you add many rows or columns at once.

1. **Click inside a cell. Choose Modify→Table→"Insert Rows or Columns".**

   The "Insert Rows or Columns" dialog box appears (see Figure 7-10).

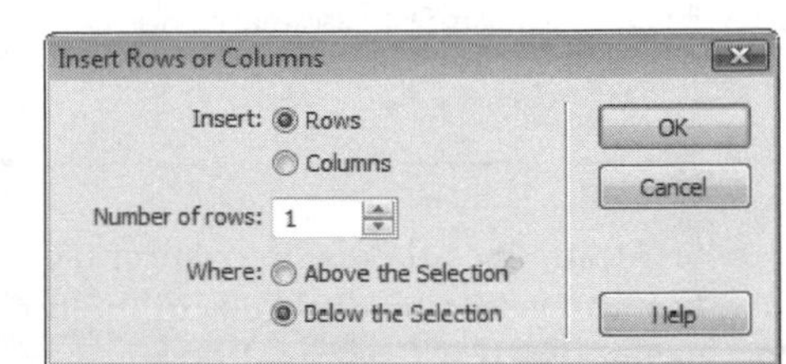

Figure 7-10:
The "Insert Rows or Columns" dialog box lets you add multiple rows or columns to a table. The wording of the options changes depending on whether you're inserting rows or columns.

2. **Click either Rows or Columns. Type the number of rows or columns you wish to add.**

   Windows users can also click the tiny up- and down-arrow buttons next to the "Number of rows" (or columns) field.

3. **Tell Dreamweaver where you want the new rows or columns to appear, relative to the cell you selected, by clicking Above or Below (for rows) or Before or After (for columns). Click OK to insert them.**

Using the dialog box gives you the advantage of choosing whether you want the new row or column to come *before* or *after* the selected information in your table, as shown in Figure 7-10.

Deleting Rows and Columns

To delete a row from your table, you can use one of the following techniques.

Tip: When you remove a row or column, Dreamweaver eliminates everything inside the cells. So before you start hacking away, it's a good idea to save a copy of the page.

- Select the row (see "Selecting Parts of a Table"); press Delete to delete all the cells—and everything in them—for the selected row.
- Click a cell. Choose Modify→Table→Delete Row, or use the keyboard shortcut Ctrl+Shift+M (⌘-Shift-M).
- Right-click (Control-click) inside a cell, and then, from the shortcut menu, choose Table→Delete Row.

Deleting a column is equally straightforward.

- Select the column ("Selecting Parts of a Table"), and then press Delete. You just eliminated all the selected cells and everything in them.
- Click a cell, and then choose Modify→Table→Delete Column, or use the keyboard shortcut Ctrl+Shift+Hyphen (⌘-Shift-Hyphen).
- Right-click (Control-click) inside a cell, and then choose Table→Delete Column from the shortcut menu.

Warning: Dreamweaver doesn't let you delete a row if you *merged* one of its cells with a cell in another row. Nor can you delete a column if it contains a cell merged with a cell in an adjacent *column*. (You'll learn about merged cells in the next section.)

Deleting a column like this is actually quite a feat. Since there's no column tag in HTML, Dreamweaver, behind the scenes, has to select individual cells in multiple rows—a task you wouldn't wish on your worst enemy if you had to do it by editing the raw HTML code.

Merging and Splitting Cells

Cells are very basic creatures with some severe limitations. For example, all the cells in a row share the same height. A cell can't be taller than the cell next to it, which can pose some serious design problems. In table-based design, designers solved this problem by combining multiple cells to form, for example, one wide banner area that spans three table columns.

Warning: If you're still using tables for page layout, be careful when merging cells; as a technique for managing a page layout, merged cells can be big trouble. For more information, go to *http://www.ap-ptools.com/rants/spans.php*. (P.S. You really don't have to use tables for layout anymore. Turn to Chapter 10 and learn how to use CSS for page layout.)

But even when your tables contain just data, there are times when you need to combine multiple cells. The table in Figure 7-11, for example, breaks down data for a single year—like 2006—into two demographic groups—men and women. Since the data in the two sets of "men" and "women" columns pertain to particular years, two table cells are merged to identify the first year, 2006, and two additional cells are merged for the year 2007. Dreamweaver provides several ways to persuade cells to work well together. The trick is to *merge* cells—combine their area—to create a larger cell that spans two or more rows or columns.

CosmoFarmer Subscriber Information by Year

Year	2006		2007	
Gender	Men	Women	Men	Women
Number	10,000	15,000	25,000	27,000
Average Age	39	34	33	30
Avg Yearly Income	$65K	$66K	$100K	$100K

Figure 7-11: *You can create cells that span multiple rows and columns by merging adjacent cells. This is one way to represent multiple related rows or columns of information with a single table header.*

To merge cells, start by selecting the cells you wish to merge, using any of the methods described in "Selecting Parts of a Table" on page 266. (You can only merge cells that form a rectangle or a square. You can't, for instance, select three cells in a column, and only one in the adjacent row, to create an L shape. Nor can you merge cells that aren't adjacent; in other words, you can't merge a cell in one corner of a table with a cell in the opposite corner.)

Then, on the Property inspector, click the Merge Cells button (Figure 7-12), or choose Modify→Table→Merge Cells. Dreamweaver joins the selected cells, forming a single new super cell.

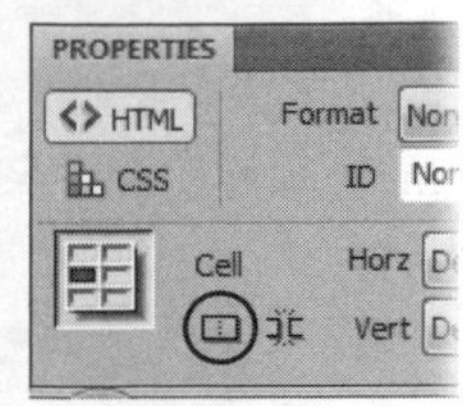

Figure 7-12:
The Merge Cells button is active only when you select multiple cells. The Split Cells button appears only when you select a single cell, or you've clicked inside a cell (see below for more on splitting cells).

Tip: Better yet, use this undocumented keyboard shortcut: the M key. Just select two or more cells, and then press M. It's much easier than the keyboard shortcut listed in the online help: Ctrl+Alt+M (⌘-Option-M).

You may also find yourself in the opposite situation: You have one cell that you want to *divide* into multiple cells. To split a cell, click, or select, a single cell. In the Property inspector, click the Split Cells button. (Once again, you can trigger this command in several ways. You can choose Modify→Table→Split Cell. And if you prefer keyboard shortcuts, you can press Ctrl+Alt+S [⌘-Option-S]. You can even right-click [Control-click] the selected cell, and then, from the shortcut menu, choose Table→Split Cell.)

When the Split Cell dialog box opens (Figure 7-13), click one of the buttons to indicate whether you want to split the cell into rows or columns. Then type the number of rows or columns you want to create; click OK.

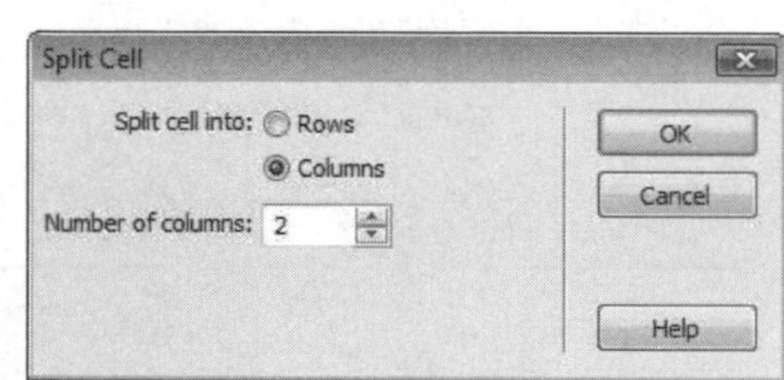

Figure 7-13:
The Split Cell dialog box lets you divide a single cell into multiple cells. You can choose whether to divide the cell into rows (multiple cells on top of one another) or columns (multiple cells side by side).

If you split a cell into columns, everything in the cell winds up in the left column, with the new, empty column or columns to the left. When you split a cell into rows, the current contents end up in the top row.

Tabular Data

Since tables are meant to display data, Dreamweaver provides useful tools to import and work with data.

Importing Data into a Table

Say your boss emails you your company's yearly sales information, which includes data on sales, profits, and expenses organized by quarter. She asks you to get this up on the Web for a board meeting she's having in half an hour.

This assignment could require a fair amount of work: building a table and then copying and pasting the correct information into each cell of the table, one at a time. Dreamweaver makes your task much easier, because you can create a table and import data into its rows and columns, all in one pass.

For this to work, the table data you want to display must begin life in a *delimited* format—a task that most spreadsheet programs, including Excel, or database programs, such as Access or FileMaker Pro, can do easily. (In most programs, you can do this by choosing File→ Export or File→Save As; then choose a tab-delimited or comma-separated text file format.)

Note: Windows users don't need to create a delimited format file if they have data in an Excel file. You can directly import Excel files into Dreamweaver for Windows, which converts the data into a well-organized table. See page 84 for details.

In a delimited file, each line of text represents one table row. That line is divided into discrete pieces of information using a special character called a delimiter—most often a tab, but possibly a comma or colon. Each discrete unit represents a single cell in the row. In a colon-delimited file, for example, Dreamweaver would convert the line *Sales:$1,000,000:$2,000,000:$567,000:$12,500* into a row of five cells, with the first cell containing the word *Sales*.

Once you save your boss's spreadsheet as a delimited file, you're ready to import it into a Dreamweaver table:

1. **Choose File→Import→Tabular Data.**

   The Import Tabular Data dialog box appears (Figure 7-14).

2. **Click Browse. In the Insert Tabular Data dialog box, find and select the delimited text file you want to import.**

   The delimited file is no longer a spreadsheet, but a plain text file. Navigate to and double-click the file in the dialog box.

3. **From the pop-up menu, select the delimiter used to separate the data in the text file.**

   The choices are Tab, Comma, Colon, Semicolon, or Other. If you select Other, an additional field appears, where you can type the character used as the delimiter.

4. **Select a table width.**

   Choose "Fit to data" if you want the table to fit itself to the information you're importing—an excellent idea when you aren't completely sure how much information the file contains. (You can always modify the table, if necessary, after you import the data.)

On the other hand, if your web page needs a table of a certain size, you can specify it by selecting the Set button, and then typing a value in the field next to it. Select pixel or percentage value (see page 264).

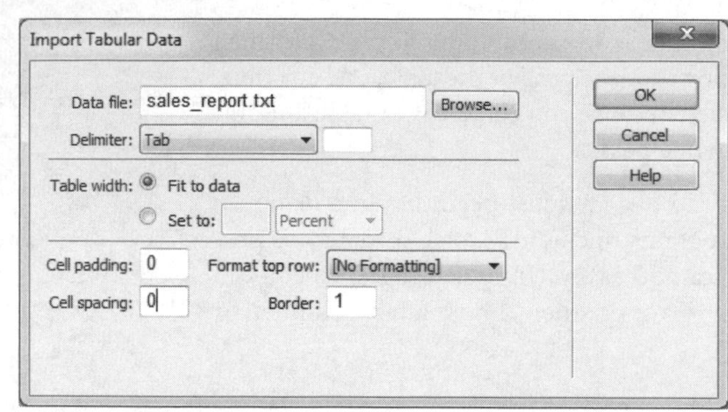

Figure 7-14: *The Import Tabular Data dialog box lets you select a text file of data to import and choose formatting options for the table.*

5. **Set values for "Cell padding", "Cell spacing", and "Border", if you like.**

   See page 263 for details.

6. **Select a formatting option for the top row of data.**

   If the first line in the text file has column headings—Quarter 1 Sales, Quarter 2 Sales, and so on—Dreamweaver lets you choose Bold, Italic, or Bold Italic to set this row apart from the rest of the table. Unfortunately, this option doesn't turn the cells in the first row into table header (<th>) tags, which is what they should be. It's best to choose no formatting, manually select the cells, and then turn them into table header (<th>) tags as described on page 272.

7. **Click OK to import the data and create the table.**

   Dreamweaver adds the table to your web page. It's a regular HTML table at this point and you can edit the contents as you normally would, or modify the table (add rows and columns, for example) using any of the techniques discussed in this chapter.

Sorting Data in a Table

If you have a table that lists employee names, you probably want to present that list in alphabetical order—or alphabetically *and* by department. Dreamweaver's Sort Table command takes a lot of the drudgery out of this task.

1. **Select the table you want to sort.**

   See "Selecting Parts of a Table" for some table-selection techniques.

2. **Choose Commands→Sort Table.**

   The Sort Table dialog box appears (Figure 7-15).

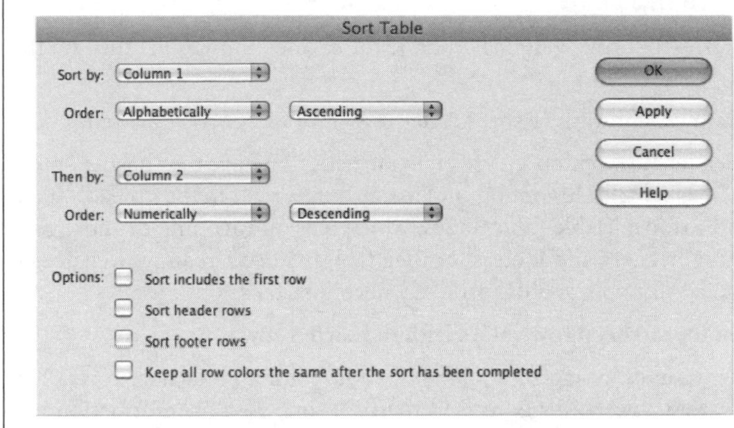

Figure 7-15:
The Sort Table command works well with Dreamweaver's Import Tabular Data feature. Imagine you get a text file listing all your company's employees. You import the data into a table, but realize that the names aren't in any particular order.

3. **Using the "Sort by" pop-up menu, choose the column by which you want to sort.**

   You can choose any column in the table. Suppose you have a table listing a bunch of products. Each row has the product name, number, and price. To see the products listed from least to most expensive, sort by the column with the product prices.

Note: The Spry Data Set tools let you create a table that your website guests can sort *interactively*. You can read about this cool tool on page 544.

---

4. **Use the next two pop-up menus to specify how you want Dreamweaver to sort the data.**

   You can sort it alphabetically or numerically. To order the product list in the example above by price, choose Numerically from the Order pop-up menu. If you're sorting a Name column, choose Alphabetically.

   Use the second pop-up menu to specify whether you want an Ascending (A–Z, 1–100) or Descending (Z–A, 100–1) sort.

5. **If you like, choose an additional column to sort by, using the "Then by" pop-up menu.**

   This secondary sort can come in handy when several cells in the *first* sorting column have the same value. If several items in your product list are priced at $100, a sort by price would place them consecutively in the table; you could then specify a secondary sort that would place the products in alphabetical order within each price group. Doing so lists all the products from least to most expensive, *and* lists all same-priced products alphabetically within their group.

6. **If the first row of the table contains data you want to sort, turn on "Sort includes the first row".**

   If, however, the first row contains *headings* for each column, don't turn on this box.

7. **Choose whether you want to sort header rows and footer rows as well.**

   The Sort Header Row option isn't referring to cells that have the "header" property set (see page 272). This option, and the next one, refer to the <thead> (table header) and <tfoot> (table footer) tags, which let you turn one or more rows into repeating headers and footers for long tables. Since Dreamweaver doesn't insert these tags for you, you'll most likely never use these options.

8. **Choose whether to keep row colors with the sorted row.**

   One way to visually organize a table is to add color to alternate rows. This every-other-row pattern helps readers focus on one row of information at a time. However, if you sort a table formatted this way, you'd wind up with some crazy pattern of colored and uncolored rows. The bottom line: If you've applied colors to your rows, and you want to keep those colors in the same order, leave this checkbox turned off.

   Dreamweaver is even in step with current web design practices, which don't assign a background color to table rows by using the outmoded *bgcolor* HTML property, but instead use CSS. A common approach to coloring table rows is to apply a CSS class style to every *other* row in a table. That class style might have the *background-color* property set so that alternating rows are colored. When you use the Sort Table command, Dreamweaver keeps the class names in the proper order. That is, it keeps the classes applied to every other row, even when you reorganize the data with the Sort Table command. This only works if you *don't* check the "Keep all row colors the same" checkbox—so don't check it!

9. **Click Apply to see the effect of the sort without closing the dialog box.**

   If the table meets with your satisfaction, click OK to sort the table and return to the document window. (Clicking Cancel, however, doesn't undo the sort. If you want to return the table to its previous sort order, choose Edit→Undo Sort Table after closing the sort window.)

Exporting Table Data

Getting data out of a table in Dreamweaver is simple. Just select the table, and then choose File→Export→Table. In the Export Table dialog box that appears, select the type of delimiter (Tab, Comma, Space, Colon, Semicolon, or Other) and the destination computer's operating system (Mac, Windows, or Unix), and then click OK. Give the file a name and save it on your computer. You can then import this delimited file into your spreadsheet or database program.

Tables Tutorial

In this tutorial, you'll create a data table containing product information. In addition, you'll use some Cascading Style Sheet magic to make the table look great (see Figure 7-25).

Note: You'll need to download files from *www.sawmac.com/dwCS5/* to complete this tutorial. See the Note on page 45 for more details.

Once you download the tutorial files and open Dreamweaver, set up a new site as described on page 37: Name the site *Tables*, and select the Chapter07 folder (inside the MM_DWCS5 folder). (In a nutshell: choose Site→New Site. In the Site Setup window, type *Tables* into the Site Name field, click the folder icon next to the Local Site Folder field, navigate to and select the Chapter07 folder, and then click Choose or Select. Finally, click OK.)

Adding a Table and Data

Once again, you'll be working on a page for the good people who run *Chia Vet*.

1. **Choose File→Open.**

   You'll work on a page similar to the ones you've built so far.

2. **Navigate to the Chapter07 folder and double-click the file named *recommend.html*. Click in the empty space, below the orange line, beneath the text "Quality products that we use ourselves".**

   You'll insert a table into this space.

3. **Choose Insert→Table.**

   You can also click the table button on the Insert panel's Common category. Either way, the Table window appears (see Figure 7-16). You need to define the table's basic characteristics.

4. **Type *3* in the Rows box and type *3* in the Columns box.**

   You'll start with a basic 3 x 3 table, but as the tutorial progresses, you'll add rows and columns. Time to set the width, spacing, and padding properties.

5. **In the Table width box, delete any value that's there and leave it blank. Type *0* in the "Border thickness", "Cell padding", and "Cell spacing" boxes.**

   Setting no width for the table will make it only as big as the content inside it. That's OK for now, since you'll use CSS later in the tutorial to apply an appropriate width. Setting the other three properties here to 0 is common. You have greater control of borders and cell padding using CSS.

6. **In the window's Header section, select the "Top" option.**

   The header setting indicates which cells Dreamweaver will mark as "table headers"—these cells contain labels that describe the kind of information in the column cells below (when you select "Top"), or the kind of information in the cells of a row (when you select "Left"). Now that you've picked "Top", the top row of cells will hold labels like "Product," "Cost," and "Manufacturer."

   You can skip the caption. It's not a requirement and the page's title makes clear what the table is all about. The window should now look like Figure 7-16.

7. **Click OK.**

   A new table appears on the page. Next, you'll add some headers to the table

8. **Click the first cell in the top-left corner of the table, and type *Product*.**

   The word appears bold and centered in the cell. That's how table header cells normally appear. You'll be able to change that look in a moment. Now add two more labels.

9. **Press Tab to jump to the next cell to the right, and type *Cost*. Press Tab again, and type *Manufacturer*.**

   Now it's time to add some actual data.

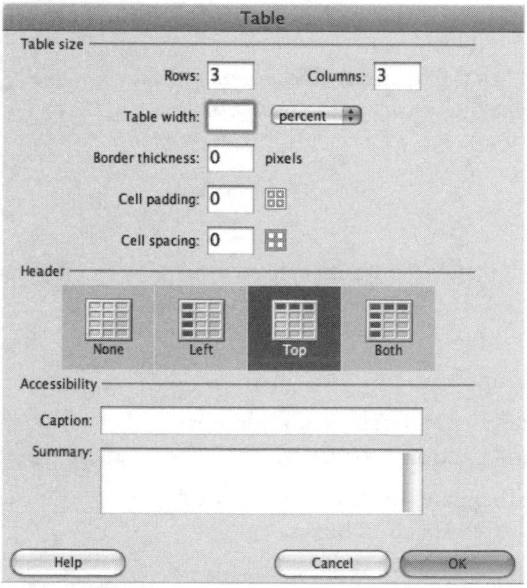

Figure 7-16:
Inserting a table into a Web page is a matter of making a few choices in the Table dialog box. Any text you type into the Summary box doesn't appear in a browser window, so you probably won't use this option frequently. It's intended to explain a particularly complicated table to non-visual web browsers (like Google's spidering software or a screen reader used by the visually impaired).

10. **Press Tab, and then type *Watering Can* in the first cell of the second row; press Tab again, and then type *$49.95*; press Tab to jump to the last cell in the second row and type *Pottery Barn*.**

    You just added the first item to the table; time for another.

11. **Press Tab to move to the first cell of the last row. Follow step 10 using the following information: *Deluxe Chia Seeds, $79.95*, and *Chia-2-U*.**

    At this point, you've filled the table with information—there aren't any more rows available. No problem; it's easy to add more.

Note: A table cell isn't limited to just a few words or numbers, as in this tutorial. You can place any HTML inside a table cell, including headlines, multiple paragraphs, images, and so on.

---

12. **If the cursor isn't already there, click in the last cell of the table (bottom right), and then press the Tab key.**

    When you reach a table's last cell, pressing the Tab key creates another row of cells. Just a little more typing to go.

13. **Using the technique above (steps 11 to 12), create the table pictured in Figure 7-17.**

    You don't need to complete the entire table if you don't want. If you've learned the technique and your fingers are tired, just add as many rows as you like.

Product	Cost	Manufacturer
Watering Can	$49.95	Pottery Barn
Delux Chia Seeds	$79.95	Chia-2-U
Rainbow Chia Seed Kit	$15.00	Chia-2-U
Seed Application Stick	$2.95	Sticks-R-Us
Terra Cotta Repair Kit	$14.95	Pots-R-Us

Figure 7-17: *Inputting data like this by hand gets the job done, but can be tedious and time-consuming. If you've got the data in a spreadsheet or a text file, you can probably use Dreamweaver's Import Tabular Data tool, described on page 280, to save your data-entering tendons.*

Modifying the Table

Just as you type the last row of information, Chia Vet headquarters calls and says they need an additional column of information added to the table. For HTML hand-coders, this would be a challenging and time-consuming task, but Dreamweaver makes the process easy.

1. **Click any cell in the third column.**

   For example, click the cell with the word "Manufacturer" in it. You'll now add a column to the table.

2. **Make sure you have the Layout category selected in the Insert Panel; click the "Insert Column to the Right" button (see Figure 7-18).**

   Dreamweaver adds a thin column to the far right side of the table. This column identifies an item's availability status.

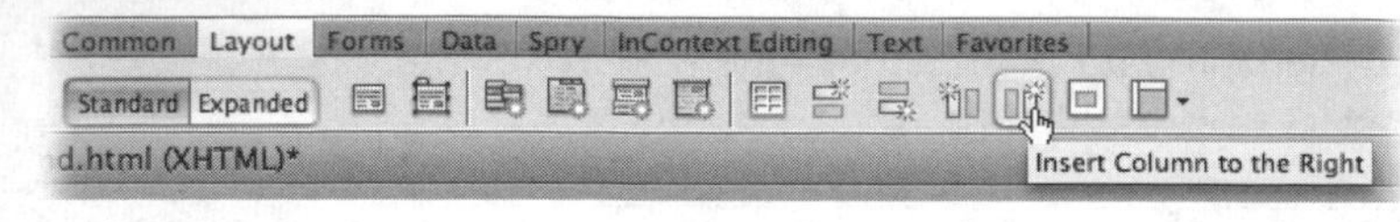

Figure 7-18:
As described in Figure 1-3, you can display the Insert panel in a variety of ways: here, it's really the Insert Bar made accessible by choosing the Classic workspace, as described on page 35.

3. **If the cursor isn't already there, click in the top cell of the new column, and then type *Availability*.**

   This is a <th> (table header) tag, so it's bold and centered. The actual data goes in the cells below.

4. **Click the cell below Availability, and then type *In stock*.**

   You can also press Tab four times to jump from the table header to this cell.

5. **Fill out the remaining cells in the column with either "In stock," "Back order," or "Silly tutorial."**

   And that's pretty much all there is to building a data table. Of course, making it look good is another story. For that, you'll turn to CSS.

Formatting the Table

Tables, like everything HTML, are drab by themselves. To make data really stand out, you need to turn to the power of Cascading Style Sheets. In this section, you'll format the table's basic font attributes, make the headers stand out, and add lines around the cells.

1. **Make sure the CSS Styles panel is open (Window→CSS Styles); in the bottom right of the panel, click the Create New Style button (the + button).**

   The New CSS Rule window appears. You'll create a class style for the table tag and store the CSS information in an already attached external style sheet. (For a recap on creating styles, turn to page 113.)

2. **Choose Class from the top menu; type *.products* in the Selector Name box; select global.css in the bottom menu, and then click OK.**

   The CSS Rule Definition window appears. Instead of creating a tag style named *table*, you're creating a class. Tag styles apply globally to every instance of the HTML tag. If this site still had some tables for layout purposes, a table tag style would probably ruin their look; in addition, by using a class style, you have the flexibility to create different designs for different types of tables.

3. **From the "Font-family" menu select "Trebuchet MS, Arial, Helvetica, sans-serif". In the "Font-size" box, type *13*.**

4. **Select the Box category and type *530* in the Width field. Click OK.**

   Here you set the width of the table to 530 pixels—that's the same amount of space available in that area of the page, so you've basically set the table to fit this space. This class style doesn't take effect until you apply it.

5. **Click the bottom border of the table to select it (or use any of the techniques described on page 266). From the Property inspector's Class menu, choose products.**

   Notice how the font changes for the table headers and regular table cells. Even though you applied these font settings to the <table> tag, the other tags inside it (<td>, <th>) use the *same* settings. This step demonstrates a useful CSS concept known as *inheritance* (you'll learn about inheritance in the next chapter on page 311).

   The table headers don't really command enough attention. You'll make them stand out by using a background graphic and increasing the space inside each cell.

6. **Click the Create New Style button. In the CSS Rule Definition window, choose Compound from the top menu (see Figure 7-19).**

   A "compound" style is usually what CSS veterans know as a descendent selector—a style name composed of two or more CSS selectors. You'll learn more about this setting in the next chapter, but for now, keep in mind that you want to create a style that affects only table headers that appear inside the table on this page—<th> tags that appear inside a table that's styled with the *products* class.

7. **Replace whatever's currently listed in the Selector Name box with .products th and make sure you have global.css selected in the bottom menu (see Figure 7-19). Click OK to create the style.**

   Here's a descendent selector, this time defining the look of every <th> tag inside another tag with the class *products* applied to it. You'll make the text white on an orange background.

8. **In the Type category, select white from the Color box; select uppercase from the "Text-transform" menu.**

   This makes the text white and all the letters uppercased. You'll use a graphic for the background.

9. **Click the Background category; set the background color to #EC6206 (a bright orange). Click the Browse button, and then, in the images folder, select the file *bgTh.jpg*.**

   Why add a background color, when you're already using a background image? Remember that in the last step, you made the text white. If you don't specify a darker background color, the column headers might be invisible. For example, if for some reason the graphic doesn't appear (the visitor has turned off graphics, or the image doesn't download properly), then the table headers appear as white text on a white background. However, by setting a dark background color too, you're covered. If the image doesn't download, the text is still readable—white text on an orange background.

Currently, Dreamweaver has centered the column headers in their cells. To match the appearance of the other cells, you'll align them to the left.

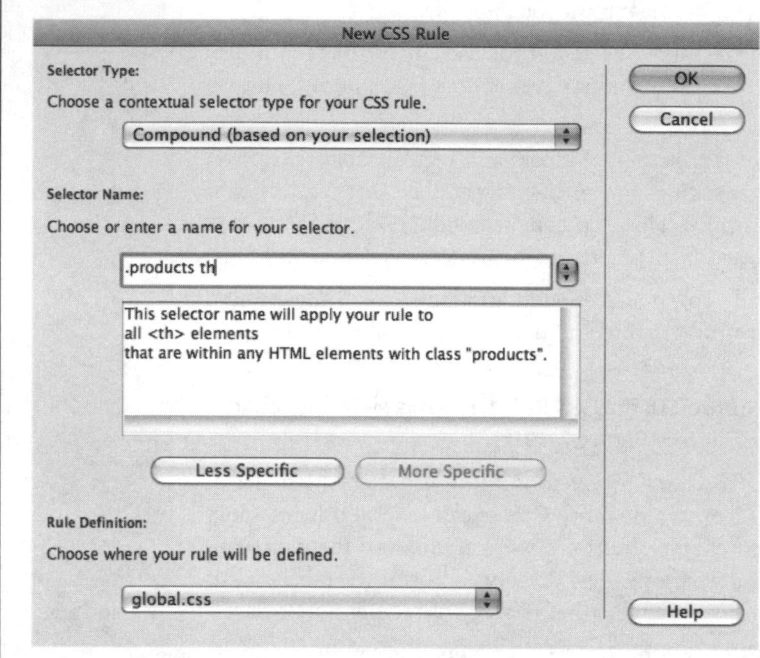

Figure 7-19: *What Dreamweaver calls a "compound" style is really just a catchall term for any type of style including class, tag, or ID styles. More significantly, Dreamweaver uses it to create one of the most important types of CSS styles: descendent selectors, like the .products th selector pictured here. This selector homes in on a very specific group of tags: <th> tags that are inside any other tag that has the class "products" applied to it.*

10. **Click the Block category, and then, from the "Text align" menu, choose Left.**

    You could also use the Property Inspector to set the horizontal alignment of each table header cell to "Left". But not only is that more work, it also adds extra HTML code to your page. The CSS method is easier and makes for faster-loading web pages.

    If you click the Apply button now, you see how this style is shaping up. The text is a bit cramped inside each cell. To add some breathing room between the edges of each cell and the text inside, you'll use the CSS Padding property.

Note: If you accidentally press the OK button before completing the style, just double-click the style's name in the CSS Styles panel to re-open the Style Definition window (see page 124 for detailed instructions).

11. **Click the Box category; turn off the "Same for all" checkbox under the Padding category. Type *4* in the Top box, *5* in the Right box, *2* in the Bottom box, and *10* in the Left box.**

    The window should look like Figure 7-20. One last touch: a border to separate each table header cell.

12. **Click the Border category; choose Solid for the style, type *1* in the Width box and make the color orange—#EC6206. Click the OK button to complete the style.**

    This adds a border around each table header. Now you'll format the regular table cells.

13. **Click the Create New Style button. In the CSS Rule Definition window, choose Compound from the top menu, type *.products td* in the Selector Name box; make sure you have global.css selected in the bottom menu, and then click OK.**

    You should be getting the hang of these descendent selectors by now: this style will apply to every <td> tag (that's an individual table cell) within another tag that has the class named *products* applied to it. You'll add padding and border lines to clearly indicate each cell.

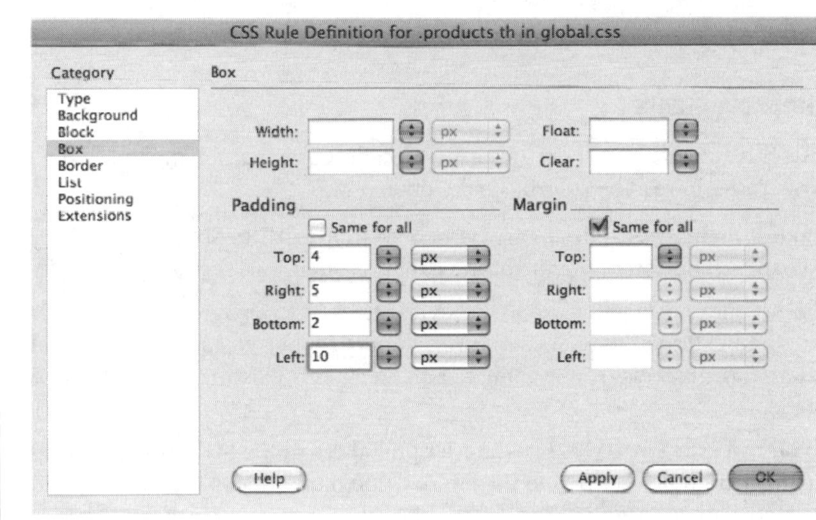

Figure 7-20: *The CSS padding property has a lot of benefits over a table's cell padding property. Not only does it eliminate unnecessary HTML for every table on your site, it lets you precisely control the amount of space around each of a cell's four sides.*

14. **Click the Box category; turn off the "Same for all" checkbox under the Padding category. Type *2* in the Top box, *2* in the Right box, *2* in the Bottom box, and *10* in the Left box.**

    Time to add some borders.

15. **Click the Border category; leave the "Same for all" checkboxes turned on; choose solid for the style, type *1* in the Width box, and make the color orange—#EC6206. Click OK to complete the style.**

    If you preview the page in a browser (F12 [Option-F12]), or click the Live View button at the top of the document window, you'll notice that, where two cells touch, the borders are a bit thick (see Figure 7-21). Because you added a border around all four sides of each cell, the border is twice as thick and looks a little chunky where two cells meet. You could edit the style and add a border to only some sides of the cell (like the left and bottom sides) so that the borders don't double up, but CSS gives you an easier way.

Note: Make sure to exit Live View when you finish viewing your page—just click the Live View button a second time. If you don't leave Live View, you can't edit your page.

PRODUCT	COST	MANUFACTURER	AVAILABLITY
Watering Can	$49.95	Pottery Barn	In stock
Delux Chia Seeds	$79.95	Chia-2-U	In stock
Rainbow Chia Seed Kit	$15.00	Chia-2-U	Back order
Seed Application Stick	$2.95	Sticks-R-Us	Silly tutorial
Terra Cotta Repair Kit	$14.95	Pots-R-Us	Back order

Figure 7-21:
Adding a border to table cells creates a slightly chunky double-border where cells touch each other. Fortunately, with a little-known CSS property, you can overcome that aesthetic nuisance.

Final Improvements

To finish this tutorial, you'll get rid of the double-border problem, and make the table rows easier to read by coloring every other row.

1. **Make sure the CSS Styles panel is open (Window→CSS Styles), and that you have the All button at the top of the panel selected.**

   The All button lets you view all the styles attached to a page. In this case, there are three external style sheets—*twoColFixRtHdr.css, global.css*, and *SpryMenuBarHorizontal.css*. You're going to edit an already existing style in the *global.css* file.

2. **If you can't see any styles listed under global.css in the Styles panel, click the + (flippy triangle on Mac) to the left of "global.css" to expand the list. Locate the style named .products, and then select it.**

   Don't double-click the style name—that opens the CSS Rule Definition window again. You're about to add a CSS property that Dreamweaver doesn't make available in that window. Instead, you need to use another technique for adding properties to a style—the Properties pane.

   The Properties pane is at the bottom of the CSS styles panel. It should look like Figure 7-22.

Note: If your Properties pane has only one property listed—*"font 13px 'Trebuchet MS', Arial, Helvetica, sans-serif"*—Dreamweaver is using CSS shorthand properties (see page 306). This doesn't affect the performance of your CSS, just the way it's written. You control this setting from the Preferences window's CSS Style category.

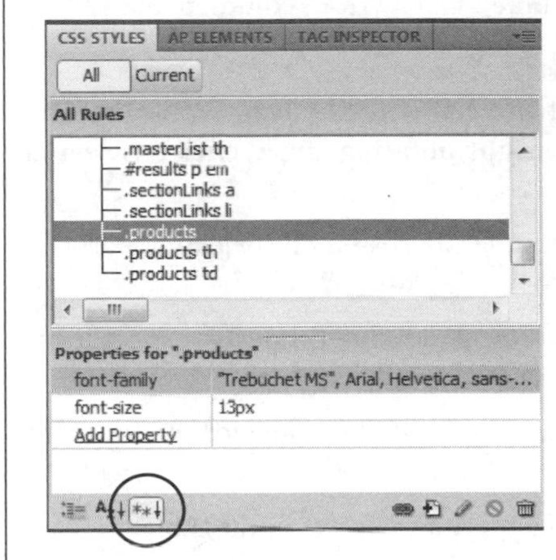

Figure 7-22:
When you select a style in the "All" view of the CSS Styles panel, the properties for that style appear in the Properties pane below. In this case, you selected the style .products and Dreamweaver displays its two properties (font-family and font-size). You can add more properties by clicking the Add Property link. There are actually three views to the Properties pane, but it's most useful to see just the currently set properties. Click the "Show only set properties" button (circled) for the view above. (You'll learn about the Properties pane in depth on page 304.)

3. **Click the Add Property link, and then, in the box, type *border-collapse*.**

   Border-collapse is a special CSS property that forces adjoining cells to "collapse" onto each other: Essentially it removes space between cells and prevents this double-border problem.

4. **From the menu to the right of the border-collapse property you just added, select "collapse" (see Figure 7-23).**

   That removes the double-border between adjacent cells (you don't see this effect in Dreamweaver's Design view, but if you click the Live View button or preview the page in a browser, you will). Now you'll highlight alternating table rows. This technique makes tables easier to scan, since your eye can easily identify all the cells in a row. To do this, you'll create two new class styles.

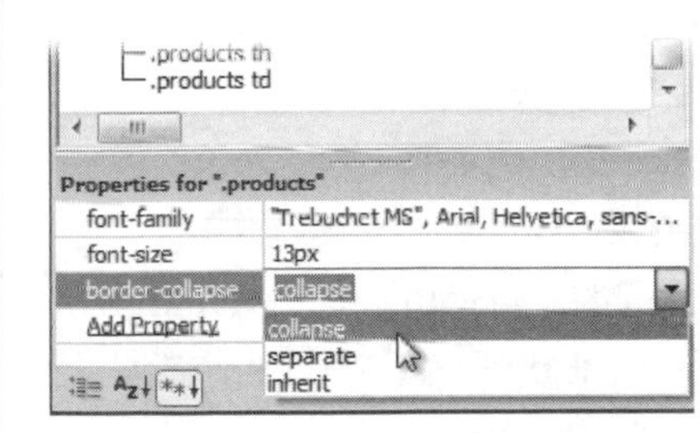

Figure 7-23:
The border-collapse property is an official CSS property, even though it doesn't appear in Dreamweaver's CSS Rule Definition window. You can, however, add it by hand using the Properties pane.

5. **Click the Create New Style button. In the CSS Rule Definition window, choose Class from the top menu, and then type *.odd* in the Selector Name box; make sure you have global.css selected in the bottom menu, and then click OK.**

   All you need to do now is define a background color.

6. **In the CSS Rule Definition window, select the Background category; set the background color to #ECF4F9 (light blue). Click OK to complete the style.**

   Now you'll apply this color to every other row.

7. **Move your mouse just to the left of the cell with the text "Watering Can". When the mouse pointer changes to a right-pointing arrow, click to select the row of cells (see Figure 7-24).**

   You can also use any of the other techniques discussed on "Selecting Parts of a Table" to select a table row. Now just apply the class style.

8. **Make sure you have the HTML button selected in the Property inspector, and then choose odd from the Class menu.**

   Every cell background in the row changes to light blue. Now for the rest of the table.

9. **Repeat steps 7 and 8 for the remaining alternating rows in the table.**

   Use Figure 7-25 for reference. You can do the same for every even row as well.

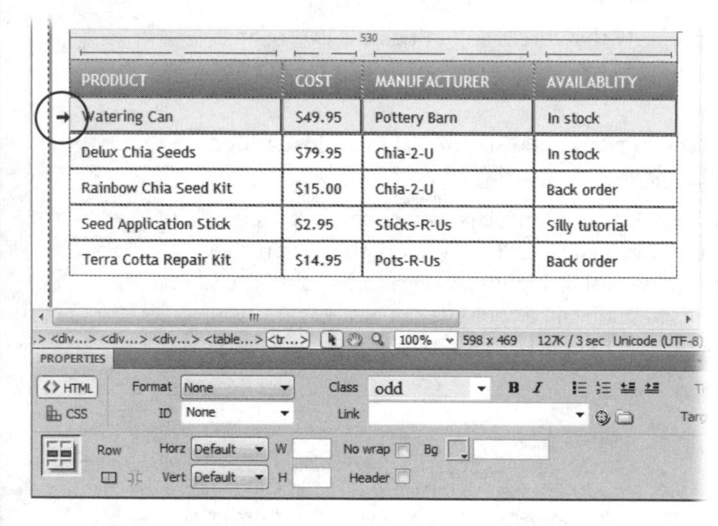

Figure 7-24: *When Dreamweaver's cursor changes to a right-pointing arrow (circled), click to select the table row. You can achieve the same thing by clicking inside any cell inside the row, and then, at the bottom of the document window, clicking the <tr> tag in the Tag selector.*

10. **Repeat steps 5–9; create a class style named** *.even* **with a background color of #F4FBD9 (a light green), and apply the even class to the unstyled, even table rows.**

    Now you have a table where every odd row has a blue background and every even row a green background, making it easy to scan across a row of data.

11. **Press the F12 (Option-F12) key to preview your hard work in a browser.**

    The complete page should look like Figure 7-25. You'll find a completed version of this tutorial in the Chapter07_finished folder that accompanies the downloaded tutorial files.

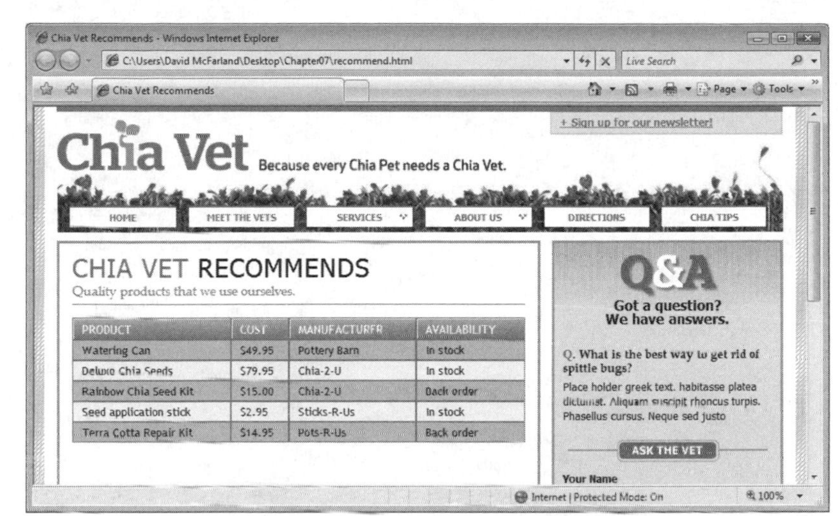

Figure 7-25: *With Dreamweaver and a little CSS, you can make elegant HTML tables.*

CHAPTER
8

Advanced CSS

Chapter 4 introduced you to the basics of Cascading Style Sheets. In other chapters, you learned how to use CSS to style links, navigation bars, text, and tables. You can go a long way in web design with just those basic techniques (many people do). However, to really become a web design expert, there are a handful of advanced CSS concepts you should grasp. Fortunately, Dreamweaver also includes tools to help you with these concepts so you can work more efficiently and avoid those head-scratching "Why the heck does my design look like that?!" moments.

Note: This chapter will help you on your journey from CSS novice to master. But keep in mind that it's the rare mortal who understands everything about CSS from reading a single chapter. If you really want to know the ins and outs of CSS, you owe it to yourself to pick up a friendly, real-world tested guide. *CSS: The Missing Manual* has gotten rave reviews on that front, and that's not marketing-speak: it's honest-to-goodness advice.

Compound Selectors

It's relatively easy to learn how to use tag, class, and ID styles. To be technically accurate, all these styles aren't really styles. In CSS lingo, they're *selectors*, instructions that tell a browser *what* it should apply the CSS formatting rules to. For example, a tag selector (not to be mistaken with Dreamweaver's time-saving selection tool, *the* Tag selector) tells a browser to apply the formatting to *any* instance of a particular tag on the page. Thus, browsers apply *h1* tag styles to *all* <h1> tags on a page. They apply class selector styles, on the other hand, only when they encounter the class name attached to an element on a page. Similarly, browsers apply ID selector styles to a tag with a matching ID name: for example, <body id="home">. (Flip back to page 112 for a review of key differences between class and ID selectors.)

Note: For a detailed discussion of selectors, visit *http://css.maxdesign.com.au/selectutorial/*.

But tag, ID, and class selectors are just the tip of the selector iceberg. CSS offers many other selector types that let you format even the smallest page element; Dreamweaver lumps these selectors together under the term *compound selectors*. "Compound selector" is a Dreamweaver term, not a CSS term, so don't go using it at your weekly web designer get-togethers. Dreamweaver uses it to describe advanced types of selectors, such as the "pseudo-class" styles you use to format different link states (*a:link, a:visited, a:hover*, and *a:active*, as described on page 181), or the descendent selectors the Spry menu bar uses (page 188).

The CSS arsenal includes a variety of these advanced selectors (you'll find a few of the most common and useful ones mentioned below), but in Dreamweaver, you create all of them the same way. Start by creating a CSS style, following the instructions on page 113. But when you get to the New CSS Rule window (Figure 8-1), instead of selecting the Class, ID, or Tag selector type, choose the Compound option.

Unless you want one of the four link state options available from the drop-down menu, you have to type the name of any advanced selector you want to use in the Selector Name box (see Figure 8-1). As described in the following sections, you need to use a different syntax (naming protocol) for each type of selector. (The rest of the process for creating the style works just like creating a tag or class style, and the process of editing or deleting the styles is also identical.)

Descendent Selectors

Tag styles have their drawbacks. While a tag style for the <p> tag makes simple work of formatting every paragraph on a page, it's also indiscriminate. You may not *want* every paragraph to look the same.

Suppose you want to divide a web page into different sections—a sidebar and a main content area—using smaller size text for the sidebar's paragraphs and headings. You *could* create two class styles—such as *sidebarText* and *mainText*—and then apply them to the appropriate paragraphs (<p class="sidebarText"> for sidebar paragraphs and <p class="mainText"> for body text). But who has that kind of time?

What you really need is a "smart" tag style, one that can adapt to its surroundings like a chameleon, and apply the appropriate format depending on where the style is located on the page. Enter *descendent selectors*.

Essentially, you use descendent selectors to format every instance of a particular tag in a similar manner (just like tag selectors)—but only when they're in a particular part of a web page. In effect, it's like saying, "Hey, you <a> tags in the navigation bar, listen up. I've got some formatting for you. All you other <a> tags, move along, there's nothing to see here." In other words, a descendent selector lets you format a tag based on its relationship to other tags. To understand how it works, you need to delve a little more deeply into HTML.

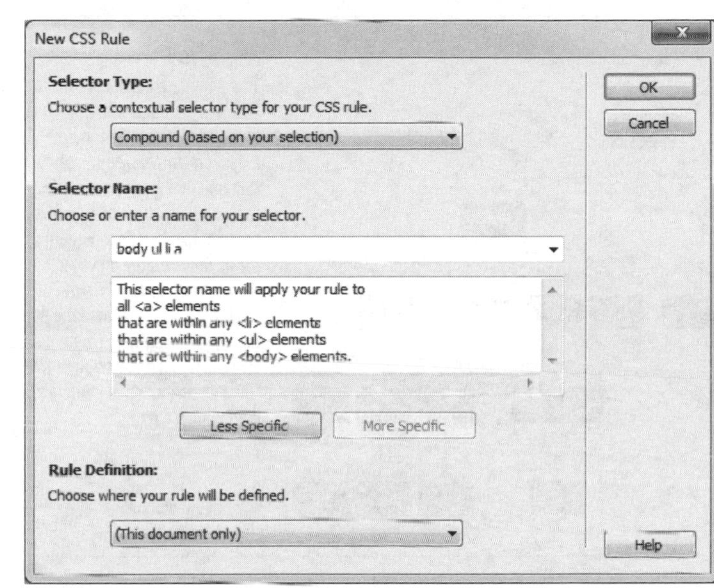

Figure 8-1:
The Compound selector option lets you type any valid CSS selector in the Selector Name box. You can even create class, tag, and ID styles after choosing the Compound selector option. For a new class, type the name of the class preceded by a period, like this: .copyright. To create a tag style, type the tag name without brackets: p for the <p> or paragraph tag, for instance. And, to create a new ID style, type the # symbol followed by the ID name: #mainContent, for example.

Think of the HTML that forms any web page as a kind of "family tree," like the one shown in Figure 8-2. The first HTML tag you use on a page—the <html> tag—is like the grandpappy of all the other tags. In essence, when a tag is *inside* another tag, it's a *descendent* of that tag. In Figure 8-2, the text "wide range of topics" is bolded in the long paragraph of text. You get that format by applying a <strong> tag to the text. Because that bolded text is inside a paragraph (inside a <p> tag, in other words), the <strong> tag is a descendent of that paragraph.

Note: The tutorial in the previous chapter includes an example of the power of descendent selectors. See steps 6 and 7 on page 289.

Descendent selectors let you take advantage of the HTML family tree by formatting tags differently when they appear inside certain other tags or styles. For example, say you have an <h1> tag on your web page, and you want to emphasize a word within that heading. One option is to select the word and press the B button on the Property inspector—that applies the <strong> tag to that word. The trouble is, most browsers boldface the words in both heading tags and <strong> tags, so your visitors won't see any difference between the emphasized word and the other words in the headline. Creating a tag selector to change the <strong> tag's color and make it stand out from the headline isn't much of a solution: you end up changing the color of *every* <strong> tag on the page, like it or not. A descendent selector lets you do what you really want: change the color of the <strong> tag *only when* it appears inside of an <h1> tag.

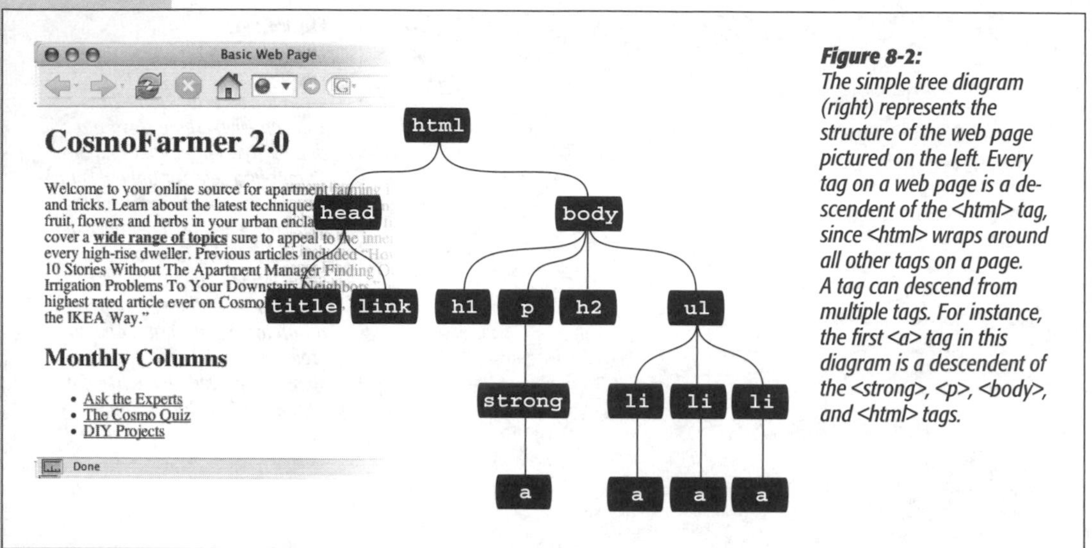

Figure 8-2: *The simple tree diagram (right) represents the structure of the web page pictured on the left. Every tag on a web page is a descendent of the <html> tag, since <html> wraps around all other tags on a page. A tag can descend from multiple tags. For instance, the first <a> tag in this diagram is a descendent of the <strong>, <p>, <body>, and <html> tags.*

Creating descendent selectors isn't much more difficult than creating any other type of style. You follow the same process as described on page 113 for creating a style—but in the New CSS Rule window, select Compound from the Selector Type menu. You then type the descendent selector's name in the Selector Name box. Figuring out how to name the selector is the tricky part.

You name a descendent selector by tacking together a series of selectors (separated by spaces) that identify the location in the family tree of the element you want to style. The most distant ancestor is on the far left and the element you wish to style is on the far right. Consider the example of the bolded word inside the headline discussed earlier. To style that bolded text (but leave any other bold text as it is), the descendent selector is *h1 strong*. You read this from right to left, so strong is the actual tag you're formatting, but only when it's inside an <h1> tag.

Figure 8-2 shows another example. There are four links (<a> tags) on the page. Three of them appear inside bulleted list items (that's the <li> tag). If you want to create a style that applied only to those three links and leave the fourth link untouched, you'd create a descendent selector like this: *li a*. Again, the actual tag you want to format—the link—appears on the far right, while the tag that wraps around the link—the <li> tag—appears to the left.

A descendent selector can contain more than just two elements. The following are all valid selectors for the <a> tags inside the bulleted lists in Figure 8-2.

- ul li a
- body li a
- html li a
- html body ul li a

These four selectors—all of which do the same thing—demonstrate that you don't have to describe the entire lineage of the tag you want to format. For instance, in the second example—*body li a—you don't need the ul.* This selector works as long as there's an <a> tag that's a descendent (somewhere up the line) of an <li> tag (which is also a descendent of the <body> tag). This selector can just as easily apply to an <a> inside an <em> tag, inside a <strong> tag, that's inside a <li> tag, and so on.

Note: One reason you might make a descendent selector longer by tacking on additional selectors is if you've written several different rules that simultaneously format a tag. The more selectors that appear in a style name, the more powerful that style is and the more likely it is to override any conflicts with other styles. More on this concept on page 312.

When you choose Compound from the Selector Type menu in the New CSS Rule window, Dreamweaver suggests a descendent selector based on what you currently have selected on the page (or where the cursor is, if nothing's selected). For example, say you had the page pictured in Figure 8-2 open in Dreamweaver. If you selected the link with the text "Ask the Experts", created a new style (for example, by clicking the New CSS Rule button on the CSS Styles panel), and then selected Compound from the Selector Type menu, you'd see something like Figure 8-1. Having Dreamweaver compose the selector for you, as you can imagine, is a brain cell-saver. In this case, Dreamweaver suggests "body ul li a". In other words, a descendent selector style that translates to format every link (a) which is inside a list item (li), which is part of an unordered list (ul) that is itself inside the body of the page (body).

Note: When you write your own descendent selectors, Dreamweaver's selector explanation box (the text box that appears below the Selector Name field) is a big help. It explains, in plain English, what elements that descendent selector will apply to (see the box below the *body ul li a* selector name in Figure 8-1 for an example).

That's a pretty long-winded style name and, as mentioned above, you don't have to have all that information to accurately target the elements on a page for a style. For example, a simpler name, *li a*, would also get the job done. Dreamweaver generally suggests the most complete descendent selector, meaning the tag you want to format and every ancestor tag (every tag wrapped around the selected element). In most cases, you won't need such complicated descendent selector names. You can replace Dreamweaver's suggestion with a simpler descendent selector; just delete what Dreamweaver provides and type in your own descendent selector name). You can also click the Less Specific button on the New CSS Rule window (see Figure 8-1). Each click of that button removes the ancestor on the far left of the list. For example, in Figure 8-1, clicking Less Specific once changes the descendent selector to *ul li a*; clicking it a second time makes it *li a*.

Descendent selectors with Class and ID styles

You're not limited to just using tag selectors in your descendent selector names, either. You can build complex descendent selectors by combining different types of selectors. Suppose you want links to appear in yellow in introductory paragraphs (which you designate with a class style named *intro*). The following selector does the trick: *.intro a*. This descendent selector formats any link (a) inside any other tag that has the *intro* class applied to it.

Web designers frequently format the same tag differently, depending on where the tag appears in the layout. For instance, you'll frequently want paragraphs in the main content area of a page to look different from paragraphs in sidebars (for example, you might use a different font and a smaller font size in the sidebar). You'll usually wrap each section of a page inside a <div> tag that has a class applied to it. For example, you might wrap the main content area in a <div> tag, and apply the class name *.content* to it. To format just the paragraphs inside the <div> tag, you'd use the descendent selector *.content p* (don't leave out the period). You'll use this technique frequently when working with CSS layouts like those discussed in the next chapter.

Tip: When you work with descendent selectors, it helps to read the selector name *backwards, from right to left*. Take, for example, the selector *.content td li*. The *li* means "This style applies to the <li> tag"; the *td* means "But only when it's inside a <td> tag"; and *.content* means "And only when that <td> tag is inside another tag that has the class *.content* applied to it."

While Dreamweaver CS5's CSS layouts create different sections of a page by applying class names to div tags, web designers also often use IDs with divs to identify unique page layout elements, such as a banner (for example, <div id="banner">). Dreamweaver itself doesn't take this approach but you can (and a lot of web designers do). In that case, you might want to target specific tags inside those divs. The process is the same as using class names, so if you want to define the look of bulleted lists wherever they appear inside a tag with an ID named *#banner*, you'd type *#banner ul* in the Selector box.

After you name the descendent selector, save it to either an internal or external style sheet as described on page 116. Then click OK in the New CSS Rule window. You're ready to start adding the CSS properties that define the format of your descendent selector style. Proceed as you normally would when you create *any* type of style (see page 116 for a refresher).

Styling Groups of Tags

Sometimes you want to apply the same formatting to several different elements. Say you'd like all headers on a page to share the same color and font. Creating a separate style for each header—*h1, h2, h3, h4, h5, h6*—is way too much work. In addition, if you later want to change the color of all the headers, you'd have to update six different styles. A more streamlined approach is to use a *group* selector, which lets you apply a style to multiple selectors at the same time.

To create a style that applies to several different elements at once, follow the steps on page 113 to create a new style, and then choose Compound from the top menu in the New CSS Rule window (see Figure 8-3). In the Selector Name box, type a list of selectors separated by commas. To style all heading tags with the same formatting options, for example, you'd create the following selector: *h1, h2, h3, h4, h5, h6*.

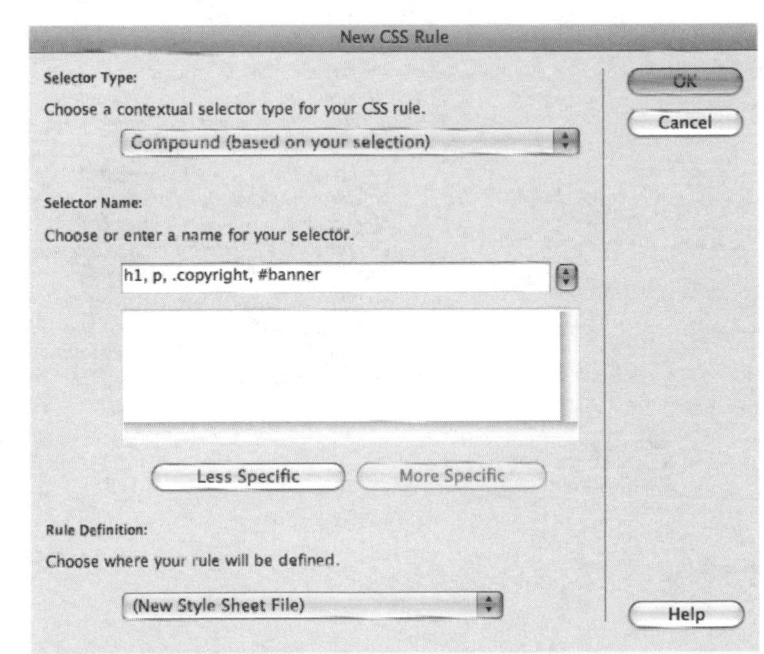

Figure 8-3: *You can apply group selectors to more than just a single tag style. You can use any valid selector (or combination of selector types) in a group selector. For example, the selector listed here applies to the <h1> tag, the <p> tag, any tag styled with the .copyright class, and the tag with the #banner ID.*

Note: At times, you may want a bunch of page elements to share *some*—but not all—of the same formatting properties. Suppose you want to use the same font for several tags, but apply different font colors to each of those tags. You can create a single style using a group selector with the shared formatting options, and separate styles with unique formatting for each individual tag. That's a perfectly valid (and common) approach: web browsers just "tally up" all the different CSS properties applied to a tag to create a kind of uber-style (see page 312).

Fast Style Editing With the Properties Pane

The CSS Rule Definition window (Figure 4-3) can be a rather tedious way to edit CSS properties. It's easy to use, but opening the window and jumping around the categories and menus may slow down experienced CSS jockeys. Fortunately, Dreamweaver offers the Properties pane (Figure 8-4) for fast CSS editing. This pane displays a selected style's currently defined properties, as well as a list of other not-yet-set CSS properties.

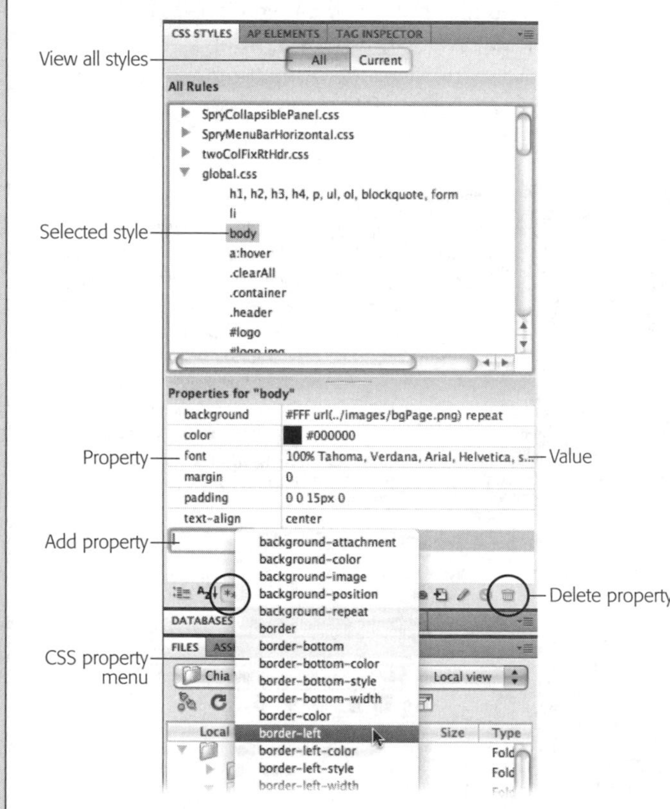

Figure 8-4: *The CSS Styles panel has two views: All (shown here) and Current. The Properties pane is available in both views, but you access it slightly differently when you're in Current view (see Figure 8-9). With the All button selected, as it is here, you can click any style from the list of CSS styles ("body" in this case) and use the Properties pane to add and edit properties. The "Show only set properties" view of the Properties pane, which you access by clicking the icon circled in this figure, provides a clear view of a particular style's properties. You can quickly see which CSS properties the style uses, and delete or edit them. You can also add a new property by clicking the Add Property link (hidden behind the pop-up menu) and selecting the new property's name from the CSS property menu.*

Start by selecting the style you wish to edit in the CSS Styles panel. The Properties pane (found in the bottom third of the Styles panel) displays CSS properties in one of three views: a "set properties" view, which displays the properties defined for the selected style only (Figure 8-4); a Category view, which groups the different CSS properties into the same seven categories used in the Rule Definition window (Figure 8-5, left); and a List view, which provides an alphabetical listing of *all* CSS properties (Figure 8-5, right). Click the view buttons at the bottom-left corner of the CSS Styles panel to switch among these three views (see the circled buttons in Figure 8-4 and Figure 8-5).

The CSS Styles panel lists property names on the left, and their values are on the right. Figure 8-4 shows an example of a style for the <body> tag, which lists six properties (such as *background-color* and *margin*) and their corresponding settings (#333333, 0px, and so on).

To add a new property, click the Add Property link below the list of properties in the Properties pane, and select the property name from the pop-up menu. You set (and can edit) the value of a particular property in the space to the right of the property name. Frequently, you don't have to type in the value. Dreamweaver provides the tools you're likely to need for each property: the ubiquitous Color box (see page 56) for any property that requires a color, like font color; a pop-up menu for properties that have a limited list of possible values, like "Repeat-y" for the *background-repeat* property; and the familiar "Browse for File" folder icon for properties that require a path to a file, such as the *background-image* property.

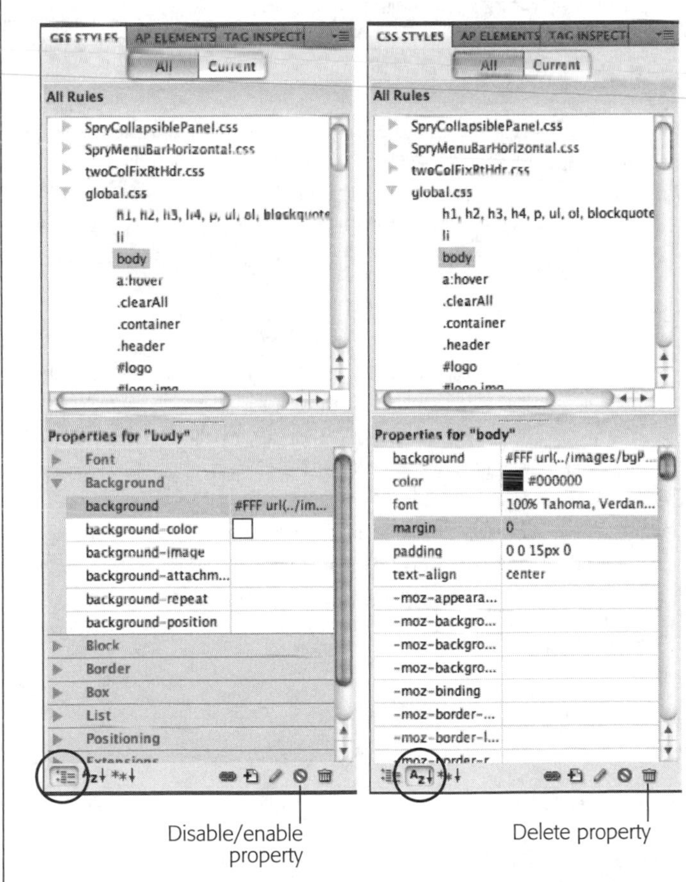

Figure 8-5:
The Properties pane's two other views aren't as streamlined or as easy to use as the "Show only set properties" view pictured in Figure 8-4. You add new properties in these views by simply typing a value in the empty box to the right of the property name—in the panel pictured here on the left, for example, type a value in the empty box to the right of "background-color". However, since these views aren't the fastest way to edit CSS, you're better off not using them. On a side note, you can click the Delete button to remove a property from a style, and the Disable/Enable button to turn a property off or on—a useful tool to quickly see how one property effects the appearance of an element on a page.

Some other properties, however, require that you know enough CSS to enter the value manually and in the correct format. That's what makes the Properties pane a good advanced option for experienced CSS gurus.

But even those not so experienced with CSS should find the Properties pane helpful. First, it's the best way to get a bird's-eye view of a style's properties. Second, for really basic editing, such as changing the colors used in a style or assigning a style a different font, the Properties pane is as fast as it gets.

To remove a property from a style, just delete its value in the right column. Dreamweaver not only removes the value from the style sheet, it deletes the property name as well. In addition, you can right-click (Control-click) a property name and then select "Delete from the pop-up menu, or simply click a property name and either press the Delete key or click the Trash can icon to banish it from your style sheet (see Figure 8-5).

FREQUENTLY ASKED QUESTION

CSS Shorthand

In the CSS Properties pane, sometimes I'll see all the font properties grouped into a single property named font; *other times, font properties are listed individually, like* font-family, font-size, *and so on. Why is that?*

Some CSS properties seem to go together: font properties, background properties (like *background-color, background-image, background-repeat*, and so on), margin, border, padding, and list-style properties. CSS supports a shorthand that combines related properties into a single property name. For example, it can combine the *font-family, font-size, font-weight, font-style*, and *line-height* properties into a single property called font. This shorthand makes writing CSS by hand faster. Instead of typing all of the above font properties—one line of CSS code per property—you can combine them into a single line like this:

```
font: italic bold 16px/150% Tahoma,
Verdana, Arial, Helvetica, sans-serif;
```

Dreamweaver uses either the shorthand or longhand method depending on your preference settings. Choose Edit→Preferences (Dreamweaver→Preferences on Macs) or use the keyboard shortcut Ctrl-U [⌘-U]); click the CSS Styles category to view the settings Dreamweaver uses when it writes CSS code. The top group of checkboxes lets you turn on and off shorthand mode.

If you hand-edit your CSS, you might want to leave the shorthand boxes turned on. If Dreamweaver writes all your CSS code, uncheck these boxes, for two reasons. First, unless you know your CSS well, shorthand versions of CSS properties are harder to edit in the Properties pane—it's very easy to make a typo, and many of the friendly pop-up menus (like a list of fonts to apply to text) that Dreamweaver displays for "longhand" versions of properties don't appear for shorthand versions. Second, with the *background* shorthand property, you can sometimes find yourself in a weird mess, where background colors and images disappear from elements on a page.

Moving and Managing Styles

In the old days, when CSS support in web browsers was new, web designers would create just a handful of styles to format headlines and text. Keeping track of a site's styles back then wasn't too hard. Today, with great CSS support in web browsers and

CSS-based layout becoming the norm, it's not uncommon to create a style sheet with hundreds of styles.

You might want to take a really long, complicated style sheet and split it up into several smaller, easier-to-read external style sheets. One common web design practice is to store styles that serve related functions in separate style sheets—for example, all the styles related to formatting forms in one style sheet, styles for text in another, and styles for page layout in yet another. You can then link each of the external style sheets to your site's pages as described on page 123.

Even if you don't have enough styles to warrant multiple style sheets, it's still useful to organize the styles *within* a style sheet. Web designers frequently use this strategy; for example, they keep all the styles for basic layout in one section of a style sheet, basic tag selectors in another section, and specific styles for text, images, and other content grouped according to the part of the page where they use them (sidebar, banner, and so on). By grouping related styles, it's a lot easier to find any particular style when it comes time to edit it.

Fortunately, you don't need to venture into Code view to move styles around in your style sheets. Dreamweaver provides a simple and logical way to do so (and to move styles from one style sheet to another, too).

- To move a style from one place to another in the same style sheet, drag the style in the CSS Styles panel (see Figure 8-6, left). Dreamweaver lists the styles in the order in which they appear in the actual CSS code—so dragging one style below another repositions the CSS code in the style sheet. (Order can be important in CSS for reasons you'll learn about starting on page 312, but in a nutshell, styles listed lower in a style sheet are given greater priority in case of conflicts with other styles.) You can select and move more than one style at a time by Ctrl-clicking (⌘-clicking) each style you wish to move and then dragging the highlighted group (Ctrl-click [⌘-click] a selected style to deselect it). Select a range of styles by clicking one style and then Shift-clicking another style: that highlights every style between the two.

Note: You'll see the full list of styles in a style sheet (and be able to rearrange those styles) only when you select the All button (circled in Figure 8-6, left) in the CSS Styles panel.

- To move one or more styles between two style sheets, drag the style from one style sheet to another in the CSS Styles panel. This works both for moving a style from an internal style sheet to an external style sheet, and for moving a style from one external style sheet to another. Say you create an internal style sheet for the current page and also attached an external style sheet to the same page. Dragging a style from the internal style sheet (represented by <style> in the CSS Styles panel) to the external style sheet (represented by its file name—*main.css*, for example) moves the style *out* of the internal style sheet and *into* the external style sheet (Figure 8-6, right). Dreamweaver then deletes the CSS code for the style from the first style sheet. You can use the same method to move a style between two attached external style sheets.

If you drag a style into another style sheet and the destination style sheet already contains a style with the same name, you can run into some confusion. For example, say you define a style for the <body> tag in an internal style sheet; in addition, you've got an external style sheet attached to the same page that also has a body tag style (perhaps with different properties). If you drag the body tag style from one style sheet into another, you're trying to add the same-named style a second time. When this happens, Dreamweaver informs you of the potential problem (see Figure 8-7).

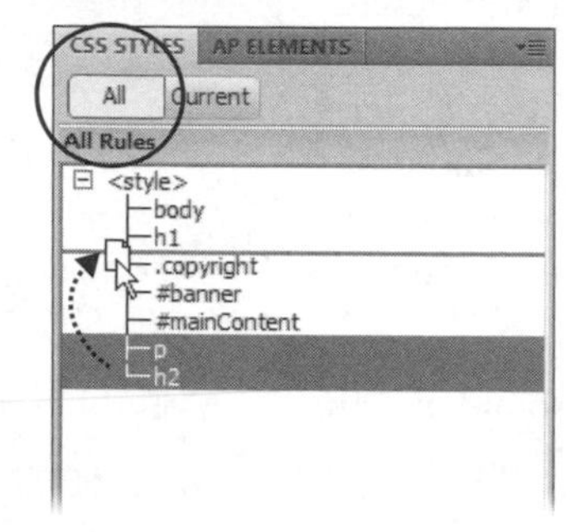

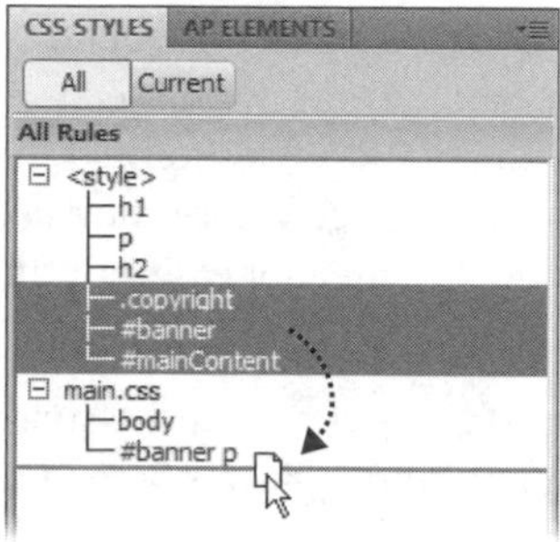

Figure 8-6: *In the CSS Styles panel, you can drag styles to different locations within a style sheet (left). In this case, dragging the styles below the h1 style groups all the basic tag selectors (body, h1, p, and h2) together. You can also drag styles between style sheets to move a style from one sheet to another. In the Styles panel on the right, you're moving three styles from an internal style sheet to a CSS file named main.css.*

Note: Unfortunately, Dreamweaver doesn't provide a way to reorder the sequence of internal and external style sheets on a page. They're attached to the page in the order in which you add them. For example, if you attached an external style sheet to a web page and then created an internal style sheet, the internal style sheet's code appears *after* the link to the external style sheet. This can have some serious effects on how the cascade works (see page 312). To change the order of the style sheets in the HTML, you have to go to Code view (see page 415) and cut and paste the code.

You have two choices at this point. You can decide not to move the style and click the No button (the Cancel button has the same effect). Dreamweaver closes the window without moving the style. Or, you can click the Yes button and Dreamweaver moves the style to the style sheet. It doesn't replace the old style, nor does it merge the properties of the two styles. It simply adds the new style to the destination style sheet—in other words, you end up with a style sheet that has two separate styles, each with the same name. Even though this is perfectly valid CSS, it's very confusing. Delete one of the styles, and, if necessary, edit the remaining one to match any properties you wanted from the deleted style.

Note: Dreamweaver says that it will place a style "adjacent" to the style with the same name when it moves like-named styles (see Figure 8-7), but it doesn't. It positions the style wherever you drop it in the list of styles in the destination style sheet.

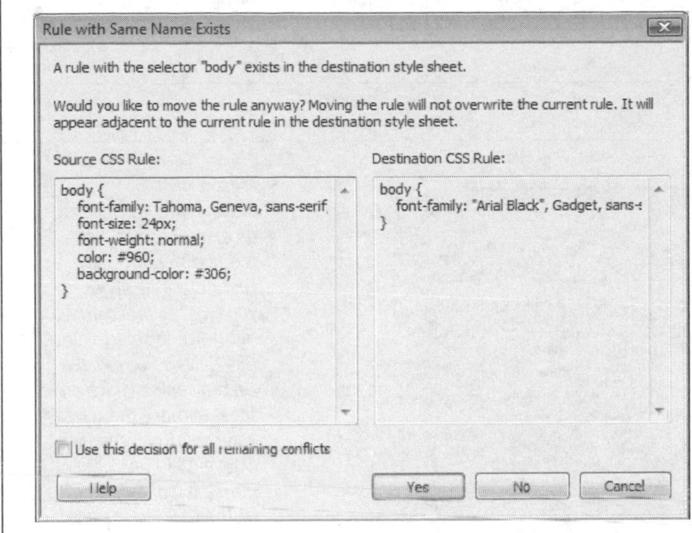

Figure 8-7:
When dragging a style from one style sheet to another, it's possible that a style by the same name already exists in the destination style sheet. When that happens, this dialog box appears, letting you either cancel the move or move the style anyway. To help you figure out what to do, Dreamweaver lists the properties in both the style you're trying to move and the one already in the destination style sheet. You can use this information to determine which of the two styles you wish to keep, or to figure out which properties from each style are most important.

- You can also move one or more styles into an external style sheet that's not attached to the current page. As discussed on page 111, external style sheets are the most efficient way to style a website's collection of pages. However, it's often easier to use an internal style sheet when you first start a design. This way, as you tweak your CSS, you only have to edit the one file (the web page with the internal style sheet) instead of two (the web page *and* the external CSS file). But once you finish your design, it's best to move the styles from the internal style sheet to an external style sheet. This process is as easy as a right-click (Control-click).

  In the CSS Styles panel, select the styles you wish to move to an external style sheet (Ctrl-click [⌘-click] each style name to select it). Right-click (Control-click) the selected styles and choose "Move CSS Rules" (see Figure 8-8, top). The "Move to External Style Sheet" window opens (Figure 8-8, bottom). You can then either add the rules to an existing external style sheet by clicking the browse button and selecting the CSS file in the site, or turn on the "A new style sheet" radio button to create a new CSS file and move the styles there. When you click OK, Dreamweaver either moves the styles to an existing CSS file, or it displays a dialog box letting you name and save a new CSS file. Either way, Dreamweaver removes the styles from the internal style sheet and places them into an external style sheet; even better, if the external CSS file isn't already attached to the current page, Dreamweaver attaches it for you, which lets you skip the manual process of attaching the style sheet, described on page 123.

Tip: If you move all the styles from an internal style sheet to an external one, Dreamweaver still leaves some useless <style> tags in your web page. To remove those, select *style* from the list of styles in the CSS Styles panel and then press the Delete key or click the Trash can icon in the lower-right corner of the Styles panel.

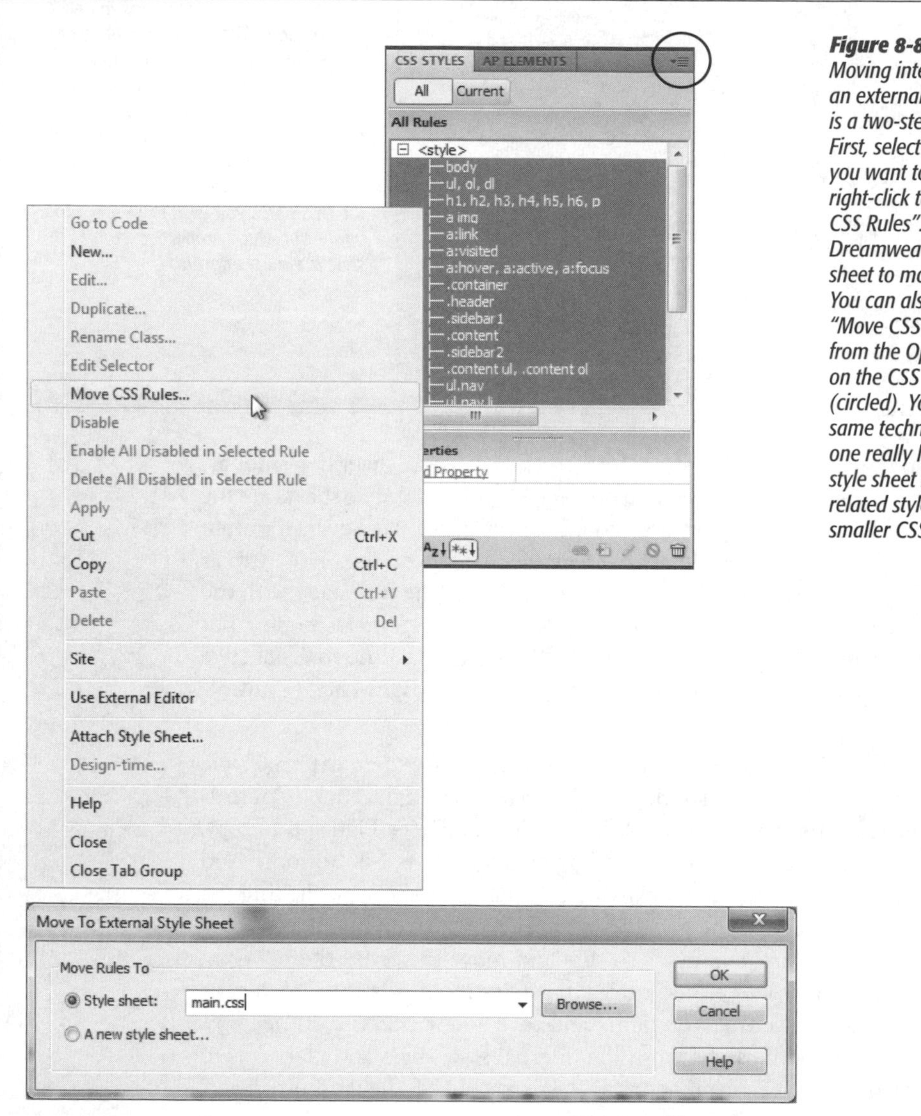

Figure 8-8: *Moving internal styles to an external style sheet is a two-step process. First, select the styles you want to move and right-click to select "Move CSS Rules". Second, tell Dreamweaver which style sheet to move the style to. You can also access the "Move CSS Rules" option from the Option menu on the CSS Styles panel (circled). You can use this same technique to take one really long external style sheet file and move related styles into several, smaller CSS files.*

More about CSS

As you begin to pile more and more styles into your pages, you may notice that a page might not look exactly as you expect. A paragraph of text might be green even though you didn't create a style for a green paragraph. Or you've styled a particular paragraph to appear with green text, but it refuses to change color. Most peculiar behaviors like these occur when styles collide. The rules governing these interactions can be complex, but they boil down to two main concepts: *inheritance* and *the cascade.*

Inheritance

Imagine you created a new style by redefining the paragraph tag (<p>). The style specifies red text displayed in the Arial font at 24 pixels tall. Then you select a single word in a paragraph and apply bold formatting to it. When you use the Property inspector's bold button to do this, Dreamweaver wraps that word in a pair of <strong> HTML tags.

When a browser loads the page, it formats all the paragraphs in red Arial text with a font size of 24 pixels, because that's how you defined the <p> tag. But what happens when the browser encounters the <strong> tag inside a paragraph? Since you didn't redefine the <strong> tag in red, Arial, 24 pixels, the browser scratches its little silicon head: Should the browser resort to its *default* font, size, and color when it gets to the <strong> tag, ignoring your style rules?

Of course not. The bolded word should look just like the rest of the paragraph—red, Arial, 24 pixels high—but boldface *too*. And indeed, that's how CSS works: The <strong> tag *inherits* the formatting of the surrounding <p> tag.

Just as human babies inherit traits like eye color from their biological parents, nested HTML tags inherit the properties of tags that surround them. In fact, a tag nested inside another tag—such as that <strong> tag nested inside the <p> tag—is called a *child*, while the enclosing tag is called the *parent*.

Note: As you read on page 298, a tag inside another tag is also called a *descendent*, while a tag that surrounds another tag is called an *ancestor*.

Inheritance passes from parent to child and ancestor to descendent. So in this example, the <p> tag (the parent) passes on the red color, Arial font, and 24-pixel size to the <strong> tag (the child). But just as children have their own unique qualities, the <strong> tag adds its own quality—boldness—to the properties it inherits from its parent.

Note: Inheritance applies to all styles, not just tag styles. For example, if you apply a class style, to the <body> tag, then all tags inside the body–paragraphs, images, and so on–inherit the properties of the class style.

Inheritance comes in quite handy at times. Say you want to display *all* the text on a page (paragraphs, headings, unordered lists, and links) in the Verdana font. You could dedicate yourself to a lengthy tagging extravaganza and redefine *every* HTML tag used to format text—<h1>, <h2>, <p>, <a>, <ul>, and so on—or create a class style and then manually apply it to all the text on the page.

However, a better and faster technique is to take advantage of inheritance. Every web page contains a <body> tag, which contains *all* the elements of your page. The <body> tag, therefore, is an ancestor of *all* the HTML you see on a page—images, paragraphs, headings, and so on. To quickly format all the text, you can create an HTML tag style for the <body> tag and set the font to Verdana, or create a class style using that font and apply it to the <body> tag. Every bit of text inside the body—all children—will inherit the Verdana font property.

Note: Actually, tags don't inherit all CSS properties. For the most part, the exclusions are logical. For example, say you create a border around an unordered list to visually set it off in its own box. If the border property were inherited, then all the elements *inside* the unordered list–like list items, links, or bolded words–would each have their own box drawn around them as well. Padding and margin are two other common properties that tags don't inherit.

The Cascade

At times, styles can conflict. Let's say you redefine the <h1> tag in an external style sheet, so that all <h1> tags show up in red Arial font. Then you attach this external style sheet to a web page that has an *internal* style sheet where you set the <h1> tag style to the Times font at 24 pixels high.

When a browser has to display a Heading 1, it runs into a little dilemma. The page has two different styles—two sets of formatting rules—for the *same tag*. To make matters even more confusing, suppose one particular <h1> tag has a class named *.highlight* applied to it. The *.highlight* class style sets the font family to Trebuchet MS and makes all the text uppercase. So which style does the browser choose: the style from the internal style sheet, the style from the external style sheet, or the class style?

The answer is "All of them." The browser adopts elements of the three styles according to these hierarchical rules (hence the term "cascade"):

- Properties that don't conflict are applied as usual. In the previous example, the red color property exists only in the external style, while only the internal style specifies a font *size*. And the class is the only style to specify uppercase text. So far, the browser knows that, for this page, text inside <h1> tags should be red, 24 pixels tall, and uppercase.
- When properties *do* conflict, the browser uses the property from the style with the greatest specificity. Specificity is just CSS jargon meaning the style with the most authority. The type of selector is one way to affect specificity: ID selectors are considered more specific than class styles, which are more specific than tag

styles. In general, this means that properties from an ID style override properties from a class style, and properties from a class style override conflicts with a tag style. For an amusing—but accurate—description of specificity, read this article: *www.stuffandnonsense.co.uk/archives/css_specificity_wars.html.* Make sure you print out the accompanying *Star Wars*-themed chart which visually explains specificity by equating class selectors with Darth Vader, and IDs with the Dark Emperor himself: *www.stuffandnonsense.co.uk/archives/images/specificitywars-05v2.jpg.* May the force be with you.

- If two styles with the same specificity conflict—like the *h1* style in the external style sheet and the *h1* style in the internal style sheet in this example—the browser chooses the properties from the styles that were added to the page last. Say you first created an internal style sheet (at which point Dreamweaver inserted the appropriate HTML and CSS code into the web page) and *then* attached an external style sheet. That means the link to the external style sheet appears *after* the internal style sheet in the web page. In this case, a style from the external style sheet with the same name as a style from the internal style sheet wins out. Similarly, if you attach the external style sheet first and then create the internal style sheet, the internal style sheet wins.

  To summarize this example, then: Once the browser sorts things out, it determines that the text inside an <h1> tag on this web page should be Trebuchet MS and uppercase (from the class style), red (from the *h1* style in the external style sheet), and 24 pixels high (the *h1* style in the internal style sheet).

Note: Descendent selectors, which include combinations of tag, class, and ID names—such as *#banner h1*, *.main p*, or *h1 strong*—have even more authority since the specificity adds up. Say you create a *p* tag style with a bright-red text color, and a descendent selector, *.sidebar p*, with purple text. Any paragraphs inside another element (like a <div> tag) that use the *.sidebar* style are purple—*not* red. Fortunately, Dreamweaver provides several ways you can decipher this confusing jumble of conflicting styles (described in the next section).

Inherited properties, however, have no specificity, so when child elements inherit properties from parent elements (as described on page 311), any style applied directly to the child element overrules properties from the parent element—no matter the specificity of the parent tag's style. Suppose you create an ID style named *#homepage* with the following properties: purple text and the Arial font. If you apply the *#homepage* ID to the <body> tag, then the child elements (anything within the <body> tag) inherit those properties. If you then redefine the paragraph tag so that paragraph text is green, paragraph text inherits the Arial font from the body, but ignores the purple color in favor of the green. Even though an ID style like *#homepage* has greater authority than a simple *p* tag selector, the inherited properties don't beat out properties applied specifically to the paragraph through the *p* tag style.

To learn more than you probably ever wanted to know about the cascade, visit *www.w3.org/TR/CSS2/cascade.html*

Note: For a really in-depth but super-illuminating explanation of confusing CSS concepts, check out *CSS: The Missing Manual*. In that book, you'll find chapters dedicated to both inheritance and the cascade.

The Other Side of the CSS Styles Panel

If you haven't yet put this book down in hopes that the swelling in your brain will subside, you've probably absorbed the notion that the application of style properties is quite complex. With all this inheritance and cascading going on, it's easy for styles to collide in hard-to-predict ways. To help you discern how styles interact and ferret out possible style conflicts, Dreamweaver includes another view in the CSS Styles panel (see Figure 8-9). By clicking the Current button, the panel switches to Current Selection mode, which tells you how a web browser formats a selected item—such as an image, paragraph, table, or <div> tag—once it takes into account inheritance and the cascade.

Current Selection mode is an invaluable tool in diagnosing weird CSS behavior associated with inheritance and cascading. But like any incredible tool, it requires a good user's manual to learn how it works. The panel crams in a lot of information; here's a quick overview of what it provides:

- The "Summary for Selection" pane gives you a summary of style properties for the currently selected item. Remember that whole thing about how parents pass on attributes to child tags, and how, as styles cascade through a page, they accumulate (which means, for example, it's possible to have an <h1> tag formatted by multiple styles from multiple style sheets)? The "Summary for Selection" pane is like the grand total at the bottom of a spreadsheet. It tells you what a selected element—a paragraph, a picture, and so on—will look like when a web browser tallies up all the styles and displays the page. For serious CSS fans, this pane is almost worth the entire price of Dreamweaver.
- The About pane displays the origin of a particular property (Figure 8-9, top). If a headline is orange, but you never created an <h1> tag with an orange color, you can find out which style from which style sheet passes the hideous orange to the heading. This pane isn't very useful, however, since you can get the same information by mousing over any property in the Summary section; in addition, when you have the About pane visible, you can't see the much more useful Rules pane, discussed next. So you're better off skipping this pane.
- The Rules pane lists the styles that apply to the current selection (Figure 8-9, bottom). Since any element can be on the receiving end of countless CSS properties handed down by parent tags, it's helpful to see a list of all the styles contributing to the current appearance of the selected object.
- The Rules pane shows you the order of the cascade (Figure 8-9, bottom). Not only are styles applied to the current selection listed here, they're also listed in a particular order, with the most general at the top and the most specific at the bottom. When the same property exists in two (or more) styles, the style listed last (farthest down the list) wins.

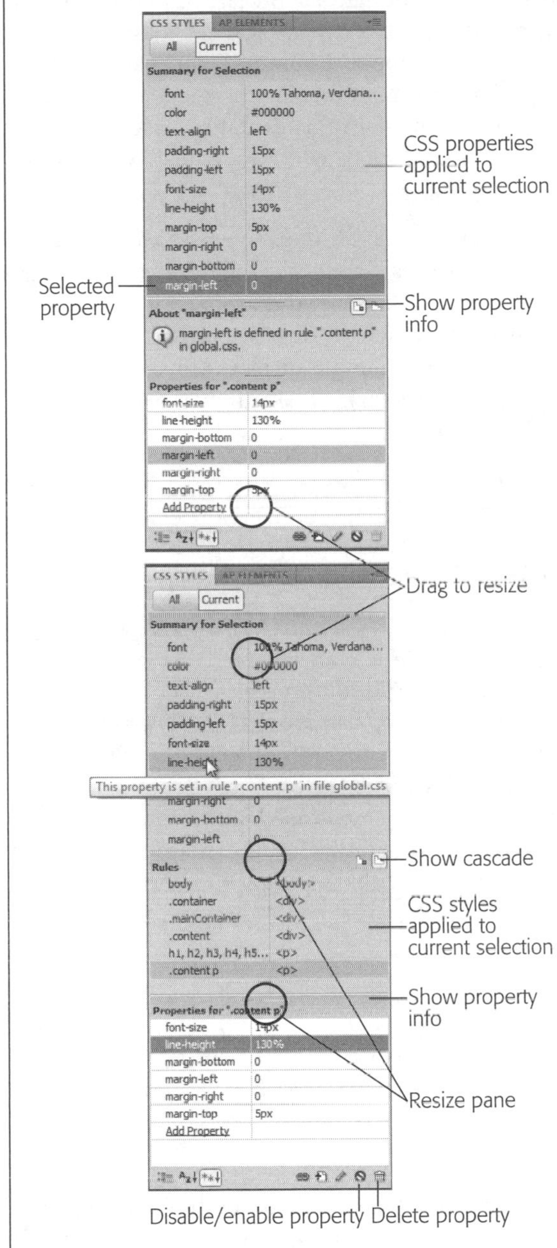

Figure 8-9:
When in Current Selection mode, you'll find that the two different views for the middle pane—Property Information (top) and Cascade (bottom)—are mostly the same. Property Information view tells you where the selected item gets its properties—that is, the style and style sheets Dreamweaver used to define the property. Cascade view, however, is by far the more useful option. You can get the same information as in the Property Information view simply by mousing over a CSS property in the Summary pane. For example, in the bottom image, hovering your mouse over the font property opens a pop-up tooltip that explains that this particular property is set in a body tag style that's defined in an external style sheet named global.css. In addition, Cascade view lists all the styles applied to the currently selected tag: in this case, six styles help format the text currently selected. Unfortunately, out of the box, Dreamweaver thinks you should be looking at the Property Information pane, so one of the first things you should do when you start working with CSS is to click the Current button at the top of the CSS Styles panel, and then click the Show Cascade button. Thankfully, Dreamweaver remembers which view you selected, so the Cascade view will remain selected even after you quit and restart Dreamweaver.

A few examples help demonstrate how to read the CSS Style panel in Current Selection mode. Figure 8-9 shows the CSS properties affecting a selection of text (in this case, a paragraph within the main content area of a web page). The "Summary for Selection" pane lets you know that if you viewed this page in a web browser, this paragraph would displayed text in the Tahoma typeface in black (#000000), left-aligned, with 15 pixels (px) of left and right padding, at a font size of 14 pixels, with a 130% line height (the space between each line of text), and with 5 pixels of space for the top margin. When you select a property from the "Summary for Selection" pane and then click the Show Property Information button (Figure 8-9, top), the About pane displays where the property comes from—in this case, the margin property settings belong to a descendent selector—*.content p*—which is defined in an external style sheet named *global.css*.

You've seen the bottom part of this pane before. It's the Properties pane, and you use it to delete, add, and edit a style's properties. Simply click in the area to the right of the property's name to change its value, or click the Add Property link to select a new property for the style. Notice that in this example, the Properties pane contains fewer properties than Summary view. That's because it displays only the properties of a single style (the *.content p* descendent selector), while Summary view shows all the properties the current selection inherits.

Note: Sometimes, it's hard to see all the information in one or more of the three panes. You can use the gray bars containing the panes' names as handles and drag them up or down to reveal more or less of each pane (see Figure 8-9), or double-click the tab of another open panel (like the Files panel) to close it and provide more room for the CSS styles panel.

Clicking the Show Cascade button (Figure 8-9, bottom) reveals a list of all the styles that affect the current selection. In this case, you can see that six styles—the body tag style, three class styles (.container, .mainContainer, .content), a group selector (*h1, h2, h3, h4, h5, h6, p*) and, finally, the descendent selector *.content p*—contribute to styling the selected paragraph. In addition, as mentioned above, the order of the styles is important. The lower the name appears in the list, the more "specific" that style is—in other words, when several styles contain the same property, the property belonging to the style *lower* on the list wins out. (See page 312 for more on conflicts caused by cascading styles.)

Tip: You can also see the cascade of rules listed in the Property inspector. First, select the text you want to analyze. Then click the CSS button on the Property inspector, and then select the Targeted Rule menu–the top group of items in the menu lists the cascade exactly as it appears in the Rules pane of the CSS Styles panel.

Clicking a style name in the Rules pane reveals that style's properties in the Properties pane below. This pane not only lists the style's properties, but also crosses out any properties that don't apply to the selected tag. A property doesn't apply to a selection for one of two reasons: either because the property is overridden by a more specific style, or because the selected tag doesn't inherit that property.

For example, Figure 8-10 shows that four styles affect the formatting of a single headline: three tag styles (<body>, <h2>, and <h2>) and one class style (*.highlight*).

In the left-hand image, the color and font-size properties for the *h2* style are crossed out—those properties don't apply to the current selection. The font-family property, on the other hand, isn't crossed out, indicating that Dreamweaver displays the current selection using the font Trebuchet MS. Because that *h2* appears near the top of the list of styles in the Rules pane, you can determine that that style is less "specific" (less powerful) than styles listed later. The style that appears last on the list—*.highlight* in this example—is most "specific" and its properties override conflicts from any other style. Selecting *.highlight* in the Rules pane (Figure 8-10, bottom right) demonstrates that, yes indeed, its font size and color properties "win" in the battle of cascading style properties.

Tip: If you mouse over a property that's crossed out in the Properties pane, Dreamweaver pops up a tooltip explaining why a browser won't apply that property. If the property is crossed out because a more specific style overrules it, Dreamweaver also tells you which style won out. For example, in Figure 8-10, mousing over the font-size property of the *h2* style opens a pop-up window explaining that a more specific class style overrides this property.

If your web pages are elegantly simple and use only a couple of styles, you may not find much need for this aspect of the CSS Styles panel. But as you become more proficient (and adventurous) with CSS, you'll find this panel a great way to untangle masses of colliding and conflicting styles.

Tip: One way to make a style more "powerful"—so that its properties override properties from conflicting styles—is to use a descendent selector (see the note on page 301). For example a *body p* descendent selector has more authority than just a plain *p* tag style, even though both styles target the exact same tags. Likewise, a *.content p* style is more powerful than a *body p* style, since it applies a class selector (which is more powerful than a tag selector) and one tag selector. You can quickly rename a style or create a more longwinded and powerful descendent selector using the CSS Styles panel: Select the name of the style in the CSS Styles panel (use the All view); click the style name a second time to edit it.

Using the Code Navigator

Dreamweaver includes yet another valuable CSS tool, this one aimed at CSS pros who like to use Code View when they write and edit CSS. The Code Navigator gives you a quick way to see all the CSS styles applied to any element you click on. It's kind of like the Rules Pane of the CSS Styles panel (discussed in the previous section), but the CSS styles appear in a pop-up menu directly in the document window (see Figure 8-11).

To access the Code Navigator, hold down the Alt key and click an element on the page (Mac owners need to press ⌘-Option and click). You can click any element whose CSS you wish to examine: an image, a heading, a paragraph, a table, and so on. For example, in Figure 8-11, clicking ⌘-Option and the "Tips" headline (that would be Alt-click for Windows) opened the Code Navigator, which lists the styles that apply to that headline.

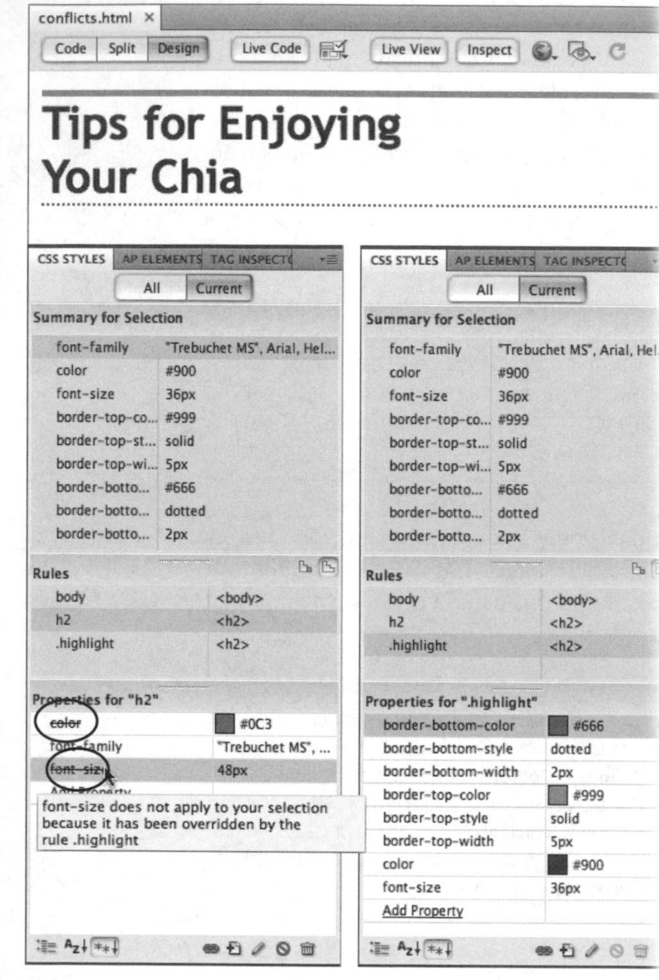

Figure 8-10:
Selecting the Current view of the CSS Styles panel lets you easily view all the properties applied to the currently selected item–in this example it's the headline (an <h2> tag) pictured at top. A line (circled in the left corner of the panel below) strikes out properties from a style that don't apply to the headline. In this case, the font-size and color properties in the.highlight class style override the same properties in the less specific h2 style (bottom left).

There are several other ways to access the Code Navigator:

- Click the Code Navigator icon (circled in Figure 8-12). This ship steering wheel icon appears next to an element you select on a page (or above an element when you put your cursor on it). It usually takes a second or so to appear, so you may want to stick with the keyboard shortcut (Alt-click or ⌘-Option-click).
- Right-click any item on the page, and choose Code Navigator from the pop-up shortcut menu.
- Select an item on a page and choose View→Code Navigator, or press Ctrl-Alt-N (Windows) or ⌘-Option-N (Mac).

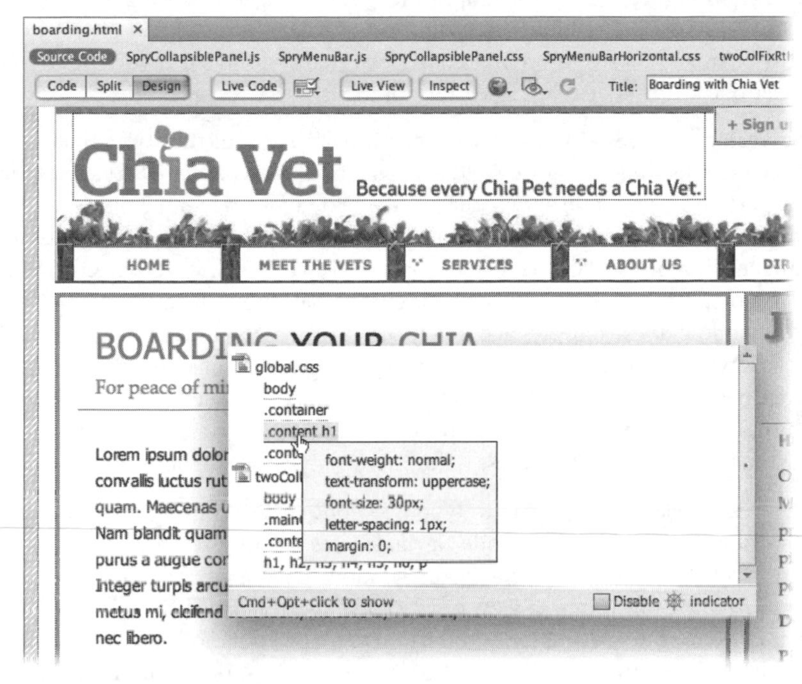

Figure 8-11: *The Code Navigator displays a list of CSS styles for any element on a page. In fact, it can show more than just CSS: If you're working with templates (see Chapter 20) or dynamic, database-driven websites (see Part Six), the Code Navigator lists other files that impact the current document, such as a template file or a file with server-side programming.*

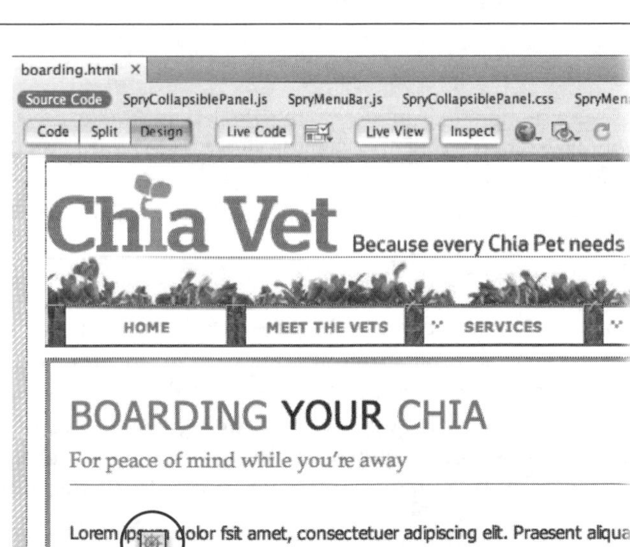

Figure 8-12: *If the Code Navigator's ever-present steering wheel icon bothers you, turn it off by turning on the Disable box in the Code Navigator window (see Figure 8-11). From that point on, you open the Code Navigator using the keyboard shortcut or one of the other methods discussed in this chapter.*

Once the Code Navigator window opens, you see all the CSS styles that affect the current item. In Figure 8-11, for example, the Code Navigator lists eight styles that impact the format for the headline "Boarding Your Chia"—four styles in the *global.css* external style sheet and five more in another external style sheet. If you move your mouse over one of the styles, you'll see a list of that style's CSS properties.

Code Navigator provides a quick way to see properties for all the styles that affect the page element as well. In Figure 8-11, hovering over the *.content h1* style lists that style's properties: normal *font-weight*, uppercase text, a *font-size* of 30 pixels, and so on. Although this is a quick way to view styles and their properties, it isn't as useful as the Current view of the CSS Styles panel (page 314), which shows you exactly which *properties* (not just which styles) apply to the current selection. In addition, the Code Navigator window doesn't always accurately display the CSS cascade (page 312)—it does list the styles in order of specificity, but it splits up the list of styles by style sheet, so if a page has more than one style sheet you may not get a clear picture of the cascade. The CSS Rules Pane (page 314), on the other hand, shows a complete list of styles from least to most specific, regardless of how many style sheets you use.

If you're a code jockey who prefers to type CSS code instead of relying on Dreamweaver's windows and panels, the Code Navigator lets you jump immediately to CSS code. Once you open the Code Navigator window, click any style listed. Dreamweaver jumps into Split mode (a view of raw code and the page's Design view) and displays the CSS for the selected style (you'll find more on Split mode on page 415). Of course, you need to know how to write CSS code for this to be useful. If you're not comfortable with that, you should stick with the CSS Styles panel and the methods discussed on pages 124 andpage 304 for editing styles.

Styling for Print

You may be surprised to see a section on print design in a book dedicated to creating beautiful on-screen presentations. However, it's common to see people print out web pages: printed directions to get to a concert, a list of product names and ratings to review while you're out shopping, or a longwinded web treatise that's easier to read on paper while reclining in a favorite chair.

Unfortunately, some web pages just don't print well. Sometimes the banner's too big to fit on one sheet of paper, so it spans two printed pages; or the heavy use of ads wastes toner. And some CSS-based layouts simply print as jumbled messes. Fortunately, CSS has an answer: *printer style sheets*. The creators of CSS realized that people might use web pages in different ways, such as printing them out. In fact, they went so far as to define a large group of potential "media types" so web designers could customize pages for different output devices, including Teletype machines, Braille readers, and more.

Basically, by specifying a media type, you can attach an external style sheet that's applied *only* when someone sends the page to a particular device. For instance, you could have a style sheet that works only when someone looks at a web page on a monitor, and another that applies only when they print the page. You can tweak a page's styles so the page looks better when printed, without affecting the page's appearance onscreen. Figure 8-13 shows the concept in action.

The basic process involves creating an external style sheet that contains styles for the particular media type, and then attaching the style sheet to a web page and assigning the appropriate media type.

You learned how to attach an external style sheet on page 123, but in a nutshell, you simply click the Attach External Style Sheet button on the CSS Styles panel (see Figure 4-1). Doing so opens the Attach External Style Sheet window (see Figure 8-14). Click the browse button and locate the proper CSS file, select the media type from the Media menu, and then click OK.

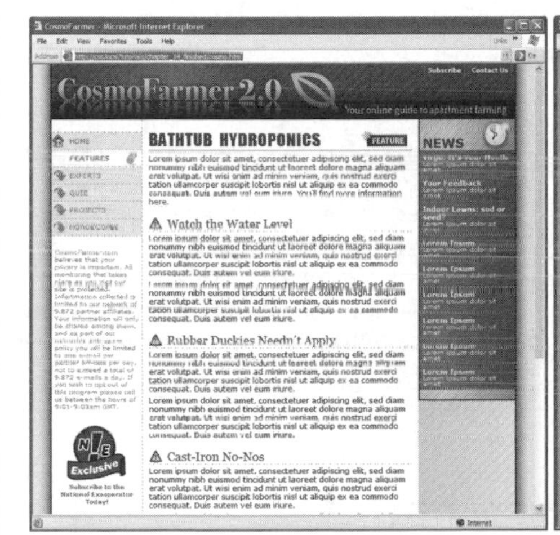

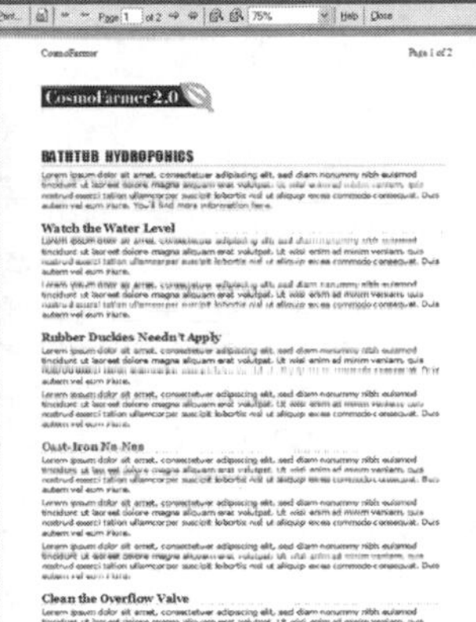

***Figure 8-13:** When you print a web page, you really don't need navigation links or information unrelated to the topic at hand (left). Create a print style sheet to eliminate unnecessary content and format the page so it prints well (right).*

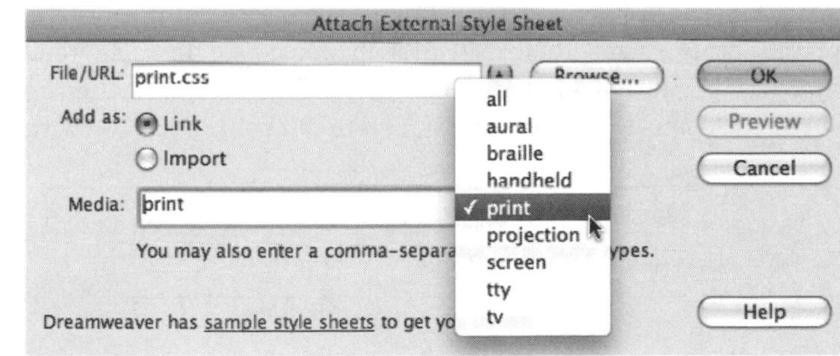

***Figure 8-14:** When you attach an external style sheet, you can assign it to a specific output device, including a printer ("print") or a monitor ("screen"). Or you can use a single style sheet no matter what the output device ("all"). Leaving this option blank is the same as selecting "all".*

Tip: If you attach an external style sheet and select a media type, Dreamweaver displays the media type name on the CSS Styles panel. For example, if you attach an external style sheet named *print.css* and specify the "print" media type, then "print.css (print)" appears in the CSS Style panel.

Although Dreamweaver lists many media types (aural, Braille, handheld, and so on), only three are widely supported: *print, screen*, and *all*. "Print" specifies that the styles apply only when someone prints the page; "screen" indicates a style sheet that takes effect only when the page appears on a monitor; and "all" is the same as not selecting anything—the style sheet applies when you print the page, viewed it on a monitor, feel it on a Braille reader, and so on. The "all" option comes in handy when you want to create a style sheet that defines the basic look of your website—such as its font, line height, and text alignment—no matter whether someone prints it or views it onscreen. You can create two additional style sheets from this basic one, one specifically designed for print, the other for monitors.

Note: Dreamweaver doesn't provide a way to create a new external style sheet *and* define its media type at the same time. One way to create and use a new printer-only style sheet is follow the steps on page 113 to create an external style sheet, unlink that style sheet from the page (page 126), and then reattach the external style sheet and select the print option from the Media menu. Alternatively, you could just create a CSS style sheet file by choosing File→New and selecting CSS from the Blank Page category of the New Document window; save the file (don't forget the .css extension), and then add styles to the file using the same methods you use when you add styles to a web page (see page 113). You can then attach this style sheet to a web page and specify a media type, as described on the previous page.

Previewing Media Styles in Dreamweaver

Web designers use Dreamweaver mainly to create pages that people view onscreen. Because of that, the program shows displays style formatting only when you either haven't selected a media type at all or when you specify the "all" or "screen" type. So how can you see what a printed version will look like when designing a print style sheet? Dreamweaver sports a fancy toolbar just for this purpose: the Style Rendering toolbar (Figure 8-15). To turn it on, choose View→ Toolbars→Style Rendering, or right-click (Control-click) the document toolbar, and then choose Style Rendering.

Note: If you're in Live View (page 578), the Style Rendering toolbar has no effect. In Live View, Dreamweaver only displays what the page will look like in a web browser.

Each button in the toolbar lets you view the page as it will look onscreen, in print, or with one of the other media types. Click the Screen button to see how Dreamweaver (and a web browser) normally display the page. Click the Print button, and any styles attached using the "print" and "all" media types appear; in other words, when you design a page for print, click the Print button.

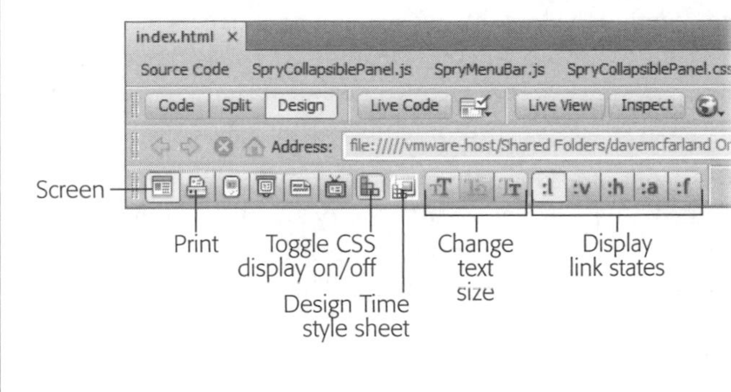

Figure 8-15: *The Style Rendering toolbar lets you see styles that match the media type you selected when you attached the style sheet to the page. The toolbar also includes buttons to attach a Design Time style sheet (see the box on page 326) and to hide all the styles. This last option is particularly useful when you create complex CSS-based designs, which can sometimes make selecting and editing HTML difficult. Click the "toggle CSS display" button to temporarily hide the styles and display just the simple, unadorned HTML.*

Note: If your CSS styles don't seem to have any effect on a page, you either have the wrong media type selected in the Style Rendering toolbar, or you might have turned off the display of CSS by clicking the Toggle CSS Display button (see Figure 8-15). Click the Toggle CSS Display again to display the CSS-styled page.

FREQUENTLY ASKED QUESTION

New Options in the Style Rendering Toolbar

Dreamweaver CS5 has added some new buttons to the Style Rendering toolbar. What do they do?

Dreamweaver CS5 has some new options for displaying some HTML elements in Design view. Three buttons control the size of text and five others let you preview links in different states (see Figure 8-15). From left to right, the three text buttons let you increase, reset, and decrease the size of text. They let you see what happens to your design when someone increases or decreases the default text size in their web browser. While this might have been a cool tool a few years back (when all browsers had an "increase text size" command), times have changed. Browsers have replaced the "increase text" command with a zoom feature—it not only increases the size of text, but of everything else on the page. In other words, these buttons aren't really useful, so skip them.

The link buttons *are* more useful—they let you preview your links in various "states." As mentioned on page 181, you can style links to look different depending on whether a visitor has not clicked a link, is currently clicking it, has already clicked it, moves her mouse over it, or tabs to it. Normally, Dreamweaver displays just the plain-vanilla link style—the way a link looks when a guest has never visited it. Clicking any link button (*:l* for the *:link* state, *:a* for the active (being clicked) state; *:v* for the *:visited* state, *:h* for the *:hover* [mouse over] state; and *:f* for the *:focus* (tabbed to) state. In other words if you create different styles for different link states as described on page 181, these buttons let you see what they look like.

Tips for Printer Style Sheets

A printer style sheet can redefine the look of any element on a page when you print it. You can change fonts, adjust type size, increase leading (the space) between lines of text, and so on. You can use any CSS property you want, and modify any style to your liking, but there are a few common tasks that most printer style sheets perform.

- **Override properties from another style sheet.** If you attach an external style sheet with the "all" media type or you didn't specify any media type at all, the printed page uses styles from that style sheet. The print style sheet may need to override some of the settings in those style sheets. The best way to do this is to simply create styles with names that match the style you wish to override. For example, if a style sheet attached to a page has a *p* tag style that specifies a font size of 12 pixels, you can create another *p* tag style in the print style sheet that changes the font size to 12 points. (Due to the rules of the cascade [page 312], the printer style sheet needs to be attached *last* to the web page for its styles to overrule similarly named styles in another sheet.)

  Another solution to this problem is to simply create two style sheets—one for print and one for the screen—and attach each with its respective media type. This way, there won't be any overlap between styles in the two sheets.

- **Text size and color.** For screen display, you'll size text using pixels, ems, or percentages (see page 133). Unfortunately, these units of measure don't make a lot of sense to an inkjet printer. If you've used Microsoft Word, you probably know the measurement of choice for printed text is points. If you don't like the size of type when you print a page, redefine font sizes using a printer-friendly size. In addition, while bright yellow type on a black background may look cool onscreen, black type on white paper is the easiest to read. If you colored your text, it may print out as a shade of gray on a black-and-white printer. Setting text to black in a print style sheet can help your visitors' weary eyes.

- **Hide unnecessary page elements.** Some parts of a web page don't really need to print out. Why, for example, do you need to see a site's navigation bar or a sidebar of links on a printed page? After all, you can't click them! Fortunately, CSS provides a property that lets you hide unwanted page elements in printed pages. Just create a style that applies to the part of the page you wish to hide—for instance, with CSS-based layouts you typically divide sections of a page into separate <div> tags, each with its own unique ID. Say you have the site's navigation bar inside a tag that has an ID named *#navbar*. To hide the nav bar when someone prints the page, create an ID style named *#navbar* in your print style sheet. In the CSS Rule Definition window (see Figure 4-3), click the Block category and then choose "None" from the Display property menu. (In Figure 8-13, right, for example, the banner and both sidebars don't appear in the printed version of the page.)

- **Adjust margins and widths.** To make a website design look more elegant, you might increase the margins around the edges of a page. But this extra space only wastes paper when printed. Remove any margins you applied to the body tag.

In addition, if you hide parts of a page when printing, it's possible that the remaining page elements won't fill the printed page. In this case, add a style to the print style sheet that changes the widths of the printed elements. For example, if you have a two-column design—a sidebar with links and other site-specific info, and a main column filled with all the useful info that should appear on a printed page—and you hide one column (the sidebar), you'd then set the width of the remaining column to 100% and remove any margins on its left and right side. That way, the printed information fills the width of the page.

- **Take advantage of !important.** As mentioned earlier, sometimes the printer style sheet needs to override certain CSS properties from another style sheet. Thanks to the cascade (page 312) a style must have greater "specificity" to overrule conflicts with another style. If you're trying to override, say, the font color used for a descendent selector named *body #wrapper #maincontent p*, you have to add the same longwinded style name to your print style sheet. Fortunately, CSS provides a simpler method: the *!important* directive. Adding *!important* to a property in a CSS style lets that property overrule any conflicting property values from other styles, even if those other styles are more specific.

  Unfortunately, Dreamweaver doesn't give you a way to easily add this option. You have to manually edit the style sheet in Code view. Say you want the text of all paragraph tags to print black. Create a *p* tag style in the print style sheet and set the *color* property to "black". Then open the print style sheet in Code view and add *!important* after the color value and before the semicolon character. Here's what that would look like in Code view:

  ```
  p {
  color: #000000 !important;
  }
  ```

  When you print the page, this style overrides any color settings for any paragraph tags in a competing style sheet—even a much more specific style.

GEM IN THE ROUGH

A Time to Design

A Dreamweaver feature called *Design Time style sheets* lets you quickly try different CSS style sheets as you develop web pages. With it, you can hide (external) style sheets you've attached to a web page and substitute new ones.

Design Time style sheets come in handy when you work on HTML that, later on, you intend to make part of a complete web page. Dreamweaver Library items are a good example; this feature (discussed in Chapter 19) lets you create a chunk of HTML that any number of pages on your site can use. When you update the Library item, Dreamweaver updates every page that uses it. A timesaving feature, for sure, but since a Library item is only *part* of a page, it doesn't include the <head> portion needed to either store styles or attach an external style sheet. So when designing a Library item, you're working in the dark (or at least without any style). By using Design Time style sheets, you can access all the styles in an external style sheet and even preview the effects directly in Design view.

You'll also turn to this feature when you work with Dreamweaver's server-side XML tools (see Chapter 27), which let you add an "XSLT fragment" to a complete web page–essentially letting you convert XML (like the kind you'd find in an RSS feed from a new website or a blog) into a chunk of HTML. But to accurately design these components, you need to use Design Time style sheets.

You can apply a Design Time style sheet by clicking the Design Time style sheet button in the Style Rendering toolbar (see Figure 8-15) or by choosing Format→CSS Styles→Design-time; the Design-Time Style Sheets window appears. Click the top + button to select an external style sheet. Note that clicking this button doesn't attach the style sheet to the page; it merely lets you access the properties of a .css file as you work on a page.

To properly view your page with this new style sheet, you may need to get an attached external style sheet out of the way. To do that, use the bottom + button to add it to the Hide list.

You can only use Design Time style sheets when you work in Dreamweaver. They have no effect on how a page looks in a web browser. That's both the good news and the bad news. Although Dreamweaver lets you apply class styles from a Design Time style sheet to your web page, it doesn't actually attach the style sheet to the page. For example, if you use a Design Time style sheet to design a Library item, Dreamweaver doesn't guarantee that the web page using the Library item has the style sheet you're using attached to it. You have to attach it yourself, or else your visitors will never see your intended result.

CHAPTER

9

Page Layout

Web design, unfortunately, isn't like most other forms of graphic design. For magazine and book projects, software like InDesign lets you place text and images anywhere you want—and even rotate and overlap them. But web designers are stuck with the basic technology of HTML, which wants to flow from the top of the window to the bottom, in one long column. To place elements around the page and create multiple columns of content, you need to resort to some fancy footwork.

For much of the Web's short life, designers have used the HTML <table> tag to control the position of elements on a page—to create columns, sidebars, banners, and so on. Unfortunately, since the <table> tag was intended to display information in a spreadsheet-like format, bending it to a web designer's will often resulted in complex HTML that downloaded slowly, displayed sluggishly, and was very difficult to modify.

Now that CSS-friendly web browsers like Internet Explorer, Firefox, Safari, and Opera rule the Web, designers can safely rely on a much better (though often frustrating) method: Cascading Style Sheets. That's right; not only is CSS great for formatting text, navigation bars, images, and other bits of a web page, it also has all the tools needed to create sophisticated designs, like the ones shown in Figure 9-1.

CSS provides two ways to lay out a web page—*absolute positioning* and *floats*. Absolute positioning lets you position an element anywhere on a page with pixel-level accuracy—or so the theory goes. This kind of control is exciting, but actually very difficult to achieve. That's why the vast majority of web pages use float-based layouts—a method that lets you create great-looking multicolumn designs.

Dreamweaver includes a starter set of 16 CSS layouts (all use the more common float-based approach). These starter pages cover the most commonly used page layouts—designs with one, two, or three columns of content, a header for a logo and banner, and a footer for a copyright notice, for example. These layout files aren't complete page designs as much as basic building blocks you can modify to match your own sensibility. Best of all, Dreamweaver's done the complex job of getting the designs to work in all current web browsers.

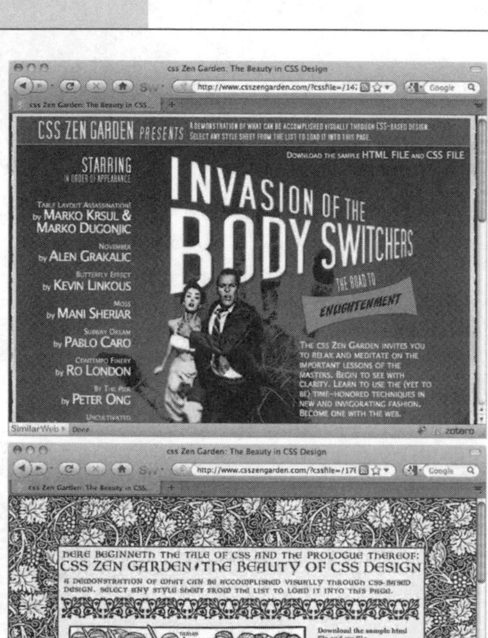

Figure 9-1:
CSS Zen Garden (www.csszengarden.com) is the original showcase for CSS layout. Although the designs haven't been updated in a while, in its day it caused many a web designer to bow down and proclaim, "I'm not worthy, I'm not worthy." The site not only demonstrates great design, it shows you the power of CSS-based layout. Each page includes the same content and the same HTML. The only difference among them is their external style sheets and graphics. Making drastic visual changes to an old table-based layout required a lot of tinkering with the underlying HTML. CSS, by contrast, lets you redesign sites without rewriting any HTML.

Note: CSS layout is one of those complex topics that is sometimes better learned by doing instead of reading. To get a taste of how CSS layout works, try the tutorial on page 374, and then flip back to the beginning of this chapter for all the messy details.

This chapter introduces the basic concepts behind float-based layouts—what they are, how they work, and how to create one; it also provides instructions for modifying Dreamweaver's CSS designs. In addition, you'll learn about absolute positioning, and how to use it to place select elements where you want them.

Types of Web Page Layouts

Being a web designer means dealing with the unknown. What kind of browsers do your visitors use? Do they have the latest Flash player installed? But perhaps the biggest challenge designers face is creating attractive designs that work across different sizes screens. Monitors vary in size and resolution: from petite 15-inch 640 × 480 pixel displays to 30-inch monstrosities displaying, oh, about 5,000,000 × 4,300,000 pixels.

Float-based layouts offer two approaches to this problem: *fixed width* or *liquid layouts* (also called *fluid layouts*). A fixed-width layout gives you the most control over how your design looks, but can inconvenience some of your visitors. Folks with really small monitors have to scroll to the right to see everything, and those with large monitors have wasted space that could display more of your excellent content. Liquid layouts make designing pages more challenging for you, but make the most effective use of your guests' screen sizes.

- **Fixed-width layout.** Many designers prefer the consistency of a set width, like the page shown in Figure 9-2, top. Regardless of how wide a browser window is, the page content's width remains the same. In some cases, the design clings to the left edge of the browser window. More often, it's centered. With the fixed-width approach, you don't have to worry about what happens to your design on a very wide (or small) monitor.

  Many fixed width designs use width of anywhere from 760 pixels to 1000 pixels. To fit a fully maximized browser window on an 800 × 600 pixel screen, use 760 pixels. These days, however, the screens on even tiny 10-inch netbooks are at least 1024 pixels wide, and all desktop computers support at least 1024 × 768 pixels, so most new site use much bigger dimensions—960 pixels wide is now common for fixed-width designs, but you'll also see 1000 pixels and even a bit more on some sites.

- **Liquid layout.** Sometimes, it's easier to roll with the tide instead of fighting it. A liquid design adjusts a page's dimensions to fit a browser's width—whatever it may be. Your page gets wider or narrower as your visitor resizes his browser window (Figure 9-2, bottom). While liquid design makes the best use of browser real estate, you have to do more work to make sure your design looks good at different window sizes. On very large monitors, these types of designs can look ridiculously wide.

Fixed-width designs are probably the most common type of layout on the Web, since they provide a consistent display and make it much easier for designers to work with.

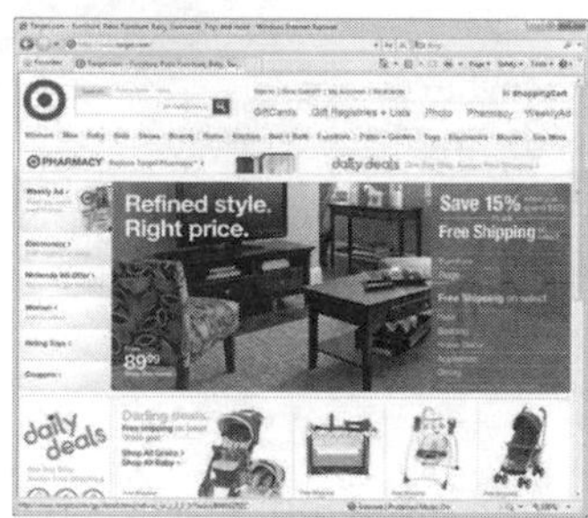

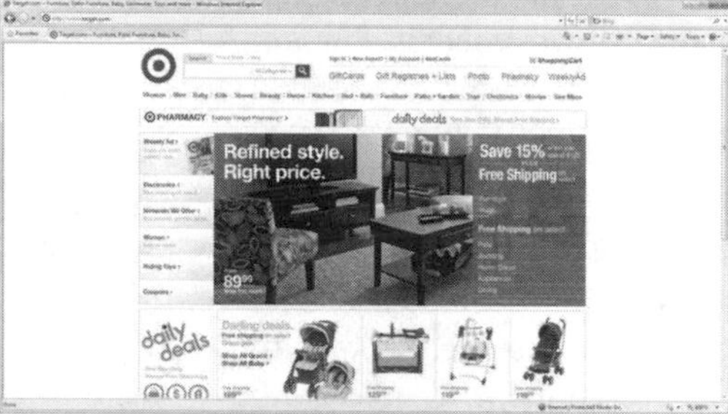

Figure 9-2:
CSS gives you several ways to deal with the uncertain widths of browser window and browser font sizes. You could simply ignore the fact that your site's visitors have different resolution monitors and force a single, unchanging width on them for your page, as the Target.com website does. As you can see in the top two images, resizing the browser window doesn't change the page–it remains the same width (but centered in the browser window) when you make the browser window wider. Most websites take this approach. Or you could create a liquid design that flows to fill whatever width window the page encounters. That's how Amazon's site works (bottom two images).

Note: A third type of layout, called "elastic," changes the width of a page based on the type size of the web browser. Increase the text size, and the page gets wider, decrease the text size and it gets smaller. This creates a sort of "zoom in" and "zoom out" effect–as both the text and page get bigger or smaller. However, since all current browsers include a "zoom" command, elastic layouts are no longer necessary.

Float Layout Basics

Float-based layouts take advantage of the CSS *float* property to position elements side by side and create columns on a page. As you read on page 228, you can float an image to make text wrap around a photograph. But it's also a powerful layout tool to move a bunch of related page elements (like a list of links that you want to appear in a left-hand column) to one side of the page or the other. In essence, the *float* property moves a page element to the left or the right. Any HTML that appears *after* the floated element moves up on the page, and hugs up against the side of the float.

Float is a CSS property, available when you create a CSS style (see page 113 for instructions on creating a style). It's listed in the CSS Rule Definition window's Box category (see Figure 9-3). Choose the "left" option, and the styled element floats to the left, choose the "right" option and the element moves to the right. For example, if you want to position a sidebar on the left side of a page, you float it to the left.

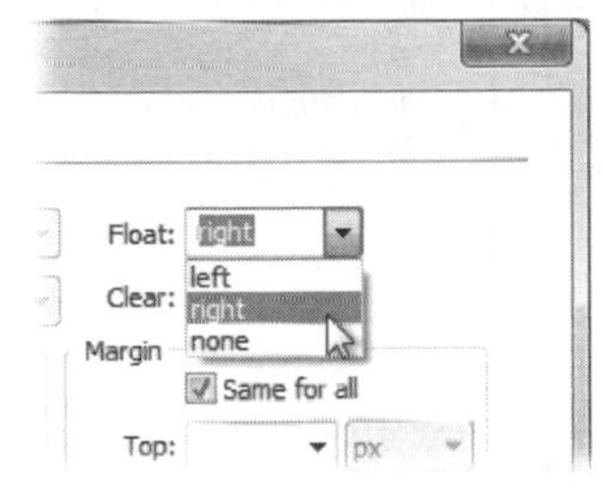

Figure 9-3: *You have just three options when you want to float an element: left, right, and none. You might never need the "none" option–it simply positions an element like a normal, unfloated element. Since this is the regular behavior of any element, you'd need this option only if you wanted to turn off a float applied by another style (see page 312 for more on how multiple styles can affect the same element).*

The Mighty <div> Tag

Whatever method you use, web page layout involves putting chunks of content into different regions of a page. With CSS, the most common way to organize content is with the <div> tag. The <div> tag is an HTML element that has no inherent formatting properties (besides the fact that browsers treat the tag as a block with a line break before and after it); you use it to mark a logical grouping of elements (a *division*) on a page.

You'll typically wrap a <div> tag around a chunk of HTML that belongs together. For example, the elements comprising the logo and navigation bar in Figure 9-4 occupy the top of the page, so it makes sense to wrap a <div> tag around them (labeled "banner div" in the figure). At the very least, you would include <div> tags for all the major regions of your page, such as the banner, main content area, sidebar, footer, and so on. But it's also possible to wrap a <div> tag around one or more *other* divs. People often wrap the HTML inside the <body> tag in another <div>. This tag, therefore, wraps around all the other divs on the page: You can set some basic page properties by applying CSS to this *wrapper* <div>. For example, you can set an overall width for the page, set left and right margins, or center all of the page's content in the middle of the screen.

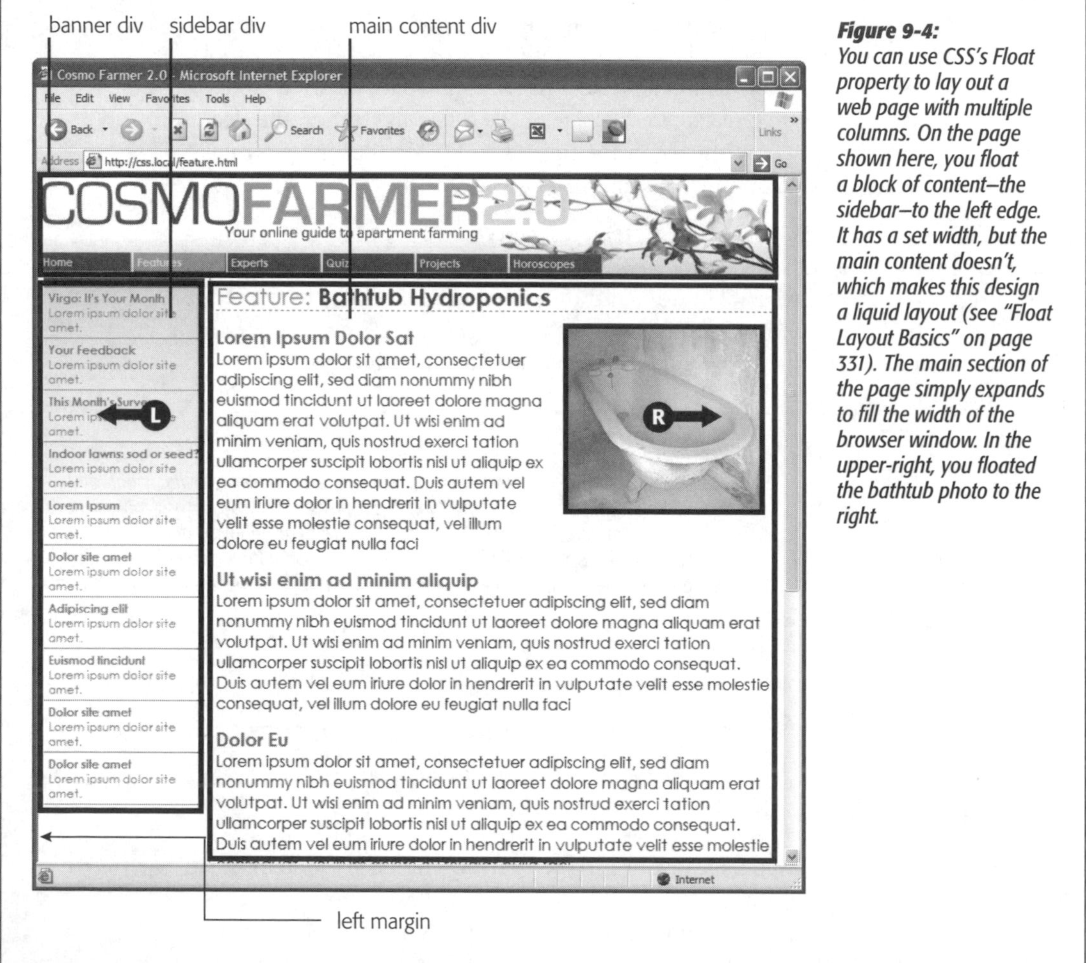

Figure 9-4: *You can use CSS's Float property to lay out a web page with multiple columns. On the page shown here, you float a block of content–the sidebar–to the left edge. It has a set width, but the main content doesn't, which makes this design a liquid layout (see "Float Layout Basics" on page 331). The main section of the page simply expands to fill the width of the browser window. In the upper-right, you floated the bathtub photo to the right.*

Once you've got your <div> tags in place, you add either a class or ID style to each one, which becomes your handle for styling each div separately. For parts of a page that form the basic building blocks of the page, designers usually apply either an ID or a class (page 112) to the div. For example, the <div> tag for a page's banner area might look like this: *<div id="banner"> or <div class="banner">*.

There are only a few differences between using a class and an ID to identify a region of a page: recall that you can use an ID only once per page, so if you have an element that appears multiple times, use a class instead. For example, if you have several divs that position photos and their captions, you wouldn't use an ID. Instead, you'd add a class to each div, like this: *<div class="photoBox">*. Another difference: ID selectors in CSS take precedence over class selectors in the case of a style conflict. For example, if you apply both an ID and a class to the same div tag, and then you create ID and class styles, any properties in the ID style that conflicted with the class would win out. This is one of the basic rules of the CSS cascade, described on page 312.

In a nutshell: if you insert a div that wraps around a unique element on a page (an element that appears only once per page), you can add either an ID or class property to it to identify it so you can style it with CSS; if you insert a div that appears multiple times on a page (like a div that holds a photograph, caption, and date for a series of photos on one page), then apply a class name to it.

Tip: If you select a <div> tag in the document window, the Property inspector provides two menus: one to apply an ID to the div, and another to apply a class style to the div.

The Insert Div Tag Tool

Because grouping parts of a page using <div> tags is such an important part of CSS layout, Dreamweaver includes a tool to simplify the process. The Insert Div Tag tool lets you wrap a <div> tag around a selection of page content, or simply drop an empty div onto a page that you can fill with images, links, paragraphs of text, or whatever.

To use this tool, either select the content you want to wrap (for example, click at the beginning of the selection and drag to the end of the selection) or click on the page where you wish to insert an empty <div> tag. Then click the Insert Div Tag button on the Layout category of the Insert panel (see Figure 9-5). You can find that button listed in the Common category, too, or you can choose Insert→Layout Objects→Div Tag. In any case, the Insert Div Tag window appears (Figure 9-6).

If you click OK, Dreamweaver wraps any selected content in a <div> tag, or, if you didn't select anything on the page, it drops a new <div> tag onto the page with the text "Content for New Div Tag Goes Here" (of course, you'll replace that with your own content). But, usually, you'll take an additional step: applying either an ID or class to the div. You do this in a couple of ways:

- **Choose a class from the Class menu or choose an ID from the ID menu.** The Class menu on the Insert Div Tag window lists all the class styles available to the current page. You usually select a class if you want to format a <div> tag the same way as all the other divs on the page. You might use a <div> tag to position an image and a caption on a page, or to create a pull-quote in the middle of an article; if you had multiple instances of photos with captions, you could create a class style (like .figure) to format each photo-caption pair. You could then select a photo and caption on the page, use the Insert Div Tag tool, and then select the class name (.figure in this example) from the class menu. You could repeat this procedure multiple times on a single page. But you can also apply a class to a div even if you use it for a unique set of elements – such as the banner at the top of the page (Dreamweaver's CSS layouts discussed on page 344, use class names and styles only).

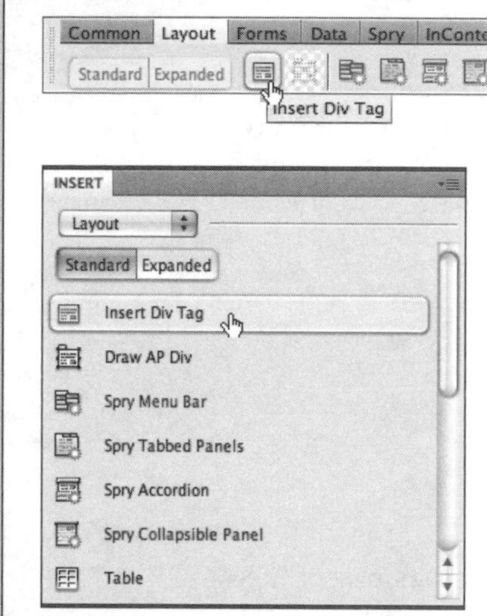

Figure 9-5:
The Layout category of the Insert panel includes buttons for adding both <div> tags and absolutely positioned divs (see page 356).

The ID menu on the Insert Div Tag window behaves a bit differently. Since you can only use an ID once per page (see page 112 for the reason) the ID menu lists IDs that exist in your style sheet, but only those you haven't yet applied to any tags. Say you create an ID style named *#banner* that you plan to apply to a <div> tag to define the banner area of your page. You select the banner content (like the site logo and navigation bar), and then click the Insert Div Tag button. At this point, you'd select *#banner* from the ID menu. If you then insert a second div on the page using the Insert Div Tag tool, *#banner* no longer appears in the ID menu.

- **Create a new class or ID.** If you haven't yet created a style to apply to the new <div> tag, you can click the New CSS Rule button (see Figure 9-6). It opens the familiar New Style Rule window, so you can create a new style. The process is the same as creating any style, as described in "Creating Styles" on page 113. Once you define the style, you'll return to the Insert Div Tag window, and the style you just created appears in the appropriate box. (In other words, if you created a class style, the name of the new class appears in the Class box; similarly, a new ID style appears in the ID box.)

After you apply a class or ID and click the OK button, Dreamweaver inserts the new <div> tag, complete with the appropriate HTML to apply the style: for example,

<div id="banner">. (Note that when you create an ID style, you add a # sign—for example, *#banner*—but when Dreamweaver inserts the HTML for the ID name, it omits the # sign. The same applies to class names: <div class="photo"> is correct, <div class=".photo"> is not.) In addition, Dreamweaver applies any styling you created for the class or ID to the div. In the case of CSS layout, that could mean sizing the div and positioning it on the page, as well as adding a background color, changing the size of text, or any other CSS formatting. You can add new content inside the div, edit what's there, or delete the div completely.

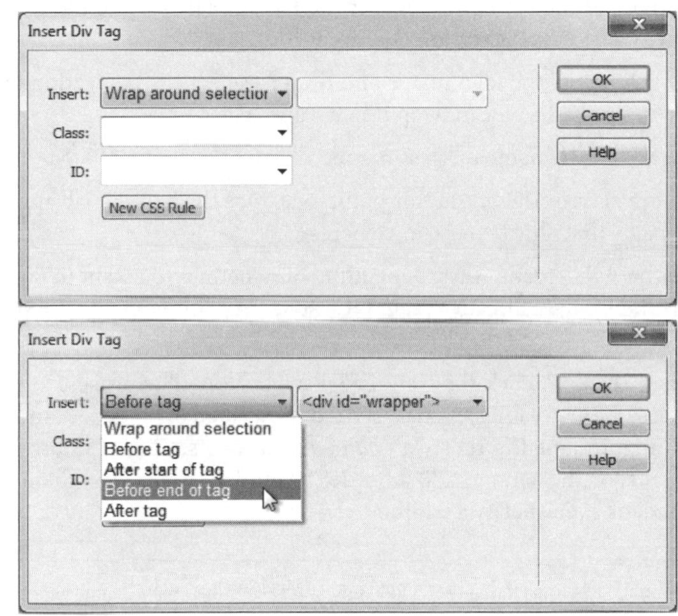

Figure 9-6: *The Insert Div Tag tool tells Dreamweaver where to place the div in relation to other tags on the page (see your choices listed in the left-hand Insert menu). The right-hand Insert menu lets you choose the precise tag for the div insertion point. That menu lets you select from tags that have an ID applied to them, or, if you chose "After start of tag" or "Before end of tag" from the left-hand menu, it lists the <body> tag. Suppose, for example, you want to insert a <div> tag to display a footer at the bottom of a page. Because you know the footer will go last on the page, you click the Insert Div Tag button, select "Before end of tag" from the Insert's left menu, and <body> from the right menu. Dreamweaver puts the <div> tag at the very end of the page's content, just before the closing </body> tag.*

Note: CSS-based layout is a big topic, worthy of a book or two by itself. For more in-depth coverage, including solutions to common float problems, pick up a copy of *CSS: The Missing Manual*.

A Simple Example

To get a better idea of how divs help with page layout, look at the layout in Figure 9-4. This design has a banner (logo and navigation bar), a left-hand sidebar (a list of story titles and links), and the main story. Figure 9-7, left, shows the order in which the HTML appears in the page: The banner elements come first, the sidebar second, and the main story (headlines, paragraphs, photo, and so on) last. (Remember, what you're seeing in Figure 9-7 demonstrates the power and the beauty of the HTML/CSS tango: Your HTML file contains your structured chunks of content, while your

CSS controls how a browser displays that content.) Viewed in a web browser, without any CSS styling, these different HTML sections would all appear stacked one on top of the other.

Note: You don't have to use this particular technique to get started with CSS layout. Dreamweaver ships with 16 premade layout designs called CSS Layouts. You can read about these starting on page 344.

To create a two-column design, you can follow these easy steps:

1. **Select the contents of the banner. Then, on the Layout category of the Insert panel, click the Insert Div Tag button (Figure 9-5).**

   For example, click before the logo image and drag to select the navigation bar. With this HTML selected, you can wrap it in a <div> tag.

2. **In the ID box, add an ID name or class name.**

   You could create a class or ID style at this point, but since the banner will appear only once per page, that's the better choice here.

   You can name the style several ways, depending on whether you want to create the style immediately, have already created the style, or want to create the style later on.

   - To create an ID style, click the New CSS Rule button. The process at this point is the same as creating any new style, as described on page 113. In this case, you might name the ID style *#banner*. You can set any CSS properties you want for the banner: add a border around all four sides, color the background, or even specify a width.

Note: When you create an ID style using the New CSS Rule box, you have to start the ID name with a # symbol, like this: *#banner*. However, when you create an ID in the Insert Div Tag window, you omit the # symbol; just type *banner*. The same applies to class styles–use a period when you create a style in the New CSS Rule box (*.pullquote*, for example), but omit it in the Insert Div dialog box.

   - Select an ID name from the ID menu, or a class name from the Class menu. The web page may already have an external style sheet attached, which contains all the necessary styles for the layout. Just select the ID or class name for the div you're inserting (for example, *banner*).
   - Type a name in the ID or Class box. If you don't want to create a style, you could just type *banner* in the ID box, and create the style later.

3. **Click OK to close the Insert Div Tag window.**

   Dreamweaver wraps the selected HTML with a <div> tag, and (if you created a new style) formats the banner region.

4. **Select the contents of the sidebar, and then, in the Insert bar, click the Insert Div Tag button. Click the New CSS Style button, and create a new ID or class style. Name it whatever you like, such as #sidebar, or .sectionNav, and then click OK.**

   This style formats and positions the left sidebar. We're finally getting to the "float" part of this design.

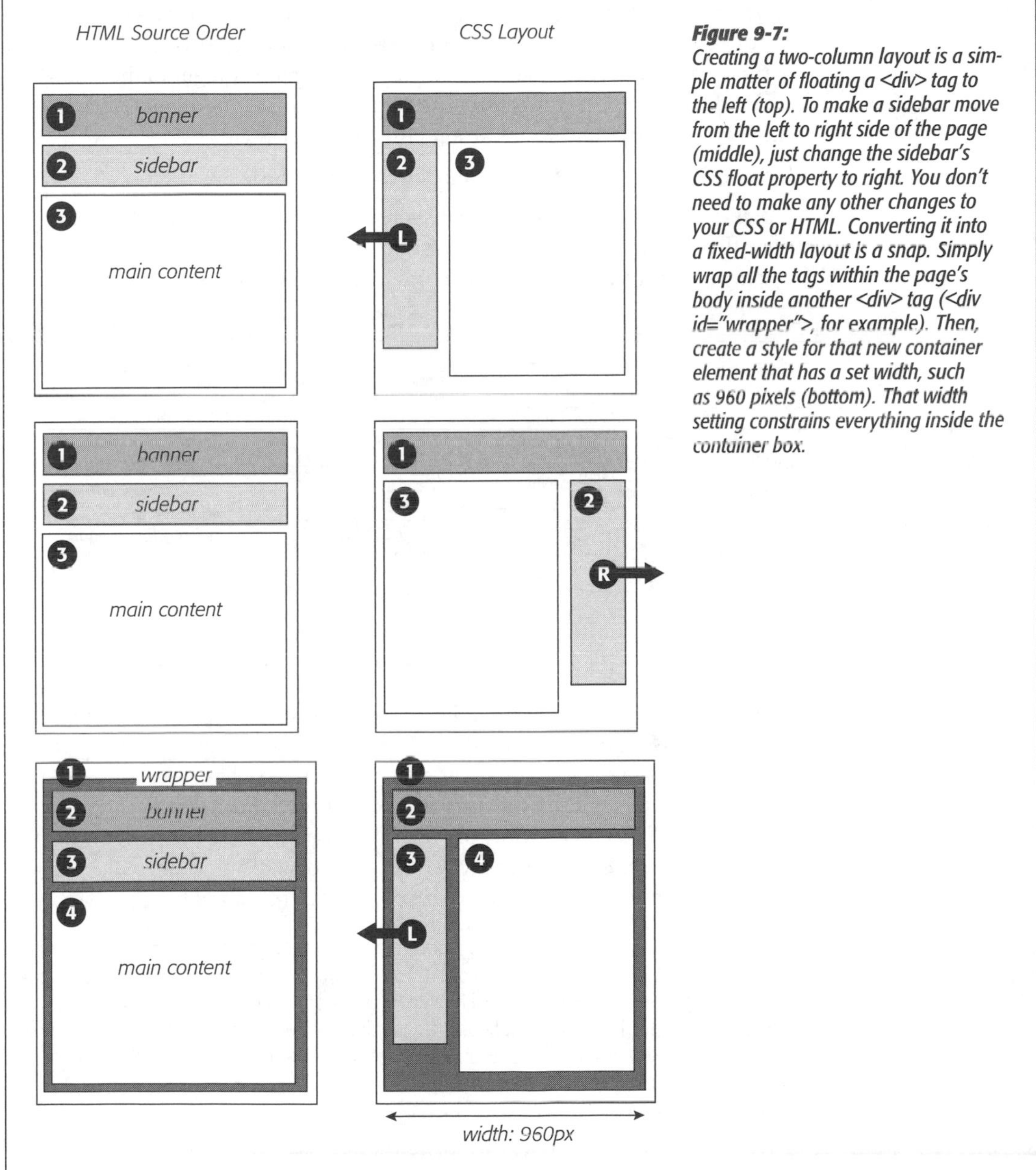

Figure 9-7:
Creating a two-column layout is a simple matter of floating a <div> tag to the left (top). To make a sidebar move from the left to right side of the page (middle), just change the sidebar's CSS float property to right. You don't need to make any other changes to your CSS or HTML. Converting it into a fixed-width layout is a snap. Simply wrap all the tags within the page's body inside another <div> tag (<div id="wrapper">, for example). Then, create a style for that new container element that has a set width, such as 960 pixels (bottom). That width setting constrains everything inside the container box.

5. **In the CSS Rule Definition window, click the Box category, and then, from the float menu, select "left" (see Figure 9-8).**

   When you work with floats, the source order (the order in which you add HTML to a file) is important. The HTML for the floated element must appear *before* the HTML for the element that wraps around it.

   Figure 9-7 shows three different two-column layouts. The diagrams on the left show the page's HTML source order: a <div> for the banner, followed by a <div> for the sidebar and, lastly, a <div> for the main content. On the right, you see the actual page layout. The sidebar comes *before* the main content in the HTML, so it can float either left (top, bottom) or right (middle). The main text area then moves up the page and wraps around the floated element.

6. **Type a value in the Width box (circled in Figure 9-8).**

   Unless you're floating an image with a predefined width, you should always give your floats a width. That way, you create a set size for the floated element, allowing the browser room to wrap other content into position.

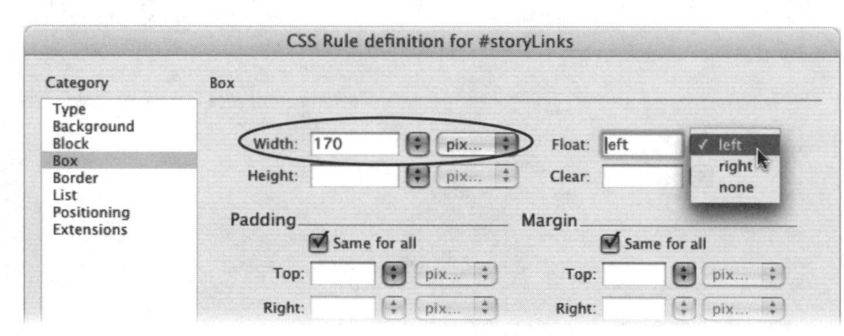

Figure 9-8: *Whenever you float an element (other than an image), always set a width. It constrains the floated element so that a browser can wrap other content around it.*

You can use a fixed width, say *170px*, or you can specify a percentage for a flexible design based on the width of the browser window (see page 329 for more about the pros and cons of set versus variable dimensions). If you set the sidebar to 20% of the width of the browser window and the latter's 700 pixels wide, the sidebar will be 140 pixels wide. But if your visitor stretches her window to 1000 pixels wide, the sidebar grows to 200 pixels. Fixed-width sidebars make page design easier, since you don't have to fret over differently sized browser windows.

Note: If you set a fixed width for your overall page design (by wrapping all the page contents in a <div> tag with its width property set), percentage width values for the sidebar are based on the fixed width-containing element–it isn't based on the window size, and doesn't change when the browser window size changes. This is true of any element whose width you specify by using percentage values: the percentage is based on the width of the tag that surrounds the element.

7. **Complete the style, and then insert the div.**

   At this point you can continue to style the sidebar: You could add a background color, set a font family, that, thanks to inheritance (see page 311), will apply to all of the text inside the div, and so on.

   When you're done, click OK in the Style Definition window; you return to the Insert Div Tag window with the ID box filled out with your freshly created style's name. Click OK to insert the div, and then watch the sidebar float.

   Now it's time to style the main column.

8. **Follow the same steps for the main content div: Select the page elements that form that main content on the page, click the Insert Div Tag button, and then create a new ID or class style for the page's main content region.**

   In this instance, you don't need to float anything. You merely have to add a left margin to the main content so that it won't try to wrap *below* the end of the sidebar. If the sidebar is shorter than the other content on the page, the text from the main column wraps underneath the sidebar. It's much like how the main text interacts with the right-floated photo in Figure 9-4. If the main content wrapped underneath the sidebar, the appearance of two side-by-side columns would be ruined. Adding a left margin that's equal to or greater than the width of the sidebar indents the main content of the page, creating the illusion of a second column.

   By the way, it's usually a good idea to make the left margin a little bigger than the width of the sidebar: That creates some empty space—a gutter—between the two elements. So if the sidebar is 170 pixels wide, adding a left margin of 185 pixels for the main content div adds an extra 15 pixels of space. If you use percentages to set the width of the sidebar, use a slightly larger percentage value for the left margin.

   In addition, avoid setting a width for the main content div. It's not necessary, since browsers simply expand it to fit the available space. Even if you want a fixed-width design, you don't need to set a width for the main content div, as described in Figure 9-7.

Expanding the two-column design into a three-column design isn't difficult either (Figure 9-9). First, add another <div> *between* the two columns, and float it to the right. Then add a right margin to the middle column, so that if the text in the middle column runs longer than the new right sidebar, it won't wrap underneath the sidebar.

Understanding the Box Model

It's no coincidence that you find the Float property in the "Box" category of the CSS Rule Definition window (Figure 9-10). To fully understand CSS layouts and how to make the most of floats, you need to understand the other CSS properties in this category: width, height, padding, margin, and clear.

- **Width and height.** You can specify the width and height for any styled object using these properties. If you want a paragraph that's 100 pixels wide, create a class style with the Width property set to 100 pixels, and then apply it to the paragraph. You'll often use the Width property in conjunction with the Float property (see the following paragraph) to do things like create a box with a set width that floats to either the left or right side of the page—a common format for pull-quotes, message boxes, and sidebars.

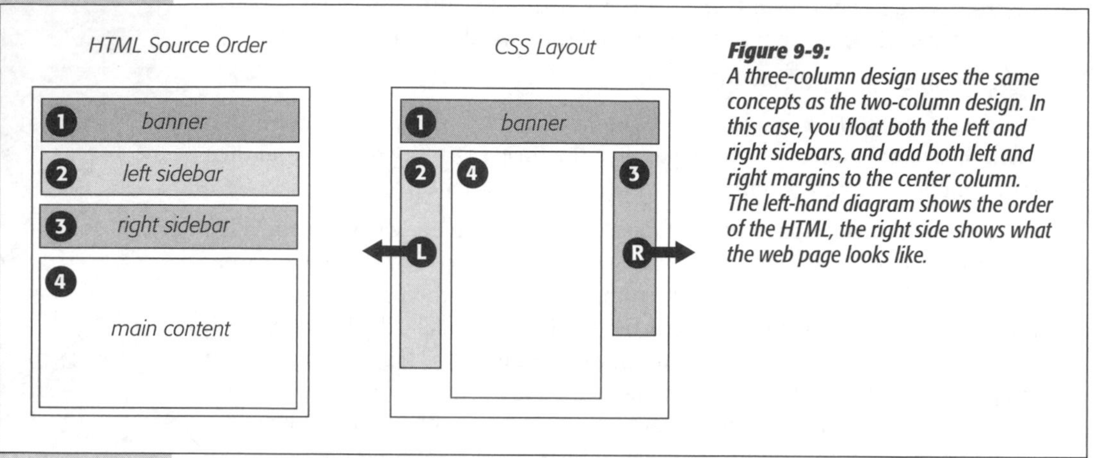

Figure 9-9: *A three-column design uses the same concepts as the two-column design. In this case, you float both the left and right sidebars, and add both left and right margins to the center column. The left-hand diagram shows the order of the HTML, the right side shows what the web page looks like.*

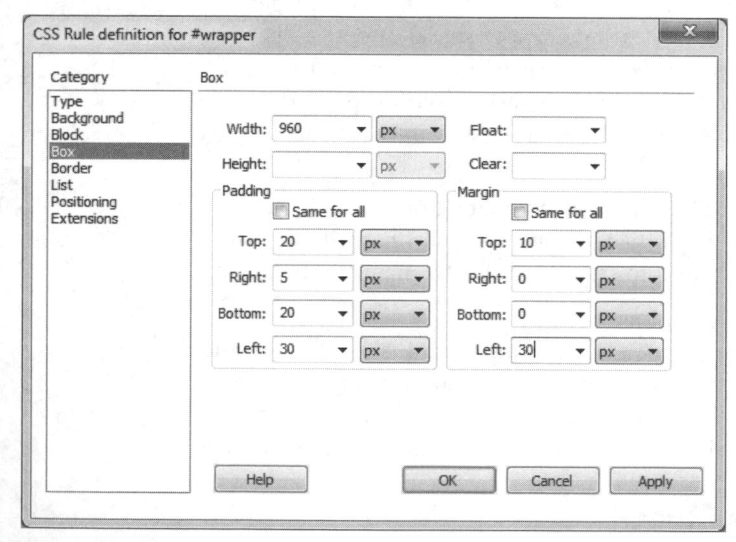

Figure 9-10: *Use the Box category to define the dimensions of a style, to position an object on the page, and to add space between the styled object and the objects around it.*

Be careful with the Height property. Many designers use it for precise control over page elements. Unfortunately, height is tricky to control. If you set a height for a sidebar that contains text, and you later add more text, you can end up with text spilling outside the sidebar—the same thing can happen if a visitor increases the text size in his browser. Because Internet Explorer 6 (and earlier versions) handles these instructions differently than other browsers, you can end up with inconsistent and strange results in different browsers. In other words, set the height of an object only if you're *sure* the content inside will never get taller—for example, if the content is an image.

- **Float.** To force an object to the left or right side of a page and have other content wrap around it, use the Float property. Of course, that's been most of the point of this chapter, so you probably understand this property by now. However, there's one important point to keep in mind: Floating an object doesn't necessarily move it to the side of the page or the browser window. A floated object merely goes to the left or right edge of what's called its "containing block." If you float a div to the left of the page to create a sidebar, and then insert an image into the sidebar and float that image right, the image goes to the right edge of the sidebar, *not* to the right edge of the page. In addition, if you float multiple elements, they can often end up sitting beside each other—you use this technique to create four-column layouts, where each column floats next to the other.
- **Clear.** Clear *prevents* an element from wrapping around any object with a right or left Float property. This property comes in handy when you want to force an element to appear *below* a floated object instead of wrapping around it. The classic example is a page's footer (the area at the bottom of the page that usually contains contact information and a copyright notice). If a page has a left-floated sidebar that's longer than the main content, the footer can move up the page and wrap around the sidebar. In this case, the bottom of the sidebar is at the bottom of the page, and the footer is somewhere in the middle. To fix this problem, set the footer's Clear property to *both*. That forces the footer to drop below both left- and right-floated elements. (If you merely want something to drop below a left-floated element, but still wrap around anything floated right, choose the *left* option; to clear a right-floated element, choose *right*.) In other words, if you ever see page content next to a floated element instead of underneath it, use the *clear* property to properly position that content.
- **Padding.** Padding is the gap that separates the content of a page element—like a paragraph of text or an image—and its border (see page 230). If you put a 1-pixel border around an image and want to add 10 pixels of space between the image itself and that border, type *10* into the top padding box, and then choose "pixels" from the pop-up menu. To set the padding around each edge separately, turn off the "Same for all" box and then type values into each of the four boxes.
- **Margin.** The margin is the amount of space *surrounding* an element (Figure 9-11). It surrounds the border and padding properties of the style, and lets you add space between elements. Use any of the values—pixels, percentages, and so on—that CSS supports.

Padding, margins, borders, and the content inside the styled tag make up what web designers call the CSS Box Model, seen in Figure 9-11. Margins and padding are invisible. They also have similar effects: 5 pixels of left padding adds 5 pixels of space to the left edge of a style; the same happens when you add a 5-pixel left margin. Most people use margins to put space between elements (for example, between the right edge of one column and left edge of an adjacent column), and padding to add space between an element's border and its content (like moving text within a column away from a surrounding borderline). Because you can't see padding or margins (just the empty space they make), it's often difficult to know if the gap between, say, the banner at the top of your page and the main area of content results from the banner's style or the main area's style.

Tip: Dreamweaver CS5 adds a new tool to help you visualize the margins and padding of elements. To learn how to use the new Inspect mode, see page 394.

You also can't always tell if the extra space comes from the padding or the margin setting. Dreamweaver includes a helpful diagnostic tool (see Figure 9-12) that lets you see these invisible properties.

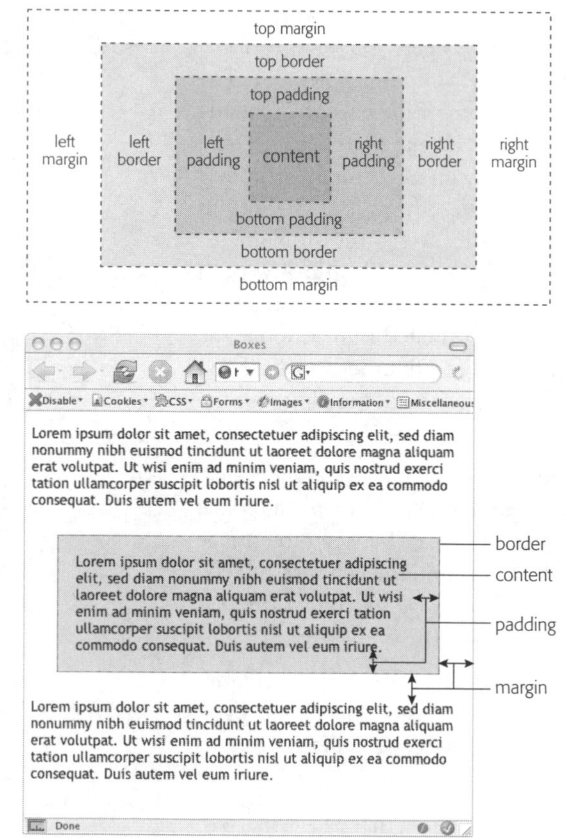

Figure 9-11:
In the CSS Box Model, every style is composed of multiple boxes, one inside the other. Each box controls certain display properties of the style. The outermost box is called the margin. It controls the space between the border of the style and any other objects around the styled object, such as images, paragraphs, or tables; padding is the space between the border and the content itself (the innermost box). The area within the border, which includes the content and the padding, may also have a background color. Actually, the background color is drawn underneath the border, so if you assign a dashed or dotted border, the background color appears in the gaps between the dots or dashes.

When you select a <div> tag with margin or padding properties set, Dreamweaver draws a box around the div, and adds slanting lines to indicate the space the margins and padding occupy (Figure 9-12 shows this box and lines in action).

Margins appear outside padding, and Dreamweaver represents them by lines that slant *downward* from left to right; padding appears inside the margin, and Dreamweaver indicates them with lines that go *upward* from left to right. In Figure 9-12, you enclosed the area with the main content in a <div> tag and applied an ID style named *mainContent* to it. When you select that div (the tag selector in the lower-left corner of the document window is great for this), Dreamweaver highlights the margins and padding values defined in that ID style. As you can see, there's a considerable amount of margin on the right edge, a smaller amount of margin at the top edge, and a small amount of padding (20 pixels' worth) applied to the top, left, and right edges.

If you find these visual aids confusing, you can turn them off via the Visual Aids menu in the document window (see Figure 9-12), or by choosing View→Visual Aids→Layout Box Model. These same steps turn the margin and padding visual aids back on.

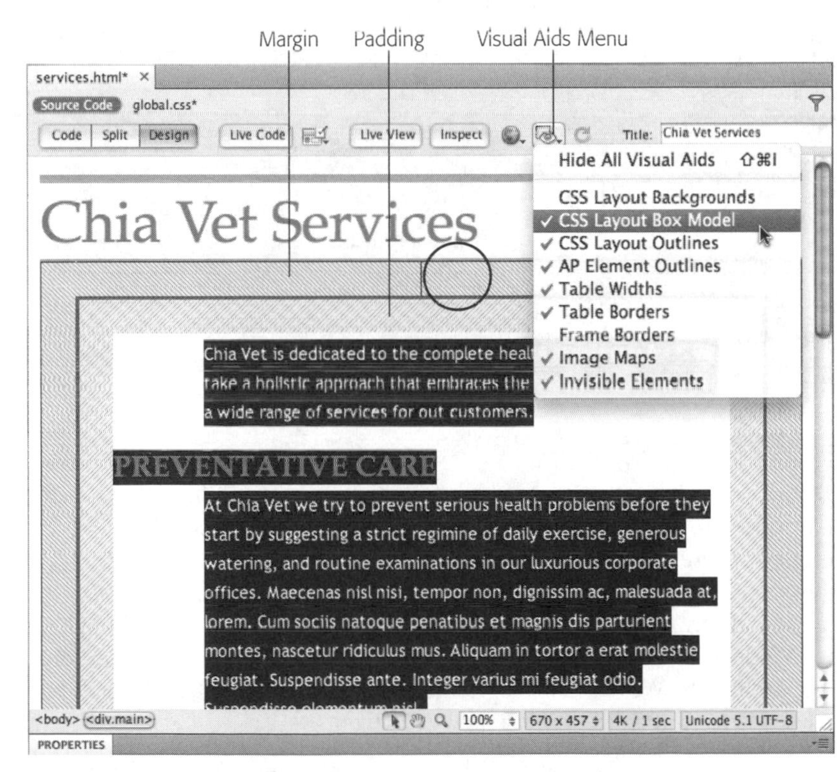

Figure 9-12: *In addition to displaying the space occupied by margins and padding, the CSS Layout Box Model's visual aids indicate the <div> tag's vertical and horizontal center point (circled in this figure).*

FREQUENTLY ASKED QUESTION

When Width Doesn't Equal Width

In my style sheet, the CSS Width *property of one of my styles is 150 pixels. But when I preview the page in a web browser, the <div> tag I applied the style to is much wider than 150 pixels. Is there a bug in my browser?*

No, you're browser's fine. The problem lies with the difference between the CSS *width* property and the final calculated width of an element onscreen. The width you see onscreen is the sum total of several separate CSS properties, not just the Width property. The Width property merely defines the width of the content area of the style–the place where the text, images, or other nested tags sit.

The actual width–that is, the amount of screen real estate assigned by the web browser–is the *total* of the widths of the left and right margins, left and right padding, left and right borders, *and* the Width property. So say you create a style with a width of 100 pixels, 10 pixels of padding on all four sides, a 2 pixel border, and 20 pixels of space in the left margin. While the space dedicated to the content inside the style is 100 pixels, any tag with this style will have an onscreen width of 144 pixels: 100 (width) + 10 (left padding) + 10 (right padding) + 2 (left border) + 2 (right border) + 20 (left margin).

This can cause problems if you're not careful. For example, in a fixed-width layout, you might create a div that wraps around all other page elements. Its width is 960 pixels, so everything inside that div must fit in that 960-pixel space. If you wanted to create a four-column layout, you might insert four divs and create styles that set the width of each to 240 pixels (960 divided by 4).

However, if you added even a 1 pixel border to one of the divs, they'd suddenly take up more than 960 pixels, and you'd find that the last column wouldn't fit–in fact, it would drop down *below* the other three columns, creating a very weird-looking layout.

So if you find yourself floating lots of elements and one of them drops below another when it should sit beside it, odds are pretty good that the elements are just too wide to sit side by side. So decrease the width, margins, padding, or borders until the elements fit (breaking out a calculator and adding up the margins, padding, borders, and widths can also help.)

The CSS Height property and the final height of a style behave the same way. The onscreen height of an element is a combination of the height, top and bottom margins, padding, and borders.

Dreamweaver's CSS Layouts

You'll find yourself contending with many details when building CSS-based layouts. You need to understand the intricacies of the CSS Box Model, as well as the sometimes-bizarre behavior of floats. In addition, different browsers handle some CSS properties different ways, which sometimes means a design that looks great in Firefox completely falls apart in Internet Explorer 6. (Remember, even though much of the Windows-loving world has upgraded to IE 8, there are still plenty of folks cruising around the Web in IE 6 jalopies.) Fortunately, Dreamweaver is ready to give you a helping hand with 16 pre-designed CSS layouts.

Dreamweaver's CSS Layouts aren't finished web page designs. They don't have graphics, fancy text, drop-down menus, or any whiz-bang features. They're simply basic designs intended to lay the foundation for your design talents. Each layout is a simple

HTML file and style sheet, each works in all current browsers, and each design's handcrafted CSS code irons out the many wrinkles in troublesome browsers (most notably Internet Explorer 6). In other words, instead of spending a day stretching and sizing your own canvas, a Dreamweaver CSS Layout is like going to the art store and buying a ready-made and primed canvas so you can get busy painting.

Note: Adobe completely revamped Dreamweaver's CSS Layouts for CS5. First, you no longer get 32 layouts to choose from, which is a good thing, since the CS4 layouts included some no-longer-popular layout techniques (such as "elastic" and absolutely positioned layouts). In addition, CS5 provides greatly simplified CSS for its layouts. In CS4, the CSS Layouts used complex collections of descendent selectors (page 298) that many people found confusing.

Creating a new CSS layout page takes just a few steps:

1. **Choose File→New.**

   This is the same first step you take when creating any new web page. The New Document window appears (Figure 9-13). You can also use the Ctrl+N (⌘-N) keyboard shortcut to open this window (however, it's possible to disable this keyboard shortcut, as described on page 44; you might want to do that if you'd rather skip this clunky window whenever you just want a new, blank web page).

2. **Choose Blank Page from the left column, and the type of page you wish to create in the Page Type column.**

   Usually, you'll select HTML from the page type category, since most of the time you'll create regular web pages. However, if you're creating one of the database-driven pages described in Part 6 of this book, choose one of the page types listed in the bottom half of this column (ASP, ColdFusion, PHP, and so on).

Note: Avoid the Page From Sample category in the left column of the New Document window (see Figure 9-13). In Dreamweaver CS4, Adobe removed most of the page designs since they used outmoded design techniques. All that's left in that category are a few CSS style sheets (you can do better), and a few designs for frame-based pages—a technology you're better off staying away from.

---

3. **From the Layout column, select a page layout.**

   This is where the fun begins. As you've read before, choose <none> here to create an empty web page. The other options, however, let you choose one of 16 prefab CSS-based layouts. Basically, you decide how many columns you want (one, two, or three), whether you want a header and footer (like a banner at the top or a copyright notice at the bottom), and the type of web page layout (fixed-width or liquid).

   This last choice relates to the kinds of web page layouts discussed on page 329. A fixed width design maintains a constant page width no matter the width of a visitor's browser window. A liquid design lets the overall width of the page change with the size of a browser window.

Dreamweaver previews each design in the top right of the New Document window. See Figure 9-14 to decipher the visual codes that help you understand how the layouts behave.

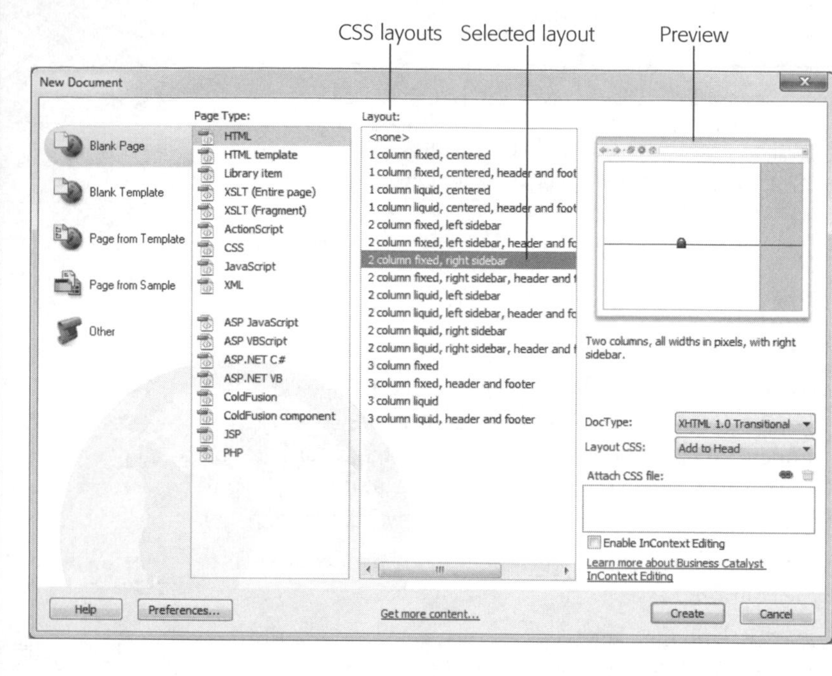

***Figure 9-13:** This dialog box lists Dreamweaver's different types of ready-made CSS Layouts. For example, "2 column fixed, right sidebar" indicates a design with 2 columns: the main content column on the left, and a thinner sidebar (for supplementary info like links) on the right. The design also sports a fixed width and has no header or footer. A preview of the selected layout appears in the top right of the window; a short description below the preview provides more detail on how the layout works.*

4. **Choose a DocType from the DocType menu.**

   Here's where you decide which type of HTML/XHTML you wish to use for the page. It's the same option you face when you create a new, blank web page, as described on page 40. You're safe going with the default option of XHTML 1.0 Transitional.

5. **From the Layout CSS menu, select where you want to store the layout's CSS code.**

   Each Dreamweaver CSS Layout requires its own style sheet of all the styles that make the layout work. When you create a new page from a CSS Layout, you can store that style sheet several places. The "Add to Head" option creates an internal style sheet in the HTML file Dreamweaver creates. Most of the time, you don't want this option, since external style sheets are more efficient (see page 111for an explanation).

   You can also store the CSS Layout styles in a new, external style sheet. Choose Create New File to let Dreamweaver store the necessary CSS rules there. You choose this option when you first use one of Dreamweaver's CSS Layouts to create a new page. This creates a separate file with all the necessary CSS to control the layout of the page. If you want to add another page to your site using a layout you've already used (for example, a 2-column fixed design with a header and footer), read on.

The "Link to Existing File" option sidesteps the entire process of creating new CSS styles. It assumes you have the appropriate styles defined in another external style sheet. If you previously created a web page using the same type of CSS layout, choose this option. Say you created a two-column fixed layout using a Dreamweaver CSS Layout. At that time, you saved the necessary styles for that layout in an external style sheet, and saved the sheet to your site. Now, you can create a *new* two-column fixed-layout page using this external style sheet. Choose "Link to Existing File", and then proceed to step 6 to link the external style sheet already on your site.

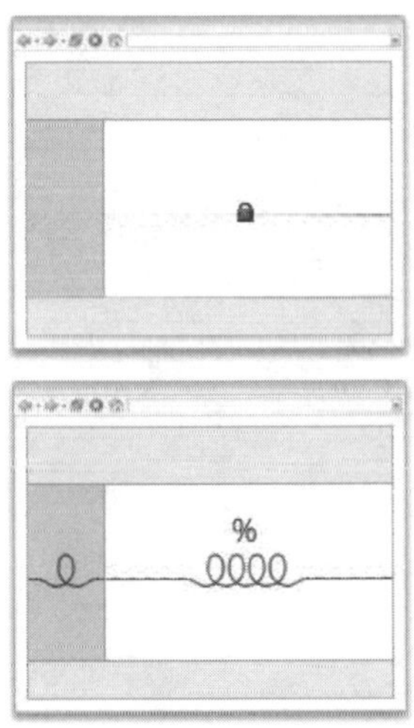

Figure 9-14:
The layout preview displayed in the New Document window visually identifies the type of CSS Layout you select. A small lock icon indicates a fixed-width design (top): the width of each column is set using pixel values, and doesn't change when a guest resizes her browser window. The % symbol indicates a liquid design (second from top): It defines column widths using percentage values that change based on the width of the browser; a wider browser window means wider columns. Liquid designs fill the entire width of the browser.

Keep in mind, however, that each CSS Layout has its *own* style sheet. So if you create a two-column fixed layout page and then want to create a three-column liquid layout page, you can't link to the style sheet Dreamweaver created for the two-column layout. In other words, whenever you create a new *type* of CSS Layout (two-column fixed, three-column liquid, and so on), choose the Create New File option, so Dreamweaver creates the appropriate CSS in a new external style sheet.

Tip: You don't need to go through these steps each time you want to create a new page using a CSS Layout you've used before. Suppose you want to build a 40-page site with two-column, fixed-layout pages. Instead of going through the New Document dialog box (and the steps listed here) 40 times, use the New Document dialog box to create the initial page, and then choose File→Save As, to save a copy of that design for the next two-column page you want to create. Better yet, use Dreamweaver's Template tool described in Chapter 20 to manage pages that have the same layout.

6. **Click the "Attach Style Sheet" button to attach any external style sheets to the page (see Figure 9-15).**

   This is an optional step, but if you already have an external style sheet you want to use to format your site, now's the time to link to it. In addition, if you chose "Link to Existing File" in the previous step, you have to link to an external style sheet to create a particular layout type. The process of linking to external style sheets is the same as with any other web page, as described in "Linking to an External Style Sheet" on page 123.

Note: If, when you create a new web page, you link to an external style sheet as described in step 6, Dreamweaver may pop up a warning message that says something about needing to save your web page in order to correctly attach the style sheet. You can safely ignore this message. In fact, turn on the "Don't show me this message again" checkbox, so you don't see this annoying message in the future.

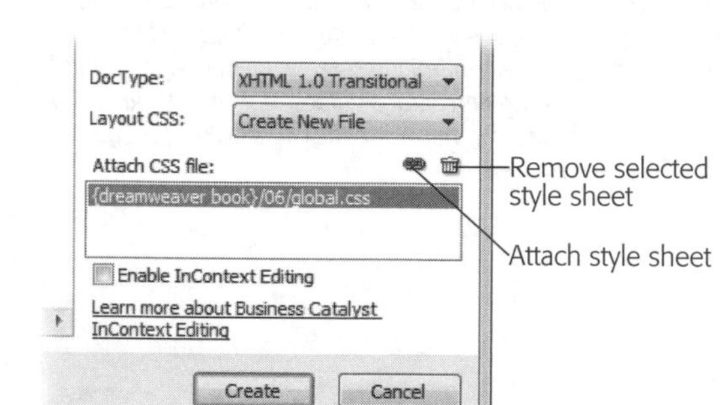

Figure 9-15:
You can attach more than one external style sheet when you create a CSS-based layout: One style sheet might define the basic look of headlines, text, images, and other elements, another might control column layout, and a third, "printer" style sheet, might dictate how the page will look when printed (see "Styling for Print" on page 320).

7. **Click the Create button to bring your new web page to life.**

   If you selected the Create New File option in step 5, Dreamweaver asks you to name the new style sheet and select where you want to save it (just like when you create a new external style sheet, as described on page 116.). Dreamweaver suggests names for the CSS files for each of its layouts—such as *twoColFixRtHdr.css* for a two column, fixed design with a right sidebar and a header and footer. You can change the name if you like, but the name Dreamweaver suggests is descriptive.

After all of that, you end up with a page with a basic structure, and some instructional text telling you to fill in the different areas of the page (see Figure 9-16). Don't forget to save and then title the page.

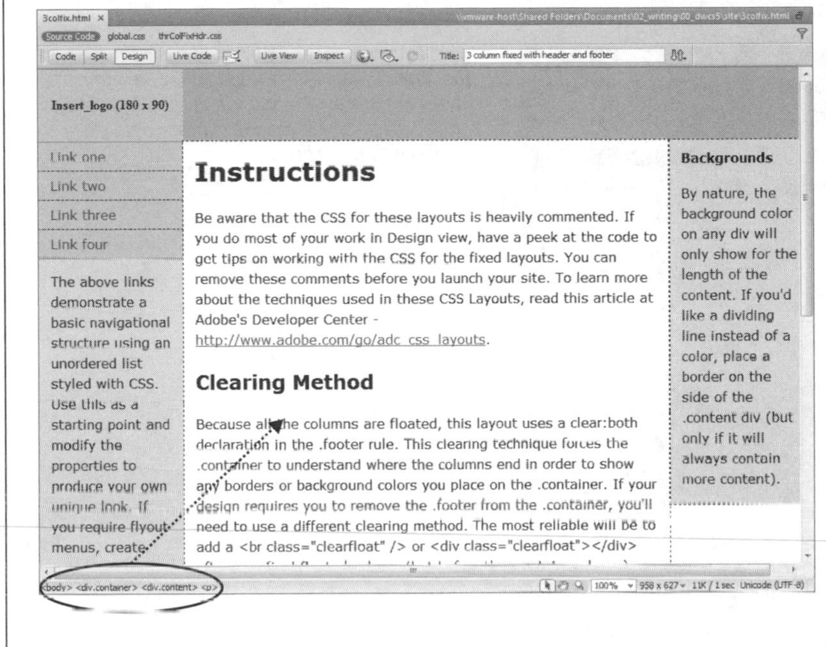

Figure 9-16: *It doesn't look like much, but a CSS Layout page has the basic scaffolding of a bona fide web page in place: <div> tags to organize the page and CSS styles to position those divs. Click inside any area of the page, and the Tag selector (circled) shows you the structure of the HTML at that point. In this case, if you click inside a paragraph in the middle column, the Tag selector shows you which tags wrap around that paragraph. You read this info from right (the <p> tag where the insertion point is) to left (the <body> tag that contains everything you see inside the document window). For this three-column design, the <p> tag is inside a div with a class of .content (that's what the <div.content> means), which is itself inside a div with a class of .container. Finally, the <body> tag encloses all the other tags.*

The Structure of Dreamweaver's CSS Layouts

Dreamweaver's CSS Layouts are made up of a handful of page elements: Some pages have a header and footer, others have one or two sidebars, and all have a section of main content. The layout circumscribes each section with a <div> tag, and each div has its own class. The layout's accompanying style sheet defines the class styles and control where a browser positions the different divs on the page.

To keep the CSS layouts consistent, Dreamweaver uses the same class names for every layout (see Figure 9-17). It calls the class for the <div> tag containing the main content *content*; if the layout has a sidebar, Dreamweaver applies the sidebar class *sidebar1* to it; if there's a second sidebar, Dreamweaver calls it *sidebar2*. Likewise, the header div has a class of *header*, while the div at the bottom of the page is *footer*. Dreamweaver uses one other <div>, and it surrounds all the other divs: Its class is *container*.

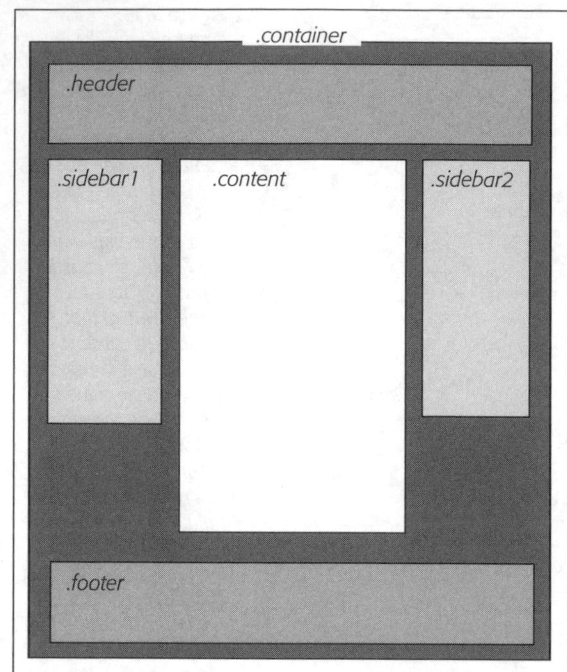

Figure 9-17: *Each Dreamweaver CSS Layout's basic structure is the same. Several <div> tags identify the various layout regions of a page. Each div has its own class name, which is then controlled by a class style in the design's style sheet.*

You may wonder: If all the CSS Layouts share the same names for their layout divs, how do you end up with different types of designs, like fixed and liquid? Each page has its own style sheet. When you create a new CSS Layout page and save those styles in an external style sheet (as described step 5 on page 346), Dreamweaver suggests a name such as thrColFixHdr.css (for a three-column, fixed design with a header and footer), or twoColLiqRt.css (for a two-column, liquid design with a right sidebar). Each style sheet has different rules for its container, content, sidebar, and header and footer styles. This means that if you plan on using more than one CSS Layout page, you need to keep separate style sheets for each type—in other words, if you attach the twoColLiqRt.css file to a three-column, fixed design, you end up with some weird results.

So what do you do if you want to, say, have the same design for all the paragraphs inside the main content div (<div class="content">) when you're using two different CSS Layouts? Create a third style sheet, named something like *global.css* or *site.css*, attach it to both types of pages, and create a descendent selector (page 298) like this: .content p. This formats just paragraphs inside another tag with the class *content*, and since it's in a style sheet shared by both pages, it works in both designs.

Modifying Dreamweaver's CSS Layouts

The basic look of a freshly minted Dreamweaver CSS Layout doesn't have much to recommend it: fixed-width layouts have a green and tan color scheme, while liquid layouts are grayish-blue. One of the first things you want to do with a CSS Layout is remove some of the Dreamweaver formatting. In addition, you might want to tweak some of the basic layout properties, like the width of a fixed-width design, or the width of sidebars and main columns.

Making General Changes to a CSS Layout

One of your first tasks should be to remove (or change) the background colors for the sidebar and other page elements of a CSS Layout page (unless you really like them, in which case your job is a lot easier). This generally means editing the styles in the Dreamweaver-supplied style sheet. You already know several ways to edit styles—like double-clicking the style's name in the CSS Styles panel (page 124) or using the Properties pane (page 304). The real trick is locating the correct style to edit. Here's the fast method:

1. **On the CSS Styles panel, click the Current button (see Figure 9-18, right).**

   If you don't have the Styles panel open, choose Window→CSS Styles. The Current view in this panel shows the styles and properties applied to whatever you select in the Document window.

2. **Make sure that, in the Rules pane, you have the Show Cascade button selected (see Figure 9-18).**

   The Show Cascade option lists all the styles that affect the current selection in the order of the "cascade"—most specific style at the bottom of the list, least specific at the top (see page 312 for a refresher on the cascade and specificity).

3. **Highlight the div you want to format.**

   For example, if you want to reformat the header, select the *header* div. You can select a div in a couple of ways:

   - Click inside the div, and then click the corresponding <div> in the Tag selector at the bottom left of the Document window (see Figure 9-18, left). For example, click inside the header and then click <div.header> in the Tag selector.

   - Click inside the div, and then press Ctrl+A (⌘-A), or choose Edit→Select All. This selects the contents of the div, and highlights the div in the Tag selector. (Pressing Ctrl+A twice selects the <div> tag itself). To highlight a <div> tag that wraps around the div you clicked in, press Ctrl+A (⌘-A) more than once. To highlight the *container* div that surrounds the header, sidebars, main content, and footer, you can click the header region, press Ctrl+A twice to select the header, and then press Ctrl+A once more to highlight the *container* div.

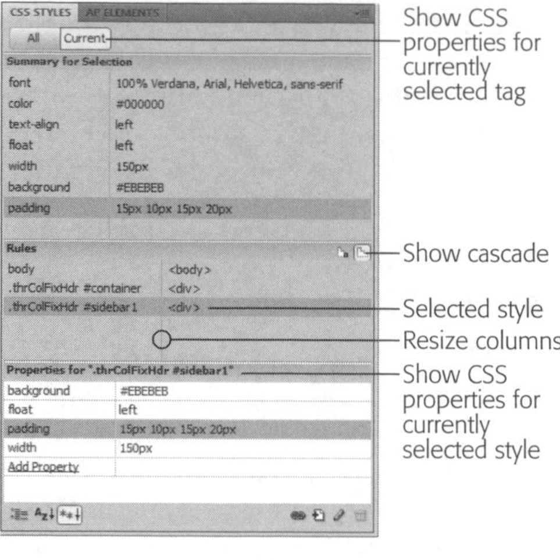

***Figure 9-18:** Finding the style that formats a particular tag can be tricky–unless you're using Dreamweaver. By combining the Tag selector and the Current view of the CSS Styles panel, you can quickly identify and edit a style applied to any tag on a page.*

After you highlight the div, its style appears in the CSS Styles panel's Rules pane. In Figure 9-18, selecting the sidebar div—*<div.sidebar1>*—from the Tag selector (left) selects that div's style—*.sidebar1* in this instance (right). At this point, you can use the Properties pane (directly below the Rules pane) to edit the style as described on page 304, or simply double-click the style name in the Rules pane to open the user-friendly Style Definition window.

Note: The styles for Dreamweaver CSS Layouts use what's called CSS "shorthand properties." These combine several CSS properties under a single property name. For example, you can combine the values for *background-color* and *background-image* into a single property named *background*, while you can specify all four margins (top, right, bottom, and left) with just one property: *margin*. This makes for more compact styles, but it also means that, to edit a shorthand property in the Properties pane, you need to know how to write the values yourself. Dreamweaver doesn't provide a color box, link button, or any other helpful tools it provides when you set the values of a "longhand" property like *background-color*. In other words, unless you know CSS well, if you want to really make changes to a style, you're better off double-clicking the style's name in the Rules pane to access the much more user-friendly Rule Definition window.

Once you select a layout region on the page (header, sidebar, and so on), you probably want to make a few common changes:

- **Background colors.** To completely remove a div's gray background, delete the value next to the *background* property in the Properties pane. You can also double-click the style's name in the CSS Styles panel to open the Rule Definition window, and then select the Background category to edit the color (see page 231).

- **Text formatting.** You can modify the text and other content of a page to your heart's content. This book's earlier chapters show you how to format headlines, paragraphs, images, and links. However, when you create styles for these elements, use an external style sheet other than the one Dreamweaver supplies for the layout styles. You can store these types of styles in a generic style sheet like *global.css*, instead of the layout-specific style sheet, such as *twoColFixLtHdr.css*. See step 5 on "The Structure of Dreamweaver's CSS Layouts" for the reason.

FREQUENTLY ASKED QUESTION

Paying Attention to Conditionals

I've noticed that when I create a page using any of Dreamweaver's two- or three-column liquid CSS Layouts, the page has some weird-looking code just above the ending </head> tag. What's that about?

If you go into Code view of any of the two- or three-column liquid layouts, you'll notice some grayed-out HTML that begins with *<!–[if lte IE 7]>* and ends with *<![endif]–>*. It's grayed out because Dreamweaver treats this code as an HTML comment. People who hand-code their pages use HTML comments to leave notes about their page like why they added a chunk of HTML or to identify which div a particular closing </div> tag belongs to. Dreamweaver and other browsers ignore HTML comments.

However, this particular HTML comment, while ignored by every other browser, has special significance for Internet Explorer. HTML comments that begin like this *<!–[if IE]>* are actually secret messages, called *conditional comments*, intended just for Internet Explorer. Conditional comments let you send HTML, CSS, and JavaScript to Internet Explorer only; you can even send special HTML to particular versions of Internet Explorer. For example, *<!–[if lte IE 7]>* sends HTML to versions 7 and earlier of Internet Explorer (the lte part stands for "less than or equal to," so it addresses Internet Explorer 7 and those "less" than 7–IE 5 and IE 6, in other words.)

Fortunately, the CSS layouts are much simpler in CS5 than they were in CS4, so you only encounter conditional comments in the two- or three-column liquid layouts. There, you find two styles squirreled away in conditional comments in the <head> of the page:

```
.content   {   margin-right:   -1px;   }

ul.nav a { zoom: 1; }
```

You might not need either of these to display your page correctly. The first helps IE determine the exact width for a percentage-based layout and only affects IE 6 and 7 (not 8). Try removing this style and testing your page in IE 6 and 7–if the column widths look and fit the same way they do in other browsers, you don't need this style. If they don't, test again with the style in place.

The second style–*ul.nav a*–only applies to the navigation buttons in the sidebar of some of these designs. If you remove the navigation bar (for example, if you have no navigation in the sidebar or use the Spry Menu [page 184] instead), remove this style.

For a short tutorial on conditional comments, visit: *www.javascriptkit.com/howto/cc2.shtml*.

Modifying Fixed Layouts

The width of any Dreamweaver fixed layout is 960 pixels. That's a common page width. It fits 1024 pixel wide screens (most netbooks, laptops, and desktop computers are at least that wide). However, that width may be too wide or too narrow for your tastes. If you're designing for the cinema-screen audience, you might want a page that takes advantage of a wider screen, so you might bump the width to 1100 pixels or more. In addition, you may want to change the widths of columns on a page. Here's how you make a few key layout changes:

- **Page width.** Dreamweaver fixes the area of the page that includes the header, sidebars, and main content at 960 pixels. This setting is defined in Dreamweaver's *container* div. Select the div and change 960 to whatever width you want.
- **Column width.** Dreamweaver makes the sidebar columns 180 pixels wide, and the main content region's width either 780 pixels for two-column designs, or 600 pixels for three-column designs. Select the sidebar you wish to make wider or narrower, and then adjust its *width* property.

  Unfortunately, you often have to do a little math if you want the three columns to sit side by side. Since the container has a set width (960 pixels by default), the width of the three columns should also add up to 960 pixels. If their total width is bigger, the content area actually drops below the two sidebars. So if you increase the size of one sidebar, you need to decrease the width of the main content area (the *.content* style) by the same amount. For example, in a two-column fixed design, if you increase the sidebar to 200 pixels wide (20 pixels more than it starts with), you need to subtract 20 pixels from the width of the content div: in other words edit the *.content* style and change its width to 760 pixels.

  Things get even trickier if you add margins, padding, or a border to the left or right side of any column. As discussed in the box on page 344, the actual horizontal space of any element is the sum of its width, left and right margins, left and right padding, and left and right border. If you add a 1-pixel right border to a sidebar, you increase the total width of all the columns to 961 pixels (1 pixel more than the container's 960-pixel width). The result? The main content area drops below the sidebar. Aye carumba! In other words, if you make a change to a sidebar, or the main content area, and the content div suddenly drops down on the page, check your math!

Note: If you use Dreamweaver CSS Layouts often, you may frequently make the same adjustments over and over again. For example, you might always remove the padding and background color, and adjust the column widths. Instead of repeatedly doing that, edit the default HTML and CSS files Dreamweaver uses when it creates a new blank CSS Layout page. In Windows, you'll find them in the C:\Program Files\Adobe\Adobe Dreamweaver CS5\configuration\BuiltIn\Layouts folder, and on the Mac, they're in the Applications→Adobe Dreamweaver CS5→configuration→BuiltIn→Layouts folder. You can also clean up this folder by deleting designs you don't use. *Just make sure you back up the folder before you do anything to the files inside. And then, back up your new designs so that if you ever have to reinstall Dreamweaver, you have a backup of your modified templates.*

Modifying Liquid Layouts

Liquid layouts adjust to the width of a browser window. Columns grow wider as visitors widen the window, and shrink when the browser window shrinks. However, you can still control the relative widths of the page:

- **Page width.** Although a page adjusts its width with a liquid layout, Dreamweaver's default styles make the page 80 percent of the window width. In other words, Dreamweaver always leaves some empty space on either side of the container div (10 percent, to be precise). To remove this space to make the page fill the entire width of the browser window, edit the *.container* style: Just delete the width entirely, don't set its width to 100 percent. (Doing so can make the page appear a little *wider* than the browser window, forcing visitors to scroll right to see all of a page's content. See the box on page 344 for an explanation.)

Note: The liquid layouts that come with Dreamweaver have built-in limits for the width of the container div. Dreamweaver sets two additional .container style properties–max-width and min-width. Max-width defines the maximum width (1260 pixels) of the div and keeps it from becoming un-readably wide on extremely large screens. The min-width property, by contrast, keeps the div from shrinking past 780 pixels. To change these values or delete them entirely, use the Properties pane (see page 304).

- **Column width.** As with fixed layouts, Dreamweaver sets the sidebar and main content widths using the Width property. The only difference is that it does so using percentages, with the combined width of the sidebars and the content div at 100%. Just as with fixed layouts, if you change the width of one div, you need to adjust the width of another. So in a three-column liquid design, to make the left sidebar, say, 25% instead of the usual 20%, you'll need to remove 5% from the content div, the right sidebar, or split that between the two: for example, change the .content type to a width of 57% (from it's normal 60%) and the .sidebar2 style to 18%.

Other Styles to Change

Dreamweaver CS5's CSS Layouts include a few other styles you might want to modify or delete.

- **Text spacing.** It's common for web designers to add some empty space between the edge of a column and the content inside it. This "white space" makes the text feel less cramped and more readable. You can add padding to the <div> that creates the column—for example the <div class="content"> element the CSS layouts use to create the main content region. However, as mentioned above, adding padding to that div increases its overall width, potentially making the column too wide to fit next to the other columns. So, instead of adding padding to the sidebars or main content styles, Dreamweaver uses a group style ("h1, h2, h3, h4, h5, h6, p") that includes left and right padding. Because it applies the padding to tags inside the column and not the column itself, the overall width of each column remains the same. You get the same visual result– added white space on either side of each column—without having to futz with width settings.

  The only downside to this approach is that it will apply to every header and paragraph on the page. What if you want a little less white space inside the left sidebar and a little more inside the main content area? The answer is descendent selectors (see page 298). For example, to create a style that affects the padding of just the headings and paragraphs in the first sidebar, you'd create this (long-winded) group style:

.sidebar1 h1, .sidebar1 h2, .sidebar1 h3, .sidebar1 h4, .sidebar1 h5, .sidebar1 h6, .sidebar1 p

Then, any left and right padding you add to the *.sidebar* style apply only to the headings and paragraphs inside the sidebar (see page 303 for instructions on creating a group style).

You'll also find a style named *.content ui, .content ol*, which Dreamweaver uses to add white space around bulleted and numbered lists inside the main content area. You may want to adjust or delete this style as well.

- **Links.** The CSS Layouts also include styles for the link states discussed on page 181 (*a:link*, *a:visited*, and so on). You may not like these, so feel free to change or delete them. And if the pages in your site use different CSS Layouts (two-column fixed and three-column fixed pages, for example) you're better off creating a shared, external style sheet (*site.css* or *global.css*, for instance), putting your link styles in that style sheet and then linking the external style sheet to all your pages (see page 123). That way, all your pages, even ones with different layouts, will have consistent link styles.
- **Navigation bar.** Some of Dreamweaver's layouts include a simple navigation bar in the sidebar. If you like this, you can change its appearance by editing the various styles that begin with ul.nav in the layout's style sheet. They control the appearance of the overall list and the links inside. If you don't plan on using the navigation bars, feel free to delete the styles entirely.

Tip: The style sheets Dreamweaver supplies with CSS Layouts are chock-full of CSS comments. This is a good thing when you're getting started, because they're like a mini-lesson in CSS layout. Read through the comments in at least one of the style sheets and you're sure to learn a few things. However, when it's time to put your site on the Web, all those comments are unnecessary bloat that slow page downloads. You can delete them by hand (CSS comments are grey in Code view and begin with /* and end with */) or you can use Dreamweaver's Find and Replace tool to quickly remove them all. For a little help, download Dreamweaver expert David Power's "Dreamweaver query" (basically a saved find-and-replace command) from *http://foundationphp.com/tools/css_comments.php*. You can read about Dreamweaver's powerful Find and Replace tool on page 801.

Absolute Positioning

Beyond float-based layouts, CSS's other main technique for placing elements on a page, absolute positioning, lets you specify an exact position on a page for any element. But before you start thinking you've found page-layout heaven, keep in mind that the Web is a fluid environment that's difficult to control with pixel-level precision. If a visitor increases the font size in her browser, the enlarged text may spill out of your carefully crafted layout. In addition, it's nearly impossible to force a footer to the bottom of a page laid out using absolute positioning (a trivial task with float-based layouts). That's why most CSS Layouts use floats and the techniques discussed at the beginning of this chapter.

Note: Dreamweaver refers to absolutely positioned divs as either AP Divs or AP Elements, *AP* meaning *absolutely positioned*. Any tag can take advantage of CSS positioning, but you'll most often apply positioning to a <div> tag that contains text, images, or other content. In this book, the term AP Div refers to any absolutely positioned div. However, because you can absolutely position any tag (a link, unordered list, or even a simple paragraph), you'll see the term AP Element used to describe any tag that's absolutely positioned.

That's not to say you shouldn't use absolute positioning. It's great for moving small elements, like a logo, image, or short set of links, to a specific position on a page; and it's the only way to have one element overlap another element (see the circled image in Figure 9-19). As long as you don't try to dictate the exact width, height, and position of every page element, you'll find absolute positioning powerful and helpful.

Figure 9-19:
One unique aspect of CSS positioning is its ability to place an element on top of other page content. That lets the Chia Kitten here break the page's "grid"–it sits to the left of the headline and even appears to be hanging off the edge of the page.

The CSS Positioning Properties

Several CSS properties position elements on a screen. You'll find them under the Positioning category of the CSS Rule Definition window (Figure 9-20).

Positioning type

Normally, browsers position elements on the screen in the order they appear in the HTML; the first element tagged in the HTML appears at the top of the browser window. Similarly, HTML at the end of web page files appears at the bottom of the browser window. In Figure 9-21, the top-left image shows a headline, followed by a paragraph of text, followed by a headline, an image, and another paragraph. This is the order in which the elements appear in the HTML, top to bottom.

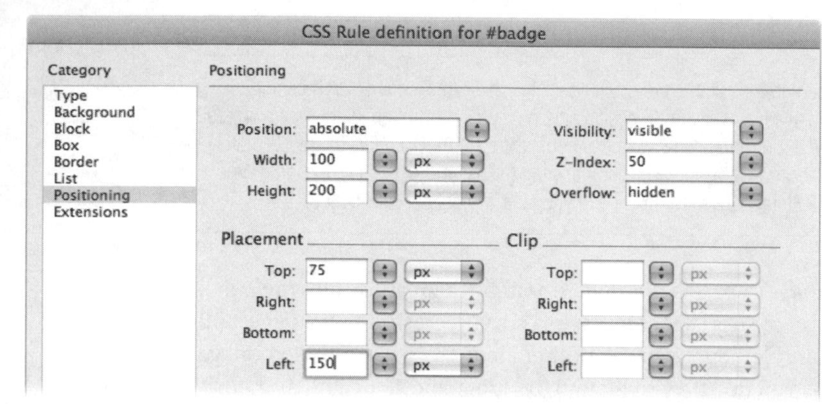

Figure 9-20: *Dreamweaver gives you easy access to its many CSS Positioning properties. You'll never need to set all of them, and web designers rarely use a few of them, like those found in the Clip section of this dialog box (see page 364 for details on the Clip section's woeful lot in life).*

The CSS *position* property, however, lets you alter the order of a styled element onscreen by assigning one of four available position types: *absolute, relative, static*, and *fixed*.

- **Absolute** is the most common option. It lets you place a tag anywhere on a page, regardless of the tag's position in the page's HTML. The top-right image in Figure 9-21 displays a graphic of a sticky note. Even though the image falls after the "Malorum Gipsum" headline in the page's HTML, it appears at the top of the page (and even a little bit off the top) because it's absolutely positioned. The space the graphic used to occupy (top-left image) is now filled by the paragraph of text beneath the second headline.

  In other words, with absolute positioning, HTML code can go *anywhere* inside a <body> tag and still appear *anywhere* on a page—its location in the code has nothing to do with its location onscreen. In addition, absolutely positioned elements are removed from the normal flow of a page—other tags on the page aren't even "aware" that the AP element exists.

  After you select the Absolute option, use the Placement properties (see page 363) to specify a position.

Browsers, however, don't always put absolutely positioned elements in relation to the page itself. If you create a style to position an element inside another element that's either positioned relatively (see the next bullet point) or absolutely, then the browser positions the first element in relation to the latter element, not in relation to the page itself. The next bullet point clarifies this confusing concept.

- The **Relative** option lets you position a tag relative to its position in the HTML. When you choose the Relative position option, the positioned element appears relative to where it appears in the HTML. The bottom left image in Figure 9-21 shows the same sticky note positioned using the Relative property. Although it has the same top and left placement values (page 363) as the top-right image, the browser now positions the sticky note relative to where its tag sits in the HTML—just below the "Malorum Gipsum" line. Even so, the note sits in the top-left position of that line, reflecting the values in the Relative property. Another side effect of relative positioning is that the space formerly taken up by the image (top-left in Figure 9-21) remains. Notice that the last paragraph doesn't try to fill up the space where the graphic was. There's still a big empty area.

  At first glance, the Relative option might seem less than useful. After all, what's the point of positioning something on a page, just to leave a big empty ("I *was* here") space? In many cases, you don't actually apply relative positioning to an *element* you want to position. You apply it to a *tag* that wraps *around* the element you want to position, in order to create a new set of coordinates for an absolutely positioned element to use.

  Say you put an image inside a headline, and you want the image to appear on the left edge of that headline. If you simply position the image in an exact spot in the browser window on the left edge of the headline tag, you're taking your chances. If the headline moves (say you add some new body text above it), the absolutely positioned image stays glued to its assigned spot. Instead, what you want to do is position the image *relative* to the headline tag, so that when the headline moves, so does the image. Look at the bottom-right image of Figure 9-21. The headline (Malorum Gipsum) is relatively positioned, and the sticky note is absolutely positioned, but it's absolutely positioned *inside the headline tag*. Even when, later on, you add a little more text to the top of the page (thereby forcing the headline to move down), the sticky note travels along for the ride.

- **Static** positioning is the normal behavior of HTML. Static simply means the content follows the normal top-down flow of HTML. Why would you want to assign an element static positioning? The short answer: You probably never will.

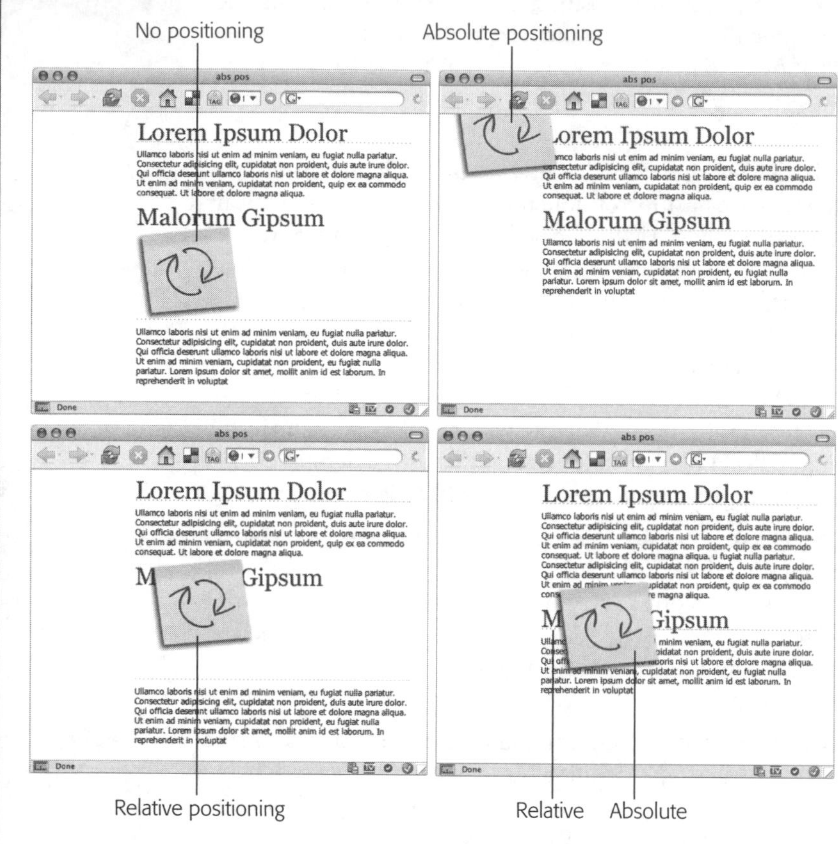

Figure 9-21: *Whenever you use absolute positioning to place an element on a page, its exact position depends on the positioning of any other tags inside which you nest the styled element. In the top-right image, the sticky note graphic is positioned relative to the browser window because it's been styled with an absolute position, and it's not inside any other tag with absolute, relative, or fixed positioning. In the bottom-right image, the graphic is absolutely positioned as well, but its placement is relative to the edges of the second headline because the HTML for the image is inside the headline, and the headline has a relative position applied to it.*

- **Fixed** positioning is similar to the "fixed" value of the CSS attachment property used to lock a background image in place (see page 231). This option "fixes" the AP div in place in the browser window. When you scroll down the page, the AP div doesn't move, it remains in an exact position in the browser window. It's a cool option with exciting possibilities …but *no* support in Internet Explorer 6. Fortunately, IE 6 continues to fade away and may represent only a small portion of your website's visitors (or maybe none at all), so you may want to experiment with the "fixed" option since Internet Explorer 7 and later, Firefox, Safari, Chrome, and Opera support it.

Width and height

These properties, logically enough, set the width and height of the element. You can use any of the available CSS measurement units, like pixels, ems, and percentages. In most cases, when you want precise control over the dimensions of your tags—that is, a page element that's *exactly* 200 pixels wide and won't change even if a visitor changes the size of his browser window—use pixels. However, if you want the element to resize as the visitor resizes his browser, use percentages. That way, you can specify a style that's 50 percent the width of the browser window, no matter the size of the window.

Note: The Width and Height properties available under the Positioning category of the CSS Rule Definition window are identical to the options of the same name under the Box category (see Figure 9-10). Also note that CSS calculates the total width of a style as the Width value *plus* any borders, margins, or padding (see the box on page 344 for more). The same is true for the height of an element.

Visibility

Left to its own devices, Dreamweaver makes the contents of all tags visible on the page, so you'll usually leave this property blank. After all, if you put something on your page, it's usually because you want people to see it. But there are situations in which you may want to make a certain tag (and its contents) invisible to your visitors.

The power of the Visibility property becomes clear when you start using Dreamweaver behaviors or do your own JavaScript programming; you can make previously hidden tags visible again, on cue. Imagine a web page where you superimpose many hidden divs on a diagram of a car engine. Moving the mouse over different parts of the image makes individual div elements visible, revealing text that describes the corresponding engine part (page 613 shows you how to create this effect).

Note: The CSS Display property also has an option to hide an element: *none* (see page 142). The benefit of using the Display property over the Visibility property is that an element whose display is set to *none* literally disappears from the page, whereas an element with *hidden* visibility can still take up space on the page—it just leaves a hole where it normally would appear. After hiding an element by setting its display property to *none*, you can make it visible again by changing the display property to *block* (using the Change Property behavior discussed on page 616, for example). That property makes the element visible again.

The options for the Visibility property let you make the AP div "visible" (which is how all tags start out anyway); make it "hidden," so it doesn't appear until you make it visible; or make it "inherit" the visibility of another AP div. (The inheritance option can be useful with nested AP divs, as discussed on page 373.)

Z-Index

Welcome to the third dimension. Absolutely positioned tags are unique in the world of web elements, because they "float" above (or even behind) a web page and can overlap each other, completely or partially.

If you were awake in high school algebra, you may remember the graphing system in which the x-axis specified where a point was in space from left to right and the y-axis specified where the point was vertically from top to bottom. And if you were awake *and* paying attention, you may remember that the z-axis denoted a point's position in *front-to-back* space. When you draw a three-dimensional object on this type of graph, you need to use all three axes: x, y, and z.

The Z-Index of an absolutely positioned element doesn't make your web page *appear* three-dimensional; it simply specifies the "front-to-backness" of overlapping AP elements. In other words, the Z-Index, represented by a number in the Z-Index field, controls the stacking order of AP elements on a page.

Note: The Z-Index setting doesn't always work when you try to overlap certain kinds of content, like pull-down menus, radio buttons, or other form elements. It also may not work with plug-in content like a Flash player. That's because web browsers let other programs control the display of these items.

The page itself lies behind all AP elements, and the AP elements stack up from there. In other words, the higher the Z-Index number, the higher the AP elements, so that an AP element with a Z-Index of 4 appears *behind* an overlapping AP div with a Z-Index of, say, 7.

Z-Index numbers have no relation to the actual number of absolutely positioned items on a page. You can have three AP elements with Z-Indexes of, say, 2, 499, and 2000, if you choose. You'd still just have three AP elements, one on top of the other in ascending order. Spacing your Z-Index numbers in this somewhat arbitrary manner is helpful, since it lets you insert divs between already positioned divs as you develop your page without having to renumber the Z-Indexes of all your AP divs.

Overflow

Suppose you create a square AP div that's 100 × 100 pixels. Then you fill it with a graphic that's 150 × 162 pixels—that is, larger than the AP div itself.

You've already seen how a table cell reacts to this situation: It simply grows to fit the content inside it. AP divs, however, are more (or less) flexible, depending on your choice of Overflow option in the Property inspector. The following choices let you decide how browsers handle the excess part of the image:

- **Visible** will display any content that doesn't fit inside the element. It doesn't actually expand the size of the element itself, however, something you'll notice if you apply a background or borders to the element. In the example above, for instance, if you added a border to the AP div, the border would only be drawn around the 100 × 100 pixel square defined by the style. The graphic would simply "pop out" of the box. This isn't true in Internet Explorer 6, however, which does expand the box to fit any content larger than the set dimensions—in other words, in IE 6, the border would grow to accommodate the graphic.
- **Hidden** chops off the excess content. In the example above, you'd only be able to see the top-left 100 × 100 pixels of the image.

- **Scroll** adds scroll bars to the AP div, so that a visitor can scroll to see all of the AP div's contents. It's like having a miniature browser window embedded in the page. This feature offers an interesting way to add a small, scrollable window within a web page: Imagine a small "Latest Company News" box, which visitors can scroll to read the text inside without disturbing anything else on the page.
- **Auto** adds scroll bars to an AP element *only* if necessary to accommodate oversize contents.

In Design view, if you select any option besides "Visible", you see the AP div's set dimensions—for example, 100 pixels by 100 pixels. Dreamweaver doesn't display any content outside that area—the overflow.

You may have content you'd like to edit that's part of the overflow—like the "Latest Company News" box mentioned above. Dreamweaver gives you an easy way to edit any of that hidden content—just double-click the AP div. Doing so expands the AP div (just as if you'd selected the Visible option) so you can edit it. To reset the AP div back to its original dimensions, right-click (Control-click) the AP div and, from the shortcut menu that appears, select Element View→Hidden.

Note: You can use the Overflow property on any element, not just absolutely positioned divs. For example, if you want to create a 100-pixel-tall div with scrollbars and lots of content inside that visitors can scroll through, just create a style with a 100 pixel height and Overflow set to Scroll and apply that style to the div. No positioning required.

Placement

These properties let you specify an absolutely positioned element's position, which is, after all, the whole point of AP divs. The four Placement properties control where each of the four edges of the AP div begin. Setting the Top box to 200 pixels positions the top of the AP div 200 pixels down the screen, whereas the Bottom option identifies where the bottom of the AP div starts. Similarly, the Left and Right properties set the beginning of the left edge and right edge of the AP div.

You'll frequently use a combination of the Width property (page 360) and the Top and Left or Right properties. To place a 150-pixel-wide sidebar 200 pixels from the top of the page and 15 pixels in from the left, you'd set the Width property to 150 pixels, the Top property to 200, and the Left property to 15 pixels.

You'll also find the Right property handy. Say you want to put a 200-pixel-wide sidebar on the right side of a page. Since you don't know the exact width of a visitor's browser—580 pixels, 1200 pixels?—you can't know ahead of time how far the AP div needs to be from the left edge of the window. So you can set the Right property to 0—if you want the sidebar to touch the right edge of the page. If you want to indent the AP div 20 pixels from the right edge of the window, type *20*.

Although it's technically possible to use Left and Right positioning simultaneously—say, placing an AP div 50 pixels from the left edge and 20 from the right—the intransigent

Internet Explorer 6 doesn't support this combination. Instead, use absolute positioning for one edge of the AP div and a margin setting (see page 341) for the other edge.

Note: Here's a cool trick: absolutely position a div and set its top, left, bottom, and right positions to 0. You'll have a div that fills the browser window–even when someone resizes the window. Works in all browsers, except IE 6, of course, so use with caution.

Positioning isn't quite as straightforward as it may seem. The exact position of a positioned div is a combination of not only these position values, but also of what type of placement you choose for the AP div—absolute or relative. As noted earlier, with relative positioning, the numbers you type for Top or Left, for instance, are calculated based on where the AP div already appears in the HTML code and on the screen. So setting the Top property to 100 pixels doesn't place the AP div 100 pixels from the top of the browser window; it places it 100 pixels from where it would appear on the screen based on the HTML code.

Absolute positioning, however, lets you place an AP div at an exact spot on a page. So setting the Top and Left properties for an absolutely positioned AP div to 100 and 150 pixels *will* place that AP div 100 pixels from the top of the browser window and 150 pixels from the left edge.

Note: There's one additional wrinkle to absolute positioning. For a div nested inside another div that has either a Relative or an Absolute position setting, the browser calculates position values based on the position of the *parent* div. If you have one AP div 300 pixels from the top of a page, an absolutely positioned AP div nested inside *that* AP div with a Top position of 20, it doesn't appear 20 pixels from the top of the page. It appears 20 pixels from the top of the parent AP div, in this case 320 pixels from the top of the page.

Clip

The Clip property can hide all but a rectangular piece of an AP div. In most cases, you should avoid this property, since it's rarely useful, and it's also a waste of precious bandwidth.

Suppose you put a large graphic into an AP div, but you want to display only one small area. You *could* use the Clip property, but a browser still has to download the *entire* graphic, not just the clipped area. You're much better off preparing the smaller graphic at the right size to begin with (see Chapter 6). The kilobytes you save may be your own.

You can use JavaScript to *move* the clipping area, creating an effect like a spotlight traveling across the AP div. Although that may be a more useful purpose for the Clip property, Dreamweaver doesn't support it, unfortunately.

The four clipping settings—top, right, bottom, and left—specify the positions of the clipping box's four edges. In other words, these indicate the borders of the visible area of the AP div.

Adding an AP Div to Your Page

In most cases, you'll position <div> tags that have a variety of HTML elements—images, paragraphs, headlines, and so on. For example, to place a series of links at the top of a page, you could wrap those links in a div tag and position that div. Dreamweaver gives you a couple of ways to insert an absolutely positioned div:

- **Use the Insert Div Tag tool discussed on page 333.** You can start out by selecting already existing content on the page, or just click where you wish to add a new absolutely positioned div. Either way, you either need to create an ID style first (with the positioning properties discussed above), and then select that style from the ID menu of the Insert Div Tag window (Figure 9-6); alternatively, you can create the ID style by clicking the New CSS Style button in the Insert Div Tag window (Figure 9-6).
- **Choose Insert→Layout Objects→AP Div.** This command inserts a <div> tag into the HTML wherever you put the cursor. The HTML looks something like this <div id="apDiv1"></div>, though the ID name will vary (it might be apDiv2, for example, if this is the second div you've inserted). In addition, it adds an internal style sheet and an ID style (matching the one used in the HTML) with some basic formatting: width, height, Z-Index, and absolute position setting.
- **Use the Draw AP Div tool.** Dreamweaver provides a tool to draw a <div> tag directly onto the document window. Ppage 368 shows you how this tool works.

Unless you add a background color or border to your AP div, it's difficult to identify its boundaries. To make working with AP divs easier, Dreamweaver provides visual cues in Design view, as shown in Figure 9-22, and explained in the following list:

- **AP element marker.** The gold shield with the letter C (huh?) represents the position in the underlying HTML where the code for the AP div actually appears.

  Dreamweaver doesn't display these markers by default. To see them, you have to turn them on in the Preferences window: Press Ctrl+U (⌘-U) to open the window, click the Invisible Elements category, and turn on the "Anchor points for AP elements" option.

  While HTML objects generally appear in the document window in a top-to-bottom sequence that mirrors their order in the HTML source code, the position of AP divs *doesn't* depend on where the AP div-creating code appears in the page's HTML. In other words, you can have an AP div in the first line in the body of the HTML page while the element appears near the bottom of the final web page (see Figure 9-22 for more detail).

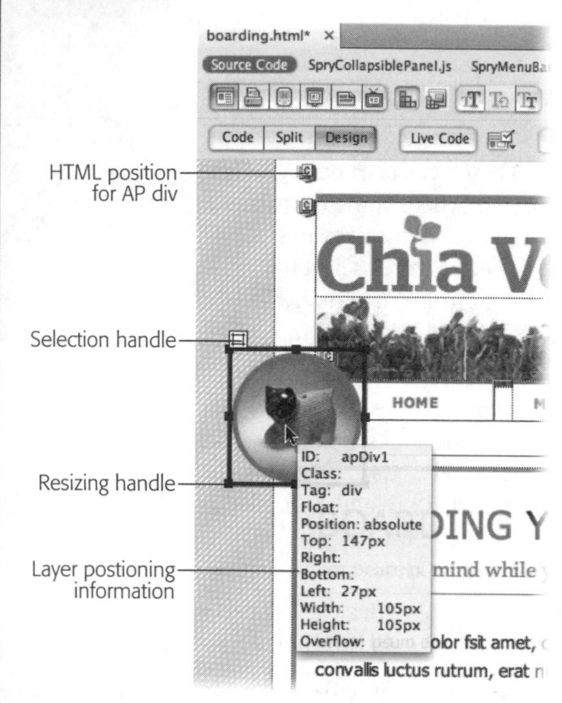

Figure 9-22: *Unlike other page elements, AP elements don't appear in the same place on the page as their HTML code. Here, a div for the Chia Kitten button hovers over a headline several hundred pixels below the top of the page. The HTML for the div, however, is the first bit of HTML on the page (and is represented by the AP element marker in the top-left corner of the page).*

To move the HTML of the AP div, drag the shield icon. Since you absolutely positioned the element, its position on the page remains the same, but its code moves to the new location in the HTML. Conversely, if you drag the selection handle of the element, it moves the element but leaves the HTML in the same location (described next).

That distinction often confuses Dreamweaver users. For instance, be careful not to drag an AP div marker (the gold shield that represents the HTML code) into a table. Putting an AP div inside a table can cause major display problems in some browsers.

That said, an AP div can *visually overlap* a table, or even appear to be inside a cell; just make sure the gold AP div marker itself isn't inside a cell.

Tip: The AP div marker (shield icon) takes up room on the screen and can push text, graphics, and other items out of the way. In fact, even the thin borders that Dreamweaver adds to divs take up space in the document window, and the space they occupy may make it difficult to place AP divs precisely. The keyboard shortcut Ctrl+Shift+I (⌘-Shift-I) hides or shows invisible items like AP div markers. The Hide All Visual Aids option from the Document toolbar does the same thing (see Figure 9-23).

- **Selection handle.** The selection handle provides a convenient way to grab and move an AP div around the page. The handle appears when you select the AP div, or when you click inside the AP div to add material to it. The handle lets you move the position of the AP div without changing the position of its code (see page 370). Behind the scenes, Dreamweaver updates the CSS code (the left and top position properties described on page 363) automatically…pretty nifty.
- **AP element outline.** Unselected absolutely positioned elements have a thin, gray, 3-D border. Like the AP div marker and selection handle, it's there only to help you see the boundaries of the AP element, and doesn't show up in web browsers. You can turn it on and off, but to turn it off, you need to make sure you turn off two options in the View→Visual Aids menu: AP Element Outlines and Layout Outlines. You can also use the Visual Aids menu in the document window (see Figure 9-23).

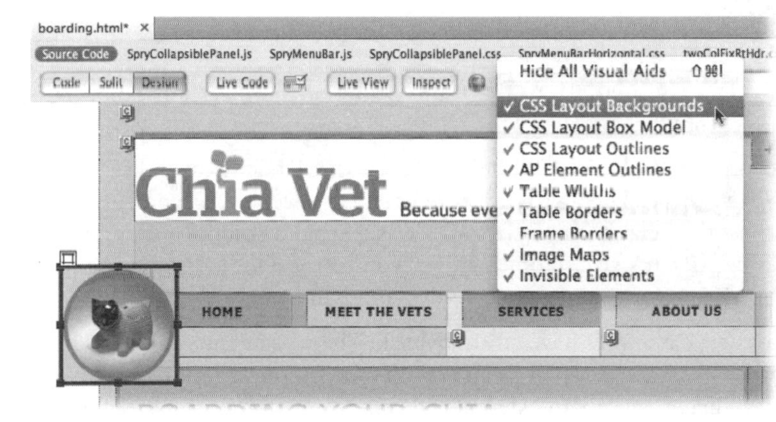

Figure 9-23: *Choices 2 to 5 in the Visual Aids menu provide visual cues to help you with CSS Layouts in Design view. The CSS Layout Backgrounds option—selected here—lights up each <div> tag on a page with a hideous, randomly selected background color. It also highlights any element whose display property you set to "block" (page 142), or that uses either absolute or relative positioning (page 356). You'll find the CSS Layout Box model option discussed in Figure 9-12.*

Note: If one AP element overlaps another, the top AP element—the one with the higher Z-Index, as described on page 361—has a solid outline; the lower element's outline appears as a dashed line where the top AP element overlaps it.

- **AP div positioning summary.** If you select an AP div and hover your mouse over that div, Dreamweaver pops up a box with information about that AP div (see Figure 9-22), including the name of the ID style or class style, what type of positioning you used, the AP div's dimensions, and so on. This box provides a quick summary of relevant positioning information, and gives you a bird's-eye view of the CSS properties defining the AP div's placement on the page.

Drawing AP Divs

Dreamweaver wouldn't be Dreamweaver if it didn't give you several ways to perform a certain task, like creating an absolutely positioned div. You can do it as described above, or turn to two methods designed specifically to help you add AP divs to a page: You can drag to create an AP div freehand, or use a menu command to insert a full-blown, complete AP div. Your choices are:

- **Use the Draw AP div tool.** You'll find the Draw AP div tool in Insert panel's Layout category (see Figure 9-5). Click the AP div button, and then drag the + cursor diagonally in the document window to create a box—the outline of the AP div.

Tip: For accurate drawing, you should hide Dreamweaver's visual aids (like the AP div border and selection handles), which take up space and move AP divs slightly out of position in Design view. Ctrl+Shift+I (⌘-Shift-I) does the trick.

- **Use a menu command.** To insert an AP div at the insertion point, choose Insert→Layout Objects→AP Div.

  If you don't like the looks of the default AP div that Dreamweaver inserts, choose Edit→Preferences (Dreamweaver→Preferences), select the AP Elements category, and adjust the default properties. Add a background color, for example, or increase the AP div's size. From then on, you can instantly create your favorite kind of AP div using the Insert→AP div command.

Dreamweaver's AP div tools have one drawback: They create internal ID styles with generic names like apDiv1, apDiv2, and so on. So you don't get to take advantage of the byte-saving virtues of an external style sheet until you move the styles to an external style sheet. Fortunately, Dreamweaver's CSS management options make this simple, as described on page 306. In addition, you have to take a second to rename these AP divs to something a little more understandable—like changing apDiv1 to *button*. (Your friend, the AP Elements panel, makes this easy to do, as shown in Figure 9-24, and explained in the next section.)

The AP Elements Panel

The AP Elements panel (Figure 9-24) helps you manage absolutely positioned elements. To open it, choose Window→AP Elements, or press F2. It's called the AP Elements panel instead of the AP Divs panel because any tag that has an ID style and has its position property set to absolute (see page 356) appears here. So if you absolutely position a single paragraph, its ID appears in this panel. The panel's three columns provide information on each element:

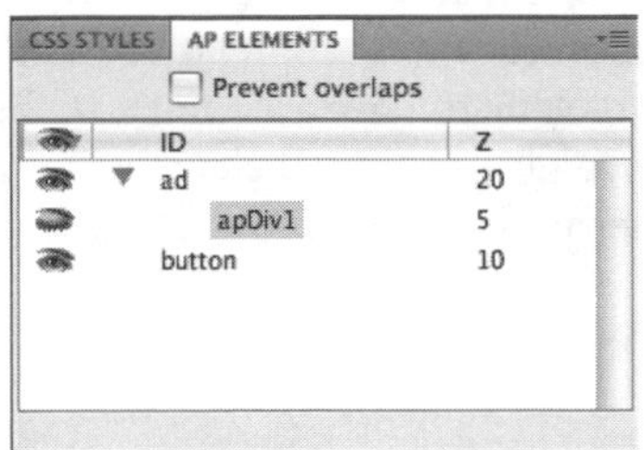

Figure 9-24:
The AP Elements panel lets you name, reorder, and change the visibility of AP elements. Turning on the "Prevent overlaps" checkbox ensures you can't position or drag one AP div on top of another. This feature is intended to make it easy to convert an AP div layout to a table-based layout using the Modify→Convert→"AP divs to Table". Don't do it! This creates horribly bloated HTML that easily falls apart as you add, edit, and adjust content on the page.

- **Visibility.** To change an absolutely positioned element's visibility property (page 361), click in the column with the eye icon next to the element's name. An open eye indicates that the property is set to visible; a closed eye, means it's hidden. No eye icon at all represents the factory setting: The element is visible on the page, but you haven't set its visibility property.
- **AP element ID.** If you use Dreamweaver's Draw AP div tool, Dreamweaver gives the AP div a generic ID name—like *apDiv1*. If you created the div yourself, you probably already came up with a pretty good ID, like *siteTools* or *signupForm*. But if you want to change that name (or provide a more descriptive name for a Dreamweaver-created AP div), double-click the AP element ID name, and then type in a new name. (AP element names are just ID names, so they must start with a letter, and can contain only letters and numbers. As Dreamweaver is quick to remind you, spaces and other punctuation aren't allowed.)

  Clicking an item in the AP Elements panel, by the way, is another way to select that element in the document window.

Warning: Don't rename an AP element's ID if you already used it in a Dreamweaver behavior like the Show/Hide Elements action (see page 613). JavaScript uses those names to "talk to" the absolutely positioned elements. If you change its ID in the AP Elements panel, Dreamweaver doesn't automatically update the name in the JavaScript code. The behavior, therefore, no longer works. In that case, you need to edit the behavior using the new ID name.

- **Z-Index.** As you read about back on page 361, the Z-Index lets you specify a third dimension to absolutely positioned elements, letting them overlap one another. To change the Z-Index of an element, double-click the space in the Z column, and then type a number.

  However, keep in mind the following slightly quirky behavior: When you place an AP element inside another AP element (page 373), the nested element shares the same Z-Index as the parent AP element. For example, Figure 9-24 shows that you put the HTML for the div with the ID *apDiv1* inside the div tag with the ID *ad*. You can tell this is the case because Dreamweaver indents *apDiv1* underneath the *ad* element in the panel. The Z-Index for the *apDiv1* element is only 5, but it will still appear *above* the button element with the Z-Index 10. That's because the *ad* element has a Z-Index of 20, and, since the *apDiv1* element's HTML is *inside* the ad element, its Z-index is also 20, relative to other elements on the page. So why does the nested element have a Z-Index at all? It doesn't have to, but if you have multiple absolutely positioned elements nested inside another AP element, the Z-Index determines how a browser stacks the nested elements relative to each other.

Modifying AP Element Properties

Once you add an AP div, you don't need to go back to the CSS Rule Definition window to edit most of the AP div's positioning properties. Using the Property inspector, you can rename it, resize it, move it, align it with other AP divs, and set many other properties.

But first, you have to select the AP div using one of these methods:

- Click the AP div's name in the AP Elements panel (see Figure 9-24).
- Click the AP div's selection handle (see Figure 9-22).
- Click the AP div's border. The border turns red when you move your mouse into the proper position.
- Click the AP element marker that indicates the HTML code for the absolutely positioned item (see Figure 9-22). (Out of the box, Dreamweaver hides these markers, since they can get in the way of your design work; to show them, see the tip on page 366.)

And if those aren't enough ways to select an AP div—Adobe's programmers never sleep—you can also Shift-click an absolutely positioned element. This Shift-click technique offers another advantage: you can select multiple AP divs simultaneously, and set the properties of (or align) many AP divs at once. If you're working in an AP div or have an AP div selected, Shift-clicking another AP div selects them both. You can continue to Shift-click to select additional AP divs. (Shift-click a second time to deselect a selected absolutely positioned element.)

Resizing Absolutely Positioned Elements

When you select an AP element, eight handles appear around the edges of the AP div (see Figure 9-22). You can drag any of them to change the AP div's dimensions. The corner handles resize both the width and height simultaneously.

You can also use the keyboard to resize an absolutely positioned element. First, select the AP element, and then do one of the following:

- Press the Ctrl (⌘) key, and then press the arrow keys to change the AP element's size by one pixel. The up and down arrow keys adjust the AP div's height; the left and right arrows affect its width.

- To change the size *10* pixels at a time, press Ctrl+Shift (⌘-Shift), and then press the arrow keys.

For better precision, use the Property inspector to set an exact width and height for the AP element (see Figure 9-25). Type values in the W and H boxes to change the width and height of the AP element, respectively. You can specify any unit of measurement that CSS understands: px (pixels), pc (picas), pt (points), in (inches), mm (millimeters), cm (centimeters), em (height of the current font), ex (height of the current font's x character), or % (percentage)—see page 133 for more on CSS measurement units. To pick your measurement unit, type its abbreviation *immediately* after you type in the size value. For example, type *100px* into the W box to make the AP div 100 pixels wide. Don't leave out the measurement unit—px, em, or %, for example—or browsers won't display the correct dimensions of the AP element.

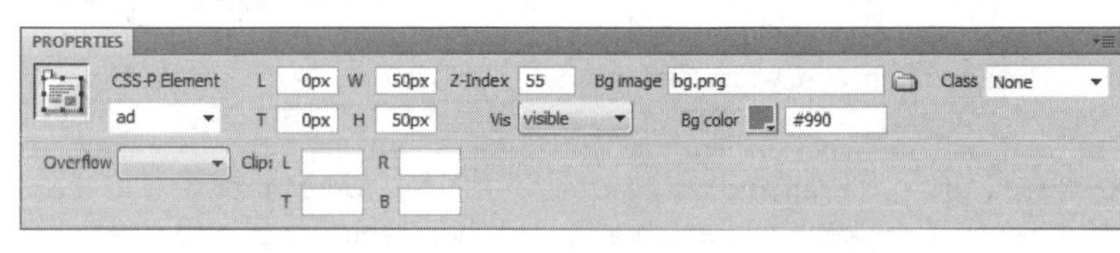

Figure 9-25: *The Property inspector controls many AP element properties (although some require editing CSS styles).*

Another benefit to using the Property inspector is that Dreamweaver lets you resize multiple AP divs at once. Shift-click two or more AP divs to select them, and then type new widths and heights. Dreamweaver sets all the selected AP divs to these dimensions.

Moving AP Elements

Moving an absolutely positioned element is just as simple as resizing it. Drag any border of the element, or the AP element's selection handle (shown in Figure 9-22). Avoid the eight resize handles, however, because they'll change the size of the AP div when you drag them.

For less speed but greater precision, you can move an AP element using the keyboard. First, select the element and then do one of the following:

- To move an AP element one pixel at a time, press the corresponding keyboard arrow key.
- Press Shift while using an arrow key to move the element 10 pixels at a time.

As you'd guess, you can also control an AP element's placement by using the Property inspector (see Figure 9-25). Dreamweaver measures an AP div's position relative to the left and top edges of the page (or, for nested AP divs, from the left and top edges of a parent div when you set the Position property to either absolute or relative). The

Property inspector provides two boxes for these values: L specifies the distance from the left edge of the page to the left edge of the selected AP div; T specifies the distance from the top edge of the page to the top of the selected AP div.

Note: You can't edit an AP div's Right or Bottom positioning properties from the Property inspector. For these properties, edit the AP Div's style using one of the methods discussed on page 124.

To position an AP div using the Property inspector, select the div (for example, by clicking the div's border or by selecting its name in the AP Elements panel), and then type distances in the L and T boxes. You can use any of the units of measurement mentioned previously. You can even use negative values to move part or all of an AP div off the page entirely (offstage, you might say), which you might want to do if you intended a subsequent animation to bring it *onstage*, into the document window (Dreamweaver no longer includes tools for creating animations, but with a little bit of JavaScript, you can add your own animations. Visit *www.viget.com/inspire/fun-with-jquerys-animation-function* for a few examples).

If you draw a 100-pixel-tall and 50-pixel-wide AP div, you can move it to the very top-left corner of the page by selecting it, and then typing *0* in both the L and T boxes. To position that same AP div so that it's just off the left edge of the page, type *-50px* in the L box.

Aligning AP Elements

At times, you may want to align several AP elements so that their left, top, bottom, or right edges line up with each other. Dreamweaver's Align command does just that; it can even make the width and height of selected AP elements the same.

To use this feature, select two or more AP divs (by Shift-clicking them), choose Modify→Arrange, and then select one of the following options from the submenu:

- Align Left aligns the left edges of all selected AP divs. In other words, it gives each AP div the same L property.
- Align Right aligns the right edges.
- Align Top aligns the top edges, so that all the T properties are the same.
- Align Bottom aligns the bottom edges of the AP divs.
- Make Same Width sets the same width for all selected AP divs (in the W box in the Property inspector). Make Same Height does the same for the height of the AP divs.

The AP div you select *last* dictates how Dreamweaver aligns the AP divs. Say you have three AP divs—A, B, and C—and you select them in order from A to C. You then align them to Left. Dreamweaver uses the left edge of AP div C (the last one you selected) as the value for the other AP divs.

Background Image and Color

To add a background image to an AP div, click the folder icon next to the Bg Image field, and then select an image from your site folder. As usual, Dreamweaver tiles the image, if necessary, to fill the entire AP div's with repeating copies of the graphic. (To adjust how or whether the image tiles, you'll need to edit the AP div's style using the normal CSS-style editing techniques; see page 124.)

Setting a background color is even easier. Just use the Bg Color box to select a color or to sample one from your screen.

Nesting AP Divs

Nesting doesn't necessarily mean that one AP div appears inside another; rather, it means that Dreamweaver writes the HTML for one AP div inside the code for another. The nested AP div itself can appear anywhere on the page. The main benefit of nested AP divs is that the *parent* AP div—the AP div that includes the HTML of one or more other AP divs—can control the behavior of its *child AP divs.*

Suppose you create one AP div, and nest two AP divs inside it. If you move the parent AP div on the screen, the two child AP divs follow it, which gives you an easy way to move several AP divs in unison. Furthermore, the parent AP div can control its children's visibility. When you hide the parent AP div (see page 361), the nested AP divs also disappear (unless you specifically set the nested AP divs' visibility property to *visible*).

Tip: Dreamweaver's factory settings hide a useful visual cue–"AP element" markers (see the "HTML position for AP div" marker in Figure 9-22). These markers identify where in a page's code the HTML for the AP div appears. Since a nested absolutely positioned element is a tag whose code appears inside another absolutely positioned element–like inside the parent's <div> tag–an AP element marker appears inside the parent AP div for each nested AP div. To turn on AP element markers, press Ctrl+U (⌘-U) to open the Preferences window, click the Invisible Elements category, and then turn on the "Anchor Points for AP Elements" checkbox. You also need to make sure you have visual aids turned on (as explained in Figure 9-23).

Here's how to create a nested AP div:

1. **Use the Insert Div Tag button on either the Common or Layout category of the Insert panel, or choose Insert→Layout Objects→Div Tag. In either case, the Insert Div Tag window appears (Figure 9-6). Select the name of the AP div you want to nest inside another AP div; choose either "After start of tag" or "Before end of tag" from the first Insert menu; and then choose the name of the parent AP div from the second menu.**
2. **Click inside an AP div, and then choose Insert→Layout Objects→AP div. You get a new, nested AP div inside it.**
3. **Drag the Draw AP Div *button* (see Figure 9-5) from the Insert panel's Layout category, and drop it inside an AP div on the page.**

Tip: You can also un-nest an AP div, and gain more control over where Dreamweaver writes the HTML for that AP div, by dragging the AP element marker to a new spot in the document window. (This AP element marker isn't always immediately visible, however; see the preceding Tip.)

CSS Layout Tutorial

In this tutorial, you'll create a page using one of Dreamweaver's CSS Layouts. You'll then add content to the page, apply styles, and modify the design to meet the exacting standards of Chia-Vet (see Figure 9-36).

Note: You need to download the tutorial files from *www.sawmac.com/dwcs5/* to complete this tutorial. See the note on page 45 for more details.

Once you download the tutorial files and open Dreamweaver, set up a new site as described on page 37. Name the site *CSS Layout*, and select the Chapter09 folder (inside the MM_DWCS5 folder). (In a nutshell: choose Site→New Site. In the Site Setup window, type *CSS Layout* into the Site Name field, click the folder icon next to the Local Site Folder field, navigate to and select the Chapter09 folder, and then click Choose or Select. Finally, click Save.)

1. **Choose File→New.**

   The New Document Window opens (see Figure 9-26).

2. **Select the "Blank Page" category in the left column; select HTML from the Page Type column, and select "2 column fixed, right sidebar, header and footer" from the Layout column. Select XHTML 1.0 Transitional from the DocType menu.**

   You selected a page design with two columns, a right-hand sidebar and a main content area on the left, with areas at the top and bottom to hold a banner and copyright notice.

   Next you need to tell Dreamweaver where to store the CSS required to make this design work.

3. **Make sure you select Create New File in the Layout CSS drop-down menu.**

   This tells Dreamweaver to create a new external style sheet with the required styles, and to link it to the new page Dreamweaver is about to create.

4. **Click the Create button.**

   The Save Style Sheet File As window appears. Before Dreamweaver creates a new web page, you first have to save the external style sheet. Dreamweaver recommends a file name—*twoColFixRtHdr.css* in this instance. You can rename this file, but the name Dreamweaver suggests is descriptive, if not particularly elegant.

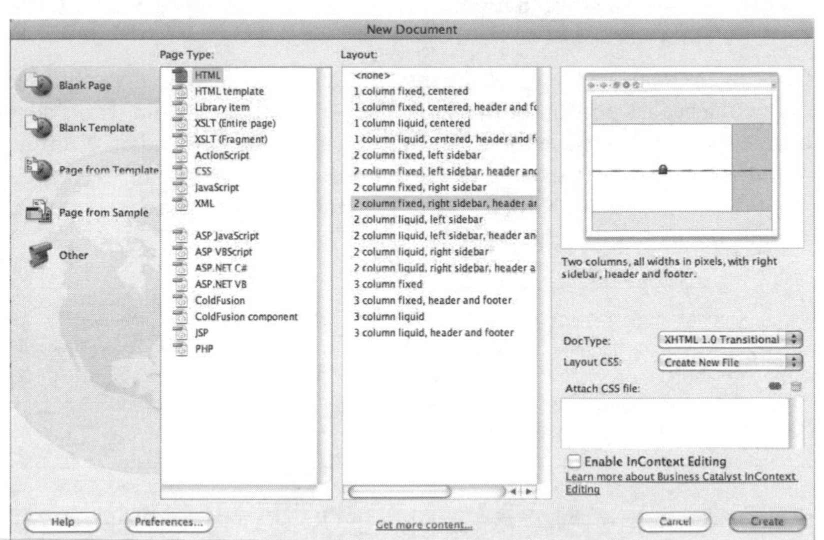

Figure 9-26: *Dreamweaver provides 16 CSS layouts organized by the number of columns each layout has.*

5. **Navigate to this site's main folder (Chapter_09), and then double-click the css folder to open it. Click Save.**

   Dreamweaver saves the file, and creates a new document. It's not much to look at yet, but you'll add your own design touches in the steps ahead.

6. **Choose File→Save; and then save the file as *tips.html* in the Chapter_09 folder.**

   Every page needs a title and the one Dreamweaver supplies—"Untitled Document"—isn't very helpful.

7. **Select and delete "Untitled document" in the Title box at the top of the Document window, and then type *Chia Tips*.**

   The first step you should take after creating a page based on a Dreamweaver CSS Layout is removing some of the formatting Dreamweaver supplies. For example, to help you easily identify the header, sidebar, and footer, Dreamweaver adds colors to each of these elements. Unless you're designing a camouflage tribute site, you should remove these colors (or at least change them to colors you like).

8. **Make sure you have the CSS Styles panel open (Window→CSS Styles), and the Current button selected at the top of the panel (see Figure 9-27). Also, make sure you have the Cascade button (labeled in Figure 9-27) pressed.**

   Dreamweaver's CSS Panel provides a quick and easy way to identify and edit a style applied to part of a page. The panel's Current view displays the styles affecting the current selection.

9. **In the document window, click the green strip at the top of the page (where the "Insert_logo" placeholder is), and then choose Edit→Select All (Ctrl+A or ⌘-A for Macs works just as well).**

   Clicking inside this area places the insertion point inside the <div> tag used to define the header portion of the page. The Select All command works slightly differently when you have the cursor inside a <div> tag. Instead of selecting *everything* on the page (probably what you'd think Select All would do), it selects all of the div's contents. Now, if you look at the CSS Styles panel, you see a style named *.header* listed in the Rules pane (see Figure 9-27).

Note: When you click inside a <div> tag and choose Edit→Select All, Dreamweaver highlights the <div> tag in the Tag selector at the bottom of the document window. A highlighted tag in the Tag selector usually means that you selected the *entire tag* (meaning the opening <div> and closing </div> tags). In this situation, however, only the *contents* inside the opening and closing div tags are selected; you must choose Edit→Select All a second time to actually select the tag.

---

10. **Make sure you have .header selected in the Rules pane (see Figure 9-27). In the Properties pane, click the Background property value—#ADB96E—press Delete, and then hit the Enter (Return) key.**

    This removes the background color and, at the same time, deletes the background property from the style sheet. You could also have changed the color to something more appropriate for the site.

    Next, you'll set the background colors for the other styles on the page.

Tip: You can delete a property from a style by selecting the property in the Properties pane and clicking the Delete (Trash can) button (see Figure 9-27).

---

11. **Repeat step 10 to remove the background color from the sidebar, footer and body.**

    For example, click inside the tan area of the sidebar, press Ctrl+A (⌘-A), and edit the *.sidebar1* style. The name of the style controlling the footer is *.footer* and the dark brown color is applied to the body tag style (one quick way to select the body tag is with the tag selector at the bottom of the document window: just click <body> to select the tag and highlight the body style in the styles panel.

    Next, you'll delete some styles you won't need. The easiest way to get to them is in the "All" view of the CSS Styles panel.

12. **In the CSS Styles panel, click the All button. Click the + (triangle on Mac) next to the *twoColFixRtHdr.css* to display the styles in the style sheet (see Figure 9-28).**

    You can select more than one style from this list and delete them all at once.

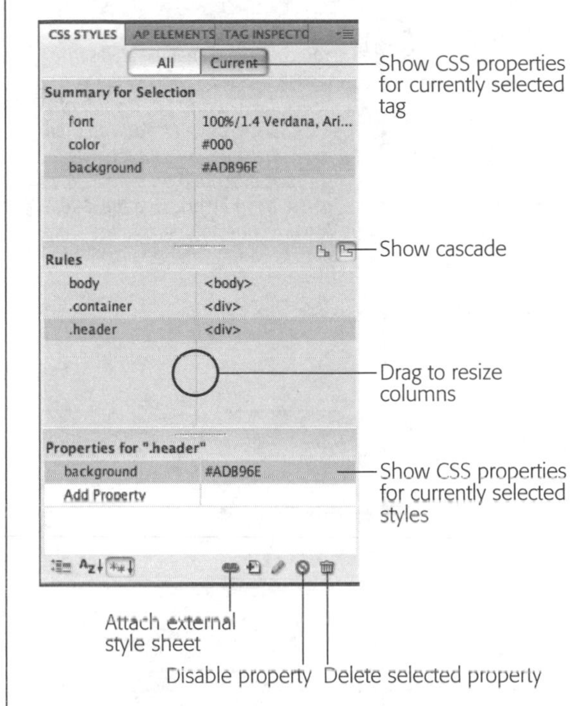

Figure 9-27:
The Current View of the CSS Styles Panel is one of Dreamweaver's greatest CSS productivity tools. It shows properties and styles that apply to any element you select in the Document window. It's most useful when you click the Show Cascade button (labeled), because you see every style that might affect the current selection in the order of their importance, with the style that has the greatest impact on the selected page element at the bottom. You can also temporarily hide the property of a style, by selecting it in the Properties pane and clicking the "disable property" button (the red strike-through symbol). To remove a property, delete its value in the right-hand column (for example, delete #ADB96E here) or select the property and click the Trash can icon. Turn to "The Other Side of the CSS Styles Panel" on page 314 to learn more about using the CSS Styles panel.

13. **Ctrl-click (⌘-click) the styles pictured in Figure 9-28, and then click the panel menu button (circled) to open a contextual menu. Select Cut from the menu to remove the styles from the style sheet.**

    Alternatively you can press the Delete key, or right-click (ctrl-click) on the styles and choose Cut. Either way, you remove the styles from the style sheet.

Adding Content

Now it's time to add the real content to this page…OK, it's not "real" content, since *Chia-Vet.com* doesn't exist, but you get the idea.

1. **Select the green "Insert_logo" placeholder and hit the delete key.**

   Alternatively, you could choose Edit→Cut. Time to add a real graphic.

Note: If you find that you can't edit the content on a page, you may be in Live View–meaning you clicked the Live View button at the top of the document window and are seeing the page as it would look in a web browser. In this state, you can't edit the page's contents. Just click the Live View button again to return to editing mode.

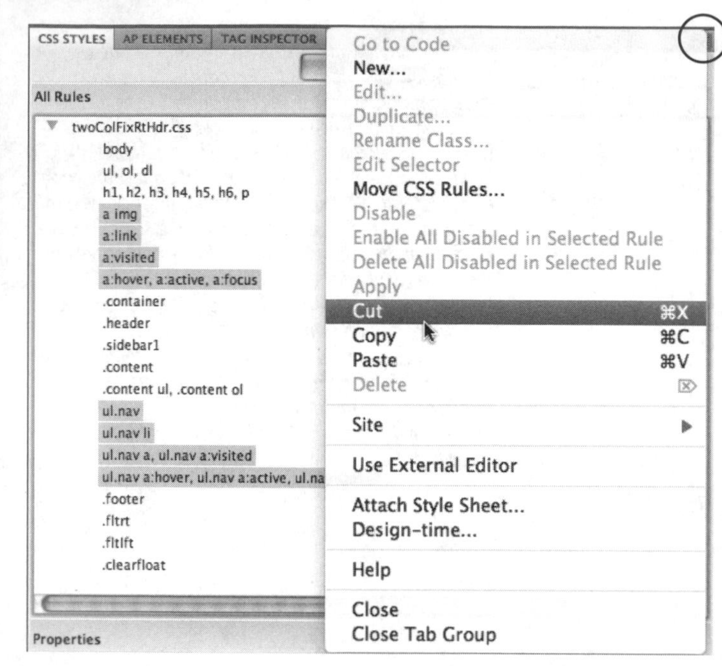

Figure 9-28:
You can select multiple styles in a style sheet–but only when you select the All button at the top of the CSS styles panel. You can then move the styles to another style sheet as described on page 306, or delete them by pressing the delete key or choosing Cut from the panel's context menu.

2. **Choose Insert→Image. In the Select Image Source window, navigate to the images folder, and then double-click the file logo.png.**

   If the Image Tag Accessibility window appears, type *Chia Vet* in the Alternate text box, and then click OK.

   The sidebar lists links to other pages related to this one. The content for that sidebar is located in another HTML file in this tutorial.

3. **In the files panel, locate the file *sidebar_content.html* in the content folder, and double-click it to open it.**

   You could also choose File→Open, navigate to the content folder in the site, and then double-click the *sidebar_content.html* file to open it. Either way, a web page opens with a headline, some text and a form. You'll copy the contents of this page and paste it into the new layout.

4. **Choose Edit→Select All, and then Edit→Copy; at the top of the document window, click the tab for tips.html to switch to that page. Click anywhere inside the right sidebar, and then choose Edit→Select All and Edit→Paste.**

   The sidebar's dummy text supplied with the layout page is replaced with not much smarter text from Chia Vet. You'll do the same for the main content area.

5. **Repeat steps 3 and 4 with the *main_content.html* file and the main content region of the page.**

   In other words, open *main_content.html*, and then paste its contents into the div with the big headline "Instructions". Now for the footer.

6. **Repeat steps 3 and 4 with the *footer.html* page and the footer region at the bottom of the page.**

   The page should look like Figure 9-29. Now it's time to adjust the layout a bit.

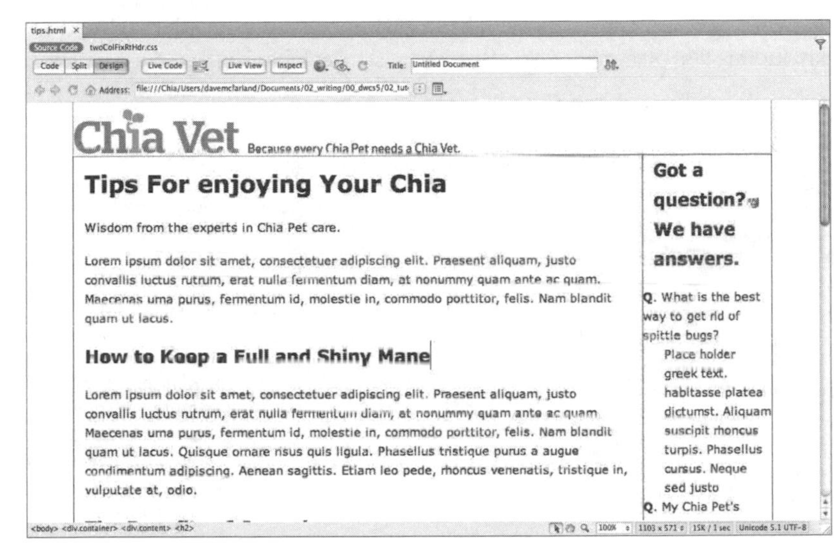

Figure 9-29: *The dotted lines that run around the different layout regions on the page represent the <div> tags that create this two-column layout. The right-hand sidebar is a right-floated div with a set width.*

Fine-Tuning the Layout

Now it's time to tune the CSS layout to make it your own. First, you'll tackle all the main components of the page: the body, header, sidebar, and so on.

1. **At the top of the CSS Styles panel, click the All button.**

   You should see a list of the styles in the attached *twoColFixRtHdr.css* style sheet. If you don't see the names of the styles, you need to expand the style sheet listing by clicking the + sign (flippy triangle on Mac) in the CSS Styles panel, to the left of the style sheet name.

   At the top of the list is a tag style for the <body> tag. You'll edit that style first.

2. **Double-click "body" in the list.**

   The CSS Rule Definition window opens. You'll change the font and a few other properties.

3. **From the Font-family menu, select "Tahoma, Geneva, sans-serif".**

   Now you'll add a background image and color to the page.

4. **Click the Background category, and then type *#CAE0EC* in the "Background-color" box; click the Browse button, and then select the file bgPage.png from the images folder (see Figure 9-30).**

   In this case, the *bgPage.png* file is a graphic that a web browser will tile seamlessly in the background.

5. **Click OK to complete the style.**

   Now it's time to readjust the overall page width. Dreamweaver's fixed-width CSS layouts are 960 pixels wide. You'll bring that down a bit for the Chia-Vet.com site.

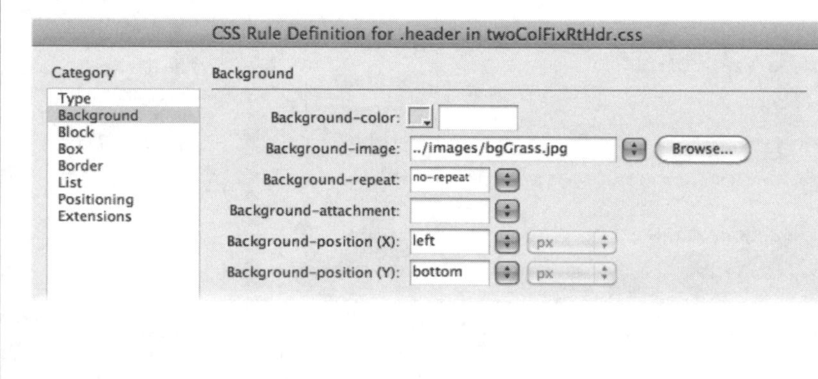

Figure 9-30: *It's a good idea to set a background color even when you assign a background image to a page. The background color should match the general tone of the image. That way, if a visitor has graphics turned off, or if, for some reason, the background image fails to load, you still have background color.*

6. **In the CSS Styles panel, double-click the style named *.container*.**

   The CSS Rule Definition window opens. The container div wraps around all other <div> tags on the page and provides the overall width of the page's content area. You'll change the width and add some padding to add some white space around the inside of this div.

7. **Click the Box category. Type 860 in the Width box; uncheck the padding's "Same for all" box and set the left and right padding values to 15px each.**

   The Rule Definition window should look like Figure 9-30.

8. **Click OK to finish editing the style.**

   Hey, what gives? The main content suddenly disappeared! Well, it didn't actually disappear; it just dropped down below the sidebar. If you scroll down you'll see it. This is one of the pitfalls of float-based layouts—as discussed on page 344, if the total width of the columns doesn't fit inside their container, you'll run into the dreaded "float drop." Basically, you just changed the container div's width to 860 pixels—the sidebar is 180 pixels, and the content div is 760 pixels; combined, the two divs require 960 pixels to fit side-by-side. The fix: decrease the widths of the sidebar and content divs so they total 860 pixels.

You may wonder what the padding values are for: the left and right 15 pixels of space indent the content inside the container, providing extra white space, a 15 pixel gutter on either side. Note, that this also affects the container's total width on the screen: it's now 890 pixels wide: 860 (the width property's value) + 15 (left padding) + 15 (right padding).

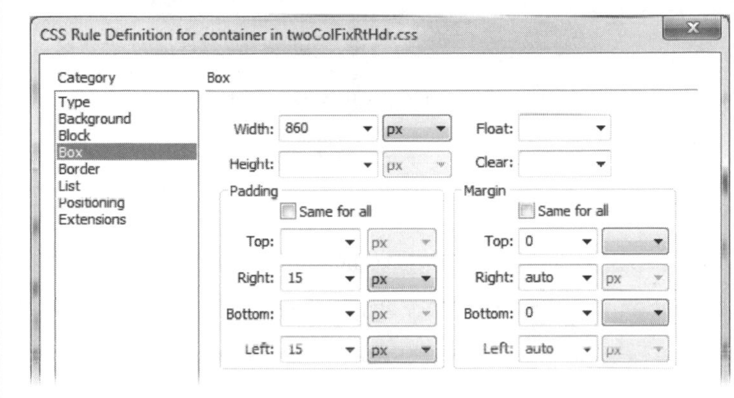

Figure 9-31: *The Rule Definition window's Box category lets you control the width of an element. It also lets you set the space that surrounds the element (margin) and the space inside the element (padding).*

9. **In the CSS styles panel, double-click the style named .content.**

   The Rule Definition window opens once again. You need to make this div a little thinner so that it can fit next to the sidebar.

10. **In the Rule Definition window, click the Box category. Type *564* in the Width box.**

    546 isn't some magic CSS number—it's just the amount that the Chia-Vet.com designer thought looked good. The width value provides 564 pixels of space for the content inside this div. While you're here, you'll add some borders.

11. **Select the Border category. Choose "solid" from the Style menu, type 3 in the Width box, and *#93BD00* in the color box.**

    The Rule Definition window should look like Figure 9-32.

12. **Click OK to complete the style.**

    The content div should now be back in place. However, the sidebar now is a bit too thin. You'll edit its style next to change its width and add borders around it as well.

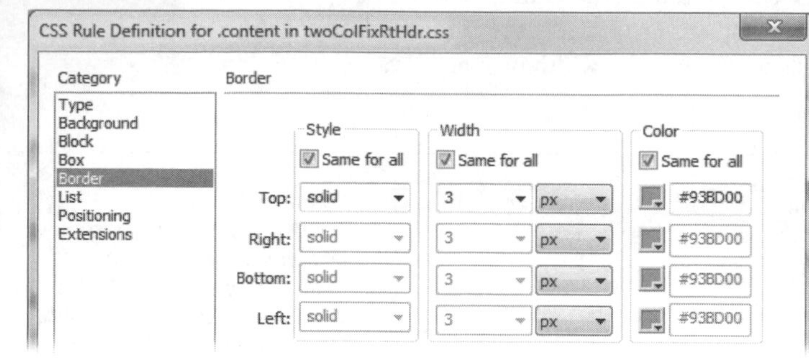

Figure 9-32: *To add a border around all four sides of an element, specify the style, width and color in the Border property window. If you want to set different borders for each site, or apply borders to only one or two sides of an element, uncheck the three "Same for all" boxes.*

13. **In the CSS styles panel, double-click the style named .sidebar1.**

    The Rule Definition window opens once again. First, you'll add borders as with the content div.

14. **Repeat step 11 to add borders to the .sidebar1 style.**

    Now, you'll set the width of this div.

15. **Click the Box category and change the width from 180 to 270 pixels; uncheck the Margin's "Same for all box" and type *14* for the left margin.**

    The 14-pixel left margin adds space between the sidebar and the content area, creating the kind of "gutter" you find between columns in a magazine.

    But why 270 for the width? Well, that's how the math works out. Yes, unfortunately, there is a little math involved, but it's no harder than adding together a few numbers. First, start with the total width available for the content and sidebar columns: that's the 860 pixels you set in step 7. Then subtract the space taken up by the content div, which is 564 pixels (the width) + 3 pixels (left border) + 3 pixels (right border), or 570 pixels total. So 860 minus 570 leaves 290 pixels for the right sidebar. The sidebar has a 3-pixel border on the left, a 3-pixel border on the right, and a 14-pixel margin on the left, for a total of 20 pixels. When you subtract that 20 from the 290 pixels available for the sidebar, you're left with 270 for the sidebar's width value. 1 pixel more and the two columns would no longer sit side-by-side. Thus endeth the math lesson—back to designing.

16. **Make sure you're still in the Box category, and type *65* in the Top padding box.**

    This step adds 65 pixels of space between the top of the sidebar and the content inside the sidebar. Why so much space—to make room for a decorative background image, which you'll add next.

17. **Click the Background category, and then, in the Background-color box, type *#EAEBE4*; click the Browse button, and then select the file *bgQnA.png*, located in the images folder. Finally, from the Background-repeat menu, choose "no-repeat"; and then position the image in the center and top using the Background-position menus X and Y respectively. Click OK to finish the style.**

Since you just expanded the sidebar to make it wider, you'll next need to make the main content area thinner—you do this by increasing the right margin for that div.

18. **In the CSS styles panel, double-click the style named *.header*.**

    First, you'll add a distinctive graphic to the background of the header.

19. **In the Rule Definition window, click the Background category. Click the Browse button, and then in the images folder, locate and double-click the file named *bgGrass.jpg*. From the "Background-repeat" menu, select "no-repeat"; from the "Background-position (X)" menu, choose "left", and from the "Background-position (Y)" menu, choose "bottom".**

    The window should now look like Figure 9-33. Now you'll control the height and bottom margin for this style.

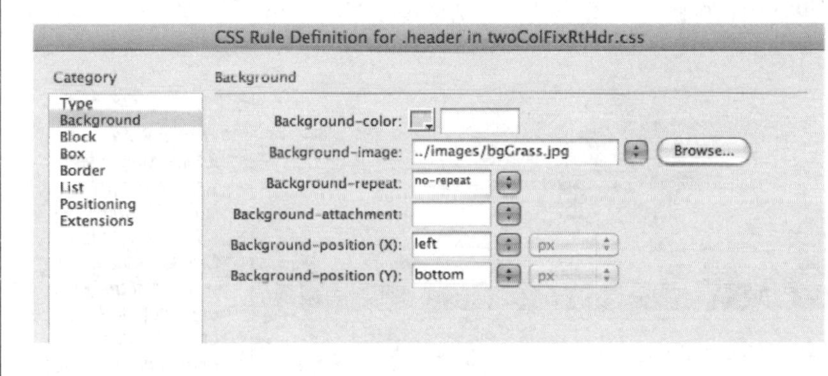

Figure 9-33: *You can use CSS to control the placement of background images as well as whether the image tiles (repeats). In this example, the image bgGrass.png appears in the background of this style. It appears only once ("no-repeat"), and at the bottom-left corner of the element.*

20. **Click the Box category, and then, in the Height box, type *142*; under Margin, uncheck the "Same for all" box, and then type *10* in the bottom margin box.**

    As mentioned on page 360, you should set the height of an element only if you're sure that the content inside the element won't be taller than the height you specify. Otherwise, content spills out of the element, and since browsers handle this situation in different ways, you end up with some weird display problems. In this case, however, you're adding only the logo image and a single-line navigation bar (which you'll do below), so you know how tall the style needs to be.

    Finally, you'll add a bold border to the top of the header.

21. **Click the Border category, and then uncheck all three "Same for all" boxes. From the top style menu, choose "solid", type *6* in the top width box, and type *#F63* in the top color box. Click OK to complete the style.**

    You should now see a bright orange border at the top of the header, as well as a green grass-like image at the bottom. At this point, the page should look like Figure 9-34.

Adding Styles and Navigation

At this point, you could create new styles to format this page using the techniques you read about earlier in this book—change the fonts and font sizes, add underlines to headlines, change the look of links, and so on. For the sake of keeping this book from rivaling the length of *War and Peace*, we assume you've already got those skills under your belt, so you'll attach a style sheet with some already created styles.

1. **In the CSS Style panel, click the Attach Style Sheet button (see Figure 9-27).**

   The Attach External Style Sheet window opens. It's a good idea to place any styles that don't directly affect the layout of one of Dreamweaver's CSS Layout pages in a separate CSS file, like the one you're about to attach. That way, one CSS file controls style elements that apply to every type of page on your site—the background color of the body, the look of headings and text, and so on. Then you can attach this global style sheet so that it shares these same styles with other pages using different types of CSS layouts—1 column, 3 column, liquid, and so on.

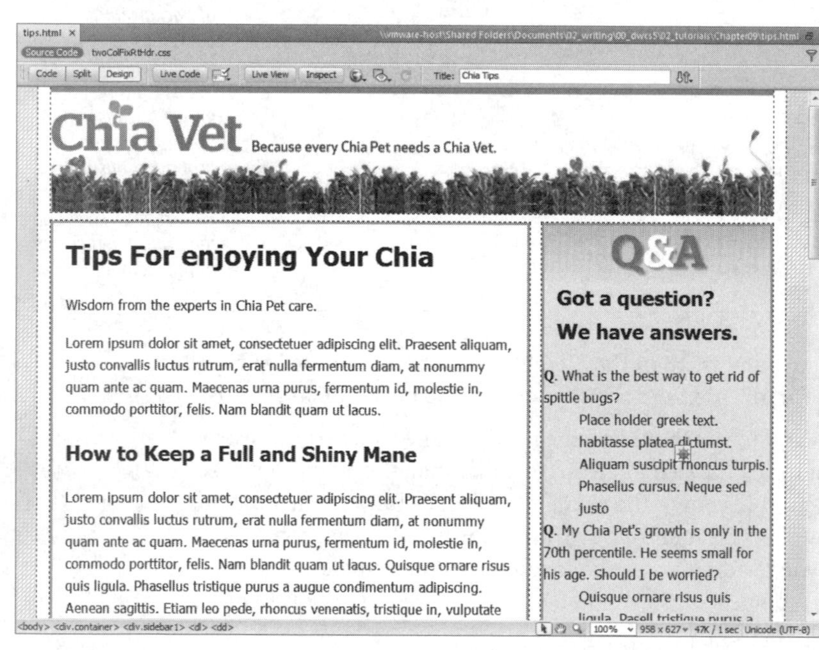

Figure 9-34: *It takes only a few steps to modify a stock Dreamweaver CSS Layout. A few tweaks to the CSS let you adjust the width of a page and the size of its columns. Most of the hard work lies in developing the individual styles to format your paragraphs, headlines, tables, lists, and so onÉbut that's the fun and creative part.*

Tip: If you only plan on using one type of CSS Layout (2 column, fixed with header and footer, for example), then you don't need a separate style sheet for the layout and another one for the site's styles. Just name the layout style sheet something generic like site.css, and put all your styles in it.

---

2. **Click the Browse button, and then navigate to the css folder; double-click the file *global.css*. In the Attach External Style Sheet window, click OK.**

   Dreamweaver links the style sheet to the page, and styles the page's content. The page is missing a navigation bar in the header. You could, of course, build that from scratch with a Spry Menu Bar (see page 184). But to save some time, a basic navigation bar has already been created for you.

3. **In the Files panel, double-click the file menubar.html.**

   Alternatively, you can choose File→Open, and then, in the site's local root folder, select the *menubar.html* file. In either case, a web page with a simple bulleted list of links appears.

4. **Click anywhere in the page, and then choose Edit→Select All; choose Edit→Copy.**

   You just copied the links. Now you'll paste them into the page you've been working on.

5. **At the top of the Document window, click the *tips.html* tab to return to the tutorial page. Click in the space below the logo (inside the grass image, for example) and then choose Edit→Paste.**

   A new navigation bar appears. You may be wondering where the bulleted list went. It's still there—it's just been transformed by the CSS stored in the *global.css* file. If you want to learn how to make a navigation bar like this one, turn to the tutorial in "Adding a Navigation Bar", page 198.

   Now you'll apply a class style from the style sheet you attached in step 2.

6. **Click inside the paragraph, below the headline "Tips For Enjoying Your Chia". In the Property inspector, make sure you have the HTML button selected, and then, from the Class menu, choose "tagline".**

   Alternatively, you can right-click (ctrl-click) inside that paragraph, and then, from the contextual menu, choose Styles→"tagline".

Fiddling with the Footer

The page is pretty much complete. However, the footer at the bottom of the page could use a little TLC. In addition, you have a good opportunity to get a taste of using the CSS *float* property to craft the design of a page. In this case, you'll create two mini columns—one to hold Chia-Vet's phone number and copyright notice, and another for its mailing address.

1. **Click inside any of the text in the footer. On the CSS Styles panel, click the "Create new style" button.**

   The New CSS Rule window appears. Dreamweaver suggests a long-winded style based on where you had the cursor. But this descendent selector is needlessly complex—you can simplify it, using the Less Specific button.

2. **Click the Less Specific button once.**

   Depending on which text you clicked inside before creating the style, in the Selector Name box you see either *.footer p* or *.footer p strong* (see Figure 9-35). Delete the strong part if you see that, so that you're just left with *.footer p*. This descendent selector affects only paragraph tags within another element (in this case a <div> tag) that has the class *footer*.

3. **At the bottom of the New CSS Rule window, from the Menu, select *global.css*, and then click OK.**

   The CSS Rule Definition window appears. You'll make the text smaller but spread out the line using the line-height property.

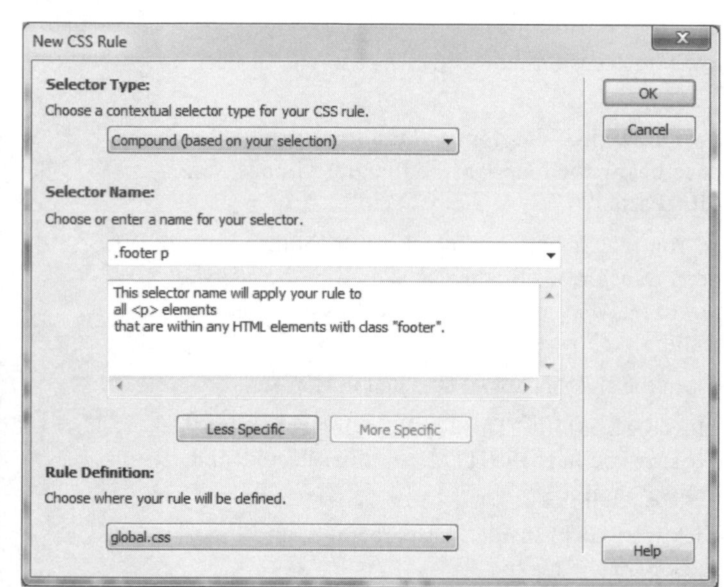

Figure 9-35: *When you have more than one style sheet attached to a page–in this case, global.css and twoCol-FixRtHdr.css–make sure to pay attention to the Rule Definition menu at the bottom of this window. You could easily accidentally store a style in the wrong style sheet.*

4. **In the Font-size box, type *12*; in the Line-height box, type *150*, and then, from the menu directly to the right, choose %. Click OK to complete the style.**

   The text in the footer shrinks and the new line-height setting increases the leading—or space between—the lines. Now you'll create a column to position some of the footer text.

5. **Click just before the M in "Make an appointment", and then drag down and to the right until you select the first five lines (stop just after "Inc.").**

   You may find it easier to click just to the right of "Inc." and drag *up* until you select the five lines of text. Next, you'll wrap this text in a div and create a style to position it.

6. **Choose Insert→Layout Objects→Div Tag.**

   This opens the Insert Div Tag window you read about on page 333. Not only will you create a div, but you'll create an ID style while you're at it.

7. **Click the New CSS Rule button. From the top menu, select ID; in the Selector Name box, type *#footerCol1*; from the Rule Definition menu at the bottom of the window, choose *global.css*, and then click OK to begin creating the style.**

   While the CSS layouts use class names to identify the divs you use to layout a web page, it's perfectly all right, as in this example, to use an ID if you want. Web designers commonly used both, and there are only a couple of functional differences between the two, as described on page 112. In this case, we use an ID to identify a unique layout element that appears only once on this page: the first footer column.

   To start, you'll add a background image to spice up the look of this div.

8. **Select the Background category; click the Browse button, and then, in the images folder, select the file vetLogo.png. From the Background-repeat menu, choose no repeat.**

   Now it's time to position the div using the float technique you learned about on page 331. In essence, you're creating the first column of a mini two-column layout within the footer div itself.

9. **Click the Box category; in the Width box, type *500*; from the Float menu, select Left.**

   These are the two basic requirements for creating a multicolumn layout: setting the width of the div, and then floating it to the left so the content that appears after it wraps around the right side of the div, creating a second column. You'll add a bit of padding to make room for the background image.

10. **Uncheck the Padding "Same for all" box. Type *0* in the Top box, *0* in the Right box, *10* in the Bottom box, and *70* in the Left box. Click OK to create the style.**

    You're returned to the Insert Div Tag window. Notice that the ID you just created—*footerCol1*—appears in the ID box menu. Click it.

11. **Click OK to wrap the selected text in a div, and apply the ID to it.**

    The first chunk of text floats to the left and the Chia-Vet address wraps around the right edge…voilà, two columns! There's one small problem—if you preview this page in a web browser (or click the Live View button) you'll notice that the last line of this new column appears to pop out of the bottom of the main page and overlap the page's background image—you'll deal with this weird situation in a moment. But first, let's spiffy up the address in the footer. The address would look better slightly farther to the right, so you'll wrap it in a div as well.

12. **Click just before the C in "*Chia-Vet.com*", and then drag down and to the right until you've selected the first four lines. Stop just after the phone number. Repeat steps 6 and 7, but name the new ID style #footerCol2.**

    You can float this column to the right to move it to the right edge of the container div.

13. **In the CSS Rule Definition window, click the Box category. Type *290* in the Width box, and choose "right" from the Float menu. Click OK once to complete the style, and then, in the Insert Div Tag window, click OK to add the <div> tag.**

    Now you have two precisely positioned side-by-side columns. However, there's still the little problem of overspill—actually it's an even bigger problem now, as you can see if you preview the page in a web browser or click the Live View button. Most of the text in the two footer columns extends outside the bottom of the container, overlapping the page's background. This problem is common with floats. When you float an element, the element containing it acts as if the floated element isn't actually there! So the main footer region grows only as large as the content it's aware of—so, the footer and the container don't really "see" either of the floated footer columns, and they just shrink in height. Fortunately, you have an easy fix to this problem.

14. **Click anywhere inside the footer, and then, in the Tag selector at the bottom of the document window, click <div.footer>.**

    This selects the div. You can quickly access its style from the Styles panel.

    At the top of the CSS Styles panel, click the Current button. Click "Show only set properties" at the bottom of the panel. In the Properties pane, click the Add Property link (see Figure 9-36). From the first column menu, choose Overflow. Click into the second column, and then, from the menu, choose "hidden".

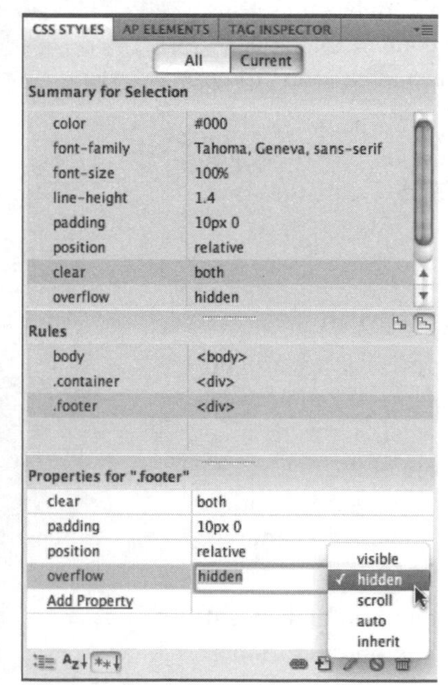

Figure 9-36:
A floated element can sometimes appear to pop out of the bottom of a tag it's inside–this phenomenon can lead to display problems like the one mentioned in step 13. You can fix this several ways. One obscure method is to simply add an overflow property to the tag that wraps around the floated element, and set that overflow to "hidden". You can read more about this weird solution at www.quirksmode.org/css/clearing.html.

15. **Save the page, and then preview it in a web browser.**

    The finished page should look like Figure 9-37. A completed version of this tutorial is in the Chapter09_finished folder included with the downloaded tutorial files.

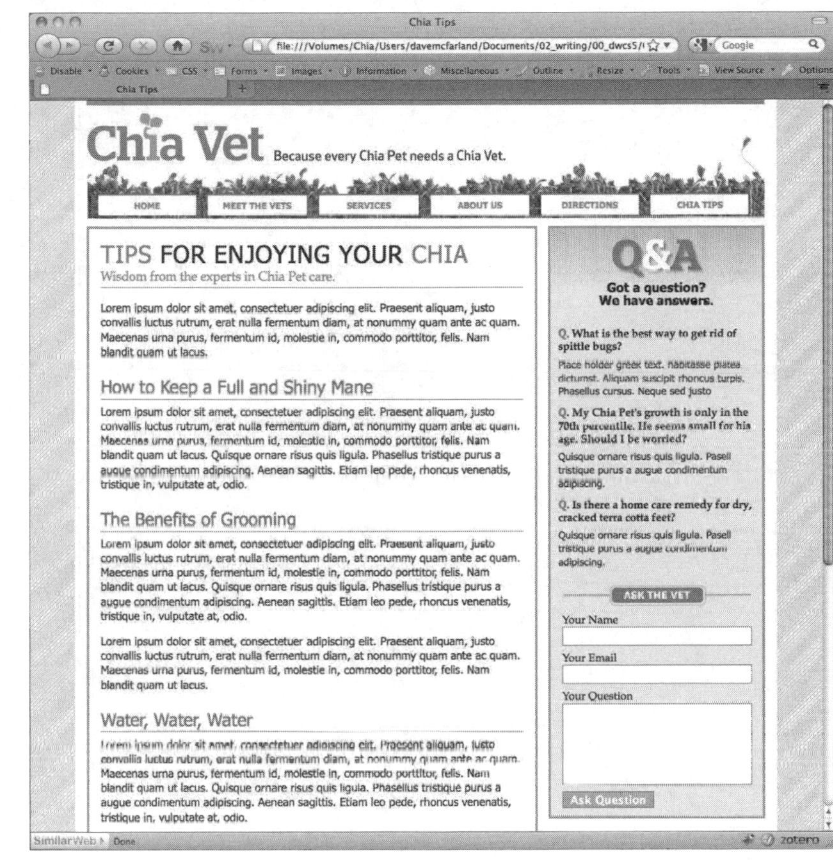

Figure 9-37: *Using Dreamweaver CS5's CSS Layouts as a starting point, you can quickly build a multicolumn web page.*

Tip: To get a full description of every Dreamweaver menu in a handy, printable PDF, go to this book's Missing CD page (*www.missingmanuals.com/cds*) and download Appendix B, "Menu by Menu Commands."

CHAPTER

10

Troubleshooting CSS

Since Cascading Style Sheets are the most important technology in a web designer's toolkit, it makes sense that many of the hair-pulling problems designers encounter relate to CSS. CSS offers many opportunities to make drab HTML beautiful, but the more beautiful your web pages, the more complex your CSS. Adding to the confusion, different browsers can display CSS differently—this is especially true with the ancient, but still widely used Internet Explorer 6.

In this chapter, we'll look at some of Dreamweaver's tools for diagnosing CSS problems, as well as common problems you'll encounter as you build the kinds of CSS layouts discussed in the previous chapter.

Analyzing CSS with Dreamweaver

Dreamweaver's CSS tools are as good as they come—you can use them to build complex designs without ever dipping your toe into code. You can manage complex style sheets easily, and quickly add external style sheets to your pages. But building and managing styles is only one part of the CSS puzzle. You also need to analyze what the CSS is doing to the tags on your page, to see why text, for example, is purple instead of the green you specified in a style. Dreamweaver provides help for this as well.

As described on page 314, the CSS Styles panel has two views: All and Current (see Figure 10-1). The All button is the best way to see all of the styles the current document has access to. When you select this button, you see not only styles in the page itself (inside an internal style sheet), but also the styles in all external style sheets linked to the page.

The Current view, however, is where you can start to analyze how styles affect a particular tag on a page. As you read on page 311, tags can inherit properties (like color and font) from tags that wrap around them. For example, if you create a body tag style with a color property of *#F00*, a browser displays the text inside the body (and even text inside other tags, such as <p>, <h1>, and <li> tags) as red. In other words, the styling of any one tag may be a combination of properties from multiple styles. The final set of properties that format a tag result from the complex interaction of styles governed by the rules of CSS inheritance (page 311) and the "cascade" (page 312).

You can view this combined, "calculated" style by selecting the tag you want to analyze (a paragraph, a div, an image, and so on), clicking the Current view in the CSS Styles panel and looking at the list of properties in the Summary pane. For example, in Figure 10-1, after the Summary pane lists properties such as *color*, *text-align*, *font-size*, *line-height*, and so on, for a paragraph on a page. If you hover the mouse over one of the properties (*color* in Figure 10-1), Dreamweaver displays a pop-up box listing the name of the style that property belongs to and which style sheet defines the style.

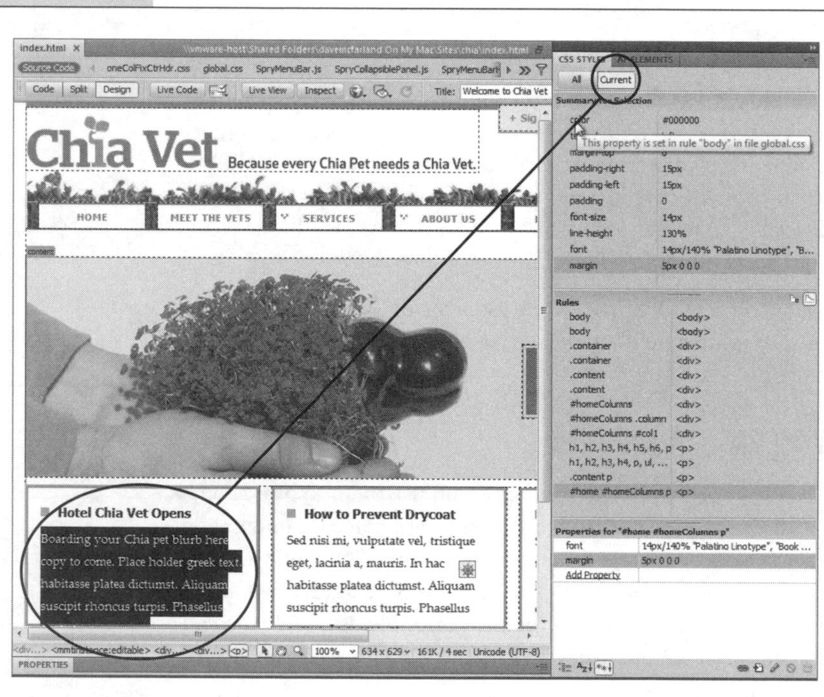

***Figure 10-1:** The Current View of the CSS Styles panel is one of Dreamweaver's greatest features. After you select a tag on a page, you see a list of all the properties that format your selection in the Summary (top) pane, and a list of all styles affecting the selection in the Cascade (middle) pane. However, you only get the Cascade view if you have the cascade button (the stair-step icon in the top-right of the middle pane) selected. Make sure you select it, since the other button (which is Dreamweaver's normal choice) isn't very useful.*

Note: While the Summary pane of the CSS Styles panel is a fantastic tool, it does make mistakes. In particular, it gets confused when one style uses a "shorthand" property (page 306) that combines several CSS properties and another uses individual property names.

For example, you can use shorthand to set top, right, bottom, and left margin values all at once, like this: margin: 5px 0 0 0. Or, you can set one margin with its individual property name: margin-top: 0. Unfortunately, Dreamweaver sees these as two separate properties and doesn't correctly determine which properties should apply.

You can see this mistake in Figure 10-1. Notice that both padding-right and padding-left properties are listed, but so is the shorthand padding property. They can't both be right, so to determine which is correct, you can click each property—the style that property belongs to will then appear in the Cascade view (middle pane). The style that appears lower in that list is the "more specific" style, and therefore its properties take precedence. In other words, that's the style you want to edit to change the padding property (for a more detailed explanation of the cascade, see page 312.) One way to avoid this problem is to set Dreamweaver to use long-hand properties when it writes CSS, as described on page 306.

Editing CSS Properties

There are lots of ways to change CSS properties and styles in Dreamweaver. For example, when you have the All button selected, a complete list of styles appears in the CSS Styles panel. Double-click the style you wish to edit and use the Rule Definition window to tweak the style's properties. If you understand CSS, you can select the style and then use the CSS Properties pane at the bottom of the Styles panel to quickly change and add properties.

Those techniques are all well and good if you know which style you need to edit, but, if you have a really long list of styles or you're working on a site for the first time in a while, you may not know which style you're after. In that case, use the Current view to home in on just the properties you want to change. Here's a quick step-by-step guide to that process:

1. **In the Document window, select the element whose style you wish to change.**

   For example, if a paragraph has green text and you want to make it blue, select that paragraph using one of the many techniques Dreamweaver offers: triple-click to select the paragraph, click once in the paragraph and then click the tag's name in the Tag selector at the bottom of the Document window, or just drag to highlight the whole paragraph.

Note: These steps work in Code view just as well as they do in Design view.

2. **Click the Current button in the CSS Styles panel.**

   This divides the panel into three panes. The top pane, the summary pane, lists all the properties a web browser will apply to the selection, even when the properties come from different styles. The middle pane lists the names of all the styles that affect the selection, with the least powerful (least "specific") at the top and the most powerful ("most specific") at the bottom—in other words, if more than one style assigns a value to the same property (for example two styles specify different text colors), then the style listed last wins (but you need to click the cascade button—top-right of the pane—to see the cascade.) Finally, the bottom pane lists all the CSS properties for the style selected in the cascade pane. This functions just like the Properties pane in All view: in it, you can edit the individual properties for the selected style.

3. **In the Summary pane, double-click the property you want to change.**

   This opens the Rule Definition window (the same window you used to create the style), where you can edit that property or any other property for the style. In the example above (the green paragraph you want to turn blue), you'd double-click the color property in the summary list to open the style that specifies the color and then change the color property from green to blue and close the style. The paragraph now reflects the new color.

   Alternatively, you can click the property in the Summary pane to select it: the Cascade pane will highlight the style that property belongs to, and the Properties pane will list all the properties (not just the one you selected) for that style. You can then edit the property in the Properties pane.

As you can see, you can go a long way tweaking a site's styles simply by selecting elements in the Document window and using the Current view of the CSS Styles panel to quickly locate and edit properties you want to change.

Tip: Even if you're not as interested in editing an existing property as you are in *adding* one, the CSS Styles panel can still be a big help. Select the element you wish to embellish with a new property–the font for the copyright notice, for example. You can look at the Cascade view to see all the styles that apply to that paragraph. If you see a style that specifically targets that paragraph (like a class selector named *.copyright* or a descendent selector like *.footer p*), you can double-click the style to add a *font-family* property. Or, if there isn't a style that formats the copyright notice's font, you can create one.

Analyzing CSS in JavaScript and Server-Side Pages

The CSS Styles panel is great at locating and editing styles that affect the elements on a page, but what about the HTML you don't normally see in the Document window. These days, lots of sites use fancy JavaScript effects to display content: the Spry tooltips (page 539), Spry form validation (page 478), and Spry Menu Bar (page 184), for example, display some page elements only when someone interacts with the page. Likewise, when you create server-side-driven pages like PHP pages that retrieve information from a database, you can only see the completed page and all its elements after the web server has processed the server-side programming and sent a completed web page to a web browser.

Note: You can edit CSS in Live View, but you can't change HTML, JavaScript, or server-side programming there. To exit Live View, click the Live View button in the document toolbar or choose View→Live View. Or, you can use the keyboard shortcut Alt-F11 (Option-F11) to turn Live view off (or on).

For these cases, Dreamweaver CS5 adds a new feature to Live View called Inspect mode. As you can read on page 578, Live View lets you see your page as it appears in a web browser (specifically, in Apple's Safari browser, since that's what Dreamweaver uses to display pages in Live View). Once in Live View, you can click the Inspect button (circled in Figure 10-2) to mouse around a page and analyze its CSS. You can even interact with JavaScript-driven page effects, such as a drop-down menu on a Spry Menu Bar (page 184), and analyze the CSS of page elements that aren't normally visible in Design view. A few things happen when you're in Inspect mode:

- **Dreamweaver highlights a tag's box, padding, and margins.** As you mouse around the page, Dreamweaver highlights the "box model" of each tag you mouse over. As you can read on page 339, every tag in HTML is basically a box with a width, height, margins, padding, and borders. When you mouse over a tag in Inspect mode, the box turns blue to reveal its dimensions; padding appears in light purple, and margins show up in light yellow. Not every element has all these properties, so you may see some but not others. In fact, since you can set padding and margin values individually for each side of a tag, you might only see padding or a margin on one side of the element. For example, in Figure 10-2, hovering over a <div> in a sidebar reveals that the designer set only the top padding and a right margin for the div.
- **The tag selector displays the HTML structure.** When you mouse over page elements, such as images, paragraphs, <div> tags, and so on, the Tag selector at the bottom of the Document window identifies the tag you're over, as well as the tags that wrap around the current one. For example, in Figure 10-1, the tag selector highlights <div.sayfalist1>, meaning your mouse is over a <div> tag that has the class sayfalist1 applied to it. The page's HTML encloses that tag in several other tags—a div with an ID of sagtaraf, another div with the ID sayfa, and finally the <body> tag.
- **The CSS Styles Panel updates.** If you select the Current view button in the Styles panel, you'll see the Summary list change as you mouse over the page in the document window, with Dreamweaver displaying the properties for each tag you hover over. The Cascade and Properties panes update as well. In other words you're getting a birds-eye view of the page's CSS by mousing over page elements. In Figure 10-2, for example, the mouse sits over a <div> tag with the class of *.sayfalist1*—a class style with that same name appears in the middle Rules pane, and a list of all of the properties for the style appears in the bottom Properties pane.

If you decide to edit the styles for a particular element, click the element while you're in Inspect mode; this selects the element and displays the CSS rules and properties in the CSS Styles panel. You can then edit the styles either in the Properties pane as described on page 304, or double-click the style name in the Rules pane to edit the style in the Rule Definition window as described on page 124.

Once you click an element, Dreamweaver exits Inspect mode (although it stays in Live view). You need to press the Inspect mode again (or use the keyboard shortcut Shift-Alt-F11 [Shift-Option-F11]) to re-enter Inspect mode.

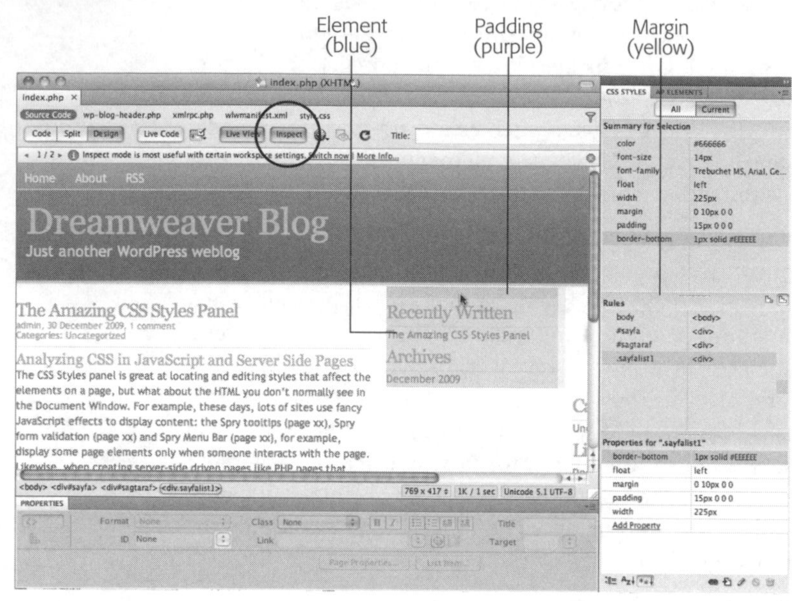

***Figure 10-2:** Dreamweaver CS5's new Inspect mode is a great way to see which CSS styles affect which elements on a page. It's especially useful for pages with a lot of JavaScript-created page elements (like drop-down menus or tooltips), or pages that include server-side programming, like PHP files. This figure shows a blog post made with the popular WordPress blogging system. In WordPress and other "content management systems" like Joomla and Drupal, web "pages" aren't individual files like the ones you've been building in this book, they're dynamically created screens that pull information from a database and construct the HTML on the spot. Live View lets you see what a page created with server-side programming looks like in a browser; Inspect mode lets you analyze the CSS that formats the different parts of the page, like the sidebar pictured here.*

Tip: In Inspect mode, it's sometimes hard to select the exact tag you wish to analyze in the Styles panel. For example, when you mouse over a div nested inside another div, Dreamweaver highlights the innermost div, and selecting the outer, parent div may not be easy. The solution? While you mouse over an element in Inspect mode, press the left arrow key to highlight the next parent (the tag wrapped around the currently highlighted tag). You can keep pressing the left arrow key to move up the nest of HTML tags. (Press the right arrow key to move back down to the original element.) Finally, when you highlight the tag you're interested in, click the mouse button and you select that tag. Dreamweaver displays all its CSS properties and styles in the Styles panel.

Following links in server-side pages

Dreamweaver CS5 adds a browse function within Live View. That is, you can actually click links in Live View to jump to different pages within your site: the linked page then appears in the document window. This is kind of cool, but not that useful for links that go out to other pages on the Web—you can't edit live pages on the Web. It's not even that useful for regular web pages within your own website—after all, you can just open those pages from the Files panel to edit them.

Note: The information in this section applies to server-side driven pages, such as pages written in the PHP programming language. You need to have a web server set up on your own computer (a.k.a. a "testing" server) or access to your server on the Internet to correctly view these pages in Live View and analyze them with the Inspect mode. Part Six of this book discusses server-side programming with Dreamweaver.

However, it's a great feature for server-side driven pages, which often require specific information passed in links to operate correctly. In other words, clicking a link sends additional information to your server, which then displays the page in a way you couldn't if you just opened the page in Dreamweaver. For example, the Web's most popular blogging system, WordPress, uses a complex set of PHP files to provide all of the program's amazing functionality. If you're using WordPress on your site, you can only see that functionality in action if you have access to your local or Internet-based server.

One peculiar feature of WordPress (well not that peculiar if you're a computer programmer) is that just one file, *index.php*, is responsible for displaying most of the pages on the site—from the home page, to an archive listing of blog posts, to an individual blog post. In other words, if you want to see your most recent blog post, you'd have to open the *index.php* page and follow a link from the home page to the post—and, strangely, that link still points to the *index.php* page. Here's the catch: the link includes information that instructs the *index.php* page to display a particular blog post. This makes editing the CSS of server-side pages the regular way—by opening the page in Design view—impossible. Instead, you need to go into Live View, click the links until you get to the page you're interested in, and then use Inspect mode (and the CSS Styles panel) to analyze and edit the styles that format the page.

To follow links on a page you need to:

1. **Enter Live view.**

   Click the Live View button in the Document toolbar, choose View→Live View, or press Alt-F11 (Option-F11).

2. **Ctrl-click (⌘-click) a link.**

   This loads the new page into Dreamweaver's Live View. In the case of some dynamic pages, like WordPress, Dreamweaver doesn't actually load a new page, it just provides a specific request to the web server and the *index.php* file, which does a bunch of behind-the-scenes magic to generate a new chunk of HTML.

While in Live view, you can also make link-following stick, so you don't have to Ctrl-Click (⌘-Click) links. Click the Live View options menu in the Browser Navigation toolbar (circled in Figure 10-3) and select Follow Links Continuously.

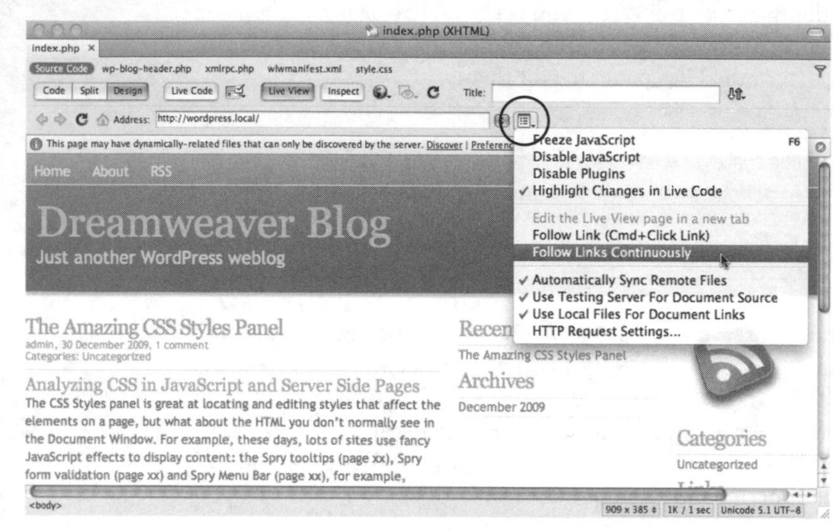

Figure 10-3: *The Browser Navigation toolbar, new in Dreamweaver CS5, acts like a web browser toolbar. You can refresh a page, go backward or forward through the links you've visited, and even type a URL in the Address bar. The toolbar is most useful for server-side pages, so it's a good idea to hide it on regular web pages. To hide or show the toolbar, choose View→Toolbars→Browser Navigation, or right-click (Option-click) on the Document toolbar and select Browser Navigation from the menu that pops up.*

Checking Browser Compatibility

As if learning Dreamweaver, HTML, and CSS weren't big enough challenges, web designers also have to contend with the fact that not all browsers display CSS the same way. What looks great in Firefox may look terrible in Internet Explorer—and vice versa. Unfortunately, a lot of CSS display problems aren't the fault of web designers or CSS, they're bugs in the browsers. This sad fact of browser life usually forces web designers to spend lots of time testing web pages in different browsers to identify and fix problems.

Fortunately for you, Dreamweaver includes yet another tool to help diagnose CSS problems. This one even provides advice on the best way to fix those problems, saving you many hours of testing and troubleshooting. The Check Browser Compatibility tool scans a page's HTML and CSS, and determines if one or more browsers are likely to have trouble displaying your page. It actually checks two things: whether you included any CSS properties or values that one or more browsers won't understand, and whether the particular combination of HTML and CSS you use might trip up a browser.

For example, neither Internet Explorer, Safari, nor Chrome supports the *blink* value of the CSS Decoration property (page 140). If you place that value in a style on a page and then use the Check Browser Compatibility tool, Dreamweaver lets you know those browsers won't do anything with the blink setting. Eradicating these types of errors is straightforward: You either change the property so that the style works in all browsers, remove the property, or live with the fact that the specified browser will ignore that style instruction.

The second type of problem is more nebulous. Dreamweaver warns you when the way you use HTML and CSS could cause browser problems. But the warning it provides isn't as clear-cut as, "Browser *X* doesn't understand the CSS property *Y*"; it's more like, "That browser *does* understand that CSS property, but in this one instance, the browser may get it horribly wrong, and mess up your web page."

For example, Internet Explorer knows what a bulleted list is; it also knows what the CSS *display* property is (see page 142). In most cases, IE has no problem displaying both bulleted lists and items styled with a *block* value for the *display* property. But in one case—when you give a link inside a list item the display value *block*—the list items appear with a mysterious extra space below them. The result: unattractive white space between an otherwise orderly stack of navigation buttons…but *only* in Internet Explorer. These are the types of obscure problems that make web designers consider new careers.

Fortunately, the Check Browser Compatibility tool knows many of the most common, hair-pulling, browser bugs, and it can save you lots of time by letting you know about potential problems. To use the tool:

1. **Open a web page you want to test.**

   You can open any page; if it has an external style sheet, Dreamweaver checks that as well. You can even open an external style sheet (.css) and run this command on it to identify CSS properties and values that some browsers might not understand.

2. **Choose File→Check Page→Browser Compatibility.**

   Alternatively, from the Check Page menu at the top-right of the document window, choose Check Browser Compatibility (see Figure 10-4). In either case, Dreamweaver analyses the HTML and CSS on the page, and spits out the results in the Results panel's Browser Compatibility tab (see Figure 10-5).

   Dreamweaver displays each issue it discovers with an icon indicating the severity of the problem, the line number in the HTML code where the problem occurs, and a short description of the issue.

   An ! mark indicates an error—a problem with the CSS, such as a property or value that's either invalid or that a particular browser doesn't understand.

   A red pie graph warns you about several types of problems, depending on how many slices you see, A single slice means that the page includes something that *might* cause a particular browser difficulty, but then again the browser may display the page just fine. You see this icon for an issue that's rare or crops up only when a very particular set of HTML and CSS are in place (and Jupiter's rising while Mars descends).

A fully red circle indicates that you're likely to see a problem in the specified browser. For example, the Internet Explorer problem related to links, lists, and the display property mentioned previously is nearly a sure trigger for a full pie. That means that if you leave your CSS and HTML as-is, you *will* see that problem in Internet Explorer.

You should always test any page that generates an error or warning, even if Dreamweaver thinks the problem is unlikely to cause problems.

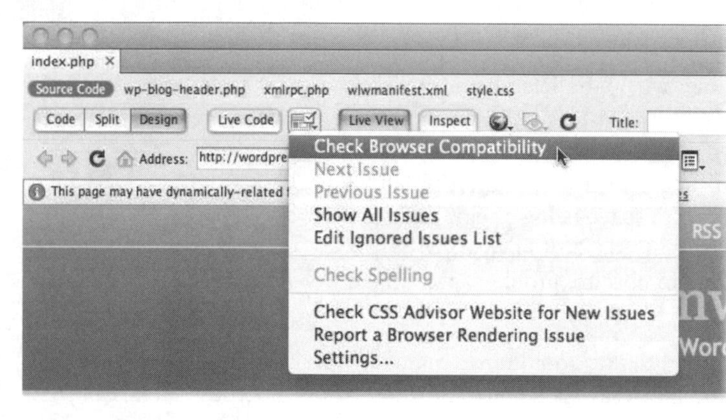

Figure 10-4:
The Check Page menu lets you examine a page and see how compatible its HTML and CSS are with a variety of web browsers. To change the browsers Dreamweaver uses for its analysis, select the Settings option. A window listing the most common browsers appears, from which you specify the earliest version of the browser you wish to check against. For example, if you don't worry about Internet Explorer 5 any longer, choose 6 from the menu. Now Dreamweaver checks only for problems that occur in version 6 or later.

3. **In the Results panel, select an issue (Figure 10-5).**

   Dreamweaver displays a detailed explanation of the problem in the right side of the panel; in addition, it lists which browsers may experience the problem, and the likelihood that the problem will trip the browser up. In Figure 10-5, the Check Page Results panel identifies an issue ("Three pixel text jog"), tells you why it's a problem (a line box sits next to a float), identifies the browser it affects (Internet Explorer 6), and tells you the likelihood of site visitors seeing the problem (you gotta fix this one).

4. **Fix the problem.**

   Dreamweaver just identifies the problem; it doesn't, alas, fix it. However, Adobe hasn't left you totally in the lurch. When you select a problem in the Results panel, a link ("View solutions") appears at the bottom-right (see Figure 10-5). Click that link to launch your web browser and open Adobe's CSS Advisor site, an ever-evolving catalog of CSS browser problems and recommended solutions. Dreamweaver "talks" to the Advisor, so the link takes you to a page that addresses the very problem you're trying to solve. Nice.

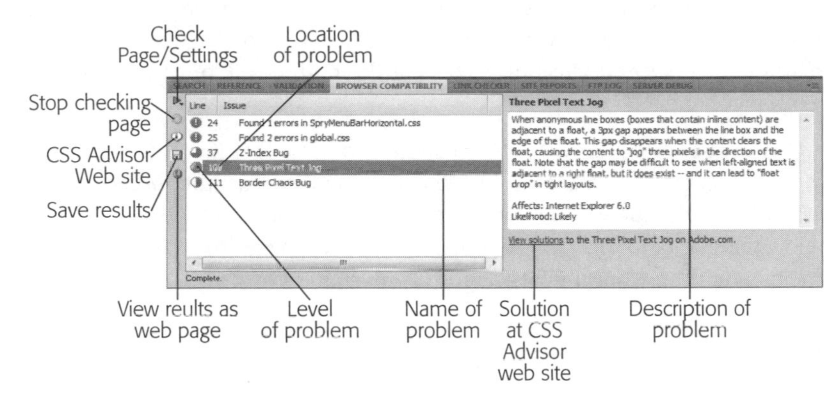

Figure 10-5: *Don't bother with the Save Results button in the left edge of the Results panel. Clicking this button creates a hard-to-read and not-so- useful XML file that lists the same information you find in the Results panel. (That said, perhaps this file could come in handy if you want to report back to your pet robot how your day went.)*

In most cases, the solution involves adding an additional style or editing an existing one. You shouldn't try to make too much sense out of the solutions—many don't make any technical sense. For example, the solution for the "Extra White Space in List Links" bug is to create two styles (both of which target the link tag inside the affected list), and apply two different display properties to it (see page 142): The first style uses the *inline-block* value, and the second applies the *block* value. It's not logical, but it does knock some sense into IE. Most of the solutions are the results of countless hours of trial and error by exasperated and industrious web designers. Be thankful the fruits of their labor are just a click away.

Overcoming Common CSS Problems

As you get more adventurous with CSS, you'll probably encounter—as many web designers have before you—some of the weird intricacies of working with floats. This section describes a few common problems and their solutions. (And if you ever stumble on a problem not listed here, you can always take it to one of the online forums listed in Appendix A.)

Note: When it comes to designing pages that work in Internet Explorer 6, you'll encounter many challenges, more so than for any other browser, including later versions of IE. In fact, IE6 is such a scofflaw that you'll find a section of this chapter dedicated to dealing with that one browser. See page 407.

Clearing and Containing Floats

As you learned in the last chapter, the CSS *Float* property is a powerful design tool. It's the only way to get content to wrap around other content: floating a photo lets text below it move up and wrap around the image. When you create float-based column designs, though, sometimes you *don't* want content to move up and next to a floated element. For example, you probably want to keep copyright notices, contact information, or other housekeeping details at the bottom of your web page, below all the other content.

In the CSS layouts discussed in the last chapter, you saw that if the main column of content is shorter than either of the floated sidebar columns, the footer moved up and around the left-floated column (Figure 10-6, left circled). To make the footer stay below the sidebars, you can use the *clear* property (page 341). It prevents an element from wrapping around floats (Figure 10-6, right circled).

Add the *clear* property to the style for any tag you want to prevent from wrapping around a floated element. You'll find the property under the Box category of the CSS Rule Definition window (see Figure 9-10). You can make an element drop below a left-floated object by selecting the left value in the Clear drop-down menu, or below a right-floated object by selecting right. For footers and other items that need to appear at the bottom of the page, select *both* to drop below left- and right-floated elements.

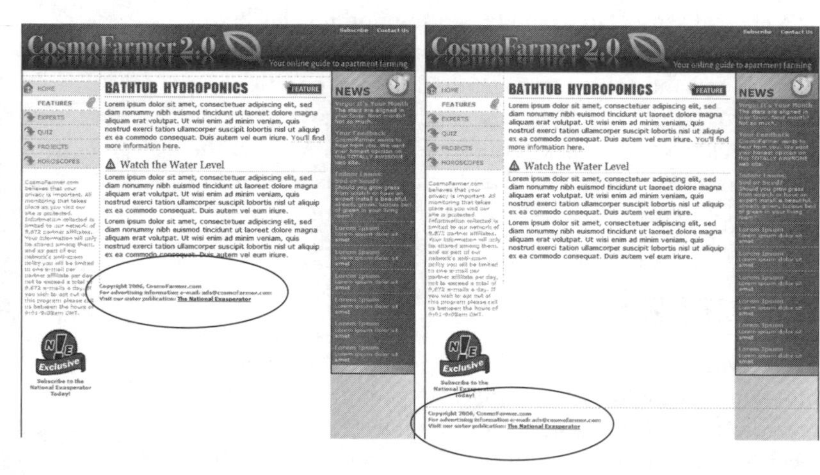

Figure 10-6: *You don't always want an item to wrap around a floated element (left). Copyright notices and other housekeeping material that belongs at the bottom of a page usually need to clear any floats they encounter. The Clear property forces the copyright notice to the bottom of the page, below any floated elements (right).*

Another problem occurs when you float one or more elements inside a non-floated containing tag, like a <div> tag. When the floated element is taller than the other content inside the div, it sticks out of the bottom of the enclosing element. This snafu is especially noticeable if that tag has a background or border. The top image in Figure 10-7 shows a <div> tag that has an <h1> tag and two columns created by floating two divs. The enclosing div's style applies background and border properties to the entire box, but they appear only around the <h1> tag. That's because the floated columns are bigger than their container. So, instead of expanding the borders of the box, the columns pop out of the bottom of it. What you really want is something like the bottom image in Figure 10-7.

Note: For a good explanation of why floated elements can pop outside of their enclosing tags, read *www.complexspiral.com/publications/containing-floats/*.

You see a similar problem with the three boxes that contain photos in the top image in Figure 10-7. In this case, the style floats each image left inside a containing <div> that has a border. Because the images are taller than their boxes, they pop out of the bottom. Unfortunately, this problem's even worse than the previous one, because each image causes the image below it to wrap to the right, creating an ugly staggered effect.

You have many ways to tackle the problem of these renegade floating elements. You'll learn several of the most common techniques below because it's good to have more than one solution under your belt.

- Add a clearing element at the bottom of the containing div. This solution's the most straightforward. Simply add a tag—like a line break or horizontal rule—as the last item in the <div> containing the floated element (that is, right before the closing </div> tag). Then use the *clear* property to force that extra tag below the float. This trick makes the enclosing div expand, revealing its background and border. You can add a line break—
 (HTML) or
 (XHTML)—*before* the closing </div> tag and add a class to it: *<br class="clearfloat">* (for HTML 4.01) or *<br class="clearfloat" />*(for XHTML). You'll most likely need to manually type this in in Code view.

  You then need to create a CSS class style (page 112) and set the Clear property to *both* (see below). If you're using Dreamweaver's CSS Layouts, the style sheets already include a class style named .clearfloat with all the proper CSS for this trick.

- Float the containing element. An easier way is to float the <div> containing the floated elements as well. A floated container <div> expands to fully contain any floated elements inside it. In Figure 10-7, top, the HTML floats the <div> containing the heading and the two floated columns to the left of the page. In the process, its entire box—background and borders—expands to fit everything inside it, including the floated elements. Strange, but true.

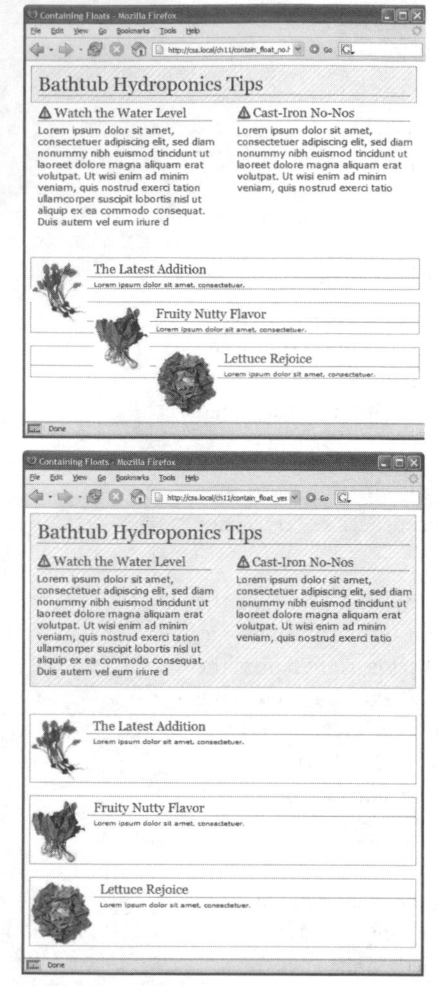

Figure 10-7:
A floated element can escape its containing <div> if it's taller than the container itself. If the containing tag includes a background or border, the escaping elements can look like they're not even part of the container (top part of top image). In addition, a floated element can bump into other elements–including other floats, thereby creating a "stair-stepped" effect (bottom part of top image) instead of the nicely stacked boxes you want (bottom image).

If you go this route, make sure you add a *Clear* property to whatever element follows the floated container so the following element drops below the container.

- **Use overflow:hidden.** Another common technique is to add the *Overflow* property (page 362) to the tag that wraps around the floated elements. Choose the "hidden" value from the Overflow menu listed in the Positioning category of the CSS Rule Definition window (see Figure 9-20).

  The *overflow:hidden* property is just another one of those weird CSS things: it forces the containing block to expand and contain the floated elements.

  In addition, you need to do one other thing for Internet Explorer 6: add *zoom:1* to the style as well. Dreamweaver doesn't have an option for this in the CSS

Rule Definition window, so you need to add it manually either using the CSS Properties pane (page 304) or by opening the style sheet in Code view and adding the following to the style:

```
zoom: 1;
```

Zoom is an IE-only property—it won't affect any other browser and has the simple task of knocking some sense into IE 6.

In general, this technique works very well. However, if you have any absolutely positioned elements (see page 356) inside the container, they may not show up. You'll experience this if you have a drop-down menu inside another tag and the drop-downs, when they appear, should be outside the container element. If that's the case, use one of the other methods described on these pages.

Avoiding Float "Drops"

Suddenly, one of your columns simply drops down below the others (see Figure 10-8). It looks like there's plenty of room for all the columns to coexist perfectly side by side, but they don't. You've got the dreaded "float drop." This can happen when you work with Dreamweaver's CSS Layouts. A floated column drops down because there's not enough room to fit it.

Be careful setting the widths for *each* column. If the available space in the browser window (or in a <div> tag that contains the columns in a fixed-width design) is less than the *total* widths of the columns, you're asking for a float drop. So, you need to make sure the math works. If you're using one of Dreamweaver's fixed-width layouts, a <div> tag with the ID *#container* wraps around the other tags on the page. Dreamweaver's stock style sheet set the div to a width of 960 pixels. In a two-column design, you'll find two other divs, one for the main content and the other for a sidebar. If the combined widths of these two divs is greater than 960 pixels, the main content div drops below the sidebar.

Also, keep the CSS box model in mind: As discussed in the box on page 344, the width of an element displayed in a browser window isn't the same as its *width property*. The displayed width of any element combines the element's width, left and right border sizes, left and right padding, and left and right margins. For the columns to fit side by side, the browser window (or containing div) must accommodate the total of all those widths.

While miscalculated column widths are the most common cause of dropping floats, they're not the only one. Here are a few others:

- **Rounding errors in percentage widths.** Be careful when you set widths in percentages. Browsers sometimes make mistakes when calculating the actual number of pixels needed to display something on the screen. That is, they can round numbers up, making elements slightly too large for the available space. So err on the side of caution and make your percentage widths total slightly less than 100 percent.

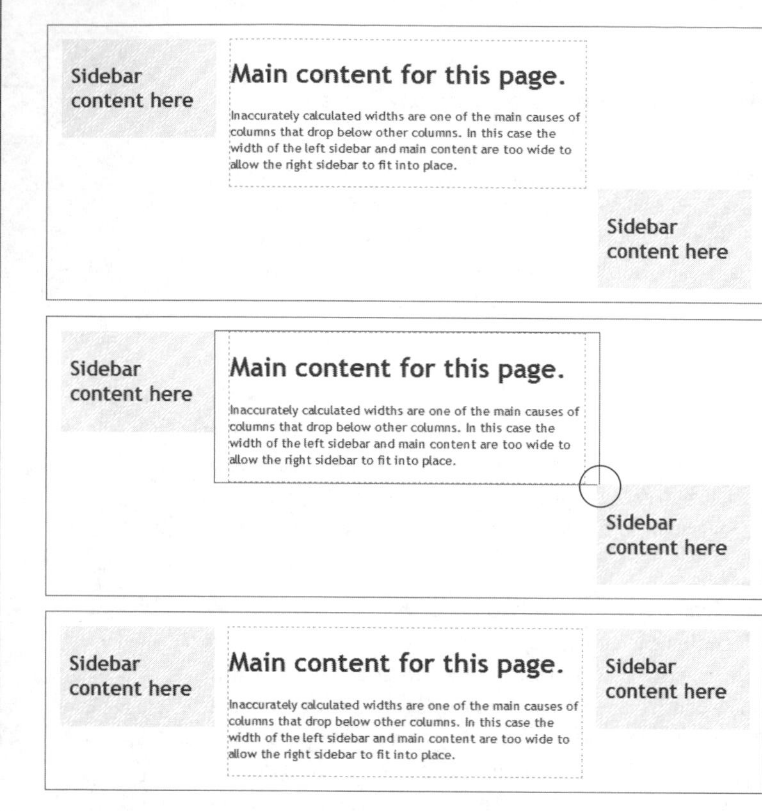

Figure 10-8: *It takes only a single pixel or two to ruin a design. When the width of floated elements is just a hair wider than their containing block (like a <div> with a set width, or even the browser window itself), the last floated element drops below the others (top). The actual width of an element combines many CSS properties. In the middle image, the outline around the main content area shows that it's a tad too wide to allow the right sidebar to fit (circled). Adjusting any of the elements by removing a bit of width, padding, or margins can solve the problem (bottom).*

- **Internet Explorer 6's double-margin bug.** Under some conditions, Internet Explorer 6 and earlier doubles the margin applied to a floated element, making the element wider than it is in other browsers. When you have a float drop in IE 6 or earlier only, this bug may be the culprit. See the next section for a solution.
- **Internet Explorer 6's 3-pixel gap.** Sometimes IE 6 and earlier add an extra 3 pixels to the side of a float. Again, if you see a float drop only in IE, this bug could be the reason. See page 408 for an explanation and solution.
- **Italic text.** IE 6 strikes again (noticing a theme here?) If a floated element contains italicized text, IE 6 sometimes makes the float wider. When there's a float drop and italic inside the float, check to see if the problem occurs in all browsers or only IE. For a solution, you can remove any italic from the sidebar, or set the *overflow property to hidden* in the style that formats the sidebar.

Bottom line: The only reason you'll see a float drop is because there's not enough room to hold all of a page's columns side by side. Rather than strive to use every last pixel of onscreen space, give your elements a little more wiggle room. Get in the habit of making the overall column widths a bit smaller than the max, and you'll spend less time troubleshooting float drops.

Handling Internet Explorer 6 Bugs

Internet Explorer 6 has a long history of CSS bugs, especially (and unfortunately) when it comes to float-based layouts. These bugs can affect the placement of floats and the overall width allotted to floated elements. If you're lucky, you may see just a slightly annoying difference in how your web page looks in Internet Explorer versus other browsers. At worst, these bugs can cause significant display problems, like the float drops discussed previously. This section tells you how to get around IE 6's most common problems.

Note: See the box on page 409 to decide how much you should worry about Internet Explorer 6.

Double-Margin Bug

Internet Explorer 6 and earlier sometimes *doubles* the size of a margin you apply to a floated element. The problem occurs only when the margin's in the same direction as the float—a left margin on a left-floated element or a right margin on a right-floated element. In Figure 10-9, you can see a left-floated sidebar holding the site's navigation links. To add a bit of space between it and the left edge of the browser window, the sidebar has a left margin of 10 pixels.

All other browsers, including Internet Explorer 7 and 8 (Figure 10-9, top) add the requested 10 pixels of space. However, Internet Explorer 6 (bottom) doubles that margin to 20 pixels. Even with relatively small margins, the visual difference in IE is significant. Furthermore, if the layout's very tight, with precisely measured floated elements sitting side by side, the doubled margin can easily trigger a float drop (page 405).

Note: Margin doubling in IE 6 only happens when the element's margin touches the edge of its containing block. If you float an element left against another left-floated element, its left margin *won't* double.

The solution's simple: for the floated element's CSS style, choose the inline option from the Display menu in the CSS Rule definition window. You'll find this option under the Block category (see Figure 4-15).

In this case, the display property doesn't do anything except fix IE's bug. Floated elements are always block-level elements, and changing a style's display to *inline* won't alter that.

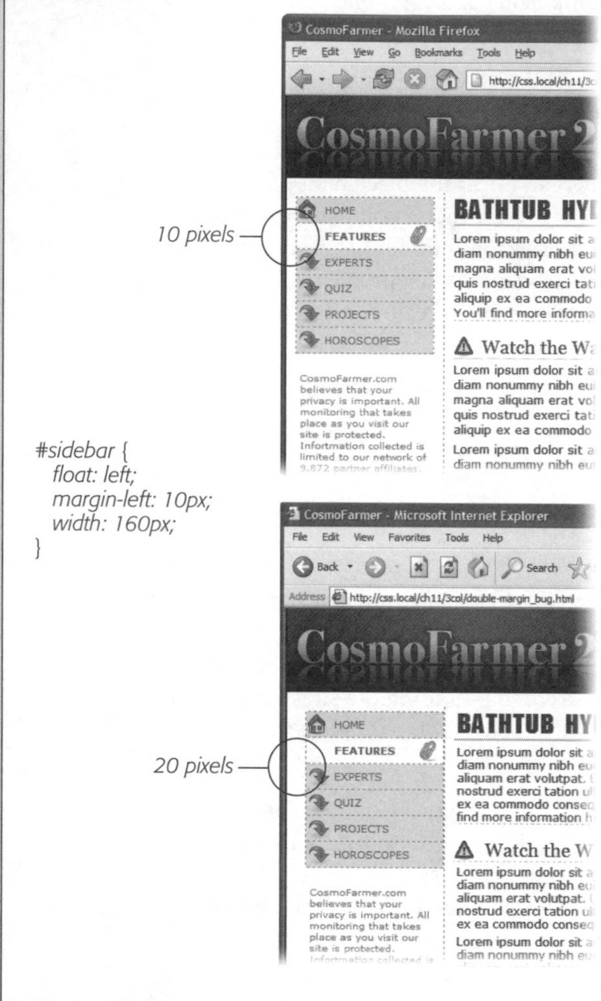

Figure 10-9:
A 10-pixel left margin applied to a left-floated element should, in theory anyway, indent the left float 10 pixels from the left edge of the page. Firefox (above) gets it right. But IE 6 (bottom) incorrectly doubles that margin. By adding 20 pixels to the left edge of the sidebar, IE 6 significantly changes the page's appearance.

Note: While Microsoft fixed a lot of bugs when it introduced IE 7, that browser still has a few. You can read about them at *http://css-discuss.incutio.com/?page=IE7*. Fortunately, IE 8, which is quickly replacing IE 7, has excellent CSS support.

Other IE Problems

A few more bugs plague float-based layouts in Internet Explorer 6. Many of them are so rare you may *never* come across them in your web projects. But just in case, here are a couple of weird things that can happen when IE 6 or earlier displays a page.

- If you get the dreaded float drop (page 405) only in IE 6, it may be the *3 pixel bug*. In some cases, IE 6 adds an extra 3 pixels of margin to a column, making it just a tad too big to fit side by side with other columns. To learn about this problem and its solution visit: *www.positioniseverything.net/explorer/threepxtest.html.*
- If the bottom part of a floated element just disappears, it may be the *guillotine bug*. For information on the cause and solution (which fortunately has nothing to do with sharp, dangerous objects), visit *www.positioniseverything.net/explorer/guillotine.html*
- If content inside a floated element doesn't appear, but sometimes reappears if you resize the browser window or scroll—this oddity is aptly called the *peek-a-boo bug*. Learn about it at *www.positioniseverything.net/explorer/peekaboo.html.*

FREQUENTLYASKED QUESTION

Should I Care About IE 6?

If you're a web designer, you've probably got the latest version of Internet Explorer, Firefox, Safari, Chrome, or Opera on your computer. Unfortunately, a surprising number of the world's web surfers still use IE 6 (otherwise known as the bane of web design). According to Net Applications, a company that tracks browser usage, around 18 percent of people were still using IE 6 in March 2010 (*http://market-share.hitslink.com/browser-market-share.aspx?qprid=0*). While that percentage will continue to drop, IE 6 will be around for a while.

Some people don't like to upgrade their software, so they stick with IE 6 even though better options exist. Corporate IT setups limit still other people; at least at work, they don't have the option to upgrade. So like it or not, unless you're building websites only for the technically savvy who upgrade their browsers frequently, you should keep an eye on IE 6 as you build your pages. There are some crippling IE 6 bugs that can destroy the look of your site in that browser—in some cases, even hiding content or making it impossible to read the web page. You'll want to fix those bugs, and this book describes how to overcome the most devastating ones (in IE 6 and 7).

But that doesn't mean that your site has to look *exactly the same* in IE 6 (or even in every other browser). Due to the slight (and sometimes not-so-slight) differences among browsers, you'll often find some small visual difference between the way your web pages look in Firefox versus Safari or IE. That's life as a web designer.

Your main goal should be to make sure that everyone has access to your site's content: if IE 6 users can get to your content, view it, read it, or download it without any hassles, you've done your job. After that, you can worry about how much you want your site to match across browsers.

CHAPTER

11

Under the Hood: HTML

Dreamweaver started life primarily as a visual web page editor, but it also hosts powerful code-editing tools that let you work on your pages' HTML, CSS, and JavaScript code directly. In fact, in recognition of the ever-multiplying types of files that today's websites use, Dreamweaver lets you edit all kinds of text-based files, including XML, Java, ActionScript, and just plain text itself.

Dreamweaver's code editor includes professional features like customizable syntax highlighting, auto indenting, line numbering, and code hints; code collapse, so you can concentrate on just the code you want; and the Code view toolbar, which provides one-click access to frequently used hand-coding commands. Dreamweaver may be the only web-page creation program that even hard-core code junkies ever need. In fact, Adobe aimed many of Dreamweaver CS5's improvements at those who use Code view to edit pages in HTML, CSS, JavaScript, and the server-side programming language PHP.

Controlling How Dreamweaver Handles HTML

Unlike many other visual HTML editors, Dreamweaver has always graciously accepted HTML written by hand (and even by other programs). In fact, Dreamweaver has always made it easy for you to jump between itself and other text-editing programs like the much-loved but retired HomeSite (for Windows) and BBEdit (for the Mac).

This openness lets you write code the way you want, without worrying that Dreamweaver will change it. For example, suppose you have a particular way of formatting your handwritten code. Maybe you insert an extra hard return after every <td> (table cell) tag, or you like to use multiple tabs to indent nested tags. In cases like these, Dreamweaver doesn't rewrite your code to fit its own style—unless you ask it to.

Auto-Fixing Your Code

That's not to say that Dreamweaver doesn't ever change your code. In fact, the program can automatically fix errors when you open a page created in another program, including:

- **Overlapping tags.** Take a look at this example:

  ```
  <p><strong>Fix your tags!</p></strong>
  ```

  This HTML is invalid, because both the opening and closing <strong> tags should appear *inside* the <p> tag. Dreamweaver rewrites this snippet correctly:

  ```
  <p><strong>Fix your tags!</strong></p>
  ```

- **Unclosed tags.** Tags usually come in pairs, like this:

  ```
  <em>This text is in italic</em>
  ```

  But if a page is missing the ending tag (<em>*This text is in italic*), Dreamweaver adds it.

- **Extra closing tags.** If a page has an *extra* closing tag (<strong>bold text </strong> </strong>), Dreamweaver helpfully removes it.

Tip: If you only use Dreamweaver's Design view to create the HTML for your web pages, you don't have to worry about these code rewriting options. Dreamweaver adds HTML correctly.

This auto-fix feature comes turned *off* in Dreamweaver. If you work on a site that was hand-coded or created by a less capable web-editing program, it's wise to turn this feature on, since all those errors are improper HTML that can cause problems for browsers. (Once upon a time, for example, some web developers deliberately omitted closing tags to save a few kilobytes in file size. Although most browsers can still interpret this kind of sloppy code, it's poor practice.)

You can turn on auto-fixing in the Code Rewriting category of Dreamweaver's Preferences window (see Figure 11-1); just turn on "Fix invalidly nested and unclosed tags" and "Remove extra closing tags". If you leave these options turned off, Dreamweaver doesn't fix the HTML, and there's no command you can run to fix these kinds of problems. Instead, Dreamweaver highlights the mistakes in Document and Code views (skip ahead to Figure 11-5 to get a glimpse of what that looks like).

Note: The "Warn when fixing or removing tags" option doesn't really warn you as much as it reports code that Dreamweaver has gone ahead and fixed. By the time you see the "Warning" message, Dreamweaver's already rewritten the code in your page. You can't undo these changes, but you can close the file without saving the changes, to retain the old (improperly written) HTML.

Dreamweaver can also change the capitalization (case) of HTML tags and properties if you want. For example, you might prefer lowercase letters for tags and properties, like this:

```
<a href="nextpage.html">Click here</a>
```

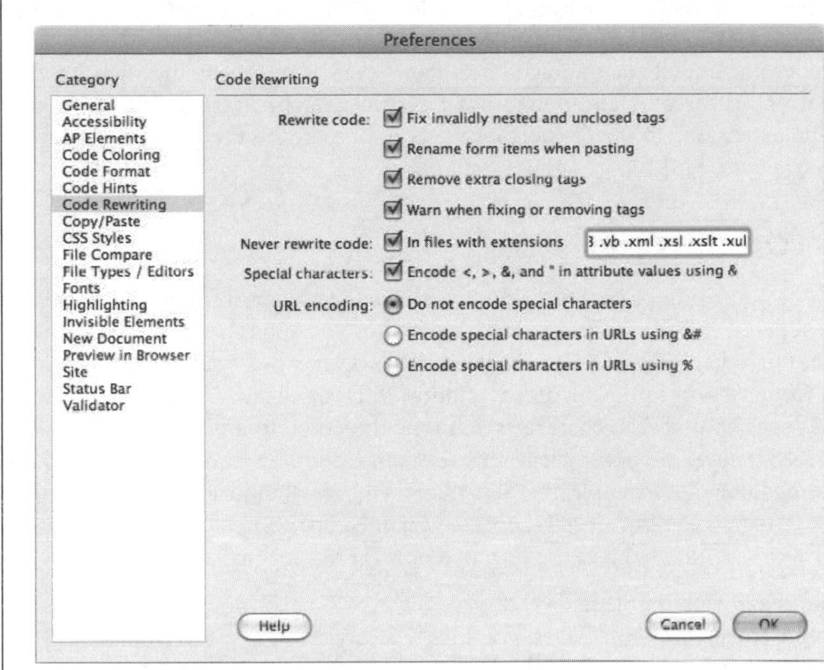

Figure 11-1: *You don't want Dreamweaver trying to "fix" some types of code. Many server-side programming languages mix HTML and server-side code in a way that confuses Dreamweaver's code rewriting tool. The box to the right of the "Never rewrite code" checkbox lists the most common server-side file extensions, such as .php, .asp, and so on. If you write pages that end in an extension not listed–for example Ruby-on-Rails files end in .rb–add the extension to this box.*

Dreamweaver can convert uppercase tags (<A HREF="next.html">) to lowercase, or vice versa, when it finds them in pages created by other programs. You can turn on this feature as described on page 431.

Note: If you're creating XHTML pages (see page 9), you don't get the option to choose between cases–by convention, XHTML tags must always be lowercase.

Web Application Server Pages

Dreamweaver can leave pages with certain file name extensions untouched—pages created for web application servers, for example. (Web application servers, covered in Part Six of this book, process web pages that access databases and other services, like shopping-cart programs and forms-processing software.) Many of these systems rely on special code within the HTML of a page—code that Dreamweaver might "fix," mistakenly interpreting it as errors in the HTML.

Unless you change its settings, Dreamweaver doesn't rewrite the code in files whose names end in .asp (Active Server Pages that run on Microsoft's IIS Web Server), .aspx (Microsoft's .NET technology), .cfm and .cfml (ColdFusion Markup Language pages that run on Adobe's ColdFusion Server), .jsp (JavaServer pages that run on any

Java Server), or .php (PHP pages), among others. Nor does it rewrite any code inside an external JavaScript file (a .js file), since it's common practice to write JavaScript that creates HTML on the fly—many times this means JavaScript coders add HTML fragments (incomplete tags and code) to their JavaScript. If you edit other types of files with Dreamweaver and don't want Dreamweaver interfering with them, add their file extensions to the "Never rewrite code" list in the Preferences window as shown in Figure 11-1.

Special Characters and Encoding

The Code Rewriting preferences window also lets you control how Dreamweaver handles special characters like <, >, and " whenever you enter them into the Property inspector or a dialog box. (This doesn't apply, however, when you type these characters in Code view or in the document window in Design view. Dreamweaver always encodes [page 87] special characters you type directly into a page in Design view; conversely, it never encodes special characters in Code view.) Some characters have special meaning. For example, the "less than" symbol (<) indicates the beginning of an HTML tag, so you can't just link to a page named *bob<zero.html*. If you typed this in, a browser would read it as the start of a new HTML tag (called *zero*).

You can avoid this problem several ways. First, whenever possible, avoid strange characters when you name pages, graphics, CSS styles, or any other object in your site. Stick to letters, numbers, hyphens, and underscores (_) to make your life easier.

You can also let Dreamweaver *encode* special characters. Encoding a character simply means using a code to represent it. For example, you can represent a space as *%20*, or a < symbol as *<*. Thus, the infamous *bob<zero.html* file becomes *bob%<zero.html*, and your link works just fine. Other characters like ™ or © are encoded as *™* and *©* respectively. To set up encoding, choose Edit→Preferences (Dreamweaver→Preferences on the Mac) and select Code Rewriting from the category list. Your options are as follows:

- **Special characters.** Turn on this checkbox to have Dreamweaver convert the less than, greater than, &, and * characters to the specially encoded format mentioned above. (This feature has no effect on code you type in Code view, nor on text that you type into the document window in Design view.)
- **Do not encode special characters.** Select this option, the first of three under "URL encoding", to tell Dreamweaver not to touch any web addresses you enter (in the Property inspector's Link box, say). (Again, selecting this option has no effect on links you add in Code view.)
- **Encode special characters in URLs using &# is the safest choice.** It's especially helpful if you use a language that has a non-Latin alphabet. If you name your files using Japanese characters, for example, choosing this option translates them into code that successfully transmits over the Internet.

- **Encode special characters in URLs using % is intended for use with older browsers** (and we're talking *old*, as in pre-Internet Explorer 4), so unless you've got a time machine and plan on going back to 1998 to build websites, skip this option.

Code View

Dreamweaver provides several ways to view a page's HTML code:

- **Code view.** In Code view, Dreamweaver displays your page's raw code, just as any text editor would.
- **Split view.** This view displays the HTML code and the visual design of the web page (Design view) side-by-side, code on the left, design on the right. You can reverse this order or stack one view on top of the other from the Code/Design View menu on the Application bar (Figure 11-2).
- **Split code view.** This option is for serious coding junkies. It lets you view the code *twice*, so you can work on two sections of a page at once. This option is really only useful for pages with lots of HTML, and can come in handy when you want to edit the CSS in the <head> region of a page while crafting HTML in the <body> section. It also works with any text file, so you can use it on long, complex external JavaScript files to view two sections of the code at once.
- **Code inspector.** The Code inspector displays your HTML in a floating window so you see your working pages in their full glory rather than have them cut in half as in Split view. To open the Code inspector, choose Window→Code Inspector, or press F10 (Option-F10). Multitasking code warriors can also use the Code inspector to look at one area of code while using the main document window to work on another area (though the Split code view works well for this too).

The rest of this chapter assumes that you're using Code view to edit your HTML.

Dreamweaver gives you three ways to select a view: From the View menu, choose Code, Design, or "Code and Design" (a.k.a. split view); click one of the buttons in the Document toolbar; or use the menu in the Application bar at the top of Dreamweaver. (The latter two options are shown in Figure 11-2.)

Tip: You can quickly jump between Code and Design view by pressing Control+` (on both Windows and the Mac). In Split view, this shortcut jumps between the two views, so you can insert an image in the design half of Split view, and then press Control+` to jump right into the HTML for that image in the Code half of the window.

Code view functions much like a text editor (only better, as you'll soon see). You can click anywhere inside the window and start typing in HTML, JavaScript, CSS, or any other programming code you want (such as ColdFusion or PHP).

You don't have to type out *everything* by hand; the Insert panel, Insert menu, and Property inspector also function in Code view. Use these sources of canned HTML blobs to combine hands-on HTML coding with convenient, easy-to-use Dreamweaver objects. This trick can be a real timesaver when you need to add a table, which would otherwise be a multiline exercise in typing accuracy.

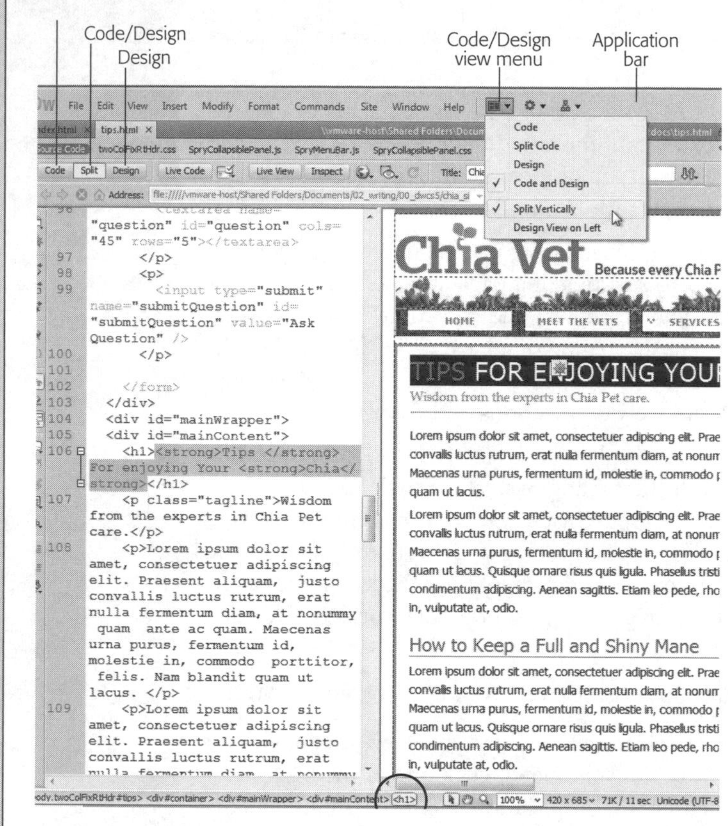

Figure 11-2: *In Split view (also called "Code and Design" view), you can display raw code side by side with the visual Design view. Normally, Dreamweaver displays the code above the design; however, from the Code/Design view menu, you can select Split Vertically. If you have a wide monitor, this is your best option, since stacking the two doesn't leave much space to work on either the code or the design. In Split view, when you select an object in the visual half (the selected "Boarding Your Chia" headline, for example) Dreamweaver selects the corresponding HTML in the code half (the highlighted <h1> tag in Code view in this figure)—a great way to identify an object in your HTML. As you work in one half of the Split view, Dreamweaver updates the other half. Use the buttons (labeled) in the Document toolbar to jump between the different views. (Notice that the Tag Selector at the bottom of the document window [circled] also identifies the selected tag.)*

You can also select a tag (like an image's <img> tag) in Code view, and use the Property inspector to modify it.

Note: When you add HTML in Code view, Dreamweaver doesn't automatically update Design view, which can be disconcerting when you work in Split view. (After all, how would Dreamweaver display a half-finished tag like this: *<table border="*?) In the Property inspector, click the Refresh button (see Figure 11-3), or press F5, to update the visual display.

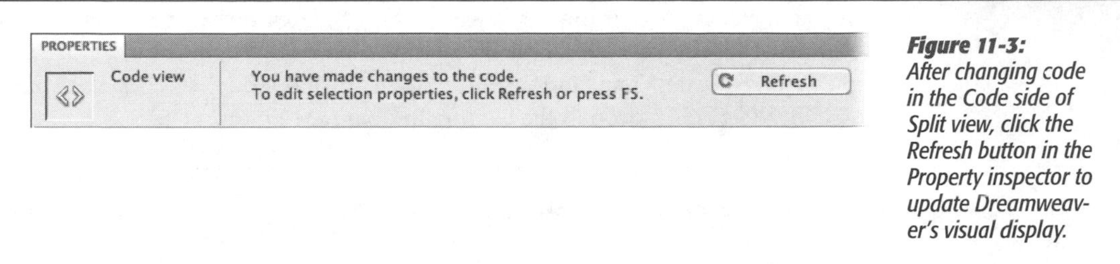

Figure 11-3: *After changing code in the Code side of Split view, click the Refresh button in the Property inspector to update Dreamweaver's visual display.*

To help you navigate your code, Code view provides several visual cues. They include:

- **Syntax coloring.** Dreamweaver displays different elements in different colors. Comments, for example, are gray. Text is black, HTML tags appear in dark blue, and HTML properties show up in a brighter blue. You can change any of these colors, and even specify unique colors for different types of tags, using the Preferences window (see Figure 11-4).

  To really make a tag stand out, you can underline, boldface, or italicize it, and even give it a background color. Dreamweaver offers separate color schemes for 24 types of documents, such as CSS, ASP, and XML files. (But do you really need different colors for HTML forms in JavaScript files, HTML pages, and PHP pages? You be the judge.)

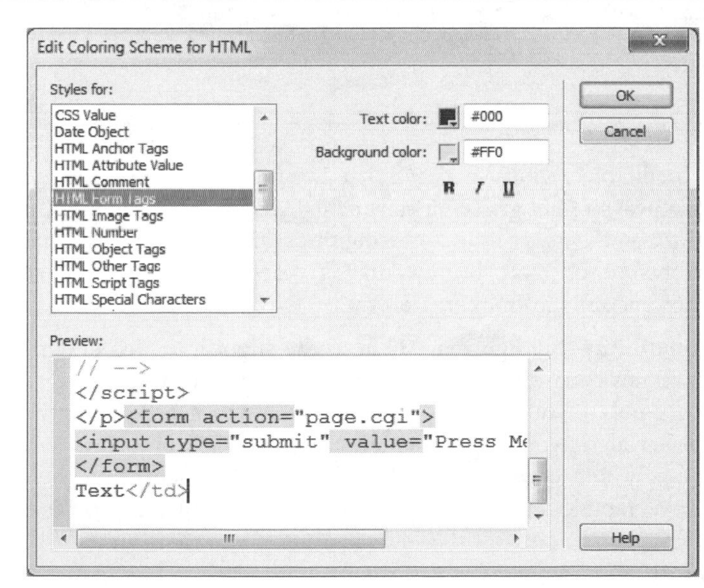

Figure 11-4: *From the Preferences window (Edit→Preferences in Windows, Dreamweaver→Preferences on a Mac), you can control the color that Dreamweaver uses to display HTML and script code in Code view. To do so, select the Code Coloring category. Then select the type of document—HTML, CSS, PHP, or whatever—and click Edit Coloring Scheme. In the Edit Coloring Scheme window (shown here), select an item whose color you want to change—Library Item or HTML Form Tags, for example—and set a text and/or background color using the color boxes. You can also make the code bold, italic, or underlined using the appropriate formatting buttons.*

- **Bad code highlighting.** When you type incorrect code (say an opening tag without a closing tag, or improperly nested tags), Dreamweaver highlights it in yellow (see Figure 11-5), but only if you turn on the Highlight Invalid Code option (View→Code View Options→Highlight Invalid Code) or click the Highlight Invalid Code button in the Coding toolbar (see Figure 11-6).

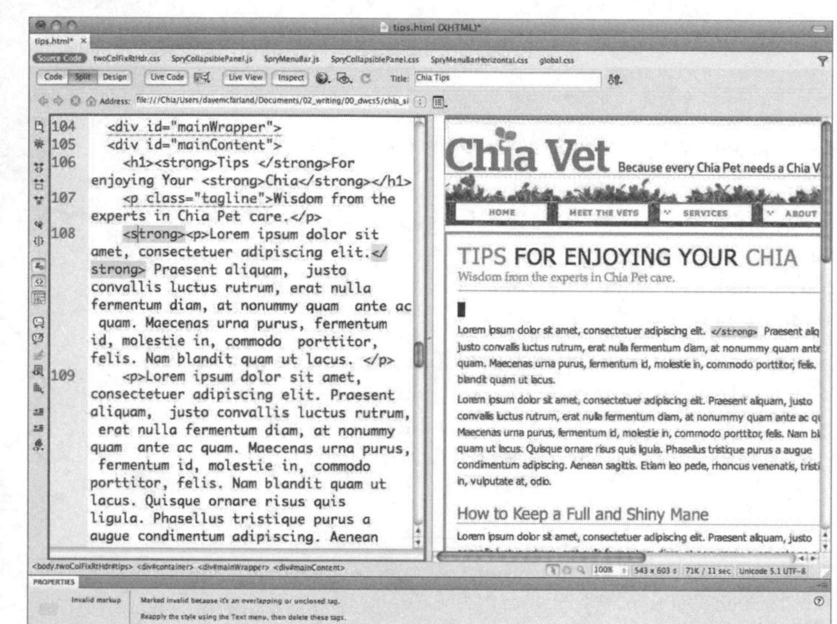

***Figure 11-5:** Dreamweaver highlights incorrect HTML in bright yellow in Code view (like the <strong> tags in this figure). If you click the yellow area, the Property inspector reveals the mistake. In this case, a tag is improperly nested—part of it lies outside the <p> tag. (In Design view, on the other hand, Dreamweaver indicates mistakes by showing the HTML tag—</strong> for example—in front of a bright yellow background.)*

- **Templates.** Uneditable regions in pages that Dreamweaver templates create (Chapter 20) appear in light gray. You can't actually change this code in Code view. This coloring scheme is a little confusing since Dreamweaver also displays HTML comments (see page 421) in gray, and you *can* edit those. You can change either color, however, as shown in Figure 11-4.
- **Browser compatibility highlighting.** Much to the anguish of web designers, browsers sometimes react differently to CSS formatting. What looks great in Firefox may crumble in Internet Explorer 6. Dreamweaver's Browser Compatibility Checker alerts you to possible cross-browser CSS problems. When you see a squiggly line underneath code—like the one underneath the tag <div id="mainWrapper"> in Figure 11-5—Dreamweaver is telling you there's a potential problem. You only see the squiggly lines if you first run the Check Browser Compatibility command as described on page 398.
- **Library Items.** Code from Library items (Chapter 19) has a light yellow background.

You can also control the following Code view display features from the View→Code View Options submenu:

- **Word Wrap.** This option makes long lines of code wrap (at the window's edge) to the next line, so you don't have to scroll horizontally to see it all. This option affects only how Dreamweaver *displays* the line; it doesn't actually change your code by introducing line breaks. Dreamweaver turns this option on by default.
- **Line Numbers.** Automatic line-numbering can come in handy when you use Dreamweaver's Browser Compatibility Checker (see page 398), or when you encounter an error in a page containing server-side code (such as the code you create in Part Six of this book). In Code view, you can also click a line number to select the entire line, which is a great way to delete or cut a line of code. Normally, Dreamweaver displays line numbers, but if you don't see them in Code view, click the "Show line numbers" button in the Coding toolbar (Figure 11-6) or choose View→Code View Options→Line Numbers to turn them on.
- **Hidden Characters.** Some characters you type on a keyboard don't show up onscreen: the end of a line, created by hitting the Enter or Return key, for example. Occasionally, these hidden characters can cause big trouble. When you work with dynamic, server-side web pages (described in Part Six), for example, you might find some cool code on the Web, and copy it to your own page. Sometimes copying and pasting code from a web page introduces hidden characters that prevent the code from working. Turning on the Hidden Characters option helps ferret out problem characters so you can eliminate them. Spaces appear as dots, paragraph breaks as paragraph symbols, and tabs as strange, lowercase *a* characters (see Figure 11-6).
- **Highlight Invalid Code.** This option is the on/off switch for highlighting bad HTML in Code view (see Figure 11-5). Dreamweaver normally turns this option off, but it's a good idea to turn it on: go to View→Code View Options→Highlight Invalid Code.
- **Syntax Coloring.** This option turns tags, comments, and text into colorful (and informative) text (see Figure 11-4). Dreamweaver turns this option on by default.
- **Auto Indent.** When you work with nested HTML tags, it's often helpful to press Tab to indent each level of nested tags, making it easier to identify large blocks of HTML (such as a table and all its contents). The Auto Indent option carries the same size indent onto the next line when you hit return or enter.

  Suppose you hit the Tab key twice, type a line of code, and then hit return. Dreamweaver puts the insertion point on the next line, indenting it two tabs. To un-indent, press the Backspace key. Dreamweaver normally turns this option on.
- **Syntax Error Alerts in Info Bar.** This feature benefits JavaScript and PHP programmers. When you turn it on, Dreamweaver highlights potential syntax errors in both languages (meaning it signals typos or improper code) and displays a yellow info bar at the top of the document window. You can also turn this feature off and on from the Coding toolbar (Figure 11-6).

Coding Toolbar

Dreamweaver includes a handy toolbar on the left edge of the document window in Code view that makes many basic hand-coding tasks go much more quickly (see Figure 11-6). If you don't see it, turn it on by choosing View→Toolbars→Coding, or by right-clicking (Control-clicking) on another toolbar, such as the Insert or Document toolbar, and then, in the pop-up menu, selecting the Coding option. Use the same technique to close the toolbar if you don't use it.

The toolbar's buttons duplicate tasks and preference settings from other parts of Dreamweaver. Here's a quick rundown, with brief explanations of what the buttons in Figure 11-6 do and, when applicable, a cross-reference to a more detailed description of the tool or action:

- **Open Documents.** This pull-down menu displays all your open documents so you can switch among them. Since it's actually easier to click a document's tab at the top of the document window, you probably won't use this button much.
- **Open code navigator.** The code navigator lets you see which CSS styles affect the currently selected HTML. If you have no HTML selected, the navigator displays the HTML tag in effect at the cursor location. It also lets you jump quickly to the code in a style sheet so you can edit the CSS. Read more about this feature on page 317.
- **Collapse Full Tag/Collapse Selection/Expand All.** These three buttons work with Dreamweaver's Code Collapse feature described on page 427. They let you collapse (and expand) multiple lines of code, essentially hiding it so you can concentrate on another piece of code.
- **Select Parent Tag.** This handy feature lets you quickly select the tag that surrounds your current selection. Say you select the text inside a link (<a>) tag, or just click inside that tag, and your cursor's blinking happily. Click this button, and Dreamweaver selects the entire <a> tag and all its contents. Click it again, and you select that link's parent tag. This button gives you a quick way to select the tag you're currently working on. If you really want to be productive, the keyboard shortcut Ctrl+[(⌘-[) is quicker.
- **Balance Braces.** If you do a lot of programming in JavaScript or a server language like PHP, ColdFusion, .NET, or Java Server Pages, this button helps you find the matching brace ({ or }) in a chunk of program code—actually this tool selects *all* of the code between an opening and closing brace, but doing so lets you identify where the braces begin and end. Just click to the right of an opening brace ({), and then click this button to find the closing brace. To find a closing brace's mate, click to the left of the brace, and then click this button. You can also find matching parentheses this way. The keyboard shortcut—Ctrl+' (⌘-')—is even faster.

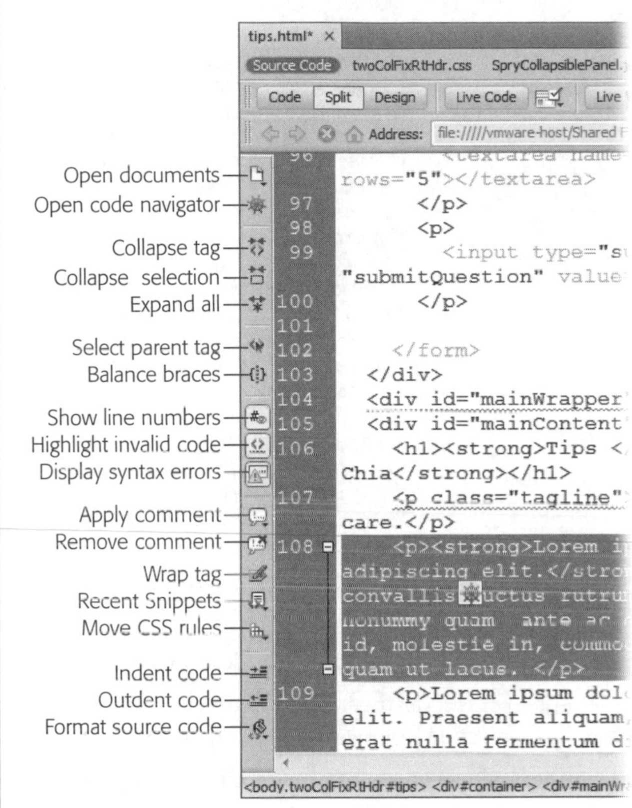

Figure 11-6: *Code view provides easy access to common code-writing commands in the Coding toolbar (left edge). Using the toolbar, it's easy to wrap a selection of HTML in an HTML comment, hide code you don't want to see or edit, or turn on and off code view options like line-numbering and highlighting invalid code.*

- **Apply/Remove Comments.** Comments let you include helpful notes in your code, which don't appear when a browser displays the page. For example, you may want to leave explanatory notes in your HTML code to help future generations of web developers. Or you might put a comment before a <div> tag (see page 331) that explains what should go inside it—"Put corporate logo and navigation bar here." People frequently use comments to mark the end of a page section— "End of navigation bar." These buttons let you add or remove comments to HTML, CSS, JavaScript, PHP, and VBScript code, as demonstrated in Figure 11-7.

Tip: You can easily turn style properties on and off in Cascading Style Sheets using "comment" behavior. Open a CSS file, select a property inside a style, and stick a pair of comment tags around it (/* at the beginning, */ at the end). When you preview a page that uses the style, you see the style minus the property you "commented out," as programmers call it. This maneuver lets you add a new style and preview it, temporarily hiding the effect of one or more other style properties without permanently deleting them. It's also a great help in debugging problematic styles. In fact, it's so useful Dreamweaver CS5 added a feature to the CSS Styles panel that makes it easy to turn style properties on and off (see Figure 9-27).

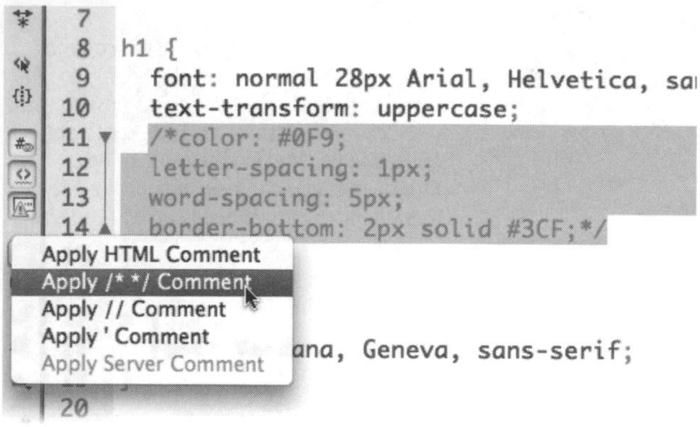

Figure 11-7:
The Coding toolbar lets you wrap HTML, CSS, JavaScript, and other programming code within comment characters. Just select the code you wish to turn into comments, click the Apply Comment button, and then select the type of comment you want to add. Use the HTML comment option to hide HTML code; the / */ option to hide multiple lines of CSS, JavaScript, or PHP code; the // option to hide each line of JavaScript or PHP code; and the ' option to hide VBScript code. The last option, Apply Server Comment, hides serve-side code like that described in Part Six; however, you should skip this option (which adds unnecessary code and just the /* */ or // options). To remove a comment, select all the code (including the comment markers), and then click the Remove Comment button (hidden in this figure; it's just below the Apply Comment button).*

- **Wrap tag.** Works the same way as the Quick Tag editor described on page 439.
- **Recent Snippets.** This pop-up menu lists all the snippets (see page 729) you recently used. Select an item from the menu and Dreamweaver inserts it into your web page.
- **Move CSS Rule.** This pop-up menu lets you move an inline CSS style to either an internal or external style sheet, or lets you move a rule from an internal to an external style sheet. You'll find more details on page 306.
- **Indent/Outdent.** These buttons indent or outdent lines of selected code, using the settings you defined in the Code Formatting preferences (see page 430).
- **Apply Source formatting.** This button lets you enforce a consistent style for your code by applying specific formatting to an entire web page, or to just a section of code. It uses the code-formatting options you set up in the Code Formatting preferences window (see page 430) and the rules defined in the type-A-uber-geek-what-a-lot-of-work Tag Library described in the box on page 433. In other words, if you want to make your HTML easier to read (by making Dreamweaver write every opening <tr> tag and closing </tr> tag separately on their own lines, for example), you can.

Code Hints

Typing code can be a chore, which is why even longtime hand-coders take advantage of anything that speeds up the process. A perfect example is Dreamweaver's Code Hints feature (shown in Figure 11-8). It lets you select tags, attributes, and even Cascading Style Sheet styles from a pop-up menu as you type.

Note: Code Hints work with other tags as well as scripting languages like PHP, ColdFusion, and ASP.NET. In addition, Dreamweaver includes CSS Code Hints, so if you write your style sheets by hand, you can take advantage of the auto-completion features of Code Hints to quickly type out CSS style properties.

Here's how it works. When you begin a new tag by typing an opening bracket (<), a menu pops up, listing all the available HTML tags. Use your mouse or arrow keys to select a tag, or type in the first few letters of it, and Dreamweaver finds the closest match. When you press Enter (Return), Dreamweaver automatically fills in the tag name. Even better, a second menu pops up, listing all the properties of that tag.

Tip: You can also open the Code Hints menu by pressing Ctrl+Space bar (in both Mac and Windows). This shortcut's very useful when you're editing code and want to add a property or edit the property of a tag you already created. For example, you could click inside the name of a class style applied to a tag—click inside the word "copyright" in the code *class="copyright"*, for instance—and then press Ctrl+Space bar. This action not only selects the name so you can change it, but also opens a menu listing all the classes available to the page. Then you can use the up and down arrow keys (or even your mouse) to select a different CSS style.

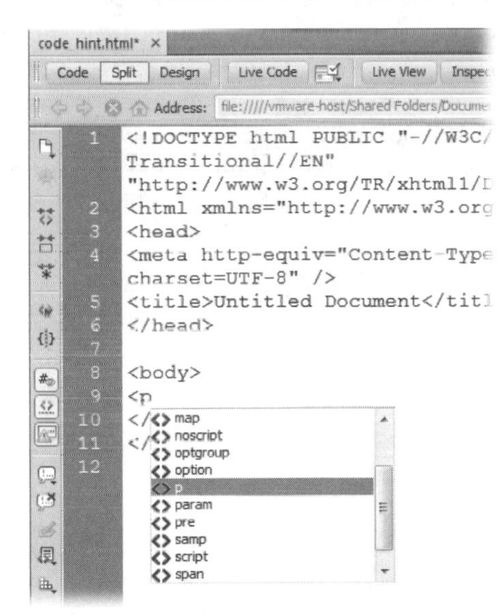

Figure 11-8: *The Code Hints feature saves your tired fingers from typing tags and tag properties. As soon as you type <, Dreamweaver displays a pop-up list of possibilities. Select the appropriate item, and Dreamweaver types it in for you. Dreamweaver's even thoughtful enough to show you all available CSS styles when you insert a class attribute in a tag.*

If the feature annoys you, you can turn off Code Hints completely, rein it in by setting a delay (so that pop-up lists don't appear immediately), or turn it off for selected types of elements (such as tag properties). To make any of these adjustments, open the Preferences window by pressing Ctrl+U (⌘-U), and then select the Code Hints category. Make your desired changes and then click OK.

Dreamweaver also simplifies writing closing tags: As soon as you type </ (the first two characters for any closing tag), Dreamweaver automatically finishes your thought by closing the tag for you. For example, after you type an opening <p> tag and add the paragraph's content, Dreamweaver finishes the closing tag—</p>—the moment you type </. For a longer tag, like the </address> tag, this feature saves your fingers a lot of work. You can change this behavior to make Dreamweaver automatically insert the closing tag immediately after you finish typing the opening tag (the way Dreamweaver 8 and earlier versions worked), or, if you just can't stand the feature at all, turn off "Enable code hints" in the Preferences window mentioned in the previous paragraph.

Note: If you like Code Hints, you'll love the Snippets panel, which makes reusing code a snap. See Chapter 19 for details.

JavaScript code hints

JavaScript programmers also have access to a wide array of code-hint features that make programming go faster. In general, JavaScript code hints work just like HTML hints. As you type in JavaScript, Dreamweaver pops up a box of suggestions that match what you're typing. But JavaScript code hints go much further than simple lists of JavaScript key words. Dreamweaver provides hints for basic JavaScript objects like arrays, dates, numbers, and strings. For example, say you create an array (gentle reader, if you have no idea what a JavaScript array is, feel free to skip this section). If you then write the array's name in your code, a hint box pops up listing all the various methods and properties of JavaScript array objects (see Figure 11-9).

In addition, Dreamweaver keeps track of JavaScript functions *you* create, and provides code hints using your own function names, as well as custom-created classes. Even better, Dreamweaver is aware of DOM (document object model; see page 581) properties, and provides hints for all the properties and methods of DOM objects. Finally, if you use either the Spry or Prototype JavaScript library, Dreamweaver has built-in code-hint support for those as well.

PHP code hints

Dreamweaver CS5 introduces sophisticated code-hinting for the server-side programming language PHP, too (but not for other server-side technologies, like ColdFusion, .NET, Ruby on Rails, and Java Server Pages). Not only does Dreamweaver support code-hinting for built-in PHP functions, it also makes note of variables, functions, and classes that you create (see Figure 11-10).

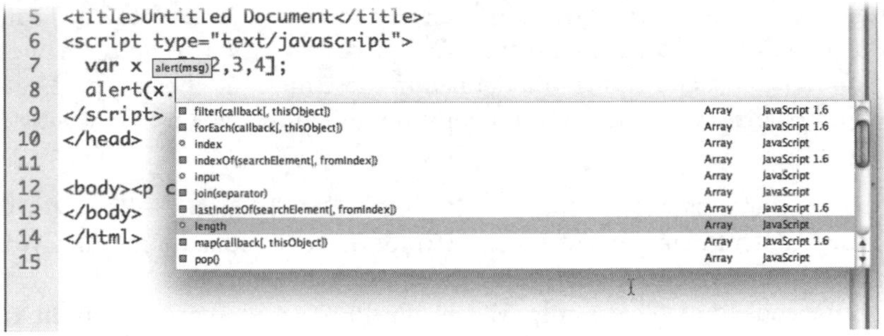

```
<title>Untitled Document</title>
<script type="text/javascript">
  var x alert(msg)2,3,4];
  alert(x.
</script>
</head>

<body><p c
</body>
</html>
```

Figure 11-9: *Code hints for JavaScript include a pop-up description tooltip—alert(msg) in this picture—that shows the basic syntax for commands. In this example, it shows that the JavaScript alert function (which opens a small window) requires one piece of information (an "argument," for you programming types), the text that should appear in the window, represented by "msg" in the tooltip.*

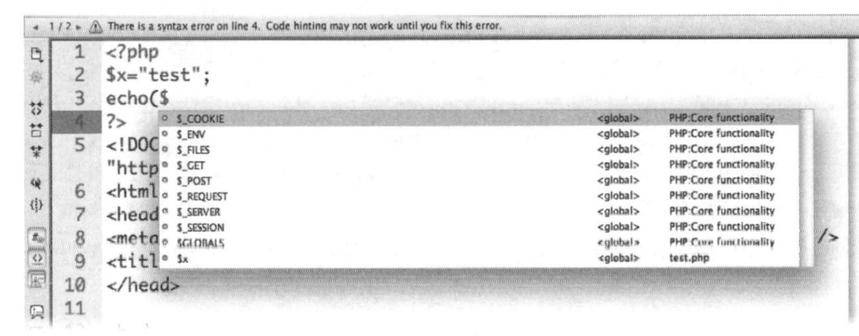

Figure 11-10: *Dreamweaver is pretty unforgiving of syntax errors (typos or missing punctuation) in PHP code. Most of the time, you'll start typing PHP code and Dreamweaver displays a yellow "there is a syntax error" bar along with a red mark at the point it thinks you made an error. Don't worry, this happens a lot as you program; the important thing is that, once you finish, there's no syntax error message. If there is, you probably left off a closing), }, ', or ".*

Since it's common for programmers to create multiple PHP files and add them all to (or include them all in) a master file, Dreamweaver CS5 searches through all the files referenced in the current working file and analyzes (or *parses*) them. That, as you type more PHP code, Dreamweaver displays code hints based on the names of variables, functions, and classes you defined in these files. In other words, Dreamweaver personalizes your code hints for your site and for the PHP programming you added to it.

In addition, since many PHP frameworks, like CakePHP and ZEND, and many PHP-based content management systems (CMSes), like Drupal, Joomla and WordPress, rely on many separate PHP files, Dreamweaver CS5 adds something called site-specific code hints. This is only available for PHP-based websites (you can read how to set up a site for PHP in Part Six of this book) and it's intended to let you identify which folders Dreamweaver scans to create its code hints for your site.

Dreamweaver's site-specific code hints have a few benefits. First, if you often include PHP files outside the root folder (for example, the Zend framework keeps its include files outside the web-accessible root folder), you can tell Dreamweaver to scan the folder above the current local root folder. Second, many CMS systems and PHP frameworks use tons of files with tons of variables, functions, and class names. Sites like these use the files internally, in the programming that drives the systems, You, as a programmer, don't ever need to see most of them, and you certainly don't want their elements cluttering up your code-hint window.

You can turn site-specific code hints on by choosing Site→Site-Specific Code Hints. This opens a new window (see Figure 11-11). If you're using either Joomla, Drupal, or WordPress, you can select your environment from the top Structure menu, and Dreamweaver automatically identifies the proper folders, files, and paths. Click OK and you're done. If, however, you're using a PHP framework or some other PHP CMS, you need to tell Dreamweaver which folders to analyze by following these steps:

1. **Pick the folder containing your site and all the PHP files you want Dreamweaver to scan by clicking the folder icon and selecting a folder.**

   If you don't have any PHP files outside your local root folder, you can skip this step because Dreamweaver automatically selects the local root folder. However, you may have PHP files one level up from the local root folder. In this case, click the folder icon and select the folder one level up that contains both the PHP files and your local site root.

2. **Click the + button.**

   The Add File/Folder window appears. You can click another icon to select either one particular PHP file, or to select a folder's worth of PHP files. If you pick a folder, check the box labeled Recursive if you want Dreamweaver to scan the files in subfolders within this main folder. You can ensure that Dreamweaver searches only .php files by clicking the + button to the right of the Extensions label and typing in *.php*. Dreamweaver won't look through any other files and, as a result, it displays code hints faster. However, if you do use other extensions for your PHP files, such as .inc, make sure to add those extensions as well.

You can prevent Dreamweaver from scanning a folder you added from the main Site-Specific Code Hints window, too (see Figure 11-11). Select the folder from the Files list, and uncheck the "Scan this folder" box. You can also turn off recursive scanning and change the file extensions from this window.

3. **Click OK to finish.**

   Dreamweaver scans the selected files and creates a list of code hints for your site.

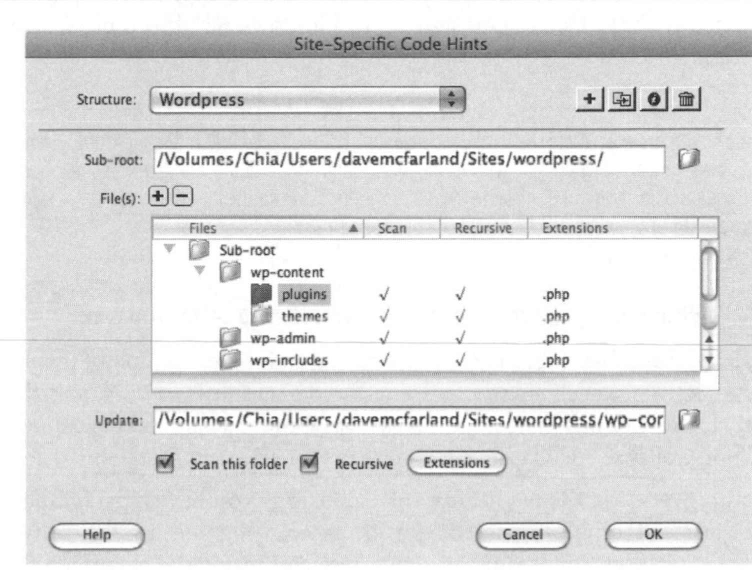

Figure 11-11: *To add the function names, class names, and variable names you use in your site's PHP code to Dreamweaver's Code Hint feature, you need to choose Site→Site-Specific Code Hints and tell Dreamweaver which files and folders to scan.*

Tip: You may find that Dreamweaver doesn't always automatically pop up a box for site-specific code hints as it does for regular PHP functions. You may need to coax Dreamweaver into displaying them by using the keyboard shortcut Ctrl-Space bar.

Code Collapse

One problem with raw HTML, CSS, JavaScript, and PHP is that, well, it's raw—a bunch of letters, numbers, and symbols that tend to blend together in a mind-numbing sea of code. This can make locating a particular bit of code needle-in-a-haystack tough. On large pages with lots of code, you can easily get lost as you scroll up and down to make a change. In many cases, you don't need to see all the code, because you're not likely to change it—for example, the top portion of a page containing the *DOCTYPE* and *html* declarations (see page 6)—or because you can't change it—like the HTML embedded in template-based pages (Chapter 20), or pages with Dreamweaver Library items (Chapter 19).

Fortunately, Dreamweaver lets you get that in-your-way code out of your face. The Code Collapse feature condenses multiple lines of code into a single highlighted box of 10 characters (Figure 11-12). The basic process is simple: Select the code you want to collapse—like all the code above the <body> tag—and then click one of the icons (Figure 11-12, top) that appears just to the left of both the first and last line you wish to collapse. In Windows, this icon is a small box with a minus sign (–); on a Mac, it's a down-pointing arrow (at the beginning of the selection) and an up-pointing arrow (at the end). The code collapses into a gray outlined box. To expand the code, just select it, and then click the icon (a plus sign [+] in Windows, a right-pointing arrow on the Mac).

Tip: To quickly select multiple lines of HTML (or any code, for that matter), click in the line-number area to the left of the code, indicating where you wish to begin the selection, and then drag to the line where you want to end the selection. (If you don't see any line numbers, you can turn them on using the Coding toolbar [see Figure 11-6] or View→Code View Options submenu.)

Dreamweaver includes a few more nuanced ways to collapse code. You can:

- **Collapse an individual tag.** Say you want to hide a long paragraph of text. Instead of selecting it, click anywhere inside the paragraph (<p>) tag, and then either click the Coding toolbar's Collapse Tag button (Figure 11-6), choose Edit→Code Collapse→Collapse Full Tag, or press Ctrl+Shift+J (⌘-Shift-J).

  This feature works on the tag nearest the cursor. Say you have a paragraph of text and, inside it, a link. If you click inside the <a> tag and use this feature, the <a> tag collapses. But if you click anywhere else inside the paragraph (but not inside any other tag), the paragraph itself collapses. This behavior is a little confusing, but it can be really useful. Say you want to hide everything inside a page's <head> tags. Instead of having to select all the lines inside the <head> tag, click anywhere between the two <head> tags (but make sure you're not inside *another* tag, like the <title> tag), and use any of the commands mentioned in the previous paragraph.

- **Collapse the code outside an individual tag.** This lets you hide everything *except* the code you want to work on. Suppose you want to see only the code inside the body tag. Click immediately after the opening <body> tag (in other words, inside the <body> tag, but not inside any other tags within the <body> tag), press the Alt (Option) key and then, on the Coding toolbar, click the Collapse Tag button. Choosing Edit→Code Collapse→Collapse Outside Full Tag, or pressing Ctrl+Alt+J (⌘-Option-J) also works.

- **Collapse the code outside the current selection.** This is another way to view only the code you want to work on. Select the code, and then either press the Alt (Option) key and click the Coding toolbar's Collapse Selection button (Figure 11-6), choose Edit→Code Collapse→Collapse Outside Selection, or press Ctrl+Alt+C (⌘-Option-C).

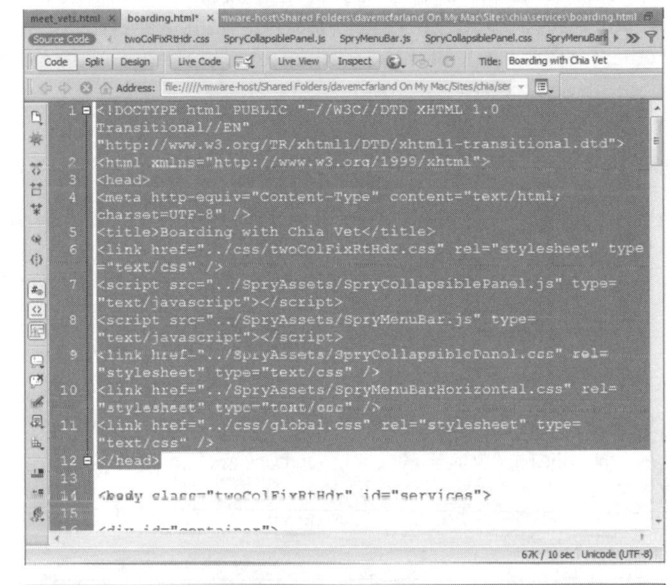

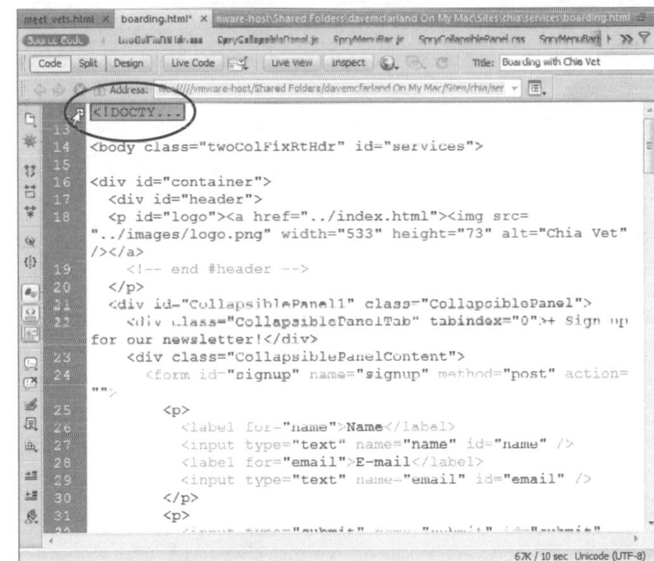

Figure 11-12: *Now you see it, now you don't. You can collapse a multiline section of code (top) into a compact little gray box (circled in the bottom image). The collapsed code is still there in your page–you haven't deleted it–but now it's conveniently tucked out of sight. If you need a reminder of what the code is, move your mouse over the gray box and a tooltip displays the hidden code.*

- **Expand All.** If you miss all that hidden code, you can quickly restore it to its full glory by clicking the Coding toolbar's Expand All button (Figure 11-6), choosing Edit→Code Collapse→Expand All, or pressing Ctrl+Alt+E (⌘-Option-E).

Note: You can only invoke Collapse Full Tag and Collapse Outside Full Tag when you work with HTML. These commands have no affect on CSS, JavaScript, or PHP pages.

You can hide any number of code regions in a page—for example, the top portion of a page, a navigation sidebar that never gets edited, or the copyright notice at the bottom of a page—so you can easily identify the code you really want to work on. Dreamweaver even remembers the state of these sections, so if you close a document and then reopen it, the collapsed sections are still collapsed.

Setting Code Formats

Whenever you use the Insert panel, Dreamweaver adds a chunk of HTML preformatted for easier reading. Dreamweaver indents the code for table rows, for instance, using two spaces; it indents the code for table *cells*, meanwhile, by four spaces. If you're particular about how your HTML is written, Dreamweaver gives you plenty of control over these settings.

Note: If you don't work in Code view frequently, you may not care a whit how your HTML is formatted in the file–and that's fine. As long as the underlying HTML is valid (and Dreamweaver writes valid HTML), web browsers can display HTML that's been formatted in many different ways. In fact, browsers simply ignore multiple spaces, empty lines, and other "white space" characters used to make HTML code more readable.

You can change basic settings in the Preferences window; to change advanced settings, see "Advanced settings" below. For obsessive coders who want to control how Dreamweaver formats individual tags, see the box on page 433.

For basic formatting settings, open the Preferences window (Edit→Preferences [Dreamweaver→Preferences] or Ctrl+U [⌘-U]), and then click the Code Format category (see Figure 11-13). While Dreamweaver's standard settings work fine, you can still configure a number of options.

Indents

To make your code easier to read, it helps to indent nested tags and other block-level elements. But if you prefer that Dreamweaver quit auto-indenting such elements, turn off the Indent checkbox. This is also your opportunity to tell Dreamweaver whether you want to indent code using spaces or tabs and to set the amount of indentation:

- If you select Spaces in the Indent menu, type in the number of spaces you want Dreamweaver to move the code over in the Indent size field. The default setting is 2, meaning that each indent will be two spaces in from the edge of the preceding code.
- If you select Tabs in the Indent menu, the number in the "Tab size" field indicates the size of each tab, measured in spaces. (The size you specify here affects only the display in Code view. In the code itself, Dreamweaver simply inserts a plain tab character.)

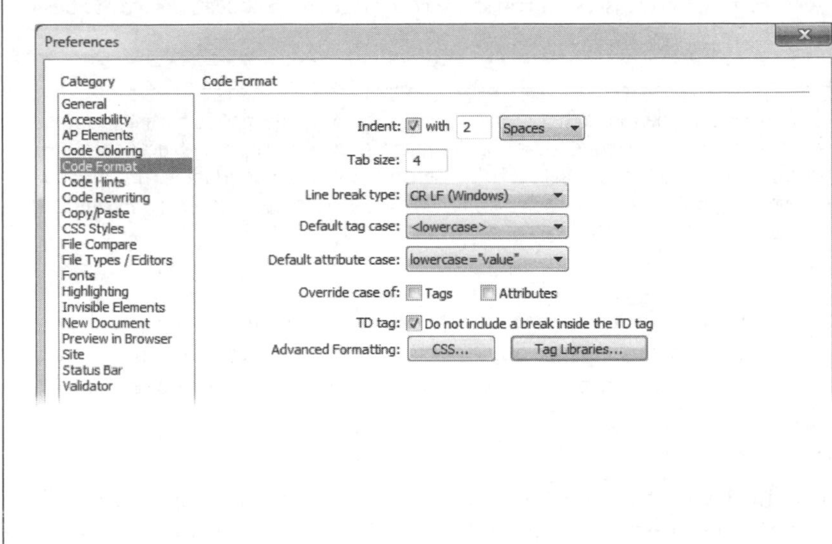

Figure 11-13: *For general control of HTML code, Dreamweaver offers the Code Format category in the Preferences window. For most people, this degree of control is overkill, but if the way HTML appears in a page's file matters to you, go wild. (These settings don't affect how the page looks in a web browser—only how the code appears when you view it in Dreamweaver's Code view, another text editor, or when you look at the page's source code in a web browser.)*

Tip: If you choose to indent using tabs you can save yourself a few bits of file size. Since Dreamweaver defaults to two space characters for each tab, switching to tabs will save you one character (that is, there will be just one tab instead of two spaces for each indent).

Line breaks

The Windows, Mac, and Unix operating systems each look for a different invisible character at the end of each line of code. This can cause problems if you create a page under one operating system and the remote server uses another OS. Fortunately, Dreamweaver fixes the problem when it transfers files to a web server.

If you plan to use another text editor to edit your Dreamweaver-built pages from a server, you should select that server's operating system from the "Line break type" pop-up menu. Doing so assures that the program on the receiving end will properly read the line breaks in Dreamweaver-produced pages.

Character case for tags and attributes

In standard HTML, you can write tag and property names using either uppercase letters (<B>bold</B>) or lowercase (<b>bold</b>); browsers don't care. However, *you* may care how they appear in Code view. Choose your preference from the two case pop-up menus, "Default tag case" and "Default attribute case". Most web developers today write tags in lowercase, so if you share your pages with colleagues, you're best off selecting lowercase (see the Note below).

Note: HTML may treat upper- and lowercase tags identically, but XML does not. Both it and the hybrid language *XHTML* require all-lowercase tag and property names. That's why many web developers now strictly use lowercase characters, even in their HTML. And that's why, if you select the XHTML option when you create a new page, Dreamweaver ignores any uppercase preferences you set—even if you turn on the "Override case of" checkboxes.

If you turn on the "Override case of" checkboxes, Dreamweaver scans tags and properties when it opens a page someone else (or some other program) created. If the case doesn't match your preference, Dreamweaver rewrites the code.

TD tag

Adding a line break after an opening <td> (table cell) tag may look good in Code view, but in some browsers it adds an unwanted extra space character in the table cell. The extra space can wreak havoc on your design, so make sure you always turn this box on.

Advanced formatting options

For real format sticklers, two advanced formatting buttons (Figure 11-13) let you control the way every aspect of your HTML and CSS code looks. The CSS button opens the CSS Source Format Options window, which lets you dictate how Dreamweaver writes your CSS code. Specify whether it indents properties, whether it uses separate lines for each property, where it puts the opening brace in CSS rules, and whether it inserts a blank line between rules to make your CSS more readable. All these options are matters of personal preference, and don't affect the performance of your web pages or CSS.

The Tag Libraries button opens the same-named dialog window, discussed in the box on page 433.

If you find yourself wading through lots of HTML and CSS code, you might want to experiment with these settings to make the code Dreamweaver produces more readable. Both the Tag and CSS format windows give you a preview of your customized HTML and CSS code.

Keep in mind that these settings don't affect how *you* write code. But if you do find that your own HTML or CSS hand-coding doesn't look as elegant as Dreamweaver's, you can turn to the Apply Source Formatting command (Commands→Apply Source Formatting) to make Dreamweaver clean up your code. That command changes a page's code—adds indents, line breaks, and so on—based on the instructions defined in these two options.

POWER USERS' CLINIC

Take Control of Code Formatting

For ultimate control over tag formatting, Dreamweaver includes the Tag Library Editor. Not only does it let you control *exactly* how Dreamweaver formats every HTML tag it inserts into a page, it lets you dictate the formatting for nine other Tag Libraries, such as ASP, PHP, JSP, and ColdFusion tags.

Even if you're using some new bleeding-edge tag language unfamiliar to Dreamweaver, you're not out of luck. You can create additional Tag Libraries, and even import custom ASP.NET and JSP tags, as well as DTD Schemas for XML. You can also add additional tags to any library; so if the HTML standard suddenly changes, you can add new or remove obsolete tags.

To control the way Dreamweaver formats tags in a library, choose Edit→Tag Libraries, which opens the Tag Library Editor window. Dreamweaver displays a list of all the tag libraries. Click the + symbol to the left of a tag library name to see a list of tags for that library. Select a tag, and then, from the Tag Format area in the bottom half of the window, select formatting options. Here's a shortcut for quickly reformatting a particular tag already present on a page: Select the tag in the Tag selector first, and then choose Edit→Tag Libraries; Dreamweaver then preselects that tag for you.

You can control where a line breaks in relation to the tag. You have four choices:

- No line breaks at all. So if you apply this option to the <a> tag, you end up with code like this:
```
<p>Here is a <a href="home.html">link</
a></p>
```
- Line breaks before and after the tag:
```
<p>Here is a
 <a href="home.html">link
</a>
</p>
```
- Line breaks before, inside, *and* after the tag:
```
<p>Here is a
 <a href="home.html">
link
</a>
</p>
```
- After the tag only:
```
<p>Here is a <a href="home.html">link</a>
</p>
```

In addition, you can choose whether Dreamweaver applies formatting rules to the contents of a tag, and choose the case–upper, lower, or mixed–that Dreamweaver uses when it adds tags to your code.

Note: Another set of preference settings affects how Dreamweaver creates its CSS code. The Preferences window's CSS Styles category tells Dreamweaver whether or not to use CSS shorthand properties. See page 306 for more on CSS shorthand properties.

Related Files

With external style sheets, JavaScript libraries like the Spry framework (Chapter 13), and server-side programming (see Part Six of this book) becoming more and more a part of the average web designer's toolbox, Dreamweaver CS5 includes a feature that make it easier for code jockeys to jump around the vast collection of files required to make a single web page work. The Related Files toolbar (see Figure 11-14) lists all the files a current web page uses (can't find the toolbar? See the Note below). This includes external style sheets, external JavaScript files (like those that create the Spry navigation bar), and server-side files such as server-side includes or other server programming files.

The first item in the toolbar—Source Code—refers to the web page you're currently editing. The other items represent linked files. For example, the page in Figure 11-14 has six related files—four external style sheets and two JavaScript files.

Note: If you don't see the Related Files toolbar, it may have gotten turned off. To turn it back on, choose Edit→Preferences (Dreamweaver→Preferences on Macs), click the General Category, and then make sure the "Enable Related Files" checkbox is turned on.

When you click the name of a related file in the toolbar, Dreamweaver displays that file's code. If you're in Design view, Dreamweaver switches to Split view and displays the web page in the Design window and the code for the related file in the other pane. If you're in Code view, Dreamweaver simply switches from the HTML of the web page to the CSS, JavaScript, or server-side code of the related file.

When you work on the related file, all the normal file operations apply only to that file. For example, if you select a CSS file from the Related Files toolbar and edit and save it, Dreamweaver saves only that file when you choose File→Save; it doesn't record these changes to the web page's code, or to any other related files (see the Tip on this page). Likewise, if you choose Site→Put to move a file to your web server, as described onpage 702, that CSS file gets whisked off to the server, but the web page itself stays put. This sequence gets a little confusing when you work on related files in Split view because the web page appears on one half of the screen while the code for a different file appears in the other half.

Note, however, that when you work on the web page in the Design view half of Split view, Dreamweaver applies all your file operations to that web page document.

Tip: When working with the Related Files feature, you may be editing multiple files (for instance, the web page, CSS, and JavaScript) at the same time. To make sure you save the changes to *all* the files, use the File→Save All Related Files command, which saves the current web page and all related files. Better yet, create a keyboard shortcut (see page 817) for this useful command.

The Related Files feature works hand in hand with the Code Navigator. As described on page 317, the Code Navigator (which appears as a small ship steering wheel icon floating above page elements) displays a pop-up list of all the CSS styles applied to the page element under your cursor. If you click one of the styles and it happens to be in an external style sheet, Dreamweaver switches to Split view, opens the CSS file, and positions your cursor on the appropriate CSS style so you can edit it. (That said, you might find the other methods of editing CSS, described on pages 124 andpage 304, easier and more error-free.)

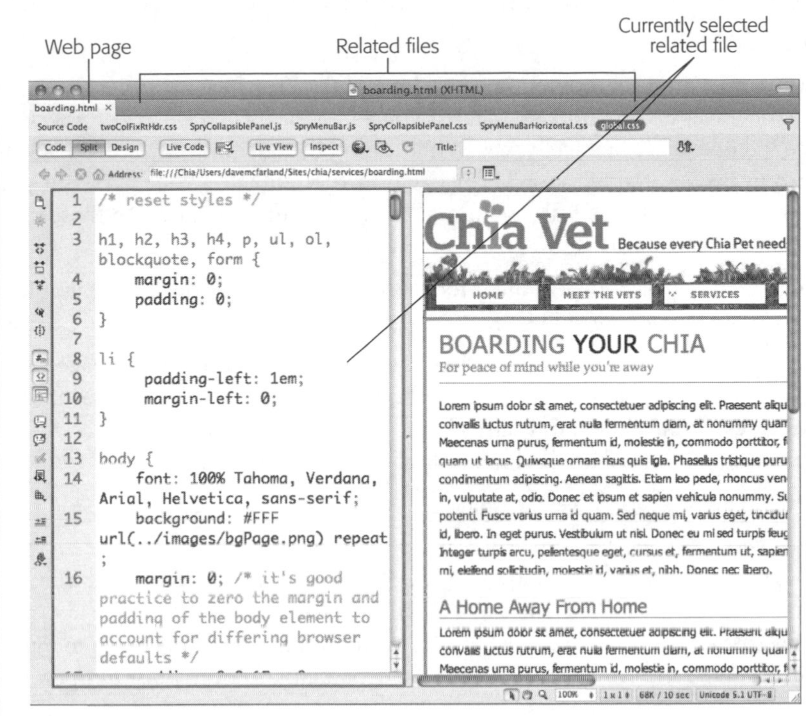

***Figure 11-14:** The Related Files toolbar is a big help for JavaScript programmers, server-side programmers, and those who like to code their CSS by hand. The toolbar gives you instant access to any CSS or programming file included in the current web page, so you can quickly summon and edit CSS, JavaScript, or server-side programming. That saves you a trip to the Open File dialog box and the need to hunt and peck through your file system to find the correct file.*

Finding nested PHP files

When programmers write code in the server-side language PHP, it's common to include several levels of programming files. For example, the popular blogging system, WordPress, uses a single file, *index.php*, to control an entire blog—this one file manages every one of the blog's pages, from the home page, to a category page, to a single blog post. To do this, the *index.php* file includes tons (really, we mean a *lot*) of other PHP files. Early versions of Dreamweaver couldn't handle multiple levels of included files, so the only way to edit them was to open each file manually. Dreamweaver CS5, however, adds the ability to "discover" all related PHP files. To do this, you need to follow a few steps:

1. **Set up a staging server.**

   A staging server (what earlier versions of Dreamweaver called a "testing server") is basically a server you set up (frequently on your own computer, or a networked computer in your office) so you can test your PHP files before moving them to the Internet for all the world to see.

   It's not too difficult to set up a testing server on your own computer. Windows users can learn how at *http://uptospeedguides.com/wamp* and Mac people can learn how at *http://uptospeedguides.com/mamp*.

After you set up a testing server, you need to edit the Site Definition to let Dreamweaver know about it. You can review that process on page 836.

2. **Open a PHP file.**

   There are a couple of different ways to "include" a PHP file in another PHP file. Dreamweaver has a command that lets you add basic includes—Insert→Server-Side Include. It automatically sees PHP files you include this way, and it displays them in the Related Files toolbar with no further effort on your part. But you might also include PHP files within *other* include files. In case like these, you need to tell Dreamweaver to "discover" them.

3. **Click the "Discover" link in the information toolbar in the document window (see top image in Figure 11-15).**

   Dreamweaver finds all the PHP files the currently open dynamic page uses. This may be just a few files, or, in the case of a complex PHP application like WordPress, quite a few. For example, in the bottom image of Figure 11-15, you can see that the Related Files toolbar is chock-full of file names.

4. **Selected a related file to work on.**

   Once Dreamweaver discovers all related PHP files, you can use the Related Files toolbar as you normally would to open a file. If there are a lot of related files, as in the case of a WordPress site, navigate through the list by clicking the left- and right-arrow buttons or click the Show More button to see a drop-down menu of all the related files (see Figure 11-15). Select a name from that list to open the file in Code view.

5. **Filter the list if necessary.**

   You may not want to see or work on some of the files in the Related Files toolbar. For example, in the case of WordPress, you'll see many PHP files listed, most of which you never want to touch since they're part of the core WordPress program and editing them might break your blog.

   Fortunately, you can filter the list of related files so you see just the ones you want. The Filter button in the top-right of the Related Files toolbar (see Figure 11-15) lets you do two things. First, clicking it pops up a menu that lets you filter by file type—meaning you can show or hide JavaScript, CSS, and PHP files, and any other file type that your web page references. By default, Dreamweaver selects all the file types, so to hide one, click the Filter button and then click the file extension (.css, .php, .js, and so on) for the file type you want to hide. To show those file types later, select them again from the Filter menu.

   You can also create a custom filter. Click the Filter button, choose Custom Filter, and a dialog box pops up. Type in the file names and/or file types you want to see. For example, with WordPress, you're interested in editing the PHP theme files—the ones WordPress uses to create your blog's look. To show the relevant files, enter their names separated by a semicolon. For example, *index.php;footer.php;header.php*, and so on. You can also filter by type. To show all JavaScript files plus *index.php*, *footer.php*, and *header.php*, type this in the Related Files toolbar: *index.php;footer.php;header.php;.js* (temporarily disable your pop-up blocker).

When you're done, click OK to close the Custom Filter. Dreamweaver displays only those files in the Related Files toolbar.

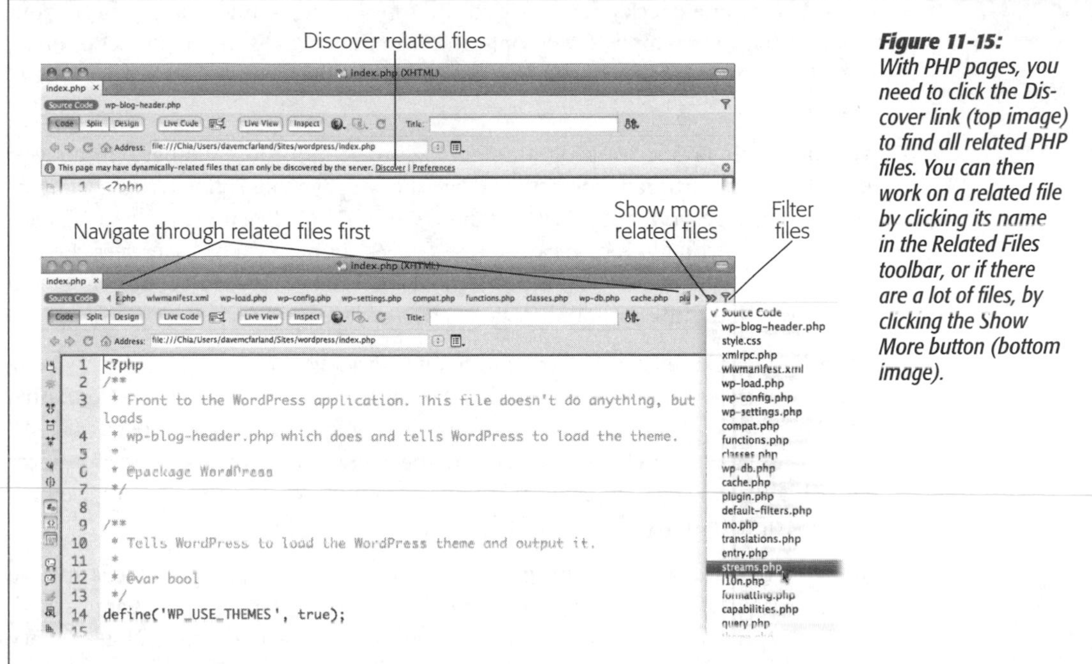

Figure 11-15: *With PHP pages, you need to click the Discover link (top image) to find all related PHP files. You can then work on a related file by clicking its name in the Related Files toolbar, or if there are a lot of files, by clicking the Show More button (bottom image).*

Note: Custom Filters are useful but, unfortunately, Dreamweaver doesn't remember a custom filter, so once you close a file, that filter is lost and you have to recreate it the next time you open the file. In addition, you can't filter by folder—all PHP files within a particular folder only—although that would be really helpful when you work with certain CMS systems like WordPress, which keep files related to the design of the site in one particular folder. Maybe next time.

Live Code

Live Code works in conjunction with the Live View option discussed in depth on page 578. (The short version: Live View lets you see what an in-progress web page actually looks like in a browser…right within Dreamweaver.)

The Live Code button (see Figure 11-16) makes Dreamweaver jump to Split view, with the page's Design view in one half of the window, and the underlying HTML in the other half. When in Live Code view, the HTML appears with a yellow background, and, as with Live View in general, you can't edit any of the HTML of the page. So what is Live Code *for*? Or, more accurately, *who* is it for?

Hear ye! Hear ye! Calling all JavaScript programmers.

Much of today's JavaScript programming manipulates the HTML of a page to make elements appear or disappear. For example, programmers often make forms more useable by adjusting the options the site displays based on selections the visitor makes. If someone checks the "married" button on a form under a question about marital status, for example, JavaScript can make the page display a *new* set of questions, ones that apply just to a married person. In other words, JavaScript actually changes the page's HTML.

Live Code gives JavaScript programmers a glimpse into those changes. It lets you see if a JavaScript program correctly changes how a page looks. If you're a JavaScript programming type, you probably know about the DOM (or Document Object Model). Live Code gives you a direct view into the DOM—into how a browser sees the underlying HTML. This view is useful when a JavaScript program doesn't change the page the way you think it should.

Activating Live Code is pretty straightforward. First, get yourself into Live View by going to the Document toolbar and then clicking the Live View button. Next, turn on its neighboring Live Code button. Now you're ready to see how a page's HTML changes based on your interaction with the page. Unfortunately, Dreamweaver doesn't highlight *what's* changed, so you have to hunt around the code to see how the JavaScript program affects the HTML.

And if you're not a JavaScript programmer? You still might have an interest in Live View. It's useful if you're using someone else's JavaScript, such as Dreamweaver's built-in Spry tools or a program you found online, like the many marvelous jQuery plug-ins (*http://plugins.jquery.com*). Using Live View, you can see the HTML, and the class and ID names it generates. Looking at JavaScript-generated HTML, it's pretty easy to figure out some of the CSS that formats the page, such as a class style (page 112) if the JavaScript adds class names to tags, an ID style (page 112) if it adds ID names to tags, or descendent selectors (page 298) that match the HTML.

For example, in Figure 11-16, you can see a page with Live View on. It captures the exact moment when a mouse hovered over a Spry drop-down menu (thanks to the Freeze JavaScript command described in the tip below). It also shows you the HTML that the JavaScript inserted. In this case, it adds a class to a menu item—*MenuBarItemHover*—whenever you move your mouse over it. That class isn't in the regular HTML; JavaScript adds it in response to the mouse's hovering over one of the link in the menu bar. With this knowledge in hand, you now know you can edit the *MenuBarItemHover* class in the Spry menu bar style sheet to change the appearance of this button when a visitor mouses over it.

Tip: The F6 key freezes any currently running JavaScript, so you can make a drop-down menu "stick" in place after you mouse over it. It's like freezing the entire page, and it's great for working with Live Code, since you can freeze a dynamic rollover effect, and see how the JavaScript programming affects the HTML of the page. You can also use the Live View menu to freeze JavaScript as pictured in Figure 11-16 (but not for any JavaScript–like a drop-down menu– you trigger by moving your mouse over it, because when you move your mouse to the Live View Menu to freeze the JavaScript, the menu disappears!)

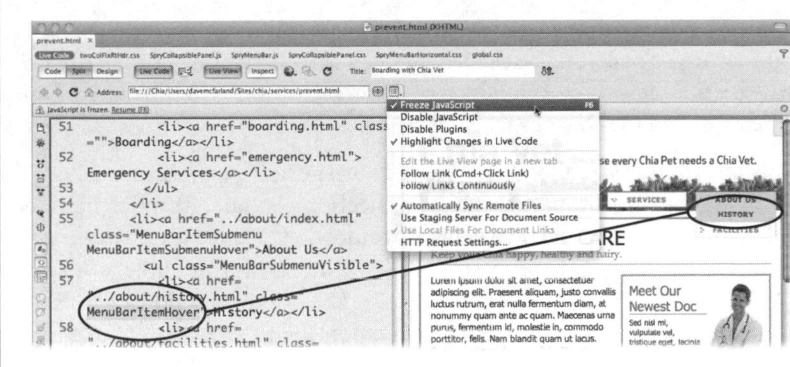

Figure 11-16: *Dreamweaver's Live View lets you preview interactive effects, such as the Spry-driven menu pictured here. In Live View, mousing over a menu item shows you how the menu will behave in a real web browser. If you want to inspect the HTML the mouseover creates, hit the F6 key—in this example, the drop-down menu sticks in place, and you can inspect the code using Live Code.*

Quick Tag Editor

Code view is great when you really need (or want) to jump into the trenches and fine-tune your HTML. But if you're visually oriented, you probably spend most of your time in Design view, enjoying the pleasures of its visual authoring environment.

Occasionally, however, you want to dip into the HTML pond, especially when you need to use some HTML that's unavailable from the Insert panel. You might wish you could type out a quick HTML tag on the spot, right there in Design view, without having to make the mental and visual shift into Code view.

That's what the Quick Tag Editor is all about. To access the Quick Tag Editor, in Design view press Ctrl+T (⌘-T)—or, if you're feeling especially mouse-driven, in the Property inspector, click the Quick Tag Editor button. Depending on what you selected in the document window, the Quick Tag Editor opens in one of the following three modes (see Figure 11-17):

- **Insert HTML.** Inserts a new tag in the page. You get this mode if you haven't selected anything in your document window.
- **Edit tag.** Lets you edit the tag for whatever element you selected in the document window (a graphic, for example). You can also edit all of that element's properties.
- **Wrap tag.** If you select a swath of text or other objects (like two images), the editor opens in this mode, which lets you easily wrap a new tag around that selection.

Tip: You can cycle through the modes by repeatedly pressing Ctrl+T (⌘-T).

Using the Quick Tag Editor

You can type tag names, properties, and property values directly into the Quick Tag Editor window. If you're editing a selected tag, you can change any of the properties listed, and even add new ones. When you're done, press Enter (Return). The Quick Tag Editor closes, and the changes take effect.

To make all this even easier, the Quick Tag Editor sports a helpful list—called *Tag Hints*—of HTML tags and properties for your selection pleasure. It's much like Code view's Code Hints (in fact, in the Preferences window, the Code Hints category also controls Tag Hints). When you're in Insert HTML mode, for example, a menu of available tags appears (top right in Figure 11-17). Use the up and down arrow keys or the scroll bar to move through the list, or type in the first few letters of a tag or property, and Dreamweaver jumps to the nearest match.

To choose the highlighted name, press Enter or Return. Dreamweaver adds that tag or property name to the Quick Tag Editor window. If you selected a tag property, Dreamweaver adds the proper punctuation (href=" ", for example), and the cursor appears between the quotation marks, waiting for you to type in the property's value.

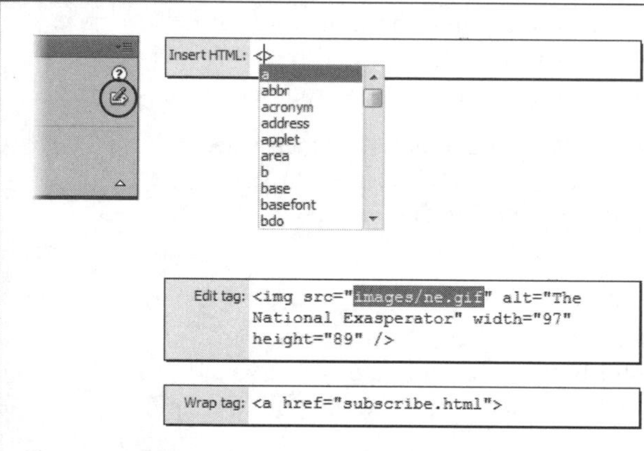

Figure 11-17:
Left: You can open the Quick Tag Editor by clicking the corresponding button in the Property inspector's upper-right corner (circled). (This button is visible only in Design view.) Right: The three modes of the Quick Tag Editor let you insert new tags, edit old tags, or wrap a new tag around a selection. The Quick Tag Editor is mobile: Drag the window by its handle (the mode name) anywhere on the screen–ideal when you want to see the part of the page you're modifying.

Tip: When editing an existing tag in the Quick Tag Editor, press Tab to select the next property or property value. You can then type a new property or value. Shift+Tab selects the *previous* property or value.

Tag Inspector

The Property inspector is a handy tool. It lets you adjust properties for all sorts of HTML tags, like a table's width or a paragraph's font. But even the Property inspector doesn't tell the whole story: Some HTML tags have additional properties that don't appear there, such as the <a> tag's *tabindex* property, which lets you control the order in which Dreamweaver highlights links as a visitor presses the Tab key.

For these hard-to-reach properties, turn to the *Tag inspector* (see Figure 11-18). Think of it as the uber-Property inspector. For hard-core HTML fanatics, it's the best way to set properties for every HTML tag. To display it, press the F9 key (Option-F9 on Mac), or choose Window→Tag Inspector (the same procedure also hides this panel).

When you select a tag on the page (in either Code or Design view), Dreamweaver displays *all* its properties in the panel. To edit any of them, click in the space to the right of the property name. You can type in a new value or, for certain properties, use a pop-up menu to choose from a list of values. For color properties, use Dreamweaver's ubiquitous color box to select the shade you want.

Note: If you don't see a list of HTML properties, you may be in the Behaviors area of this panel. Just click the Attributes button at the top of the panel (see Figure 11-18) to use the Tag Selector. Oddly, the Behaviors button adds Dreamweaver Behaviors (see Chapter 14) and isn't really used to inspect tags at all.

Unfortunately, you need to understand HTML fairly well to set values correctly; Dreamweaver doesn't make the process foolproof, so you could enter an invalid property. (To learn more about HTML tags and their properties, turn to Dreamweaver's built-in HTML reference, described on page 448.)

Comparing Versions of a Web Page

Sometimes you make a change to a page, save it, preview it, close it, and move along to the next assignment for the day. Only later, when you take a second look at your day's changes before moving pages to the web server, do you see that one of them has a problem you didn't notice at first. Perhaps the left sidebar is suddenly wider than it was before. Since you already closed the file, you can't use the Undo feature to remove whatever pesky mistake you made. You could, of course, retrieve the current version of the page from the server (see page 706), thus overwriting your changes. But what if you did a lot of good work on the page—added text, graphics, and links—that you don't want to lose? Ideally, you'd like to see all the changes you made to the page, and selectively undo the mistake you accidentally introduced to the sidebar.

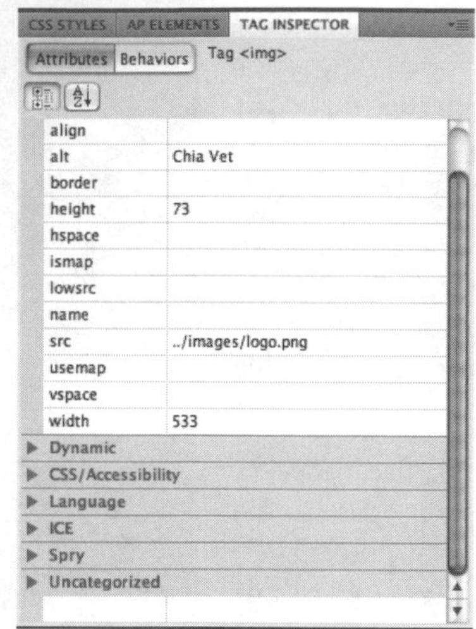

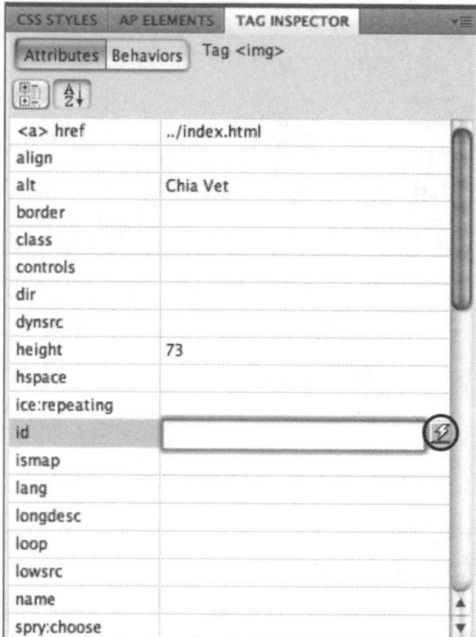

Figure 11-18: *Dreamweaver's Tag inspector lets you edit every property of every tag on a page. What it lacks in user-friendliness–you need to know a lot about HTML to use it correctly–it makes up for in comprehensiveness. It has two faces: Category view (left) and List view (right). The List view is just that: a list of all properties for the selected tag. The Category view imposes a bit of order on this mess, by organizing the different properties into related categories. You can even set a property value dynamically, based on information retrieved from a database, using the lightning bolt button (circled). (Of course, you must first learn how to build dynamic websites by reading Part Six of this book.)*

Enter the Compare File command. With it, you can compare two files and identify lines of code that differ between them. This tool is a perfect solution for problems like the unintentionally botched sidebar above. Compare the local file (the one with the messed-up sidebar) with the remote file (the live version of the website page that works, but is missing the fine new pictures and words you added). You can then identify any changes you made and smoke out your mistake.

Dreamweaver doesn't actually have this tool built into it. Instead, it just passes the files to a separate file-comparison utility (often called a "diff" tool, since it identifies *differences* between files). The first time you compare files, you need to download this utility, and you have a lot to choose from. Fortunately, you can download several free utilities for both Windows and Mac PCs (see the following boxes).

After you download and install the file-comparison utility, you need to tell Dreamweaver where to find it:

1. **Open the Preferences panel, by choosing Edit→Preferences (Dreamweaver→Preferences on the Mac), or pressing Ctrl+U (⌘-U), and then click the File Compare category.**

   There's not much to this Preferences category, just a single box and a Browse button.

2. **Click the Browse button, and then navigate to and select the file-comparison utility.**

   For example, on Windows you might find your utility here: *C:\Program Files\WinMerge\WinMergeU.exe.*

WINDOWS ONLY

Getting Your Hands on the Goodies

You can find lots of file-comparison tools for Windows. Beyond Compare from Scooter Software (*www.scooter-software.com*) is a commercial product ($30) that offers a wide range of comparison options. For a free alternative, check out WinMerge (*http://winmerge.org*). This open source software provides all the basic options you need. Here's how you get it. Go to *http://winmerge.org*. Click the "Download Now" button. At this point you're asked to save the file to your computer—of course, if you're using Internet Explorer, one of those yellow "Warning, warning, enemy attack" banners appears at the top of the page—you need to click that, and then choose "Download File" to actually download the file to your computer.

Once you download the program, the process for installing it is like most other Windows programs. Double-click the file to launch an installer, and follow the step-by-step instructions. You have several options along the way, but just accept the suggested settings and you'll be fine. Once you install it, you're ready to proceed as described below.

   On a Mac, it's slightly different. Instead of selecting the text-editing program Text Wrangler or BBEdit, you need to specify the proper "diff" tool, which is stored in a special location on your computer. Navigate to the */usr/bin* folder (fortunately Dreamweaver drops you there automatically when you browse for the file-comparison tool)—something like this: *Macintosh HD:usr:bin*—and select the correct file. For Text Wrangler, it's *twdiff*; for BBEdit, it's *bbdiff*; and for FileMerge, it's *opendiff*.

3. **Click OK to close the Preferences window.**

   Dreamweaver's been notified of the location of the utility, so you're ready to begin comparing files.

MACS ONLY

What Difference Does It Make?

The Mac version of Dreamweaver supports only three file comparison tools: File Merge (which is a Mac developer program that comes with the XCode tools on your Mac OS X installation disc), BBEdit (the powerful, $125 commercial text editor), and Text Wrangler (the free little brother of BBEdit). Bare Bones Software (*www.barebones.com*) produces both BBEdit and Text Wrangler, but since Text Wrangler's free, it's the best place to begin.

Point your Web browser to *www.barebones.com/products/textwrangler/download.html*, and click any of the download links to get the program onto your computer. As with many Mac applications, this download opens a disk image—just like a folder—with the program inside it. Just drag it to your Applications folder to install it.

The Compare File command works with either two local files that you select in the Files panel (see the Note on page 445 for an explanation), or, more commonly, for a local file and a remote file, so you need to have a site defined with both local and remote root folders (see Chapter 18 for details on how to do this). In addition, since you're comparing two files, you need to make sure you've got a version of the same file on both your local computer and on your remote site—for example, a copy of your home page both locally and on your server. To compare the files, follow these steps:

1. **In the Files panel, select the location of the file you want to compare.**

   Use the drop-down menu in the top-right of the panel to choose either Local View or Live Server View (see Figure 18-6).

2. **Right-click (Control-click) the file, and then, from the pop-up menu that appears, select "Compare with Live Server" (if you're in the Live Server view, this menu says "Compare with Local").**

   Dreamweaver does a little behind-the-scenes trickery before passing the files off to the file comparison program. It first creates a folder (if it's not already created) named *_compareTemp* in the local root folder of your site. Dreamweaver then creates a temporary file with all the code from the remote-site file, and stores that in the new folder. So, you don't actually compare the live file on the server with the local file on your computer; you compare a *copy* of the remote file with the local file. This distinction is important if you want to incorporate changes to the live file, as described in step 3.

   At any rate, your selected file-comparison program—for example, WinMerge or Text Wrangler—starts up and compares the two files. If it finds no differences—if they're *exactly* the same—you'll most likely get a message saying something like "The Selected Files are Identical." Your work is done. If there *is* a difference, the file-comparison program displays the two files, and identifies the code that differs between the two (see Figure 11-19 and Figure 11-20).

3. **Evaluate the differences, and incorporate any changes into your local file.**

All file-comparison programs generally work the same way. When they compare two files, you see the code for each side by side. In addition, the program highlights the differences in some way. You can then review the differences and merge the changes into one file or the other. For example, say you accidentally deleted a table from your local file; a comparison of this file with the remote file shows the table intact in the remote file, but missing in the local file. You can copy the table code from the remote file into the local file. If, however, you deleted the table purposefully, then do nothing, and move on to evaluate the next difference.

Here's where Dreamweaver's little bait-and-switch mentioned in step 2 becomes important. You're not actually comparing the remote file with the local file; you're comparing a *copy* of the remote file saved locally in the *_compare Temp* folder. As a result, you want to move changes in only one direction—from the temporary file to your local file. That's because any changes you make to the temporary file have no effect on the live file on your web server.

So how do you update the remote file? Make changes to your local file, save it, return to Dreamweaver, and upload the local file to your remote site folder. Then pour yourself a cup of tea and be thankful you don't have to do *that* very often.

4. **Save any changes, return to Dreamweaver, and then move your newly updated local file to your web server.**

   The exact process varies from program to program, but see the next two sections for examples using WinMerge and Text Wrangler.

Note: Dreamweaver lets you compare two files on your local hard drive (the home page of the site you're working on vs. a backup of that page you made last week, for example). To do this, go to the Files panel and then, from the site list, select your hard drive (instead of a defined site). In this mode, the Files panel acts just like Windows Explorer or the Mac Finder. You just need to wade through all of the folders until you can see both files at once. Ctrl-click (⌘-click) each file to select them both, right-click (Control-click) one of the files, and then, from the pop-up menu, choose Compare Local Files. The process from that point on is the same as comparing a local and remote file.

Using WinMerge to Compare Files

If you've got a Windows PC and you want to take Dreamweaver's Compare Files command for a test drive, see the box on page 443 for instructions on downloading WinMerge, and then follow these steps:

1. **Once you download and install WinMerge, follow the steps on page 443 to set up Dreamweaver to work with WinMerge.**

   You need to make sure Dreamweaver knows that you want to use WinMerge for file comparisons.

2. **Follow steps 1 and 2 on the opposite page to select a file and tell Dreamweaver to compare it with its sibling on the remote web server.**

   WinMerge launches, and if there are any differences between the files, the program shows the code for the two files side by side, with the differences highlighted (see Figure 11-19).

   WinMerge highlights differences using one or more yellow bars in the left Location pane (circled in Figure 11-19), and the *code* is highlighted either in yellow or gray indicating areas where the code in the files are different.

3. **Click anywhere in either file's code, and then click any of the "diff" navigation buttons—next diff, previous diff, first diff, or last diff—to move from one code difference to another (see Figure 11-19).**

   "Diff" stands for difference. WinMerge automatically selects the differing code and highlights it in red. It also displays the exact spot in the code where the difference is in the Diff Pane below the files. You can now see which code you wish to keep.

4. **If the code in the live server file looks correct, click the Copy Right button.**

   The live server file (a temporary file with a name like TMP4wr997.html) appears on the left and the local file appears on the right. Remember you only want to make changes to your local file. Hitting the Copy Right button copies the code from the live server file to the local file.

   You don't need to do anything if the code in the local file looks OK.

Note: The "diff" pane gives a clear picture of how the code differs between the files. To view it, choose View→Diff Pane.

---

5. **Continue with steps 3 and 4 until you evaluate all the code differences in the two pages.**

   At this point, the "perfect" copy is your local file. It has all the correct code from the live server file, and all the correct code from the local file. Now you just need to move it to your web server.

6. **Move your local file to your server using one of the techniques described on page 702.**

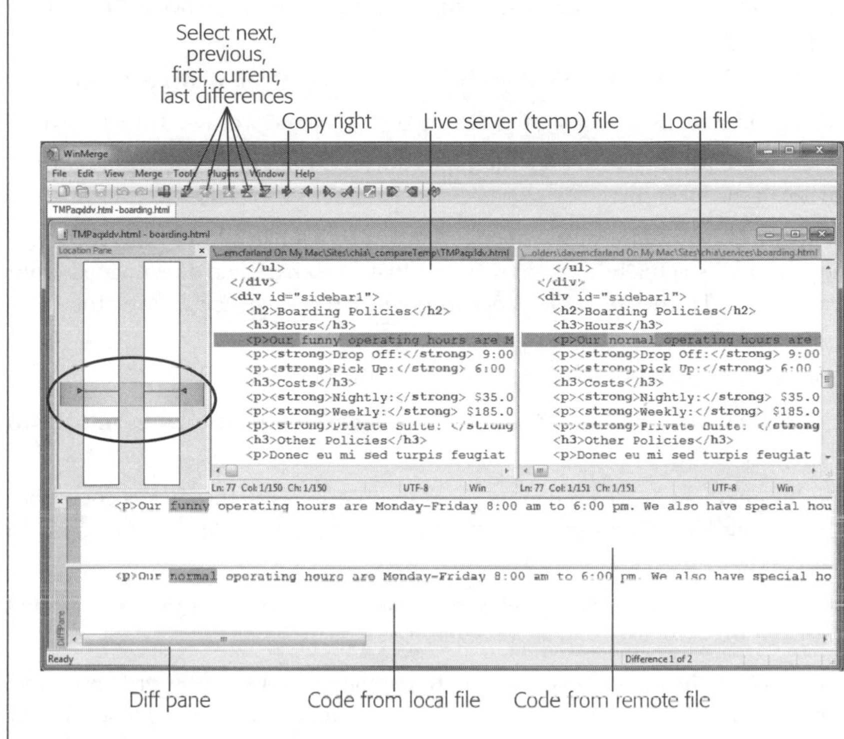

Figure 11-19: *WinMerge includes a kind of bird's-eye view of code differences in the far-left Location pane. Click near any yellow bands (circled) to jump to code that differs between the two files. The temp file (from the live server) is on the left. You can tell by looking at the file path just above the page's code, or by locating the file with _compareTemp in the name. In this example the temporary file's name is TMP4wr997.html.*

Using Text Wrangler to Compare Files

Mac owners can download the free Text Wrangler to compare files (see the box on page 444). And since BBEdit is a more powerful version of Text Wrangler, these steps work for that program as well:

1. **Once you install Text Wrangler, follow the steps on page 443 to set up Dreamweaver's preferences.**

   You need to tell Dreamweaver you want to compare files using Text Wrangler.

2. **Follow steps 1 and 2 on page 444 to select a file and tell Dreamweaver to compare it with its sibling on the remote web server.**

   Text Wrangler launches and displays any code differences for the two files side by side (see Figure 11-20). It also breaks out the problematic code in the Differences panel below the two pages.

   Text Wrangler tells you how the lines differ: For example, "Nonmatching lines" means the lines are similar (some of the code is the same) but not identical, while "Extra lines before line 678" means that one file uses a line of code that's completely different from the other file.

If the files are identical, Dreamweaver pops up a "No difference found between these files" message (although sometimes, if there's no difference, you don't see any message at all).

3. **In the Differences panel, double-click the difference you want to inspect.**

   It's a good strategy to just start at the top of the list and work your way down.

4. **If the code in the live server file looks correct, then click the Apply button beneath the local file.**

   Remember, you only want to make changes to your local file, since the "live server" file is actually a temporary file that Dreamweaver downloaded from your server. The live server file appears on the left, and the local file on the right, so make sure to hit the Apply button on the *right* side.

   You don't need to do anything if the code in the local file looks OK.

5. **Continue with steps 3 and 4 until you evaluate all the differences in the two pages.**

   At this point, the "perfect" copy is your local file. It has all the correct code from the remote file, and all the correct code from the local file. You just need to move it to your server.

6. **Move your local file to your Web server, using one of the techniques described on page 702.**

You can also use the file-compare feature to compare two local files or two remote files, but the steps are so convoluted that it's a lot easier to just bypass Dreamweaver and go directly to WinMerge, Text Wrangler, or the file-comparison utility of your choice. In the case of two remote files, download them first, and then compare them.

Reference Panel

When it comes to building websites, there's a lot to know. After all, HTML, Cascading Style Sheets, and JavaScript are filled with cryptic terms and subtle nuances. Dreamweaver provides a Reference panel to make your search for knowledge a little bit easier. Unfortunately, the references supplied are so out-of-date that none but the HTML Reference has any relevance, which, since HTML hasn't changed in years, still provides a good guide to tags and properties (though you won't find any information on HTML 5 there).

To open the Reference panel, choose Help→Reference, or press Shift+F1. The Reference panel appears at the bottom of the screen, docked with the Results panel group (see Figure 11-21). The first menu at the top of the panel lets you choose the "book" you want. Again, only the HTML reference is any good. Once you select it, choose a particular HTML tag from the menu to the right of the Book menu. A description of that item appears in the main window. A secondary menu to the right, the Attribute menu, lets you access additional information about a property or tag. For example, if you want to see information about the <a> tag's *tabindex* property, choose "a" from the Tag menu and, from the Attribute menu, click "tabindex".

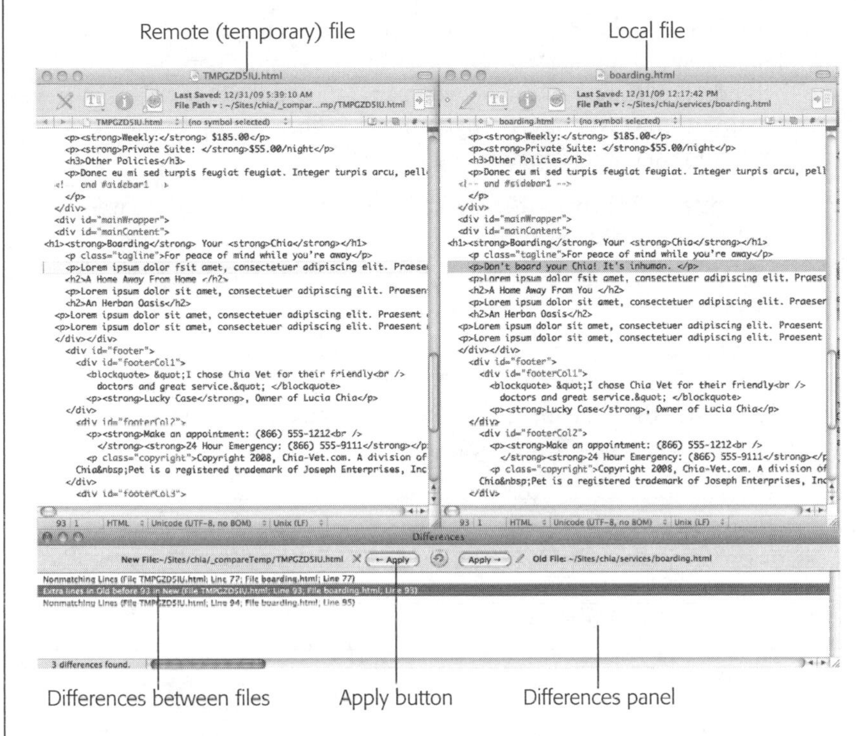

***Figure 11-20:** Text Wrangler in action. The live server file's code appears on the left. To move code from it to the local file, click the Apply button on the right (the one underneath the local file). You can identify the remote file by the letters "TMP" in its name. In this example, TMP579J0M.html is the temporary copy of the remote file that Dreamweaver created.*

For information on other topics, you're better off turning to the Web and Google. Here are a few good resources:

- For CSS help, SitePoint.com's free, online reference to CSS is great: *http://reference.sitepoint.com/css*
- For JavaScript, W3Schools.com provides an in-depth reference: *www.w3schools.com/jsref/default.asp*
- For PHP, you can't beat the Source. The official PHP site has excellent documentation on every aspect of PHP: *www.php.net/manual/en/*

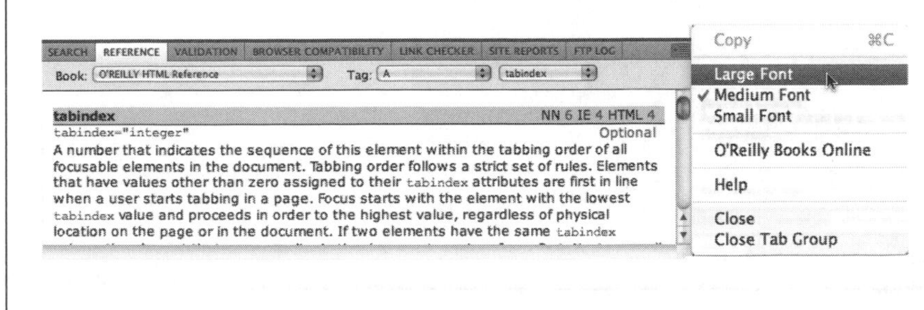

***Figure 11-21:** If the print in the Reference panel is too small or too large, use the panel's shortcut menu (click the arrow in the panel's upper-right corner), as shown here, and select a different size.*

Inserting JavaScript

Dreamweaver includes many fun and useful interactive effects—Spry Menus, Spry Form Validation, Spry Effects, Dreamweaver behaviors, and so on. JavaScript is the "engine" behind all of them. Of course, you can do a lot of other cool things with JavaScript that Dreamweaver hasn't programmed. In these cases, you need to wade into the depths of JavaScript programming yourself.

The most straightforward approach, especially if you're familiar with JavaScript, is to simply switch into Code view (Ctrl+` [Option-`]), and then type away. Or, if you prefer, you can use Dreamweaver's Script window to add your JavaScript code (see Figure 11-22).

To add JavaScript code, click in either the head or body section of a page and then choose Insert→HTML→Script Objects→Script. In the Script window that appears (Figure 11-22), from the Type menu, choose "text/javascript" (you have a bewildering array of options, but only "text/javascript" is useful for JavaScript).

Note: You can use the Insert Script command in Design view also, but to add a script to the <head> of a page, first choose View→Head Content, which opens a small bar below the Document toolbar that lists all the different tags like <title>, <script>, and <meta> that appear in the head of a page. Click here, and follow the preceding recipe for inserting a script.

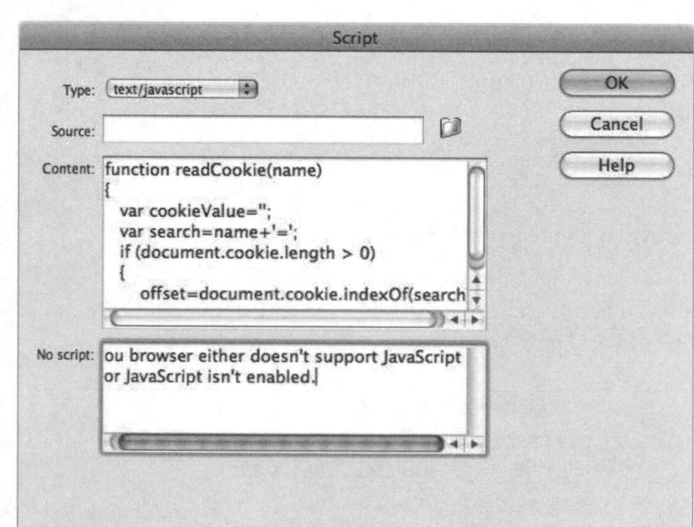

***Figure 11-22:** Unlike Code view, the Script window doesn't respond to the Tab key; if you're accustomed to indenting your code, you need to use spaces. You can also insert a message in the "No script" box, which appears if the web browser doesn't understand JavaScript.*

In the Content section, type in your script (no need to include <script> tags, as Dreamweaver handles that part), and then click OK. If you insert the script in the body of the document, a small gold icon (indicating an invisible element on the page) marks its location.

You can edit your script in Code view, of course. In Design view, select the script icon, and then, in the Property inspector, click Edit.

If you use external JavaScript files, you can link to them directly in the Script window. Instead of typing in any code, click the familiar "Browse for File" icon (to the right of the Source box), locate the external JavaScript file, and then click OK. Dreamweaver adds the appropriate code to link the script file to the web page (see Figure 11-22).

Dreamweaver also lets you open and work on external JavaScript files (.js files) right in Code view and with the Related Files toolbar discussed on page 433, you can easily jump right to the JavaScript code in an external JavaScript file. You can use the built-in text-editing capabilities of Code view to write your JavaScript programs.

Note: JavaScript programming is no walk in the park. Although it's certainly easier to learn than full-featured languages like Java or C++, it can still be challenging. If you want to get your feet wet, here's a great resource for basic tutorials and information on JavaScript: *http://www.w3school.com/js/*. For a more in-depth coverage, check out *JavaScript: The Missing Manual.*

GEM IN THE ROUGH

JavaScript Extractor

For JavaScript programmers, it's generally considered best practice to put as much of your JavaScript code as possible into an external file. An external JavaScript file has the same benefits as an external CSS file. First, you need to download the code only once, so your site loads faster. Second, with most of the code in an external file, you can easily make site-wide changes to your programs by editing just a single file.

Unfortunately, Dreamweaver doesn't follow this philosophy when it comes to much of the code it creates. Dreamweaver behaviors (covered in Chapter 14), for example, insert JavaScript code directly into a web page. If you use the same behavior throughout your site, you're unnecessarily repeating code in every page, when it would be much more efficient to store that code in a separate file and just attach that file to each web page.

Dreamweaver CS5 includes the JavaScript Extractor, which lets you strip chunks of JavaScript from your web pages and store them in an external file. To use the Extractor, open a page with JavaScript code in it–for example, a page with a Spry menu (page 184) or one that uses Dreamweaver's image rollover tool (page 246). Then choose Commands→Externalize JavaScript. The Externalize JavaScript window appears, listing all the changes Dreamweaver will make. You can uncheck the box next to a proposed change you don't like to prevent Dreamweaver from making that change.

You can also choose how Dreamweaver moves the code from the page: The "Only externalize JavaScript" option leaves what are called inline event handlers in place (this is code embedded in a tag, like an <a> tag that triggers the JavaScript); while the "attach unobtrusively" option removes that code. The first option is good if you're just using the Dreamweaver behaviors described in Chapter 14 (but not the Spry effects). In that case, Dreamweaver removes the JavaScript, but you can still edit the behaviors as you normally would (page 586).

The second option isn't very useful, so skip it. It's intended to achieve one of the goals of a good JavaScript program–keeping JavaScript out of your HTML–but it doesn't achieve any of the other goals of unobtrusive JavaScript (like making sure your page works even with JavaScript turned off). To learn more about unobtrusive JavaScript, visit *www.onlinetools.org/articles/unobtrusivejavascript/*.

Unfortunately, either option makes any Spry effects, widgets, or datasets you add to a page uneditable. Well, actually, they're still editable, but you have to do it yourself in Code view! In other words, if you use the JavaScript Extractor, you can't use Dreamweaver's friendly interface to change your Spry widgets. In addition, if you choose the second export option–"attach unobtrusively"–even normal Dreamweaver behaviors become uneditable. The bottom line: If you ever want to update a Spry widget or Dreamweaver behavior you add to a page, you're better off skipping this tool altogether.

CHAPTER 12

Forms

A website is a great way to broadcast a message, announce a new product, post late-breaking news, or just rant about the state of the world. But that's all *one-way* communication, which you may find a bit limiting. You may be curious to get some feedback from your audience. Or you may want to build your business by selling your product online, and you need a way to gather vital stats from customers. If you want to *receive* information as well as deliver it, it's time to add *forms* to your web design repertoire (see Figure 12-1 for a simple example). Whatever type of information you need to collect on your site, Dreamweaver's *form objects* make the task easy.

Form Basics

A form begins and ends with the HTML <form> tag. The opening tag (<form>) indicates the beginning of the form, and sets its properties; the closing tag (</form>), of course, marks the form's end.

You add different objects between these tags to deck out your pages with the elements your visitors interact with—radio buttons, text fields, and pull-down menus are just a few ways you can gather input. It's perfectly OK to include other HTML elements inside a form, too. In fact, your visitors would be lost if you didn't also add (and format) text that explains each element's purpose. And if you don't use a table or Cascading Style Sheets to lay out a form in an organized way, it can quickly become an unreadable mess (see the box on page 473).

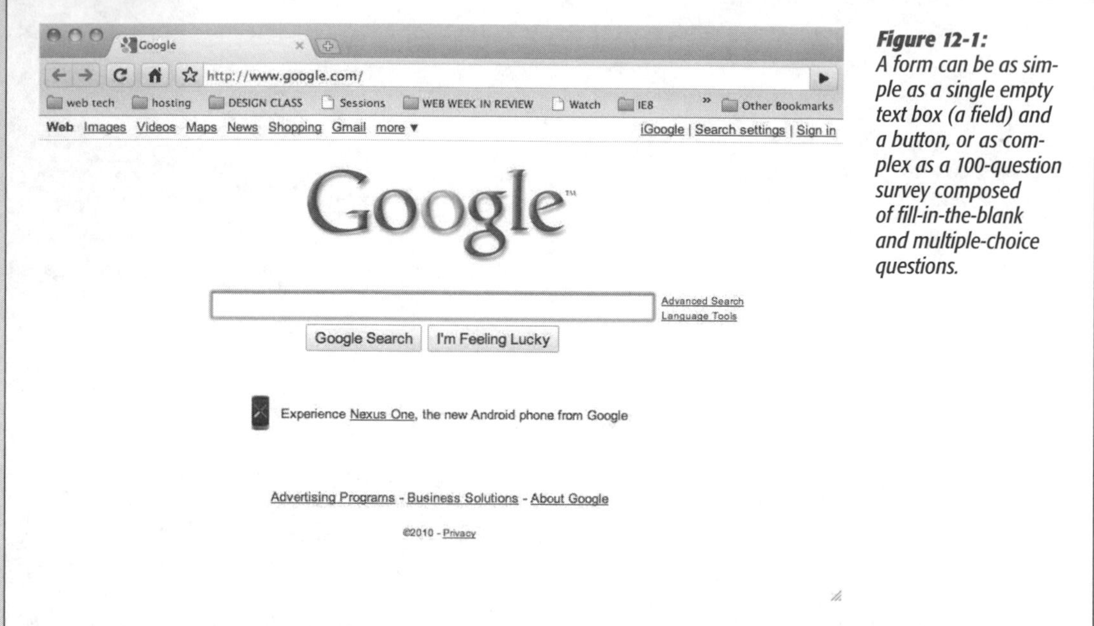

Figure 12-1: *A form can be as simple as a single empty text box (a field) and a button, or as complex as a 100-question survey composed of fill-in-the-blank and multiple-choice questions.*

Every form element, whether it's a text field or a checkbox, has a *name* and a *value*. You supply the name, which should reflect the information you're trying to collect. For example, if you want visitors to type their email addresses into a text field, you might name that field *email*. The value, on the other hand, is what the visitors' actually type in—the text they enter into a text field, for example, or the selections they make from a pull-down menu.

After your visitors fill out a form and click the Submit button to transmit their responses, the browser transmits each form element as a name/value pair like this: *email=bob@bobville.com*. Submitting both pieces of information helps the program that processes the form figure out what the input means. After all, without a name, a value of "39" doesn't mean much (39 what? Potatoes, steps, days until Christmas?). The name/value pair (*age=39*) provides context for your visitor's input.

The Code Backstage

Creating a form is just the first step in collecting information from your visitors. You also need to *connect* the form to a program that actually *does* something with the information. The program may simply take the data from the form and email it to you. But it could also do something as complex as contacting a bank, processing a credit card payment, creating an invoice item, or notifying a shipping department to deliver the latest Stephen King novel to someone in Nova Scotia.

A form is pretty useless without a form-processing program on the other end of things—running on your web server. These information-crunching programs come in a variety of languages—Perl, C, C#, Visual Basic, VBScript, Java, ColdFusion Markup Language, PHP—and may be part of a dedicated application server like Adobe's ColdFusion Server or Microsoft's .NET technology.

Writing the necessary behind-the-scenes processing software can be complex, but the concepts behind the forms themselves are straightforward:

1. **First, someone fills out a form on your website and clicks the Submit button (or Search, Buy, or whatever you actually label the button that transmits information).**
2. **Next, the browser transmits the form data over the Internet to a processing program on your web server.**
3. **The form-processing program collects the data and does something with it—whatever you and the programmer decide it should do. It could, for example, send the data off as an email to you, search a vast database of information, or store the information in a database.**
4. **Finally, the server returns a page to the browser, which your visitor sees. It may be a standard web page with a message like "Thanks for the info", or a page the program generates on the fly that includes information like a detailed invoice or the results of a search.**

So how do you create the processing half of the forms equation if you're not a programmer? You can use Dreamweaver, of course. Part Six of this book describes Dreamweaver's dynamic web-building tools for creating pages that use information collected from forms. If your web server accommodates PHP, for example, Dreamweaver can create form-processing programs for you. If you're part of a web development team in a company, you may already have programmers on staff who can create the processing program.

Furthermore, even if your web hosting company doesn't tolerate any of the application servers that work with Dreamweaver, they probably offer free form-processing programs as part of their services. Contact your host and ask about this; most companies provide basic instructions on how to use these programs.

If you feel adventurous, many form-processing programs are available free on the Web. For a thorough sampling, see the CGI Resource Index at *http://cgi.resourceindex.com*. Using these free programs can be tricky, however, because you need to download the appropriate program and install it on your web server—something not every web host allows.

Lastly, you can use a form-processing service like Wufoo (*http://wufoo.com/*), which handles all the complicated parts of collecting and storing information from forms and provides tools for retrieving that information in a variety of formats.

Creating a Form

In Dreamweaver, you can build forms with one-click ease using the Insert panel's Forms category (see Figure 12-2).

To begin, you need to insert a <form> tag on your web page to indicate the boundaries of a form:

1. **In the document window, click the location where you want to insert the form.**

   You might decide to place it after a paragraph of introductory text, for example, or into a <div> tag that holds the page's main content.

Note: If you plan on using an HTML table to organize a form's fields, insert the form first, then insert the table inside the <form> tag.

---

2. **On the Insert panel, select the Forms category.**

   The tab reveals 22 form-building tools.

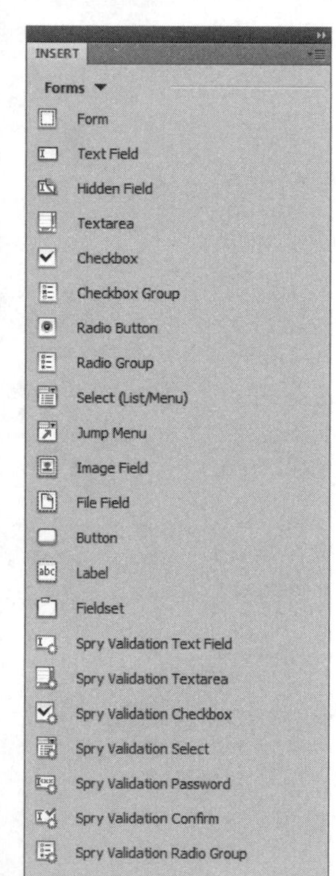

Figure 12-2:
The Insert panel's Forms category gives you one-click access to all the different form elements–buttons, text fields, checkboxes, and more. Since the Forms category has so many buttons, you might want to turn off the labels that appear next to each icon as described on page 34. This step lets you see all the form buttons without taking up your monitor's entire height. Another option is to choose the "Classic" view from the Workspace switcher as described in the note on page 35. This moves the insert panel into a toolbar that runs along the top of the application (see Figure 12-28). (You can also just drag the Insert panel up to the top of the screen to turn it into a toolbar.)

3. **Click the Form icon (the very first square in the 22-icon list—or the far-left square if you're in the "Hide Labels" mode described on page 34).**

   Alternatively, if you're a menu-driven person, choose Insert→Form→Form.

   Either way, a red, dashed-line rectangle appears in the document window, indicating the form's boundaries. (If you don't see it, choose View→Visual Aids→Invisible Elements.) The top line represents the opening <form> tag; the bottom represents the closing tag. Make sure you always insert form objects, like buttons and menus, *inside* these lines. Otherwise, Dreamweaver thinks you're trying to create a second form on the page. (It's perfectly valid to include more than one form per page [as long as you don't try to insert a form inside *another* form], but your visitor can submit only one form—and its data—at a time.)

Tip: An even faster way to insert a <form> tag is to bypass step 3 and just insert a form element—like a text field or radio button; Dreamweaver asks if you want to add the <form> tag at the same time.

   Since you can place so many other HTML elements inside a form, you'll often find it easier to insert the form first, and add tables, graphics, text, and form objects later.

4. **If it isn't already selected, click the dotted red line to select the form.**

   This step not only selects the form, but it highlights everything inside the red lines, too. The Property inspector displays the "Form ID" label at the upper-left corner, as shown in Figure 12-3.

5. **If you like, type a name for your form into the "Form ID" field.**

   This step is optional. Dreamweaver supplies a generic ID name—*form1*—but you don't need to name a form for it to work. A name is useful if you use the JavaScript or the Spry form validation tools discussed below because they both interact with the form or its fields, and the tools need a way to uniquely identify each form. But you don't have to change the name Dreamweaver supplies, and the name doesn't appear anywhere on the page, so you can leave the default name in place if you wish.

6. **Into the Action field, type a URL, or select a file by clicking the tiny folder icon.**

   Your mission here is to specify the location of the program that will process the form. If someone else is responsible for the programming, ask that person what to enter here. It's a standard web address—either an absolute URL (one that begins with *http://*) or the path to the server's form-processing program (see page 159 for more on these different kinds of links). If you use Dreamweaver's dynamic page-building tools, then you usually leave this field blank. When you apply a server behavior—the programming code that makes the page "dynamic"—Dreamweaver automatically inserts the correct URL.

   Either way, the file name you add to the Action field *doesn't* end in *.html*. The path might, for example, be *.../cgi-bin/forms.pl*. In this case, .pl extension indicates a program written in the Perl programming language. Other common file extensions for web programs include .cfm (for ColdFusion Markup Language pages), *.aspx* (for .NET pages), *.php* (for PHP pages), *.jsp* (for Java Server Pages), or *.cgi* (for CGI programs).

7. **Using the Method pop-up menu, specify how you want the browser to transmit the form data to the processing program (see Figure 12-3).**

   Basically, browsers can transmit form data to a web server in either of two ways. You'll use the more common method, called POST, most often. It sends the form data in two steps. First, the browser contacts the form-processing program at the URL you specified in the previous step; then, it sends the data to the server. This method gives your data a bit more security, and it can easily handle forms with lots of information.

   The GET method, on the other hand, adds the form data to the destination URL, like this: *http://search.yahoo.com/bin/search?p=dogs*. (Even though the GET method *sends* data, it's named GET; that's because its purpose in life is to *receive* information—such as the results of a search.) The characters following the *?* in the address represent the form data. This code submits a single form field—named *p*, with the value *dogs*—to the server. If a form has lots of fields and accepts lots of user input, a GET URL can become extremely long. Some servers can't handle very long URLs, so don't use the GET method if your forms collect a lot of data.

Note: The GET method has one big benefit: You can *bookmark* it, which is great if you want to save and reuse a common search request for Google, for example, or you want to send someone Google Maps driving directions. That's why search engines use the GET method for form submissions.

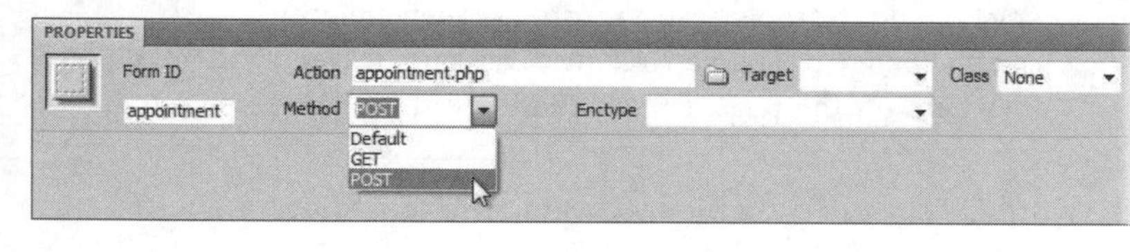

***Figure 12-3:** Unless you're creating a search form, you'll generally want to use the POST method of sending data to the server. See step 7 for more details.*

8. **If you're using frames, select a Target option.**

   You'll most likely skip this menu. Frames are so 1998 web design, and pose serious problems for web designers and search engines. However, even if you're not using frames, you can choose the "_blank" option to open a new browser window to display the results. (See page 172 for more on the Target property.)

9. **Select an encoding type, if you like.**

   You usually don't have to select anything from the Enctype menu. Leaving this box empty is almost always correct, and is the same as selecting the much more long-winded "application/x-www-form-urlencoded" option.

   But if you use the File Field button (see page 473) to let visitors upload files to your site, you should use the "multipart/form-data" option. In fact, Dreamweaver automatically selects this option when you add a File Field to a form. See the box on the opposite page for more info on potential problems with File Field forms.

   You've laid the foundation for your form. Now you're ready to add the input controls—menus, checkboxes, and so on—as described in the next section.

FREQUENTLY ASKED QUESTION

Using a Form to Upload Files

I want to let visitors upload photos to my site, but when I add a Form Field button to one of my forms, I get an error from the server whenever I try to submit the form. Why?

To upload files from a web page, you need to do two things: Change the encoding method (see step 9 on page 459) to "multipart/form-data", and set up your server to receive files. Dreamweaver automatically takes care of the first part: whenever you insert a form field, Dreamweaver changes the form's encoding method to "multipart/form-data".

The second part is up to you (or your web hosting company). Many web servers have this option turned off for security reasons. Check to see if your web host lets you use forms to upload files to your server. If it doesn't, then find a hosting company that does.

In addition, you have to program the form-processing script to accept data in the "multipart/form-data" format. Since this task is challenging, you might want to enlist some help. The box on page 475 provides several resources for commercial Dreamweaver extensions that can help with this task.

If you decide that's too much trouble and you delete the Form Field button, you're still in trouble. Dreamweaver doesn't reset the encoding method to the original "application/x-www-form-urlencoded" setting, so when visitors try to submit the form (even without the Form Field), they'll get a nasty error message from the server. You must remedy the situation manually by selecting the form, and then using the Property inspector to change the encoding method back to "application/x-www-form-urlencoded".

Adding Form Elements

Unless you've never used a computer before, the different user interface elements available for HTML forms should look familiar (Figure 12-4): text fields where people can type in information (their names, addresses, phone numbers, and so on); checkboxes for making multiple-choice selections; and menus for picking items from a list. The Insert panel's Forms category (Figure 12-2) lets you create all these elements and more.

Dreamweaver includes some special form elements, called Spry Validation widgets. They're like the regular form elements discussed below, but have the added ability to *verify* the contents of a form field, which prevents visitors from submitting forms if they don't fill them out correctly. The Spry Validation widgets are discussed on page 478.

What All Form Elements Have in Common

Adding form elements to your document always follows the same pattern:

1. **In the document window, insert a form (see page 456).**

   Or, if the page already has a form, click inside its red border.

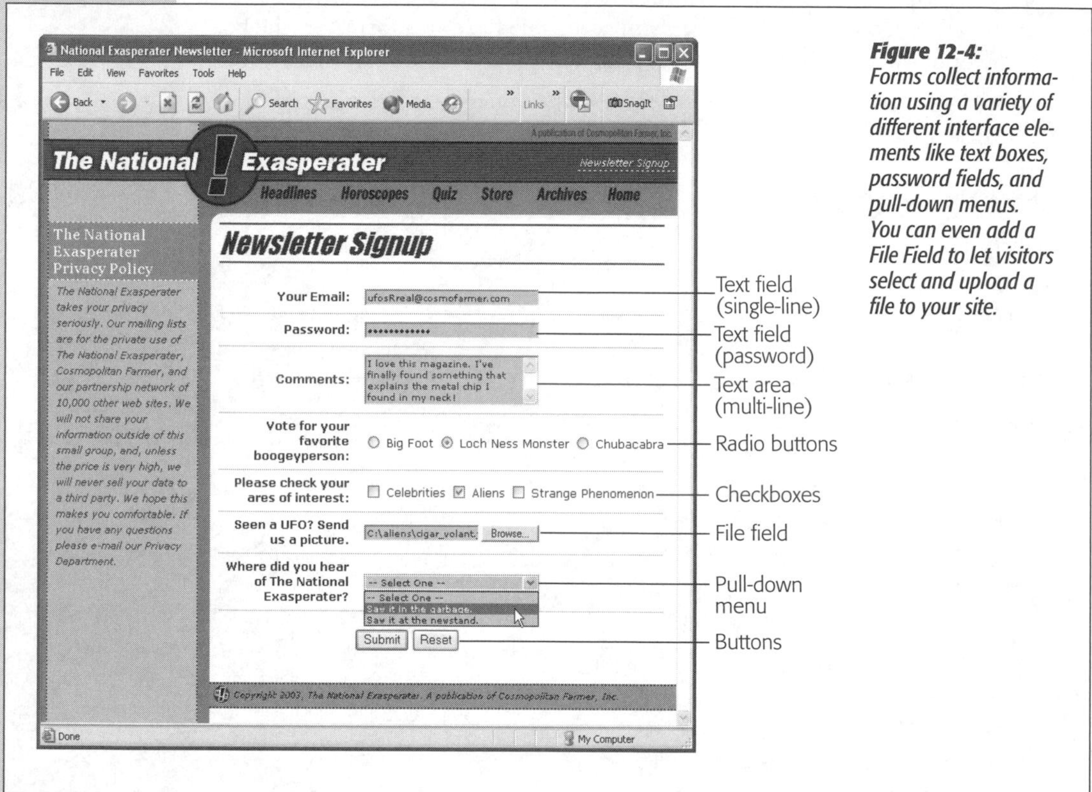

Figure 12-4: *Forms collect information using a variety of different interface elements like text boxes, password fields, and pull-down menus. You can even add a File Field to let visitors select and upload a file to your site.*

Tip: You can skip step 1 and have Dreamweaver add a form element when you first add the form field to a page. When you insert a field (step 2) and there's no form yet, Dreamweaver asks if you'd like to add the proper <form> tag. Click Yes and Dreamweaver automatically creates the red dotted-line form boundaries (and, behind the scenes, inserts the corresponding <form> tags). You should *always* click the Yes button. A form field that isn't surrounded by the proper form tag doesn't work in all browsers.

---

2. **In the Insert panel's Forms category, click the appropriate button (see Figure 12-2).**

   Alternatively, use the Insert→Form submenu. You'll soon discover that Dreamweaver represents every form object on the Insert panel by a command on the Insert menu, too (for example, Insert→Form→Text Field).

3. **In the Input Tag Accessibility Attributes window, type an ID (see Figure 12-5).**

   This window serves a couple of functions. It lets you assign an ID (this step) and set a few accessibility options. These options add information and tools for the benefit of those who surf using *assistive technologies*—like screen readers—or those who use their keyboard (rather than their mouse) to jump from form field to form field.

   The ID you type in this field also determines the *name* of the field. Remember, each field has a name so that the form-processing program can identify the information it receives (see page 453). Say you add a text field to a page that collects a visitor's town name. In the ID box, if you type *town*, then when Dreamweaver inserts the text field onto the page, the underlying HTML Dreamweaver writes looks like this: <input type="text" name="town" id="town">.

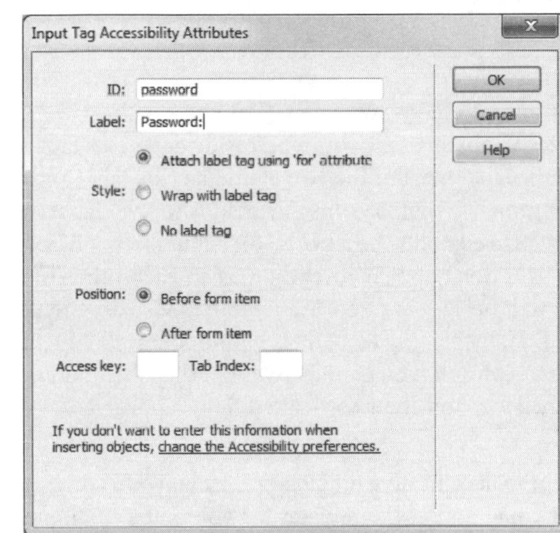

Figure 12-5:
This window appears when you're inserting a form element. If you don't see it, you or someone else has turned off Dreamweaver's factory setting to automatically launch this window. To summon it, choose Edit→Preferences (Dreamweaver→Preferences), click the Accessibility category, and then turn on the Form Objects checkbox.

   Be sure to follow the same naming conventions you use for CSS ID names: Begin with a letter, use only numbers, letters, hyphens, or underscores, and skip spaces, punctuation, and other characters. (Keep in mind that adding an ID to an HTML tag doesn't create a CSS ID style—but if you want to create a special look just for that one field, you *can* create an ID style using the name you supply for the form element.)

Note: The ID value you type in step 3 has a slightly different effect when you add radio buttons. What you type becomes the radio button's ID value, but Dreamweaver sets its name to "radio". That's because you can only use an ID once per tag on a page, but radio buttons that form part of a group (like answers to a multiple-choice question) must share the same name. Using the same name for more than one button tells a web browser that a visitor can select one and only one radio button from the group (see page 469). Therefore, make sure you rename your radio button using the Property inspector as described on page 469.

4. **Type a label, and then select label options (see Figure 12-5).**

The label option lets you add text that identifies the form element's purpose. In fact, Dreamweaver wraps whatever text you type in an HTML tag, named, logically enough, the <label> tag. This tag identifies the form field's purpose, and your visitors see the text you enter here as they fill out the form. The label usually appears either to the left or right of the form field. For example, if you add a text field to collect someone's name, you might use the label *Name:*. Someone filling out the form then sees the word "Name:" followed by a box where they can type in their name. It's always a good idea to add a label. (You can read more about the <label> tag on page 477.)

Tip: Sometimes you don't need or want a label. For example, Dreamweaver's stock buttons–like Submit or Reset– already have a label, so you don't need to add another. In this case, either click the Cancel button, which adds the form field without any of these *accessibility* properties, or leave the label box empty, and select the "No label tag" radio button.

You can attach a label to a form element two ways. The first method, "Attach label tag using 'for' attribute", wraps the text you type inside a <label> tag. The form field itself isn't inside the label tag, but the two elements (the label and the field) are connected by a *for* property that Dreamweaver adds to the <label> tag, which tells a browser which form element the label is "for." This is a good option when a label and its form field don't appear directly next to each other in the HTML code. For example, web designers often use a table to visually organize forms (see the box on page 473). By placing text labels in one column of the table and form fields in an adjacent column, you can neatly align the labels and their corresponding fields, but the label and their associated fields appear in far different places in the HTML

Here's an example that might make this all a bit clearer: Say you add a text field that lets someone enter her email address to register for your site's email newsletter. If, when you insert the field, you use the ID *email*, the label "Your email address:", and the "Attach label tag using the 'for' attribute" option, you end up with this HTML code:

```
<label for="email">Your email address:</label>
<input type="text" name="email" id="email" />
```

At this point, you can move the <label> tag (or the text field) to any other location on your web page, and the label remains related to the field. Of course, if you place the label at the top of the page and the field at the bottom, your visitors don't know they're related, so it makes sense to keep the two tags in close visual proximity. However, people often put the <label> tag in one table cell of a row, and the field in a table cell to the right. (The label tag has one added benefit: click it and you select the associated form field, ready for the visitor to type in a response.)

The second way to attach a label, "Wrap with label tag" (Figure 12-5), wraps the <label> tag around both the text you type and the form element itself. This method keeps the two together and easily identifies which label goes with each form field. However, although wrapping a field with the <label> tag produces valid HTML, it isn't considered as accessible (to screen readers, for example) so the "Attach label tag using 'for' attribute" is generally considered the best way to go.

Note: You can skip the <label> tag entirely simply by choosing "No label tag." Any text you type in the label field is just dumped onto the page as regular text positioned next to the form field.

---

5. **Optionally, type an "Access key" and a Tab Index number, and then press OK.**

   These steps let visitors hop to form fields using the keyboard. The "Access key" option lets visitors use a keyboard shortcut to jump immediately into or select a field. If you enter *M*, for example, for a form element's access key, visitors can jump to that element by using Alt+M (Windows) or Control-M (Mac). While this feature seems to be a great way to make your forms more usable, it has a couple of drawbacks. First, not all browsers support this feature. In addition, since it's not at all obvious to your visitors what keyboard shortcuts work where, you need to list the shortcuts next to the form elements, or create a "user's manual" of sorts that explains the shortcuts. You're probably best off leaving the Access key blank.

   Browsers support the Tab Index more often than the "Access key" property. The Tab Index lets you number each form field and, in the process, set the order in which the fields will be selected as a visitor presses the Tab key. Number 1 indicates the first field selected, and each number after that—2, 3, 4, and so on—dictates the rest of the selection order. You don't usually need to go to this extreme, since most browsers automatically jump to the next form field when you press the Tab key, but it sometimes comes in handy when you have a particularly complex form and you use either tables or CSS to lay it out. In some cases, the order in which the fields are selected by default doesn't match the visual presentation of the form. If this is the case, setting the Tab Index lets you correctly specify the tab order.

6. **In the Property inspector, set the form element's properties (Figure 12-6).**

   For instance, some elements let you specify things like width, height, and other variables. The following descriptions indicate the options available for each form element.

Text Fields

When you need to collect a specific piece of information, like a person's name, phone number, or address, use a text field (shown in Figure 12-4). Text fields accept typed responses, and they're great for open-ended questions. They come in three different flavors: *single-line* fields for short responses, *password* fields to hide people's input from snooping eyes, and *multiline* fields for longer replies.

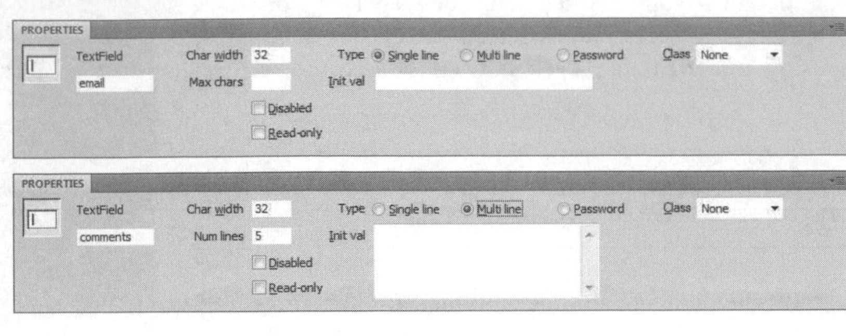

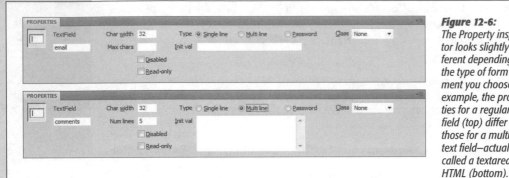

Figure 12-6: *The Property inspector looks slightly different depending on the type of form element you choose. For example, the properties for a regular text field (top) differ from those for a multiline text field–actually called a textarea in HTML (bottom).*

Once you insert a text field, you can adjust the following settings in the Property inspector (see Figure 12-6):

- **Char Width.** The width of a text field is measured in characters; so if you type *20* for the Char Width (character width) setting, Dreamweaver creates a text field that holds 20 typed letters. Be aware, however, that the *physical* width of the field (how many inches or pixels wide it is) can vary from browser to browser. (You can use Cascading Style Sheets to set an exact width using the *width* property described on page 360.)
- **Type.** You can choose from three types of text fields:
  - — A *single-line* text field, of course, holds just one line of text. This is the most common text field; use it for collecting small pieces of information, like a last name, Social Security number, or credit card number.
  - — *Multiline* fields let guests type in multiple lines of text. You need this kind of field when you let visitors type in longer notes, such as those for a "Let us know what you think!" or "Nature of problem:" field.

Note: Dreamweaver includes a separate button for adding multiline text fields–called *textarea* in HTML (see Figure 12-2).

  - — *Password* fields hide a password a guest types from the prying eyes of passing spies. Whatever your web visitor types in appears as asterisks (*** in Windows) or bullets (•••• on a Mac) on-screen. (However, the information in the password field isn't completely secret: it's still transmitted as plain text, just like any other form field. The masking action takes place only in your visitor's browser. See the Frequently Asked Question on page 466 for more on this.)
- **Max Chars/Num Lines.** Max Chars (maximum characters) lets you limit the number of characters the field accepts. It's a good way to help ensure that guests type in the right information in the right place. For instance, if you use a field

to collect a visitor's age, odds are you don't need more than three characters to do it; very few 1,000-year-olds surf the Web these days (and those who do don't like to reveal their ages).

When you specify a multiline text field, the Max Chars box morphs into the Num Lines box. In this case, you can't limit the amount of text someone types into the field. Instead, you specify the height of the text field. (You can, however, use Spry Text Area to limit the number of characters a multiline text field accepts, as described on page 493.)

Note: The limit you specify here affects only how tall the field is *onscreen*. Your visitors can type as many lines of information as they want (a scroll bar appears if the number of lines exceeds the size of the box).

- **Init val.** Here, you can specify the Initial Value of the field—starter text that automatically appears in the field so that it isn't empty when a visitor begins completing the form. You can use this feature to include explanatory text inside the field itself, such as "Type your name in this box" or "Example: (212) 555-1212". Another common use for the "Init val" box: when you create an *update form*—a form for editing previously entered information. For example, if you want to update your Facebook profile, then you go to a page that presents all your current information. You can change that information and then submit the form to update your profile. An update form requires a database and some server-side programming—you'll learn how to build this type of form in Chapter 25.

Note: If your form page is one of the dynamic file types with which Dreamweaver works–ASP, PHP, or ColdFusion–you also see a small lightning bolt to the right of the "Init val" box. This button lets you add *dynamic data*–information drawn from a database–to the text field. (In-depth coverage of this feature starts on page 939.)

- **Disabled and Read-only.** You probably won't ever have any reason to use these two options. Adobe added them in Dreamweaver CS4, and both make the text field uneditable. The Disabled option grays out the text field and prevents visitors from clicking into it, or even selecting any text that's already there (from the Init Val property discussed above). In addition, when you disable a field, a browser doesn't submit any data in it when it submits the form itself.

  The Read-only option lets a visitor select and copy anything in the text field, but doesn't let him change it.

  Since forms are meant to collect information from visitors, don't taunt them with uneditable fields. Leave both options alone. So why do they exist? People usually use these options in conjunction with JavaScript programming—for example, to disable a text field until a visitor selects another option.

FREQUENTLY ASKED QUESTION

Using the Password Field for Credit Card Numbers

Can I use the Password field type for credit card numbers and other sensitive information?

Yes, but it doesn't give the information any extra security.

The Password field does one thing: It hides people's input on the screen. Someone looking over your visitor's shoulder can't read what he's typing–it looks like a bunch of dots–but once a browser submits that information over the Internet, it's just as visible as a regular text field.

To provide real security for form information, you need an encrypted connection between your web server and the visitor's computer. Most website creators use SSL (Secure Socket Layer) technology for this purpose.

Web browsers understand this technology, but your web server must be specially configured to work in this mode. Contact your web host to see if you can use SSL on your server (the answer is usually yes). If so, they can tell you how to set it up. You don't have to make any special changes to your web pages to take advantage of SSL; once the server is set up, you put your web pages on it as you would for a non-secure website (Chapter 18 covers moving your web files onto the Web).

Checkboxes and Checkbox Groups

Checkboxes (see Figure 12-4) are simple and to the point; a guest either checks them or not. They're great for questions that can have more than one answer. Suppose you offer visitors their choice of three different email newsletters you send out each month. In your form, you might include some text—"Check the boxes for the newsletters you want to receive"—and three corresponding checkboxes with labels that indicate the name of each newsletter.

Once you add a checkbox to a form, you can set up these options in the Property inspector (see Figure 12-7):

- **Checked value.** Here's where you specify the information the browser sends to your form-processing program when a visitor selects the checkbox. Since visitors never actually see this information, it doesn't have to match the checkbox's label; it could transmit a coded response.
- **Initial state.** If you like, you can have a checkbox already filled in when your web page first loads. You've probably seen this setup if you've ever signed up for something on a commercial site. There's usually a checkbox—already checked—near the bottom of the form with fine print like this: "Check here if you want to get daily, unsolicited email from our marketing department."

Note: As with many form elements, the state of your checkbox (checked or unchecked) can reflect information it retrieves from a database. The Property inspector's Dynamic button–available only when you work on a dynamic page (ASP, PHP, or ColdFusion)–lets you set the checkbox state based on data in a database. (See page 941 for details.)

After you set these options, if you don't use Dreamweaver's accessibility options (discussed on page 461), return to the document window to add a text label next to the field. You want to let people know what the checkbox is for: "Yes, sign me up!", for example.

Checkboxes don't have to come in groups, but they often do, as in "yes" and "no" boxes. Dreamweaver includes a tool to make inserting multiple checkboxes easier as discussed next.

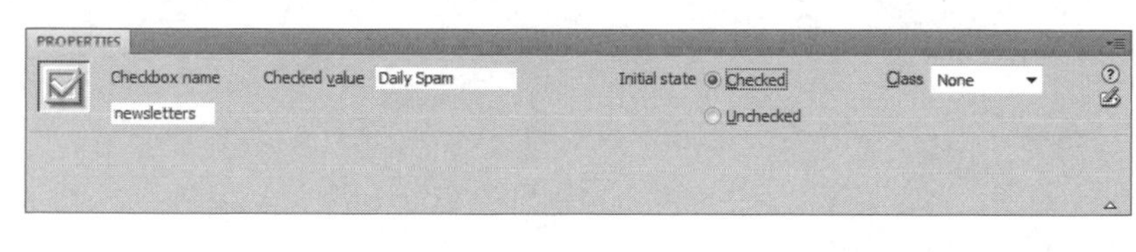

Figure 12-7: *The "Checked value" property defines the checkbox's actual value–that is, the value that's sent to the form processing application when the form is submitted.*

Checkbox Groups

Checkboxes frequently travel in groups—"What activities do you like? Check all that apply." Here's how you set them up.

1. **On the Insert panel, click the Checkbox Group button.**

   The Checkbox Group window appears (see Figure 12-8).

2. **In the Name field, type a name.**

   This name applies to all the checkboxes in the group, saving you the trouble of typing the name for each checkbox yourself. The name you type is the name the browser submits to your web server, so follow the formatting rules that apply to all form fields: letters and numbers, no spaces or other funny characters except an underscore or a hyphen. (To see how Dreamweaver differentiates checkboxes that all have the same name, see the Note on page 469.) Although each checkbox shares the same name, if someone selects multiple checkboxes, the browser sends the data from *all* the checked boxes to the server.

3. **In the Label column, click "Checkbox" and type in a label for the first box.**

   For example, if you're adding a set of checkboxes so visitors can sign up for one or more newsletters, you might type the name of the newsletter—like "Our Design Newsletter". This label will appear next to the checkbox.

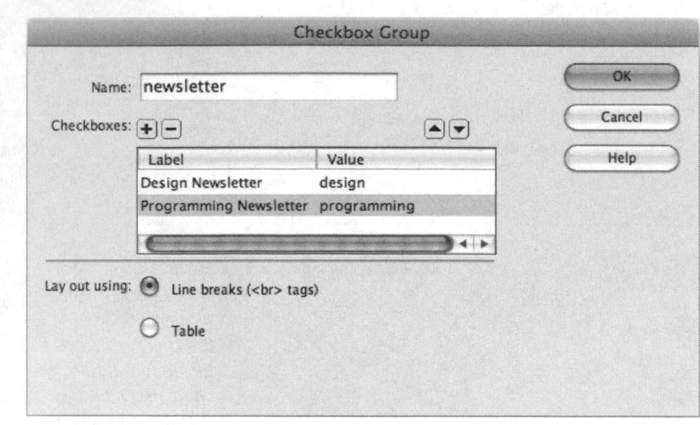

***Figure 12-8:** The Checkbox Group dialog box lets you quickly add multiple checkboxes to a page.*

Note: If you use the Checkbox Group tool, Dreamweaver skips the Accessibility Attributes window (Figure 12-5). You don't have any control over how Dreamweaver inserts the <label> tag; it just wraps the tag around the checkbox–the same as if you'd selected the "Wrap with label tag" option described in step 4 on page 462.

4. **Hit the Tab key to jump to the Value column for that checkbox, and then type in a value.**

   This is the value the browser passes to the web server when somebody selects the checkbox and submits the form—for example, "design" for the "Design Newsletter" option.

5. **Repeat steps 3 and 4 for the second checkbox in the group.**

   You can create additional checkboxes by clicking the + button. Follow steps 3 and 4 for each checkbox you want to add.

6. **Select a layout for the group.**

   Dreamweaver puts each checkbox on its own line. Choose whether you want Dreamweaver to do so using a line break (
 tag) to separate each line or by creating a table with one checkbox per row.

   Don't care for either of these options? Pick the "Line breaks" option—it's easier to modify—and read the Note below.

Note: If you want a group of checkboxes to appear side by side instead of stacked one on top of the other, choose the "Line breaks" option in the Checkbox Group dialog box. Then, with Dreamweaver set to display the invisible line break character (see page 76), click the line break's gold shield in Design view, and hit Backspace or Delete to move the lower checkbox onto the same line as the current checkbox.

7. **Click OK to add the group of checkboxes to your page.**

   The checkboxes and their labels are essentially text (or buttons) on the screen. You can move the checkboxes around, change their labels, and, in the Property inspector, alter each checkbox's properties.

Note: When you insert checkboxes using the Checkbox Group tool, Dreamweaver inserts all the checkboxes with the same name, but gives each a unique ID. For example, if you insert two checkboxes with this tool, you might end up with HTML that looks like this:

```
<label>
<input type="checkbox" name="newsletter" value="design" id="newsletter_0" />
Design newsletter</label>
<br />
<label><input type="checkbox" name="newsletter" value="programming"
id="newsletter_1" /> Programming newsletter
</label>
```

Notice that the two boxes have the same name—newsletter—but, since you need unique ID names to differentiate the checkboxes, Dreamweaver creates them by tacking _0, _1, and so on to the end of each ID.

It's perfectly valid to use the same name for multiple checkboxes—however, keep in mind (and tell your programmer) that the data is submitted as an *array*—a data format common to programming languages that lets you store multiple items under a single name. So, the values of every checked box are sent together in one group using the name you supplied in step 2, but using the unique ID that Dreamweaver added.

Radio Buttons and Radio Groups

Radio buttons, like checkboxes, are simple page elements (see Figure 12-4); they appear either selected (represented by a solid circle) or not (an empty circle).

But unlike checkboxes, radio buttons restrict your visitor to making only a single choice from a group, just like the radio buttons on old cars (or, if you're too young to remember those car radios, like the buttons on a blender). Radio buttons are ideal for multiple-choice questions that require a single answer, like, "What is your income: A. $10–35,000, B. $35–70,000, C. $70–100,000, D. None of your business."

In the Property inspector, set the following options for a radio button (Figure 12-9):

- **Name.** Dreamweaver supplies the generic name *radio* (or radio2, radio3, and so on) when you insert a radio button. Make sure you change it to something more descriptive, and, when you insert a group of related radio buttons, give them all the *same name*. Given a group of radio buttons, your visitors should be able to select only one button in the group. To make sure that's the case, every button in the same group needs to share the same name (although they should have different "Checked values"; see the next bullet point).

If, when you test your page, you notice that you can select more than one radio button at a time, you must have given them different names. (Consider using Dreamweaver's Radio Group object, described next. It acts like a wizard that simplifies the process of creating group radio buttons.)

- **Checked value.** This is the information your form submits to the server when your visitor selects this button. Once again, it doesn't have to match the radio button's onscreen label. If you filled out the accessibility window's ID box (see Figure 12-5), Dreamweaver uses the ID you supplied there as the checked value. If you don't like it, change it here.
- **Initial state.** When you create a radio-button form, you can set a button as pre-checked when the page loads. To do your visitors this timesaving courtesy, turn on Checked for the button that holds the default value—the one they'll choose most often.

  Of course, if making a choice here is optional, leave all the buttons unselected by setting their initial state to Unchecked. However, once somebody *does* select a radio button, only the Reset button (if you add one) can unselect them *all* again (see page 475 for information on creating a Reset button).

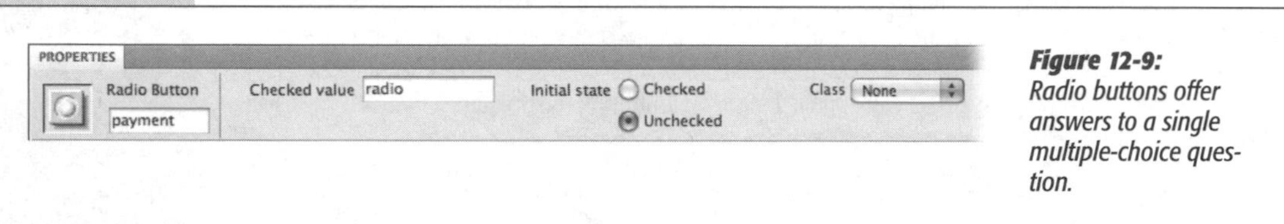

***Figure 12-9:** Radio buttons offer answers to a single multiple-choice question.*

Finally, you should add a text description for the entire group. For example, if you've added radio buttons intended to let a visitor choose how she wishes to pay for a purchase, you'd want to have introductory text such as "How would you like to pay?" There isn't any special HTML for creating a label for an entire group, so you just type this descriptive text next to the radio buttons.

Radio Group

Although you can easily create a group of radio buttons using the Radio Button object, Dreamweaver makes it even simpler with the Radio Group object, a single dialog box that creates a group of radio buttons and their labels in one fell swoop. It works the same way as the Checkbox Group tool discussed on page 467, the only difference being that Dreamweaver inserts radio button form objects instead of checkboxes.

Pull-Down Menus and Lists

While checkboxes and radio buttons both provide ways to offer multiple choices, use them when your form questions offer relatively few answer choices. Otherwise, your form can quickly become overcrowded with buttons and boxes. The beauty of lists and pull-down menus (usually called *pop-up menus* on the Mac) is that they offer many choices without taking up a lot of screen space. (Figure 12-10 shows an example.)

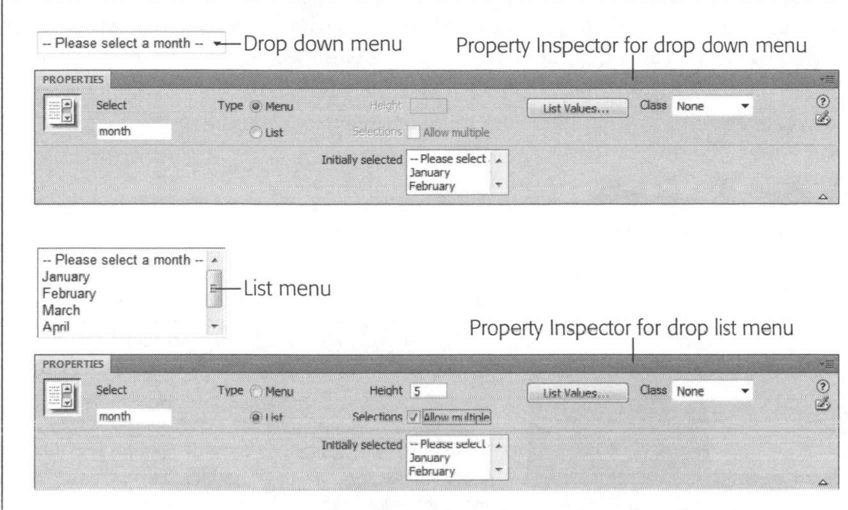

Figure 12-10: *A menu (top) is a single compact line; a list (bottom) can take up any number of lines on the page. Use the first menu or list item to tell visitors what to do. For example, "--Please select a month--" or "--Select One--".*

Once you insert a menu or list object into your document, adjust its settings in the Property inspector.

- **Type.** Menus and lists differ both in appearance and function (see Figure 12-10), as described in a moment. Click the one you want (Menu or List).
- **Height.** In the Height box (available only for lists), type in the number of lines you want the list to take up on the page. That can vary from a single line (in which case you might as well use a menu) to many lines (displaying a number of choices at once). Dreamweaver adds a vertical scroll bar if the height you specify is smaller than the number of items in the list.
- **Allow multiple.** Here's a key difference between menus and lists: If you turn on this option, a visitor can select more than one item from a list, just by pressing the Ctrl (⌘) key while clicking items in the list. (If you do choose this option, tell your visitors that they can select multiple items.)
- **List Values.** This button opens a dialog box (see Figure 12-11) where you type in the items that make up your menu or list. You specify two pieces of information for each item: a *label* (the text that appears in the menu or list on the web page) and the *value* (the information your form submits to the web server, which isn't necessarily the same thing as the label).

  To use this dialog box, type an item label. Press Tab (or click in the Value column), and then type a value, if you like (see Figure 12-11 for details).

Note: A menu item's label isn't the same as the HTML <label> tag discussed on page 477. It's just the text that appears for an item in the menu.

Values are optional; if you don't specify one, the form submits the item's label *as* the value. Still, you'll often find a separate value useful Imagine you've designed a pull-down menu on an e-commerce site so your visitors can select their credit cards' expiration months. Figure 12-11 shows what the items for such a pull-down menu might look like. The menu displays the names of the months, but the form actually transmits the *number* of the month to your form-processing program When a visitor selects "April," the form submits 4.

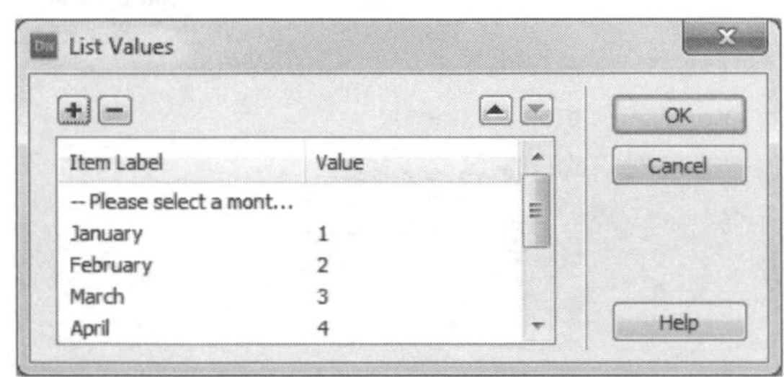

Figure 12-11: *Using the + button, you can add an item to the end of a list; when you click in the list's last item's Value column, pressing Tab creates a new list item. To delete an item, select it, and then click the minus sign (_) button. You can move an item higher or lower in the list of options by selecting the item, and then clicking the up or down arrow buttons. Like radio buttons, pop-up menu and list items always flock together–nobody ever creates just one.*

Computer programs often work more easily with numbers than with names, while humans do the opposite. So when you offer visitors a pop-up menu of products, the label might use the human-friendly name of the product ("Blue Wool Cap"), while the value reflects a model number that your form-processing program readily understands (XSD1278, say).

- **Dynamic values.** Dreamweaver can also create *dynamic menus*, where the menu's labels and values come from a database. This option—available only when you insert a menu into one of the dynamic page types described in Part Six of this book—is great when the menu items change frequently, as they would in a list of employee or product names. Read more about this feature on page 944.

Click OK when you finish building your menu or list. You can always return to this screen and edit the list of options. To do so, in the document window, click the menu or list and then, in the Property inspector, click the List Values button. You return to the dialog box shown in Figure 12-11.

As with other form elements, you can, and probably should, add some explanatory text alongside the menu or list in the document window. One easy method: You can automatically add a label to a menu or list using Dreamweaver's accessibility features as described on page 461.

Note: Styling form fields with CSS can be frustrating. Not all browsers format form fields the same way, and some browsers limit what kind of styling you can apply. For a good introduction to styling form fields, visit *www.456bereastreet.com/archive/200701/styling_form_controls_with_css_revisited*. And for comprehensive coverage, check out the free appendix (164 pages on CSS and forms alone!) from Christopher Schmitt's *CSS Cookbook*: *http://cdn.oreilly.com/books/9780596527419/appd.pdf*.

POWER USERS' CLINIC

Giving Order to Your Forms

If you're not careful, creating forms can quickly lead to visual chaos. The different shapes and sizes of text boxes, radio buttons, and other form objects don't naturally align well with text. One solution: Use tables to control your forms' appearance.

The page designer of the left-hand form below added text boxes directly beside the label on each line, forcing your eye to follow an ungainly zigzag pattern created by the form's text boxes. The result is not only ugly, but hard to read.

In the form on the right, the designer organized the form using a table made of two columns and 13 rows (one row for each question); one column holds the label, the other the text box. Notice that the text next to each form element aligns to the right, creating a clean edge that effectively mirrors the edge created by the form fields.

To make this table-based solution work most effectively, set each text field to the same width, using the *Char Width* property (page 464) or Cascading Style Sheets and the CSS *width* property (page 360).

Add the <form> tag first, insert the table inside the form's dotted red boundaries, and then add form elements inside the cells of the table. If you make a table first and then try to insert a form, Dreamweaver lets you add it to only a single cell of the table. See Chapter 7 for more on creating tables.

You can also use CSS to lay out a form. This technique is a bit more complex, but if you're interested, you can find a good tutorial on CSS-based form layout at *http://articles.sitepoint.com/article/fancy-form-design-css*.

File Field

Receiving responses to checkboxes, radio buttons, and pull-down menus is all well and good, but what if you want your visitors to submit something a little meatier—like an entire file? Imagine a bulletin board system that lets guests post JPEG images of themselves, or upload word processing documents to share with others. They can do just that thanks to File Field (see Figure 12-4)—and a little magic from your web server.

Before you get carried away with the possibilities the File Field offers, you need to do a little research to see whether you can use it on your website. Although Dreamweaver lets you easily *add* a field for uploading image files, text files, and other documents, you need to check your web server administrator to see if it permits anonymous file uploads (some don't for fear of receiving viruses or performance-choking large files). Then, of course, you have to ensure that the program that processes the form actually *does* something with the incoming file—stores it on the server, for instance. Dreamweaver doesn't have any built-in functions that help with this, but you can enlist some third-party solutions as described in the box on page 475.

When you click the File Field button on the Insert panel's Forms category (or choose Insert→Form Objects→File Field), Dreamweaver inserts a text field *and* a Browse button; together, they constitute a single File Field. When you click either one, you highlight both.

The Browse button, once it appears in somebody's browser, opens the standard Windows or Macintosh Open File dialog box, letting your visitor navigate to and select a file to upload.

The Property inspector offers only two settings (other than specifying a more creative name):

- **Char width.** Dreamweaver measures the width of text fields in characters; type *20* in the character width box and Dreamweaver creates a field 20 characters wide.
- **Max chars.** Leave this blank, as explained in Figure 12-12.

You haven't finished the File Field until you add instructions or a label in the document window, something like "Click the Browse button to select a file to upload" (again, Dreamweaver simplifies this task with the Label option in the form's Accessibility window described on page 462).

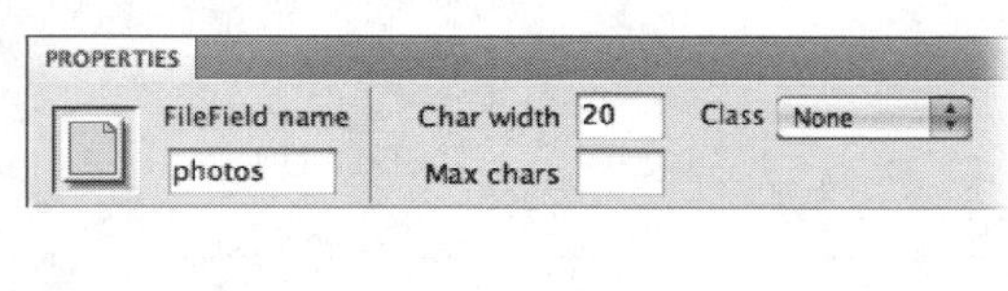

Figure 12-12: *Avoid the "Max chars" field. It's intended to limit the number of characters that the field accepts, but doesn't have any effect on the File Field, which selects the full path to the file regardless of how many characters long it is.*

Hidden Field

Most form elements are designed to accept input from your visitors: click a radio button, type into a text field, and make a choice from a menu, for example. But visitors don't even know about, and don't ever see, one kind of form field: the *hidden* field.

Note: Hidden fields aren't exactly hidden–it's true that visitors don't see them in a browser, but they (and their data) are visible if a visitor checks the page's HTML (using the browser's View→View Source or View Page Source command), In other words, despite their name, don't put anything into a hidden field that you wouldn't want someone to see.

Why, you're probably asking, would you need to submit a value you already know? Because hidden fields supply information to the programs that process forms—information that the program has no other way of knowing. Most web hosting services, for example, offer a generic form-processing program that collects information submitted with a form and emails it to the site's administrator. But how does the program know where to email the data? After all, it's a *generic* program that hundreds of other people use. The solution: A hidden field that stores the information required for the program to properly process the form—like *email=me@mydomain.com*.

To insert a hidden field, click the Insert panel's Hidden Field button (under the Forms category), or choose Insert→Form→Hidden Field. A gold shield icon appears on the page (this is Dreamweaver's symbol for HTML that you can't see in web browsers). Use the Property inspector to give the field a name and a *value*—that is, the value that gets submitted to your form-processing program (in the example above, that value would be your email address).

Note: Gold shields indicating a hidden field appear only if, in the Preferences window's Invisible Elements category, you turn on the Hidden Form Fields checkbox (see page 76), and, in the View menu, you turn on Invisible Elements (View→Visual Aids→Invisible Elements).

EXTENSION ALERT

Adding File Upload Ability to Your Site

Imagine adding a "Job Application" page to your site, where applicants can upload their resumes for review. Or a web-based way for clients to submit graphics files and word processing documents.

Dreamweaver lets you add a File Field to a form, but doesn't provide the tools you need to make this useful feature function on your site. To compensate for that glaring omission, you can turn to extensions that add this missing power to Dreamweaver when you build a dynamic site (described in Part Six of this book). But before you shell out any hard-earned cash on the extensions listed next, make sure your web hosting company allows anonymous file uploads from a web form–some don't.

DMXZone (*www.dmxzone.com/index?3/1019*) offers two fee-based extensions for ASP and PHP. The Pure Upload extension offers many different settings to manage the process of uploading files to a site, including the ability to rename duplicate files and to add file information to databases.

WebAssist (one of the big players in the Dreamweaver extensions market) offers a commercial product, Digital File Pro, for uploading *and* downloading files from a server (*www.webassist.com/dreamweaver-extensions/digital-file-pro*). This extension works for PHP.

Buttons

No form is complete without a Submit button for your visitors to click as a final step (see Figure 12-4). Only then do their responses set out on their way to your form-processing application. People sometimes add a Reset button, which visitors can click if they make an error. The Reset button clears all the form entries, and resets all the form fields to their original values.

To add either type of button, use the Insert panel's Forms category (see Figure 12-2), or choose Insert→Form→Button. If the Accessibility window appears (see page 461), you don't need to add a label, since the button itself has "Submit", "Reset", or whatever text you wish emblazoned across its face, so just click the Cancel button.

The Property inspector controls (Figure 12-13) for a freshly inserted button are:

- **Button name.** The button's name provides the first half of the "name/value" pair that a form sends to your server (see page 453).

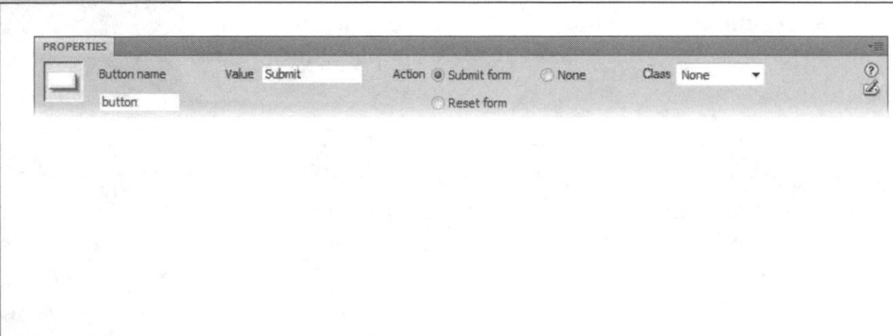

Figure 12-13: *Buttons have just three properties: Name, Value, and Action. Like other form elements and HTML tags, Dreamweaver also lets you apply a CSS class style to improve your form's design.*

- **Value.** The value is the label that appears on the button. Dreamweaver proposes *Submit*, but you're free to substitute *Do It, Make It So*, or *Send my data on its merry way*.

  What your visitors see printed on the button—for example, "Click Me"—is the value transmitted along with the button's name when the form is submitted. This characteristic opens up some interesting possibilities. You could, for example, include *several* Submit buttons, each with a different label. If you create a form for a database application, one button might say Delete, while another says Edit. Depending on which button your visitor clicks, the program processing the form either deletes the record from the database or modifies it.

- **Action.** These three buttons govern what happens when somebody clicks your button. A "Submit form" button transmits the form data over the Internet to your form-processing program. A "Reset form" button sets all the fields back to their original values. (The fields, checkboxes, or menu items aren't left blank or unselected, they return to their *initial* state, which you specified when you created the control. So, for example, if you set the Initial State property of a checkbox to Checked, and your visitor unchecked the box and then clicked the Reset button, the box becomes Checked once again.)

  The Reset button used to appear on nearly every form on the Web; these days it's much less frequent, mainly because it's unlikely that anyone would want to *completely* erase *everything* she's typed into a form. In addition, its presence offers the unfortunate possibility that a visitor, after painstakingly filling out a form, will mistake the Reset button for the Submit button, and click it—erasing everything she's typed. If you do add a Reset button, make sure you don't put it right next to the Submit button.

Note: A Reset button can come in handy on a page intended to *update* information. An update form contains previously recorded information (like the shipping address for your *Amazon.com* account). In this case, a Reset button lets you erase any mistakes you made when you updated your account information. Click the Reset button and the form goes back to displaying the original information. You'll learn how to create an update form for a database-driven site in Chapter 25.

Setting the button's action to None means that clicking the button has no effect on the *form*. "Gee *that's* useful," you're probably thinking. But while the button doesn't trigger an action related to the form, you *can* use it to program one of Dreamweaver's built-in behaviors (see the Chapter 14). The only way to do that is to make the button available for programming by choosing None. This way, you get a common user interface element—the cool 3-D look of a beveled form button—that can trigger any of many different actions, like opening a new browser window or popping up a message on the screen. If you're a JavaScript programmer, you can use the button to activate your own programs.

Note: You can also use a graphic as a Submit button, thanks to something called an Image Field, thus freeing you to be more creative with the look of the button itself. On the Insert panel, click the Image Field button (see Figure 12-2), or choose Insert→Form→Image Field, to select the graphic you want to use as a button. When a visitor clicks the image, it submits the form and all its data. (Image Fields do only one thing: Submit form data. You can't use them for Reset buttons.)

<label> Tag

As discussed on page 462, the <label> tag lets you associate a label with a particular form element, like a checkbox or text field. Of course, you can always place plain text next to a form element on a page. But because a <label> tag is "attached" to a particular form element, it's more helpful in explaining the function and layout of your form to people who use assistive technologies like screen-reading software for the blind.

On the Insert panel's Forms category, the Label tag button (see Figure 12-2) doesn't do much more than switch you into Code view and drop the <label> tag into your HTML. You're much better off inserting labels with Dreamweaver's form accessibility option, as described on page 462. However, there are some cases where you don't want to put the label directly next to the form field; for example, when you use tables to lay out a form, you usually put the label in one table cell, and the form element in another. In such a case, you need to jump into Code view to add a label anyway, and this button can save you a little typing.

<fieldset> Tag

The <fieldset> tag is a form organization tool intended to let you group related form fields. For example, if you create an online order form, you can organize all the "ship to" information—address, city, state, Zip code, and so on—into a single set. Again, this arrangement can help those using assistive technology to understand the organization and intent of a form.

The <fieldset> tag also has a visual benefit. Browsers display an attractive border around fieldsets. In addition, the Legend tag (which Dreamweaver automatically adds whenever you insert a fieldset) lets you identify the fields grouped inside a fieldset with a descriptive label. The legend appears at the top of the fieldset.

To use this tag, select the related form fields. You have to position the form fields next to each other onscreen, and you can organize them within other HTML elements like a table. Then, on the Insert panel's Forms category, click the Fieldset button (see Figure 12-2). In the Label window that appears, type a label (called, somewhat dramatically, a "Legend") for the fieldset, and then click OK.

In addition to displaying the label you type, Dreamweaver creates a simple border around the group of fields you select. Because different browsers display this border differently, make sure you preview the page (F12, or Option-F12 on a Mac) in a recent version of Internet Explorer, Firefox, Opera, and Safari to see both the label and the surrounding border.

Validating Forms

You might get frustrated when you review feedback submitted via a form on your web page, only to notice that your visitor failed to provide a name, email address, or some other critical piece of information. That's why, depending on the type of form you create, you might want to make certain information *mandatory*.

For instance, a form used for subscribing to an email newsletter isn't much use if the would-be reader doesn't type in an email address. Likewise, if you need a shipping address to deliver a brochure or product, you want to be sure that the visitor includes his address on the form.

Luckily, Dreamweaver includes a set of validation options that do exactly this: Spry Validation "widgets." (The term *widget* refers to any of the Spry-based, interactive web page element that Dreamweaver helps you create, such as the Spry Menu Bar, Spry Validation Text Field, and Spry Tabbed Panels.) With a Spry Validation widget, you can display a friendly "Hey, please fill out this box" message when someone tries to submit a form that's missing important information. You can specify that visitors can't leave a particular field blank, or that a field must contain information in a specific format, such as a phone number, email address, or credit card number. If someone tries to submit a form without the correct information, your message appears. And instead of an annoying and amateurish JavaScript error window popping up, Spry form validation widgets display error messages right on the web page, and right next to the faulty form field. You can even change the field's look to highlight a problem (add a red background to the field, for example).

FREQUENTLY ASKED QUESTION

Emailing Form Results

I don't want to store form submissions in a database or anything fancy like that. I just want to get an email with the information from each form submitted. How do I do that?

This common function–available on countless websites–may seem like an easy task, but Dreamweaver doesn't supply a tool to automate the process. Basically, you need a program to collect the data and send it off in an email. Most web hosting companies provide just such a program. They generally work like this: You build a form, set the form's Action property (see page 457) to point to the URL of the server's form-emailing program, and then add one or more hidden fields. The hidden fields contain information that the program uses–your email address, for example, and the URL of the page the browser should load after it submits the form. Since this form-emailing program varies from server to server, you need to contact your hosting company for details.

Many commercial extensions can help you, too. For basic form mailing, the Mail Form extension for ASP and PHP is available from Felix One for $40 (*www.felixone.it/extensions/prod/mxmfen.asp?offset=15*). Two other extensions offer much more advanced emailing features, including the ability to mass-mail newsletters to email addresses stored in a database: WA Universal Email ($99) from WebAssist (*www.webassist.com/professional/products/ProductDetails.asp?PID=134*) works for PHP pages, and DMXZone sells both an ASP (*www.dmxzone.com/go?5578*) and a PHP (*www.dmxzone.com/go?5628*) version of its Smart Mailer extension ($99).

For all these extensions, however, you need to install a program on your web server, and your server has to support the programming language (ASP or PHP)–Part Six of this book has more on server-side programming.

Spry Validation Basics

Spry Validation widgets let you verify input in a text field, a text area, a pull-down menu, a checkbox, or a group of radio buttons. You can make sure a field is filled out, a checkbox turned on, a list selection made, or a button clicked. You can limit input to a specific type of information, such as a date or a phone number, and even limit the number of letters someone can type into a text box.

The basic process for all form validation widgets is the same:

1. **Insert the Spry widget.**

   Buttons for inserting the seven types of Spry Validation form fields appear in three places: on the Insert panel's Forms menu (see Figure 12-2), in the dedicated Spry menu (Figure 13-2), and from the Insert→Form submenu. The initial steps are the same as those for inserting any form field. The Input Tag Accessibility window appears (Figure 12-5), and you follow steps 3, 4, and 5 on page 461.

   If you've already inserted a text field, multiline text box, checkbox, or pull-down menu, you can add Spry Validation to it by selecting the form element on the page, and then, on the Insert panel, clicking the appropriate Spry form button. If you want to validate a text field, select the text field, and then click the Spry Validation Text Field button. You can't add validation to a group of already placed radio buttons, however. To do that, you have to create them as part of the Spry Validation Radio Group widget (page 501).

When you insert a widget, Dreamweaver adds more than just the HTML needed for the form field: It also inserts a <span> tag that surrounds the form field, a label, and additional HTML necessary to display one or more error messages. A Spry Validation widget also adds JavaScript programming (to make sure the form field receives valid information), and CSS (to style the appearance of the field and the validation error messages).

Note: When you save a web page after inserting a Spry widget, Dreamweaver pops up a window letting you know that it's added JavaScript and CSS files to the SpryAssets folder in the site's root folder (see the Tip on page 188).

2. **Rename the widget (optional).**

   Once you insert a widget, you can rename it using the Property inspector (see Figure 12-14). Dreamweaver assigns every Spry widget a generic ID like *spry-textfield1, sprytextfield2*, and so on. You can change this to something more descriptive, but for clarity's sake leave "spry" in the ID name. If you insert a Spry text field to collect a person's email address, for example, you might name the widget *spryEmail*. Dreamweaver applies this ID to a <span> tag that wraps around the actual form field, form label, and error messages that Spry creates. Don't get this ID confused with the ID you assigned to the form field—that's a different tag that requires its own ID. That's why it's a good idea to include "spry" in the new ID you assign to the widget. If this all sounds confusing, then do yourself a favor and don't bother renaming the widget. Dreamweaver can track the IDs just fine, and since the generic name Dreamweaver assigns is never visible on the form, no one visiting your site knows the difference.

3. **Assign a validation requirement.**

   Use the Property inspector to assign the type of validation you want to apply. The most basic form is simply requiring input into the form field. That is, ensuring that a guest's typed *something* in the text box or text area, made a selection from a pull-down menu, turned on a checkbox, or selected a radio button. But each type of form field has additional validation options. For example, you can make sure a visitor fills out a text field with numbers in the correct format for a credit card. The options for each field are discussed below.

Note: Properties for a Spry widget appear in the Property inspector only when you select the widget (as opposed to selecting the form field itself). To do so, mouse anywhere over the form field until a blue Spry tab appears (see Figure 12-15), and then click the tab to select the widget.

4. **Select when the validation occurs.**

   A browser validates form fields as soon as a visitor submits the form. So, when someone clicks the Submit button, the JavaScript in the web page checks to make sure your guest filled out everything correctly. If not, the form does not pass Go and one or more error messages appear, letting the visitor know what went wrong. In fact, Spry tools always validate information when a browser submits the form, and you can't turn this behavior off (that's why, in the Property inspector, the Submit checkbox is checked and grayed out [see Figure 12-14]).

   However, to provide more responsive feedback, you can also check to make sure the form has the right info immediately after your visitor interacts with it. Say you add a text field to collect a visitor's email address, and some wisenheimer types in, "I'm not telling" instead of his email address. You could present an error message—like "This is not a valid email address"—when he tries to submit the form. Or you could display an error message the moment he moves onto the next field. This kind of instant feedback can make it easier for your site visitors: They can immediately see and fix their mistakes instead of waiting until they submit the form.

   You dictate *when* a field is valid by turning on one or both of the Property inspector's "Validate on" checkboxes (circled in Figure 12-14). Dreamweaver lets you validate a form field when the field is "blurred," "changed," or both. "Blur" doesn't mean the field suddenly gets fuzzy; it refers to the moment when a visitor clicks on another field or another part of the page. If you type something into a text box and then click the Tab key to jump to another field, the browser considers the text box "blurred." The same is true if you type into a text box, and then click somewhere else on the page. This blurred state is a great time to validate a text field, because you know the visitor is done with that field.

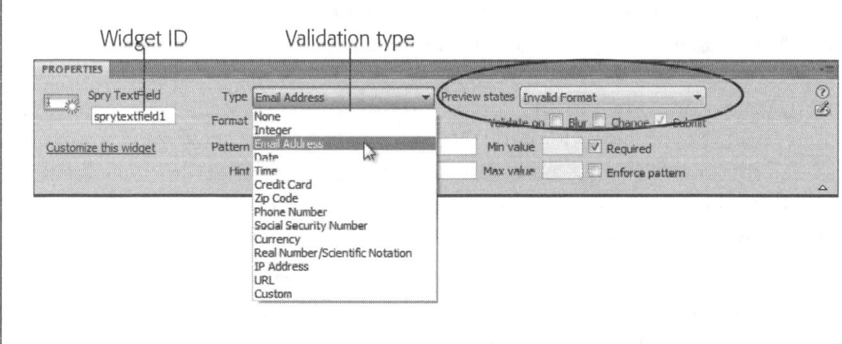

***Figure 12-14:** Depending on the type of form field, Spry Validation can check for different types of input. In the case of a text field, pictured here, Dreamweaver lets you verify that the visitor input text conforms to one of 14 different formats.*

   You can also validate a field when the field "changes." In this case, "change" means anything entered in the field. If someone types into a text field, for example, each letter the person types represents a "change" to the field, so the browser validates the field following each keystroke. This can be a bit annoying, since an error message might appear the moment you start typing. For example, if you validate email addresses, the JavaScript looks for text in the form of *bob@somewhere.com*. So say Bob clicks in the field and starts to type. The moment he hits the 'b' key, he changes the field and JavaScript validates its contents. But since 'b' isn't a proper email address format, Bob gets an "Invalid Format" message. That's a bit rude. In a case like this, the "blur" option is better, since it waits until the visitor finishes filling out the field.

On the other hand, validating a pull-down menu field when it changes can be quite useful. Say you add a pull-down field to a form, and the first option is "Please make a selection". Obviously, you want people filling out the form to select something other than that the initial "Please make a selection" option. Imagine that someone starts to fill out the form, and she scrolls down to an item on the pull-down menu; then, for whatever reason, she changes her selection to "Please make a selection". This option isn't valid, and the browsers should notify her immediately. If you validate the form when it changes, that's what will happen. But if you validate the page when the menu is "blurred," the browser notifies your guest only after she's clicked somewhere else on the page—a few moments later, rather than immediately.

In general, "blur" works best for text fields and text areas, while "change" is better for checkboxes, radio buttons and pull-down menus.

5. **Set other options for the widget.**

   Some widgets have other settings that can come in handy. For instance, with a text validation widget, you can limit the number of letters someone can type into a text area, and you can add "hints", like "Type your name in this box" in the text field of a text field widget. These options are discussed below.

6. **Modify error messages.**

   Preventing incomplete visitor input solves only part of the problem of user input. When a visitor leaves a required field blank, or types incorrect information into a field, you need to let him know what went wrong so he can fix it. Every form validation widget includes one or more error messages. An error message appears next to an invalid form field entry, and different error messages appear under different circumstances. For example, a Spry Validation Text Field left blank displays the message "A value is required", or "Invalid format" if the field isn't empty but has the wrong type of response—a word instead of a year in a "What year were you born?" field, for instance.

   You can customize each of these error messages from the Property inspector, by selecting, the proper "preview state" (see Figure 12-15). After you select a preview state, Dreamweaver changes the display of the page in Design view. In Figure 12-15, selecting "Required" displays the error message that appears if a guest leaves a field blank.

   To change the message, select the text in Design view and type in a new error message. It's generally a good idea to come up with a friendly and descriptive message. If a text field is programmed to accept a date in a particular format, you might change the "invalid format" error message to something like "Please enter a date in this format: 02/27/2011."

Tip: Be careful when you select a Spry error message; you can inadvertently delete it and the <span> tag that the Spry programming relies on. Without that <span> tag, the validation won't work. A good precaution is to select everything up to (but not including) the final period in the error message and then type the new error message.

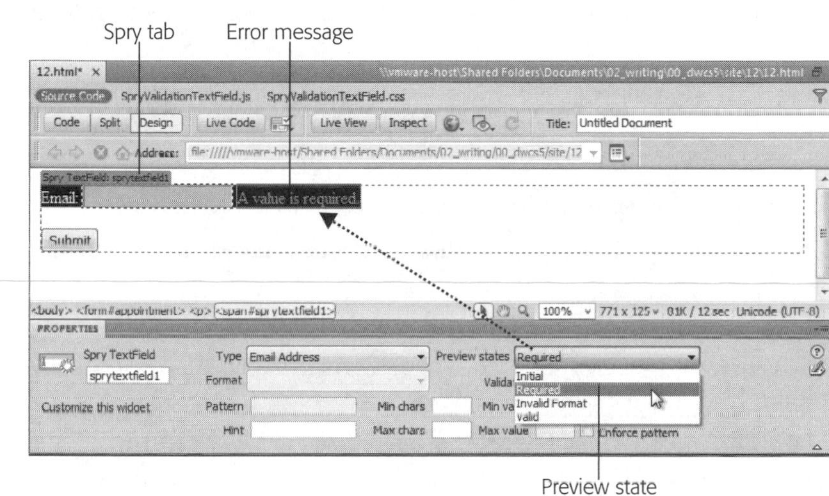

Figure 12-15: *Click the blue Spry tab to select a Spry Validation widget. This way is the only way to display the widget's properties in the Property inspector. If you click the form field (text box, checkbox, or pull-down menu), you see just the regular form field properties, discussed on page 463.*

Most validation widgets have more than one error message, so make sure you preview each of the different "states." Some preview states have no error message, so you're just previewing the page in the selected state. For example, no error message appears when a form first loads, so the "Initial" option in the preview state menu just shows what the form field looks like when the browser first loads the page. Every other widget (except for the checkbox widget) also includes a "Valid" preview state. This is how the form field looks when it receives input. There's no error message in this instance, but the form field's background changes to green. You create this green formatting with CSS, which you'll learn to modify next.

Note: You can change the placement of a Spry form field error message by going into Code view, and then moving the <span> containing the error message—it'll look something like *<span class="textfieldInvalidFormat Msg">Invalid format</span>*. Because each form field can have multiple error messages (for Required and Invalid formats, and so on), there may be more than one <span> element. However, keep in mind that each Spry form widget has *another* <span> that surrounds the label, the field, and the error messages—it looks something like *<span id="sprytextfield1">*. You can move the <span> tags only for the error messages to another location *within* the surrounding widget's <span> tag. If you move them outside that, the error messages no longer work.

Formatting Spry Error Messages and Fields

Spry's error messages appear in red with a red outline. Fortunately, you're not stuck with this factory setting. CSS controls the display of the Spry widgets, and a single style controls the "invalid" error message format. When you insert a Spry Validation widget, Dreamweaver adds the style sheet to the SpryAssets folder in your site's root folder (see page 188). Each Spry Validation widget (text boxes, text areas, menus, and checkboxes) has its own external style sheet. Dreamweaver names the style sheet after the type of widget: For example, the style sheet for a Spry Validation text field is named SpryValidationTextField.css. If you add several types of Spry Validation fields, you have to edit several different style sheets to change the look of the error messages.

Fortunately, you don't have to hunt and peck through the .css file to modify an error message style. By using Dreamweaver's CSS Styles panel's Current view, you can easily identify the proper style, and then edit it. Here's how:

1. **Open the CSS Styles panel (see Figure 12-16), if it's not already open.**

   Choose Window→CSS Styles in either Windows or on a Mac, or Shift-F11 on Windows.

2. **At the top of the panel, click the Current button.**

   The Current view shows the styles and properties that Dreamweaver applies to the selection in the document window.

3. **Make sure you select the Cascade button (circled in Figure 12-16).**

   The Cascade button activates the Rules pane in the middle of the CSS Styles panel. It displays all the CSS styles that Dreamweaver applies to the selection in the order of their specificity—least specific on top, most specific at the bottom (see page 312 for a refresher on specificity). The style that most directly applies to the given selection is listed last.

4. **Select the Spry Validation widget.**

   To select the widget, mouse anywhere over the form field in Design view until a blue Spry tab appears (see Figure 12-15); click the tab to select the Spry widget.

5. **From the Property inspector's "Preview states" menu, select the preview state you want to format.**

   Dreamweaver displays the error message that appears for the selected state. In addition, it displays any formatting it applies to the form field in that state; for example, a text field in its "Valid" state has a green background. You can adjust the formatting of the form field as well.

6. **In the document window, click the error message or the form field you wish to format.**

   The Styles panel displays the style in the Rules pane (see Figure 12-16). Its name is a rather long-winded descendent selector (like *.textfieldRequiredState, .textfieldRequiredMsg*). In addition, Dreamweaver usually lumps together several descendent selectors in a group style (see page 303 for details on group styles). You don't really need to pay attention to the name, however, since you already selected the style you want to edit.

Note: When you format an error message, just click inside the text. Don't try to select the entire message by double-clicking it–if you do, you'll select more than the error message, and the CSS Styles panel won't display the message's style.

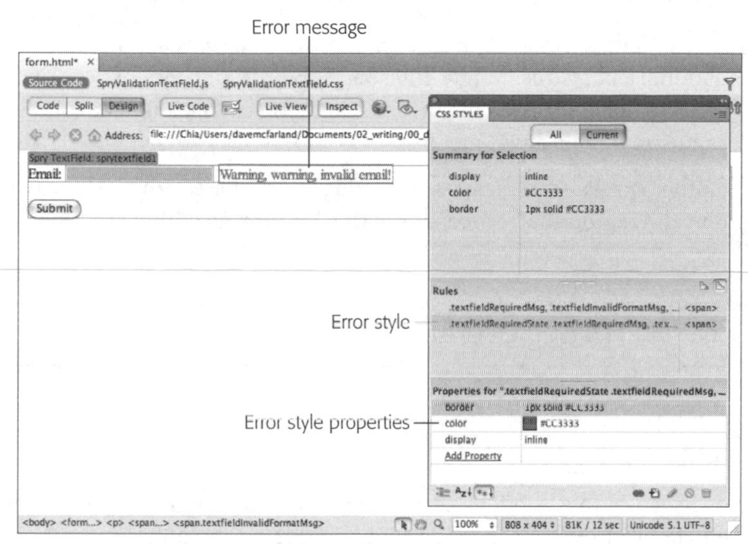

Figure 12-16: *You can adjust the formatting of a Spry Validation error message easily by clicking inside the error message, identifying the style in the Rules pane, and, in the Properties pane, editing the style properties. Or, just double click the style name to open the friendly CSS Rule Definition window.*

7. **Edit the style's properties.**

   You can do this most easily by double-clicking the style's name in the Rules pane; that opens the CSS Rule Definition window, where you can edit CSS properties just as you would any other style, as described on page 124. You can also use the Properties pane for a more rapid edit: To quickly change the text color, for instance (see page 304 for more on how to use the Properties pane to edit and set CSS properties).

Note: Dreamweaver puts Spry error messages inside <span> tags, and displays them inline (meaning on the same line as the form field). If you want to put the error message on its own line, change the *display* property from *inline* to *block* (the tutorial at the end of this chapter includes an example of this trick; see step 15 on page 506).

In addition, you can move the <span> tags containing the error messages, and even change them from a <span> tag to a <div> or <p> tag. The exact tag type doesn't matter–but if you change the tag type (from <span> to <p>, for instance), make sure the class name remains the same. Spry depends on the proper class name to identify the error message. If you move the error message, it must remain inside the outer <span> tag that forms the Spry Validation widget.

A few other styles affect the appearance of Spry form fields, but you can't preview or adjust them using the method just described. For example, when you click in a Spry-enabled text field, its background color changes to yellow; when you click a Spry menu, its background also changes to yellow. Dreamweaver applies these different colors to what's called the field's "focus state"—that's the moment when a visitor interacts with the field. The styles to control these focus states are:

- **Text field focus style:** *.textfieldFocusState input, input.textfieldFocusState*. You'll find it in the SpryValidationTextField.css file.
- **Text area focus style:** *.textareaFocusState textarea, textarea.textareaFocusState*. Located in the SpryValidationTextarea.css file.
- **Menu focus style:** *.selectFocusState select, select.selectFocusState*. Found in the SpryValidationSelect.css file. While Internet Explorer and Firefox let you use nearly any CSS style to format a menu, Safari lets you change only the font family, color, and size of pull-down menus.

In addition, another special style formats text fields and text area boxes when a visitor presses an invalid key on the keyboard (see the Tip on page 491).

Note: Dreamweaver's Live View can also help you style CSS elements controlled by JavaScript (like the Spry Validation widgets). Ppage 394 has more information.

Spry Text Field

Spry text fields have the most options of any Spry form validation widget. Dreamweaver lets you choose from 14 validation types, and lets you control several other settings, such as limiting the minimum and maximum number of characters allowed.

First, decide whether you want to require that your visitor enter information in the field; if so, turn on the Required box in the Property inspector (circled in Figure 12-17). A form almost always requires *some* information (an email address to sign up for a newsletter, for instance). But sometimes you want to make a response optional, such as when you ask for a phone number. In a case like that, you don't want to turn on the Required box, but do want your guest to format the information accurately. That's where validation types come in.

Validation types

To make sure your visitors supply answers in the appropriate format on your forms, you validate the contents of a field. Use the Type menu (see Figure 12-17) in the Property inspector to assign one of 14 validation options:

- **None.** This option is the default setting: no validation. The JavaScript code Dreamweaver creates doesn't inspect the contents of the field to make sure it matches a particular format. Use this setting, in combination with the "Required" checkbox, when you don't care what someone types, just so long as they enter something. You might use these settings to capture the reason a customer wants to return a product, for example.

Note: When you assign any validation option other than "None", Dreamweaver adds an "Invalid Format" error message to the page. You can change this error message as described in step 6 on page 482.

- **Integer.** Use this option to verify that your guest entered a whole number into a field, like one asking for someone's age or year of birth. If someone types in 1.25, JavaScript doesn't validate the field or submit the form; it displays an "Invalid format" error message. (If you *do* want to allow decimal values, use the Real Number option discussed below.)

  If you specify integer validation, you can also assign minimum and maximum allowed values as discussed on page 491.

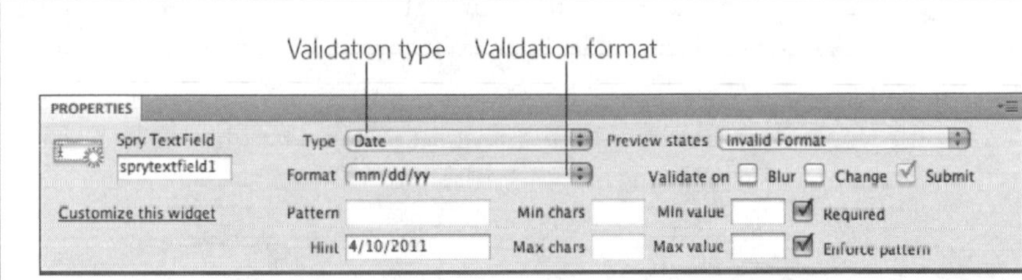

Figure 12-17: *Spry Validation text fields provide multiple options for managing user input.*

- **Email.** This option looks for a validly formatted email address (like *missing@sawmac.com*). It can't verify that the email address is real, so someone could enter a fake address (like *nobody@nowhere.com*), but this option at least makes sure an honest visitor doesn't enter a typo.
- **Date.** When you require visitors to enter a specific date, use this option. If you create a form that schedules the use of a meeting room, for example, you could add a "Date needed" field. Dates comprise a month, day of the month, and year, which can be formatted in many different ways: 12-02-2011, 12/02/11, 02.12.11, and so on. To specify the format you want, use the Property inspector's Format menu (see Figure 12-17).

Note: With date validation, the option *yyyy* means visitors have to enter the full year (2011) to pass validation. However, *mm* and *dd* both allow single-digit values, like 1 for January, or 2 for the second day of the month-guests don't need to enter an initial zero (01 or 02, for example).

You specify the format for a month by *mm*, a day by *dd*, and the year by either *yy* (for just the last two digits of the year: 11) or *yyyy* (for a complete year: 2011).

You should also indicate the kind of separator you want, like a backslash (/) and a hyphen (–), between the month, day, and year values. So, for example, the option *mm/dd/yyyy* means that 1/2/2009 and 12/15/2009 would both be valid inputs, but 1-2-2009 or 12/15/09 would not.

Note: If you'll eventually store the responses from a date form field in a MySQL DATE field, choose yyyy-mm-dd as the format option since it matches the format MySQL uses.

- **Time.** This option validates time entries in one of several formats, such as 12:15 PM or 23:15. You can use it along with a date field to capture the exact time of an event: You could include time fields so guests can specify a beginning and an ending time on a meeting room scheduling form. As with the Date format, Time validation requires that you specify a format using the Property inspector's Format menu. *HH* indicates the hour using 24-hour time—13 for 1 p.m., for example; *hh* is the hour using nonmilitary time; *mm* represents minutes; *ss* indicates seconds; *tt* means before noon and after noon in AM or PM format, and *t* indicates it using just a single letter, A or P.

  So, the HH:MM option validates 13:35, but not 01:35 PM (guests must enter a zero for single-digit hours, minutes, and seconds). The hh:mm:ss tt option requires visitors to format time like this: 01:35:48 PM.

Tip: Whenever you require a visitor to type information in a specific format—12:45 PM, for instance—be sure to include clear instructions. Something like, "Please enter the time you'd like to reserve, using this format: 12:45 PM." You can also take advantage of a Spry text field's Hint setting, as described on page 491.

- **Credit Card.** An e-commerce site isn't much good if you don't give people a way to pay for your products. To make sure visitors enter a validly formatted credit card number, choose this option. If you accept only one type of credit card—like Visa or MasterCard—you can specify it using the Property inspector's Format menu. As with email addresses, the validation checks only that someone has correctly formatted the number—it doesn't actually check to see if this is a real (and not stolen!) credit card.

Note: Be careful if you accept credit card numbers online. An awful lot of responsibility goes along with taking someone's credit card number, including potential liability if the card was stolen, or someone manages to steal credit card numbers you collect. For an introduction to online payment processing, check out *http://particletree.com/notebook/processing-online-credit-card-transactions/*.

- **Zip Code.** To mail a brochure, t-shirt, book, or any other product, you need a Zip code. Use the Zip Code validation format to make sure guests format it correctly. The Format menu lets you specify a Zip code type and country. For example, US-5 means you want to see a five-digit US Zip code, like 97213, whereas

US-9 is the nine-digit US Zip code format, composed of five digits, a hyphen, and four more numbers: 97213-1234. Dreamweaver also offers Canadian and UK Zip code formats, and you can create your own by specifying a custom pattern (see the next section).

- **Phone Number.** The US/Canada phone number format looks like this: (555) 555-1234, with the parentheses, space, and hyphen required. Or, you can define a custom pattern in the Pattern field, as described in the next section. For an alternative style, see page 490.
- **Social Security Number.** This option requires three numbers, a hyphen, two numbers, a hyphen, and three more numbers, like this: 555-12-4888. You might want to avoid requesting Social Security numbers. Many people are reluctant to disclose them for reasons of privacy and fear of identity theft, and by law, they don't have to.
- **Currency.** If you require someone to specify a monetary amount in a field—"How much money would you like to contribute to the home for wayward web designers?"—then choose the currency option to validate their responses. You can choose US or European formatting. US format appears like 1,000.00, while the same value in European format is expressed as 1.000,00. The comma (period for the European value) that indicates a "thousands" position (1,000) is optional. JavaScript considers both 1000.00 and 1,000.00 valid. However, it doesn't accept an opening dollar sign; if a visitor enters $1,000.00 into a currency field, she gets an "Invalid format" error message.
- **Real number/Scientific Notation.** To allow decimal points in a field intended to capture numeric values, use this option. For a serious, scientific audience, this format even allows scientific notation: 1.231e10.
- **IP Address.** Since we all like having people type the unique set of numbers that identify a computer on the Internet, you can make sure a form accepts only properly formatted IP addresses (like 192.168.1.1). The Format menu lets you choose between the current IPv4 and (the newer, not yet fully implemented) IPv6, or both—oh, please, do people really go around asking for people's IP addresses?
- **URL.** Make sure visitors enter proper web addresses using this option. The address has to include the protocol (http://). So *http://www.sawmac.com/* is valid, but *www.sawmac.com* isn't.
- **Custom.** If you're unhappy with the validation options Dreamweaver offers, you can create your own as described next.

Custom validation

If you need to make information entered in a very precise way and none of Dreamweaver's predefined validation types fit the bill, you can create your own custom validation format. Say your company has an internal ID system for employees. Each employee is assigned an ID composed of three numbers, a hyphen, and the first three letters (in uppercase) of the person's last name: like 348-MCF. You can create your own custom validation "pattern" to enforce this format. If a visitor's input matches the pattern, JavaScript considers the information valid and submits the form. If the input doesn't match the pattern, it displays an error message.

A pattern is just a series of symbols that indicate acceptable input; each letter in the pattern has a special meaning that defines the valid character type. AAA means "Accept three uppercase letters in a row as valid."

To create your own custom validation, select a Spry text field widget and, from the Property inspector's Type menu, choose Custom. Then, in the Pattern field, type the pattern you want (see Figure 12-18). Here's a key to the symbols you use to create a pattern:

- 0 means a whole number between 0 and 9. If you want to make sure that someone enters five digits, type *00000* in the Property inspector's Pattern field. This pattern is the same as a five-digit Zip code.
- Type *A* to indicate a single uppercase alphabetic character. The pattern, A0A, for instance, is good for an uppercase letter, followed by a number, followed by another uppercase letter, like U5U.
- A lowercase *a* identifies a lowercase alphabetic character. The pattern *aaa*, then, matches *abc*, but not *ABC*.
- To accept either an uppercase *or* a lowercase letter, use B. The pattern *BBB* matches both *abc* and *ABC*.
- To include numbers along with uppercase letters, use X; the letter *x* matches both numbers and lowercase alphabetical characters. Use Y for a case-insensitive match for numbers and letters. *XXX* matches *B2B*, *BBB* and *123*, but not *b2b* or *bbb*. To match b2B or bb1 use YYY as the pattern.
- Finally, use ? as a kind of wild card. It stands in for any character whatsoever, and you should use it when a character other than a letter or number (like a period, !, or $ symbol) is also valid.

You can include any required symbol, like a period, comma, or hyphen, as part of the pattern. In the employee ID example discussed at the beginning of this section, the pattern to match that format is 000-AAA. In other words, three numbers, a hyphen, and three uppercase letters. To match a phone number like this: 503-555-1234, use the pattern 000-000-0000. To match the MySQL DATETIME format, use 0000-00-00 00:00:00.

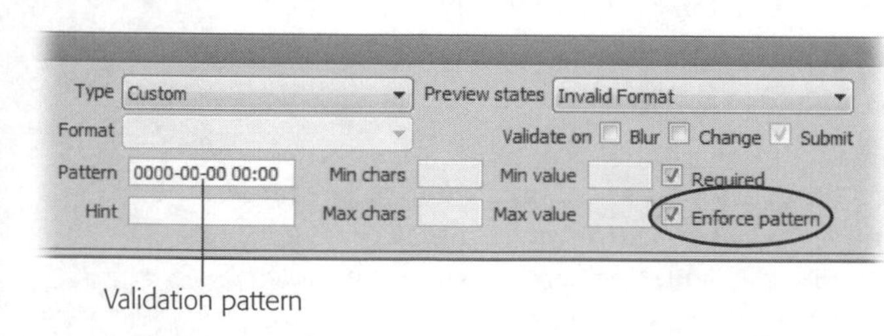

Figure 12-18:
Are Spry's validation types not enough for you? Create your own by creating a pattern that a form field's input must match in order to validate.

Enforcing a pattern

You can make sure visitors can't even type in incorrect characters by turning on the "Enforce pattern" checkbox in the Property inspector (circled in Figure 12-18). When you select this option, JavaScript prevents guests from entering invalid characters in the form field.

For example, suppose you add a Spry text field and set its validation type to Zip code, using the US-Zip5 format. That box can accept only digits, and only five digits at that. If you turn on the "Enforce pattern" option for this field, a visitor could type only five numbers into the field. If a visitor types the letter A, nothing happens. If the visitor types five numbers, and then any other character (like another number or even a letter), that sixth character never appears.

You can choose the "Enforce pattern" option for any validation type except *None*. It even works with custom patterns.

Tip: When someone types invalid characters into a form field that has the "Enforce pattern" option set, any text inside the box flashes bright red to indicate a problem. If you want to change that color, you can edit the styles responsible. For text fields, in the SpryValidateTextField.css file, the style is a group selector named *".textfieldFlashText input, input.textfieldFlashText"*. In the SpryValidationTextarea.css file, a similar style named *".textareaFlashState textarea, textarea.textareaFlashState"* applies to text area fields.

Supplying a hint

When you require a very specific format for a form field, you should provide clear instructions on how visitors should fill it out. You can have these instructions appear next to the label or below the form field.

Dreamweaver also lets you add a short "hint" inside a Spry text field. This hint appears when the form first loads, but the moment a visitor clicks into the field, it disappears; visitors are then free to type in a response.

To add a hint, select the Spry widget, and then, in the Property inspector's Hint field, enter what you want to appear (see Figure 12-17).

Since text fields are relatively short, you don't have much room for instructions. A better use of the hint is an example of the format the field requires. If you want to collect an email address, make the form field hint something like *your_email@your_site.com*. If you're looking for a phone number and use the phone number validation type ("Custom validation"), add a sample phone number example, like this: (555) 555-1234. This lets visitors know that they should include the parentheses and hyphen.

Limiting characters and enforcing a range of values

At times, you may want to control the amount of text someone types into a field. If you create a member profile form as part of your "members-only" website, you might want to collect a person's age—so you want an integer that's at least two numbers long (no babies allowed!), but no more than three numbers long (and no immortals either!). As you've read, you can control the maximum number of characters in a text field with HTML's "Max chars" property (see page 464). However, HTML gives you no way to require *a minimum* number of characters. In addition, setting the "Max chars" property doesn't alert a visitor when she's typed the maximum number of allowable characters.

With Spry text fields, you can set both, using the Property inspector's "Min chars" and "Max chars" fields (see Figure 12-19). Select the Spry widget by clicking the blue Spry tab that appears when you mouse over the Spry text field, and then set the minimum and maximum number of characters in the "Min chars" and, in the "Max chars" fields. You can fill in either field, both fields, or neither field. In the age example above, in the "Min chars" box, you'd type *2* in "Min chars box and *3* in the "Max chars" box.

Each setting has its own error message. You can view and edit by choosing the appropriate state from the Preview States menu (see step 6 on page 482). For example, while the error message for the minimum number of characters reads "Minimum number of characters not met", you can change it to something more descriptive, like "You're too young to join our club."

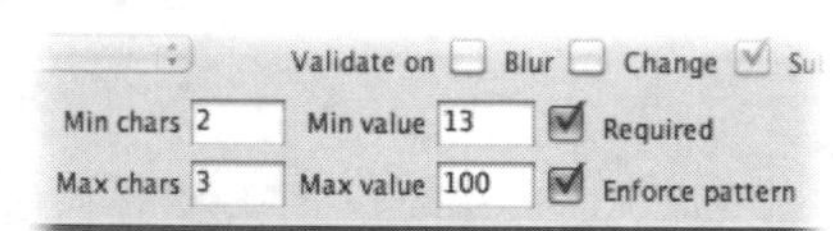

Figure 12-19:
Go ahead, be a dictator. The Spry text field validation widget even lets you control how many characters someone can type into a field.

Some validation fields also let you enforce a *range* of values. If you select the Integer validation type (see page 487), the "Min value" and "Max value" boxes (see Figure 12-19) become active in the Property inspector. Say you include a question on a form that reads, "Please rate our service quality from 1 to 10," and supply a text box for a response. In this case, set the "Min value" to *1* and the "Max value" to *10*; that way, JavaScript won't allow answers like 100, or –10.

You can set Min and Max values for other numeric validation types, like currency (page 489) and real numbers (page 489). These two settings even work with the date and time validation types (page 487). Say you offer rebates to anyone who buys your product before a certain date—08/05/2012, for instance; the online rebate form includes a "Date purchased" field. In this instance, you can choose the Date validation type from the Format menu, select mm/dd/yyyy, and then, in the "Max value" field, type *08/05/2012*. If someone who buys the product on September 15, 2012, tries to claim the rebate, he gets an error message when he fills out the form.

Note: Setting a minimum and maximum value for a text field that uses Time validation works reliably only if you use 24-hour time (like 18:00 for 6:00 PM). If you use one of the formats that requires the AM or PM notation, you can end up with inaccurate results. Spry treats 12:00 PM (noon) as later than 5:00 PM, and 8:00 AM as earlier than 12:00 AM (midnight).

Spry Text Area

A Spry text area has far fewer validation options than a normal text field. You can't select a type of validation or enforce a pattern on the text box's contents. However, the Property inspector does let you specify whether content is required; dictate the minimum and maximum number of characters allowed; and supply a hint that appears inside the text box when the form page loads (see Figure 12-20). (These options works just like those for a text field, described on page 486.)

In addition, you can include a counter alongside the text area that tells your guest either how many characters they've entered (turn on the "Chars count" radio button you see in Figure 12-20), or how many more they *can* enter before they hit the limit ("Chars remaining"). That's helpful if you limit the amount of feedback a visitor can type in; you can include a message like "Please limit your feedback to under 300 letters" and either tally up the number of characters your guest enters or counts down the number of characters to zero (Figure 12-21).

Both of these counters are helpful, but neither gives your guest a context for the number: 300? 300 what? Letters remaining, or letters already typed into the box? To add a clarifying message next to the number, you have to go into Code view. The best method is to select the text area field in Design view; click the Code or Split view button; then look for a <span> tag that looks something like: <span id="countsprytextarea2"> </span>. In this example, "sprytextarea2" is the Spry widget's name. You must add your message either before or after the <span> tag, but not *inside* the tag. The code above could be changed to

```
<span id="countsprytextarea2"> </span> characters remaining
```

for a text area with the "Chars remaining" option turned on. This way, a visitor sees something like "300 characters remaining".

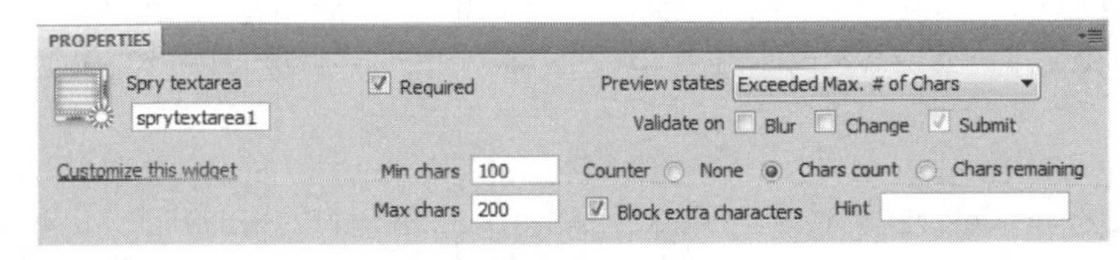

***Figure 12-20:** If you turn on the "Block extra characters" checkbox after you set a value in the "Max chars" field, anything someone types beyond the maximum character limit doesn't appear. HTML gives you no way to limit the amount someone can type into a multiline text box, so this Spry feature offers a nice workaround.*

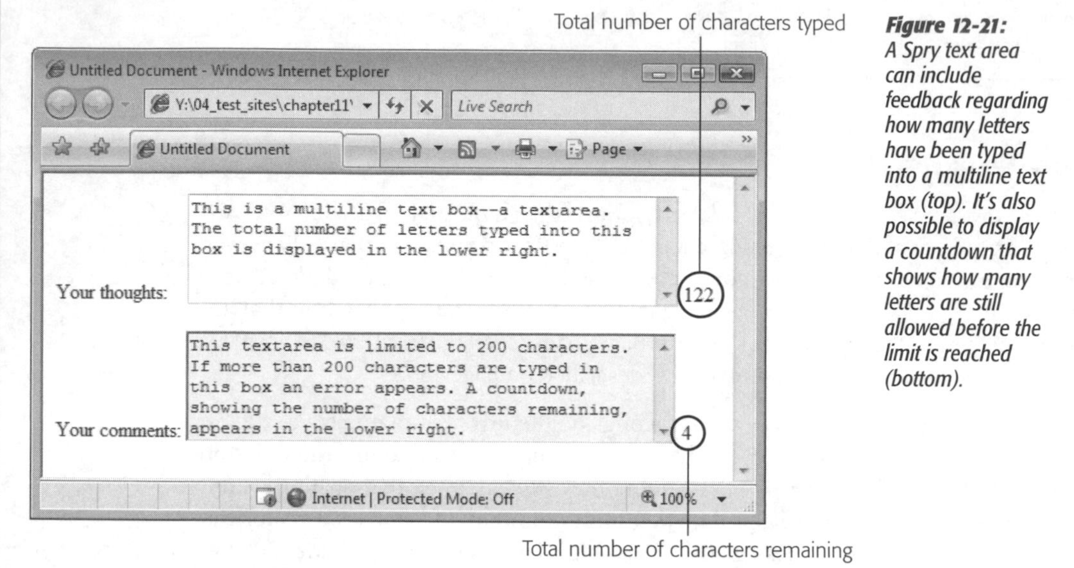

***Figure 12-21:** A Spry text area can include feedback regarding how many letters have been typed into a multiline text box (top). It's also possible to display a countdown that shows how many letters are still allowed before the limit is reached (bottom).*

Spry Checkbox

The Spry Validation checkbox lets you make sure that a visitor turns on a checkbox, an especially handy tool for those ubiquitous "I agree to your rules and conditions" checkboxes. In addition, you can add several checkboxes as a group, and require that your guest select a minimum number ("Please make at least two choices") or a maximum number ("Please choose no more than two") of options.

To add a single Spry checkbox, choose Insert→Form→Spry Validation Checkbox, or, on the Insert panel's Forms category, click the Spry Validation Checkbox button (Figure 12-22). The Spry checkbox that appears on the page already has the "Required" option selected in the Property inspector (see Figure 12-22). If you want just a single checkbox, you're done. But beyond the kind of "You must turn on this checkbox to free us from all legal responsibility" scenario, a single, required checkbox isn't so useful. After all, checkboxes more commonly come in groups as part of a multiple-choice question.

Unfortunately, Dreamweaver doesn't include a simple "Add a group of checkboxes" tool. If you insert several Spry checkboxes in a row, Dreamweaver creates a Spry widget, for each one and JavaScript validates each box separately, rather than as a group. Nor can you insert a bunch of regular checkboxes, select them all, and then apply the Spry Validation Checkbox to them.

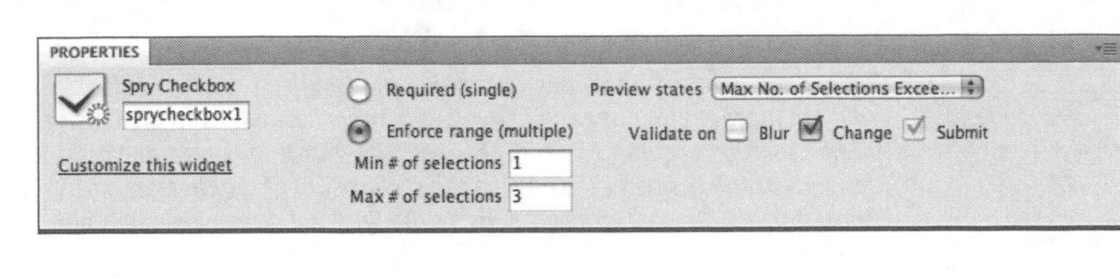

Figure 12-22: *Use the Spry Validation Checkbox widget to make sure your site visitors turn on a checkbox (in cases where you want this to happen, of course).*

To create a group of related Spry checkboxes, you either need to go into Code view or execute a delicate keyboard dance to get all the code just right. If you want to stay in Design view, here's a way to insert a group of checkboxes that JavaScript validates together:

1. **Insert a Spry checkbox.**

   Use either the Insert→Form menu or the Insert bar. Dreamweaver inserts a checkbox with the familiar blue Spry tab. Add a label in the text field to the right of the checkbox. Now, say you want to add another checkbox to the right of the one you just inserted.

2. **Click the label text (see top image in Figure 12-23).**

   In Code view or Split view, Dreamweaver highlights the current label. Your goal is to make sure your cursor is *outside* the <label> tag for the current checkbox. If you simply click to the right of the label and insert the next checkbox, one of two (bad) things can happen: You insert another checkbox inside the first checkbox's <label> tag—when this happens, Dreamweaver gets really confused and omits a <label> tag for the new checkbox. Or, you insert the checkbox outside the Spry widget, meaning the new checkbox won't be validated along with the first checkbox.

3. **Press the right arrow key until the <label> tag disappears from the Tag selector at the bottom of the document window, but you still see something like <span#sprycheckbox1> (Figure 12-23, bottom image).**

   When you no longer see <label> in the Tag selector, your cursor is outside the label and you can insert another checkbox. The <span#sprycheckbox1> identifies the tag responsible for the Spry checkbox widget. As long as you see that in the Tag selector, the next checkbox you insert receives Spry Validation.

4. **Insert a *regular (non-Spry)* checkbox as described on page 466.**

   The cursor is already inside a Spry checkbox widget, so don't insert a Spry checkbox.

5. **Repeat steps 2 to 4 to insert as many checkboxes as you need.**

   You can add as many checkboxes as you want. As long as you insert them inside the Spry widget, they'll be part of the validation process.

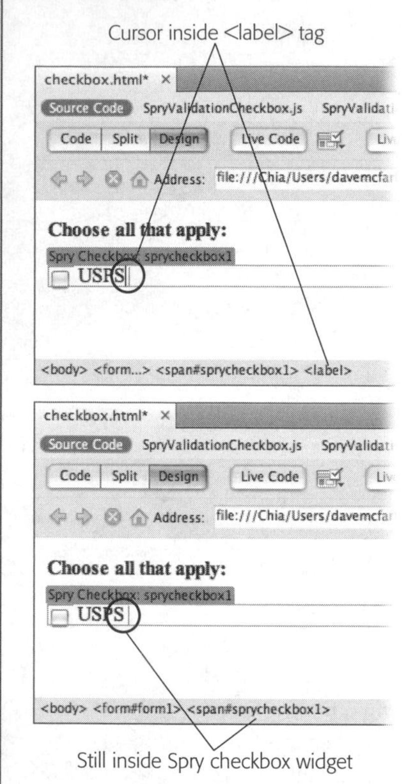

Figure 12-23:
If you want to include multiple checkboxes in a single Spry Checkbox Validation widget, you need to first insert a Spry checkbox, and then insert additional regular (non-Spry) checkboxes. The trick is making sure you don't insert the new checkbox inside the <label> tag of another checkbox (top). But you do want to insert it inside the Spry Validation widget's code (bottom).

Note: If you want to put each checkbox in its own paragraph, change the <span> tag that the Spry checkbox validation widget uses to a <div> tag. According to the rules of HTML, you can't wrap a <span> tag around block-level elements like a paragraph. Go into Code view, locate the opening span tag (it should look something like <span id="sprycheckbox1">), and change *span* to *div*. Then locate the closing tag, </span>, and change it to </div>.

---

6. **Click the blue Spry tab to select the widget; in the Property inspector, select the "Enforce range" button, and then, in the "Min # of selections" and the "Max # of selections" fields, type *numbers* (see Figure 12-22).**

   You don't have to fill out both the Min and Max fields. If you have a question like "What type of food do you like (select as many as apply)", you might choose 1 for "Min # of selections" but leave the Max field blank. This way, you require at least one choice, but your visitor can choose as many other options as she wants.

   Or, you might have a question like "Select your four favorite foods". In this case, you'd type *4* in the Max field if you don't want more than four answers. (You could also type *4* in the Min field if you want to make sure you get exactly four choices.)

Spry Select

The Spry Validation Select widget validates the choices in pull-down menus, and has two options to determine whether or not a selection in the menu is valid (see Figure 12-24). Remember that a pull-down menu (which Dreamweaver creates using the <select> tag) consists of a label and a value (see page 470). The label is what someone sees when he makes a selection from the menu, and the value is what the browsers sends over the Internet when it submits the form.

With a Spry menu, if a guest makes no selection, or if she's makes an invalid selection, you can prevent JavaScript from submitting the form, and have it display an error message instead. Say you have a menu listing all the months of the year. The label is the month's name and its value is a number (see Figure 12-11). Suppose you added "Please select a month" as the first item on the menu. This common technique lets visitors know that the menu's a list of months they should select from. Of course, when the browser submits the form, you want it to send the value for a month and *not* "Please select a month".

Note: Although Dreamweaver inserts a pull-down menu when you add a Spry Validation Select widget, you can convert the menu to a static list, as described on page 470. The same validation options apply.

To make sure this is the case, leave the value for "Please select a month" blank and, in the "Do not allow" section of the Property inspector, turn on "Blank value" (see Figure 12-24).

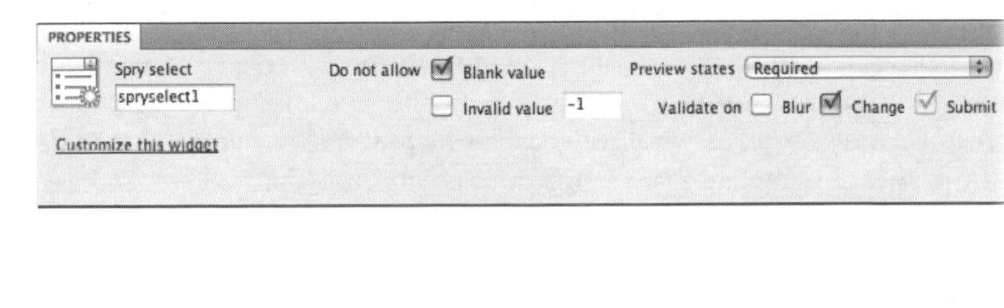

***Figure 12-24:** Clicking the "Customize this widget" link that appears when a Spry widget is selected launches the Adobe Help program, and displays documentation that tells you which CSS styles affect the appearance of the particular widget. You can use this information to edit the supplied widget styles to make them match the look of your site.*

Sometimes a label and a value are the same. For example, on a menu with a list of years ("In what year were you born?"), for example, the label ("1967") is the same as the value ("1967"). In cases like this, it would be frustrating to have to set both the label and value for each menu item. Fortunately, you don't have to. As you read on page 470, a label doesn't require a value, and if you don't specify a value, JavaScript submits the label *as* the value.

If you have a list without values, the "Blank value" validation option won't work. After all, even valid selections (the selected label) won't have a value explicitly set. In cases like this, use the "Invalid value" option in the Property inspector to ensure that the form gets submitted. Here's how you set this option up: First, identify the invalid selection(s). There's just one in the example above, the label at the top of the menu ("In what year were you born?"). Assign an arbitrary value to the illegitimate selection(s). In this case, assign a value of -1 to "In what year were you born?" (see Figure 12-11). Then select the Spry widget and, in the Property inspector, turn on the checkbox for "Invalid value" and enter -1 in the field next to it (see Figure 12-24). Should a guest select "In what year were you born?" from the list, JavaScript recognizes its value as invalid and prevents the form from winging its way to your server. (If this sounds confusing, you'll find a hands-on example in the tutorial on page 512.)

Tip: If your form menu has a long list of options, you might add a separator (like a row of hyphens, ---------) as a label, to demarcate groups of options. You could either forego assigning a value to that separator and use the "Blank value" validation option, or assign it an invalid value (like -1) and use the "Invalid value" setting. In this way, if someone accidentally selects the separator, she can't submit the form.

Spry Password

A password like "sesame," "password," or "bob" isn't very secure. Any hacker with a dictionary (or access to an infinite number of monkeys) can easily infiltrate a password-protected web page, or gain access to someone's personal information. If you ever add a sign-up form that requires someone to come up with a password, use Dreamweaver's Spry Password widget. This helpful tool lets you enforce a set of rules for password names so that visitors don't create easily hacked credentials. For example, you can say that a password must be at least eight characters long, have at least three numbers, and contain a minimum of two uppercase letters. This kind of password-naming strategy means visitors have to come up with hard-to-crack passwords like AB3859kirI.

Note: Use the Spry Password widget only for forms where a visitor *creates* a password. Don't use it for a form where a visitor logs in with an already created password. After all, there's no point in telling a visitor that she needs a certain number of letters or numbers in her password if she already has a valid password.

To add a Spry password field, click the area in the form where you want to add the password field, and then, on the Insert Panel's Forms category, select the

Spry Validation Password button (Figure 12-2), or choose Insert→Form→Spry Validation Password. Then, just as with any form field you insert, the Input Tag Accessibility window opens (Figure 12-5); follow steps 3-5 on page 461 to insert the field.

Tip: If you want to turn a text field in a form into a Spry password field, you first need to make sure the password option is turned on for that field (see page 463). Then select the field and click the Spry Validation Password button in the Insert Panel or choose Insert→Form→Spry Validation Password.

Once inserted, the password field has a blue Spry Password tab, and the Property inspector shows the options for validating the field (see Figure 12-25). Since one of the goals of a good password is to make it hard to figure out, the validation options for the password widget try to enforce a pattern that's essentially a random collection of numbers, letter, and characters. The Min and Max characters options let you specify the length of a password. You can set either or both of these options, but at the very least, you should specify a minimum number of characters—8 is a solid amount—so that no one creates an easily hacked password like 1, A, or A1.

In addition, you can specify the *types* of characters visitors must include in their password. For example, you might decide that passwords should have at least four letters, two numbers, and one special character (like an exclamation point). That rule would make a password like ABCDE38! valid, but wouldn't let someone create a password like ABCDEFGH, or 12345678. You can even dictate that passwords have a certain number of uppercase letters as well, just to mix things up. For example, say you type *6* in the Min letters box; this rule means a valid password needs at least six letters in it. But to make sure there's a good mix of upper and lowercase letters, you could set the "Min uppercase" value to 2, and the "Max uppercase" value to 4. This would mean that a visitor has to include at least a few uppercase and lowercase letters in the password.

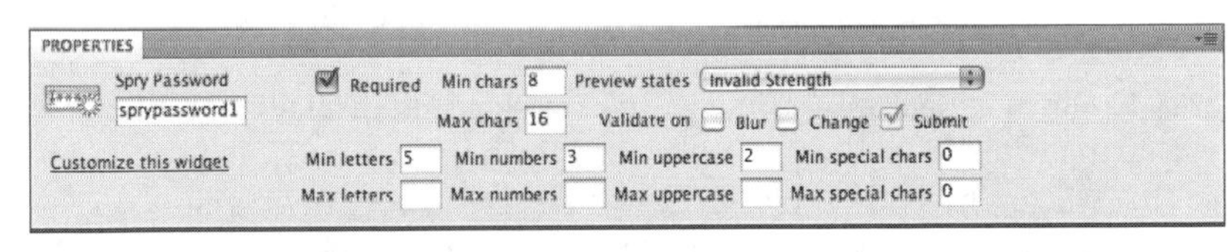

Figure 12-25: *Use Dreamweaver's Spry Password Validation widget to make sure that new visitors creating a password for your site make it suitably random and difficult to crack.*

Depending on which validation options you select for the password widget, you can customize up to four different error messages: the "Required" message, which your page displays when a visitor leaves the password field blank and tries to submit the form; the "Min # of characters" message that appears when you specify a value in the "Min chars" box and your guest creates a password with fewer than that number of characters; the "Max # of characters" message that appears when your visitor exceeds the number of characters in the Max chars box; and, finally, if you set values for any of the other options ("Min letters" or "Min numbers" for example), an "Invalid Strength" message that appears if a guest types in a password that doesn't match the options you set.

The "Invalid Strength" error message that Dreamweaver supplies—"The password doesn't meet the specified strength"—doesn't really tell your visitor what he did wrong. So either change this message to something like "Please type a password that's at least 8 characters long and which contains letters, numbers, and at least one special character, like a period, question mark, or exclamation point" or, even better, provide those instructions on the form to begin with. That way, a visitor won't waste his time trying to decode the runes of your password requirements. (See step 6 on page 482 for instructions on editing Spry form validation error messages.)

Spry Confirm

The Spry Confirm validation widget comes in handy when you want to make sure someone correctly enters important information. For example, if you create a form for people to sign up for your email newsletter, you want to make sure they give you their correct email addresses. One way to do this is to have a visitor enter the same information twice, by adding a second field that asks her to confirm her address by typing it again.

Tip: You can also use this double-checking maneuver with a "Create a password" field. Remember, a password field (see page 464) displays what the visitor types as dots or asterisks, so it's easy to make a mistake without ever realizing it. Adding a second, confirmation field can help make sure the visitor gets it right.

The Spry Confirm widget works only with text fields, and displays an error message if the value in the text field doesn't match the value in another text field on the page. To use this widget, first add a text field—either a Spry text field, a Spry password field, or just a regular text field. That field is the original "Type your email" or "Create a password" box. Next, from the Insert Panel's Forms category, add the Spry Confirm widget (Figure 12-2), or choose Insert→Form →Spry Validation Confirm. (It's best to put this field directly after the original field, and use a label like "Please confirm your password".)

The options for a Spry Confirm widget are simple (see Figure 12-26). From the "Validate against" menu, simply select the name of the field you're comparing. For example, say you add a Spry Password validation widget, and you named that field *password1*. When you insert the Spry Confirm field, in the Property inspector's "Validate against" menu, select *password1*. Then, when someone fills out the form, she must type a password in the password1 field. That password becomes *password1*'s value. Then, in the confirmation field, she types the same password. The Spry Confirm widget compares the two values. If they're different, the widget displays an error message, letting the visitor know she made a typo.

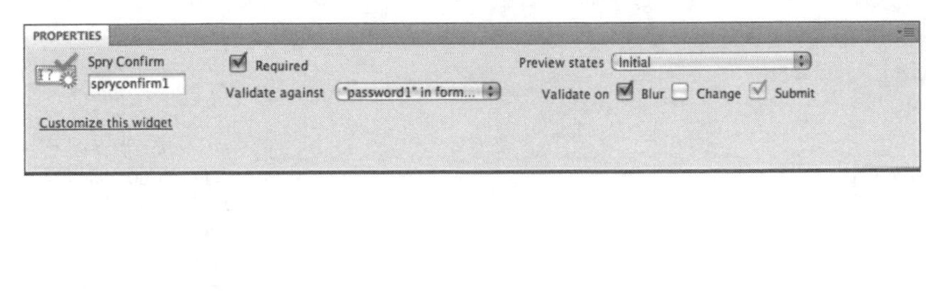

Figure 12-26: *If the field you're comparing against is required, then make sure the "Required" box is turned on for the confirmation field as well. Since the information is so important that you need a second field to confirm it, odds are that it's required anyway, so you almost always leave the Required box checked.*

Spry Radio Group

Sometimes you want to make sure a radio button is selected before a browser submits a form. For example, say you have an e-commerce site and you collect shipping information from a customer. For the shipping method, you want the customer to select either USPS, FedEx, or UPS. Since visitors have to choose a delivery method in order for you to ship a package, it's a good idea to make sure they click one of the radio buttons before submitting the form. This is where the Spry Radio Group comes in handy. Essentially, it's just like the radio group described on page 470, except that it displays an error message if a guest tries to submit a form without a button selected.

To add a Spry Radio Group, use the Insert panel's Forms category or choose Insert→Form→Spry Validation Radio Group. The process is the same as inserting a regular radio group or a checkbox group. Once you add the group of buttons to a page, use the Property inspector to set the validation options (see Figure 12-27). Dreamweaver gives you several ways to validate a radio group, but only one is really useful: The "Required" checkbox simply means that a radio button must be selected (and it doesn't matter which one).

The other two options—Empty Value and Invalid Value—produce error messages should a visitor selects a radio button that you specify. In either of the boxes beside these options, enter the same value you used when you created the buttons. If a guest selects a button with the specified value, he sees one of two error messages when he tries to submit the form. In the case of Empty Value, the error message tells the visitor that he *hasn't* made a selection (huh?); and for the Invalid Value, the error message announces that the choice he made was invalid. Neither of these options seem like they would ever be useful: After all, do you really want to display an error message when someone clicks a radio button that says, in effect, "Ha, ha, you fool, you just released the hounds!"

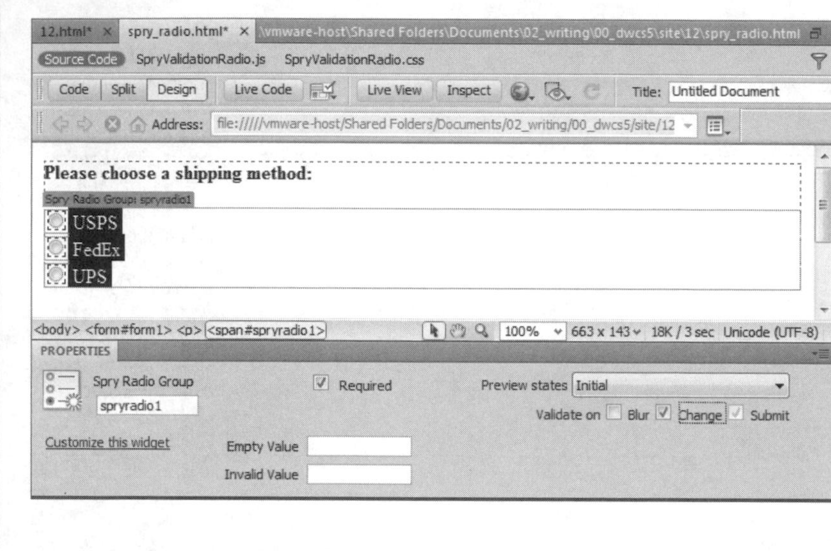

Figure 12-27: *The Spry Radio Group's Property inspector's only useful validation option is Required, which makes sure that site visitors select a button within a group of radio buttons. The Empty and Invalid Value boxes are just plain silly—even Adobe's online documentation doesn't provide a good use for these options. If you come up with one, send an email to missing@sawmac.com.*

Forms Tutorial

In this tutorial, you'll build a simple appointment sign-up form for *the Chia Vet* website (see Figure 12-37). To make sure the folks at Chia Vet get the right information, you'll use the Spry form validation tools.

Note: You'll need to download the tutorial files from *www.sawmac.com/dwcs5/* to complete this tutorial. See the Note on page 45 for more details.

Once you download the tutorial files, open Dreamweaver and define a new site as described on page 37. Name the site *Forms*, and then select the Chapter12 folder (inside the MM_DWCS4 folder). (In a nutshell: Choose Site→New Site. In the Site Definition window, type *Forms* into the Site Name field, click the folder icon next to the Local Site Folder field, navigate to and select the chapter12 folder, and then click Choose or Select. Finally, click OK.)

Insert a Form and Add a Form Field

The first step in building a form is inserting a <form> tag. This tag encloses all the fields within the form, and indicates where the form begins and ends. As noted earlier in this chapter, you can insert other HTML elements, too, like text elements and <div> tags.

1. **Choose File→Open; click the Site Root button (at the bottom-left of the open file window). Double-click the file *appointment.html* to open it.**

   If you have the Files panel open (Window→Files), just double-click *appointment.html* in the panel. The page is partly designed, with a banner, sidebar, and footer.

2. **Click the empty white space directly below the paragraph that begins with "Make an appointment with *Chia-Vet.com* 24 hours a day." On the Insert panel, select the Forms category (see Figure 12-2).**

   The Insert panel shows you the Forms icons you need.

3. **Click the Insert panel's Form button (see Figure 12-28), or choose Insert→Form→Form.**

   A red, dashed rectangle appears in the document window, indicating the boundaries of the form.

4. **In the "Form ID" field of the Property inspector, replace form1 with *appointment* (see Figure 12-29).**

   You just added an ID to your form.

5. **In the Action field, type *http://chia-vet.com/make.php*.**

   As shown in Figure 12-29, leave off the period after the URL in the sentence above (we had to add it to make our copy editors happy).

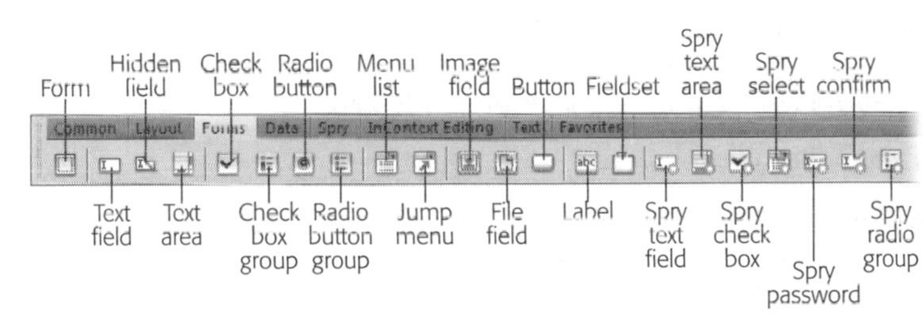

Figure 12-28: *When you choose the "Classic" workspace layout as described on page 35, the Insert panel (pictured in Figure 12-2) becomes the Insert bar and moves out of the right hand panels. Click the "Forms" tab displays all of the Form objects. If you're monitor is big enough, the classic view is usually the better way to go—moving the Insert panel makes the panels on the right side of the monitor less crowded.*

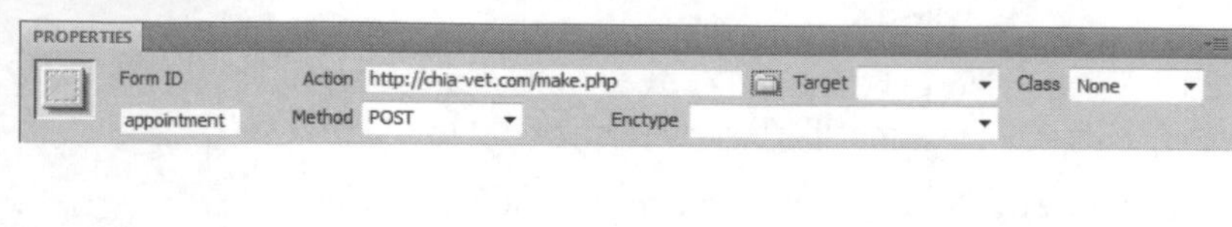

***Figure 12-29:** The Action property of a form is simply a URL pointing to the program that processes the form.*

A form's Action property identifies the address of the program that processes the form's submitted data. In this case, you've been spared the effort of writing (or hiring a programmer to write) the required form-processing software. Such a program already exists on the website whose address you've just specified, and it's waiting to process the form you're about to design.

You may be creating your own form-processing programs if you're using Dreamweaver's dynamic web-building tools described in Part Six. See the tutorial on page 949 for an example.

6. **In the Method menu, make sure you see POST selected. Leave the Target and Enctype fields blank.**

   The Method specifies how a form sends information to a form-processing program and the POST option is the most common (see page 458).

   Now you're ready to insert a text field.

7. **In the document window, click inside the form—anywhere within the red dashed lines. On the Insert panel, click the Text Field button (see Figure 12-28 or Figure 12-2) or choose Insert→Form→Text Field.**

   Dreamweaver displays the Input Tag Accessibility window (see Figure 12-30). If you don't see it, choose Edit→Undo to remove the Text Field you just entered; use the Preferences window to turn on the accessibility options for form objects as described in Figure 12-5; and then repeat this step.

8. **In the ID box, type *clientName*.**

   The widget adds the name you type to both the *name* and *ID* properties of the field's HTML. The form-processing program uses the *name* property to connect an ID with the value a visitor types in. In this case, when a client types his name into the text field, the form-processing program receives information (*clientName=Bob*, for instance) in what's called a name/value pair (see page 453).

   The ID uniquely identifies the form element. If you want, you can create an ID style to format this particular form field—for example, to assign a width or background color to this one field. Next you'll add the text label that appears along with the text field on the web page.

9. **In the Label box, type *Your name* and select "Attach label tag using 'for' attribute"; then select the "Before form item" button.**

   The window should now look like the one in Figure 12-30.

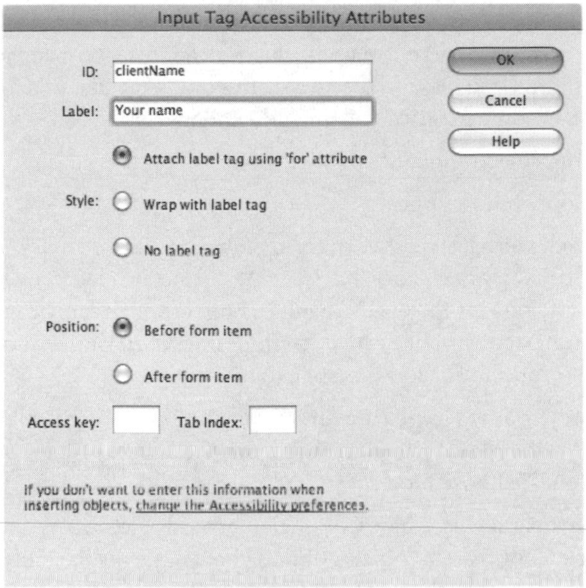

Figure 12-30:
The Input Tag Accessibility Attributes window gives you a great way to quickly insert a bunch of form-related HTML.

10. **Click OK to insert the text field.**

    The label and text field appear side by side on the page. The label's text is wrapped inside the HTML <label> tag (page 477). Your first order of business is to dictate how wide you want the field to be.

11. **Click inside the newly inserted field (the box on the page); in the Property inspector's "Char width" field, type *35*.**

    This action defines the box's onscreen width in characters, so this box displays up to 35 letters (though a visitor can actually type in more than 35 letters, as described on page 464).

    Now it's time to add some style.

12. **Make sure you have the CSS Styles panel open (choose Window→ CSS Styles); on the Styles panel, click the + button to create a new style.**

    Alternatively, you can choose Format→CSS Styles→New. Either way, the New CSS Style window opens. (If you need a refresher on creating styles, see page 113.)

13. **If it's not already selected, choose Compound from the top menu. Delete whatever is currently in the Selector Name box, and type in *#appointment .question*.**

    #appointment .question is a descendent selector (page 113) that contains a new class style named *.question*. The point of this style is to let you create a unique look for each label in this particular form. The formatting you're about to assign applies only to an element with the *.question* class applied to it that also happens to be inside *another* tag with an ID of *appointment*. Since, in step 4 above, you gave the form itself the ID *appointment*, this style applies only to tags with the *.question* class that are inside this form. If you want to use this style on other forms, you can simply create a class style named *.question* and use it throughout the site. But in this instance, you want to create a distinct look for just this form (and you also want to get some practice creating descendent selectors).

14. **From the bottom menu, select "global.css"; click OK.**

    The CSS Rule Definition window appears.

    This page already has an external style sheet named global.css. In fact, it has several style sheets—one for a Spry navigation bar (page 184), one for a Spry collapsible menu (page 534), and one for the page's layout (using one of Dreamweaver's CSS layouts, described on page 344.) The *global.css* file defines the basic format for the pages on the site, so you should add this style to it.

15. **In the Rule Definition window's Type category, from the Font-weight menu, choose bold; then select the Block category, and, from the Display menu near the bottom of the window, choose block.**

    The block option formats a tag as a block-level element—it adds a line break above and below the element. You use this option to change the display of a tag that would normally appear "inline" (side by side) with other elements. For example, the <label> tag is an inline element and, in the form you're working on, the label "Your name" appears directly to the left of the text field. By applying this style, with its *block* format, to that label, you force the label to appear above the field. Positioning the label this way isn't any kind of requirement for forms; it's just a design choice to make the form more readable.

    Next, you'll add a border above the label to visually separate it from the element above it.

16. **Select the Border category, and turn off the three "Same for all" checkboxes. From the Top Style menu, choose "dashed"; in the top Width box, type *1*; and then, in the top Color box, type *#9BBF13*.**

    Finally, you'll add a bit of padding to separate the border and the label. You'll also add a top margin to create a bit more space between form elements.

17. **Select the Box category. Turn off the two "Same for all" checkboxes and, in the Padding's Top box, type *5*; in the Top Margin box, type *15*. Click OK to complete the style.**

    Because this is a class style, you must apply it manually.

18. **In the document window, click anywhere inside the label "Your name". In the Tag selector, click <label> (circled in Figure 12-31) to select the label tag; in the Property inspector, make sure the HTML button is selected, and then, from the Class menu, choose question (see Figure 12-31).**

    The form field drops below the label. Next you'll add a field to collect the patient's name.

Note: After step 17, you might be wondering why you didn't just create a tag style for the <label> tag, instead of a class style that you had to manually apply to the tag. Good question. In some cases you can, but if you add checkboxes or radio buttons to a form, you can't always go that route. That's because these form fields usually have their own label (the text that appears next to it)–for example, "Select a shipping method" or "Pick your 4 favorite fruits". That text isn't in a <label> tag since it's not associated with any single form field. So creating a class style–*.question*–lets you apply the same CSS style–and therefore the same format–to different types of tags.

19. **In the document window, click to the right of the text field you added in the last part of this tutorial. Hit Enter (Return) to create a new paragraph.**

    The form field drops below the label. Next, you'll add a form field to collect the name of the Chia pet.

20. **On the Insert panel, click the Text Field button (see Figure 12-28 or Figure 12-2) or choose Insert→Form→Text Field. Repeat steps 8-11 to insert this new field. Type patient for the field ID, and Your Chia Pet's Name for the label.**

    You've added a second text field—now it's time to add a little style.

21. **Repeat step 17 to apply the question class to the new field's label.**

    So much for regular text fields; now it's time to add a little Spry Validation.

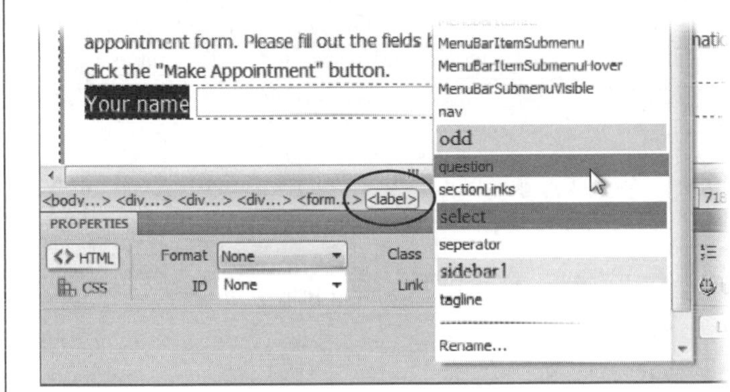

Figure 12-31: *The Tag selector and the style menu are a great one-two punch for precisely applying a CSS class style to any tag.*

Adding a Spry Validation Text Field

Next up for this form: a phone number field. The vets at Chia Vet need a way to contact clients in case they have to reschedule an appointment, so it's important that clients fill in this field. In addition, you want to make sure the customer doesn't mistype and enter too few or too many numbers. A Spry Validation text field is the perfect solution.

1. **In the document window, click to the right of the text field you added in the last part of this tutorial. Hit Enter (Return) to create a new paragraph. On the Insert panel's Forms tab, click the Spry Validation Text Field button (see Figure 12-28 or Figure 12-2).**

   Alternatively, you could choose Insert→Form→Spry Validation Text Field. Either way, the Input Tag Accessibility window appears just as it does when you're inserting a regular text field. You fill it out the same way, too.

2. **In the ID field, type phone; in the Label field, type Your phone number; make sure the "Attach label tag using 'for' attribute" and the "Before form item" radio buttons are selected (they should be); and then click OK to insert the text field.**

   A new text field and label appear. A blue tab also appears, identifying this field as a Spry widget. If you look at the Property inspector, you see all the properties available for Spry Text Fields. You'll choose a few options in a minute, but first you'll format this field like the one you inserted earlier.

3. **Repeat step 11 on page 505 to set the Char width of the new field to 35.**

   The label also needs some formatting.

4. **Repeat step 18 on page 506 to format the "Your phone number" label.**

   When you use the Property inspector's style menu to apply the *question* class, you see a whole bunch of new classes listed. Those classes come from another external style sheet that Dreamweaver quietly attached to this page after you inserted the Spry form field.

5. **Choose File→Save.**

   Dreamweaver opens the Copy Dependent Files dialog box, letting you know the page now requires both a style sheet file and a JavaScript file for the new Spry Validation field.

6. **Click OK to close the Copy Dependent Files window.**

   If you look at the Files panel (Window→Files), then you see a folder named SpryAssets where Dreamweaver just saved the two new files (see the Note on page 480 for an explanation). You see other files in there as well, for two other Spry widgets on this page—a Spry menu bar (page 184) and a Spry Collapsible panel (discussed in the next chapter on page 534).

7. **Move your mouse over the phone form field in Design view; click the blue Spry tab when it appears.**

   The Property inspector displays the Spry field's properties (see Figure 12-31). Now you'll assign a validation type to this widget.

Note: Dreamweaver automatically creates an ID for the Spry widget. The Spry widget you just inserted has an ID *sprytextfield1*. You can change the ID to something more descriptive like *spryPhone*, but you don't have to. The name doesn't ever appear on your web page; the Spry programming uses it to identify this particular validation widget.

8. **From the Property inspector's Type menu, select Phone Number, and then turn on the Blur checkbox (see Figure 12-31).**

   The Type menu defines the type of information the widget allows in the field. In this case, only a validly formatted US or Canadian phone number works. The Blur box determines when the widget validates the contents of the field. For example, if a visitor types "not telling" into the field and presses the Tab key to jump to the next field, he receives an error message.

   If you look at the document window now, you see that the phone field has a red background and a red "Invalid format" message to the right of it. Every Spry Validation field has several "preview" states. You can preview the field at the various points a visitor interacts with the field—for example, when she's typed invalid information, or simply left a required field blank. You'll tweak this error message now.

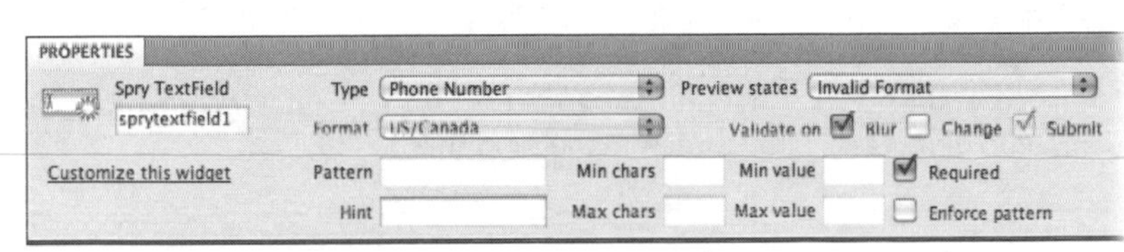

Figure 12-32: *Select a Spry Validation widget in the document window, and then use the Property inspector to assign validation options.*

9. **In the document window, replace the text "Invalid format", and type *Format the # like this: (555) 555-1212.***

   The Spry Validation widget requires that guests enter a phone number in a specific format—(555) 555-1212—so it's helpful to tell visitors what it is in the error message. Now, when some wise guy types "xxxxxxxxx," (or some innocent person types 555-555-5555), he gets an error message telling him how to format the number. An error message also appears if a guest leaves the field blank. You can adjust this message as well, but first you have to switch to a different "preview state."

Note: When you replace the error message in step 9, don't delete the "Invalid format." message before you type in the new message. If you do, you actually delete the <span> responsible for making the error message work. Just select the text "Invalid format" (without the period), and then type in the new error message. As an added precaution, select all the text except for the period after the words "Invalid format." It's not common, but occasionally if you select all of the text, Dreamweaver actually deletes the <span> tag as well.

---

10. **Click the blue Spry tab again; from the Property inspector's "Preview states" menu, select Required.**

    A new error message appears: "A value is required." This message appears when visitors leave the field blank and try to submit the form.

11. **Repeat step 9, replacing the "A value is required" with "We need your number to contact you."**

    The red outline surrounding the error message doesn't fit the look of *Chia-Vet.com*. Fortunately, you can easily update the look of a Spry widget.

12. **Click anywhere inside the error message text you added in the last step; make sure you have the CSS Styles panel open (Window→CSS Styles). At the top of the panel, select the Current button, and make sure the Cascade button is selected (circled in Figure 12-33). Alternatively, click CSS in the Property inspector and then click the Edit Rule button.**

    A long-winded group selector (page 303), made up of a bunch of descendent selectors (page 298) controls the error message's styling. The style you want is the last one listed in the Styles panel's Rules pane; it begins with "*.textfieldRequiredState .textfieldRequiredMsg*" (the middle pane in Figure 12-33).

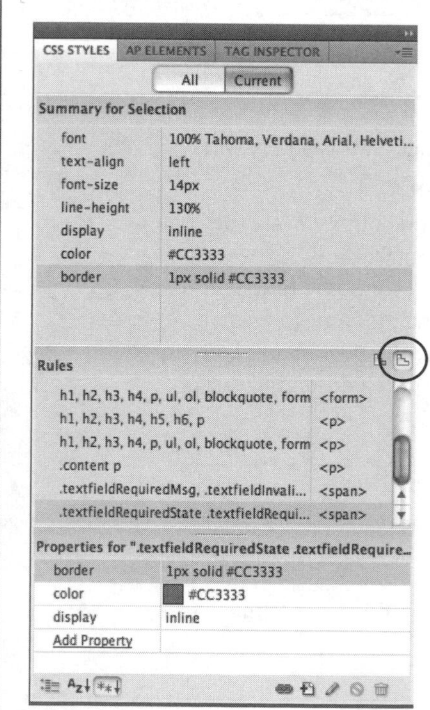

Figure 12-33: *When formatting Spry widgets, you can most easily use the CSS Styles panel's Current view. If the Cascade button is selected (circled), then you merely need to click the element whose style you want to change. In this case, selecting the error message for a Spry Validation Text field highlights the appropriate style's name. Double-click the name to open the CSS Rule Definition window, and style away!*

13. **In the Rules pane, double-click the style beginning with "*.textfieldRequired-State .textfield-RequiredMsg*" to open the CSS Rule Definition window.**

    You'll make the error message bold and remove the border.

14. **In the Rule Definition window, from the "font-weight" menu, choose "Bold". Click the Border category, and then delete the contents of the top row of boxes.**

    Deleting the contents of the type, width, and color boxes removes the border entirely.

15. **Click OK to complete the style.**

    Notice that the error message next to the Spry form field is bold, but no longer has a border. Time to insert another form field.

    Repeat steps 1–4 to add another Spry text validation field. Use the ID *date*, and, for the label, type *Please specify the date you'd like.*

    Make sure you click to the right of the phone number widget's error message before hitting Return to insert the new field.

    This field collects the day, month, and year of the appointment. Since you want to make sure you receive properly formatted dates, add that validation option next.

16. **Select the Spry widget by moving your mouse over the new field, and then click the blue "Spry TextField" tab. In the Property inspector, choose Date from the Type menu, and then choose "mm/dd/yyyy" from the Format menu.**

    You just specified that visitors need to enter a date in a format like "9/22/2009". If they don't, they get an error message. Of course, people filling out this form might not know that, so you should give them a hint. And while you're at it, make sure that the validation check occurs the moment a visitor exits the form field.

17. **In the Hint box of the Property inspector, type *3/22/2011* and then select the Blur box.**

    The Property inspector should now look like Figure 12-34. Time to change the error message.

18. **From the "Preview states" menu in the Property inspector, select "Invalid Format". On the web page, change the text "Invalid format" to "Please enter a date."**

    Notice that the error message shares the same style as the one you added for the phone number; that's because you modified the look of error messages for *all* Spry text fields in step 14. Now, you just need to make the label and field match the others in this form.

19. **Repeat step 11 on page 505 to set the width of the field and step 18 on page 506 to format the label.**

    Dreamweaver supplies Spry widgets for other types of form fields as well. You'll add a Spry Form Menu next.

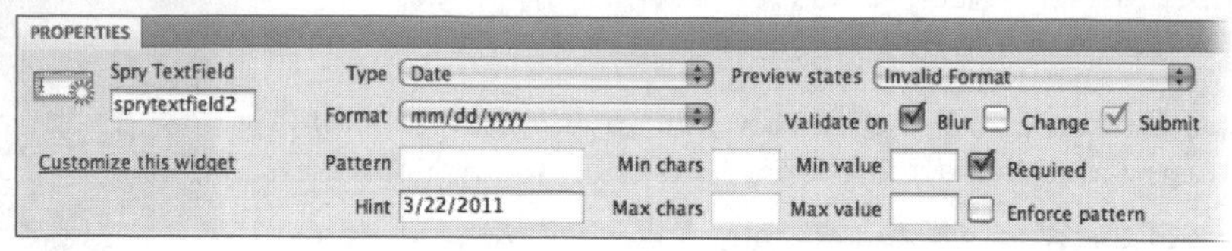

***Figure 12-34:** You have many different ways to type a date—12/31/2009 or 12.31.2009, for example—so if you use the Spry text validation widget to collect a date, you should always provide a hint or other instruction that tells visitors how they should correctly type that date.*

Adding a Spry Form Menu

Text boxes aren't the only form fields you can validate. You can make sure someone's made a selection from a pull-down menu by adding a Spry menu to a form.

1. **Click to the right of the error message you just added (after "Please enter a date."), and then press Enter or Return to insert a new empty paragraph.**

   Make sure you click to the right of the Spry widget's blue outline before you press Return. If you hit Return immediately after you type in the error message (step 19 in the previous section of this tutorial), you're still inside the Spry Text Field widget, and the next steps won't work.

2. **Choose Insert→Form→Spry Validation Select, or, on the Insert panel, click the Spry Validation Select button (see Figure 12-2 or Figure 12-28).**

   As with any form field, the Input Tag Accessibility window appears.

3. **In the ID field, type *time*; in the label box, type *Time of Appointment*; click OK to insert the menu.**

   A form menu appears on the page.

4. **Choose File→Save.**

   Another window appears, letting you know that you need an additional JavaScript file and CSS file to make this Spry Validation widget work. Click OK to dismiss that window. Time to style the label.

5. **Repeat step 18 on page 506 to format the "Time of Appointment" label.**

   In other words, use the tag selector to select the <label> tag and select the *question* style from the Class menu in the Property inspector. At this point, the pull-down form menu is empty, so your next step is to add a few options.

6. **In the document window, click the newly inserted menu to select it. In the Property inspector, click the List Values button.**

   The List Values window opens (see Figure 12-35), where you can add options for the menu.

7. **Type --** ***Select a Time*** **--; press the Tab key, and then type** ***-1.***

   The text ("Select a Time") appears at the top of the menu. It's an instruction telling your visitor what to do. Of course, you want your guest to choose an option *other* than this text. If he does select it, the –1 serves as a kind of secret message that flags the Spry Validation program that this option isn't valid. Before you get to that, though, add the valid selections for this form.

8. **Press the Tab key, and then type** ***8:00am*****; press the Tab key twice to create another list option, and then type** ***9:00am*****. Continue adding options in this way until you add** ***5:00pm*** **(or until you've got the hang of adding menu items).**

   The List Values window should look like Figure 12-35.

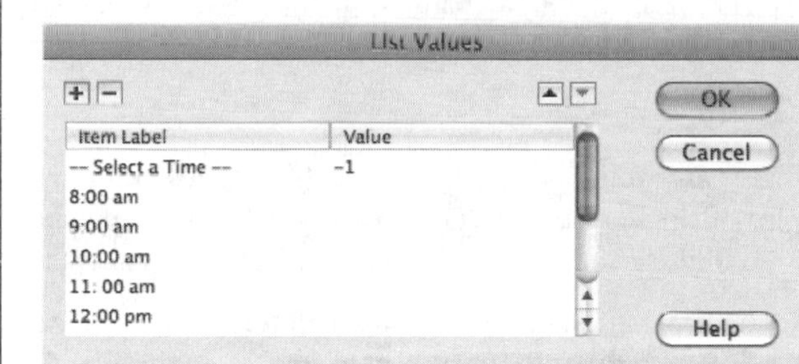

Figure 12-35: *The Item Label column displays what appears in the menu on the web page, while the Value column contains the value that's actually submitted (–1 in the first row, for example). If you don't specify a value (as with all of the time ranges here), then the label's text is submitted as the value.*

9. **Click OK to insert the menu. Move your mouse over the menu, and then click the blue Spry tab to select it.**

   You need to specify invalid menu selections.

10. **In the Property inspector, turn off the "Blank value" box, turn on the "Invalid value" box, and then make sure** ***-1*** **appears in the field. Then turn on the Change checkbox.**

    The Property inspector should look like Figure 12-36. In the "Preview states" menu, make sure you have "Invalid" selected. In the document window, to the right of the form menu, you should see a red error message, "Please select a valid item."

11. **Choose File→Save.**

    Another window appears, letting you know that you need an additional JavaScript file and a CSS file to make this new Spry Validation widget work (click OK to close that window).

    You'll change the error message and its style next.

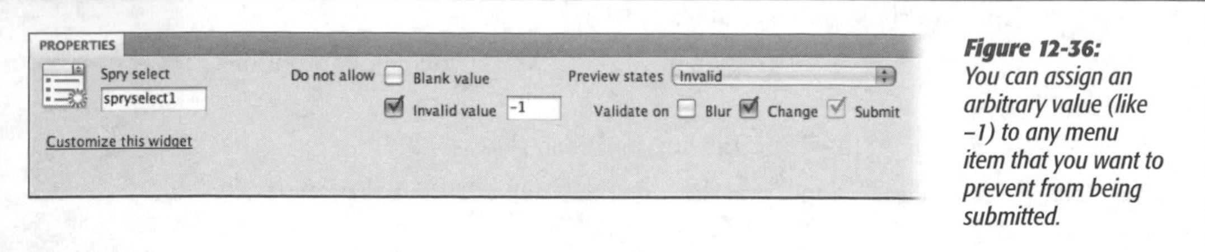

***Figure 12-36:** You can assign an arbitrary value (like –1) to any menu item that you want to prevent from being submitted.*

12. **Replace the text *Please select a valid item* with *Please select a time*. Repeat steps 12–15 on page 510 to make the error message bold and remove the borderline.**

    Each type of Spry Validation widget (text field, menu, checkbox, text area) has its own CSS styles to format error messages. So, unfortunately, if you use more than one type of validation in a form, you have to repeat the same formatting steps to get error messages that match. In the case of a pull-down menu error message, the style name begins with "*.selectRequiredState .selectRequiredMsg*", and it's in an external style sheet named SpryValidationSelect.css.

Adding a Spry Radio Group

Just a couple more form fields and you'll be done. Now it's time to ask a multiple-choice question that requires a single response. This task is perfect for a group of radio buttons, but since you require an answer, you'll use Spry Validation as well.

1. **Click to the right of the error message you just formatted (after "Select a time"), and then press Enter (Return) to insert a new empty paragraph. Type *Please select a reason for this appointment.***

   If you no longer see the error message you created in step 11 in the previous section, you probably just clicked somewhere else on the page and deselected the Spry widget. Time to format the question.

2. **From the Property inspector's Class menu, select "question".**

   If you don't see the Class menu in the Property inspector, make sure you have the HTML button selected. The Class menu formats the paragraph so that it looks like the labels for other questions on the form. Next you'll add a few checkboxes.

3. **Press the Enter (Return) key to create a blank paragraph.**

   The new paragraph also has the *question* class applied to it. You need to remove that style.

4. **From the Property inspector's Class menu, choose None (it's at the top of the list). Choose Insert→Form→Spry Validation Radio Group.**

   Under the Insert panel's Forms category, you can also click the Spry Radio Group button (see Figure 12-2 or Figure 12-28). Either way, the Spry Validation Radio Group window appears (Figure 12-37).

5. **In the Name field, type appointmentType.**

   This names the group of radio buttons—each button shares the same name, but obviously the label and value of each button should be unique. You'll add those next.

6. **In the Label column, click the first instance of the word Radio; type *Routine check-up*. Press Tab to jump to the value column, and then type *cv767*.**

   The label is the text that appears next to the button, while the value is the data the form transmits to the forms-processing program—in this case, "cv767" is Chia Vet's internal code for "Routine check up" (yeah, sure it is).

7. **Press Tab again to jump to the label column for the second radio button, type *Weed dip*, press Tab, and then type *cv524*.**

   You've now changed the labels and values for the two generic buttons supplied in this window. To add another, you need to use the + button.

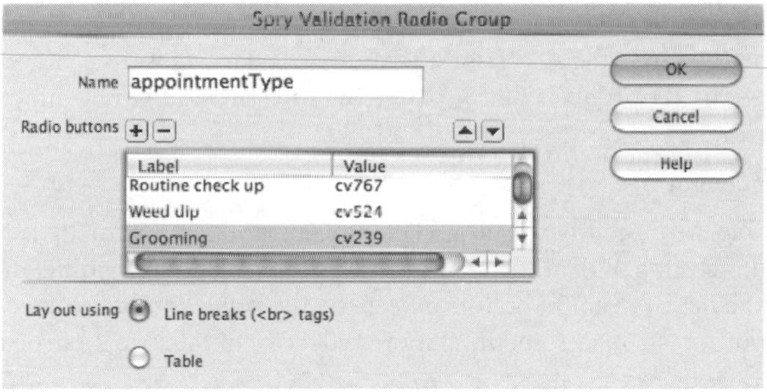

Figure 12-37: *When you insert a Spry Validation Radio Group, you can choose whether to put the group of buttons and labels in a table or on single lines separated by line breaks (
 tags). Choose the line breaks option—it gives you the most flexibility for controlling the display of your radio buttons.*

8. **Press the + button to add another pair of label and value options. Type *Grooming* for the label, and *cv239* for the value.**

   The window should now look like Figure 12-37.

9. **Make sure you select the "Line breaks" button, and then click OK to insert the group of three radio buttons.**

   Three rows of radio buttons appear on the page, along with the now-familiar blue Spry tab. In the Property inspector, you don't have to make any validation choices because you always want the default option "Required"—so, someone requesting an appointment can't submit this form until she's clicked one of the three radio buttons.

   You should, however, make sure the style of the error message matches the others on the page.

10. **From the Preview States menu in the Property inspector, choose Required. Repeat steps 12-15 on page 510 to format the "Please make a selection" error message.**

11. **Choose File→Save.**

    Another window appears, letting you know that you need an additional JavaScript file and a CSS file to make this new Spry Validation widget work (click OK to close that window).

Completing and Testing the Form

At this point, nobody can submit the form after they fill it out—you need to add a Submit button.

1. **Click to the right of the "Please make a selection" message for the radio group. Hit Return to create a new paragraph. From the Property inspector's Class menu, choose *question*.**

   A green line and a little extra space appear above the paragraph. This look matches the look of the other parts of the form.

2. **Choose Insert→Form→Button or, on the Insert panel, click the Button icon (Figure 12-2 or Figure 12-28).**

   Your old friend the Input Tag Accessibility window appears. This time, however, you don't need an ID or label. Buttons (like Submit) already have a message printed on them, so you don't need to add a label.

3. **Click the Cancel button.**

   In the Input Tag Accessibility window, clicking Cancel doesn't actually cancel the process of inserting a form field—it just skips the steps of providing an ID and label for the field. A Submit button appears on the page. You can change the generic "Submit" message to something more reflective of the form's purpose.

4. **Click the button on the page; in the Property inspector's Value field, type *Make appointment*.**

   The form is done. Now take it for a test drive.

5. **Choose File→Save All, and then press the F12 (Option-F12) key.**

   A web browser opens with the new form.

6. **Click the "Make appointment" button.**

   The form doesn't submit (see Figure 12-38). Instead, several error messages appear. Fill out the form correctly, and try to submit it again.

Note: If, after you submit the form, you notice that some of the information you entered doesn't show up on the form-processing page ("Appointment Scheduled"), you may not have typed the name of the field exactly as specified in the tutorial. Form-processing programs are very particular: if you don't provide the exact name it's expecting it won't correctly capture the form data. You can change the names of form elements by selecting them and using the Property inspector.

Figure 12-38: *Dreamweaver's Spry Validation Form widgets can help ensure that your forms collect the information you want. Professional-looking error messages, placed next to the offending responses, give visitors clear feedback.*

CHAPTER
13

Spry: Creating Interactive Web Pages

As a web designer, you can count on one thing: The Web is always changing. Yesterday's technology is yesterday's news—remember Java applets, frames, and messages that scroll in your browser's status bar (if you don't, you're lucky!)? You can see the most recent web design innovations on sites like Google Maps, Flickr, and Facebook, all of which offer a high degree of interactivity without resorting to multimedia plug-ins like Flash. Google Maps, for example, lets you zoom in, zoom out, and scroll across a map of the world without loading a new web page for each view. Many of the most cutting-edge websites almost feel like the kinds of complex programs you run right on your computer.

JavaScript—which has grown from a simple little language that helped create pop-up windows and image rollovers to a full-blown programming tool that can change the content of a web page as you look at it—is the key to this interactivity. JavaScript can even update a page with new data that gets downloaded behind the scenes (that's why you can scroll to new sections of that Google map without loading new pages). Dreamweaver, which has always tried to provide tools to meet web designers' current needs, includes a set of JavaScript tools that let you add interactive page elements like drop-down navigation menus, tabbed panels, pop-up tooltips, and data-driven, sortable tables. That's what this chapter is all about.

What is Spry?

You've already seen Spry in action in Chapters 5 and 12, where you learned about the Spry Menu Bar and Spry Validation widgets. But what exactly is Spry? It isn't just a Dreamweaver tool; it's a technology developed by Adobe, and distributed freely and independently on the Adobe Labs website (*http://labs.adobe.com/technologies/spry/*).

It's officially called the "Spry framework for Ajax" and it's a collection of JavaScript programs that let you, the web designer, offer sophisticated control of a web page to your visitors through *widgets, effects*, and *data sets*. A widget is an interface element like a menu bar, form validation message, or set of tabbed panels that generally makes a site easier to use. For example, the Spry Menu Bar adds a lot of links to a compact navigation bar, so you can easily find your way around a site.

An effect is a visual treat that doesn't necessarily improve how a web page works, but adds cool eye candy. You can use a Spry effect to fade page elements in and out of view (you'll learn all about effects in the next chapter).

Finally, a Spry data set is a data presentation format that's more interactive than a standard HTML table. Imagine you have a table listing products your company sells. The table displays one product per row, with columns for product name, price, and availability. A visitor can sort a Spry data table by any of these columns, simply by clicking the name of the column. And that all happens without the browser ever having to reload the web page.

In addition, a Spry data set can suck down the contents of an XML file or even a garden-variety HTML table, and then update a web page with that file's content; see page 548 for the full scoop on XML, an increasingly popular and extremely flexible data format. But because not all web designers use XML, Dreamweaver lets you put data into a common HTML table and use that as the basis for an interactive table. This Spry-data set tango is the "Ajax" part of the "Spry framework for Ajax." Ajax is a term coined in 2005 to describe a timesaving system for transferring information from a web server to a web page (and vice versa). The revolutionary advantage of Ajax, as highlighted in the Google Maps example, is that it lets a page's contents change quickly without having to reload a new page from the server.

Note: Ajax originally stood for "Asynchronous JavaScript and XML," since most original Ajax examples used XML. Nowadays the term more commonly describes the use of JavaScript to send and receive data (XML or any other text format) to and from a web server, and update the contents of a page based on that data.

Tabbed Panels

Some website visitors are loath to scroll; if they don't see what they want when a page first loads, they move on. Because of this, some web designers divide long passages of information into multiple pages so that each page presents small, easy-to-digest chunks. Of course, that means building several pages instead of just one, and forces visitors to click through (and wait for) a series of pages. Spry Tabbed Panels provides an alternative (see Figure 13-1). Instead of creating one long page, or several smaller pages, you can organize information into separate tabbed panels. That way, your content is always front and center, and your visitors can easily access different sections by clicking a tab above each panel.

Adding a Tabbed Panel

You can place Spry tabbed panels anywhere on a web page. But since the tabs form a single row at the top of the group of panels, you need enough horizontal space to accommodate all the tabs (see page 527 for an exception to this limitation). Unless you have only a couple of tabs with one-word text labels, you should place the tabbed panels in a fairly wide space, such as the main column of a web page, or across the entire width of the page. Just follow these steps:

1. **In the document window, click where you wish to insert the panels.**

   For example, inside a div tag (page 331).

2. **Choose Insert→Spry→Spry Tabbed Panels, or, on the Insert panel's Spry category, click one of the Spry Tabbed Panel's buttons (see Figure 13-2).**

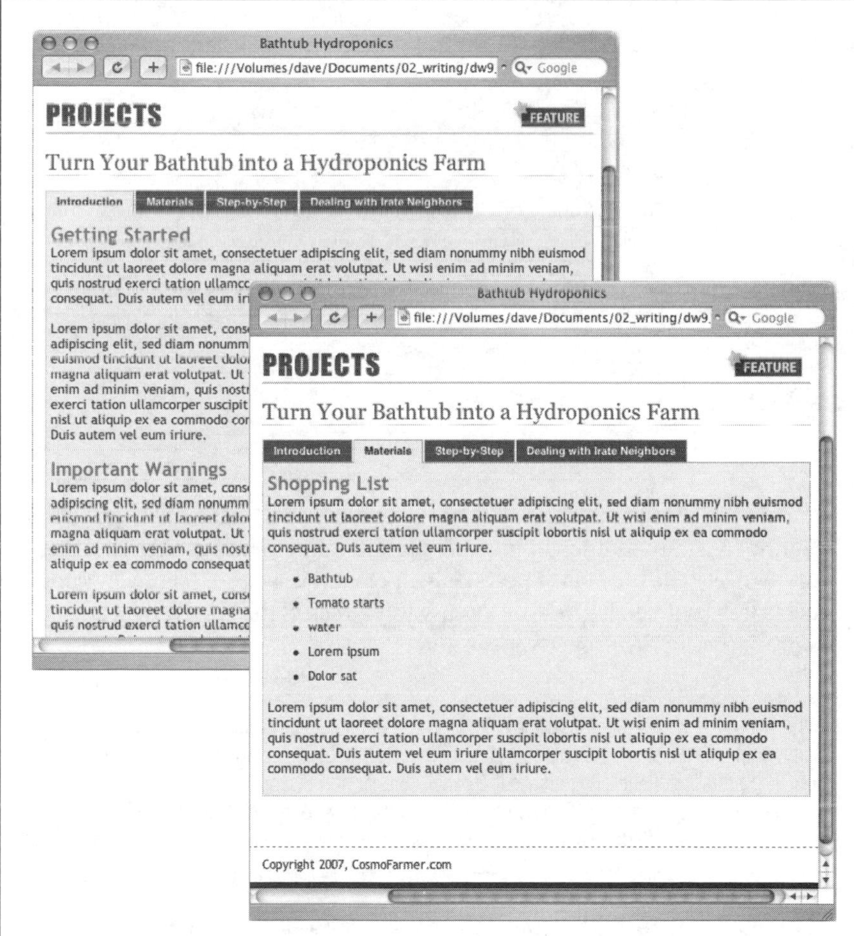

***Figure 13-1:** Organize your page's content into easily accessible panels with the Spry Tabbed Panels widget. Clicking a tab opens a new panel's worth of information without the browser having to load a new web page.*

You can find all the Spry goodies on the Insert panel's Spry category (Figure 13-2, left); you'll also find several Spry widgets (including tabbed panels) listed under the Layout category (Figure 13-2, right), and other Spry buttons grouped under other tabs (form validation Spry widgets appear under the Forms tab, for example).

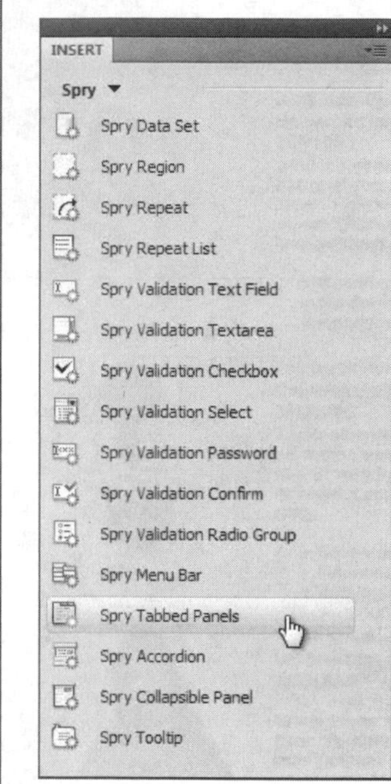

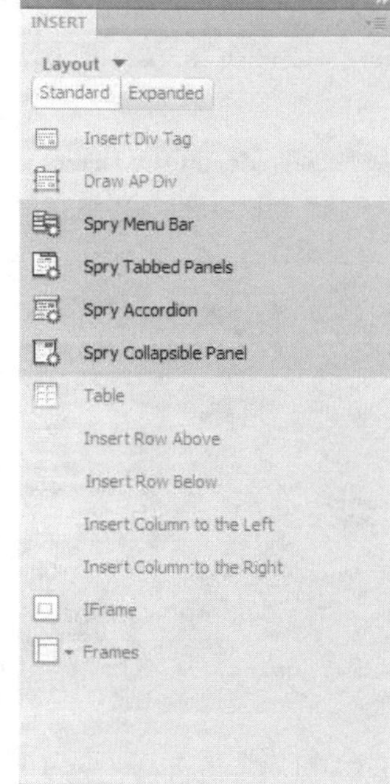

Figure 13-2:
In the Insert panel, you can identify a Spry icon by the starburst in the button's lower-right corner. It's even easier to distinguish them from other buttons if, from the Insert Panel's category menu, you choose Color Icons–this changes the drab gray starburst to a bright orange. (You can also display the Insert Panel as a toolbar at the top of your screen as described in the note on page 527.)

After you insert a tabbed panel, you see two tabs and two panels on the page (Figure 13-3); in addition, a blue tab appears above the panels indicating the Spry widget. The blue tab appears only in Dreamweaver's Design view, not in a guest's web browser. It gives you an easy way to select the Spry widget and access its properties in the Property inspector.

Note: When you save a page after inserting a Spry Tabbed Panel, Dreamweaver notifies you that it has added two files to the site: a CSS file (SpryTabbedPanels.css) for formatting the panel group, and a JavaScript file (SpryTabbedPanels.js) to make the panels appear and disappear when visitors click the tabs. Dreamweaver saves both files in the SpryAssets folder in your site's root folder (see the tip on page 188). Make sure you upload this folder when you move your site onto your web server.

3. **In the Property inspector, name the panel group (Figure 13-3).**

   This step is optional. Dreamweaver provides a generic name (TabbedPanels1, for example) for the group of panels. You don't really have to change this name;

it never appears in a browser window. But if you ever take the plunge into manually modifying your Spry widgets in Code view, you may want to change the Spry panel group's name to something more descriptive. If you create a group of tabbed panels to house information about a product, for example, you might name the panel group *productPanels*. A descriptive name helps you identify code related to the panel group if you work in Code view to enhance or change the functionality of the panels (see the box on page 527).

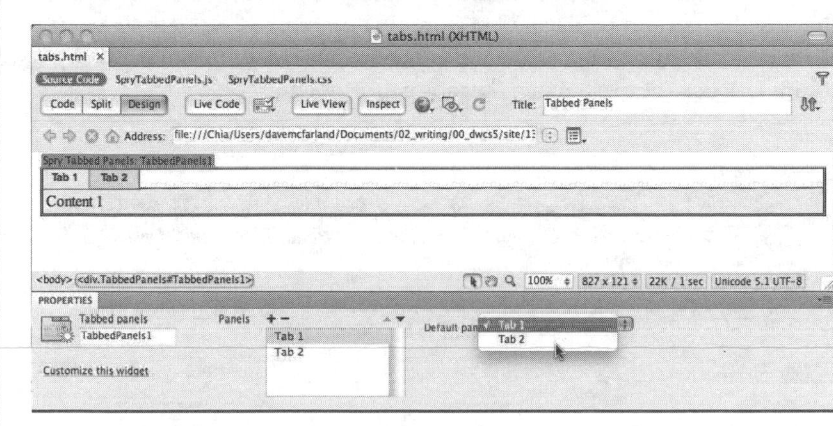

Figure 13-3: *Normally, when a browser downloads a page containing Spry panels, it highlights the first tab and panel. However, if you'd rather open another panel when the page loads, select the relevant tab's name in the Property inspector's "Default panel" menu.*

4. **Add additional panels.**

   If two panels aren't enough for your needs, use the Property inspector to add more. Above the list of tab names, click the + button (see Figure 13-3) to add a new panel. To remove a panel, in the same list, click the name of a tab, and then click the minus (-) button. You can also reorder the panels by selecting a tab from the list, and then clicking the up or down arrow button. The up arrow moves a panel to the left, while the down arrow moves a panel to the right.

Note: A Spry widget's properties appear in the Property inspector only when you select the widget. To do so, click the blue tab above the elements inside the widget (see Figure 13-3).

Adding and Editing Panel Content

Each tabbed panel has two parts: a labeled tab and a panel containing content associated with the tab. In Figure 13-1, "Introduction", "Materials," "Step-by-Step", and "Dealing with Irate Neighbors" are each tabs, while the area of the page beginning with the "Shopping List" headline is the panel for the "Materials" tab.

To change the label on a tab, just select and replace the tab's text in Design view. The label is normal HTML text, so you can just triple-click to select it as you would any block of text.

Dreamweaver stores the text for the panel itself inside a <div> tag, so you can select it by clicking anywhere inside the panel, and then choosing Edit→Select All (or Ctrl+A [⌘-A]). You can place any combination of HTML inside a panel: headlines, paragraphs, bulleted lists, forms, images, and Flash movies (you can even insert *another* Spry Tabbed Panel if you like that kind of circus-sideshow-hall-of-mirrors effect).

To edit a panel's contents, you need to make the panel visible first. Since the entire point of the Spry Tabbed Panels is to present a lot of information within overlapping panels, you see only one panel at a time. Fortunately, Dreamweaver offers a simple way to close the current panel and open another one so you can edit it: Move your mouse over a hidden panel's tab, and an eye icon appears at the tab's right edge (see Figure 13-4). Click the eye to open the tab's panel for editing.

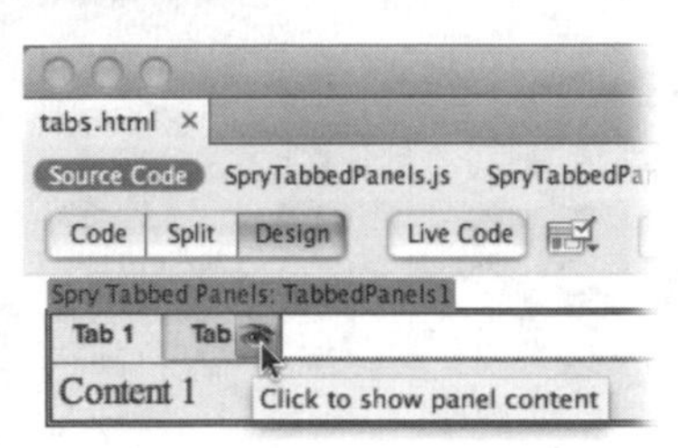

Figure 13-4:
Dreamweaver displays an eye icon for all Spry widgets that include tabs and panels. Clicking the eye makes a currently hidden panel visible and ready to edit.

Formatting Tabbed Panels

The tabbed panels and the content inside them are just basic HTML, made to look good with a generous dose of CSS. The tab buttons are a simple bulleted list, while each panel is a separate div; Dreamweaver wraps all the panels together in another div. An external style sheet in the root folder's SpryAssets folder, SpryTabbedPanels.css, controls all the fancy formatting—tab buttons sitting side by side, borders, and background colors.

Note: Dreamweaver stores Spry support files (the external CSS and JavaScript files that make Spry so spry) in a folder named SpryAssets in your site's root folder. If you don't like the name of that folder or want to store those files elsewhere on your site, you can do that as described on page 188.

Dreamweaver supplies different CSS styles to format the panels, the currently selected tab, and the tabs whose panels aren't currently visible. The general process of modifying the look of any element in a panel group is simple: Identify the element you want to modify (like a panel or tab), locate the style that controls that element, and then edit that style. If you want to change the text color of the currently selected tab, for example, in the SpryTabbedPanels.css file, you need to open the *.TabbedPanelsTabSelected* class style. The basic steps are as follows:

1. **Open the CSS Styles panel (Window®CSS Styles).**

   At the top of the Styles panel, make sure you have the All button selected.

2. **Expand the list of styles for the SpryTabbedPanels.css style sheet.**

   Just click the + (arrow on a Mac) symbol next to the file's name to reveal all the styles for tabbed panels.

3. **In the Styles panel, double-click the style's name.**

   The Style Definition window for that style opens.

4. **Make the changes, and then, in the Style Definition window, click OK to finish editing the style.**

   You can use the CSS Properties pane (page 527) to edit the styles as well. For a recap on editing CSS styles, see page 124.

To help guide you in the process of modifying Spry panels, here's a list of panel elements and the styles that control them:

- **Spry Tabbed Panel group:** *.TabbedPanels*

  Normally, the width of a collection of panels and tabs stretches to fit the available space. So if you place a panel group on an empty page, it stretches to fit the entire width of the browser window. Placed inside a div with a set width, the group of panels stretches to match the div's width. If you wish to make the group of panels thinner, change the width property of the *.TabbedPanels* style. Normally it's set to 100%, but you could change this to 50% or a set pixel amount. The *.TabbedPanels* style floats the entire group of panels and tabs to the left, so any content that appears after the panel group wraps around the right side of the panels (see page 331 for more on floats). (To adjust the height of a group of panels, see the "Panels" bullet point, below.)

- **All tabs:** *.TabbedPanelsTab*

  The Spry Tabbed Panels widget uses two types of tabs: one for the currently displayed panel, and one for tabs that aren't active. The *.TabbedPanelsTab* style controls both types of tabs. If you want to change the font on all tabs, edit the *.TabbedPanelsTab* style, and then choose a new font family. To change the borders around the tabs, edit this style's Border property. To adjust the amount of space between the edge of the tab and the text label inside it, edit the style's Padding property (page 341); to change the space between tabs, edit the style's Margin property (page 341).

- **Not selected tab:** *.TabbedPanelsTab* and *.TabbedPanelsTabHover*

  The *.TabbedPanelsTab* also dictates the basic look of an unselected tab, like its background color. In addition, a non-selected tab has a hover style—*.TabbedPanelsTabHover*—so that when a mouse moves over it, the tab highlights to indicate that you can click it. The basic style sheet supplied with Dreamweaver merely changes the tab's background color when a mouse moves over it, but you're free to change other settings, such as the font color.

Note: Dreamweaver's Live View lets you instantly preview style changes without leaving Dreamweaver. For example, with the CSS Styles panel open and your web page in Live view, you can make changes to the *.TabbedPanelsTabHover* style (change the background color, for instance) and immediately test that change by moving your mouse over the tab in Design view. See page 578 for more on Live View.

- **Currently selected tab:** *.TabbedPanelsTabSelected*

  The *.TabbedPanelsTabSelected* style applies to the tab for a currently displayed panel. This style essentially overwrites the style properties inherited from the *.TabbedPanelsTab* style, which all the tabs share. The background color and text color differ from the other tab style, but, again, you're free to modify the style (by picking a new font, for instance).

  With this style, be aware of a couple of things. First, it has a set bottom border. You shouldn't eliminate it, unless you eliminate bottom borders on the *.TabbedPanelsTab* as well. Otherwise, you see a noticeable line separating the tab from its panel. In addition, if you change the background color of the tab and the panel (they're usually set to the same color to make it appear that they form a unified element), then set the color of the bottom border for this style to match. If you don't, you end up with a line separating the tab from the panel.

Note: If you make the text size for one type of tab larger or smaller than the other tab type, you end up with different heights for the different tabs. What's worse, the shorter tab no longer touches the top of the panel group. To fix this, add a *line-height* property (page 360) to the *.TabbedPanelsTab* style that's large enough to force the two tabs to occupy the same height—use a pixel value so that you can guarantee that different tabs will be the same height. You'll probably need to conduct some trial-and-error testing to get this right.

- **Panels:** *.TabbedPanelsContentGroup* or *.TabbedPanelsContent*

  Two styles affect the panels. The first, *.TabbedPanelsContentGroup*, is applied to a <div> tag that wraps around the HTML of *all* the panels. The second wraps the content of each panel itself in a <div> tag with the *.TabbedPanelsContent* class applied to it. You can edit either style to adjust basic properties like font color, size, and so on. However, the *.TabbedPanelsContentGroup* controls the borders and background color for the panels; edit that style to change the panels' borders or backgrounds. Out of the box, the *.TabbedPanelsContent* style sheet just has the Padding property set (page 341)—it adds space inside each panel so its contents don't butt right up against the borders of the panel.

  Each panel is only as tall as the content inside it. If one panel has a lot of information and another just a little, the panels grow or shrink wildly as you switch among them. If you're a stickler for consistency, you can set a uniform height for all the panels: Edit the *.TabbedPanelsContent* style, and add a *height* property (see page 360). Be careful with height, however; before building a web page, it's difficult to judge how much content a panel will have (and thus how tall it needs to be). If the content inside a panel grows taller than the panel's height setting, you get some weird display problems, as explained on page 340.

Note: In Firefox, when you click a tab, you see a fuzzy, dotted outline around it. That's because the browser applies a "focus" state to the tab (see page 182). To remove it, you need to create a compound style named *.TabbedPanelsTab:focus*. Then you need to set the CSS *outline* property to *none*. Unfortunately, you can't do this with Dreamweaver's Rule Definition Window. To add this property, first create the *.TabbedPanelsTab:focus* style (make sure to save this new style in the SpryTabbedPanels.css style sheet); when the CSS Rule Definition window appears, just click OK. This creates a style with no properties. Next, in the CSS Styles panel, find the style, and select it. Then, in the Properties pane (see page 527), click the Add Property link, type *outline*, hit Tab, and then type *none*. You're done.

- **Content inside the panel.** Dreamweaver doesn't start you off with any styles that control the tags inside a panel. Although headlines and paragraphs inherit (see page 311) any text properties you add to the panel styles, you might want to define a different look for headlines, paragraphs, lists, and other tags inside the panel. This situation is perfect for a descendent selector. A descendent selector, as you read on page 298, lets you specify the look of a tag when it's inside another tag, and thus lets you pinpoint the look of page elements based on where they appear on the page.

  In this case, say you want the paragraphs inside a panel to look different from other paragraphs on the page. Create a descendent selector style named *.TabbedPanelsContent p*, and then add any CSS properties you'd like. Or, to format the look of Heading 2 tags inside a panel, create a style named *.TabbedPanelsContent h2*. In other words, to control the look of any particular tag inside a panel, create an advanced style, and then tack on *.TabbedPanelsContent*, followed by a space before the name of the tag you want to look different when it appears inside a panel (see page 113 for more on creating styles).

FREQUENTLY ASKED QUESTION

.VTabbedPanels Explained

In the SpryTabbedPanels.css style sheet, what do all the styles whose names begin with .VTabbedPanels *do?*

The short answer: Nothing. The longer answer: Nothing, unless you want vertical tabbed panels. Like the accordion panels discussed above, a browser stacks vertical tabbed panels one on top of the other, except that this time the browser truncates the tabs, so they take up just a little room along the left edge of the panels, and the panels open to the right of them. They don't look particularly good, and if that weren't reason enough to avoid them, they're difficult to manage. To see one in action, visit: *http://labs.adobe.com/technologies/spry/samples/tabbedpanels/tabbed_panel_sample.htm*.

If you feel like experimenting, you can turn a regular tabbed group of panels into vertical tabs by applying a *.VTabbedPanels* class to the <div> tag that surrounds the entire Spry Tabbed Panel group. (This <div> tag looks something like <div.TabbedPanels#TabbedPanels1> in the Tag selector). The exact ID—*#TabbedPanels1* in this example—depends on the ID you (or Dreamweaver) set in step 3 on page 522. You can most easily change this div's ID with the Tag selector method described on page 123.

Accordions

A Spry Accordion is another space-saving widget that lets you stuff lots of content into a multi-paneled display (Figure 13-5). Like Spry Tabbed Panels, a Spry Accordion contains panels of information, each with a labeled tab. But in this case, a web browser stacks the tabs on top of each other instead of side by side. When you click the tab of a panel that's not currently visible, that panel rises with a smooth animated effect. In addition, you must set each panel's height, so if the content inside a panel is taller than the panel itself, a browser adds a scroll bar to the panel's right edge. It's kind of like having a browser window inside a browser window. Dreamweaver's stock style sheet sets the height of each panel to 200 pixels, but you can change that (see the bullet point "Panels" on page 533).

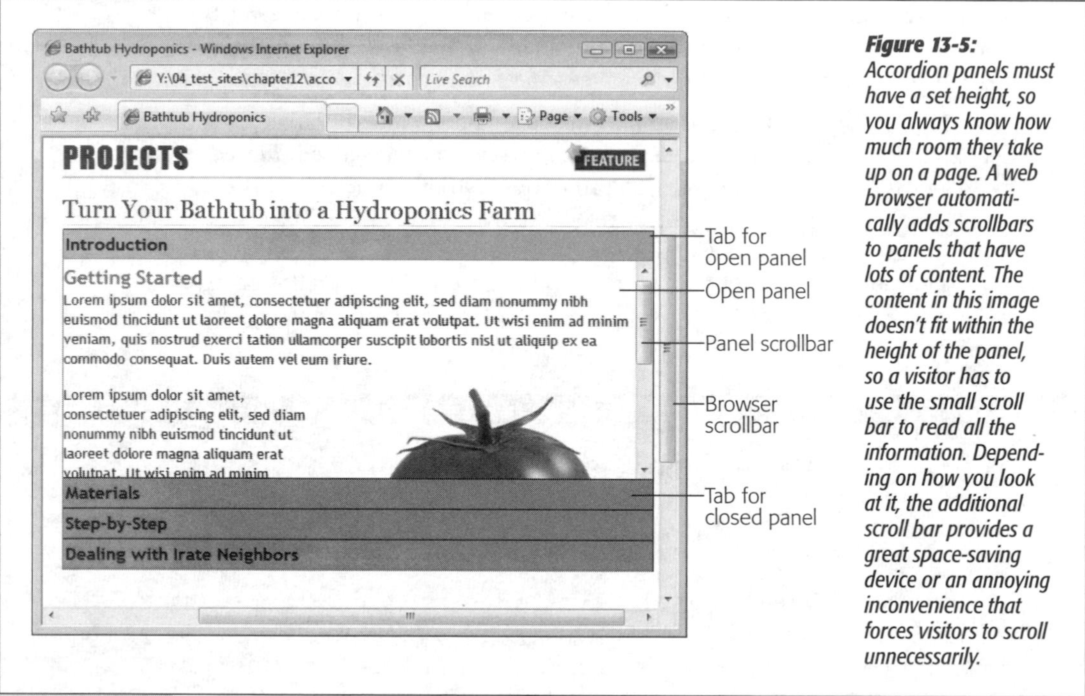

Figure 13-5: *Accordion panels must have a set height, so you always know how much room they take up on a page. A web browser automatically adds scrollbars to panels that have lots of content. The content in this image doesn't fit within the height of the panel, so a visitor has to use the small scroll bar to read all the information. Depending on how you look at it, the additional scroll bar provides a great space-saving device or an annoying inconvenience that forces visitors to scroll unnecessarily.*

Adding an Accordion

You can place a Spry Accordion anywhere on a web page—on an empty page, inside a <div> tag, and so on.

1. **In the document window, click the area where you wish to insert the accordion.**

   For example, inside a <div> tag.

2. **Choose Insert→Spry→Spry Accordion, or, on the Insert panel, click one of the Spry Accordion buttons (see Figure 13-2).**

   After inserting an accordion, you see a tab (named "Label 1"), an open panel (with "Content 1" inside it) and another tab ("Label 2") at the bottom (see Figure 13-6); in addition, a blue Spry tab appears above the top tab, and the Property inspector displays the accordion's properties (Figure 13-6).

Note: You can insert any Spry widget by dragging its icon from the Insert panel to anywhere on a web page.

---

3. **In the Property inspector, name the accordion.**

   As with Spry Tabbed Panels, this step is optional (see step 3 on page 522).

4. **Add additional tabs and panels to the accordion.**

   If two panels aren't enough for your needs, use the Property inspector to add more. Click the + button above the list of tab names (see Figure 13-6). To remove a panel, click the name of the tab in the panels list, and then click the minus (–) button. (You can also reorder the panels by selecting a tab from the list, and then, in the Property inspector, clicking the up or down arrow button.)

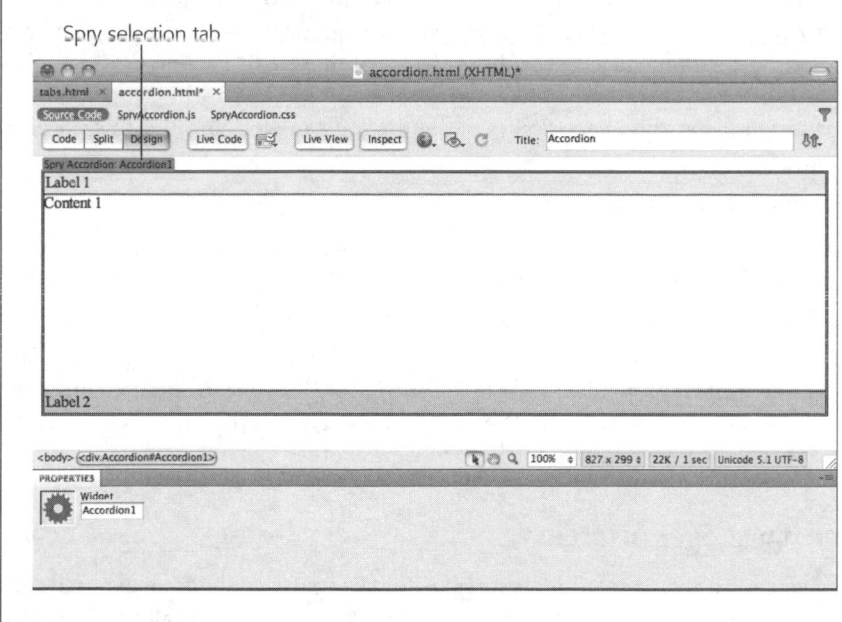

Figure 13-6: *To edit a Spry Widget's properties, select it. In Design view, click the blue Spry tab on top of the widget. The blue tab is an internal Dreamweaver control, and doesn't appear in a guest's browser.*

Adding and Editing Accordion Content

Dreamweaver divides accordions into sections, composed of a labeled tab and a content panel associated with that tab. It embeds each tab in its own <div> tag, and the content for each tab's panel inside another <div> tag. Dreamweaver then encloses each tab/panel pair in yet another div (and wraps the entire accordion [all tab/panel groups] in one final div).

To edit a tab's label, select its text in Design view, and then type in a new label. (Since Dreamweaver enclosed the label in a <div> tag, you can also just click the tab, and then press Ctrl+A [⌘-A] to select all the label's text.) Since accordion tabs span the width of the accordion, you can put a lot more words on an accordion tab than you can on the tabs you read about earlier in this chapter.

As with those Spry Tabbed Panels, you have to make a panel visible to edit it: Mouse over the tab of a hidden panel, and then, at the right edge of the tab, click the eye icon to open the panel for editing. It's the same procedure (and same eye icon) you used with tabbed panels (see Figure 13-4). To select all the text inside a panel, click the panel, and then choose Edit→Select All (or Ctrl+A [⌘-A]). You can place any combination of HTML inside a panel: headlines, paragraphs, bulleted lists, forms, images, and Flash movies.

You'll run into one big problem if you add more content than fits inside an accordion panel's height: You can't see all the content in Dreamweaver! Remember, accordion panels occupy a fixed height: When you view the accordion in a browser, you can just scroll inside the panel to see any content that doesn't fit (see Figure 13-5). But you don't get any scroll bars in Dreamweaver's Design view, so when you add more content than fits in the panel, you can't edit it. You can work around this problem two ways:

- Double-click the panel.
- Right-click (Control-click) the panel, and then, from the contextual menu, choose Element View→Full (see Figure 13-7).

Either way, the panel fully expands so you can see and edit all the content. In fact, all the panels in the accordion expand when you do either of these things. This "full" view is visible in Dreamweaver only in order to make it easier to edit content in the accordion panels: When someone views the page in a web browser, he sees only the top panel, and he must click another tab to view another panel's content.

Formatting a Spry Accordion

When you add a Spry Accordion to a web page, Dreamweaver links an external style sheet named SpryAccordion.css to the page. This CSS file contains all the styles that control the look of the accordion's tabs and panels. The process of modifying the appearance of those tabs follows the same general sequence described on page 524 for Spry Tabbed Panels: Identify the element you wish to format, and then open and edit that element's style to match your page's overall design.

To help you modify Spry Accordions, here's a list of accordion elements and the styles that control them:

- **The Accordion** (all tabs and panels): *.Accordion*

  The *.Accordion* class style controls the overall settings for the accordion. Dreamweaver applies the class to the <div> that surrounds the tabs and panels. If you add basic font formatting to this style, such as font color, size, and font family, the other tabs and panels inherit these same settings (see page 311).

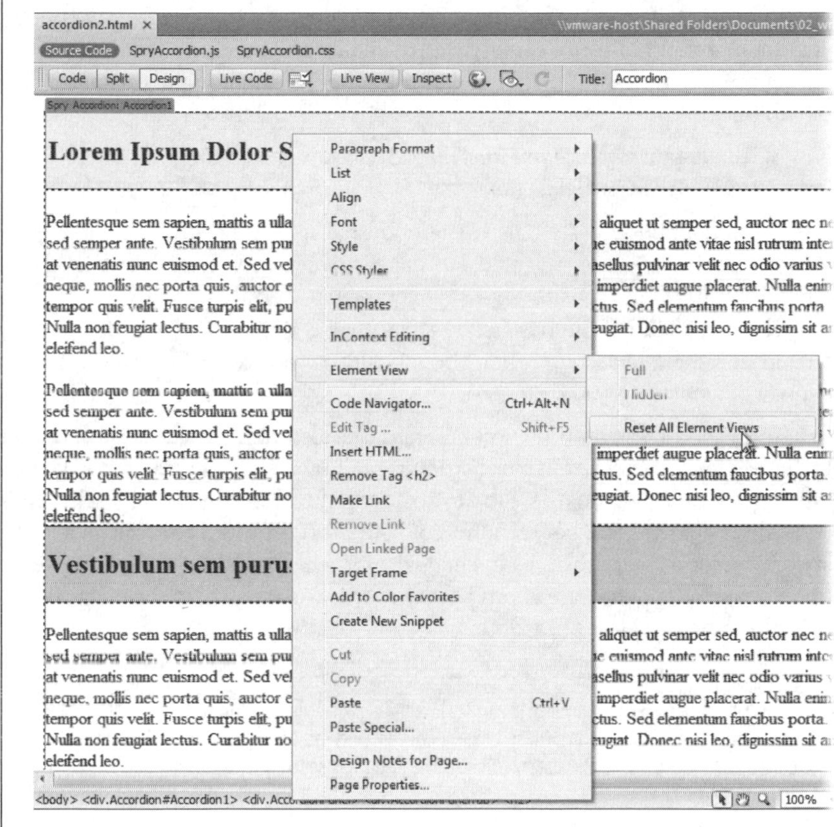

***Figure 13-7:** Dreamweaver's "Full" view shows all the content for all the panels of a Spry Accordion widget. Double-click any panel whose content is taller than the panel's height to enter Full view, or right click (Control-click) anywhere on the panel, and then, from the Element View submenu, choose Full. To return the accordion back to its collapsed state (the way it appears in a web browser), right-click (Control-click) anywhere on the page, and then, from the Element View submenu, choose **Reset All Element Views**.*

  In addition, you set the left, right, and bottom borders that appear around the accordion in this style.

- **All tabs:** *.AccordionPanelTab*

  A web browser displays tabs inside a Spry Accordion four possible ways (some design-inspired Adobe engineer got a little wild): As with a Spry tabbed panel, you see both a selected tab (the tab for the currently displayed panel) and a non-selected tab (the tab eagerly waiting to be clicked to reveal the hidden contents of its panel).

In addition, both the selected and nonselected tabs have "focus" states that kick into action to format *all* tabs when you click any *one* tab (*.AccordionFocused .AccordionPanelTab*, and *.AccordionFocused .AccordionPanelOpen .AccordionPanelTab*). In other words, click a single tab, and all the tabs change their appearance—"Yes sir, my tabs-in-arms and I are ready for your command!" Overall, the focus tabs are visually distracting (especially since the background colors are two shades of electric blue). They aim to aid someone using a keyboard instead of a mouse to navigate the accordion panels (you can actually tab to the accordion, and then use the up and down arrow keys to hide and reveal panels).

To alter the basic appearance of all tabs, edit the *.AccordionPanelTab* style. If you define a font family for this style, then all tabs use that font. In addition, you define the padding inside each tab, and the borders that appear around each tab, in this style.

- **Not selected tab:** *.AccordionPanelTab, .AccordionPanelTabHover, and .AccordionFocused .AccordionPanelTab*

  The *.AccordionPanelTab* style also dictates the background color for non-selected tabs. In addition, a non-selected tab has a hover style—*.AccordionPanelTabHover*—so that when a visitor mouses over the tab, the tab highlights to indicate that she can click it. The basic style sheet that Dreamweaver supplies merely changes the tab's text color when the mouse moves over it, but you're free to change other settings as well.

  When guests click any tab, all non-selected tags also change appearance, thanks to the *.AccordionFocused .AccordionPanelTab*. Tabs also use this style when a visitor presses his keyboard's Tab key to access the accordion panels. The stock style sheet changes the background color to a bright blue. You can delete the style if you don't want the tabs to change color when clicked. (At the very least, for the sake of all who care about beauty in this world, change the electric blue color to something less obnoxious.)

Tip: The same Tip on page 527, regarding the fuzzy line that Firefox places around focused tabs, applies to the Spry accordion, but in this case, the fuzzy line appears around the entire accordion. To remove this outline, create an advanced style called *.Accordion:focus*, and then set that style's *outline* property to *none*.

- **Currently selected tab:** *.AccordionPanelOpen .AccordionPanelTab, .Accordion-PanelOpen .AccordionPanelTabHover, and .AccordionFocused .AccordionPanelTab*

  The *.AccordionPanelOpen .AccordionPanelTab* style applies to the tab associated with the currently opened panel. This style essentially overwrites style properties inherited from the *.AccordionPanelTab* style that all tabs share. In the stock style sheet, only the background color differs from the other tab style, but, again, you're free to modify this. In addition, the text on a selected tab also changes color when a visitor mouses over it, thanks to the *.AccordionPanelOpen .AccordionPanelTabHover* style. This subtle "you can click me" cue is useful for a non-selected tab (since clicking one of those tabs actually does something). But since clicking an already opened tab doesn't do anything, this hover style is actually a needless distraction.

A selected tab also changes color when you click its tab, or press the keyboard's Tab key to access the accordion (again, you see that hideous electric blue). The *.AccordionFocused .AccordionPanelTab* style is the culprit.

- **Panels:** *.AccordionPanelContent*

  Dreamweaver adds the *.AccordionPanelContent* class to the <div> tag that surrounds the HTML in an accordion panel. You can adjust the font settings for this style to affect only the text inside the panel. In addition, this style defines each panel's height. Dreamweaver sets the CSS *height* property to 200 pixels at first, but you can make this value larger to display a bigger panel, or smaller for a shorter one. Unfortunately, you can't make the panels automatically adjust to fit whatever content is inside them; you have to set the height for the accordion panels to work.

- **Content inside the panel.** Dreamweaver supplies no styles to control the HTML tags in an accordion panel. You can follow the process described for Spry Tabbed Panels (under the bullet point "Content inside the panel" on page 527) to create descendent selectors that affect only tags inside accordion panels. Just use *.Accordion* as the first part of the selector. For example, *.Accordion p* is a descendent selector that formats paragraphs inside an accordion panel.

  Also note that content inside an accordion panel butts directly up against the panel's left and right edges. If you apply padding directly to the panel (in the *.AccordionPanelContent* style), then the opening and closing panel animation isn't very smooth. It's a bit more work, but it's better to add padding to the tags that appear inside the panel. For example, if you want all Heading 2 tags to indent 5 pixels from both the left and right sides of the panel, create a descendent selector like *.Accordion h2*, and then set the left and right margin properties to 5 pixels.

Note: When creating descendent selectors, always keep in mind the *cascade* (page 312). This CSS concept provides a set of rules for handling styles that conflict. You can easily create some confusing conflicts as you add multiple descendent selectors to a page.

For example, say you create the main content region of a page using a div with an ID named *mainContent*. If you want to create a descendent selector to format the paragraphs *inside* that main content region, you might name it *#mainContent p*. Now, say you insert a Spry Accordion, and you want to create a unique look for the paragraphs inside it. You could then create a style named *.Accordion p*. Unfortunately, since the *#mainContent p* style is more specific (has greater power) than the *.Accordion p* style, if you pick a font size for both, the size in the *#mainContent p* wins. In other words, it would be impossible to change the size of paragraphs inside the accordion...unless you create a more specific style for the accordion, something like *#mainContent .Accordion p*. You'll find all the messy details of this kind of problem (and how to fix them) described on page 312.

POWER USERS' CLINIC

Get the Most from Spry

Spry isn't just a Dreamweaver tool; it's a separate JavaScript-based toolset with a lot of bells and whistles beyond what's available from Dreamweaver's Insert bar and Property inspector. You can do things like change the speed of most effects (like how fast collapsible panels open and close). You can even program other ways to make an accordion panel open–by clicking another link on a page, or simply mousing over a tab, for example. You can even change the underlying HTML for most Spry widgets. For example, you could change the <span> tags Dreamweaver usually uses for Spry Validation error messages to a <p> tag.

To modify the Spry widgets that Dreamweaver inserts into a web page, you need to dip into Code view and make some changes. This sounds scarier than it actually is. Adobe made Spry easy for nonprogrammers to learn and use. The complex programming that makes Spry work its magic is hidden; you need to learn only a few basic concepts, and have a handy guidebook nearby, to take control of your Spry widgets.

To learn more about Spry and how to modify it, check out the online manual at *http://livedocs.adobe.com/en_US/Spry/SDG/index.html*.

Collapsible Panels

A Spry Collapsible Panel is like an accordion panel, except that it consists of just a single tab-and-panel pair (see Figure 13-8). The tab toggles the panel's display; each click of the tab either opens or closes the panel. You decide whether the panel is opened or closed when the web page first loads. A closed collapsible panel is great for keeping information out of a visitor's face until she wants it—like a form for signing up for an email newsletter, or driving directions to your business. Add an opened panel to your page when you want to make an important announcement that, once read, can be quickly hidden with a click of the mouse.

Adding a Collapsible Panel

You can place a Spry Collapsible Panel anywhere on a web page—on an empty page, inside a <div> tag, and so on.

1. **In the document window, click the place you wish to insert the collapsible panel.**

   For example, inside a <div> tag.

2. **Choose Insert→Spry→Spry Collapsible Panel, or, on the Insert panel, click one of the Spry Collapsible Panel buttons (see Figure 13-2).**

   After you insert a panel, you see a tab in the document window labeled "Tab", and an open panel labeled "Content"; in addition, a blue Spry tab appears above the top tab, and the Property inspector displays the properties for the collapsible panel (Figure 13-9).

3. **In the Property inspector, name the collapsible panel.**

   As with Spry Tabbed Panels, this step is optional (see step 3 on page 522).

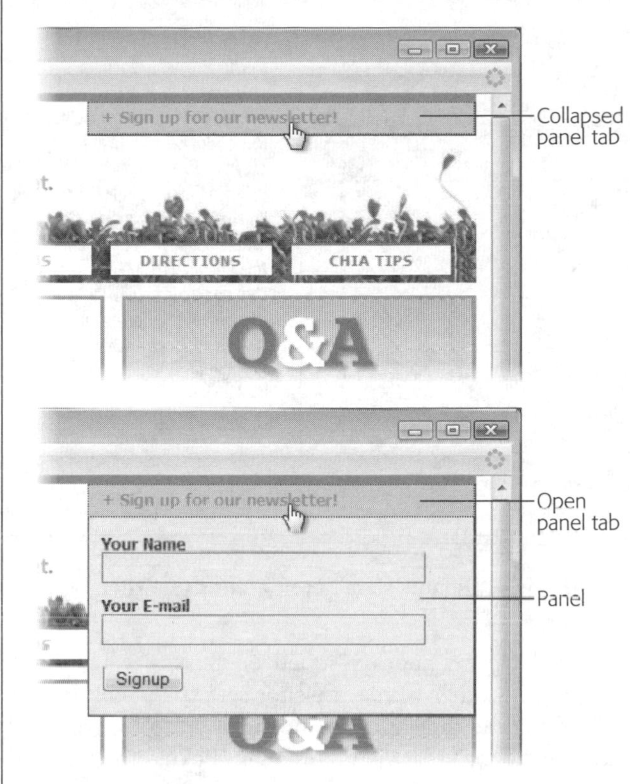

Figure 13-8:
Collapsible panels work especially well as absolutely positioned divs (see page 356). Here, you positioned the collapsible panel at the top of the page overlapping an empty area on the page's banner (top). Since you absolutely positioned the panel, it floats above other content on the page. When a visitor clicks the tab and the panel expands (bottom), it doesn't push other page content out of the way; it merely sits above the page, like a sheet of paper on a desktop. Clicking the tab above the panel hides the panel once again.

Unlike tabbed panels and accordions, a collapsible panel is just a single tab/panel pair. You can't add additional tabs or panels. You can, however, place multiple collapsible panels on a page, stacked one on top of the next. This has two distinct advantages over an accordion. First, you don't have to have a panel open when the page loads. You can have three collapsible panels on a page with all three closed. A visitor clicks the tab of one panel, and it opens, leaving the other collapsible panels unaffected.

In addition, because each collapsible panel works independent of the others, a visitor can have all of the panels open at once.

4. **From the Property inspector's Display menu, choose either Open or Closed (see Figure 13-9).**

   The Display menu controls whether the panel is opened or closed *in Design view only*. In other words, this setting is just to help you while you work within Dreamweaver; it doesn't affect how the panel appears when a visitor gets to the page.

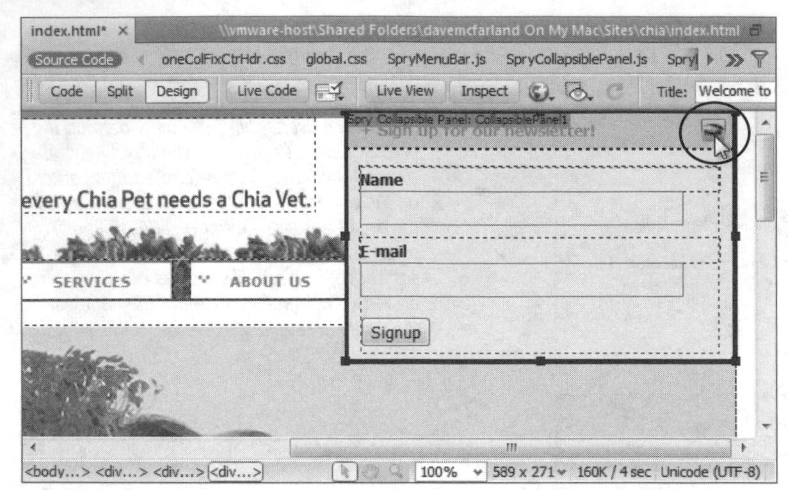

Figure 13-9:
In the Property inspector, you can skip the Display menu, and open and close the collapsible panel by clicking the eye icon (to open a closed panel) or the shut-eye icon (circled–to hide an open panel). Like the Display menu options, this controls only whether the panel is opened or closed in Dreamweaver's Design view.

5. **From the Property inspector's "Default state" menu, choose either Open or Closed (see Figure 13-9).**

   This menu controls how the panel appears—open or closed—when a web browser first loads the page. In other words, a visitor sees the panel this way when he visits the page: Either the panel is open and visible, or closed and hidden. Of course, a visitor can change that view simply by clicking the tab when he views the page.

   If you start with the panel closed, you should somehow inform visitors that they need to click the tab to see the panel's content. For example, you could simply add a + sign to the tab text like this "+ Sign up for our newsletter". Web designers commonly use the + sign to indicate that there's more information a click away. Or you could use text to let visitors know what to do: "Click here to sign up for our newsletter."

6. **Enable or disable animation.**

   Turn on the Property inspector's "Enable animation" checkbox (see Figure 13-9) if you want the panel to move in and out of view in a smooth "window-blind" effect. Uncheck this box if you simply want the panel to instantly appear and disappear from view with each tab click. The choice is purely aesthetic, so choose according to your design preferences.

Adding Content to a Collapsible Panel

A collapsible panel consists of a simple combination of <div> tags: one <div> tag marks the beginning and end of the widget, and it wraps around two other <div> tags (one for the tab, followed by another for the panel).

To edit a tab's label, in Design view, select its text, and then type in a new label. Since Dreamweaver encloses the label in a <div> tag, you can also just click inside the tab, and then press Ctrl+A (⌘-A) to select all of the label's text.

To edit the panel's content, you have to make the panel visible, and you control it either with the Property inspector's Display menu (step 4 on page 535) or on the panel's tab by clicking the eye icon (Figure 13-9). To select all the text inside a panel, click anywhere inside the panel, and then choose Edit→Select All (or Ctrl+A [⌘-A]). You can place any combination of HTML inside a panel: headlines, paragraphs, bulleted lists, forms, images, and Flash movies.

Formatting a Collapsible Panel

When you add a Spry Collapsible Panel to a web page, Dreamweaver links the page to an external style sheet named *SpryCollapsiblePanel.css*, which contains all the styles that control the look of the tab and panel. You edit the styles the same way you edit Spry Tabbed Panels (see page 524): namely, identify the element you wish to format, and then open and edit that element's style to match your page's overall design.

To help guide you in the process of modifying Spry Collapsible Panel styles, here's a list of the panel elements and the styles that control them:

- **The Collapsible Panel:** *.CollapsiblePanel*

  This style controls the border that appears around a collapsible panel. You can alter the color or style of the border, or remove it completely.

- **All tabs:** *.CollapsiblePanelTab*

  Four styles control how browsers display a collapsible panel's tab. Each style applies to the tab under different circumstances: when the panel is open, when it's closed, when a mouse moves over a tab, and when a guest clicks the tab (this last action gives the tab "focus").

  To alter the basic appearance of all tabs, edit the *.CollapsiblePanelTab* style. For example, define a font family for this style, and all tabs use that font. In addition, this style dictates the padding inside each tab, and the border that separates the tab and the panel beneath it.

- **Tab when panel is closed:** *.CollapsiblePanelTab*

  The *.CollapsiblePanelTab* style also dictates the properties, such as the background color, for the tab when the panel is closed.

Tip: The same Tip on "Accordions," regarding the fuzzy line that Firefox places around focused tabs, applies to the Spry Collapsible Panel. To remove this outline, create an advanced style called *.CollapsiblePanel: focus*, and then set that style's *outline* property to *none*.

- **Tab when moused over:** *.CollapsiblePanelTabHover, .CollapsiblePanelOpen .CollapsiblePanelTabHover*

This long group selector applies to the hover state for tabs—both when the panel is open and when it's closed. If you want to define a different hover style for a tab when the panel is open, create two styles: *.CollapsiblePanelTabHover* for a tab when the panel is closed, and *.CollapsiblePanelOpen .CollapsiblePanelTabHover* for a tab that a visitor mouses over when the panel is closed. (If you go this route, you should either delete the supplied group selector style—"*.CollapsiblePanelTabHover, .CollapsiblePanelOpen .CollapsiblePanelTabHover*"—or change its name as described on page 126 so that it applies only to one of the tab states.)

- **Tab when panel is opened:** *.CollapsiblePanelOpen .CollapsiblePanelTab, .CollapsiblePanelFocused .CollapsiblePanelTab*

  The *.CollapsiblePanelOpen .CollapsiblePanelTab* descendent selector style applies to a tab when the panel is opened. This style overwrites style properties inherited from the *.CollapsiblePanelTab* style. In Dreamweaver's stock style sheet, only the background color differs from the other tab style, but, again, you're free to modify this style.

  A tab also changes color when a visitor clicks it, or presses the Tab key to access it. The *.CollapsiblePanelFocused .CollapsiblePanelTab* style is the culprit here, so you want to edit it if you don't want this color change to take place.

- **Panel:** *.CollapsiblePanelContent*

  The *.CollapsiblePanelContent* class is applied to the <div> tag that surrounds the HTML contained in an accordion panel. You can adjust font settings for this style to affect only the text inside the panel, or add a background color to make the panel stand out from other page content.

- **Content inside the panel.** As with the panels for Spry Tabbed Panels and Spry Accordions, Dreamweaver doesn't start you out with any styles that control specific tags inside a collapsible panel. You can use the same general process described for Spry Tabbed Panels (under the bullet point "Content inside the panels" on page 527) to create descendent selectors that affect only tags inside a collapsible panel. Just use *.CollapsiblePanel*, followed by a space as the first part of the selector: For example, the style *.CollapsiblePanel p* formats paragraphs inside an accordion panel.

  Also note that content inside a collapsible panel butts directly up against the panel's left and right edges. Avoid adding padding directly to the panel (the *.CollapsiblePanelContent* style), since the animation of the panel opening and closing isn't very smooth and the second time the panel is opened it's actually taller than when it started. Instead, add padding to the tags inside the panel. For example, if you want all Heading 2 tags to indent 5 pixels from both the left and right sides of the panel, create a descendent selector (like *.CollapsiblePanelContent h2*), and then set the left and right margin properties to 5 pixels.

Spry Tooltips

Pop-up tooltips are a great way to provide supplementary information without visually overloading a web page (see Figure 13-10.) A tooltip waits in hiding, until a visitor mouses over a word, sentence, or image, then...bam!...the tooltip appears. You can use a tooltip to define a web page feature, to display pictures and text, or even to point to a web link containing extra information. *Netflix.com*, for example, provides simple listings of the DVDs they rent—just pictures, ratings, and a way to quickly add the DVD to a "to rent" list. However, when you mouse over the DVD listing, a tooltip appears featuring a detailed summary of the DVD. Dreamweaver includes a Spry tool for creating these kinds of useful pop-up boxes.

Adding a Spry Tooltip

A Spry tooltip widget consists of a *trigger*—text or an image that your visitor mouses over—and the *tooltip* itself—the pop-up box. To add one:

1. **Select a word, sentence, image, or block-level element.**

   You can turn any block-level element into a trigger, such as a paragraph, a headline, or an entire <div> tag; or you can turn a single word, sentence, or image into a trigger. Which way you go depends on the tooltip's purpose: For example, if you want to define important words in a document, select a single word to trigger the tooltip.

2. **Choose Insert ›Spry ›Spry Tooltip or, on the Insert panel, click the Spry Tooltip icon (Figure 13-2).**

   When you insert a tooltip, Dreamweaver first adds an ID to the trigger—if you select an entire paragraph, for example, Dreamweaver adds the ID name to the <p> tag like this: <p id="spryTrigger1">. If you select just a single word, Dreamweaver wraps the word in a <span> tag with the proper ID name: <span id="spryTrigger1">*word*</span>. The exact name Dreamweaver assigns depends on whether you already added tooltips to the page. You might have various IDs on the same page—spryTrigger1, spryTrigger2, and so on.

Note: You don't have to select anything to insert a tooltip. You can just place the cursor anywhere on a page, and complete step 2 here. Dreamweaver then inserts a <span> tag into the document at the location of your cursor, along with the text "Tooltip trigger goes here." You can then change the text to something more appropriate–"Move your mouse here for a pop-up list of directions"–and even move the span to another location on the page (just cut and paste the tag). You can even delete the <span> tag. This action lets you assign the tooltip to another tag, as described in step 4 on page 541.

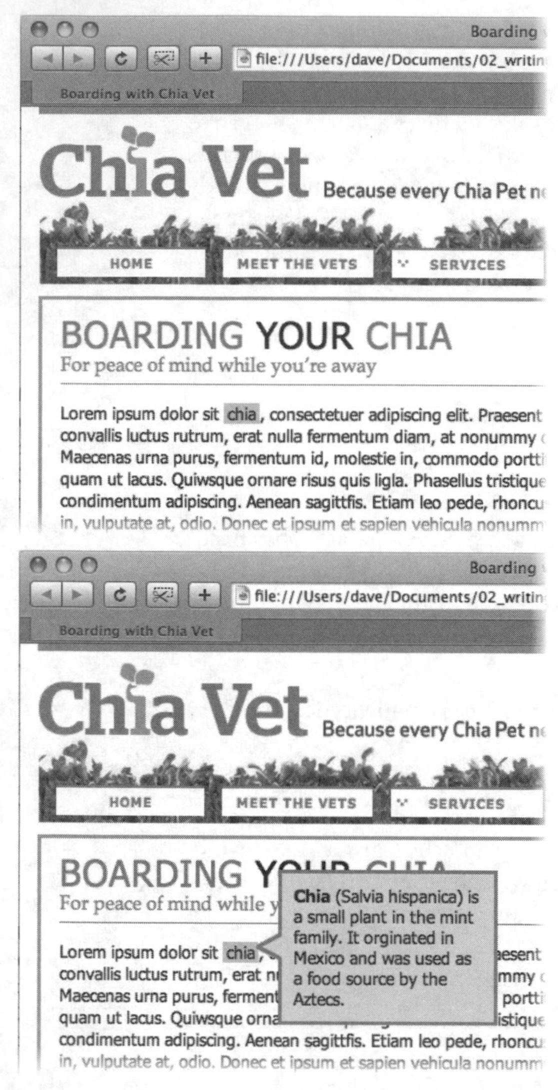

Figure 13-10:
Now you don't see it, now you do. A Spry tooltip lets you add an informative pop-up bubble that appears when a visitor mouses over a particular word, picture, or chunk of HTML.

Dreamweaver also inserts a new <div> tag containing some placeholder text—"Tooltip content goes here." This is the tooltip itself and, depending on how big your web page is, you may not actually see it at first. That's because Dreamweaver adds tooltips to the very end of the web page, after all the other content. So if you have many paragraphs of text, images, and so on, you may need to scroll down to the bottom of the page to see and edit your tooltip text. By default, the tooltip has a light yellow background, but you can change that as described in "Formatting a Tooltip" on page 544.

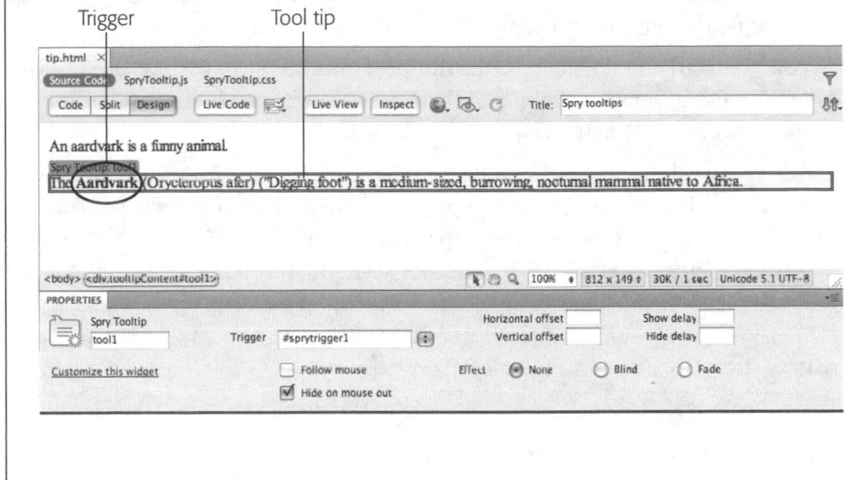

Figure 13-11: *Spry tooltips can be confusing. Unlike a lot of other Spry elements, nothing on a page identifies a tooltip trigger. The telltale blue Spry tab you see with all other Spry widgets appears only above the tooltip box itself. In this figure, for example, the word "aardvark" in the top paragraph is the trigger—mousing over it pops open the tooltip below. But unless you remember that you tooltip-ified that word, simply scanning the page doesn't make you aware of its existence. In addition, in the Property inspector, to make any changes to the tooltip's settings, you have to click the blue tab above the tooltip <div>. You can't access the tooltip settings from the tooltip trigger text.*

Note: Dreamweaver always makes tooltips visible so you can edit their content. However, when you view the page in a browser (or click the Live View button [page 578]), the tooltips remain hidden until you hover over a tooltip trigger.

3. **In the Property inspector, name the tooltip.**

   As with the other Spry widgets, this step is optional (see step 3 on page 522). Changing the name alters the ID Dreamweaver applied to the tooltip <div> tag.

4. **If you want to change the ID name Dreamweaver applies to the tooltip trigger, click anywhere inside the trigger text. In the Property inspector, type a new name in the ID box.**

In most cases, you'll skip this step. When you insert a tooltip, Dreamweaver correctly prepares all the HTML you need. But if you don't like the generic name Dreamweaver supplies (sprytrigger1, for example), you can change it.

5. **If you changed the trigger's ID in the previous step, then click the tooltip's blue Spry tab to select it again, and then, from the Property inspector's Trigger menu, select the ID name you typed in step 2.**

   This step is optional as well, so you'll probably skip it. However, you might want to select the ID name of an existing page element. For example, say you have an image on your page and you gave it the ID name logo. You can use this element as a trigger. First, insert a tooltip (without selecting any text, as described in the Note on page 539) and then, from the Property inspector's Trigger menu, select the ID of the element—for example #logo. (Don't forget to delete the original trigger <span> that Dreamweaver inserted.)

6. **In the Property inspector, set one or more of the display options (Figure 13-11).**

   The placement of the tooltip on your final web page depends on where the visitor's mouse is when he moves over the trigger element. That is, if the trigger is an entire paragraph of text and a visitor moves his mouse into the top line of the paragraph, the tooltip appears near the top of the paragraph; if he mouses up into the paragraph, the tooltip appears near the bottom of the paragraph. You can fine-tune these settings in the Property inspector, with the additional tooltip options. Here's how they work:

   - **Follow mouse.** With this option selected, the tooltip following the mouse if your visitor moves her cursor around the trigger element. For example, say a visitor triggers a tooltip when she mouses over a large picture of the Eiffel Tower. If the visitor moves the mouse around the picture, the tooltip follows along. Since this can induce sea-sickness, you might want to leave this box unchecked, in which case, once the tooltip appears, it doesn't move.
   - **Hide on mouse out.** This confusingly named option lets you keep a tooltip open as long as the mouse is over *either* the trigger element or the tooltip box itself. Normally, a tooltip disappears when you mouse off the trigger element. In general, this is a good idea, since you don't want tooltips cluttering up the page. However, if the tooltip has content that a visitor might click—such as a set of links—turn this option on. If you don't, as soon as someone moves her mouse toward one of the links in the tooltips—at the same time moving the mouse off the trigger element—the tooltip disappears, and the visitor can never click the link! Turn on this option, and the tooltip remains visible while the mouse hovers over the trigger element or the tooltip; it disappears only when the mouse is no longer over either.
   - **Horizontal and Vertical Offset.** Dreamweaver normally places tooltips 20 pixels to the right and 20 pixels down from the position where the mouse moves over the trigger element. If you want the tooltip to appear in a different location, you can type either a pixel or percentage value in the "Horizontal offset" box (to control its placement from left and right) or the "Vertical offset" box (to

control the placement from top to bottom). You can even use a negative value. For example, in Figure 13-10 the tooltip's vertical offset is set to –60%. This positions a little more than half of the tooltip above the mouse's position. By using a negative value for both offsets, you can make a tooltip appear directly over the trigger element.

- **Delay.** If you don't want a tooltip to appear immediately, type a number in the "Show delay" box. Browsers register the value in milliseconds, so if you type *1000*, the tooltip appears 1 second after a visitor mouses over the trigger. This feature may not seem very useful—after all, by the time one second passes a visitor has probably moved his mouse off the trigger, and the tooltip never appears. However, a smaller value, like 100, serves a good purpose: it prevents a tooltip from appearing if the mouse momentarily travels over a trigger. This keeps your tooltips from suddenly flashing on and off as someone mouses over the trigger on his way to somewhere else.

  The "Hide delay" option determines how long the tooltip hangs around *after* your guest moves her mouse off the trigger.

- **Effect.** You can also add visual effects to the appearance and disappearance of the tooltip. Turn on the None option if you want the tooltip to appear or disappear in a blink. But for a fancier display, choose Blind (the tooltip wipes into and out of existence like a window shade) or Fade (the tooltip fades in and out like a ghost).

Adding Content to a Tooltip

The HTML for a tooltip is very basic: It's just a single <div> tag placed at the end of your page's HTML. After you insert a tooltip, click inside the div, and then press Ctrl-A (⌘-A) to select the dummy text Dreamweaver supplies. Then add your own content. You can insert a simple paragraph, or a complex combination of HTML, including images, Flash movies, and other divs. If you want, you can even turn a tooltip into a mini-web page—just make sure you don't add so much content that the tooltip doesn't fit in the browser window.

You can also edit the tooltip's trigger element—the text, paragraph, div, or image you selected before adding the tooltip. As mentioned above, Dreamweaver adds an ID to the trigger's HTML (or, if you selected just a word or two, wraps the selection in a <span> tag, and then adds an ID to that span). Unfortunately, you have no immediate way to identify a particular tooltip's trigger element—it doesn't highlight, for example, when you select the tooltip. You need to either remember where the trigger is, or select the tooltip and then, in the Property inspector, look for the ID name applied to it (see Figure 13-11). Once you know the ID, execute a search for that name using Dreamweaver's excellent Find and Replace tool, described on page 801.

Formatting a Tooltip

When you add a Spry Tooltip to a web page, Dreamweaver links the page to an external style sheet named SpryTooltip.css, which contains only two styles. Leave the first one—*.iframeTooltip*—alone. That style overcomes some browser display bugs related to the tooltip. The second style—*.toolTipContent*—defines the look of the pop-up. Out of the box, the style has just a single property—a light yellow background. However, you'll probably want to change the background color, add some padding (page 341) to move the content away from the edges of the tooltip, and so on.

In addition, you may want to create styles that apply just to tags inside the tooltip—for example, to provide a unique look for paragraphs or a heading inside a tooltip. Here, again, descendent selectors come to the rescue (see page 298). Since all tooltip content goes inside a <div> tag with the class *tooltipContent* applied to it, you can create special styles that apply only to the content. For example, the descendent selector *.tooltipContent p* affects only paragraphs inside a tooltip.

You might also want to create a style to format a tooltip trigger. Dreamweaver doesn't help you out with this—the program doesn't supply a style to make a tooltip trigger stand out. In fact, unless you do something to alter the look of a trigger element, it's difficult for anyone to figure out that any particular element has a tooltip attached to it! For example, say you select a single word on a page, and then add a tooltip to it—perhaps the tooltip provides a definition of the word. When viewed in a web browser, that word doesn't look any different from any other word, so the visitor has no way of knowing that she should mouse over it.

One way to solve this problem is to create a class style—*.trigger*, for example—and apply it to the HTML tag for the trigger (see page 119 for instructions on applying a class to a tag). If you add tooltips to single words (as in the definition example), you might want to add a light background color to highlight the word. You could also change the cursor style used for that class. For example, if you set the *cursor* property to "Help", then the cursor changes to a question mark when a visitor mouses over the particular trigger.

Of course, if the trigger is obvious—for example, if it has the text "Mouse over me to see …"—you might not want or need to create any special style for the trigger.

Spry Data Sets

Dreamweaver includes a way to display data more dynamically than a plain-vanilla HTML table. Spry data sets provide several ways to present data from a variety of sources, including basic HTML tables or XML files. With a Spry data set, for example, you can create an interactive table that visitors can sort just by clicking the top of a table column (Figure 13-12).

Say a page has a table that lists all the employees in a company. The table includes each employee's name, the region of the country in which he or she works, the phone number, and other important data. Sometimes you probably want to see the list of employees alphabetized by last name; other times you want to sort the list by the regions in which they work (northeast, southeast, and so on). Normally, you'd have to create two web pages: one with a table of employees listed by last name, and another with employees listed by region.

With a Spry data set, you need only one page and one table, no matter how many columns you have. That's because a Spry table is interactive, just like a regular old Excel spreadsheet. Want to see employees organized by last name? Click the "Name" column. To group employees by region, just click the "Region" column. A Spry table is interactive, instantaneous, and doesn't require loading another web page.

In addition, Spry data sets let you display detailed data on a single item in the table. Suppose you have a simple table that just lists employees' names and the regions in which they work. With Spry, you can add an "Up Close and Personal" section to the page, so that when you click an employee name in a table row, detailed information, such as the employee's phone number, photo, and email address, appear in another part of the page. Once again, this little trick doesn't require the browser to download a different web page. All this information appears on the same page and with a simple mouse click.

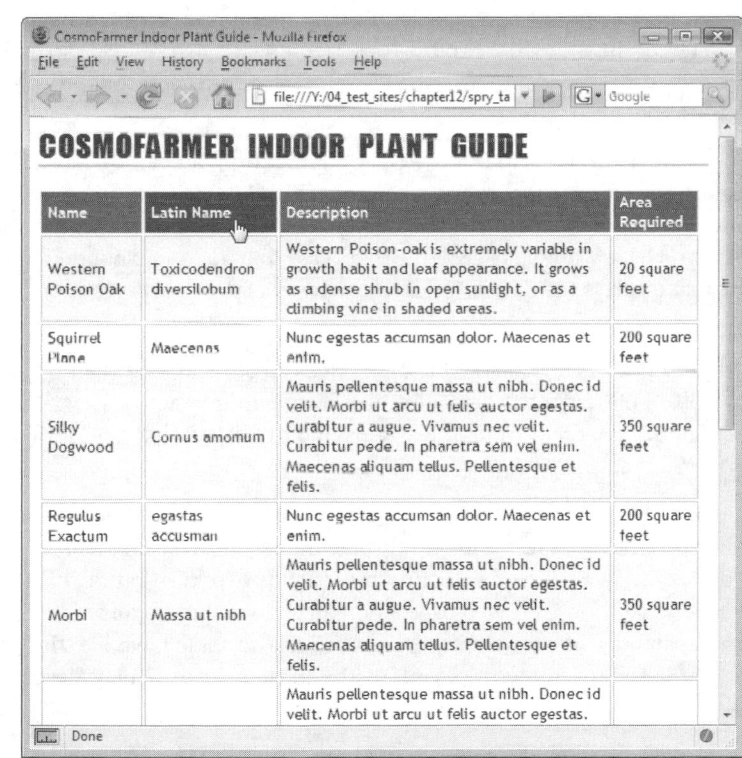

Figure 13-12: *A Spry data table lets visitors interact with your data. Clicking a column header sorts the column in ascending order; click the column again, and data is sorted in descending order. Here, if you wish to view the plants in alphabetical order by their Latin names, then click the Latin Name column header. The table's data is sorted instantly, without loading a new web page.*

If you often add data tables to your site, or simply have large amounts of related data that you want to display in an interactive format, the Spry data set is the perfect tool for you. You can store the data you want to make interactive in either a plain HTML table, like those you read about in Chapter 7, or in a more, computer-friendly format called XML. The JavaScript programming included in the Spry data set reads the data from an HTML table or an XML file and reformats it for presentation. If you have an HTML table, you can either create a separate page that displays the HTML table, or include the table directly inside the page with the Spry data set. If you use XML data, Dreamweaver stores it in a separate file. When the page that includes the table loads, the Spry programming downloads the XML file, extracts the required data, and displays it on the page.

Keep in mind that Adobe wrote Spry data sets primarily to display repeating rows of information. Although an HTML or XML file can hold any type of information, you should use it with Spry for tables that contain lists of information, like product catalogs, employee records, and so on.

Storing Data in an HTML File

To get started with Spry data sets, you need a file containing data. You can store the data in a basic HTML file or in an XML file (described next). If you don't normally deal with geek-friendly formats like XML, HTML files offer the easiest approach to Spry data sets.

Dreamweaver provides two ways to create a Spry data set from an HTML table. The first is to create a separate file that contains a basic HTML table with all your data in it. You can then use Spry to load that file and its data, and then display it on your site. This means you have a simple HTML file that's easy to update, and another, fully designed page that displays the data using Dreamweaver's Spry data set tools.

The second method is to add the HTML table to the same page as the Spry data set. In other words, insert a basic HTML table on a page in your site, and then use the Spry data set tools to massage that data, and turn it into an interactive super-table. (The Spry programming actually hides the original table of data if that table is on the same page as the Spry data set.)

This second approach might sound a bit weird. After all, why add a table to a page, and then add some fancy JavaScript just to display data from the same table? If all you want to do is display a table of data, this approach is overkill—rather, create a nice-looking HTML table on your web page, and you're done. But if you want to tap the interactive capabilities of a Spry data set—to create a sortable table like the one discussed on page 563, for example, or the interactive master/detail display discussed on page 566—this approach has a couple of advantages.

First, Spry uses JavaScript to load data into a data set. If the HTML table is in a separate file and a visitor has JavaScript turned off, then that separate HTML file never loads, and the visitor never sees the data—just an empty space where the data should be. In addition, search engines don't use JavaScript either, so any data that JavaScript loads is lost to a search engine. By putting the HTML table on the same page, search engines and visitors without JavaScript can still access the data (although they lose all the fancy interactivity JavaScript provides).

Which method to use? If you want search engines to index the data you display, or you want to make sure the data's visible even for people who have JavaScript turned off, use the second approach: Add the HTML data table to the same page that displays the data. The first approach is good if your data comes from a source other than the page that displays it—for example, if another program exports the data as an HTML table—or if you want someone who's not Dreamweaver-savvy to have a simple way to update the data in the table.

In either case, you start by adding a basic HTML table containing all your data. The table doesn't have to be fancy—your site's visitors don't actually see this web page; they just see the data pulled from the table, and either placed onto *another* web page or completely reformatted and displayed on the same page that Dreamweaver enhances with interactive Spry effects. In fact, the table should be as simple as possible (see Figure 13-13). You don't need to worry, for example, about the table's width, the cell padding and spacing, or any of the other formatting choices you make when you design regular HTML tables. Also, do yourself a favor and avoid merged cells and rowspans (page 279), which produce inconsistent results in your data. Finally, don't apply any styles to the rows, columns, or the table itself. This table, if it hasn't sunk in by now, is just for the data—you format the data's appearance when you add it to a web page using a Spry data set, as described on page 554.

Make sure the top row of the table is a header row (see page 272) that includes descriptions of each column's data. In the table in Figure 13-13, for example, the top row of cells contains table headers. Column 1 has the header named "thumb", column 2 is "large", and so on. With descriptive header names, it's easier for you, later on, to identify and select the data you want to use in a Spry data set.

Tip: You can also put images in table cells; use the same procedure you would for inserting an image into a web page (page 211). However, for those images to show up correctly on a web page that uses the Spry data tools, you need to make sure that, if you create a separate file for the HTML table, that file is in the same folder as the web page using the data. Otherwise, the path to the images is different, and they don't display on the final web page. Alternatively, you can use site root-relative links for your images (see page 161) and keep your HTML data file anywhere in your site. Any page on the site can display those images correctly, using the Spry data tools.

Finally, you need to give the table an ID. The Spry programming requires this, and if you don't provide an ID, you can't extract the data from the table. To add an ID, select the table (click the table border, for example, or use one of the other methods mentioned on page 266), and then, in the Property inspector, in the ID box (circled in Figure 13-13), type a name—a simple ID name, like *data*, works just fine.

Dreamweaver also lets you store data in tags other than HTML tables. For example, you could create a series of <div> tags that store the data you wish to display. If you go this route, you need to have one <div> tag that surrounds all your data—it has to have an ID applied to it. You also need separate divs for each row and for each column within a row, and you must apply a class to each of the row divs and another class to each of the column divs. For example, the basic HTML for a data file using divs might look like this:

```
<div id="data">
  <div class="row">
    <div class="column">Godzilla Chia</div>
    <div class="column">1955</div>
  </div>
<div class="row">
    <div class="column">Bambi Chia</div>
    <div class="column">1960</div>
  </div>
</div>
```

You need the class names—*row* and *column* in this example—to let Dreamweaver know which divs hold one row of information, and how many columns are in each row. Of course, if you go to all this trouble, you might as well create an XML file. Unless you already have data set up in the format described in this paragraph, stick to HTML tables for storing data—they're a lot easier to create and maintain.

Note: Because the Spry programming actually downloads the entire data file (the HTML or XML file) and stores it in a browser's memory, Spry data sets work best with relatively few rows of data. If you build an HTML table with 1,000 rows of information, you're better off using a database instead. Otherwise you'll find that your Spry-driven data sets run slowly in a web browser.

Storing Data in an XML File

Although the HTML table method of storing data is a simple and straightforward way to pipe data into a Spry data set, an XML file can also serve as your data source.

What is XML?

XML is a common way to store information, and it's routinely used for exchanging data between computers. You might already have XML files generated out of the computer systems at work: Databases can easily save information as XML files, for example. In addition, one of the most common web-related uses of XML is for RSS feeds—you find them at every news website, and if you run a blog on your site, you probably have an RSS feed as well. If so, you can easily post a listing of stories and articles from your site's blog directly onto any page of your website, using the Spry data set tools.

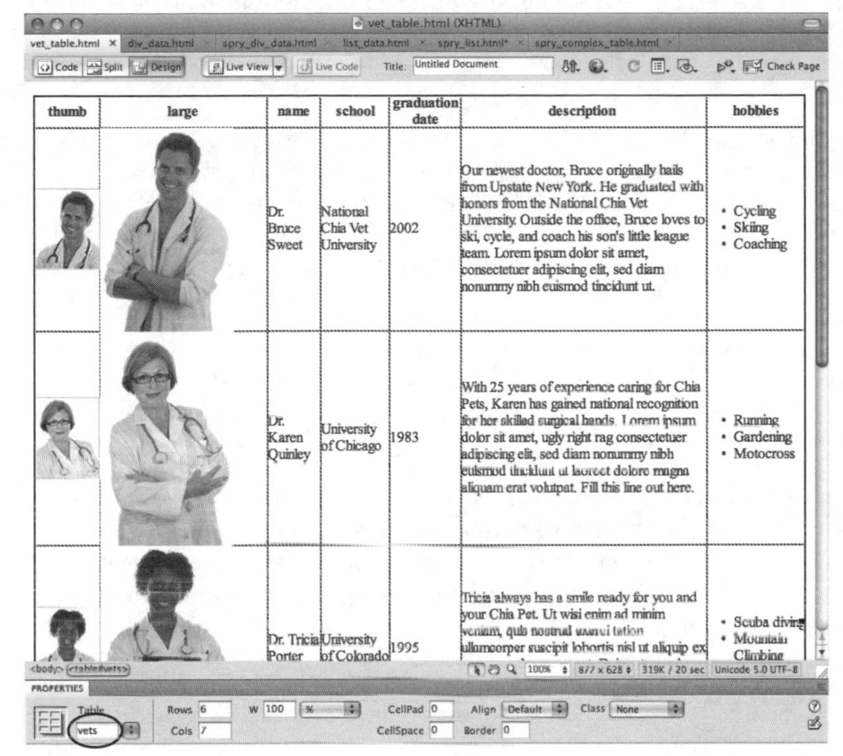

Figure 13-13: *The Spry data set tool lets you extract data from a basic HTML table and manipulate it in fun, interesting, and interactive ways. You can even suck data from an existing table on your site (a nice way to reuse content that's already on your site). The only condition is that any table you want to use for Spry data must have an ID assigned to it. See "Applying IDs to a Tag" on page 123 for details.*

Note: Spry lets you access HTML or XML files from the Web for use in Spry data sets. For example, if you want to use your blog's RSS feed to list your blog postings on other pages of your site, you can use the RSS feed from your server as the XML source for a Spry data set. Unfortunately, due to security restrictions in web browsers, you can access HTML and XML files in this way only if both your web pages (with the Spry data programming on it) and the HTML or XML file are on the same server. In other words, you can't use Spry to list the top 10 news stories from *CNN.com*. (You can, however, use Dreamweaver's server-side programming tools to do that, as described in Chapter 27.)

XML, or Extensible Markup Language, has many similarities to HTML. Like HTML, it's a tag-based language used to identify different pieces of information, and structure data into a meaningful document. For example, HTML has the <h1> tag to identify the most important headline, or the <ul> tag to denote a bulleted list. But HTML has only a handful of tags, and, in many cases, they don't always meaningfully identify the information you're presenting. You can format a news title like "Bigfoot to Wed Super Model" with an <h1> tag, but you could also use the <h1> tag to format the name of a product you're selling, the title of a book, or an event on a calendar. In these cases, you're using the same tag to identify different *types* of information. Technically speaking, there's nothing wrong with using <h1> tags that way. But you can introduce some awfully messy organizational problems into your document, as you'll learn in a moment. Instead, it would be much more informative to use a tag that accurately identifies the type of information, like <product>, <title>, or <event>.

That's where the "X" in XML comes in. XML is not really a markup language like HTML, as much as it is a set of guidelines for creating your own markup languages. The X, or *extensible*, part of XML lets you define your own types of tags—or "extend" the language to fit your needs. In this way, you can create very specific tags to describe different types of information, like invoices, books, personnel, and so on.

Note: To learn more about XML, check out *www.w3schools.com/xml*, grab a copy of *Learning XML*, (O'Reilly, 2003) by Erik T. Ray, or visit the XMLTopic Center on the Adobe website: *www.adobe.com/devnet/topics/xml.html*.

Suppose *Chia-Vet.com* wants to use XML to store data about Chia Pets, and so decides to come up with an XML format for storing their list of favorite Chia Pets. That list consists of each Chia Pet's name, when it was issued, how rare it is, a short description of its features, and a path to an image file on the site. In HTML, this information might look like this:

```
<h2>Chia Godzilla <em>1955</em></h2>
<p><img src="images/godzilla.jpg">Chia Godzilla was produced in a limited run
following the release of the classic 1954 movie, Godzilla. <strong>Very rare.
</strong></p>
```

This code is all well and good for display in a web browser, but it doesn't give you any sense of what *kind* of information it is. This quality is particularly important when you keep in mind that XML was invented as a way to exchange data between computers. So if another computer encounters this HTML, it doesn't understand the purpose of the text inside the <h2> tag. In fact, even a human viewing this code might not easily discern what the "1955" means; it's a number, but without some descriptive label, you can't tell that this number refers to the year the product was sold. XML provides a much clearer way to define the structure and meaning of content.

Chia-Vet.com's IT staff could come up with its own XML format to store this data. They might write the same information in XML like this:

```
<pets>
<pet>
<name>Chia Godzilla</name>
<issuedate availability="very rare">1955</issuedate>
<description>Chia Godzilla was produced in a limited run following the
release of the classic 1954 movie, Godzilla.</description>
<image>images/godzilla.jpg</image>
</pet>
</pets>
```

Kind of like HTML, right? But with a completely different set of tags. This new markup makes the meaning of each chunk of information clearer. You can easily tell that this data describes a Chia Pet (the <pet> tag) with a name, a description, and so on. In a nutshell, that's what XML offers: Tags that meaningfully identify the information inside them.

Rules of the road

Since XML is intended as an easy way to exchange data between computers, operating systems, programs, institutions, and people, it has some fairly strict requirements to ensure that everyone's playing by the same rules. If you've done your fair share of writing raw HTML code, much of this will be familiar. In fact, if you've written XHTML code (see page 527), then you've already been writing XML. XHTML is an XML version of HTML that just has a few more rules than plain old HTML.

- **Every XML document must have a single "root" element.** A root element is a tag that surrounds all other tags in a document, and appears only once in that document. In an XHTML (and an HTML) document, this is the <html> tag. In the example XML format introduced above, this tag is <pets>. If you're creating your own XML-formatted file, you can make this root element whatever you want: <events>, <employees>, and so on. It makes sense for this tag to describe whatever content you store inside the file.
- **All tags must be nested properly, with no overlapping tags.** This rule works just as it does in HTML. You can't have code like this: <b><i>Bold and italics</b></i>. Since the opening <i> tag appears after the opening <b> tag, its closing tag—</i>—must appear before (or "inside of") the closing <b> tag, like this: <b><i>Bold and italics</i></b>.
- **All tags must have both an opening and closing tag, or be self-closing.** In HTML, you indicate a paragraph of text by both an opening <p> and a closing </p>. Some HTML tags, however, don't hold content, like the <img> tag or the line break (<br>) tag. The XML version of these tags include a forward slash at the end of the tag, like this: <br />. This type of tag is called an *empty element*.
- **The property values of all tags must be quoted.** In regular old HTML, you could get away with this line as a way to add a link to a page: <a href=index.html>Home</a>. In XML, this doesn't fly. You need to quote the *href* property's value like this: <a href="index.html">Home</a>. You're probably used to doing this already, and if you've been using Dreamweaver, the program always does it for you. But when you write your own XML files, make sure to include quotes around a tag's property values.

If your XML file meets these conditions, it's known as (to use the official XML designation) "well-formed." In other words, your XML code is written properly. If you write more complex XML documents, you need to follow additional rules, but those are the basic requirements.

In many cases, you also include what's called a *prolog*—an introduction of sorts that appears at the very top of the document and announces what kind of document it is. In its most basic form, the prolog looks like this:

```
<?xml version="1.0"?>
```

The prolog can also include the type of encoding (useful for indicating different characters for different languages) the document uses.

Here, then, is a basic, complete, and well-formed XML document:

```
<?xml version="1.0" encoding="utf-8"?>
<pets>

<pet>
    <name>Chia Godzilla</name>
    <issuedate availability="very rare">1955</issuedate>
    <description>Chia Godzilla was produced in a limited run following the
release of the classic 1954 movie, Godzilla.</description>
    <image>images/godzilla.jpg</image>
</pet>

<pet>
    <name>Chia Bambi</name>
    <issuedate availability="very rare">1960</issuedate>
    <description>Chia Bambi was produced in a limited run and some units were
packaged as a set with Chia Godzilla.</description>
    <image>images/bambi.jpg</image>
</pet>

</pets>
```

Note: Dreamweaver can verify whether or not an XML file is well-formed. Open the file in Dreamweaver, and then choose File→Validate→As XML. The Results panel opens. If nothing appears inside the Validation panel, the file is OK. If there's an error, then a message explaining the problem appears. Fix the error, and then try to validate the document again. Dreamweaver can even validate XML using a DTD file (see the box below).

If you want to use XML as a data source, you need to either create an XML file like the one listed above (but hopefully not about Chia Pets or Godzilla), or export data in an XML file format from another program, such as a database or Microsoft Excel. Place that XML file (with the file extension .xml) with the other files in your local site.

Inserting a Spry Data Set

Dreamweaver provides an easy-to-follow wizard that lets you create both a complete Spry data set *and* all the HTML needed to display the data using one of four canned layouts. (You can also create your own data set layouts, as described on page 571.

To begin using a Spry data set, open a web page you want to add Spry data to, and then click in the area of the page where you want to insert the data. Next, insert the Spry data set object from the Insert panel's Data category (Figure 13-14) or by choosing Insert→Spry→Spry Data Set. The new Spry Data Set wizard opens. The process has three basic steps:

1. **Choose a data source.**

   The data source is the HTML or XML file containing your data (described on pagespage546andpage548). You can specify a file on your computer, or even use an absolute URL pointing to a file on your web server. (Due to security limitations of web browsers, you have to have the data source file and the web page that displays the Spry data on the same server.)

UP TO SPEED

Taming the Tower of Babel: DTDs and XML Schema

You may be wondering: If anyone can make up her own tags to create her own types of XML files, how can XML help computers, people, and organizations exchange data? After all, if you come up with one way of formatting invoices using XML, and your buddy in accounting uses his own set of tags to create invoices, you'll end up with two different and incompatible types of files for tracking the same information. It's like the Tower of Babel–everyone speaking his own language and unable to talk to one another. Fortunately, XML provides two solutions to this problem: *DTDs* (or Document Type Definitions) and *XML Schemas*. Both create a common vocabulary, so everyone can use the same language to talk about the same things.

In fact, you already use a DTD when you build web pages in Dreamweaver. When you create a new web page, Dreamweaver adds a line of code at the beginning of the page, like this:

```
<!DOCTYPE html PUBLIC "-//W3C//DTD XHTML
1.0 Transitional//EN" "http://www.w3.org/
TR/xhtml1/DTD/xhtml1-transitional.dtd">
```

This line varies depending on the type of HTML or XHTML you use, but the concept is the same. The entire line defines the document type for the page–in this example, XHTML 1.0 Transitional–and points to a URL where the DTD can be found–here, it's *www.w3.org/TR/xhtml1/DTD/xhtml1-transitional.dtd*.

Essentially, the DTD for each type of HTML or XHTML defines what tags the language allows, and how coders should write them. If you don't follow the rules, the page is considered invalid.

XML Schemas are just another way to enforce a language for a particular XML format, with a few bells and whistles that DTDs lack. DTDs have been around a long time and are more common; schemas are a newer concept, but will probably eventually replace DTDs. Both XML Schemas and DTDs are very confusing beasts–difficult to read, and difficult to create. There are many DTDs and Schemas, and they describe a wide range of different types of information. A consortium of businesses that agrees to a single way of describing information often creates these DTDs and Schemas, so they can easily share data with each other. You probably won't create your own anytime soon, but keep in mind that they exist, and they're a common way to make sure everyone speaks the same tongue.

Dreamweaver includes a nice feature related to both DTDs and Schemas: If you include a DTD or Schema in an XML file and then edit that XML file in Code view, Dreamweaver displays Code Hints for the various XML tags as you type. Code Hints are shortcuts for typing an entire tag or tag property; as you begin to type a tag, Dreamweaver pops up a small window displaying tags that match what you've typed so far. At that point, you can select the correct tag, instead of typing it all out. This feature is also available when you work with HTML in Code view, and you'll find it described on page 422.

The exact process of choosing a data source differs depending on whether you have the data in an HTML table or an XML file. See the specifics for each file type below.

2. **Set data options.**

   In this step, you choose various options, such as how to sort the data. Again, since the exact options differ between HTML and XML data, you'll learn below about the specifics for each file type.

3. **Choose insert options.**

   This step is the same for both HTML and XML data files. You choose from four ready-to-use layouts. In other words, the wizard inserts all the necessary HTML and CSS required to display your data. You'll see these layout options discussed on page 562. You can also tell Dreamweaver to just create the data set, leaving you free to manually apply your own design—page 571 has the full scoop.

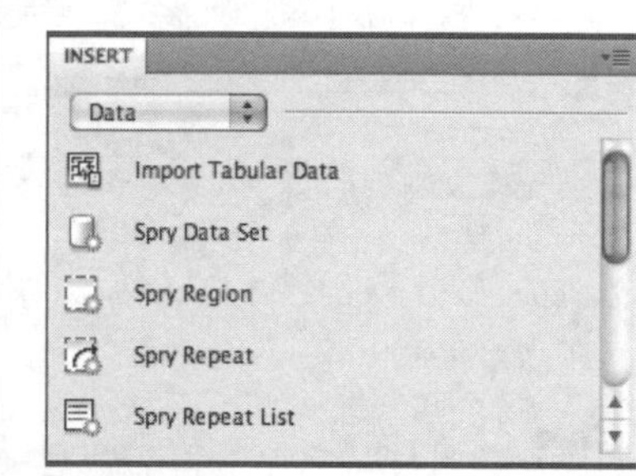

Figure 13-14:
You can insert Spry data set objects using the button in the Insert panel's Data category.(Many of these buttons also hang out in the Spry category.

Inserting HTML Data

The Spry Data Set window takes you step by step through the process of selecting an HTML data file, and then inserting it into your web page (see Figure 13-15). This window's many choices can make it a little intimidating, but setting the options correctly is a pretty simple process:

1. **From the Select Data Type menu, choose HTML.**

2. **In the Data Set Name field, type a name.**

   Dreamweaver supplies a generic name—like *ds1*—but change it to something more descriptive. If you add multiple data sets to a page, distinguishing among *ds1, ds2, ds3* isn't as easy as among, say, *dsEvents, dsEmployees*, and *dsProducts.*

   However, keep *ds* prefix—*dsEvents*, for example. If you ever go into Code view, this small step makes it easy for you to identify a reference to a Spry data set.

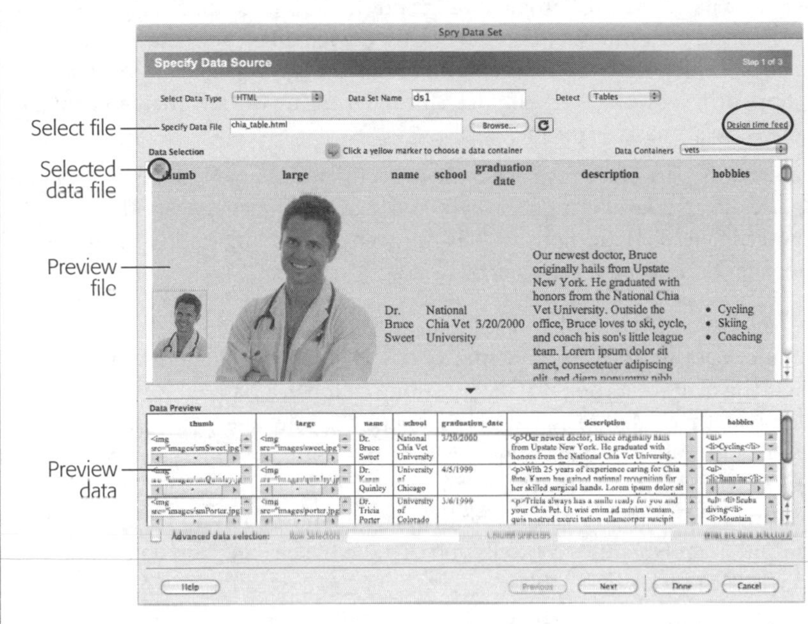

***Figure 13-15:** When you choose an HTML file as a Spry data source, Dreamweaver shows you a preview of the web page file, and lets you specify which table on the page to use. You can specify a complete web page, including a banner, footer, and logo (as well as the HTML table whose data you want), but you're better off creating a plain, simple web page that contains only the table and the data you want. That way, you let the Spry programming just load the data (and not any unnecessary HTML) it needs. The result is a faster-loading web page.*

3. **From the Detect menu, select Tables.**

   You can actually select Divs, List, or Custom from this menu, too. As mentioned earlier, you can store data inside any nested group of HTML tags, such as a group of <div> tags or even a nested unordered list (the Detect menu lets you specify the HTML tag you used in the data file). However, HTML tables really are the most straightforward way to store data, so you're better off sticking with the Tables option.

4. **Click the Browse button, and locate and select an HTML file.**

   You can choose a separate file with a table, or even the same file you're working on if it has the data table you want to "Spry-ify." You can also type in an absolute URL that points to an HTML file—like *http://www.chia-vet.com/vets/table.php*. This is handy if you're not pulling data from an actual HTML file, but from a program that generates the HTML (for example, from a database on your web server). In that case, use the URL of the server-side program that generates the data.

Note: If you specify a URL for the data file, you can choose a temporary local file while you construct the data set. Click the "Design Time feed" link (circled in top right of Figure 13-15), and then, from your hard drive, select an HTML file. You might choose this option if you're not connected to the Internet and Dreamweaver can't communicate with your web server, or if the programming that generates the data isn't ready. You need a file that duplicates the HTML the server will produce for this to work. You can also use the Design Time feed for XML files.

Keep in mind a couple of caveats when you work with absolute URLs. First, for the Spry data set to work, the data file and the web page that displays the data have to be on the same site. In other words, if you add a Spry data set that specifies an XML file on *www.chia-vet.com*, to a web page at *www.cosmofarmer.com*, the Spry data set won't work. In fact, a browser trying to view that Spry-enabled page displays a nasty error message.

That error is part of a browser's built-in security system. When a page on one site tries to use JavaScript to access and display data from another site, the browser smells something fishy—"Is this web page trying to pretend it's on another site?"—and spits out an error message.

5. **Identify the data container.**

   The Spry data set tools let you specify any HTML page, including the page to which you're adding the Spry data (as long as it has a data table); you can also specify another fully designed HTML page on your site that just happens to have a table on it. The page might even have a couple of different tables, so you need to tell Dreamweaver which one to use. As mentioned earlier, when you build an HTML data table for use with Spry, you must apply an ID to the table. If you don't, then Dreamweaver tells you that the file has no valid data containers, and you can't pick a data table.

   You can identify a data container two ways. The middle part of the Spry Data Set wizard window shows a preview of the HTML file containing the table (see Figure 13-15). A yellow arrow indicates a valid table (that is, any HTML table with an ID). Click the yellow arrow, and it turns green indicating that Dreamweaver will use the information from that table for the Spry data set (circled on left side of Figure 13-15). If you know the name of the ID you applied to the HTML table, then, in the top right of the window, you can select it from the Data Containers menu.

   After you select a table, in the bottom portion of the window, Dreamweaver previews the table's data (see Figure 13-15). If the table has a row of table headers at the top, then the text in that row's cells appears as the name at the top of each column. For example, in Figure 13-15 the text "thumb" appears in the Data Preview pane at the top of the first column, because the same text is inside a table header cell in the actual HTML file. (See the HTML preview in the middle of Figure 13-15.)

6. **Optionally specify advanced data selection rules.**

   If you use HTML tables for data, then, at the bottom of the Specify Data Source window, you probably never need to turn on the "Advanced data selection" checkbox (see Figure 13-15). However, if you're using nested <div> or <ul> tags to store data, then you *have to* choose this option, and then specify which tags are rows and which are columns. For instance, in the earlier nested div example, each <div> tag that acts as a single row has the class name *row* applied to it; likewise, divs that act as single "cells" of information have the class name *column*. So, to use the nested div example, you would need to turn on the "Advanced data selection" box, and in the Row Selectors box, type *.row*, and in the Column Selectors box, type *.column*. (Dreamweaver uses the same syntax as CSS to specify a class selector.)

Or, even better, just use HTML tables and skip this entire step!

7. **Click the Next button.**

   The Set Data Options window appears (see Figure 13-16), previewing the data, and providing tools for setting various options for the data display.

8. **Set column data types.**

   Click each column, and then, from the Type menu, choose an option. This step is necessary only if you want to sort the table before a browser displays the data (see the next step) or if you want to give your visitors the ability to sort the table by column. You can choose one of four types of data:

   - **String.** Choose *string* for text. For example, if the column contains people's names, choose this option.
   - **Number.** Choose *number* if a column contains, uh, numbers, of course. For example, if the column displays how many units of a particular product you have in stock, then, from the Type menu, choose *number*. For a sortable table (like the kind described on page 563), a visitor can then click the Units column and view product listings in the order of how many units are in stock.
   - **Date.** Use this option if the column holds dates in the form of 3/29/2009—in other words, the month, followed by a forward slash, the day, another forward slash, and the year. You can specify the month and day with either one or two digits—03 and 3 both work—and the year with either two or four digits—11 and 2011 both work. However, if the column includes just years (such as 1977), then use the *number* option.
   - **HTML.** Finally, if the column contains HTML markup (such as <img src="photo.jpg">), then you can choose this option. You don't actually have to, though, because Dreamweaver strips out the HTML anyway if you choose the *string* option.

9. **Set additional options.**

   The Set Data Options window's bottom portion has several options that control how Spry displays the data from the HTML file:

   - **Sort column.** If you want to sort the data before it's displayed on the page, choose a column from this menu. For example, if you have an HTML table listing employee names and information, you could choose the employee name column to make sure the employees are listed in alphabetical order. From the menu to the right, choose Ascending if you want the data to be sorted A–Z or 1–100; choose Descending to put the data in the opposite order: Z–A or 100–1

- **Use first row as header.** Dreamweaver automatically turns on this box if the first row of the table contains table header (<th> tags). If the first row of table cells contains real data that you want displayed, make sure this box is unchecked.

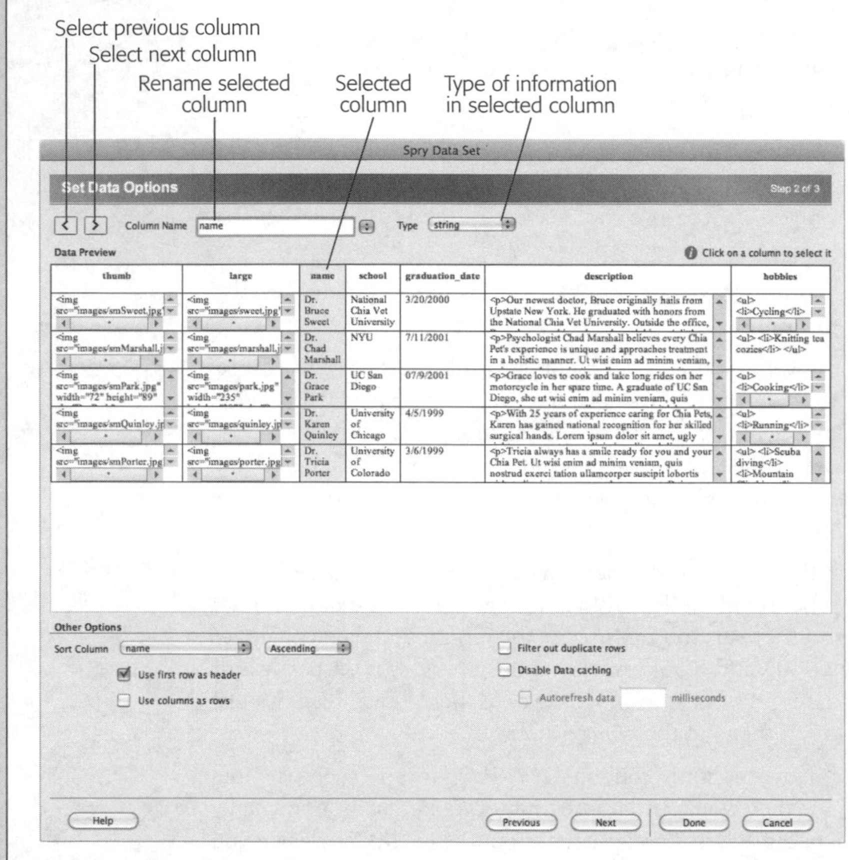

Figure 13-16: *Use the Set Data Options window to assign data types to each column. You only need to do this, however, if you plan on either making your table sortable (page 563), or if you use the Sort Column option at the bottom of the window; in addition, you need to assign a data type only to the columns that you want to sort, and the ones you want your visitors to be able to sort. (As you'll see on page 564, you don't have to make every column sortable.)*

- **Use columns as rows.** If you organized your table so each column contains data on a single record, turn on this checkbox. This configuration is common on pages that compare products. To give guests an easy-to-read, side-by-side comparison, each table row holds data for *different* records (for example, a row might display the prices of four different cellphones). If you set up your table like this, turn on this checkbox to make sure the data for each record remains grouped together.

- **Filter out duplicate rows.** Turn on this box only if your table has the same record with the identical data listed twice.

- **Disable Data caching.** Sometimes, data needs to be as fresh as bread from the bakery. Stock prices, sports scores, and other time-sensitive info needs to be up-to-date. Since web browsers tend to download and store files in a cache (see page 689), when you load a Spry data set page, you may be looking at data downloaded a week earlier. Turn on this checkbox to force the Spry programming to download the HTML data file every time it downloads the web page. This is especially true if the data comes from a frequently updated database.

  However, if you modify the HTML data table only every now and again, keep this box unchecked. The web page performs more quickly if the browser doesn't have to constantly download the HTML data file.

- **Autorefresh data.** This option is available only if you select the "Disable Data caching" box. Put a check in this box if your data changes *really* frequently—as in every few seconds or so. With this option set, a browser downloads the data file according to the schedule you specify in the milliseconds box. For example, if you type 1000 in the milliseconds box (see Figure 13-16), the browser downloads the HTML data file every second. Normally, you use this option only when the HTML data comes from a server program that receives constantly updated information.

10. **Click Next, and then select a method for inserting the Spry data.**

    The Choose Insert Options screen gives you the same option for HTML and XML data files. Details on how to use it start on page 562.

Inserting XML Data

The process for using an XML file with a Spry data set is similar to the HTML file method just described: Open the web page to which you want to add Spry data, click in the region on the page where the data should go, and then choose Insert→Spry→Spry Data Set or use the Insert Panel to open the Spry Data Set wizard (Figure 13-17). Then follow these steps:

1. **From the Select Data Type menu, choose XML.**
2. **In the Data Set Name field, type a name.**

   As with HTML data sets (page 554), change the generic name Dreamweaver supplies—*ds1*, for example—to something more descriptive—like *dsEvents.*
3. **Click the Browse button, and then locate and select an XML file.**

   You can also type an absolute URL that points to an XML file—like *www.chiavet.com/rss/*. This is handy for dynamically generated XML files, such as an RSS feed on a blog. In that case, you don't have a real file you can point to on your computer; just use the URL of the server-side program that generates the data.

Note: If you specify a URL for the data file, the same security restrictions that apply to HTML data (described on page 554) apply to XML data: The URL to the XML file must come from the same domain as the web page that displays the XML data. In addition, see the note on page 555.

Dreamweaver loads the XML schema—the structure of the XML file. You can see this structure pictured in the large "Row element" box. In Figure 13-17, a nested list of names indicates the different tags in the XML file. Each < > icon represents a tag. The topmost item (rss) is the root element (see page 551). Inside the root element, you find other nested tags.

The XML file usually has at least one repeated element, which has a + symbol to the right of its < > icon. In Figure 13-17, the repeated element is named "item". (This XML file contains a list of items from an RSS feed.) Within a repeated element, you can have other elements as well, such as the *title, link, comments*, and *pubDate* tags pictured in this example. The @ symbol indicates an attribute of an element (like a tag's property). In this example, *isPermalink* is an attribute of the <guid> tag. (One example of this tag in the XML file might look like this: <guid isPermalink="false">*http://www.sawmac.com/etc/2010/07/25/dreamweaverCS5.*</guid>.)

4. **From the list of XML tags, select a Row element.**

   The Spry data set tools can display multiple instances of similar data, such as a list of employee phone numbers, or a list of events. So your job is to tell Dreamweaver which XML tag indicates a repeating item. Basically, you just select an element that has a + symbol. In Figure 13-17, that's the *item* element.

   After you select a row element, Dreamweaver fills out the Spry Data Set window's XPath field (see Figure 13-17). A preview of the data appears in the lower portion of the window. Each tag that's nested inside the row element tag is treated like a column in a table. In Figure 13-17, the "item" element is like a table row; the "title", "link", "comment", and "pubDate" elements are each like the data you'd find in that row's columns.

5. **Click the Next button to move to the Set Data options screen (see Figure 13-18).**

   The options listed here are similar to those for an HTML table: Assign data types to the columns of data, choose a sorting option, and then assign caching options for the XML file as described in steps 8 and 9 on page 557.

6. **Click Next, and then select a method for inserting the Spry data.**

   The Choose Insert Options screen provides the same option for HTML and XML data files, and is discussed next.

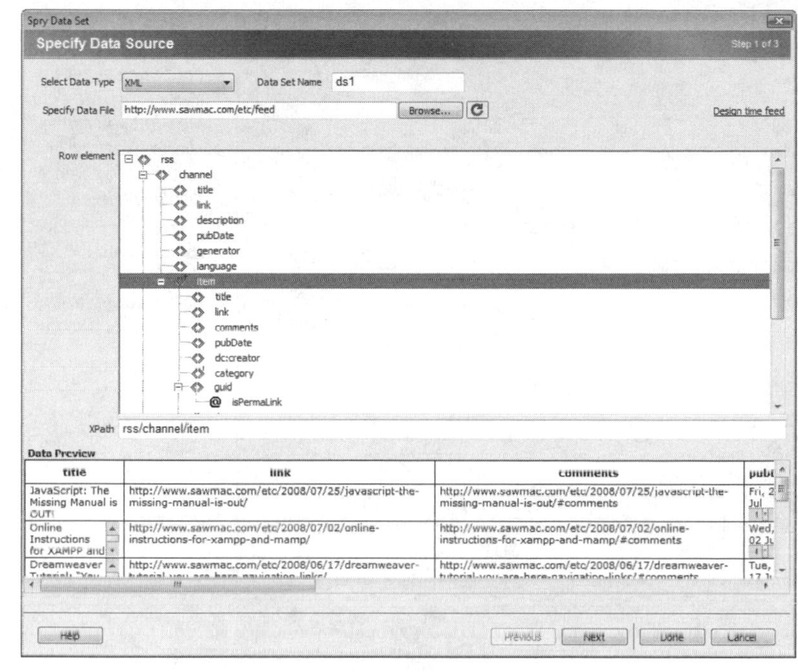

Figure 13-17: *Unless you're an XML pro, don't fill out the XPath field. Dreamweaver automatically does that for you when you identify a repeating row. XPath is a language that identifies particular elements or tags in an XML file. You use XPath to create what's called an "XPath expression," which is kind of like a trail of cookie crumbs that leads from one part of a document (frequently the beginning tag, or "root element") to the particular "node"–tag or tag property–you wish to select. In its most basic form, XPath works very much like the document window's Tag selector: It pinpoints a tag nested in any number of other tags. For instance, in this example, the XPath expression "rss/channel/item" means: Start at the rss element (that's the root element of this particular XML file), move to the channel element, and then find a nested tag named "item". Chapter 27 has more about XPaths.*

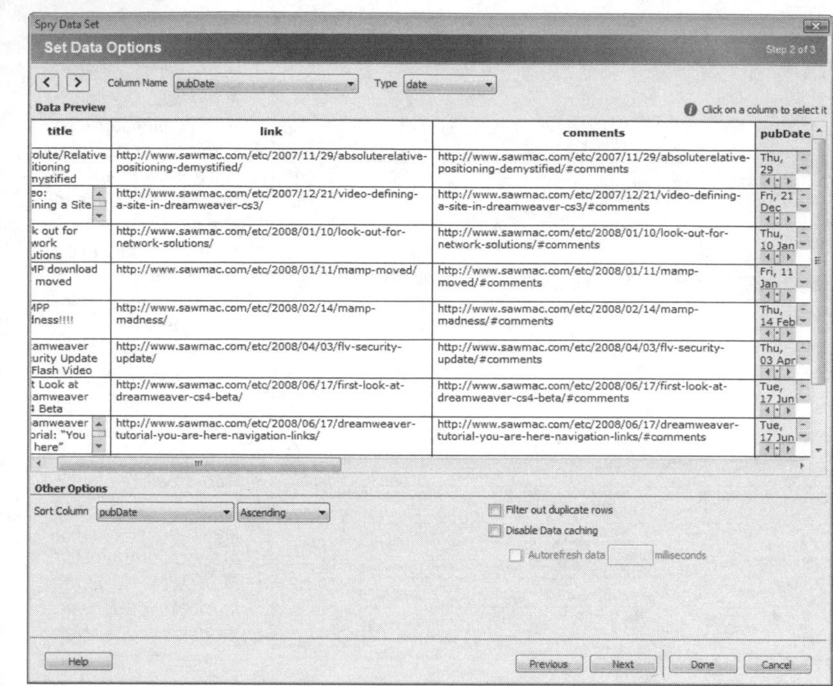

***Figure 13-18:** The options for XML data are simpler than those for HTML data files, but you can still choose whether to sort the data before displaying it and instruct the page to re-download the XML data at set intervals—perfect for up-to-the-minute sports scores.*

Choosing a Data Layout

The last step for the Spry Data Set wizard is selecting how you wish to insert the data into your web page (see Figure 13-19). To make the process easier, Dreamweaver includes four ready-to-use layouts which insert the necessary HTML tags, add the data, attach an external CSS file with some basic formatting, and essentially perform all the heavy lifting so that you just need to massage the CSS to match the look of your site. You'll read about each of these four options in the following sections.

Alternatively, you can just add the data set programming as described in the previous sections, and then add the data to your page by hand, using a panel just for this purpose: the Bindings panel (you'll learn this method on page 573). This provides the greatest amount of layout flexibility at a cost of more time, effort, and brain cells.

Note that once you finish with the Spry Data Set wizard and select one of the four layouts, you can't return to the wizard and change the layout, or alter any of the layout options you selected when you first inserted the layout into the page. You can, however, delete any of the Spry layouts on the page (for example, the Spry table the wizard inserted). You can then reinsert a different layout (or choose different layout options) by editing the Spry data set as described on page 573.

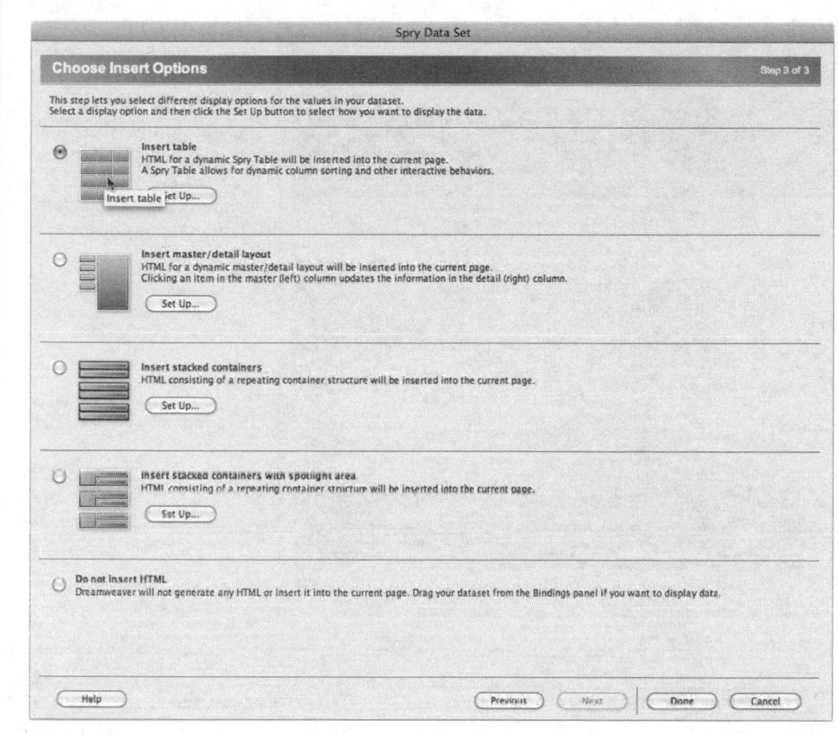

Figure 13-19: *Dreamweaver's Spry Data Set wizard makes it easy to insert all the code necessary to create one of four canned layouts for your data. If you don't like the four that come with Dreamweaver, choose the "Do not insert HTML" button, and then insert the data the way you'd like it.*

Spry Table

The first choice in the Choose Insert Options window (see Figure 13-19) is the easiest way to present rows of information from an XML file in a quick and orderly fashion (see Figure 13-20). While the information might look like a regular HTML table, it's actually interactive, letting visitors click column headers to sort the data and mouse over rows to highlight them.

To add this kind of Spry table, click the "Insert table" button in the Choose Insert Options window (Figure 13-19) and then:

1. **Click the Set Up button.**

   The Insert Table window opens (see Figure 13-21).

2. **Remove and rearrange your table's columns.**

   Dreamweaver lists all the columns from the data set. Each column appears inside a single table cell. If you don't want one of the elements to appear in the table, click its name in the Columns list, and then press the minus (-) button to remove it. (If you want to bring back a column you deleted, press the + button, and then select the column name in the window that appears.)

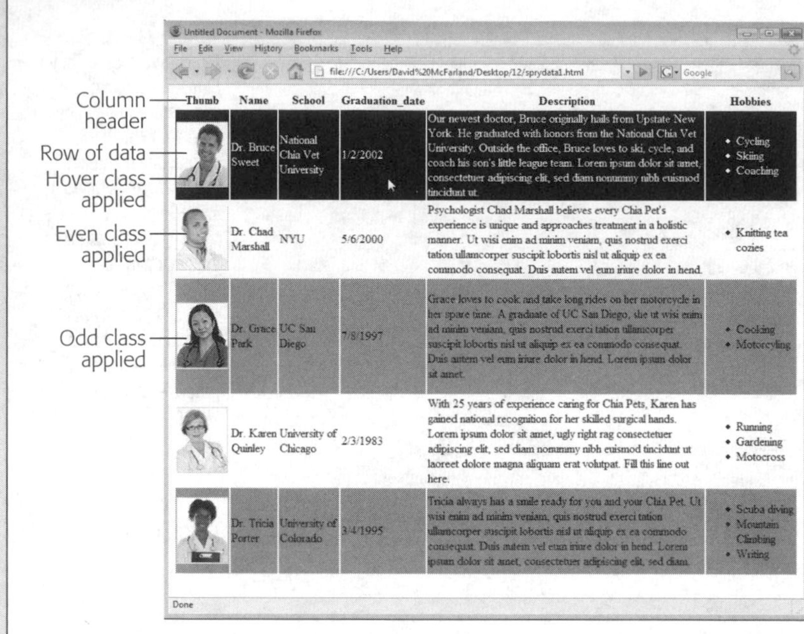

Figure 13-20: *This is the basic, out-of-the-box look of a Spry Data Table. Dreamweaver adds a style sheet with a couple of CSS styles to identify every other row and highlight a row as a visitor mouses over it.*

Removing an element from the column list means only that Dreamweaver won't add the column to the table it's about to create. You're free to use the Bindings panel (discussed on page 573) after you insert the table to drag missing elements into the table.

You can also rearrange the columns so that they appear in a different order in the table. The name at the top of the list is the table's left-most column; the name at the bottom is the column on the far right. To rearrange a column, click its name, and then press the up-arrow button (to move its column of data to the left in the final table) or the down-arrow button (to move the column to the right).

3. **Assign sortable columns.**

   One of a Spry table's coolest features is its ability to instantly re-sort table data simply by clicking a column's header. If someone visiting your web page wants to sort the information in a Spry table differently from the way you presented it, he just needs to click a different header.

   Columns aren't normally sortable—the Insert Spry Table window defaults to listing all columns as non-sortable. To make a column sortable, in the Column list, select its name, and then turn on the "Sort column when header is clicked" checkbox (see Figure 13-21).

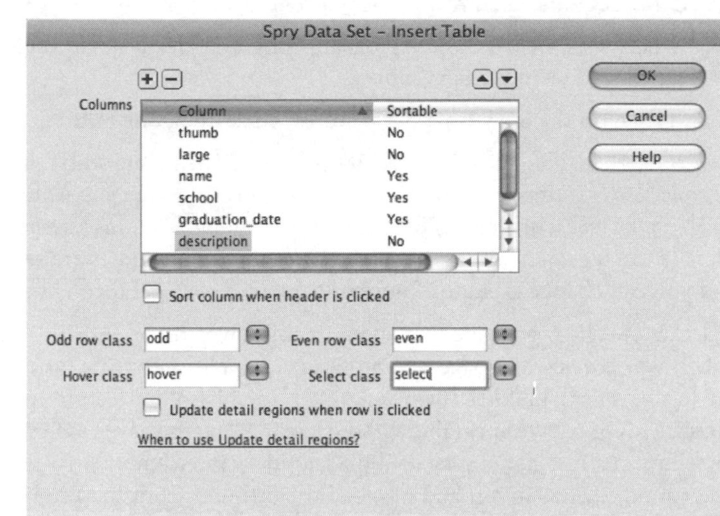

Figure 13-21: *It doesn't always make sense to make a column sortable. For example, it's not useful to sort a column full of descriptive paragraphs (who wants to see a list of items based on whether their description begins with "A", "The", or "This"?), nor would you want to sort a column based on the name of thumbnail images.*

4. **Assign CSS classes to table rows.**

   A Spry table provides helpful visual feedback that makes it easier for you to read and interact with a table of data. You can more easily scan all the columns in a single, wide row of data if every other row has a distinct background color (see the Spry table in Figure 13-20). Dreamweaver lets you assign a class style to a table's odd rows and another class style to its even rows. For a simple approach, create two classes, *.odd* and *.even*, each with different background colors. Then, in the Insert Spry Table window, select the appropriate class from the "Odd row class" menu and the "Even row class" menu.

   Similarly, you can assign classes to rows based on how someone interacts with a row. For example, you can make a row change color when someone mouses over any column in the row. Or you can change a row's color when someone clicks it (a kind of "this row is now selected" indicator). The *hover* class controls the look of a row when a mouse passes over it, while the Spry programming applies the *select* class when someone clicks a row. Both are useful for master/detail layouts, but since Dreamweaver has a simple tool for creating those types of layouts, you'll probably skip these options (unless you like the eye candy).

   If you haven't yet created any class styles for these rows, then just type in a class name (without the period). Even if you're not sure you want to change the look of the table's rows, assign classes to all four options (*odd*, *even*, *hover*, and *select*) anyway. Dreamweaver provides no way to return to the Insert Spry Table window, so if you later decide to add styles to the rows, then you have to go into Code view and add them by hand using specific Spry syntax (see page 534). Save yourself this hardship by assigning the classes while you've got an easy-to-use dialog box.

5. **If you plan to include a detail region with your table (discussed next), turn on the "Update detail regions when row is clicked" checkbox.**

   This option makes sure that the Spry programming changes a detail region when a visitor clicks a row in the Spry table.

6. **Click OK, and then, in the Spry Data Set window, click the Done button.**

   Dreamweaver inserts a table into the page. It's just an HTML table with a little extra Spry code. You can resize the table, and then adjust it just as you would a regular HTML table (see Chapter 7). The top row of the table contains a series of table headers (<th> tags) containing each column's name. The names are regular text, and you can change them to a more understandable label if you like.

   The second row of cells represents the data. Dreamweaver represents just one row, but when you preview the page in a browser, a table row appears for each row of data in the HTML or XML file. Even better, the Live View feature (page 578) lets you quickly preview a Spry table without leaving Dreamweaver. In Design view, each cell in this row has a Spry data placeholder (the element's name on a blue background) just as if you had dragged the element from the Bindings panel (page 573) into the table cell. You can select a format for the Spry data placeholder as if it were regular HTML (for example, apply a CSS style to it or make it bold).

Master/detail layout

One of the most exciting uses for Spry data is the so-called master/detail layout. When you select this option from the Choose Insert Options window (Figure 13-19), you can create a page that provides a list of all the rows in a data set (the *master* list) accompanied by a region of the page that displays more details from a single, selected row (detailed information for the selected item). For example, in Figure 13-22, clicking Dr. Chad Marshall's box on the left, fills the area on the right with detailed information about the good doctor.

To create a master/detail layout, click the "Insert master/detail layout" button in the Choose Insert Options screen (Figure 13-19) and then:

1. **Click the Set Up button.**

   The Insert Master/Detail Layout window opens (see Figure 13-23).

2. **Remove and rearrange the "master" columns.**

   The top portion of the window lets you specify which columns of data appear in the master list. For example, in Figure 13-22, the master columns are the ones with the thumbnail image and the name of each doctor in the list on the left side of the page. To add a column of data, click the + button, and then, in the window that appears, select a column name. If you don't want one of the elements to appear in the table, click its name in the Columns list, and then press the minus (–) button to remove it. You can also rearrange the columns by using the up and down arrows, so that they appear in a different order in the list.

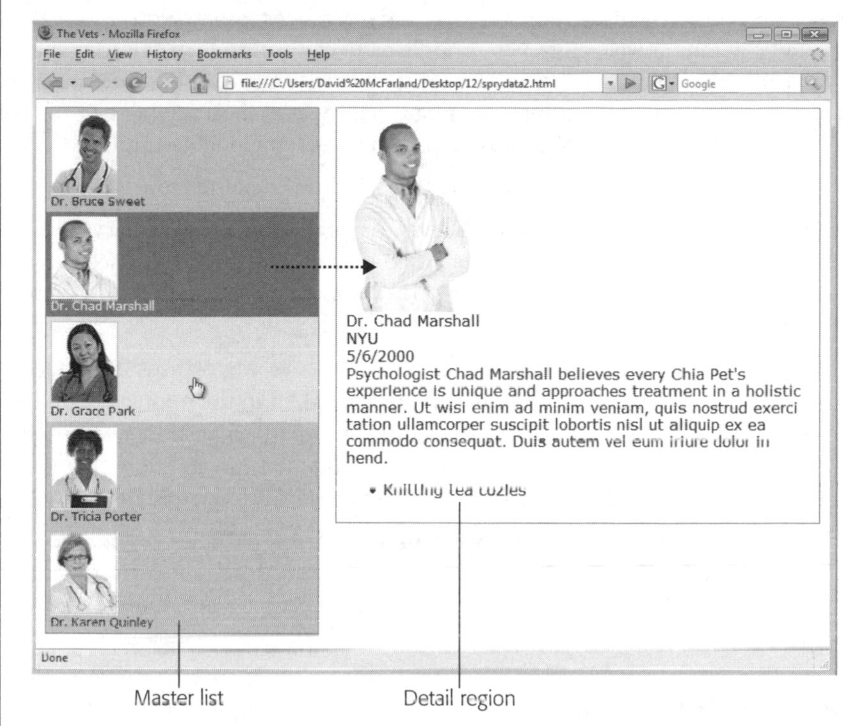

Figure 13-22: *Here's the plain, out-of-the-box design Dreamweaver supplies for a Spry master/detail layout. You can edit the supplied CSS (thankfully) to match the look of your site.*

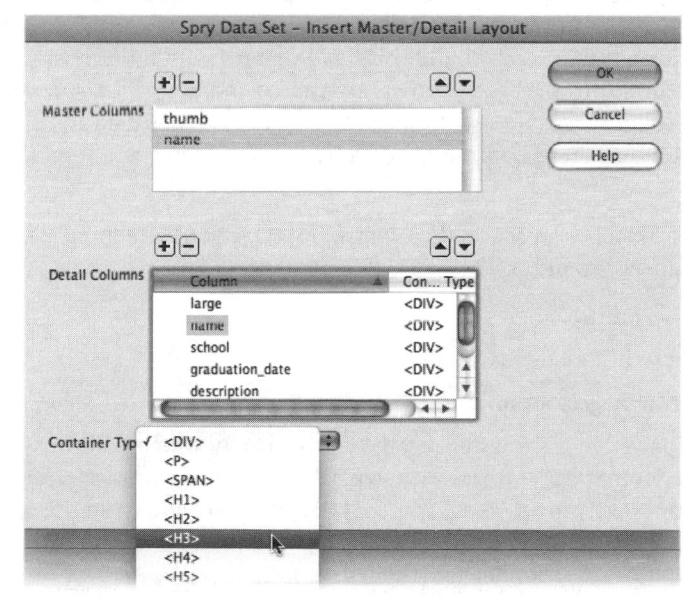

Figure 13-23: *When you add column data to the detail region, you can specify the type of HTML tag Spry should use for the data. The normal setting is a <div> tag, which means that each data item appears in its own div. However, once you insert the master/detail layout, you can move the Spry data elements around, change the tags they're in, and formatting them with additional CSS styles.*

3. **Remove and rearrange detail columns.**

   The procedure you use to add, remove, and rearrange master columns works for detail columns as well. However, in addition to choosing which columns should appear in the detail region, you can also specify which HTML tag you want Spry to put the data in. For example, you might want to use a heading (a <h2> tag, for example) to list the title of an article, or a <p> tag for a long description.

4. **Click OK, and then, in the Spry Data Set window, click the Done button.**

   Dreamweaver inserts all the HTML and Spry programming necessary to create the master/detail layout. In addition, it attaches an external style sheet—SpryMasterDetail.css—that provides basic formatting for the different elements on the page.

   Basically, Dreamweaver creates the master list with a series of <div> tags stacked one on top of the other. The program puts each item in the master list in a div and applies the class *MasterColumn* to it. If you want to change the look of each of those boxes (for example, add a top borderline to separate each item in the list), edit the descendent selector style *.MasterDetail .MasterColumn.*

   Likewise, Dreamweaver creates the detail region using a single div with the class *DetailContainer*, while it puts each piece of data in the detail region within a different HTML tag (see step 3), and applies the class *DetailColumn* to each of them.

Stacked Containers

The third option in the Choose Insert Options window (Figure 13-19) lets you create a series of stacked <div> tags with information from a Spry data set; Figure 13-24 shows you what this rather pedestrian layout looks like. This layout option really isn't that useful. It doesn't offer any of the interactivity of a Spry table or the master/detail layout. You could just as easily build this table yourself without imposing all the download overhead—in the form of the data source and Spry files—on your visitors. However, you may want to use this layout if you can't get the data any other way—for example, if a database spits out the data from a web server, and it gets updated frequently.

To create a stacked container layout, in the Choose Insert Options screen, select the "Insert stacked containers" button (Figure 13-19), and then:

1. **Click the Set Up button.**

   The Insert Stacked Containers window opens.

2. **Remove and rearrange columns.**

   As with the Spry table and master/detail layouts, specify which columns you want to appear on the page. Also, as with step 3 (previously) in the master/detail layouts, you can specify in which HTML tag Dreamweaver should put the data. For example, you might want to use a heading (an <h2> tag, for example) to list the title of an article, or a <p> tag for a long description.

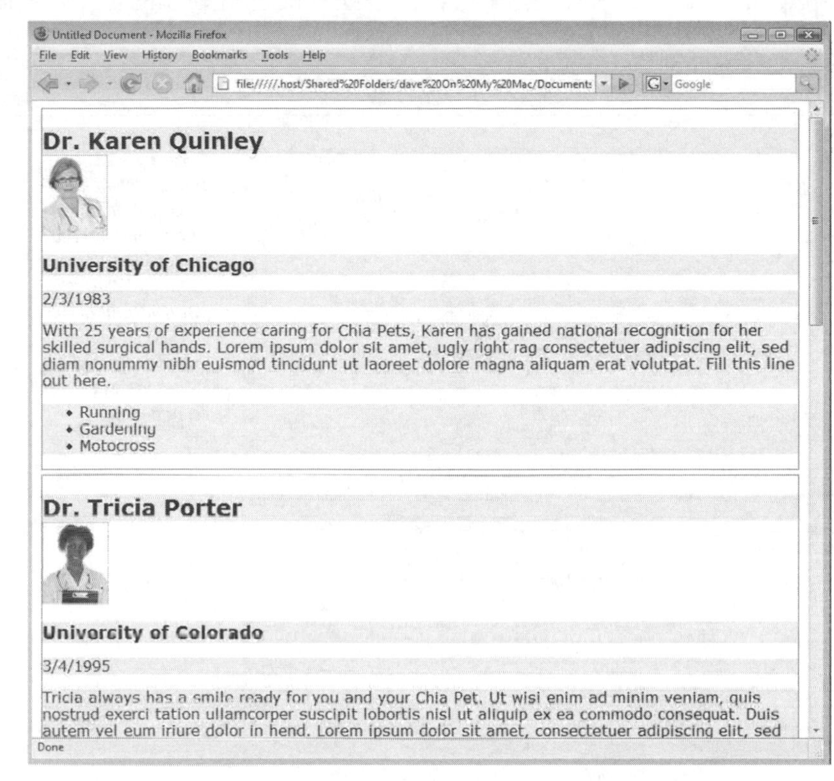

Figure 13-24: *The stacked container layout for Spry data doesn't look like much. Here's an example right out of the box with Dreamweaver's stock CSS applied to it. On top of these design shortcomings, the data isn't interactive, as it is with a Spry table or master/detail layout. If you're going for a design like this, you might want to think about using plain old HTML and a little elbow grease.*

3. **Click OK, and then, in the Spry Data Set window, click the Done button.**

   Dreamweaver inserts all the HTML and Spry programming necessary to create the layout. In addition, it attaches an external style sheet—SpryStackedContainers.css—that provides basic formatting for the elements on the page. The style sheet comes with just three styles, and they control the formatting for the overall div container (a class style named *.StackedContainers*), the div containing one row's worth of data (a descendent selector style named *.StackedContainers .RowContainer*) and a class style applied to the tag wrapped around each column of information (a descendent selector style named *.StackedContainers .RowColumn*).

Stacked Containers with Spotlight Area

Since variety is the spice of life, Dreamweaver includes yet a fourth way to lay out your Spry data. The lovingly named Stacked Container with Spotlight Area layout works much like the stacked container layout just discussed, with the addition of one area that floats to the left of the main data. As you can see in Figure 13-25, this design is best suited for data that includes paths to image files, so you can display a large image on the left (like an employee photograph or a product image), and detailed information on the right.

As with the stacked container option, you could just as easily build this layout without Spry, but, since you asked, here's how you create one of these babies: First, click the "Insert stacked containers with spotlight area" button in the Choose Insert Options screen (Figure 13-19), and then:

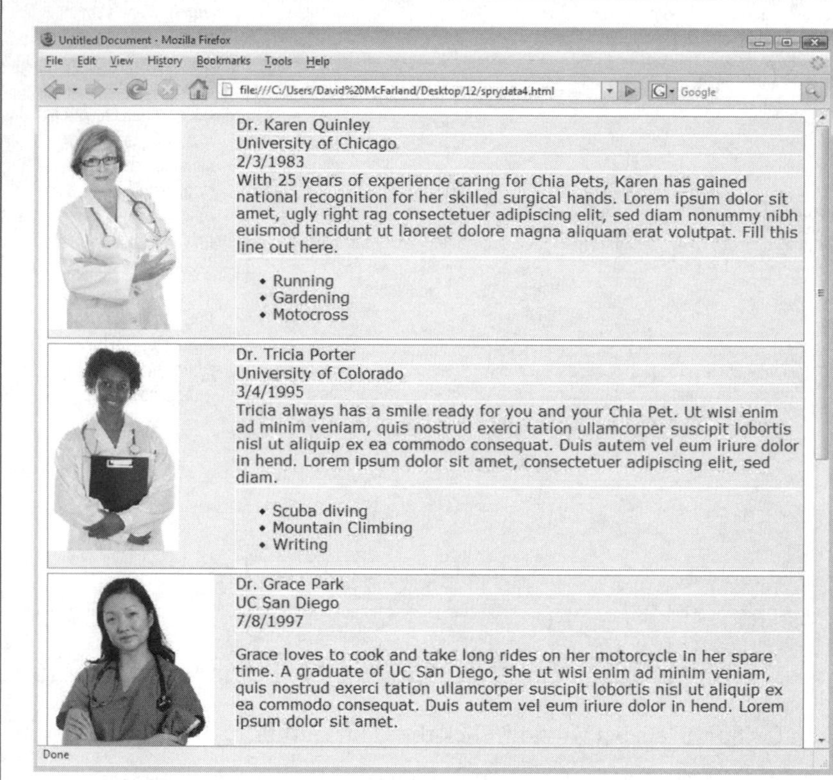

Figure 13-25: *The long-winded Stacked Container with Spotlight Area layout (also know as the SCWSA) is just a variant of the stacked container layout discussed in "Stacked Containers" on page 568.*

1. **Click the Set Up button.**

   The Insert Spotlight Area window opens. This window has two sections, one that lets you specify which columns should appear in the spotlight (left) side of the table and which should appear in the stacked column (right) side of the design.

2. **Remove, rearrange, and assign HTML tags to columns.**

   As with the Spry table and master/detail layouts, you specify which columns you want to appear on the page. Since the left-hand area (the spotlight) is small and tall, a path to an image file is a good bet here, and you want only one or two columns of data . You should display the longer, more detailed data in the right-hand area, the stacked column region. Also, as with step 3 (page 571) in the master/detail layouts, you can specify which HTML tag the Spry programming puts the data in. For example, you might want to use a heading (an <h2> tag, for example) to list the title of an article, or a <p> tag for a long description.

3. **Click OK, and then, in the Spry Data Set window, click the Done button.**

   Dreamweaver inserts all the HTML and Spry programming necessary to create the layout. In addition, it attaches an external style sheet—SprySpotlightColumn.css—that provides basic formatting for the different elements on the page.

Creating a Spry Region

If you're not a fan of the four prepackaged layouts the Spry Data Set wizard offers, you can manually create a layout using a combination of Spry data (the information drawn from the HTML table cells or an XML file) and HTML. Even if you do use one of the stock layouts, you can refine the design, layout, and data using the do-it-yourself Spry tools the Insert panel's Data or Spry category offer. But first you need to get the data loaded onto your web page from the data file. To do that, follow the steps presented for HTML files (page 554) or XML files (page 559); when you get to the last step (Figure 13-19), select the "Do not insert HTML" option, and then click the Done button. Dreamweaver adds all the necessary programming to access the data in the data file, but none of the HTML. You'll do that yourself in the following pages.

At this point you've told Dreamweaver which HTML or XML file to use for the data, and how to process it; none of the information from the file actually appears on the web page until you add it. You can display multiple items from a data file using one of the Spry tools dedicated to this task: a Spry Repeat List, or a Spry Repeat Region. Each tool provides a different way to display multiple records from an HTML table or an XML file. If you want to display a list of employee names, for instance, you can present them in a simple bulleted list, or in a bunch of repeating <div> tags.

But before you use one of these tools, you first need to insert a Spry Region. A Spry Region is simply a tag that marks the beginning and end of a portion of a web page dedicated to displaying Spry data. You then add the data from your data source—the HTML table or the XML data—inside the region you create.

To insert a Spry Region:

1. **Click the spot in web page where you wish to insert the Spry Region.**

   This area might be inside a div used for laying out the web page, such as inside a sidebar or on the main content region of a page. In addition, you can select any HTML already on the page, and either replace it with a Spry Region, or wrap the Spry Region around it, as described in step 6.

2. **On the Insert panel's Data or Spry category, click the Spry Region button.**

   You can also choose Insert→Spry→Spry Region. Either way, the Insert Spry Region window opens (Figure 13-26).

3. **Choose a type of container—div or span.**

   A Spry Region uses either a <div> or <span> tag to hold Spry data. Div is the most common selection, since a <div> tag can hold block-level elements like tables, bulleted lists, and other divs. In other words, a <div> tag provides plenty of room to insert content.

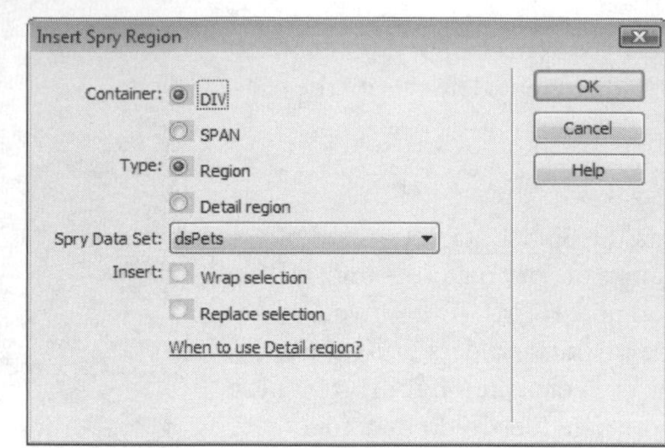

Figure 13-26:
A detail region lets you display more detailed information about individual records from the XML file. It works in conjunction with a Spry table, as described on page 563.

4. **Choose the type of region.**

   To display multiple records from a data file (like a list of employee names, or a catalog of all of your company's products), choose the Region option.

   You'll find the "Detail region" button useful when you want to display extra information about one particular record in the data file (like a photo and extra statistics about a particular product), just as in the master/detail layout the Spry Data wizard provided. This detail information appears when a visitor clicks a row in a Spry table or a row in a Spry repeating region; Spry updates the detail region with whatever extra data you want to grab from the data file.

5. **From the Spry Data Set menu, choose a data set.**

   If you added multiple data sets to a page, use this menu to specify the data set whose data you want to insert into the region. Dreamweaver lets you insert data from more than one data set into the same Spry Region: from the Bindings panel (page 573), simply drag an element from the different data sets into the Spry Region.

6. **If you selected content on the page before inserting the Spry Region, then choose either "Wrap selection" or "Replace selection."**

   Choose "Wrap selection" if you want to include elements already on the page within a Spry Region. Say you want to add a bunch of information from a data file to various locations in the main content area of a page (like inside a div), but you already had some content in that div. Just click the div, click Ctrl+A (⌘-A) to select everything inside it, insert a Spry Region, and then click the "Wrap selection" button. Dreamweaver then "spry-ifies" that div.

   Be careful of the "Replace selection" option: It deletes anything you selected, and replaces it with an empty Spry Region.

7. **Click OK to insert the Spry Region.**

   Dreamweaver inserts the <div> (or <span>, depending upon your choice in step 2) tag in the page, and then adds the proper code to mark it as a Spry Region. You can insert anything inside this region, even non-Spry stuff, such as tables, other divs, images, and so on. In addition, you've now enabled that area so that it's ready to accept Spry data using the Bindings panel—or one of the Spry data tools discussed in the following pages.

Warning: Spry data sets add invalid HTML to a web page. To make all the Spry data magic happen, Dreamweaver inserts invalid HTML attributes like *spry:repeat* and *spry:region* to <div> and <span> tags. The web page no longer passes muster as proper HTML. It still works in web browsers, but it's harder for you to locate other invalid HTML that might actually affect how your page displays in a web browser. Note that the other Spry widgets discussed in this chapter, as well as Spry Effects, Spry Menu Bars, and Spry Validation widgets, do not insert invalid HTML. The Spry data set is the only scofflaw.

The Bindings Panel

The bindings panel lists the Spry data sets attached to the current web page (see Figure 13-27). It also lists all the elements for a particular data set. You can drag an element from the Bindings panel into any Spry Region on a page. In Design view, the element is just a placeholder for either a table cell (for an HTML data file) or XML element (for an XML data file)—Dreamweaver surrounds its name with braces, like this: {employee} (see Figure 13-28). The program also adds a blue background to the placeholder so you can easily identify it as a special Spry element. When you view the page in a web browser, Dreamweaver replaces the placeholder with data from the HTML or XML file—like "Frank Jones".

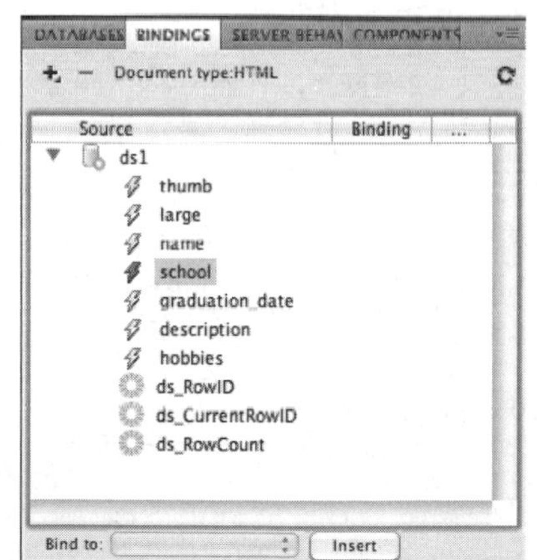

Figure 13-27: *The Bindings panel adds three elements to the bottom of each data set: ds_RowID, ds_CurrentRowID, and ds_RowCount. ds_RowCount defines the number of items in the data set. Each item has its own ds_RowID number, and the fs indicates the currently active row, which comes into play when you use the Master/Detail layout described on page 566.*

You can select a data set element on a web page, style it with CSS, include it inside other HTML (such as a paragraph or Heading 1), and even move it around the page (as long as it remains inside a Spry Region). To delete the element, just select it, and then press Delete.

However, if you insert a Spry Region and then immediately drag an element from the Bindings panel, you see only the first item from the data set—for example, the first employee listed, not a list of all employees. To see all the records in a data set, you must use one of Spry's repeating region tools, discussed next.

You also use the Bindings panel to edit a Spry data set. Just double-click the data set's name in the Bindings panel to return to the Spry Data Set window you encountered when you first added the data set (Figure 13-15 and Figure 13-17). You can rename the data set, and even choose a different file for the data source—however, don't do either of these things if you already added Spry data from the data set to your web page; you'll end up with an ugly error message when you view the page. However, you can safely change the initial sort order of data and any of the other options mentioned in step 9 on page 557.

Spry Repeating Region

Dreamweaver provides several ways to insert multiple rows of information from a data set. The simplest, though least flexible, are the four stock layouts available from the Spry Data Set wizard. However, there are two do-it-yourself tools as well. The most flexible is the Spry Repeating Region. A Spry Repeating Region is a <div> or <span> tag in which you insert any combination of HTML and Spry Data (using the Bindings panel as described above). Dreamweaver repeats the tag and its contents once per row in the HTML table or the XML file (see Figure 13-29).

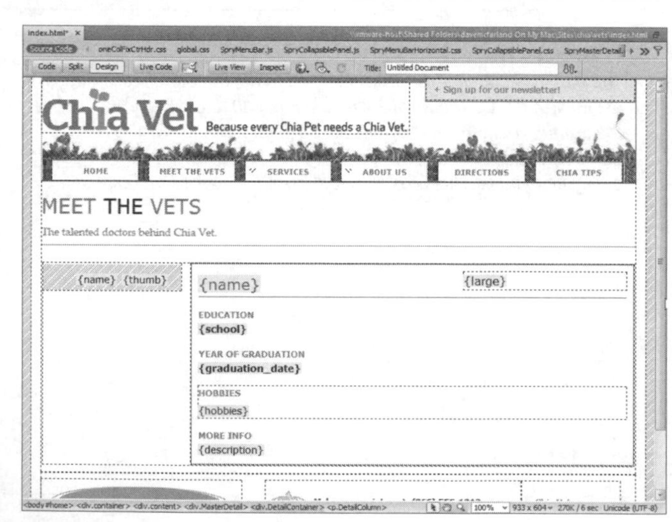

Figure 13-28:
In Dreamweaver's Design view, a Spry Data Set page isn't much to look at. Dreamweaver surrounded the data element names with braces a blue background, and their names are. In this case, {name}, {thumb}, {large}, {school}, {graduation_date}, {hobbies}, and {description} represent data that Dreamweaver will replace from the data file. This page shows a master/detail layout (see page 566). The left-hand block (the one with {name} and {thumb}) is actually a repeating region (see below) that will list a name and display a small picture for every record in the data file. The right-hand area is a detail region that will display detailed information about a single record.

To create a repeating region:

1. **Click anywhere inside a Spry Region.**

   You have to insert anything related to Spry data sets inside a Spry Region. You can click inside an empty area, or even select HTML inside the Spry Region that you want included as part of the repeated region.

2. **On the Insert panel's Data or Spry category, click the Spry Repeat button (Figure 13-14).**

   Alternatively, choose Insert→Spry→Spry Repeat. The Insert Spry Repeat window opens (see Figure 13-30).

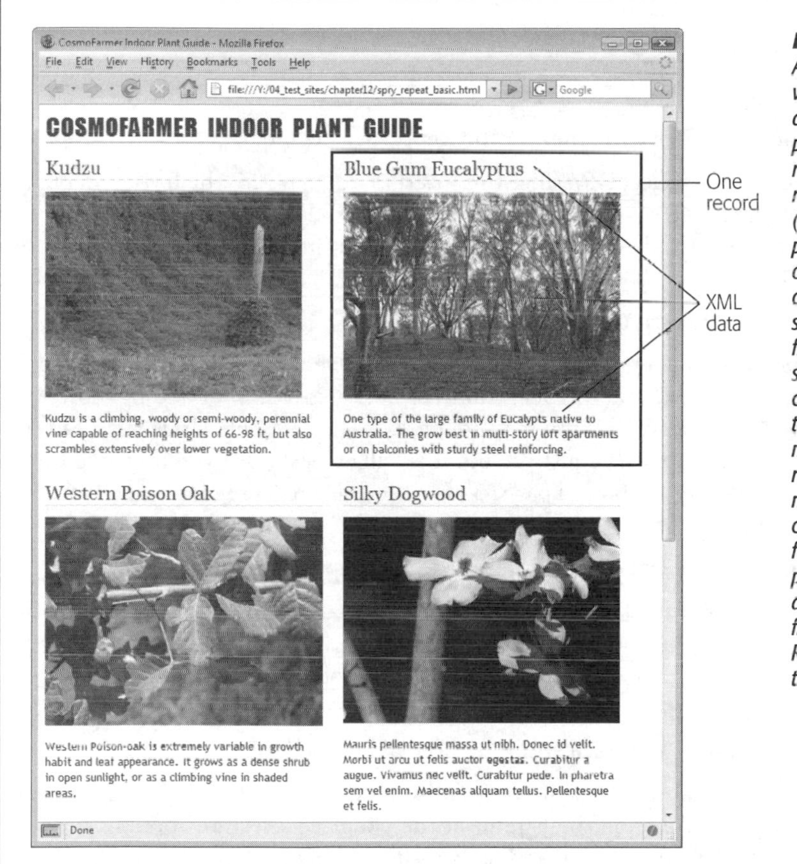

Figure 13-29: *A Spry Repeating Region provides a flexible way to display data from a data file. This particular page includes four records from an XML file. The repeating region is a <div> tag (outlined), containing three pieces of information from one XML record. However, you could just as easily create this same design using an HTML file with a table as the data source. In that case, each record would actually be a single table row, and each data element would be one cell in that row. For example, this design might be based on a table containing three columns: one for the plant name, one for a photo of the plant, and one for a description of the plant. The flexibility of the Spry Repeating Region means you can lay out this data any way you like.*

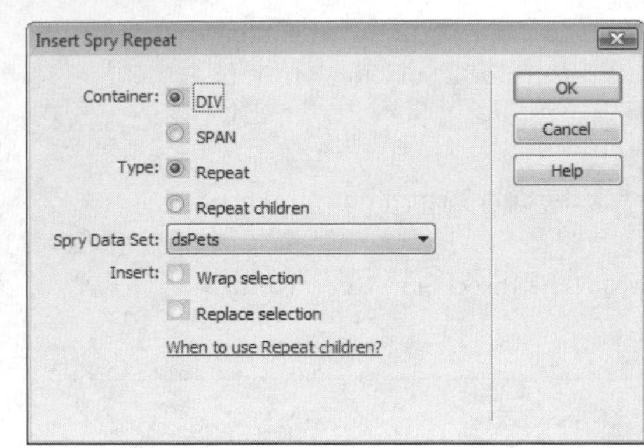

Figure 13-30:
A Spry Repeat Region is the most flexible way to insert multiple records from a data file. However, unlike the layouts available from the Spry Data Set wizard or a Spry Repeat List (discussed next), this tool doesn't insert data automatically; you need to decide which data elements to include, and drag them from the Bindings panel into the Spry Repeat Region.

3. **Choose a type of container for the Repeating Region.**

   In most cases, select DIV, since this inserts a <div> tag in which you can put lots of other HTML elements, such as paragraphs and other divs. The SPAN option can come in handy when you wish to display a single row of data elements side by side.

4. **Select the "Repeat children" button.**

   In practice, you'll find no difference between the Repeat and "Repeat children" options. However, the "Repeat children" option is useful for adding more complex logic to Spry data. You may not be ready to jump into Code view and start hand-coding Spry data just yet, but this will at least leave you prepared for the day you do (see the box on page 534 for more on enhancing Dreamweaver's Spry offerings).

5. **From the Spry Data Set menu, choose a data set.**

   If you're inserting data from multiple data files, then your page has several data sets. Choose the one whose data you want to display. Remember, this is a Repeating Region, so each record in the data file appears in its own div.

6. **If you selected content on the page before inserting the Spry Region, then choose either "Wrap selection" or "Replace selection".**

   Choose "Wrap selection" if you want to include elements already on the page within a Spry Region. Be careful of the "Replace selection" option: It deletes anything that you selected and replaces it with an empty Spry Region.

7. **Click OK to insert the Spry Region.**

   Dreamweaver inserts the <div> (or <span>, depending upon your choice in step 3) in the page, and then adds the proper code to mark it as a Spry Repeat Region.

At this point, you can add any HTML to the Repeat Region. In addition, to include data (which is, after all, the whole point), drag elements from the data set in the Bindings panel (page 573) into this region. Spry repeats everything inside the region once for each row in the data file.

Spry Repeat Lists

If you simply want to list a bunch of repeating elements from an XML file, the Spry Repeat list gives you the simplest solution. It inserts either a bulleted list, a numbered list, a form menu, or a definition list full of data (see Figure 13-32). Here's how you add one:

1. **Click inside a Spry Region where you wish to insert a list of repeating elements.**
2. **On the Insert panel's Data category, click the Spry Repeat List button.**

   Alternatively, choose Insert→Spry→Spry Repeat List. The Insert Spry Repeat List window opens (see Figure 13-31).
3. **From the "Container tag" menu, choose the type of container you want for the Repeating Region.**

   Pick from any of the four list types: bulleted lists, numbered lists, form menus, or definition lists.
4. **Choose the data set whose data you want to repeat.**

   Make your choice from the Spry Data Set menu.

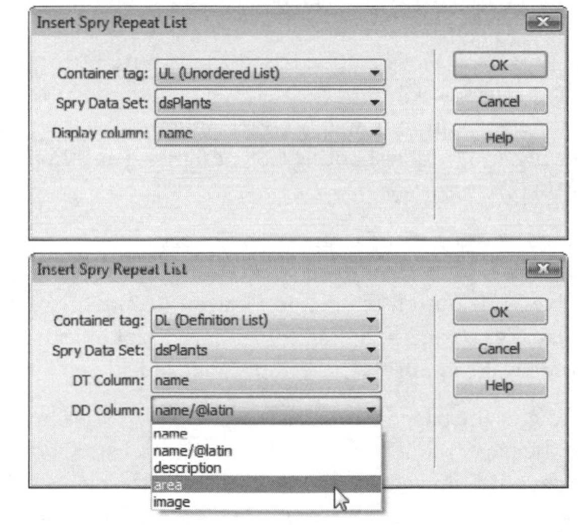

Figure 13-31:
A Spry Repeat List provides four ways to display repeating data from an HTML table or XML file.

5. **Choose the column or columns you want to display.**

   If you're going with a bulleted or numbered list, you only get to pick one column (Figure 13-31, top). If you're using a form menu or a definition list, you can pick two data elements (Figure 13-31, bottom). For a menu, you can select one element for the label (what the visitor sees when she views the menu) and another for the value (the information submitted to the web server when the form is processed). Definition lists include one term (like a word in a glossary) represented by the <DT> tag, and one definition represented by the <DD> tag.

6. **Click OK to insert the list.**

   Dreamweaver inserts the list into the page. In Design view, you don't actually see the entire list of items. You see only one bulleted or numbered item. You have to preview the page, or click the Live View button (see Figure 13-33), to see the final effect with all the items listed.

Tip: To get a full description of every Dreamweaver menu in a handy, printable PDF, go to this book's Missing CD page (*www.missingmanuals.com/cds*) and download Appendix B, "Menu by Menu Commands."

You can select and style a Spry Repeat List just as you would a regular chunk of HTML, and you can even move it (as long as it remains inside the Spry Region).

Live View

Dreamweaver includes a built-in web browser-like view of your web pages. Called Live View, this new feature lets you view a web page just as you would in a web browser; you can interact with the page and preview your designs without leaving Dreamweaver. It's not perfect, however. Since Adobe based the feature on Apple's WebKit (the engine behind the Safari and Chrome web browsers), you don't really see how the page will look in the most common web browser: Internet Explorer. So it's not the best tool for previewing and troubleshooting CSS designs—you still need to test using real browsers for that.

However, Live View is perfect for working with Dreamweaver's Spry widgets, and in particular, seeing how Spry Data pages look and work. To activate Live View, in the document toolbar, click the Live View button (circled in Figure 13-33). Once activated, the page functions like a real web page—you can try out JavaScript objects like Spry widgets, see how CSS-based rollover effects (page 180) look, and so on.

You can't, however, continue to edit the page in Live View—you can't, for example, select or move HTML around the page. But if you're comfortable with hand coding, you can choose Split view (see page 415) and get a side-by-side view of the raw HTML and the design's Live View. You can also edit HTML in Code view, click back to the live Design view, and immediately see how the changes you made affect the final design.

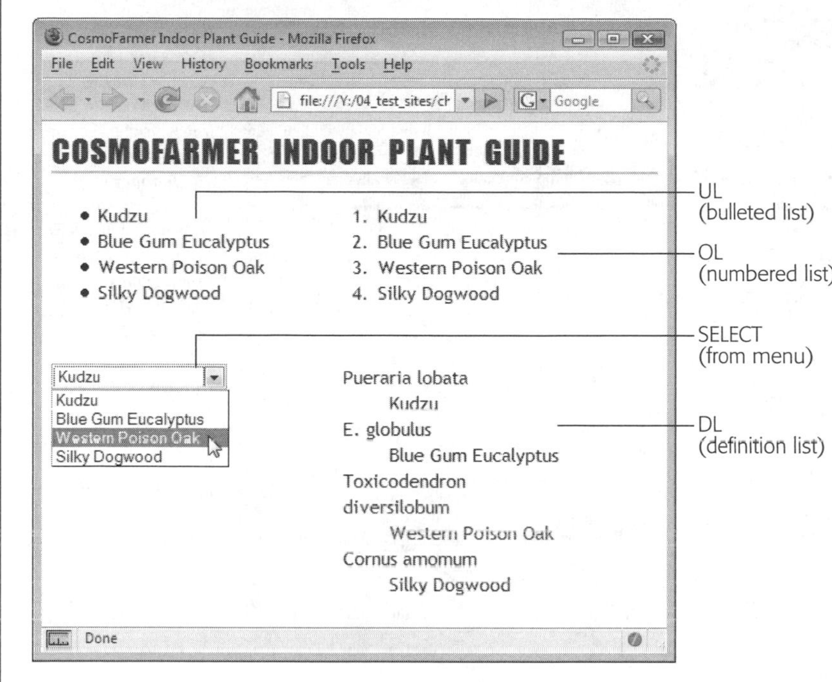

***Figure 13-32:** Dreamweaver provides different options for a Spry Repeat List, depending on the type of list you insert. For a numbered or bulleted list, you choose just one data element to display from the "Display column" menu (top); form menus and definition lists require two data elements (bottom). Once you insert the list, you can use the Bindings panel to add more data elements to it. If you want a bulleted list of employee names but also want to include the employee's phone extension as part of the list item—"Bob Jones (x456)"—insert the Spry list using the employee name, and then, from the Bindings panel, drag the phone extension number.*

In addition, you can edit CSS in Live View. In fact, one of Live View's best attributes is that you can tweak the CSS styles that format dynamic elements like Spry navigation menus, Spry tabbed panels, and Spry data sets. You can use the CSS Styles panel (page 124) to open and edit styles, and immediately see how those changes will look in a web browser. In fact, you can use the Current view of the CSS Styles panel (see page 314) to identify the styles that affect dynamically generated HTML (like Spry navigation menus, Spry Repeat Regions, and so on). Just turn on Live View, click inside an element on the page, and then see which CSS styles control its formatting using the CSS Styles panel. (See page 527 for complete directions on how to use the CSS Styles panel's Current view for troubleshooting and editing styles.)

When you're done previewing a page in Live View, make sure you click the Live View button again to return to Dreamweaver's regular Design view.

Figure 13-33: *Here's the Live View of a Spry master/detail layout. In fact, this is how the page pictured in Figure 13-28 appears in a web browser, complete with all of the JavaScript magic that lets you see a complete design. You can even interact with the page within Dreamweaver's Live View—mouse over rows of data, click a record, and see the updated detail information for the selected row.*

CHAPTER
14

Dreamweaver Behaviors

Chapter 6 makes clear how easy it is to add mouse rollover effects by using Dreamweaver's Rollover Image object. That and other interactive features rely on *scripts* (small programs) written in the JavaScript programming language. You've already seen some JavaScript-powered tools like the Spry menu, Spry form validation, and all the cool Spry tricks discussed in the previous chapter.

You *could* create the same effects without Dreamweaver, but you'd need to take a few extra steps: buy a book on JavaScript; read it from cover to cover; learn concepts like arrays, functions, and the Document Object Model; and spend weeks discovering the eccentric rules governing how different browsers interpret JavaScript code differently.

But Dreamweaver's behaviors let you add dynamic JavaScript programs to your Web pages without doing a lick of programming. Most Dreamweaver behaviors have been around for a long while, but Dreamweaver CS3 added a new set of behaviors called Spry Effects that let you add dazzling visual touches like fading a photo in or out, highlighting a portion of a page with a flash of color, and making a <div> tag appear to shake to catch a visitor's attention.

Tip: What's that you say? You'd like to read a book on JavaScript? Happy to oblige: *JavaScript: The Missing Manual*, written by yours truly.

Understanding Behaviors

Dreamweaver behaviors are prepackaged JavaScript programs that let you add interactivity to your Web pages with ease, even if you don't know the first thing about JavaScript. By adding behaviors, you can make your Web pages do things like:

- Make portions of a page appear and disappear.
- Open a new browser window to a specified size, with or without scroll bars, a status bar, a location bar, and other Web browser "chrome."
- Change the background color of any element on a page.
- Pop open an alert box with an important message for your site's visitors.

Behavior Elements

To use a behavior, you bring together three elements: an HTML tag, an action, and an event:

- First, you select an HTML tag to apply the behavior to.
- Next, pick an action. The action is whatever the behavior is supposed to *do*—such as open a new browser window or hide an element on the page.
- Finally, you assign an event to the behavior. The event *triggers* the action, which usually involves a visitor interacting with your site, like clicking a Submit button on a form, moving the mouse over a link, or even simply loading the web page into the browser.

For instance, say that, when a visitor clicks a link, instead of just sending them to another page, you want a new browser window to pop up and load that linked page. In this case, the HTML tag is the link itself—an <a> tag; the *action* is opening another browser window and loading a Web page in it; and the *event* brings the two together so that, when your visitor clicks the link, his browser opens a new window and loads the new page. Voilà—interactivity!

More About Events

When people visit a Web page, they do more than just read it—they interact with it, in all sorts of ways. You already know that when someone clicks a link, the browser reacts by loading a new Web page or jumping to a named anchor.

But visitors can interact with a Web page in a variety of other ways. They may resize the browser window, move the mouse around the screen, make a selection from a pop-up menu, click an image, type inside a form field, or click a form's Reset button. Web browsers "listen to" and react to these triggering events with actions.

In JavaScript and Dreamweaver, events always begin with the word "on," which essentially means "when." For example, the *onLoad* event refers to the moment when an object fully loads into a browser—that is, when a web page, its images, and other linked files have downloaded. Events also include the various ways someone can interact with a particular HTML tag (element). For instance, when someone moves a mouse over a link or clicks a link, the corresponding events are called *onMouseOver* and *onClick* events.

FREQUENTLY ASKED QUESTION

Behaviors and Added Code

I hear the JavaScript that Dreamweaver produces adds excessive lines of code, unnecessarily adding to a page's file size. Is this true, and should I therefore avoid behaviors?

It's true that a seasoned JavaScript programmer could write a program that mimics Dreamweaver behaviors using less code. But Adobe developed Dreamweaver behaviors to work with as many browsers as possible. JavaScript, on the other hand, doesn't work the same in all browsers, or even in all versions of the same browser; indeed, many browsers understand JavaScript so differently that programmers have resorted to elaborate workarounds that require a lot of experience, practice, and patience.

Accordingly, the engineers at Adobe used their vast understanding of JavaScript, HTML, and web browsers to ensure that Dreamweaver behaviors work in as many browsers as possible. This cross-browser compatibility can, at times, lead to larger files of more lines of code, but it also assures that your pages appear as you intended for the broadest possible audience.

In addition, while Dreamweaver stores the programming code for most behaviors directly within the web pages it creates, it stores most Spry Effects and other Spry tools in an external JavaScript file. This design works in your favor. The file for Spry Effects alone is a whopping 67k in size, but your visitors only need to download the file once, and it can remain in their browsers' caches.

Applying Behaviors

Dreamweaver makes adding behaviors as easy as selecting a tag and choosing an action from a drop-down menu in the Behaviors panel.

The Behaviors Panel

The Behaviors panel is your control center for Dreamweaver's behaviors (Figure 14-1). On it, you can see behaviors that are applied to a tag, add more behaviors, and edit behaviors that you've already applied.

You can open the Behaviors panel three ways:

- Choose Window→Tag Inspector and click the Behaviors button.
- Press Shift+F4 to open the Tag Inspector and click the Behaviors button.
- If the Tag inspector is open, click the Behaviors button.

Note: Dreamweaver includes two types of behaviors, and it's important not to confuse them. This chapter describes JavaScript programs (that is, *behaviors*) that run in your visitors' web browsers–for that reason, they're called "client-side" programs. Another type of behavior, called *server behaviors* (they're listed in the Application panel group), run on your website's *server* and let you access information you store in a database on the server. You'll learn about server-side behaviors in Part Six of this book.

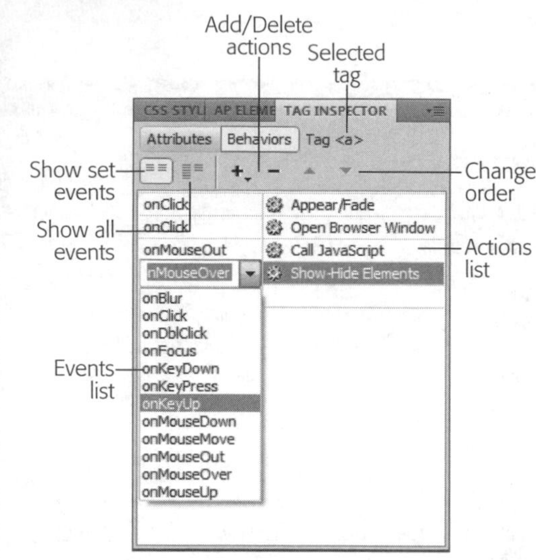

Figure 14-1: *Dreamweaver's Behaviors panel lists all the behaviors you applied to the currently selected HTML tag. Because the same event can trigger multiple actions, Dreamweaver groups the actions by event. In this example, the onClick event for an <a> tag (a hyperlink) triggers two actions. When a visitor clicks this hyperlink, a page element appears or fades away (the Appear/Fade effect), and a new browser window opens. The order in which the behaviors occur is determined by their order in this panel. For instance, when a visitor clicks the link in this example, she sees the Appear/Fade effect first, and then a browser window opens. To change the order of these events, use the up- and down-pointing arrows. To change the type of event, click the event name and select a different event from the pull-down menu. If different events trigger all the actions, the order in which they appear in this panel is irrelevant, since the event itself determines when the action takes place, not the order of the event in this panel.*

The currently selected tag is indicated at the top of the Behaviors panel; a list of the behaviors applied to that tag, if any, appears below. Each behavior is listed in two parts: Events and Actions, as described earlier.

The Behaviors panel offers two different views. Switch between them, using the buttons at the upper-left of the panel:

- "Show set events" (pictured in Figure 14-1) gets down to the specifics: which behaviors you've applied to a tag and which events trigger them. When you work on a web page, this view moves extraneous information out of your way.
- "Show all events" lists all the events *available* to a particular tag. This view isn't that useful, since you see a complete list of events for that tag when you select the tag and add an action (see the left side of Figure 14-1).

Applying Behaviors, Step by Step

Open the Behaviors panel, and then proceed as follows:

1. **Select the object or tag you want to assign a behavior.**

   You have to attach a behavior to an HTML tag, such as a link (indicated by the <a> tag) or the page's body (<body> tag). Take care, however: It's easy to accidentally apply a behavior to the wrong tag. Form elements, like checkboxes and text fields, are easy to target—just click one to select it. For other kinds of tags, consider using the Tag selector, as described on page 23, for more precision.

Tip: You can be sure which tag you've applied a behavior to by looking at the Tag inspector's header (beside the Behaviors button). For example in Figure 14-1, "Tag <a>" indicates that you applied the behaviors listed to an <a>, or link, tag.

2. **In the Behaviors panel, add an action.**

   Click the + button in the Behaviors panel and, from the Add Action menu, select the action you wish to add (see Figure 14-2). You'll find a list of these behaviors and what they do beginning on page 592.

   Some actions are dimmed in the menu because your web page doesn't include an element that the action can affect. If your page lacks a form, for instance, you won't be able to select the Validate Form behavior. Other behaviors are grayed out because you have to apply them to a particular page element. For example, Jump Menu is off limits until you add a list/menu field to the page and select it.

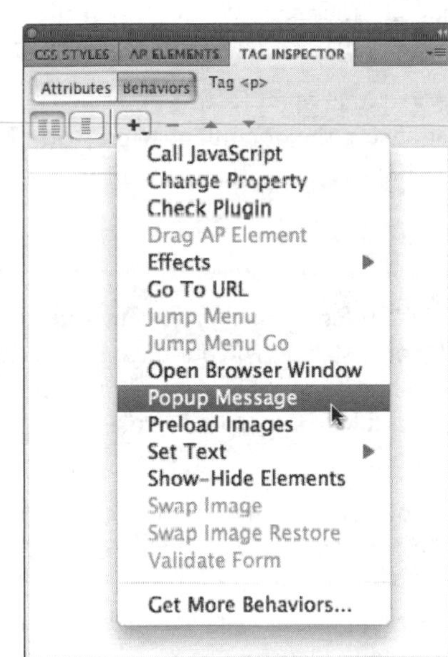

Figure 14-2:
Dreamweaver grays out behaviors you can't apply to a currently selected tag. The reason? Your page is either missing a necessary object, or you've selected an object that can't exhibit that behavior. For example, you can't apply the Show-Hide Elements behavior if your page doesn't have at least one tag with an ID applied to it.

3. **In the dialog box that opens, set options for the action.**

   Each action has properties specific to that action, and you set them to your liking in the dialog box that now appears. For instance, when you choose the Go To URL action, Dreamweaver asks what Web page you want to load. (Once again, the following pages describe each of these actions.)

4. **Click OK to apply the action.**

   At this point, Dreamweaver adds the HTML and JavaScript required to invoke the behavior to your page's underlying code. The behavior's action appears in the Behaviors panel.

Unlike HTML objects, behaviors usually add code to two different places in a document. For behaviors, Dreamweaver usually adds JavaScript code to the head of the document *and* to the HTML tag of the target behavior to the body of the page.

5. **Change the event, if desired.**

   When your newly created action shows up in the Behaviors panel, Dreamweaver displays—in the Events column of the panel—a default event (trigger) for the selected tag and action. For example, if you add an Open Browser Window behavior to a link, Dreamweaver suggests the *onClick* event.

   However, this default event may not be the only one available. Links, for instance, can handle many events. An action could begin when your visitor's cursor moves *over* the link (the *onMouseOver* event), *clicks* the link (the *onClick* event), and so on.

   To change the event for a particular behavior, click the event's name, and the Events pop-up menu appears (see Figure 14-2). Select the event you want from the list of available events for that particular tag. (See page 587 for a list of all available events in current versions of the most popular browsers.)

When you're done, you can leave the Behaviors panel open to add more behaviors to the tag, or to other tags. Select another tag, using the document window or Tag selector, and repeat steps 2 through 5.

Adding Multiple Behaviors

You can have more than one behavior per HTML tag. In fact, you can, and often will, apply several behaviors to the same tag. For instance, when a page loads—the onLoad event of the <body> tag—it can preload images to be used in rollover effects, open a small browser window displaying a (shudder) pop-up advertisement, *and* highlight a message on a page with a flash of color.

Nor are you limited to a single *event* per tag—you can add any number of actions to a link triggered by different events, such as *onMouseOver, onMouseOut*, and *onClick*. For example, if you set things up for a link as shown in Figure 13-1, when you click the selected link in the browser window, some element on the page fades into view, and then a new browser window opens, and finally a custom JavaScript program runs. The link also responds to other events, like moving the mouse over it—in this example, making an invisible element appear on the page.

Editing Behaviors

Once you apply a behavior, you can edit it any time. Double-click the behavior in the Behaviors panel to reopen the Settings dialog box, as described in step 3 of the previous instructions. Make any changes you like, and then click OK.

To remove a behavior from your Web page, select it in the Behaviors panel and click the minus sign (–) button or press Delete. (If you *accidentally* delete a behavior, just choose Edit→Undo Remove Behavior.)

A Quick Example

The brief example below shows you the behavior-creation process. In it, you'll use a behavior that makes an important message appear automatically when a web page opens.

1. **Choose File→New to create a new untitled document.**

   You'll start with a new page.

2. **Choose File→Save and save the file to your computer.**

   It doesn't matter where you save the page, since you won't be including any graphics or linking to any pages.

   You start the process of adding a behavior by selecting a specific tag—in this case, the page's <body> tag.

3. **In the Tag selector in the lower-left corner of the document window, click <body>.**

   Once you select a tag, you can apply one or more behaviors to it. But first, make sure you have the Behaviors panel open. If you don't see it, choose Window→Tag Inspector or press Shift+F4, and then click the Behaviors button.

4. **Click the + button on the Behaviors panel. From the Add Action menu, choose Popup Message (see Figure 14-2).**

   The Popup Message dialog box appears.

5. **In the message box, type "Visit our store for great gifts!" Then click OK.**

   Dreamweaver adds the required JavaScript code to the page. Notice that the Behaviors panel lists the *action* called Popup Message next to the *event* called *onLoad*. The *onLoad* event triggers an action *after* a page and everything on it—graphics and so on—have loaded.

   To see the page in action, preview it in a web browser by pressing the F12 (Option-F12) key. (You can also use the Live View feature, described on page 578, to see this behavior without leaving Dreamweaver.)

Note: Dreamweaver behaviors rely on little JavaScript programs that run inside a web browser. For security reasons, Internet Explorer doesn't always like running JavaScript programs from your own computer. If the JavaScript you add to a page doesn't work when you preview it in IE, look for a narrow yellow bar just above the page. Click it and follow the instructions to allow the JavaScript on the page to run.

Events

Events are at the heart of interactive web pages. They trigger behaviors based on your visitors' actions, like clicking a link, mousing over an image, or simply loading the page. But not all events work with all tags. For example, the *onLoad* event only works with Web pages and images, not paragraphs, divs, or any other page element. The Event menu in the Behaviors panel can help: It lists only those events available for the tag you're targeting.

Current browsers—Firefox, Safari, Google Chrome, and Internet Explorer 8—support a wide range of events for many HTML tags. In most cases, you'll find that many of the events listed in the following pages work with all of the tags pictured in Figure 14-3. Many events work with other tags as well, such as headline, paragraph, and div tags. However, don't go crazy. Making an alert message appear when someone double-clicks a paragraph is more likely to win your site the Hard-To-Use Website of the Month award than a loyal group of visitors.

To help you select a good combination of event and HTML tags, the following pages list and explain the most common and useful HTML tags and events.

Each section shows you the name of the event as you'll see it listed in the Behaviors panel, a plain-English description of what that event really means, and the list of tags to which this event is most commonly applied. See Figure 14-3 for the visual representations of those HTML tags. For example, you'll see that the <select> tag represents a pull-down menu.

Mouse Events

Web designers most often use mouse *movement* events to trigger actions (like the familiar rollover image). But mouse *clicks*—on checkboxes, radio buttons, and other clickable form elements—also qualify as mouse events. All current web browsers respond to many of these events when you apply them to most tags—for example, you can trigger a behavior when a visitor moves her mouse over a paragraph of text. Of course, just because you *can* trigger a behavior doesn't mean you *should*. Most web surfers aren't accustomed to having things happen when they click on a paragraph or mouse over a headline, for example (but if you want to add an *onclick* event to a paragraph, check out the tip on page 590).

Note: In the following list, you'll see the many different types of *input* form elements listed like this: <input type="button | checkbox | radio | reset | submit">. This notation simply means that *any* of these form elements–button, checkbox, radio button, reset button, or submit button–react to the listed event. Also, when you see an <area> tag, it refers to the hotspots on an image map (see page 244).

---

onMouseOver

Gets triggered: When the cursor moves over the tag.

Commonly used with these tags: <a>, <area>, <img>

onMouseout

Gets triggered: When the cursor moves off of the tag.

Commonly used with these tags: <a>, <area>, <img>

onMouseMove

Gets triggered: When the cursor moves anywhere inside the tag. Works similarly to *onMouseOver*, but *onMouseOver* is triggered only once—when the mouse first moves over the tag. *onMouseMove* is triggered continually, whenever the mouse moves over the tag. The possibilities for an annoying Web page are endless.

Commonly used with this tag: <body>

onClick

Gets triggered: When a visitor clicks the tag and releases the mouse button.

Commonly used with these tags: <a>, <area>, <input type="button | checkbox | radio | reset | submit*onDblClick*">

Gets triggered: When a visitor double-clicks the tag.

Commonly used with these tags: <a>, <area>, <input type="button | checkbox | radio | reset | submit">

onMouseDown

Gets triggered: When a visitor clicks the tag. Visitors don't need to release the mouse button for this event to occur (note the contrast with *onClick*).

Commonly used with these tags: <a>, <img>, <input type="button | checkbox | radio | reset | submit">

onMouseUp

Gets triggered: When a visitor releases the mouse button while the cursor is over the tag. The effect is the same as the *onClick* event.

Commonly used with these tags: <a>, <img>, <input type="button | checkbox | radio | reset | submit">

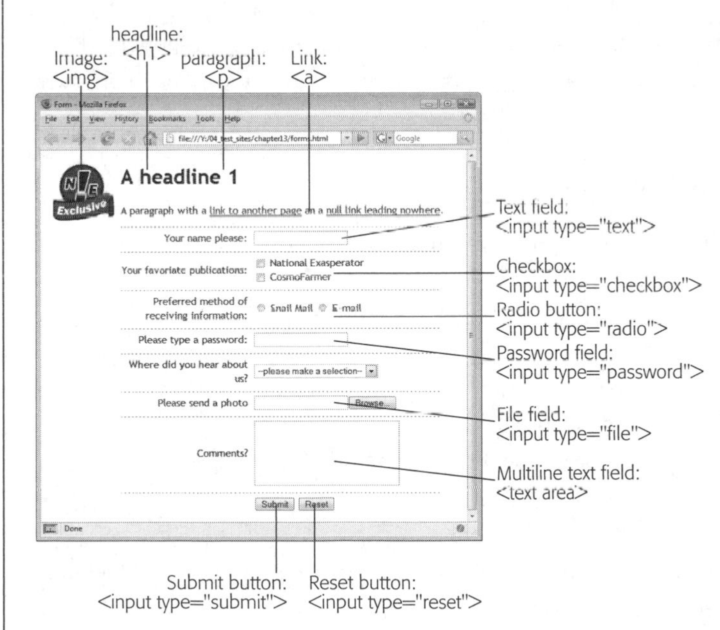

Figure 14-3: *This sample web page illustrates HTML tags to which you can attach events. Not shown is the body of the page (the page in its entirety, in other words), whose tag is <body>, and the form portion of the page (see Chapter 12), whose tag is <form>. Whenever you set up a behavior, you should attach it to one of the tags shown here. Today's browsers add events to every tag, so you could add a behavior to a page's level 1 heading or to a paragraph of text, but since those tags usually aren't associated with user interactions (like clicking on a link or mousing over an image), visitors to your site probably won't interact with them.*

Tip: If you *do* want to add an *onmouseover*, *onclick*, or any other mouse event to a tag that people aren't used to clicking on (for example a heading, paragraph, or div) you can create a CSS style for the element and set its cursor property to "pointer" in the Extensions category of the CSS Rule Definition window. This turns the mouse turn into a pointing finger when it's over the element (it's the same icon you see when you mouse over a link).

Keyboard Events

Keyboard events respond to key presses and releases. Most Web designers use them in association with form elements that accept text, such as password or text fields. (See Chapter 12 for more on forms.)

onKeyPress

Gets triggered: When a visitor presses and releases a key while the tag is highlighted.

Commonly used with these tags: <textarea>, <input type="file | password | text">, <a>

onKeyDown

Gets triggered: When a visitor presses a key while the tag is highlighted. The key doesn't need to be released for this event to occur.

Commonly used with these tags: <textarea>, <input type="file | password | text">, <a>

onKeyUp

Gets triggered: When a visitor releases a key while the tag is highlighted.

Commonly used with these tags: <textarea>, <input type="file | password | text">, <a>

Body and Frameset Events

Several events relate to actions involving an entire Web page or frameset.

onLoad

Gets triggered: When a web page *and* any embedded elements—like images and Flash and QuickTime movies—load. Frequently used to trigger actions when a visitor first loads a page; you can also use it with an image tag to signal when that image has finished loading.

Commonly used with these tags:<body>, <frameset>, <image>

onUnload

Gets triggered: When a web page is about to be replaced by a new page—for instance, just before a browser loads a new page after a visitor clicks a link.

Commonly used with these tags: <body>, <frameset>

onResize

Gets triggered: When a visitor resizes the browser window.

Commonly used with these tags: <body>, <frameset>

onError

Gets triggered: When an error occurs while a browser tries to load a web page or image.

Commonly used with these tags: <body>, <img>

Note: The *onFocus* and *onBlur* events described in the following section also apply to the <body> and <frameset> tags.

Selection and Highlighting Events

Some events occur when the visitor focuses on different parts of a Web page, selects text, or chooses from a menu.

onChange

Gets triggered: When a visitor changes the text in a form field.

Commonly used with these tags: <textarea>, <input type="file | password | text">, <select>

onFocus

Gets triggered: When an element becomes the focus of the visitor's attention. For instance, clicking in a form text field or tabbing to it gives the text field focus. Also applies to a link when a visitor presses the tab key to reach the link (see the Note on page 182).

Commonly used with these tags: <a>, <body>, <frameset>, <textarea>, <input type="button | checkbox | file | password | radio | reset | submit | text">, <select>

onBlur

Gets triggered: When an element loses focus. For instance, if a visitor types into a form text field and then clicks outside of that field, the onBlur event occurs. The Spry Validation tools (see page 478) can use this event to validate text fields. The onBlur event is also triggered when a visitor sends a window to the background. Suppose your visitor is reading your Website in one window and has another one open in the background. If he clicks the background window, the current page loses focus and an *onBlur* event occurs.

Commonly used with these tags: <body>, <frameset>, <textarea>, <input type="button | checkbox | file | password | radio | reset | submit | text">, <select>

Form Events

While each element of a form (radio button, text field, checkbox) can respond to a variety of events, the whole form—the entire collection of elements—can respond to only two events:

onSubmit

Gets triggered: When a visitor clicks the Submit button on a form.

Commonly used with this tag: <form>

onReset

Gets triggered: When a visitor clicks the Reset button on a form.

Commonly used with this tag: <form>

The Actions, One by One

While events get the ball rolling, actions are, yes, where the action is. Whether it's opening a 200 × 200 pixel browser window or slowly fading in a photograph, you'll find an action for almost every interactivity need.

In some cases, alas, the actions aren't very good. Dreamweaver CS5 is still saddled with behaviors that were created for (and haven't been updated since) Dreamweaver 4. Although Spry Effects—part of the much newer Spry Framework discussed in the last chapter—offer a fresh set of behaviors to play with, Adobe has only weeded out a few behaviors that aren't very useful or that don't work well. This book makes clear which are the rotten eggs you want to steer clear of.

After you complete the steps required to set up an action as described on page 584, the new action appears in the Behaviors panel, and your Web page is ready to test. At that point, you can click the behavior's name in the Behaviors panel, where—by clicking the Events pop-up menu, as shown in Figure 14-1—you can change the event that triggers it.

Spry Effects

Spry Effects are a relatively new addition to Dreamweaver's arsenal of behaviors. They first appeared in Dreamweaver CS3 and are sophisticated visual effects that can do things like highlight elements on a page, make a photo fade in, or shake an entire sidebar of information like an earthquake. They're mostly eye candy and work well when you want to draw attention to an element on a page, or create a dramatic introduction. It's easy to abuse these fun effects, however: If every part of your page blinks, shrinks, shakes, and flashes, most visitors will quickly grow tired of your page's nonstop action.

Spry Effects are part of Adobe's Spry Framework, which you read about in-depth in the previous chapter and have encountered when learning about the Spry menu bar and Spry Validation widgets. To use a Spry Effect, you first have to apply an ID to the "target" element—the part of the page you wish to affect. Every effect, except Slide, can target any element (an <img> tag, for instance, for an image). (The Slide effect can target only a <div> tag.)

You're probably thinking of IDs as something you'd use when creating the kinds of CSS layouts discussed in Chapter 9. True, IDs are often associated with Cascading Style Sheets as a way of formatting a unique element on a page. However, IDs are also handy when you want to use JavaScript to add interactivity to a page. In fact, you can add IDs to HTML without ever creating any associated ID styles using CSS.

Recall that the HTML ID attribute marks a tag with a unique name. You can apply CSS to that tag using an ID style, but you can also control that tag using JavaScript. How you apply an ID to a tag differs depending on the tag, but here are the most common techniques:

- **Div tags.** Assign an ID to a div using the Property inspector. Just select the <div> tag and then use the ID field in the Property inspector to give it a unique name. In addition, you can wrap any collection of HTML tags (or even a single element, like an image) inside a <div> tag and apply an ID at the same time using the Insert Div Tag tool (see page 333).
- **Images.** When you select an image in the document window, you can type an ID for that image in the Property inspector's ID box (see Figure 6-7).
- **Forms.** Select the form and type an ID in the ID field on the left edge of the Property inspector (see Figure 12-3).
- **Form fields.** When you insert a form field, you can set the field's ID in the Input Tag Accessibility Options window (see Figure 12-5). You can later set or change a field's ID by selecting it and then using the ID field on the left edge of the Property inspector.
- **Other elements.** To add an ID to paragraphs, headlines, bulleted lists, and other tags, select the tag and then type a name in the ID field (see Figure 4-5).

After you apply an ID to the target, you then add a Spry Effect behavior to a tag (usually some tag other than the target) which then triggers the effect. For example, you may want the site's banner image to emerge on the page after the Web page loads. The target is the banner image, but you apply the Spry Effect behavior to the <body> tag using the onLoad event (page 590). Any of the tag/event combinations discussed in "Events" on page 587 will work.

Appear/Fade

To make an element fade in or out, use the Appear/Fade effect. To add a dramatic introduction to your site, you can fade in a large photograph on your site's home page after the page loads. Or you can have an "Important Announcement" box disappear when a visitor clicks it.

To use this effect:

1. **Select the tag that you want to trigger the fade in or out.**

   For example, you could pick a link that triggers the effect, or you could use the <body> tag coupled with the onLoad event (page 590).

2. **From the Actions list on the Behavior panel, choose Effects→Appear/Fade.**

   The Appear/Fade window appears (see Figure 14-4).

3. **Select a target element from the first menu.**

   Here's where you specify which page element should appear or fade away. The menu lists every tag on the page that has an ID applied to it. In addition, you may see <Current Selection> listed, which refers to the tag you selected in step 1. Choose this option if you want to apply the behavior to any that contains some kind of message—like "We'll be closed February 2nd to celebrate Groundhog's Day!" When a visitor clicks this <div> tag, it fades away.

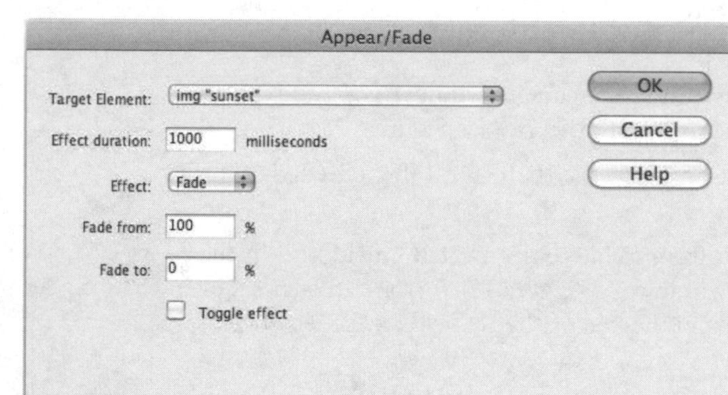

Figure 14-4: *Use the Appear/Fade effect to make an element fade from a page, or have a photograph fade into view on your site's home page.*

4. **Type an amount in the "Effect duration" field.**

   This setting controls how long the fade in or out lasts. The duration is measured in milliseconds, so entering *1000* gets you 1 second. If you want the target element to appear or disappear immediately, enter *0*.

Tip: If you're just after a simple hide/show type of effect without the fancy animation (and large file size) of the Spry Effects, see the instructions for the Show/Hide behavior on page 613.

---

5. **Choose the type of effect—Fade or Appear—from the Effect menu.**

   If you want the target element to fade into view, it must be hidden to begin with. Otherwise the fade in effect looks really weird: first you see the photo, then you don't, and *then* it fades in. To make the element invisible, add (or edit) a style for the target element, and then use the CSS *display* property (page 142). Set the display property to *none*.

6. **Type a percentage amount in the "from" and "to" fields.**

   Depending on which type of effect (Appear or Fade) you selected, you'll see either "Appear from" or "Fade from" and "Appear to" or "Fade to" in the Appear/Fade window. These two fields let you define the opacity of the target element. You'll commonly type *100* in the "Fade from" field and *0* in the "Fade to" field. Doing so makes the image fade completely out of view. However, if you like ghostly apparitions, you can fade from 100 percent to 25 percent, which makes a solid element become transparent.

7. **Optionally, turn on the "Toggle effect" checkbox.**

   This option turns the trigger tag into a kind of light switch that lets you fade the element in and out. Say you added an absolutely positioned div to a page that contains helpful hints on getting the most out of your website. You could then add a link that said "Show/hide hints." Add the Appear/Fade effect, target the AP div, and turn on the "Toggle effect" checkbox. Now, when a visitor clicks that link, the div fades into view (if it were hidden) or fades out of view (if it were visible).

8. **Click OK to apply the behavior.**

   Once you add the effect to a tag, you can edit or delete it just as you can any other behavior; see page 586 for details.

Blind

Don't worry: The Blind effect won't hurt your eyes. It's actually just a way of simulating a window blind—either being drawn closed over an element to hide it or opened to reveal an element. The basic concept and functionality is the same as the Appear/Fade effect: It lets you hide or reveal an element on a page. Follow the basic steps described in the previous section for Appear/Fade.

Once you select Blind from the Effects menu in the Behaviors panel, you can control all the basic elements of this effect from the Blind dialog box (Figure 14-5).

Use the Effect pull-down menu to choose in which direction the blind moves. If you want to display a hidden element on the page, choose "Blind down". To make an element disappear, choose "Blind up". This behavior is totally counterintuitive—you'd think raising a blind upward would actually reveal something. Fortunately, you can choose either direction for both revealing or hiding an element; the key is entering the correct percentage values in the "from" and "to" fields (Figure 14-5). If you wish to hide an already visible element, then type *100* in the "from" field and *0* in the "to" field.

To make an element appear, you first need to set its *display* property (page 142) to *none* by creating a CSS style for the target element. Next, apply the Blind effect to a tag (for example, a link or the <body> tag), and then select the direction you wish the blind to move (up or down) from the Effect menu. Finally, type *0* in the "from" field and *100* in the "to" field. The "Toggle effect" checkbox reverses the effect when a guest triggers the event again. For example, a link clicked for the first time might reveal a photo on the page; when clicked again, the photo disappears.

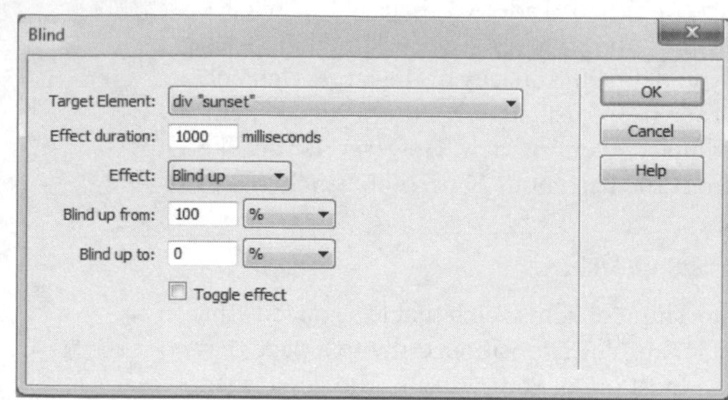

Figure 14-5:
The "from" and "to" fields can also hide or reveal just a portion of a div. If you set "Blind down from" to 0 percent and "Blind down to" to 50 percent, the effect will begin to reveal the contents of the div starting at the top and then it stops at the halfway mark–in other words, the bottom half of the div will still be invisible.

Grow/Shrink

The Grow/Shrink effect is another "now you see it, now you don't" type of effect. With it, you can make a photo, a paragraph, or a div full of content grow from a tiny speck on the screen to its full size, or you can make an element disappear by shrinking it into nothingness. The basic setup is the same as with the Appear/Fade effect described on page 593. The Grow/Shrink window (Figure 14-6) lets you target any element with an ID, set a duration for the effect, and then select whether to make the element appear (grow) or disappear (shrink). You can also have an element grow or shrink to a percentage of its full size. However, unless you target an image, displaying an element at less than its full size is usually unattractive and unreadable.

Tip: You can combine multiple types of effects for a single target element. For example, you could make a photo fade into view when a page loads, shake when a visitor moves his mouse over it, and even slide out of view when your visitor clicks a link. However, be careful when you assign multiple effects to the same event on the same element. If you add a Grow/Shrink effect *and* a Shake effect, both targeting the same element and using the same event, you won't see the element grow and *then* shake–you'll see it shake *as it grows*. In other words, the effects happen simultaneously (and usually bizarrely) instead of one after the other.

Highlight

Adding a background color to a paragraph, headline, or div is one way to create visual contrast and make an important piece of information stand out. A red box with white type will draw the eye quicker than a sea of black type on a white page. But if you really want to draw someone's attention, use the Highlight effect. Highlighting an element lets you add a flash of bright background color to it. For instance, on a form, you may have an important instruction for a particular form field ("Your password must be 10 characters long and not have !, # , or $ in it"). You could add the Highlight effect to the form field so that when a visitor clicks in the field, the instruction's background color quickly flashes, ensuring that the visitor sees the important information.

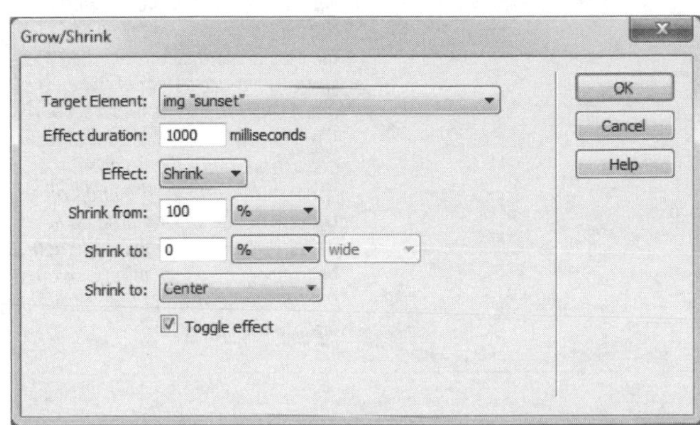

Figure 14-6: *The "Grow from" menu ("Shrink from" if you selected the Shrink effect) determines the point on the page from which the element begins its growth on its way to achieving its full size. You can either make the element grow from its center or from its top-left corner. The "center" option makes the element appear to come straight at you (or recede straight from you when you select Shrink).*

As with other Spry Effects, you use the Behaviors panel to apply the Highlight effect to some triggering element (like a form field you click in, or a link you mouse over). Then set options in the Highlight window (see Figure 14-7): a target element (any tag with an ID), the duration of the effect, and background colors.

Colors work like this: The Start Color is the background color of the target element when the effect begins. The background subsequently fades from the Start Color to the End Color (time the duration of the fade using the "Effect duration" setting). Finally, the End Color abruptly disappears and the Color After Effect replaces it. The general settings suggested by Dreamweaver when you apply the effect aren't so good: white, red, white. Assuming the background color of your page is white, you don't get so much of a flash effect as a "fade-to-a-color-that-immediately-disappears" effect. The effect looks a lot better if you set the Start Color to some bright, attention-grabbing, highlight color, and the End Color to match the background of the target element. Then the effect looks like a bright flash that gradually fades away.

However, instead of a flash, you may want an element's background to slowly fade to a different color and stay that color. In that case, set the Start Color to match the target element's current background, and use the same color for both End Color and Color After Effect.

Shake

The Shake effect is like adding an earthquake to a web page. The target element shakes violently left to right for a second or so. And that's all there is to it. When you apply this behavior, you have just one option: which element on the page to shake. You can shake any element with an ID—a div or even just a paragraph. It's kind of a fun effect...once...and maybe just for kids.

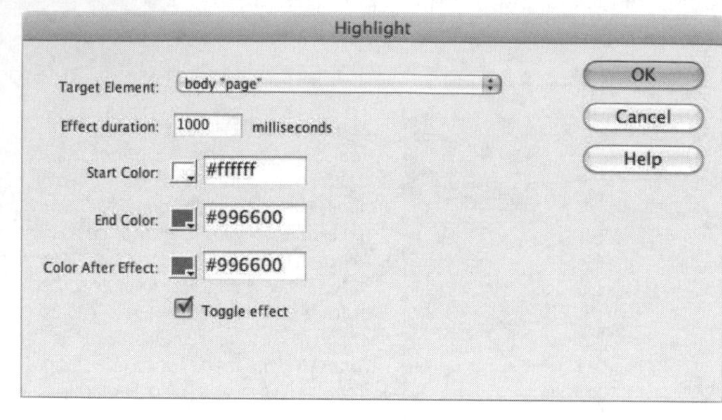

Figure 14-7: *The "Toggle effect" checkbox lets you fade in a background color with a single action (for example, the click of a link) and then fade the background color out when the same event occurs again (when a guest clicks the same link a second time, for instance). But for it to look good, make sure the Color After Effect is the same as the End Color. Otherwise, the second time your visitor triggers the highlight (when he toggles the effect, in other words) the background won't fade smoothly back to the start color.*

Slide

The Slide effect is just like the Blind effect. But instead of a "blind" moving over an element to hide it, or moving off an element to reveal it, the element itself moves. Say you have a <div> tag that contains a gallery of photos. If you target that div with a "slide up" effect, the images all move upwards and disappear at the top edge of the div. Think of the <div> as a kind of window looking out onto the photos. When the photos move up past the "window", you can't see them any longer.

Note: You can only use the slide effect on div tags that have IDs. You can't use it on, for example, just an image with an ID.

You can make an element slide up or slide down using the Effect menu in the Slide window (Figure 14-8). And, as with the Blind effect, to make an element disappear, type *100* in the "from" field and *0* in the "to" field. To make an element slide either up or down and *appear* on the page, first create a style for the element's ID, and then apply the Slide behavior to some other element (a link or the body tag, for instance). Finally, type *0* in the "from" field and *100* in the "to" field.

Squish

The Squish effect offers no options other than selecting a target element. The effect hides an element by shrinking it down until it disappears. It behaves exactly like the Grow/Shrink effect (page 596) with the Shrink effect selected (see Figure 14-6). Since it doesn't provide any timing controls, you're better off sticking with the more versatile Grow/Shrink effect.

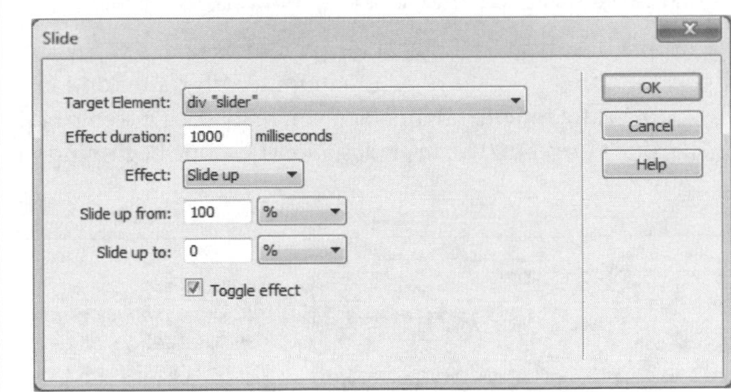

Figure 14-8: *The Slide effect works just like the Blind effect described on page 595. The only difference is that the element itself moves and disappears (as opposed to a blind being drawn over the element).*

Navigation Actions

Dreamweaver offers a host of navigational aids you can add to your pages to give visitors customized alternatives to the simple click-and-load approach of getting around a basic site.

Open Browser Window

Sometimes, when a visitor action opens a new browser window, you want to dictate the size of that window. If you have a link to a "Sign up for our newsletter form", for example, you may want to open the sign-up page in a window that matches the exact width and height of the form. Or, when a visitor clicks on a thumbnail image, you may want to open a new window with the exact dimensions of the full-size photo—and skip all the distracting browser "chrome," like the location bar, status bar, toolbar, and so on.

Enter Dreamweaver's Open Browser Window action (Figure 14-9). Use this behavior to tell your visitor's browser to open a new window to a height and width *you* desire. In fact, you can even dictate what elements the browser window includes. Don't want the toolbar, location bar, or status bar? No problem; this action lets you include or exclude the frills.

To open a new browser window, you start, as always, by selecting the tag to which you want to attach the behavior. You can attach it to any of the tags discussed on page 587, but you usually want to add it to a link with an *onClick* event, or to the <body> tag with the *onLoad* event.

Note: Most browsers have pop-up blockers. This nifty feature prevents a browser from opening a new browser window unless the visitor initiates the request. In other words, you probably won't be able to open a new browser window when a page loads in the current window, but you can open a new browser window based on a visitor's action–like clicking a link.

Once you select this action from the + menu in the Behaviors panel, you see the dialog box shown in Figure 14-10. Specify the following options:

- **URL to display.** In this box, type in the URL or path of the page you want to load, or click Browse and find the page on your computer (the latter option is a near-foolproof way to ensure functional links). If you're loading a web page on somebody else's site, don't forget to type in an *absolute* URL, one beginning with *http://* (see page 160).

Figure 14-9: *You, too, can annoy your friends, neighbors, and website customers with these unruly pop-up windows. Just add the Open Browser Window action to the <body> tag of your document. Now, when that page loads, a new browser window opens with the ad, announcement, or picture you specify. To be even more annoying, use the onUnload event of the <body> tag to open a new browser window—with the same web page—when your visitors try to exit the page. They won't be able to get to a different page, and may even encounter system crashes. Now that's annoying! Fortunately, most current web browsers prevent these kinds of automatic window-opening tricks, and will only open a new browser window when your visitor clicks a link.*

- **Window width, Window height**. Next, define the width and height of the new window. Specify these values in pixels; most browsers require a minimum window size of 100 × 100 pixels. Also, if the width and height you specify are larger than the available space on the visitor's monitor, the window fills the monitor (but won't ever generate a wider or taller window).

- **Attributes**. Turn on the checkboxes for the elements you want the new window to include. Figure 14-11 shows the different pieces of a standard browser window. Note that in most browsers, you can't really get rid of the resize handle, so even if you leave that option unchecked it still appears and a visitor will still be able to resize the window.

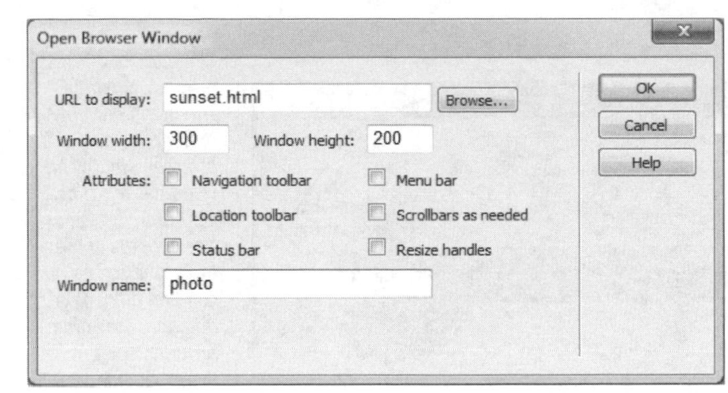

Figure 14-10: *Here, you can define the properties of the new window, including what Web page loads into it, its dimensions, and so on. If you leave the "Window width" and "Window height" properties blank, you'll get different results in different browsers. In Firefox, Opera, and Google Chrome, you won't get a new window; the page will open up a new tab. In Safari and Internet Explorer, you'll get a new window that is the same size as the window it opens from.*

- **Window name**. Give the new window a name (using letters and numbers only). If you include spaces or other symbols, Dreamweaver displays an error message and lets you correct the mistake. The name won't actually appear on your web page, but it's useful for targeting links or actions from the original window.

Once you set up the Open Browser Window action, you can load web pages into the new window from the original page; simply use the name of the new window as the link's target. For example, you could add the Open Browser Window behavior to a link labeled "Open photo gallery" that, when clicked, opens a small new window showcasing a photo. You could include additional links on the main page that load additional photos into the small window.

If you use more than one Open Browser Window behavior on a single page, make sure you give each new window a unique name. If you use the same name, your page might retain the first new window's settings and you might not get the width, height, or other settings you want in the new window.

When you click OK, your newly created behavior appears in the Actions list in the Behaviors panel.

Go to URL

The Go to URL action works just like a link does—it loads a new web page. However, while links work only when you click them, Go to URL can load a page based on an event *other than* clicking. For instance, you may want to load a page when your visitor's cursor merely moves over an image, or when she turns on a particular radio button.

Once you select a tag and choose this action's name from the + menu in the Behaviors panel, set these options in the resulting dialog box:

- **Open in**. If you aren't using frames, Dreamweaver lists only "Main Window" here. But if you're working in a *frameset* file and have named each of your frames, they're listed in the "Open in" list box. Click the name of the target frame.

Figure 14-11: *The parts of a browser window. Note: The menu bar only appears as part of the browser window on Windows machines. On Macs, the menu bar appears at the top of the screen and can't be hidden; in addition, the Safari browser won't hide the resize handle or the scroll bars (if they're needed).*

- **URL**. Fill in the URL of the page you wish to load. You can use any of the link-specifying tricks described in "Adding a Link" on page 165: type in a path or an absolute URL starting with *http://*, or click the Browse button and select a page from your site.

Tip: You can use the Go to URL behavior as a way to redirect users from one page to another. For example, say the marketing department sent out a flyer saying "Sign up for free goodies" and used an incorrect web address–for instance, *http://mysite.com/sinup.html*, instead of *signup.html*. Rather than rename the signup.html page to *sinup.html*, just create a new page–*sinup.html*–and add the Go To URL behavior to that page's <body> tag. That way, when someone visits *sinup.html*, they'll be instantly carried away to the correct page, *signup.html*. (Also make sure the marketing department always checks with you BEFORE advertising a web address on your site.)

Jump Menu and Jump Menu Go

Conserving precious visual space on a web page is a constant challenge for designers. Put too many buttons, icons, and navigation controls on a page, and you clutter your presentation and muddle a page's meaning. As sites get larger, so do navigation bars, which can engulf a page in a long column of buttons.

The Spry menu bar is one solution to this problem, but you may not want to go through the lengthy process of creating and styling a Spry menu as described on page 184. A simpler way to add detailed navigation to a site without wasting pixels is to use Dreamweaver's Jump Menu behavior. A *jump menu* is a form pop-up that lets visitors navigate by choosing from a list of links.

Dreamweaver lists the Jump Menu behavior in the Behaviors panel, but for a simpler, happier life, don't insert it into your page that way. Instead, use the Insert panel or Insert menu command, like this:

1. **Click where you want the jump menu to appear on your Web page.**

   It could be in a table cell at the top of the page, or along the left edge, for example.

2. **Under the Forms category on the Insert panel, click the Jump Menu icon (see Figure 12-2). Or choose Insert→Form→Jump Menu.**

   If you had used the Behaviors panel instead, you'd first have to add a form and insert a menu into it. The Insert Jump Menu object saves you those steps.

Note: Even though the Jump Menu behavior uses a pop-up menu, which is a component of a *form*, you don't have to create a form first, as described in Chapter 12. Dreamweaver automatically creates one when you insert a jump menu.

   The Insert Jump Menu dialog box opens, as shown in Figure 14-12.

3. **Type an instructive label, like "Select a Destination", in the Text box.**

   What you enter in the Text box sets the menu's default choice—the first item listed in the menu when the page loads. Dreamweaver gives you two ways to trigger the Jump Menu behavior: when a visitor makes a selection from the list—which is an *onChange* event, since the visitor changes the menu by selecting a new option—or when the visitor clicks an added "Go" menu button after making his selection. The second method requires extra effort on the visitor's part—he has to make a selection *and* click a button. The first method, therefore, offers a better visitor experience. But it means that you can't include an actual link in the first menu item in the menu; after all, that item is selected by default and a visitor only triggers the jump behavior when he selects an item *other than* the one currently listed.

   If you intend to add a Go button, skip to Step 6.

4. **Leave the "When selected, go to URL" box empty.**

   Since the first item in the list is just an instruction, you don't want to link it to a page.

5. **To add a link, click the + button.**

   This adds another item to the menu.

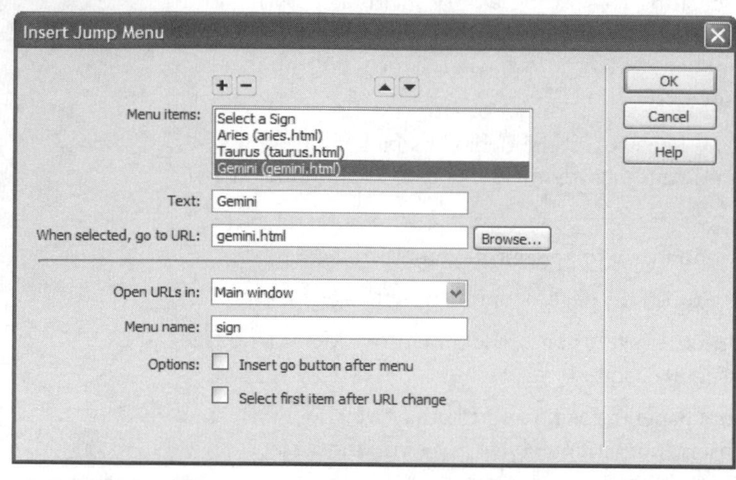

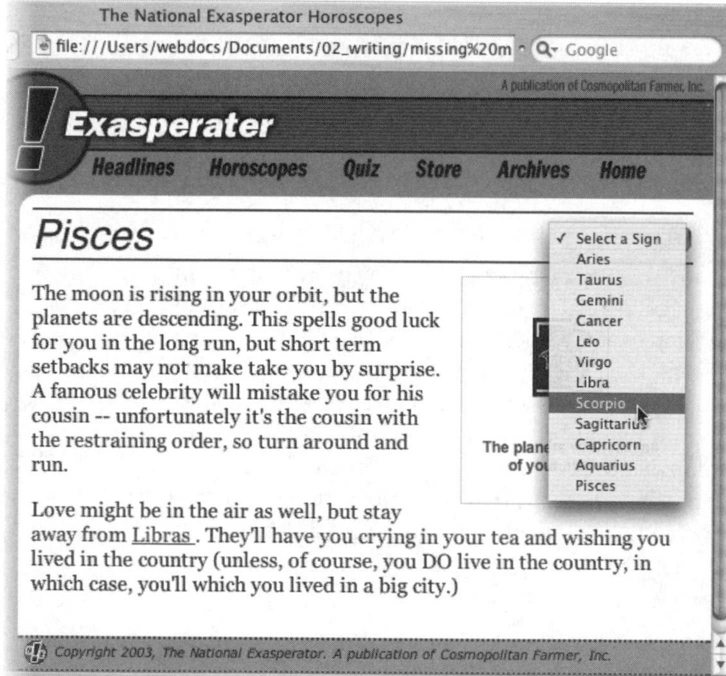

Figure 14-12:
Top: The Insert Jump Menu dialog box is set up so that the onChange event of the <select> tag triggers the Jump Menu action. That is, the Jump Menu behavior works when your visitor selects an item other than the one currently listed.

Bottom: Unless you turn on the "Insert go button after menu" checkbox, you should never use the first item of a jump menu as a link. Instead, use some descriptive text–such as "Select a Page to Visit"–to let visitors know what the menu does. Then leave the URL blank in the Insert Jump Menu dialog box. When placed on a page, the resulting menu is very compact, but it can offer a long list of pages.

6. **Type the name of the link in the Text field.**

   Specify the first link in your pop-up menu. The name doesn't have to match the page title or the anchor name; you can make it descriptive. For instance, you can call a menu choice *Home* even if the title of your home page is "Welcome to XYZ Corp."

7. **Enter a URL for this link in the "When selected, go to URL" field.**

   As mentioned earlier, the most error-free way to select a target file is to use the Browse button. However, if you're linking to another site, you have to type in an absolute URL, starting with *http://*.

8. **To add the next link in your pop-up menu, click the + button and repeat Steps 6 and 7. Continue until you add all the links.**

   To remove a link, select it from the "Menu items" list and then click the minus sign (–) button. To reorder your list, click a link name and then click the up and down arrow buttons.

9. **If you're using frames (which you really shouldn't be, for the reasons described on page 15), use the "Open URLs in" pop-up menu to specify a target frame for the web page.**

   Otherwise, the "Main window" option loads links into the entire browser window.

10. **In the "Menu name" box, give the menu a name.**

    This step is optional; you can also accept the name Dreamweaver proposes. Since Dreamweaver uses this name just for the JavaScript that drives the behavior, it doesn't appear anywhere on your page.

11. **If you want a Go button to appear beside your jump menu, turn on the "Insert go button after menu" checkbox.**

    Use this option only when you want to make the first item in your jump menu a link instead of an instruction, or when the jump menu is in one frame and loads pages into another.

    When you include a Go button, Dreamweaver adds a small standardized button next to the menu, which your visitor can click to jump to a selected link. But most of the time, your visitors won't get a chance to click the button; the browser loads the new page as soon as our visitor selects a link.

    The Go button's handy, however, when there's no selection to make. For example, if the first item in the menu is a link, your visitors won't be able to select it; it's *already* selected when the menu page loads. In this case, a Go button is the only way to trigger the "jump."

12. **If you want to reset the menu after each jump (so that it once again shows the first menu command), turn on "Select first item after URL change."**

    You're best off skipping this option. It's only useful if you use the really outdated HTML frames technology (page 15).

13. **Click OK to apply the action and close the Jump Menu dialog box.**

    Your new pop-up menu appears on your web page, and the new behavior appears in the Actions list in the Behaviors panel.

Note: To edit a jump menu, click the menu in your document and then, in the Behaviors panel, double-click the Jump Menu action in the Actions list. The settings dialog box reappears. At this point, you can change any of the options described in the previous steps, though you can't add a Go button to a jump menu that didn't have one to begin with. Click OK when you're finished.

The Jump Menu Go action (available on the Behaviors panel) is useful only if you didn't add a Go button in Step 11. In this case, if there's a jump menu on the page and you want to add a Go button to it, click next to the menu, add a form button, and then attach this behavior to it. (For more on working with forms, see Chapter 12.)

Check Plugin

You wouldn't be reading a Missing Manual if you didn't appreciate our candid advice. This behavior is useless, so skip it! It just doesn't work on all browsers, and if all you want to do is see if your visitor has a Flash plug-in, Dreamweaver has a better tool for that. Best of all, you don't need to do anything to take advantage of this tool. When you insert a Flash movie, Dreamweaver automatically adds code that not only checks whether your visitor has the Flash plug-in, it even verifies that he has the correct *version* of the plug-in (see page 629 for details). If either is missing, your page displays a message to that effect and provides a quick and easy way to download and install the plug-in.

Image Actions

Images make web pages stand out, but using Dreamweaver behaviors with images can make them come to life.

Preload Images

It takes time for images to load over the Internet. A 64 KB image, for instance, takes about 1 second to download over a DSL modem. Add 10 images of this size to a page, and it can take a while to actually load the page. However, once a browser loads an image, it stores that image in its *cache*, as described on page 689, so that if the page requires that same graphic again, it loads extremely quickly. The Preload Images action takes advantage of this concept by downloading images and storing them in the browser's cache *even before* they're actually needed.

Preloading is especially important when you use mouse rollover effects on a page. When a visitor moves her mouse over a button, it may, for example, appear to light up. If the rollover image weren't preloaded, the light-up graphic wouldn't appear when your visitor rolled over the button; in fact, it wouldn't even begin to download until she rolled her cursor over the button. The resulting delay would make your button feel less like a rollover and more like a layover.

If you use the Insert Rollover Image command (see page 246), you don't need to apply the Preload Images action by hand because Dreamweaver adds it automatically. But there are exceptions. For example, when you use the CSS *background* property (page 231) to add an image to the hover state of a link (see page 180), a new background image appears when a visitor mouses over a link. But the browser loads that image only when a visitor triggers the hover state, not before. In a case like this, you want to add the Preload Images action to the event.

To do so, select the <body> tag. You can apply the Preload Images behavior to any tag, but it really only makes sense to attach it to the <body> tag using an onLoad event, so that when the page loads, the browser begins downloading the images.

If you add rollover images to your page, this behavior may already be in the <body>. If that's the case, just select the body tag (click <body> in the Tag selector) and then double-click the Preload Images action that should already be listed in the Behaviors panel. If it isn't, just choose Preload Images from the + menu in the Behaviors panel. Either way, Dreamweaver displays the Preload Images dialog box.

Click the Browse button and navigate to the graphics file you want to preload, or type in the path or (if the graphic is already on the web) the absolute URL. Dreamweaver adds the image to the Preload Images list. To preload another image, click the + button and repeat the process. Continue until you add all the images you want to preload.

You can remove an image from the list by selecting it and then clicking the minus sign (–) button. (Be careful not to delete any images required for a rollover effect you've already created—the Undo command doesn't work here.)

When you click OK, you return to your document and your new action appears in the Behaviors panel. You can edit it, if you like, by changing the event that triggers it. But unless you're trying to achieve some special effect, you usually use the *onLoad* event of the <body> That's all there is to it. When your page loads in a browser, the browser continues to load and store the graphics you specified quietly in the background. They'll appear almost instantly when they're called by a rollover action or even by a shift to another page that incorporates the graphics.

Swap Image

The Swap Image action exchanges one image on your page for another. (See the end of this section for detail on Swap Image's sibling behavior, Swap Image Restore.)

Simple as that process may sound, swapping images is one of the most visually exciting things you can do on a web page. Swapping images works something like rollover images, except that you don't have to trigger them with a mouse click or mouse pass. You can use *any* tag-and-event combination. For instance, you can create a mini slideshow by listing the names of pictures down the left side of a web page and inserting an image in the middle of the page. Add a Swap Image action to each slide name, and the appropriate picture replaces the center image when a visitor clicks on a new name.

To make this behavior work, your page has to include a *starter image*, and the images you want to swap in have to match the width and height of that starter graphic. If they don't, the browser resizes and distorts the swapped pictures to fit the "frame" dictated by the original image.

To add the Swap Image behavior, first identify the starter image (choose Insert→Image, or use any of the other techniques described in Chapter 6.) Give your image an ID in the Property inspector, so that JavaScript knows which image to swap out. (JavaScript doesn't really care about the original graphic image itself, but rather about the space that it occupies on the page.)

Tip: You can swap more than one image using a single Swap Image behavior (Figure 14-13). Using this trick, not only can a button change to another graphic when you mouse over it, but any number of other graphics on the page can also change at the same time. An asterisk (*) next to the name of an image in the Swap Image dialog box (see Figure 14-14) indicates that the behavior will swap in a new image for that particular graphic. In the example in Figure 14-14, you can see that two images–*horoscope* and *ad*, both marked by asterisks–swap as a result of a single action.

Now select the tag you want to associate with the Swap Image behavior—you can choose a link, a paragraph, another image, or even the starter image itself. When you choose this action's name from the Behaviors panel, the Swap Image dialog box appears, as shown in Figure 14-14.

- **Images**. From the list, click the name of the starter image.
- **Set source to**. Here's where you specify the *image* file you want to swap in. If it's a graphics file in your site folder, click Browse to find and open it. You can also specify a path or an absolute URL to another website, as described in "Absolute Links" (page 160).
- **Preload images**. Preloading ensures that image downloads don't slow down the swap-in.
- **Restore images onMouseOut**. You get this option only when you apply the Swap Image behavior to a link. When you turn this checkbox on, the previous image reappears when a visitor moves *off* the link.

Swap Image Restore

The Swap Image Restore action returns the last set of swapped images to its original state. Most designers use it in conjunction with a rollover button so that the button returns to its original appearance when the visitor moves his cursor off a button.

You'll probably never find a need to add this behavior yourself; Dreamweaver automatically adds it when you insert a rollover image and choose the "Restore images onMouseOut" option when you set up a regular Swap Image behavior (see Figure 14-14). But, if you prefer, you can add the Swap Restore Image behavior to other tag-and-event combinations, using the routine described on page 584. (The Swap Image Restore dialog box offers no options to set.)

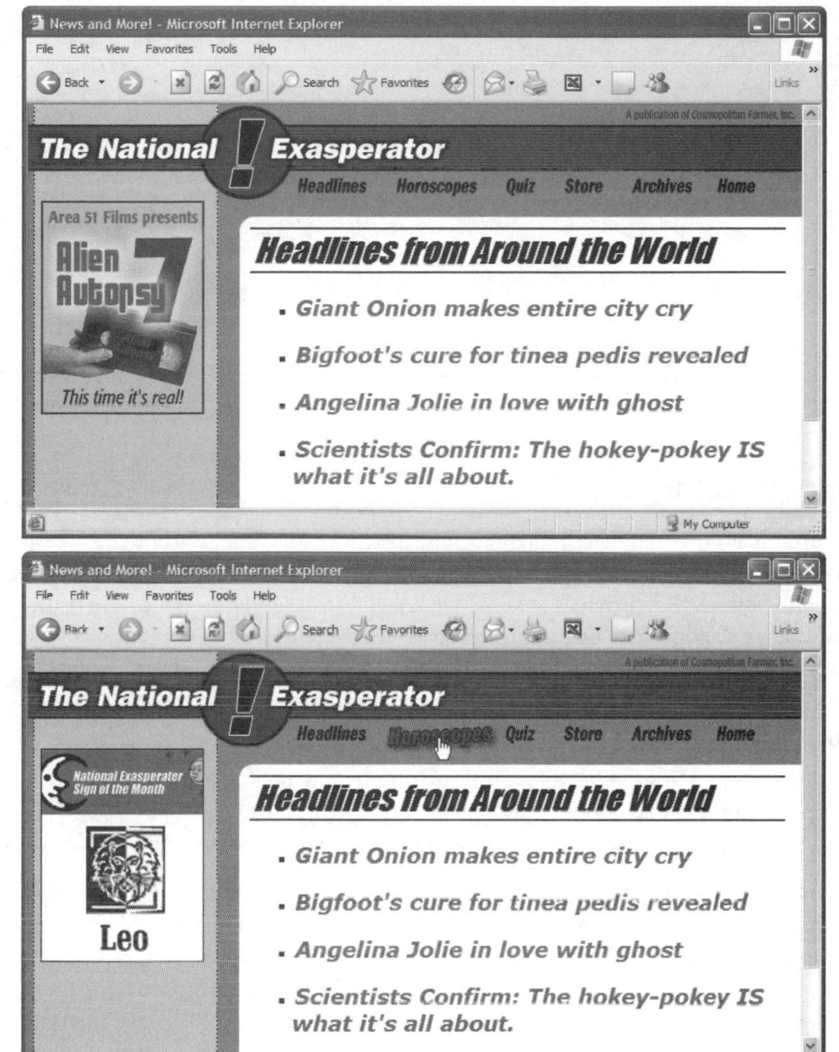

Figure 14-13: *You can use the Swap Image behavior to simultaneously change multiple graphics with a single mouseover. A humble web page (top) comes to life when a visitor moves her mouse over the Horoscopes button (bottom). Not only does the graphic for the Horoscopes button change, but so does the ad on the left sidebar; it's replaced with a tantalizing look at the "Sign of the Month." The Swap Image action lets you easily get this type of effect, sometimes called a disjoint rollover.*

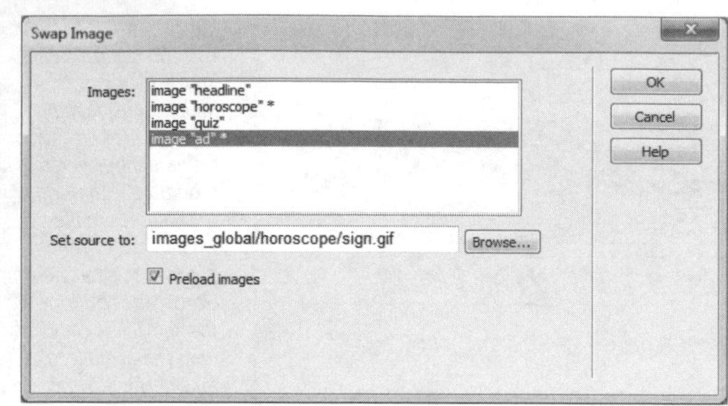

Figure 14-14: *Some actions, like the Swap Image action, can automatically add behaviors to a web page. In this case, the "Preload images" and "Restore images onMouse-Out" options actually add a Swap Image Restore action to the onMouseOut event of the currently selected tag, and a Preload Images action to the onLoad event of the <body> tag.*

Message Actions

Communication is why we build websites: to tell a story, sell a product, or provide information that entertains and informs. Dreamweaver can enhance this communication with actions that provide dynamic feedback. From subtle messages in a browser's status bar to dialog boxes that command a visitor's attention, Dreamweaver offers numerous ways to respond, in words, to the things your visitors do on your pages.

Popup Message

Use the Popup Message behavior to send important messages to your visitors, as shown in Figure 14-15. Your visitor must click OK to close the dialog box. But because a pop-up message demands immediate attention, reserve this behavior for important announcements.

To create a pop-up message, select the tag that you want to trigger the behavior. For example, adding this action to the <body> tag with an *onLoad* event makes a message appear when a visitor first loads the page; adding the same behavior to a link with an *onClick* event makes the message appear when the visitor clicks the link.

From the Add Action menu (+ button) in the Behaviors panel, choose Popup Message. In the Popup Message dialog box, type the message that you want to appear. (Check the spelling and punctuation carefully; nothing says "amateur" like poorly written error messages, and Dreamweaver's spell-checker isn't smart enough to examine these messages.) Then click OK.

Note: JavaScript programmers, your message can also include any valid JavaScript expression. To embed JavaScript code in a message, place it inside braces ({ }). If you want to include the current time and date in a message, for example, add this: {*new Date()*}. If you just want to display a brace in the message, add a backslash, like this: \{. The backslash lets Dreamweaver know that you *really* do want a { character—and not just a bunch of JavaScript—to appear in the dialog box.

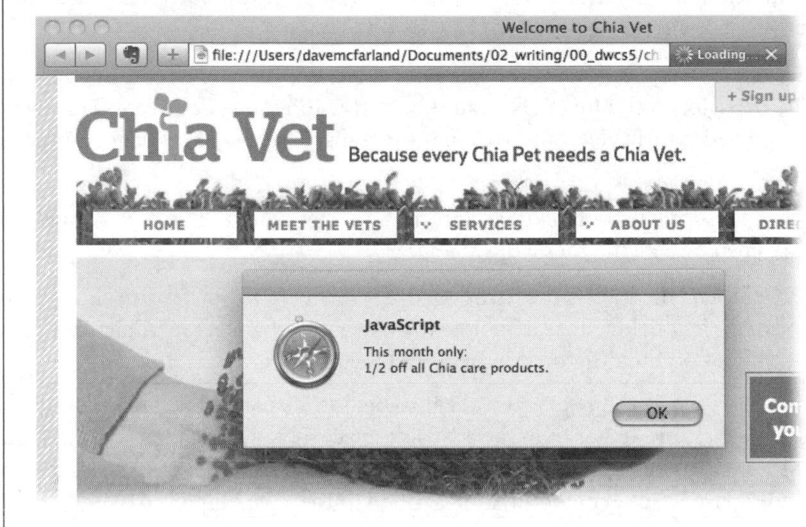

Figure 14-15: *Here, a pop-up message indicates a sale going on at Chia-Vet.com. While the Popup Message behavior is easy to use, you can't customize the look of the dialog box. That's controlled by the browser, and it looks different from browser to browser. For a better look, you could create an absolutely positioned <div> (see page 356) containing a nicely styled message, and then add one of the Spry Effects (like Fade, Blind, or Shrink) to a "close" button inside the div, so that when a visitor clicks the button, the div disappears.*

Set Text of Status Bar

Skip this action—it's intended to display a message in the status bar at the bottom of a browser window. Few people look for messages there, and many browsers don't display the status bar unless a visitor actually turns that option on. And many browsers, including Opera, Safari, Firefox, and Chrome, won't let you change the text in the status bar anyway.

Set Text of Text Field

Normally, a text field in a form (see page 463) is blank. It sits on a page and waits for a guest to type in it. The Set Text of Text Field behavior, by contrast, can save your visitors time by automatically filling in form fields with obvious answers.

For instance, if you create a visitor survey page, the first question might require a yes or no answer, along the lines of "Do you own a computer?" You provide radio buttons labeled "Yes" and "No". The second question might be "What brand is it?" followed by a text field, where your visitors type in the answer.

But if someone answers "No" to question 1, there's no point in answering the second question. To keep things moving along, you can have the question's text field display "Please skip to Question 3." To do so, simply add the Set Text of Text Field action to the *onClick* event of the "No" radio button.

To apply the Set Text of Text Field action, make sure your page includes a form and at least one text field; since this behavior changes the text in a form text field, you won't get very far without the proper HTML on the page.

Select the tag to which you want the behavior attached. In the example above, you attach the behavior to the form's No radio button with an *onClick* event. However, you aren't limited to form elements. Any of the tags discussed on pages page 587–page 592 work.

When you choose Set Text of Text Field from the + menu in the Behaviors panel, its dialog box opens. Make the following changes:

- **Text field**. The menu lists the names of every text field in your form; choose the name of the text field whose default text you want to change. (See Chapter 12 for the full story on building online forms in Dreamweaver.)
- **New text**. Type in the text you want that field to display. Make sure you don't make the message longer than the available space. If you leave the New text field blank, the contents of the field will be erased. Once again, your message can include a JavaScript expression, as described in the note on page 610.

Set Text of Container

Another way to get your message across is to change the text that appears inside any element that has an ID. For example, you might change the text in a <div> tag, an absolutely positioned element (see page 356), or just a paragraph with its ID property set. This action also lets you use HTML code to *format* the message. (Actually, the "Set Text" part of this action's name is a bit misleading, since the action lets you include HTML code, images, forms, and other objects in the tag, not just text.)

As always, start by selecting a tag. For example, you could select a link so that moving a mouse over the link changes the text inside a <div> to read, "Click here to see our exclusive photos of collectable Chia Pets."

When you choose this action's name from the + menu in the Behaviors panel, you get these controls in a dialog box:

- **Container**. The menu lists the names of every element on the web page that has an assigned ID (see page 112 for more on IDs); choose the name of the container whose text you want to set.
- **New HTML**. In this field, type in the text you wish to add to the layer. You can type in a plain-text message or use HTML code to control the content's formatting.

  For instance, if you want a word to appear bold, place the word inside a pair of strong tags like this: <strong>important</strong>. If you'd rather not mess around with HTML, you can design the content using Dreamweaver's Design view—that is, right out there in your document window. Copy the HTML source from the Code view (Chapter 11), and then paste it into this action's New HTML field.

Tip: You can use the Set Text of Container to both set and erase the text in a container. For example, say you wanted text to appear inside a div when you mouse over a photo, but disappear when you move the mouse off of the photo. Select the photo and apply the Set Text of Container behavior twice: the first time, add your message and set the event to *onMouseOver*; the second time, leave the HTML box empty (in other words, without a message) and set the event to *onMouseOut*.

Text of Frame

Here's another holdover from the dark ages of website design. Like the Set Text of Container action, the Set Text of Frame action replaces the content of a specified frame with HTML you specify. As mentioned on page 15, frames just aren't used professionally (and haven't been for years), so skip them and this behavior.

Element Actions

Dreamweaver includes several tools that let you manipulate the appearance and placement of any element on a page.

Show-Hide Elements

Do you ever stare in awe when a magician makes a handkerchief disappear into thin air? Now you, too, can perform sleight of hand on your own web pages, making HTML disappear and reappear with ease. Dreamweaver's Show-Hide Elements behavior is a piece of JavaScript programming that lets you create your own magic. It works a lot like the Spry Effects (page 592), but there's no fancy animation or fading out of view—the element just pops out of view or pops into view. (And it does so with a lot less code, so if you want a simple appear/disappear effect, this is the behavior to use.)

Show-Hide Elements takes advantage of the CSS Visibility property (page 361). You can use it for things like adding pop-up tooltips to your Web page, so that when a visitor mouses over a link, a paragraph appears offering a detailed explanation of where the link goes (see Figure 14-16).

The following steps show how to create this effect:

1. **Add absolutely positioned divs to your web page using the techniques described on page 356. Use the Visibility setting (page 361) to specify how you want each div to look when the page loads.**

   If you want a tag to be visible at first and then to disappear when a visitor performs an action, set the layer to Visible. If you want the layer to appear only *after* a specific event, set it to Hidden.

Note: You don't have to use an absolutely positioned div to take advantage of the Show-Hide behavior. Any element with an ID applied to it can be hidden or shown, but AP divs work best because they don't take up any room on a page and they float above other content on the page. If you make a regular element disappear, there's a large empty spot on the page where it once was.

2. **In the Tag selector, click the tag to which you want the behavior attached.**

   Web designers often attach behaviors to link (<a>) tags, but you can also attach them to paragraphs, headlines, div tags, images or, as in Figure 14-16, to an image map, which defines hotspots on a single graphic.

   To create this effect, attach two behaviors to each hotspot in the document window (that is, to each <area> tag in HTML): one to show the div, using the *onMouseOver* event, and one to hide the div, using the *onMouseOut* event.

Note: If this is all Greek to you, see page 244 for more on image maps and hotspots.

---

3. **If it isn't already open, choose Window→Tag Inspector. Then click the Behaviors button in the Tag Inspector window to open the Behaviors panel.**

   The Behaviors panel (pictured in Figure 14-1) appears. It lets you add, remove, and modify behaviors.

4. **Click the + button on the panel. Select Show-Hide Elements from the menu.**

   The Show-Hide Elements window appears (see Figure 14-17). You'll use this window to tell Dreamweaver what div you intend to work with first.

5. **Click an element from the list.**

   It's useful to give your elements descriptive ID names so you can easily distinguish them in lists like this.

6. **Choose a Visibility setting for the elements by clicking one of three buttons: Show, Hide, or Default.**

   You're determining what happens to the element when someone interacts with the tag you selected in Step 2. "Show" makes the element visible, "Hide" hides it, and "Default" sets the element's Visibility property to the browser's default value (usually the same as the Inherit value described on page 361).

   Your choice appears in parentheses next to the element's name, as shown in Figure 14-17.

7. **If you like, select another element and apply another visibility option.**

   A single Show-Hide Elements action can affect several elements at once. It can even make some elements visible and others invisible simultaneously. (If you apply an action to an element by mistake, select the same option again to remove it from that element.)

8. **Click OK to apply the behavior.**

   The Show-Hide Elements action now appears in the Behaviors panel, as does the event that triggers it.

Figure 14-16: *Using Dreamweaver's Show-Hide Elements behavior, you can make page elements appear and disappear. In this example, several elements lay hidden on a page. When a visitor moves his mouse over different parts of the tree cross-section, informative graphics (each placed in a hidden element) suddenly appear. Moving the mouse away returns the element to its hidden state. Notice how the information bubble overlaps the tree image and the text above it–a dead giveaway that this page uses absolutely positioned divs.*

Once you add Show-Hide Elements, you can preview the behavior in a browser or click the Live View button in the Document toolbar (see page 578 for more on Live View). Like other Dreamweaver behaviors, you can edit or delete this action as described on page 586.

Draggable Divs

The Drag AP Div behavior lets you create pages with absolutely positioned divs (page 356) that a visitor can freely position on the page (think interactive jigsaw puzzle). This was kind of a cool behavior in its day, but it hasn't been updated in years. It adds lots of JavaScript code that really weighs down your page, and because it's based on really old code, it isn't guaranteed to work in new browsers.

Advanced Behaviors

Dreamweaver has two advanced behaviors that let you call (invoke) custom JavaScript functions and change the properties of various HTML elements on a page. Both of them require familiarity with JavaScript and HTML. Unlike the other Dreamweaver behaviors, these two can easily generate browser errors if you use them incorrectly.

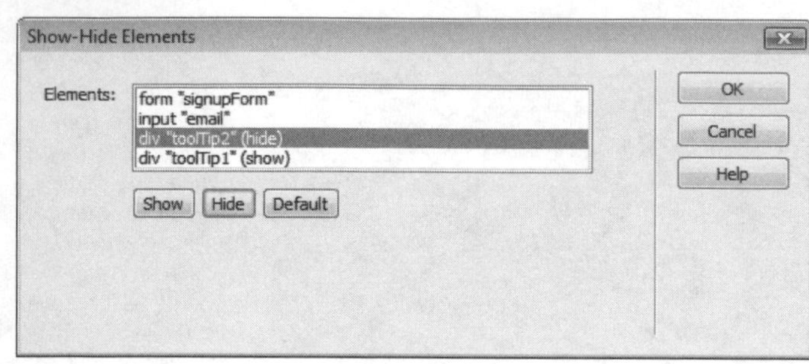

Figure 14-17: *This box lets you hide or show any element on a page. In fact, you can control multiple elements at once. Here, the "toolTip1" div appears, while the div "toolTip2" disappears, when a visitor triggers the behavior. Other elements–like an HTML form and a form field (both have IDs so they appear here)–are unaffected by this particular action.*

Call JavaScript

You can use the Call JavaScript behavior to execute a single line of JavaScript code or to call a JavaScript function that you add to the <head> section of your web page.

When you select a tag and choose this behavior's name from the Behaviors panel, the Call JavaScript dialog box opens. If you want to execute a single line of JavaScript code, simply type it in. For instance, if you want to make the browser window close, type *window.close()*. If you want to call a JavaScript function, type the function name, like this: *myFunction()*.

Change Property

The Change Property behavior can dynamically alter the value of a property or change the style of any of the following HTML tags: <div>, <span>, <p>, <tr>, <td>, <img>, <form>, <textarea>, or <select>. It can also change properties for radio buttons, checkboxes, text fields, and password fields on forms (see Chapter 12). As with the previous behavior, this one requires a working knowledge of HTML, CSS, and JavaScript.

Select a tag, choose this behavior's name from the + menu in the Behaviors panel, and then fill in the following parts of the Change Property dialog box (see Figure 14-18):

- **Type of element**. This pop-up menu lists the 13 HTML tags that this behavior can control. Choose the type of element whose property you wish to change.
- **Element ID**. From this pop-up menu, choose the ID of the object you want to modify. You'll only see elements of the type you selected from the first menu (for example, <div> or <p> tags). Dreamweaver will list any tag of the selected type that doesn't have an ID applied to it, but it will have the label "unidentified" next to it. Dreamweaver only lets you choose an element that has an ID.
- **Property**. Choose the property you want to change (or, if you know enough about JavaScript and CSS, just type the property's name into the Enter field). All the options in the menu refer to various CSS properties. For example, "color" refers to the *color* property, which sets text color, as discussed on page 128.

POWER USERS' CLINIC

Closing Browser Windows with the Call JavaScript Behavior

Suppose you add an Open Browser Window behavior to your home page so that, when visitors come to your site, a small window opens, displaying a web page that advertises a new site feature.

After they read the ad, your visitors will want to close the window and continue browsing your site. Why not make it easy for them by adding a "Close this Window" button?

To do so, simply add a graphic button–text works fine, too. Next, add the Call JavaScript behavior; in the Call JavaScript window that appears, type the following line of JavaScript code: *window.close()*.

Finally, after you click OK, make sure that the event is set to onClick in the Behaviors panel.

That's all there is to it. The link you add to the pop-up window offers a working close button.

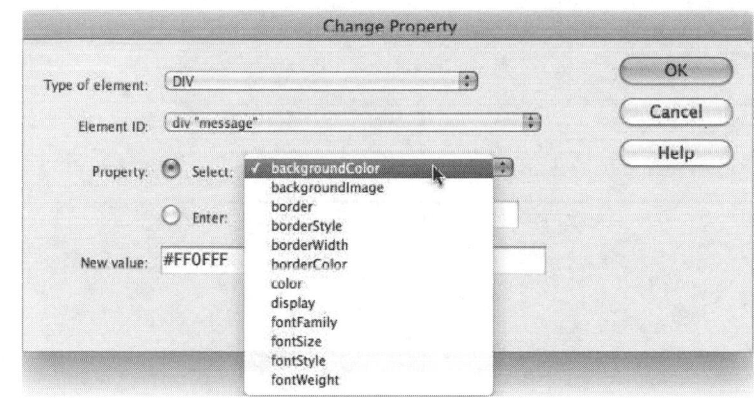

Figure 14-18:
Caution: The Change Property behavior requires some knowledge of HTML, JavaScript, and CSS. All the options in the menu refer to various CSS properties.

- **New value**. Type the new value for this property. It should be appropriate to the type of property you're changing. For example, if you're changing a background color, the value should be a color, like *#FF0066*. The options in the Property menu refer to CSS properties, so you'll find that the values listed for the different CSS properties in Chapters 4, 5, and 6 should work. For example, the *fontWeight* property is the CSS Font Weight property (page 128), so you could enter a value of *bold* to change text in an object (inside a <div> tag, for instance) to bold.

Tip: As with the Set Text of Container behavior (see the tip on page 613), the Change Property behavior works well in pairs. You can add the behavior once to an element by using the *onMouseOver* event to change the property, and then add the behavior a second time to the same element with the *onMouseOut* event to change the property back to its original setting

Adding More Behaviors

Dreamweaver's behaviors can open a whole new world of interactivity. Even if you don't understand the complexities of JavaScript and cross-browser programming, you can easily add powerful and interesting effects that add spice to your pages.

While Dreamweaver comes with the preprogrammed behaviors described in this chapter, you can download many additional behaviors from Adobe's Exchange Website (*www.adobe.com/exchange*) or any of the sites mentioned on page 825. Once you download them, you can easily add them to Dreamweaver, as described in Chapter 22.

CHAPTER

15

Add Flash and Other Multimedia

As you learned in previous chapters, you can bring your website to life with interactivity and animation using Cascading Style Sheets (Chapter 4), Spry widgets (Chapter 13), Dreamweaver effects and behaviors (Chapter 14), and images (Chapter 6). But as you've probably seen by now, today's web pages go even further—they blink, sing, and dance with sound, video, and advanced animation.

You can create these effects too, but you'll need some outside help. Programs like Flash (see Figure 15-1) let you create and display complex multimedia presentations, such as slick animations, interactive games, and video tutorials.

In this chapter, you'll learn how to embed these media files in your pages. And you'll see why Flash, a versatile program that lets you both develop and play back multimedia, has become the standard for web animation, complex visual interaction, and what has become known as "Rich Internet Applications," a fancy way of saying programs that give websites the visual richness and feature set of desktop programs.

Flash: An Introduction

One big reason for Flash's widespread adoption by the web development community is its sophisticated technology. Flash produces high-quality animations—known as Flash movies—in a relatively small file size, a boon when you want to distribute complex multimedia over the Web. Flash performs this magic by storing images as *vector graphics*. Instead of recording every pixel in an image and then redrawing that image in every frame of a movie, Flash represents the image as a compact mathematical formula. And that's the key to Flash's advantage: redrawing the same image in each frame of a movie would require considerable storage space and processing power, but storing it as a mathematical expression results in a far slimmer file of little more than a set of calculations.

***Figure 15-1:** Some web pages, like the Disney (http://disney.com) home page, are created almost entirely with Flash. The interactivity, animation, and video playback abilities of Flash make it a great technology for entertainment websites. Ultimately, however, you still need an HTML file to display the Flash movie.*

By contrast, with *bitmap* technologies, like GIF and JPEG images, every pixel of an image is a piece of information that must be stored, gobbling up precious bytes and adding to download time.

Note: Flash supports bitmap images, too, so a Flash movie can have GIF, PNG, and JEG files in it, in addition to (or in place of) vector-based graphics. Therefore, it's possible to create a Flash movie that downloads at a glacial pace and plays back like molasses.

Another reason for Flash's popularity is its flexibility. Flash plays not only natively created animations, but third-party audio and video files as well. And its advanced programming features let you add a level of sound, video, and interactivity that can make plain HTML pages look dull by comparison. For example, sophisticated Flash gurus can build automatic score-tracking into an online game or add a cannon-firing animation each time a player clicks his mouse. While JavaScript (see Chapter 14) has, in some ways, caught up with Flash—letting you animate elements on a page, send information to a Web server, and create powerful Internet applications—Flash movies offer a wider range of effects and much better control over animation.

Note: These multimedia effects are so cool you can easily become smitten with them, to the point of overuse. Blink and flash too much, and you'll find your audience beating a hasty retreat for the cyber-door.

Third, Flash movies look and work exactly the same in every browser, whether you use a Windows, Mac, or even Linux PC. That kind of cross-platform compatibility is rare.

And finally, the ubiquity of Flash on the Web means that nearly every browser—in fact, 90 percent of them—have a Flash player installed. So the chance of a visitor being unable to enjoy your site is small. (and if it does happen, Dreamweaver automatically points your visitors to the file they need to download; see "Automate the Flash Download" below for details.)

However, that 90 percent figure covers desktop computers only. One of the most popular devices for surfing the Web, the iPhone, doesn't support Flash at all (neither does the amazingly popular iPad). So if you think you'll have visitors using their iPhones to search for your business's hours of operation, street address, and phone number, make sure you at least provide your most crucial information in HTML format. This means, don't make your site's home page one big Flash movie (as some sites do). Otherwise iPhone/iPad visitors will be staring at a blank page.

Of course, all this power comes at a price. You need Adobe Flash or a similar program, like Swish (*www.swishzone.com*), Toon Boom (*www.toonboom.com/*), or Anime Studio (*http://my.smithmicro.com/win/anime/*), to produce full-fledged movies. And although these programs aren't necessarily difficult to get started with, they represent one more expense and one more technology you have to learn.

Note: Creating external movies, animations, and applications is an art (and a book or two) unto itself. This chapter is a guide to *inserting* these goodies into your web page and assumes that a cheerful programmer near you has already *created* them. For the full scoop on creating Flash files, pick up a copy of *Flash CS5: The Missing Manual*.

Insert a Flash Movie

To add a Flash movie to a page, position your cursor where you want the movie to appear and then choose Insert→Media→SWF (.swf is the file extension for Flash movies) or, in the Common category of the Insert panel, choose SWF from the Media menu (circled in Figure 15-2). Either way, the Select File dialog box appears. Navigate to the Flash file (look for the .swf extension) and double-click it. Dreamweaver automatically recognizes the width and height of the movie and generates the appropriate HTML to embed in your page. You'll see a gray rectangular placeholder with the Flash logo in the center; you can adjust the movie's settings as described in the next section.

Tip: You can also drag a Flash movie file from the Files panel into the document window. Dreamweaver automatically adds the correct code.

To preview Flash files directly in Dreamweaver, select the movie (click it) and then click the Play button in the Property inspector (see Figure 15-3). To stop the movie, click the same button—it toggles between a Play and a Stop button.

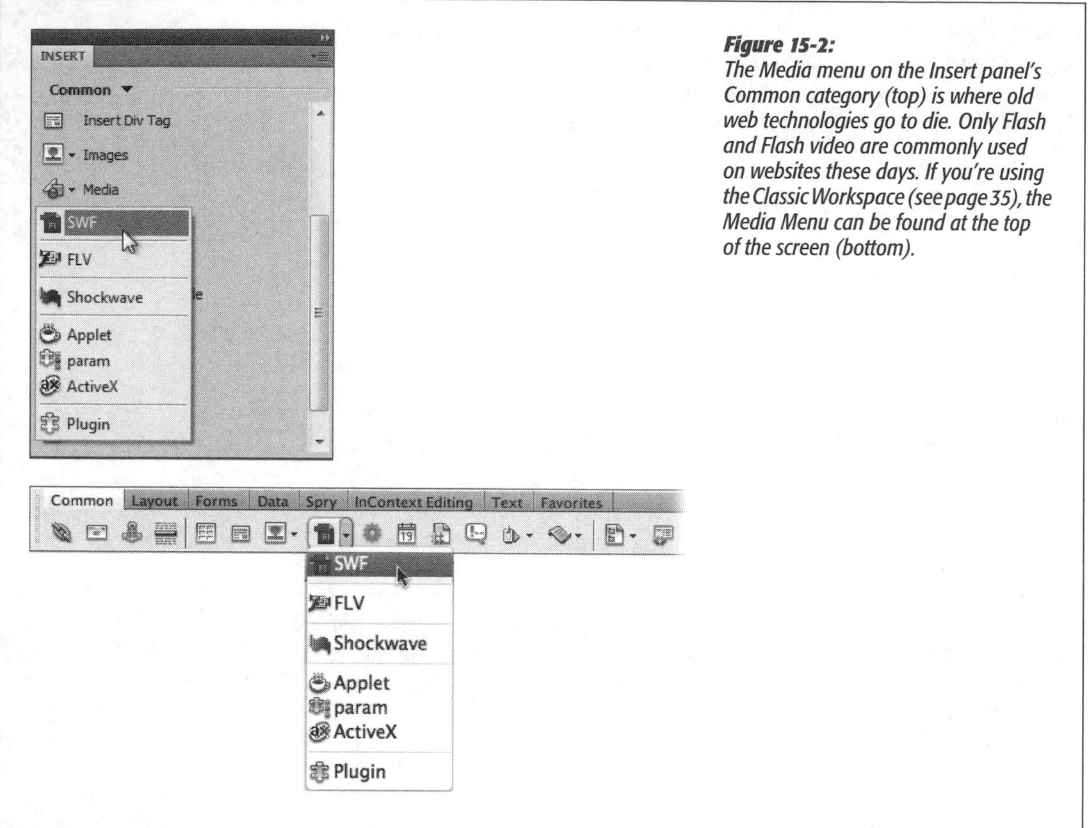

Figure 15-2:
The Media menu on the Insert panel's Common category (top) is where old web technologies go to die. Only Flash and Flash video are commonly used on websites these days. If you're using the Classic Workspace (see page 35), the Media Menu can be found at the top of the screen (bottom).

Note: When inserting a Flash movie, an Object Tag Accessibility Options window appears. This window lets you set options that are intended to make accessing the Flash content easier, but they don't really work in most browsers. If you don't want to set these options, just click Cancel, and Dreamweaver still inserts the Flash movie. To permanently turn off this window, open the Preferences window–Edit→Preferences (Dreamweaver→Preferences on a Mac)–click the Accessibility category, and then turn off the Media checkbox.

If your page has lots of Flash movies—numerous animated buttons, say—you can play all of them at once by pressing Ctrl+Shift+Alt+P (⌘-Shift-Option-P). Then sit back and watch the show. To stop all the movies, press Ctrl+Shift+Alt+X (⌘-Shift-Option-X).

POWER USERS' CLINIC

The Two Lives of the <object> Tag

If you choose View→Code after inserting a Flash movie, you may be surprised by the amount of HTML Dreamweaver deposits in your page. You may also encounter some HTML tags you've never heard of, including <object>, and <param>. These tags provide browsers with the information they need to launch the Flash Player and play a Flash movie.

Due to differences between Internet Explorer and all the other browsers, Dreamweaver has to insert the <object> tag twice: once for IE (with all the proper settings for that browser) and once for the other browsers. To do this, Dreamweaver uses IE conditional statements–HTML comments that are only interpreted by Internet Explorer and are used to send special instructions to just IE (and even to just specific versions of IE). You can learn more about conditional comments at *www.javascriptkit.com/howto/cc2.shtml*.

Using the <object> tag like this was added in Dreamweaver CS4 and replaces the method used in previous versions of Dreamweaver, which inserted two tags: the <object> and the <embed> tags. This new method is completely standards-compliant, which means that any page where you use Dreamweaver CS5 to add a movie will pass W3C validation. That wasn't true in versions of Dreamweaver prior to CS4 which produced invalid HTML that failed the W3C validator.

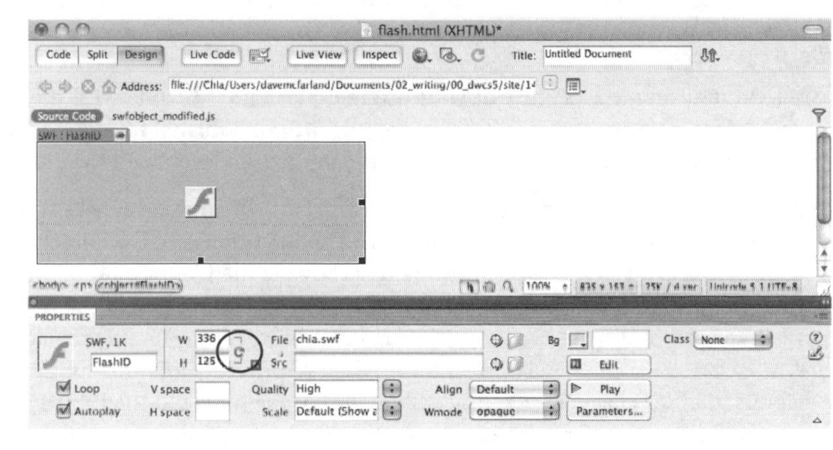

***Figure 15-3:** Use the Property inspector to set the display and playback controls for a Flash movie. Avoid the V space, H space, and align settings. Those same formatting options are better handled with CSS.*

Note: When you save a web page after inserting a Flash movie, Dreamweaver pops up a dialog box informing you that it needs to save two files–*expressInstall.swf* and *swfobject_modified.js*–to your site. These files make it possible to notify your visitors that they need to download a new version of the Flash plug-in (see page 629).

Change Movie Properties

You'll rarely have to change the default properties Dreamweaver assigns Flash movies. But if you need to—say you resize a movie and want to change it back to its original size, or you want to swap in a different movie altogether—the Property inspector is the place to go.

Rename your movie

Just as you learned that JavaScript can control images and buttons, so it can control Flash movies. Dreamweaver assigns a generic name to each movie you embed—*FlashID*, *FlashID2*, *FlashID3*, and so on. This act of naming your movie is important—the auto install option discussed on page 629 requires a name—but the exact name isn't. If you want, you can change the name in the Name field, the box directly below "SWF" at the top-left of the Property inspector (see Figure 15-3). However, there's no real need to do so since no one visiting the page will ever see it.

Relace your movie

The File box specifies your movie's location on your hard drive. To swap out the current movie, type a new path into the File field, or click the nearby folder icon and browse to the new movie.

Set the Src property

The Src field indicates the location of your original Flash file (the one with the .fla *extension*), When you first insert a Flash movie, the Src box is blank. It's a good idea to tell Dreamweaver where to find the original file in case you ever need to edit it.

To do that, click the Edit button in the Property inspector. Dreamweaver asks you to locate the original file; you're looking for a file with an .fla extension. Double-click it and Dreamweaver launches the Flash program and opens the file for editing. Make any changes you wish (or not) and, in Flash, click Done. Flash *renders* the movie (prepares it for playback) and exports the updated .swf file into your site, replacing the previous version of the movie. In addition, the Src property box now points to your original .fla file. That way, if you need to work on the movie in the future, you just press the Edit button. Dreamweaver launches Flash, and it opens your original movie for editing.

Change your movie's size

Although enlarging GIF or JPEG images by dragging them usually results in a pixelated mess, you can resize Flash movies without a problem. They use vector-based images, and vectors' mathematical formulas scale nicely. (The only exception is Flash movies that contain bitmap images, such as GIFs, PNGs, or JPEGs. Resize a movie with bitmaps, and the images distort and pixelate just as they would on their own.)

To resize a movie, do one of the following:

- Select the movie in the document window and drag one of the three resizing handles that appear at the edges of the movie. To maintain the movie's proportions, press Shift as you drag the lower-right corner handle.
- Select the movie in the document window and type new width and height values into the W and H boxes in the Property inspector. You can also use percentage values, in which case your movie scales to fit the browser window.

If you make a complete mess of your page by resizing your movie beyond recognition, just click the Reset Size button in the Property inspector (circled in Figure 15-3).

Tip: If you want to insert a Flash movie that fills 100 percent of a browser window, you first need to set the movie's height and width to 100%. Then you need to create a few CSS styles. First, create a tag style for the <body> tag with *padding* (page 341) and *margin* (page 341) set to 0, and *height* and *width* (page 360) set to 100%. Next, create a tag style for the <html> tag with the same settings as the <body> tag (a group selector—discussed on page 303—makes the process of creating the styles more efficient). If the Flash movie is contained within other tags, like a <div> or a <p> tag, then you need to remove the padding and margin for those tags and set their heights and widths to 100% as well. Finally, choose an appropriate Scaling setting for the movie, as discussed on the next page.

Set playback options

The Loop and Autoplay checkboxes control how your movie plays back. When you turn on Loop, the movie plays over and over endlessly, an approach advertisers often use in animated banner ads. The Autoplay option starts playback as soon as a page loads into a browser.

Neither of these options overrides any programming instructions you embed in the Flash movie, however. For instance, if you add a Stop command to the final frame of a movie, the movie stops at that frame regardless of the Loop setting.

Leave margins unspecified

Skip the V space and H settings in the Property inspector. They're intended to add space to the top and bottom (V) and left and right (H) edges of your movie, but they produce invalid HTML code for strict document types (see page 7 for more on doctypes). In addition, you can't control each of the four margins individually.

Instead, use Cascading Style Sheets and the CSS *margin* property (discussed on page 341) to add space around your movie. You can create an ID style (page 112) using the movie's name. For example, you might create an ID style named *#FlashID*.

Select a quality setting

If your Flash movie requires a lot of processing muscle—if it's heavy on animation and action, for example—it may overwhelm computers of lesser pedigree, making playback slow and choppy. Not every computer has a three gigahertz processor and two gigabytes of memory (not yet, anyway). Until that day, you may need to adjust the quality settings of your Flash movie so it looks good on all computers, from the sluggish to the speedy.

By default, Dreamweaver sets movie quality to High, but you can choose any of the following four settings from the Quality menu in the Property inspector:

- **High** provides the best quality, but the movie may run slower on older computers.
- **Low** looks terrible. This setting sacrifices quality by eliminating all *antialiasing* (edge smoothing) in the movie, leaving harsh, jaggy lines on the edges of every image. Movies set to low quality look bad on *all* computers.
- **Auto Low** forces the movie to start in low-quality mode, but switches automatically to high-quality playback if the visitor's computer is fast enough.
- **Auto High** makes the movie switch to low-quality mode only if the visitor's computer requires it. This way, you can deliver a high-quality image to most visitors, while still letting those with slow computers view the movie. This mode is the best choice if you want to provide a high-quality image but still make your movie accessible to those with older computers.

Adjust your movie's scale

Scaling only becomes an issue when you've specified *relative* dimensions for your movie, setting it to, say, 90 percent of a browser window's width. That's because the movie grows or shrinks as your visitor's browser grows or shrinks, and you have no control over what your visitors does with her browser—one person may prefer a small horizontal browser at the bottom of her screen, while another may use a tall, narrow window.

Enter Dreamweaver's Scale property. It lets you determine *how* Flash scales your movie. For example, in Figure 15-4, the top movie's original size is 334 pixels high × 113 pixels wide. If you resize the movie using the W and H attributes so that it's *350* pixels high × 113 pixels wide, one of three things will happen, depending on your Scale setting:

- **Show All**. This setting, the default, maintains the original aspect ratio (proportions) of your movie (second from top in Figure 15-4). In other words, although the overall *size* of the movie may change as a visitor fusses with his browser, its width-to-height ratio won't. Show All keeps your movie from distorting (but it may also cause white borders on the top, bottom, or either side of your movie; to hide them, make the movie's background color the same color as the page).

- **No Border**. This setting resizes a movie according to your specifications *and* maintains its aspect ratio, but it may also crop the sides of the movie. Notice how the top and bottom of the Chia Vet logo are chopped off in Figure 15-4 (third image from top).
- **Exact Fit**. This option may stretch your movie's picture either horizontally or vertically. In Figure 15-4 (bottom), "Chia Vet" is stretched wider.

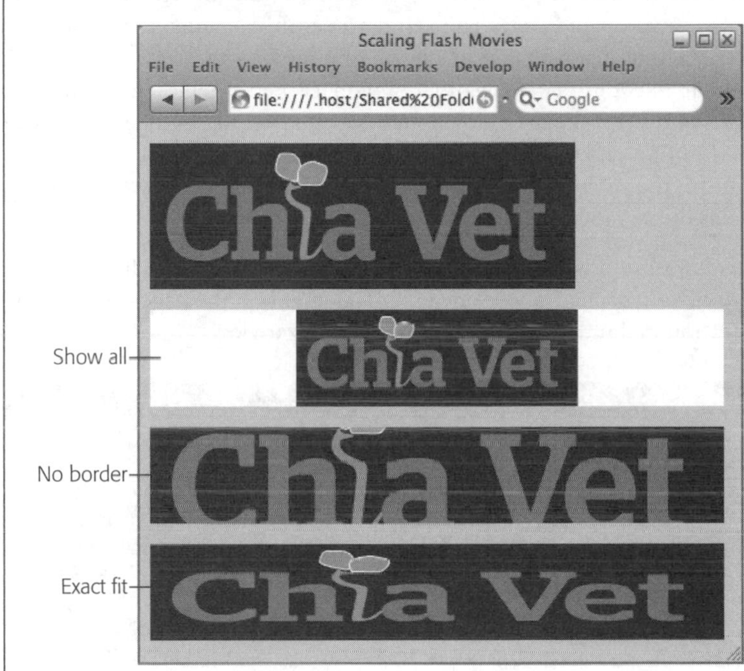

Figure 15-4: *This browser window shows the results of your different choices in the Scale menu on the Property inspector. A Flash movie's Scale property specifies how a movie should be scaled when its width and height properties are set differently than the original movie. If you resize a movie, press F12 (Option-F12) to see how it looks in a Web browser, and then, if necessary, choose a different setting from the Scale pop-up menu in the Property inspector.*

Align your movie

You can align Flash movies relative to the paragraphs around them just as you can align images relative to the surrounding text. In fact, the Property inspector's movie alignment options work exactly the same way as its text alignment properties. For example, when you choose Right from the Align menu, Dreamweaver positions the movie at the right edge of the screen and wraps text around its left side. (If the movie is inside a cell, Align Right moves the movie to the right edge of the cell.) However, for strict document types (page 7), the Align property is invalid. As with the margin settings discussed above, you're better off using CSS properties, such as the *float* property described on page 228.

Background color

To set a background color for a Flash movie, use the Bg Color box in the Property inspector. This color overrides any background color set in the movie itself, and it provides the movie's placeholder color when the page loads but the movie hasn't.

Wmode

Wmode stands for "Window mode" and it controls how your movie interacts with other HTML elements on the page. The standard setting, *opaque*, is useful when you include HTML that needs to appear on top of a movie—the classic example is a drop-down menu like the Spry Navigation Bar you learned about on page 184. The opaque setting ensures that the drop-down menu appears on top of the Flash movie. The *transparent* option lets HTML appear above a movie, too, but it also lets any HTML *underneath* the movie—like a page's background color—show through any transparent areas of the movie.

Finally, the *window* option is the exact opposite of the opaque option: It makes sure the Flash movie always appears above any HTML element on the page—even above a pop-up navigation menu that should display over the movie.

UP TO SPEED

The Land of Obsolete Web Technology

Dreamweaver CS5 includes several other options in the Media menu of the Insert panel (see Figure 15-2). Some have been around since Dreamweaver was in training pants, and most of them don't see much use on today's Web; they either don't work for many users, or creating the content to work with these technologies is so hard that few web designers bother. In addition, some of these technologies look like they're being phased out by their creators.

Shockwave is a web technology that's been around a long time. It's the Internet-ready form of movies created with Macromedia Director. Historically, Director was a program for creating CD-ROMs. But when the Web exploded onto the scene, Director quickly morphed into a web authoring tool, and its movie-creation tool was called Shockwave. As a result of its CD background, Shockwave offers complex programming possibilities, which makes it ideal for detailed, interactive presentations.

However, most people won't find a use for it. Flash provides much of the same functionality for websites using simpler programming and, consequently, it's the much more common choice for web designers. In addition, the Shockwave plug-in isn't installed with Web browsers, so visitors have to download the plug-in, which weighs in at a hefty 4.08 MB for Windows and 3.68 MB for Mac.

But if you just can't do without Shockwave, you can insert a Shockwave movie into a web page just as you would any other multimedia file. Choose where you want to insert the movie, and then choose Insert→Media→Shockwave, or choose Shockwave from the Media menu on the Common category of the Insert panel. Either way, a Select File dialog box appears. Find and double-click the Shockwave movie file (look for the .dcr extension).

Dreamweaver also includes tools for inserting other multimedia and plug-in files. In fact, these tools have been around since much earlier incarnations of Dreamweaver, when there really *were* other media types like Java applets, ActiveX controls, and other plug-in technology. However, Java applets never really took off (their performance never quite lived up to the hype), and ActiveX controls are limited to Internet Explorer for Windows.

Automate the Flash Download

Even though the Flash plug-in is nearly universal, you can't be sure that every visitor has it installed. In addition, you may have created a Flash movie that only runs in the latest version of the plug-in, so a visitor might have the Flash plug-in, but not the correct *version*. The result? A movie that either doesn't play back at all or doesn't play back as it should. Guests who fall into this category have to choose from three equally unpalatable options: go to a different website to download the plug-in, skip the multimedia show (if you've built a second, plug-in-free version of your site), or skip your website entirely.

Fortunately, Dreamweaver CS5 provides a built-in solution for both scenarios. When you embed a movie in a page, Dreamweaver includes additional code that detects your visitor's plug-in status. If a visitor either doesn't have the Flash plug-in or doesn't have the right version of it, the page displays a message alerting the visitor to the problem (see Figure 15-5) and offering a link button (labeled "Get Adobe Flash Player") to the plug-in. If the visitors has at least version 6 of the plug-in, she can take advantage of the plug-in's "express install" feature, which lets her upgrade to the latest version with just a mouse click.

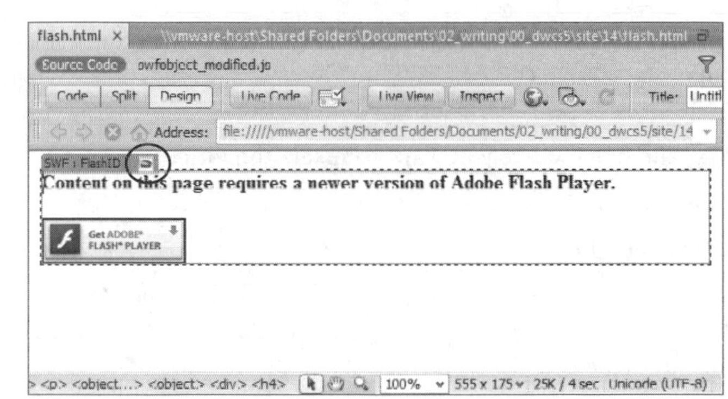

Figure 15-5: *Here's the normal message that a Web browser displays if a visitor doesn't have the Flash player installed, or has an old version of the player. You can customize this message by changing the text. However, it's a good idea to leave the Flash Player icon in place–it includes a link to a page on http://Adobe.com where the visitor can download the player.*

In practice, most of your visitors will never see this message. In fact, in Design view, you won't see it either; Dreamweaver keeps it hidden. But you can see and edit the message by clicking the eye icon (circled in Figure 15-5).

To make all this happen, Dreamweaver adds two files to your website inside a folder named Scripts: *expressInstall.swf* and *swfobject_modified.js*. When you move your finished web pages and Flash movies to your web server (see Chapter 17), be sure to move the Scripts folder as well.

Note to Dreamweaver CS3 Users: Dreamweaver CS3 used to add a JavaScript file to your site when you added a Flash movie to a page. This file, named *AC_RunActiveContent.js*, was necessary to overcome some relationship problems between Internet Explorer and Flash movies. Microsoft has since worked out those problems in IE 6 and IE 7 (browser therapy?), so you no longer need that file.

Add Flash videos

In addition to playing back animations and hosting games, the Flash player plays back videos, too. In fact, *Flash video*, as this feature is called, is likely the most common way to play video on the Web. If you've visited a little site called YouTube, you've seen Flash video in action. High among this format's advantages—compared to competing standards like QuickTime or Windows Media Video—is that you can reasonably count on every visitor having the new Flash program to view your videos.

Dreamweaver makes it a snap to embed videos. Unfortunately, Flash can't play back videos in just any old format, like MPEG or AVI. And Dreamweaver can't transform videos in these formats to the Flash video format (which has the extension .flv). Instead, you need one of several Adobe products to create Flash video files. If you bought the Creative Suite, you're in business; it includes the Flash video Encoder. Otherwise, you need Flash CS5 Pro or Flash CS4 Pro.

Note: For a quick intro to creating Flash videos, visit *www.adobe.com/devnet/flash/quickstart/video_encoder/*. Adobe also dedicates an entire section of their site to Flash video: *www.adobe.com/devnet/video/*.

Fortunately, creating the .flv file is the hard part. Dreamweaver makes the rest easy. Follow these few simple steps to inserts a Flash video into your page, complete with DVD-like playback controls.

1. **Click the place on the page where you want to insert the video.**

   Like other Flash movies, you'll want an open area of your page.

2. **Choose Insert→Media→FLV.**

   Or, from the Common category of the Insert panel, select FLV from the Media menu (see Figure 15-2), and the Insert FLV window appears (see Figure 15-6). You can also just drag the .flv file from the Files panel and drop it onto the document window.

3. **Select Progressive Download Video from the "Video type" menu.**

   Dreamweaver provides two download options, Progressive Download Video and Streaming Video. The latter requires you to have some expensive software (a Flash server) or a Flash video streaming service, which can run you anywhere from $10 a month to a couple of hundred dollars a month. Streaming Video is usually used for live events or to handle very large numbers of viewers. That's why websites for TV networks like *http://ABC.com* use streaming servers—it's an efficient way to distribute video when thousands of people watch the same video at the same time.

   If you choose Progressive Download, your video doesn't have to download completely before it begins playing back, so viewers don't have to wait, say, 30 minutes while your 40 MB movie downloads. Instead, the video starts as soon as the first section of the file arrives on their machine, and plays back as the rest of the movie downloads. This is how YouTube video works.

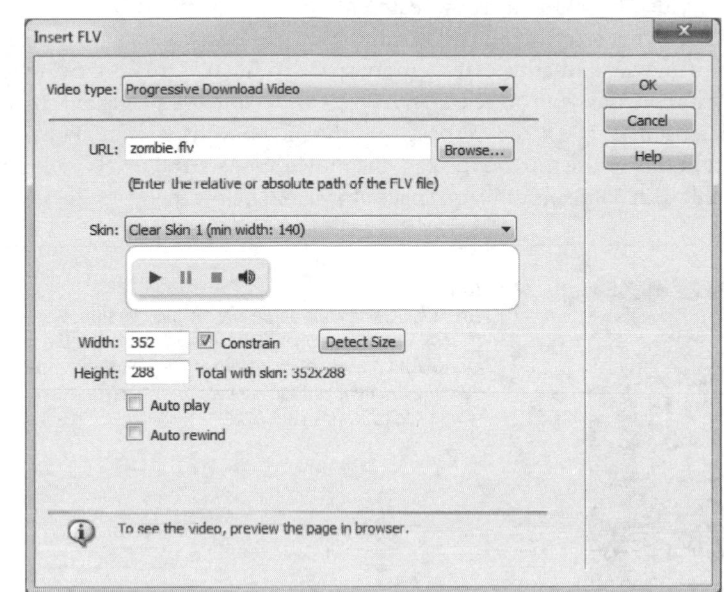

Figure 15-6: *The Insert Flash video command is probably the easiest way to add video to your website. All your visitors need is the Flash Player, which in many cases comes preinstalled with their browser.*

4. **Click the Browse button and select the Flash video (.flv) file you wish to add to the page.**

   Due to differences in how operating systems work, you're best off putting your Flash video file in the same folder as your web page. If you want to put it elsewhere (in a dedicated Flash video folder, for instance, or even on a different Web server), then use absolute links (see page 160).

5. **Select a skin.**

   A *skin* is a set of playback controls for your video: buttons that start, pause, and stop the video; a progress bar; and various volume-adjustment controls (see Figure 15-7).

   Dreamweaver adds the controls to your video, and offers nine styles—actually, three types of controllers, each with three different graphical styles.

6. **Click the Detect Size button.**

   Flash videos contain *metadata*—information embedded inside the video file that describes its features, like its dimensions, file size, and so on. The Flash video encoder adds this metadata when you create a video file. Clicking the Detect Size button extracts the movie's width and height measurements, adds the width and height of the playback controls, and then automatically fills in the width and height boxes in the Insert Flash video window (see Figure 15-6).

   If, for whatever reason, your file doesn't include metadata, you have to enter the width and height values yourself—these settings specify how much space the video occupies on the page. Note that entering these dimensions won't actually distort your video—making it really, really thin or really, really wide, for example. No matter what size you enter, Dreamweaver preserves the original aspect ratio of your movie, and adds extra, empty space to fill any area not occupied by it. For example, say your movie is 352 pixels wide and 288 pixels tall. If you enter a dimension of 100 x 288, respectively, the movie won't stretch like you're watching it in fun-house mirror. Instead, the movie appears 100 pixels wide and 82 pixels tall, with 53 pixels of blank space above and below it.

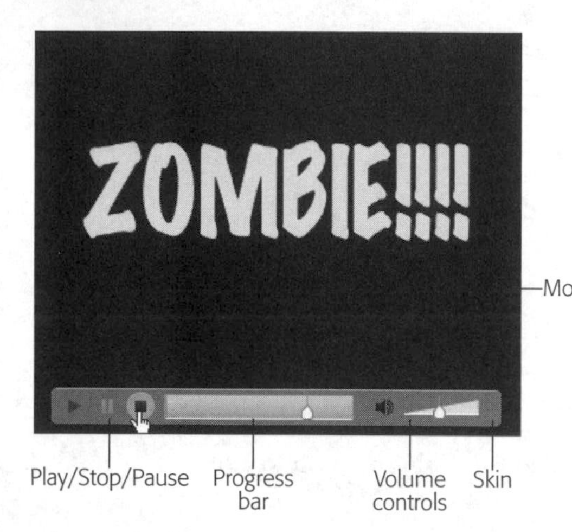

Figure 15-7: *The "Clear" skin controls lie directly over your movie ("Clear Skin 3" is shown here). They disappear if the mouse isn't anywhere inside the movie, but they reappear the moment you mouse over the video. Try each skin to see which fits your taste.*

7. **If you want, turn on the "Autoplay" checkbox.**

   Doing so makes the movie play as soon as enough video data's been downloaded from the Web. Otherwise, a visitor has to press the play button to begin the movie.

8. **If you want, turn on the "Auto rewind" checkbox.**

   Your movie automatically "rewinds" to the first frame if you turn on this checkbox. But you may not always want to abide by the old video-store credo "Be Kind, Rewind." If your movie ends with a dramatic message—"Stay tuned for the next exciting installment of Blind Mole Rats from Mars!"—you might prefer to leave the movie on its last frame when it's complete.

9. **Click OK to add the Flash video to your page.**

   This step installs the necessary code not only for the video, but for detecting the Flash plug-in as well (see page 629). You can check out the newly inserted video by pressing F12 (Option-F12) to preview the page in a browser.

Note: When you upload your web page and Flash video to your site (see Chapter 18), you need to upload four additional files that Dreamweaver secretly adds to your site: the two files (and the *Scripts* folder) discussed on page 629, the FLVPlayer_progressive.swf file, and the .swf (Flash movie) file for the skin you selected. That last file is named after the skin you chose—for example, Clear_Skin_1.swf. Save yourself some work: When uploading your Flash-filled web page (uploading details are on page 702) choose to include "dependent files"; that way Dreamweaver grabs these three files for you.

FREQUENTLY ASKED QUESTION

Adding Sound to Web Pages

Hey man, I'm a rock star-in-training, and I want to surprise the world with my cool tunes. How do I put my music on my website?

Lots of different technologies let you add music and sound to your site. Most require plug-ins, which limit your audience because few people are going to rush off to another website to download and install more software just to enjoy your site—unless you're U2 or Miley Cyrus.

As a result, the ubiquitous Flash provides the best and fastest way to add sound to your site. Flash supports several audio formats, such as MP3, WAV (Windows), and AIFF (Mac) files, and if you have QuickTime installed, even more formats. You'll have to dip into the Flash Help files to learn how to import audio, but it's not too hard. If you just want ambient background music on a page, you can even create a very small (like 1 pixel x 1 pixel) Flash movie that simply plays back music. Follow the steps on "Inserting a Flash Movie" for inserting the Flash movie into a Web page.

There are also a few Dreamweaver extensions that let you add sound and music to your site as well: Speaker from HotDreamweaver (*www.hotdreamweaver.com/speaker*; $19.99) lets you insert MP3 files on your page that play back when you click a small icon. Trio Solutions (*http://components.developers4web.com/*) sells more than a dozen MP3 player extensions; each lets you insert CD-player-like controls (play, pause, stop, fast-forward) to control playback and some let you create a playlist of multiple songs.

CHAPTER 16

Introducing Site Management

As the dull-sounding name *site management* implies, organizing and tracking your website's files is one of the least glamorous, most time-consuming, error-prone aspects of being a web designer. On the Web, your site may look beautiful, run smoothly, and appear as a gloriously unified whole, but behind the scenes, it's nothing more than a collection of various files—HTML pages, images, Cascading Style Sheets, JavaScript code, Flash movies, and so on—that must all work together. The more files you have to keep track of, the more apt you are to misplace one. A single broken link or missing graphic can interfere with the operation of your entire site, causing personal—even professional—embarrassment.

Fortunately, computers excel at tedious organizational tasks. Dreamweaver's site management features take care of the complexities of dealing with a website's many files, freeing you to concentrate on the creative aspects of the site. In fact, even if you're a hand-coding HTML junkie and you turn your nose up at all visual web page editors, you may find Dreamweaver worth its weight in gold just for the features described in this and the next two chapters.

Where the first three parts of this book describe how to create, lay out, and embellish your site, this part offers a bird's-eye view of the production process as you see your site through to completion and, ultimately, upload it to the Internet.

To get the most out of Dreamweaver's site management features, you need to be familiar with some basic principles for organizing web files, as discussed in the next section.

The Structure of a Website

When you build a website, you probably spend hours providing visitors with carefully planned links, helpful labels, and clear, informative navigation tools. You want your *site architecture*—the structure of your site—to make it easy for visitors to understand where they are, where they can go, and how to return to where they came from (see Figure 16-1). Behind the scenes, it's equally important to organize your site's files with just as much clarity and care, so you can find *your* way around when you update or modify the site later. And, just as on your computer, a website's main organizational tool is the humble *folder*.

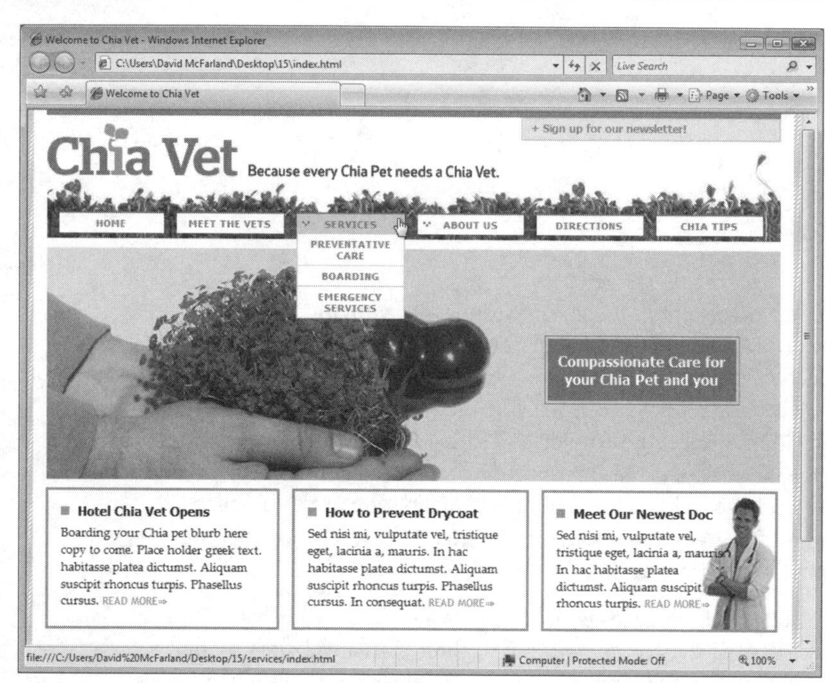

Figure 16-1: *A good site has an easy-to-understand structure. It divides content into logical sections, and includes a prominent navigation bar—the row of buttons below the Chia-Vet logo in this image—to give visitors quick access to that content. When you building a site, the site's "architecture" provides a useful model for naming and creating the behind-the-scenes folders that hold the site's files.*

You probably organize files on your computer every day, creating, say, a folder called Personal, within which are folders called Financial Planning and Vacation Pictures. Inside the Vacation Pictures folder, you might have separate folders for memories of Maui, Yosemite, and the Mall of America.

The same principle applies to the folders that make up a website: All websites have one primary folder—the *root folder*—that holds all of the site's web pages, graphics, and other files. The root folder usually contains additional folders where you further subdivide and organize your site's files.

A sensible site structure (see Figure 16-2) makes it easy for you to maintain your site because it's logically organized—it gives you quick access to whatever graphic, style sheet, or Flash movie you're looking for. But don't fall into the trap of becoming so obsessed with bins that you put every graphic or web page you create in its own folder; adding structure to your site should make your job easier, not harder.

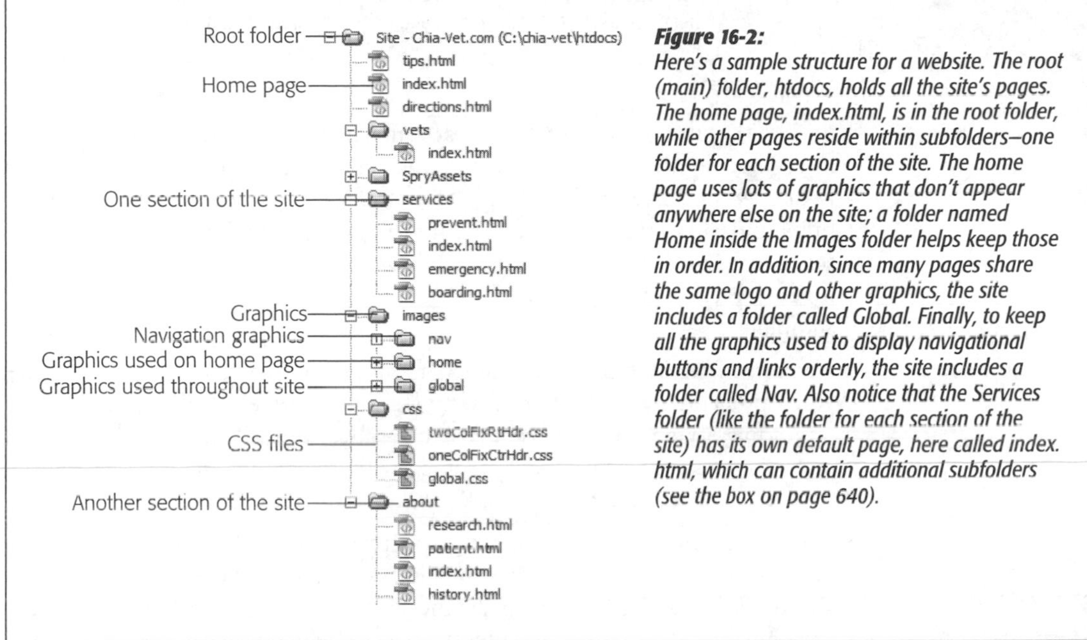

Figure 16-2:
Here's a sample structure for a website. The root (main) folder, htdocs, holds all the site's pages. The home page, index.html, is in the root folder, while other pages reside within subfolders–one folder for each section of the site. The home page uses lots of graphics that don't appear anywhere else on the site; a folder named Home inside the Images folder helps keep those in order. In addition, since many pages share the same logo and other graphics, the site includes a folder called Global. Finally, to keep all the graphics used to display navigational buttons and links orderly, the site includes a folder called Nav. Also notice that the Services folder (like the folder for each section of the site) has its own default page, here called index.html, which can contain additional subfolders (see the box on page 640).

Tip: If you already have a website that suffers from lack of organization, it's not too late. Dreamweaver can help you reorganize your files quickly and accurately. Take the following rules to heart and then turn to "Organizing Site Files" on page 648 to learn how Dreamweaver can whip your current site into shape.

Here, then, are some guidelines for effective site organization:

- **Plan for future growth.** Like ever-spreading grapevines, websites grow. Today you may have only enough words and pictures for 10 web pages, but tomorrow you'll put the finishing touches on your new 1,000-page online catalog. It may seem like overkill to create a lot of folders for a small site, but better to start with a solid structure today than find yourself knee-deep in files tomorrow.

  For instance, it's useful to create separate folders for graphics files that appear within each section of the site. If a section of your site is dedicated to promoting your company's products, for example, create a folder called *products* for your product web pages. Create an additional folder called *images* to store the pictures of those products. Then, when you add more products or images, you know right where to put them.

Note: While you can start with no organization plan and later use Dreamweaver to bring it all into shape (see page 648), you may run into unforeseen problems if your site is already on the Internet. If your site's been up and running for a while, search engines may have indexed your site, and other websites may have linked to your pages. If you suddenly rearrange your site, those cherished links from the outside world may no longer work, and people who try to access your site from a search engine may be foiled. If that's the case, you're better off leaving the site as it is, and begin the organization process with new files only.

- **Follow the site's architecture.** Take advantage of the work you've already done in organizing the content on your site. For instance, the Chia Vet site content is divided into five main sections: Meet the Vets, Services, About Us, Directions, and Chia Tips, as shown in Figure 16-1. Following this structure, it makes sense to create folders—*vets, services, about*, and so on—in the site's root folder for each section's respective web pages. If one section is particularly large, add subfolders.
- **Organize files by type.** After you create folders for each section of your site, you'll probably need to add folders to store other types of files, like graphics, Cascading Style Sheets, external JavaScript files, and PDF files. Most sites, for instance, make extensive use of graphics, with several graphics on each page. If that's the case for you, file those images neatly and efficiently.

  One way to organize your graphics is to create a folder for images that appear on your home page and another for images that appear elsewhere in the site. Often, the home page is visually distinct from other pages on the site and contains graphics that are not only unique to it, but which might change frequently. You can create a folder—such as *images_home*—in the root folder for images that appear on your home page only. Create another folder—*images_global*, for example—to store graphics that appear on all or most of the other pages, images like the company logo, navigation buttons, and other frequently used icons. When you add these images to other pages of your site, you'll know to look for them in this folder. Alternatively, you could create an *images* folder in the root of your site and add subfolders such as *home, global*, and *nav* (see Figure 16-2). The choice of an organizational system is yours; just make sure you have one.
- **Use understandable names.** While file names like *1a.gif, zDS.html*, and *f.css* are compact, they aren't very explanatory. Make sure file names mean something. Clear, descriptive names like *site_logo.gif* or *directions.html* make it a lot easier to locate files and update pages.

  This principle is especially important if you work as part of a team. If you're constantly explaining to coworkers that *345g.gif* is the banner for the home page, changing the file name to *home_banner.gif* could save you some aggravation. There's a tradeoff here, however, as long file names can waste precious bytes. For instance, a site full of file names like *this_is_the_image_that_goes_in_the_upper_right_corner_of_the_home_page.gif* is probably not a good idea.

Note: Dreamweaver employs the industry-standard .html extension for web pages—as in *index.html*. Another common extension is .htm (a holdover from the days when Windows could only use three-letter extensions). It doesn't really matter which you use, and if you're used to .htm, you can easily change the extension Dreamweaver uses. Just choose Edit Preferences (Dreamweaver Preferences on a Mac) to open the Preferences window, select the New Document category, and then type *.htm* in the default extension box.

It's also helpful to add a prefix to related files. For example, use *nav_* at the beginning of a graphic name to indicate that it's a navigation button. This way, you can quickly identify *nav_projects.png*, *nav_quiz.png*, and *nav_horoscopes.png* as graphics used in a page's navigation bar, or *bg_body.png* and *bg_column.png* for graphics used as backgrounds. As a bonus, when you view the files on your computer or in Dreamweaver's Files panel (see Figure 16-6), they appear neatly sorted by name; in other words, all the *nav_* files cluster together in the file list. Likewise, if you have rollover versions of your navigation graphics, give them names like *nav_projects_over.gif* or *nav_ horoscopes_high.gif* to indicate that they're the highlighted (or rollover) state of the navigation button. (If you use Fireworks, its button-creation tools automatically use names like *nav_projects_f1.gif* and *nav_projects_f2.gif* to indicate two different versions of the same button.)

- **Be consistent.** Once you come up with an organization that works for you, follow it. Always. If you name one folder *images*, for instance, don't name another *graphics* and a third *pretty_pictures*. And certainly don't put web pages in a folder named *images* or Flash movies in a folder named *style_sheets*.

  In fact, if you work on more than one website, you may want to use a single naming convention and folder structure for all your sites, so that switching among them goes more smoothly. If you name all your graphics folders *images*, then no matter what site you're working on, you know where to look for GIFs and JPEGs.

UP TO SPEED

Naming Your Files and Folders

The rules for naming files and folders in Windows and on the Mac are fairly flexible. You can use letters, numbers, spaces, and even symbols like $, #, and ! in folder and file names.

Web servers, on the other hand, are far less accommodating. Because many symbols—such as &, @, and ?—have special significance on the Web, using them in file names can confuse web servers and cause errors.

The precise list of no-no's varies from web server to web server, but you'll be safe if you stick to letters, numbers, the hyphen (-), and the underscore (_) character when you name files and folders. Stay away from spaces. File names like *company logo.gif* or *This company's president.html* may or may not work on a web server. Replace spaces with underscores or inner caps—*company_logo.gif* or *companyLogo.gif*—and remove all punctuation marks.

Sure, some operating systems and web servers permit strange naming conventions, but why take the chance? Someday you may need to move your site to another, less forgiving server. Play it safe: keep your file names simple.

Note: It's usually best to put only files that go on your website in the root folder and its subfolders. Keep your source files–the original Photoshop, Fireworks, Flash, or Word documents–stored elsewhere on your computer. This way, you're much less likely to accidentally transfer a 14.5 MB Photoshop file to your web server (a move that would *not* gain you friends in the IT department). That said, if you do like keeping all your files together, check out Dreamweaver's *cloaking* feature (described on page 708). Using it, you can prevent Dreamweaver from transferring certain file types to your web server when you use its FTP feature.

FREQUENTLY ASKED QUESTION

All Those Index Pages

Why are so many web pages named index.html (*or* index.htm)?

If you type a URL like *www.missingmanuals.com* into a web browser, the Missing Manuals home page opens on your screen. But how did the web server know which page from the site to send to your browser? After all, you didn't ask for a particular web page, like *www.missingmanuals.com/index.html*.

When a web server gets a request that doesn't specify a particular page, it looks for a default web page–often named *index.html* or *index.htm*. It does the same thing even when the URL you type specifies (with a slash) a folder inside the site root, like this: *www.missingmanuals.com/cds/*. In this case, the server looks for a file called *index.html* inside the cds folder and–if it finds the file–sends it to your browser.

If the web server doesn't find an *index.html* file, two things can happen, both undesirable: the browser can display either an ugly error message or a listing of all the files inside the folder. Neither result is helpful to your visitors.

While your site still functions if you don't give the main page inside each folder a default page name, it's good form to name that file index.html. This avoids the "404 File Not Found error" when someone requests just a folder name and not a specific file inside that folder.

Web servers can use different names for these default pages–*default.html*, for example–although *index.html* works on most web servers. In fact, you can specify any page as a default, so long as you set up your web server to look for that default page. So if you create a dynamic site like those discussed in Part Six, you can set up a server to look for a default dynamic page like *index.asp* or *index.php*. Most web servers already predefine multiple default page names, so if it doesn't find a file named *index.html*, it may automatically look for a file called *index.php*.

Setting Up a Site

Organizing and maintaining a website—creating new folders and web pages; moving, renaming, and deleting files and folders; and transferring pages to a web server—can require going back and forth between a couple of different programs. With Dreamweaver's site management features, however, you can do it all from within one program. But to take advantage of these features, you must first make Dreamweaver aware of the site; in other words, you need to give Dreamweaver some basic information about it.

Setting up a site in Dreamweaver involves showing the program which folder contains your website files (the *root folder*) and setting a few other options. You already know the very basics of setting up a site using Dreamweaver's Site Setup window (page 37). Here, you'll get a more detailed explanation of the options available in Site Setup.

Start by choosing Site→New Site. This opens the Site Setup window (see Figure 16-3). It includes four categories of options where you specify the details of your site—Dreamweaver labels them Site, Servers, and Version Control, and a drop-down menu of Advanced Settings.

You've encountered the Site category several times already (page 37): it's where you tell Dreamweaver where on your computer it can find your website files. The Servers and Version Control settings help Dreamweaver work with your remote server; you'll learn about these settings in Chapter 18 (see pagespage 691 andpage 713).

You'll find the Advanced Settings options useful for different situations, described below. You'll learn about the Local Info options next, the Cloaking options on page 721, the Design Notes category on page 708, the File View Columns options on page 41, the Contribute option on page 41, the Templates option in Chapter 20, and the Spry option on page 188. They're called "Advanced" for a reason and you may not ever feel a need to visit or change these settings.

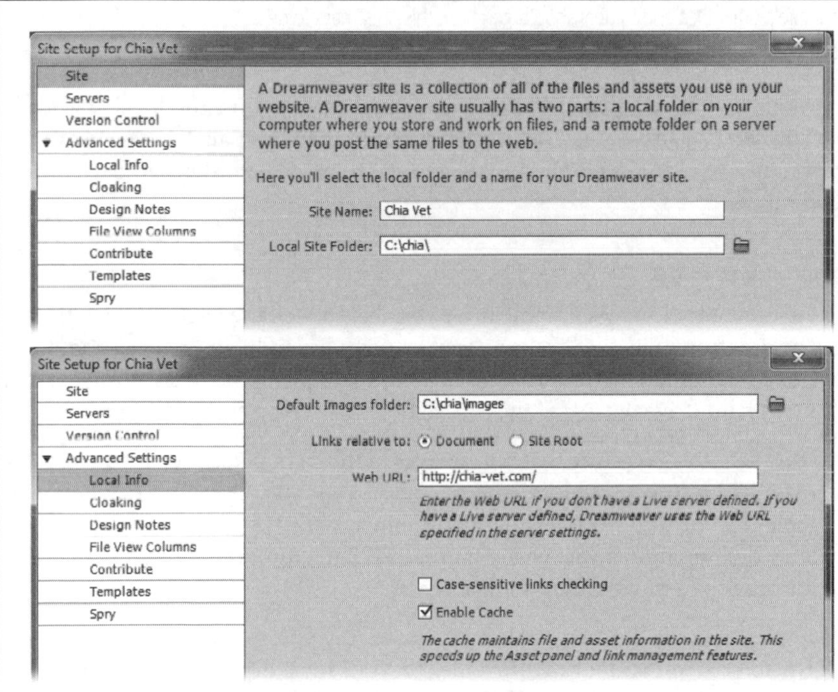

Figure 16-3: *Dreamweaver CS5 introduces a new site setup process that replaces the old "Site Definition Window" with a simpler (but sometimes more confusing) Site Setup window.*

The most important category in the Site Setup window is the first: Site (top image in Figure 16-3). Filling out the following two options are all you need to get started using Dreamweaver effectively.

Site name

In the "Site name" field, type a name that briefly identifies the site for you—and Dreamweaver. This is the name that appears, among other places, on the Site pop-up menu on the Files panel (skip ahead to Figure 16-6 for a glimpse of that), so that you can tell what site you're working on. It's just for identifying your site while you work in Dreamweaver—it doesn't appear on the actual pages of your site.

Local site folder

Identify your site's local site folder—the folder on your computer that contains all the files belonging to your site. (This is also known as a local "root" folder.) Click the folder icon to the right of the "Local site folder" box to find the folder. See the box on page 646 for more information on local site folders.

Tip: If you're confused about which folder should be the local site folder, just ask yourself this question: "Which folder on my computer contains (or will contain) my site's home page?" That's the local site folder. All your site's other files and folders should go inside this one, main folder.

The Dreamweaver tools that manage your sites' files rely on the local site folder. Once you set up a site, you see all its files listed in the Files panel. Under Advanced Settings, the Local Info tells Dreamweaver how to work with the web page files on your computer.

Default images folder

When you want to display a graphic in a web page, you tell the page where to find the image by pointing to its file location. That location has to be in the local root folder or one of its subfolders. In other words, if you link to a graphic that's sitting on your computer's hard drive *outside* of the root folder, the web browser will never find it.

Dreamweaver offers a feature that puts images in the right place even if you forget to. When you add a stray graphics file to a page on your site, Dreamweaver automatically copies the file into your default images folder. In fact, even if you drag a graphic from your desktop onto a web page-in-progress, Dreamweaver copies the file to the default images folder without missing a beat.

You identify the default images folder the same way you select the local site folder. Click the folder icon and locate the folder on your local drive. If you haven't set up the folder yet, click the "New Folder" button to create it on the spot. (For example, you might name the folder named *images* or *images_global* in your local root folder.)

Links relative to

As discussed on page 159, you can set up links in your web pages in a variety of ways. When you link to another page in your site, Dreamweaver lets you create *document-relative* or *root-relative* links. As explained on page 160, document-relative links are often the easiest way to go, but Dreamweaver offers you the flexibility to choose. Click either the Document or Site Root radio button. Then, whenever you embed a link in your pages, Dreamweaver creates the link using that setting.

Tip: You can override this setting and use whichever type of link you wish–site root-relative or document-relative–when you create the link, as described in step 4 on page 167.

FREQUENTLY ASKED QUESTION

Bringing Your Own Website

I already have a website. Will Dreamweaver work with it?

Yes. In fact, Dreamweaver's site management features are an invaluable aid in organizing the files of an existing site. As you can read in "Organizing Site Files" on page 648, you can use Dreamweaver to rearrange, rename, and reorganize files–tasks that are extremely difficult and time-consuming to do by hand.

Furthermore, Dreamweaver lets you clean up and reorganize a site without breaking links. So Dreamweaver is just as useful for working with a completed site as it is for creating one from scratch.

To work on an existing site, make sure the site has its own root folder–in other words, its home page, graphics, CSS files, other web pages, and any subfolders all in one main site folder. Then set up a new site in Dreamweaver as described above, and choose this folder as the local site folder.

HTTP address

This option serves two functions: first, if you use absolute URLs to link to pages within your site (see page 160), you must fill out the "HTTP address" field for Dreamweaver's link-management features to work properly. Type in your site's full URL, beginning with *http://*. Dreamweaver uses this address to check for broken links within your site and to correctly rewrite links if you move pages around. For example, maybe your webmaster told you to link a form to *http://www.yourdomain.com/cgi/formscript.php* instead of using a document-relative link. In this case, you'd type *http://www.yourdomain.com* in the "HTTP address" box. Now, if you move or rename the *formscript.php* page from within Dreamweaver, the program is smart enough to update the absolute link in the form.

This setting is also incredibly valuable for one particular situation: if you use site root-relative links, but the site you're working on isn't actually located in the site root on the web server. For example, say you run the marketing department at International ToolCo. You manage just the web pages for the marketing department, and they're located in a folder called *marketing* on the web server. In essence, you manage a sub-site, which acts as an independent site within the larger International ToolCo site. Maybe your webmaster demands that you use site root-relative links—man, is that guy bossy.

This is a potentially tricky situation. Here's why: site root-relative links always begin with a /, indicating the root folder on the web server (for a refresher on this concept, see page 161). Normally, if you add a root-relative link, say, to the main page in a folder named *personnel* located inside the local root folder, Dreamweaver would write the link like this: */personnel/index.html*. But in this case, that wouldn't work. The *personnel* folder is actually located (on the web server) inside the *marketing* folder. So the link should be */marketing/personnel/index.html*. In other words, Dreamweaver normally thinks that the local root folder maps exactly to the web server's root folder.

You can solve this dilemma by adding a URL that points to the "sub-site" in the Site Definition window's "HTTP address" box. In this example, you'd type *http://www.intltoolco.com/marketing/* in the box. Then, whenever you add a root–relative link, Dreamweaver begins it with */marketing/* and then adds the rest of the path to the URL. In summary, *if* you use site root-relative links *and* you're working solely on pages located inside a subdirectory on the actual server, *then* fill out the absolute URL to that subdirectory. Finally, add this whole rigmarole to the list of reasons why document-relative links are easier to manage in Dreamweaver.

Note: Strangely, the first use of the HTTP address box mentioned above—that is, managing absolute URLs pointing to files in your site—doesn't work with the second option—sub-sites. For example, if you specify a subdirectory like *www.intltoolco.com/marketing/* in the HTTP address box, Dreamweaver isn't able to keep track of absolute links within this site. So if you had to use the URL *www.intltoolco.com/marketing/cgi/form.php* to point to a form page within your site, and then you move that form page, Dreamweaver won't update the page using that absolute link.

Case-sensitive links

Some web servers (namely, those of the Unix and Linux variety) are sensitive to the case you use in file names. For example, both OSes consider *INDEX.html* and *index.html* different files. If your server uses either OS, turn on the "Use case-sensitive link checking" box to make sure Dreamweaver doesn't mistake one file for another when it checks links. Say you link to a file named *INDEX.html*, but change the name of another file named *index.html* to *contact.html*. Without this option turned on, Dreamweaver may mistakenly update links to *INDEX.html* because it considers the file the same as *index.html*.

In real-world use, you probably won't need this option. First, it's not possible to have two files with the same name but different combinations of upper- and lowercase letters in the same folder on a Windows or Mac machine. So if your local root folder is on a Windows or Mac computer, you'll never be able to get into this situation. In addition, it's confusing (and just plain weird) to use the same name but different cases for your files. Revisit the rules of file naming (see page 639) if you find yourself tempted to do this.

Cache

The cache is a small database of information about the files in your site. It helps Dreamweaver's site management features work more efficiently; leave this checkbox turned on.

In almost all cases, you'll want to keep this checkbox turned on. However, if you have a really large site, composed of tens of thousands of web pages, Dreamweaver might act pretty sluggishly when you perform basic tasks like moving files around within the site, or checking for broken links.

Once you provide the local information for your site, click Save to close the Site Definition window and begin working.

Editing or Removing Sites

Sometimes you need to edit the information associated with a site. Perhaps you want to rename the site, or you reorganized your hard drive and moved the local root folder, so you want to let Dreamweaver know the new location.

To edit a site, open the Manage Sites dialog box (choose Site→Manage Sites or, in the Files panel, choose Manage Sites from the bottom of the Site pop-up menu) and double-click the name of the site you want to edit. The Site Definition window opens (Figure 16-3). Now you can type a new name in the Site Name box, choose a new local root folder, or make any other changes. Click OK to close the dialog box when you're done.

Note: If you want to edit the current site's information, there's a shortcut. In the Files panel (Figure 16-6), just double-click the name of the site in the Sites menu. (Mac owners need to click once to select the name in the menu, and then click again to open the Site Definition window.)

Once you finish designing a site, you may want to remove it from Dreamweaver's list of sites. Open the Manage Sites dialog box as described above, click to select the site you wish to delete, and then click Remove.

A warning appears telling you that you can't undo this action. Don't worry; deleting the site here doesn't actually *delete* the site's web pages, images, or other files from your computer. It merely removes the site from Dreamweaver's list of sites. (You can always go back and set up the site again, by following the steps on page 640.) Click Done to close the Manage Sites window.

Note: If you do, in fact, want to delete the actual web pages, graphics, and other site components, you can either switch to the desktop (Windows Explorer or the Finder, for example) and delete them manually, or delete them from within Dreamweaver's Files panel, described on page 657.

UP TO SPEED

Local vs. Live Site Folders

A site folder (also called a root *folder*) is a site's main, hold-everything folder. It contains every component that makes up the site: all web page documents, graphics images, CSS style sheets, Flash movies, and so on.

The word "site" in the name "site folder" implies that this folder holds your entire site. It's the master, outer, main folder, in other words, the folder in which you may have plenty of subfolders. Remember that, in most cases, your website exists in two locations: on your computer as you work on it, and on the Internet where people can enjoy the fruits of your labor. In fact, most websites in the universe live in two places at once–one copy on the Internet and the original on some web designer's hard drive. (In some cases, you'll also have what's called a "testing server" often used to test dynamic, database-driven websites, before publishing them to the Internet–you'll learn about testing servers on page 836.)

The copy on your own computer is called the *local site.* Think of it as a sort of development area, where you build your site, test it, and modify it. (With database-driven sites, you do your testing on the testing server, and use the local site to store the files as you work on them. As you'll read on page 837, it's common for the files on your local site and testing server to be one and the same.)

Because the local site isn't on a web server, and the public can't see it, you can freely edit and add to it without affecting the pages your visitors see. The folder for the version of the site you keep on your computer, therefore, is called the *local site folder*.

After you add or update a file, you move it from the local site to the *remote server*. The remote server mirrors the local site. Because you create a remote site by uploading your local site to a server, it has the same folder structure as your local site and contains the same polished, fully functional web pages The local site also includes all the half-finished, typo-ridden drafts you're working on. Chapter 18 explains how to use Dreamweaver's FTP features to upload only your ready-for-prime-time local site and how to work with a remote server.

Exporting and Importing Sites

When you define a site, Dreamweaver stores that site's information in its own private files. If you want to work on your site using a different computer, therefore, you must re-set up the site for *that* copy of Dreamweaver. In a design firm where several people work on many different sites, that's a lot of extra set-up. In fact, even if there's just one of you working on two computers, duplicating your efforts takes extra work.

Dreamweaver lets you import and export site setups so you can put your time to better use. For example, you can back up your site set-up files in case you have to reinstall Dreamweaver, and you can export a site definition for others to use.

Note: Exporting a site in Dreamweaver doesn't actually export your site files–all of the web pages, folders, and other files–just the setup options you used when you set up the site. In other words, you just export and import the information that lets Dreamweaver work with your site's files.

To export a site setup:

1. **Choose Site→Manage Sites.**

   The Manage Sites window appears, listing all the sites you've defined (Figure 16-4).

Figure 16-4:
The Manage Sites window is the control center for managing your sites. Add new sites, edit old ones, duplicate a site definition, and even export site definitions for use on another computer, or as a precautionary backup.

2. **Select a site from the list, and then click Export.**

   If the site setup includes server information (so you can have Dreamweaver connect to your server to move files onto it as described on page 702), you'll see a dialog box called "Exporting site" (Figure 16-5). If you simply want to make a backup of your site definition because you need to reinstall Dreamweaver, select the "Back up my settings" radio button. (The other option, "Share settings," is useful when, for example, your local site folder is on the C: drive, but the site folder is on the E: drive on someone else's computer, so your setup information doesn't apply to them. It's also handy when you don't want to give someone your user name and password to the web server.)

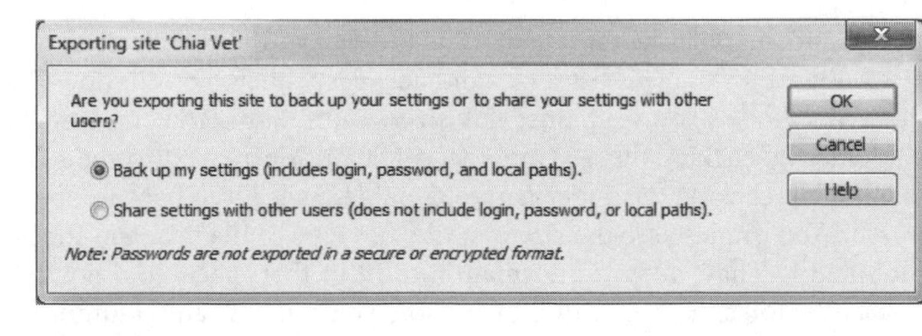

Figure 16-5:
This dialog box lets you back up your settings or share them (minus your login information) with other people.

3. **Click OK.**

   The Export Site panel appears.

Tip: You can export multiple sites in a single step. Just select all the sites you want to export (Ctrl-click [⌘-click] the names of the sites), and then click the Export button.

4. **In the Export Site panel, specify where you want to save the file and give it a name.**

   If you're making a backup, save the file outside the local root folder (for example, with the Photoshop, Fireworks, and Word source files for your site). Because the export file can potentially contain the username and password you use to move files to your remote site, you don't want to keep the file anywhere in your local root folder—you might mistakenly upload it to the web server, where someone might find it and wreak havoc with your site.

   Dreamweaver uses the extension *.ste* for site definition files.

Once you create a site set-up file, you can import it into Dreamweaver as follows:

5. **Choose Site→Manage Sites.**

   The Manage Sites panel appears.

6. **Click Import.**

   The Import Site panel appears. Navigate to the set-up file—look for a file ending in .ste. Select it, and then click OK.

If you import the site set-up to a computer other than the one you used to export it, you may need to perform a few more steps. If Dreamweaver can't find the location of the local site folder in the site set-up file, it asks you to select a local site folder on the new computer, as well as a new default images folder.

Organizing Site Files

Once you set up your local site, you can use the Files panel as your command center for organizing your files, creating folders, and adding new web pages to your site. To open the Files panel, choose Window→Files, or just press F8 (Shift-⌘-F).

In its most basic incarnation, the Files panel lists the files in the current site's local root folder (see Figure 16-6). This list looks and acts very much like Windows Explorer or the Mac's Finder; you see names, file sizes, and folders. You can view the files inside a folder by clicking the + symbol (triangle on Macs) next to the folder (or simply by double-clicking the folder name). Double-click a web page to open it in Dreamweaver. You can also see the size of a file, the type of file it is, and the last time you modified it. That's a lot of information to fit in that space, so if you find this new view a little too crammed with information, you can hide any columns you don't like—see page 650.

Note: You can open certain types of files in an outside program of your choice by defining an external editor for that file type. For example, you can tell Dreamweaver to open GIF files in Fireworks, Photoshop, or another image editor. See page 238 for more on this feature.

You can view your site's files four ways, using the View pop-up menu (shown in Figure 16-6):

- Local view lists the files in your local root folder. Dreamweaver displays folders in this view as green.
- Remote server displays the list of files in your remote site folder, which itself mirrors the list of files on your web server (see page 646). Of course, before you post your site to the Web, this list is empty. Dreamweaver adds files to this folder only after you set up a connection to a remote server (see page 691). Dreamweaver displays folders in this view yellow on Windows and blue on Macs.
- Testing server view is useful when you create the dynamic, database-driven sites discussed in Part Six of this book. No files appear in this view until you set up a testing server (see page 836) and connect Dreamweaver to it. Dreamweaver displays folders in this view in red.
- Repository view gives you a peek inside a file versioning system called Subversion. You'll learn about this advanced file-management tool on page 713.

Note: If you've got a small monitor, the Files panel (and other panel groups) might take up too much space to let you comfortably work on a web page. You can hide (and show) all panels, including the Property inspector and the Insert bar, by pressing F4.

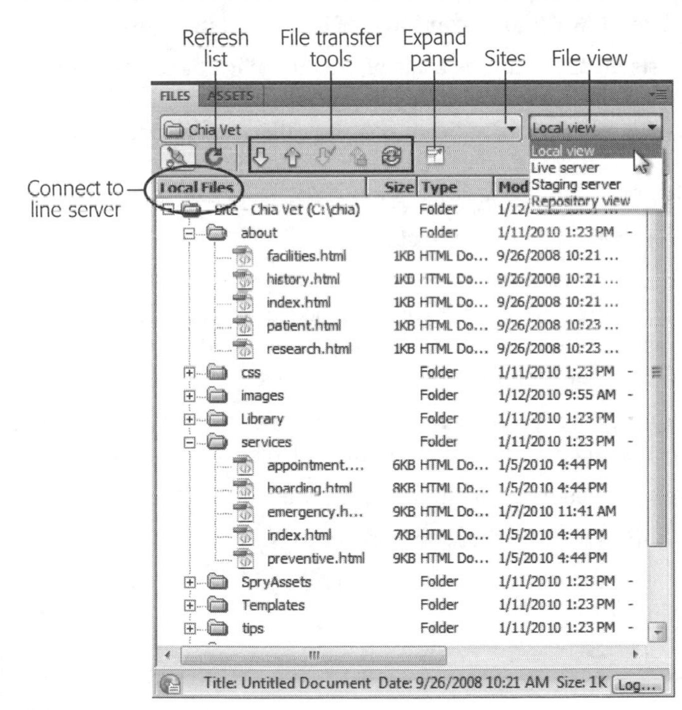

Figure 16-6: *The Files panel, logically enough, lists files in the currently active website. A list of all the websites you defined in Dreamweaver appears in the Sites pop-up menu. To work on a different site, select its name (but be aware that you can also select files in your local file system, potentially tripping up Dreamweaver's Site Management tools–see the box on page 658). You can use the Files panel to connect to a web server and transfer files back and forth between your local and remote sites, as described on page 702. You can tell whether you're looking at the files on your computer, the web server, the testing server, or a Subversion repository by looking at the name that appears at the top of the file column. In this figure, for example, you're looking at files on your computer since the file view pane lists "Local view" (circled).*

Modifying the Files Panel View

Dreamweaver stocks the Files panel with loads of information: the file name, the size of the file, the type of file (web page, graphic, and so on), and the date you last modified it. This is all useful to know, but if you have a relatively small monitor, you may not be able display everything without having to scroll left and right. What's worse, the filenames themselves often get clipped by other columns of information.

There are a couple of things you can do to fix this. First, you can resize the width of each column by dragging one of the dividers that separates each column name (see Figure 16-6). Using this technique, you can at least display the full name of each file.

If you don't like the number of columns Dreamweaver displays, you can hide any or all of them. After all, how useful is listing the type of each file? The folder icon clearly indicates when you're looking at a folder; a file name ending in .html is a web page; and a JPEG file's extension, .jpg, is clearly visible as part of the file's name. For most folks, that's enough.

Unfortunately, there's no program-wide setting to control which columns appear. You have to define the visible columns on a site-by-site basis:

1. **Choose Site→Manage sites, and double-click the name of the site whose files panel you want to modify.**

   This opens the Site Setup window (see Figure 16-3).

2. **Click the Advanced Settings category to expand the list of advanced options, and select the File View Columns option (see top image in Figure 16-7).**

   Dreamweaver lists all the columns available for the Files panel, and indicates which it displays ("Show") or hides ("Hide"). Under the Type heading, all the files initially say "Built In" to indicate columns that are preprogrammed in Dreamweaver. As you'll read on page 721, you can add your own customized columns to this list.

3. **Double-click the column you want to change.**

   For example, double-clicking the Type column displays the options you see in Figure 16-7 (bottom): Column Name, "Associate with Design Notes", and "Share with all users". In this case, most of the options are dimmed out because they only apply to custom columns, described on page 724.

4. **Change the alignment of the column (Left, Right, or Center) from the Align menu, and select or uncheck the Show checkbox to show or hide a column.**

   For example, to hide a column, uncheck the Show box.

5. **Click the Save button to close that column's settings.**

   Repeat steps 3–5 for any other columns you wish to edit, and when you're done click the Save button on the Site Setup window.

You can change the order of the columns, too—perhaps the Modified date information is more important to you than the file size. Select a column and click the up or down arrow. The up arrow moves the column to the left in the Files panel, while the down arrow scoots a column over to the right.

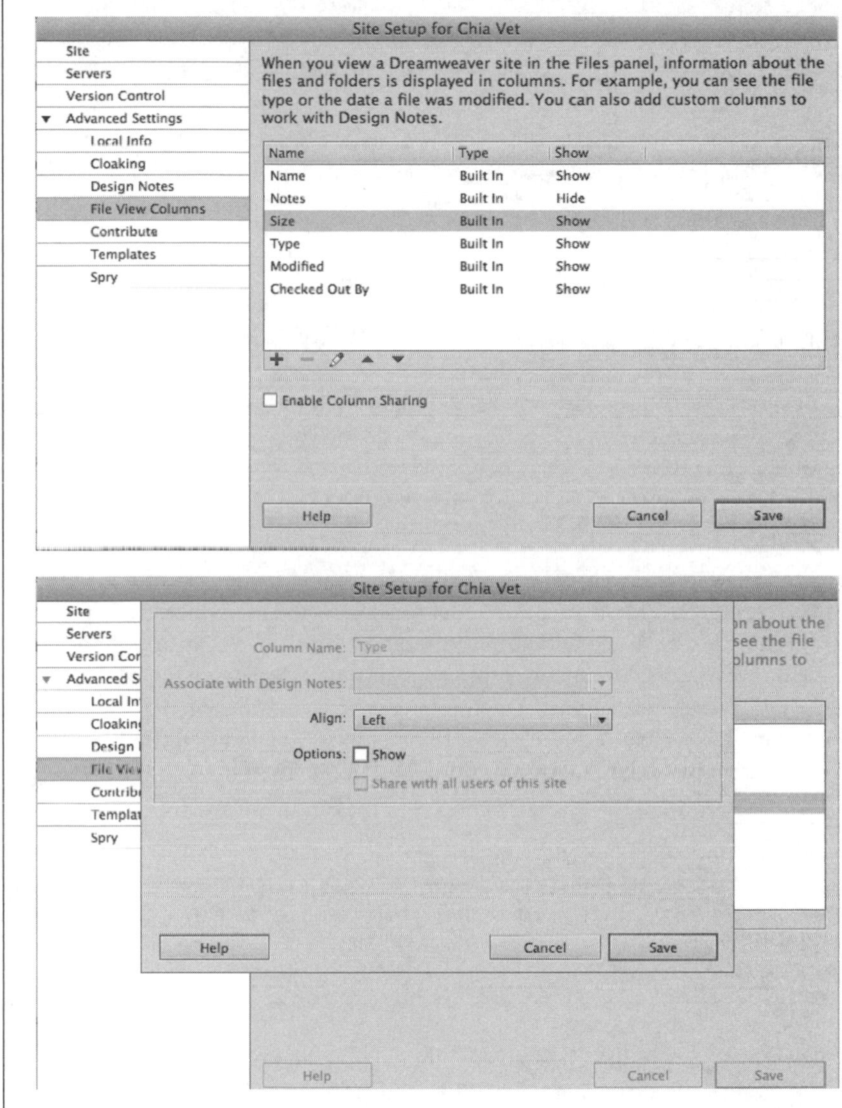

Figure 16-7: *Use the File View Columns category to show or hide columns of information in the Files panel. You can rearrange the columns by selecting one and clicking the up or down arrow (pictured in top image). The up arrow moves the column to the left in the Files panel, while the down arrow scoots it over to the right. You can also use the Files View Columns category to work with Dreamweaver's collaborative note-sharing feature called Design Notes. Instructions on using Design Notes start on page 721.*

FOR WINDOWS PCS

The Expanded Files Panel

If you'd like to expand the Files panel so you can see the *remote server* files and *local site* files side by side, click the Expand/Collapse button (labeled in Figure 16-6). The Files panel fills the screen as shown in Figure 16-8. The obvious drawback is that you can't work on a web page with the Site window maximized, because you can't even see it. Click the Expand/Collapse button again to minimize the Files panel and uncover the document window.

To get around this limitation, you can undock the Files panel before you click the Expand button: Grab the Files panel group by its grip–the tiny column of dots to the left of the word "Files"–and drag it toward the middle of the screen. (Stay away from the edges of the screen when you do this; touching there may simply re-dock the panel group.) The panel group now floats. Press the Expand button to get the side-by-side files view. You can resize the Files panel even after you expand it.

Adding New Folders and Files

The Files panel provides a fast way to add blank web pages to your site. With one click, you can create a new page in any folder, saving you several steps compared to using the File menu.

Adding files

To create a new, blank web page, open the Files panel using one of the methods described on page 27, click on a file or folder to select it, and then right-click (Control-click) on the selected file or folder. In the shortcut menu that appears, choose New File. Dreamweaver creates a new, empty page in the folder where the selected page resides or, if you selected a folder, Dreamweaver adds a new page to it. (Actually, the page Dreamweaver creates doesn't have to be empty; you can edit the file Dreamweaver uses as its default new page, as described in the box below.)

Note: The type of file Dreamweaver creates depends on the type of site you're creating. For a plain HTML site, Dreamweaver creates a blank HTML page. If you're building a dynamic, database-driven site, however (like those described in Part Six), Dreamweaver creates a blank page based on the type of server model you selected. For example, if you're building a site using PHP and MySQL, the page is a blank PHP page (named *untitled.php*).

The new file appears in the Files panel with a highlighted naming rectangle next to it; type a name for the page here. Don't forget to add the appropriate HTML extension (.htm or .html) to the end of the name—if you do forget, Dreamweaver creates a completely empty file, no starter HTML included (and changing the name by adding the .html extension won't fix the problem). If this happens, delete the file and create a new one. (If you're creating a PHP file, as described in the note above, make sure the file name ends in .php.)

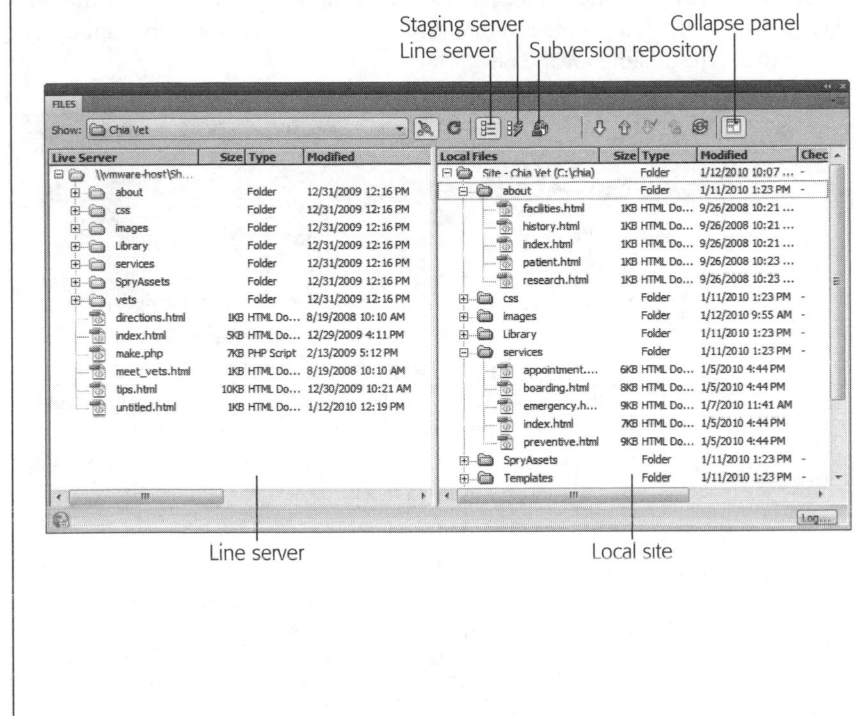

Figure 16-8: *Click the Expand/Collapse button shown back in Figure 16-6 to maximize the Files panel and display two views simultaneously. This way, you can view both your remote server and local site at the same time. Local files normally appear on the right, but might be on the left, depending on the preference you set under the Site category of the Preferences window. (If you want to change this, press Ctrl+U [⌘-U] to open Preferences and then click the Site category.) The view that appears opposite the local files view—Remote Server, Testing, or Repository—depends on which view you selected before clicking the Expand button. To change views, click a different view button.*

Tip: If, immediately after creating a new file in the Files panel, you rename that file and add a new extension, the contents of the file update to reflect the new file type. For example, changing *untitled.html* to *global.css* erases all the HTML code in the file and turns it into an empty CSS file.

Adding folders

You can add folders to your site directly in Dreamweaver using the Files panel. Just click to select a file or folder, and then right-click (Control-click) on that file or folder. From the shortcut menu, choose New Folder. If you click a file, Dreamweaver creates the new folder in the same folder as that file; if you click a folder, you get a new folder inside it.

If you crave variety, you can add a folder another way. Select a file or folder in the Files panel and then click the contextual menu button (at the top right of the Files panel) and select File→New Folder. Finally, in the naming rectangle that appears in the Files panel, type a name for the new folder.

POWER USERS' CLINIC

Changing the Default New Page

Whenever you create a new web page–by choosing File→New or by right-clicking (Control-clicking) an existing file in the Files panel–Dreamweaver gives you a blank, white document window. But what if you always want your pages to have special HTML comments indicating that your company created the page, or you always want to include a link to the same external style sheet?

Every new web page you create is actually an untitled copy of a default template document called Default.html. You can find this file in the Dreamweaver configuration folder. On Windows it's in *C:\Program Files\Adobe\Adobe Dreamweaver CS5\configuration\DocumentTypes\NewDocuments*. On a Mac, you can find it in *Applications→Adobe Dreamweaver CS5→Configuration→DocumentTypes→New-Documents* folder.

Save a copy of this folder to your user folder (so you can always return to the original, Dreamweaver-supplied file). In Windows XP, use the folder name *C:\Documents and Settings\[your user name]\Application Data\Adobe\Dreamweaver CS5\en_US\Configuration*. In Windows Vista, use *C:\Users\[your user name]\AppData\Roaming\Adobe\Dreamweaver CS5\en_US\Configuration*. On a Mac, try *Volume Name→Users→[your user name]→Library→Application Support→Adobe→Dreamweaver CS5→en_US→Configuration*.

You can then open a file from the NewDocument folders in your personal configuration folder and edit it however you like: change or add HTML comments, meta tags, precanned links to a style sheet or whatever, so that all subsequent new pages inherit these settings. Consider making a backup of this file before you edit it, however, so you can return to the factory settings if you accidentally make a mess of it. (Also, make sure you don't touch an HTML fragment that probably appears to you to be incorrect: namely, the *charset="* snippet, which appears at the end of the <meta> tag. This fragment of HTML is indeed incomplete, but when you create a new page, Dreamweaver correctly completes the code according to the alphabet your page uses–Chinese, Korean, or Western European, for example.)

You'll notice lots of other files in this folder. Since Dreamweaver can create lots of different file types–Cascading Style Sheets, Active Server Pages, and so on–you'll find a default blank file for each. You can edit any of these–but don't, unless you're sure of what you're doing. You can easily damage some of the more complex file types, especially those that involve dynamic websites.

Moving files and folders

Because the Dreamweaver Files panel looks and acts so much like Windows Explorer and the Macintosh Finder, you may think it does nothing more than let you move and rename files and folders on your computer. You may even be tempted to work with your site files directly on the your Windows or Mac desktop, thinking that you're saving time. Think again. When it comes to moving files and folders in your site, Dreamweaver does more than your computer's desktop ever could.

In your Web travels, you've probably encountered the dreaded "404: File Not Found" error. This "broken link" message doesn't necessarily mean that the page doesn't exist; it means that your web browser didn't find the page at the location (URL) specified by the link you just clicked. In short, someone working on the website probably moved or renamed a file without updating the link. Because website files are interrelated in such complex ways—pages link to other pages, which include paths to graphics, which in turn appear on other pages—an action as simple as moving one file can wreak havoc on an entire site. That's why you shouldn't drag website files around on your desktop or rename them in Windows Explorer or the Macintosh Finder.

In fact, moving and reorganizing website files is so headache-ridden and error-prone that some web designers avoid it altogether, leaving their sites straining under the weight of thousands of poorly organized files. But you don't have to be one of them: Dreamweaver makes reorganizing a site easy and error-free. When you use the Files panel to move files, Dreamweaver looks for actions that could break your site's links and automatically rewrites the paths of links, images, and other media (see the cautionary box on page 658).

Note to JavaScript programmers: If your custom JavaScript programs include paths to web pages, images, or other files in your site, Dreamweaver can't help you. When you reorganize your site with the Files panel, the program updates *links* it created, but not *paths* in your JavaScript programs.

Just be sure to do your moving from within Dreamweaver, like this: In the Files panel, drag the file or folder into its new folder (see Figure 16-9). To move multiple files, Ctrl-click (⌘-click) each and then drag them as a group; to deselect a file, Ctrl-click or ⌘-click it again. You can also select one file or folder and Shift-click another to select all files and folders in between the two.

Note: Close *all* your web documents *before* you reorganize your files this way. Dreamweaver has been known to not always correctly update links in open files. But if you do end up with malfunctioning links, you can always use Dreamweaver's Find Broken Links tool (see page 671) to ferret out and fix any broken links.

When you release the mouse button, the Update Files dialog box appears (Figure 16-9); just click Update. Dreamweaver updates all the links for you.

Tip: If you accidentally drag a file or folder to the wrong location, click Don't Update. Then drag the file back to its original location and, if Dreamweaver asks, click Don't Update once again.

Renaming files and folders

Renaming files and folders poses the same problems as moving them. Because links include file and folder names, altering a file or folder name can break a link just as easily as moving or deleting a file or folder.

For example, say you create a new site with a home page named *home.html*. You cheerfully continue building the other pages of your site, linking them to *home.html* as you go along. But after reading this chapter and checking the default file name your web server requires (see page 640), you find you need to rename your home page *index.html*. If you were to rename the file *index.html* using Windows Explorer or the Macintosh Finder, every link to *home.html* would result in a "File not found" error!

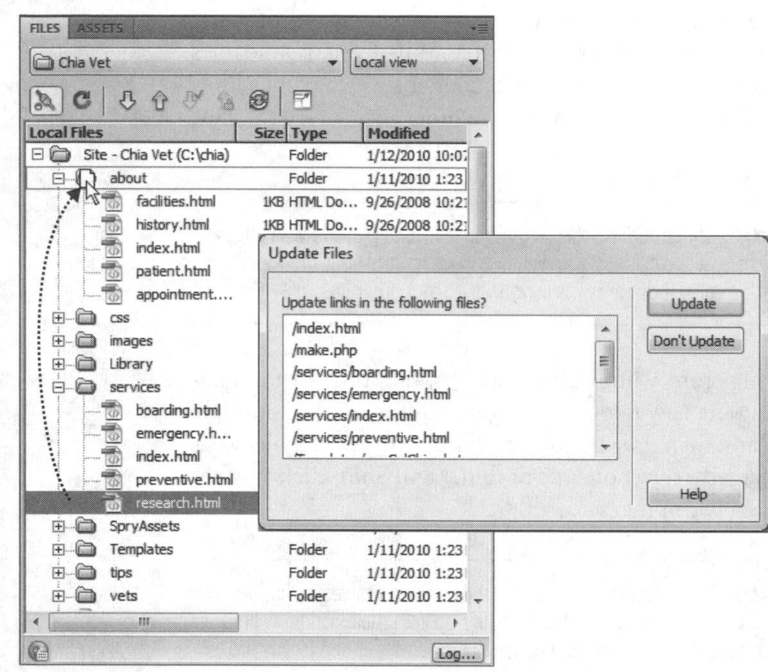

Figure 16-9: *You can move files and folders within the Files panel just as you would in Windows Explorer or the Macintosh Finder. Simply drag the file into (or out of) a folder. But unlike your computer's file system, Dreamweaver constantly monitors the links between web pages, graphics, and other files. If you move a file using Windows Explorer or the Finder, you'll most likely end up breaking links to that file or, if it's a web page, breaking links within that file. By contrast, Dreamweaver is smart enough to know when moving files will cause problems. The Update Files dialog box lets you update links to and from the files you move so your site keeps working properly.*

Dreamweaver, on the other hand, handles this potential disaster effortlessly, as long as you rename the file in the Files panel. To do so, click the file or folder name in the panel. Pause a moment, and click the *name* of the file or folder. (The pause ensures that Dreamweaver won't think you just double-clicked the file to edit it.)

A renaming rectangle appears; type the new name. Be sure to include the proper extension for the type of file you're renaming. For example, GIFs end with .gif and Cascading Style Sheets end with .css. Although Dreamweaver lets you name files without using an extension, extension-less files won't work when you move them to a web server.

Finally, in the Update Files dialog box (Figure 16-9), click Update. Dreamweaver updates all the links to the file or folder to reflect the new name.

Warning: It bears repeating: never rename or move files and folders *outside* of Dreamweaver. If you use Windows Explorer or the Macintosh Finder to reorganize your site's files, links will break, images will disappear, and the earth will open underneath your feet. (Well, that last thing won't happen, but it can *feel* that way when your boss comes in and says, "What happened to our website? Nothing works!")

If you move files outside of Dreamweaver by accident, see page 671 to learn how to find and fix broken links.

Deleting files and folders

It's a good idea to clean up your site from time to time by deleting old and unused files. Just as with moving and renaming files, you delete them from the Files panel.

To delete a file or folder, click to select it in the Files panel and press Backspace or Delete. (To select multiple files or folders, Ctrl-click [⌘-click] them.) If no other page references the doomed file or folder, a simple "Are you sure you want to delete this file?" warning appears; click Yes.

However, if other files link to the file or to files within the folder you want to delete, Dreamweaver displays a warning dialog box (Figure 16-10) informing you that you're about to break links on one or more pages in your site.

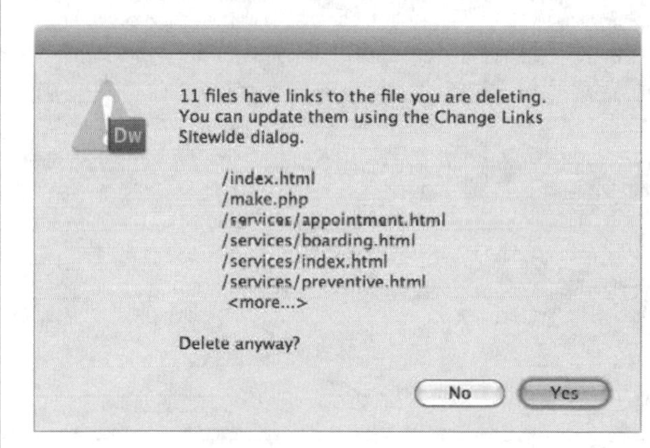

Figure 16-10: *When you delete files in the Files panel, Dreamweaver tells you if other pages reference (link to) the file. If they do, you'll need to repair the links. Dreamweaver makes it easy to do so via the Change Links Sitewide command (see "Changing a Link Throughout a Site" on page 678)—and it reminds you of the feature in this dialog box.*

The message even lists the first few pages that use the file. If you made a mistake, click No to leave your site untouched.

If you're sure you want to delete the file or folder, click Yes. And yes, this move does *break links* in all the pages listed. Repairing those links, which usually means linking them to a new page, requires a separate step: using the Site→Change Links Sitewide command, as described on page 671.

Note: If you have moved files into your site folder using Windows Explorer, or the Mac Finder, Dreamweaver might not be aware of those files, or links between those files and others in your site. If that's the case, when you move or delete files, Dreamweaver may not correctly update links or warn you of broken links caused by deleting necessary file. To make Dreamweaver aware of the new files you've added, choose Site→Advanced→Recreate Site Cache—Dreamweaver will scan all the files in the local site folder and update the cache (its database of files and links in the site).

Site Assets

Web pages integrate lots of different elements: PNGs, GIFs, JPEGs, links, colors, JavaScript files, and Flash movies, to name just a few. In a large site with lots of files, it's a challenge to locate a particular image or remember an exact color.

To simplify the process, Dreamweaver provides the Assets panel. For want of a better generic term, Dreamweaver defines the term *asset* to mean any element you use on a web page, such as a GIF, a link, or even an individual color.

FREQUENTLY ASKED QUESTION

Beware "Site-less" Web Design

Why doesn't Dreamweaver warn me when I delete or move a file?

Dreamweaver's site management tools are always watching your back—unless you're not working within a site. Dreamweaver tries to be a flexible tool for all situations. Some developers don't like the whole notion of sites and prefer to just work on their pages in the old (unmonitored) way of most programs. And in cases where you just want to edit a single page and don't want to go through the whole business of defining a site, Dreamweaver's Files panel lets you browse your files, just like Windows Explorer or the Mac Finder does. If you click the Sites menu (where you normally switch between sites) and scroll to the top of the list, you see a list of hard drives and other networked storage devices. For example, you could select your main drive (C: or Macintosh HD, for example). The Files panel then displays all of the files on that drive. Unfortunately, this flexibility can also cause a lot of trouble.

Sometimes people accidentally select their hard drive instead of their site in the Sites menu, and *then* navigate to the folder holding their site's files. Then they begin working, blissfully unaware that they're working without Dreamweaver's safety net. When you work with your files this way, Dreamweaver doesn't monitor changes you make to your existing site files—like moving, deleting, or renaming—it figures you know best). Similarly, all of Dreamweaver's other site-management features, like Libraries (Chapter 19), templates (Chapter 20), and file transfers (Chapter 18), don't work when you're off in un-site-managed-land. In other words, it's best to always set up a local site, and always make sure you select the site's name in the Files panel, to work on your site.

Viewing the Assets Panel

Dreamweaver lists your site's assets on the nine category "pages" of the Assets panel (Figure 16-11). To open the panel, choose Window→Assets.

Select an asset by clicking its name; Dreamweaver displays a miniature preview of the asset above the Assets list. To preview a movie, click the green arrow that appears in the preview window.

Dreamweaver divides your site's assets into nine categories, represented by icons on the left of the Assets panel. To view the assets in a particular category, click its icon:

- The Images category lists all the GIF, JPEG, and PNG files in your site. Dreamweaver lists the dimensions of each image next to its name, so you can quickly identify whether *logo1.gif* or *logo2.gif* is your 728 × 90 pixel banner logo. You can also see the images' sizes, types, and locations in the list (you may need to scroll to the right to see all this).
- The Colors category shows you all the colors specified in your site's pages and style sheets. These include link colors, background colors, and text colors.
- The Links category lists all *external* links—and not just standard http:// links, but also email links, FTP addresses, and JavaScript links.
- The three multimedia categories—SWF (meaning Flash movies), Shockwave, and Movies (meaning Flash or QuickTime movies)—are roughly equivalent. They each display movie files with their corresponding extensions: .swf (Flash), .dcr (Shockwave), .flv (Flash video), and .mov or .mpg (QuickTime and MPEG).
- The Scripts category lists JavaScript files. This category only includes external script files your web pages link to. You won't see scripts embedded *in* a web page—like those that Dreamweaver behaviors create.
- The last two categories—Templates and Library—are advanced assets that streamline website production. They're discussed in Chapters 19 and 20.

You can switch between two views for each asset category—Site and Favorites—by clicking the radio buttons near the top of the Assets panel. The Site option lists all the assets in your site for the chosen category. Favorites lets you create a select list of your most important and frequently used assets (see page 662).

If you add additional assets as you work on a site—for example, if you create a new GIF image in Fireworks and import it into your site—you need to update the Assets panel. To do so, click the Refresh Site List button (see Figure 16-11).

Inserting Assets

The Assets panel's prime mission is to make it easy for you to add assets to your site by dragging the asset from the panel into your document window. For example, you can add graphics, colors, and links to your pages with a simple drag-and-drop operation. Note that most of the categories on the panel refer to external files you commonly find on web pages: images, Flash, Shockwave, movies, and scripts.

You can drop an asset anywhere on a page you'd normally insert an object—in a table cell, a <div> tag, at the beginning or end of a page, or within a paragraph. You can add script assets to the head of a page (see Figure 16-12).

(If you're billing by the hour, you may prefer the long way: click in the document window to plant the insertion point, click the asset's name, and then click Insert at the bottom of the Assets panel.)

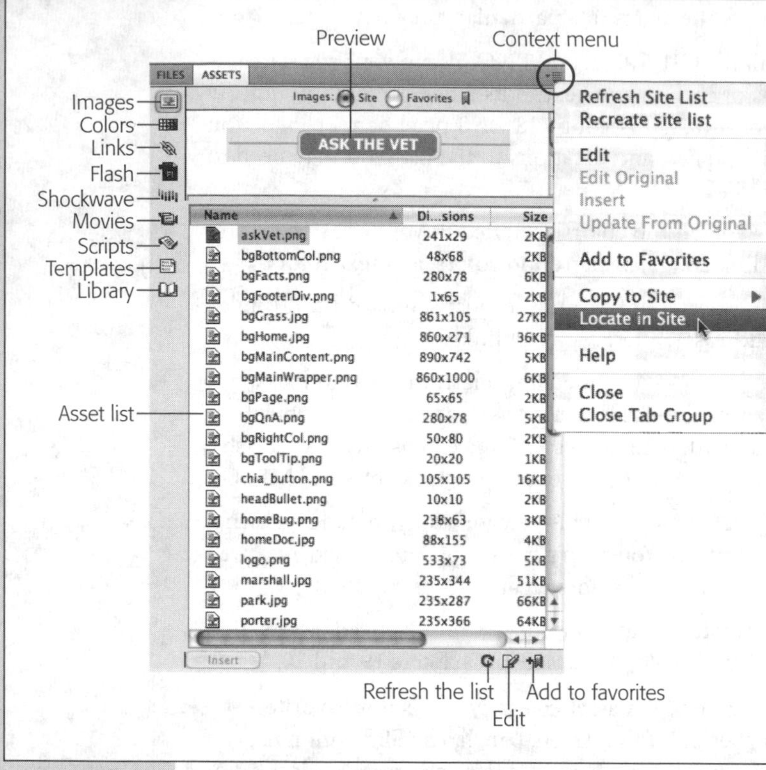

Figure 16-11: *Most of the commands in the Assets panel's contextual menu are duplicated in the panel itself, but three options appear only on this menu. "Recreate Site List" comes in handy if you add or delete files without Dreamweaver's help using Windows Explorer or the Mac Finder. It rebuilds the site cache and updates the list of assets. "Copy to Site" copies the selected asset to another site. "Locate in Site" switches to the Files panel and selects the file. You can also open the contextual menu by right-clicking (Control-clicking) any asset in the list.*

POWER USERS' CLINIC

The Return of Root-Relative Paths

Chapter 5 explains the different types of link paths—absolute, document-relative, and root-relative (see page 159). While, in many cases, it's best to use document-relative paths to link to pages within your own site or to add images and other media to a page, you may notice that Dreamweaver frequently displays root-relative paths in its site management tools.

For instance, the list in the Assets panel includes the full root-relative path of each asset—*/images_home/banner.png*, for example. The initial "/" indicates the site folder (the "root") of the site, and the information that follows indicates the rest of the path to that asset. In this example, the graphic asset *banner.png* is in a folder called *images_home*, which is itself in the site's local folder. Dreamweaver needs to look no further than the root folder to find the asset in question.

Root-relative paths indicate a precise location within a site and let Dreamweaver know where to find a file. This doesn't mean, however, that when you use the Assets panel to insert an image or other file, that Dreamweaver uses site root-relative links. Dreamweaver uses the type of link you specified for the site as described on page 642.

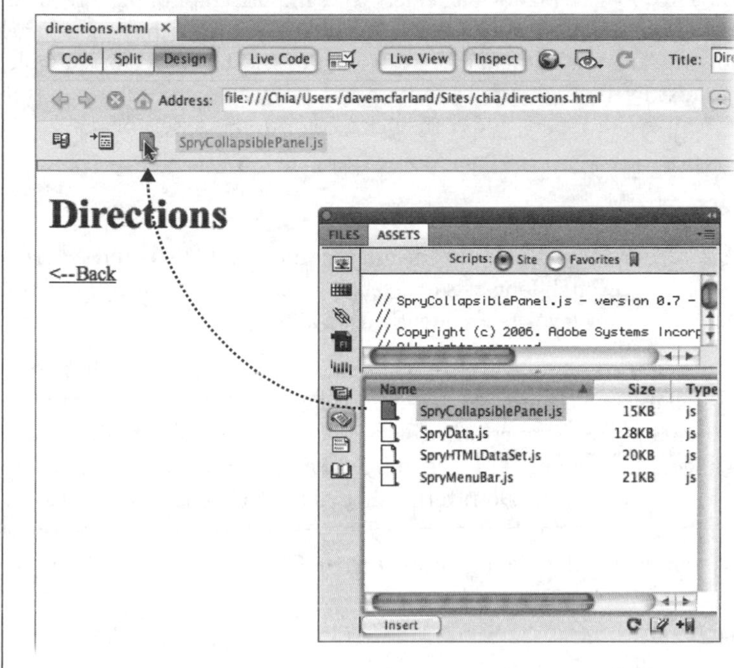

Figure 16-12: *Although you'll insert most assets into the body of a web page, you can (and usually should) place script files in the head of the page. To do this, choose View→Show Head Content. Then drag the script from the Assets panel into the head pane, as shown here. (Adding a script asset doesn't copy the JavaScript code into the web page. Instead, just as with external style sheets, Dreamweaver links to the script file so that when a web browser loads the page, it looks for and then loads the JavaScript file from the website.)*

Adding color and link assets

Color and link assets work a bit differently than other asset files. Instead of standing on their own, they *add* color or a link to text or images you select in the document window. (You can add colors to any text selection, or add links to images and text.) This makes it easy to quickly add a frequently used link—the URL to download the Flash player or Adobe Reader, for example.

To do so, start by highlighting the text (to change its color or turn it into a link) or image (to turn it into a link). In the Assets panel, click the appropriate category button—Colors or Links. Click the color or link you want, and then click Apply. Alternatively, you can drag the color or link asset from the panel to the selected text or image.

In the case of a link, Dreamweaver simply adds an <a> tag to the selection, with the proper external link. For color, Dreamweaver pops-up the New CSS Rule window (Figure 4-2) and asks you to create a new CSS style—you then need to go through the whole rigmarole described on page 113 to do so. Unfortunately, Dreamweaver's not smart enough to update the text color of any style that's currently applied to the selected text. In other words, applying colors with the Assets panel is more trouble than it's worth.

However, there is one way to use the color assets effectively, sort of. As you'll recall from page 56, the Dreamweaver color-picker lets you sample a color of the screen. So if you want to use a color from the Assets panel, make sure you have the Assets panel open and the color assets visible; then, when you want to select a color (for example, to add a color to text in the CSS Rule Definition window), click the color box (the cursor changes to an eye dropper), and then click a color in the Assets panel.

Favorite Assets

On a large site, you may have thousands of images, movies, colors, and external links. Because scrolling through long lists of assets is a chore, Dreamweaver lets you create a compact list of your favorite, frequently used assets.

For example, you might come up with five main colors that define your site's color scheme, which you'll use much more often than the other miscellaneous colors on the Assets list. Add them to your list of favorite colors. Likewise, adding graphics you use over and over—logos, for example—to a list of favorites makes it easy to locate and insert those files into your pages. (Don't forget that you can also use Dreamweaver's Library and template features for this function. They're similar but more powerful tools to keep frequently used items at the ready. Turn to Chapter 19 for the details.)

Identifying your Favorites

If the color, graphic, or other element you want to add to your Favorites list already appears on your Assets panel, highlight it in the list and then click the "Add to Favorites" button (see Figure 16-11).

Even quicker, you can add Favorites as you go, snagging them right from your web page. If you're working on your site's home page and you insert a company logo, for example, that's a perfect time to make the logo a favorite asset.

Simply right-click (Control-click) the image. From the shortcut menu, choose "Add Image to Favorites"; Dreamweaver instantly adds the graphic to your list of favorites *within that asset category*—meaning that you'll see the file when you're in the Favorites view *and* you have the Image category selected. You can use the same shortcut for Flash, Shockwave, and QuickTime files, and for links. (Unfortunately, it doesn't work for colors and script files.)

When it comes to colors and links, you can turn them into Favorites another way. In the Assets panel, select the Color or URLs category, click the Favorites radio button, and then click the New Asset button (see Figure 16-13). Then:

- If you're adding a favorite color, the Dreamweaver color box appears. Select a color using the eyedropper (see page 56).
- If you're adding a favorite link, the Add URL window opens. Type either an absolute URL in the first field (a web address starting with *http://*) or an email link (for instance, *mailto:subscriptions@nationalexasperator.com*). Next, type a name for the link—such as *Acrobat Download* or *Subscription Email*—in the Nickname field and then click OK.

Your new color or link appears in the Favorites list.

Using your Favorites

You insert assets from the Favorites list into your web pages just as you would any other assets; see page 659.

Removing Favorites

Removing an asset from the Favorites list is just as straightforward as adding one: select it in the Favorites list of your Assets panel and then press Delete. The "Remove from Favorites" button (see Figure 16-13) on the Assets panel does the same thing. Yet another approach is to use the contextual menu (Figure 16-11).

Don't worry; removing an asset from your Favorites list *doesn't* delete that asset from the Assets panel (or your site). You can still find it listed by clicking the Site radio button.

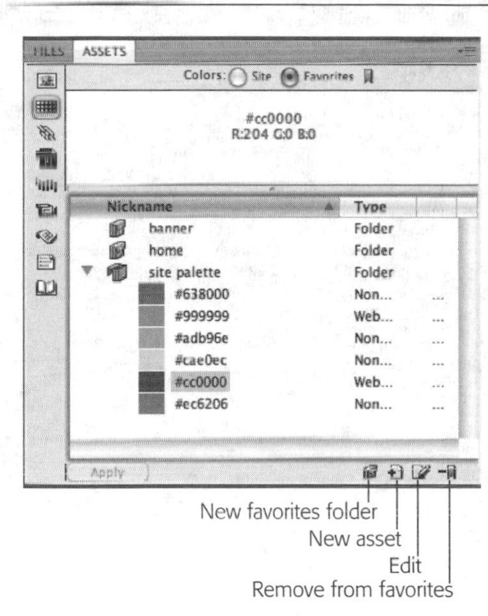

Figure 16-13:
In addition to using folders to organize your Favorites, you can give a Favorite asset an easily identifiable nickname. Instead of listing a favorite image using its file name—148593.gif, for instance—use an easily understood name like New Product. Naming favorite colors is particularly helpful; a nickname like Page Background is more descriptive than #FF6633. To name a Favorite asset, click to select it; pause a moment, and then click again to edit its name. (These nicknames only apply in the Assets panel; they don't rename or retitle your files.)

Organizing Favorite assets

On a large site with lots of important assets, even a Favorites list can get unwieldy. That's why you can set up folders within the asset categories of the Favorites panel to organize your assets. For example, if you use lots of ads on a site, create a folder in the Image assets category of your Favorites list called Ads or, for even greater precision, create multiple folders for different types of ads: Banner Ads, Half Banner Ads, and so on.

You can then drag assets into the appropriate folders, and expand or contract the folder to show or hide the assets inside (see Figure 16-13). These folders simply help you organize your Assets panel; they don't actually appear anywhere within the structure of your site. Moving a Favorite asset into a folder doesn't change the location of files within your site.

To create a Favorites folder, click the appropriate asset category button at the left edge of the Assets panel (any except the bottom two, since, alas, you can't create folders for templates and Library items). Click Favorites at the top of the Assets panel (you can't create folders in Site view). Finally, click the New Favorites Folder button (see Figure 16-13) at the bottom of the Assets panel. When Dreamweaver displays the new folder with its naming rectangle highlighted, type a new name for the folder and then press Enter (but don't use the same name for more than one folder).

To put an asset into a folder, just drag it there from the list. And if you're really obsessive, you can even create subfolders by dragging one folder onto another.

EXTENSION ALERT

Nothing Could Be Kuler

Adobe's Kuler web tool (*http://kuler.adobe.com/*) is an online gallery of color palettes. It lets you build your own favorite sets of colors and offers tools based on the science of color theory to create harmonious color combinations for your site. Even better, you can see thousands of palettes created by *other* web designers, showcasing everything from cool and subtle schemes, to loud and vibrant color mixes. It's a great site if you're eager for a little color inspiration.

To make it even easier for you to use this site, the extension developer WebAssist has a free Dreamweaver extension named PalettePicker. This simple add-on is essentially a floating palette within Dreamweaver that lets you browse or search Kuler's large collection of color palettes. When you find colors you like, you can use Dreamweaver's color box and eye-dropper tool to sample a color from the PalletePicker palette just as you'd sample a color from a picture on a web page. You can find the extension at *www.webassist.com/free-downloads/dreamweaver-extensions/palettepicker.* To learn how to use and install extensions, turn to page 822.

CHAPTER

17

Testing Your Site

As you've no doubt realized by now, building a website involves quite a few steps. At any point in the process, you can easily introduce errors that affect the performance of your pages. Both small mistakes, like typos, and site-shattering errors, like broken links, occur frequently in the web development cycle.

Unfortunately, web designers often don't develop a good procedure for testing their sites. This chapter offers helpful techniques for testing your site, including using Dreamweaver's wide array of site-testing tools.

Site Launch Checklist

Don't wait until you finish your site before developing a thorough strategy for regular testing. By that time, serious design errors may have so completely infested your site's pages that you may have to start over, or at least spend many hours fixing problems you could have prevented early on.

- **Preview early and often.** The single best way to make sure a page looks and functions the way you want it to is to preview it in as many browsers as possible. For a quick test, click the Live View button (page 578) in Dreamweaver's Document toolbar. This is a great way to quickly check JavaScript components and view complex CSS. However, since Dreamweaver's built-in browser is WebKit (a.k.a Apple's Safari browser), Live View doesn't necessarily show you how your page will look in another browser, like Internet Explorer.

  To see how your layouts, CSS, and JavaScript hold up elsewhere, use Dreamweaver's Preview command (File→Preview in Browser) to test your pages in every browser you can get your hands on (Dreamweaver lists your installed browsers when you click Preview, and you select a browser from that list). Make sure the graphics look right, your layout remains intact, and Cascading Style Sheets and Dreamweaver behaviors work as you intended.

For a thorough evaluation, however, you should preview your pages using every combination of browser *and* operating system you think your site's visitors may use. At the very least, try to test your pages using Internet Explorer 6, 7, and 8 on Windows, Firefox on Windows or Mac, and Safari on the Mac. According to the Market Share website (*http://marketshare.hitslink.com/browser-market-share.aspx?qprid=0*) Internet Explorer 6 for Windows is the most popular web browser, followed very closely by IE 8, Firefox, Chrome, Safari, and others. Including all versions, Internet Explorer claims over 60.percent of the world market for browsers (as of December 2009).

Tip: If you already have a site up and running, you can find useful browser information in your site's *log files*. These files track information about visits to your site, including which browsers and platforms your visitors use. Most web hosting companies provide access to these files, as well as software to analyze the confusing code inside them. You can use this information, for example, to see whether *anyone* who visits your site still uses Internet Explorer 6. If no one does, that's one less browser you have to design for.

Unfortunately, you'll discover that what works on one browser/operating system combination may not work on another. That's why you should preview your designs *early* in the process of constructing your site. If you design a page that doesn't work well in Internet Explorer 6 on Windows, for example, it's better to catch and fix that problem immediately than to discover it after you build 100 pages based on that design. In other words, once you create a design you like, don't plow ahead and continue building your site! Check that page in multiple browsers, fix any problems, and then, grasshopper, begin to build.

To test your pages, enroll your friends and family to check your pages on as many browsers and operating systems as possible. You can also use Dreamweaver CS5's built-in support for Adobe's BrowserLab (see below) to get screenshots of your designs.

Note: Internet Explorer 6 is usually where most Web pages fall apart. This old and crotchety browser is full of bugs that often cause hair-pulling bouts of hysteria among web designers. Most of these problems are related to using CSS for layout (see Chapter 9). An approach recommended by professional web designers is to preview your page in Firefox, Safari, or Internet Explorer 8 first. Get the page working in those browsers, and then preview it in IE 6 to fix the bugs. If you design with just IE 6 in mind, you'll find that your site doesn't work in Firefox, Safari, and, in many cases, the ever-growing population of IE 8 browsers. Dreamweaver's Check Browser Compatibility tool gives you one way to track down nasty CSS bugs (see page 398), and if you use Dreamweaver's CSS Layouts (Chapter 9), you'll find that Adobe has already solved many cross-browser problems.

- **Validate your pages.** Previous versions of Dreamweaver included a tool that let you compare your web pages against agreed-upon standards for HTML and other web languages. It wasn't completely reliable, so Adobe removed that feature from Dreamweaver CS5.

Of course, creating valid web pages is still important. Valid pages are more likely to work in a predictable way on all browsers. And if you envision your site on mobile devices such as smartphones and cellphones, valid pages are again your best bet. In addition, one possible cause of page layout problems is invalid HTML, so using a validator can help spot otherwise hard-to-find errors.

You can validate pages in a couple of ways. You can use the W3C's online validator (*http://validator.w3.org*), and since the W3C makes up the rules for HTML, you know the validator's going to be right. You can type in the URL of a page on the web, upload a file from your computer, or copy and paste HTML into a form field. The validator checks the page and lets you know of any errors. If you use Firefox, the Web Developer Toolbar extension makes quick work of testing a web page using the W3C validator. Just launch Firefox and install the extension from *http://chrispederick.com/work/web-developer/*. Restart Firefox, and the newly installed toolbar appears near the top of the browser window (if you don't see it, choose View→Toolbars→Web Developer Toolbar). Now, whenever you preview a page in Firefox, just choose Tools→Validate Local HTML and Firefox will contact the W3C server, feed it your HTML, and then display the results in a new tab.

While you do the bulk of your checking during page development, you should do some troubleshooting at the end of the process, just before you move a page (or entire site) to your web server:

- **Check the spelling on your pages.** Amazingly, people often overlook this simple step. As a result, you can easily find otherwise professional-looking pages undermined by sloppy spelling. To learn how to use Dreamweaver's built-in spell-checker, see page 86.
- **Check your links.** A website can be a complex and twisted collection of interconnected files. Web pages, graphics, Flash movies, and other types of files all work together. Unfortunately, if one file is moved or deleted, problems can ripple through the entire site. Use Dreamweaver's Check Links command to identify and fix broken links (see below).
- **Run site reports.** It's always the little things. When you build a website, small errors inevitably creep into your pages. While not necessarily life-threatening, forgetting to title a page or to add an Alt property to an image does diminish the quality and professionalism of a site. Use Dreamweaver's site-reporting feature to quickly identify these problems (see page 683).

Previewing Web Pages in BrowserLab

Adobe's BrowserLab service is like having a legion of Macintoshes and PCs with various browser types and versions at your beck and call. Basically, BrowserLab provides screenshots of your web pages so you can see how your designs hold up in different browsers. If you're on Windows and don't have access to a Mac, or vice versa, BrowserLab is a simple way to cross-browser test. You can even test interactive page elements, like Spry drop-down menus.

Note: As of this writing BrowserLab is still in a beta-testing phase and is free. However, Adobe ultimately plans to turn this into a pay service, probably with a monthly service contract. They haven't released any details on pricing yet, but they indicated that they want to offer it at a price that's lower than similar commercial services, like the ones described in the FAQ on page 673.

BrowserLab Setup

Dreamweaver lets you access BrowserLab as if you were previewing your page in a web browser, by choosing File→Preview In Browser→BrowserLab. However, you need to do a little setup before you can get it to work:

1. **Get an Adobe Account at *www.adobe.com/cfusion/membership*.**

   To use BrowserLab you need an Adobe account: it's free and you only need to supply a few pieces of information, like your name, email address, city, country, and Zip code. Once you have an account, you can sign up for BrowserLab

2. **Visit *https://browserlab.adobe.com* and click the Sign In button in the top right of the page.**

   A form appears asking for your Adobe membership ID (that's your email address) and the password you supplied when you signed up for the Adobe account.

3. **Type your email address and Adobe member password, and click the Sign In button.**

   The first time you sign in you have to accept the "Terms of Use" statement. You know these things: lots of legal mumbo-jumbo that nobody ever reads.

   Once you sign in, you go to the main Adobe BrowserLab screen…there's not much too it, but this is where you'll be able to preview your web pages from Dreamweaver. But before you do that, you should set up a "Browser Set."

4. **Click the Browser Sets button (see Figure 17-1) and check off the browsers in which you wish to test your pages.**

   That becomes your browser set. As of this writing, BrowserLab supports 14 browsers, and they add more as more browsers come out. The more browsers you choose, the slower the service, since it must take a separate screenshot for each browser, so here's one strategy to streamline the testing process: first, choose only a handful of browsers for the Default Browser Set. Pick the popular browsers that you don't have easy access to. For example, if you're on Windows, you may have Internet Explorer 8, Firefox, and Chrome installed, but not IE 6 or 7, or any of the Mac browsers. In that case, select IE 6 and 7, and Safari 3 and 4 for Mac. If you're on a Mac, choose all the Internet Explorer versions, but since Firefox is pretty much the same on Mac and Windows, just test your page in Firefox for Mac. You should use this basic browser set for your routine testing as you build your pages.

Then, create a second browser set (click the Add New Browser Set button as pictured in Figure 17-1). Name it something like "Complete Set," and check all the browsers you don't have access to. Most likely, this will include quite a few browsers, and it'll take some time to test this set, so use it after you finish testing with your Default Browser Set. In other words, get your pages to look good in the Default Browser Set, and then, as one last check, use the complete browser set to check your pages.

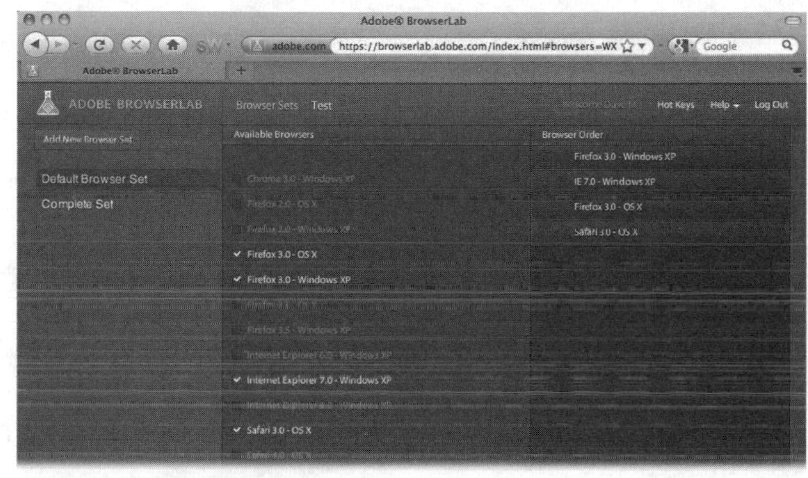

Figure 17-1: *Adobe's BrowserLab service creates screenshots of your web pages in a variety of browser brands, browser versions, and operating systems. Click the Browser Sets button at the top of the screen to define which browsers you want to preview in, and create different browser sets. Once you tell BrowserLab which browsers to use, click the Test button at the top of the screen to return to the view for testing your Web pages.*

Testing Pages in BrowserLab

Once you set up an account and create your browser sets, you're ready to start testing your pages. BrowserLab lets you test directly from Dreamweaver, or you can test pages directly within BrowserLab so long as BrowserLab can grab those pages from the Web (as described in Figure 17-2 and in the note on the next page).

To view a page from within Dreamweaver, open the page you want to check, and then choose File→Preview In Browser→BrowserLab. Dreamweaver opens a small, floating Adobe BrowserLab panel (see Figure 17-2). If you don't have a web browser open, Dreamweaver launches one and goes to the BrowserLab website. If you're not logged in, you have to do so using your Adobe Membership credentials as described in step 3 on page 668.

The BrowserLab site displays a message asking you to wait, letting you know it's busy creating screenshots of the tested page. This can take a while (30 seconds or more), so be patient. Once BrowserLab's done, it displays a screenshot of your page (see Figure 17-3).

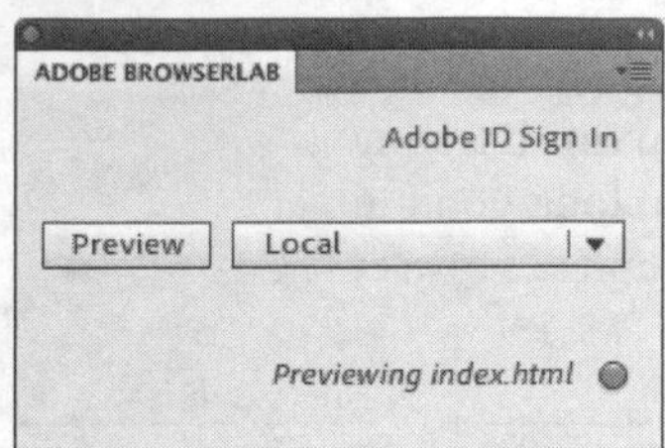

Figure 17-2:
The Adobe BrowserLab panel opens when you preview a page in Adobe BrowserLab. You can also access it by choosing Window‣Extensions‣Adobe BrowserLab or from the CS Live menu in the application toolbar (see Figure 1-6). Clicking the Preview button is the same as choosing File→Preview In Browser→BrowserLab. The file location menu (the one listed Local in this screenshot) is described in the Note below.

Note: The Adobe BrowserLab panel (Figure 17-2) lets you choose whether to preview a Local page (meaning the page you're currently working on in Dreamweaver) or a page from your web Server. Usually, the Local option is the best way to go. You'll only want to use the server option for database-driven pages (like those discussed in Part Six of this book) and other pages that depend on information coming from your web server. And even if you create those kinds of sites, you can still use the Local option if you set up a testing server on your system (see page 836 to learn how). However, to test local dynamic pages in the BrowserLab, you must first click the Live View button (page 578).

You can use the BrowserLab's browser menu to see screenshots from different browser (see Figure 17-3) or to switch browser sets (after which BrowserLab will create screenshots for all the browsers listed in the new browser set).

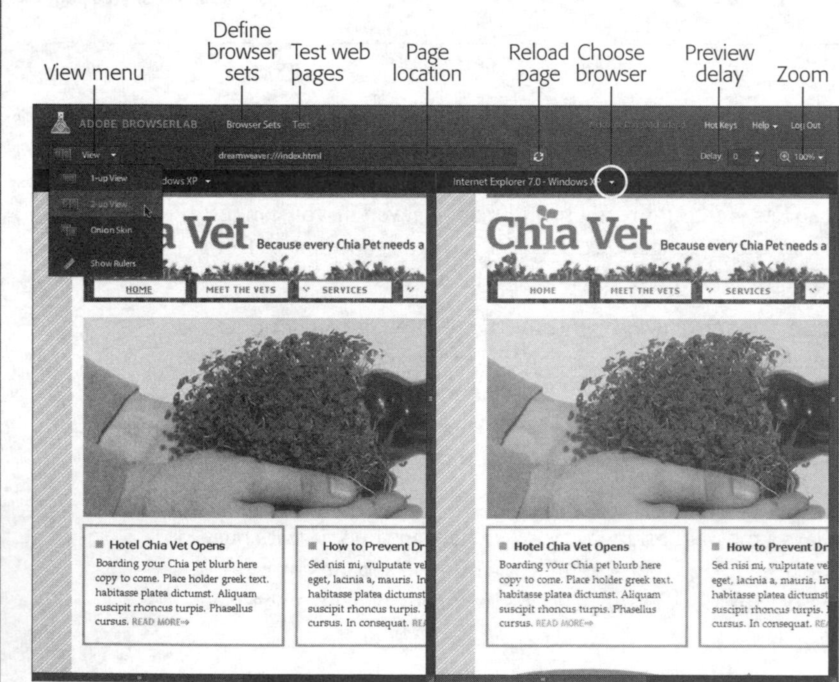

Figure 17-3:
Use the View menu to select different views. This is a 2-up view, meaning you'll see two screenshots from two different browsers side-by-side. Use the browser menu (circled) to display the screenshot from another one of the browsers in a browser set. In the page location field, you can type in an absolute URL pointing to a page that already exists on the Web, and have BrowserLab test that page.

Use BrowserLab's View menu to see two screenshots side-by-side (select "2-Up"), or use the Onion Skin view to see the different screenshots superimposed on top of each other (see Figure 17-3). The latter can help you identify page elements that appear at different widths in different browsers and it can highlight differences in how different browsers interpret margin and padding settings.

Tip: BrowserLab includes a "Preview delay" setting (see Figure 17-3) that forestalls the screen capture for a specified number of seconds. This is useful if a page has to download a lot of files, like a Flash movie, or if you have JavaScript that runs when the page loads and alters the look of the page. If your previews don't look right, try changing the setting to 5 seconds and previewing again.

Unfortunately, BrowserLab can't tell you *why* your page looks different in different browsers. For that, you'll have to brush up on your CSS, use Dreamweaver's "Check Browser Compatibility" tool (page 398), and learn about some common CSS problems (and solutions) on page 401.

Capturing JavaScript interactivity

Some screenshot services can only take a picture of a page when it first loads. Because these services are just automated screenshots of a page's HTML, they can't capture effects that your visitors might trigger, like a menu that drops down when your guest mouses over it. BrowserLab, with the aid of Dreamweaver's Live View, can capture screenshots of most kinds of JavaScript interactivity, such as the drop-down menu in the Spry menu bar (page 184), or the look of a validation error in a Spry validation field (page 478).

To do this, you need to use Dreamweaver's Live View (discussed on page 578), which lets you preview a page, complete with interactivity, directly in Dreamweaver. Just click the Live View button in the Document window (see Figure 17-4), which displays your page using the WebKit rendering engine (the same program behind the Safari and Chrome browsers). You can move your mouse over a JavaScript-powered Spry menu bar and see a drop-down menu, or click on a Spry collapsible panel to display a normally hidden <div> tag (page 534).

If you want to see what a JavaScript effect looks like in other browsers, you need to "freeze" the page once you trigger the effect and then preview it in BrowserLab. To "freeze" JavaScript in Live View, hit the F6 key or choose "Freeze JavaScript" from the Live View Options menu (see Figure 17-4). Once you do so, choose File→Preview In Browser→BrowserLab. BrowserLab captures a screenshots of the page in the chosen browser in that state.

Find and Fix Broken Links

Broken links are inevitable. If you delete a file from your site, move a page or graphic outside Dreamweaver, or simply type an incorrect path name to a file, you may end up with broken links and missing graphics. In the B.D. era (Before Dreamweaver), you could fix such problems only by methodically examining every link on every page on your site. Fortunately, Dreamweaver's link-checking features automate the process.

Note: In this context, a link doesn't mean just a hyperlink connecting one page to another. Dreamweaver checks links to external files, such as PNGs, GIFs, JPEGs that reside in a different folder, external CSS style sheets, and Flash movies. For example, if a graphic is missing or isn't in the place your page specifies, Dreamweaver reports a broken link.

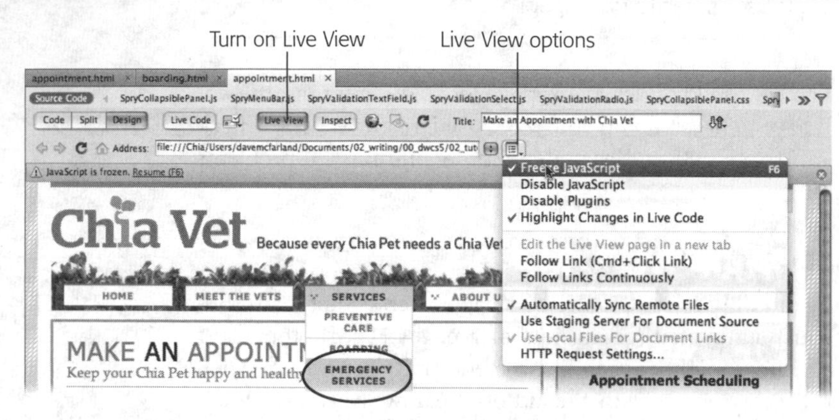

***Figure 17-4:** When you're in Live View, Dreamweaver lets you "freeze" a JavaScript effect, like a drop-down menu, by pressing the F6 key or choosing Freeze JavaScript from the Live View Options menu. Use this feature with BrowserLab preview to see how a dynamic JavaScript effect (like the drop down menu circled here) looks in different browsers.*

Finding Broken Links

Dreamweaver's Check Links Sitewide command scans an entire site's worth of files, and reports all links and paths that don't lead to a file. (It's one of Dreamweaver's site management features, meaning that you have to set up a local site before you can use this command; see page 640 for instructions on how to do that.) Note that Dreamweaver checks only links and paths *within* the local site folder; it doesn't check links that lead to other people's sites (see the Note later for a tool that can help with *that* annoying chore).

Note: If your local site contains a lot of pages, you may not want to check links in one or more folders whose pages *you know* have no broken links. You can exclude files from the Check Links Sitewide operation using the Cloaking feature described on page 708. Doing so also makes the link-checking operation go faster.

Checking just one page

To check links on an open page, save it in your local site folder and choose File→Check Page→Links (or press Shift+F8 [shift-F8]). Dreamweaver scans the page and opens the Link Checker window, which lists any broken links (see Figure 17-5). If Dreamweaver doesn't find any—you HTML god, you—the window comes up empty.

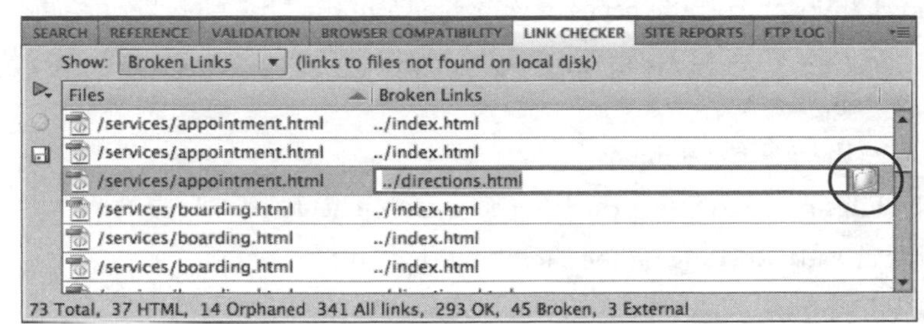

Figure 17-5:
The Check Links Sitewide command generates a list of all external links and orphaned files (files with no links to them). If you wish, click the Save (floppy disk) button to save all this information into a tab-delimited text file. You can also fix a broken link directly inside this panel using the "Browse for File" button (circled).

FREQUENTLY ASKED QUESTION

Testing Your Sites in Multiple Browsers

How can I test my website if I have only a couple of the most common browsers on my computer?

If you don't have every browser ever created installed on your Mac, Windows, and Linux machines (you *do* have all three, don't you?), you can use Adobe's BrowserLab service as discussed on page 667.

But you can find other alternatives as well, such as the testing service at the commercial website *www.browsercam.com*. This service takes screenshots of your site using a variety of browsers and operating systems. The downside: it's $40 a month (ouch). Another service, *CrossBrowserTesting.com* is $19.95 a month for 150 minutes of use and offers an added benefit: interactive testing. You get to see your page running remotely on a PC under your control—you can test features that a screenshot can't capture, like Flash movie playback, animation, and JavaScript interactions.

Browsershots (*www.browsershots.org*) is a free alternative, which provides screenshots for a wide range of browsers on Linux and Windows.

Windows users can try out a program named IETester (*www.my-debugbar.com/wiki/IETester/HomePage*). It lets you see how your pages look in multiple versions of IE including 6, 7, and 8.

If you're a Mac person with an Intel chip at the heart of your system, you can install Windows on your machine using Apple's Boot-camp technology (*www.apple.com/bootcamp*) or use third-party "virtualization" software that runs Mac OS X and Windows simultaneously on the same computer (and believe it or not, the universe does *not* implode). VMWare Fusion for Mac (*www.vmware.com/products/fusion/*) and Parallels Desktop (*www.parallels.com/products/desktop/*), for example, lets you run multiple versions of Windows (XP, Vista, and Windows 7) as well as Mac OS X.

Note: Although Dreamweaver can't check links to the outside world, a free tool from the W3C can. You can find its link checker at *http://validator.w3.org/checklink*. This tool checks both internal links (among pages on the same site) and external links (to other sites). The only possible downside: The pages you wish to check must already be on the Web. Windows users find that Xenu's Link Sleuth, a free, automated link checker, can help speed up the process of checking external links (*http://home.snafu.de/tilman/xenulink.html*). In addition, Firefox users can download the LinkChecker extension at *www.kevinfreitas.net/extensions/linkchecker/*.

Checking specific pages

You can check links on specific pages of your site from the Link Checker panel:

1. **Choose Window→Results to open the Results panel, and then click the Link Checker tab.**

   The Link Checker panel opens.

2. **Use the Files panel to select the site you wish to check (see Figure 16-6).**

   If you're already working on the site, skip this step.

3. **In the Files panel, select the files you want to check.**

   For techniques on selecting files and folders in the Files panel, see the box on the opposite page.

Tip: Selecting a folder in the Files panel makes Dreamweaver scan all the files in that folder.

---

4. **In the Link Checker panel, click the green-arrow icon. From the menu that appears, choose "Check Links for Selected Files/Folders in Site".**

   Alternatively, you can right-click (Control-click) the selected files, and then from the shortcut menu, choose Check Links→Selected Files.

   Either way, Dreamweaver scans the pages and displays any broken links in the Link Checker panel (Figure 17-5).

UP TO SPEED

Selection Shortcuts for the Files Panel

You'll often want to use the tools in the Results panel on more than one page in your website. Fortunately, most of these tools can work on multiple pages in the Files panel.

You know that you click a file to select it, but you can also select several consecutively listed files at once: Click the first one, scroll if necessary, and then Shift-click the last one. Dreamweaver highlights all the files between your first and final clicks.

If you want to select files nonconsecutive files, click each one while pressing the Ctrl (⌘) key.

Once you select one or more files, you can deselect any single one by Ctrl-clicking (⌘-clicking) it once again.

Dreamweaver also includes a snazzy command for selecting recently modified files in the Files panel. Suppose you want to select all the files you created or changed today (to see if the links work or to upload them to your web server). To use this command, in the upper-right corner of the Files panel, you need to click the panel's contextual-menu button. From the menu that appears, select Edit→Select Recently Modified.

The Select Recently Modified window appears. You can either specify a range of dates (for example, files you created or changed between February 1, 2009, and February 7, 2009) or a number of days (to specify all the files you modified in, say, the last 30 days). (The last option–Modified By–works only with Adobe's Contribute program.) Set the options, click OK, and Dreamweaver selects the appropriate files in the Files panel.

Checking an entire website

You can check all the links on all the pages in your site in any of three ways. For all three techniques, you have to have your website selected in the Files panel (press F8 [Shift-⌘-F] to open the Files panel, and then use the panel's menu to select your site).

- Choose Site→Check Links Sitewide or use the keyboard shortcut Ctrl+F8 (⌘-F8).
- Open the Files panel, and then right-click (Control-click) any file. From the shortcut menu, choose Check Links→Entire Local Site.
- Open the Link Checker panel (Window→Results to open the Results panel, and then click the Link Checker tab), click the green-arrow icon, and then, from its menu, choose "Check Links for Entire Current Local Site".

Once again, Dreamweaver scans your site and opens the Link Checker panel, which lists files containing broken links (Figure 17-5).

Fixing Broken Links

Of course, simply finding broken links is only half the battle. You also need to *fix* them. The Link Checker panel provides a quick and easy way to do so:

1. **In the Link Checker panel, click a path in the Broken Links column.**

   Dreamweaver highlights the path, and displays a tiny folder icon to the right (circled in Figure 17-5).

Note: The Link Checker panel shows you which pages *contain* broken links, but doesn't show you the text or images of the broken links themselves, which can make it difficult to figure out how to fix them ("Was that a button that links to the home page?"). In cases like that, *double-click* the file name in the Link Checker panel's left column. Dreamweaver opens the Web page and, even better, highlights the link on the page.

Once you determine where the link should lead ("Oh yeah. That's the button to the haggis buffet menu."), you can fix the link right on the page (see page 165) or go back to the Link Checker panel and make the change as described in the next step.

---

2. **Click the tiny folder icon.**

   The Select File dialog box opens. From here, you can navigate to and (in the next step) select the correct page—the one that the link *should* have opened.

   If you prefer, you can type a path directly in the Link Checker panel. Doing so usually isn't a good idea, however, since it's difficult to understand the path from one page to another just by looking at the Link Checker panel. Searching for the proper page using the Select File dialog box is a much more accurate and trouble-free method.

3. **In the Select File dialog box, double-click a web page.**

   The dialog box disappears, and Dreamweaver fixes the link.

If your site contains other links pointing to the same missing file, Dreamweaver asks if you'd like to fix the same broken link on those pages, too—an amazing timesaver that can quickly repair broken links on dozens of pages.

Note: Dreamweaver's behavior is a bit odd when it comes to fixing the same broken link, however. Once you fix one link, it remains selected in the Link Checker panel. You must click another broken link, or one of the buttons in the window, before Dreamweaver asks if you'd like to fix that same broken link on other pages.

---

4. **Continue to fix broken links, following steps 1 to 3.**

   When you repair all the broken links, you can close the Results panel by double-clicking anywhere along the top row of tabs (for example, double-click the Link Checker tab). Double-clicking any tab reopens the Results panel.

Listing External Links

Although Dreamweaver doesn't verify links to other websites on your pages, it does show you a list of such external links when you run the link checker. To see this list, choose External Links from the Link Checker panel's Show menu (see Figure 17-6). The list includes absolute URLs leading to other sites (like *http://www.yahoo.com*) as well as email links (like *mailto:appointment@chia-vet.com*).

This window is especially useful if you created a link to a certain external website several times throughout your site, and you've decided to change the link. For example, if you discovered through testing (or through the W3C Link Checker mentioned in the note on page 673) that an external link you've peppered throughout your site no longer works, then:

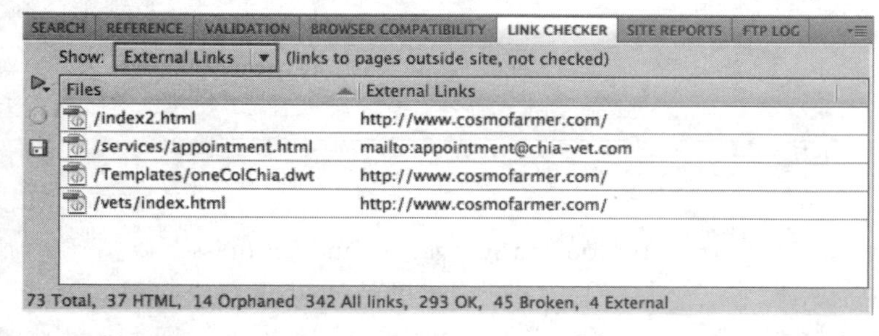

Figure 17-6: *Although Dreamweaver can't check external links, you can use this window to change the URL of an external link.*

1. **Choose Site→Check Links Sitewide (or press Ctrl+F8 [⌘-F8]).**

   Dreamweaver scans your site, and then opens the Link Checker panel.

2. **From the Show pop-up menu, choose External Links.**

   The window lists links you created to sites outside your own.

3. **Click the external link you want to change.**

   Dreamweaver highlights the link, indicating that you can now edit it.

4. **Type in the new URL, and then press Enter (Return).**

   If other pages contain the old URL, Dreamweaver asks if you want to fix them as well. If so, click Yes; the deed is done.

Orphaned Files

The Link Checker panel also provides a list of files that aren't used by any page in your site—*orphaned files*, as they're called. You wind up with an orphaned file when, for example, you save a GIF to your site folder but then never use it on a web page. Or suppose you eliminate the only link to an old page that you don't need anymore, making it an orphaned file. Unless you think you may link to it in the future, you can delete it to clean up unnecessary clutter.

In fact, that's the primary purpose of this feature: to locate old and unused files, and delete them. Here's how it works:

1. **Choose Site→Check Links Sitewide, or press Ctrl+F8 (⌘-F8).**

   Dreamweaver opens the Link Checker panel.

2. **From the Show menu, choose Orphaned Files.**

   The list of orphaned files appears (see Figure 17-7).

3. **Select the files you want to delete.**

   For example, by Ctrl-clicking (⌘-clicking) the files.

4. **Press Delete.**

   Dreamweaver asks if you really want to delete the files. Click OK if you do or Cancel if you suddenly get cold feet.

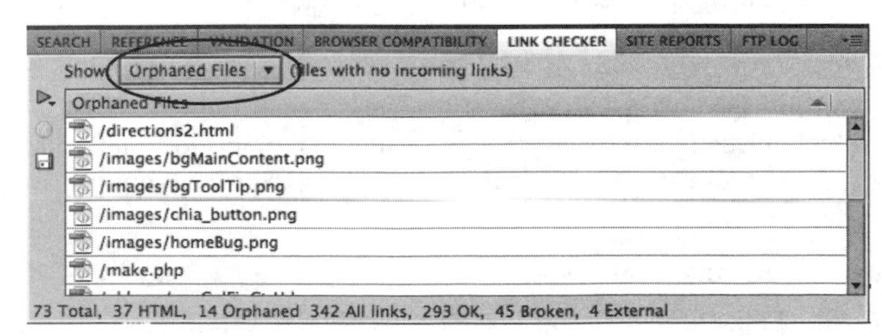

Figure 17-7: *Identify (and delete) unused files with Dreamweaver's Link Checker panel. This panel lists external links and orphaned files as well as broken links; use the Show menu (circled) to isolate the different types of link.*

Before you get spring-cleaning fever and delete all orphaned files in your site, however, keep a few pointers in mind:

- Just because a file isn't *currently* in use doesn't mean you won't need it again later. For example, say you have an employee-of-the-month page. In March, you included a photo of Robin Albert, your best salesperson. In April, someone else got the award, so you removed Robin's photo from the page. The photos still resides on your computer; it's just that no web page currently uses it, making it an orphaned file. But next month you may need the photo again, when Robin develops a spurt of motivation. So make sure a file is really useless before deleting it.
- More important, Dreamweaver may flag files your site actually *needs* as orphaned. For example, some sites include what's called a *splash page*: an introductory page that first appears when someone comes to the site. It can be a page with a bold graphic and the text "Click here to enter the site". Or it may be a fancy Flash movie intended to make a big impact on your visitors. Usually, this page is nothing more than a welcome mat that leads to the *real* home page. Since it's simply an introductory page, no other page in the site links to it. Unfortunately, that's precisely what Dreamweaver considers an orphaned file.
- If you write your own JavaScript code, you may reference graphic files and web pages. Dreamweaver doesn't keep track of references in your JavaScript code, and identifies those files as orphans (unless you insert or link them elsewhere in the page or site).

  On the other hand, Dreamweaver is somewhat smarter when it comes to Spry widgets and Dreamweaver Behaviors. It can track files referenced as part of its own JavaScript programs—for example, graphic files you use in a rollover effect—and doesn't list them as orphaned.

The bottom line is that while this report can be useful, use it cautiously when deleting files.

Changing a Link Throughout a Site

Suppose you create a page to teach your visitors about the basics of the HTML language. You think this page would be really, really helpful to your visitors, so you create links to it from every page on your site. After a while, you realize that you just don't have the time to keep this page up-to-date, but you still want to help your visitors get this information. Why not change the link so it points to a more current and informative source? Using Dreamweaver's Change Link Sitewide command, you can do just that:

1. **Choose Site→Change Link Sitewide.**

   The Change Link Sitewide dialog box opens (see Figure 17-8).

   This dialog box offers two fields: "Change all links to" and "Into links to". Understanding what you're supposed to do at this point is easier if you imagine that the first label actually says Change All Links That *Currently* Point To. In other words, you first indicate where those links point now; then you'll indicate where you'd like them to point instead.

Type the old web address in the "Change all links to" field. For example, if your aim is to round up every link that now points to Yahoo and redirect it to Google, you could start by typing *http://www.yahoo.com* here.

If the links you're trying to change refer to a page in your own site, however, proceed to step 2.

2. **To the right of the Change All Links To field, click the folder icon.**

   The "Select Link to Change" dialog box opens. You're about to specify the file that the links should point to *now*.

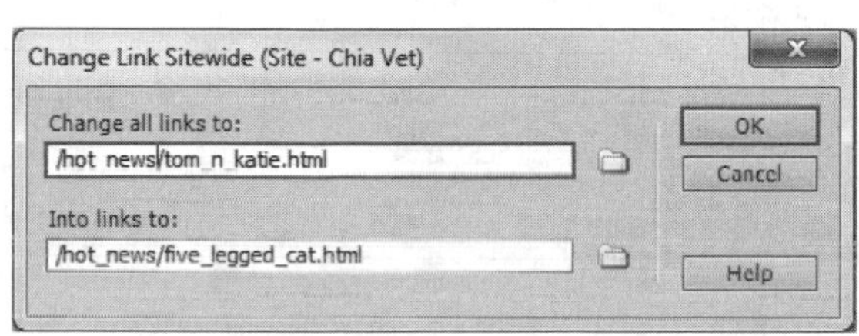

Figure 17-8: *Dreamweaver uses a root-relative link to specify the page whose URL you want to change, as indicated by the slash (/). Don't worry: This doesn't mean that Dreamweaver makes the link root-relative. It's just how Dreamweaver identifies the location of the page in the site. See page 161 for more on root-relative links.*

3. **Select a file in the local site folder; click OK (Windows) or Choose (Mac).**

   In the following steps, Dreamweaver changes every link that should lead to *this file*, whether it's a graphic, Cascading Style Sheet file, or any other external file that can be part of a web page.

Note: As a shortcut to following steps 1, 2, and 3, in the Files panel, you can select a file, and *then* choose Site→Change Link Sitewide. Dreamweaver automatically adds the selected file's path to the "Change all links to" field.

Now it's time to substitute the new URL or file—the one to which all those links will be redirected. If you're reassigning them to a different website, you can type its URL directly into the "Change all links to" field. For example, in the previous example, you can type in *http://www.google.com*.

Note: For another way to change one external link into another, see Figure 17-6.

If you'd like the changed links to point to a file on your own site instead, proceed to step 4.

4. **To the right of the "Into links to" field, click the folder icon.**

   The "Select Link to Change" dialog box opens.

5. **Select a file in the local site, and then click OK (Windows) or Choose (Mac).**

   You just selected the new file to which you want to link. In other words, every link that once led to the file you selected in step 3 now links to this file. You can select graphics, Cascading Style Sheets, or any other external file you can include in a web page.

   You'll get unpredictable results, however, if you change a link that points to a graphic file into, say, a link that points to a web page, or vice versa. Make sure the "before" and "after" links share the same file type: web page, style sheet, or graphic.

6. **Click OK to make the change.**

   The same Update Files dialog box you encountered in the last chapter appears, listing every page that the change will affect.

7. **Click Update to update the pages.**

   Dreamweaver scans your site, and updates the pages.

Cleaning Up HTML (and XHTML)

You've been reading about what great HTML code Dreamweaver writes, and how, no matter what doctype you pick (XHTML 1 or HTML 4.01, for example), Dreamweaver adds the correct tags in the correct order. But there are exceptions to every rule. In the process of formatting text, deleting elements, and—in general—building a web page, it's quite possible to end up with less-than-optimal HTML coding. While Dreamweaver usually catches potentially sloppy HTML, you may nonetheless run across instances of empty tags, redundant tags, and nested tags in your Dreamweaver pages.

For example, in the normal course of adding, editing, and deleting content on a page (either by hand or even in Dreamweaver's Design view), you can occasionally end up with code like this:

```
<div align="center"> </div>
```

This empty tag doesn't serve any purpose, and only adds unnecessary HTML to your page. Remember, the less code your page uses, the faster it loads. Eliminating redundant tags can improve your site's download speed.

Another possible source of errors is you. When you type HTML in Code view or open pages created by another program, you may introduce errors that you need to clean up later.

Note: The Clean Up HTML command doesn't fix really bad errors, like missing closing tags, or improperly nested tags. You can have Dreamweaver automatically fix these types of problems when opening a file (see page 412).

Aware of its own limitations (and yours), Dreamweaver provides a command that's designed to streamline the code in your pages: Clean Up HTML (if you're using Dreamweaver's XHTML mode, the command is called Clean Up XHTML). This command not only improves the HTML in your page, it can also strip out other nonessential code, such as comments and special Dreamweaver markup code, and it can eliminate a specific tag or tags.

Note: The Clean Up HTML command is extremely useful. Once you try it a few times, you'll probably want to use it on all your pages. Unfortunately, it doesn't come with a keyboard shortcut. This is a classic example, where Dreamweaver's *keyboard-shortcut editor* is just the white knight you need; using it, you can add a keystroke combination to trigger this command from the keyboard. See page 817 for details.

To use this command:

1. **Open a web page you want to clean up.**

   Unfortunately, this great feature works only on one page at a time. No cleaning up a site's worth of pages in one fell swoop! Accordingly, it's best to first use the Site Reports feature (see page 683) to identify problem pages. *Then* open them in Dreamweaver and run this command.

2. **Choose Commands→Clean Up HTML (or Clean Up XHTML).**

   The Clean Up HTML/XHTML window appears (see Figure 17-9).

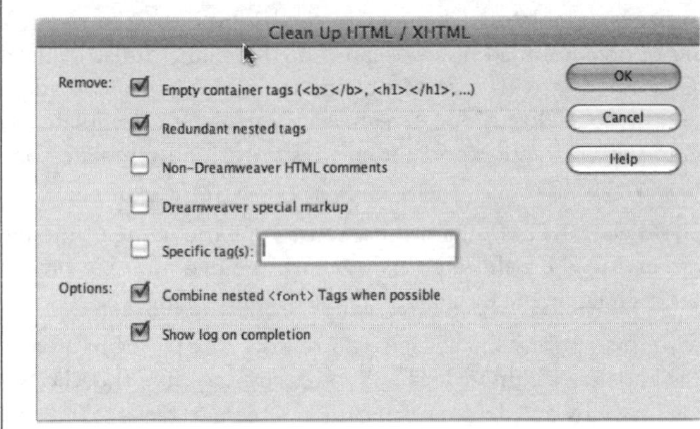

***Figure 17-9:** The Clean Up HTML/XHTML command lets you strip out redundant and useless code. You can even use it to strip out unnecessary tags by specifying a tag in the "Specific tag(s)" field (although the "Find and Replace" command provides a much more powerful way to identify and remove HTML tags; see page 801).*

3. **Turn on the checkboxes for the options you want.**

   Here's a rundown:

   - **Empty Container Tags** deletes any tags that don't actually contain anything. For example, you may have deleted text you set in boldface, leaving behind opening and closing bold tags without any text in between: <b></b>. Or you may have deleted an image within a link, leaving behind a useless pair of <a> tags. It's always a good idea to turn on this option.

- **Redundant Nested Tags** deletes tags that appear within other tags of the same type, like this: <b>You can't get any <b>bolder</b> than bold</b>. The inner set of bold tags does no good, so choosing this option would produce this HTML: <b> You can't get any bolder than bold</b>. This option is extremely useful.

  Non-Dreamweaver HTML Comments deletes any comments *not* inserted by Dreamweaver as part of its site management tools. For example, the Dreamweaver Template tool (Chapter 20) inserts HTML comments to help you identify different parts of the template. But web designers also place notes within code as instructions or to explain parts of the code. (These comments are invisible in a browser, by the way. They appear only in the Code view, or in Dreamweaver's document window as a gold comment icon.) However, if the page is finished and you doubt you'll need the information the comments contain, you can decrease the file size of a page a little bit by using this option.

Note: Dreamweaver's Clean Up HTML command doesn't strip out CSS comments. If you use Dreamweaver's CSS Layouts, you'll find the style sheets loaded with CSS comments. For a quick way to remove those types of comments, visit *www.foundationphp.com/tools/css_comments.php*. There, you can download a "stored query" (a reusable search) to use with Dreamweaver's "Find and Replace" tool (page 801).

- **Dreamweaver Special Markup** deletes any special code that Dreamweaver inserts. Dreamweaver relies on certain code in some of its features, including tracing images, templates (Chapter 20), and Libraries (Chapter 19). Choosing this option eliminates the special code that makes those features work, so use this option with care. (Since the template feature can add a fair amount of this specialized code, Dreamweaver includes a Template Export command that lets you export an entire site with all template code removed. See page 787.)
- **Specific Tag(s)** deletes HTML tags you specify. Type the name of the tag (without brackets) in the field like this: *font*. To remove multiple tags at once, separate each tag name by a comma, like this: *font, blink*.

  Be careful with this option. Since it lets you remove *any* tag from a page, you could easily delete an important and necessary tag (like the <body> tag) from your page by accident. Furthermore, Dreamweaver's "Find and Replace" command provides a much more powerful tool for doing this kind of surgery (see page 801).
- **Combine Nested <font> Tags When Possible** combines multiple *font* properties into a single tag. Hopefully, you've moved to CSS for all of your text formatting needs, so you don't use the <font> tag and don't need this option.
- If you want to see a report of all the changes Dreamweaver makes to a page, turn on **Show Log on Completion**.

4. **Click OK to clean up the page.**

   If you selected "Show Log on Completion", a dialog box appears, listing the types and number of changes that Dreamweaver made to the page.

Note: When running this command on an XHTML page, Dreamweaver also checks to make sure the syntax of the page matches the requirements of an XHTML document. Among other concerns, in XHTML, all tags must be lowercase, and any empty tags must be terminated correctly <br /> for the line break tag, for example. Dreamweaver fixes such problems.

As long as you keep the page open, you can undo changes Dreamweaver made. Suppose you asked Dreamweaver to remove comments, and then suddenly realized you really did need them. Ctrl+Z (⌘-Z) does the trick.

Site Reporting

The Clean Up HTML command is a great way to make sure your code is well-written. But what if you forget about it until after you've built all 500 pages of your site? Do you have to open each page and run the command—whether there's a problem or not?

Fortunately, no. Dreamweaver's Site Reports feature makes identifying problems throughout a site a snap. Dreamweaver not only locates the problems fixed by the Clean Up HTML command, it checks your pages for other problems, such as missing titles, empty Alt properties for images, and other issues that can make your site less accessible to disabled web surfers.

Tip: To save time when running a report, you can exclude selected folders from a Site Report using the cloaking feature described on page 708.

After you run a report, Dreamweaver displays a list of pages with problems. Unfortunately, the Site Reports feature only *finds* problems, it doesn't fix them. (To see the full life cycle of an HTML error, jump ahead to Figure 17-12.) You have to open and fix each page individually.

To run a report on one or more web pages, proceed like this:

1. **Choose Site ›Reports.**

   The Reports window opens (see Figure 17-10).

2. **From the "Report on" menu, select the files you want to analyze.**

   Dreamweaver can report on a single web page, on multiple pages, or even on an entire site. Choose Current Document to check the web page you have open at the moment. Entire Current Local Site" checks every web page in the local site folder, including folders within the site folder. This option is great when you want to check your entire site prior to uploading it to a web server and making it "live" (more on that in Chapter 18).

Selected Files in Site checks only the files you choose in the Files panel. You need to open the Files panel and then select files in the local file list for this option to work. See the box on page 674 for ways to select files in the Files panel. Choose this option when you modified or added pages on a site, and you're ready to move them to the web server.

Folder checks all Web pages in a selected folder. After you choose this option, an empty field and a folder icon appear. Click the folder icon; a dialog box gives you the opportunity to locate and select the folder you want to check, including any folders inside it. You can also use this option when you wish to check pages that aren't actually part of the current site.

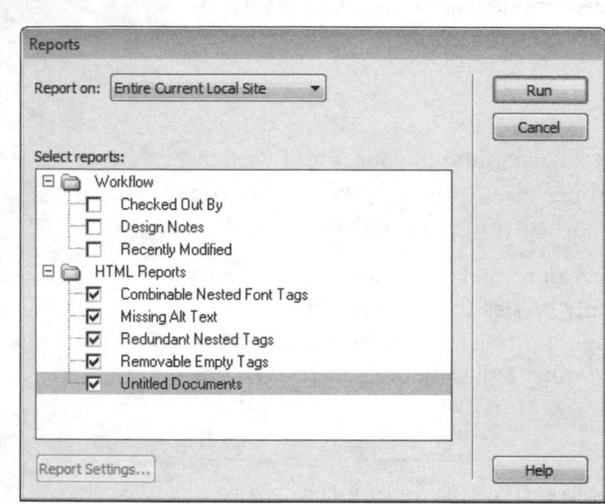

Figure 17-10:
Dreamweaver's Site Reports feature makes quick work of finding common page errors. You won't use all these options, but at the very least make sure you check for missing Alt text (page 224) and any untitled documents before you put a new website up on the Internet.

3. **Select the types of reports you want Dreamweaver to generate.**

   Dreamweaver displays two kinds of reports in the Reports window. The first set, Workflow Reports, deals mostly with features that facilitate working with others as part of a production team (see the following chapter). The last option in this group—Recently Modified—generates a list of files that you either created or modified within a certain number of days or within a range of dates (February 1 of last year to the present, say). When you run this type of report, Dreamweaver lists the files in the Site Reports panel *and* opens a Web page listing the files in your browser.

Note: The Recently Modified site report looks for files created or changed in the last seven days, but you can adjust that time frame. In the Reports window, select Recently Modified, and click the Report Settings button (Figure 17-10). A window appears where you can change the range of dates to check.

In fact, you'll find the technique described on page 674 more useful. It not only identifies recently modified files, it also selects them in the Files panel, giving you many more options for acting on this information. For example, with those files selected, you can upload them to your server, run find-and-replace operations on just those files, or apply many other tools.

The second type of report, HTML Reports, is useful for locating common errors, such as forgetting to title a web page or forgetting to add an Alt property to an image.

Three of the HTML Report options—Combinable Nested Font Tags, Redundant Nested Tags, and Removable Empty Tags—search for pages with common code mistakes. These problems are the same ones fixed by the Clean Up HTML command (see page 680).

Turn on Missing Alt Text to search for pages with images without a text description (see page 224).

Finally, turn on Untitled Documents to identify pages that are either missing a title or still have Dreamweaver's default title.

Note: The Site Report command doesn't identify XHTML syntax errors like those fixed by the Clean Up XHTML command (see page 680).

---

4. **Click Run.**

   Dreamweaver analyzes the pages you specified, and then it produces a report that lists pages that match your report settings (see Figure 17-11). Each line in the Results window displays the name of the file, the line number where the error occurs, and a description of the error.

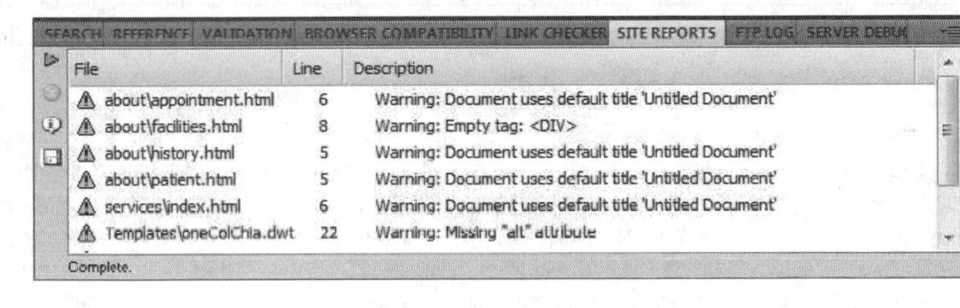

Figure 17-11: *If you decide that it's taking too long for Dreamweaver to generate the report, you can always stop it. In the Results panel's left-hand toolbar, click the icon that looks like a red stop sign with an X through it.*

5. **In the Results panel, double-click the file to open it.**

   Dreamweaver opens the file, and automatically highlights the offending code.

6. **Fix the problem according to its type.**

   For a page containing Combinable Nested Font Tags, Redundant Nested Tags, or Removable Empty Tags errors, use the Clean Up HTML command as described on page 680.

   For pages missing a title, add one by using the technique described on page 44.

You can add missing Alt properties using the Property inspector, as described on page 224, but, if the same image on several pages is missing its Alt property, you may find it faster to use Dreamweaver's powerful Find and Replace command (see page 801).

7. **Continue opening files from the Results window and fixing them until you correct each mistake.**

   Unfortunately, Dreamweaver doesn't provide a quick, one-step method to fix any of these problems. Except when using the "Find and Replace" command for adding missing Alt text, you must open and fix each page individually.

If you want to save the results of your report, click the Save Report button. Dreamweaver opens a Save As dialog box, and lets you save the report as an XML file (so you can file it in the "Files I don't really need" folder on your desktop).

Download Statistics

Remember the old joke that WWW really stands for "World Wide Wait"? Even as more and more people upgrade to speedy DSL and cable modems, file size is a web designer's constant foe. What takes only a moment to load from your computer's hard drive could take minutes to travel across the Internet. The more information you put into a web page, the more time it takes to load.

You can judge how big your page is, and therefore how long it'll take to load, by looking at the bottom of the document window, in the status bar, and reading the download stats. You'll see something like this: *9k/2 sec*. This term indicates the file size of the page (9k in this instance) and how long it'll take a visitor to download the page (2 seconds) using a 56 Kbps modem.

Note: Because many people now have cable modems or DSL, to get a more realistic view of a visitor's download time you might want to change this 56 Kbps default setting. To do so, choose Edit→Preferences (Dreamweaver→Preferences), click the Status Bar category, and then, from the Connection Speed menu at the bottom of the window, choose a higher setting–a setting of 128 Kbps is a faster, but still conservative setting. You can also manually type in a connection speed (256 Kbps, for instance) to get a setting that Dreamweaver's menu doesn't list. Be conservative in which value you pick: the download time Dreamweaver displays is the ideal time for that speed and won't account for all real-world variables, like high volumes of Internet traffic, which can slow down web surfing.

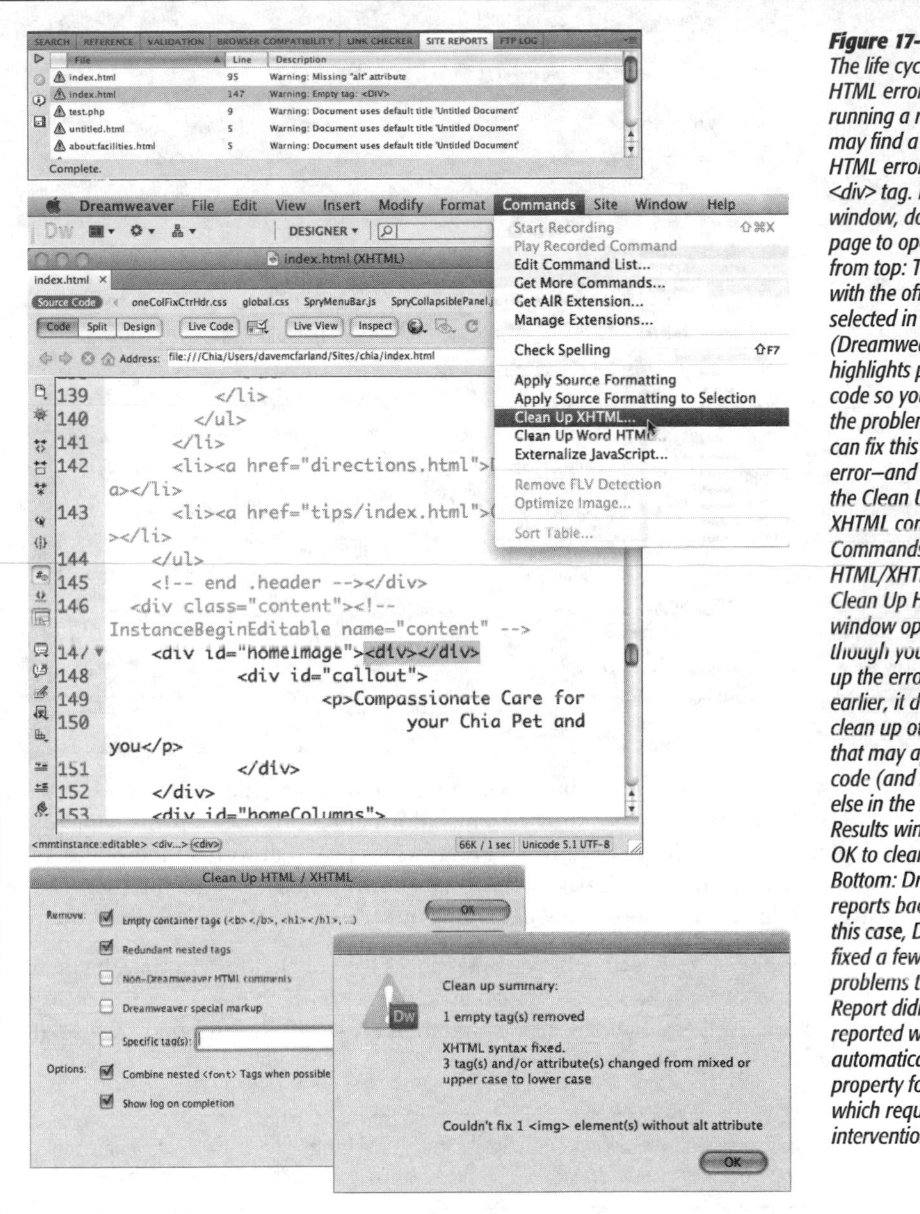

Figure 17-12:
The life cycle of a typical HTML error. Top: After running a report, you may find a common HTML error, like an empty <div> tag. In the Results window, double-click the page to open it. Second from top: The page opens with the offending code selected in Code view. (Dreamweaver often highlights problem HTML code so you can identify the problem.) Since you can fix this particular error—and more—with the Clean Up HTML/XHTML command, choose Commands→Clean Up HTML/XHTML. Third: The Clean Up HTML/XHTML window opens. Even though you can just clean up the error you identified earlier, it doesn't hurt to clean up other problems that may appear in your code (and somewhere else in the Site Report Results window). Click OK to clean up the HTML. Bottom: Dreamweaver reports back to you. In this case, Dreamweaver fixed a few other XHTML problems that the Site Report didn't catch, and reported what it couldn't automatically fix: the Alt property for an image, which requires human intervention to fix.

POWER USERS' CLINIC

Making Accessible Websites

Building websites that meet everyone's requirements is a daunting task. Unless you have screen-reader software to simulate the experience of a visually impaired visitor, or a crew of people with a variety of impairments (from color-blindness to repetitive stress injury) to test your site, how do you know what it takes to build a fully accessible site?

Previous versions of Dreamweaver included an "Accessibility Report" which scanned a site's files for accessibility problems. However, it was outdated and unreliable, so Adobe removed it from Dreamweaver CS5.

Nevertheless, creating websites that reach the widest possible audience is still important. Fortunately, you can find plenty of resources. The best place to start is at the Web Accessibility Initiative's website, especially their accessibility resources page: *http://www.w3.org/WAI/Resources*. You'll find lots of information, including examples of different disabilities some web surfers face, plus tips, checklists, and techniques for making your site accessible. You should also check out Dive Into Accessibility (*http://diveintoaccessibility.org*), a site dedicated to teaching web designers the whys and hows of accessibility. For a short checklist that provides information for a basic accessibility evaluation, check out *www.tomjewett.com/accessibility/basiceval.html*.

And if you do want to see how screen readers work with your site, you can download a demo of JAWS, one of the most popular screen readers, at *www.freedomscientific.com/fs_downloads/jaws.asp*. A free alternative is a Firefox extension named Fangs, which displays (in text) what a screen reader like JAWS reads aloud. You can download it from *www.standards-schmandards.com/projects/fangs*.

Finally, Adobe dedicates an entire section of its site to accessibility issues: *www.adobe.com/accessibility/*. Here, you'll find explanations of the issues in accessible design, tips for using Adobe products, and a showcase of model accessible sites.

The file size and download time takes into account linked files like images, external CSS style sheets, and Flash movies. This information provides a realistic picture of download speed, since not only does a browser have to download these files, but it has to fetch any files that a page uses (like a photo) from across the Internet. The file size and download time can be misleading, however.

If you use the same external files on *other* pages in your site (for example, if you use a common external style sheet or a logo that appears on each page), your site's visitors may have already "cached" those files and their browsers don't need to download the files again (see the box on the next page).

Tip: To get a full description of every Dreamweaver menu in a handy, printable PDF, go to this book's Missing CD page (*www.missingmanuals.com/cds*) and download Appendix B, "Menu by Menu Commands."

GEM IN THE ROUGH

Caching In

Behind the scenes, web browsers store the graphics they download in a part of your computer's hard drive called a *cache*. This is a speed trick. If you click your Back button to return to a web page whose graphics files the browser has already downloaded, the browser simply pulls them out of the cache–off the hard drive, in other words–instead of re-downloading them. This system makes the page load more quickly, since retrieving information from a hard drive is generally much faster than getting it through a modem.

As a web designer, you can capitalize on this standard browser feature by reusing the same graphics files on more than one page of your site. For instance, you can create a navigation bar composed of small graphic buttons (Home, Contact Us, Products, and so on). If you reuse those buttons on other pages of the site, those pages appear to download more quickly.

This same trick works for external CSS style sheets. A browser needs to download a complete style sheet with hundreds of formatting commands only once, and any page on your site can reuse it. By putting all your formatting into one or more external files, you can keep your web pages tidy and lean.

Note: People hate to wait. You may think that the graphic design of your site is so compelling that even if it takes a full minute to download that zippy new Flash home page, people will stick around.

Think again. Research shows that 10 seconds is the maximum amount of time that someone stays focused on a task while waiting. That means that if you're designing a website for people to view over DSL, you should keep your pages below a few hundred kilobytes (KB)—and that's if you want it to take 10 seconds for your page to appear. Most site owners want their site to load a lot faster than that.

A Firefox plug-in called YSlow is a great tool for testing your download times. It can analyze bottlenecks and help you determine why a page downloads slowly. You can get the plug-in at *http://developer.yahoo.com/yslow/*. It even had a tool that compresses graphics even more than tools like Photoshop or Fireworks.

CHAPTER 18

Moving Your Site to the Internet

Building web pages on your computer is a big accomplishment, but it's not the whole job. Your beautifully designed and informative site will languish in obscurity unless you move it from your hard drive to a web server.

Fortunately, once your site is ready for prime time, you can put it on a server without ever leaving the comfort of Dreamweaver. The program includes simple commands for transferring files back and forth between the server and your desktop.

Depending on how you operate, choose one of these two methods to transfer your files:

- If you're the sole developer for a site, Dreamweaver's Get and Put commands are the easiest way to go.
- If, on the other hand, a group of people work on your site, Dreamweaver's Check Out and Check In tools let you move files at will without wiping out others' hard work. In addition, this group feature integrates seamlessly with WebDAV, an open-source file management tool that's common at universities.

Either way, you begin by adding a "remote server" to your site.

Adding a Remote Server

As you create your website on your computer, you keep it in a *local root folder* (see page 42), often called a *local site* for short. You can think of the local site as a work-in-progress. As you shape your site—whether you're building it from scratch or adding and modifying pages—you'll routinely have partially finished documents sitting on your computer.

Then, after you perfect and test your pages by using the techniques described in Chapter 17, you're ready to transfer them to a server that's connected to the Internet. Dreamweaver calls the web server copy of your files the *remote server*, and gives you five ways to transfer files to it from your local site:

- **FTP.** By far, the most common method is *FTP*, or File Transfer Protocol. Just as HTTP is the process by which web pages are transferred from servers to web browsers, so FTP is the traditional way to transfer files over the Internet. If your site resides at a web hosting company or your Internet Service Provider (ISP) you'll use this option or, even better, the SFTP option discussed next.
- **SFTP** stands for Secure FTP. This transfer method encrypts *all* your data, not just your user name and password, so information you transfer this way is unintelligible to Internet snoops. It's the ideal way to connect to a web server, since normal FTP connections send your user name and password unencrypted, susceptible to Internet creeps; in many cases, Secure FTP is also faster. Unfortunately, not all web hosting companies offer this advanced option, so you may be stuck with regular FTP. If you're not sure if you can use SFTP, just try it—Dreamweaver will tell you if it's unable to connect to the server. In that case, just switch to FTP.
- **Local/network.** If you're working on an intranet, or if your company's web server is connected to the company network, you may also be able to transfer files just as you would any files on your office network (using the Network Neighborhood, My Network Places, or "Connect to Server" command, depending on your operating system).
- The last two options—**WebDAV and RDS** —are advanced file-management systems used for collaborative web development. You'll learn about them on page 699.

FREQUENTLY ASKED QUESTION

Beyond Dreamweaver

Do I have to use Dreamweaver to move my files to the Web?

No. If you use another program to FTP files, like CuteFTP (Windows) or RBrowser (Mac), you can continue to use it and ignore Dreamweaver's Remote Site feature.

However, if you've never before used Dreamweaver to move files to a server, you may want to at least try it because it simplifies much of the process. For example, when you want to move a file from your computer to the web server using a regular FTP program, you must first browse for the file on your local machine and then navigate to the proper folder on the server. Dreamweaver saves you both steps; when you select the file in the Files panel and click the Put button, Dreamweaver automatically locates the file on your computer and transfers it to the correct folder on your server.

Setting Up a Remote Server with FTP or SFTP

You can set up a remote server only if you first set up a *local* site on your computer. Even if you're just putting up a temporary site while working on your *real* one, you must at least have the temporary site constructed and set up in Dreamweaver (see page 37). Once that's done, here's how you go about creating an Internet-based mirror of your local site:

1. **Choose Site→Manage Sites.**

   The Manage Sites dialog box opens, listing all the sites you've defined so far. You're about to tell Dreamweaver how to connect to a web server so you can create a living, Internet-based *copy* of one of these hard drive–based local sites.

2. **Click the name of the site you want to post on the Internet, and then click Edit.**

   Alternatively, just double-click the site name in the list. The Site Setup window appears for the selected site, as shown in Figure 18-1.

Note: You can set up your local site and remote server simultaneously, when you first begin creating your site (as described on page 37). Even then, however, Dreamweaver requires that you first give the site a name and choose a local site folder. At that point, you rejoin the steps described here.

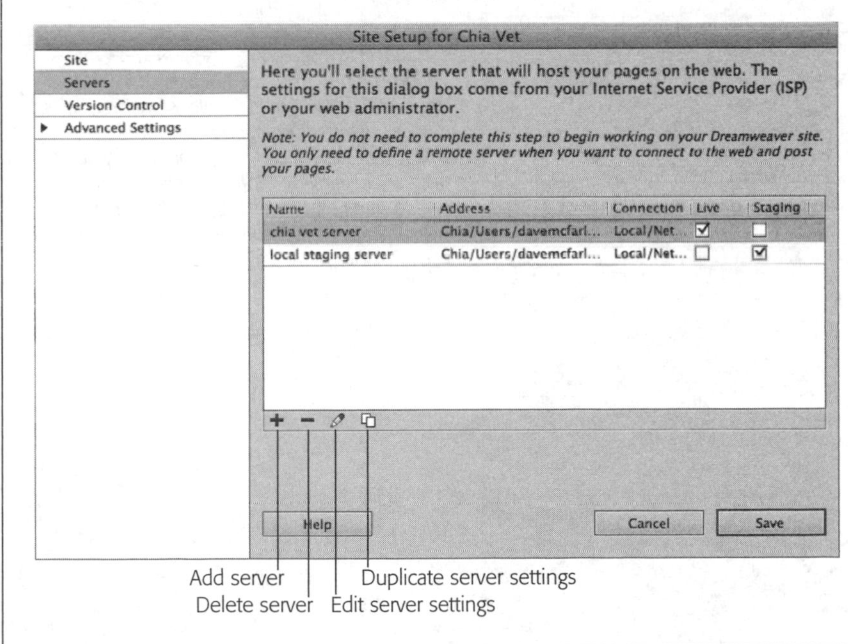

Figure 18-1: *Adobe has reorganized the site set-up procedure in Dreamweaver CS5. Dreamweaver now lists both remote and testing servers in the same "Server" category.*

3. **Click the Servers option.**

   The Servers category of the Site Setup window lists your "remote" and "testing" servers. The remote server is the one containing the site the world can see, while the testing server acts as a test area—you use it to test pages before you put them up on a remote server. Web developers usually use testing servers only when they create dynamic, database-driven sites, like those discussed in Part Six of this book, so if you're building a regular website without using PHP, ASP, Cold Fusion, or some other server-side programming language, you won't need to set up a testing server.

   Initially, the Servers category is empty: you need to add a remote server.

Note: Dreamweaver lets you define as many remote and testing servers as you want, but you probably won't ever have to take advantage of that. But if you do find that you need to have the same site uploaded to two different web servers (perhaps you have a high-traffic website and put the site on several servers to balance the load), you can define a second, third, and even a fourth remote server. However, you can only "turn on" one remote server at a time. In other words, you can only upload and download to one remote server–the one with the Remote checkbox selected (see Figure 18-1).

---

4. **Click the + button to add a new server.**

   A new pane pops up (see Figure 18-2). Here you supply the information necessary for Dreamweaver to connect to the server.

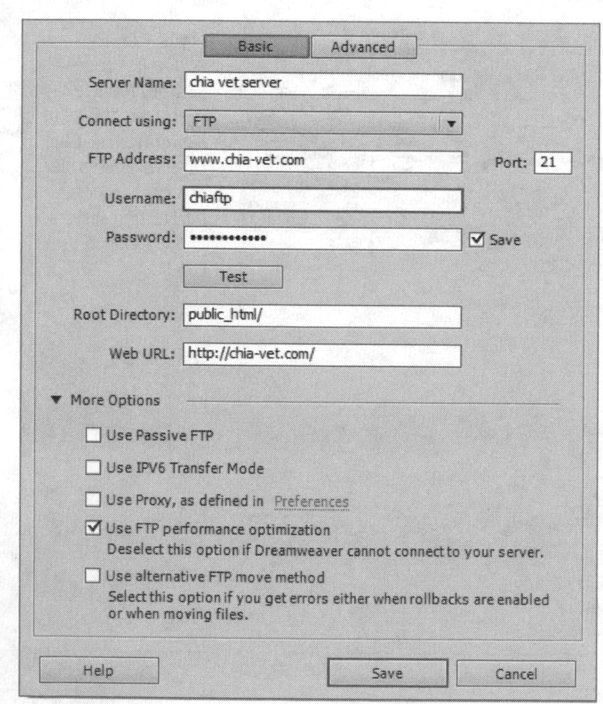

Figure 18-2:
To connect to a server, you need to know the address of the server, the FTP username and password, and where the server stores your files. You get all this information when you sign up with a web hosting company. You usually don't need to change the "More Options" settings when using FTP, though they can help if you're having connectivity problems (see page 697). (If you use SFTP the "More Options" don't appear.)

5. **Type a name in the Server Name field.**

   Dreamweaver only uses this name internally; it's not something anyone else will see, so name it anything you like, such as "My Server" or "Hosting Company."

6. **From the "Connect using" pop-up menu, choose either FTP or SFTP.**

   Ideally, you'd like to use SFTP—it's more secure and usually faster, but your web hosting company may not offer SFTP, so you'll have to choose FTP.

Tip: If you're not sure whether your server supports SFTP, try it out. Follow these set up instructions using SFTP as the "Connect using" option, then click the Test button. If Dreamweaver can't connect, try regular FTP. If you still can't connect, you probably typed the wrong user name, password, or FTP address.

---

7. **Fill in the "FTP address" field.**

   This is the address of the web server computer. It's usually something like *www.chia-vet.com*. It never includes directories, folders, or slashes (like *www.chia-vet.com/vets*); never includes codes for the FTP protocol (*ftp://ftp.cosmofarmer.com*) or HTTP protocol (*http://www.chia-vet.com*); and it may simply just be a domain name, such as (*chia-vet.com*). It can also be an IP address, like *64.226.43.116*. In most cases, it's the address you would type in a web browser's address window (minus the *http://*) to get to your site's home page.

   If you don't know the host name, there's only one way to find out: call or email your web hosting company or ISP, or check its website.

8. **In the Username field, type your user name, and then type your password in the Password field.**

   Dreamweaver uses bullets (••••) to display your password so that office evildoers can't see what you're typing. If you want Dreamweaver to remember your password each time you use the program, turn on the Save checkbox. This way, you won't have to type your password each time you connect to the server.

Warning: For security reasons, don't turn on the Save box if you access the Web using computers at, say, your local library, or anywhere else where people you don't trust may use the machine. Otherwise, you might just awaken one morning to find the following splattered across your home page: "Hi there! Welcome to Jack's house of illegally acquired and unlawfully distributed music, featuring Metallica's greatest hits."

---

9. **In the "Root Directory" field, type the path to the root directory.**

   Here you specify which *folder* on the server will contain your web page files and serve as the root folder for your site.

   Just as all your website's files on your hard drive reside in a master folder, so they do on the server, in a master folder known as the *root folder*. But when you connect to your server using FTP, you're rarely connected to the root folder itself.

Instead, you usually connect to a folder that most people never see—an administrative folder for your web account, which your host often fills with folders for log reports of your site's traffic, and other housekeeping files.

You need to make sure Dreamweaver places your site's files in the site's root folder, and that's why you're typing its name here. Common names for the root folder at ISPs and web hosting companies include *docs, www, htdocs, public_html, httpdocs, or virtual_html.* (Call or email your web host or ISP to find out.)

The information you give Dreamweaver here represents the path from the folder Dreamweaver connects to with FTP to the site's root folder on the server. It may look like this: *site_files/htdocs*. In effect, you're telling Dreamweaver: "After you connect to the web server, you'll find a folder named *site_files*. Inside *this* folder is another folder, named *htdocs*. Put my site files in there." In other words, *htdocs* is your website's root folder on this particular remote hosting account.

10. **Type the web address for your site in the Web URL box.**

    This is simply what you'd type in your web browser's address line to get to your site: *www.chia-vet.com/*, for example. Sometimes, though, you might work on files in a subdirectory of the site's root folder. For example, if you work in corporate web design, you might oversee a self-contained site for the marketing department, which means the URL to reach the files you work on might be *www.mycompany.com/marketing/*. If that's the case, then also include the subdirectory's name: *www.chia-vet.com/marketing/*.

Note: the value you type into the Web URL box when you set up a remote server can affect how Dreamweaver checks and updates links (see page 643).

11. **Click the Test button.**

    Dreamweaver attempts to connect to your web server. If it succeeds you'll see a box that says, "Dreamweaver connected to your Web server successfully." If it didn't succeed, you'll get an error message. See the box on the opposite page for the most common problems and solutions.

Note: When Dreamweaver can't connect to a web server, one of the first things you should try is turning on the "Use passive FTP" checkbox. See the box on the opposite page for more.

12. **Click Save to save these settings.**

    Dreamweaver returns to the Servers category of the Site Setup window (Figure 18-1).

13. **Click Save once again to return to the Manage Sites window, and then click Done.**

At this point, you're ready to connect to the web server and transfer files. If you're the only person working on the site, Dreamweaver's Get and Put commands will do the trick (page 702). If, however, you're part of a development team, use Dreamweaver's Check In and Check Out feature, described on page 711.

FREQUENTLY ASKED QUESTION

When Your Remote Site Is Too Remote

Help! I can't connect to my web server. What should I do?

Things don't always go smoothly. That's doubly true when you try to connect to a web server, since you depend on a variety of things–your Internet connection, the networks connecting you to the server, the server itself, and the FTP software that runs the show–working together in harmony. Dreamweaver presents an error message if you can't successfully establish an FTP connection with your server. The error box frequently contains useful information that can help you determine the problem. Here are some of the most common:

- Remote host cannot be found usually means that you typed in an incorrect FTP Host address (step 7 on page 695).
- Your login or password is incorrect means just that–you've typed in the wrong user name or password (step 8 on page 695).
- Cannot open remote folder usually means you mistyped the name of the root directory, or you've got the wrong name for it (step 9 on page 695).

Unfortunately, there are lots of reasons Dreamweaver may not be able to connect, so sometimes the error message isn't particularly helpful. Here are a few other suggestions for troubleshooting: make sure you're connected to the Internet (open a web browser and see if you can visit a site); return to the Site Setup window for the site, open the Remote server settings, and turn on the "Use passive FTP" option (sometimes this just makes things work); turn off the "Use FTP performance optimization" box; and if you have another FTP program, like CuteFTP or RBrowser, see if you can connect to your server using the same settings you gave Dreamweaver. If all these steps fail, you can visit this page on the Adobe website for additional troubleshooting tips: *www.adobe.com/cfusion/knowledgebase/index.cfm?id=tn_14834*.

More Remote Server Options for FTP

The steps discussed above will be probably be all you'll ever need to FTP your files, but Dreamweaver offers a few more options when you set up a FTP connection, as well as some advanced settings that apply to all types of connections (see page 701).

Note: The options listed below aren't available (or necessary) when you connect using SFTP.

To see additional options for FTP connections, click the More Options arrow (see Figure 18-2). Most of these should remain unchecked, but here's what they do:

- **Use Passive FTP.** Select this if you're unable to make an FTP connection and you know you correctly typed your FTP address, user name, password, and root directory name (see steps 7 to 9 on page 695). This option can overcome problems encountered with firewalls: hardware- or software-based gateways that control incoming and outgoing traffic through a network. Firewalls protect your company's network or your personal computer from outside hackers; unfortunately, they also limit how computers inside the network—behind the firewall—connect to the outside world.
- **Use IPV6 Transfer Mode.** You probably won't need to turn on this checkbox for several years to come. It's intended for the day when we run out of IP addresses, and web servers switch from IP addresses that look like 192.168.1.1 to ones that look like this: 1A23:120B:0000:0000:0000:7634:AD01:004D. Egads.
- **Use Proxy.** If you can't connect to the remote server and your company's system administrator confirms that you have a firewall, check the Use Proxy box, and click the "Preferences" link to open the Site category of the Preferences window. Here you'll need to enter the name of the firewall host computer and its port number. Your firewall configuration may also require passive FTP—a method of connecting using your local software, rather than the firewall server. Check with your administrator to see if this is the case, and, if so, turn on the "Use passive FTP" checkbox.
- **Use FTP performance optimization.** Dreamweaver normally checks this box because it helps speed up file transfers between your computer and your web server. However, it can also be the source of connection problems. If you can't connect to your server, try unchecking this box.
- **Use Alternative FTP move method.** If everything's okay when you connect to your server, but you're getting errors when you move files there, turn on this option. This transfer method is slower but more reliable. It's also handy if you use Adobe's Contribute program and take advantage of its "rollback" feature (to learn more about Contribute, visit *www.adobe.com/contribute/*).

Setting Up a Remote Server over a Local Network

If you work on an intranet, or if your company's web server is connected to the company network, you may be able to transfer site files just as you'd move any files from machine to machine. Dreamweaver provides the same file-transfer functions as with FTP, but the setup is simpler.

Follow steps 1 to 5 from the previous instructions, but in step 6, choose Local/Network from the "Connect using" menu. This brings up menus and fields for collecting your connection information in the Site Definition box (see Figure 18-3).

Click the folder icon next to the "Remote folder" field. In the resulting dialog box, navigate to and select your site's remote site folder. On a local network, this folder isn't *truly* remote, because your company's web server is still within the walls of your building. But you get the idea,

Wrap up with steps 10, 12, and 13 of the previous instructions. At this point, you're ready to connect to the "remote" server and transfer files.

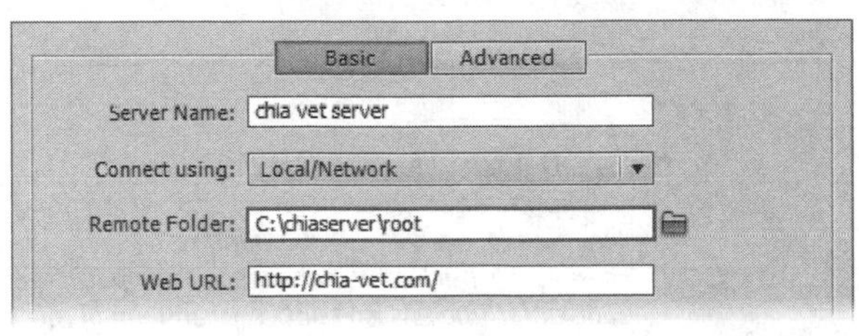

Figure 18-3:
If your company keeps its web server in your office, the "remote site" might not be that remote: In a case like this, choose a folder on your local network as the remote site.

Setting Up a Remote Server with WebDAV

Dreamweaver also allows access to a remote site using *WebDAV*, short for Web-based Distributed Authoring and Versioning. Like FTP, it's a standard, or *protocol*, for transferring files. Like SFTP, it uses a secure connection (called SSL or Secure Socket Layer) that encrypts all your data as it passes back and forth between your computer and your web server. But unlike both of those technologies, WebDAV addresses the kinds of problems you encounter when you collaborate on a website with other people.

For instance, all kinds of havoc can result if two people edit a page simultaneously; whoever uploads the page to the server *second* winds up wiping out the changes made by the first person. WebDAV supports a check-in and check-out system that works similarly to Dreamweaver's Check In/Check Out tool (see page 711) to make sure only one person works on a file at a time and no one tramples on anyone else's files. In fact, Dreamweaver's Check In and Check Out tools work seamlessly with WebDAV.

Both Microsoft Internet Information Server (IIS) and Apache Web Server work with WebDAV. Colleges and universities commonly use WebDAV, but that's not the case with web hosting companies. To find out if your server can handle WebDAV (and to find out the necessary connection information), consult your web server's administrator (for example, call or email your web hosting company.)

Setting up WebDAV access to a remote site is similar to setting up FTP access. Follow steps 1 through 5 on page 693, and then:

1. **Click the Remote Info category, and then choose WebDAV from the "Connect using" menu.**

   The Site Definition window displays the WebDAV settings (Figure 18-4).

2. **In the URL box, type in the URL of the WebDAV server.**

   In most cases, this is the URL of your website, so it begins with either *http://* or *https://*. The "s" in *https* means you'll connect securely to the server using SSL. The normal *http://* method doesn't use any encryption, which means that, just as with regular FTP, your computer sends your user name, password, and data "in the open" as it travels across the Internet. Note that just adding an "s" won't suddenly make your file transfers secure; the receiving server needs to be set up to accept *https* connections (a technically challenging task).

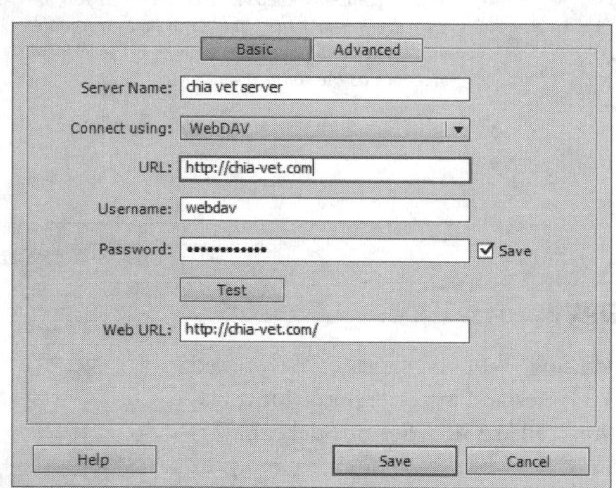

Figure 18-4: *WebDAV, short for Web-based Distributed Authoring and Versioning, is a powerful tool for working on a site in collaboration with other people. It's built into several web server packages but, unfortunately, isn't not very common at most web hosting companies.*

3. **In the Username field, type your user name, and then type your password in the Password field.**

   Turn on the Save checkbox to save yourself the hassle of having to type in your password each time you move files to your server (but heed the Warning on page 695).

4. **Click the Test button to see if your connection works.**

   If Dreamweaver succeeds, it proudly tells you. Unfortunately, if it fails, you'll get an error message that isn't exactly helpful. WebDAV isn't nearly as finicky as FTP, so if there's an error, you most likely just typed the URL, password, or login incorrectly, or WebDAV just isn't available for the server.

Note: However, due to the different possible server configurations for WebDAV, Dreamweaver may not be able to connect at all. If this is the case, you'll need to use FTP or another method to connect to your server.

The rest of the process is identical to the FTP setup process, so follow steps 10, 12, and 13, starting on page 696. At that point, you're ready to connect to your server and transfer files, as described on page 702.

Setting Up a Remote Server with RDS

RDS (Remote Development Services) is a feature of Adobe's ColdFusion Server. It lets designers work on web files and databases in conjunction with a ColdFusion application server. If you aren't using ColdFusion, then this option isn't for you.

To create a remote site in Dreamweaver that works with RDS, follow steps 1 through 5 on page 693. In step 6, choose RDS from the "Connect using" pop-up menu.

The Site Definition window displays a version number, a short description, and a Settings button. Click Settings to open the Configure RDS Server window. Fill in the dialog box as directed by your server administrator or help desk.

Advanced Remote Server Settings

No matter which connection method you use (FTP, local/network, and so on) each remote server has a set of advanced options that you access by clicking the Advanced button in the Remote Server setup window (see Figure 18-5):

- **If you don't want to synchronize files, turn off the "Maintain synchronization information" box.** Dreamweaver's synchronization feature is useful to keep your site up-to-date. It helps you maintain the most recent versions of your files on the remote server, by keeping track of when you change a file on your computer. When you synchronize a site, Dreamweaver moves the more recent files onto your server (you'll learn about this feature in detail on page 717). If you don't want Dreamweaver to synchronize your files, definitely turn off this checkbox. When it's on, Dreamweaver inserts little files named *dwsync.xml* throughout your site in folders named *_notes*. These items store synchronization information about each file in your site, but there's no need to clutter up your site with them if you don't use synchronization. In addition, Dreamweaver spends time determining the synch information for each file, so your file transfers go more quickly with this turned off.
- **Don't turn on "Automatically upload files to server on Save".** Not only will this slow things down—Dreamweaver has to connect and move the saved file to the server every time you press Ctrl-S (⌘-S)—but it also means you may save half-finished pages on your remote server.
- **If you work with a team of developers, you may want to use Dreamweaver's Check In/Check Out tools discussed on page 711.** If you do, then turn on "Enable file check in and check out". Then fill in the corresponding options as explained in Figure 18-5. If you do wind up using the "check out" feature (see page 712), you can save yourself some clicks by turning on "Check out files when opening". (Fill in your name and email address, too, as shown in Figure 18-5.) Now you can "check out" a file from the remote server just by double-clicking its name in the Site Files list. If you're not working with other developers on the site, *do not* turn on this setting, since it slows down the process of moving files back and forth from the server and adds unnecessary files (used to determine who has what file checked out) to both your server and your own computer.

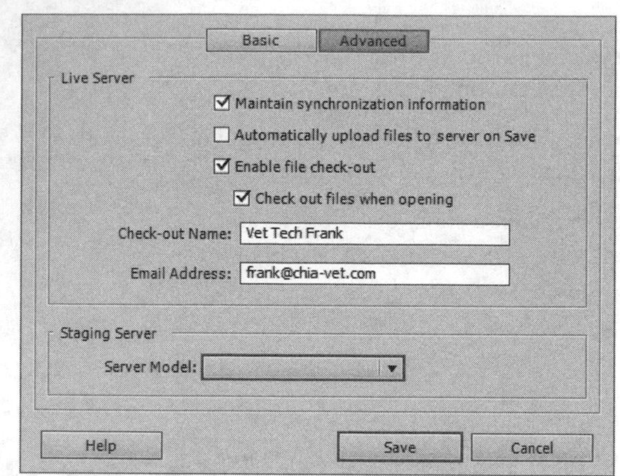

Figure 18-5:
If you use Dreamweaver's Check In/Check Out feature and you work on your site in several different locations (for example, from home and your office), use a different name for each location (BobAtHome and BobAtWork, for example). That way, you know which files you checked out to your home computer and which to your computer at work.

Transferring Files

Once you tell Dreamweaver *how* to ship your web pages off to the Net, you can set about actually *doing* so. Thanks to Dreamweaver's Files panel, the whole process takes only a few steps.

Moving Files to the Web Server

To transfer files to your web server:

1. **Open the Files panel (Figure 18-6).**

   Choose Window→Files (keyboard shortcut: F8 [Shift-⌘-F]).

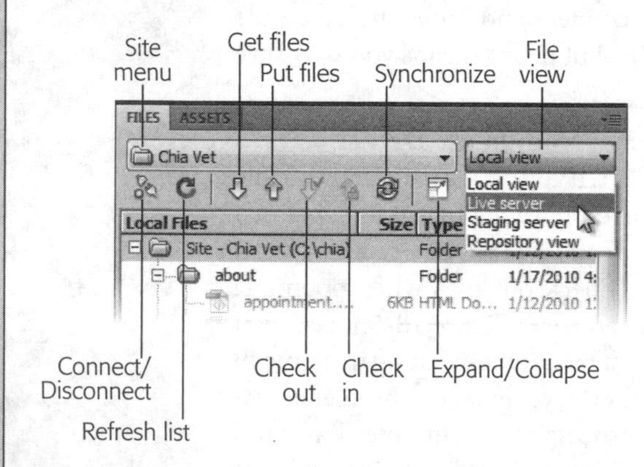

Figure 18-6:
The Files panel offers toolbar buttons for uploading and downloading your web files to and from the web server that actually dishes them out to your site's adoring public. (See Chapter 16 for much more on this important window.)

2. **From the Site menu, choose the name of the site whose files you wish to move (if it isn't already selected).**

   The Files panel displays files for the selected site. You can use the File View pop-up menu to access either a list of the local files or the files on the remote server (see Figure 18-6). You can also see both local and remote server files side by side if you first choose "Remote server" from the File View pop-up menu and then click the Expand button on the Files panel, as described in Figure 16-8.

Note: The color of the folders in the Site panel lets you know which view you're currently in: green folders mean Local view (your computer), beige (blue on the Mac) folders mean Remote view, and red folders indicate the Testing view if you have a testing server, as described on page 836.

---

3. **From the file list in the Files panel, select the files you wish to upload to the server.**

   To move a folder and every file inside it, just select the folder. (In other words, you can transfer your *entire* website to the server by simply selecting the local site folder—the folder listed at the very top of the Local Files list.) When you've changed only a few files on your site, you can selectively upload files or folders using any of the techniques described on page 674.

Note: If you don't see the files you want to upload in the Site Files list, you may have selected "Remote server". Select "Local view" to see only those files on your computer and then click the Refresh button on the Files panel (Figure 18-6).

When you use do-it-yourself FTP programs like WS_FTP or Fetch, you have to specify a folder location for every file you transfer to the web server. But here's one of the great advantages of letting Dreamweaver do your file shuffling; it already *knows* where your files should go on the remote server. The local and remote sites are, after all, mirror images, so Dreamweaver simply puts your local files in the corresponding folders on the remote server.

For example, suppose you select the file *mayo.html*, which is in a folder called Condiments, which is itself stored in the local root folder. When you transfer the file, Dreamweaver knows to put this file in the Condiments folder in the root folder on the remote server. In fact, if the folder Condiments doesn't exist on the remote server, Dreamweaver creates it and *then* puts the file into it. Now that's service!

You're now ready to go live with your web page.

1. **Click the "Put files" button—the up-arrow icon identified in Figure 16-6—on the Files panel.**

   Alternatively, you can use the keyboard shortcut Ctrl+Shift+U (⌘-Shift-U).

Several things happen when you do this: First, if you're using an FTP connection, Dreamweaver attempts to connect to your server. As you can see in the status window that opens, it may take a moment or so to establish the connection; once it is, the Connect button (see Figure 18-6) displays a bright green light.

Next, if any of the files you're transferring are currently open and have unsaved changes, Dreamweaver asks if you want to save the files before transferring them to the server. Click Yes to save the file, or, if there are multiple unsaved files, click the Yes To All button to save all of them before posting them online.

In addition, as Dreamweaver transfers your pages, it asks if you want to transfer any *dependent files* (see Figure 18-7). Dependent files include graphics, external CSS files, or Flash movies that a browser needs to display your pages properly.

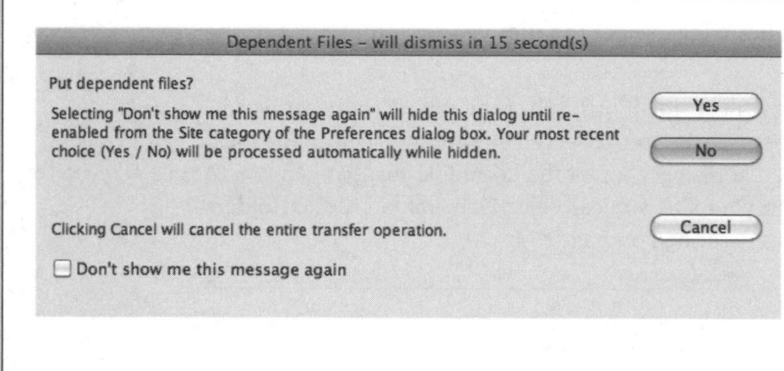

Figure 18-7: *Dreamweaver's Dependent Files feature of its File Transfer command makes sure that Dreamweaver copies to the server all the files a browser needs to display a web page correctly–graphics, external style sheets, Flash movies, and so on. The feature also includes a time limit–you'll see a "will dismiss in xx seconds" message. If you don't click a button within 30 seconds, Dreamweaver assumes you mean "No" and uploads just the files you selected.*

The dependent files feature can save you considerable time and hassle; no need to hunt for and upload each graphic file or external style sheet yourself. On the other hand, if all the dependent files are *already* on the server, having Dreamweaver transfer the same files again is a waste of time. Fortunately, Dreamweaver prevents this wasted effort as described in the next step.

Note: If you turn on the "Don't show me this message again" box in the Dependent Files dialog box (see Figure 18-7) and then click Yes, from that moment forward, Dreamweaver copies dependent files without asking. On the other hand, if you turn on the "Don't show me this message again" box and click No, Dreamweaver *never* copies dependent files.

If you want to get the Dependent Files dialog box back after you've turned it off, hold down the Alt (Option) key when you transfer a file (using any method except a keyboard shortcut). Or choose Edit→Preferences→Site Category (Dreamweaver→Preferences→Site Category) to turn this feature on or off.

2. **Click Yes to transfer dependent files, or No to transfer only the files you selected.**

   Dreamweaver copies the files to the server. If you copy a file that's inside a folder that doesn't exist on the remote server, Dreamweaver creates the folder in the same step. In fact, Dreamweaver creates as many subfolders as necessary to make sure it transfers every local file to a mirror folder location on the remote site. (Try doing *that* with a regular FTP program.)

   If you choose to transfer dependent files as well, Dreamweaver may or may not put the dependent file on the server, depending on your settings. If you turned on the "Maintain Synchronization Information" checkbox when you defined your remote site (see page 701), Dreamweaver determines whether the dependent file already exists on the server and, if it does, whether your local copy is a newer version. If the dependent file doesn't exist on the server or your local copy is newer (meaning you made changes to it locally but haven't moved it to the Web), Dreamweaver sends it when you tell it to transfer dependent files.

   However, if Dreamweaver thinks that it's the same file, or that the copy of the file on the server is newer, it won't transfer the file. This behavior is a huge timesaver, since you won't have to repeatedly upload the same 50 navigation buttons each time you say "Yes" to transferring dependent files; but, best of all, Dreamweaver still transfers those dependent files that really *are* new.

Note: Dreamweaver's ability to correctly determine whether a dependent file on your computer is the same as a file on the server depends on its Site Synchronization feature, described on page 717. Dreamweaver's accuracy with this tool is good, but it has been known to get it wrong. If Dreamweaver isn't moving a dependent file that you want moved to the server, you can just select that file and upload it manually (for example, select it in the Files panel and then click the Put button). Dreamweaver always obeys a direct order to move a selected file to your remote site.

---

3. **Continue using the Put button to transfer all the files in your website to the remote site.**

   Depending on the number of files you transfer, this operation can take some time. Transferring files over the Internet using FTP isn't nearly as fast as copying files from one hard drive to another (see the box below).

Other ways to move files to your web server

To copy your current document to your server without using the Files panel at all, you can go directly to the Put command. Say you finish building or modifying a page and want to immediately move it to the Web. Just choose Site→Put or press Ctrl+Shift+U (⌘-Shift-U); Dreamweaver automatically copies the fresh page to the proper folder online.

The toolbar also provides a quick menu shortcut for this operation, as shown in Figure 18-8.

POWER USERS' CLINIC

A Little More Background on File Transfers

Dreamweaver lets you keep working as it dutifully moves files in the background. You can edit a web page, create a new style sheet, and so on, while the program busily transfers files over the Internet. However, there are some things you *can't* do while Dreamweaver transfers files. These are mostly logical restrictions: you can't edit the site definition (since this could affect how you connect to the remote server), you can't Put or Get other files (since Dreamweaver's already busy doing that), and you can't delete a file on the local or remote server (since you may be transferring that file). Dreamweaver lets you know if you try to take a forbidden action while it's working with the server.

If you find Dreamweaver's background activity window a nuisance, click the Hide button and it temporarily disappears. In addition, if you accidentally start uploading a 10,000-page website, you probably won't want to wait until Dreamweaver is finished. Click the Cancel button to stop the process.

When Dreamweaver finishes moving files around, you can see a record of its actions by clicking the Log button that appears at the bottom-right corner of the Files panel. This log differs from the raw FTP log discussed in the box on page 708. This plain-language report lets you know what (and how) Dreamweaver did—"Put successful," "Get successful," and so on. If you see a "Not transferred" message, Dreamweaver tried to Get or Put a file, but both the local and remote server copies were identical, so it didn't do anything. See the previous Note for more information.

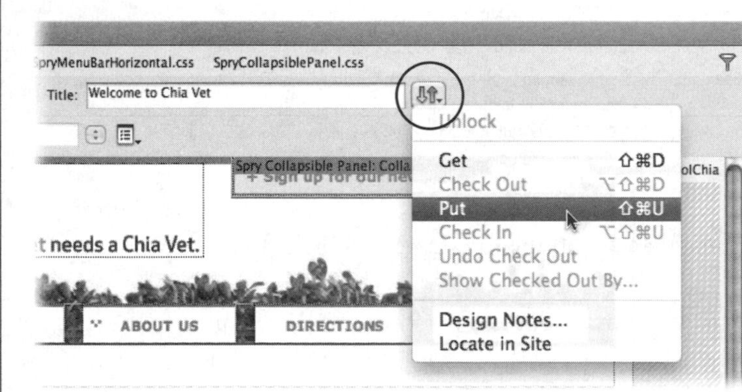

Figure 18-8: *Click the File Status button (circled) and choose Put to quickly move a file to your web server. You can also use this menu to retrieve a copy of this file from the server (Get), use Check In and Out features (page 711), or review Design Notes (page 721) for the page. To select this file in the Files panel, choose "Locate in Site".*

Getting Files *from* Your Web Server

So far, this chapter has described getting your hard drive-based pages to the Internet. Sometimes, however, you want to download one or more files *from* the Web server. Perhaps you made a horrible (and irreversible) mistake on the local copy of a file and you want to retrieve the last version from the Web, using the remote server as a last-ditch backup system. Or perhaps someone else uploaded some files to the site, and you want to download a copy to your own computer (although the Synchronize feature described on page 717 would also work).

To get files from the remote site, open the Files panel (press F8 [Shift-⌘-F]) and proceed as follows:

1. **From the Site pop-up menu, choose the site whose files you wish to retrieve.**

   As with all of Dreamweaver's site management features, downloading files from a Web server depends on first defining a site.

2. **From the Files panel's View menu (see Figure 18-6), choose "Remote server".**

   Dreamweaver tells you that it's attempting to connect to the web server. Once it makes the connection, it lists the files and folders on the live server, and turns the Connect button a bright green. (Dreamweaver automatically disconnects you after 30 minutes of inactivity, at which point the green dot turns black.)

Note: To change the disconnect-after-30-minutes-of-inactivity setting, press Ctrl+U (⌘-U) to open the Preferences window. Click the Site category and change the number listed in the "Minutes Idle" box. Be aware, however, that some web servers have their own settings and may disconnect you sooner than you specify.

---

3. **From the Live Server file list, select the files you want to download.**

   For techniques on selecting files in the Files panel, see page 674. To download a folder and every file inside it, just click the folder. This technique also lets you get your *entire* website from the server; just click the remote server root folder, which appears at the very top of the Live Server file list.

TROUBLESHOOTING MOMENT

Don't Replace the Wrong File

One strange feature of the Files panel's Get and Put commands may get you in trouble. Suppose, having just added new information to the home page (*index.html*), you want to transfer it to the web server. You select it in the Local Folder list—but then you accidentally click Get instead of Put.

Not knowing your true intention, Dreamweaver dutifully retrieves the file from the server and prepares to replace (wipe out) the newly updated home page on your computer.

Fortunately, Dreamweaver also opens a warning message asking if you really want to overwrite the local file. Click No or Cancel to save your hard work.

There may be times when you *do* want to wipe out your local copy—if, for example, your cat walks across your keyboard, types illegible code, presses Ctrl+S to save the ruined page, and Ctrl+Q to quit Dreamweaver (keeping you from using Undo to fix the mistakes). In this common situation, you'll want to replace your local copy with the remote server copy. To do so, press the Yes key to wipe out your cat's errors. Oh yeah, this is also a useful trick if *you* ever make a mistake on a page you can't fix and want to return to the working copy on your Web server.

Dreamweaver also includes a useful Compare button to help you sort out the differences between the local and remote server file. Clicking this button compares the two files so you can identify which changes you made. This way, you can salvage changes you made to the local copy and discard errors you (or your cat) may have introduced to the page. You'll learn more about this feature on page 441.

4. **Click the Get files button (the down arrow).**

   Alternatively, you can use the keyboard shortcut Ctrl+Shift+D (⌘-Shift-D).

   If you have the *local* version of a file you're getting from the remote server open with unsaved changes, Dreamweaver warns you that you'll lose those changes. (No surprise there; copying a file from the remote server automatically replaces the same file on the local site, whether it's open or not.) Dreamweaver also warns you if you're about to replace a local file that's *newer* than the remote one.

   Dreamweaver also offers to transfer any dependent files, as described in Figure 18-7.

5. **Click Yes to transfer dependent files, or No to transfer only the files you selected.**

   Dreamweaver copies the files to your local site folder, creating any folders necessary to replicate the structure of the remote site.

POWER USERS' CLINIC

Troubleshoot with the FTP Log

If you have problems moving files using Dreamweaver's FTP command, you may be able to find some clues in the records Dreamweaver keeps when it transfers files. If you've used other FTP programs, you may have seen little messages that the web server and FTP program send back and forth, like this:

```
200 PORT command successful. LIST 150
Opening ASCII mode data connection for
/bin/ls.
```

Dreamweaver also sends and receives this information, but it keeps it hidden. To see the FTP log, choose Window→Results, and then click the FTP Log tab. Any errors Dreamweaver encounters appear here.

For example, if you encounter a →cannot put file" error, it may mean that you're out of space on your web server. Contact your ISP or your server administrator for help. WebDAV connections also produce a log of file-transfer activity, but it's not very easy to decipher.

And Secure FTP (SFTP) produces no log in Dreamweaver—hush, hush, it's a secret.

Cloaking Files

You may not want *all* your files transferred to and from your remote site. For example, as part of its Library and Template tools, Dreamweaver creates folders inside your local root folder. These folders don't do you any good on the web server; their sole purpose is to help you build your site locally. Likewise, you may have Photoshop (.psd), Flash (.fla), or Illustrator (.ai) files in your local site folder. They're inaccessible from a web browser and can take up a lot of disk space, so you shouldn't transfer them to your server when you move your site online.

Note: If you work on a website with other people, you probably *will* want to have the Library and templates folders on the server. That way, others who work on the site can access them as well.

To meet such challenges, Dreamweaver includes a feature called *cloaking*. It lets you hide folders and specific file types from many file-transfer operations, including Get/Put, the Check In/Check Out feature (page 711), and site synchronization (page 717). In fact, you can even hide files from many site-wide Dreamweaver actions, including reports (see page 683), search and replace (page 801) functions, the ability to check and change links site-wide (page 671), and the Assets panel (page 658). There's one exception: files linked to library items (see Chapter 19) or templates (Chapter 20) can still "see" items even in cloaked Library and template folders.

Dreamweaver lets you cloak folders and file types (those that end with a specific extension such as .fla or .psd). In addition, Dreamweaver CS5 even lets you cloak a single file anywhere on your site. Each type of cloak requires a different technique.

To hide specific types of files:

1. **Choose Site→Manage Sites.**

   The Manage Sites window opens, listing all sites you've defined in Dreamweaver.

2. **Select the site of interest and click Edit.**

   That site's Site Setup window opens.

3. **Click the arrow next to Advanced Settings to expand that list of options. Click the Cloaking category.**

   The cloaking settings appear (see Figure 18-9). The factory setting is On for every site you define. (If you want to turn it off, just turn off the "Enable cloaking" box.)

Tip: You can quickly turn cloaking on and off by right-clicking (Control-clicking) any file or folder in the Files panel and selecting Cloaking→Enable Cloaking from the shortcut menu. A checkmark next to Enable Cloaking means that cloaking is turned on.

---

4. **Turn on the "Cloak files ending with" checkbox.**

   Dreamweaver identifies file types by their extensions—.fla for Flash files, for example. If you use Fireworks, don't add the .png extension to this box. Even though you might not want to have your byte-heavy Fireworks files moved to your web server, cloaking files with the .png extension means that you'll keep Dreamweaver from transferring graphic files saved in the very common and useful compressed PNG file format (page 217) to your server.

Note: Mac programs don't always add these file name suffixes, but without them, Dreamweaver can't cloak, so if you use a Mac, make sure you add an extension when you save a file. Some programs have a "Hide File Extension" checkbox that appears when you save a file—make sure you have this *unchecked*.

---

5. **In the text box, type the extensions you wish to cloak.**

   Each extension should start with a period followed by three or four letters. To type multiple extensions in the box, separate them with a space.

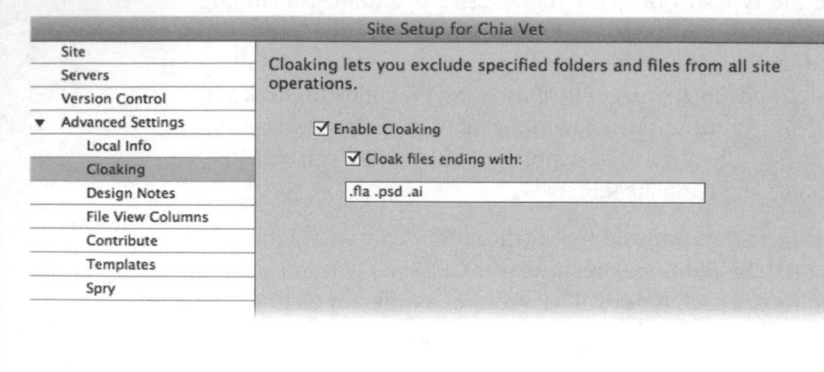

Figure 18-9: *The Cloaking category of the Site Definition window lets you turn cloaking on and off—a feature that lets you hide folders, specific file types, and individual files from sitewide operations like transferring files to a web server or searching and replacing text. In this window, you can specify which types of files to hide by listing their extensions (.psd for Photoshop files, for example).*

6. **Click Save and then Done to close this and the Manage Sites window.**

   In the Files panel, you'll see that all cloaked files have a red slash through them.

You can also cloak a single folder or file using the Files panel like this:

1. **Open the Files panel by pressing F8 (Shift-⌘-F).**

   Alternatively, choose Window→Files.

2. **Right-click (Control-click) any folder or file in the Local Files view.**

   A shortcut menu appears with many site-related options.

3. **Select Cloaking→Cloak.**

   Dreamweaver adds a red slash through the folder or file's icon in the Files panel. When you cloak a folder, Dreamweaver hides all files and folders within it as well, as indicated by the red slashes through their icons.

Once you cloak a folder, it and any folders inside it disappear from Dreamweaver's file-transfer functions. Dreamweaver also hides individual files you cloaked, and any files with an extension you specified in the Preferences window.

As with everything in life, there are exceptions, however. You can override the cloaking, for example, by selecting a cloaked folder or file and then using the Get or Put file buttons as described on page 702. Dreamweaver assumes that since you specifically selected that file or folder, you want to override the cloaking feature.

Dreamweaver also ignores cloaking if you answer Yes in the Dependent Files message box (Figure 18-7) when you put or get files. In that case, Dreamweaver transfers all dependent files, even if you cloaked them (this applies to Library and template files as well).

Check In and Check Out

If you're the sole developer for a website, the Files panel's Get and Put buttons are fine for transferring your files. But if you're on a team of developers, those simple tools can get you in trouble.

For example, suppose your boss emails you an important announcement that she wants posted on the home page immediately. So you download the home page from the web server and start to edit it. At the same time, your co-worker Bob notices a typo on the home page. He downloads it, too.

You're a much faster worker than Bob, so you add the critical news to the home page and move it back to the server. But then Bob transfers *his* corrected home page, *overwriting* your edits and eliminating that urgent notice you just uploaded. (An hour later, your phone rings. It's the boss.)

Without some kind of system to monitor who has what file and to prevent people from overwriting each other's work, collaborative web development is a chaotic mess. Fortunately, Dreamweaver's Check In and Check Out system provides a civilized answer to the problem, specifically designed for group web development. It works like your local public library: When you check out a file, no one else can have it. When you're finished, you check the file back in, releasing control of it, and allowing someone else on the team to check it out and work on it.

To use the Check In/Check Out feature effectively, keep a few things in mind:

- When you develop a website solo, your local site usually contains the most recent versions of your files. You make any modifications or additions to the pages on your computer and *then* transfer the edited pages to your web server.

  But in a collaborative environment where many people work on the site at once, the files on your hard drive may not be the latest ones. After all, your co-workers, like you, have been updating pages and transferring them to the server. The home page sitting in the local site folder on your computer may be several days older than the file on the remote site, which is why checking out a file from the *remote server*, rather than editing the copy on your computer, is so important. It guarantees that you have the latest version of the file.

- In a collaborative environment, nobody should post files to the web server using any method except Dreamweaver's Check In and Check Out system.

  The reason is technical, but worth slogging through: When Dreamweaver checks out a file, it doesn't actually *lock* the file. Instead, it places a small, invisible text file (with the three-letter suffix .lck) on both the remote server and in your local site folder. This text file indicates who has checked out the file. When Dreamweaver connects to a remote server, it uses these files to know which web files are in use by others.

  But only Dreamweaver understands the .lck files. Other FTP programs, like WS_FTP (Windows) or Fetch (Mac), gladly ignore them and can easily overwrite any checked-out files. This risk also applies when you simply copy files back and forth over the office network.

Note: Adobe's word processor-like web-page editing program, Contribute, also takes advantage of the Check In/Check Out feature, so you can use the two programs on the same site.

- All Dreamweaver-using team members must configure their remote site to use Check In and Check Out (see page 711). If just one person doesn't do it, you risk overwritten files.

Note: WebDAV people are free of these last two constraints. As long as everyone working on the site uses programs that support the WebDAV protocol, they can work seamlessly with Dreamweaver people, and vice versa.

Checking Out Files

When you want to work on a file on a collaborative site, you check it out from the web server. Doing so makes sure that *you* have the latest version of the file, and that nobody else can make changes to it.

Warning: Dreamweaver's Check In/Check Out feature only works if everyone on the team uses it. They must all have Dreamweaver and must all turn on this feature, as described in "Setting Up a Remote Site over a Local Network." If one person doesn't use the system, you could run into problems.

If you're used to creating sites by yourself, this business may feel a little strange; after all, your local site (the files on your computer) contains the latest versions of all files. When you work with a group, however, you should consider the *remote server*—where everyone can access, edit, and add new web pages—the master repository of your site's files.

Note: There's nothing to check out when you create a new page. Since the only version of the file in the universe lies on your computer, have no fear that someone else may work on it at the same time as you. In this case, you only need to check the file *into* the site when you're done.

You check out a file using the Files panel; if it's not open, press F8 (Shift-⌘-F) or choose Window→Files. Then select the site you want to work on from the Site pop-up menu (shown at the top of Figure 18-10).

Now you're ready to begin. From the Local Files list in the Files panel, select the files you wish to check out from the server—or, to check out an entire folder and every file inside it, select the folder.

POWER USERS' GEM IN THE ROUGH

Subversion in Dreamweaver

Dreamweaver CS5 expands on its support for a popular version control system called *Subversion*. Well, at least it's popular among programmers and open-source aficionados. Subversion is a free, open-source program that developers usually use to manage files as part of a large programming project. It has powerful features to make sure that multiple users don't overwrite each others' changes, and to make it easy to "roll-back" to previous versions of a file if something goes wrong.

To take advantage of Dreamweaver's Subversion support, first you need to set up a *Subversion server*—a separate piece of software running on either your own computer, on a server on your network, or even on a server somewhere on the Internet. You can download the software at *http://subversion.tigris.org/getting.html*. You can also find companies that offer free or cheap Subversion hosting (in other words, they take care of the mess of setting up a Subversion server for you). Next, you need to create what's called a Subversion *repository*—a way of identifying a set of files that belong to a particular project. For example, each web project would probably be its own repository. You can learn more about how to set up Subversion at *http://svnbook.red-bean.com/*.

For Dreamweaver users, it's important to keep in mind that a Subversion repository is independent of the website running on your web server. In other words, you'll have a Subversion repository, local files on your computer, and another set of files out on the Web (that is, your remote website).

You can set up Subversion support for a site in Dreamweaver by choosing Site→ Manage Sites, and choosing a site to edit. In the Site Definition window, select the Version Control category and choose Subversion from the Access menu. Then fill out the other settings, such as the server address, repository path, your username, and password.

Once you do this, you'll connect to the repository when you choose Repository View from the File View menu (see Figure 16-8). In addition, when you use the Check Out and Check In buttons on the Files panel, you'll check files out and in from the Subversion repository. Dreamweaver CS5 adds the ability to copy, move, delete, and revert (go back to a previous version of) files in the repository. (Dreamweaver CS5 also fixes a major problem with CS4—out-of-date Subversion software. Now you can update your Subversion program to new versions as they come out.)

Unfortunately, if you want to perform site-wide changes like updating templates or changing the footer information throughout your site, you need to check out the *entire* website from the repository.

If you develop websites on your own, Subversion is definitely overkill. Even if you toil in a small workgroup, unless you have someone with the system administrator know-how to set up a Subversion server and repository, you're probably better off with something simpler, like Dreamweaver's Check-in/Check-out system or even WebDAV. Probably the most important feature of Subversion is the ability to go back to a previous version of a file that has somehow been wrecked.

If you're not going to use Subversion, it's definitely worth investing in some basic backup software like Retrospect Remote or Apple's Time Machine. Even most simple backup software lets you keep hourly, daily, weekly, or monthly file backups, and lets you go back in time to retrieve older versions. Or, for the low-tech approach, just back up your site every day and store the copied files in a folder named something like *June_10_2011*. That way, you'll have a daily backup you can turn to if you need to recover a lost file.

However, if your company or organization does use Subversion, you can get in-depth information on using Dreamweaver with it at *http://help.adobe.com/en_US/Dreamweaver/10.0_Using/WS80FE60AC-15F8-45a2-842E-52D29F540FED.html*.

In some instances, you may want to select a file from the Live Server list as well. For example, you might need to modify a page you didn't create and which you've never checked out before. In such a case, the file isn't *in* your local site, so you must select it from the live server list. Select "Remote server" from the Files panel (see Figure 18-6); Dreamweaver connects to and then displays the remote server files in the Files panel. Select the ones you want to check out.

Tip: If, when you set up your remote server (see page 701), you select the "Check Out File when Opening" option, you can also check out (and open) a file by double-clicking it in the Files panel. This is a quick way to open a page you want to edit while still using Dreamweaver's Check Out feature.

In any case, now just click the Check Out files button on the Files panel (see Figure 18-10), or use the keyboard shortcut Ctrl+Alt+Shift+D (⌘-Option-Shift-D). (Not enough fingers? See page 817 to learn how to change Dreamweaver's shortcuts.)

Dreamweaver asks if you want to check out dependent files, too. Click Yes if you think the page you're checking out uses files you haven't downloaded. Dreamweaver then copies the dependent files to your computer, so the page you check out displays its current images, CSS style sheets, and other linked files. It doesn't *check out* a dependent file, however, so if you do want to *edit* the dependent file—if, for example, you need to edit the styles in a linked external style sheet, too—you must also check out that dependent file.

Note: When you edit a web page you've checked out, you may run into a weird problem if you edit the CSS tags on that page. If the page uses an external style sheet and you didn't check out the style sheet, you won't be able to edit any styles in the page. Instead, you'll get a message saying that the file is locked and Dreamweaver will ask if you want to check it out. Click the Check Out button and Dreamweaver tries to check it out. If Dreamweaver informs you that someone else has checked out the external style sheet, click cancel, and wait until the other person checks the style sheet back in. Then check it out and make your changes. Bottom line: check out your site's external style sheets if you want to edit the CSS in your pages.

When you check out files, Dreamweaver copies them to your computer and marks them as checked out so others can't change them. Like uploading and downloading files, checking out files can take time, depending on the speed of your Internet connection.

After you check out a file, Dreamweaver displays a green "checked-out" checkmark in the Files panel next to its name (see Figure 18-10). You can now open and edit the file, and, when you're done, check the file back

If you attempt to check out a file that someone else has already checked out, Dreamweaver tells you as much. It also gives you the option to override the person's checkout—but unless you're the boss, resist the temptation, for two reasons. First, your colleagues may have made some important changes to the page, which you'll wipe out with your shenanigans. Second, because you so rudely stole the file, they may stop bringing you donuts in the morning.

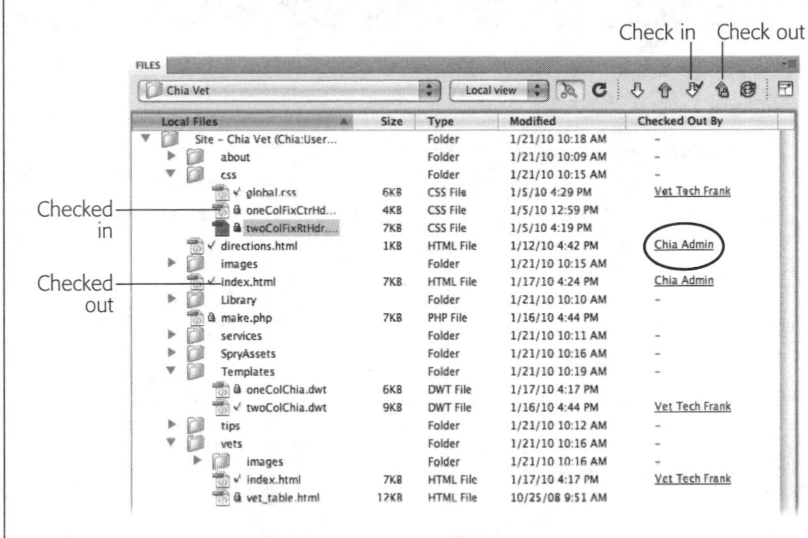

Figure 18-10:
The Check In/Out buttons transfer files between your local site and web server. A padlock identifies files checked into the remote site. Confusingly, the lock means that the file is open for anyone to check out and edit. If someone has checked out a file, a checkmark appears next to its name. A green checkmark indicates you've checked out the file; a red checkmark means someone else has.

A better way to work with someone who's checked out a file that you need is to use Dreamweaver's email feature. You can see who checked out the file by consulting Dreamweaver's Checked Out By column (see the circled entry in Figure 18-10). Even better, if you click the name, Dreamweaver opens your email program and addresses an email to that person, so you can say: "Hey Bob, you've had the home page checked out for two days! I need to work on it, so check it back in!"

The name and email address Dreamweaver uses depends on the information your co-workers provided when they configured their computers for remote site use (you provided this same information when you configured your computer). See the Advanced options on page 701 for more detail.

Checking In Files

When you're ready to move a page you edited back onto the server, you check it in. (You also check in *new* files you create.)

To check in files, open the Files panel (press F8 [Shift-⌘-F]), choose the relevant site from the Site pop-up menu, and (using the Local Folder file list in the Files panel) select the files you want to check in to your server. As always, you can click a folder to check *it* in, along with every file inside it.

The files you check in should be files you've checked out, or brand-new files that have never been on the server. If you attempt to check in a file that someone else has checked out, Dreamweaver warns you with a message box. Click Cancel to stop the check-in procedure, so you won't overwrite the checked-out file on the server. Dreamweaver also warns you if you try to check in a file that's older than the copy on the server. Again, unless you're sure this is what you want to do, click Cancel.

WORKAROUND WORKSHOP

Manual Checkout Override

Occasionally, you may want to erase the checked-out status of a file. Suppose, for example, someone who's checked out a lot of files suddenly catches the plague and can't continue working on the site. To free those files so others can work on them, you have to undo his checkout (and quarantine his cubicle).

To do the former, make sure you have the Files panel in remote server view (this trick won't work with the local files displayed). Then, right-click (Control-click) the checked-out file and select Undo Checkout from the menu that appears.

Dreamweaver warns you that whoever checked out the file won't be able to check it back in. (This is, in fact, false. That person can still check in the file, overwriting whatever's on the web server. So you can see why you should override the checkout only when the person who checked it out is very unlikely to check it back in–stranded on a deserted island, perhaps.)

When the operation's complete, a padlock icon appears next to the file.

You can also use this technique on a file *you've* checked out. For example, if, after checking out a file, you make a horrible mistake on the page and wish to revert to the copy on the server.

Tip: If you want to check in the page you're currently working on to the remote site, use the toolbar in the document window (see Figure 18-8).

You can check in the selected files in any of the usual ways:

- Click the Check In files button on the Files panel (see Figure 18-10).
- Use the keyboard shortcut Ctrl+Alt+Shift+U (⌘-Option-Shift-U). (See page 817to learn how to change the Dreamweaver shortcut to something less cumbersome.)

Dreamweaver asks if you want to check in any dependent files at the same time (see Figure 18-7). You should transfer dependent files only if you first checked them out, or if the dependent files are new and have never been uploaded to the server. If you attempt to check in a dependent file that someone else has checked out, Dreamweaver warns you with a message box—click the No button in this box, so that you don't overwrite someone's checked out file.

After you click through all the message boxes, Dreamweaver copies the files to the remote server. Once you check in a file, a padlock icon appears next to its name in the Local Files list of the Files panel (see Figure 18-10); checking in locks the file so you don't accidentally change the local copy. If you wish to modify the file in some way, check it out from the server.

Note: Dreamweaver's Site Report feature (page 683) lets you see which files are checked out and by whom. Skip it. On a large site, the report can take a long time to run, it isn't always accurate, and you can't do the things you're most likely to do with checked-out files (like checking them back in) from the Reports panel.

FREQUENTLY ASKED QUESTION

Get and Put, In and Out

I'm using Dreamweaver's Check In and Check Out buttons to transfer my files. What do the Get and Put buttons do if I use the Check In/Out feature?

If you use Check In and Out, the Get and Put commands function slightly differently than described on page 702. *Get*, in this case, copies the selected file or files to your local site. However, Dreamweaver draws a small lock icon next to each of the "gotten" files in your Local Folder list. The files are locked, and you shouldn't edit them. Remember, checking out a file is the only way to prevent others from working on it simultaneously. If you edit a locked file on your computer, nothing stops someone else from checking out the page, editing it, and checking it back in.

But you may still find the Get command useful in such a situation. For example, suppose someone just updated the site's external style sheet. The pages you're editing use this style sheet, so you want to get the latest version. You don't want to edit the style sheet itself, so you don't need to check it out. If you use Get instead of checking out the pages, you can keep a reference copy on your computer without locking it for anyone else and without having to check it back in later.

Put, on the other hand, simply–and blindly–transfers the file on your local site to the remote site. If you use the Check In/ Check Out feature and you haven't also checked out the file, using Put is a bad idea. The remote site should be your reference copy; several rounds of revisions may have been made to a file since you last checked it out. Your local copy will be hopelessly out-of-date, and moving it to the server using Put destroys the most recent version of the file.

However, if you *do* have the file checked out, you can use Put to transfer your local copy to the server so your site's visitors see it. For example, say you're updating the home page with 20 new news items. To keep your site Dup-to-the-minute" fresh, you can Put the home page after you add each news item. Then the whole world will see each item as soon as possible. When you completely finish editing the home page, check it in.

Synchronizing Site Files

As you may suspect, when you keep two sets of files—local site and remote server—it's easy to lose track of which files are the most recent. For example, say you finish your website and move all the files to the server. The next day, you notice mistakes on a bunch of pages, so you make corrections on the copies in your local site. But in your rush to fix the pages, you didn't keep track of which ones you corrected. So although you're ready to move the corrected pages to the server, you're not sure *which* ones you need to transfer.

When you use the Check In/Check Out feature described on page 711, you avoid this problem altogether. Using this system, the version on the server is *always* considered the latest and most definitive copy—*unless* you or someone else has checked out that file. In that case, whoever checked out the file has the most recent version.

But if you're operating solo and don't use the Check In/Check Out feature, you may get good mileage from Dreamweaver's Synchronize command, which lets you compare the remote and local sites and transfer only the newer files in either direction.

(In fact, since the Synchronize command uses the Get and Put methods of transferring files, you may not get the results you expect if you synchronize your site while also using Check In and Check Out [as described in the box on the opposite page].)

To synchronize your sites:

1. **Make sure you turn on the "Maintain synchronization information" checkbox when you set the server options (see the Advanced options mentioned on page 701).**

   Dreamweaver automatically turns this option on when you set up the server (see Figure 18-5).

2. **Choose Site→Synchronize Sitewide.**

   Alternatively, you can right-click anywhere inside the Files panel. From the shortcut menu that appears, select Synchronize. In either case, the Synchronize Files dialog box appears (see Figure 18-11).

3. **Using the Synchronize pop-up menu, specify the files to update.**

   You can either synchronize all files in the current site, or just the files you select from the Local site list. This last option is good when you have a really big site and want to limit this operation to just a single section of the site—one folder, for example.

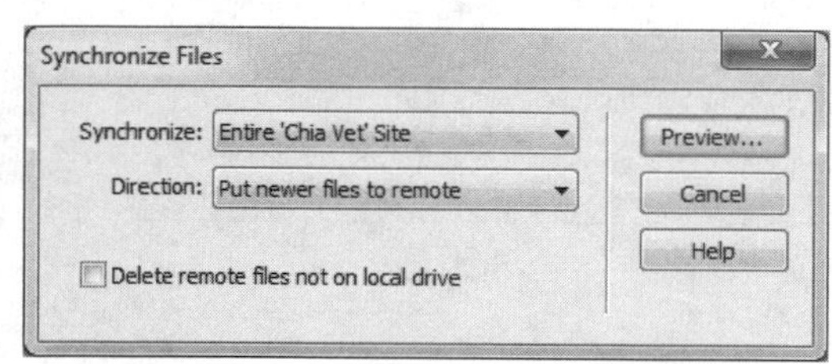

Figure 18-11: *Using the Synchronization command, you can copy newer files from your computer to the web server, or get newer files from the remote site.*

4. **Using the Direction pop-up menu, choose the destination for newer files.**

   You have three choices. *Put newer files to remote* updates the web server with any newer files from your local site folder. It also copies any *new* files on the local site to the remote server. Use this option when you've done heavy editing to the local site and want to move all new or modified pages to the server.

   Get newer files from remote does the reverse: it updates your local site folder with any newer (or new) files from the remote site. Here's one instance where the synchronize feature comes in handy in team-design situations. If you've been out of the office for a while, click this option to download copies of the latest site files. (Note that this doesn't check out any files; it merely makes sure you have the latest files on your computer. This is one example where synchronization works well with Check In/Check Out, since it refreshes your local copy of the site with the latest files, including graphics and external CSS style sheets, that your checked-out pages may depend on.)

Get and put newer files is a two-way synchronization. Dreamweaver transfers any new files on the local site to the remote site and vice versa. For example, if you update a page on your computer, Dreamweaver moves that file to the web server; if someone has made changes to a file on the server that is more recently than the copy on your computer, Dreamweaver downloads that file to your hard drive. The result is that both "sides" contain the latest files.

5. **Turn on the Delete checkbox, if desired.**

   The way Dreamweaver words this option reflects the option you selected in the previous step. If you move newer files to the remote site, it says, "Delete remote files not on local drive". It's a useful option when, for example, you spent the afternoon cleaning up the local copy of your site, deleting old, orphaned graphics files and web pages, and you want Dreamweaver to update the web server to match.

   If you chose to transfer newer files *from* the remote site, Dreamweaver lets you "Delete local files not on remote server". Use this feature when your local site is hopelessly out-of-date with the remote site. Perhaps you work on the site with a team, but you've been on vacation for two months (this is, of course, a hypothetical example). The site may have changed so significantly that you want to get your local copy in line with the website.

Warning: Of course, you should proceed with caution when using *any* command that automatically deletes files. There's no Undo for these delete operations, and you don't want to accidentally delete the only copy of a particular page, graphic, or external Cascading Style Sheet.

   If you chose the "Get and put newer files" option in step 4, Dreamweaver dims and makes unavailable the Delete checkbox. This option truly synchronizes the two; Dreamweaver copies newer files on the remote site (including files that exist on the server but not on your computer) to your local site, and vice versa.

6. **Click Preview to begin the synchronization process.**

   Dreamweaver connects to the remote site and compares the two sets of files—if your site is large, this comparison is a time-consuming process. When it finishes, the Synchronize preview window appears (Figure 18-12), listing which files Dreamweaver will delete and which it will transfer, and providing an additional set of options for working with the listed files.

Note: Synchronization is not a fast process. Dreamweaver needs to connect to the remote server, and then compare the remote server files with your local files. On a site with even a dozen or so pages and lots of graphics, the synchronization process can take minutes to complete. This is one reason why, if you only need to synchronize files in one folder, you should first select that folder in the Files panel, and then, in step 3 above, choose Selected files only.

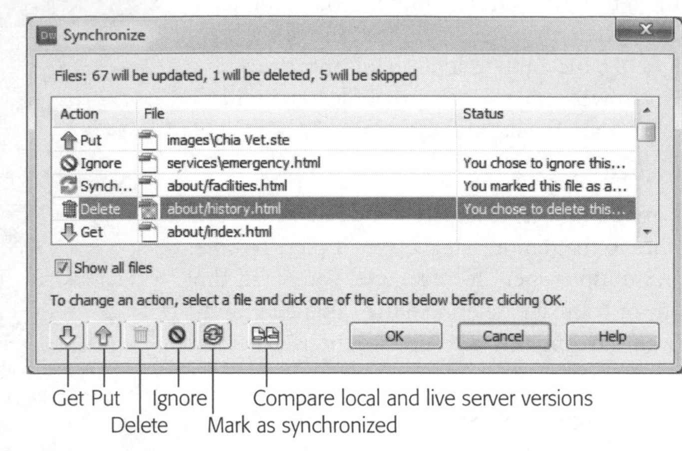

Figure 18-12: *The Synchronize window lets you preview any actions Dreamweaver intends to take to synchronize the files on your local and remote server sites. You can change this action on a file-by-file basis. Turn on the "Show all files" checkbox to list all files, including ones Dreamweaver believes are identical on both the remote and local copies of the site: these files are marked Synchronized in the Action column.*

7. **Change the action Dreamweaver takes on the listed files.**

   The preview box tells you what Dreamweaver plans to do with a file—get it, put it, or delete it. You can override these actions by selecting a file from the list and clicking one of the action buttons at the bottom of the window. For example, if you realize that Dreamweaver is going to delete a file that you *know* you need, select the file in the list and click the "Ignore file" button (the red circle with a line through it).

   Most of these options are useful only if you know Dreamweaver made a mistake: for example, when the program says you should get a file, but you know your local copy is identical to the server's copy. In that case, you could select the file and click the "Mark as synchronized" button, to tell Dreamweaver that they're identical. However, if you knew exactly which files were identical and which ones needed updating, you wouldn't need to use the synchronize feature in the first place, right?

   One option can come in quite handy. The "Compare local and remote versions" button lets you compare the code in the local file to the code in the remote file so you can identify exactly what differs between the two. You can use this feature to, for example, see exactly what changes were made to the remote copy of the file. You'll learn about this feature in detail on "Comparing Versions of a Web Page" on page 441.

8. **Click OK to proceed, or Cancel to stop the synchronization.**

   If you click OK, Dreamweaver commences copying and deleting the chosen files. If you want to stop the process, click the Cancel button in the Background File Activity window (see the box on page 706).

9. **Click Close.**

Note: If you just want to *identify* newer files on the local site without synchronizing them (to run a report on them, for example), click the contextual menu in the top-right corner of the Files panel and choose Edit→Select Newer Local. Dreamweaver connects to the remote server and compares the files, and then, in the Files panel's "Local view" list, highlights files on the local site that are newer than their remote counterparts.

You can also identify newer files on the remote server: Choose Edit→Select Newer on Remote server from the Files panel's contextual menu.

Finally, you can identify files on your computer you either created or modified within a given date range, using the Select Recently Modified command described in the box on page 674.

Communicating with Design Notes

Lots of questions arise when a team works on a website: Has this page been proofread? Who is the author of the page? Where did this graphic come from? Usually, you must rely on a flurry of emails to ferret out the answers.

But Dreamweaver's Design Notes dialog box (Figure 18-13) eliminates much of that hassle by letting you attach information, such as a web page's status or author, to a file.

You can open these notes (from the Files panel, from a currently open document, or automatically [see Figure 18-13]), edit them, and even share them with others. This way, it's easy to leave notes for other people—such as, "Hey Bob, can you make sure that this is the most recent photo of Brad and Angelina?" You can even add notes to files other than web pages, including folders, images, Flash movies, and external Cascading Style Sheets—anything, in fact, that appears in the Files panel.

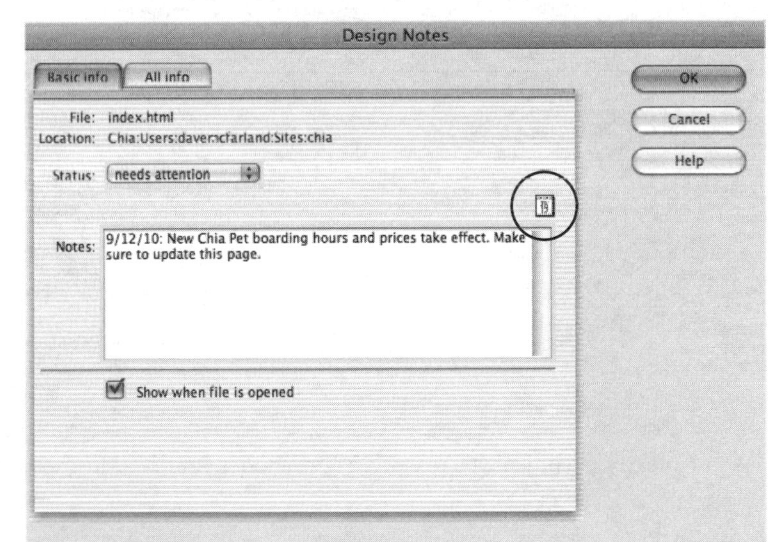

Figure 18-13: *If you want the Design Notes window to open whenever someone opens a page, turn on the "Show when file is opened" checkbox. This option makes sure that no one misses an important note attached to a page, because Dreamweaver automatically opens the note at the same time it opens the page. (This option has no effect when you add notes to GIFs, JPEGs, Flash movies, or anything other than a file that Dreamweaver can open and edit, such as a web page or an external style sheet.)*

Setting Up Design Notes

You can't use Design Notes unless you turn the feature itself on. To find out if it is turned on, open the Site Setup dialog box by double-clicking the site's name in the Manage Sites dialog box (choose Manage Sites from the Site menu or the pop-up menu in the Files panel). In the Advanced setting category list, click Design Notes; as shown in Figure 18-14, two checkboxes pertain to the notes feature:

- **Maintain Design Notes.** This checkbox lets you create and read notes using Dreamweaver's File→Design Notes command (see "Viewing Design Notes" on page 723).
- **Enable Upload Design Notes for sharing.** If you use Design Notes as part of a team, turn on this checkbox, which makes Dreamweaver upload design notes to the remote site, so that your fellow team members can read them.

Tip: Design Notes are especially useful for keeping track of pages built and maintained by a team of web developers. But if you're a solo operator and still want to use them—maybe you're the type with a hundred Post-it notes taped to the edges of your monitor—then turn off "Upload Design Notes for sharing." You'll save time and server space by preventing Dreamweaver from transferring note files to the server.

Click OK to close the Site Definition dialog box. You can double-click another site in the Manage Sites dialog box to turn on its Design Notes feature, or click Done.

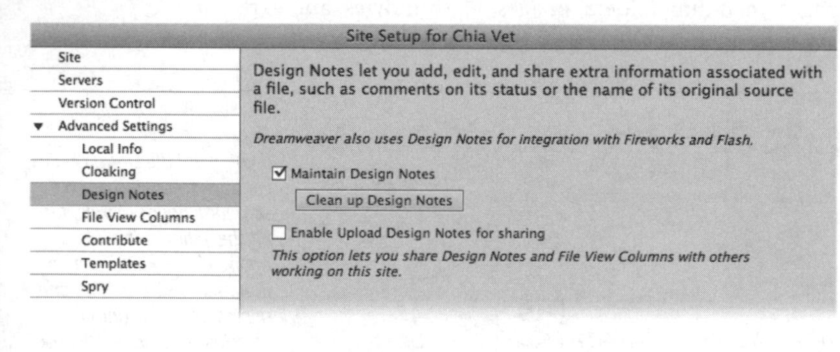

Figure 18-14: *The Clean Up button deletes any notes that were attached to now-deleted files. (To avoid stray notes files in the first place, always delete pages in Dreamweaver's Files panel, as opposed to Windows Explorer or the Mac's Finder.) If you turn off the Maintain Design Notes checkbox, clicking Clean Up removes all Design Notes files from the site.*

To add a Design Note to a document you're working on, choose your favorite method:

- Choose File→Design Notes.
- From the File Status menu in the document toolbar, choose Design Notes (see Figure 18-8).

- Right-click (Control-click) a file in the Files panel (or an external object, such as a graphic or Flash movie, in the document window), and choose Design Notes from the shortcut menu.

In any case, the Design Notes window opens (Figure 18-13). If you like, you can use the Status pop-up menu to let your team members know where the file stands. For example, is it ready to move to the server? Is it just a draft version? Or is there something wrong with it that requires attention? Dreamweaver provides eight different options: "draft," "revision1," "revision2," "revision3," "alpha," "beta," "final," and "needs attention."

The note itself, which you type into the Note box, could be a simple question you have for the author of the page ("Are you sure 'Coldplay: Defining a New Musical Language for the Modern Age' is an appropriate title for this article?") or more information about the status of the page ("Still need studio shot for Chia Pet bad hair days article").

Tip: Click the calendar icon (circled in Figure 18-3) to pop the date into your note—a great way to keep a running tally of notes and the dates they were written.

When you click OK, Dreamweaver creates a file with all the note information in it. This file ends with the extension .mno and begins with the name of the file; for the file *index.html*, for example, Dreamweaver would name the note *index.html.mno*.

Dreamweaver stores notes in a folder called *_notes* that it keeps in the same folder as the relevant page or file. For example, if you add notes to the home page, Dreamweaver stores the *_notes* folder inside the root folder.

Viewing Design Notes

You can view Design Notes in a number of ways. If the note's author turned on "Show when file is opened" (see Figure 18-3), of course, the Design Notes window opens automatically when you open that page (subject to the limitations explained in Figure 18-14).

Otherwise, to look at a note, you have any number of options:

- Choose File→Design Notes.
- Choose Design Notes from the File Status drop-down menu in the document window's toolbar (see Figure 18-8).
- Double-click the small yellow balloon icon in the Notes column of the Files panel. (You'll only see this column if you've turned on this option in the Site Definition window, as described below.)
- Right-click (Control-click) an embedded object, like a graphic or Flash movie, right in the document window, and choose Design Notes from the shortcut menu.

- Right-click (Control-click) a file in the Files panel and choose Design Notes from the shortcut menu.

Organizing the Columns in the Files Panel

Columns in the Files panel identify a file's name, size, modification date, type, and so on.

This may be more information than you're interested in—or it may not be enough. So remember that Dreamweaver lets you show or hide columns, change their order, or even create new ones with information it retrieves from a file's Design Notes.

Note: You can adjust the relative width of these columns by dragging the dividing line between the column names. You can also sort all the pages listed in this window by clicking the relevant column's name. Click "Modified", for example, to sort the files so the newest appear first. Click a second time to reverse the sort, placing oldest files first.

When you set up a website in the Site Definition window, you can view the column setup by clicking the File View Columns category (Figure 18-15).

Once you're looking at the display shown in Figure 18-15, you can perform any of these stunts:

- **Reorder columns.** Click a column name in the Site Definition window to select it. Then click the up and down arrow buttons to move the column one spot to the left or right, respectively, in the Files panel.
- **Deleting columns.** Click the column name, and then click the minus (–) button to delete the column. (Dreamweaver doesn't let you delete the built-in columns: Name, Notes, Type, Modified, and so on.)
- **Adding Columns.** You can add columns of your own, as described next.

To hide a column (or show a hidden column), select the column in the File View Options category of the Site Setup window (Figure 18-15), and then click the Edit button (circled in Figure 18-15). In the window that opens, you can hide the column by unchecking the Show box. You can also change how Dreamweaver aligns the text in the column (left, right, or center) using the Align menu. It's a good idea to hide columns you don't need, since they take up space in the Files panel, often hiding parts of file names.

"All Info" Design Notes in Column Views

Your Files panel offers columns for all the usual information bits: Name, Checked Out, and so on. But you may someday wish there were a column that showed each page's status, so that your Files panel could show you which files need proofreading, or who wrote each article, or which pages are being held until a certain blackout date.

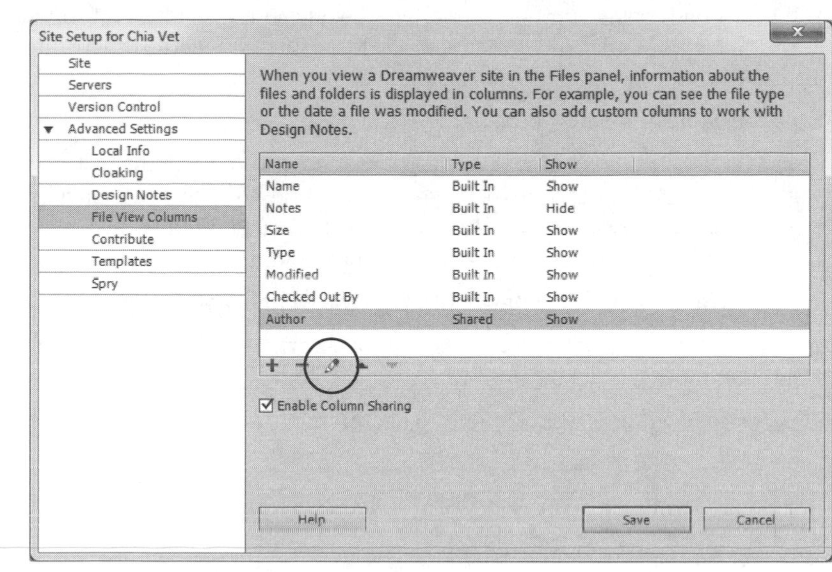

***Figure 18-15:** Dreamweaver's Files panel has a handful of set columns: Name, Notes, Size, Type, Modified, and Checked Out By. You can't delete these columns, but you can hide them as described below after clicking the Edit button (circled). You can also create custom columns to display information that matches your work requirements (for example, a column listing the author of each web article).*

You can indeed add columns of your own design, although the process isn't streamlined by any means. It involves two broad efforts: First, using an offshoot of the Design Notes feature described earlier, you set up the new columns you want to display. Then, using the column-manipulation dialog box shown in Figure 18-15, you make the new columns visible in the Files panel.

Phase 1: Defining the new information types

You create new kinds of informational flags—primarily for use as new columns in the Files panel—using the Design Notes dialog box. Here's the rundown:

1. **Choose File→Design Notes.**

   The Design Notes window appears. (You can summon it in various other ways, as described on page 723.)

2. **Click the "All info" tab.**

   This peculiar window shows the programmery underbelly of the Dreamweaver Notes feature (see Figure 18-16). It turns out that it stores every kind of note as a name/value pair. If you used the main Notes screen (Figure 18-12) to choose Beta from the Status pop-up menu, for example, you'll see a notation here that says "status=beta". (*Status* is the name of the info nugget; *beta* is the value.) If you turn on the option called "Show when file is opened", you'll see "showOnOpen=true". And if you typed *Badly needs updating* as the note itself, you'll see "notes=Badly needs updating" on this screen.

   But those are just the built-in info types; you're free to create your own.

3. **Click the + button.**

   You may wonder why you'd do this; after all, you can type a lot of information in the Notes box under the Basic Info tab. The primary benefit is that you can display the information in the Files panel.

4. **Type the name of the new note in the Name field.**

   It may be *Author*, for example, so that you can note who wrote the text of each page. Or it could be *Artist*, if you wish to add a note to each image specifying who created it. Maybe you need a column called *Hold Until*, which lets you know when certain information is OK to publish online.

5. **Press Tab (to jump to the Value field); type the contents of the note.**

   You can enter the actual name of the author or artist—Jennifer Jones, for example—or the actual "Hold Until" date.

   Repeat steps 3 through 5 if you want to add more notes.

Note: Keep the value short–one or two words. Otherwise, the narrow Files panel column chops off the latter part of it. If you've got enough screen real estate, you can resize the columns by dragging the divider bars between column names.

---

6. **Click OK.**

   The dialog box closes.

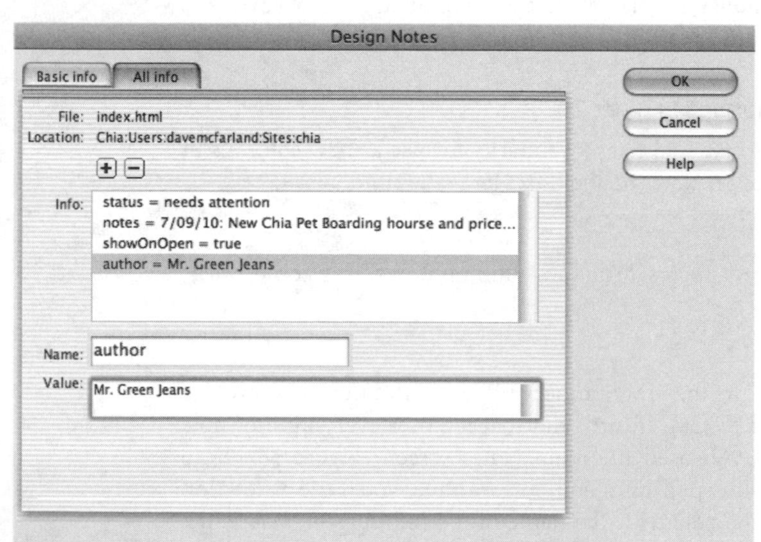

Figure 18-16: *Dreamweaver lets you create your own types of notes in the "All info" tab of the Design Notes window. This lets you add more information to a page, such as its author or designer. Deleting a note you added is a simple matter of clicking on the note in the Info box and then clicking the minus (-) button.*

Phase 2: Adding the column

Just creating a new note type gets you only halfway home; now you have to tell Dreamweaver to display that information in the Files panel.

To add a column:

1. **Open the Site Setup window for the particular site and select the File View Columns category under the Advanced Setting Options.**

   To edit a site, choose Site→Manage Sites, then double-click the name of the site from the Manage Sites window. The File View Columns options appear (Figure 18-15).

2. **Click the + button.**

   A pane appears (Figure 18-17) for adding the information for the new column.

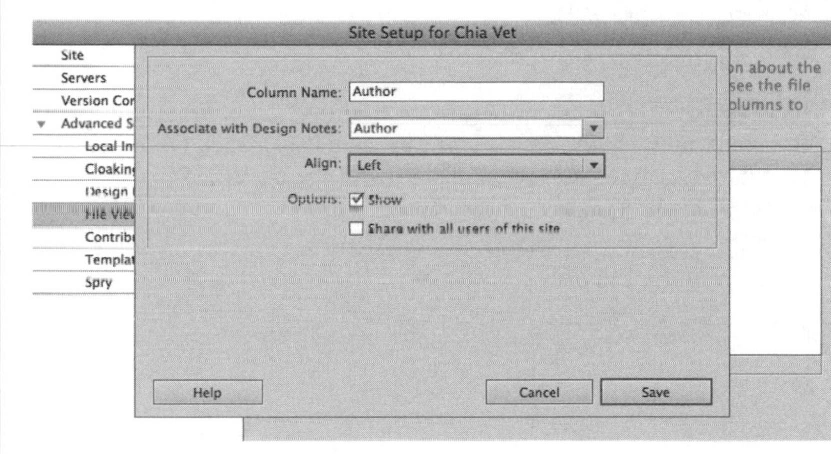

***Figure 18-17:** Creating your own columns is definitely for the hyper-organized. If you want to keep special information about your pages always visible in the Files panel (such as an author name, or a "hold until" date), then this feature may be worth the trouble of setting up special design notes and columns.*

3. **In the Column Name box, type the column heading you want to appear in the Files panel.**

   Make it short and descriptive. If possible, it should match the note type (*Author, Artist, Hold Until*, or whatever).

4. **Press Tab. Type the name of the Design Note you wish to use for this column.**

   This is the name part of the name/value pair described in step 4 of the previous instructions. For example, if you add a note named Author to a file, you would type *Author* here. Capitalization matters; so if you named the Design Note *Author*, type it with a capital A.

   There's a pop-up menu here, too, but it always lists the same four options: Status, Assigned, Due, and Priority. If you choose Status, you'll get a column that reflects your choice from the Status pop-up menu. The other three options do nothing *unless* you create a matching note type in step 4 of the previous instructions. (It would be nice if this pop-up menu listed *all* the note names you've created, so you didn't have to remember them.)

Before you wrap up the column-adding procedure, you can, if you wish, choose an alignment option for the text in the column (left, right, or center). Check to make sure that the Show checkbox is turned on (otherwise, your new column won't appear, and you've just defeated the purpose of this whole exercise). Finally, turn on "Share with all users of this site" if you like.

The Share feature works like this: The next time you connect to the remote server, Dreamweaver uploads a file containing your newly defined column information. The next time another member of the team connects to the remote site, *his* copy of Dreamweaver downloads this file, so that his Files panel shows the same columns yours does.

Note: The column-sharing feature can be very handy; it lets everyone working on a site share the same note information. But it works properly only if everyone on the team has the "Enable column sharing" checkbox turned on (see Figure 18-15).

---

5. **Click OK.**

   You should now see the new column in your Files panel. (You may need to widen the panel to see all the columns. You can also click the Expand Files Panel button [Figure 16-8] to expand the Panel.)

CHAPTER

19

Snippets and Libraries

You've finished the design for your company's new website. It looks great and your boss is ecstatic. But you've really only just begun. You have to build hundreds of pages before you launch. And once the site's online, you'll need to make endless updates to keep it fresh and inviting.

This is where Dreamweaver's Snippets and Library features come in, streamlining the sometimes tedious work of building and updating web pages.

As you build more and more web pages (and more and more websites), you may find yourself creating the same web page elements over and over again. Many of your pages may share common elements that always stay the same: a copyright notice, a navigation bar, or a logo, for example. And you may find yourself frequently using more complex components, such as a pull-down menu that lists all the countries you ship products to, or a particular design for photos and their captions.

Recreating the same page elements time after time is tiresome and—thanks to Dreamweaver—unnecessary. Dreamweaver provides two subtly different tools for reusing common page elements: *Snippets* and *Library items*.

Snippets Basics

Snippets aren't fancy or complex, but they sure save time. A snippet is simply a chunk of code you store away and then plunk into your web pages as necessary. The can be as simple as boilerplate legal text, or as complex as HTML, CSS, or JavaScript code (or code from any other programming language you encounter). For example, say you always use the same table design to list product specifications in your company's catalog. Each time you want to create a similar table, you could go through all the same steps to build it—or you could turn that table into a snippet, and then, with a simple double-click, add it to page after page of your site.

You keep these code chunks in the Snippets panel (see Figure 19-1), and you summon them in a couple of ways:

- Choose Window→Snippets.
- Windows people can press Shift-F9. (There's no Mac keyboard shortcut for opening the Snippets panel, but you can create your own if you want, as described on page 817.)

Once open, the Snippets panel appears grouped with the Files and Assets panels. Above and beyond Dreamweaver's preinstalled snippets, you can quickly build a collection of your own.

Using Snippets

Snippets come in two varieties: those that are a simple block of code, and those that wrap around your current selection in a document. For example, in the Snippets panel's Text folder, you'll find a snippet called Service Mark. Adding this snippet to a page instantly inserts the code *^{sm}*, creating a superscript service mark (^{SM}) symbol.

But on occasion, you'll want to wrap code around something you've already typed. You may, for example, want to add an HTML comment to your page (a message that won't appear in a web browser, but that helps you or other web designers decipher the page). The "Comment, multi-line" snippet (in the Comments folder) can help you quickly add such a note. It wraps whatever you select with opening (<!--) and closing HTML comments (-->). Adding an HTML comment is as easy as typing the comment in your page, selecting it, and then double-clicking this snippet. This may sound a lot like the Apply Comment button in the Coding toolbar described inFigure 11-7, but the cool thing about this snippet is that it works in Design view, too, not just Code view.

Note: Unfortunately, unless the snippet's description (which you find in the Snippet Panel's Description column) specifies that the snippet wraps, you can't tell whether it will or not. You either have to try out the snippet or open the snippet in Editing mode to find out. (And while you have the snippet open, you can add a note to its description indicating its ability, or inability, to wrap.)

To add a snippet to a web page, click in the document where you want the item to go, or select the object you wish to wrap with a snippet. Then do one of the following:

- On the Snippet's panel, double-click the name of the snippet.
- On the Snippets panel, select the snippet, and then click the panel's Insert button.
- Drag the snippet from the panel into the document window. (If the snippet is supposed to wrap a selection, then drag the snippet *onto* the selected object.)

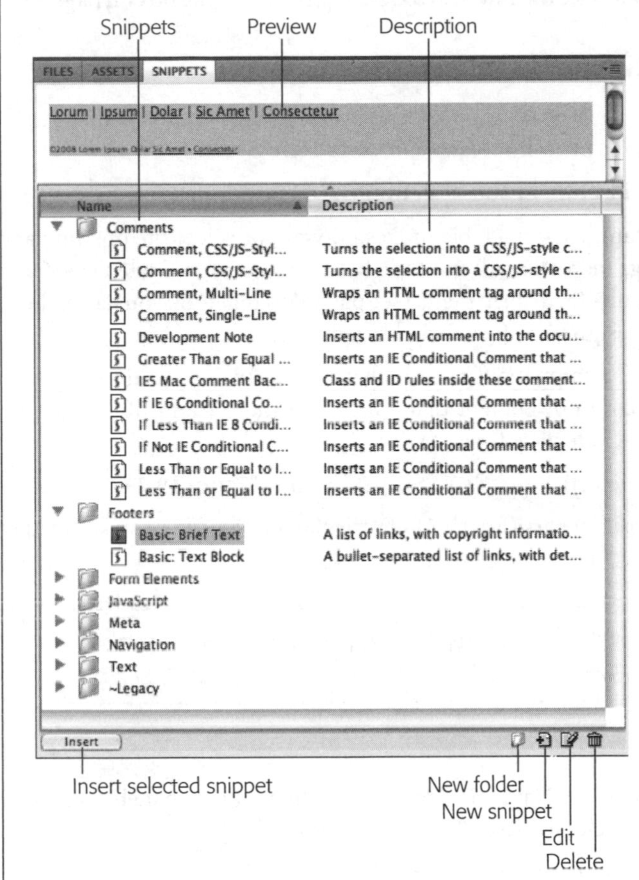

Figure 19-1: *The Snippets panel contains reusable chunks of code–snippets–which you can organize into folders. After selecting a snippet from the list, a preview appears in the Preview pane. In this example, you can see a preview of a simple footer with a colored background, and dummy text and links. Snippets can have either a graphic preview (as in this example), called Design preview, or a Code preview, which shows you the snippet's raw code. You'll find Code previews useful for snippets such as JavaScript code that you can't see in Design view. (When you create your own snippets, you specify the preview type.)*

While you can use snippets in either Design or Code view, some make sense only in Code view. For example, you typically have to insert the JavaScript snippets that come with Dreamweaver in the <head> section of a page, inside <script> tags. To use them, you must switch to Code view, insert the <script> tags, and then put the snippets inside.

Note: To quickly insert a snippet you recently used, select the snippet's name from the Insert→Recent Snippets menu. Better yet, create a keyboard shortcut for your favorite snippets, and then insert them with a quick keystroke, as described on page 817.

Snippets simply dump their contents into a document—essentially copying the snippet code and pasting it into your web page; Dreamweaver doesn't step in to make sure that you're adding the code correctly. Unless you're careful—and have some knowledge of HTML—you may end up adding snippets that make your web page impossible to view. (For advice on how to avoid such pitfalls, see the box on page 735.)

Creating Snippets

Dreamweaver comes with a lot of snippets, and you may find many of them irrelevant. No problem—you can easily create your own. Here's how:

1. **Create and select the content you wish to turn into a snippet.**

   You could, for instance, select a table in Design view, or select the opening and closing <table> tags (as well as all the code between them) in Code view. Or, if you want to save a pull-down form menu (see page 470) that took you half an hour to build, then, in Design view, just click the form menu.

   If you want to make a snippet out of code that isn't visible in Design view, such as a JavaScript program or content that appears in the <head> of a page, you need to switch into Code view first.

2. **In the Snippets panel, click the New Snippet button (Figure 19-1).**

   The Snippet window appears (Figure 19-2), displaying the code you selected in the Insert field.

Note: If you skip step 1 and just click the New Snippet button, you can either type the code or, in the Insert box, paste a previously copied selection (see step 6).

---

3. **Title the snippet.**

   The name you type in the Name field appears in the Snippets panel. Make sure to give it a name that clearly describes what it does.

4. **In the Description field, type identifying details.**

   This step is optional, but useful. Use this field to describe when and how to use the snippet, and whether or not the snippet wraps a selection.

5. **Select a Snippet type.**

   "Wrap selection" makes the code wrap around a selection when you use the snippet. The "Insert block" option is for a snippet that's a single block of code inserted into the document—for example, a copyright notice or a form menu.

6. **If necessary, add the code for the snippet.**

   If you initially selected code in the document window, then it already appears in the "Insert before" field for a snippet that wraps around other code. For snippets that are just a single block of code, the code appears in the "Insert code" box.

   If you create a wrapping snippet, you need to add some code in the "before" field and some in the "after" field. For example, say you create a lot of photo galleries, and you want to wrap each photo in its own <div> tag (see page 331) with some room for a caption. Instead of adding that HTML manually over and over again, you can create a snippet that wraps the image with the appropriate HTML. For example, the code that goes before the image might include an opening <div> tag with a class applied to it, and the code that goes after the image includes the HTML for the caption and the closing </div> tag. In this case, in the "Insert before" field you might type <div class="galleryItem">, and in the "Insert after" field, you'd type the HTML that goes after the image; maybe something like <p>Caption goes here</p></div>.

7. **Select a "Preview type".**

   The preview type determines how the snippet appears in the Snippets panel's Preview pane (see Figure 19-1). *Design* means the snippet looks as it would in Design view—a snippet of a table appears as a table, for instance. *Code* means the code itself appears in the Preview pane, so a snippet for a horizontal rule would preview like this: <hr>. Use Code preview for snippets like JavaScript code that isn't visible in Design view.

8. **Click OK.**

   Dreamweaver adds the snippet to the Snippets panel; you can then drop it in your web pages using any of the techniques described on page 730.

If you need to go back and edit a snippet—change the code, type, description, or name—in the Snippets panel, select the snippet, and then click Edit Snippet (Figure 19-1). You can also right-click (Control-click) the snippet name, and then, from the shortcut menu, select Edit.

Whichever method you choose, the Snippet window (Figure 19-2) opens. Make your changes, and then click OK.

Organizing Snippets

To keep your snippets organized, you can create folders to store them by category. To add a folder to the Snippets panel, click the New Folder button (see Figure 19-1). An untitled folder appears; type in a name for it. If you select a folder before clicking New Folder, Dreamweaver creates the new folder *inside* that folder. You can move folders around by dragging them into other folders.

Note: To drag a folder or snippet to the top level of the Snippets list, you have to drag it all the way to the *bottom* of the Snippets panel, below any other folders. If you try to drag it to the top, Dreamweaver puts the folder or snippet inside the list's top folder.

To move a snippet into or out of its folder, simply drag it. If you drag a snippet over a closed folder without releasing the mouse, that folder expands to reveal the folders and snippets inside, if any.

To delete a snippet, from the Snippets panel, select it, and then click the Delete Snippet (Trash can) button (see Figure 19-1). Quicker yet, press Delete.

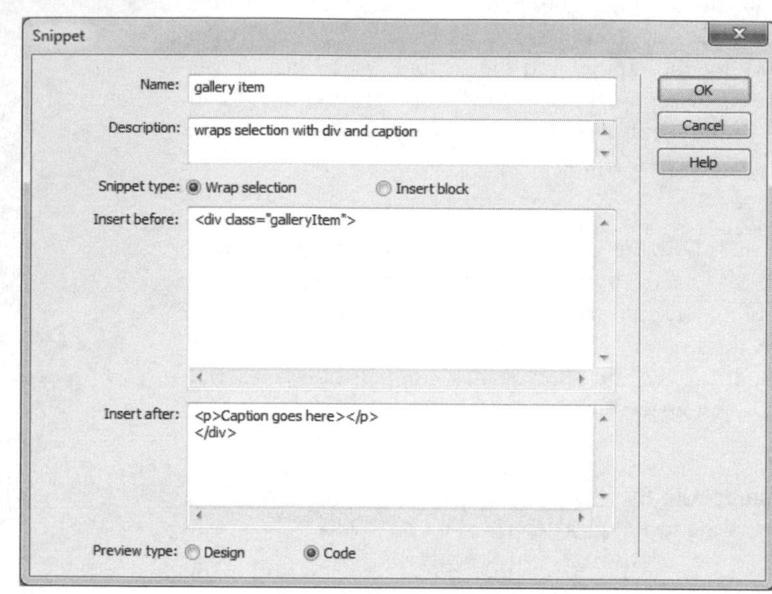

Figure 19-2: *The Snippet window lets you create reusable chunks of HTML called snippets. For snippets that wrap around a currently selected object on the page–for example, a snippet that adds a link to any selected text or graphic–you put code in the two Insert boxes. The code that appears before the selected object goes in the top box, and the code that goes after the object appears in the bottom box. In this example, the snippet wraps the current selection in a <div> tag (see page 331) with a predefined class applied to it.*

Note: Storing lots of snippets slows down the Snippets panel. You'll probably never use many of the snippets that come with the program, so it's best to remove the ones you don't use. An excellent candidate is the ~Legacy folder listed at the bottom of the panel. This folder, which really should be called the Old Garbage folder, is full of out-of-date, you-really-shouldn't-use-them snippets Adobe added to much earlier versions of Dreamweaver. If you don't want to permanently delete these snippets, you can move them out of the main Adobe Dreamweaver CS5→configuration→Snippets folder, and then store them in a separate folder on your hard drive. (For more on the configuration folder and how to find it, see the box on page 828.)

Built-In Snippets

Many of Dreamweaver's stock snippets offer solutions to problems you may never encounter, like a page footer containing two lists of links and a copyright notice. In addition, many use older design techniques (like tables to lay out content) that are best avoided. However, most web developers find at least a few snippets worth using. Here are some highlights:

- **Close Window Button.** When you create a pop-up window (page 599), this snippet lets you add a Close button to let people dismiss the window. The Close Window Button snippet (in the Form Elements folder) places a form button with the words "Close Window" on the window, complete with the JavaScript necessary to close the window when your visitor clicks the button.

- **Dropdown Menus.** If you create a lot of forms for your sites (see Chapter 12), you'll find some useful snippets in the Form Elements folder, especially in the Dropdown Menus subfolder. For example, the "Numbers 1–12" snippet inserts a menu with the numbers 1–12 already coded into it—great for capturing credit card expiration dates on an e-commerce site. (To create an even more useful drop-down snippet, see the tutorial at the end of the chapter.)
- **HTML Comments.** You can use the Comment Multi-Line snippet (in the Comments folder) to "comment-out" or hide HTML. And this works in Design view, so just select the element you want to hide and apply this comment. This is a good if you want to temporarily hide some HTML—for example to test what a page looks like with or without different chunks of HTML. To make the HTML visible again, go into Code view because the Coding toolbar has a handy tool for quickly un-commenting HTML (see Figure 11-7).
- **IE Conditional Comments.** Sometimes Internet Explorer just doesn't get things right. This is frequently the case with CSS. To overcome browser differences, you sometimes need to provide IE with CSS code (or HTML or JavaScript) that differs from the code you send to other browsers. You can insert special code (in the form of so-called conditional comments) that only IE understands. Dreamweaver provides a handful of code snippets (the last five listed in the Snippets panel's Comments folder) that create the necessary code for adding IE-oriented conditional comments. (For more information on why and how to use IE Conditional Comments visit *www.javascriptkit.com/howto/cc.shtml.*)

TROUBLESHOOTING MOMENT

A Snippet of Caution

Snippets aren't as smart as other Dreamweaver features. Dreamweaver is usually good about warning you before you make a mistake, but it doesn't make a peep if you're incorrectly adding a snippet.

For instance, when you use one of the program's form snippets to add, say, a text field to a page, Dreamweaver doesn't check to see if you're really putting the snippet into a form. Dreamweaver doesn't let you know if you're missing the required <form> tag, and certainly doesn't add it itself. Furthermore, if you're working in Code view, Dreamweaver lets you add snippets to the <head> (or even outside the <html> tags altogether), which is useful for creating dynamic web pages that include server-side programming code, but just creates messy and invalid HTML on normal web pages.

Furthermore, snippets don't take advantage of Dreamweaver's site management features to keep track of links or paths to images. Suppose you create a snippet that includes an image. If you insert that snippet into another page, the image may not show up correctly. If you create a snippet that includes a link from one page to another on your site, that link is also unlikely to work in the destination page.

So it's best to create snippets without images or links–but there are workarounds. For instance, you can create snippets with fake links–use nothing but the # symbol for the link, for example–and update the link after you insert the snippet into a page. For images, you can use Dreamweaver's Image Placeholder object to simulate a graphic in a snippet (choose Insert→Image Objects→Image Placeholder). After you add the snippet to the page, update the placeholder with the real image file.

If you want to create reusable content that can keep track of links and images, see Dreamweaver's Library feature, described below.

Library Basics

Imagine this situation: You manage a relatively large website consisting of thousands of web pages. At the bottom of each page is a simple copyright notice: "Copyright MyBigCompany. We reserve all rights—national, international, commercial, non-commercial, and mineral—to the content contained on these pages."

Each time you add another page to the site, you *could* retype the copyright message, but this approach invites both typographic errors and carpal tunnel syndrome. And if you must *format* this text too, you're in for even more work.

Fortunately, Dreamweaver's Library can turn any selection in the document window (a paragraph, an image, a table) into a reusable chunk of HTML that you can easily drop into any Dreamweaver document. The Library, in other words, is a great place to store copyright notices, navigation bars, or any other chunks of HTML you use frequently.

So far, this description sounds pretty much like the snippets described in the previous section. But Library items have added power: When you add HTML to a web page using a Library item, that code remains linked to the original Library item, the one stored in Dreamweaver. Thanks to this link, whenever you update the original Library item, you get a chance to update every page that uses that item.

Suppose your company is bought, and the legal department orders you to change the copyright notice to "Copyright MyBigCompany, a subsidiary of aMuchBiggerCompany" on each of the website's *10,000 pages*. If you had cleverly inserted the original copyright notice as a Library item, you could take care of this task in the blink of an eye. Just open the item in the Library, make the required changes, save it, and then let Dreamweaver update all the pages for you (see Figure 19-3).

Compared to Snippets, Library items are much smarter. They possess the unique ability to update the same material on an entire site's worth of files in seconds, and can successfully deal with links and images. Unlike Snippets, however, Dreamweaver's Library feature is site-specific. In other words, each site you define in Dreamweaver has its own Library. You can't use a Library item from another site on a page you're working on.

Creating and Using Library Items

To create a Library item, start by opening the Library window. Click the Assets tab (to the right of the Files panel) or choose Window→Assets, and then click the Library Items button (it looks like an open book, circled in Figure 19-4) to reveal the Library category.

Now select the part of your document that you wish to save as a Library item: a blob of text, a graphic, or whatever.

Note: however, that Library items can contain only page elements that appear in the document window–in other words, only HTML from the <body> of a web page. You can't include anything that appears in the <head> of a page, like Cascading Style Sheets, Spry widgets (Chapter 13) or meta tags. This means you can't store Dreamweaver behaviors or Spry widgets in your Library (but you can include them with a Dreamweaver Template, discussed in the next chapter). Furthermore, Library items must include a complete set of HTML tags–both an opening and a closing tag–as well as all the tags necessary to complete the original object. For example, Dreamweaver doesn't let you turn just a single cell, row, or column of a table into a Library item. If you try, then Dreamweaver adds the *entire* table to the Library

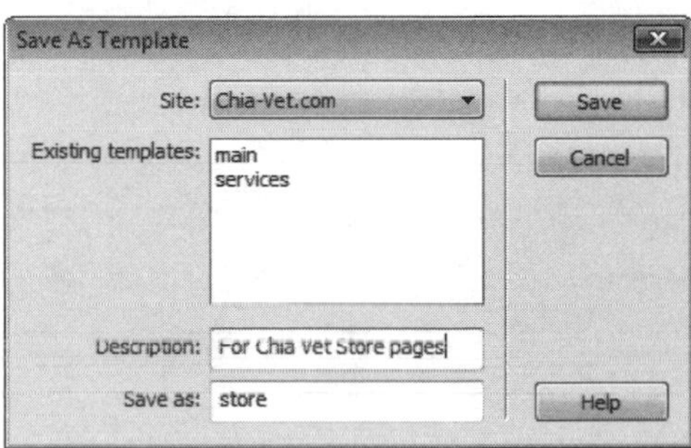

Figure 19-3:
Library items are great for small chunks of HTML that you use frequently on a site. Here, on an old version of The Museum of Modern Art's home page, many of the navigation options on the page (circled) are Library items. If the Museum needed to add or remove a navigation link, they could update the Library item to change every page on the site in one simple step. In fact, since a Library item is a chunk of HTML, the left-hand navigation bar could be replaced with a Flash movie, plain-text links (instead of graphics), or any other valid HTML code.

Note: Use the Tag selector (see page 23) to make sure you choose the precise tag information you want. But sometimes you want the content inside a tag. For example, to select the contents of a cell, click at the beginning of the content, and drag until you select everything in the cell.

Next, add the selection to the Library. As you may expect, Dreamweaver provides several ways to do this:

- Drag the highlighted selection into the list of Library items.
- Click the New Item button (Figure 19-4).
- Choose Modify→Library→"Add Object to Library".

The new item appears in the Assets panel, bearing the jaunty name "Untitled". Type in a more useful name, such as *Copyright notice* or *Logo*. (Avoid hyphens in your Library item's name. Hyphens tend to trip up the Firefox web browser, as described in the box on page 742.) Your new Library element is now ready to use.

Note: Even though you can't turn a CSS style into a Library item, you *can* turn HTML that you've styled with CSS into a Library item. For example, you can add to the Library a paragraph that has a CSS class style applied to it. When you attempt to add this paragraph to the Library, Dreamweaver warns you that the item may not look the same when you place it in other documents–because the style sheet information doesn't come along for the ride. To make sure the Library item appears correctly, make sure you attach the same style sheet to any page where you use that item. External style sheets (see page 111) make this easy.

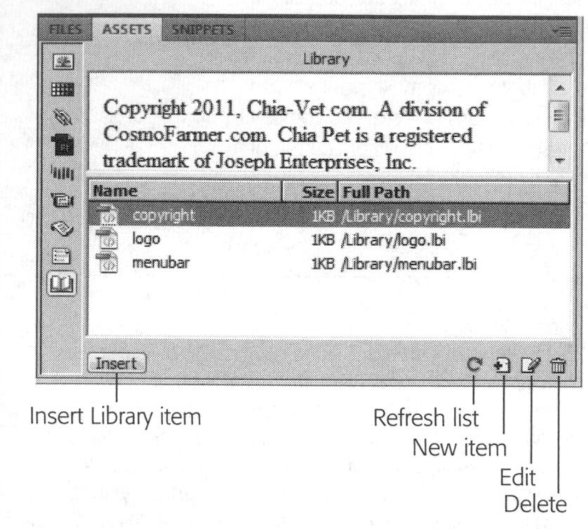

Figure 19-4:
The Assets panel's Library category lists the name, file size, and location of each Library item in the currently opened site. When you select a Library item from the list, you see a small preview. In this example, the Library item "copyright" is, shockingly, a copyright notice.

Adding Library Items to a Page

To add a Library item to a web page, drag it directly out of the Assets panel's Library items list onto your page. (The long way: Click to plant your insertion point on the web page, click the Library item you want in the Assets panel, and then, on the Assets panel, click the Insert button, shown in Figure 19-4.)

Note: Library items (.lbi files) also appear in the Files panel in a site's Library folder. Dragging a Library item from the Files panel to a page, however, *doesn't* insert it into the page. It adds the name of the Library item file (not its contents) with a link to the .lbi file—not something you want to do.

When you insert a Library item into a page (or turn a selected item *into* a Library item), it sprouts a light yellow background. The highlighting indicates that Dreamweaver intends to treat the Library item as a single object, even though it may be made of many different HTML elements. You can select it or drag it around, but you can't edit it. (Unfortunately, if you turn a nontransparent graphic into a Library item—like a logo, for example—Dreamweaver doesn't give you the helpful yellow background.)

Remember, too, that the placed Library item links to the original copy in the Library. The copy in your document automatically changes to reflect any changes you make to the copy in the Library, using the technique described next.

Tip: At some point, you may want to sever the connection between the Library and a Library item you placed on a page–to modify a copyright notice on just a single page, for example. Select the item on the page, and then, in the Property inspector, click "Detach from original" (Figure 19-5). Dreamweaver removes the comment tags (see the box on page 742), thus breaking the link to the Library.

You can also insert the HTML of a Library item *without* maintaining a link to the Library by pressing the Ctrl (Option) key when you add it to your document. This treats the HTML more like a snippet, since Dreamweaver doesn't update the HTML on this page when you change the original Library file.

Editing Library Items

You'll appreciate the real power of Library items when it's time to make a change. When you update the original file in the Library, all the pages graced with that linked item update, too.

Start by opening the Library, as described on page 736. Then:

1. **Open the Library item you want to edit.**

   You can do this by double-clicking the Assets panel's Library item, by highlighting it and then clicking the Edit button (Figure 19-4), or by highlighting a Library item on a web page, and then, in the Property inspector, clicking the Open button (Figure 19-5). (You can also open the Library item file—an .lbi file—in the Library folder of your site's root directly from the Files panel.)

   Dreamweaver opens what looks like a normal web page, but it contains only the text, graphics, or other elements of the Library file.

Figure 19-5: *The selected Library item (an .lbi file) is in the site's Library folder. (The path appears after the word "Src".)*

2. **Edit away.**

   A Library item is only a selection of HTML; it's not a complete web page. That means you shouldn't add *page* properties like the title or background color. (Dreamweaver actually lets you do this, but that adds invalid HTML code to the Library item as well as to every page that uses that Library item.) Also, you can insert Library items only in the body of a web page, so stick with objects that would normally appear in the document window, such as links, images, tables, and text. Don't add any code that appears in the head of a web page, such as Cascading Style Sheets, meta tags, behaviors, or Spry widgets.

Since Library items can't contain style sheets, if the HTML in your Library item relies on a style, then you'll have trouble previewing it correctly. Dreamweaver's Design-Time Style Sheet tool comes in handy here. It lets you temporarily "add" a style sheet while you design a page, without actually adding the CSS code to the page. For more on this useful feature, turn to page 326.

Note: Don't turn any of Dreamweaver's Spry widgets into Library items. For example, if you use the Spry Menu Bar (page 184), you might be tempted to turn the menu into a Library item you can reuse on other pages of your site. Problem is, all Spry features combine HTML, JavaScript, and CSS code placed in different parts of a page's code. When you select the Spry widget on the page, and then turn it into a Library item, only the HTML goes along for the ride–the CSS, which makes the widget look good, and the JavaScript, which make the widget work, aren't included. The solution? Use Dreamweaver templates instead (see the next chapter).

---

3. **Choose File→Save.**

   Dreamweaver checks to see if it can find any pages that use the Library item, and, if it does, it opens the Update Library Items window. A list of pages in the site that use that item appears.

4. **Click Update.**

   Dreamweaver opens the Update Pages window, updates the HTML in all the pages that use the Library item, and then lists all the files that it changed.

   On the other hand, you don't necessarily have to click Update. Perhaps you have a lot of changes to make to the Library item, and you just want to save the work you've done so far. You're not done editing it yet, so you don't want to waste time updating pages you'll just have to update again later. You can always update them another time (see the box on page 786); to do that, click Don't Update. (Once you finish making changes and save the file for the final time, *then* you can update the site.)

5. **Click Done.**

   As you can see, the Library is an incredible timesaver that greatly simplifies the process of changing common page elements.

Renaming Library Elements

To rename something in your Library, on the Assets panel, click its name (Figure 19-4). Pause briefly, click again, and the name highlights, ready for your edit. Type the new name, and then press Enter (Return).

If you already added the item to your web pages, Dreamweaver prompts you to update those pages. Click Update. Otherwise, the link between those pages and the Library breaks.

Note: If you accidentally click Don't Update, don't panic. Simply change the Library item back to its original name, and then *re*-rename it. Don't forget to click Update this time!

Deleting Library Elements

You can delete unnecessary elements from your Library any time, but use caution. When you delete something from the Library, Dreamweaver leaves behind every copy of it you placed on your pages—complete with links to the now-deleted Library item.

In other words, you can't edit the copies on your web pages until you break those links. If you do indeed want to edit them, you have to break the links manually on each page where the Library item appears by selecting the item, and then clicking the "Detach from original" button (see Figure 19-5).

Now that you've been warned, here are the instructions. To get rid of a Library item, in the Assets panel, click the item, and then do one of the following:

- In the Assets panel, click the trash can icon.
- Press Delete.
- Right-click (Control-click) the item's name, and then, from the shortcut menu, choose Delete.

Tip: If you ever accidentally delete an item from the Library, you can recreate it, provided you used it on one of the web pages in your site.

Open the page containing the Library item, and then click the item to select it. On the Property inspector, click Recreate (Figure 19-5) to make it anew. A new Library item appears in the Library, using the name and HTML from the item you selected.

Snippets and Library Tutorial

In this tutorial, you'll do two things: First, create a useful form pull-down menu snippet, and, second, turn a Chia Vet announcement into a reusable Library item, and then add it to several pages in the site.

Note: You need to download the tutorial files from *www.sawmac.com/dwcs5/* to complete this tutorial. See the note on page 45.

Once you download the tutorial files and opened Dreamweaver, define a new site as described on page 37: Name the site *Snippets and Library*, and then select the Chapter19 folder (inside the MM_DWCS5 folder). (In a nutshell: choose Site→New Site. In the Site Setup window, type *Snippets and Library* into the Site Name field, click the folder icon next to the Local Site Folder field, navigate to and select the Chapter19 folder, and then click Choose or Select. Finally, click OK.)

TROUBLESHOOTING MOMENT

Under the Hood of Library Items

Behind the scenes, Dreamweaver stores the HTML for Library items in basic text files. Those files' names end with the extension .lbi, and they stay in the Library folder inside your local site folder.

When you insert a Library item into a web page, Dreamweaver inserts the item's HTML, and adds a set of comment tags. These tags refer to the original Library file, and help Dreamweaver remember where the Library item begins and ends. For instance, if you turn the text "Copyright 2011" into a Library item called *copyright*, and insert it into a web page, Dreamweaver adds the following HTML to the page:

```
<!-- #BeginLibraryItem "/Library/
copyright.lbi" -->Copyright 2011<!--
#EndLibraryItem-->
```

Avoid using hyphens in Library item names. Why? Since HTML comments use hyphens, <!-- -->, Firefox gets tripped up by additional hyphens, and responds by hiding the contents of the item or displaying raw HTML code instead.

In addition, although you can't edit a Library item on a page in Design view, you can muck around with the code in Code view. In the example above, you could change 2011 to 2012 in Code view. Don't do it! Dreamweaver obliterates any changes you make the next time you update the original Library item. If you want to make a change to a Library item, then edit the *original* Library item, or detach the item from the Library (as described in the tip on page 739), and then edit it.

Creating a Snippet

1. **With your site freshly defined, make sure you have the Files panel open.**

   If it isn't, press the F8 key (Shift-⌘-F) or choose Window→Files.

2. **In the Files panel, double-click the file *snippet.html*.**

   A page with several form pull-down menus opens. The page includes menus for the months of the year, names of US states, and the numbers 1 to 31. You can use these menus to specify dates when something needs to be done, states for order shipments, or simply to select a month for your astrological sign. Dreamweaver's own Snippets don't include these useful menus, but, fortunately, you can add them yourself.

3. **At the top of the page, click the first form menu.**

   This menu appears to the right of the words "Months of the year". You've selected the menu (and its underlying HTML code). To add this as a snippet, you need to open the Snippets panel.

4. **Choose Window→Snippets.**

   The Snippets panel (Figure 19-1) is your control center for adding, editing, and deleting Snippets.

5. **At the bottom of the panel, click the New Snippet button (Figure 19-1).**

   The Snippet window opens. Dreamweaver automatically copies the code for the menu into the window. You just need to name the snippet, and add a few more details.

6. **In the Name box, type *Month Menu*, and in the description box, type *A list of month names, with numeric values* as pictured in Figure 19-6.**

   The name and description appear in the Snippets panel. In this case, the description identifies what appears in the menu on the page (a list of month names) and what value the snippet applies when a visitor selects a month from the list—in other words, the name/value pair for this form field. (See Chapter 12 for more information on how forms work.)

7. **Select the "Insert block" radio button.**

   This button identifies the snippet as a chunk of HTML that's simply plopped down on a page, as opposed to HTML that wraps around a selected graphic or text, like a link or table cell (if you wanted to do that the latter, you'd select the "Wrap selection" button).

8. **At the bottom of the window, select the Design button.**

   You just told Dreamweaver to display the snippet visually when you select it in the Snippets panel. In other words, when you select this snippet in the panel, you see a preview of the form menu, not a bunch of HTML code.

9. **The window should now look like Figure 19-6. Click the OK button to create your new snippet.**

   The snippet should now appear in the Snippets panel, ready for you to insert it into a page.

10. **Select the Files panel by clicking the Files tab or by pressing the F8 key (Shift-⌘-F), and then double-click the file *preventative.html*.**

    This step opens a page from the Chia Vet website. You'll insert the new snippet as part of the "Make an appointment online" form in the right sidebar. Depending on the size of your monitor, you may need to scroll down a little to see the Month area in the form on the right side of the page.

11. **Return to the Snippet panel once again by clicking the Snippets tab or by choosing Window→Snippets.**

    Now for the moment of truth.

12. **Drag your new snippet—Month Menu—from the Snippets panel to the space just below the bolded word "Month" in the right sidebar.**

    Ta-da, Dreamweaver adds the new menu. Now, whenever you need to add a menu listing the months of the year, don't bother creating it from scratch. Just use the snippet!

Note: If you select a folder in the Snippets panel when you create a snippet, Dreamweaver stores it in that folder. To move it out of the folder and up to the top-level list of snippets, drag the snippet–Month Menu–to the very bottom of the Snippets panel.

13. **At the top of the document window, click the *snippet.html* tab. Click the third menu (the one with days of the month), and then repeat steps 4–12.**

    Name this new snippet *Days of month* and, as a description for the snippet, type *numerical days of the month.* Insert this new snippet in the empty space directly below the word "Day" in the form. You can close the file *snippet.html* when you're done.

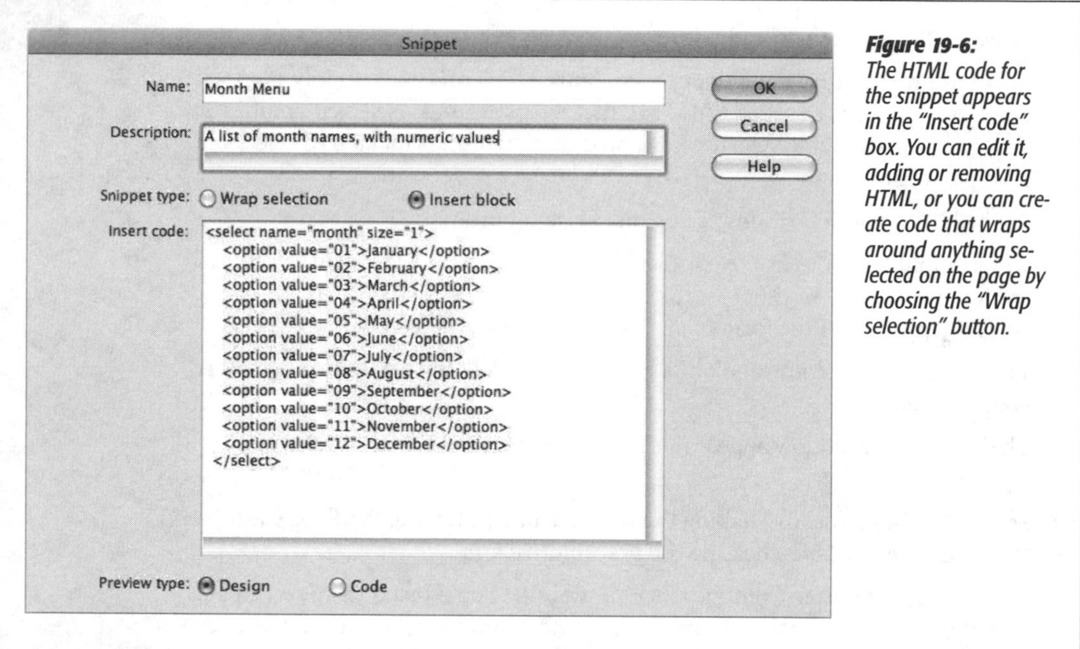

Figure 19-6: *The HTML code for the snippet appears in the "Insert code" box. You can edit it, adding or removing HTML, or you can create code that wraps around anything selected on the page by choosing the "Wrap selection" button.*

Creating a Library Item

Now you'll see one way in which Dreamweaver's powerful site management tools can help you create and update your websites more effectively:

1. **Make sure you have the file *preventative.html* open.**

   This is the same page you added the snippet to in the last section. Here you're going to work on the box with the headline "Meet Our Newest Doc". This box is a simple <div> element with a headline, paragraph, and image inside it. Chia Vet uses this box for recent announcements, and it appears on various pages of the site. Since you need to keep these announcements up to date, creating an easily updated Library item is an efficient choice.

2. **Click anywhere inside the box (for example, on the headline), and then, in the Tag selector, click <div.announcement> (Figure 19-7).**

   Alternatively, you can click anywhere inside the div, and then choose Edit→Select All *twice* (pressing Ctrl-A or ⌘-A two times also works). You need to use Select All twice because you want to select the actual <div> tag—when the cursor is inside a div, the first Select All grabs all the *contents* of the div, while the second one additionally selects the opening and closing <div> tags.

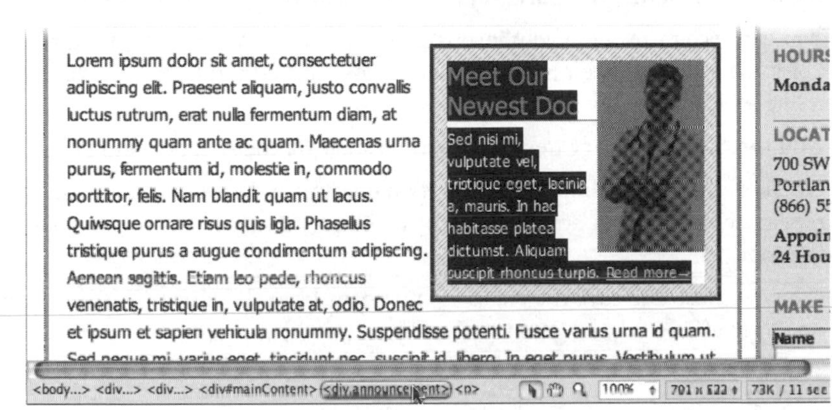

Figure 19-7: *Click <div.announcement> to select the <div> tag containing recent Chia Vet announcements.*

3. **Choose Window→Assets, and then click the Library button.**

   The Assets panel opens, and displays the Library category.

4. **On the Assets panel, click the New Library Item button (Figure 19-4).**

   A warning message appears, saying that the Library item may not look the same in other pages. Dreamweaver's trying to tell you that Library items can contain only HTML from the body of a web page—not Cascading Style Sheets. (You can still include HTML, such as this <div> tag, that has a style applied to it, as long as you make sure that any *pages* to which you add the Library item have the appropriate style sheets.)

   The text in this example *is* formatted using a style sheet, so, sure enough, it won't look the same in pages that don't have the same style sheet. In this exercise, however, this isn't a problem, since all the pages on the site share the same linked external style sheet.

   Click OK to dismiss the warning. The announcement item appears in the Library list, with the "Untitled" name highlighted for editing.

5. **Type *news* to name the new item on the Assets panel, and then press Enter.**

   You just checked this standard blob of text into your Library. It's ready to use anywhere else on your site. Notice that the div's background has changed to yellow in the document window—Dreamweaver's way of letting you know that this is a Library item.

6. **In the Files panel, double-click the file called *tips.html*.**

   You'll frequently jump between the Files panel and the Assets panel, so the keyboard shortcut to open the Files panel comes in handy: click the F8 key (Shift-⌘-F). The Assets panel doesn't have a keyboard shortcut, but you can create your own to open and close the panel as described on page 817.

   The Tips page doesn't have an announcement box, so you'll add one.

7. **Switch back to the Assets panel, and drag the "news" Library item to the left of the letter "L" in the first paragraph of text, as pictured in Figure 19-8.**

   You can recognize the newly inserted Library item by its yellow background. Click the text in the item, and notice that you can't edit it; Dreamweaver treats it like a single object.

8. **Add the "news" Library item to one other page on the site: boarding.html.**

   Open the page (by double-clicking its name in the Files window), and then repeat step 7. You can actually insert this Library item anywhere you want on the page.

   (You can close and save the pages as you go, or leave them open. Leave at least one open at the end and go on to step 9.)

9. **This just in!**

   New things are happening at Chia Vet all the time, so it's time to update this announcement. Fortunately, you used a Library item, so it's easy to make the change.

10. **In the Library in the Assets panel, double-click the "news" item.**

    The Library item opens up, ready for editing. Notice that it doesn't have any of the formatting you saw on the web page—that's because there's no CSS file attached to the Library item, so you see only the plain HTML version of this announcement box.

11. **Delete the picture of the vet, and change the headline to Chia Vet nominated for horticulture award of excellence. Save the file.**

    The Update Library Items dialog box appears, listing the three pages in the site that use this announcement box.

12. **Click Update.**

    Dreamweaver opens the Update Pages dialog box, and then updates all the pages that use the "news" item.

13. **Click Close to close the Update Pages dialog box.**

    And now if you open *preventative.html, tips.html*, and *boarding.html*, you find that Dreamweaver has updated the announcement box on all three pages.

    Now imagine that you just used this auto-update feature on a 10,000-page site. Sit back and smile.

Tip: If you use a particular Library item on some pages of your site but not all, you'll want to know which pages you changed so you can move them up to your web server. You won't want to, after all, upload your entire website when you update just a handful of pages. Dreamweaver's Select Recently Modified command can help (see the box on page 674). You can also use Dreamweaver's synchronization feature to make sure you get the most recent pages from your computer onto your server (see page 717).

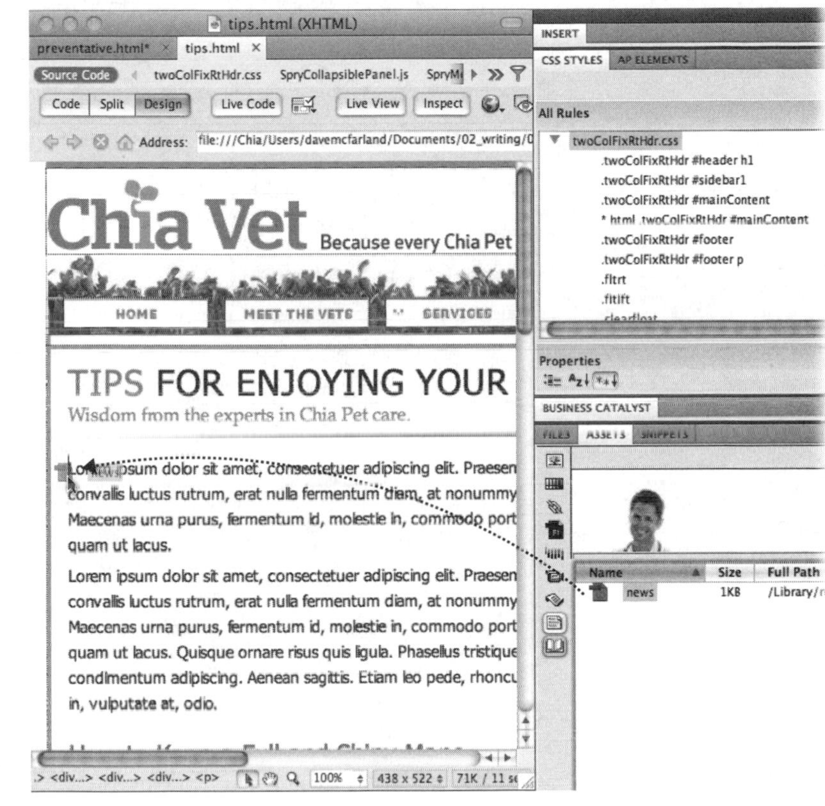

Figure 19-8: *In addition to dragging a Library item into the document window, you can insert the item by finding the insertion point in the document window, and then, on the Assets panel, clicking the Insert button.*

CHAPTER

20

Templates

Some web designers handcraft their sites with loving care, changing layouts, colors, fonts, banners, and navigation page by page. But that approach isn't always practical—or desirable. Consistency is a good thing. Web pages that look and act similarly reassure visitors; they can concentrate on each page's unique content when the navigation bar and left sidebar stay the same. But even more important, a handcrafted approach to web design is often unrealistic when you need to crank out content on a deadline.

That's where *templates* come in. Frequently, the underlying design of many website pages is identical (see Figure 20-1). An employee directory at a company site, for instance, may consist of individual pages dedicated to each employee. Each page has the same navigation bar, banner, footer, and layout. Only a few particulars change from page to page, like the employee's name, photograph, and contact information. This is a perfect case for templates. This chapter shows you how templates can make quick work of building pages where most, if not all, the pages use repetitive elements.

Template Basics

Templates let you build pages that share a similar structure and graphic identity, quickly and without having to worry about accidentally deleting or changing elements. Templates come in very handy when you design a site where other, less Dreamweaver-savvy, individuals will build the individual pages. By using a template, you, the godlike Dreamweaver guru, can limit the areas that these underlings can modify in each page.

Note: Adobe Contribute, a simple, word processor–like program for updating websites, works very well with sites built using Dreamweaver templates. If you build sites that people who don't know the first thing about Dreamweaver or building web pages will update, Contribute can help. Contribute even lets novices update pages on their sites through their own web browser. You can learn more about Contribute at Adobe's website: *www.adobe.com/products/contribute*.

A new page based on a template—also called a *template instance*, or *child page*—looks just like the template, except that page authors can edit only designated areas of the page, called, logically enough, *editable regions*. In the example in Figure 20-1, you can see that the question-and-answer text is an editable region; the rest of the page remains consistent (and is, in fact, locked).

A Dreamweaver template can be very basic: you can create one where a page author can change one or more areas of a page built from the template (the editable regions), but he can't edit other areas (the *locked regions*). At the same time, Dreamweaver lets you build templates that give page authors an impressive amount of flexibility in the pages they build. Here's an overview of the features you can tap when you create and use templates:

- **Editable regions.** These are the basic building blocks of a template. An editable region is that part of a page—a paragraph, the contents of a <div> element, or a headline, for example—that page authors can change as they build template-based pages. Templates can include multiple editable regions—a sidebar and the main content section of a page, for example.
- **Editable tag attributes.** There may be times when you want to make a particular tag *property* editable. For example, say you have a banner ad at the top of a page--the banner ad's just a basic image file, and each page should have a different ad. You want to make sure that no one can delete the image (after all, those ads are paying for your site), but you do want them to be able to swap in a new image file. In other words, no one should mess with the <img> tag; they should only be able to assign a new file by changing the <img> tag's *src* attribute. To keep someone from deleting the image but still allow them to swap in a new image, just make the *src* property editable. (You could also make the image's *alt* property editable, and if the *Width* and *Height* properties vary from image to image, you can make those attributes editable as well)"

  Or you might want a unique headline design for each section of your site. To get that, when you build the site template, assign an ID to the <body> tag and make the ID name editable. Then, when you create pages for each section of the site, you add an ID name specific to that section. For example, for a site's "About Us" page, you could set the body's ID to *about.* Once you do, you can use a descendent selector (like *#about h1*) to create a custom style for all the headlines on just that page. On template-based pages showcasing your company's products, change the ID to products, and then add a descendent selector style #product h1 to your style sheet and you'll have a unique look for all h1 tags on product pages.

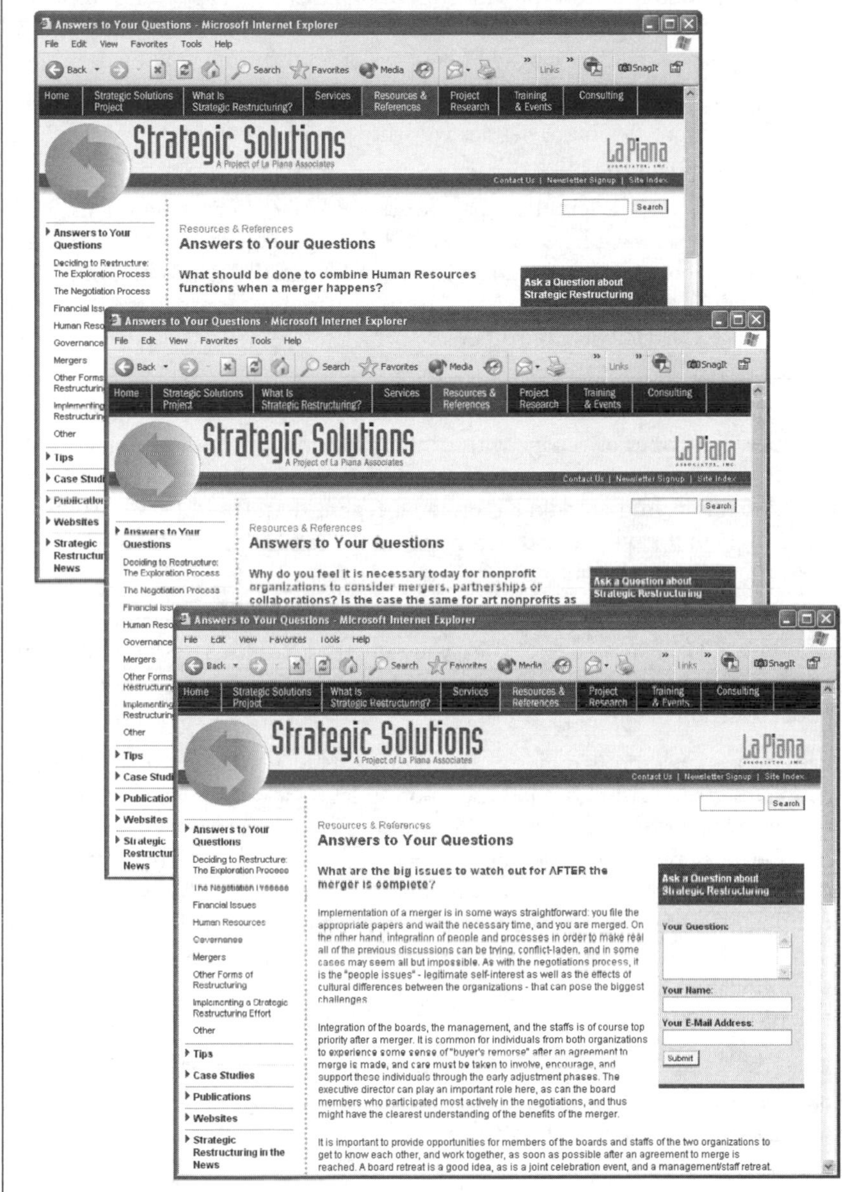

Figure 20-1: These three web pages are part of a section of a website dedicated to answering frequently asked questions. The pages each provide the answer to a different question, but are otherwise identical, sharing the same banner, navigation buttons, sidebar, and footer. Why rebuild the design for each one? Enter one of Dreamweaver's greatest timesaving features—Templates—which help you quickly build similar-looking pages, and make updating page designs a snap.

- **Repeating regions and repeating tables.** Some web pages, like product catalogs and news sites that post article headlines, include *lists* of items. For pages like these, Dreamweaver lets you define *repeatable regions* in your template. For example, your design for a page of product listings might include each product's picture, name, and price, organized using a table with multiple rows (Chapter 7).

As the template builder, you may not know in advance how many products the page will eventually list, so you can't fully design the page. However, you can use Dreamweaver to define a row—or any selection of HTML—as a repeating region, so that page authors can add new rows of product information as needed.

- **Optional regions and editable optional regions.** *Optional regions* make templates even more flexible. They let you show or hide content—from a single paragraph to an entire <div> full of tags—on a page-by-page basis.

  Suppose you create a template that displays your company's products. Some products go on sale while others remain full price, so you add an *optional region* to the product descriptions that displays a big "On Sale!" logo. When you create a new product page, you could *show* the optional region for products that are on sale and keep it *hidden* for the others.

  Editable optional regions are similar, but have the added benefit of being editable. Maybe you're creating a template for an employee directory, giving each employee his or her own page with contact information. Some employees also want their picture displayed on the page, while others don't (you know the type). Solution: Add an editable optional region that would let you show the space for a photo and add a different photo for each page. For the shyer types, you'd simply hide the photo area entirely.

Dreamweaver can also create *nested* templates, which inherit design elements from a master template. Using nested templates, you can create a unified design throughout a site, along with unique (nested) templates for individual sections. You'll find this feature described in detail on page 774.

Facilitating page creation is only one of the benefits of templates. You'll also find that templates greatly simplify the process of updating a website's design. Like Library items (Chapter 19), pages based on templates retain a reference to the original template file. Dreamweaver passes any changes you make to that template to all the pages created from it, which can save you hours of time and trouble when it comes time to update the look or structure of your site. Imagine how much time you'll save when your boss asks you to add "just one more" button to a site's navigation bar. Instead of updating thousands of pages by hand, you need to update only a single template file.

Note: Templates aren't just for building regular, static web pages. You can also create templates for the dynamic, database-driven web pages discussed in Part Six of this book.

Creating a Template

The first step in creating a template is to build a basic web page and tell Dreamweaver that you'd like to use it as a template. You go about this in two ways: build a web page and turn it into a template, or create a blank, empty template file and add text, graphics, tables, and other content.

Turning a Web Page into a Template

The easiest way to create a template is to base it on a web page in your current site folder. Although you can create templates based on web pages that *aren't* part of your current local site, you may run into problems with links and paths to images, as described in a moment.

Once you open the page, choose File→Save As Template or, on the Common category of the Insert panel (see Figure 20-2), click the Templates button and then select Make Template from the menu. In the Save As Template window (Figure 20-3), the name of the current local site appears in the Site pop-up menu; meanwhile, all templates for that site show up in the Existing Templates field.

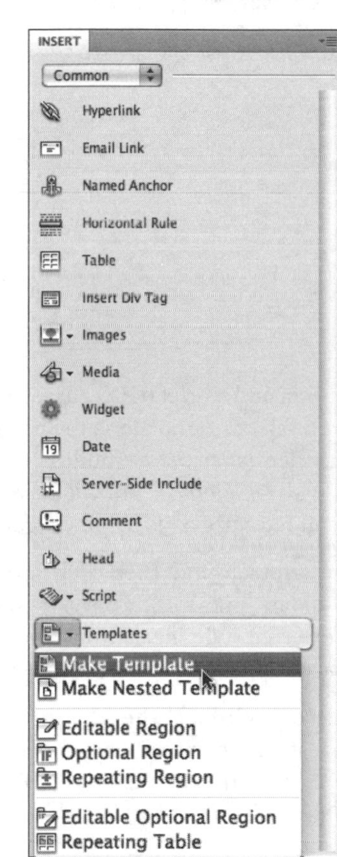

Figure 20-2:
The Templates menu on the Common category of the Insert panel provides access to tools for creating templates and setting up a variety of Dreamweaver template features.

Note: At this point, you could theoretically use the Site menu to save a template into any local site folder you've set up (see Chapter 16 for a discussion of local sites), but be careful with this option. If your page contains images, external style sheets, and links, and you save it as a template for another local site, Dreamweaver doesn't copy the images or style sheets from the first site folder into the other one. As a result, the paths to the image files and links don't work correctly, and the page won't show any styling.

If you must use a page from one site as a template for another, copy the web page, *graphics and style sheets* into the new site's root folder, open the page from there, and then create a template as described here.

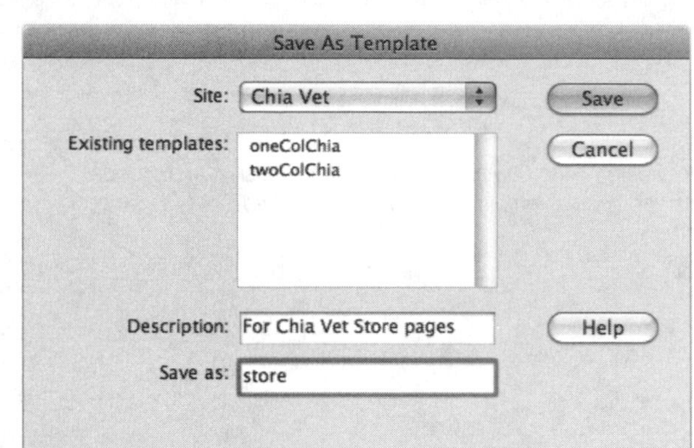

Figure 20-3: *The Save As Template dialog box lets you save your template into any of the local site folders you defined in Dreamweaver. Stick to your current local site to avoid broken links and similar problems.*

Dreamweaver includes a Description field where you can add a brief note characterizing the template. This description appears when you select a template as the basis for new pages you create. The description is useful when *other* people build a site using your templates and aren't sure whether *templateA1*, *templateA2*, or *templateA3* is the correct choice; a simple "Use this template for all FAQ pages" is much clearer.

Finally, in the "Save as" box, type a name for the new template, and then click Save. Choose Yes when Dreamweaver asks if you want to update links for the page. If you choose No, all page-relative links break, styles from external style sheets won't work, and all the images on the page appear as broken-image icons.

Dreamweaver saves the page in the Templates folder of your local site root folder. It adds the extension .dwt to the file to indicate that it's a Dreamweaver template. (For dynamic web pages, Dreamweaver adds the .dwt *before* the file's extension. For example, a PHP template may have a name like *maintemplate.dwt.php*.)

Note: Don't get carried away building too many templates for a site. It doesn't make any sense to create 20 templates for a 20-page site. You should only need a handful of templates to cover the different types of pages you have on a site. In fact, you might just need a single template to dictate the look of all the pages on your site.

Building a Template from Scratch

It's easiest to create a web page first and then save it as a template, but you can also build one from scratch. Open the Asset panel's Templates category by choosing Window→Assets and then click the Template assets icon (see Figure 20-4). Then click the New Template button at the bottom of the Assets panel. Once Dreamweaver adds a new, untitled template to the list, give it a new name. Something descriptive like "Press release" or "Employee page" helps you keep track of your templates.

After you create a blank template, open it by double-clicking its name in the Assets panel (or selecting its name and then clicking the Edit button at the bottom of the Assets panel). It opens just like any web page, so that you can get busy designing it with the unchanging elements of your site—logo, navigation bar, and so on. You'll learn how to add editable regions to your template in the next section.

Defining Editable Regions

Your next task is to specify which parts of your template you want locked and which you want editable. By default, *everything* on a page is locked. After all, the main reason to use a template is to maintain a consistent, unchanging design and structure among pages. To make a template usable, you must define the area or areas page authors *can* change.

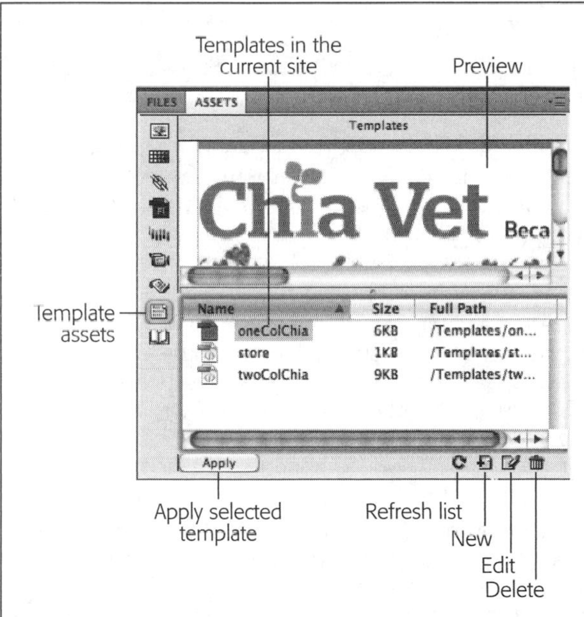

Figure 20-4: *The Templates category of the Assets panel lists the name, file size, and location of each template in the current local site. The Apply button applies a template to the current open web page. The Refresh Site List button updates the list of templates: If you just created a template and don't see it listed, click this button. The New Template button creates a new blank template in the Templates folder. Select a template from the list and click the Edit Template button to open the template for editing.*

Adding a Basic Editable Region

To add an editable region to a template, start by selecting the part of the page you want to make changeable. You can designate as editable anything in the document window (that is, any HTML between the <body> tags).

Note: You can always add Cascading Style Sheets, JavaScript code, and meta tag information to the <head> of a template-based page. Any <head> content in the original template files stays put in the page you create from it, however. For example, you can't remove an external style sheet applied to a template from a page based on that template.

For templates you created from scratch, place your cursor at the point where you want to insert an editable region. For templates you built from an existing page, drag across your page to select the elements you wish to make editable, or, for greater precision, use the Tag selector (see page 23) to make sure you select the exact HTML you want.

Now tell Dreamweaver that you want to make the selected elements editable. You can use any of these techniques:

- In the Common category of the Insert panel (Figure 20-2), select Editable Region from the Template menu.
- Choose Insert→Template Objects→Editable Region.
- Press Ctrl+Alt+V (⌘-Option-V).
- Right-click (Control-click) the selection and then choose Templates→New Editable Region from the shortcut menu.

When the New Editable Region dialog box appears, type a name for the region (you can't use the same name twice) and then click OK. You return to your template, where the name you gave the region appears in a small blue tab above the editable region, outlined in blue (see Figure 20-5).

Note: If you use tables to lay out your pages (see Chapter 7), you'll often assign one table cell as the main area to hold the primary content of the page. For example, in the pages shown in Figure 20-1, the Frequently Asked Question and its answer appear in a single cell on the page. This cell makes a perfect editable region for a template. In the Tag selector, just click the <td> tag associated with that cell and use any of the techniques discussed here to convert the contents of that cell into an editable region. (By the way, if you're still using tables for layout, please read Chaer 910–CSS layout is by far the preferred method for controlling page design.)

If you use CSS, on the other hand, you can create a separate <div> tag (see page 331) for the main content area. In this case, select just the *contents* of the <div> tag, not the tag itself. Here's one instance where you want to *avoid* the Tag selector (page 23), which selects the entire <div> element, tags and all. If you turn the <div> tag into an editable region, it's possible for someone modifying the page to delete the tag entirely, which could wreak untold havoc on your CSS-based layout.

Fortunately, Dreamweaver has a handy shortcut for selecting just the contents of a <div> tag. Click anywhere inside the <div> tag, and then press Ctrl+A (⌘-A) or choose Edit→Select All. Then, turn this selection into an editable region, and the <div> tags will remain *outside* the editable region, so no one can inadvertently delete them.

FREQUENTLY ASKED QUESTION

The Broken-Link Blues

Why aren't the links in my templates working?

When you created the link in the template file, you probably typed a path into the Property inspector's Link field—a recipe for heartbreak. Instead, always select the target web page for a link by clicking the folder icon in the Property inspector, or by pressing Ctrl+L (⌘-L). In other words, when you add links to a template, always link to pages within the site by browsing to the desired file.

Dreamweaver saves templates in the Templates folder inside the local root folder; all document-relative links need to be relative to this location. (Absolute links, like those to other websites, aren't a problem; neither are root-relative links; see page 159 to learn the difference.) The reason you should browse to, rather than type in, your links is so that Dreamweaver can create a proper relative link.

Imagine this situation: You create a template for all the classified ads that appear on your site. You store all the ads for April 2001 inside a series of folders like this: classifieds→2001→april, as shown in the site diagram here.

A link from a page in the *april* folder to the home page would follow the path marked 1 here. So when you create a link in your template, you can create a link to the home page by typing the path *../../../index.html*.

That choice is logical if you're thinking about the page (in the *april* folder) you'll create from the template—but it won't work. Dreamweaver stores templates in the Templates folder, so the correct path would be path 2, or *../index.html*. When you create a new page based on the template and save it in the *april* folder, Dreamweaver, in its wisdom, automatically rewrites all paths in the page so that the links function correctly.

The beauty of Dreamweaver is that you don't have to understand how all this works. Just remember to use document-relative links in your templates and create them by clicking the folder icon in the Property inspector.

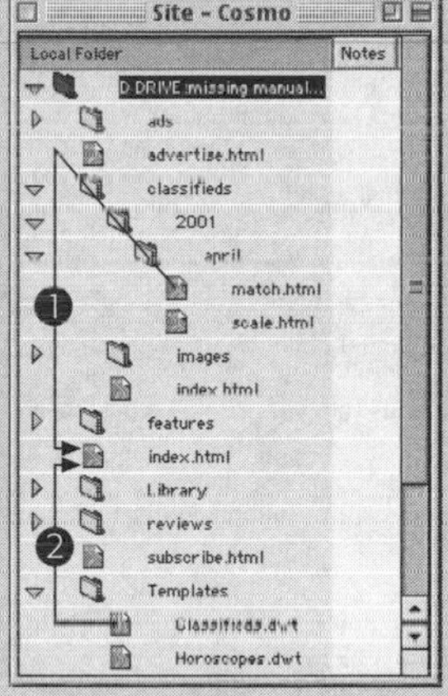

You may find that a single editable region is all you need—for example, when you put text for a product review in just a single area of a page (a section of a page enclosed by a <div> tag, for example). However, if you need to be able to edit *multiple* areas of a page, just add more editable regions to the template. For instance, when you create a template for an employee page, you can create editable regions for the employee's name, telephone number, and photo. If you change your mind and want to lock a region, select the editable region and then choose Modify→Templates→Remove Template Markup. Dreamweaver removes the code that makes the region editable. You can do the same thing with other types of template regions, like repeating and optional regions.

FREQUENTLY ASKED QUESTION

When Save Won't Behave

I keep getting an error message when I save my template. What's going on?

If you add an editable region *inside* certain block-level elements, like a paragraph or a heading, Dreamweaver pops up a warning message when you save the template, explaining that you can't create additional paragraphs or headings inside this region on any pages you build from this template. This just means that you selected the *contents* of a paragraph or heading (not the actual paragraph or heading tag itself) when you made the region editable. Dreamweaver considers anything outside of the editable region locked, so you can't change those tags. Since it's improper HTML to have a paragraph, heading, or other block-level elements inside *another* paragraph or heading, Dreamweaver won't let you add a paragraph, a heading, a bulleted list, or any other block-level element inside the editable contents of the locked paragraph or heading. This characteristic may not be such a bad thing, however. Imagine you're creating a template to be used by other people building a website. You have a Heading 1 with a style applied to it, and you want to make sure it looks the same on every page. You wouldn't want anyone changing the heading tag, and possibly erasing the style. In addition, you don't want them to change the Heading 1 to a Heading 2 or a Heading 3; nor do you want them to completely erase the <h1> tag and type paragraph after paragraph of their random thoughts. You just want them to type in new text for the page title. Selecting just the text inside the heading (as opposed to the <h1> tag *and* the text) and turning it into an editable region does just that. Viva micro-management!

If this is in fact what you want to do, you can save yourself the bother of having to constantly see the "You place an editable region inside a block tag" warning box each time you save the template by simply turning on the "Don't show me this message again" checkbox. However, if you made a mistake and *do* want to allow people to change the heading, or add more headings and paragraphs in this region, you need to do two things: First, unlock the editable region you created (see below); then, select the text *and* tag (the Tag selector [page 23] is the best way to make sure you select a tag), and then turn that into an editable region.

Warning: You can rename an editable region by clicking the blue tab on the template page and typing a new name into the Property inspector. However, if you've already built pages based on this template, that's not a good idea. Because template-based pages identify regions by their name, Dreamweaver can lose track of where content should go when you rename a region. See Figure 20-18 for a workaround.

Adding a Repeating Region

Some web pages have types of content that repeat over and over on a page. For example, a catalog page may display row after row of the same product information—product picture, name, price, and description. An index of Frequently Asked Questions may list questions and the dates visitors posted them. Dreamweaver provides a couple of ways to turn content like that into an editable region in a template.

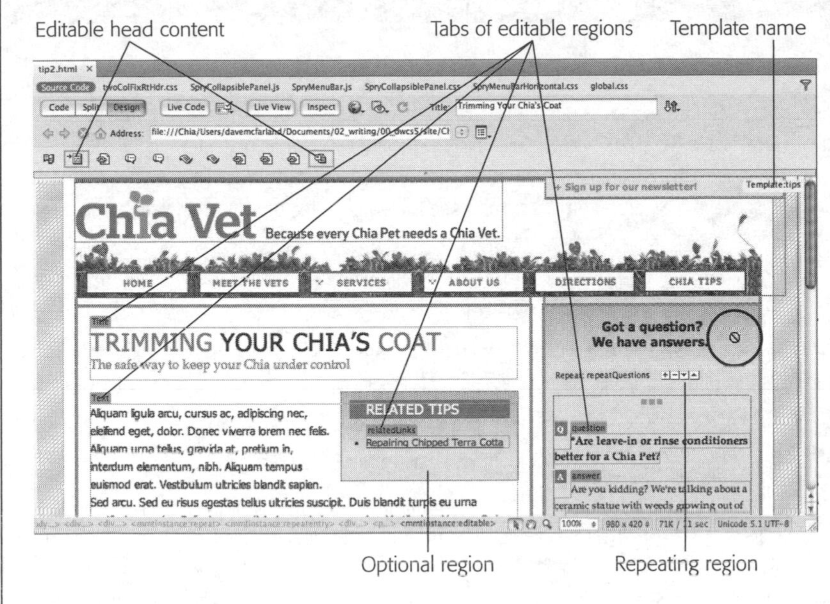

Figure 20-5: *This page is based on a template called "tips", as you can tell from the little tab in the document window's upper-right corner. You can modify this page's editable regions, which Dreamweaver labels with small tabs. In this example, one editable region is called "Title". Two additional editable regions (named "question" and "answer") appear within a repeating region (labeled "repeatQuestions") that lets you duplicate editable regions to create a list of questions and answers. Optional regions don't have any clear identifier on a template-based page; you can identify them only in the Template Properties window, as described on page 780. You can also edit the title of any page created from a template. All other parts of the page are locked (circled); you can make changes to these parts only in the original template file.*

You could, of course, make the entire area where the repeating content appears editable. For example, you could use one of Dreamweaver's CSS layouts (see Chapter 9) to build a template for a FAQ page. The list of questions and answers go inside the page's main <div> tag. You can turn this div into an editable region. The downside to this approach is that you won't have any ability to enforce (or easily update) the HTML used to lay out the questions and answers, since another designer could edit or delete everything in the div.

POWER USERS' CLINIC

Under the Hood of Templates

Dreamweaver saves templates as HTML files in the Templates folder inside your current local site folder (see Chapter 16 for information on local sites). Each template bears the file extension .dwt to distinguish template pages from regular web pages.

Dreamweaver treats files in the Templates folder differently from normal web pages, so don't save anything but .dwt files there. In addition, since Dreamweaver expects to find the Templates folder in the local root folder of your site, don't move it or change its name in any way (don't even change the capital "T" in Templates, even if you're a low-key type of person). If you do, your templates won't work.

As with Library items, Dreamweaver uses HTML comment tags to indicate the name of a template. If you inspect the HTML code of a template-based document, you'll see that, immediately following the opening <html> tag, Dreamweaver inserts a comment tag with the text "InstanceBegin" followed by the location and name of the template. Additional comment tags indicate areas of the page that you can modify, plus special template features like template parameters used for optional regions. For instance, the title of a page based on a template is always editable; its comment tag might look like this:

```
<!-- InstanceBeginEditable
name="doctitle" -->
<title>My New Page</title>
<!-- InstanceEndEditable -->
```

The first comment indicates the editable region's beginning and also includes the editable region's name. When you edit pages based on the template, you can change only the HTML between these comment tags. Everything else on the page is locked, even when you're working in Code view.

Fortunately, Dreamweaver provides a pair of template tools to address the problem: *repeating regions* and *repeating tables*. Both let you create areas of a page that include editable (and uneditable) regions that you can repeat any number of times (see Figure 20-6).

You add a repeating region the same way you add an editable region. Select the area of the template page where you want to repeat information, which usually contains at least one element that you have made editable. It could be a single list item (the <li> tag), a table row (<tr> tag), or even an entire <div> tag.

Tip: You can make a repeating region that *doesn't* include an editable region. For example, a template for a movie review web page could include a repeating region that's simply a graphic of a star. A page author adding a new movie review could repeat the star graphic to match the movie's rating–four stars, for example. (There's just one caveat–see the tip on page 780.)

Next, tell Dreamweaver that the elements you selected represent a repeating region. You can use any of these techniques:

- On the Common category of the Insert panel (Figure 20-2), select the Repeating Region option from the Templates menu.
- Choose Insert→Template Objects→Repeating Region.
- Right-click (Control-click) the selection and choose Templates→New Repeating Region from the shortcut menu.

FREQUENTLY ASKED QUESTION

Hindered by Highlighting

I'm distracted by the tabs and background colors that Dreamweaver uses to indicate Library items and Templates. How do I get rid of them?

When you use Templates or Library items, you see blue tabs and yellow backgrounds, respectively, to indicate editable regions and Library items. Although these visual cues don't appear in a web browser, they can make your page hard to read while you work in Dreamweaver. Fortunately, you can alter the background color of these items and even turn highlighting off altogether.

Choose Edit→Preferences, or press Ctrl+U (⌘-U). In the Preferences Category list, click Highlighting. To change the background color of editable regions, locked regions, and Library items, use the color box (see page 56) or type in a hexadecimal color value (see page 56). To remove the highlighting, turn off the Show box next to the appropriate item.

Often, it's useful to keep highlighting on to help you keep track of Library items and editable regions. If you want to turn off highlighting temporarily, simply choose View→Visual Aids→Invisible Elements, or use the keyboard shortcut Ctrl+Shift+I (⌘-Shift-I) to toggle these visual cues off and on. This technique has the added benefit of hiding table borders, layer borders, and image maps, as well as other invisible elements.

When the New Repeating Region dialog box appears, type a name for the region and then click OK. You return to your template, where the name you gave the region appears in a small blue tab above it (see Figure 20-6). (See page 779 for a discussion of using a repeating region when building a new template-based page.)

Warning: Dreamweaver lets you name a repeating region with a name already in use by an editable region. But don't, ahem, repeat names—multiple template areas with the same name make Dreamweaver act unpredictably.

Repeating Tables

Dreamweaver's *repeating table* tool is essentially a shortcut to creating a table with repeating rows. If you had time on your hands, you could achieve the same effect by adding a table to the page, selecting one or more rows, and applying a repeating region to the selection.

To use the repeating table tool:

1. **Click the in template page where you want to insert the table.**

   You can't insert a repeating table into an editable, repeating, or optional region, as explained in "Making a Tag Attribute Editable" coming up on page 764. You must be in an empty, locked area of the template.

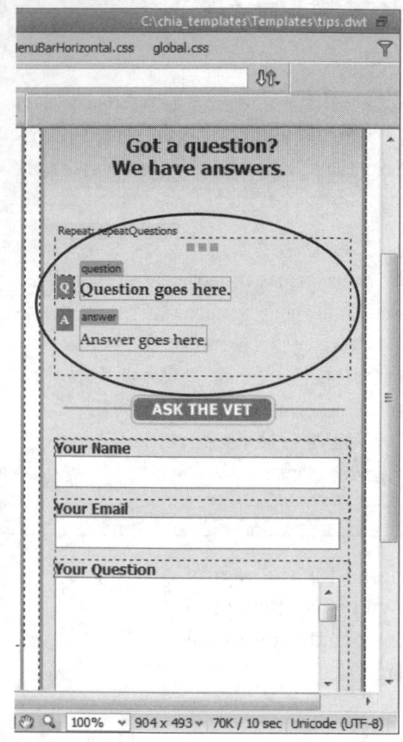

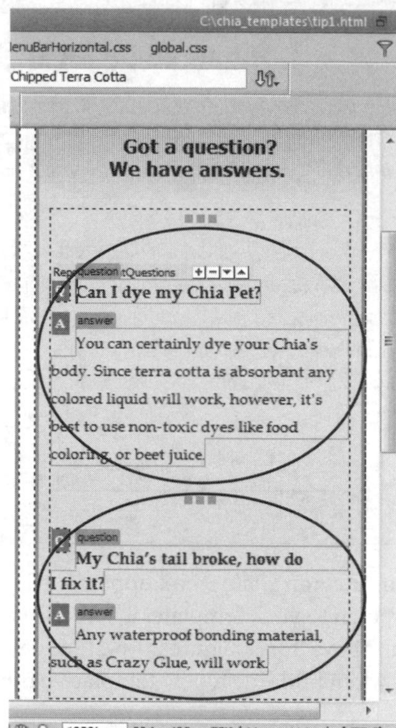

Figure 20-6: *A repeating region lets page authors add multiple instances of repeating information. Left: In this template, you see a repeating region, labeled "repeatQuestion" (circled). Right: A complete page based on this template includes two repeated editable regions (circled). If another page requires more question/answer pairs, you can easily add additional ones to each list by clicking the + button at the top of the repeating region in the template-based page (right). Even with the ability to dictate how many repeating regions appear on a template-based page, the master template still controls the page's basic design. That means page authors can't change the repeating region's underlying HTML—for example, they can't change the "Q" to "Question or the "A" to "Answer" because both these elements reside in the uneditable part of the template page. If you, however, go into the master template and make these changes, Dreamweaver automatically changes the same elements in all the pages the template created.*

2. **On the Common category of the Insert panel (Figure 20-2), select the Repeating Table option from the Templates menu.**

   Alternatively, you can choose Insert→Template Objects→Repeating Table. Either way, the Insert Repeating Table window appears (Figure 20-7).

3. **Fill out the basic properties of the table.**

   The top part of the window lets you set up the basic structure of the table: rows, columns, cell padding, cell spacing, width, and border. Basically, it's the same information you provide when you create any table, as described on page 263. You usually start a repeating table with two rows—one for a heading, another to contain the information you want to repeat.

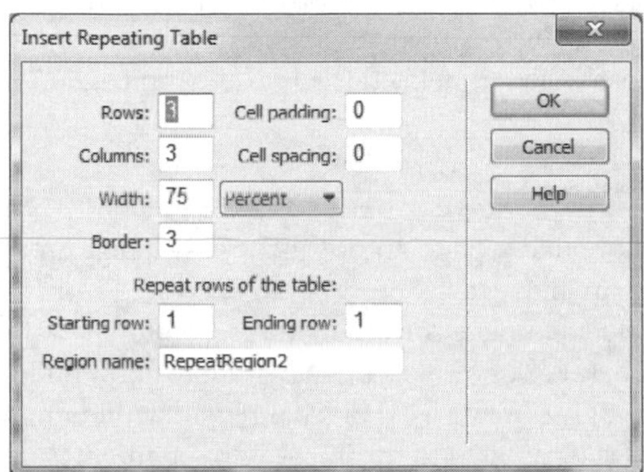

Figure 20-7: *The Insert Repeating Table dialog box lets you kill three birds with one stone: it adds a table to a page, turns one or more rows into a repeating region, and adds editable regions into each table cell inside the repeating region.*

4. **In the "Starting row" box, type the number of the row where the repeating region should begin.**

   Often 'll have just one repeating row: one row of product information, for example. You may want to use the top row for labels indicating the information contained in the rows below. If that's the case, enter *2* at this step, leaving the first row as an uneditable part of the template.

   It's conceivable, however, that you may want each entry to take up *two* rows. The first would list Product Name and Description; the second would contain a cell for a photo and a cell for the price. You set up this effect in this step and the next.

5. **In the "Ending row" box, type the number of the last repeating row.**

   If you wish to repeat only a single row, enter the same number you provided for step 4. If you want to create a double repeating row, add 1 to the number you provided in step 4. For example, if you need three rows for each repeating entry, add 2 to the number from step 4.

6. **Type a name for this repeating region.**

   Don't use the same name as another template region. You'll run the risk of unpredictable results on template-based pages.

7. **Click OK.**

   Dreamweaver inserts a table into the page. A blue tab with the name of the repeating region appears (see Figure 20-6), as do blue tabs in each cell of each repeated row. These tabs indicate new editable regions—one per cell.

   Since these new editable regions have uninformative names like EditRegion4, you may want to rename them. Click the blue tab and type a new name in the Property inspector. (But do so *before* you create any pages based on the template—see the warning on page 758.)

To remove a repeating region, select it by clicking the blue Repeat tab, and then choose Modify→Templates→Remove Template Markup. A more accurate way to select a repeating region is to click anywhere inside the region, and then click <mmtemplate: repeat> in the Tag selector (see page 23). Note that removing a repeating region doesn't remove any editable regions you added inside the repeating region. If you want to rename a repeating region, heed the Warning on page 758.

Making a Tag Attribute Editable

An editable region lets you—or, more likely, page-author jockeys—change areas of HTML, like a paragraph, image, or an entire table, on new pages created from your template. However, when you create a template for others to use, you may want to limit the page authors' editing abilities. For example, you may want to allow budding web designers to change the source of the image used in a banner ad without letting them change the width, height, and class applied to the image. Or you might want to use templates but still let others assign a class or ID to the <body> tag—a move that's normally forbidden on template-based pages. You can use Dreamweaver's Editable Tag Attribute to specify which tag properties your successors can change.

Note: Before you make a tag attribute editable, first set that property to a default value in the template: for example, add an ID to the <body> tag if you want to make the ID editable. Doing so inserts a default value and makes the attribute appear in the Editable Tag Attribute window (see steps 3 and 7 in the following instructions).

To make a tag attribute editable:

1. **Select the tag whose property you want to make editable.**

   Using the Tag selector (see page 23) is the most accurate way.

2. **Choose Modify→Templates→Make Attribute Editable.**

   The Editable Tag Attributes window opens (Figure 20-8).

FREQUENTLY ASKED QUESTION

Editable Regions, Repeating Regions, and Errors

When I try to insert an editable region inside a repeating region, I get the following error: "The selection is already in an editable, repeating, or optional region." *What's that about?*

This error message essentially means you're trying to add a template region where it doesn't belong. It appears most often when you attempt to put a repeating or optional region inside an editable region. That kind of nesting is a no-no; anything inside an editable region can be changed on template-based pages, and as such, Dreamweaver can't touch it.

However, you may get this error message seemingly by mistake. For instance, it's perfectly OK to add an editable region inside a repeating region, and it's even OK to add a repeating region inside an optional region, and vice versa.

But say one day you select text inside a repeating region and try to turn it into an editable region, and boom—error message. What probably happened was, when you selected the text, Dreamweaver actually selected part of the hidden code used to define a template region (see the box Under the Hood of Templates" on page 760) and thought you were trying to put an editable region inside it. To avoid confusion, use the Tag selector to select the page element you want to turn into an editable region. In the Tag selector, you can click <p> to select the paragraph inside the repeating region. Alternatively, go into Code view (see page 415), and then select whatever part of the code inside the repeating region you wish to make editable.

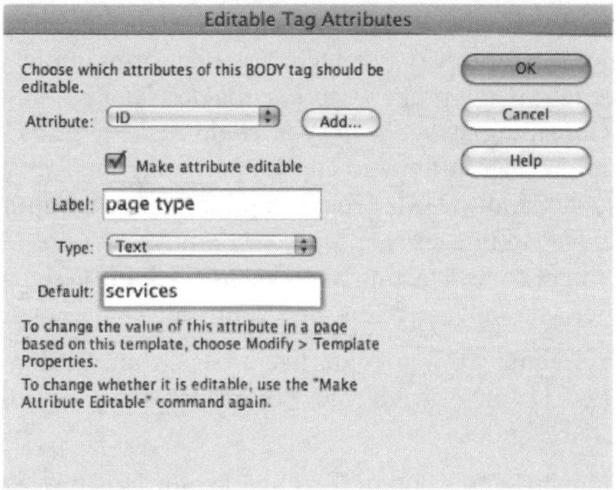

Figure 20-8:
Dreamweaver provides detailed control for template pages. To make just a single property of a single tag editable on pages based on your template, turn on the "Make attribute editable" checkbox. In this case, the "id" attribute of the body tag is editable, allowing page designers the freedom to apply different CSS styles to the body of each template-based page. They could change the ID name from page to page, and use descendent selectors to target styles that apply only to elements within pages that have that specific ID.

3. **Select an attribute from the menu or add a new attribute with the Add button.**

   The Attribute menu displays only those properties you already set for the selected tag. In other words, if you select an image, you probably see the *Src, Width*, and *Height* properties listed. But unless you set the image's alternative text, the *alt* property won't appear.

To add a property, click the Add button. In the window that appears, type in the appropriate property name. For example, to make the *alt* (alternate text) attribute of a graphic editable, you'd type *alt* in here. (If you're not sure of the attribute's name, check out Dreamweaver's built-in HTML reference, described in "Reference Panel" on page 448.)

Note: If you want page editors to be able to change a CSS class or ID applied to the <body> tag on template-based pages–to apply different fonts, background colors, or any of the many CSS formatting options to each template-based page–you *have* to make the Class or ID attribute editable. (See page 112 for more on CSS classes and IDs.)

---

4. **Make sure you turn on the "Make attribute editable" checkbox.**

   If you decide at some point that you no longer want people to be able to edit this property, you can return to this dialog box and turn off editing, as described in a moment.

5. **Type a name in the Label field.**

   What you type here should be a simple description of the editable tag and property, which helps page authors correctly identify editable properties. For example, you could use *Product Image* if you're making a particular image's *source* (*src*) property editable.

6. **Choose a value type from the menu.**

   Your choices are:

   - **Text.** Use this option when a property's value is a word. For example, you can change the image tag's *Align* property to *top, middle, baseline*, and so on. Or, when using Cascading Style Sheets, you could make a tag's *Class* property editable to allow page authors to apply a particular custom style to the tag—*content, footer*, and so URL. Use this option to let page authors edit the path to a file, like an image's *src* property or a link's *href* property. Using its site management tools, Dreamweaver keeps track of these paths and updates them when you move pages around your site.
   - **Color.** If the property requires a web color, like a background color, select this option. It makes Dreamweaver's color box available to people who build pages from the template.
   - **True/False.** You shouldn't use this option. It's intended for Dreamweaver's Optional Regions feature (discussed below), and it doesn't apply to *HTML* properties.
   - **Number.** Use this choice for properties that require a numeric value, like an image's *Height* and *Width* properties.

7. **Type a default value into the Default field.**

   This step is optional. The default value defines the initial value for this property, when people first create a page based on the template. They can then modify this value for that particular page. If you already set this property in the template, its value automatically appears in this box.

8. **Click OK to close the window.**

   Dreamweaver adds code to the template page that allows page authors control of the attribute. To set this attribute on pages created from the template, see the instructions on page 780.

If you later decide that you *don't* want a particular tag property to be editable, Dreamweaver can help. Open the template file, select the tag with the editable attribute, and choose Modify→Templates→Make Attribute Editable. In the window that appears, turn off the "Make attribute editable" checkbox (Figure 20-8). Unfortunately, doing so doesn't remove *all* of the template code Dreamweaver added. Even after you turn off editing for an attribute, Dreamweaver leaves behind the parameter used to control the tag's property. To eliminate *this* extra code, see the box on page 774.

Adding Optional Regions

Templates provide consistent design. While consistency is generally a good thing, it can also get boring. Furthermore, there may be times when you want the flexibility to include information on some template-based pages but not on others.

Dreamweaver provides a fairly foolproof way to vary page design: *optional regions*. An optional region is simply part of a template you can hide or display on each template-based page (see Figure 20-9). When a page author creates a new page based on the template, she can turn the region on or off.

Creating an optional region is a snap. Just select the HTML code you wish to make optional and do one of the following:

- On the Common category of the Insert panel (Figure 20-2), select the Optional Region option from the Templates menu.
- Choose Insert→Template Objects→Optional Region.
- Right-click (Control-click) the selection and choose Templates→New Optional Region from the shortcut menu.

In the New Optional Region window, type a name (Figure 20-10). Make sure not to use the same name as any other region on the page, and—although Dreamweaver lets you—don't use spaces or other punctuation marks. (Following the rules for naming files as described on page 639 ensures that the optional region works properly.) Click OK to close the window and create the new optional region. Dreamweaver adds a light blue tab with the word "If," followed by the name you gave the region (Figure 20-9).

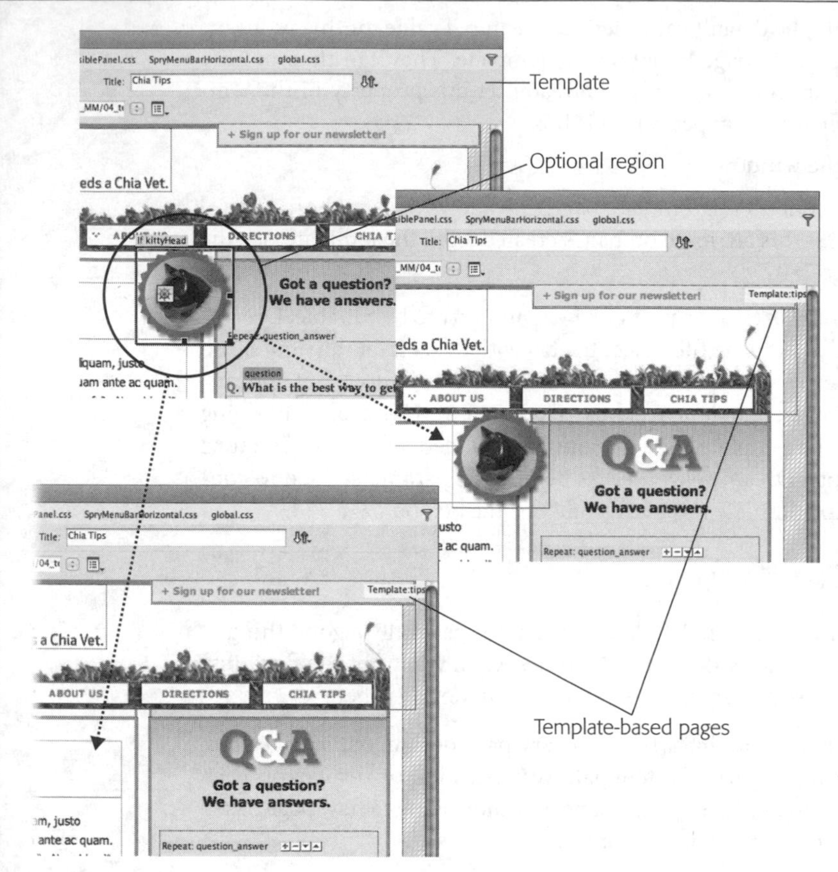

Figure 20-9: *Now you see it, now you don't. Optional regions let you show or hide content on a page-by-page basis. In these examples, the template page (top) has an optional region containing a "Chia Kitten" icon (circled). When you create a page from this template, you can either display the optional region (middle) or hide it (bottom).*

Locking Optional Regions

An optional region can include editable regions, repeating regions, *and* locked regions. For example, if you want to allow a page editor to turn on or off a graphic ("This item on sale!!!!"), insert the graphic outside an editable region on the page, and then make it an optional region as described above. Since anything not inside an editable region is locked, a page editor can't change the graphic or ruin its formatting—he can only make it visible or hidden.

Repeating Optional Regions

An optional region can also include repeating regions. For example, suppose you create a repeating region (see page 768) that lets a page editor add row after row of links to a list of related articles. You could then turn this repeating region into an optional region, as described above, so that if a particular page had no related articles, the page editor could simply hide the entire "related articles" section of the page.

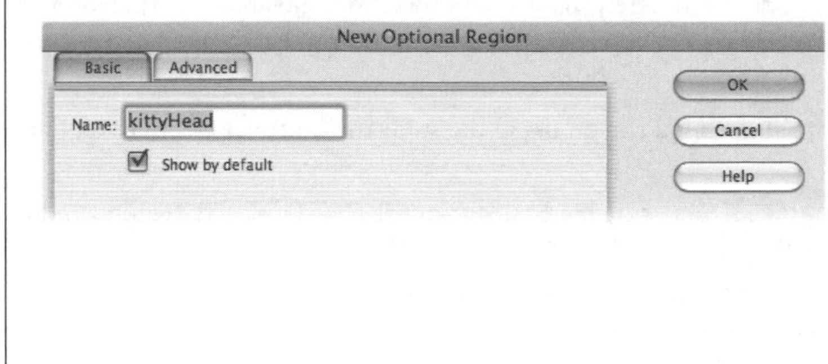

Figure 20-10: *The Optional Regions feature lets you show or hide specific content on template-based pages. Turning on "Show by default" tells Dreamweaver to display the region when a page editor first creates a template-based page. Turn this box on if you want to display the optional region on most pages. You'll save someone the effort of doing so each time she creates a new template-based page.*

Optional Editable Regions

Dreamweaver's Optional Editable Region command inserts an optional region with an editable region *inside* of it. To use it, click on the spot in the template where you'd like to add it, and then choose Insert→Template Objects→Optional Editable Region (alternatively, you can choose this option from the Templates menu on the Common category of the Insert panel). The New Optional Region window appears; give it a name, and then follow the same steps for adding an optional region (see page 767).

This technique doesn't offer a lot of control; it's hard to insert HTML *outside* the editable region, for example. So if you want an image or table that's optional but *not* editable, it's usually better to just create the editable region as described on page 755and turn it (and any other HTML you wish to include) into an optional region.

Note: The Optional Editable Region command doesn't let you name the editable region; it automatically assigns a generic name like *EditRegion7*. You can select the editable region and change its name in the Property inspector, but do so *before* you build any pages based on this template (see the Warning on page 758).

Advanced Optional Regions

A basic optional region is a rather simple affair: It either appears or it doesn't. But Dreamweaver offers more complex logic for controlling optional regions. For example, you may want several different areas of a page to be either hidden or visible at the same time—perhaps an "On Sale Now!" icon at the top of a page *and* a "Call 1-800-SHIZZLE to order" message at the bottom of the page. When one appears, so does the other.

Because these objects are in different areas of the page, you have to create two separate optional regions. Fortunately, using Dreamweaver's advanced settings for optional regions, you can easily have a single region control the display of one or more additional areas of a page. Here's how:

1. **Create the first optional region using the steps in "Adding Optional Regions" on page 767.**

   Give the region a name using the Basic tab of the New Optional Region window (Figure 20-10).

2. **Select the part of the page—an image, paragraph, or table—you want to turn into a second optional region.**

   In this case, you make the display of this region dependent on the optional region added in step 1. If the first region is visible on the page, this second region also shows.

3. **On the Common category of the Insert panel (Figure 20-2), choose the Optional Region item from the Templates menu.**

   The New Optional Region window appears.

4. **Click the Advanced tab.**

   The optional region's advanced options appear (see Figure 20-11). In this case, you want the first optional region you created to control the display of this new region. So instead of giving this region a name, you simply select the name of the first optional region in the next step.

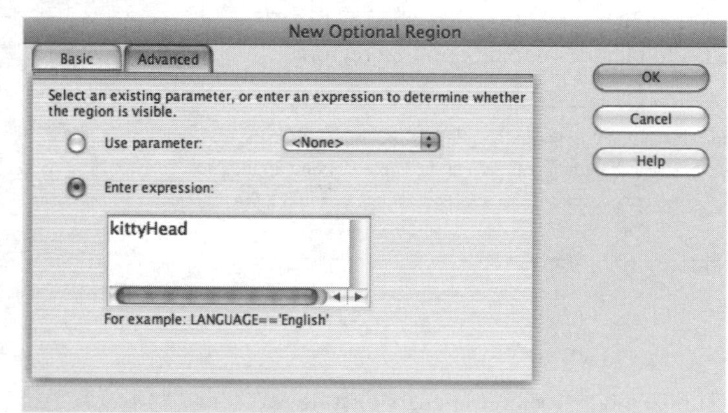

Figure 20-11: *The New Optional Region box lets you more precisely control the display of an optional region. You can make the region appear only when another region is visible, or use Dreamweaver's template expression language to create a more complex behavior. In this case, the selected region appears only when another region–named "kittyHead"–is not visible (the ! is the programming equivalent of "is not").*

5. **Click the "Use parameter" button and select the name of the first optional region from the menu.**

   This step is what makes the first optional region control this region. If a page displays the first region, it also displays this second region.

6. **Click OK to close the window and create the new optional region.**

   You can continue adding optional regions this way, using the Advanced tab and selecting the name of the first optional region from the menu. As a result, the first optional region controls the display of many other areas of the page.

Even fancier tricks

You can use these advanced controls for even more elaborate web page stunts. For example, say your site has several sections. When a visitor is in one section of the site, its navigation button is attractively highlighted and a secondary navigation bar miraculously appears, offering links to other pages in that section.

Using a template, you can add an optional region with the highlighted section button in it. When you add the secondary navigation bar to the page, you make *it* an optional region controlled by the highlighted navigation button. Then, when you add a page to that section of the site, you simply show the optional region containing the highlighted button, causing the secondary navigation bar to appear as well (see Figure 20-12 for a look at how this works).

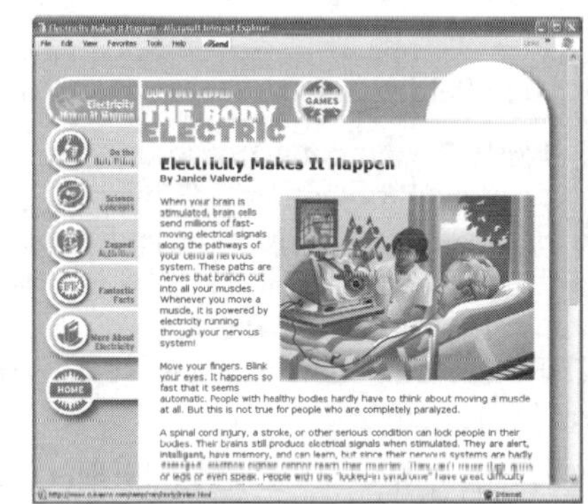

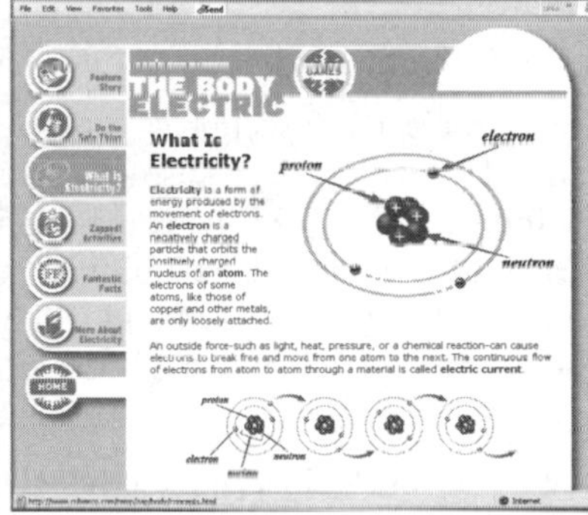

Figure 20-12: *An optional region on the page at left highlights the top navigation button (Electricity Makes It Happen). By turning on a different optional region (right), the navigation system can highlight the site's current section—"What is Electricity?" (the third button from the top).*

Controlling regions with expressions

You can program even more complex behaviors using a basic *expression language*, loosely based on JavaScript, that Dreamweaver understands. For example, instead of having an optional region appear when another optional region is visible (as in the previous example), suppose you want to have a region appear when another region is *in*visible. This arrangement can come in handy when you create a navigation bar unique to only one part of your site. For example, if a visitor is in one section of your site, she sees a highlighted, "you are here" navigation button for that section, but if she's in another section, the regular, non-highlighted button appears.

In other words, you can build a single template for all the sections of a site, but control the appearance of the navigation bar separately for pages in each individual section (see Figure 20-12).

Here's how you control the navigation bar:

1. **Click the page where you wish to insert the navigation buttons.**
2. **Insert the highlighted ("You are in this section") navigation button.**

   This button could be a rollover image (see page 246) or just a single graphic. If you have multiple pages in the section, you probably also want to link this graphic to the main page for that section.
3. **Click next to the highlighted button and insert the plain ("You can go here") navigation button.**

   The button could also be a rollover image with a link to the main page for this section (for example, a main Products page).
4. **In the Property inspector, select the highlighted navigation button and its link (if it has one).**

   This button appears on any template-based page for this section.
5. **On the Common category of the Insert panel (Figure 20-2), choose Optional Region from the Template menu.**

   The New Optional Region window appears. Make sure you have the Basic tab selected.
6. **Type the name of the section into the Name field. Click OK.**

   For example, if this section of your site advertises your company's products, you can call it *products*. Don't use any spaces or punctuation other than hyphens (-) or underscores (_) for the name. Also, make sure the "Show by default" box is turned *off*. Since you'll be building template-based pages for all the sections of your site, most pages you build will be in other sections of the site. Your work goes faster if this highlighted button starts out hidden. In the next steps, you make the plain navigation button appear by default.
7. **Use the Property inspector to select the plain button and link, and then click the Optional Region button on the Insert bar.**

   The New Optional Region window appears again, but this time you'll use the advanced options.
8. **Click the Advanced tab; select "Enter expression" (Figure 20-11).**

   You're going to type an *expression* in the Expression field. An expression is a programming statement that's either true or false. (For an obvious example, it's true that 2 is always equal to 2, but it's obviously false to say, "2 is equal to 4." In programming, you express equality using a *pair* of = signs. So 2==2 is true, but 2==4 is false.) The important thing to remember here is that when an expression is true, the optional region is visible; when it's false, it's hidden.

9. **Type an exclamation point (!) followed by the name you entered in step 6—*!products*, for example.**

   Dreamweaver's template expression language is based on the JavaScript programming language. An exclamation mark means "not," so this code means *not products*. Translation into non-propeller-head language: when the *products* region (remember, that's the highlighted button) is *not* displayed, this region (the button) appears on the page.

   The logic gets a little complicated, but have faith. When you add a new page based on this template, the optional region you added in step 6 is *not* visible (because you turned off the "Show by default" box). In other words, because the region—*products* in this example—is *not* showing, this region, the one with the plain navigation button, appears on the page by default. Turning the *products* region on *hides* the plain navigation button. In other words, the first optional region works like a light switch, alternately turning on one or the other navigation button.

10. **Click OK to close the window and add the additional optional regions.**

    Repeat this process for each button in the navigation bar. Now your template is perfectly suited for displaying customized navigation bars for each section of your site. When you create a new template-based page, simply turn on the region for the particular section in which the page is located. (Hiding and showing optional regions is described on page 781.)

As you can see, optional regions are very powerful—and potentially confusing. But using even basic optional regions, you can exert a great deal of control over your template-based pages. For more information on template expressions and optional regions, take a look in Dreamweaver's Help sysem. (Choose Help→Dreamweaver Help to open the Adobe Help system; then, in the search box, type *template expressions*, open the Search Options section, choose Local Help from the Search Location, and then hit Enter (Return). You'll then get a page that lists several articles related to templates and template expressions.

Editing and Removing Optional Regions

After you insert an optional region, you can always return to the New Optional Region dialog box to change the region's name, alter its default settings, or use advanced options. To edit an optional region, first select it using one of these techniques:

- Click the region's blue tab in the document window (Figure 20-9).
- Click anywhere inside the optional region in the document window and then click the <mmtemplate:if> tag in the Tag selector (see page 23 for details on the Tag selector).

When you select an optional region, Dreamweaver displays an Edit button in the Property inspector. Click it to reopen the New Optional Region window. You can then change the region's properties.

To remove an optional region, select it by using one of the techniques listed previously and choose Modify→Templates→ Remove Template Markup. Dreamweaver removes most of the code associated with the optional region (but see the box below).

POWER USERS' CLINIC

Understanding Template Parameters

When you insert an optional region, Dreamweaver adds special code to the head of the web page. Called a *template parameter*, this code is responsible for showing or hiding an optional region.

In fact, Dreamweaver uses parameters when you make a tag attribute editable, too. A typical parameter for an optional region might look like this:

```
<!-- TemplateParam name="SaleBug"
type="boolean" value="true" -->
```

The <!-- and --> are HTML comments that hide this code from web browsers. TemplateParam tells Dreamweaver that the comment is actually part of the program's Template features–specifically, a template parameter.

A parameter has three parts: name, type, and value. The name is the name you give the editable region. The type–Boolean above–indicates that the value of this parameter can be only one of two options: true or false. In this example, the value is "true," which simply means that the optional region called SaleBug is visible. (Don't worry; you don't have to actually edit this code by hand to turn optional regions on and off, as you'll see on page 781.)

In programming jargon, a template parameter is known as a *variable*. In simpler terms, it's just a way to store information that can change. Dreamweaver reacts differently depending on the parameter's value: show the region if the parameter's true, or hide it if the parameter's false.

Editable tag attributes also use parameters to store the values you enter for tag attributes. For example:

```
<!-- TemplateParam name="PageColor"
type="color" value="#FFFFFF" -->
```

On template-based pages, you can change the value of an editable tag's parameter using the Modify→Template Parameters menu (see page 780).

Unfortunately, when you delete an optional region from a template, or remove the ability to edit a tag attribute, Dreamweaver always leaves these parameter tags hanging around in the head of the template document. Keeping in mind that Dreamweaver adds these parameter tags directly before the closing </head> tag, you can find and remove them in Code view (see Chapter 11).

Nested Templates

Large sites may have many different sections or types of pages. Each section or type of page may have its own unique look. A Frequently Asked Questions page may have distinct areas for a question, an answer, and links to further resources, while a product page may have a picture, a product description, and ordering information. You could create different templates for each type of page, but even that may be more work than necessary.

Note: Nested templates are a somewhat advanced and potentially confusing concept. Many people happily use Dreamweaver templates without ever using the nested template feature.

While many pages in a site may have subtle differences, they usually share very basic design features. The overall structure of every page, for example, may be the same: same logo, banner, and navigation bar. Even the basic layout may be the same (sidebar on the left, main content in the middle, for example). And therein lies the problem with creating individual templates for each section of a website: if you need to make a very basic sitewide change, like adding a new button to the navigation bar or altering a sitewide banner, you need to edit *each* template individually, adding extra time, effort, and the chance of making a mistake.

Good news—Dreamweaver offers a tool to solve just this problem: nested templates. A *nested template* is one you make from an existing template, which then becomes the *master* template (see Figure 20-13).

Imagine a basic software company website with three sections: Support, Our Products, and Downloads. Each section has its own kind of information and specific layout needs. However, all three sections share the same banner and navigation bar.

To create a template for this site, you first create a very basic template that includes the site's common elements (including any editable regions)—this is your master template. You can then create nested templates based on this master template. In the nested templates, you can add design refinements and additional editable regions unique to each of the site's sections.

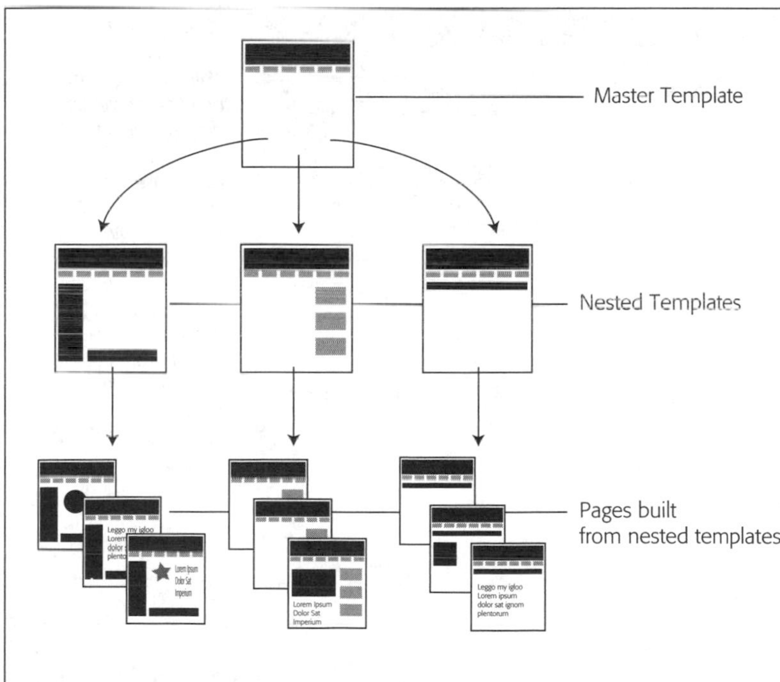

Figure 20-13: *Nested templates (middle row) let you build templates that share common, sitewide design elements while giving you precise control over pages unique to each section of the site. A page built from a nested template (bottom row) contains both elements from your master template (top row)–like a banner and a sitewide navigation bar–in addition to elements specific to the nested template–like a section-specific secondary navigation bar. Dreamweaver passes changes you make to the master template on to all of the site's pages, including those created from the nested templates. Changes you make to a nested template, by contrast, end up on only the pages you build with that nested template.*

To create a nested template:

1. **Build a template as described on page 752.**

   This page acts as your master template and it controls all your nested templates. It should include the elements you want on all of your pages, like your logo and email links. It should also include editable regions that you want to customize for each section of your site, like div tags that hold blocks of text and images. That way, when you create a nested template from this master, you (or a page author) have the flexibility to put unique content in these areas of your pages,

2. **Name and save this template (File→Save as Template), and then close it.**

   Your template is safe on our hard drive.

3. **Choose File→New.**

   The window for creating new documents and template-based pages opens (see Figure 20-14).

4. **On the left side of the New Document window, click the Page from Template button. In the Site list, select the site on which you're working.**

   You can open templates from any site you've defined in Dreamweaver, but this is generally not a good idea, as Figure 20-14 explains.

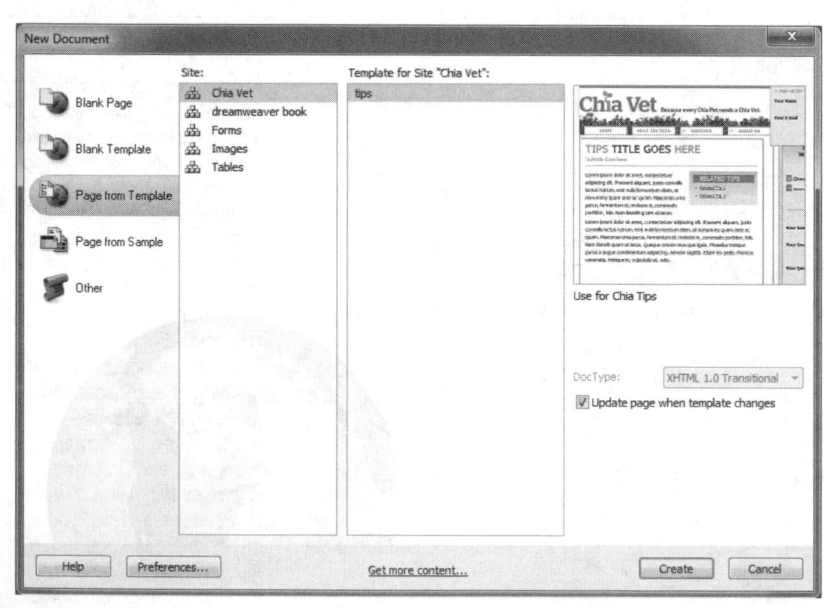

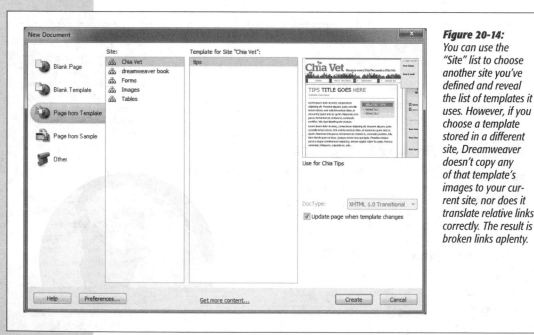

***Figure 20-14:** You can use the "Site" list to choose another site you've defined and reveal the list of templates it uses. However, if you choose a template stored in a different site, Dreamweaver doesn't copy any of that template's images to your current site, nor does it translate relative links correctly. The result is broken links aplenty.*

5. **From the list of templates, select the name of the master template file you created in step 1.**

   Make sure you have the "Update page when template changes" box turned on. Otherwise, your nested templates won't update when you edit the master template.

6. **Click OK.**

   Dreamweaver creates a new template-based page. At this point, it's simply a basic web page based on your original template. Next, you'll turn this into a *nested template.*

7. **Choose File→"Save as Template." Or, on the Common category of the Insert panel (Figure 20-2), select Make Nested Template from the Templates menu.**

   The Save As Template window appears (see Figure 20-3).

8. **Type in a name for the template and click the Save button.**

   Voilà! A nested template. What? It doesn't look like a nested template? In truth, it isn't. Right now, there's no difference between it and your master template. They share the same design, content, and template regions. You'll turn it into a nested template by following the steps below.

Customizing Nested Templates

After you create a nested template file, the next step is to add the design elements that make the template unique (and a true nested template). For example, you can add a special type of table to display a set of product photos, descriptions, prices, and other information. This table will appear only in pages you build with this nested template, not those you build with the master template or any other nested template.

There are a few things you should keep in mind when planning your template development strategy:

- When you create pages from templates, you can add content only to editable regions. That's true not only for template-based pages, but for nested templates, too. If the master template has *no* editable regions, you won't be able to change *anything* on the nested template you create from it.
- When you work on a nested template, you can insert an editable region only into an editable region supplied by the master template. For example, say you create a master template to provide a consistent banner and navigation bar on the site, all in a locked region of the master template. Then you add a large empty area at the bottom of the page and turn it into an editable region. After you create a nested template from the master, you can add new, additional editable regions to this open area. In fact, you can add any template region—editable, optional, or repeating—to this area.
- If, when you work on a nested template, you insert a template region (editable, optional, or repeating) into an editable region supplied by the master template, you can modify *only* these newly added regions in the pages you create based on that nested template. The rest of the editable region supplied by the master template isn't editable on the pages based on the nested template.

  Using the example in the previous paragraph, if you add a repeating table to your nested template (see page 761 for more about repeating tables), you can change *only* the editable areas of that repeating table on any pages you create based on the nested template. Of course, the other side of the coin is that if you add an editable region to the master template and then refrain from adding any particular template regions when you create the nested template, all the HTML inside that region is editable in the nested template *and* in all the pages based on that template.

Using Nested Templates

Here's an example of how you can use nested templates. Suppose you want to create a uniform design for your site where every page of the site has a logo as well as a sitewide navigation bar. Each page within one section of the site also has a sidebar containing a *secondary* navigation bar with navigation buttons for just that section. Finally, every page has a large content area to hold the information specific to that page.

Using nested templates, creating a website like this couldn't be easier (really!). Create a master template that includes the site banner and the navigation bar, and then add editable regions for a sidebar and a main content area.

Next, create a nested template for one *section* of the site, leaving the content area as it is—as an editable area. Since each page will have unique content in this area, you don't need to do anything to this region (like define optional or repeating regions).

Then add the secondary navigation bar to the nested template's sidebar area. To lock this region so no one can tinker with it (in pages built from the nested template), add an empty editable region, or see the Tip on the next page.

If you want, you can build similar nested templates for the other sections of the site.

Now you're ready to start building the pages of your site. Create a new page based on one of the section templates. Add text or graphics to the editable content area of the page. Should you need to change the site logo or add a button to the sie-wide navigation bar, open the master template, make the changes, save the file, and let Dreamweaver update all the pages of your site with the new look. If you simply need to change the secondary navigation for one section of the site, open the appropriate nested template, change the sidebar, save the template, and let Dreamweaver update all the pages built using that nested template.

Tip: You can lock an editable region passed from a master template to a nested template so that page builders can't change this region in pages based on the nested template. In the nested template, go into Code view, and then locate the beginning of the editable region, which looks something like, <!--InstanceBeginEditable name="regionName" -->. Then insert the text @@("")@@ directly after the -->.

If you find yourself typing this code often, think about creating a snippet (see page 732) containing the text @@("")@@.

Building Pages Based on a Template

Building a template is only a prelude to the actual work of building your site. Once you finish your template, it's time to produce pages.

To create a new document based on a template, choose File→New to open the New Document window (see Figure 20-14). Click the "Page from Template" button, and then, from the Site list, select the site you're working on. All the templates for the selected site appear in the right-hand column. Select the template you wish to use, and then click Create.

Note: If you don't want your new web page linked to a template (so that future changes to the template won't affect the web page), turn off the "Update page when template changes" checkbox. The result is a new page that looks just like the template, but has no locked regions; you can edit the entire page. This is a useful technique to use when you want to create a new template starting with the general design and structure of an existing template. (Be aware that Dreamweaver remembers this choice the next time you create a new template-based page. In other words, future pages you create from a template will *also* be unlinked—unless you remember to turn the "Update page" box back on.)

A new web page document opens, based on the template, bearing a tab in the upper-right corner that identifies the underlying template name. Dreamweaver outlines any editable regions in blue; a small blue tab displays each region's name (Figure 20-5).

Dreamweaver makes it obvious which areas of a page are off-limits; your cursor changes to a "forbidden" symbol (a circle with a line through it) when you venture into a locked area.

To add content to an editable region, click anywhere inside the region. You can type inside it, add graphics, or add any other object or HTML you can normally add to a document. You can also change the document's title and add a Spry Menu bar (Chapter 5), Spry widget (Chapter 13), Behavior (Chapter 14), Cascading Style Sheet (see Chapter 4), and meta tag information (items that go in the <head> of an HTML document).

Working with Repeating Regions

Repeating regions work a bit differently from editable regions. In most cases, a repeating region includes one or more editable regions (which you can edit using the instructions above). However, Dreamweaver provides special controls to let you add, remove, and rearrange repeating entries (see Figure 20-15).

These regions let page editors add repeated page elements—like rows of product information in a list of products. To add a repeating entry, click the + button that appears to the right of the Repeat region's blue tab. You can then edit any editable regions within the entry. Click inside an editable region inside a repeating entry and click + again to add a new entry *after* it.

Deleting a repeating entry is just as easy. Click inside an editable region within the entry you want to delete and click the minus sign button (-).

Tip: You can create repeating regions that don't have any editable regions–for example, you can create a repeating region with a star in it; repeat the region several times to indicate the rating for a product. Although you can use the + button to repeat such regions, you can't delete those regions with the minus sign (–) button. In other words, you're stuck with any extra stars you added. The only workaround is to add an editable region to the repeating region. Then Dreamweaver lets you remove the repeating regions.

To rearrange entries in the list, click inside an entry's editable region. Click the up or down arrows to move the entry up or down in the list (to alphabetize it, for example).

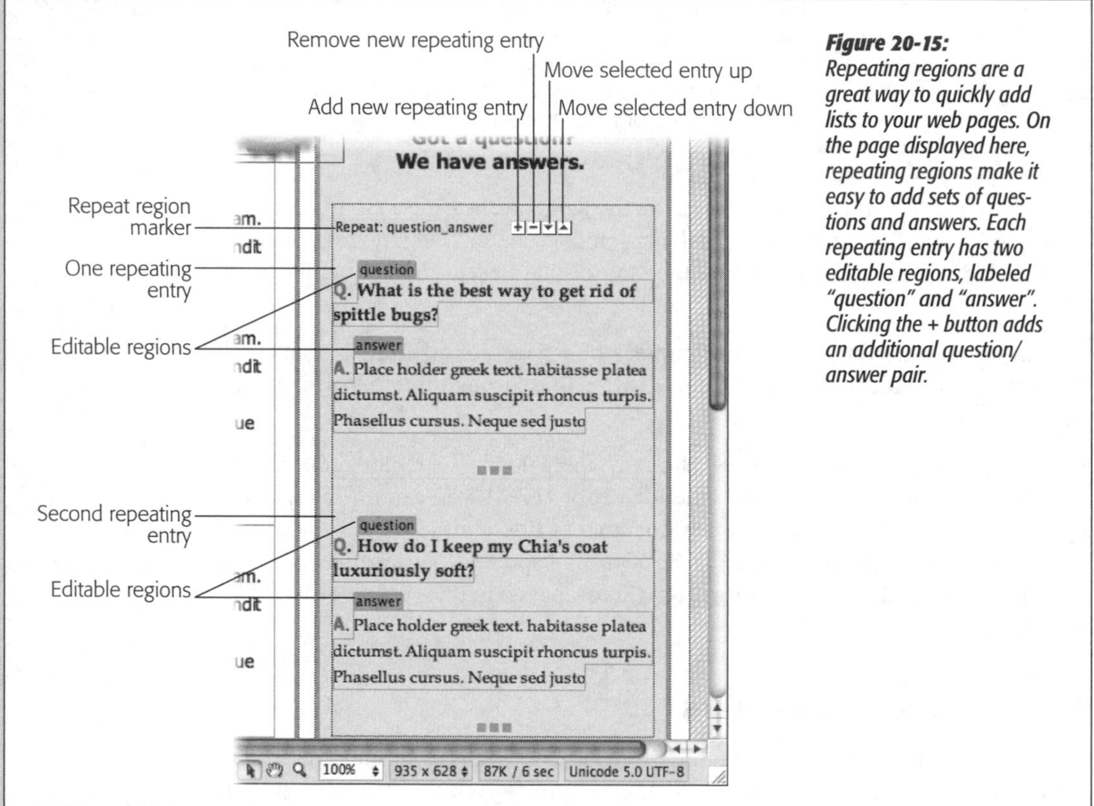

Figure 20-15: *Repeating regions are a great way to quickly add lists to your web pages. On the page displayed here, repeating regions make it easy to add sets of questions and answers. Each repeating entry has two editable regions, labeled "question" and "answer". Clicking the + button adds an additional question/ answer pair.*

Changing Properties of Editable Tag Attributes

Unlike editable or repeating regions, you can't readily see an editable tag attribute on template-based pages. There's no blue tab that identifies them, as there are for editable regions; in fact, nothing appears in Design view to indicate that there are *any* editable *tag* properties on the page. The only way to find out is to choose Modify→Template Properties to open the Template Properties dialog box (see Figure 20-16).

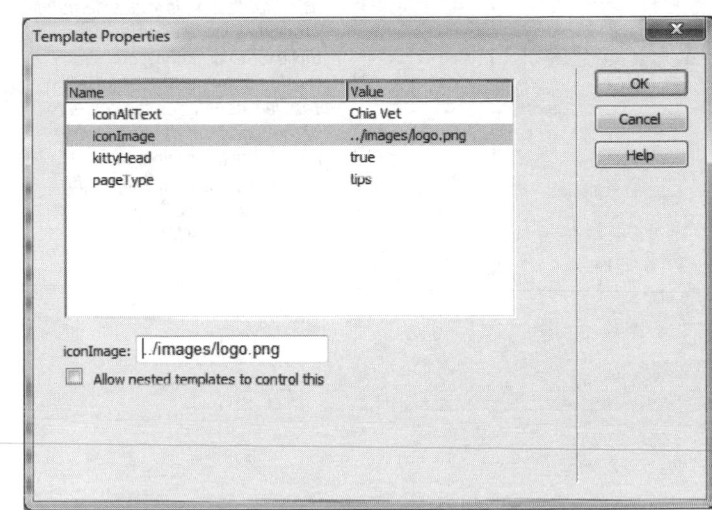

Figure 20-16: *The Template Properties window lets you control editable tag attributes and other parameters for optional regions. Depending on which parameter you select, the options at the bottom of the window change. In this case, the src property of an image tag has been made editable. To change the image tag's src property, click Dreamweaver's familiar "Browse for File" button and select a new graphic file.*

Dreamweaver displays all the editable tag attributes for this page in this window. In addition, it displays all the parameters defined for this page, including optional regions, as discussed in the box on page 774.

To change the value of a template property—in other words, to edit the property of an editable tag—select its name from the list and fill out the option that appears at the bottom of the window. For example, in the case of color properties, use the color box to pick a color. If the property is a path (like a link or an image's *src* property), click the "select a file" folder icon to browse to the file.

Once you finish setting the editable properties for the page, click OK to close the window.

Hiding and Showing Optional Regions

As with Editable Tag Attributes, you use the Template Properties window to control the display of optional regions. On template-based pages, you can show or hide an optional region by choosing Modify→Template Properties to open this dialog box (see Figure 20-17). Next, select the name of the optional region. To make all the page elements in the region visible, turn on the "Show" checkbox at the bottom of the window. To hide all the optional regions, turn off this box.

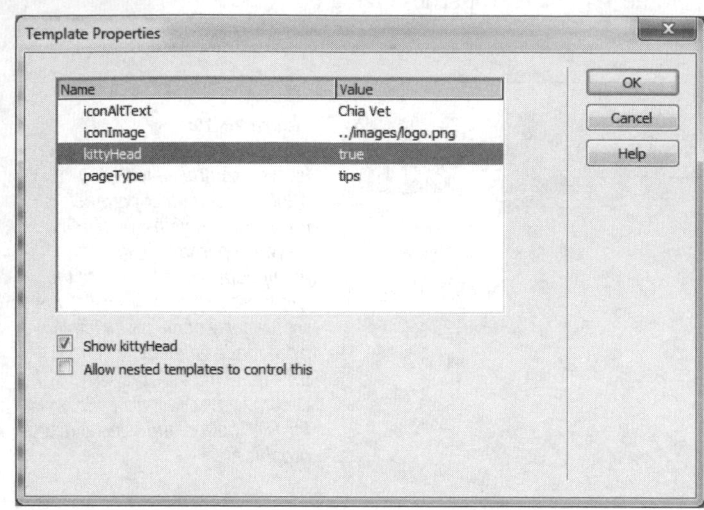

Figure 20-17: *The Template Properties window displays optional regions as well as editable tag attributes. Template properties for optional regions–in this example, "kittyHead"–have a value of either true or false. True lets people see the contents of the region on the page, while false hides the region. (The "Allow nested templates to control this" option is described in the box "Controlling the Nest".)*

Applying Templates to Existing Pages

What happens if you create a web page, and *then* decide you want it to share the look of a template? No problem. Dreamweaver lets you apply a template to any web page in your site. You can even swap one template for another by applying a new template to a page based on a different template.

To apply a template to a page you already created:

1. **Choose File→Open to open the page you want to alter.**

   The page opens.

2. **Choose Window→Assets. Click the Assets panel's Templates button (see Figure 20-4).**

   The Assets panel appears and reveals a list of your site's templates.

Note: You can also apply a template to a page by choosing Modify→Templates→ Apply Template to Page. Select the name of the template from the window that appears and skip to step 5.

---

3. **Click a template in the list on the Assets panel, and then click Apply.**

   The Inconsistent Region Names dialog box opens (Figure 20-18).

FREQUENTLY ASKED QUESTION

Controlling the Nest

The Template Properties dialog box includes a checkbox labeled "Allow nested templates to control this.". *What does it do?*

First off, this only applies if you use nested templates as described on page 774. If you never use them, this box has no effect on your pages. However, if you do use (or plan on using) nested templates, here's how that box works.

Imagine you create a template and add several optional regions and editable tag attributes to it. You then use this template as the basic design for more refined templates for each section of your site using the nested template feature. When you create one of these nested templates based on the master template, it has access to the Template Properties window, where page authors can modify any of the *template* properties in the original, master template.

For example, to better identify each section of a site, you might assign a different class style to the <body> tag of a section's pages. The class might apply a different background color to each page within a section: blue for the products section, orange for the support section, and so on. In the master template, you make the <body> tag's *class* property editable. Now, when you create a nested template for the products section, you simply open the Template Properties dialog box, and then assign a class style with a blue page background. For the support section's nested template, apply a class that sets the background to orange. Now, when you create a template-based page for the support section, its background is orange, while a page for the products section has a blue background.

However, to let your site's color palette go really wild, you may want every page in the site to have its own unique background color, each defined by a different class style. In this case, you want to let every page based on a nested template have an editable *class* property.

To do so, open the nested template, open the Template Properties window, select the property you want to make editable in pages built from this template (*color* in this case), and turn on the "Allow nested templates to control this" checkbox. Now this property is uneditable in the nested template, but editable in all the pages you create from it.

You've probably realized by now that the phrase "Allow nested templates to control this" doesn't make much sense. Turning it on actually *prevents* the nested template from controlling the property. A better way to think of it is "Allow pages created from this nested template to control this property." The bottom line: Turning on this box makes the attribute uneditable on that page. If the page is a nested template, it lets the template property "pass through" to all pages based on this template. In other words, you can't set the background color in the template, but you can change it in pages you create from the template.

4. **In the list under "Editable regions," choose "Documentbody.".**

   To the right, in the Resolved column, you see <Not resolved>. This is Dreamweaver's way of saying it doesn't know what to do with the contents of the current page. You need to pick one of the template's editable regions.

5. **From the "Move content to new region" menu, select an editable region.**

   If you want to keep the material, select the name of an editable region in which to place it from the list; otherwise, choose Nowhere, which, in effect, creates a new blank page based on the template.

   Unfortunately, you can only select a single editable region. If the original page has several content regions, Dreamweaver pushes them all into a single editable region.

6. **If "Document head" also appears in the window, select it and choose "head" from the "Move content to new region" menu.**

   This step preserves any special information you added to the head of your page, like Cascading Style Sheets, meta tags, and custom JavaScript programs. Unfortunately, Dreamweaver always replaces the title of your original page with the default title of the template. You have to reenter the title (see page 44) after you apply the template.

7. **Click OK.**

   Your new page appears.

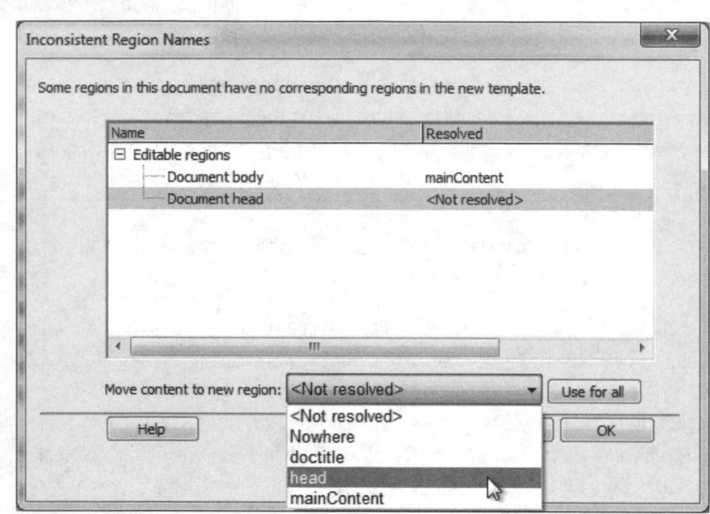

Figure 20-18: *When you apply a template to an existing page, you must tell Dreamweaver what to do with the material already on the page. You do that by selecting one of the template's editable regions from a pop-up menu, which takes charge of all editable regions in the page you're converting.*

Updating a Template

Templates aren't just useful for rapidly building pages; they also make quick work of site updates. Template-based pages maintain a link to the original template; Dreamweaver automatically passes changes you make to the original template along to every page built from it. If you used templates to build your site, you probably won't cry on your keyboard when the boss asks you to add an additional button and a link to the navigation bar. Instead of editing every page, you can simply open the template file, update the navigation bar, and let Dreamweaver apply the update to all the pages.

You update a template (and all the pages based on it) like this:

1. **Choose Window→Assets.**

   The Assets panel appears.

2. **Click the Templates button (see Figure 20-4).**

   A list of the site's templates appears.

3. **Double-click the template's name to open it.**

   Alternatively, you can select the template in the Assets panel, and then click the Edit button to open the original template (.dwt) file (see Figure 20-4). The template opens.

Tip: You can also open a template by double-clicking the appropriate template file (.dwt) in the Templates folder in the Files panel.

---

4. **Edit the template as you would any web page.**

   Since this is the original template file, you can edit any of the HTML in the document, including Cascading Style Sheets, meta tags, and layers. You can also add or remove editable regions.

   Take care, however, to edit *only* the areas that you did *not* mark as editable regions. The reason: When you update your pages, any region marked as editable in a template file isn't passed on to pages based on that template. After all, the template dictates only the design of those pages' *non*-editable regions.

Note: Be careful when you remove editable regions from a template. If you already built some pages based on the template, Dreamweaver warns you when you save the template. As described below, you can either *delete* the content you added to that region in each of the pages you created, or you can move it to another editable region in the page.

---

5. **Choose File→Save.**

   If you already created pages based on this template, Dreamweaver opens the Update Template Files dialog box. It lists all the files that use the template.

6. **Click Update to update all the files based on the template.**

   Dreamweaver automatically applies the changes you make to the pages based on the template. Then, the Update Pages dialog box opens. If you want to see a list of all the files Dreamweaver changed, turn on the "Show log" box.

   On a large site, this automatic update feature can be an incredible time-saver, but you may *not* want to click Update, at least not right now. Perhaps you're just saving some of your hard work on the template but aren't quite finished perfecting it—why waste your time updating all those pages more than once? In such a scenario, click the Don't Update button. Remember, you can always update the pages later (see the box "Wait to Update" on page 786).

7. **Click Close.**

   The Update Pages dialog box closes.

Remember that you need to update all your files, even if you make a simple change to the template, like changing its name.

Updating Nested Templates

When you build a website using nested templates, you often end up with multiple templates. The master template controls the design elements of nested templates, which in turn control the pages based on those nested templates. (You can even make nested templates *out of* nested templates, but for sanity's sake, you'd better not.) With this level of complexity, updates to nested templates can get confusing fast.

In a nutshell, here's how it works:

- If you edit a locked region in a master template and then update your site, Dreamweaver updates not only the nested templates, but all pages built from them.
- If you edit a locked region in a nested template and then update your site, Dreamweaver passes those changes on only to pages built from that nested template.

However, changes you make to an *editable* region of a master template don't pass on to any page. Neither do changes you make to editable regions of a nested template.

POWER USERS' CLINIC

Wait to Update

Whenever you modify and save a template, Dreamweaver gives you the option of updating any pages in the site that are descended from the template. The same holds true of Library items; if you change a Library item, Dreamweaver asks if you want to pass that change to all the pages with that item. Very often, you'll say Yes.

But there are times when you want to wait to update your site. If you're making a lot of changes to templates or multiple Library items, you may wish to wait until you finish all your edits before you let the changes ripple through your pages. After all, it can take some time to update large sites.

Dreamweaver lets you update pages that use templates and Library items any time. Just choose Modify→Templates→Update Pages or Modify→Library→Update Pages.

Both menu options open the same window, the Update Pages dialog box.

At this point, you can update pages that use a specific template or Library item by going to the "Look in" menu, choosing "Files that Use," and then selecting the appropriate name from the pop-up menu. If you want to update all the pages in a site, choose Entire Site, and then, from the pop-up menu, select the name of the local site. Turn on both the Templates and "Library items" checkboxes to update all pages.

To see the results of Dreamweaver's work, turn on the "Show log" checkbox, which displays all the files Dreamweaver updated.

Note: Sometimes, after you make changes to a master template, Dreamweaver doesn't update the pages based on those templates. To safely verify that Dreamweaver updated all the templates, recreate the Site Cache (Site→Advanced→Recreate Site Cache), choose Modify→Template →Update Pages, and then select the "Entire Site" option.

Unlinking a Page from a Template

If you're confident that you won't make any further changes to a page's template and you want to edit a page's locked regions, you can break the link between the page and its template by choosing Modify→Templates→Detach from Template.

You can now edit all the HTML in the page, just as you can on a regular web page—which is, in fact, what it now is. You removed all references to the original template, so changes to the template no longer affect this page.

Note: If you unlink a nested template from its master template, Dreamweaver removes only the code provided by the original master template. Any editable regions you added to the nested template remain.

Exporting a Template-Based Site

The good news about Dreamweaver's sophisticated templating features is that they let you build complex web pages that are easy to create and update. The not-so-good news is that you need some behind-the-scenes code to achieve this ease of use. Dreamweaver's template features rely on HTML comment tags to identify editable, optional, and repeating page regions, as well as nested template and editable tag attributes (see the box on page 760).

Although this code is only for Dreamweaver's use and has no effect on how a web browser displays the page, it does increase, by a small amount, the size of your pages. That's probably why Dreamweaver includes a feature that lets you export an entire site into a new folder on your computer *without* any template markup code—to give you the leanest HTML possible. The following steps show you how.

Note: While it's certainly possible to perform this file-slimming procedure, truth be told, it's not really necessary—the code Dreamweaver adds is minimal, so it won't have much affect on the download speed of your site.

1. **Choose Modify→Templates→Export Without Markup.**

   Dreamweaver uses the currently active site, so make sure you've selected the site you wish to export in the Files panel. The Export Site Without Template Markup window appears (see Figure 20-19).

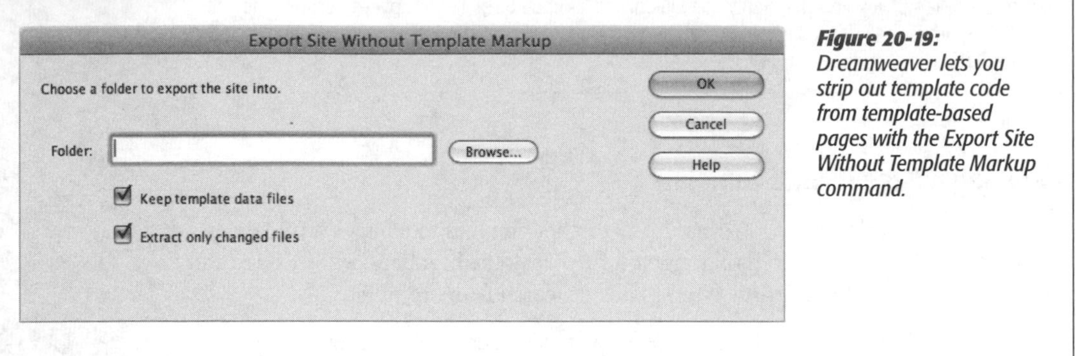

***Figure 20-19:** Dreamweaver lets you strip out template code from template-based pages with the Export Site Without Template Markup command.*

2. **Click the Browse button, and then select a destination folder for the exported site.**

   Select a folder *other* than the current local site folder. You always want to keep the original files in the local folder, since they're the ones that retain the template markup, making future updates possible.

3. **Turn on the export options you want.**

   The Export window includes two options. The first, "Keep template data files," creates an XML file for each template-based page. In other words, when you export the site, there's one HTML page (without any template code) and an XML file (which includes all the template code as well as the page contents).

   Theoretically, you could then go back and choose the File→Import→"XML into Template" to recreate the page, complete with the original template information. However, in practice, you probably won't. This process creates lots of additional files that you wouldn't want to move to a website for one thing. Also, when you want to work on the site to edit and update it, you should use the original files in the site's local foldr, since they have the useful template code in them.

   The "Extract only changed files" option speeds up the process of exporting a large template-based site. This option forces Dreamweaver to export only pages you changed since the last export. Unfortunately, it doesn't tell you *which* files it exports until after the fact. So, to make sure you get those newly exported files to your server, you need to keep track of the changed files by hand.

4. **Click OK to export the site.**

   Dreamweaver goes through each page of the site, stripping out template code and exporting it to the folder you specified.

   You can use Dreamweaver's FTP feature to upload the files to your server (see page 702), but you need to create a new site and define the folder with the *exported* files as a local root folder. Whenever you need to add or update template-based pages, use the original site files, and then export the changed files. You can then switch to the site containing the exported files and transfer the new or updated files to your server. If that sounds like a lot of work, it is. Every change you make means exporting the site again. You're better off just leaving the template code in your pages, or use this command only if you're absolutely sure that you're done using templates for your site.

Template Tutorial

In this tutorial, you'll create a template for the Chia Vet website. Then you'll build a page based on that template and enjoy an easy sitewide update courtesy of Dreamweaver's templates feature.

Note: You'll need to download the tutorial files from *www.sawmac.com/dwcs5/* to complete this tutorial. See the note on page 45 for more details.

Once you download the tutorial files and open Dreamweaver, setup a new site as described on page 37: Name the site *Templates*, and then select the Chapter20 folder (inside the MM_DWCS5 folder). (In a nutshell: Choose Site→New Site. In the Site Setup window, type *Templates* into the Site Name field, click the folder icon next to the Local Site Folder field, navigate to and select the Chapter20 folder, and then click Choose or Select. Finally, click OK.)

Creating a Template

1. **Open the Files panel by pressing the F8 key (Shift-⌘-F).**

   Of course, if it was already open, you just closed it. Press F8 (Shift-⌘-F) again.

2. **In the Files panel, find and double-click the page *tips.html*.**

   It's usually easier to create a template from an existing web page (rather than from scratch), which you then save as a template. For the purpose of getting to bed before midnight tonight, pretend that you've just designed this beautiful page.

3. **Choose File→Save As Template.**

   The Save As Template dialog box opens.

4. **In the description field, type Use for Chia tips.**

   This description appears in the New Template window when you create a page based on this template.

5. **Name the template *Tips*; click Save. In the Update Links window, click Yes.**

   Behind the scenes, Dreamweaver creates a new folder—Templates—in the site's root folder, and saves the file as Tips.dwt inside it. A new template is born. You can see it in the newly created Templates folder in the Files panel and in the Templates page of the Assets panel (see the Note below).

The template is a model for other pages. But although they'll be *based* on its design, they won't be identical. The next step is to identify those areas of the design you want to change from page to page—the editable regions.

Note: Templates don't always immediately show up in the Templates category of the Assets panel. Sometimes you need to click the Refresh Site List button (the circular arrow in the bottom right of the Assets panel) to see a newly added template.

---

6. **Select the text from the "T" in the heading "Tips Title" to the right of the "e" for "here" in "Subtitle goes here".**

   You just selected the title and subtitle for the page. As people add new tips to the Chia Vet site, you'll want them to add specific titles for each tip, so you should make these two paragraphs editable.

7. **Choose Insert→Template Objects→Editable Region.**

   The New Editable Region dialog box appears. Here, as in the following steps, you can also, from the Insert panel's Common category, go to the Templates menu and choose the Editable Region option (Figure 20-2), or just press Ctrl+Alt+V (⌘-Option-V).

8. **Type *Title*; click OK.**

   A small blue tab, labeled *Title*, appears above the headline. You've just added one editable region—the most basic type of template region. You'll make the main text area editable as well.

9. **Select the two paragraphs of text beneath "Title". Repeat steps 7 and 8; name the region *Text*.**

   Another small blue tab, labeled *Text*, appears above the paragraphs. You might wonder why you did this in two chunks. Why not select the title, subtitle, and paragraphs in one fell swoop and turn them into a single editable region? Because of the "Related Tips" box. That's a bit of HTML that appears *between* the subtitle and the first paragraph of text. If you created just a single editable region, you also would have been able to edit that tip box (since you would have inadvertently selected its HTML, too).

   However, you've got bigger plans for that box. You want it to list web pages with related information. But what if there *are* no related tips for a particular page? In that case, you don't want the box to appear at all—a perfect case for an optional region.

10. **Click anywhere inside the "Related Tips" box (inside the bulleted list, for example) and choose Edit→Select All, twice.**

    The first time you choose Edit→Select All (Ctl-+A, or ⌘-A works too), you select the contents of the box; the second time you invoke Select All, you grab the <div> tag that creates the box.

You'll turn this <div> into an optional region so you can hide it on most pages, but display it when you can point visitors to related web pages.

11. **Choose Insert→Template Objects→Optional Region.**

    The New Optional Region window appears. (Again, this same option is available in the Common category of the Insert Panel [Figure 20-2].)

12. **Type *relatedTips* in the name field, turn off the "Show by Default" checkbox, and then click OK.**

    From now on, when you create a new template-based page, you won't see this box. When you build a page where you can point to related tips, however, you can make the box visible.

    You see a blue tab labeled "If relatedTips" above the "Related Tips" box (see Figure 20-20): this part is the optional region, and represents where the HTML code with the div is located.

    Of course, to let someone add links to related pages, you need to add an editable region as well.

13. **Click anywhere inside the two links—for example in the text "Related Tip 1" or "Related Tip 2". In the Tag selector at the bottom of the document window, click the <ul> tag (circled in Figure 20-20). Choose Insert→Template Objects→Editable Region. Name the new region *relatedLinks*.**

    Now you can edit the links inside the optional region.

    Next, you'll add a repeating region to the right sidebar, so you can add multiple sets of questions and answers. You'll then make the text editable, so you can add story titles and links.

14. **In the right sidebar, click inside the text "Question goes here".**

    Both the question and answer are contained inside a <div> tag. You'll turn that entire <div> tag into a repeating region.

15. **At the bottom of the window, in the Tag selector, click the <div.qa> tag to select that div.**

    Choosing Edit→Select All twice will also select the div. The .qa part means that you applied a class named *qa* to that div. You just selected the <div> tag and the two paragraphs inside it. Because you may want to add any number of question/answer pairs, you'll turn this into a repeating region.

16. **Choose Insert→Template Objects→Repeating Region. In the window that appears, type *repeatQuestions*. Click OK.**

    Dreamweaver inserts a new repeating region with the familiar blue tab. The tab reads "Repeat: repeatQuestions," indicating that it isn't any ordinary template region—it's a repeating region. However, turning a part of the page into a repeating region doesn't automatically make it editable. Since you want to edit the text and add new names to each page, you need to add an editable region *inside* this repeating region.

Figure 20-20: *When you create optional, editable, and repeating template regions, the Tag selector is your best friend. Click a tag (<ul> in this case) to accurately select a piece of content. You'll also see Dreamweaver-specific tags listed on template files. Here, <mmtemplate:editable> indicates the editable region you created in step 13. Because the <ul> tag appears to the right of the <mmtemplate:editable> tag, you know that page authors can edit and change the <ul> tag and everything inside it when they create template-based pages.*

17. **Select the text "Question goes here". (Don't select the orange "Q." that marks the beginning of the question, however.) Choose Insert→Template Objects→ Editable Region. In the Name field, type *question*, and then click OK.**

    Another blue tab, labeled "question," appears inside the repeating region. On template-based pages, you can now change this text. You don't select the "Q." at the beginning of the paragraph because you don't want that to be editable. That's part of your design, and at some point you might want to change it (for example, you might want to spell it out and add a colon: "Question:"). Because it's not part of an editable region, you can make that change once in the template and have every page based on that template reflect the change.

18. **Choose File→Save.**

    A Dreamweaver dialog box appears, saying that the editable region you just created is inside a block tag and that you won't be able to add new blocks in this region. The reason for this dialog box is discussed on page 758, but in a nutshell it simply means that you won't be able to add additional paragraphs inside this area. Since this editable region is only intended for a single-line question and not multiple paragraphs, this is OK. (If you don't see this warning dialog box, you or someone using your computer may have already turned off that type of warning, as described in the next step.)

19. **Put a check inside the "Don't show me this message again" box and click OK.**

    You may see another dialog box saying that you've changed a template and asking if you want to update pages on the site. Well, since you haven't yet created any pages from this template, there's nothing to update, so click the No button.

    Dreamweaver saves the file. You'll add another editable region for the answer.

20. **Repeat Step 18 for the text "Answer goes here." Name the editable region, *answer*.**

    The template should now look like Figure 20-21.

21. **Choose File→Save, and close this File.**

    Congratulations! You've created your first template.

Creating a Page Based on a Template

Now it's time to get down to business and build some web pages. Look at the Files panel and make sure you selected the site you defined in step 1. Then proceed as follows:

1. **Choose File→New.**

   The New Document window opens.

2. **On the window's far left side, click the "Page from Template" button.**

   A list of all defined sites appears in the Site list.

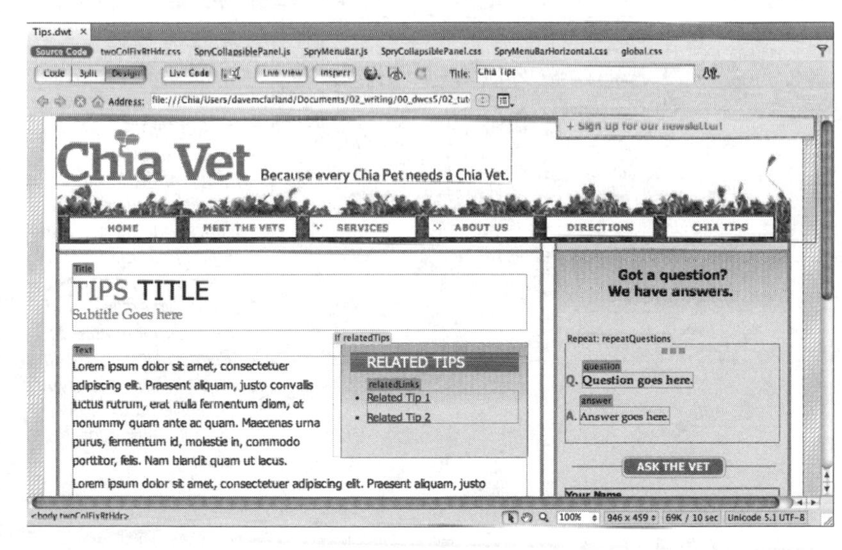

Figure 20-21: *A template file. If you don't see the blue boxes representing editable, optional, and repeatable regions, you may have turned them off. To show them, choose View→Visual Aids and make sure you have Invisible Elements checked.*

3. **Make sure you have the site you set up for this tutorial ("Templates") selected in the Site column; also make sure the "Update page when template changes" checkbox (in the right of the window) is turned on.**

   If you don't turn on the "Update page" box, the new page doesn't link to the original template file—and doesn't update when you make changes to the template.

4. **From the templates list, select Tips, and then click Create.**

   And lo, a new, untitled web page document appears, one that looks (almost) exactly like the template (Figure 20-22).

5. **Choose File→Save. Click the Site Root button and save the file as *tip1.html* in the root folder. In the Document toolbar's Title field (at the top of the document window), type *Repairing Chipped Terra Cotta.***

   To indicate that it's your template's offspring, the document window has a yellow tab in the upper-right corner that reads Template:Tips. You can see your editable and repeating regions indicated by blue tabs. Now it's time to add some content.

6. **Choose File→Open; in the Open file window, click the Site Root button; double-click the file *tip1_text.html.***

   You can also open this file by double-clicking its name in the Files panel. The *tip1_text.html* page contains the content for the new template-based page. It's just a matter of copying and pasting the text from one page to the other.

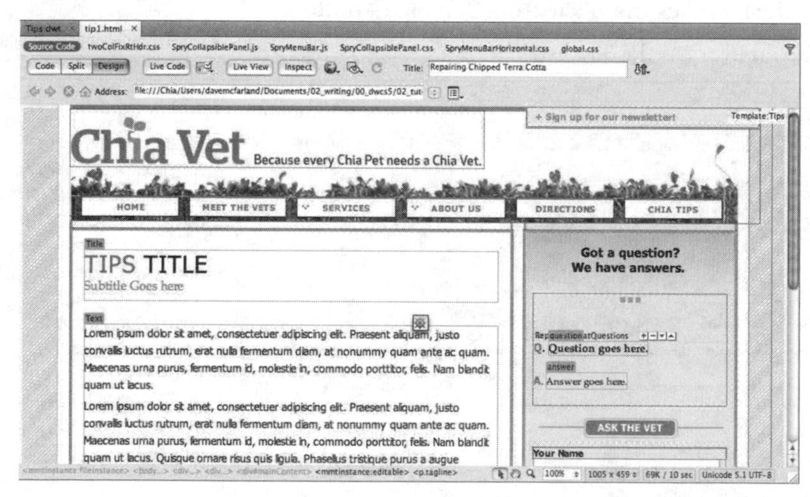

***Figure 20-22:** In template-based pages, blue tabs identify editable areas, and the yellow tab at the top right lists the template's name. In some cases, template tabs may overlap. Here, the tab for the editable region "question" sits on top of the tab for the repeatable region. Notice that the repeating region has small control buttons (+, -, and up and down arrows) and the optional region–the "Related Tips" box–is invisible. (Remember, you deselected the "Show by Default" option for this region.)*

7. **Select the headline and the paragraph immediately following it at the top of the page and choose Edit→Copy. At the top of the document window, click the *tip1.html* tab to switch to the template-based page.**

   Remember that you can add content only to an editable region. If you move your mouse over the banner, navigation, or footer areas of the page, you see a black "forbidden" symbol. You can't insert the cursor anywhere but inside an editable region.

8. **Click the blue tab labeled "Title" (the label is just above the headline "Tips Title Goes Here").**

   This selects everything inside that region. Since it's just placeholder text anyway, you'll replace it with the two paragraphs you just copied.

9. **Choose Edit→Paste.**

   Dreamweaver replaces the dummy content with the title and subtitle for this Chia Tip page. (If the two lines of text look like plain paragraphs, turn the top line into a Heading 1 using the Format menu in the Property inspector, and add the class *tagline* to the second paragraph.) Now you'll add the main content of the tip.

10. **Click the *tip1_text.html* tab at the top of the Document window. Repeat steps7–9, copying the remaining text on the *tip1_text.html* page and pasting it into the Text editable region on the *tip1.html* page.**

    The main tip is in place. This particular page doesn't have any related tips, so you'll leave the hidden optional region hidden (you'll show it on the next page you build).

    Time for some questions and answers.

Note: If, at a later time, *Chia-Vet.com* does add another page with a tip that's related to this web page, you can make the Related Tips box visible simply by choosing Modify→Template Properties and then turning on the "Show relatedTips" checkbox. You'll see this process in action in step 5 on page 796.

---

11. **In the page's right sidebar, delete the text "Question goes here" and type, "*Can I dye my Chia Pet?*"**

    You've added a question in one editable area, now time for the answer.

12. **Click the "answer" tab and type some suitably silly answer in keeping with the Chia Vet website.**

    For example: "You can certainly dye your Chia's body. Since terra cotta is absorbent, any colored liquid will work. However, it's best to use non-toxic dyes like food coloring or beet juice." As it happens, there's another important question for this page. Since you're using a repeating region, it's easy to add another question/answer pair.

13. **Click the + button just to the right of the blue "Repeat: repeatQuestions" tab.**

    You've added another pair of question and answer editable regions to the page, as shown in Figure 20-23.

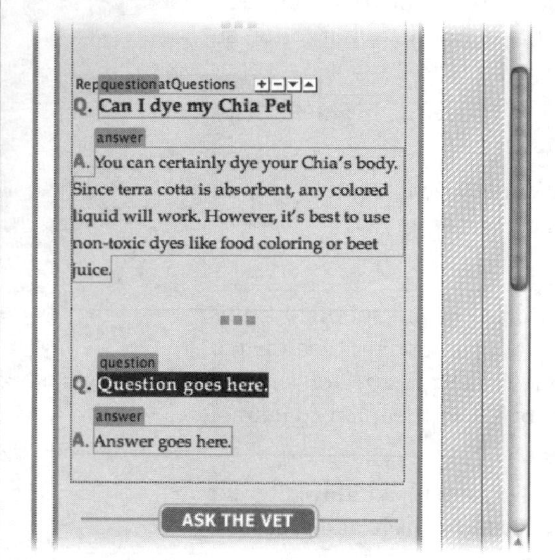

Figure 20-23:
If a page has a lot of elements crowded together–tables, images, text, and so on–Dreamweaver sometimes can't display the small buttons that let you add and remove repeating entries. In this case, you can also use the Modify menu. Click a repeating region, and then choose Modify→Templates→New Entry After Selection to add a new entry after the current one, or New Entry Before Selection to add a new entry before the current one.

14. **Repeat steps 11 and 12, adding an even sillier question and answer.**

    Congratulations, you've just completed a web page for *Chia-Vet.com*. Save this page and preview it in a Web browser (press F12 [Option-F12]). Return to Dreamweaver and close this page. Now you'll add another page to the site.

Creating Another Template-Based Page

Templates are useful only if you use them to build lots of pages. You'll build one more template-based page for this tutorial, and see how optional template regions let you create very adaptive web pages.

1. **Choose File→New. In the New Document window, click the "Page from Template" button; from the templates list, select Tips, and then click Create.**

   Another new web page is born.

2. **Choose File→Save. Save the file as *tip2.html* in the root folder. In the Title field in the Document toolbar (at the top of the document window), type *Trimming Your Chia's Coat.***

   You'll add some already created content to this page.

3. **Repeat steps 6–10 on page 792 in "Creating a Page Based on a Template". Use the file *tip2_text.html* located in the root folder.**

   Because trimming a Chia Pet's mane with sharp scissors is a recipe for chipped terra cotta, you've decided that you should provide a link from this page to the one you created previously. Fortunately, the optional region you created earlier is ready to be used.

4. **Choose Modify→Template Properties.**

   The Template Properties window appears (see Figure 20-24). It lists the optional region you wish to make visible.

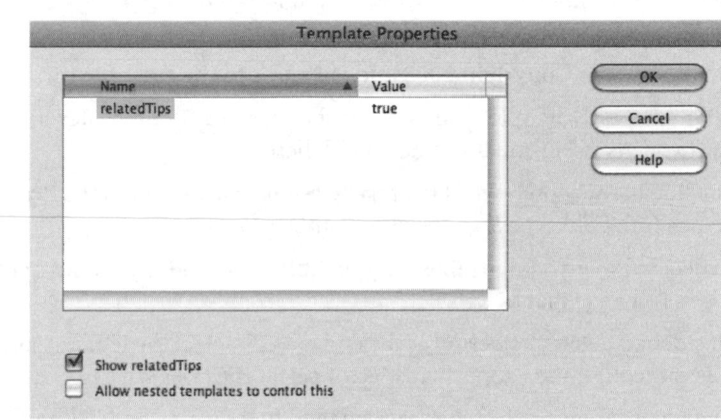

Figure 20-24: *The Template Properties window does double duty. It let you hide or show optional regions, and it lets you set values for editable tag attributes.*

5. **Turn on the "Show relatedTips" checkbox and then click OK to close the window.**

   The Related Tips box suddenly appears. There's only one related page, so you don't need both bulleted items.

6. **Delete second bullet point ("Related Tip 2") and change the text of the first bullet to "*Repairing Chipped Terra Cotta*". Link that text to the *tip1.html* page (use any of the link-creation techniques discussed on page 165).**

   This page is nearly complete: just one final item.

7. **Repeat step 14 on page 796.**

   You're almost done.

8. **Preview the page in a web browser.**

   While most of the page looks the same as the first template-based page you created, the optional region let you add special content to this page without having to create another template. Next you'll edit the template file and update the website.

   Close this page and *tip1.html* when you're ready to move onto the next step.

Updating a Template

Now the fun begins. Remember, this page maintains a reference to the original template. In the final phase, you're going to make a few changes to the template. Choose Window→Assets to open the Assets panel, and then click the Template button to reveal the templates for this site (see Figure 20-4):

1. **Return to Dreamweaver, and in the Assets panel, click the Templates button (see Figure 15-11), and double-click the Tips template to open it.**

   The original template, the Tips.dwt file, opens. You can also open the .dwt file by double-clicking its name inside the Templates folder in the Files panel.

   There are a couple of things that need changing; first the copyright needs to be updated.

2. **In the footer, locate the Copyright 2008 and change it to the current year.**

   If it's still 2008 (you early-adopter you), change the year to 2010 or whatever the current year happens to be. You'll also add a link here.

3. **On the same line in the footer, select the text "*Cosmofarmer.com*". In the Property inspector's link field type *http://www.cosmofarmer.com/*.**

   You've also decided that you don't like the look of the "Q." and "A." in the right sidebar, so you'll change that as well.

4. **In the right sidebar, delete the period at the end of "Q."; select the letter Q, and from the Class menu in the Property inspector select the class style *q*.**

   The Q changes appearance—the letter gets smaller, turns white, and has an orange box around it.

Note: If you don't see a Class menu in the Property inspector, you're in CSS view. Click the HTML button on the left side of the Property inspector to reveal the Class menu.

---

5. **Repeat step 4, replacing the "A." with just "A" and applying the class *a* to it.**

   The A changes appearance—the letter gets smaller, turns white, and a green box surrounds it. Because both the Q and A are outside of the editable regions (that is, the area with the blue tabs "question" and "answer"), the changes you just made will pass on to template-based pages.

6. **Choose File→Save.**

   Dreamweaver displays the Update Template Files window. This is the moment of truth.

7. **Click Update.**

   Dreamweaver opens the Update Pages dialog box and updates the appropriate web pages, adding the copyright year, the link, and new Q and A icons to each one. In this case, you based only two pages on the template, so Dreamweaver updates only two pages—as indicated by the list of changes Dreamweaver shows when it's finished.

Note: If, after you update pages based on a template, you don't see the number of updated pages listed in the Update Pages window, turn on the Show Log checkbox.

---

8. **Click Close to close the Update Pages dialog box. Finally, open the files *tip1.html* and *tip2.html*.**

   Notice that Dreamweaver updated the copyright and question/answer sections in both (see Figure 20-25). This series of events happened because you changed the template to which the page was genetically linked. Ah, the power!

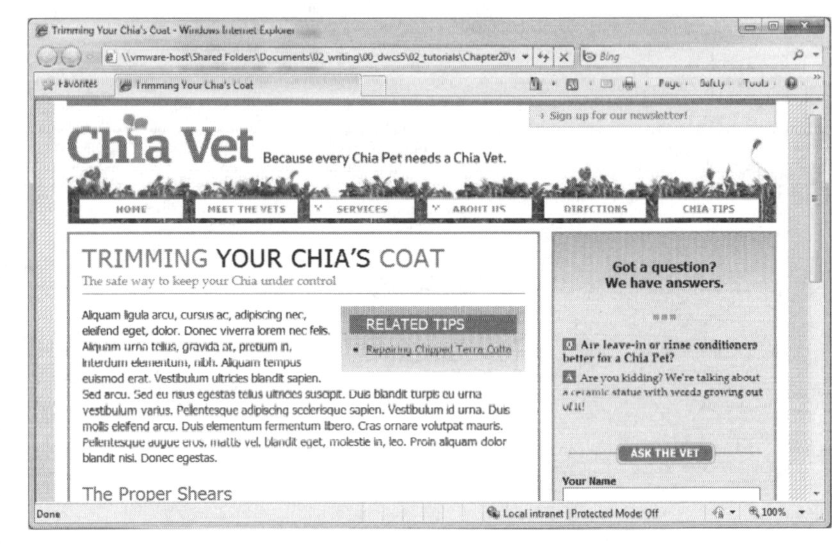

Figure 20-25: *The finished tutorial page, complete with a useful Chia tip, a box with a link to a related web page, and a helpful question and answer.*

CHAPTER 21

Automating Dreamweaver

One of Dreamweaver's greatest selling points is that it makes you more productive. You know this firsthand if you've ever labored over tables in an HTML text editor and then built the same tables in Dreamweaver. What once took many keystrokes now takes one click of the Insert panel's Table object.

If you want to cut even more time off your work day, Dreamweaver doesn't disappoint. In addition to its Snippets, Library, and Template features (see Chapters 19 and 20), the program offers two tools that let you automate common and time-consuming tasks: the History panel and the "Find and Replace" command.

Find and Replace

You've probably encountered find-and-replace tools in word processing programs and even some graphics programs. As the name implies, the command finds a piece of text (*webmaster*, for example) and *replaces* it with another piece of text (*webmistress*). Like Microsoft Word, Dreamweaver can search and replace text in the body of your web pages. But it also offers variations on this feature that enhance your ability to work within the tag-based world of HTML.

What's more, Dreamweaver lets you find and replace text on *every* page of your site simultaneously, not just the current, open document. In addition, you can *remove* every appearance of a particular HTML tag, or search and replace text that matches very specific criteria. For example, you can find every instance of the word "Aardvark" that appears within a paragraph styled with the class named *animal*. These advanced find-and-replace maneuvers are some of the most powerful—and underappreciated—tools in Dreamweaver. If you learn how to use them, you can make changes to your pages in a fraction of the time it would take using other methods.

Tip: You can use "Find and Replace" to search an entire site's worth of files. This is powerful, but it can also be slow, especially if some folders hold files you don't want to search–old archives, for example. You can use Dreamweaver's cloaking feature to hide files from find-and-replace operations. See page 708 for more details.

Find and Replace Basics

To start a search, press Ctrl+F (⌘-F), or choose Edit→Find and Replace. The "Find and Replace" window opens (see Figure 21-1). Now all you have to do is fill in the blanks and set up the search.

Whether you perform a simple text search or a complex, tag-based search-and-replace, the procedure for using the "Find and Replace" command is basically the same. First, you need to tell Dreamweaver *where* to search (within highlighted text on a page, in a file, a folder, or on your entire website). Next, tell it *what* to search for (text, HTML, or a particular tag with a specific attribute). Finally, you dictate what the replacement item is. This last step is optional; you can use the "Find and Replace" window as a way to locate an item on a page or on your site, without changing it to anything.

Tip: After you enter the "Find and Replace" criteria, click the Save Query button (see Figure 21-1). A Save dialog box appears; you can type in a name for your query, which Dreamweaver saves as a .dwr (Dreamweaver replace query) file. You can save this file anywhere on your computer. If it's a query you'll use for a particular site, you might want to save it with those files. To reuse a query, click the Load Query button and locate the .dwr file. After the search-and-replace criteria load, you can click any of the four action buttons–Find Next, Find All, Replace, or Replace All.

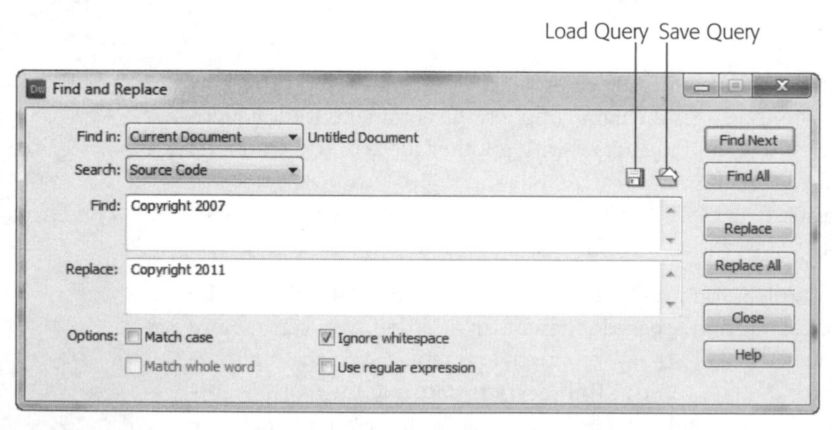

***Figure 21-1:** Dreamweaver's "Find and Replace" feature lets you replace text and HTML quickly and accurately. By using the Load Query and Save Query buttons, you can even save complex searches to use in the future.*

Basic Text and HTML Searches

Dreamweaver can search all the source code in a page or focus on text that appears in the document window.

- Source code searches let you find and replace any code on a page, including words, letters, and symbols. This means *anything* you see in Code view, such as HTML, CSS, or server-side programming code used to create the dynamic database-driven sites described in Part Six of this book. Code searches are the only type of search allowed on files that aren't web pages, such as external JavaScript files or external CSS files.
- Text searches are more refined. They only look for text that appears within the <body> element of a page. That is, Dreamweaver ignores HTML tags, properties, and comments when it searches—in short, it ignores anything that doesn't appear as actual words in the document window. By using a text search when you want to change the word "table" to "elegant wood table," for example, you won't accidentally change the very useful HTML <table> tag into a browser-choking <elegant wood table> tag.

If you've used "Find and Replace" in other programs, the following routine will be familiar.

Phase 1: Determine the scope of your search

Using the "Find in" pull-down menu (see Figure 21-2), choose any of these options:

- **Selected Text.** Searches only the highlighted section of the page you're working on. This can be useful if you're working in Code view and you want to search the code in just a certain section of the page, such as the head of the document. But it can also come in handy if you have a large HTML table full of data, and you want to search and replace just the content inside that table—just select the table (for example click <table> in tag selector [see page 23] or use any of the techniques described on page 266), and then choose the "Selected Text" option when executing a Find and Replace.
- **Current Document.** Searches the Web page you're working on.
- **Open Documents.** Searches all currently open Dreamweaver documents. This option is handy if you're working on a bunch of pages at once and you realize you made the same typo on each.
- **Folder.** Search all Web pages in a particular folder. Dreamweaver also searches Web pages in all folders *within* the selected folder. You can use this option to search pages that aren't part of the current site.
- **Selected Files in Site.** To use this option, open the Files panel and select the files you want to search in the local file list (see page 674 for details).

- **Entire Current Local Site.** Searches every Web page in the current site folder, including pages in folders *inside* the site folder. This option is invaluable when a basic piece of information changes throughout your site. For instance, if your company hires a new boss, you can replace every instance of "Mark Jones" with "Joe Smith."

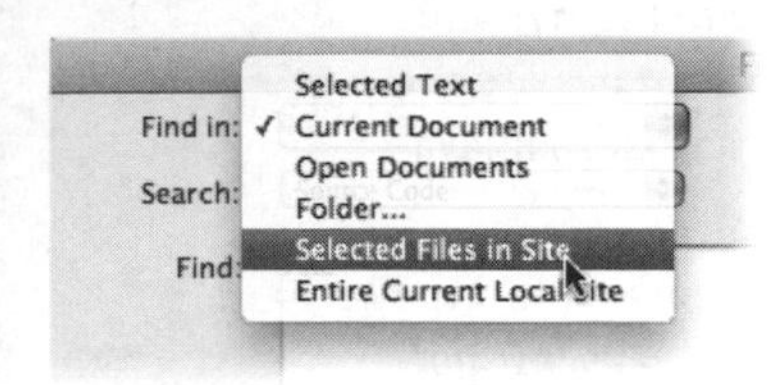

Figure 21-2:
The effect of the "Find and Replace" command isn't limited to the current document. You can also search multiple Web pages, or even an entire site.

Note: Using the "Find and Replace" command is one of the best ways to quickly make changes to an entire site, but it's also one of the easiest ways to wreck a site's worth of Web pages. Dreamweaver *can't* undo changes made by the "Find and Replace" command to files that aren't open in Dreamweaver. So be careful. If you plan on making extensive changes, make a backup copy of your files first!

Phase 2: Specify what to search for

For your next trick, you'll tell Dreamweaver what you want to search for. Use the Search pop-up menu to choose one of these two options:

- **Text.** This makes Dreamweaver search for a certain word or phrase that appears in the *body* of the documents you specified. Type the text you want to find into the Search field. If you're searching for a pattern in your text, enter a *regular expression* here and turn on the "Use regular expression" checkbox. (See the box on page 811 for more on regular expressions.)
- **Source Code.** Basic text searches are useful, but they're limited to text that appears in the body of a page (what you see in the document window). If you want to search and replace *code*, you need the Source Code option.

  Source-code searches work identically to text searches, except that Dreamweaver searches *everything* within the file—text, HTML, JavaScript, CSS, and so on—and replaces any part of the file. Using this option, you could search for any instance of the tag <img src="mark_jones_photo.jpg">, for example, and then replace it with <img src="joe_smith_photo.jpg">.

  (If you're in Code view, Dreamweaver automatically selects the Source Code option.)

  As you fill in the Search field, be aware that some plain-English words are also special words in HTML, JavaScript, or CSS. If you replace *table* with *desk* using a source-code find and replace by mistake, you'll completely destroy any <table> tags on the page.

You can also enter a regular expression to search for patterns in your HTML source code (see the box on page 811).

Phase 3: Provide the replacement text

If you want to change the text that Dreamweaver finds, type the replacement text into the Replace box. It may be the word or words you want to swap in (for a text search), or actual HTML code for a source-code search.

Note: Dreamweaver won't let you create a new line in the Search or Replace boxes–for example, if you want to replace some source code with two lines of HTML. At least it won't let you do it the normal way. If you hit the Enter key, Dreamweaver begins the search rather than inserting a new line. To add another line, use Shift-Enter (Shift-Return).

If you just want to find text without replacing it, skip this step.

Tip: If you want to find the specified text and replace it with *nothing* (that is, deleting every occurrence of the text), leave the Replace field blank and perform a replace operation, described in Phase 5.

Phase 4: Choose the search settings

Dreamweaver gives you three options that govern its search and replace; some of them are quite complex:

- The **Match Case** option limits the Find command to text that exactly matches the case (capitalization and lowercase) of the text in the Search field. If you search for the text *The End* with the Match Case box turned on, Dreamweaver finds a match in "The End is near," but not in "You're almost at the end." Use this trick to find every instance of *Web* and replace it with *web*.
- **Match Whole Word** searches for an entire word—not a portion of a larger word. For example, if you turn this option on, a search for *Rob* matches only "Rob," and not any parts of "Robert," "robbery," or "problem." If you don't select this option, Dreamweaver stops on "rob" in all four instances, and could cause serious problems if you also *replace* "Rob" with something like "Bob" (unless, of course, you've come up with a new word for thefts committed by people named Bob: Bobbery). (Note that if you selected the Match Case option, Dreamweaver matches *Rob* in "Rob" and "Robert," but *not* in "robbery" and "problem," since they don't include a capital R.)
- The **Ignore Whitespace** option treats multiple spaces, tabs, non-breaking spaces, and carriage returns as single spaces when searching. For instance, if you search for *the dog* and turn on this option, Dreamweaver matches "the   dog", as well as "the dog"—even if the multiple spaces are actually the HTML non-breaking space character * * (see page 76).

Note to Mac users: Unfortunately, in the Mac version of Dreamweaver, the "Find and Replace" function does not treat nonbreaking space characters as spaces, so if you have *the dog* in your HTML and search for *the dog*, even with the Ignore Whitespace box checked, the search will find nothing.

Unless you have a good reason, always leave this option turned on. The HTML of a page can contain lots of extra spaces, line breaks, and tabs that don't appear in a Web browser or in Dreamweaver's document window. For example, in the HTML of a document, it's possible to have two lines of code that look like this:

```
<p>This sentence will appear on one
line in a Web browser</p>
```

Even though this text would appear on a single line in the document window, a search for "one line" *without* the Ignore Whitespace box turned on would find no match; the carriage return after "one" is not an exact match for the space character in "one line."

Note: You can't turn on the Ignore Whitespace option when you have the Use Regular Expression checkbox turned on.

- The **Use Regular Expression** option is matches patterns in text. For a discussion of this advanced technique, see the box on page 811.

Phase 5: Take action

Finally, you're ready to set the search in motion by clicking one of the four action buttons in the "Find and Replace" window (see Figure 21-3):

- **Find Next** locates the next instance of your search term. If you're searching the current document, Dreamweaver highlights the matching text. If you're searching an entire website or a folder of pages, Dreamweaver opens the file *and* highlights the match. You can cycle through each instance of the search term by clicking this button repeatedly.

Tip: As in other programs (notably Microsoft Word), you can press Enter to repeat the Find Next function (Windows only). If you click in the document window—or even closed the Find window—you can press F3 (⌘-G) to repeat the Find Next function.

- **Find All** locates every instance of the search terms, all at once, and shows them to you in a list in the Search tab of the Results panel (Figure 21-4). The name and location of each file (if you searched multiple files) appear to the left, and the matched text appears to the right. Dreamweaver displays part of the sentence in which the matched word or words appear. It underlines the exact match with a squiggly red line, so you can see the search in context and identify text you may *not* want to replace.

Unlike the Find Next action, Find All doesn't automatically open any of the Web pages containing matches. To open a matched page, double-click its name in the results list. Only then does Dreamweaver open the Web page and highlight the match.

- **Replace** locates the next instance of the search term *and* replaces it with the text in the Replace field, leaving the replaced text highlighted for your inspection.

  You can use this button in combination with Find Next to selectively replace text. First, click Find Next. Dreamweaver locates and highlights the next match. To replace the text, click Replace. Otherwise, click Find Next to search for the next match, and repeat the cycle. This cautious approach lets you supervise the replacement process and avoid making changes you didn't intend.

- **Replace All** is the ultimate power tool. It finds every instance of the search term and replaces it with the text in the Replace field. Coupled with the "Find in Entire Local Site" option, you can quickly make sitewide changes (and mistakes—so back up all your files before you Replace All!).

  When you click this button, Dreamweaver warns that you can't undo this operation on any closed files. You can erase mistakes you make with the "Find and Replace" in *open* documents, by choosing Edit→Undo in each document, but Dreamweaver *permanently* alters closed files that you search and replace. So be careful! (On the other hand, changes to open documents aren't permanent until you save those files.)

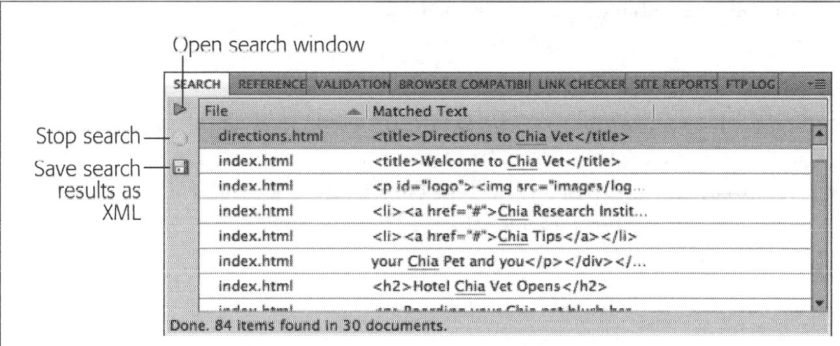

Figure 21-3: *The green-arrow button reopens the "Find and Replace" window. Click the red Stop button to abort the current search (for example, when you inadvertently begin a search for "the" in a 10,000-page Web site). You can also save a rather useless XML file that provides a report of the results of the find-and-replace command (remember the old adage: Just because you can doesn't mean you should).*

Tip: Before you take the plunge and click the Replace All button, it's a good precautionary step to click Find All first and then preview the results in the Results panel (Figure 21-4). This way, you can be sure that you're going to change exactly what you *want* to change.

If you use the Find All or Replace All commands, the "Find and Replace" window closes, and the results of the search appear in the Search tab (see Figure 21-4). You can reopen the "Find and Replace" window (with all your previous search criteria still in place) by clicking the green arrow on the Search tab (called the "Find and Replace" button), but only if you haven't selected anything else—like text on a page—first.

Advanced Text Searches

If you want greater control over a text search, use the "Find and Replace" command's *advanced* text search option, which lets you confine a search to text either inside or outside a specific tag.

For example, when Dreamweaver creates a new blank document, it sets the page's *Title* property to *Untitled Document*. Unfortunately, if you forget to change it, a site can quickly fill up with untitled web pages. A basic text search doesn't identify this problem, because it searches only the body of a page; titles appear in the head. And a source-code search for *Untitled Document* would turn up the words "untitled document" *wherever* they appeared in the page, not just inside the <title> tag.

In cases like this, an advanced text search is your best choice. Simply set the "Find and Replace" command to search for *Untitled Document* whenever it appears within the <title> tag. To use advanced text search, follow the same general routine as described on the previous pages. But before using one of the action buttons, you make a few additional setup changes to the dialog box.

Limiting the search by tag

Choose Text (Advanced) from the Search pop-up menu to make the expanded controls appear (see Figure 21-4). Now, from the menu next to the + and – buttons, choose either Inside Tag or Not Inside Tag. For example, consider this line of code: "Stupid is as <strong>stupid</strong> does." The first instance of "stupid" isn't inside the <strong> tag, but the second one is.

Note: A more descriptive name for the first option would be "*Enclosed* By Tag"; Dreamweaver actually searches for text that's between *opening and closing* tags. In fact, an advanced text search using this option doesn't identify text that's literally inside a tag. For example, it won't find "Aliens" in this line of code: <img src="ufo.jpg" alt="Aliens live among us.">, but it would find "Aliens" in this one: <strong>Aliens live among us.</strong>. In the first example, *Aliens* appears as part of the <img> tag, while in the second, *Aliens* is enclosed by the opening and closing <strong> tags.

Once you specify whether you're looking for text inside or outside tags, you can choose a specific HTML tag from the Tag menu identified in Figure 21-4. The menu lists all HTML tags—not just those with both an opening and closing tag. So the image tag (<img>) still appears, even though Dreamweaver doesn't identify text inside it.

Tip: A great way to search for text in both the title and body of a Web page is to choose the Inside Tag option and then select *html* from the Tag menu. That way, you can search for any text that appears within the opening <html> and closing </html> of the page—which, since those tags start and end any Web document, is *all* text on a page. This trick is handy when you want to change text that might appear in the body *and* the title of a page (for example, a company name).

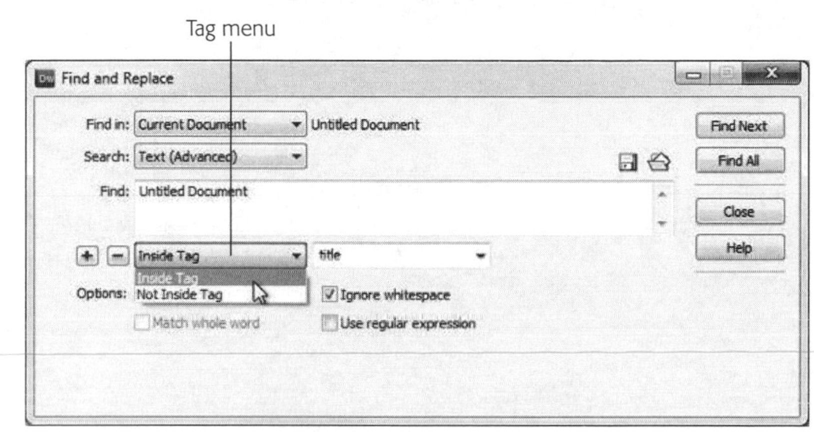

Figure 21-4: *Use an advanced text search to limit your search to text that appears within a particular HTML tag. Or, conversely, use it to search for text that doesn't appear within a tag.*

Limiting the search by attribute

To limit the search further, click the + button (see Figure 21-5); yet another set of fields appears. Using the Tag Modifier menu—next to the + and – buttons (Figure 21-5)—you can choose from any of six options that break down into three groups:

- **With Attribute/Without Attribute.** To limit the search, you can specify that a tag must either have (With Attribute) or not have (Without Attribute) a specific property.

  For example, say the following lines of code appear throughout a website:

```
<p>For assistance, please email
<a href="mailto:mail@chia-vet.com">
Chia Vet.</a></p>
```

  Now, for the sake of argument, say you need to change it to read "For assistance, please email Customer Service." A basic text find-and-replace would incorrectly change the words "Chia Vet" to "Customer Service" *everywhere* on the site.

  However, an advanced text search using the With Attribute option lets you specifically target the text "Chia Vet" wherever it appears inside an <a> tag whose *href* attribute is set to *mailto:mail@chia-vet.com*. You could then just change that text to "Customer Service" while leaving all other instances of "Chia Vet" alone. (To learn about the different HTML tags and attributes, use Dreamweaver's built-in code reference; see page 448.)

After you choose With Attribute, use the menu on the right to select *which* of the tag's properties you want to find. (Dreamweaver automatically lists properties appropriate for the tag you specify.) For example, if you search inside a <table> tag, the menu lists properties such as *align, background, bgcolor*, and so on.

Figure 21-5: *When you click the + button in the "Find and Replace" window, a new set of fields appears. Use these options to carefully hone your "Find and Replace" commands, and zero in on text that matches precise criteria.*

Advance to the next pop-up menu to choose a type of comparison: = (equal to), != (not equal to), > (greater than), or < (less than). You'll only use these options when a property's value is a number, such as the *width* property of a table cell. For example, you could use the comparison option to locate all table cells wider than 100 pixels (width > 100). (This setting has no effect on values that are words, such as *center* in this example: <td align="center">.)

Finally, type the value of the property in the last field. If you were searching for a black-colored background, the value would be *#000000* (the hex value for black).

You can also click the menu and choose "[any value]"—a useful option when you want to find tags that have a certain property, but you're not interested in the property's value. For example, if you want to find all <table> tags with a background color (no matter whether the color's #336699, #000000, or #FFFFFF), choose the *bgcolor* attribute and "[any value]".

- **Containing/Not Containing.** These options let you specify whether the tag contains (or doesn't contain) specific text or a particular tag.

  When you choose this option, a different set of fields appears. Choose either Text or Specific Tag from the menu to the right, and then either enter some text or select a tag in the last field in the row. For example, another (less error-proof) solution to the problem above would be to search for the text "Chia Vet" wherever it appears inside a <p> (paragraph) tag that *also contains* the text "please email."

- **Inside Tag/Not Inside Tag.** These last two choices are identical to those described in "Limiting the search by tag" above. They let you specify whether the tag is inside—or not inside—a specific tag. Use these to limit a search, for example, to text that appears only within a <span> tag that's *inside* an <h1> tag.

If you like, you can add even more restrictions to your search, adding new rules by clicking the + button and repeating the setup just described. When you're really on a roll, it's even possible to add so many modifiers that the "Find and Replace" window actually grows past the bottom of your monitor. To remove a modifier, click the minus sign (–) button.

POWER USERS' CLINIC

Turbocharge Your Searches

If you want to find the phone number 555-123-5473 on your site, no problem; just type *555-123-5473* into the search field. But what if you want to find *every* phone number—555-987-0938, 555-102-8870, and so on—on a web page or across a site?

In such a case, you need to use *regular expressions*, the geeky name for a delightfully flexible search language carried over from early UNIX days, which consists of wildcard characters that let you search for patterns of text instead of actual letters or numbers. Each phone number above follows a simple pattern: three numbers, a dash, three more numbers, another dash, and four more numbers.

To search for a pattern, you use a variety of symbols combined with regular text characters to tell Dreamweaver what to find. For example, in the world of regular expressions, "\d" stands for "any number." To find three numbers in a row, you could search for \d\d\d, which would find 555, 747, 007, and so on. There's even shorthand for this: \d{3}. The number between the braces ({}) indicates how many times in a row the preceding character must appear to match. To finish up the example of the phone numbers, you could use a regular expression like this: \d{3}-\d{3}-\d{4}. The \d{3} finds three numbers, while the hyphen (-) following it is just the hyphen in the phone number, and \d{4} finds four numbers.

Here are some of the other symbols you'll encounter when using regular expressions:

- . (period) stands for any character, letter, number, space, and so on.
- \w stands for any letter or number (but not spaces, tabs, , or line breaks.)
- * (asterisk) represents the preceding character, zero or more times (and is always used after another character). This is best explained with an example: The regular expression colou*r, for instance, matches both colour and color—the * following the u indicates that the u is optional (it can appear zero times). This would also match colouuuuur (handy for those times when you've fallen asleep on the keyboard).

To see a complete list of regular-expression characters Dreamweaver understands as wells as a short tutorial on regular expressions, visit. *www.adobe.com/devnet/dreamweaver/articles/regular_expressions_03.html*. A full-length discussion of regular expressions could—and does—fill a book of its own; check out *Mastering Regular Expressions*, Third Edition (O'Reilly, 2006) by Jeffrey E. F. Friedl or, for made-to-order regular expressions, visit the Regular Expression Library at *http://regexlib.com/*.

For an example of using regular expressions in Dreamweaver, see page 813.

Advanced Tag Searches

If you find the number of options an advanced text search offers overwhelming, you haven't seen anything yet. Dreamweaver's tag search adds more choices to help you quickly search for, and modify, HTML tags. You can use a tag search to strip out unwanted HTML tags (for example, if you're migrating an old site to CSS, you could remove the <font> tag), transform one tag into another (you could turn old-style *bold* [<b>] into the more widely accepted *strong* [<strong>] tag), and perform a host of other powerful actions.

In its basic outline, a tag search is much like the regular text search described on page 803. But this time, from the Search menu, you should choose Specific Tag. Now a Tag menu appears next to the Search menu, and the dialog box expands to display a new set of fields (see Figure 21-6). Some of them are the same as the controls you see when you do an advanced text search (page 808), such as the Tag Modifier menu and the + button that lets you add additional restrictions to the search.

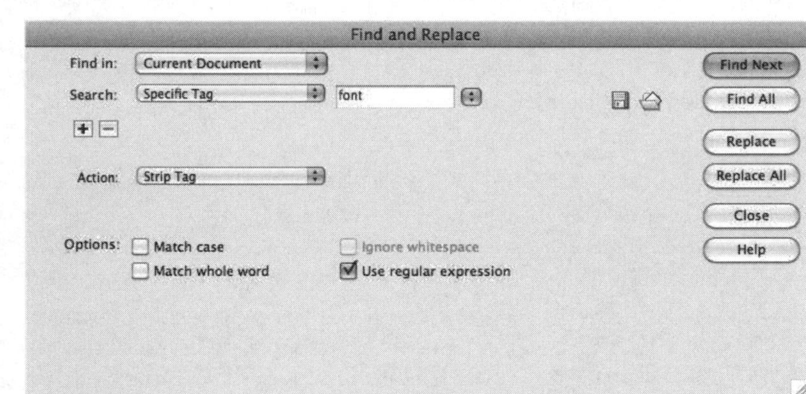

Figure 21-6: *It's a snap to remove tags when you use the Specific Tag option in Dreamweaver's "Find and Replace" command—just select the Strip Tag action. This option is handy if you want to replace old-style text formatting with Cascading Style Sheets. Use it to strip out unwanted <font> tags from old sites, for example.*

But a key difference here is the Action menu (Figure 21-7), which lets you specify the action Dreamweaver performs on tags that match the search criteria when you click Replace or Replace All (if you intend to search, but not replace, then these options don't apply):

- **Replace Tag & Contents.** Replaces the tag, and anything enclosed by the tag (including other tags), with whatever you put into the With box to the right of this menu. You can either type or paste text or HTML here.
- **Replace Contents**. Only replaces everything enclosed by the tag with text or HTML that you specify. The tag itself remains untouched.

Note: Depending on which tag you're searching for, you might not see all the actions listed here. For example, the <img> tag doesn't have both an opening and a closing tag like the <p> tag does, so you won't see any of the options such as "Replace Contents Only" that affect the content between an opening and closing tag.

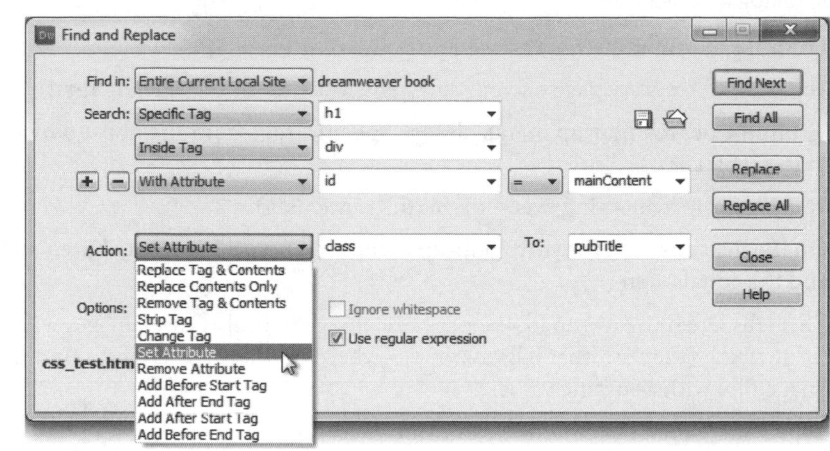

Figure 21-7: *Once Dreamweaver finds a specific tag, it can perform any of 11 different actions on the tag or its contents.*

- **Remove Tag & Contents.** Deletes the tag and *everything* inside.
- **Strip Tag.** Deletes the tag from the page, but leaves anything enclosed by the tag untouched. The outmoded <font> tag is a perfect candidate for this action.
- **Set Attribute.** Adds an attribute to the tag. For example, you could set the *alt* property of an image this way (see the example in the next section).
- **Remove Attribute.** Removes an attribute from a tag. You could remove the not-at-all-useful *lowsrc* attribute from all image tags on your pages, for example.
- **Add Before (After) Start (End) Tag.** The last four actions in the menu simply offer variations on the same theme. Each lets you place content in a Web page just before or after the tag for which you're searching.

  To understand how this works, remember that most HTML tags come in pairs. The paragraph tag, for example, has an opening tag (<p>) and a closing tag (</p>). Say you searched for a paragraph tag; you could add text or HTML *before* or *after* the start tag (<p>), or *before* or *after* the end tag (</p>). (For an example of when you might use this feature, see the box on page 816.)

A Powerful Example: Adding Alt Text Fast

You've just put the finishing touches on the last page of your brand-new, 1,000-page site. You sit back and smile—and then snap bolt upright when you notice you forgot to add an Alt description for the site's banner graphic (see page 224). This graphic, called *site_banner.gif*, appears on every single one of those 1,000 pages. With rising dread, you realize you have to open each page, select the graphic, and add the *alt* property by hand.

And then you remember Dreamweaver's advanced tag-based "Find and Replace" feature.

Here's what you do. Press Ctrl+F (⌘-F) to open the "Find and Replace" window. Set up the dialog box like this:

1. **From the "Find in" menu, choose Entire Current Local Site.**

   You want to fix *every* page on your site (remember to make a backup first!)

2. **From the Search pop-up menu, choose Specific Tag; from the pop-up menu to its right, choose "img".**

   You'll start by identifying every image (the <img> tag).

3. **On the next row, use the three pop-up menus to choose With Attribute, "src", and the equals sign (=).**

   This tells Dreamweaver to look for specific images—in this case, images with a *src* attribute (the path that tells a browser where on the web server to find the image file) with a specific value.

4. **Type .*site_banner\.gif in the box next to the = sign.**

   For this exercise, assume you stored the graphics file in a folder called *images* located in the root folder of the site. The name *site_banner.gif* is the name of the image file. The .* is the magic, and you'll learn its purpose in a moment (ditto the backslash hanging out before the second period).

5. **Click the + button.**

   Another row of Tag Modifier menus appears.

6. **From this new row of menus, choose Without Attribute and "alt".**

   You've further limited Dreamweaver's search to only those images that don't already have the *alt* attribute. (After all, why bother setting the *alt* property on an image that already has it?)

7. **From the Action menu, choose Set Attribute; from the Tag menu, choose "alt".**

   You've just told Dreamweaver what to do when you click the Replace or Replace All button. When Dreamweaver finds an <img> tag that matches the search criteria, it will then *add* an *alt* property to that tag.

   In this example, you might type *Chia Vet* in the To field; you've just specified the Alt text for Dreamweaver to add to the image.

8. **Turn on "Use regular expressions".**

   Regular expressions, described on "Advanced Tag Searches", let you search for specific patterns of characters and, in this case, help you accurately identify the banner graphic file everywhere it appears.

   You know you're looking for the file *site_banner.gif* wherever it appears on the site. Unfortunately, if you just type *site_banner.gif* as the value of the *src* property in step 3, Dreamweaver can't succeed in its task. That's because the *src* attribute—the part of the <img> tag that includes the name of the file—varies from page to page. Depending on where a page is relative to the graphic, the src might be *site_banner.gif*, *images/site_banner.gif*, or even *../../../images/site_banner.gif*. What you need is a way to match every *src* attribute that ends in *site_banner.gif*.

A simple regular expression, *.*site_banner\.gif*, does the trick. The period stands for *any* character (6, g, or even %, for example), while the * (asterisk) means "zero or more times." When you add these codes to the graphic name, *site_banner.gif*, you instruct Dreamweaver to find every *src* value that ends in *site_banner.gif*.

In other words .* will match *../../images/*, *images/*, and so on. It will even match nothing at all in the case where the Web page is actually inside the *images* folder and the *src* property is then just *site_banner.gif*.

Note the backslash before the last period: \.*gif*. In the world of regular expressions, a period means "any character," so simply using *site_banner.gif* would not only match *site_banner.gif*, but also *site_banner1gif*, *site_bannerZgif*, and so on—in other words, any character that sits between *site_banner* and *gif*. The backslash tells Dreamweaver to treat the next character literally; it's just a period with no special regular-expression power.

The dialog box should look like the one in Figure 21-8.

9. **Click the Replace All button and sit back.**

   In a matter of moments, Dreamweaver updates all 1,000 pages.

   To test this out first, you might try a more cautious approach: Click the Find Next button to locate the first instance of the missing *alt* property; verify that it's correct by looking in the Search box (see Figure 21-8); and then click the Replace button to add the proper *alt* value. Double-check the newly updated page to make sure everything worked as planned. You can continue updating pages one at a time this way, or, once you're sure it works correctly, press Replace All.

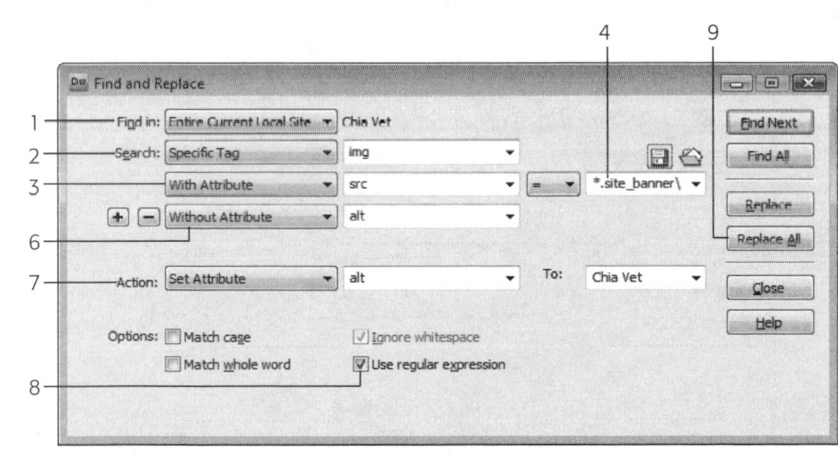

***Figure 21-8:** The numbers shown here correspond to the steps in this example, in which you want to add an <alt> tag to every occurrence of the banner logo for the benefit of people who can't, or don't want to, see graphics in their browsers.*

FREQUENTLY ASKED QUESTION

Convenient Copyright Notices

I want to add a copyright notice to the bottom of each page in my website. Is there a way to automate this process so I don't have to edit every page in my site by hand?

You bet. Use Dreamweaver's "Find and Replace" command to add text or HTML to the bottom of any Web page. The trick is knowing how to use the command's Specific Tag option.

First, choose Edit→Find and Replace to open the "Find and Replace" window. Next, choose Entire Current Local Site from the "Find in" menu, and choose Specific Tag from the Search menu. Choose "body" from the Tag menu. Remember, the <body> tag in HTML encloses everything that appears inside a browser window; it's equivalent to what you see in the document window.

From the Action menu, choose Add Before End Tag. The end tag in this case is </body>. Since </body> marks the end of any content in a web page, whatever appears directly before this closing tag will appear at the bottom of the page (you can probably see where this is going).

Now, in the text field next to the Action menu, type (or paste) the copyright notice you want on each page. You may want to first design the copyright message using Dreamweaver, and then copy and paste the HTML into this field.

Click Replace All. Dreamweaver handles the rest.

You may not want to put the copyright notice at the *very end* of the page's HTML, as in this example. You might want it to go inside a particular <div> tag that's already on the page. Let's say that that div has an ID of *footer*. In that case, you would search for a <div> tag from the Tag menu and then select "With attribute" ID equal to "footer." Then you could use either the "Add Before End Tag" or "Add After Start Tag" options to place the copyright notice either at the end or beginning of that div.

Tip: To get a full description of every Dreamweaver menu in a handy, printable PDF, go to this book's Missing CD page (*www.missingmanuals.com/cds*) and download Appendix B, "Menu by Menu Commands."

CHAPTER

22

Customizing Dreamweaver

Whether you're a hard-core HTML jockey who prefers to be knee-deep in Code view, or a visually oriented, drag-and-drop type who never strays from Design view, Dreamweaver lets you work whichever way you want.

By now, you're probably already using the Favorites tab on the Insert panel to store your most frequently used objects in one place, as discussed on page 28. But don't stop there. Dreamweaver gives you the power to add, change, and share keyboard shortcuts—it's a simple way to tailor the program to your needs. And if that's not enough of an efficiency boost, you can add features that even Adobe's engineers never imagined, from simple productivity add-ons like QuickLink (see page 174) to advanced Server Behaviors that help power a complete e-commerce website. Dreamweaver's design allows amateur and professional programmers alike to write new features and functions using HTML, JavaScript, and XML (Extensible Markup Language). There are hundreds of these extras, called *extensions*, for you to explore. Best of all, you can try many of them for free.

Keyboard Shortcuts

As you use Dreamweaver, you'll hit the same keyboard shortcuts and travel to the same palettes and menus time and again; perhaps your site uses a lot of graphics and Flash movies, for example, and you're constantly using the keyboard shortcuts to insert them. But you may find that, after the thousandth time, Ctrl+Alt+F (⌘-Option-F) hurts your pinkie and uses too many keys to be truly efficient. On the other hand, the things you do all the time—like inserting text fields into forms or adding rollover images—may not have shortcuts at all, so you're forced to go to a menu.

To speed up your work and save your tendons, Dreamweaver comes with a keyboard-shortcut editor that lets you define or redefine shortcuts for most of the program's commands.

Dreamweaver stores its keyboard shortcuts in sets. It's easy to switch between them—a useful feature when you share your computer with someone who likes different keystrokes. Four sets of shortcuts come with the program:

- **Dreamweaver Standard.** When you first fire up Dreamweaver, the program turns on this set of keyboard shortcuts. It's the same one available since Dreamweaver 8, and it matches the keyboard shortcuts found in Fireworks.
- **Dreamweaver MX 2004.** Some keyboard shortcuts have changed since Dreamweaver MX 2004—for example, Shift+F5 now opens the Tag Editor window, instead of Ctrl+F5. But the changes are so minor, it's not really necessary to use this set.
- **BBEdit.** If you're a Mac user with a code-editing past, you may have spent a lot of time learning shortcuts for Bare Bones Software's popular BBEdit. If so, you can choose this set.
- **HomeSite.** Likewise, if you're adept at the Windows HTML text editor HomeSite, you may want to use its keyboard shortcuts. Don't remember HomeSite? That's because it hasn't been available for years, so you probably won't ever see a need for this.

You access the shortcut sets from the Keyboard Shortcuts dialog box. Choose Edit→Keyboard Shortcuts (Dreamweaver→Keyboard Shortcuts on Macs). Be patient—the sets can take some time to load. Once the dialog box appears, you can switch sets by choosing a new one from the Current Set menu (see Figure 22-1).

Make Your Own Shortcut Set

What if you want a set that *combines* BBEdit shortcuts with the ones you use most from Dreamweaver ones? Or you're a radical individualist who wants to remap *every* command to keys of your liking? No problem. Since Dreamweaver doesn't let you alter any of the four standard shortcut sets, you first want to make a copy of one of them.

Choose Edit→Keyboard Shortcuts (on the Mac, it's Dreamweaver→Keyboard Shortcuts). In the Keyboard Shortcuts window, use the Current Set pop-up menu to choose the set you wish to copy, and then click the Duplicate Set button (see Figure 22-1). Dreamweaver asks you to name the new set; once you do, click OK.

You can delete or rename any set you create—once you figure out that the first button in the Shortcuts window, the one with the cryptic dual-page icon, is the Rename Set button (see Figure 22-1). The Trash Can button, of course, lets you delete a set.

Note: Dreamweaver lets you delete the four main keyboard shortcut sets. If you want one of them back, don't worry. The actual file isn't gone. You just need to edit a file called *mm_deleted_files.xml* in your Dreamweaver configuration folder. Remove the line that lists the keyboard shortcut set you want to get back and save the file. Then quit and restart Dreamweaver. (Note that each account holder on Windows and Mac OS X maintains a separate Configuration folder. See the box on page 821 for more details.)

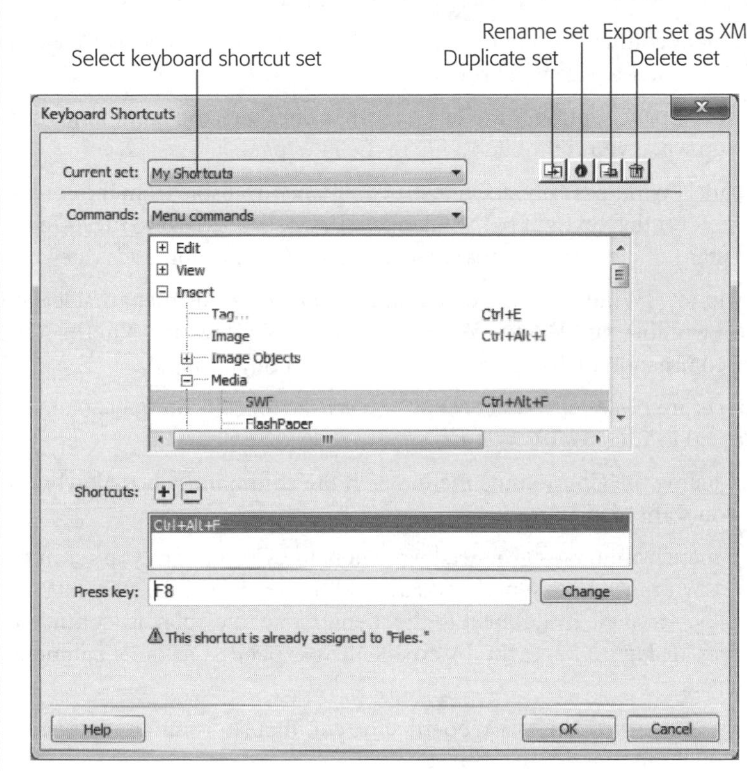

Figure 22-1: *The Keyboard Shortcuts window lets you select or duplicate a shortcut set, as well as add and remove keyboard shortcuts for every menu item in Dreamweaver. You can also create keyboard shortcuts for Snippets (see Chapter 19). When you attempt to create a shortcut that another command already uses, Dreamweaver warns you. If you wish, you can ignore the warning and reassign the keys to the new command.*

Changing Keyboard Shortcuts

Once you duplicate a set of shortcuts, you can select any command and alter its shortcut. Start by choosing Edit→Keyboard Shortcuts (Dreamweaver→Keyboard Shortcuts) to open the Shortcuts window, if it's not already open. Then:

1. **From the Commands pop-up menu, choose the command type.**

   Dreamweaver organizes shortcuts into seven (Windows) or four (Macintosh) primary categories. They don't always make sense: For example, Copy and Paste appear under the Code Editing category, even though you use them at least as frequently while editing a document in the visual Design view. In addition, you'll find quite a few commands listed under multiple categories (you only need to change a keyboard shortcut once for Dreamweaver to change all instances).

Browse to see which commands have (or could have) keyboard shortcuts associated with them:

- Menu commands are those that appear in Dreamweaver's menus, such as Insert→Image.
- You might use the Code editing commands when you edit HTML. However, you could just as easily use them in Design view—they include Cut, Paste, and "Move to Top of Page"" to name a few.
- Document editing commands let you select text and objects on a page, as well as preview a page in a browser.
- The "Files panel options" menu (Windows only) are the commands that show up when you right-click a file in the Files panel.
- Site panel (Windows only) include the commands available from the contextual menu at the top right of the Files panel, such as Site→New Site. (On the Mac, many of these commands are listed in the Menu Commands category.)
- Site window (Windows only) commands are an odd assortment that let you close a window, quit Dreamweaver, or cancel an FTP session. On the Mac, these commands are listed in the Document Editing group.
- Snippets are pieces of reusable code you select from the Snippets panel, as discussed in Chapter 19.

2. **In the list below the Commands menu, click the command whose keyboard shortcut you want to change.**

   You'll find menu commands grouped by menu name: Commands you see in the File drop-down menu, like Open and Save, fall under File. Click the + (Windows) or flippy triangle (Mac) next to the menu name to display its command. For example, in Figure 22-1, the Insert menu is expanded as is its submenu, Image Objects.

   If the command already has a keyboard shortcut, that shortcut appears in the right-hand column. If it doesn't, you see an empty space.

3. **Click inside the "Press key" field, and then press the new keystroke.**

   Unless you assign the shortcut to an F-key or the Esc key, you must begin your shortcut with the Ctrl key (⌘-key). For example, the F8 key is a valid shortcut, but the letter R isn't; press Ctrl+R (⌘-R) instead.

Note: Some keyboard shortcuts may already be in use by your operating system, so assigning them in Dreamweaver may have no effect. For example, in Windows, Ctrl+Esc opens the Start Menu, while in Mac OS 10.4 and above, Dashboard uses the F12 key.

Of course, many commands already have shortcuts. If you choose a key combination that's in use, Dreamweaver tells you which command has dibs. You can pick a different key combination, or you can click the Change button to reassign the shortcut to your command. The original command now has no shortcut.

4. **Click the Change button.**

   Dreamweaver saves the new shortcut in your custom set.

   Repeat the steps above to make other keystroke reassignments. When you finish, click OK to close the dialog box.

FREQUENTLY ASKED QUESTION

Sharing Shortcuts

How do I share my keyboard set with other people?.

Dreamweaver stores your keyboard shortcuts as XML files–but in Dreamweaver, finding them can be tricky. These files are in different locations depending on your operating system. Each keyboard set lives in an XML file; the file's name ends with the extension .xml. For example, if you create a new set of keyboard shortcuts name My Shortcuts, the XML file would be named *My Shortcuts.xml*.

In Windows XP, you'll find the custom keyboard set on your main hard drive in *Documents and Settings→[Your Name]→Application Data→Adobe Dreamweaver CS5→en_US→Configuration→Menus→Custom Sets*. In Windows Vista and 7, they're in *C:\Users\[your user name]\AppData\Roaming\Adobe\Dreamweaver CS5\en_US\Configuration\Menus\Custom Sets*. (Note that Windows hides these files from you normally (see the note on page 822 to get around this little problem).

In Mac OS X, these files are squirreled away in your *Home folder Library→Application Support→Adobe→Dreamweaver CS5→en_US→Configuration→ Menus→Custom Sets*.

Depending on the language you use, you might see something other than "en US" (which stands for English), such as "de_DE" for German, or "ja_JP" for Japanese.

You can copy these files and place them in the Custom Sets folder on other computers. Once you do so, Dreamweaver users on those machines can use the Keyboard Shortcuts window (Edit→Keyboard Shortcuts or, on the Mac, Dreamweaver Keyboard Shortcuts) to select the new set, just as though you created it in that copy of Dreamweaver.

What if a command you use often doesn't have a shortcut at all? It's no problem to create one. As a matter of fact, Dreamweaver lets you assign *two* keyboard shortcuts to every command—one for you, and one for your left-handed spouse, for example.

To give a command a first or additional shortcut:

1. **Choose the command.**

   Follow the first two steps of the preceding instructions.

2. **Click the + button next to the word "Shortcuts".**

   The cursor automatically pops into the "Press key" field.

3. **Press the keys for the shortcut, and then click the Change button again.**

   Repeat these steps to assign another set of keystrokes; when you finish, click OK.

Deleting shortcuts is just as easy. Simply click the command in the list, and then click the minus sign (–) button next to the word "Shortcuts".

Create a Shortcut Cheat Sheet

Unless your brain is equipped with a 400-gig hard drive, you'll probably find it hard to remember all of Dreamweaver's keyboard shortcuts.

Fortunately, Dreamweaver offers a printable cheat sheet for your reference. At the top of the Shortcuts window, there's a handy "Export Set as HTML" button (labeled with an odd icon; see Figure 22-1). Click this button to name and save a simple HTML page that lists all the commands and keyboard shortcuts for the currently selected command set. Once you save the file, print it out or use it as an online reference—a great way to keep a record of your shortcuts for yourself or a team of designers.

For Windows Users: Windows normally hides certain files, such as important system files, from sight. This includes the Configuration folder discussed in the box on page 828, and the Menus folder discussed in the box on page 821. To access these folders, you need to make hidden files visible. XP users should visit this page: *www.howtogeek.com/howto/windows/display-hidden-folders-in-xp/*, and Windows Vista and 7 should follow the steps on this page *www.howtogeek.com/howto/windows-vista/show-hidden-files-and-folders-in-windows-vista/*.

Dreamweaver Extensions

While keyboard shortcuts give you an easy way to access frequently used commands, they're not much help if the command you want doesn't exist. Suppose, for example, you use Dreamweaver's Open Browser Window behavior (page 599) to load a new web page into a window that's exactly 200 X 300 pixels. What if you want to center the window in the middle of your visitor's monitor? Dreamweaver's behavior doesn't do that. What's a web designer to do? You could go to the Adobe site and request the new feature (*www.adobe.com/cfusion/mmform/index.cfm?name=wishform&product=12*) in hopes that the bustling team of programmers will add the command to the next version. But you'd have to wait—and there's no guarantee that Adobe would add it.

The legions of hard-core Dreamweaver fans have taken this feature wish-list issue into their own hands. As it turns out, amateur (and pro) programmers can enhance Dreamweaver relatively easily by writing new feature modules using the basic languages of the Web: HTML, JavaScript, and XML. (In fact, HTML forms, JavaScript programs, and XML documents constitute much of Dreamweaver's functionality. The objects in the Insert panel, for example, are actually HTML pages stored within Dreamweaver's Configuration folder, and Adobe wrote all of Dreamweaver's menus as an XML file.)

Because of this "open architecture," you can add new functions and commands—called *extensions*—to Dreamweaver by downloading the work of one of those programmers and installing it in your own copy of the program. A Dreamweaver extension can take many forms and work in a variety of ways to change how the program works. It can be an icon on the Insert panel, a behavior listed on the Behaviors panel, or a command in the Commands menu. It might even be an entirely new floating window, like the Property inspector, that you use to alter some aspect of your page.

Best of all, whereas programming ability may be required to *create* extensions, none at all is necessary to use them. You can download hundreds of extensions from the Web for free and install them on your computer. In addition, you can find many sophisticated extensions, like those for creating e-commerce sites, commercially available.

Note: Extensions have been around for many versions of Dreamweaver. Unfortunately, each version added a few kinks for extension developers, so not all work with Dreamweaver CS5. (Many extensions that were compatible with Dreamweaver CS4 *do* work with Dreamweaver CS5.) Most extension developers list which versions of Dreamweaver their extensions work with, and you can also check for version compatibility on the Dreamweaver Exchange (see Figure 22-2).

Browse the Exchange

The largest collection of extensions awaits you at the Adobe Exchange website, where you'll find hundreds of free and commercial extensions. Although some come from Adobe itself, an army of talented Dreamweaver users write the vast majority of them.

Using the Exchange is straightforward:

1. **In your browser, go to *www.adobe.com/exchange* and then click the Dreamweaver link under the list of →Exchanges by Product".**

   You can also get to the Exchange from within Dreamweaver by choosing Commands→Get More Commands.

2. **Sign in (see Figure 22-2).**

   You can *browse* the site without signing in, but to *download* any of the extensions, you need to get a free Adobe ID and sign in, using the Exchange Sign In form—click the *Your account* link in the top-left corner of the web page.

3. **Browse the extensions.**

   Once you log into the site, the home page highlights new and popular extensions. A list of extension categories—Accessibility, DHTML/Layers, Navigation, and so on—appears on the right. Click any of them to see a list of extensions in that category. Click one of the sorting tabs (circled in Figure 22-2) to view staff picks, the newest, most popular, or the highest rated extensions.

   Use the menu to the right of "License type" to view extensions that match a particular license—for example, if you want free stuff, select Open Source or Freeware and then click the Filter button.

   If you're looking for a *particular* extension, the Search command is your best bet. Type the extension's name or a few descriptive words into the Search Dreamweaver field, and then click Search.

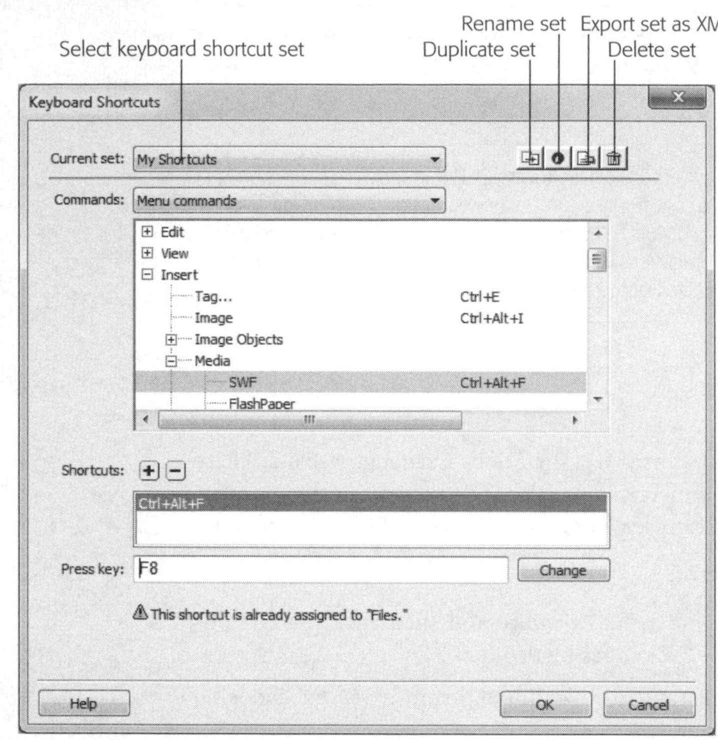

Figure 22-2: *You can peruse the Dreamweaver Exchange freely, check out the offerings, and even buy commercial third-party extensions. However, if you want to download a free extension, you must get an Adobe ID and log into the site. Unfortunately, the marketing machine must be appeased, so you'll need to provide personal information and face a (fortunately optional) survey of your Web development habits.*

4. **Click an extension's name to go to its web page.**

   You'll find lots of information about the extension, including a description of how it works, a button to either purchase or download the extension, information about which version of Dreamweaver and which operating system (Windows or Mac) it works with, and buttons to add the extension to Favorites and Alerts lists. The Favorites option lets you create a personal list of the extensions you like best; the Alerts list feature means the author sends you an email whenever she updates the extension.

   When you click the Download button for an extension, your browser either starts downloading the extension or shuttles you off to the author's website. A Buy button, on the other hand, always sends you to the site where you buy the extension directly from its creator.

Find a Good Extension

How do you figure out which extensions are worth checking out? First, you can find recommendations of the best ones scattered through this book in special boxes labeled Extension Alert (see pages 174 andpage 475, for instance).

The Exchange also provides information to help you separate the wheat from the chaff. Adobe tests each extension before posting it. Extensions that pass a basic set of tests—it installs OK, it works, it doesn't blow up your computer—get a Basic approval rating. Some extensions pass a more rigorous test that determines if the extension works in a way that's "Dreamweaver-like." In other words, these extensions look, feel, and act like the program, so you won't need to learn a new interface. Adobe gives them an Adobe Approved rating, indicated by the word "Adobe" in the approval section of an extension's details page.

Of course, these approval ratings only let you know if an extension works; they don't tell you whether it's *useful*. As an extra aid, Dreamweaver aficionados (including you) can rate each extension on a scale of 1 (worst) to 5 (best). An extension's average rating gives you a good indication of how handy it is. When you browse the Exchange, look for the star rating at the bottom of each extension (see Figure 22-2). You can also click the Highest Rated link to sort the list of extensions from most to least number of stars.

Other Extension Sources

Unfortunately, the glory days of totally free extensions are mostly over. You can still find plenty of extensions offered free of charge, but many developers realize they can't survive by giving away their work. The upside is that there are now more excellent, polished, well-documented commercial extensions than ever—many even with customer support. Here are a few highlights:

- **WebAssist** (*www.webassist.com*) is one of the largest and most professional extension development companies. They offer a wide variety of high-quality extensions, including a few free onlf PHP or ASP is your bag, then you'll find an impressive collection of extensions at Felix One (*http://www.felixone.it/extensions/dwextensionsen.asp*).
- **Project Seven** (*hwww.projectseven.com*) offers free extensions and several excellent commercial extensions that let you create animated HTML and CSS menus, scrolling areas of text, CSS-based page layouts, photo galleries, and more.
- **Trent Pastrana** (*www.fourlevel.com*) sells extensions that build photo galleries, whiz-bang effects (like menus that slide onto the page), or scrollers that move text up and down (or left and right) across a web page.
- **Trio Solutions** (*http://components.developers4web.com/*) sells lots of inexpensive extensions that let you add CSS-style calendars, insert Flash music players into a page, and much more.
- **Hot Dreamweaver** (*www.hotdreamweaver.com/*) sells extensions for server-side needs like sending form submissions as e-mails, adding Captcha (those little hard-to-read pictures of letters and numbers that you have to type into a form to prove you're a human), and uploading files to a web server.

Download and Install Extensions

Once you find a great extension, download it to your computer. You can save the downloaded file anywhere on your computer, but you may want to create a special folder. That way, if you ever need to reinstall Dreamweaver, you can quickly find and add your collection of extensions.

Extension file names end with *.mxp*, which stands for Macromedia Exchange Package (from the days before Adobe bought Macromedia). That's a special file format that works with Adobe's Extension Manager—the program, described next, that actually installs the extension in Dreamweaver.

Extension Manager

To add or remove a Dreamweaver extension, use the Extension Manager, a standalone program integrated into Dreamweaver. The Extension Manager handles add-ons for many Adobe programs, not just Dreamweaver. It lets you install extensions, turn them on and off, and remove them. It's handy if you also use Adobe's Flash or Fireworks programs—you get a single place to manage all your extensions.

You can launch the Extension Manager from within Dreamweaver by choosing Help→Manage Extensions, or Commands→Manage Extensions (see Figure 21-4).

To add an extension:

1. **Download an extension package (.mxp file) from the Exchange or another website.**

   See instructions above.

2. **From Dreamweaver, choose Help→Manage Extensions (or Commands→ Manage Extensions).**

   You can also select Extension Manager from the Extension menu in the Application Bar (see Figure 1-6). Either way, the Extension Manager launches. It lists all currently installed extensions (see Figure 22-3).

3. **Choose Dreamweaver CS5 from the left-hand list of Adobe Products.**

   Since the Extension Manager handles extensions for several different programs, you need to specify which program you're using. If you don't have any other Adobe products installed on your machine, Dreamweaver CS5 and Bridge CS5 (installed alongside Dreamweaver) are your only options.

4. **Choose File→Install Extension.**

   You can also click the Install Extension button. The Select Extension window appears, listing the folders on your hard drive.

5. **Navigate to and select the extension package (.mxp file) you wish to add.**

   A disclaimer appears with a lot of legal text. In brief, it frees Adobe from liability if your computer melts down as a result of installing the extension.

6. **Click Accept in the Disclaimer window.**

   A message may appear that asks you to quit and restart Dreamweaver. If so, follow the directions.

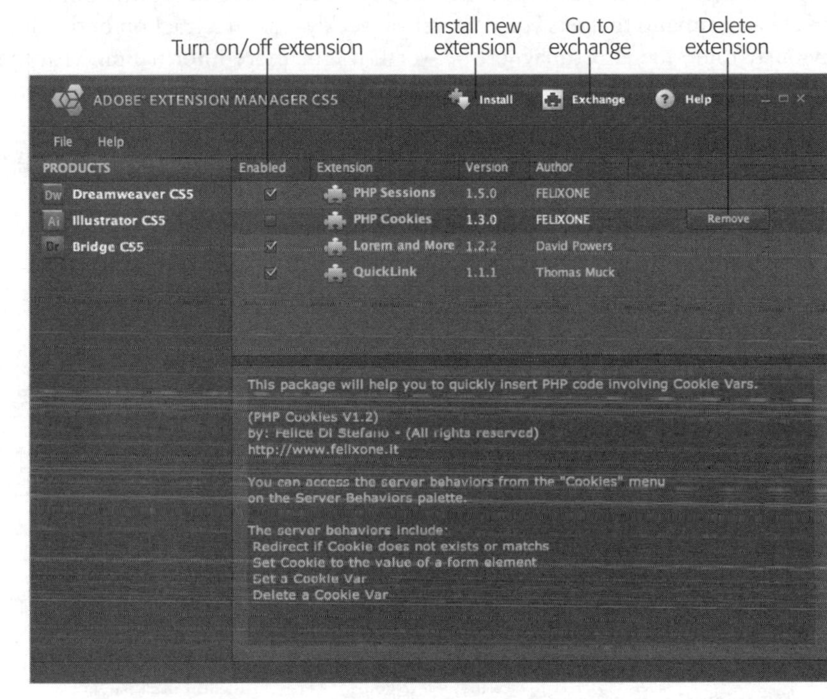

Figure 22-3: *The Extension Manager window lists each extension you install, along with its version number, type, and author. If you select an extension from the list, a description appears in the bottom half of the window. Adobe Bridge (listed here on the left) is a program for managing visual "assets" among the various programs that make up Adobe's Creative Suite, like Photoshop and Illustrator. Since Bridge's emphasis is on visual media—not web pages—it's not as useful for web developers as it is for graphics designers. If you want to learn more about Bridge visit* www.adobe.com/products/creativesuite/bridge/.

Tip: A faster way to install an extension is to simply double-click the .mxp file after you download it.aunchslaunches the Extension Manager and installs the extension.

To remove an extension, select it from the list and choose File→Remove Extension, or click the Remove button.

Note: If you install a lot of extensions, Dreamweaver may take longer than usual to load; it needs to process every extension file as it opens. If you want to temporarily turn off an extension (as opposed to deleting it), open the Extension Manager and turn off the Enable box next to the extension's name. To turn it back on, simply turn on the checkbox again. You may need to restart Dreamweaver to make the extension available again.

Make Your Own Extensions

The Exchange is a great resource for finding useful extensions. But what if you can't find the extension you need? Create your own.

Writing extensions requires in-depth knowledge of JavaScript and HTML. But when you create a command that lets you complete a weekly task in a fraction of the time it previously took, the effort may just be worth it. For more information, visit the Dreamweaver support center at *www.adobe.com/support/dreamweaver/extend.html.*

POWER USERS' CLINIC

The Secret Life of Extensions

Where do extensions go? The basic answer is: inside the Dreamweaver Configuration folder. But Dreamweaver actually supplies you with multiple configuration folders: a main folder located with the program itself, and account-specific folders for each user account on a computer. Windows and Macs let multiple users have an account on a single computer–one for you, your spouse, and your pet ferret, say. Of course, you may be the only one using your computer, so in that case there'd be just one configuration folder.

On a Windows machine, the main configuration folder is in *C:\Program Files\Adobe\Adobe Dreamweaver CS5\en_US\configuration* (assuming the C:\ drive is your main drive). On a Mac, you can find it here: *Applications→Adobe Dreamweaver CS5en_US→Configuration*. The individual account configuration folders are located in folders dedicated to each user. In Windows XP: *C:\Documents and Settings\[your user name]\Application Data\Adobe\Dreamweaver CS5\en_US\Configuration*. In Windows Vista and Windows 7: *C:\Users\[your user name]\AppData\Roaming\Adobe\Dreamweaver CS5\en_US\Configuration*. On a Mac: *Volume Name→Users→[your user name]→Library→Application Support→Adobe→Dreamweaver CS5→en_US→Configuration*. (As mentioned in the box on page 821, "en_US" means English. If you installed Dreamweaver using a different language, this folder will be named something else, such as "de_DE" for German.)

Some changes you make to Dreamweaver are recorded in your personal configuration folder, such as when you add an extension, delete a keyboard shortcut set (see page 817), or save a workspace layout (see page 34).

The main Configuration folder holds many of the files that control Dreamweaver's look and operation. For instance, the entire menu structure, including menu items and submenus, is described in a file called *menus.xml*. When Dreamweaver starts, it reads this file and uses the information inside it to draw the menus on the screen.

The Configuration folder holds many subfolders, each with a special purpose. For example, the Objects folder contains files that tell Dreamweaver which icon buttons appear on the Insert bar and how each one works.

Depending on the type of extension you downoaded—-command, object, behavior, or whatever—-the Extension Manager stores the file (or files) required by the extension in one or more folders inside the Configuration folder. Because all of the files inside the Configuration folder are crucial to the way Dreamweaver works, don't delete the folder or any of the files inside it. In fact, because the Extension Manager automatically makes any required changes to the Configuration folder, there's no reason for you to even look inside it.

(The only exception is when you want to copy your keyboard shortcut set to another computer [see page 821].)

CHAPTER

23

Getting Started with Dynamic Web Sites

So far in this book, you've learned to build and maintain websites by using Dreamweaver's powerful design, coding, and site management tools. The pages you've created use straightforward HTML, which you can immediately preview in a web browser to see a finished design. The web cognoscenti often call these kinds of pages *static*, since they don't change once you finish building them (unless you edit them later, of course). For many websites, especially ones where you carefully handcraft the design and content on a page-by-page basis, static web pages are the way to go.

But imagine landing a contract to build an online catalog of 10,000 products. After the initial excitement disappears (along with your plans for that trip to Hawaii), you realize that even using Dreamweaver's Template tool (Chapter 20), building 10,000 pages is a lot of work!

Fortunately, Dreamweaver offers a better and faster way to deal with this problem. Its dynamic website creation tools let you take advantage of a variety of powerful techniques that would be difficult or impossible with plain HTML. With Dreamweaver, you can build pages that:

- Display listings of products or other items, like your record collection, your company's staff directory, or your mother's library of prized recipes.
- Search through a database of information and display the results.
- Require site login so you can hide particular areas from prying eyes.
- Collect and store information from visitors to your site.
- Personalize your visitors' experience: "Hello Dave, it's been a while since you've visited. Did you miss us?—Hal."

Visit *www.Amazon.com*, for example, and you'll find more books than you could read in a lifetime. In fact, you'll find more products—DVDs, CDs, and even outdoor lawn furniture—than could fit inside a Wal-Mart. In just an hour, you could browse through hundreds of products, each with its own web page. Do you really think Amazon hired an army of web developers to create each page for every product they sell? Not a chance.

Note: Luckily you aren't limited to *either* static" *or* dynamic" web pages. Websites frequently use both–static pages for custom designs and handcrafted content, and dynamic pages for mass production of a thousand catalog pages.

Instead, when you search for a book on Amazon.com, your search triggers a computer program, running on what's called an *application server*, which searches a large database of products. When the program finds products that match your search criteria, it merges that information with HTML elements (banner, navigation buttons, copyright notice, and so on) to create a page on the fly. You see a web page that's been created, perhaps for the first time ever (Figure 23-1).

Figure 23-1: *An infinite number of monkeys couldn't create all the web pages for all the products Amazon.com sells. The solution? A dynamic website, which takes your programmed instructions and automatically creates pages made up of content chunks pulled from a database. That's the way to go if you've got a site with loads of pages that all present similar information.*

Dynamic websites are usually the realm of professional programmers, but Dreamweaver can simplify routine tasks like viewing information from a database and adding, updating, and deleting data. Even if you don't have a programmer's bone in your body, this chapter and the next few give you the basics.

Pieces of the Puzzle

You may be thinking, "Yeah, that sounds fantastic, but so did that time-share in the Bahamas. What's the catch?"

The catch is that dynamic websites are more complex and require more technologies to get off the ground. Simple static websites require only the computer you use to build them and a web server to dish them out. In fact, as you can see by previewing your site with a web browser on your own computer, you don't even need a web server to effectively view a static website.

Dynamic web pages, by contrast, require more horsepower (see Figure 23-2). Not only is there a web server that handles requests for web pages, two other types of servers enter the equation: an *application server* and a *database server*.

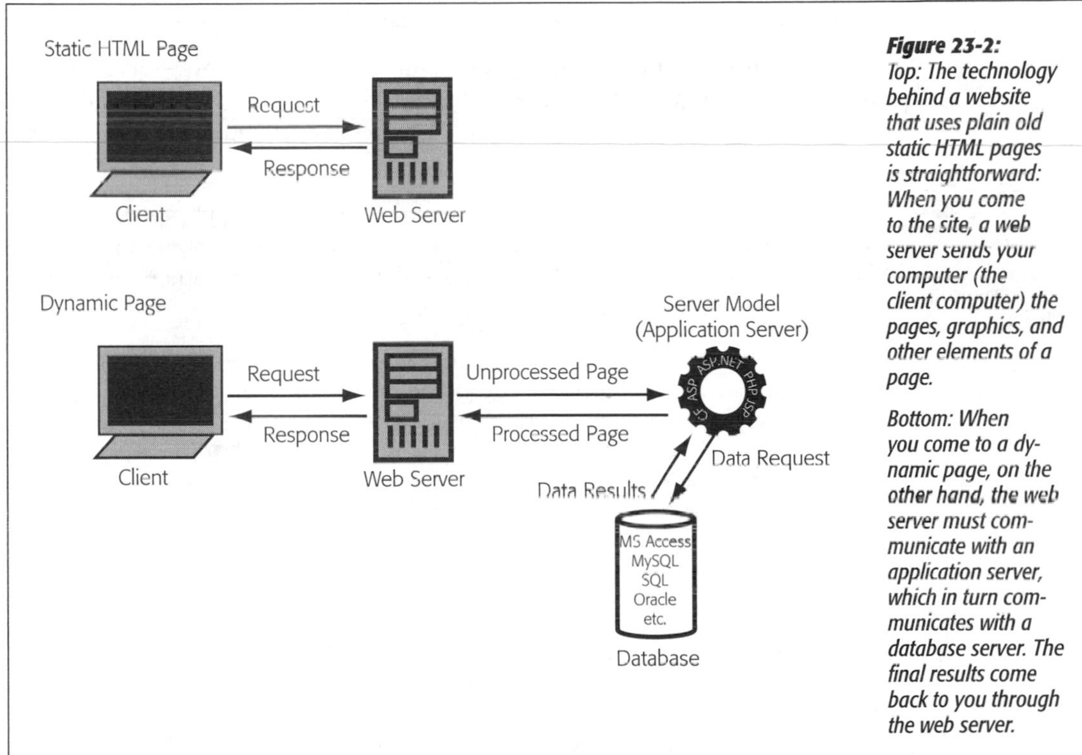

Figure 23-2: *Top: The technology behind a website that uses plain old static HTML pages is straightforward: When you come to the site, a web server sends your computer (the client computer) the pages, graphics, and other elements of a page.*

Bottom: When you come to a dynamic page, on the other hand, the web server must communicate with an application server, which in turn communicates with a database server. The final results come back to you through the web server.

You'll still be using a lot of HTML (and CSS) to build a dynamic site—for example, to provide the layout, add banner graphics, and display navigation bars. But you'll augment this mix with some form of programming code. The application server processes this code and sends a complete HTML page to the web server, which, in turn, sends that page on to the site visitor. In many cases, the programming code requires the application server to retrieve information from a database, and then merges it with the HTML of a page.

Note: When you talk about websites, a *server* refers to the software that dishes out particular types of information—web pages, database queries, or a program's output. It doesn't necessarily mean a separate computer; web hosting firms can (and frequently do) have web, database, and application servers all running happily together on a single machine.

Because dynamic websites require more technology, as you're building these sites you can't just open their pages in your web browser as you can with a regular web page. You must view a dynamic page through a web server that has an appropriate application server running.

You also have to set up a database, and connect that database to your application server. Although this can be quite complex, it's not difficult to set up a basic web server, application server, and database on your own computer, so you can build and test database-driven web pages. It's also easy to connect to remote computers that are already configured to serve up dynamic, database-driven web pages.

And once you or your company's system administrator set up a web server and the other assorted components necessary for a dynamic website, Dreamweaver can easily create complex web pages that access databases and let you build powerful web applications, all without ever learning any programming.

Even so, there are literally hundreds of combinations of web, application, and database servers, and Dreamweaver doesn't work with all of them. However, it's capable of working with three of the most popular and powerful combinations, using three different programming languages!

Note: The term *web application* refers to web pages that work together to complete a task. All the various pages that come together to form an online shopping site—which lets visitors do things like search a database of products, view individual product pages, and add products to a shopping cart—would be considered a web application.

Understanding Server Models

When an application server works with a programming language to create dynamic web pages, Dreamweaver calls that a *server model*. Dreamweaver recognizes several server models, including those based on the technologies ASP, ColdFusion, and PHP. Each server model has its own set of unique requirements, and its own methods of performing identical tasks.

Each server model also works with one programming language. For example, you can create an ASP page using VBScript. PHP can refer both to a programming language named PHP *and* to the application server. Likewise, CFML, or ColdFusion Markup Language, is a programming language, and a ColdFusion server is an application server. If your head is hurting trying to make sense of all this, just keep this in mind: An application server processes programming code and carries out various actions, like talking to a database or spitting out a web page.

Dreamweaver once supported more server models, including ASP.NET and Java Server Pages. However, keeping up with advances in those technologies was just too much work for the Adobe team, so they removed them in Dreamweaver CS4. In fact, Adobe has put a lot of effort into making Dreamweaver work with PHP, which is the most widely used server-side programming language (even Facebook uses PHP). While Dreamweaver still has tools for quickly creating dynamic pages in ASP and ColdFusion, if you're new to the game of database-driven websites you should start with PHP—ASP is very old (Microsoft doesn't even support it anymore), and Adobe provides other tools for programming ColdFusion pages. However, for the sake of completeness here's a brief description of the three server models.

FREQUENTLY ASKED QUESTION

The Dynamic Duo

How does a dynamic website differ from dynamic HTML?

Dynamic is a word that's thrown around a lot in web circles, and it has a variety of uses.

For starters, *dynamic* sometimes refers to the power of JavaScript. For example, Dreamweaver CS5's Spry Framework uses JavaScript to create interactive page elements such as the Spry menu bar discussed on page 184, or the animated effects described on page 592. The result is sometimes called "Dynamic HTML," because the elements on the page *change*.

However, in this section of the book, *dynamic* refers to any web page that an application server processes–pages that undergo some form of transformation on the web server side of the Internet, like connecting to a database, or collecting information from a form.

What's important to remember is that JavaScript, used for Dynamic HTML, Spry, and Dreamweaver Behaviors (Chapter 14), is a *client-side* programming language. It runs in someone's web browser, and is limited to changing the way a web page looks and behaves *after* it's been downloaded over the Internet.

Dynamic websites, on the other hand, use *server-side* programs–those that run on an application server, out there on the Web somewhere. The dynamic part (where a site responds to a form or accesses a database, for example) happens *on the web server*. The visitors to your site never see any programming code, and their computers never have to run the program. They merely enjoy the results of the application server's hard work: a finished HTML page.

PHP

PHP (PHP Hypertext Preprocessor) is a programming language created specifically to build dynamic web pages. It's the most popular and widely available option at web hosting companies—in other words, when it comes time to place your finished website on the Internet, you're most likely to find a hosting company that supports PHP. (PHP is also quite often the least expensive hosting option.) The PHP *interpreter*—that's the application server—works in conjunction with a variety of web servers, including Microsoft's Internet Information Server (IIS), but was initially created for the Apache web server. PHP can also work with a variety of different database servers, but Dreamweaver understands only the MySQL database server (also available at nearly every web hosting company).

Note: Because Apache, PHP, and MySQL are so commonly used together, you may encounter an acronym frequently used to describe them: AMP.

Apache, PHP, and MySQL are free (that's one of the reasons they're so popular), and you can find simple installation programs—see page 836 for suggestions—that let you install all three programs on your own desktop computer. The tutorials for this section of the book use the PHP server model.

ASP

ASP (Active Server Pages) used to be one of the most common ways to build database-driven websites. It's a bit long in the tooth now. Microsoft no longer supports ASP, since the company replaced it with ASP.NET. ASP isn't the best choice if you're just starting with database-driven sites. It works with Microsoft's Web Server—IIS—and can work with a variety of databases. For small projects, you can use Microsoft Access (the database program that comes with some versions of Microsoft Office), since it's fairly easy to use. For more demanding projects, where you need to store lots of data and host lots of visitors, Microsoft's SQL Server is a better choice.

ColdFusion

ColdFusion is an application server from Adobe (the maker of Dreamweaver) that's programmed using CFML (ColdFusion Markup Language). ColdFusion works in conjunction with several web servers, including IIS and Apache, and uses its own programming language, which resembles HTML. For this reason, some web designers find it easier to learn than other programming languages.

The downside is that this application isn't free. You *can* download a developer's edition—a free version that runs on your computer—so you can build and test ColdFusion web pages. But if you want to host the website on the Internet, you have to either buy the ColdFusion Server package (which isn't cheap) or find a hosting company that offers ColdFusion hosting. But, for testing purposes, you can get the Developer Edition of ColdFusion for free at *www.adobe.com/go/devcenter_cf_try*.

Like ASP, ColdFusion works with many different databases.

Adobe has another tool intended for working with ColdFusion—Adobe ColdFusion Builder (*http://labs.adobe.com/technologies/coldfusionbuilder/*). This dedicated programming environment is intended just for building ColdFusion applications.

Picking a Server Model

In Dreamweaver CS5, Adobe added lots of tools for PHP programmers (like the PHP CodeHints described on page 422). In fact, their own research indicates that PHP is far and away the most popular server-side programming language used by those who use Dreamweaver.

You can easily set up a fully operational web server (Apache), application server (PHP), and database server (MySQL) on your desktop computer, and quickly begin building dynamic pages with Dreamweaver.

In fact, since PHP is so popular, and it's the easiest server model to set up, this book's tutorials concentrate on building PHP pages.

However, when you're building a real-world website, the final decision on which server model to use may be out of your hands. You may work for a company that already uses ColdFusion for its website. Or, if you've already got a website up and running, but want to add some database-driven content, you have to use what's installed on that server. If you use a web hosting company to serve up your site, contact the company to find out which operating system, web server, and databases it uses. If they're Windows-based, odds are they use IIS, meaning that you can use ASP, and either Access or SQL Server databases (although PHP and MySQL are also available for Windows). On the other hand, if they're a Unix operation, you'll most likely find the Apache web server, PHP, and MySQL database.

Fortunately, the tools Dreamweaver provides for the different server models are largely the same. Essentially, you start to build dynamic pages using the same techniques you learned in the earlier sections of this book. For the heavy lifting (like retrieving data from a database or password-protecting a web page), you'll turn to Dreamweaver's menu-driven database tools. They'll help you add the programming code necessary to make an application server do all the server-side magic needed to work with databases to generate dynamic web pages. Once you learn Dreamweaver, you can build pages for any of the server models with which it works.

Note: Just because Dreamweaver doesn't have built-in tools for ASP.NET, Java Server pages, or any other server-side programming languages (like Ruby on Rails), doesn't mean you can't use Dreamweaver for these types of sites. Dreamweaver is a fully capable text-editor that you can use to program in any server-side programming language you wish. In fact, experienced PHP programmers will probably skip all of Dreamweaver's menu-driven PHP tools in favor of simply programming PHP by hand. This section of the book is dedicated to those non-programmers who want to get started building database-driven websites (and even if you are a PHP programmer, you might like to try out Dreamweaver's tools for rapidly building basic dynamic sites).

Dynamic Web Sites: The Setup

Now that your head is spinning, and you're considering some noble career alternative like farmer, firefighter, or carpenter, it's time to set up Dreamweaver to work with an application server and database.

You can configure your setup several ways. One involves using what Dreamweaver calls a *testing server*. Remember how you can create a website on your own computer (the *local site*) before posting it online for all to see (the *remote site*)? Here, the concept is similar. When you build web applications, it's a good idea to keep all your "work in progress" pages on your own computer, just as you did when you created static pages. After all, you don't want to fill up an online database with test data, or put half-finished product pages on the Internet. But because dynamic websites require an application server and a database, you need to set up a *testing server* to store and preview your dynamic pages-in-progress: a real web server, application server, and database—all running on your own computer.

Then, when you finished building your site, you transfer the pages to the remote site using Dreamweaver's built-in FTP feature (see Chapter 18). If you are working in a group setting, with other web developers, you can set up the testing server on a machine that's part of your group's local network. Each developer can then connect to the testing server and retrieve files to work on. (Using Dreamweaver's Check In/Check Out feature is a good idea when a group of people work on the same site.)

Note: You can always use your remote site as a testing server, as long as it has one of the application servers and databases that Dreamweaver works with. While this method is an easy way to get started, you must contact your web host to see what application server it uses, and whether it can handle databases. In addition, you should have a fast Internet connection to the server. Otherwise, testing your dynamic pages may just test your patience.

Finally, whenever you work on dynamic files directly on a remote server, be aware that mistakes you make along the way may affect a database that *other* dynamic pages use. If, while hurriedly trying to complete your website, you accidentally create a page that deletes records from your database, important information may no longer be available on your site. So whenever possible, keep your testing server separate from the server that stores your finished and perfected site.

In the next four chapters, you'll build a dynamic website using PHP and a MySQL database. The concepts you learn work for all of the other server models as well, although some of the details may be different. Significant differences among various server models are mentioned where applicable.

Setting Up a Testing Server

To get started with the tutorials in this section of the book, you need to install Apache, PHP, MySQL, and a database-administration tool called phpMyAdmin. Don't worry, it's a lot easier than it sounds. There are several simple installers available for both Windows and Macs that make this step a snap.

Windows

For Windows, WAMP is a good choice. WAMP is a simple installer for putting Apache, PHP, and MySQL on your computer. It's free and works on Windows XP, Windows Vista, and Windows 7. You can find the software at *www.wampserver.com/en/*. Because the software changes somewhat frequently, you'll find instructions online at *www.uptospeedguides.com/wamp* (temporarily disable your pop-up blocker) that match changes to the WAMP installer.

Macs

For the Mac, MAMP provides a simple way to get Apache, PHP, and MySQL up and running. MAMP is free and available from *www.mamp.info*. The MAMP software changes (as does the website) frequently, so make sure you get the most up-to-date directions at *www.uptospeedguides.com/mamp*.

If you plan to follow along with the tutorials in this section of the book, it's a good idea to download and install WAMP or MAMP now.

localhost and the htdocs Folder

If you followed the previous instructions and installed a testing server on your computer, you've already visited a web page at either *http://localhost/* or *http://localhost/MAMP* (the home pages for WAMP or MAMP). You may be wondering, what's this *localhost* thing? For a computer, "localhost" is just another way of saying "me." When you instruct a browser to go to *http://localhost*, you're merely telling it to look for a web server running on the same computer as the browser is. Normally, when you visit a website, you type a web address like *http://www.google.com/*. That sends your browser out over the Internet looking for a web page located on some computer identified as *www.google.com*. When you set up a web server on your own computer and want to view the Web pages you create there, your browser need look no further than your own computer.

But once the browser asks the local web server to give it a web page, where does the web server find that page on your computer? When you work with static Web pages (like the ones you built earlier in this book), you can keep your website files pretty much anywhere you want: on your desktop, in your Documents folder, on an external hard drive, and so on. Dynamic pages, on the other hand, work only with a web server, and must reside in a particular location on your computer in order for the server to find them.

That folder is called the *site root* folder (you may also hear it referred to as the *document root*). The exact name and location of the site root folder varies from system to system. For example, different web hosting companies have different setups, and might name the folder *htdocs, webdocs*, or *public_html*. WAMP uses a folder named *www* as the site root folder, while MAMP uses a folder named *htdocs*. For WAMP users, that folder is located in the *www* folder in your WAMP installation (*C:\WAMP\www*, for example); for MAMP folks, head over to Applications→MAMP→*htdocs*.

In the case of WAMP, if you type *http://localhost/my_page.html* into your browser, the browser requests a file named *my_page.html* from the web server running on your computer. The server then looks inside *C:\Program Files\WAMP\www* for a file named *my_page.html*; if it finds it, the server sends the file back to the browser. On a Mac running MAMP, the web server looks in Applications→MAMP→htdocs for the file *my_page.html*.

Note: If you don't specify a particular file—for example, you just surf to *http://localhost/*—the web server looks for a "default file" (usually named *index.html* or *index.php*), as described on page 640.

Remember, when you work on a dynamic, database-driven site, you need to keep your website files inside the site root folder of your testing server. If you don't, Dreamweaver doesn't let you start building database-driven pages.

Note: You can also put your site files in a folder *inside* the site root folder. If you placed a folder named *store* in the *www (WAMP) or htdocs (MAMP)* folder, you could visit a web page named *products.php* inside that folder by browsing to *http://localhost/store/products.php*.

In addition, as you start to build more dynamic sites, you might want to have separate names for each site. For example, you could put the site files for clientX in a folder named *clientX* inside the *www or htdocs* folder. Then you could test that client's web pages by typing *http://localhost/clientX/* into a browser. However, it's more elegant to have separate local sites for each client; that way, you can type something like *http://clientX/* into a web browser and your local web server would find the files just for that one client. To do this, you create what are called *virtualhosts* for each site. You can learn how to do that by following the instructions at *www.uptospeedguides.com/WAMP/virtualhosts* or *http://www.uptospeedguide.com/mamp/virtualhosts* (temporarily disable your pop-up blocker). MAMP users can also buy MAMP Pro ($60), which provides a simple program for creating and managing separate websites on the same server.

Setting Up Dreamweaver

To learn how to use Dreamweaver's dynamic features, you'll be building a small web application for the fictitious website CosmoFarmer.com (see Figure 23-3). In fact, you'll turn the site's online store into a group of dynamic web pages that retrieve information from a database and merge it with existing HTML code.

Before you begin building the page, download the tutorial files. As always, you can find them at *www.sawmac.com/dwCS5/*; click the Tutorials link to go to the tutorials page and download the files. If you did any of the previous tutorials, you already downloaded the necessary files. The files for this section of the book are inside the *php_dynamic* folder, which is inside the MM_DWCS5 folder. Inside the *php_dynamic* folder you'll find another folder named *cosmo_shop*, and a file named *cosmofarmer.sql*.

To begin, move the *cosmo_shop* folder into the newly installed web server's root folder. If you followed the previous directions, the root folder on Windows should be in *C:\WAMP\www*, while the root folder for Macs is in Applications→MAMP→*htdocs*. Place *cosmo_shop* inside the *www or htdocs* folder. To make sure you set this up right, open a browser, and then, in the address bar, type *http://localhost/cosmo_shop/*. If a web page appears, your server is set up correctly.

The first step in working on this dynamic web application is setting up a site. The process of setting up a dynamic site, as outlined in the following steps, is slightly different than that for a static site, but no harder:

1. **Start Dreamweaver, and then choose Site→New Site.**

   The Site Setup window opens (See Figure 23-4). First, you need to give this new site a name and tell Dreamweaver where it can find the site files.

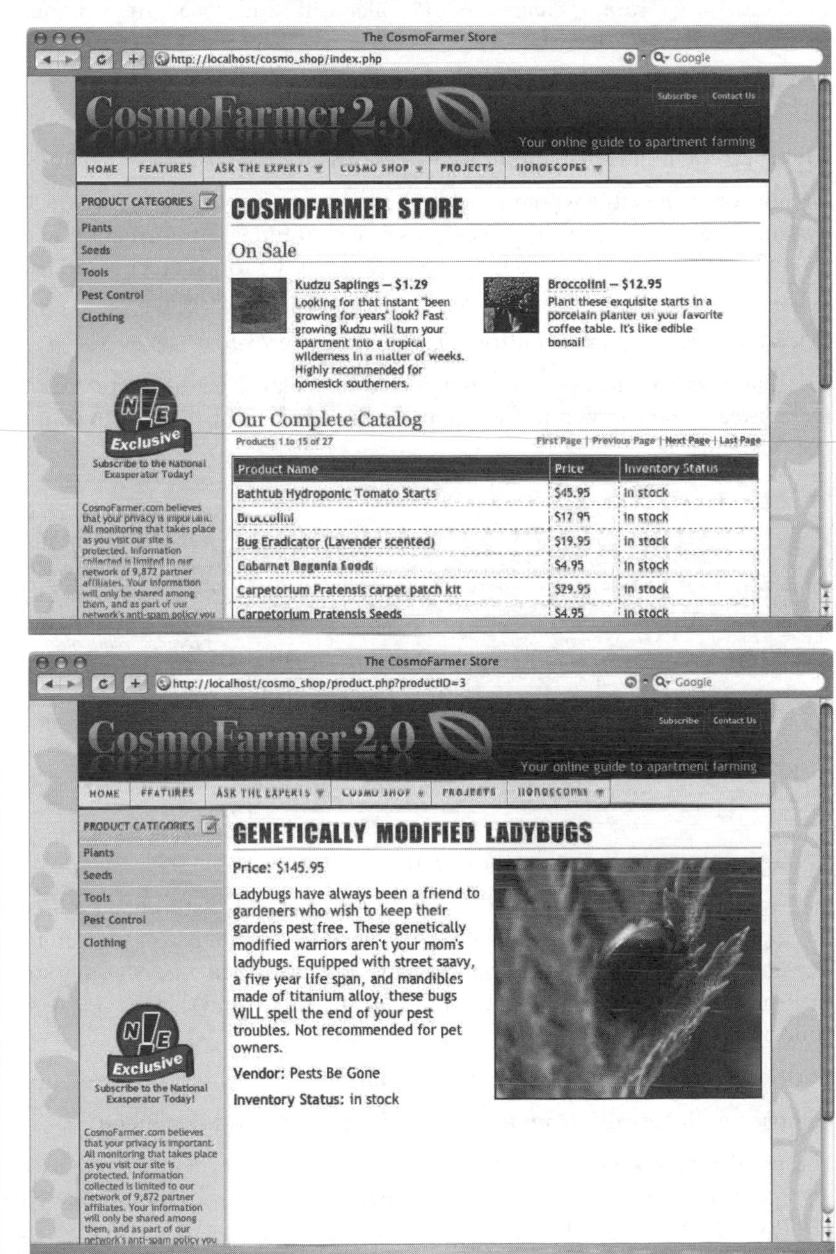

Figure 23-3: *Whenever you need to display lots of similar information, dynamic web pages may be the answer. Dynamic pages at the CosmoFarmer online store list many products. Because the site stores all the product information in a database, it takes only two dynamic pages to display a complete list of products (top), as well as detailed information for individual products (bottom).*

2. **Type *Cosmo Shop* in the first box. Click the folder at the right side of the middle of the window; navigate to and select the *cosmo_shop* folder on the testing server.**

   If you're following along using WAMP, you'll find the *cosmo_shop* folder at *C:\WAMP\www\cosmo_shop*; MAMP folks can find it at Applications→MAMP→*htdocs*→*cosmo_shop*.

   You just told Dreamweaver the name you want to use as well as selected the local site folder.

3. **Click Servers in the left-hand list of categories (see Figure 23-4).**

   Dreamweaver uses this screen to set up both remote and testing servers for the dynamic site. In other words, you use this screen to add FTP information so you can upload your site files to your live web server (as described on page 691), and you use this screen to tell Dreamweaver about your local testing server.

4. **Click the Add New Server button (circled in Figure 23-5).**

   The Basic server settings window appears (see Figure 23-6). Here, you tell Dreamweaver how to connect to your testing server and where it can find the files for your site.

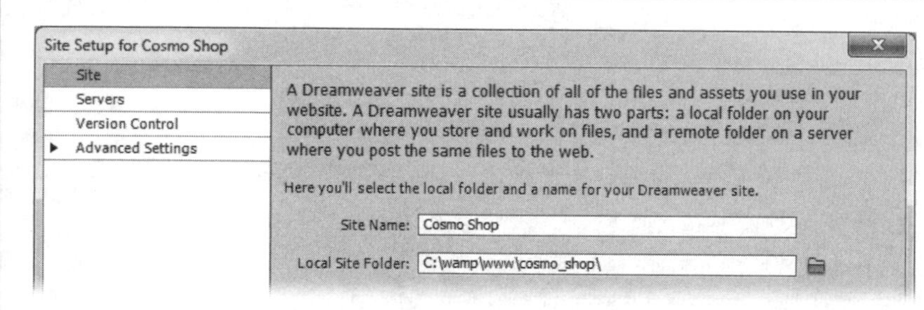

Figure 23-4: *Setting up a dynamic site starts the same way as setting up a regular, plain old HTML site: name the site and tell Dreamweaver where to find its files.*

5. **In the Server Name box, type local testing.**

   It doesn't really matter what you type here—the name is just to make it easier for you to identify the server in the Servers window (Figure 23-5). You can type any name that makes sense to you—in this case, you're using *local testing* since that makes clear that we're both adding a testing server and that it's "local" (on your own computer.)

   The next step tells Dreamweaver how to connect to the server.

6. **Choose Local/Network from the "Connect using" drop-down menu.**

   You use the same window to set up connections to both local and remote servers, so, even though you're setting up a local site, you'll see options like FTP, SFTP, WebDAV and RDS here (see page 691 for more on these). However, because you're working with a local testing server, choose Local/Network.

7. **Click the folder icon and select your local site folder (basically the same as step 2).**

   In other words, if you are using WAMP, select the *cosmo_shop* folder at *C:\WAMP\www\cosmo_shop*; if you use MAMP, select Applications→MAMP→*htdocs*→*cosmo_shop*. Next, you need to provide a web address to connect to your testing server.

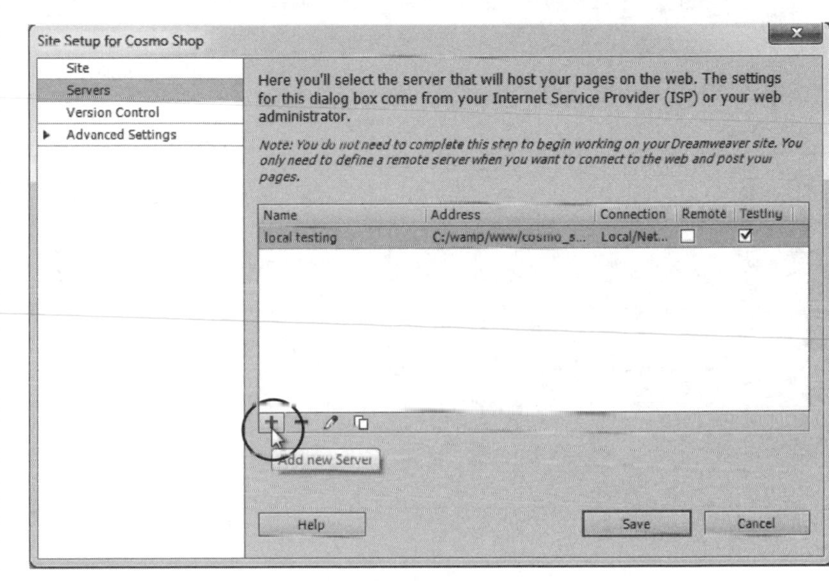

Figure 23-5: *Dreamweaver CS5 lets you add more than one server to a site, a crucial feature for testing dynamic sites. For example, to upload files to your site, you need a web server, and you have to tell Dreamweaver how to connect to it via FTP (this is discussed in Chapter 18). If you're building dynamic, database-driven pages, as you are in this section of the book, you also need a testing server, and you have to give Dreamweaver the connection details.*

8. **Type *http://localhost/cosmo_shop/* in the Web URL box.**

   Although Dreamweaver asks for a "Web URL," don't type in the address for your site out on the Web. Dynamic pages only work when you have a web server, and you just set up a server (a testing server) on your own computer. Therefore, you have to tell Dreamweaver to direct a web browser to your own, local testing server. Therefore, the URL you type in should point to your own computer and the cosmo_shop folder. That way, when you use Dreamweaver's File→Preview in Browser command, Dreamweaver opens a browser and tell it to load the page through the web server at *http://localhost/cosmo_shop/*.

   The Site Setup window should now look like Figure 23-6. Lastly, you'll tell Dreamweaver that you want to create PHP pages.

Note: If you run MAMP and can't change the port Apache uses as described in the MAMP setup instructions at *www.uptospeedguides.com/mamp/*, you need to add the port number 8888 to the URL, like this: *http://localhost:8888/cosmo_shop/*.

9. **Click the Advanced tab and choose PHP MySQL from the Server Model menu (see Figure 23-7).**

   This lets Dreamweaver know which types of pages you'll create.

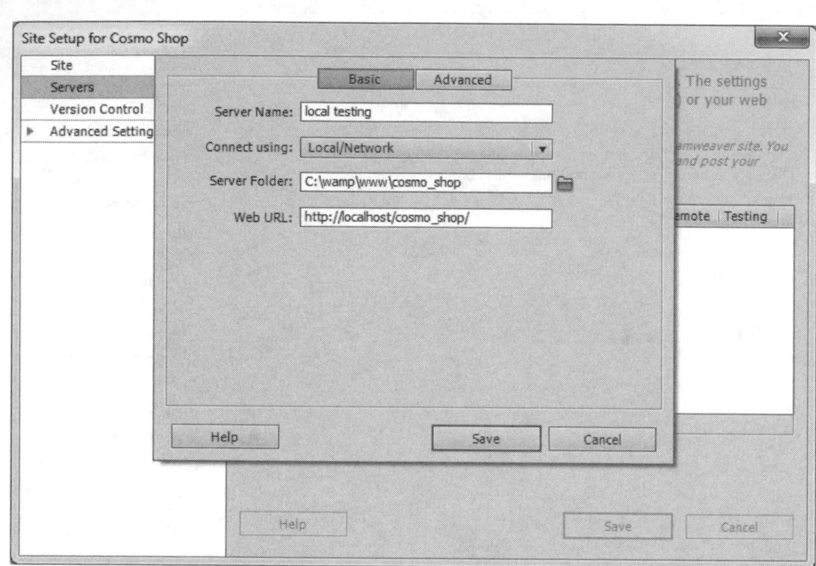

***Figure 23-6:** You want to test your dynamic site locally (on your own computer) before you upload your files to a live server on the Web. To do that, you need to tell Dreamweaver where to find the local testing server. Your setup window should look like this when you're done.*

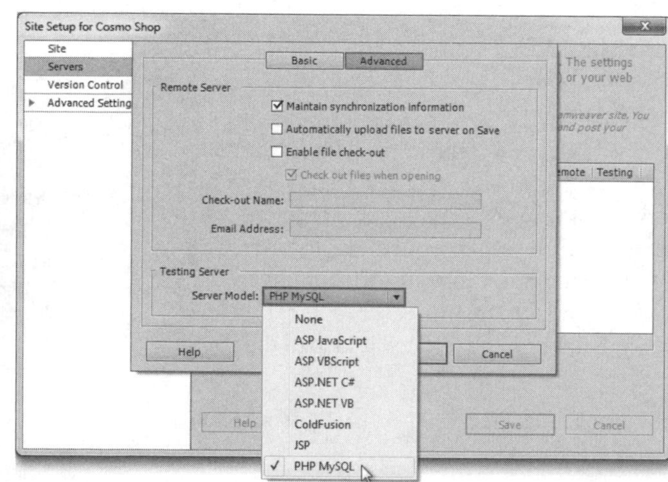

***Figure 23-7:** The Advanced server settings in the Site Setup window let you choose options related to your live web server on the Internet (a.k.a. "Remote server" options), and pick the server model you'll use when you build your pages. Although the list includes JSP, ASP.NET C#, ASP.NET VB, and ASP JavaScript, none of these models let you tap into Dreamweaver's easy-to-use server-side programming tools. The only effect these options have is when you build a new, blank web page—Dreamweaver creates a file with the correct file extension (.jsp, .aspx, for example), but that's about it.*

10. **Click the Save button. In the Site Setup window uncheck the "Remote" box and check the "Testing" box (see Figure 23-5).**

    This last step identifies this server as the testing server and, when Dreamweaver previews your pages in a browser, it will load the page from this server. You're just about done.

Note: If you forget to check the "Testing" box as described in step 10, Dreamweaver pops up an error message when you try to use the Preview in Browser command with a PHP page. Dreamweaver will tell you that you need to set up a testing server in order to preview the page and give you the option to go to the Site Setup window to add a testing server. If this happens, click Yes, and just check the Testing box, for the appropriate server.

---

11. **Click Save to save the new site.**

    Whew! That took a few steps, but you've now successfully set up your site for building and viewing dynamic pages. You're now ready to learn about databases, and set up a new database using the MySQL server.

Creating a Dynamic Page

Once you set up an application server and a database server, you're ready to connect to a database, retrieve information, and display it on a web page.

You already know how to handle the first step: Design an HTML page to display the database information. Dynamic pages differ from regular HTML pages in a couple ways. For starters, the name of a dynamic file doesn't end with .html. Depending on which server model you use, dynamic pages end in .php (for PHP pages), .asp (ASP), or .cfm or cfml (ColdFusion). The file extension you use is important: A web server uses it to identify the type of page requested. If a server gets a request for an .html file, it simply finds it and sends it to the web browser. But if it gets a request for a page that ends in, say, .php, it will send the page to the application server to sort out all the messy programming.

The good news is that the basic process of creating a new, blank, dynamic page is the same as with a regular HTML page:

- Choose File→New to open the New Document window. Select the Blank Page category; from the Page Type list, choose a dynamic page type (PHP, for example). From the Layout list, choose a layout (or none if you wish to start with a fresh, blank page), and then click the Create button.

  When you save the file, Dreamweaver automatically adds the proper extension: .asp for ASP pages, .cfm for ColdFusion, or .php for PHP pages.

Note: When you create a new page from the New Document window, Dreamweaver lets you select many different types of dynamic pages, including JSP, ASP.NET, and ASP JavaScript. However, only the PHP, ASP VBScript, and ColdFusion types work with Dreamweaver's built-in tools for automatically creating database-driven pages.

- Or, more simply, just right-click (Control-click) in the Site panel; choose New File from the shortcut menu.

  Dreamweaver creates a file in the correct server model format, with the proper extension.

Note: For ASP pages, just renaming a file in the Sites panel (from *about.html* to *about.asp*, for example) does *not* give the file the code necessary to apply the correct server model to the page. However, PHP and ColdFusion pages don't start life within any special code, so you could start with an .html page, change the extension to .php, and then add PHP programming. More importantly, changing the file's extension (from .asp to .php, for example) doesn't change the page to the new server model, either, and usually ends up "breaking" the page.

Once you created the page, you can use any of the page-building tools described in this book—Cascading Style Sheets, Spry Widgets, Library items, or whatever—to design the page. Even though the file's officially a PHP page (or ASP or ColdFusion), it still contains lots of HTML. Unlike a plain-vanilla HTML page, though, this one can also contain the server-side programming code that lets the page communicate with a database.

Finally, you can also edit your newly created page in Design view as well as Split view or Code view. But before you can add dynamic content to a page, you need to create a connection to a database.

Databases: A Quick Introduction

Simply put, databases store information. You encounter them every day in one way or another, whether searching Amazon.com for new books, or updating your Facebook profile.

A database is like an electronic filing cabinet that stores related information. At home, you might have a filing cabinet that stores the bits and pieces of your life: a folder labeled "Insurance," for example, in which you keep information about the various insurance policies you carry. Other folders might contain information on phone bills, car service records, and so on. Databases work more or less the same way, as the following sections explain.

Tables and Records

Databases use an electronic equivalent to filing folders: tables. A *table* is a container that holds information about a set of similar items. In the CosmoFarmer online store database, one table stores information on all the products the site sells, for example.

This Products table tracks certain information—the name of the product for sale, its price, a short description, and a few other items. The table stores each piece of information, like price, in a column. All the information for each product (all the columns taken together, in other words) makes up a single *record*, which the table stores in a row (see Figure 23-8).

Column

Row

productID	productName	price	description	vendorID	categoryID	image
1	Kudzu Saplings	1.29	Looking for...	1	1	kudzu.jpg
2	CosmoFarmer Tee	20.00	Celebrate...	4	5	cosmo_tee.jpg
3	Indoor Tractor	375.00	The ultimate...	2	3	tractor.jpg
4	Gotcha Cucaracha	2.95	Let this urban...	2	2	cockroach.jpg

Figure 23-8: *This diagram shows part of CosmoFarmer's Products table's structure, with information for four records. Each row in the table represents a single record, or item, while each piece of information for a record is stored in a single field, or cell.*

If you were designing a database, you'd try to model a table on some real-world item you needed to track. If you use a database to generate invoices for your business, for example, you might have a table called Invoices in which you store information such as the invoice number, date, amount owed, and so on. Since your customers are another source of data that needs tracking, you'd also create a table called Customers to store information about them.

Tip: If you're designing a database to track a business process that you already track on paper, a good place to start is with the paper forms you use. If your company uses a personnel form to collect information on each employee, you've got a ready-made database table. Each box on the form is the equivalent of a column in a table.

In addition to the Products table, CosmoFarmer also tracks the vendors who manufacture the products. (After all, after they run out of inventory, the staff will need to order more products from their vendors.) Because a product and a vendor are really two different things, the database has a *second* table, called Vendors, that lists all the companies that make the products that CosmoFarmer sells.

Note: Some databases are extremely picky about the names you give your tables and database columns (also called fields). For example, Microsoft Access databases won't let you name a column "Date."

You might think, "Hey, let's just put all that information into a single table." After all, you could consider the vendor's information part of the information for each product. Although it seems like this might simplify things (because you'd have one table instead of two), it can actually create a lot of problems.

Imagine a scenario where CosmoFarmer stores both product and vendor information in a single table: CosmoFarmer begins selling a hot new item, *Kudzu seeds*, that it gets from its vendor Seeds 'R' Us. All the product information, including the name and price of the plant, as well as the phone number and mailing address for Seeds 'R' Us, are stored in a single table row. Next month, Seeds 'R' Us offers another new product, Eucalyptus Saplings, as part of its Invasive Plant of the Month club. But, in the meantime, Seeds 'R' Us has moved locations and changed its phone number. So when someone at CosmoFarmer adds the new plant to the Products database, she adds the new phone number and address as part of the new plant's record.

Now the database contains *two* sets of contact information for Seeds 'R' Us—one for each plant. Not only does this redundant data take up extra space, but the contact information in one record is now wrong.

You could run into an even worse problem when you delete a record. Suppose that the online store decides to discontinue the two plants from Seeds 'R' Us. If a CosmoFarmer staffer removes those two records from the database, she also deletes any contact information for Seeds 'R' Us. If the *CosmoFarmer* staff ever decides to stock up on kudzu again, they have no way to contact the vendor.

So you can see why it's prudent to keep separate classes of information in different tables. With two tables, when Seeds 'R' Us moves, you have to update only the information in the Vendors table, without touching the Products table at all. This way, if the staff deletes a product, they still have a way to contact the vendor to learn about new products.

You may wonder, with a setup like this, how to tell which vendor makes which product. All you have are two distinct tables—one with just product information and one with just vendor information. How do you know which vendor is connected to which product?

Note: For a great book on database design, check out *Database Design for Mere Mortals* (Addison-Wesley Professional) by Michael J. Hernandez. For a concise, online introduction to database design, visit *www.geekgirls.com/databases_from_scratch_1.htm*.

Relational Databases

To connect information between tables, you create a *relationship* between them. In fact, databases that use multiple related tables are called *relational databases*.

The most common way to connect tables is by using what's called a *primary key*—a serial number or some other unique identifying flag for each record in the table. In the case of the *CosmoFarmer* database, the Products table includes a field named *productID*, each product's identification number (see Figure 23-9). When the staff adds a product to the database, it gets a new number (usually issued by the database server itself). But you can assign numbers as well. For example, if you build a database that contains a table about employees, you might use each employee's Social Security number as a primary key, or an internal employee ID number based on your company's own cryptic method of identifying employees.

Products table

Primary key — Foreign key

productID	productName	price	description	vendorID	categoryID	image
1	Kudzu Saplings	1.29	Looking for...	1	1	kudzu.jpg
2	CosmoFarmer Tee	20.00	Celebrate...	4	5	cosmo_tee.jpg
3	Indoor Tractor	375.00	The ultimate...	2	3	tractor.jpg
4	Gotcha Cucaracha	2.95	Let this urban...	2	2	cockroach.jpg

Vendors table

Primary key

vendorID	vendorName	vendorStreet	vendorCity	vendorState	vendorZip	vendorPhone
1	Seeds 'R Us	8538 5th Ave.	New York	NV	89173	702-555-1212
2	Gap Plants	237 5th St	New York	NY	21222	212-555-1232
3	Burpee	4578 A St	Portland	OR	97213	503-555-2983
4	John Dear	9900 C Ave	Wilmington	OH	88437	706-555-9348

Figure 23-9: *Each table in your database should have a primary key—a column that contains a unique identifier for each record in a table. To relate information from one table to another, people often add an additional column with information pertaining to another table. In this case, a column called vendorID in the Products table contains a primary key from the Vendors table. To determine which vendor distributes, say, the Gotcha Cucarache, look at the fifth column in the Products table, which identifies the vendor's ID number as 2. When you check the Vendors table, you see that vendor 2 is Gap Plants. A column that contains the primary key of another table is called a" foreign key."*

The Vendors table has a primary key named, not so creatively, *vendorID*. Whenever a staffer adds a vendor to the database, the database assigns the vendor a primary key.

To join these two tables, you'd add another column called vendorID to the Products table (see Figure 23-9). Instead of storing *all* the contact information for a vendor within the Products table, you simply store the vendor's ID number. To find out which vendor makes which product, you can look up the product in the Products table, find the vendor's ID number in the vendorID column, and use *that* information to look up the vendor in the Vendors table.

While this hopscotch approach of accessing database tables is a bit confusing at first, it has many benefits. Not only does it prevent the kinds of errors mentioned earlier, it also simplifies the process of adding a new product from a vendor. When Seeds 'R' Us adds a third plant to their collection, a store staff person determines whether any of Seeds 'R' Us' info has changed (by checking it against the Vendors table). If not, she simply adds the information for the new product, and leaves the vendor's contact info untouched. Thus, relational databases not only prevent errors, they also make data entry faster.

Databases, of course, can be much more complicated than this simple example. It can take many tables to accurately hold the data needed to run a complex e-commerce site such as Amazon.com. In some cases, you may already be working with a previously created database, so you won't have to worry about creating one or even learning more than what's described above. For the tutorials in this section of the book, you'll use the already created CosmoFarmer database.

Loading a Database

To continue with the tutorial, you need to install the data for the CosmoFarmer store in your new MySQL server. That process requires a few steps. First you'll create a new database; next, you'll load the data into this new database; finally, you'll create a new *user* for the database (a special account that you'll use to access and update the database). The following steps lead you through everything.

1. **In any Web browser, type *http://localhost/phpmyadmin on Windows*. (On a Mac, type *http://localhost/MAMP*), and then click the phpMyAdmin button.**

   This opens the phpMyAdmin home page. phpMyAdmin is a web-based tool (written in PHP) that lets you easily manage MySQL databases.

Tip: If you're using WAMP, you'll find a menu in the right side of your Windows taskbar at the bottom of the screen. From this menu you can select phpMyAdmin to open a Web browser to start using phpMyAdmin. This menu also lets you stop and start the servers, as well as providing a quick shortcut to C:\WAMP\www–the local root folder for the web server.

---

2. **In the "Create new database" box, type *cosmofarmer* and then press the Create button (see Figure 23-10).**

   This step actually creates a new database on the MySQL server. In addition, it takes you to a new page that includes a row of buttons for working with the new database.

   Next, you'll load a SQL file that creates the required tables, and adds the actual data to the database. →SQL" stands for Structured Query Language, and it's the language you use to communicate with databases: to read, edit, update, and generally manipulate the structure and information in a database. You'll learn more about how to use SQL on page 870.

3. **In phpMyAdmin's top navigation bar, click the Import button.**

   Doing so takes you to a page that lets you type in a SQL query or load a text file that has SQL commands in it. You'll do the latter—load a text file that contains all the SQL necessary to create the tables and data for the database.

4. **Click the Browse button in WAMP or the Choose File button in MAMP (circled in Figure 23-11). In the File Upload window that appears, navigate to and select the file *cosmofarmer.sql* in the *php_dynamic* folder you downloaded with the tutorial files.**

   As explained in the previous step, this file contains all the goodies that will appear in your database.

5. **Click the Go button (Figure 23-11, lower-right corner).**

   The MySQL server slurps down the SQL file, and executes the instructions found within it. The result? Four new tables (see the list of tables that just appeared on the left side of the phpMyAdmin window), and a bunch of data added to them. Your last step in prepping the database: Create a new MySQL user that has permission to add to and update the CosmoFarmer database.

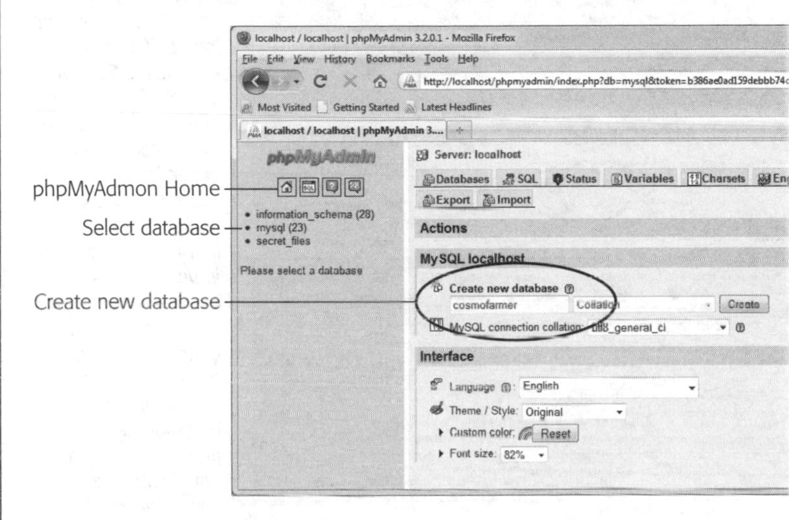

Figure 23-10: *The phpMyAdmin main page. Here, you can create a new database, select an already created database to work with, and handle many administrative tasks for MySQL.*

6. **Click the Privileges link in the top row of phpMyAdmin navigation buttons (see Figure 23-11).**

   This step opens a page listing all users who have access to the CosmoFarmer database. In this case, the only user listed is the *root* user. The root user has total control of your database, and you should never use it in any of your PHP programming. Instead, you should create a new user who only has access to this one database.

7. **Click the "Add a new user" link.**

   The link appears under the list of current users. Clicking it opens the →Add a new User" page (see Figure 23-12).

8. **Type *cosmo* for the user name and choose *local* from the Host menu. In the password field, type *cosmo*, and in the re-type box, type *cosmo* again. The screen should look like Figure 23-12).**

   This step creates a user whose name is *cosmo*, whose password is *cosmo*, and who can access the database only locally from the server. This means someone out on the Internet can't try to log in to your MySQL server using the cosmo account; only local access—for example, PHP pages run on the same computer—is allowed.

In general, it's a bad idea to make a password the same as a user name (as in this example), or to use any word that you can find in a dictionary, since it doesn't take much imagination for a hacker to figure this out and suddenly gain control of your database. But for this example application, it's best to keep things simple so you can quickly get to the more interesting stuff (actually using Dreamweaver, for instance!).

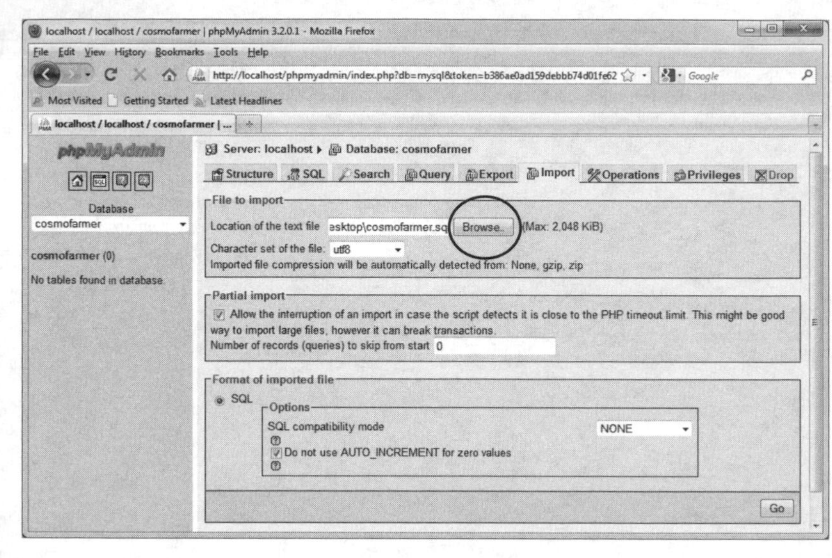

Figure 23-11: *phpMyAdmin lets you load a SQL file, and execute the SQL code inside it. Translation: phpMyAdmin talks to the database server and tells it to create tables and fields, and add data to them. phpMyAdmin's import feature is a great way to replicate data from another database. In addition, you can get data out of your database by exporting all the tables and data from any database to which phpMyAdmin has access.*

9. **Scroll to the bottom of the page, and then, in the lower-right corner, click the Go button.**

   phpMyAdmin creates a new user, cosmo, and takes you to another web page so you can tweak that user's privileges. In MySQL, you can limit which users have access to which databases, and how much power they have to work with those databases. You could give a user the ability to read, update, and add data to a database, but prevent him from changing the structure of the database by adding or deleting tables, for example. At this point, the cosmo user has access just to the CosmoFarmer database—exactly what you want here. The last step is to reload the privileges so that MySQL recognizes the new user.

10. **Click the Privileges button once again, then scroll down to the bottom of the page. Click the "reload the privileges" link (circled in Figure 23-13).**

    This step takes you back to the user's page. A "the privileges were reloaded successfully" message should appear inside a green box.

    All right, let's take stock of what you've done: set up a database, added data, and created a new user. Wow. That was a lot of work, and you barely touched Dreamweaver in this tutorial. Don't worry, all the hard work is behind you. Now it's time to use Dreamweaver to build your site.

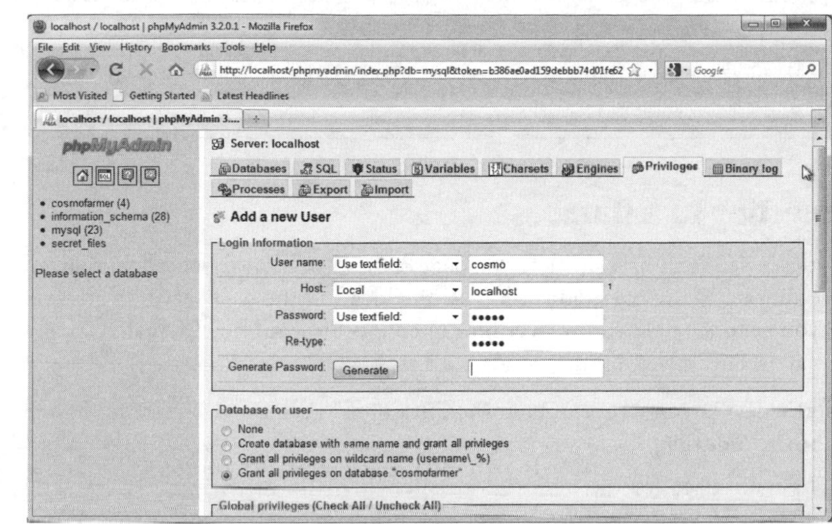

Figure 23-12: *To create a new database user, just supply a name, choose where the user can access the database from (usually localhost), and then type a password.*

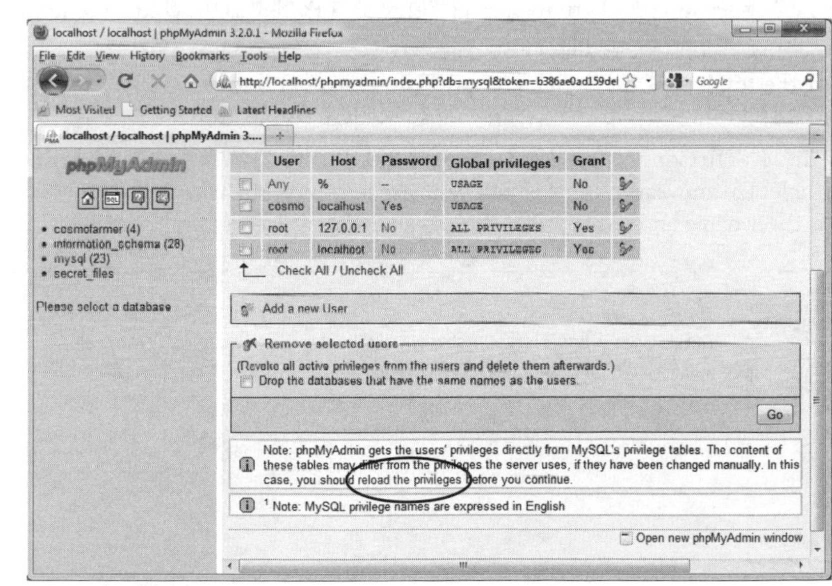

Figure 23-13: *When you add users to the MySQL server, they don't actually have any power until you "reload the privileges," which basically just reloads MySQL. Don't forget this step: if you do, you'll never be able to connect to the database with that user name and password.*

Note: In many cases, when you set up an account with a web hosting company, they supply you with an already-created database and user account. Frequently, the database is named after your domain name or your account name. When setting up MySQL on your machine as part of your testing environment, you should use the same user name and database name supplied by your hosting company. That way, when you perfect your site on the testing server, you can simply transfer it to your web host's server and the database connections should work perfectly.

Connecting to a Database

You already defined a new site (back on page 838), so Dreamweaver knows that you'll be working on PHP pages, and it knows the location the web server's root folder. Now, you need to tell Dreamweaver how to connect to your newly created database. Fortunately, Dreamweaver makes this a snap.

1. **Return to Dreamweaver. From the Files Panel (Window® Files), double-click the file *index.php*.**

   The main page for the online store opens. This is a dynamic PHP page; you must have a PHP page (or ASP or ColdFusion, depending on your server model) open in order to connect Dreamweaver to a database.

2. **Open the Databases panel by choosing Window→Databases.**

   The Application panel group opens (Figure 23-14). This is the control center for building dynamic web pages.

3. **At the top left of the panel, click the plus sign (+) button (circled in Figure 23-14). From the pop-up menu, choose MySQL connection.**

   The MySQL Connection window opens (see Figure 23-15). In this dialog box, you let Dreamweaver know which database to connect to, where it's located, and the user name and password of the account that can access the database.

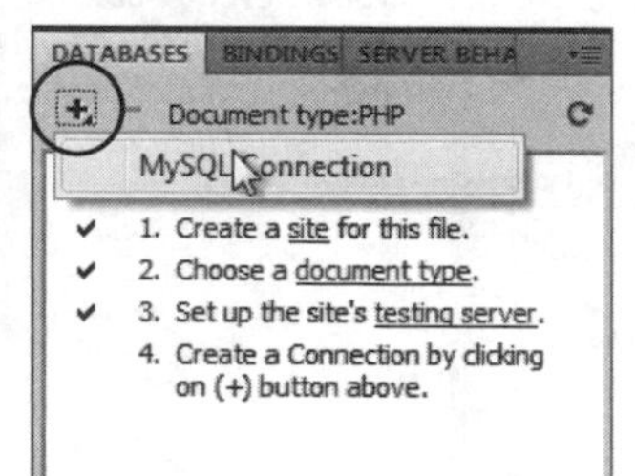

Figure 23-14: *The databases panel lets you connect to databases, and will display the tables and field names of any you already connect to.*

4. **In the "Connection name" box, type *connCosmo*.**

   You can use any name you want as long as it doesn't start with a number and doesn't contain any characters other than letters, numbers, and the underscore character. In this case, *conn* is a helpful indicator that this is a database connection, and makes identifying it easier if you ever need to look into the underlying code of the page.

   Next, you tell Dreamweaver where to find the database.

5. **In the MySQL server box, type *localhost*.**

   In this case, you set up both the web server and MySQL server on the same computer (namely, yours). So when you run a dynamic page on the testing server that tries to connect to the MySQL database, the application server needs to look only on the same computer—"localhost"—to find the database.

   In many cases, the MySQL server your web hosting company provides is also located on your remote web server, so when you start building "real" PHP pages to put up on your own site, you can use *localhost* when you create the connection on your remote server. This attribute is helpful, because it means you can develop your sites locally on your computer, move them onto the Internet, and they should be able to connect to the database without you having to go in and edit any settings.

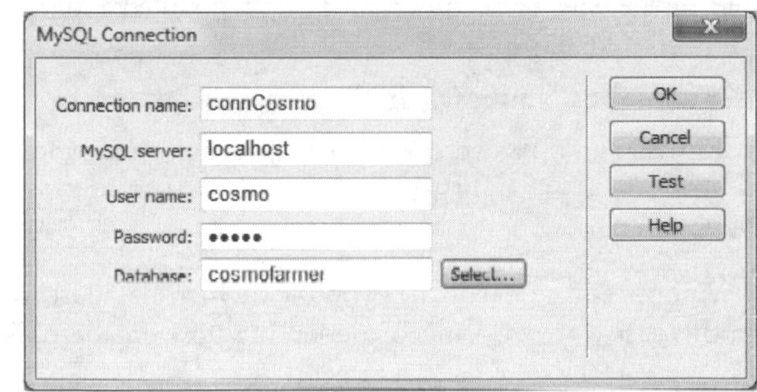

Figure 23-15: *Setting up a Dreamweaver-to-MySQL-database connection requires just a few easy steps.*

   However, some web hosts put their databases on separate machines, ones dedicated to the task of managing databases. If that's true for you, the database connection you set up on your local computer won't work when you upload files to your web server. You need to edit the database connection information, replacing *localhost*, which works for development and testing on your own computer, with the address of the your web host's MySQL server—which might be something like *mysql.webhost.com* or even a basic IP address like *192.168.1.2* (don't use *http://*, or anything besides the server's address in either case). Your Web hosting company can supply the connection information.

Unfortunately, this means that when you upload your dynamic site to the remote server, you need to change the connection file that Dreamweaver creates so that it points to your host's MySQL server (instead of your own, local MySQL server). Here's how you do that: Before you upload your site, open the connection file. You do that either from the Databases panel (double-click the connection name—*connCosmo* in this case—to open the connection file, or look in a folder named *Connections* in the local root folder of your site. In that folder, you'll find a file named after the connection name you supplied when you created the connection in step 4 above—that's *connCosmo.php* in this tutorial. Double-click this file, and then change *localhost* to your web host's MySQL server address (see the paragraph above for examples). Then upload this file to your site (see page 702 for information on uploading web files).

You can then open the connection file again, and then change the database address back to *localhost* so you can continue to work and test on your local computer (just make sure you don't upload this file to your web server, or you'll wipe out the connection file you customized for the remote server, and your dynamic pages won't be able to connect to the database).

This all assumes, of course, that the database and user name you set up on your testing server is the same as the one you use at your web hosting company (see the note on page 852). If not, you need to change the user name and password in the connection file, too, before you transfer it to your web server.

Okay, with all *that* out of the way, back to our regularly scheduled programming: the MySQL Connection dialog box.

6. **Type *cosmo* in the user name box, and *cosmo* in the password box.**

   This is the MySQL user name and password you created earlier, when you set up the database.

7. **Click the Select button.**

   The Select Database window appears. This lets you pick which database you wish to connect to. In this case it's the CosmoFarmer online store database.

   If you get an error instead, check that you spelled *localhost* correctly, and that you supplied the right user name and password.

8. **Select *cosmofarmer*, and then click OK.**

   The dialog box closes, and *cosmofarmer* appears in the Database box at the bottom of the window. Click the Test button.

   A window saying "Connection was made successfully" should appear.

9. **Click OK to close the window that appeared when you tested the connection; click OK once more to close the MySQL Connection box.**

   Behind the scenes, Dreamweaver creates a small PHP file and stores it in a folder called Connections in your site's root folder. Whenever you create a dynamic page that communicates with a database, Dreamweaver adds a line of code pointing to this connection file. (The file's name reflects the connection name you typed in step 4—here it's *connCosmo.php*.)

Warning: Don't delete the Connections folder. It holds a script that lets your pages connect to your database. If, while cleaning your site, you throw this folder away, you'll break the database connection for all your site's dynamic pages. If this happens, recreate the connection by following steps 3–9.

Exploring the Databases Panel

The Databases panel (Figure 23-16) lets you do more than just connect databases to your site. It also lets you explore a database's structure and data. Of the three items—Stored Procedures, Tables, and Views—only the Tables option actually does anything with MySQL.

By clicking the + sign button (flippy triangle on Macs) next to Tables, you'll see a list of all the tables in the database. Expanding a table displays all the columns for that table.

The Views and Stored procedures options are always empty, but if you're curious, a view is a selection of information in the database—a slice of its data. Think of a view as a saved search. Only MySQL version 5 and later supports this feature, and on top of that if you do create a view in MySQL, it will actually appear as a table under the list of Tables. Although MySQL 5 lets you create stored procedures (programs that access and manipulate information in the database), Dreamweaver doesn't recognize or display them.

Tip: To get a quick peek at the data in a database table, in the Databases panel, right-click (Control-click) the table's name. From the shortcut menu, choose View Data. A window appears, displaying a table of data extracted directly from da2316.tiff

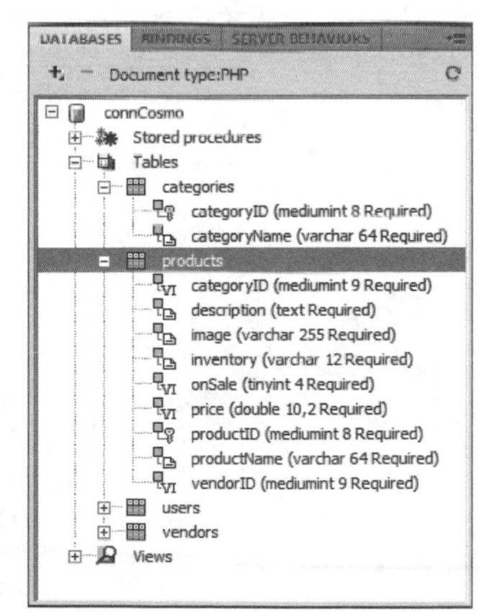

Figure 23-16:
Along with the Databases panel, both the Bindings and the Server Behavior panels provide a quick way to work with dynamic database-driven websites.

In this chapter, you've laid the foundation for a dynamic website. In the next chapter, you'll start adding data from a database to the page you created in the preceding tutorial—and building a real, dynamic web application.

FREQUENTLY ASKED QUESTION

Parenthetical Puzzler

In the Databases panel, I see some weird information in parentheses next to the column names–mediumint 8 Required, *for example. What's that about?*

You're right–there's a notation next to each column name. For example, Figure 23-16 shows a column called *categoryID*, which is followed by (*mediumint 8 Required*).

The information in parentheses denotes the *type* of data in that column. In this instance, it's an *integer* (a whole number like 1, 3, or 5), it's *8* bytes of data long (meaning it can be a very, very large number), and it's *required* (meaning that every new record *must* have a value stored in this field). Within each of these categories, you might see subtypes like timestamp, decimal number, and so on. Different databases recognize different data types, so there's a long list of possible data types for all the server models Dreamweaver supports.

These notations may appear cryptic, but they can come in handy. For example, if you create a form to update or insert a record in a database (as described in Chapter 25), the data type and length can help you figure out what kind of information you're looking for and how long it could be, and help you when you add Spry Validation to your form (as described on page 478).

The categoryName column pictured in Figure 23-16 contains text (that's what "varchar" stands for) and is 64 characters long. It's also "required," meaning you can't add a record to the categories table and leave the categoryName field empty. So if you create a form to add records to this table, you want to create a required text field that accepts at most 64 characters (you learned how to do this back on page 464).

CHAPTER

24

Adding Dynamic Data to Your Pages

A database is different from a mere pile of facts because it can selectively retrieve information. After all, when you visit Amazon.com, you don't want to see every single book and product they sell. You probably just want to see a list of books on a certain subject or by a particular author, and then view more detail about the books that pique your interest.

This chapter shows you how to use Dreamweaver to display database information on your Web pages. Because these concepts can be tricky, you may prefer to get some hands-on experience by completing the tutorial on page 902 before reading the rest of the chapter.

Retrieving Information

Since databases can contain lots of information, you need a way to find just the data you want to display on a particular web page. Even though your company keeps information about its products, customers, suppliers, and so on in one database, you may want to see only, say, an alphabetical list of your customers. After grabbing that list, you might want to display a particular customer's contact information, or perhaps the list of products that person bought.

Understanding Recordsets

To retrieve specific information from a database, you start by creating what's called a *recordset*. A recordset—also called a *database query*—is a command you send to a database asking for particular information: "Hey Database, show me all the customers listed in the Customers table." Executing commands like this is the heart of many database operations you'll ask Dreamweaver to perform (and a piece of jargon you can't escape in the dynamic web page business).

Recordsets let you retrieve specified columns in a database. They can also sort their results alphabetically or in numerical order, so you can, for example, view a list of products from least expensive to most expensive. In addition, a recordset can zero in on a specific record based on information a visitor submits to the site or on information that comes packaged as part of a URL. In essence, recordsets let you winnow down massive amounts of database information in a fraction of a second—a powerful benefit, indeed.

Creating Recordsets

Database queries can range from quite simple to extremely complex. Dreamweaver provides tools to get novice database developers up and running quickly, while supplying the necessary technology to create more advanced recordsets. Whatever your level of expertise, you start by opening (or creating) a web page on which you want to display database information; then you open the Recordset dialog box using one of the following methods (each of which assumes you've set up a server model, as described in Chapter 23):

- In the Data category of the Insert panel, click the Recordset button (see Figure 24-1).
- Choose Insert→Data Objects→Recordset.
- On either the Bindings or Server Behaviors panels, click the + sign button (skip ahead to Figure 24-9 for a screen shot), and then, from the menu that appears, select Recordset.

Whichever technique you choose, the Recordset dialog box opens (Figure 24-2). It lets you create a database query (a.k.a. a recordset), and gives you both simple and advanced modes of operation.

To create a simple query, make sure you're in the *Simple* mode. (If a button labeled Simple appears at the right edge of the dialog box, click it to make it say Advanced. Now you're in Simple mode.)

1. **In the Name field, type a name for the recordset.**

   You can use any name you want, as long as it doesn't start with a number, and doesn't contain any characters other than letters, numbers, and underscores (_).

Tip: People often begin database query names with *rs (rsProducts*, for example). The *rs* helps you identify a recordset if you work in Code view.

---

2. **From the Connection menu, select a database connection.**

   The menu lists all the database connections you defined for the site. If you haven't yet created a connection, do so now by clicking Define and following the instructions on page 852.

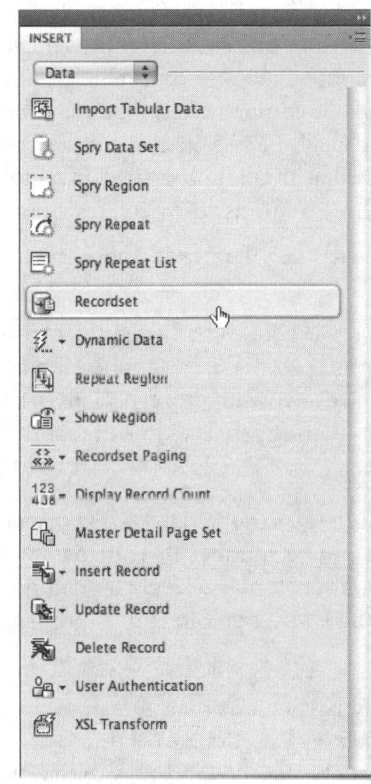

Figure 24-1:
The Insert panel's Data category gives you one-click access to many powerful "application objects," which automate common dynamic-web-page-building tasks. Actually, the first five buttons don't require dynamic web pages: The first lets you import data from a text file and creates a table from it in your document (described on page 280), while the next four are Spry Data objects (seepage 544). (You'll learn about the Data category's Insert, Update, and Delete Records buttons in the next chapter, the User Authentication features in Chapter 26, and XSL Transformation, the last option, in Chapter 27.)

Note: You have to have your testing server running to create a recordset—in other words, in addition to setting up a dynamic site in Dreamweaver, you must have WAMP (page 836) or MAMP (page 837) running so that Dreamweaver can "see" the database tables to create a recordset.

---

3. **From the Table menu, select the table that'll supply the data.**

   Relational databases usually store information in different tables, each of which holds a particular type of information, such as customer data or product data. For example, to get a list of products from the CosmoFarmer database, you'd select the Products table. Choose that table from the drop-down list now.

Note: To retrieve data from more than one table at a time, you need to create an *advanced* recordset (see page 870).

4. **To select columns from which you want to extract data, click the All or Selected button. If you choose Selected, then click the columns whose data you want to import.**

   By default, Dreamweaver highlights the All button, but you may not want the data from *all* the columns in your table. For example, suppose your table contains lots of detailed information for each product your company sells. You may want to create a basic product listing that simply displays names, prices, and descriptions. For this list, you don't need all the details, like SKU number, sizes, inventory status, and so on. Therefore, you'd select the three columns you're interested in.

   To select multiple columns, Ctrl-click (⌘-click) their names in the Recordset dialog box's list.

   It's always best to limit your recordset to just those columns whose information you need. The more data you retrieve, the more you make the application and database servers work, and the more you slow down your site, especially when the database is large and the recordset you're creating retrieves lots of records.

5. **Choose a Filter option, if you like.**

   In many cases, you don't want to retrieve *every* record in a table. For example, if you're looking for a particular customer's phone number in your database, you don't want the details on every one of your customers. *Filters* let you limit the records a recordset retrieves. (Details on how to set up filters in a moment.)

6. **Choose a Sort option, if desired.**

   Data from a database may not appear in any particular order. Dreamweaver's Sort options let you arrange information based on a particular column. For example, you might create a recordset that gathers the title and release date for every CD you own, sorted in alphabetical order by album title, or chronologically by release date.

   To sort database records, from the first Sort menu, choose a column to sort by (Figure 24-2). Then select the sort order: either Ascending (A–Z, 0–10, earliest to latest) or Descending (Z–A, 10–0, latest to earliest).

   The Simple recordset mode lets you sort by one column only. To continue with the previous example, that means that if you want to sort records by date (so your most recent CDs appear first), and then by name (so CDs with the same date are *then* listed in alphabetical order), you have to use the Advanced mode (see page 870).

   To view the results of the recordset, click Test to open the Test SQL Statement window, which contains all records that match that query. If more than 25 matches exist, you can see the next group of results by clicking Next 25 at the bottom of the window. When you finish looking at the test results, click OK to return to the Recordset window.

If the test results look right, click OK to close the Recordset window, and then add the code into the currently opened page.

Note: Unlike a database connection, which Dreamweaver lists in the Databases panel and makes available to every page on the site, a recordset is specific to a particular page. (See page 876 to learn how to reuse recordsets on other pages.)

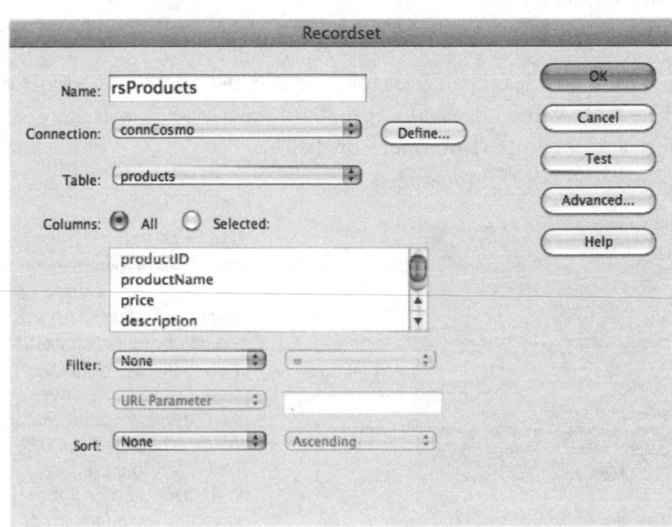

Figure 24-2: *The Recordset window lets you retrieve data from a database. The Simple window (pictured here) lets beginners search and sort databases for specific information. Advanced options (accessed by clicking the Advanced button) let seasoned database programmers create more complex database queries as described on page 870.*

Filtering Information

Although you may select a limited number of columns when you create a basic recordset, the final results of the recordset still include *all* the records within the table. That's fine when you want a list of all the items in a database, like when you create a list of all your company's products. But it's not so useful when you want a particular subset of those records, like a list of just the red toupees your company sells, or when you want details on a *single* record—the "Flaming Inferno 78B toupee," for example.

To have Dreamweaver cull *specific* records from a table, use the Filter option in the Recordset window (see Figure 24-3). A *filter* compares the information in one database column with a particular value, and then selects records that match—in other words, it searches through the database for particular records. Suppose, for example, that your toupee products database table contains a column named *price* that contains a product's price. To find all the toupees that cost less than $35, you create a filter that looks for all records where the price column holds a value of less than 35.

It only takes a few steps to set up a filter:

1. **Create a recordset as described on page 858.**

   To create a filter, you must fill out the Recordset window's Filter options' four form fields—three menus and one text field.

2. **From the first Filter menu, select a column name.**

   Dreamweaver will compare the entries in this column to a particular value. In the previous example, you'd select "price" from the menu to indicate the table's price column (see Figure 24-3).

3. **From the next menu, choose a comparison operator (=, < or >, for example).**

   To find products that cost less than $35, for example, use the < (less than) operator. To find an exact value (all products that are exactly $35), use the = sign. You'll learn more about comparison operators below.

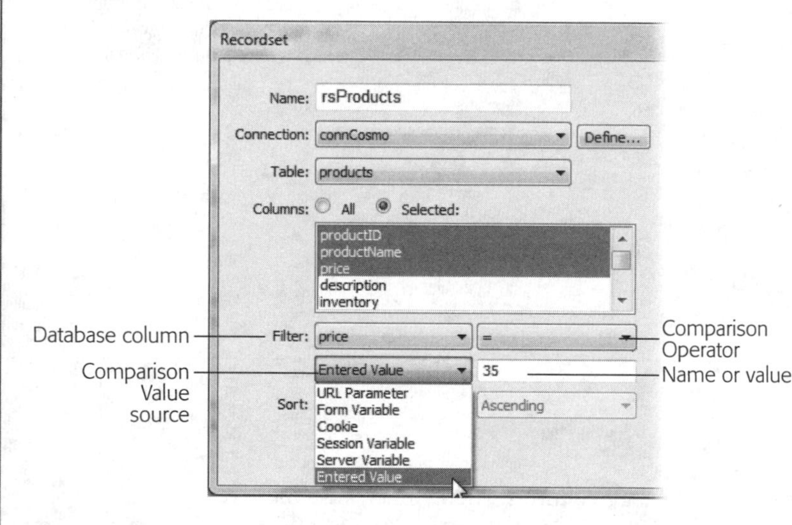

Figure 24-3: *Use a filter to identify and retrieve data for a single record or collection of records in a database. Dreamweaver gives you several ways to apply filters. The three most common are: filter criteria embedded in a URL (click a link to a product on Amazon's home page and you'll see a long list of cryptic characters tacked onto the end of the URL); via a form a visitor submits to your site; or simply based on a value you type into the recordset window. (You'll find out about three other, more advanced filter options–cookies, session variables, and server variables–on page 981.)*

4. **Using the third Filter pop-up menu, select a source for the comparison value.**

   A filter compares the information in a table column against some other value. It can get that value from many sources. For example, a page that lists the details for a single product.

   If you built a Search page for the Chia Vet site, you'd create a form that lets visitors type in a search term, and then click a Search button. In this case, the comparison value would come from a form. To set up this kind of filter, you, the designer, would select Form Variable from this menu.

For complete information on selecting the source for a comparison value, see the section "Getting Comparison Values" on page 864.

Note: Sometimes, you must choose URL Parameter, even when the filter receives information from a form. As discussed on page 458, a form's *method* property determines how a web browser submits information to a web server. The *Get* method puts the form information in the URL. It's a common choice for search forms, since a search often produce results that you'd like to bookmark. If you assign the *Get* method to the form, then choose URL Parameter for the filter; if the form uses the second method, *Post*, then choose Form variable.

5. **Type a name or value into the lower-right Filter box.**

   The value you enter in this field depends on the source you selected in the last step; type in the name of the form variable, cookie, session variable, or whatever. The one exception: If you selected Entered Value in the previous step, then type a specific value into this field. For instance, if you want to find items that cost $35, select Entered Value here, and then, in the next field, type *35*. The Recordset window then looks like Figure 24-3.

6. **Complete the Recordset window by choosing a sort option (if desired), and then clicking OK.**

   You can test the recordset and filter by clicking Test. If you selected anything other than Entered Value from the source menu, a message prompts you to type in a test value for the source—URL parameter, form variable, and so on.

Comparison Operators for Filters

Dreamweaver gives you many ways to compare information in a database column with a value from another source, such as a form, cookie, or simply a value you type into the Recordset window. The *type* of comparison you choose depends on whether you want to compare text or numbers.

Comparing text values

You'll often want to create recordsets that find database matches to particular words. For example, a recordset could filter a list of products to find only those whose descriptions contain the word "green," or you could filter a database of clients to search for a record for "Craig McCord."

Dreamweaver provides the following types of text comparisons:

- **Equality.** To check whether the information in a column is *exactly* the same as another value, select the = sign from the comparison menu.
- **Inequality.** To find records that match everything *but* a particular piece of text, select the <> (doesn't match) operator from the menu. Use this to, say, search a database of clothing for items that do *not* match a particular phrase (like "winter" in the Season column).

- **Begins With, Ends With, and Contains.** The last three comparison operators are ideal for locating one or more words within text. For example, a database of movies might have a column containing a short review of each movie. To locate reviews that include the words "horrible acting," you could choose the Contains option, which finds any movie that includes the phrase "horrible acting" anywhere in its review.

  The Begins With and Ends With options are more selective. The former finds records only when the text matches the very beginning of a particular record; the latter works only when the text appears at the end. You probably won't use these options very often, but they come in handy if you want to search a database for people whose names are Bob or Bobby, but not Joe-Bob. In this example, you use the "Begins With" option, and use Bob as the comparison value.

You won't find the other comparison operators (<, >, <=, >=) very useful for searching text in a database. They're intended to compare numbers, as described next.

Comparing numbers

Filters are particularly useful for honing in on numbers: finding products that cost less than $35, albums that were released in 1967, products with more than 3,000 items in stock, and so on. If you've taken basic algebra, these options for comparing numbers should be familiar: = (equal to), <> (not equal to), < (less than), > (greater than), <= (less than or equal to), or >= (greater than or equal to).

Getting Comparison Values

By now it should be clear that the Recordset window's Filter option lets you compare data in one column with some other value. But you're probably wondering where this "other value" comes from. The answer is, it depends on which option you select in the third drop-down menu—the Comparison Value Source menu (see Figure 24-3).

The most straightforward option in the menu is the last item: Entered Value. When you select this option and specify a value in the next field, the application server searches the database for records that exactly match that value. This value could be a number (like 35 in the toupee example above), a letter, or one or more words (like "Craig McCord" in the client database example above). So, to create a recordset that finds a product whose price is more than $50, you tell Dreamweaver to search the price column only (by selecting "price" in the Filter drop-down menu), to find only prices that are higher than (select the > (greater than) symbol in the next drop-down menu) $50 (select the Entered Value option in the third drop-down menu, and type *50* into the value field.

Unfortunately, this kind of recordset is rather limited. The comparison value you specify (50) is hardwired into the search, making it very inflexible. What if a visitor wants to see products that cost more than $15, $30, or $100? No joy. You limited the search results to what you, the designer, entered as a value.

You're better off creating the filter criteria on the fly, based on information that a visitor supplies via his browser. That way, site guests can search your databases for a variety of pieces of information, not just the *one* value *you* selected. (After all, how good a search engine would Google be if the *programmers* determined the search criteria? No matter what you searched for—*web design, used cars*—it would always find websites about Java, Burning Man, and Google's stock valuation.)

Dreamweaver can also extract filter values from forms, cookies, and URLs. The process is always the same: From the filter's Comparison Value Source menu (Figure 24-3), select the source you want, and then type the name of the appropriate source item. For example, if you select Form Variable from the source menu, then, in the box to the right, you'd type the name of the form field. The application server uses the value a guest types into this form field to search the databases.

In most cases, you need more than one web page to let visitors execute a search on your site. One page has to have two components: a search field into which your visitor types her search terms (you might label it something like "Enter the maximum dollar amount you want to spend") and a Submit button so she can send the search criteria to your site; once the application server executes the search, it generates a second page that displays the search results. In this example, the form on one page sends information (the search terms) to another page (the results page), which uses those search terms to mine the database. In essence, Dreamweaver uses the words your visitor typed into the search form on one page to create the recordset that appears on the other page.

The two most common ways to pass information from one page to another are forms and URLs. (You'll find out about three advanced sources of information—cookies, session variables, and application variables—on page 984.)

Form variables

A *form variable* is simply the information a visitor types into a form field (or the value of a selected radio button, menu item, or checkbox). You learned about forms in depth in Chapter 12, but the way you use them in recordset filters is straightforward:

1. **Create a form page.**

   It can include a text field, pop-up menu, radio button, or some other form element. Make sure you *name* the form element. If you use a *simple* recordset filter, you can only let visitors search one type of information (price, for example). To let guests filter results by more than one element (price and color, for example), you need to use an *advanced* recordset (see page 870) and include more than one form field in your form page.

   If you want to give your visitors a chance to look at differently priced products, for example, you can create a drop-down menu that includes the values 10, 50, 100, 500, and so on. People can then choose one of those options to look at products below the selected price. (Also be sure to give the menu a name, such as "price," as described on page 453.)

Tip: Give the form field the same name as the database column it refers to. For example, if you let your visitors search for a product by name, the search taps the table's *productName* column, so you'd name the form field *productName*. By doing so, Dreamweaver automatically fills out the correct form field name in step 6 below.

2. **Set the Action property of the form (see page 457).**

   You want it to point to the results page.

Note: For these steps to work, you have to set the form's method to *Post* in the Property inspector (see page 458). If you select *Get*, the form information appears in the URL of the page your visitor submits to run the search, and that information isn't available as a form variable. (You can, however, use the *Get* method in conjunction with the URL parameters option discussed next.)

3. **Open (or create) the results page.**

   This page displays the results of the recordset Dreamweaver creates based on the information in the form. You need to make this a dynamic page based on the server model you chose—ASP, PHP, and so on. (See page 843 for information on how to create a dynamic page.)

4. **Add a recordset to the page, using the directions on page 858.**

   You'll also create a filter using a form variable.

5. **From the Filter menu, select a database column. Then choose a type of comparison, as described on page 861.**

   All this is the standard filter-creation routine.

6. **From the Source pop-up menu, select Form Variable. In the box to the right of the source menu, type the name of the form field that contains the value for comparison.**

   In keeping with the previous example, type *price* into the box, since that's the name of the menu on the form page.

7. **Add a sort option, if you like, and then click OK to create the recordset.**

   Remember that the recordset results depend on the search criteria sent from the form page. If a visitor just stumbles across the results page without using the form, the recordset most likely produces no results (for a workaround to this problem, see the box on page 868). That's why the initial form page should provide the only way a visitor can arrive at the results page—in other words, you should link to the results page only by using a form's *Action* property (see page 457).

URL parameters

In your Web travels, you've probably encountered URLs that look kind of strange, along the lines of *www.cosmofarmer.com/cart.php?productID=34&quantity=4*. Everything up to the ? probably looks familiar, but you might be wondering what the *?productID=34&quantity=4* means.

Forms aren't the only way you can pass information to a dynamic web page; URLs can do it, too, thanks to information tidbits called *parameters*. Dynamic websites can read parameters and use them to create a recordset, among other things. (In fact, using the *Get* method for a form puts the form's information into the URL.)

You can manually add a URL parameter to a link, but it's even more common to dynamically create a URL parameter from another recordset. This technique is common when you want to link from a long list of items to a single, dynamic page that displays information about a single item. For example, say you have a page that displays all of your store's products—this products page represents a recordset, the set of all the products you offer. If a visitor clicks on one of the products, the link pointing to the individual product page contains the product ID in the URL; that page extracts the ID from the URL, and searches the database for a product that matches. The results are a new page profiling just that one product, listing its name, description, price, and photograph.

By sending a URL parameter along with a link to a dynamic page, a dynamic page can use that parameter as a filter to search a database. To identify a single record in a database, for instance, the URL could contain a number identifying the record's *primary key* (see page 846 for a definition). You'll find an example of this trick in the tutorial starting at step 4 on page 909.

The steps for using URL parameters to filter recordsets are similar to those for using form variables. You need two pages, one with a link containing the URL parameter, and another, dynamically created page, containing the recordset.

Creating a link with a URL parameter

You can create a link that contains a URL parameter in several ways. The simplest is to highlight the item you wish to turn into a link—usually text or a graphic. Then, in the Property inspector's link box, type the link followed by a ?, a parameter name, an =, and the value (for example: *products.php?category=7*).

However, you'll probably find it easier to browse for the file, and let Dreamweaver write all the complex stuff. To do so, follow these steps:

1. **In Design view, highlight the item you want to turn into a link.**

   In other words, select a graphic or text on the page.

2. **On the Property inspector, click the folder icon (browse button).**

   The Select File window appears. (For more on creating links, see Chapter 5.)

3. **Browse to and select the page containing the recordset.**

   This page displays the results of the database search.

4. **In the Select File window's lower-right corner (the middle of the window on Macs), click the Parameters box.**

   The Parameters window appears (see Figure 24-4).

5. **Click in the space below the Name column, and then type the name of the URL parameter.**

   Use a name of your choosing that describes the data you're searching for. Avoid spaces and any punctuation characters for the name, since you're likely to run into trouble when you try to use such a name in the recordset filter. You could use the name of the table column that the application server will search to create the recordset. For example, say you create a link to lead to a page listing all the products in a certain category (for instance, plants). Each product might have a column named *categoryID*, which identifies the category to which the product belongs. In this case, name the parameter *categoryID*.

TROUBLESHOOTING MOMENT

The Default Value for a Filter Source

Using a variable as the search criteria for a filter presents a problem. If the filter requires information from a form or URL parameter, what happens if someone comes to the results page without first filling out the form or clicking a link that has a URL parameter? In most cases, the resulting recordset is empty, and the results page displays no records. You can, however, set a *default* value for the form variable or URL parameter, so that at least some records always appear.

Using the steps outlined on page 858, create a basic recordset; include a filter using a form variable or URL parameter. Then, in the Recordset window, click the Advanced button.

Now you get a more complex view of the recordset. The Variables list has a single entry: *colname*. Select *colname*, and then click the Edit button to open the Edit Variable window. The "Default value" box indicates the value the page uses to filter the recordset if none is supplied (in other words, when a visitor and his browser don't submit a form or URL variable). The page just uses the value *-1*, which probably doesn't match anything in your database.

Change this value to something that will. For example, if you filter on a primary key (to identify one record in the database), just type a value that you KNOW exists in the primary key field for one particular record. For example, *1*.

You could type a value that matches *all* the records in the database. For example, if the recordset finds products under a certain price, then type a value (price) that's larger than the most expensive product in your database. This way, the recordset retrieves all the items below that price—in other words, all the products. (This trick also works for the other sources discussed on page 984: cookies, application variables, and session variables.)

One last word of warning: If you switch back to the basic recordset view by clicking the Simple button, Dreamweaver resets the recordset variable to the default value of *-1*. So, if you change the default value in the Advanced view, then *don't* switch back to the basic recordset view.

Finally, you may want a recordset that returns no results—for example, if a visitor searches for a particular product that's not in your database, you want to let him know that there are no products that match his search. In that case, you can use the "show if" server behaviors described on page 991 to create two distinct regions on a page with a recordset: one region displays a message like "No results found", and the other displays whatever you choose if the page can't find any records. With the "show if" server behaviors, you can show one region of the page if the page returns no records and the other region if it does find records.

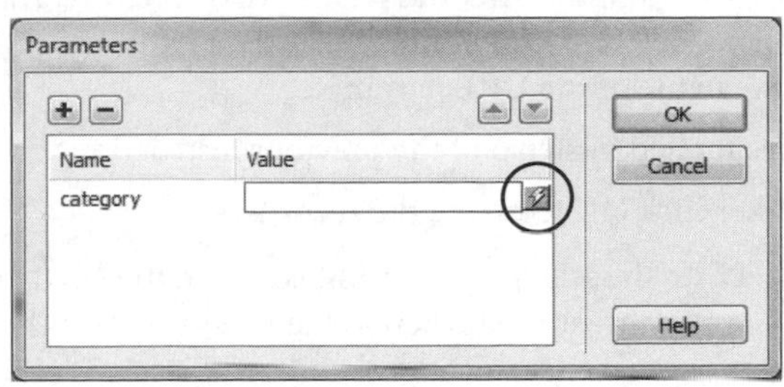

Figure 24-4:
The Parameters window lets you add URL parameters to a link. Recordsets can then use these pieces of information to filter a database, as discussed in "Filtering Information". The lightning bolt button (circled) is used to retrieve dynamic data, such as information from a recordset, a cookie, or a server variable, and it's especially useful for passing a primary key value to a page that provides detailed information on a single database record.

6. **Click the space below the Value column, and then type in the value for the URL parameter.**

   This value is the search term the filter uses to match records in the database.

   Usually this value is a simple one like *17, blue*, or *yes*. But you can also use spaces and punctuation marks in the value—for example, *Bob Jones*, in order to search for "Bob Jones" in the database. However, you need to make sure you set Dreamweaver's Preferences accordingly: Choose Edit→Preferences (Dreamweaver→Preferences), click the Code Rewriting category, and then make sure you have the "Encode special characters using &#" option selected (the "Encode special characters using %" option also works, but it can have trouble with some characters from some languages). Either of these options rewrites invalid characters in a form that works in a URL. For example, it converts a space in a search term to *%20*.

Note: Forms using the *Post* method don't suffer from any of these problems, and they can accept all types of punctuation and space characters.

7. **Click OK to close the Parameters window. Click OK to close the Select File window and apply the link.**

Creating the recordset for the results page

Once you create the link containing a parameter, you need to create an appropriate recordset for the results page. Here's how:

1. **Open (or create) the results page.**

   This page displays the results of the recordset created using information from the URL parameter.

2. **Add a recordset to the page, using the directions on page 858.**

   You'll also create a filter using a URL parameter.

3. **From the Filter menu, select a database column. Choose a type of comparison, as described on page 863 (for example, = to find records that match a certain value). From the source menu, select URL Parameter. In the box to the right of the source menu, type the name of the URL parameter.**

   This name is the name you supplied in step 5 of the previous instructions.

4. **Add a sort option, if you like; click OK to create the recordset.**

Like form variables, this recordset uses the search criteria embedded in the URL that triggers the database search. If a visitor just stumbles across the results page without using a link with a URL parameter, the recordset most probably produces no results. So make sure you link to this kind of page only via a link with a parameter. Otherwise, in the recordset, modify the default value for the URL parameter, as described in the box on page 868.

Tip: Using URL parameters (as opposed to form variables) to retrieve records has an added benefit: since the parameter is embedded in the URL–*http://www.cosmofarmer.com/products.php?productID=20*, for example–you can bookmark or email a link that matches a particular results page. This way, you can bookmark, say, a page displaying all the products under $50. Then, when you want to see if any new products (under $50) have been added to a site, you don't have to search the site again; just revisit the bookmarked page.

Advanced Recordsets and SQL

Sometimes you need more power than Dreamweaver's simple recordset tool gives you. For example, say you build an online classified ads system. On one page, you want to present various pieces of information: the name of the sale item, its price, who's selling it, and how to contact the seller, for example. Your database uses two tables to store this information,—one containing information on the products for sale (the ads, in other words), and one containing information about the sellers.

To present the ad, you need to simultaneously access both tables. In addition, you need to connect the records of those two tables so that each item is associated with the correct seller—John Smith selling the Whirligig 2007, for example. You have only one way to create this kind of complex query: using the advanced options of the Recordset window.

To display these options, insert a recordset using the steps described on page 858. Then, in the Recordset window, click the Advanced button. The Advanced Recordset window should appear (see Figure 24-5). (If you see a Simple button, then you're looking at the advanced options.)

Unfortunately, putting together advanced database queries isn't as easy as most other operations in Dreamweaver. The Advanced Recordset window is basically just a way to type in commands, using a database programming language called *SQL* (Structured Query Language). SQL is the language most database servers use to access, update, delete, and add information to their records.

To create an advanced recordset, in the window's SQL box, type an SQL statement.

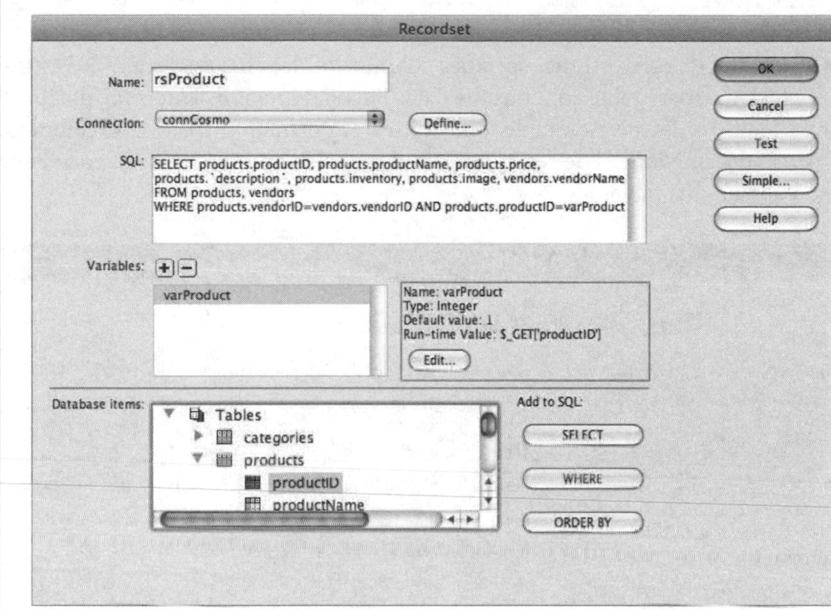

Figure 24-5: *The Recordset window's advanced options aren't for the uninitiated. You need to have a good grasp of SQL—the standard database programming language—to create complex database queries.*

SQL: The very basics

SQL lets you communicate with a database in order to find, add, update, and delete records. It actually supports even more advanced database work, such as adding new tables to a database, and deleting tables and databases. But in the context of the Advanced Recordset window, you just need to understand how SQL *retrieves* information. After all, a recordset is just a selection of data pulled from the database.

To make an SQL query (called an SQL statement), you must first specify:

- **Which columns of data you want to retrieve.** For example, item price, item name, seller name, and seller contact information.
- **Which tables will supply this data.** In the earlier example, the information is stored in two tables: Ads and Sellers.
- **How you want to limit the search.** You might want to display just the products less than $10 or whose seller is Zachariah Smith. Or you might want to let visitors make these choices themselves, via a form.
- **The sort order.** You could sort items using the Price column to view a list of items from least to most expensive, for example.

Only the first two pieces of information are absolutely necessary. A very basic SQL statement looks like this:

```
SELECT itemPrice, itemName
FROM ads
```

SELECT is an SQL keyword that specifies columns of data for retrieval; FROM indicates which database table contains the data. This statement instructs the database server to look inside the Ads table, and retrieve information from two columns: itemPrice and itemName. The result is a list of the price and the name of each item in the database's Ads table.

UP TO SPEED

Getting Your Feet Wet in SQL

SQL isn't difficult to pick up. While you can create very complex SQL queries, a basic SQL statement is straightforward. Once you reach the limits of Dreamweaver's basic recordset, you may want to expand your skills beyond that simple tool.

Dreamweaver itself is a great place to start learning how to write SQL statements. After you create a simple recordset (see page 858), click the Advanced button. You'll see the SQL statement Dreamweaver created in the SQL box.

This chapter introduces the very basics of SQL. For a more complete introduction, check out *SQLCourse.com* (*http://www.sqlcourse.com*). Or pick up a book like *SQL Queries for Mere Mortals* (Addison-Wesley Professional) by Michael Hernandez, or *Simply SQL* (Sitepoint) by Rudy Limeback.

Note: Developers write SQL keywords in capital letters–SELECT, for example. This is just a convention, not a hard and fast rule; "select" also works. But since you can more easily identify the keywords if they're capitalized, it's best to stick with this practice.

Of course, you may not always want *every* record in a table. You may want to limit a search to a select number of items, such as products under $10. The WHERE keyword lets you do just that:

```
SELECT itemPrice, itemName
FROM ads
WHERE itemPrice < 10
```

Now the SQL statement retrieves only the price and the name of products that cost less than $10. Finally, SQL can sort records in order. In the example here, you could sort the results from least to most expensive, like this:

```
SELECT itemPrice, itemName
FROM ads
WHERE itemPrice < 10
ORDER BY itemPrice ASC
```

The ORDER BY keywords indicate which column the recordset should use to sort the records. Specifying the prodPrice column sorts the items by price. ASC is short for *ascending*, meaning that the records appear in low-to-high price order. (DESC sorts records into *descending* order, Z–A, or high-to-low.) You can even sort by multiple columns. If, for example, you want a list of all products sorted by price, and *then* alphabetically by product name, you simply change the above ORDER BY keyword to read like this:

```
ORDER BY prodPrice ASC, prodName ASC
```

This way, the recordset presents all the products with the same price (for example, all $10) in alphabetical order (A–Z).

Using the Data Tree view

Although you need to know SQL to use the Recordset window's advanced options, you can get a little help from the data tree in the "Database items" list at the bottom of the window (see Figure 24-5). This area functions just like the Databases panel, letting you view the tables, columns, views, and stored procedures in the database.

Click the + (arrow) button next to the word "Tables" to see a list of all the database's tables. Click the + (arrow) next to a table *name* to see all the columns within the table. This resource is very helpful when you build SQL statements, because you may not remember the exact names of every table and column in your database.

To build an SQL statement, select a column name, and then click one of the three command buttons—SELECT, WHERE, or ORDER BY. The SQL command and column name appear in the SQL box.

Suppose, for example, you want to create the following SQL statement:

```
SELECT productID, productName
FROM products
```

To build this statement using the data tree, click the + button next to the table named Products, which expands to show a list of all the table's columns. Then click the column named productID, and then click SELECT. Next, click the productName column, and then click SELECT again.

Actually, when you use the Data Tree to insert SQL, Dreamweaver doesn't write its SQL statements exactly as listed above. What you get after following the previous instructions is:

```
SELECT products.productID, products.productName
FROM products
```

Dreamweaver inserts "qualified" column names, those that identify not only the column, but the column's source table, too. For example, *products.productID* indicates the products table's productID column. When you build a SQL query that involves more than one table, fully qualifying the column name by preceding it with the table name is good practice. If the same column name appears in two tables you're searching, your SQL doesn't work. For example, say the Products and the Vendors table both have columns called *name*. Each column refers to different types of data—the item for sale, and the name of the vendor respectively. Without differentiating the two columns (by "pointing to" them, for example, as *products.name* and *vendors.name*), the database doesn't know which column you mean, and you end up with a SQL error when you try to test the recordset.

Although these buttons can save you time, they don't check to see whether the SQL statement is valid. Unless you've got a decent grasp of SQL, you can easily create a statement that generates errors when you test it.

Creating variables for filtering data

Variables let you filter data using information from sources such as forms, URLs, cookies, session variables, and application variables. If you use the basic Recordset window's filtering option, Dreamweaver creates a variable for you behind the scenes. But in the advanced Recordset window, you must create them yourself.

To add a variable to an SQL query, follow these steps:

1. **In the Recordset window, next to Variables, click the + button (see Figure 24-5).**

   The Add Variable window opens (see Figure 24-6).

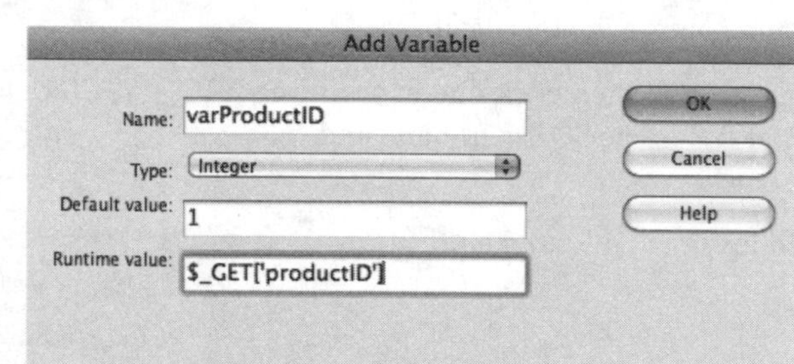

Figure 24-6: *This dialog box lets you create variables to customize an SQL statement. You're not limited to the filter part of an SQL statement (the WHERE clause) when you use variables, either. You can include them as any part of the statement. For example, one variable might determine the order of a sort operation: ASC or DESC.*

2. **In the Name box, type a name for the variable.**

   The name shouldn't include spaces or other punctuation marks.

Tip: As with database connections and recordsets, it's a good idea to add a prefix to the variable's name so you can more easily identify it in Code view. For example, you could begin the variable name with *var–for example, varPrice*–just as you begin a recordset name with *rs* (*rsProducts*, for example).

3. **From the Type menu, choose a data type.**

   Your options are Integer, Text, Date, and "Floating point number". If you'll use the variable as part of a filtering operation, then the type you choose depends on the type of data stored in the column you want to filter. For example, if you use the variable as part of a search on the name of a product, choose Text.

   The integer and text options are, of course, for numbers and text. Use Date when the variable contains a date type. This date isn't just any old date, however—it's the type of date defined by your database. Each database represents dates differently (to find out how MySQL handles date types, visit *http://dev.mysql.com/doc/refman/5.0/en/date-and-time-types.html*). Finally, SQL reserves the "Floating point number" option for numbers stored with decimal places—for example, a monetary value like 10.25 or 9.99.

Tip: You can easily determine the type of data stored in a column using the Databases panel, as described in the box on page 855.

---

4. **In the "Default value" box, type a value.**

   A default value comes in handy should you get an empty value from a form, URL, cookie, session variable, or application variable. The recordset uses the default value to filter the database records. See page 868 for more on when and why this might happen.

5. **Press Tab to jump to the "Runtime value" box; type the appropriate code.**

   The exact code you use depends on the server model you selected. For example, to retrieve the value of a form field named *price*, type *$_POST['price']* for PHP; to retrieve information from a URL parameter named *productID* (for example, *http://www.cosmofarmer.com/product.php?productID=2*), type *$_GET['productID']*. You can best learn how to create variables when you use the Recordset window's filter tool in the Simple menu (see instructions on page 861), and then switch to the advanced Recordset window, select the variable, and click the Edit button. The proper code for collecting information from forms, URLs, cookies, and so on appears in the variables' "Runtime value" field.

Note: If you add more than one SQL variable in the advanced Recordset window, you can't switch back to the Simple view.

Once you create a variable, you can include it in your SQL statement. Since variables help filter information, you'll often add them to the SQL *WHERE* keyword.

For example, if you create a variable named *varPrice* that retrieves information from a form, you can add it to the SQL statement like this:

```
SELECT ads.itemPrice, ads.itemName
FROM ads
WHERE ads.itemPrice < varPrice
```

In this example, the information the form passes to the page gets stored in the *varPrice* variable; the database query then compares the variable value to the price stored in the *itemPrice* column in the database's *ads* table.

If you ever need to edit a variable, select its name from advanced Recordset window's Variables list, and then click the Edit button. That opens the Edit Variable window, which looks just like the Add Variable window (Figure 24-6).

Reusing Recordsets

You create recordsets on a page-by-page basis. In other words, when you create a recordset, Dreamweaver adds it to only the current document. If you create another web page that requires the same recordset, you have to add the proper code to the new page. You can do this either by recreating the recordset—a potentially laborious process—or simply by copying the recordset from one page and pasting it into another.

Here's how:

1. **Open the Bindings panel by choosing Window→ Bindings.**

   Ctrl+F10 (⌘-F10) also works. You can also copy and paste from the Server Behaviors panel.

2. **Right-click (Control-click) the name of the recordset you want to copy. From the shortcut menu that appears, choose Copy.**

   In the Server Behaviors panel, recordsets appear like this: *Recordset (rsName)*, with the name of the recordset inside the parentheses.

Now switch to the document into which you'll paste the recordset. Right-click (Control-click) in the Bindings (or Server Behaviors) panel, and then, from the shortcut menu, choose Paste.

Tip: If you need a recordset that's similar but not identical to a recordset you created, you can copy the original recordset, paste it into a new document, and then edit it, following the instructions in the next section.

Editing Recordsets

What if you have to edit a recordset? Maybe you forgot an important column of information when you originally created the recordset, or perhaps you want to modify a recordset you copied from another page. The process is easy: Simply open either the Bindings panel (Ctrl+F10 [⌘-F10]) or Server Behaviors panel (Ctrl+F9 [⌘-F9]), and then double-click the name of the recordset you wish to edit.

The Recordset window appears, looking just as it did when you first created the recordset (see Figure 24-2). Make any changes to the recordset, and then click OK.

Note: Dreamweaver lets you change the name of a recordset after you create it and even after you use its data on a page. Just double-click the recordset name in the Bindings panel, and change the name in the Recordset window. However, this clunky procedure requires using "Find and Replace" (see page 801) to locate and update every instance of the recordset's name. Dreamweaver opens the "Find and Replace" window for you when you click OK, but it's up to you to make sure Dreamweaver makes the changes.

However, you shouldn't change names. Here's one area where Dreamweaver can really make mistakes. Sometimes Dreamweaver rewrites the recordset code, adding it a second time and subtly making it impossible to edit the recordset later.

The safest (although slowest) way to change a recordset's name is to recreate it. Of course, that's extra effort–a good argument for making sure you're satisfied with a recordset's name when you *first* create it. (If you do find yourself with a page that's no longer working you might be able to return to a working version following the tips in the box on page 878.)

Deleting Recordsets

If you add a recordset to a page and later realize that the page isn't using any of the information the recordset retrieves, you should delete it. Each recordset forces the database server to do some work. Unnecessary recordsets only make your pages work harder and assemble more slowly.

You can delete a recordset using either the Bindings or Server Behaviors panel. Select the name of the recordset in either panel, and then, at the top of the panel, click the minus sign (–) button (pressing Delete on your keyboard has the same effect). However, if you've added dynamic data from that recordset to a page (described next) and then you delete the recordset, Dreamweaver doesn't remove the references to it. In most cases, this action breaks the functionality of the page, so it doesn't work when viewed in a browser. You need to make sure you delete that dynamic information from the page (as described on page 881) and remove from the Server Behavior panel any server behaviors that rely on that recordset.

Adding Dynamic Information

Once you create a recordset, it's a snap to add information retrieved from the recordset to a web page. In fact, Dreamweaver gives you several ways to add dynamic information. Start in the document window by clicking on the spot where you want to add recordset information. Then do one of the following:

- Choose Insert→Data→Dynamic Data→Dynamic Text.
- In the Insert panel's Data category, click the Dynamic Data button, and then, from the menu, select Dynamic Text (see Figure 24-7).

Either way, the Dynamic Text window appears (see Figure 24-8), listing the recordsets on the current page. Click the + sign button next to the recordset from which you want to get information. This recordset expands to show all the columns retrieved in it. Pick the database column (also called Field) containing the information you want to add to the page. You can pick only one column at a time, but you can repeat this process to add multiple columns to the page.

TROUBLESHOOTING MOMENT

Look Out For Multiplying Recordsets

Unfortunately, Dreamweaver has one serious bug related to recordsets and the recordset navigation toolbar. Sometimes, Dreamweaver adds a duplicate version of a recordset (as well as some other duplicate code related to the recordset navigation bar). Frequently the page will work anyway (however it does the database work twice, which is just a waste of server power), but sometimes the page breaks. The duplicate recordsets can appear after you edit an existing recordset as discussed on page 876, and usually when the page includes a recordset navigation bar (page 887.)

There's no really good way around this except to be careful when you edit a recordset. It's a good idea to immediately test a web page after you add or edit a recordset to make sure it still works. If the page stops working, you can go back to Dreamweaver and choose Edit→Undo. (Dreamweaver's History panel provides another great way to step backwards in time to the point before Dreamweaver broke the page!)

It also helps to know what the code for a recordset looks like: it's usually 5 lines long and begins with *mysql_select_db* followed by some other stuff, and ends with a line that starts with *$totalRows*. Here's a simple recordset:

```
mysql_select_db($database_connCosmo,
$connCosmo);

$query_rsTest = "SELECT * FROM categories
ORDER BY categoryName ASC";

$rsTest = mysql_query($query_rsTest,
$connCosmo) or die(mysql_error());

$row_rsTest = mysql_fetch_assoc($rsTest);

$totalRows_rsTest = mysql_num_
rows($rsTest);
```

Dreamweaver often not only duplicates an edited recordset, but it doubles up on other server code, too, such as the programming that makes the recordset navigation bar work. Basically, once this happens it's very tricky to manually remove the code causing the problem.

The best way to avoid this problem? First, if you see the problem (test often!), undo any changes until the page works again. Then delete the recordset navigation bar, edit the recordset, and then add the recordset navigation bar back in. What fun!

Figure 24-7: *On the Insert panel's Data category, the Dynamic Data button (circled) lets you add a variety of dynamic data to a web page–from form fields filled in with information retrieved from a database to a complete table based on a recordset. (As discussed on page 23, you have many ways to control the placement and appearance of the Insert Panel, so your setup might not exactly match this figure.)*

Note: *Dynamic Text* is a bit of a misnomer. This tool can also insert dates, numbers, and dollar values, not just text.

The format menu lets you format the data, like making a date appear as *January 17, 2009*. You'll learn about formatting in depth below.

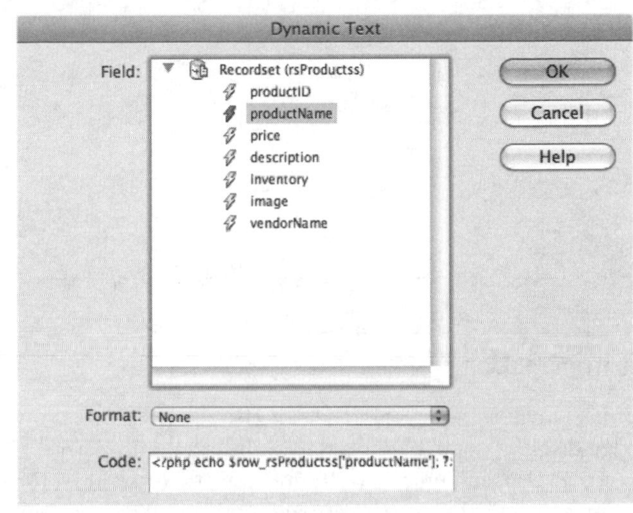

Figure 24-8: *After you select a database field to add to a page, Dreamweaver displays the necessary code in the Code box. For example, <?php echo $row_rsProducts['productName']; ?> means write the value in the productName column of a record from the rsProducts recordset. This code is the programming code that makes the data appear on your page. Dreamweaver writes this code using whichever programming language is compatible with the server model you chose.*

The Bindings Panel

The Bindings panel (Figure 24-9) gives you two other ways to add data from a recordset to a page. (It's called Bindings because the panel provides a mechanism to "bind," or attach, data from a database to a particular spot on a web page.) Recordsets appear in the Bindings panel. To open this panel, choose Window→Bindings or press Ctrl+F10 (⌘-F10).

To add data from the Bindings panel to a page, click the spot in the document window where you want to insert the dynamic data. Then, in the Bindings panel, select the column you wish to add, and click Insert (circled in Figure 24-9). That said, the best and fastest method is to just drag a column's name from the Bindings panel directly into the document window—into a paragraph or table cell, for example. You'll probably use this method most of the time.

After adding dynamic information to a page, it looks something like this: *{rsProducts.productName}*. That tells you the name of the recordset (*rsProducts*) and the name of the data column (*productName*). (You can make "real" data appear—instead of this code—when you use Dreamweaver's Live View, as described on page 898.)

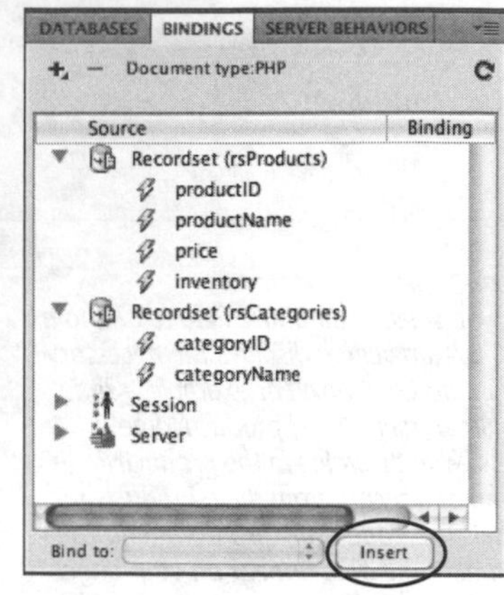

Figure 24-9:
The Bindings panel lists the types of dynamic data you can add to your page. Recordsets (and the columns of data they retrieve) appear here, but any URL, Form, Cookie, or Session variables (as described on page 984) you added will appear here as well.

Formatting Dynamic Information

Not only does the Bindings panel list your Recordsets, it also provides tools so you can change the way a page displays the dynamic data you inserted into a page. Unfortunately, the options for PHP (see Figure 24-10) aren't all that useful: you can capitalize all the letters in any text the search retrieved or capitalize first letters only…yippee! Well, you can do that with CSS, so these choices are pretty useless. As described in Figure 24-10, a few choices make working with HTML that's embedded into database records easier, but other than that, PHP users don't have many useful choices here.

What would really be useful is the ability to take a number like 8 or 10.9 that's stored in a database column for a product's price and format it like 8.00 or 10.90—the way we humans are used to seeing prices. To do that, you need to turn to a very useful, even indispensable Dreamweaver Extension named PHP Server Formats. It's offered free by its author, J. Andres Cayon from his website at *http://www.tecnorama.org/document.php?id_doc=51*. Click the PHP Server Formats 1.3.1 download link (even though it currently says it supports only CS3 and CS4, it does work with Dreamweaver CS5). Once you download the files, double-click the .mxp file to open the Extensions Manager and install it in Dreamweaver. Then quit and restart Dreamweaver (you can find a lot more information on Dreamweaver Extensions in Chapter 22.) The Bindings panel now reveals a completely new set of formatting options (see Figure 24-11*)*.

Whether you use Dreamweaver's built-in formatting options or the PHP Server Formats extension, you format dynamic text the same way: choose a formatting option when using the Insert Dynamic Text window (Figure 24-8), or apply, remove, or change a formatting option using the Bindings panel.

To set a format using the Bindings panel (Ctrl+F10 [⌘-F10]), proceed as follows:

1. **In the document window, click the dynamic item you want to format.**

   A down-pointing arrow appears in the Bindings panel, under the Format column.

Note: To format dynamic text using the Bindings panel, you have to select an instance of the dynamic text on the web page—dynamic text that's been placed onto the page. If you just click the column name in the recordset, no formatting options appear.

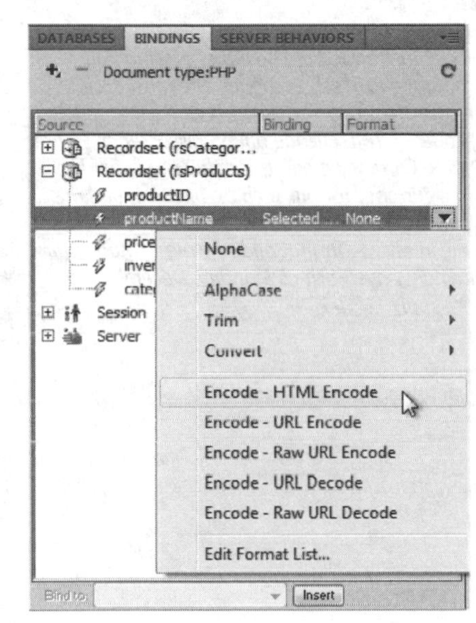

Figure 24-10: *The PHP server model doesn't have too many useful formatting options; however, one of them, "Encode _ HTML Encode", may come in handy if your database stores HTML code (this option is called "Encode– Server.HTML Encode" in the ASP server model). For example, maybe you created a bulletin board whose messages are stored in a database. When you add one of those messages to a page, applying the "Encode _ HTML Encode" format ensures that web browsers don't render any code in a message as part of your page. Instead, any HTML in that dynamic text appears to visitors as code. Similarly, if there's any chance a data field might store a bracket like this <, the Encode formatting option prevents a browser from thinking that the opening bracket is the start of an HTML tag—a situation that could make your page not appear at all!*

2. **In the Bindings panel, under the Format column, click the down-pointing arrow and then, from the menu, select a formatting option (Figure 24-11).**

   Pick an option that's appropriate to the selected piece of data: currency formatting for the price of a product, for example. If you try to apply a formatting option that isn't appropriate for the selected item (Currency to a text description, say), the page may produce an error when you preview it on the testing server.

You can also format selected dynamic data just as you would other text on a page by applying CSS styles, headings, bulleted lists, and so on.

Deleting Dynamic Information

Dynamic information added to a page behaves like a single object. Just click to select it. You can also drag it to another location on the page, copy and paste it, remove it from a page by selecting it and pressing Delete, and so on.

If you remove all the dynamic information from a page, and don't plan on using any information from the recordset, make sure you delete the recordset, too, as described on page 877. Even though you may not display any dynamic information on the page, if a page contains a recordset, it must still communicate with the database server, which slows down your pages.

You can find dynamic data listed in the Server Behaviors panel, too. You remove it just like you would any other server behavior, by selecting it from the Server Behaviors panel, and then clicking the minus (–) sign button (see Figure 24-15).

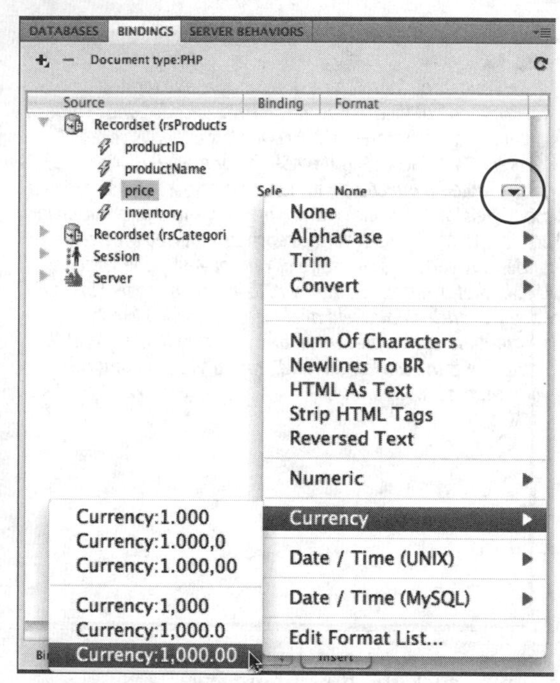

Figure 24-11:
The PHP Server Formats extension is really the only useful way to use the Binding panel's formatting options for the PHP server model. The most useful options are "HTML to Text" (which works the same as the Encode _ HTML Encode option discussed in Figure 24-10); the Currency menu to display a number like 1200 in a currency format such as 1,200.00; and the Date/Time (MySQL) menu which lets you take a date and time in MySQL format and re-write in many more user-friendly ways, such as Monday, December 31, 2010 or simply 12/31/2010.

Note: You may notice that the same piece of dynamic text is listed more than once in the Server Behaviors panel—for example, something like Dynamic Text (rsProducts.price) listed twice. That means you inserted the same column of information more than once on the page—each time you insert dynamic text onto a page, Dreamweaver lists it as a new entry in the Server Behaviors panel.

Displaying Multiple Records

Often, you'll want to create a web page that displays multiple records, such as a page that lists all the products in your company's catalog.

So far, the techniques you learned for inserting dynamic data insert information from only a single record. Even if you created a recordset that retrieves a thousand records, you still just see information from the very first record in the recordset when you simply drag data from the Bindings panel onto a dynamic Web page. You need a bit of extra programming if you want to see information from more than one record (like a long list of all company employees) on a single page. Fortunately, Dreamweaver gives you two tools to display multiple records: the Dynamic Table and Repeat Region objects.

Creating a Repeating Table

You use HTML tables (see Chapter 7) to display data. The columns and rows provide tidy compartments for individual pieces of information. It's not surprising, then, that in database terminology, *row* often refers to a single record in a database, and column indicates a single type of information in a record. Where a row and *column* meet, they form a "cell" that holds one piece of data from a single record.

Dreamweaver's Dynamic Table tool lets you display the results of a recordset in an HTML table. When you insert a dynamic table, it consists of two rows. The top row displays the name of each database column so you can identify the data in the rows below. The bottom row includes the code for the actual dynamic data—one database column item per table column (Figure 24-12).

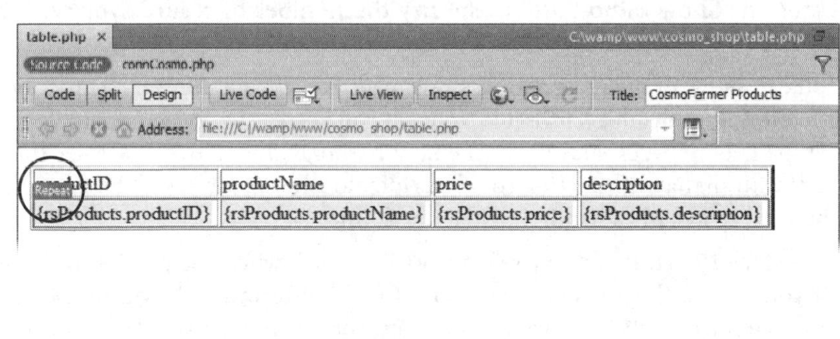

***Figure 24-12:** Although the Dynamic Table tool creates a table that displays multiple records, you see only one table row's worth of dynamic data. The Repeat tab (circled in this figure) that appears above the row indicates that this row will repeat, once for each record in the recordset. To see the effect, click the Live View button as describedonpage898.*

The magic of this tool is that it duplicates the bottom row for each record in the recordset. In other words, the table displays multiple records, one record per table row. Here's how to use it:

1. **Create a recordset (see page 858). In the Insert panel's Data category, from the Dynamic Data button menu, select Dynamic Table (see Figure 24-7).**

   You can also choose Insert→Data Objects→Dynamic Data→Dynamic Table. Either way, the Dynamic Table window opens (see Figure 24-13).

2. **From the Recordset menu, choose the recordset you want to use.**

   Since a page can contain more than one recordset, you have to indicate which records you want to display.

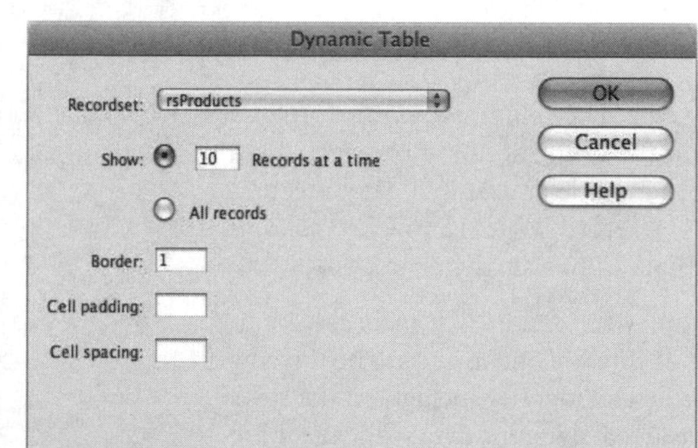

Figure 24-13: *The Dynamic Table tool lets you quickly create a table to display all or some of the records in a recordset.*

3. **Using the Show radio buttons, specify the number of records you wish to display.**

   You can show all the records on a single page by clicking the "All records" button. However, if your recordset is huge—if you're creating a web page to display company employees, and your company has 10,000 employees, say—a single page with all that information could be ridiculously long. In cases like these, you should display only a handful of items at a time.

   If you type *10* in this box, you see at most 10 records when you preview the page. (If you choose this method, make sure to add a Recordset Navigation bar, as described on page 887, to give visitors a way to page through the full list of results.)

4. **Set the Border, Cell Padding, and Cell Spacing values for the table.**

   These HTML table properties are described on page 268. All you're creating here is a plain old HTML table. You can dress it up later in Design view by changing the border, cell padding, cell spacing, background cell color, and other table properties, as well as creating CSS styles to format the table, rows, and cells.

Note: If you insert a Dynamic table and later alter the recordset used in the table–for example, by adding a column of information to your query–Dreamweaver doesn't update the repeating table as a result of this change. In fact, if you remove a column of information from a query, you get an error when you try to preview the repeating table. If you edit the recordset and change the number of columns it retrieves (see page 876), it's usually easiest to delete the current repeating table and replace it with a new one.

5. Click OK.

   Dreamweaver inserts a table into the page. The top row contains the names of each column from the recordset—one name per table cell. You can, and probably should, edit these names to make them more understandable. After all, *productID* probably doesn't mean anything to your visitors.

   The bottom row of the table contains the dynamic data from the recordset and represents one record. Each table cell in that row simply holds dynamic text for each field in the recordset. You can select each of these placeholders and style them as you would any dynamic text—for example, using the Property inspector's style menu to apply a CSS style. The table row has a Repeat Region object applied to it, which you can edit or delete as described in the next section.

Creating a Repeat Region

While the Repeating Table is easy to use, it doesn't give you the flexibility you might require. For example, what if your dynamic information needs to be presented in a bulleted list (one record per bulleted item) or in individual paragraphs (one paragraph per record)? In these cases, you need to create a *repeating region*—a chunk of HTML that repeats once for each record in a recordset.

Here's an example that can help you understand how to use the Repeat Region object. Imagine you're creating a directory of your company's staff. This page would include the name, telephone number, email address, and department of each employee. Of course, all this information is stored in a table in a database—one column for each piece of information, and one record for each employee.

In Dreamweaver, you create the basic design of the page, and then add a recordset that retrieves the required information about each employee in the company. The page layout presents each employee's information in a single paragraph, so the finalized page has many paragraphs—one for each employee.

Since this is a dynamic page, you can't predict how many paragraphs you'll need. After all, your company may hire many new employees, which would add records to the database. To allow for this uncertainty, create a single paragraph by adding the dynamic information you want in it, following the steps on page 877. Then tell Dreamweaver to *repeat* that paragraph using information from each record the recordset retrieves.

Just follow these steps:

1. **Using the Bindings panel or one of the techniques described on page 877, insert dynamic text onto the page.**

   You should put these items together on the page, maybe in a single paragraph, in a bulleted or numbered list, or in a <div> tag.

2. **Select the dynamic text and any HTML code you wish to repeat.**

   For example, select the paragraph (in the document window's Tag selector, click the <p>) containing the dynamic data. If you're using a bulleted list to present this information, select the list item (<li> tag) containing the dynamic data. For data in a table row, select the table row (<tr> tag).

Note: You need to be very precise when you select the HTML in a Repeating Region. If you aren't, the page may not look or work as you expect. For example, if you select the dynamic data in a bulleted list, but don't include the <li> tag representing the list item, when you insert a repeating region, the records will repeat within a single bulleted list. In other words, you end up with a bunch of words (data from multiple records) as part of a single bullet. Use the Tag selector (see page 23) to accurately select an HTML tag.

---

3. **In the Insert panel's Data category, click the Repeat Region button (see Figure 24-1).**

   You can also choose Insert→Data Objects→Repeated Region. Either way, the Repeat Region window appears (Figure 24-14).

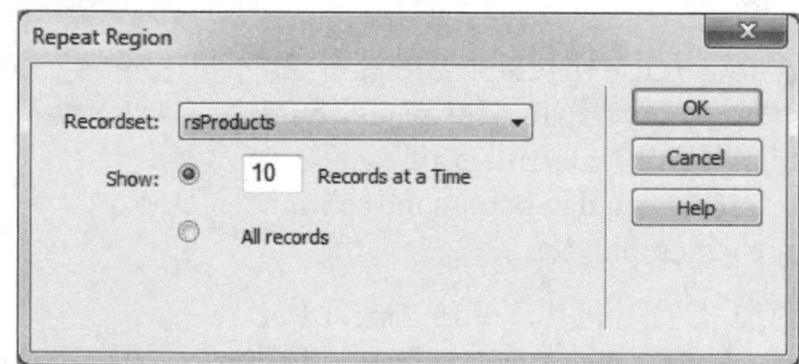

Figure 24-14:
In a Repeat Region that reveals only a limited number of records at a time (in this case, 10), add a Recordset Navigation bar (see the next page). Otherwise, visitors to the page see the first 10 records of a recordset, but don't have any way to view additional records!

4. **From the Recordset menu, choose the recordset you want the page to work with.**

   Since it's possible to have more than one recordset per page, be sure to select the recordset that includes the data identified in the bottom row of the Dynamic Table.

5. **Choose the number of records you want to display.**

   If you decide not to use the "All records" option, make sure that you add a Recordset Navigation bar, as described below, to let visitors page through the list of results.

6. **Click OK.**

   Dreamweaver adds the proper programming code to the page.

Editing and Removing a Repeat Region

If you selected the wrong recordset, or want to increase the number of records displayed at a time, you can easily edit a Repeating Region. Simply open the Server Behaviors panel (Ctrl+F9 [⌘-F9] or Window→Server Behaviors), and then double-click Repeat Region from the list. In the Repeat Region window (Figure 24-14), make any changes, and then click OK.

To remove a Repeat Region, open the Server Behaviors panel (see Figure 24-15). From the list, select Repeat Region, and then click the minus sign (–) button (or press the Delete key).

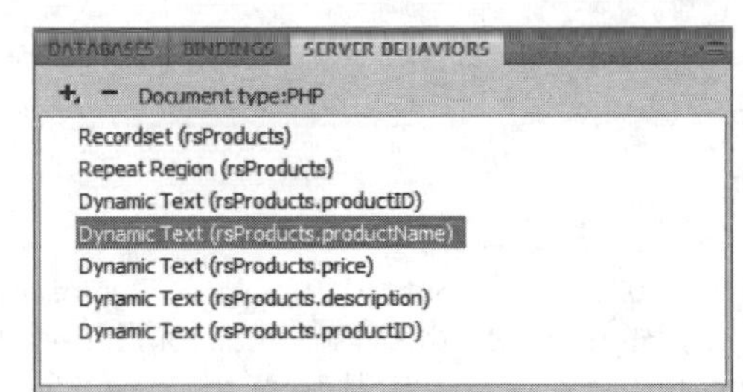

Figure 24-15:
The Server Behaviors panel lists every dynamic element you add to a page, from recordsets to Repeat Regions. Even when you drag a column from the Bindings panel to add dynamic data to a page, you create a server behavior. In this example, the highlighted element Dynamic Text (rsProducts.productName) represents data from a recordset that'll appear somewhere on the web page. You can delete any server behavior by selecting it from the list and then clicking the minus (-) button.

Recordset Navigation

Dreamweaver's Repeating Region tool lets you display multiple database records on a single web page. But a recordset with large amounts of data—like 1,000 employee records—can quickly choke a page. A large amount of information takes a long time to download, and forces visitors to scroll down many screens to see it all.

Fortunately, the Repeating Region tool also lets you limit the number of records displayed at once. Of course, this limit presents its own set of problems: How do visitors see additional records, and how do you let them know where they are among all the records in the recordset?

To solve this dilemma, Dreamweaver comes with two handy commands for adding navigation to a recordset—and providing useful feedback about the recordset.

FREQUENTLY ASKED QUESTION

A Little Less Repetition

I applied the Repeat Region object, and when I preview the page, the same record repeats over and over. That's not what I wanted to do! What's going on?

This scenario can happen when you apply a Repeat Region object, and, from the Repeat Region window, inadvertently select the wrong recordset (see Figure 24-13)—a mistake you can easily make if you include more than one recordset on a page.

The Repeat Region object adds programming code that steps through each record of a recordset. So, in practice, the Repeat Region object should get the information from the first record in a recordset and write it to the web page, and then go to the second record and add its info to the page. This process should continue until it's either gone through all the records in the recordset or reached the limit specified in the "Records at a Time" box.

However, if the information you want repeated is retrieved by a recordset different from the one selected in the Repeat Region window, this system breaks down. Instead, the code continues to cycle through each record from the selected recordset, but doesn't cycle through each record from the recordset containing the dynamic information you want repeated. The result: You get the same information over and over again. The first record of the recordset (the one you want repeated) is repeated for each record in the *other* recordset (the one you don't want repeated).

In other words, to ensure that Repeat Region works, select the recordset whose data is contained in the area you want *repeated*.

Recordset Navigation Bar

Suppose a page contains a recordset of 100 records, but the Repeating Region on the page limits the display to 10 records at a time. In this case, you should insert a Recordset Navigation Bar to add either text links or graphic buttons to a page. These navigation bars let your audience view the next 10 records in the recordset, jump to the last records in the recordset (see Figure 24-16), jump back to the first record, or move to previous records.

To add a Recordset Navigation Bar, follow these steps:

1. **Click in the document window at the location where you want to insert the navigation bar. In the Insert panel's Data category, click the Recordset Paging button, and then, from the menu, select Recordset Navigation Bar (see Figure 24-17).**

   You can also choose Insert→Data Objects→Recordset Paging→Recordset Navigation Bar. In either case, the Recordset Navigation Bar window appears.

2. **From the Recordset menu, select the recordset to navigate.**

   If the page contains more than one recordset, select the one you used when you created the dynamic table or added the Repeating Region.

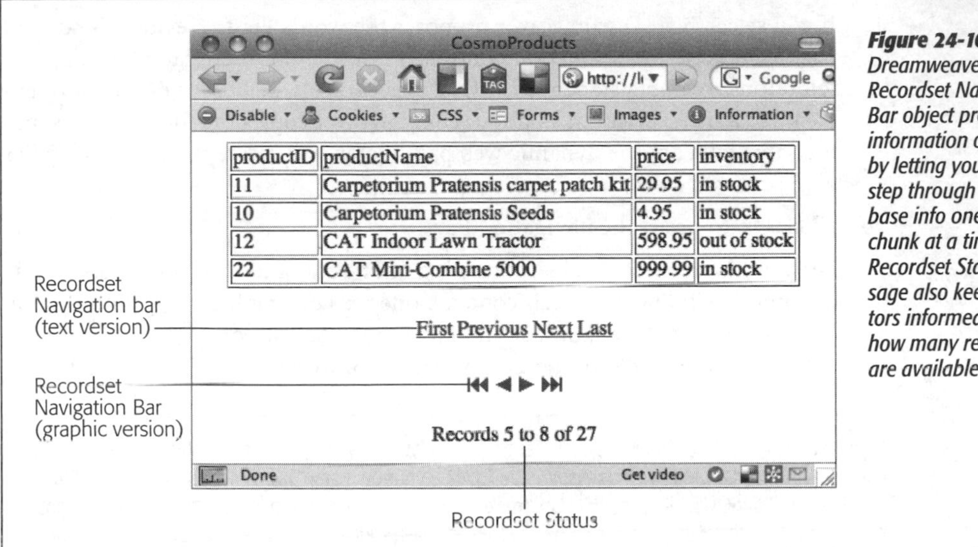

Figure 24-16: *Dreamweaver's Recordset Navigation Bar object prevents information overload by letting your visitors step through database info one small chunk at a time. The Recordset Status message also keeps visitors informed about how many records are available.*

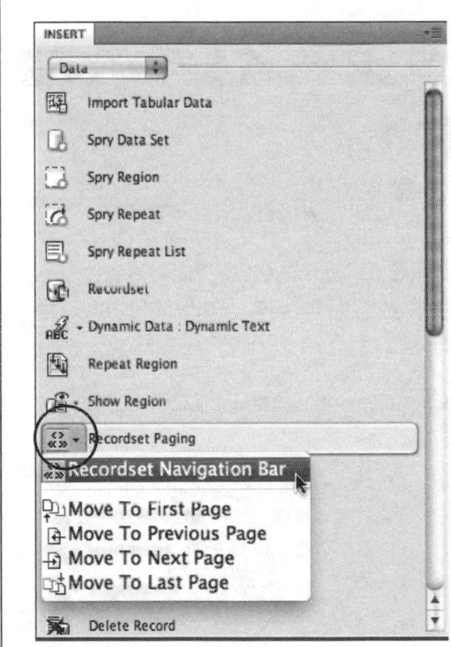

Figure 24-17: *The Recordset Paging button lets you insert a navigation bar so visitors can navigate a long list of records. In addition, if you want to build your own recordset navigation system, you can individually apply server behaviors like "Move to First Page" and "Move to Next Page". You'll find these server behaviors discussed on page 990.*

3. **Select whether you want to use text or graphic buttons for the navigation bar.**

   If you select Text, Dreamweaver proposes the words First, Previous, Next, and Last to indicate the navigation controls. (You can edit them later.) The graphic buttons resemble standard DVD player controls, representing forward and backward. If you select this option, Dreamweaver copies the four GIF files into the same folder as the dynamic web page. Later, you can replace these graphics with ones you create.

4. **Click OK to insert the navigation bar.**

   Dreamweaver inserts a table, consisting of one row and four columns, into the document window. Each cell contains one text or graphic navigation button. You can change the alignment and any other property of the table to fit your design (see Chapter 7 for more information on working with HTML tables).

Tip: If you use the Recordset Navigation Bar frequently, you may long to permanently replace the DVD-control graphics that Dreamweaver displays. Just create your own graphics, and then name them FIRST.GIF, Last.gif, PREVIOUS.GIF, and NEXT.GIF (make sure you capitalize them inconsistently just like Adobe has done). Place these graphic files in the *C:\Program Files\Adobe\Adobe Dreamweaver CS5\configuration\Shared\UltraDev\Images* folder (Applications→Adobe Dreamweaver CS5→Configuration→Shared→UltraDev→Images folder).

FREQUENTLY ASKED QUESTION

Behaviors That Serve You Well

What's the difference between Dreamweaver Behaviors (Chapter 14) *and a server behavior?*

Both are prewritten programs created by Dreamweaver's engineers. They differ mainly in where the programs run and what they attempt to accomplish.

A Dreamweaver Behavior is a JavaScript program that runs in a web browser. It usually affects the interaction between a visitor and a web page. For instance, the Swap Image behavior makes a browser exchange one image for another when a visitor mouses over a link. The behavior itself runs in the visitor's browser, and anyone can see the program by looking at the page's source code.

A server behavior, on the other hand, always runs on the *application server*—that is, on the web server side of the Internet. You can write server behaviors in a variety of languages—VBScript, PHP, and so on, depending on the server model (page 834) your site uses. Server behaviors specifically let you create connections to databases and display, edit, and delete information from databases. Furthermore, since these programs run on the application server, your site's visitors never see the actual programming code. All they see if they look at the source code is plain old HTML (the results of the server program).

In a nutshell, Dreamweaver Behaviors add interactive elements, like rollovers and JavaScript alert boxes, to a web page,. Server behaviors supply the programming code you need to build complex database-driven websites.

Recordset Navigation Status

When you have hundreds of records to view, it's nice to know where you are in the list and how many records there are in all. The Recordset Navigation Status tool adds just such information to your pages, as shown in Figure 24-16. Dreamweaver presents the status message in the form of "Records 1 to 10 of 18", indicating which records the visitor is currently viewing, and the total number of records.

Here's how to add a Recordset Navigation Status message:

1. **Click in the document window at the location you want to insert the status message. In the Insert panel's Data category, click the Display Record Count button (circled in Figure 24-18).**

   You can also choose Insert→Data Objects→Display Record Count→Recordset Navigation Status. In either case, the Recordset Navigation Status window appears.

2. **From the menu, select a Recordset.**

   If the page contains more than one recordset, select the one you used when you inserted the Recordset Navigation Bar.

   Click OK to close the window and insert the status message.

   The Recordset Navigation Status message is simply text with the three dynamic text items (see page 877 for more on dynamic text). Change the words "Records", "to", and "of" to anything you like, such as in "Products 1-10. 149 total products retrieved."

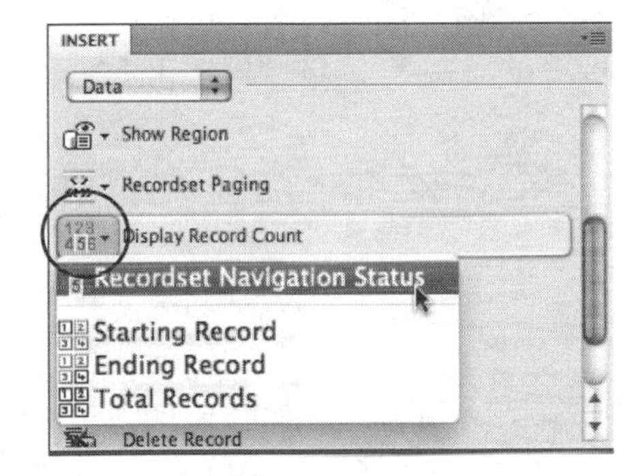

Figure 24-18: *Use the Display Record Count menu to insert status information about a recordset, including the helpful message ("Records 1 to 10 of 18") provided by the Recordset Navigation Status server behavior.*

You can easily build your own recordset navigation status bar using the last three options in the Data tab's Display Record Count menu (see Figure 24-18). Just click in the document window where you want to insert the status information, and then, from the menu, select an option.

The Starting Record option displays the number of the first record in a Repeated Region. The exact number depends on where the visitor is within the recordset. For example, say you add a Repeated Region that displays 10 records at a time; you then add a Recordset Navigation Bar (page 887) so visitors can view all the records in the recordset by paging through 10 records at a time. On the first page, the starting record number is 1, but when someone clicks the "next page" button in the Recordset Navigation Bar, the starting record on that page is 11. In other words the starting record number is the "11" in "Showing records 11 to 20 of 100".

The same is true with the Ending Record option. It displays the number of the last record displayed on the page. Again, the exact value depends on the recordset, and which page of records your guest is viewing. The ending record number is the "20" in "Showing records 11 to 20 of 100".

Finally, the Total Records option is simple: It's just the total number of records retrieved in a recordset. You'll find yourself using this useful option even without a Recordset Navigation Bar. For example, say you want to know how many employees are listed in your database. Create a recordset that retrieves every employee (in other words, don't use a filter [page 861]), and then, from the Record Count menu, use the Total Records option.

Master Detail Page Set

When you build a database-driven website, you often want to give your visitors both an overview and a detailed view of information. Usually, it takes two separate web pages to do the job: one that lists limited information about all the records in a recordset, and one that links to a second page with detailed information about a single record. Dreamweaver calls these *master* and *detail* pages, and gives you a tool to make quick work of creating them. Figure 24-19 shows how these pages work together.

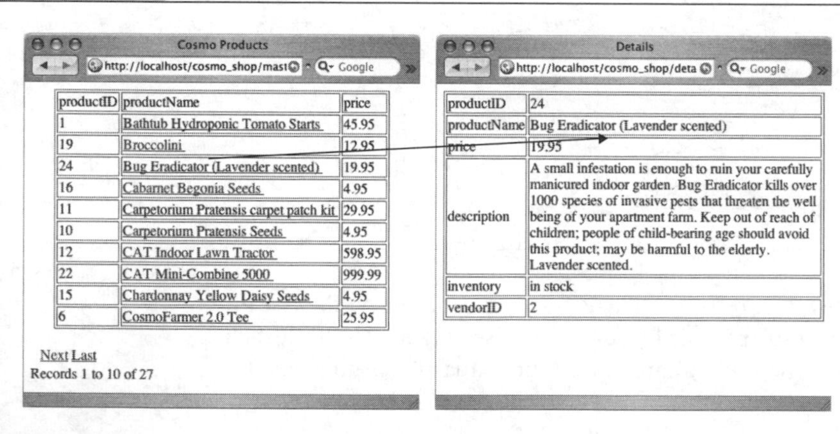

***Figure 24-19:** Here's an example of Dreamweaver's Master Detail Page Set. The screen on the left represents a master page—a list of items retrieved from a recordset. Clicking a link on this page opens a detail page (right), which displays the details of a single record.*

The Master Detail Page Set object automates the process of creating dynamic tables and Recordset Navigation Bars, as well as adding many different server behaviors to your pages. In fact, there's nothing this tool does that you can't do (albeit more slowly) with the other tools you learned about in this chapter.

To create a Master Detail Page Set, follow these steps:

1. **Create two web pages—one for the master page and another for the detail page.**

   The pages can be new, blank pages or existing pages that require dynamic information from a database. It helps to use descriptive names for these pages, such as *productIndex.php* and *productDetails.php*. (Save each page with an extension appropriate to the server model you're using: .asp, .cfm, or .php.)

2. **Open the master page—the one listing all the records—and add a recordset to it.**

   This recordset must include not only all the columns you want displayed on the master page, but also all the columns you want to appear on the detail page. Both pages use the same recordset, so this one recordset must retrieve *all* the information you want on both pages. Also, make sure you select the primary key for the table (the ID used to identify each record). Even if you won't display this key on the page, you need it to link the information in the master page to that in the detail page.

3. **In the Data category of the Insert panel, click the Master Detail Page Set button (see Figure 24-1).**

   You can also choose Insert→Data Objects→Master Detail Page Set. Either method opens the Insert Master Detail Page Set window (see Figure 24-20).

4. **From the Recordset pop-up menu, choose the name of the recordset you created in step 2.**

5. **Select the fields (database columns) you wish to appear on the master page.**

   You'll probably remove a bunch of columns from the "Master page fields" box, since most of the information is reserved for the detail page. To remove a column, click its name to select it, and then click the minus (–) button. (If you accidentally delete a column, click the + button to add it back in.) You can also change the order of the columns by selecting a column name, and then clicking the up or down arrow buttons. The order of the fields the box dictates the order in which they appear on the master page.

Note: It's OK to remove the primary key from the Master page fields list. This list is only for the columns you want to see on the page. If you remove the primary key field, it's still part of the recordset you created in step 2, and Dreamweaver will use it to link the master and detail pages.

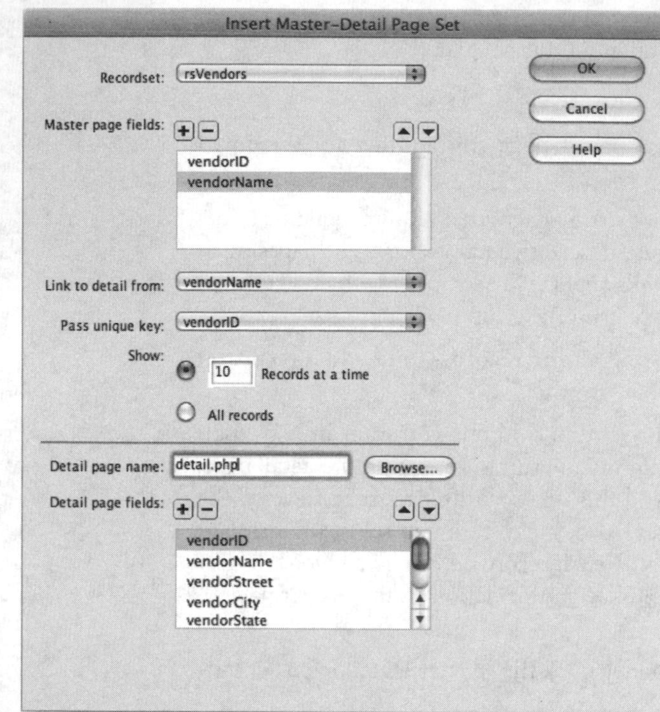

Figure 24-20:
The Insert Master Detail Page Set window lets you quickly create two common types of dynamic pages: one that lists many records in a database, and another that shows detailed information about a single database record.

6. **From the "Link to detail from" pop-up menu, choose a column.**

   Here you determine which item on the master page links to the detail page. In Figure 24-19, each product's name has a link to the detail page. If you're creating a staff directory, you might select the column that contains each staff member's name. That way, visitors can click a name to see a page with that staff person's details.

7. **Using the "Pass unique key" field, select a column.**

   Choose a column that uniquely identifies a single record in the database, such as a product identification number or Social Security number. In most cases, this is the *primary key* in a database table (see page 846 for more on primary keys). (If you want the primary key info to appear in this menu, you must include the "unique key" column in the recordset you create in step 2.)

8. **Select how many records you wish to show.**

   You can either type a number into the "Records at a time" box or select "All records".

9. **Click Browse. Select the detail page you created in step 1.**

   In this step and the next, you define the detail page and the information that appears on it.

10. **Select the fields you want to display on the detail page.**

    The process is the same as step 5, but in this case, you'll probably include most, if not all, of the columns. After all, that's the purpose of a detail page—to display detailed information.

11. **Click OK to close the window and finish programming the pages.**

    It may take a few moments for Dreamweaver to complete this step. It's adding a lot of code to both the master and detail pages.

Once that's done, you can (and should) modify the tables, format the dynamic items, and design the page to your liking. Because the Master Detail Page Set tool just automates the process of adding Repeating Regions, Recordset Navigation Bars, and other server behaviors, you must edit those items individually on the page. In other words, you can't return to the Insert Master Detail Page Set window (Figure 24-20) to alter items on either page. For example, if you decide to remove a piece of dynamic information from the detail page, you must make this change on the detail page itself.

While the Master Detail Page Set tool makes building these types of pages a snap, it does have its drawbacks. The primary problem is that Dreamweaver creates the same recordset for both the master and detail pages. This feature can slow down the works, because even though you may want to display only a few columns of data on the master page (the vendorName field in Figure 24-20), the recordset added to the page must retrieve *all* the information the detail page needs. The database server does extra work retrieving unused data. However, you have a workaround: After you create the master and details pages, return to the master page, edit the recordset, and then select *only* the fields that that page uses—and don't remove the primary key field, since it's necessary for linking the master and detail pages. (You'll find editing recordsets described on page 876.)

Although the Master Detail Page Set makes quick work of creating these types of pages, you can do all the same tasks using the tools you've already learned—Repeating Regions, Recordset Navigation Bars, and so on—with the added benefit of greater design flexibility. For an example of creating a more complex master and detail page set by hand, complete the tutorial at the end of this chapter.

Passing Information Between Pages

Every now and then, you'll want to pass a piece of information from one page to another. The Master Detail Page Set described in the previous section uses this concept: A link on the master page not only points to the detail page, but also passes along the unique ID used to create a filtered recordset on the detail page. In other words, the master page lists a bunch of records from a database. Each record not only links to its own detail page, but also passes along its unique ID. The link might be something like *productDetails.php?productID=7.*

The information after the *?* in the above URL is a *URL parameter*, which the detail page uses to build a recordset. In this example, the detail page would find only one record—the one whose *productID* is *7*—and display its details on the page. The key to the success of the Master Detail Page Set, then, is the ability to pass information to another page, and then use that information to filter a recordset (see page 861 for details on filtering database records).

To retrieve the details for only one record, the detail page must include a recordset that filters the records of a database table based on some unique identifier—usually a record's primary key. For example, if every ad in a database of advertisements has its own unique ad ID, to find info on just a single ad, you simply search for the one record that matches a particular ID number. In other words, you create a recordset that filters the data based on that ID number.

Dreamweaver lets you pass information from a recordset in the URL of a link—for example, *productDetails.php?productID=4*—when you create a link using Dreamweaver's "Browse for file" feature. Just follow these steps:

1. **Create a page with a recordset and a Repeating Region.**

   This page might be one that lists all the products your company sells, or it might be a list of all the company employees.

2. **Select an element on the page to serve as a link to a detail page.**

   To show the details of a particular product or employee, you'll add a link to each row in a Repeating Region—for example, add a link to the product name's or employee name's detail page. With a Repeating Region, you need to add this link only a single time, since Dreamweaver's programming takes care of the process of actually displaying the multiple rows of repeating information (and therefore the link attached to each row).

3. **In the Property inspector, click the Folder icon.**

   The Select File window appears (Figure 24-21). This method of creating a link is probably very familiar by now.

4. **Select the file you want to link to, but don't close this window yet.**

   In this step, select the file you wish to pass additional information *to*. Most likely, this file is a detail page that'll use the data supplied in the URL to search a database, and then return detailed information about a single record in the database.

5. **Click the Parameters button (circled in Figure 24-21).**

   The Parameters window opens (see Figure 24-4). You read about this window on page 867 as a way to add URL parameters to a link. The basic process described on page 867 applies here, but you'll be using dynamic data from a recordset as the value of the URL parameter

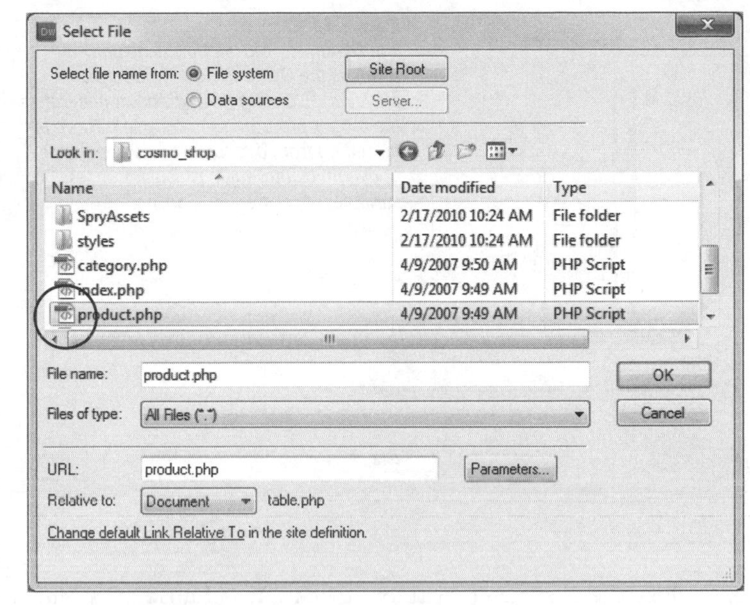

***Figure 24-21:** The Select File window provides a quick and error-free way to link to a page. When working with dynamic pages, you can also click the Parameters button (circled) to tack additional information onto the link that dynamic pages can use to search a database. On Macs, the Parameters window appears just to the right of the URL field.*

6. **Click in the space below the Name column, and then type the name of the URL parameter.**

   Since the URL provides data to another web page (like a detail page), the name you provide here should match the filter name on the detail page's recordset (see page 861 for more on filtering recordsets). In many cases, the name you provide should match the name of the primary key field the detail page uses to retrieve a record. For example, if you link to a page that provides detailed information on an individual product in your catalog, the name might be *productID* to indicate the ID number for the product.

7. **Click the space below the Value column, and then click the lightning bolt button.**

   The Dynamic Data window opens (Figure 24-22). This window lets you select information from a recordset. For example, you can use it to add a record's primary key value to a link. That way, you pass the primary key to another page (like a detail page), which uses that information to retrieve detailed information for that record.

8. **From the Dynamic Data window, select an item, and then click OK.**

   Dreamweaver adds the programming code necessary to grab that bit of dynamic data and attach it to the URL.

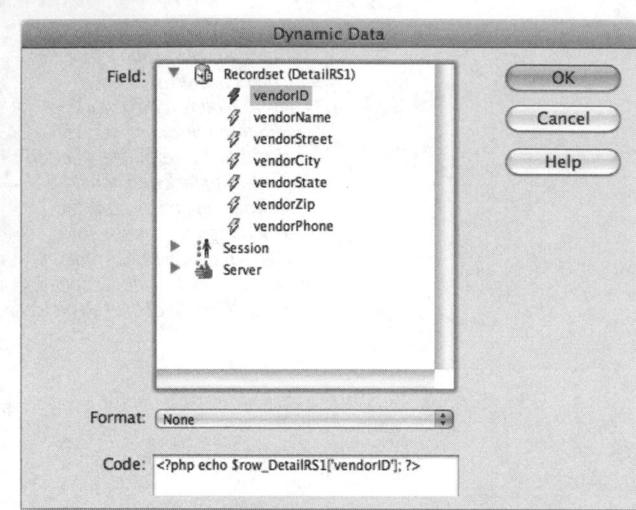

Figure 24-22: *The Dynamic Data window is actually the same as the Dynamic Text window displayed in "Deleting Recordsets". It generates the proper programming code to retrieve information from a recordset or other source of dynamic data, such as cookies or session variables, discussed in "Cookies".*

9. **Click OK to close the Parameters window. Click OK (Choose on a Mac) to close the Select File window and apply the link.**

   Now, when you view this page, the link points to the page you specified with the addition of a dynamically generated URL parameter.

Tip: A handy extension simplifies this laborious process. The free PHP Missing Tools extension by Felix One (*www.felixone.it/extensions/freeextdetailen.asp?IDProdotto=FX_PHPMissing*) includes a Go To Detail Page server behavior that makes the preceding nine-step process a matter of a few clicks.

Viewing Live Data

After you add dynamic information to a web page, you see something like this in the document window: *{rsProducts.productID}*. That gives you an idea of what the information is—in this example, the database column *productID* from a recordset named *rsProducts*—but it doesn't show any real database information, which can make designing a page difficult. You're especially far from seeing the actual result when a page contains a Repeating Region: what appears as a single row of dynamic text will actually show up as multiple rows or records when someone views it in a browser.

You've already encountered one way to simulate the browser-view of a page: Live View (discussed on page 898). You can use Live View for dynamic pages as well as the JavaScript-enabled pages you learned about in this chapter. Just click the Live View button (see Figure 24-23) to see what the page looks like, complete with data directly from your database.

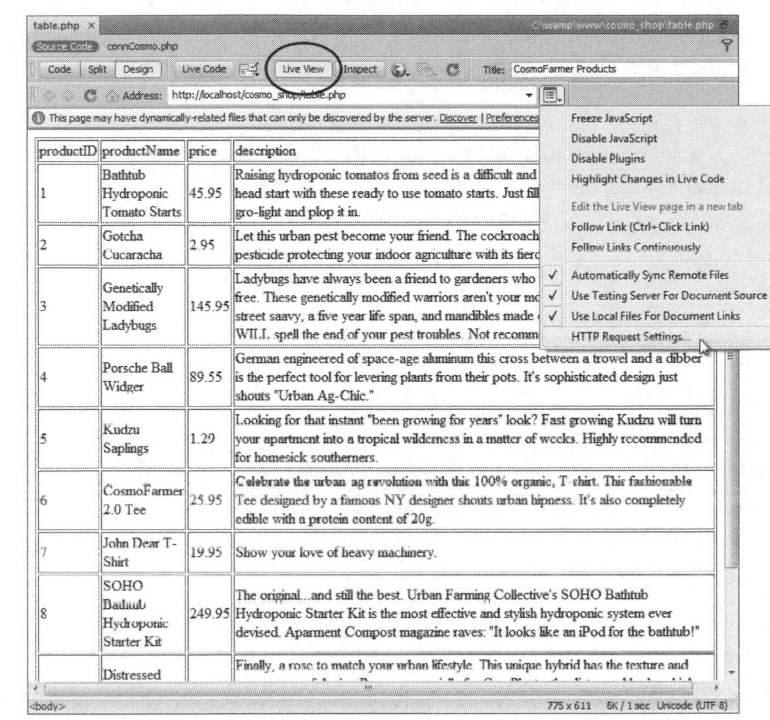

***Figure 24-23:** This is the Live View of the dynamic table pictured in Figure 24-12. When you see the Live View button highlighted (it looks like it's pressed on Windows, and highlighted in blue on Macs), Dreamweaver is displaying the page in Live View. You can't make any changes to the document until you leave Live View by pressing the Live View button again. One handy supplement to Live View is the HTTP Request Settings option in the Live View menu available from the Browser Navigation toolbar–it lets you set up test URL or Form variables to see how the page reacts when you pass it data. This feature is discussed next.*

HTTP Request Settings

Some recordsets depend on information provided by a form or URL. Often when you use the filter option, for instance, a recordset searches a database for records that match information from a form or URL.

This feature can come in handy for pages that provide detailed information about a single record. Frequently, for these types of pages, the URL might appear something like this: *product.php?productID=38*, where the name of the page *(product.php)* is followed by a URL parameter that includes a name *(productID)* and value *(38)*. The recordset then looks for the product whose ID *(productID)* matches 38.

Pages like this can't show up properly without a little outside help, so you need to provide extra information in the Live View Settings window, like this:

1. **In the Browser Navigation toolbar, click Live View Settings menu and select HTTP Request Settings button (see Figure 24-23).**

   You can also choose View→Live View Options→HTTP Request Settings. Either way, the Live View Settings window appears (Figure 24-24). Click the + button to add a new name and value pair.

   Dreamweaver refers to each name value pair in this window as a "URL request", but essentially it means either a form variable (see page 984) or a URL parameter (see page 983).

2. **Click the Name column, and then type a name for the new "URL request" item.**

   If you use the "URL request" to filter data in a recordset, use the name you used when you created the filter in the Recordset window (see step 5 on page 863). For example, a URL like *http://www.cosmofarmer.com/product.php?productID=24* passes a primary key value to the detail page in a master/detail page set (page 892) In this case, you'd type the name *productID*.

3. **Click the Value column, and then type in a value.**

   This value may be a number or text, but the value must retrieve at least one record from the database, according to the filter options you set up in the recordset. For example, if you create a filter to find products under a certain price, then you might type *price* as the name of the URL request, and *10* as its value. Or, in the example in step 2, you'd type *24*—the value part of the URL parameter *productID=24*.

4. **From the Method menu, select either *GET* or *POST*.**

5. **If the filter in your recordset uses a *form* variable, select *POST*; if it uses a URL parameter, select *GET*.**

6. **Click OK to close the Live View Settings window.**

   If you selected the *GET* method in step 4, the name and value you supplied in the Live View Settings window appears in the Browser Navigation toolbar, following the URL of the page.

Note: The Recordset Navigation Bar and Status message objects react differently, depending on which records in a recordset Dreamweaver displays. To see this effect in action, in the Live Data Settings window, add a new URL request item named *pageNum_rsName* (where *rsName* is the name of the recordset used in the Repeating Region). Set the value to something other than zero. Click OK to return to the Live View.

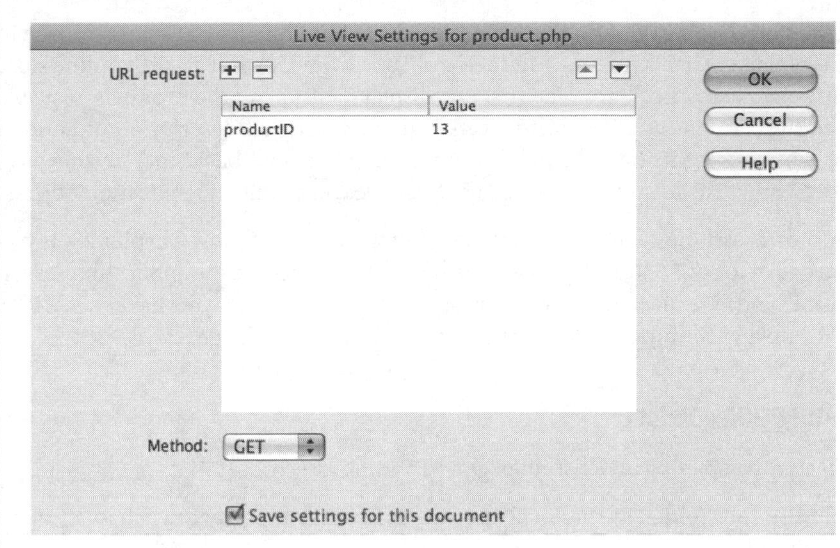

Figure 24-24: *The Live View Settings window lets you define information that the dynamic page needs to operate correctly. For example, the page may use information embedded in a URL to search records in a database .*

Navigating Live View

Dreamweaver CS5 adds a new feature to Dreamweaver's Live View—live navigation. When you view a page using Live View, you can now follow the links on the page. In other words you can view a page in Live View, mouse over a Spry navigation menu, click on a drop-down menu, and Dreamweaver display the linked-to file in Live View.

This is especially useful with dynamic pages like the ones you built in this section of the book. As you read on page 866, oftentimes dynamic pages rely on other dynamic pages to work. For example, in the master/detail page set, the detail page only knows which record to display because a link on the master page passes along a record ID—*product.php?productID=12*, for instance.

However, you'll normally find this Live View link feature turned off. To turn it on, first open a web page, then click the Live View button (or choose View→Live View), and then either select Follow Links or Follow Links Continuously from the Live View Settings menu (Figure 24-24). (Alternatively, choose View→Live View Options→Follow Links). The Follow Links option is just a one-time thing—once you turn it on and click one link, Dreamweaver turns off the link-following feature. To keep it on indefinitely so you can click around to preview the different pages of your site at will, choose the Follow Links Continuously option.

Tutorial: Displaying Database Info

In this tutorial, you'll continue the work you started on the CosmoFarmer website in the last chapter. Displaying the products available from CosmoFarmer's online store requires two dynamic pages. The first one displays a list of all the products available on the site. From that page, visitors can jump to a detailed description of an item for sale by clicking its name. You'll learn how to create both basic and advanced recordsets, and take advantage of some of Dreamweaver's built-in application objects.

This tutorial assumes you've done all the setup work described in Chapter 23. If you haven't, turn to page 836 and follow the instructions to prepare the application server, database, and Dreamweaver for this project. (Also make sure you have WAMP or MAMP up and running, as described on pagespage 836 andpage 837.)

Creating a Recordset

You'll start by opening an existing page and adding a recordset to it:

1. **In the root folder of the local site you defined in the previous chapter, open *index.php*.**

   Either choose File→Open and navigate to and select *index.php*, or, in the Files panel, double-click the file name.

   The basic structure of this page is already complete. It was built using CSS layout, the Spry Navigation Bar, a table, Cascading Style Sheets, and the other HTML features you've already learned. Nothing about this page is dynamic yet, so you'll need to create a recordset and insert database information into the page.

2. **Open the Bindings panel (Windows→Bindings or Ctrl+F10 [⌘-F10]).**

   The Bindings panel is control center for retrieving and using information from a database. It lets you create new recordsets and add dynamic data to a page.

3. **In the Bindings panel, click the + button, and then choose Recordset.**

   You can also use the Server Behaviors panel (on that panel, click the + button, and then select Recordset); on the Insert panel's Data category, click the Insert Recordset button (see Figure 24-1); or choose Insert→Data Objects→Recordset. Choose whichever method feels easiest for you. In any case, you should now see the Recordset box. (Make sure you use the *simple* mode—you should see a button on the right labeled "Advanced", as shown in Figure 24-25.)

   Next, select the information you want to retrieve.

4. **In the Name box, type *rsProducts*.**

   Since Dreamweaver lets you connect to more than one database, you must now indicate *which* database you want to use.

5. **From the Connections pop-up menu, select "connCosmo".**

   This is the name of the connection you created in the last chapter. The CosmoFarmer database contains several tables. For this page, you'll create an index of all the products CosmoFarmer sells. That information is in the Products table.

6. **From the Tables menu, choose "products". Click Selected.**

   You don't need to retrieve *all* the information from the Products table. Since this dynamic page will present a listing of all of the products, you need only basic information, like the name of the product, its price, and its inventory status. More details about each product will appear on a second page, the detail page, which you'll create later in this tutorial.

7. **In the Columns list, Ctrl-click (⌘-click) "productName", "price", and "inventory".**

   You want the page to get these columns of data from the database. You don't have to filter this recordset (meaning you're not trying to search the database for a particular product), so you can ignore those controls in the dialog box. However, it would be nice if the product names appeared in alphabetical order.

8. **From the first Sort pop-up menu, choose "productName". From the second menu, choose Ascending.**

   The Ascending option makes certain the records start with products whose names begin with A and end with names that begin with Z. The Recordset window should look like Figure 24-25.

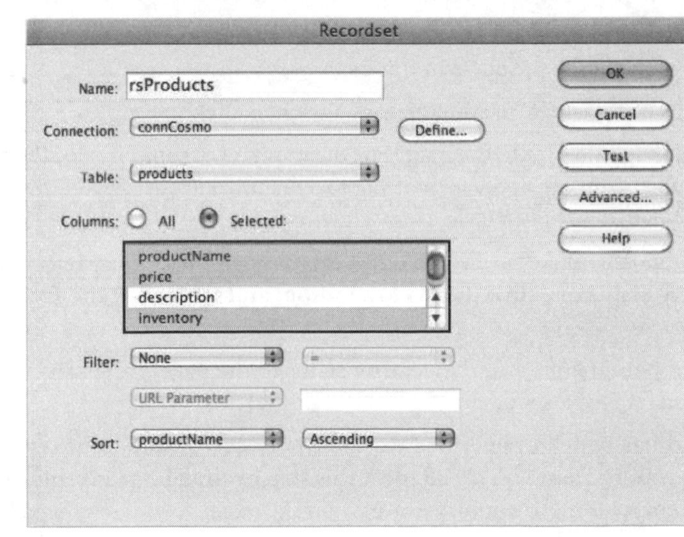

***Figure 24-25:** Recordsets let you retrieve information from a database, so you can display it on a page. This simple recordset retrieves the product name, price, and inventory status of every product in the CosmoFarmer database.*

9. **Click OK to close the Recordset dialog box.**

   The new recordset appears in the Bindings panel. To see the database columns in the recordset, you may need to expand the recordset list.

10. **In the Bindings panel, next to the Recordset icon, click the + icon (flippy triangle on Mac).**

    The Bindings panel should look like Figure 24-26. The page already has an HTML table—below the CosmoFarmer Online Store headline—waiting for the product information.

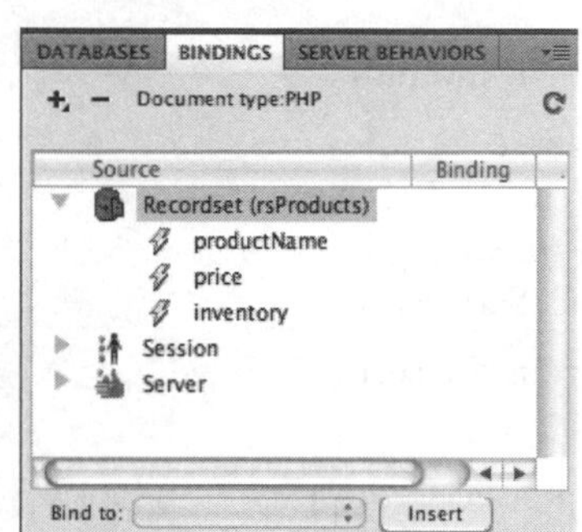

Figure 24-26: *The Bindings panel provides a list of a page's recordsets and data fields. You can use these fields to add dynamic text to a page.*

11. **In the document window, click inside the table cell directly below the one labeled "Product".**

    You'll add the name of the products in this cell.

12. **In the Bindings panel, click "productName", and then click Insert.**

    You just added dynamic data to the page. For the moment, it looks like *{rsProducts.productName}*. You can apply formatting to dynamic data just as you would to regular HTML text—apply a style, change the font, make it bold, and so on.

13. **In the page's table cell, make sure you have *{rsProducts.productName}* selected. In the Property inspector, click the HTML button, and then click the B button.**

    Now you'll add both the price and inventory status to the page. Here's an even easier way to insert recordset data.

14. **From the Bindings panel, drag "price" to the empty cell on the web page—below the cell with the label "Price". Repeat this step by dragging "inventory" into the third empty cell ("Inventory Status") on the page.**

    At this point, your page should look like Figure 24-27.

Live View and Creating Repeating Regions

When you add dynamic data to a page, it doesn't look like much. All you see is the recordset and column name between braces (*{rsProducts.productName}*, for example). Not only can this interfere with your design, it certainly doesn't give you a clear picture of what your web page will actually look like.

FREQUENTLY ASKED QUESTION

"Discovering" Dynamic Files

Whenever I open a PHP page, a bar appears just above the document, saying "This page may have dynamically-related files that can only be discovered by the server." What does that mean?

It's not uncommon for an application server to build a dynamic page from a collection of other dynamic files. Using something called "server-side includes," you can reuse chunks of programming code on multiple pages (kind of like how Dreamweaver Library Items work as discussed in Chapter 19). For example, content management systems like Drupal, Joomla, or the blogging software WordPress, might use dozens of separate files to complete the display of a single page—each file contributes some part of the page or programming to display the page, such as getting a list of the blogger's latest posts, or displaying comments in a forum.

In addition, unlike the types of related files Dreamweaver uses for static pages, such as external CSS and JavaScript files, dynamically attached files aren't automatically displayed in Dreamweaver's Related Files toolbar (see page 433). To see all the related files for a dynamic page, just click the "Discover" button—Dreamweaver then loads any other files used by the current page. Dreamweaver lists those files in the Related Files toolbar and you can access the code in them simply by clicking their associated tab (just like regular related files).

Basically, this is a pretty advanced option intended for serious PHP programmers. You won't need to use this feature with the basic database and server programming tools you learn about in this chapter.

Thank goodness for Dreamweaver's Live View:

1. **Choose View→Live View.**

   Alternatively you can use the keyboard shortcut: Alt-F11 (Option-F11). In either case, Dreamweaver connects to the testing server and database to retrieve the data requested by the recordset (this step may take a few seconds). For the first time, you get to see the page as it'll appear on the Web. But you have a problem: Only one item is listed. This page is meant to show listings for *all* products. To show more products, you have to add a Repeating Region—a part of the page that repeats for each record in a recordset.

2. **Choose View→Live View to turn off Live View.**

   You can't work on the page in Live View, so turn it on when you want to get an accurate view of a page, then turn it off when you're ready to keep editing the page.

3. **Move your cursor to the left of the table cell with** ***{rsProducts.productName}*** **(you want your cursor to be over the left edge of the table); click when the right-pointing arrow appears.**

   That's how you select the bottom row of the table. (For other ways to selecting a table row, see page 266.) Since this row displays the info for a single product, it's a perfect candidate for a Repeating Region, where an additional row appears in the table for each product.

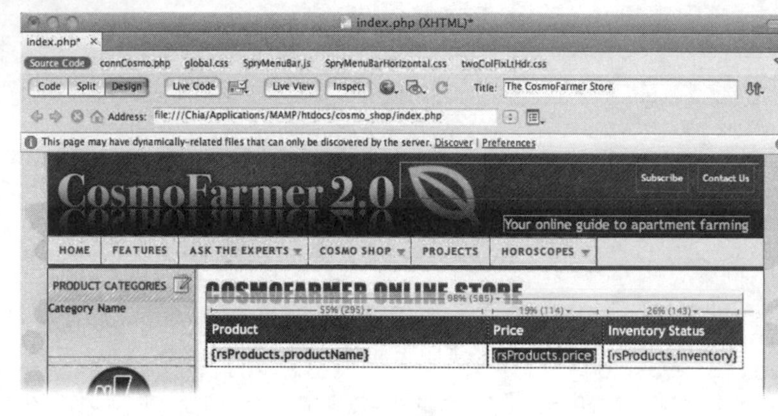

Figure 24-27: *After you add dynamic information to a page, its table and column name appear with a blue background. Here, three pieces of dynamic data appear on the page from the rsProducts recordset: rsProducts.productName, rsProducts.price, and rsProducts.inventory. To change this background color, choose Edit→Preferences (Dreamweaver→Preferences). Click the Highlighting category, and then, at the bottom of the window, change the Live Data colors.*

4. **On the Insert panel's Data category, click the Repeated Region button (see Figure 24-1).**

   The Repeat Region dialog box (Figure 24-14) appears, so you can select which recordset to use (if the page has more than one) and how many records you want to display. In this case, since you have only one recordset, you just have to tell Dreamweaver how many records to show.

5. **In the "Records at a Time" box, type** ***12*****. Click OK.**

   You don't know how many products the CosmoFarmer store offers at any time. If it's a lot, you don't want to show them all on a single page—a thousand listings would make for a pretty long web page. In this case, just list 12 records at a time.

   If the database has more than 12 products, you need to give people a way to see the other items. You'll do that next.

6. **Click to the right of the table that lists the products. Then, in the Insert panel's Data category, click the Recordset Paging button, and, from the menu, select Recordset Navigation Bar (see Figure 24-17).**

   The Recordset Navigation dialog box appears. You can do only one thing here.

7. **Make sure you have the Text button selected; click OK.**

   Dreamweaver plops a table containing four columns onto the page. The columns contain links that let visitors navigate through the product listings.

   The table will look better once you apply some CSS style to it.

8. **In the document window, select the navigation bar table (for example, click anywhere inside the table then click <table> in the tag selector at the bottom left of the Document window). In the Property inspector, from the class pop-up menu, choose "paging".**

   For other techniques on selecting a table, see page 266.

9. **Click at the end of the headline "CosmoFarmer Online Store", and then press Enter to create a new, empty paragraph; from the Display Record Count menu, choose Recordset Navigation Status (see Figure 24-16). Click OK when the Recordset Navigation Status window appears.**

   Dreamweaver inserts something that looks like this: *Records {rsProducts.FirstRecord} to {rsProducts.LastRecord} of {rsProducts.TotalRecords}*. That's place holder code for this notation: "Records 1 to 10 of 27". In fact, if you choose View→Live View, that's exactly what you see.

   Now to rework the message a little bit.

10. **Select the word "Records", and then change it to *Products*; select each of the placeholders (*{rsProducts.FirstRecord}*, and so on), and then, in the Property inspector, click the B button to make them bold.**

    You can add or remove any of the non-dynamic text in the navigation status bar. Now to see the results of your hard work.

11. **Press F12 (Option-F12) to preview the page in your web browser.**

    The page opens in a browser, displaying 12 records (see Figure 24-28).

Editing a Recordset and Linking to a Detail Page

Now that the main product listings page is complete, you need to create a link for the name of each product so that, when a guest clicks that link, the web browser retrieves a page with the details for that item. How does the detail page know which product to display? You need to add some additional information to the link for each product—the product's ID number. In other words, while all the product links point to the same page, they pass some additional (and unique) information that tells the detail page which product to display.

Unfortunately, Dreamweaver doesn't provide a simple, one-click way to add a URL parameter to tell a detail page which recordset's details to display. You have to create that yourself, but first you need to add a primary key to the product's recordset.

1. **Open the Server Behaviors panel by pressing Ctrl+F9 (⌘-F9), or, in the Application panel group, by clicking the Server Behaviors tab.**

   A list of all the different server behaviors appears; you added these behaviors when you created a recordset, put dynamic text on the page, and used Dreamweaver's other dynamic page creation tools. Instead of adding another server behavior at this point, you can edit one you already created: the recordset. When you first added this recordset, an important piece of information was missing—the product's ID number. (Actually, it was omitted from the tutorial intentionally, so that you now have the engaging educational opportunity to learn how to edit a recordset.)

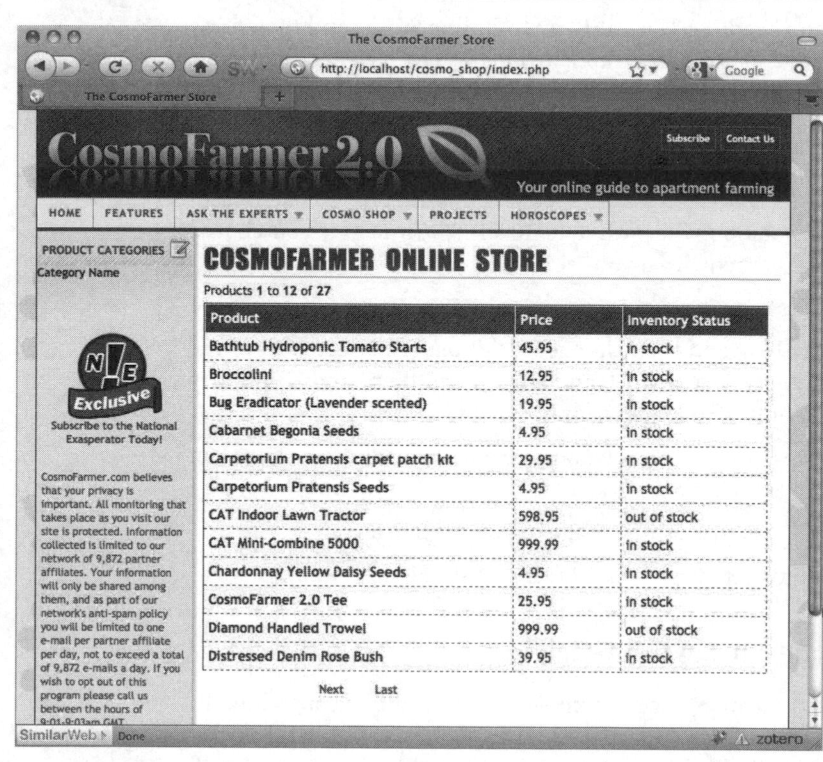

Figure 24-28: *You can easily build dynamic web pages in Dreamweaver. In just a few short steps–all right, 25 steps– you can create pages that display database records. (At the bottom of the page, you can click the Next link to jump to the next set of product listings.)*

   Each product has its own ID number, which you'll use to tell the Details page which item to display.

2. **In the Server Behaviors panel, double-click "Recordset (rsProducts)" to open the Recordset dialog box.**

   You'll just add one additional column to the recordset.

3. **Ctrl-click (⌘-click) "productID" in the columns list, and then click OK.**

   You just added one additional column (productID) to the recordset. Now the recordset not only retrieves the name, price, and inventory status for each product, it also picks up its unique ID number.

4. **In the document window, select the dynamic data containing the product's name: "{rsProducts.prodName}".**

   A simple link to an already created web page doesn't work here. Since the page containing a product's details is dynamic—it changes based on which product your guest decides to view—you need one of Dreamweaver's server behaviors.

5. **In the Property inspector, click the "Browse for file" icon.**

   The Select File window appears. This process is the same as creating a regular link.

6. **Locate and select the file *product.php*, located in the site's root folder.**

   This page displays the detailed records for each product. Next, you'll add a little dynamic information to the link, so that the page can pass each product's unique ID number to the details page.

7. **On the right side of the Select File window, click the Parameters button (it's just to the right of the URL box).**

   The Parameters window opens (see Figure 24-29).

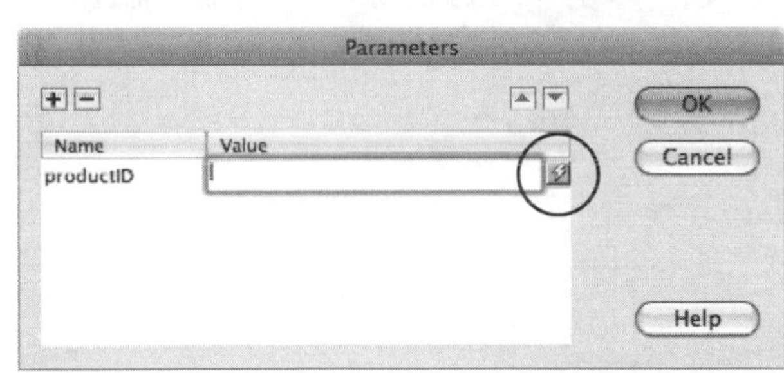

Figure 24-29:
The Parameters window lets you tack dynamic information onto the end of a link. In this way, you can pass information (for example, a product's ID number) off to another dynamic page that uses that information to display dynamic data.

8. **In the Name column, type *productID*, and then press the Tab key twice to jump to the Value column. On the right side of the Value column, click the dynamic value button (circled in Figure 24-29).**

   The Dynamic Data window appears (see Figure 24-30). "productID" is the name Dreamweaver will add to the link. It identifies the category of information the details page will look in. In a moment, you'll identify a value, which uniquely identifies a single item in that category so the detail page can display a full set of information on just that one item.

9. **Expand the Recordset list (click the + or arrow buttons to the left of the Recordset); select "productID", and then click OK to close the Dynamic Data window.**

   This step selects the "productID" column from the recordset. In other words, this indicates that each link should have the unique ID for a particular product.

10. **Click OK to close the Parameters window, and finally click the OK (Windows) or Choose (Mac) button in the Select File window to finish creating the link.**

    You've just created a dynamic link. Now, preview it.

11. **Press the F12 (Option-F12) key to preview the page in your browser. Click the Bathtub Hydroponic Tomato Starts link.**

    The detail page loads…without any details! You'll get to that step in a moment. In the meantime, look at the URL in your browser's address bar. It should look something like this: *http://localhost/cosmo_shop/product.php?productID=1*. Notice the *?productID=1* tagged onto the page *product.php*. That's the information the details page needs in order to retrieve the proper product information. The two pieces of information—*productID* and *1*—are called a *key/value pair*. The key (*productID*) tells the details page which field to look in, while the value *(1)* identifies a particular product with an ID of *1*. Hit your browser's back button, click a different product's link, and you'll see that the ID number is now different.

12. **Save and close this page.**

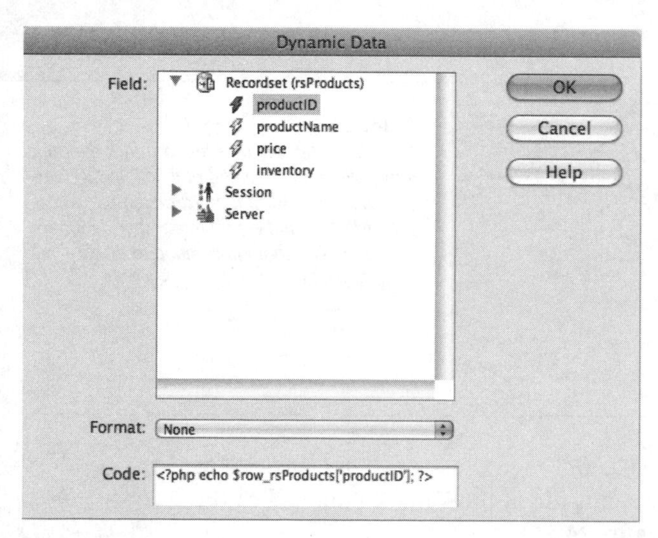

Figure 24-30: *The Dynamic Data window lets you select data from a database recordset that becomes part of a link's URL.*

Building the Detailed Product Page

In this part of the tutorial, you'll build a detail page that displays all the details for a particular product. In addition, you'll create an advanced recordset that combines information from two separate database tables:

1. **Open the file called *product.php* in the site's root folder.**

   Either choose File→Open and navigate to and select *product.php*, or, in the Files panel, double-click the file name.

   Since this page displays the details for a product, it must retrieve data from the database. To set this up, start by creating a recordset.

2. **From the Insert panel's Data category, click the Recordset button (see Figure 24-1).**

   You can also choose Insert→Data Objects→Recordset. Or, click the + button on either the Bindings panel or Server Behaviors panel, and then, from the pop-up menu, select *recordset*. In any case, the Recordset dialog box should now be open.

   The CosmoFarmer database contains several database tables—one for product information, one for vendor information, one that lists the different product categories, and one that contains user information (user names and passwords). The details page will list not only information from the Products table (such as the product's name and price) but also the name of the product's vendor. Unfortunately, the Products table contains only the vendor's ID number, not its name, so the recordset must incorporate information from both tables. Since the basic panel of the Recordset dialog box doesn't let you retrieve information from more than a single database table, you have to use the advanced setting.

3. **On the right side of the Recordset window, click the Advanced button.**

   The Advanced Recordset dialog box appears. Unfortunately, Dreamweaver isn't particularly user-friendly in this area. It helps to understand SQL (see page 870)—or you can just take the following steps.

4. **In the Name field, type *rsDetails*. From the Connection menu, choose "connCosmo".**

   In the next few steps, you'll create an SQL query—essentially a line of programming code that asks the database for particular information that matches specific criteria. In this case, it's the information for a particular product.

5. **If there's any text inside the big SQL text box, delete it. Click the + icon (flippy triangle) in the Database Items list, next to the word "Tables" (at the bottom of the dialog box).**

   It expands to reveal the four tables in the database: Category, Products, Users, and Vendors.

6. **Click the + icon (flippy triangle) to expand the Products table.**

   Your job is to select the information from this table that you want to display on the page.

7. **Select "productID"; click the Select button to the right.**

   Notice that Dreamweaver writes *SELECT products.productID FROM products* in the SQL box. This is SQL code for selecting a particular column of data from a table. You can now choose the other pieces of information.

8. **Repeat step 7 for the following items in the Products table: productName, price, description, inventory, image.**

   These items are all the ones you need to retrieve from the Products table. Now you can choose data from the Vendors table.

Note: If you understand SQL, then you can bypass this point-and-click approach, and simply write a SQL query directly in the SQL box.

---

9. **Click the + icon (flippy triangle) to expand the Vendors table. Repeat step 7 for the "vendorName" item in that table.**

   The dialog box should now look like Figure 24-31. Congratulations, you just created a SQL query.

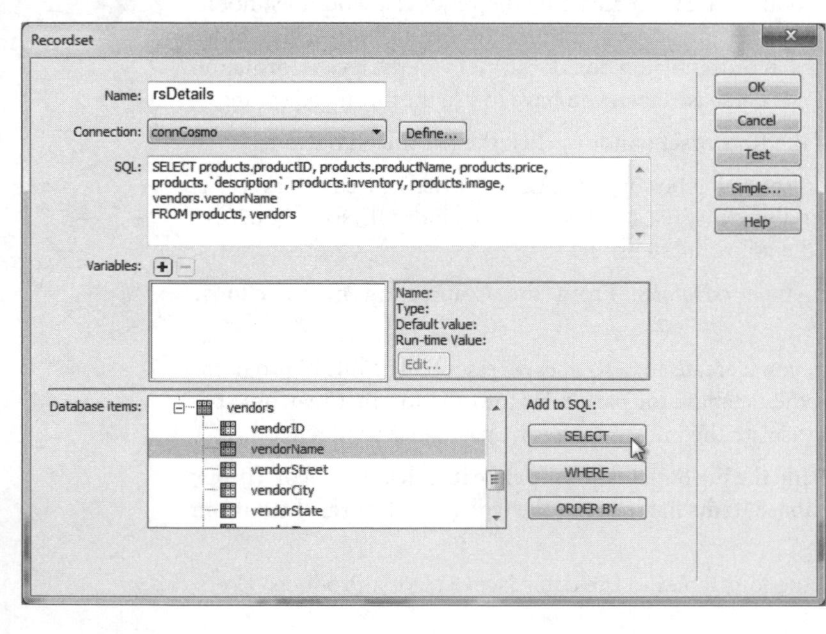

Figure 24-31: *The Recordset window's advanced mode lets you use a data tree (the bottom half of the window) to build an SQL statement. By selecting a column name, and then clicking either the SELECT, WHERE, or ORDER BY buttons, you can get Dreamweaver to do some of the heavy lifting. Unfortunately, you still need to understand a little bit of SQL to create functioning database queries using these advanced options. See "SQL: The Very Basics" on page 871 for a brief introduction to SQL.*

But you have a problem here: Because of this query's structure, it retrieves *all* the records for both tables (click the Test button to see for yourself). To remedy the situation, you must do two things: First, combine information from two tables so that you get the vendor information for the corresponding product; and second, retrieve only the information for the particular product specified by the link you created in the last part of this tutorial.

10. **Click inside the SQL box after the word "vendors" in the last line. Press Enter or Return.**

    Now you have to dive into typing out SQL code.

11. **Type *WHERE products.vendorID = vendors.vendorID*. (Don't include the sentence-ending period put there by our grammar-oriented copy editor.)**

    This little bit of code is called a *WHERE clause*, and it helps filter information in a database. In this instance, you create what's called a *join*—a statement that joins two or more tables together. When you retrieve product information, you also want to retrieve the name of the vendor who manufactures that product. By matching the vendor ID from the Products table to the identical vendor ID in the Vendors table, the database can produce the proper vendor name.

    If your eyes are glazing over, go get a cup of coffee before plunging ahead.

12. **To the right of the word "Variables", click the + button.**

    The Add Variable window appears (see Figure 24-32).

    You're about to expand on the WHERE clause you just wrote. Not only do you need to get the details of a product (plus the vendor's name), you also want to retrieve just a single record—the particular product whose details the visitor wants to review.

13. **Click in the Name box, and then type *varProduct*. Type *1* for "Default value". Type *$_GET['productID'] for the "Runtime value"*.**

    The Add Variable box should now look like Figure 24-32. Look back to step 8 on page 909. Remember that the ID number for the product is embedded in the URL that links to this page. In other words, when someone clicks a link on the main product listings page, the ID number for the product is passed along like this: *product.php?productID=12*.

    In this step, you're retrieving that information from the URL—that's the *$_GET ['productID']* part—and storing it in a variable that you'll use in the rest of the SQL query.

14. **Click OK to add the new variable. In the SQL box, click at the end of the WHERE clause (after "vendors.vendorID"), and then type *AND products.productID = varProduct*.**

    The Recordset window should now look like Figure 24-33.

15. **Click the Test button to see if the SQL query works.**

    A Test SQL Statement window opens, containing a single record. Hallelujah: It includes not only product details but also the vendor's name. (If Dreamweaver spits out an error message instead of a record, there's probably a typo somewhere in the SQL. Either try to identify the problem, or delete the SQL query, and then start again at step 5 above.)

16. **Click OK to close the Test SQL Statement window. Click OK again to complete the recordset. Choose File→Save to save your changes.**

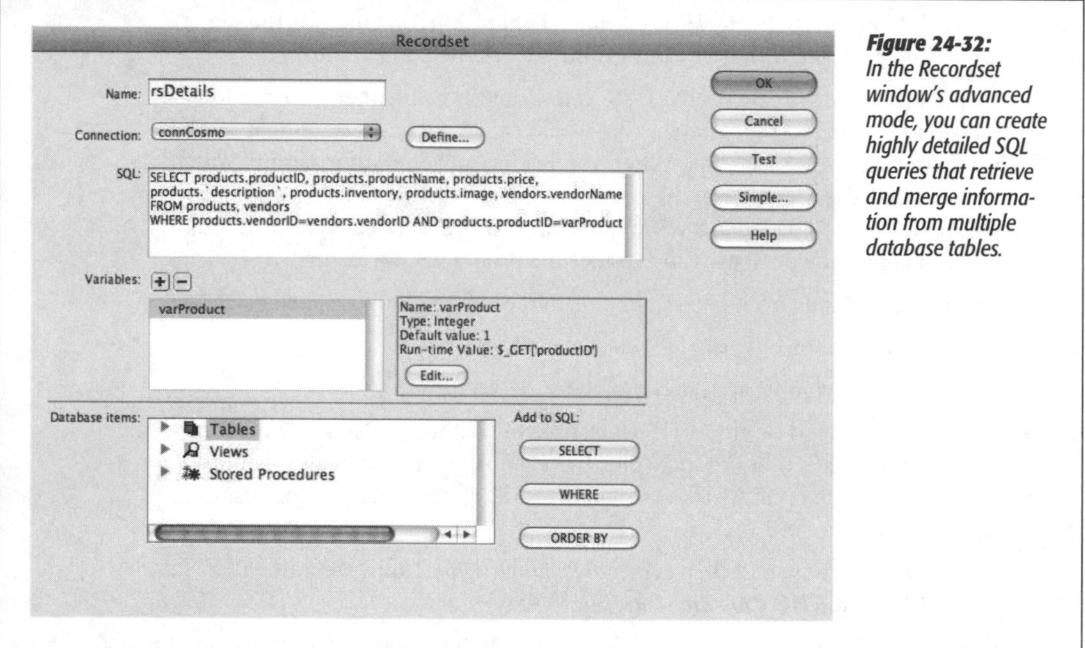

Figure 24-32: *In the Recordset window's advanced mode, you can create highly detailed SQL queries that retrieve and merge information from multiple database tables.*

Filling in the Details

Now you just have to add the information retrieved in the recordset to the detail page:

1. **In the document window, select the words "Product name".**

   You'll add the name of the product here.

2. **Open the Bindings panel.**

   Either press Ctrl+F10 (⌘-F10) or, in the Application panel group, click the Bindings tab.

3. **In the Bindings panel, click the + icon (flippy triangle) next to the recordset to display all the columns retrieved in the recordset. Select "productName", and then click Insert.**

   The placeholder for the dynamic data—*{rsDetails.productName}*—appears in the document window. Next, you'll try the drag-and-drop method of inserting dynamic data.

4. **In the Bindings panel, drag "description" into the empty, blank line just below the product name.**

   Now it's just a matter of adding the additional data to the page.

5. **Continue adding content to this page using these same steps.**

   Add the price, vendor name, and inventory status in the appropriate places in the document window. You might want to add some additional text, such as "Price: $", "Vendor:" and "Inventory Status:" to the page as labels to described the information, and then drag the appropriate dynamic text into place.

   To finish off this page, add a photo.

6. **Click just to the left of the product description (just before *{rsDetails.description}*). Choose Insert ›Image.**

   The Insert Image window appears. You've encountered this dialog box many times before when you inserted a graphic (see Chapter 6). However, in this case, you'll retrieve the image's file name from the database.

7. **Select the Data Sources button.**

   In Windows, this button is at the top of the Insert Image window; on a Mac, it's at the bottom. At this point, depending on whether you use Windows PC or a Mac, you'll see either the Select Image Source window or the Dynamic Data window (see Figure 24-33).

   A list of all of the different data items from the recordset appears. See the item labeled "image"? The database stores the *name* of the image file for each product in the database. But the image file itself isn't stored there. Although some databases do let you store the actual image data—called binary data—in a database, if you merely want to display an image on a web page, that's a big waste of database space and processing power. A better method, and the one used here, is to just store the name of an image file that's already on the website (for example, in a folder named *images*). In the next two steps, you'll craft a path to an already existing file on the web server.

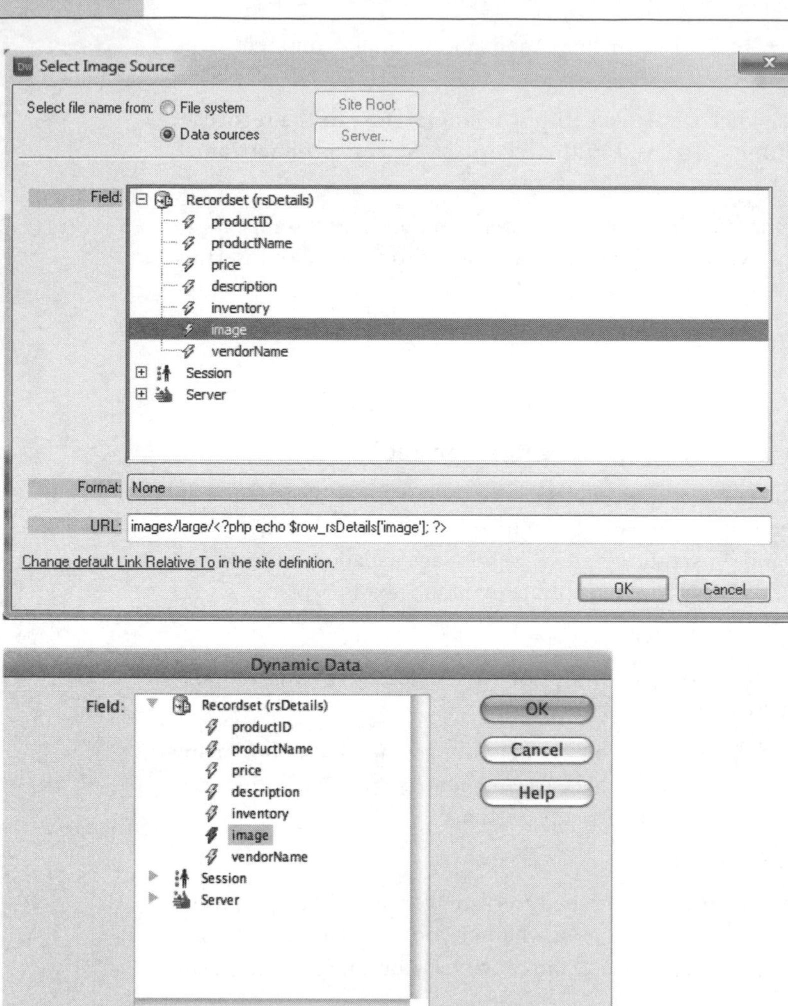

Figure 24-33: *You don't need to hardwire paths for links and images into a web page. You can craft custom paths and links using information retrieved from a database. A good technique when you work with images and a database is to store just the name of the image file in the database. Then, when you insert an image using the database as a data source, you select the field that contains the image's file name, and then precede the PHP code that appears in the URL (Windows, top) or Code (Mac, bottom) box with the information necessary to create a complete path to the image.*

8. **Select "image".**

   At the bottom of the window (in the URL box [Windows] and the Code box [Mac]), you see some PHP programming code that looks like this: *<?php echo $row_rsDetails['image']; ?>*. It looks scary, but it simply mirrors whatever's stored in the image column for the particular recordset. Since the image column in this table stores the name of a file, this code would print something like *tomatoes.jpg*. This value appears as the *src* property of the image—in other words, specifying where a browser should look for the file. (You learned about the *src* property in Chapter 6.)

Tip: One benefit of this only-store-the-file-name-in-the-database approach is that you can store different size images for the same record in different locations, yet still use the same recordset field for each. For example, say you have a dynamic page that displays thumbnails of all the products in your database. And you also have a page that displays a larger picture of the same product. Use the same file name in each case (*tomato.jpg* for example) but store the thumbnail file in one location (perhaps *images/small/*) and the larger file in another folder (*images/large/*). When you want to insert a thumbnail, you use the database field used to store the image, but add the appropriate path (for example, *images/small/*). When you want to insert the larger image, you use the same database field (*image*, for example), but supply the path that points to the larger file (*images/large/*).

For the CosmoFarmer store, the images are actually stored inside a folder named large, which is inside the images folder. (Thumbnails for each image are stored in the small folder.) For the image to appear correctly, you need to add a little information to this window.

9. **In the URL (Code) box, click before the text "<?php", and then type *images/large/* as pictured in Figure 24-34.**

   Don't omit the forward slash after the word large. You'll then have this code: `images/large/<?php echo $row_rsDetails['image']; ?>`.

10. **Click OK. (If the Image Tag Accessibility Attributes window appears, just click OK to dismiss it.)**

    A little square icon appears in the document window. This icon is an image placeholder icon, and represents the space where an image appears when a visitor views the page in a browser. Next you'll add a style to this graphic.

11. **Make sure you still have the little square icon selected (if not, click it), and then, from the Class menu, choose "productImage".**

    The image placeholder floats to the right side of the page. One last thing to do: Since you're a web design expert (or at least an aspiring one), you know that images should always have their *alt* properties (page 224) set. But since the exact image that appears varies based on which product your guest views—it might be a tomato or a picture of an indoor lawn mower—how can you specify alt text that matches the picture? As with most things in this section of the book, the answer is, "You do it dynamically, of course!"

    To set alt text dynamically you need to use the Tag inspector window.

12. **Make sure you still have the image placeholder selected, and then choose Window→Tag Inspector (or press F9).**

    The Tag inspector is a kind of super Property inspector. It lets you set every conceivable HTML property for a particular tag (not just the most common ones listed in the Property inspector).

13. **Click the Show List View button (the icon with A-Z on it), and then, to the right of "alt", click the empty area.**

    You could just type the alt text here, but notice that our friend, the lightning bolt icon, appears. This is your clue that we can access some dynamic data.

14. **Click the lighting bolt icon to open the Dynamic Data window.**

    The Dynamic Data window works just like the Dynamic Text window pictured back in Figure 24-8. It lets you insert information from a field in a recordset. In this case, the appropriate text description for each product's photo is the product's name.

15. **In the Dynamic Data window, click "productName"; click OK.**

    Now, whenever a guest views the page, the alt text for the image matches the product in the image. Time to see how it looks.

16. **Choose View→Live View or click the Live View button in the top of the Document window. If everything looks good (Figure 24-35), choose File→Save.**

    To see the results of your hard work, open the *index.php* page in Dreamweaver, and then press the F12 key (Option-F12) to preview the page in a browser. Now click a link to see the details for that product.

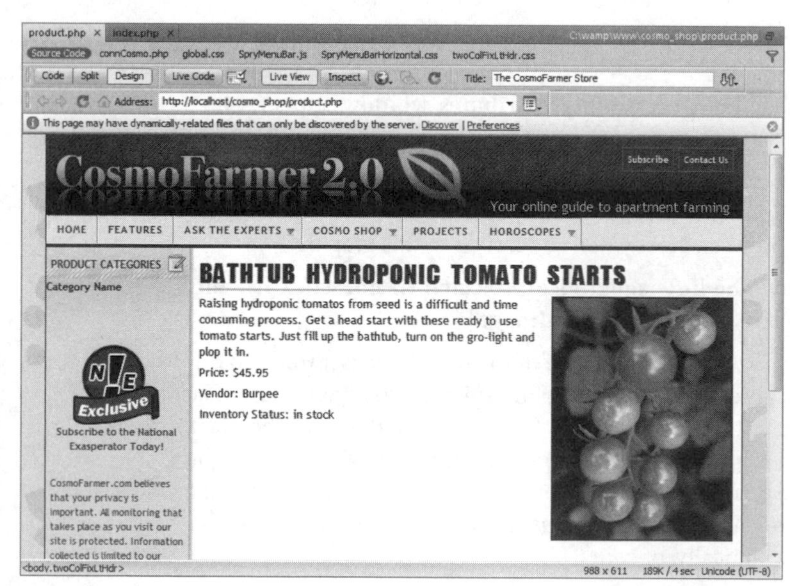

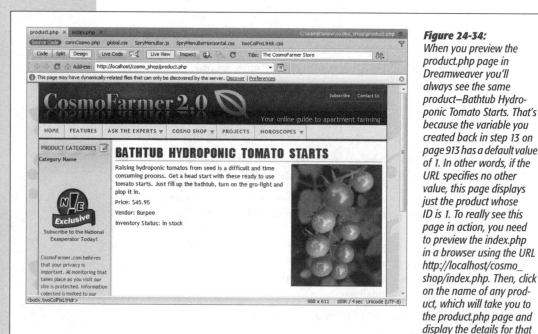

Figure 24-34: *When you preview the product.php page in Dreamweaver you'll always see the same product–Bathtub Hydroponic Tomato Starts. That's because the variable you created back in step 13 on page 913 has a default value of 1. In other words, if the URL specifies no other value, this page displays just the product whose ID is 1. To really see this page in action, you need to preview the index.php in a browser using the URL http://localhost/cosmo_shop/index.php. Then, click on the name of any product, which will take you to the product.php page and display the details for that particular product. (You can even use Live View to navigate pages in your site as described on page 901.)*

Operators Standing By

One final touch would make the products page perfect. Each product sold at the CosmoFarmer online store belongs to a category—plants, seeds, pest control, and so on. Shoppers might find it useful to view a list of products in a particular category—just the plants, for instance.

Since the database also stores category information, you can use this info to create such a feature. In this final part of the tutorial, you'll add a category navigation bar along the left side of the products page, so that when a visitor clicks a category name, a list of the products within that category appears:

1. **Open the *index.php* page.**

   This is the page to which you add the category links. The first step is to add a new recordset that retrieves all the category names from the database.

2. **If it's not open, open the Bindings panel (press Ctrl+F10 [⌘-F10], click the big + button, and then, from the pop-up menu, select Recordset.**

   You can also, on the Insert panel's Data category (see Figure 24-1), click the Insert Recordset button; choose Insert→Data Objects→Recordset; or, on the Server Behaviors panel, click the + button, and then, from the pop-up menu, select Recordset. In any case, the Recordset dialog box opens. (You may need to click the Simple button to switch the Recordset dialog box out of Advanced mode.)

3. **Type *rsCategories* into the Name box.**

   The *CosmoFarmer* database includes a table with the names of each category of products it sells. You use this table to dynamically generate the list of category names.

4. **From the Connections pop-up menu, select "connCosmo".**

   This is the same connection you've used throughout this tutorial. In this case, you're going to retrieve information from a different table in that database.

5. **From the Table menu, select *categories*.**

   The Categories table is very basic: just a name and ID number. It identifies a category by using a Category ID number—the table's "categoryID" field. You may wonder why a separate table is even necessary. Why not just store the category name with the product information?

   This design has two advantages. First, because the table is just a list of category names, you can easily retrieve an alphabetized list of those names by creating a recordset. That ability is useful, for example, when you want to add a list of categories to a page—as in these tutorial steps. In addition, the separate category table makes changes to categories easier. If you decide you want to change a name—say "Pest Control" to "Pest and Weed Control"—you need to update it only in one record in the Category table. If "Pest Control" were stored in the Products table, you would have to change the name to "Pest and Weed Control" in potentially hundreds of records.

6. **Make sure you have the All radio button selected, and then, from the Sort box, choose "categoryName".**

   At this point, the dialog box should look like Figure 24-36.

7. **Click OK to apply the recordset to the page.**

   Now the page has two recordsets—one to retrieve product info, the other to retrieve the list of categories. You'll add the category name to the page next.

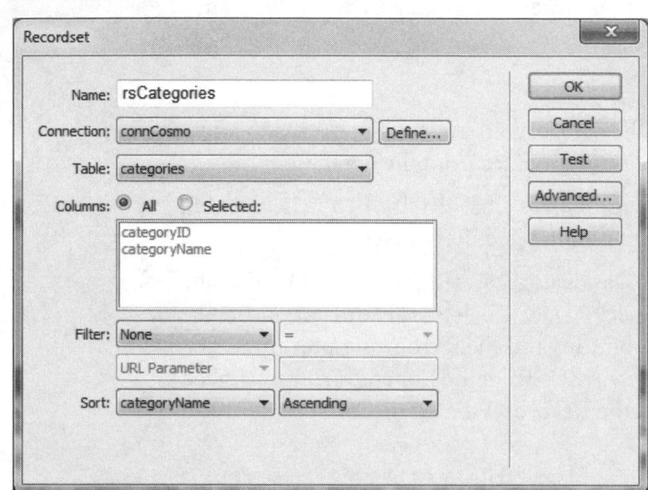

Figure 24-35:
By storing all the product category names in a single table, you can build a dynamic category navigation bar with the help of a simple recordset.

The Bindings panel should look like Figure 24-37. The list of category links will appear in the left-hand sidebar on the page; currently the text "Product Categories" appears in that space. You'll add the links below that.

8. **In the left-hand sidebar on the web page (below the headline "Product Categories"), select the text "Category Name".**

   The text you just selected is "dummy" text—a simple placeholder for the dynamic text you'll add now.

9. **From the Bindings panel, select "categoryName" (click the triangle to the left of the recordset name if you don't see the list of columns). Click the Insert button.**

   This step replaces the dummy text with dynamic text. Next, you'll add a link that points to the categories page.

10. **In the document window, select the dynamic text *{rsCategories.categoryName}*. In the Property inspector, click the "Browse for File" icon.**

    The Select File window appears. This is the same process as creating a regular link.

11. **Locate and select the file *category.php*, located in the site's root folder.**

    This page will display the list of products within a particular category. You'll next add a little dynamic information to the link, so that Dreamweaver can pass along each category's unique ID number.

12. **On the right side of the Select File window, click the Parameters button (it's just to the right of the URL box).**

    The Parameters window opens.

13. **In the Name column, type *categoryID*, click the Value column to the right, and then click the Dynamic Value button (the lightning bolt).**

    The Dynamic Data window opens (see Figure 24-30). *categoryID* is the name you want to add to the link. It helps the details page identify the purpose of the value (which you'll select next).

14. **Expand the "rsCategories" recordset list (click the + or arrow buttons to the left of the Recordset); select "categoryID", and then click OK to close the Dynamic Data window.**

    This step selects the "categoryID" column from the recordset. In other words, it indicates that each link should have the unique ID for each product category.

15. **Click OK to close the Parameters window and, finally, in the Select File window, click the OK (Windows) or Choose (Mac) button to finish creating the link.**

    You just created a dynamic link. Finally, you'll add a Repeating Region so that *all* the category names appear.

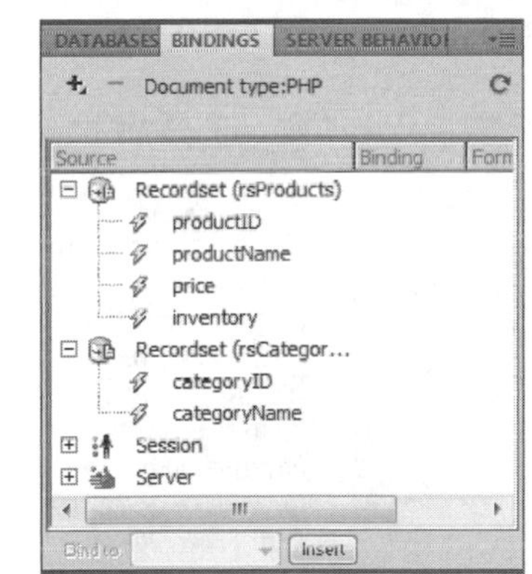

Figure 24-36:
The Bindings panel displays all recordsets currently applied to a page. To hide the recordset's field names, to the left of the recordset icon, click the minus (-) sign (arrow on the Mac).

16. **At the bottom of the document window, in the Tag selector, click the <li> tag.**

    The Tag selector (page 23) is the most accurate way to select an HTML tag. When working with Dreamweaver's Repeat Region server behavior, you have to be particularly careful to select exactly what you want to repeat for each record in a recordset. In this case, you want each category name to appear as its own bulleted item in the list—that means you need to select the <li> tag (or list item) before applying the Repeat Region server behavior.

17. **On the Insert panel's Data category, click the Repeat Region button (see Figure 24-1).**

    The Repeat Region window appears.

18. **From the menu, select "rsCategories". Click the All records radio button, and then click the OK button to create the Repeating Region.**

    Because you now have two recordsets on this page—*rsProducts* and *rsCategories*—it's important to choose the recordset whose records you wish to repeat: in this case, it's the Categories recordset. If you preview the page at this point, you see a list of categories along the left side of the page.

19. **Press F12 (Option-F12). When the page opens, click any of the category names at the left side of the page.**

    A new page should open, listing all the products within a particular category, as shown in Figure 24-38. If you're feeling adventurous, open the *product.php* page and follow steps 2 through 19 above to add the same category list to that page.

    Congratulations! You just built two powerful, complex, dynamic web pages (and probably watched three presidential administrations pass). As you can see, Dreamweaver has an impressive array of tools to build dynamic pages. And even though there were some twists and turns to negotiate, you never once had to resort to Code view.

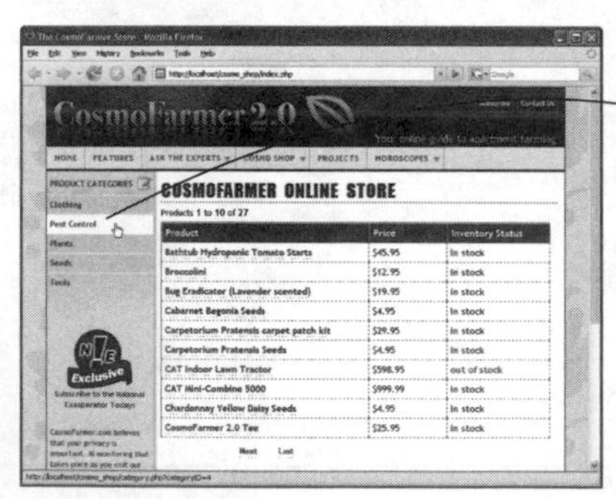

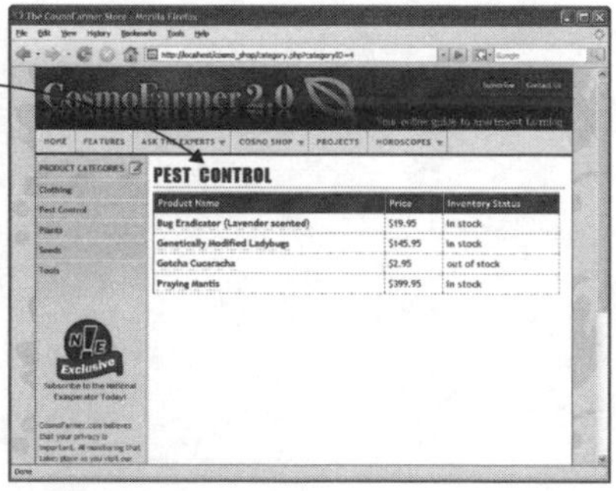

***Figure 24-37:** URL parameters can do more than link to a page with the details of a single record. You can use them to pass any information needed to search a database. In this case, the link on the products page (left) provides an ID number to the categories page (right), so that just the products within a particular category appear.*

CHAPTER

25

Web Pages that Manipulate Database Records

Displaying database information on a web page is useful, but you may be more interested in the opposite kind of communication—*collecting* information from your site's visitors (see Figure 25-1). Maybe you want them to do something as simple as register with your site. Other times, you may have something more ambitious in mind—like accepting and processing product orders using a full-fledged e-commerce system.

Both of these kinds of transactions require that you have some way to change the information stored in your database—to add a new visitor's user name and password in the former case and to add or delete products and change prices in the latter. In short, once you have data in a database, you need a way to maintain it—to update and delete information. After all, you'll change prices, discontinue products, and remove any record of "Harvey the Wise Guy" from your site's online guestbook. Thankfully, Dreamweaver makes changing information in a database simple and painless.

Note: You may feel more comfortable learning these concepts by *doing* them. If so, turn to the tutorial on page 949 before you read the next section.

Adding Data

As noted in Chapter 12, the primary way you collect information over the Internet is through an *HTML form*. Its basic elements—text boxes, radio buttons, pop-up menus, and so on—give you all kinds of ways to collect a wide assortment of data.

But to *record* this information, you either need to write your own program or, more simply, use Dreamweaver's built-in tools to funnel data into a database. Dreamweaver's Record Insertion Form Wizard and Insert Record server behavior make adding data a simple process.

Warning: You might not want just anyone adding, editing, or deleting database information. To control access to these types of pages—or any page, for that matter—use Dreamweaver's User Authentication server behaviors, as discussed on page 971.

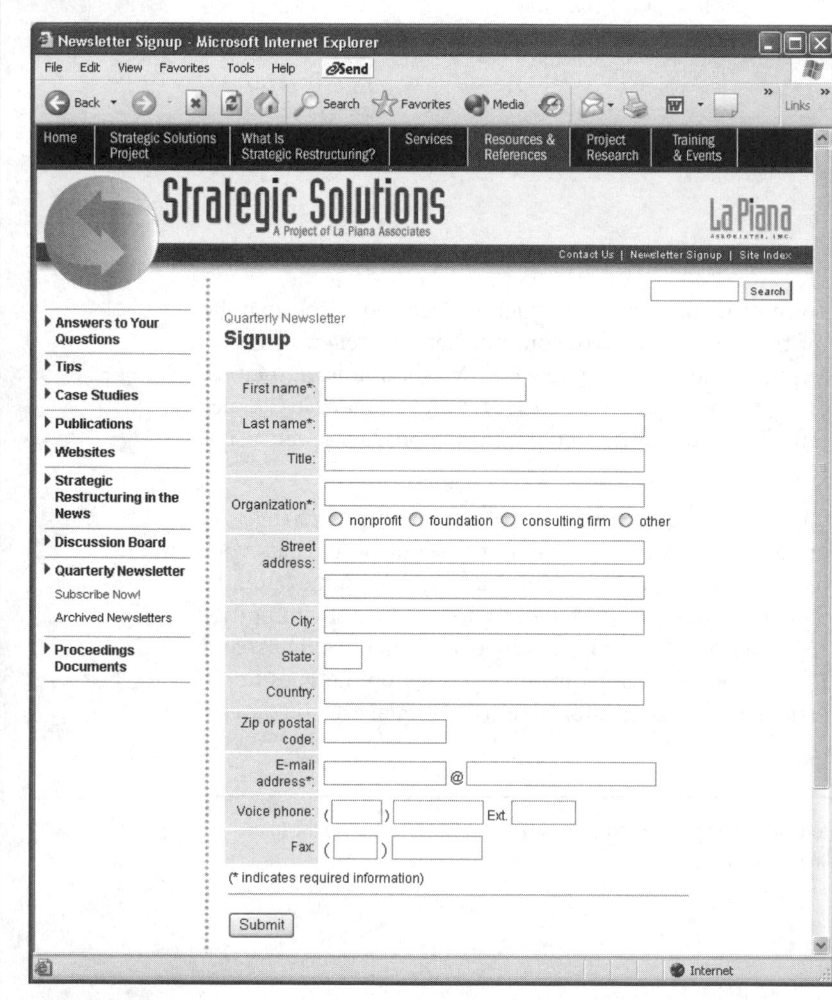

***Figure 25-1:** Whether you want to accept credit cards on an e-commerce site or gather sign-up information for an online newsletter, Dreamweaver simplifies the process of creating forms that funnel info into a database.*

Dreamweaver's Record Insertion Form Wizard

Dreamweaver's Record Insertion Form Wizard is the quickest way to add records to a database. It builds a form, creates a table, and then adds all the necessary programming code in just a couple of steps. To use it:

1. **Create a new web page, and save it to your site (or open a dynamic page you've already created).**

   Make sure the page uses the extension (.asp, .cfm, .php) that matches your site's server model (page 834). (See page 843 for info on creating new dynamic pages.)

2. **In the document window, click the spot where you want the form to appear. Choose Insert→Data Objects→Insert Record→Record Insertion Form Wizard.**

   You can also select Record Insertion Form Wizard from the Insert Record menu on the Insert panel's Data category. Either way, the Record Insertion Form window opens (Figure 25-2).

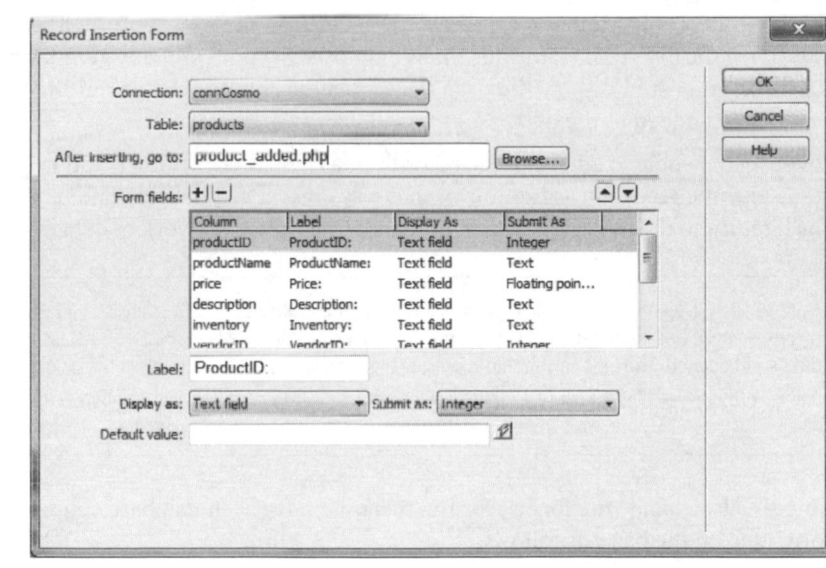

Figure 25-2: *When you create a web page form, remove the columns the database creates for its own use, such as the one for record IDs. Here, the column "productID" holds a unique number the database creates when someone adds a new record. You wouldn't want anyone to manually enter a record number, so leave the column off the form.*

3. **From the Connection menu, select the database connection.**

   You need to tell Dreamweaver where to put the data that your forms collect. Select the connection to the destination database. (You'll find database connections described on page 852.)

4. **From the Table menu, choose a table.**

   This drop-down menu lists all the tables in the selected database. Dreamweaver lets you insert data into only one table at a time. You can, however, add multiple record-insertion forms to a single web page. So you can create one "add data" page that has several forms, each of which inserts data into a different table. You still have to input records one at a time for each table, but at least your guests could add all their information from a single page. (Of course, if your database has 20 tables, you probably want to create several "add record" pages so you don't end up with one gigantic web page with 20 different forms.)

Tip: You can use Dreamweaver's Spry Tabs to display multiple insert forms on a single page without wasting a lot of precious screen real estate. The tutorial starting on page 949 has an example of this.

---

5. **Click the Browse button and select a file from your site.**

   Choose the page you want your visitors to see after they add a record to the database. It could simply be a page saying, "Thanks for signing up with our site." Or, if the insertion form adds a new employee to your company's employee database, you could display the page that lists all the employees (including the one you just added to the database).

   If you want people to add multiple records, one right after the other, you might re-display the record insertion form; that way, once a visitor adds one record, she'll return to the form, ready to continue the very pleasant work of data entry.

Note: Unfortunately, Dreamweaver doesn't give you a way to immediately display the details of a newly added record. So once a visitor enters information, you can't direct him to a page that lists the details of the record he just entered. The best you can do is present a page showing *all* the records in the database table (in other words, a Master page, as described on page 892). His newly added record will appear on that page.

   You can also change the format for the menu item for each database column is formatted on the page, as follows.

6. **In the "Form fields" box, select a database column, and change its settings, if you like.**

   Your options include:

   - Remove the field. Click the minus (–) button to remove the field from the form. It doesn't appear on the form page, and visitors can't manually submit a value for this field. You should remove any fields that the database automatically fills out, such as a primary key field (see page 846). (If you accidentally delete a field, click the + button to add it back in.)

Note: Use the up and down arrow buttons (see Figure 25-2) to rearrange the order in which the fields appear on the form.

- Label is the text Dreamweaver adds next to the form field on the page. It identifies what someone should type into the field, like First Name. Dreamweaver just uses the name of the column in the database—"fName", for instance—so it's usually best to change this text to something more understandable.
- The "Display as" menu lets you select the *type* of form element you want to use to collect the column's information. If the column is someone's first name, select Text Field. This adds a text box to the form, so visitors can type in their names. On the other hand, if you want people to make a selection from a limited number of choices (like *U.S. Postal Service, FedEx–2 day*, or *FedEx–next morning*, for example), you might select "Radio group".

  Radio buttons and pop-up menus ensure consistency and rule out typos. On a form that asks visitors to indicate the state they live in, you could offer a pop up menu of the 50 states. If you provided a text box instead, your visitors could type in every conceivable abbreviation and misspelling. (For a description of the different types of form elements, see page 459.)

Note: Dreamweaver can also create *dynamic* menus, which display data taken from a database. See page 944

- Dreamweaver automatically fills in the "Submit as" menu based on the kind of data you told Dreamweaver to collect in the field, so you don't need to change anything here.
- The Default value text box lets you preload a form field with information. It's actually the same as a text field's *initial value*, described on page 465. You can also add a dynamic value that your server model's programming language generates. For example, if you have a field called *date*, you can have Dreamweaver automatically insert the current date by typing *<?php echo date("Y-m-d") ?>* here (for the PHP/MySQL server model).

  Depending on what type of field you select for the "Display as" menu, Dreamweaver will replace the Default value box with one of three controls: If you selected "Check box" from the "Display as" drop-down menu, Dreamweaver gives you the option to have the boxes checked or unchecked in the form it creates; if you selected Menu or "Radio group" from the "Display as" menu, Dreamweaver displays a Properties button, which lets you set the options that appear in the drop-down menu or radio group on the Insert form—the process is the same as adding a dynamic menu or dynamic radio button group, as described on page 944.

  In most cases, you'll change the label of every column. But for now, leave the other options alone.

7. **Click OK to close the window and create the form.**

   Dreamweaver inserts a table, form, form elements, and the programming code to the page. At this point, the page is complete and ready to add records to the database table you specified. Unfortunately, Dreamweaver doesn't let you return to this window to make any changes. (If you quickly realize you made a mistake, you can always use Ctrl+Z [⌘-Z] to undo the operation, and then bring up the Insert Record Form Wizard again. (Otherwise, you have to delete the table and the form, and remove the Insert Record server behavior from the Server Behaviors panel. Do that by selecting Insert Record Server behavior in the panel and then press the Delete key. You can then go back to the Insert Record Form Wizard.)

To ensure that your form works correctly when guests submit it, add form validation. The powerful Spry validation tools make this easy (see page 478).

Warning: Once you add the form, don't rename any form fields. You'll break the programming code responsible for inserting the record. If you forget and rename a form field, here's what you need to do: edit the Insert Record sever behavior by double-clicking Insert Record on the Server Behaviors panel. This reopens the Insert Record window. You can make changes in this window, like associating a database column to the form field you renamed.

Using the Insert Record Behavior

Dreamweaver's Record Insertion Form Wizard makes quick work of adding the table, form, and programming code required to create a web page that adds data to a database table. At times, though, you want a more customized approach. Perhaps you already designed a form that you want to use, or you created a beautiful CSS-based design for your form. Rather than rely on Dreamweaver's rather pedestrian table and form design, you can supercharge your own design with the Insert Record server behavior.

To build a page like the one above, start by creating a dynamic web page ending in .php. Add a form to the page (see Chapter 12). Make sure it has one form field for every column to which you wish to add data. Every time a visitor fills out the form, the database acquires a new record.

In some cases, you don't include certain form fields. For example, databases usually automatically create a table's primary key (a unique identifier for each new record), so you wouldn't add a field for this column.

In other cases, you might add *hidden* fields (see page 474) that your guests can't see. Suppose someone signs up for your online newsletter and you want to store the date they registered. Instead of letting the visitor fill in the date, add a hidden form field that records the current date.

Once you create the form, add the Insert Record server behavior like this:

1. **Choose Window→Server Behaviors to open the Server Behaviors panel.**

   The keyboard shortcut is Ctrl+F9 (⌘-F9). You can also use the Insert Record menu (circled in Figure 25-3).

2. **Click the + button on the panel, and then select Insert Record.**

   The Insert Record window opens (see Figure 25-4). It's similar to the Insert Record Form window, except that you have to manually associate a form element with the correct database column. (If you name your form fields after the corresponding fields in your database, Dreamweaver helps you out here.) Another difference is that you can't define default values for each form element in this window. You can, however, apply default values to a form field using the Property inspector, as described on page 465.

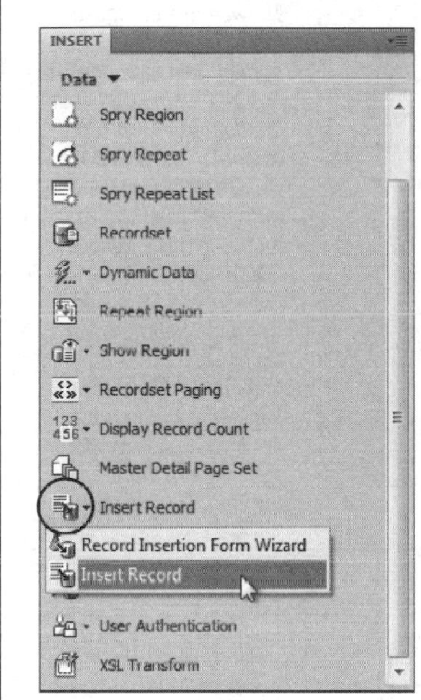

Figure 25-3:
The Insert Record menu (found in the Insert panel's Data category) lets you use either an automated wizard (Record Insertion Form Wizard) or a basic server behavior (Insert Record) to add a record to a database.

3. **Choose the name of the form that will collect the information for the new record.**

   If there's only a single form on your web page, you don't have an option here. If you have multiple forms (like a search box at the top of the page and a form to insert a new record), make sure you select the name of the form that adds data to the database.

4. **Choose a database connection and table.**

   These are the same options described in steps 3 and 4 for the Record Insertion Form Wizard (see page 925). Here, you tell Dreamweaver which database to use and which table to add data to.

5. **From the Columns list, select a database column. From the Value menu, choose the name of the form field that collects data for that column.**

   To make sure the form's information ends up in the proper database columns, tell Dreamweaver which form field will collect the data for which database column. You can let Dreamweaver choose the proper type from the "Submit as" pop-up menu. As with step 6 on page 926, this choice depends on how you set up your database (which Dreamweaver can figure out).

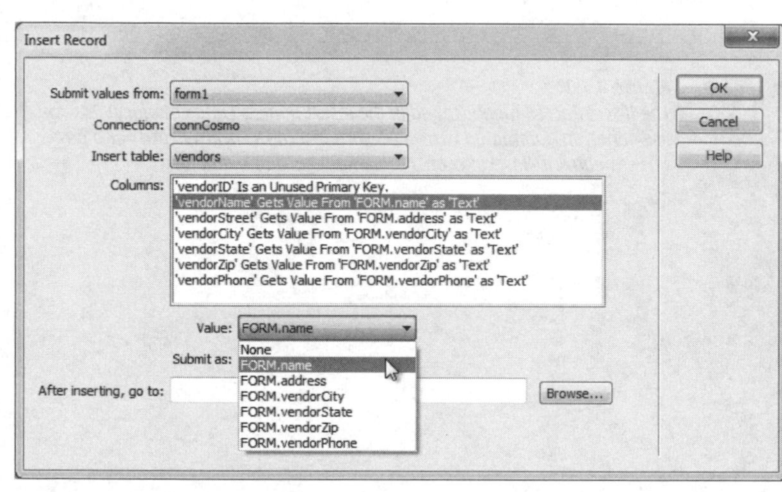

Figure 25-4: *The Vendors database table contains a column named "vendorName". To ensure that the page adds the data to the correct column in the database, choose the corresponding form field from the Value menu–in this example, FORM.name. (The actual name of the form field is "name;" Dreamweaver, for whatever reason, tacks on FORM at the beginning.) (You may not have to worry about selecting anything; see the Tip following step 5.)*

Note: You need to follow step 5 only if the names of the form fields *differ* from the names of the columns in the database. If you name a form field "productName" and there's a database column named "productName", Dreamweaver automatically connects the two in the Insert Record window.

6. **Click the Browse button and then select a web page.**

   This step is the same as step 5 on page 926, and indicates which page someone sees after they add a new record to the database.

7. **Click OK to close the window and apply the server behavior.**

   The page can now add information directly to the database.

If you change the name of a form field, add a form field, or want to change any of the settings for this behavior, you can edit the Insert Record server behavior by double-clicking Insert Record on the Server Behaviors panel. This opens the Insert Record window once again.

Updating Database Records

Maybe someone made an error while entering info into the database. Maybe the price of your product changes. Or maybe you want to provide a way for your visitors to update their email addresses. In any case, the time will come when you have to edit your online database.

Creating Update Record Forms in Dreamweaver is similar to creating Insert Record Forms. Both require an HTML form that your audience can fill out and submit. The primary difference is that an update form is *already* filled out with information from the database. It's like a combination of an Insert Record Form and a record detail page (such as the one the Master Detail Page set created, described on page 892).

The first step in creating an update form is to add a *recordset* to the update page (page 858). The recordset retrieves the data in each field of the update form.

The recordset should contain only a single record—the one you or your visitor wants to update. Therefore, you have to filter the overall recordset using a form or URL parameter (see page 861 for more on filtering). For example, if you have a page that lists company employees, you could add an Edit button that links to a page containing the update form. To retrieve a specific record (the employee's detail page), use the technique discussed on page 867 to add a URL parameter to a link. In this case, you pass the employee record's primary key to link to the update page. The update page, in turn, uses that key to filter the database and find a single record, the one with the employee's detail information in it. (If all this sounds confusing on paper, try the tutorial on page 919, which takes you step by step through the process.)

After you add the recordset to the update form page, you have two options to build an update form. You can let Dreamweaver automate the process with its Insert Update Record Form Wizard, or you can build the form yourself, and then add Update Record server behavior. The following pages cover both methods.

The Update Record Form Wizard

Dreamweaver can automate most of the steps involved in creating an update form:

1. **Open a dynamic page with a recordset already added.**

   Remember, the recordset should contain only a single record—the one you want to update. So you must use a filter to create the recordset (see page 861 for more on filtering recordsets).

2. **In the document window, click where on the page you want the insertion form to appear. Choose Insert→Data Objects→Update Record→Record Update Form Wizard.**

   You can also select Record Update Form Wizard from the Update Record menu on the Insert panel's Data category (Figure 25-5). Either way, Dreamweaver opens the Record Update Form window (Figure 25-6).

3. **From the Connection menu, select the database connection.**

   If your site works with several databases, select the connection to the database you want to edit.

4. **From the "Table to update" menu, choose a table that matches the recordset you created in step 1.**

   This menu displays a list of the tables in the database. You can only edit data from a single table at a time, so select the table that matches the filtered recordset.

Note: You can include multiple update forms on a single page, so you can create a single page to update all the tables in a database. You'll need to add filtered recordsets for each table you want to edit and provide links that identify which table you're updating. In one case, a URL may include the primary key for a table (*update.php?productID=2*, for example). Meanwhile, another link passes a different primary key (*update.php?categoryID=1*) to the same page so you can update a record in a different table.

One way to keep a page like this from appearing overly cluttered with forms is to use the "Show if Recordset Not Empty" server behavior (see page 991). Select an update form, apply the server behavior, and in the "Show if Recordset Not Empty" dialog box, select the recordset that matches the update form. That way, the update page only displays one form–the one that updates the record from the specified recordset.

---

5. **In the "Select record from" menu, make sure you see the recordset you created earlier.**

   Dreamweaver should display this recordset by default. If not, you must have created another recordset after you created the first one.

6. **In the "Unique key column" pop-up menu, make sure you see the table's primary key column selected. If the column contains a number—and it usually does—verify that the Numeric checkbox is turned on.**

   The "Unique key column" is used to identify which record to change during the update process. (For a description of primary keys, see page 846.)

7. **To fill out the "After updating, go to" box, click the Browse button and select a file from your site.**

   This file represents the page that appears after you or a visitor updates a record. A good choice here is a page that lists the details of the edited record (like the detail page in the master/detail pages discussed on page 892). Then, after a visitor updates her page, she sees the results of her changes.

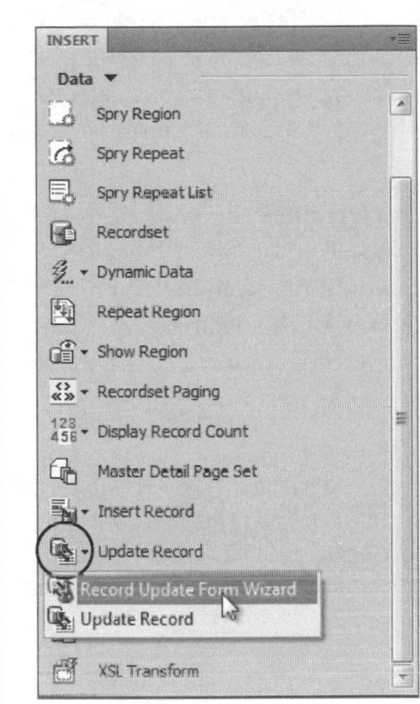

Figure 25-5:
As discussed in "The Insert Panel", you can call up the Insert Panel several ways. Shown here is Dreamweaver's standard, out-of-the-box Insert Panel icons. To save screen space, click the category menu (for example, Data, in this case) and choose Hide Labels. Only the small icons remain in the menu, freeing up lots of space for other important panels–or that YouTube video you've been meaning to watch.

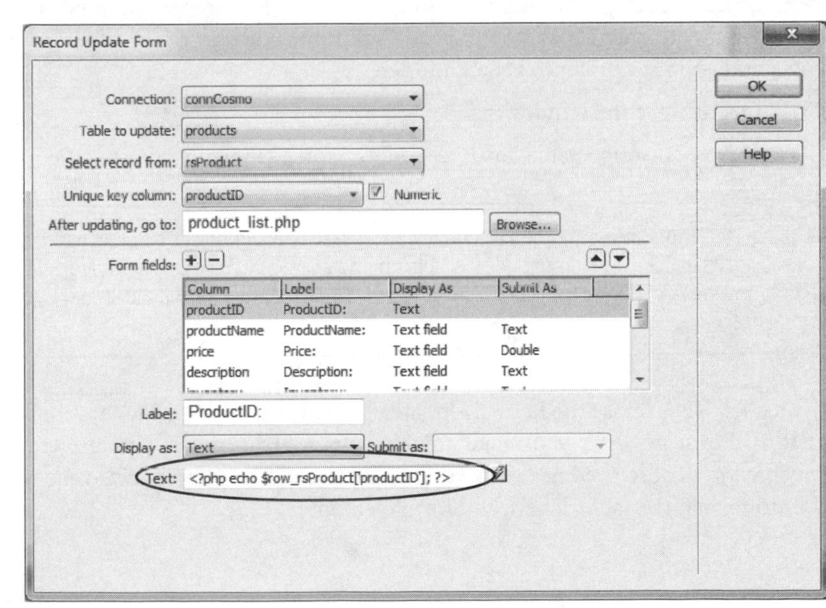

Figure 25-6:
A form field's default value is what you see on the web page. When you update a form using the Update Record Form Wizard, Dreamweaver fills out the default value (circled) for each form field using the proper information from the database.

8. **If you like, change a column's settings.**

   After clicking a row in the "Form fields" list, you can change the Label and "Display as" properties in the database column, described in step 6 on page 926. If the table includes a Description column that holds a fair amount of text, select Text Area from the "Display as" menu. That way, the form includes a larger text box that can accommodate a lengthy description.

   Don't change the "Submit as" option, which determines the kind of data you submit—text, a number, and so on—Dreamweaver automatically gets this information from the database. In addition, you would rarely change the "Default value" property. This represents the data pulled out of the database for a particular record, and modifying it *always* changes that information in the database.

Note: Sometimes, you might want to change the "Default value" for a column. Say you have a column that records the date a record was created, but now you want to know when the record was last updated. To do that, you'd change the default value from the date stored in the database to the current date. That way, when someone updates a record, the database records the current date in the "last update" field. In PHP, you do that by typing <?php echo date("Y:m:d");?> in the "Default value" field–this creates a value that matches the date expected for a MySQL Date field.

   To delete a field so it doesn't appear in the form, click the Remove (minus sign [–]) button. For example, you might want to remove the primary key column—the column you selected in step 5. Dreamweaver doesn't create an editable form field for the primary key because it uniquely identifies a record, and editing it could overwrite data for another record. But it does display the number on the page, and you may prefer to keep it hidden.

9. **Click OK to close the window.**

   Dreamweaver inserts a table, form, and all the form elements you specified.

Note: If you get the error, "Please choose a unique key from the selected Recordset, or Click Cancel", the recordset you added to the page didn't include the table's primary key. Cancel the Update wizard, edit the recordset, and then click the "All" button next to the word "Columns". Then call up the Record Update Form Wizard again.

Once you click OK to close the Record Update Form dialog box, you can never again return to it. From now on, you make any changes by editing the Update Record server behavior, as described next. You're also free to use any of Dreamweaver's editing tools to format the table, labels, and form elements.

Note: After you edit a record with the Update wizard, don't change the name of the form or any of its fields. The program that updates the database relies on these names, and changing them stops the update code from working. If for some reason you do change a form or field name, you can edit the Update Record sever behavior by double-clicking Update Record on the Server Behaviors panel. That opens the Update Record window once again. You can make changes in this window, like associating a database column to a form field that you renamed.

The Update Record Server Behavior

Dreamweaver's Record Update Form Wizard makes it delightfully easy to add the table, form, and programming code required to create a web page for editing database records. But when you need more flexibility—if you already designed a form you want to use or you created a CSS-based design for the form—the Update Record server behavior lets you keep your own beautiful design and give it the power to update a database.

You must start with a page that has a filtered recordset, as described on page 861. Then you add a form to the page (see Chapter 12). Make sure the form has one form field for every database column you want to edit. Don't include an editable form field for the primary key, however. Allowing anyone to change the primary key could have disastrous effects on your database. But you will want to add a hidden field containing the primary key, as described in step 6 below.

Tip: Give your form fields the same names you used for the database table's columns to speed up the process of adding the Update Record server behavior.

At this point, the form is full of empty fields. If you preview the page, none of the data you retrieved from the recordset appears. To fill the form with data, you must *bind* data from the recordset to each form field, as follows:

1. **In the document window, select a form field.**

   Click a form field to select it.

Note: These instructions apply to both text and hidden fields. Information on binding data to radio buttons, checkboxes, and menus appears on page 939.

2. **In the Property inspector, click the dynamic data button (the lightning bolt) to the right of the "Init val" box.**

   The Dynamic Data window appears (Figure 25-7).

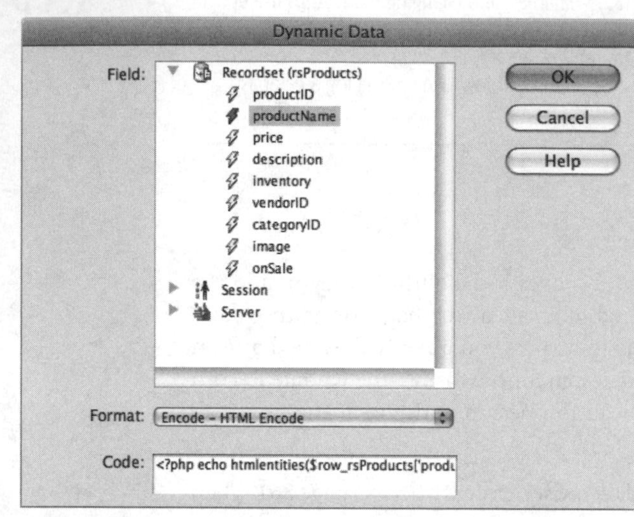

Figure 25-7:
The Dynamic Data window lets you add information from a recordset to form fields, so parts of a form can be pre-filled out. This ability is exactly what you want when updating information already in the database. In fact, the Dynamic Data window displays and lets you use additional data sources (like URL variables) that you've added to the page (see "Additional Data Sources" on page 981).

3. **Click the + button next to the recordset you used for the update page.**

   A list of all columns retrieved by the recordset appears.

4. **Select the name of the table column you want to bind to the form field.**

   To make sure the page displays correctly, you need to change the format for the data.

5. **Select "Encode—HTML Encode" from the Format menu. Click OK.**

   This step is necessary only when you insert database content that includes text that a web browser might misinterpret as HTML (so skip ahead to step 6 if the database field holds only numbers). For example, if you had "I think 5<3" in a database field, a browser will interpret the less-than sign (<) as the beginning of an HTML tag. If that text was output as-is to the update page, the browser might completely mess up its design. By choosing the HTML Encode formatting option, you're telling Dreamweaver to change HTML characters like < or > to their safe-to-display equivalents such as *<* or *>*.

   Ignore the Code box (which just displays the PHP code that Dreamweaver adds to the page). The form field is now set to display information from the recordset.

Note: If you installed the PHP Server Formats extension as discussed on page 880, you won't have an "Encode–HTML Encode" option in the Dynamic Data window as mentioned in step 5. Instead choose the "HTML as TEXT" option–it does the same thing.

---

6. **Repeat steps 1–5 for each field in the form.**

   There's one final step—providing the record's primary key. Although you don't want to let anyone edit this number, you need to include it so that Dreamweaver knows which record to update.

Tip: You can also bind data from a recordset to a form field by dragging the database column from the Bindings panel (see page 879), and dropping it onto the form field. Then use the Bindings Panel's Format menu (page 880) to set the format to "Encode–HTML Encode" (see step 5 above).

---

7. **Click somewhere inside the form (between the dashed red lines) and then choose Insert→Form→Hidden Field.**

   You can also use the Forms category of the Insert Panel to insert a hidden field, as described on page 474. Dreamweaver adds a hidden form field—which it represents with a gold shield—to the form. Now you need to give it a name and a value.

8. **In the Property inspector, change the name of the hidden field to match the name of the primary key field in the appropriate table.**

   For example, if you named the field "productID" in the database table, name the hidden field "productID" as well (see page 474 for more on naming hidden fields). Next, give the hidden field a value.

9. **Click the dynamic data button (the lightning bolt) in the Property inspector and, from the Dynamic Data window (Figure 25-7), choose the recordset's primary key field.**

   In other words, tell Dreamweaver to make the hidden field match the primary key of the record that will be updated.

   Once you create the form and add recordset information to each field, add the Update Record server behavior with the following steps.

10. **Choose Window→Server Behaviors to open the Server Behaviors panel.**

    The keyboard shortcut is Ctrl+F9 (⌘-F9).

11. **Click the + button on the panel, and then select Update Record.**

    The Update Record window opens (see Figure 25-8).

12. **From the "Submit values from" menu, select the name of the form.**

    You can have multiple forms on a single page: one to edit a record and one to search the site, for example. Select the name of the form whose data you want to edit.

13. **Select the database connection and the table you want to update.**

    They're the same as described in steps 3 and 4 for the Record Update Form Wizard on page 931. They tell Dreamweaver which database to use, and which table to update.

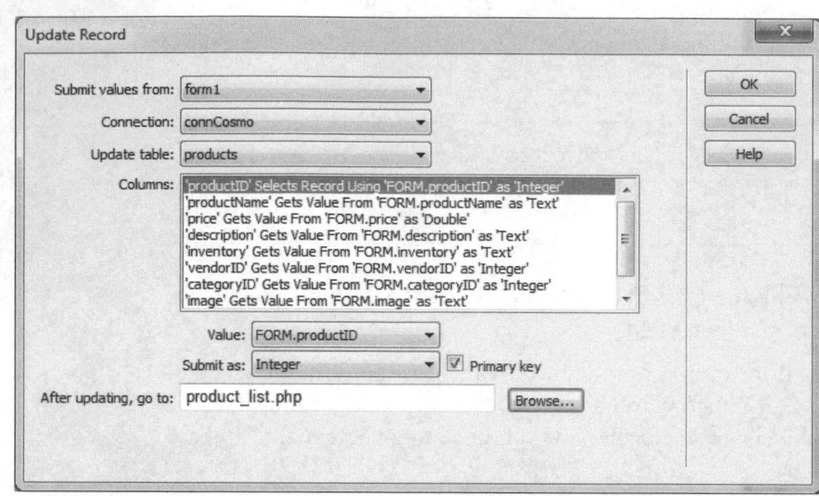

Figure 25-8: *The Update Record window is similar to the Record Update Form window (Figure 25-6). Here, though, you must manually associate a form element with the correct database column.*

14. **Select a form element from the list and then, from the Columns menu, select the matching database.**

    To get the form's information in the proper database columns, you must tell Dreamweaver the destination column for the selected form field's information.

Note: If you use the name of your database columns to name the form fields too, Dreamweaver automatically associates the two, so you can skip this step.

    From the "Submit as" menu, let Dreamweaver choose the proper input type. As with step 6 on page 926, this choice depends on how you set up your database (which Dreamweaver can figure out).

15. **For the "After updating, go to" box, click the Browse button and select a file from your site.**

    This file appears after you or a guest update a record. Select a page that lists the details of the record edited (like the detail page in the master/detail pages, discussed on page 892).

16. **Click OK to close the window and apply the server behavior.**

    The page now lets you edit information in the database.

As with any server behavior, double-clicking its name on the Server Behaviors panel—in this case, Update Record—opens the behavior's dialog box so you can change its properties.

Dynamic Form Fields

Form fields don't necessarily have to be empty. For example, Dreamweaver automatically fills out the record update forms covered in the previous section with data it pulls from the database. Likewise, you don't necessarily have to manually create the options in a pull-down menu; they could come from information in a database.

Imagine you create an Employee Directory section of your company's website. On the Insert New Employee page, you build a pop-up menu that lets you select a department for the new employee.

You, the designer, *could* create a menu by manually typing in the name of each department (as described in the Forms chapter on page 470). But what if the names of the departments change, or your company adds new departments? You'd have to reopen the page and edit the form field each time this happened. But if you use a dynamic menu instead, the page automatically builds the Departments pop-up menu by retrieving the current list of departments from the database. Figure 25-9 shows a similar example of a dynamically created pull-down menu.

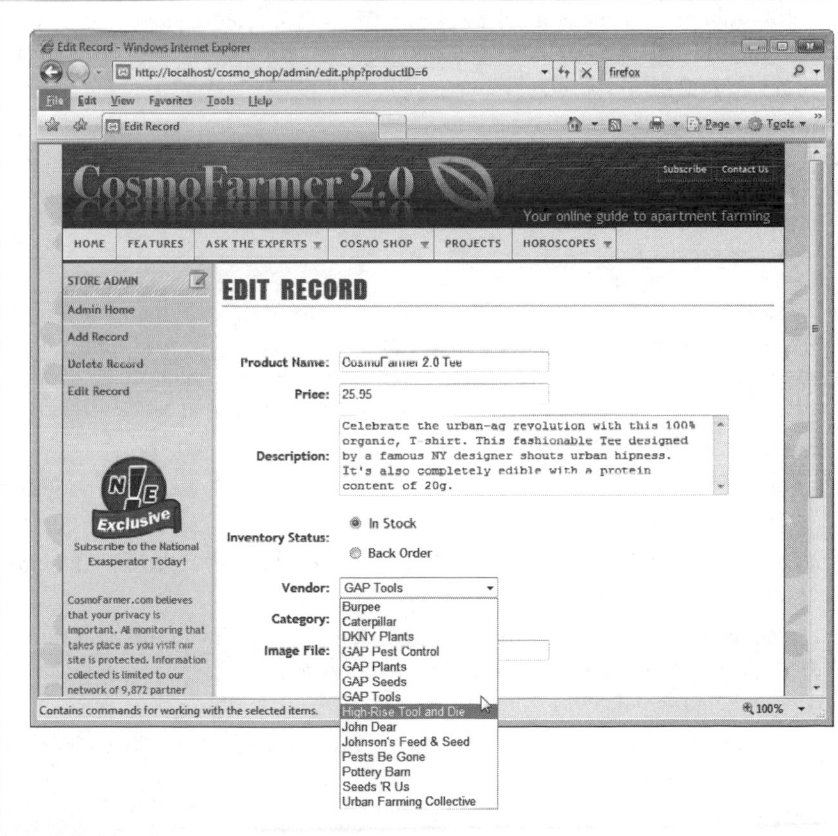

Figure 25-9: *Dynamic form fields come in handy for update forms. Dreamweaver automatically fills in the fields with database information that's ready to be edited. You can also dynamically generate menus from records in a recordset. The Vendor shown open here lists records retrieved from a database table containing the names of all the vendors who supply the CosmoFarmer online store.*

In essence, a dynamic form field is a form element whose value, labels, and other settings come from dynamic data in the Bindings panel. The dynamic data can come from a recordset (as it does for an update form), a form or URL parameter, or even a cookie or session variable (see page 984).

Whenever you wish to use a dynamic form field, start by creating a form. Add all the form fields that might include dynamic content. (Not all the fields have to be dynamic, however. In the employee directory example discussed above, only the Department menu on the Insert New Employee form would be dynamic. The other employee information fields would initially be empty.)

Next, add a recordset, request variable, session variable, or application variable to the Bindings panel (see page 981 for information on those last three choices). Then, finally, attach the dynamic data to the form field. The process for binding dynamic data depends on the type of form field.

Dynamic Text Form Fields

You can make any form field that accepts typed-in data—text, text area, and password fields—dynamic. For example, if a site requires a user login, you could include a "Remember me" feature, so that when a visitor who's previously signed into a site returns, the signup form already lists his username and password.

Note: If you like the idea of a "Remember me" feature for password-protected pages, try the free Save Password Login Form extension, which works with ASP, PHP, and ColdFusion. You can find it at *www.felixone.it/extensions/freeextdetailen.asp?IDProdotto=FX_SavePassLF*.

You can add dynamic data (also called *binding* data) to a text field using any of the methods described below. (Remember, you must first have the form field on the page and have added the dynamic data to the Bindings panel, which means adding a recordset to a page as described on page 858, or creating additional data sources [like cookies or session variables], as described on page 981.)

- In Design view, drag the dynamic data item from the Bindings panel, and drop it onto the form field.
- In Design view, select the text field. In the Bindings panel, select the dynamic data item, and then click the Bind button.
- Select the text field. In the Property inspector, click the dynamic data button (the lightning bolt). The Dynamic Data window appears (see Figure 25-7); select the dynamic data item from the list, and then click OK.
- In the Server Behaviors panel, click the + button, and then select Dynamic Form Elements→Dynamic Text Field. In the window that appears, you see a text field menu. Select the text field to which you wish to add dynamic data, and then click the lightning bolt button to open the dynamic data window.

Select the dynamic data item from the list, and then click OK. (Insert→Data Objects→Dynamic Data→Dynamic Text Field works, too.)

Note: You can bind dynamic data to a *hidden* field using these same steps (for an example, see steps 9–12 on page 967.).

After binding the data to a field, the name of the data item appears inside the field—*{rsDetails.adName}*, for example. If you switch to Live Vew (page 898), you'll see the actual data from the database in the field.

Note: Dreamweaver lets you format dynamic data in a form field just like you can format dynamic text you add to a page, as described on page 880. As mentioned in step 5 on page 936, if there's a chance the database field contains text that has special meaning for a web browser, like a greater-than or less-than sign, use the "Encode–HTML Encode" formatting option (or "HTML as Text" if you have the PHP Server Format extension [page 880]). This translates those special characters in a way the browser can properly handle, without ruining the page's look.

To remove dynamic data from a text field, just select the field, and then, in the Bindings panel, click the Unbind button. (Deleting the contents of the field's "Init val" box in the Property inspector also works.)

Dynamic Checkboxes and Radio Buttons

As you saw above, you can dynamically change the *value* of a text field. With checkboxes and radio buttons, however, you can dynamically control only their status (checked or unchecked).

You can select one radio button in a group based on a value in the database. As part of a product ordering system, shoppers could select a particular shipping option: USPS, FedEx, or UPS. But after reviewing her orders, what if a customer changes her mind and chooses a different option? When she returns to the order page, you want the Shipping Option radio button to reflect the choice she made earlier. In other words, you want the page to read the shipping option from the database, and highlight the radio button that matches it. (See an example of this in the "Building a Page for Editing Database Records" section of the tutorial starting on page 958.)

Dynamic radio buttons

You add dynamic radio buttons like this:

1. **Add a group of radio buttons to the page.**

   You should have as many radio buttons as there are possible values stored in the database column. Remember, if you wish to create a group of related radio buttons, you must give every button in the group the same name (see page 469).

Note, too, that the value of each radio button must exactly match the values stored in the database. If a Shipping column in the database stores USPS, FedEx, or UPS, then the radio group should have three buttons. Each button would share the same name—*shipping*, for instance—but their checked values would match the different values stored in the database: USPS, FedEx, and UPS. Capitalization counts, so if the value in the database is UPS, the radio button value must be UPS, not Ups, ups, or UpS.

2. **Open the Server Behaviors panel (Window→Server Behaviors). Click the + button, and then select Dynamic Form Elements→Dynamic Radio Group.**

   You can also find this option under Insert→Data Objects→Dynamic Data, or under the Dynamic Data menu in the Data category of the Insert bar (Figure 24-1). The Dynamic Radio Group window appears (see Figure 25-10).

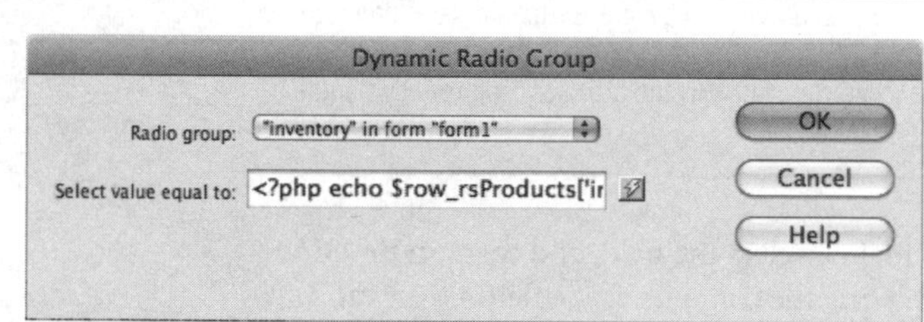

Figure 25-10: *The Dynamic Radio Group window lists the values of each button in the group. By selecting a button from the list, you can change its value in the Value field.*

3. **From the first menu, choose the radio button group.**

   In other words, select the name assigned to every button in the group. If your form has more than one group of radio buttons, select the one you want to make dynamic.

4. **Click the dynamic data button (the lightning bolt) to the right of the "Select value equal to" field.**

   The Dynamic Data window opens (see Figure 25-7). Select the dynamic data item for this radio group. In a nutshell, the radio button whose value matches the dynamic data is selected. If no radio buttons contain the same value, then no buttons are selected.

Note: You set the "Select value equal to" field only once per radio group (not once per button in the group).

5. **Click OK to close the window.**

   Dreamweaver adds a Dynamic Radio Buttons server behavior to the page. If you change the value of one of the buttons in the radio group, you need to reapply the server behavior like this: Open the Server Behaviors panel and then double click the Dynamic Radio Group item. This opens the Dynamic Radio Group window again (Figure 25-10). Click the OK button and Dreamweaver updates the code to reflect the change you made to the button's value.

Note: If you find that the Dynamic Radio button doesn't highlight correctly when you preview the web page in a browser, odds are that you didn't type the correct value for one of the buttons. Double-check the radio button values to make sure they match the data in the database (including the case of the letters). You then need to reapply the Dynamic Radio Group server behavior as described in step 5 above.

Dynamic checkboxes

Dynamic checkboxes work almost the same way:

1. **Add a checkbox to the page.**

   This process is described on page 466.

2. **Select the checkbox, and in the Property inspector, click the Dynamic button.**

   The Dynamic CheckBox window appears (Figure 25-11).

Tip: You can also open the Dynamic CheckBox from the Server Behaviors panel under Dynamic Form Elements→Dynamic CheckBox, or in the Dynamic Data menu in the Data category of the Insert Panel (Figure 24-1). Heck, you can even open the window by choosing Insert→Data Objects→Dynamic Data→Dynamic CheckBox.

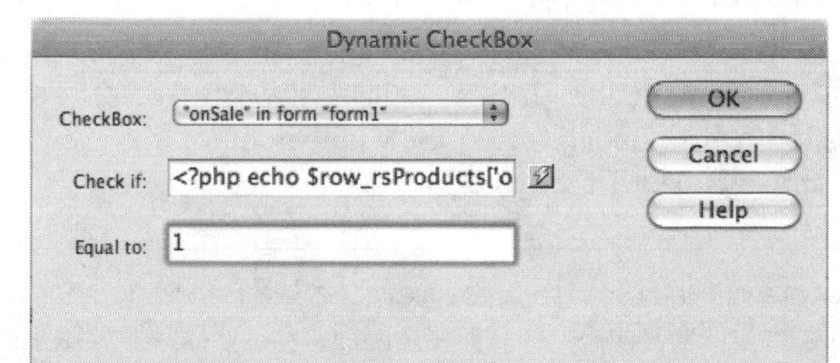

***Figure 25-11:** The Dynamic CheckBox server behavior lets you control whether or not a checkbox is turned on, based on information from a database, cookie, URL parameter, or other piece of dynamic data.*

3. **Select a checkbox.**

   If the form has more than one checkbox, select the one you want to control dynamically from the first menu.

4. **Click the dynamic data button (the lightning bolt) to the right of the "Check if" field.**

   The Dynamic Data window opens (see Figure 25-7). Select the dynamic data item for this checkbox.

5. **Type a value into the "Equal to" box.**

   If the value from the dynamic data (in the previous step) matches the value you provide here, the checkbox is turned on. (If the checkbox is part of an update form, this should match the value you gave the checkbox in step 1.)

6. **Click OK to close the window.**

   Dreamweaver adds a Dynamic CheckBox server behavior to the page.

To *remove* the dynamic properties from a group of radio buttons or a checkbox, open the Server Behaviors panel (Window→Server Behaviors). Among the list of server behaviors, find the dynamic radio button or checkbox behavior. It looks something like "Dynamic Radio Buttons(group_name)" or "Dynamic Check Box(checkbox_name)"—where *group_name* or *checkbox_name* reflects the name you gave the buttons or checkbox. Select it, and then click the Remove (minus sign [–]) button. (Pressing the Delete key does the same thing.)

Dynamic Menus and Lists

Dynamic menus and lists are among the most helpful form elements. You can use them for more than just updating forms. Even a form you use to add information to a database can have a dynamic menu that displays a list of options stored in the database. They save you the effort of rebuilding traditional menus or lists every time your company opens a store in a new state, adds a new employee department, or adds a new category to its product line.

To create a dynamic menu or list, proceed as follows:

1. **Create a form, and then add a menu or list to the page.**

   For example, choose Insert→Form→Form, and then Insert→Form→List/Menu. This process is the same as adding a menu or list as described on page 470. Don't add any items to the list, though. That's the whole point of this exercise: Dreamweaver builds the menu or list for you.

Tip: If the dynamic menu is part of a form that updates or adds a record to a database, give the menu the same name as the corresponding field in the database table. For example, if the database table has a field named "employeeCategoryID", name the menu in the form "employeeCategoryID". This makes it easier for Dreamweaver to associate the menu with the database field you want to update.

---

2. **Add a recordset to the page, which includes the information you want in the menu or list.**

   Perhaps you want to create a menu listing the different categories of product your company sells—books, DVDs, CDs, lederhosen, clogs, and so on. If the database has a table containing the categories, you could then create a recordset that retrieves the name of each category. (In most cases, you also retrieve a primary key, like the category ID field. The name of the category appears in the menu, while the primary key is the value Dreamweaver submits with the form.)

3. **In the document window, select the menu or list, and then, on the Property inspector, click the Dynamic button.**

   The Dynamic List/Menu window opens (see Figure 25-12). The name of the menu or list you selected appears in the Menu box.

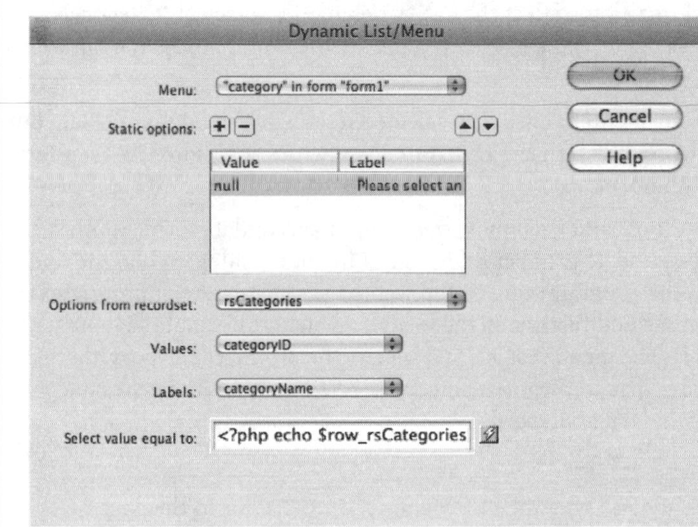

Figure 25-12: *Dreamweaver simplifies the process of creating automatically generated menus like the one pictured in Using information pulled from a database, you may never have to create another menu by hand.*

4. **If you like, add some static options to the menu or list.**

   A *static option* is simply a value and a label you enter by hand—menu or list items, appearing at the top of the list, that don't change. Dreamweaver doesn't pull this information from the recordset you created.

   You could use the static option feature for options not likely to change—Amazon.com may begin to sell hors d'oeuvres, and dermatology services, but chances are good that books will always be among its categories. You can also use it to provide instructions for the menu: "Pick a state," or "Choose an option from this list," for example. But this step is optional—the menu options can come entirely from the database. (Adding static options works just like it does in a regular menu's List Values box, as described on page 470.)

Note: Any static options you add to a dynamic menu appear at the top of the menu. You can't mix the static options with the recordset's records–in other words, you can't alphabetize a list that includes both static options and records.

5. **From the Options From Recordset menu, choose the recordset you created in step 2.**

   This identifies the source for the menu items.

6. **Choose a table column from the Values menu; choose another column from the Labels menu.**

   Menu and list items consist of a *label* (what someone actually sees in the menu) and a *value* (the information the web browser transmits when a visitor submits the form). For example, in Figure 25-12, "categoryID" is the recordset's primary key, so that's what you select from the Values menu. You want the label that appears in the menu to reflect the categories name, so select "categoryName" from the Labels menu. If the label and value are the same, choose the same table column from both menus.

7. **If you want your menu to have a preselected item, click the dynamic data button (the lightning bolt). In the Dynamic Data window (Figure 25-7), select a dynamic data item.**

   This step is optional and used most frequently in an update form. Suppose you create a form to update product information in your catalog. When the update page loads in the programming in the web page, it pulls the appropriate data from the database and fills out all the form fields with information about a particular product. The menu that lets you specify the product's category, therefore, should have the correct category name preselected because it matches the product's category in database record.

8. **Click OK.**

   Dreamweaver adds a Dynamic List/Menu server behavior to the page.

You can remove the dynamic menu or list by selecting and deleting it. To leave the menu but remove its dynamic properties, open the Server Behaviors panel (Window→Server Behaviors). Here, you see the dynamic list/menu behavior; it's listed as "Dynamic List/Menu(menu_name)," where "menu_name" is your name for the menu or list. Select it, and then click the Remove (minus sign [–]) button or press the Delete key.

To edit the behavior, select the menu in the document window, and then, once again, click the dynamic data button in the Property inspector.

Deleting Records

The Delete Record server behavior offers a lot of flexibility, so you can implement it in a variety of ways. You don't have to add a recordset to a page to delete a record, nor do you have to add a form with a delete button.

The main requirement: The page with the Delete Record server behavior must have some way to retrieve the primary key for the record you want to delete. This can be a form, a URL, a cookie, a session variable, or any of the other data sources discussed on page 981.

On a page that lists the details of a particular record, for example, you could include a link to a delete page and pass the ID of that record in the URL of a delete page (see page 867). The delete page could then use the ID number in the URL to delete the record, and then send the visitor off to another page—perhaps a page verifying that Dreamweaver successfully deleted the record.

Note: Because of this flexibility, you could put a Delete Record server behavior on a blank dynamic page. All the page would do is delete the specified record, and then send the visitor off to another page on the site.

There are many ways, therefore, to delete a record in this server model. Here's one that creates a delete page with a confirmation button:

1. **On one of the pages in your site, add a link to the delete page.**

   On a page that provides the details of a single record, you could add a link to the delete page—maybe the word "Delete" or a button with a picture of a trash can. Alternatively, you could add a "Delete this record" link as part of a repeating region (see page 885). This way, you would have multiple records on a single page, each with its own link to the delete page. In both cases, you attach the record's primary key to the link, as described on page 867.

Note: Unfortunately, Dreamweaver doesn't provide a tool to delete more than one record at a time.

---

2. **Create a dynamic page—the delete page—containing a filtered recordset.**

   This recordset should retrieve a single record—the one you want to delete. You don't need to retrieve *all* the columns for the record. At a minimum, the recordset must retrieve the record's primary key, since the Delete Record server behavior needs it to know which record to remove. You may want to include some identifying information, such as the name of the item to be deleted, so your visitors can see what they're about to delete.

3. **Add a form to the page consisting of a single Submit button (as described on page 456).**

   When you create the button, change its label to reflect what it does—"Delete This Record", for example.

4. **Select the form. Then, in the Property inspector's Action box, type the page's file name.**

   If the page is called *delete.php*, type *delete.php*.

The *Action* property tells a web browser where to send the form (see page 457). In this case, when a visitor clicks the Submit button, the form information goes *back* to the same page.

This kind of trickery is common in dynamic pages. When your visitor clicks the Delete button, the browser sends the form to the same page—but this time the form doesn't show up. Instead, the Delete Record server behavior (which you'll add in step 6) deletes the record, and then sends the visitor off to another page.

5. **Add a hidden field to the form (page 474). Name this field whatever you wish, but bind (attach) to it the primary key from the recordset you created in step 2.**

   This hidden field tells the Delete Record server behavior which record to delete. (For instructions on binding dynamic data to a form field, see page 939.)

6. **Open the Server Behaviors panel (Window→Server Behaviors). Click the + button, and then, from the list of server behaviors, select Delete Record.**

   The Delete Record window appears (Figure 25-13).

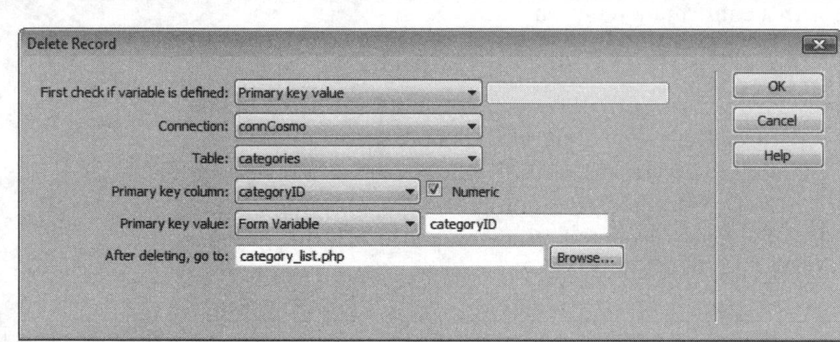

***Figure 25-13:** Dreamweaver's Delete Record window differs slightly from its ColdFusion counterpart. ColdFusion lets you specify a username and password for the database.*

7. **From the "First check if variable is defined" menu, choose "Primary key value".**

   This step may seem like putting the cart before the horse, because you won't define the primary key value until step 10. However, this option lets you control *when* the page deletes the record by making sure you define the proper variable *before* the server behavior deletes the record. In this case, the record doesn't go away until the visitor clicks the Delete button, which causes the server to send a form variable containing the record's primary key.

   This precaution is necessary; without it, the application server would delete the record whenever the page loads. Since the page really serves two functions—letting visitors confirm that they wish to delete the record and actually deleting the record from the database—you need to make sure the visitor has first visited the page, and *then* clicked the Submit button you added in step 3.

8. **From the Connection menu, select a database. From the Table menu, select the table that has the record you want to delete.**

   These steps should be familiar by now. The table you select should be the same one you used when you created the detail recordset for this page.

9. **From the "Primary key column" menu, select the table's primary key.**

   This tells Dreamweaver which database field contains the unique key that identifies which record to zap from the table.

10. **From the "Primary key value" menu, select Form Variable. In the box just to the right of that menu, type the name of the hidden field you added in step 5.**

    This step is the final piece of the puzzle. It tells the server behavior where to find the ID number for the doomed record. In this case, the form with its hidden field supplies the ID number.

Warning: In step 10 above, *don't select the URL Parameter option*. If you do, the application server will *immediately* delete the record when someone visits the page. Since the page passes the primary key value to this page in the URL (to create the filtered recordset from step 2), the Delete Record server behavior will have all the information it needs to delete the record, skipping over the "are you sure you want to delete this record?" part.

---

11. **Click the Browse button; navigate to your confirmation page.**

    The confirmation page appears after a visitor deletes a record. It's a page you create in advance—either a page with a confirmation message ("The Record has been successfully deleted"), or a page that lists the records of the database—a *master* page.

12. **Click OK.**

    Dreamweaver inserts the code necessary to remove a record from the database.

As with any of the other server behaviors that change content in a database, you should carefully control who has access to the delete page. Going to work one morning and finding that someone has deleted all the products from your company's e-commerce site is enough to ruin your whole day. Dreamweaver's User Authentication behaviors, discussed in the next chapter, can help.

If you ever need to change any of the properties of the Record Delete action, such as picking a different page to go to after the page deletes a record, you can go to the Server Behaviors panel, and then double-click Delete Record. The Delete Record window opens; make any changes, and then click OK.

Tutorial: Inserting and Updating Data

In this tutorial, you'll continue working on CosmoFarmer's online store. You'll work on two administrative pages that let CosmoFarmer employees add new products to the database and edit products already there.

This tutorial assumes you completed the tutorials in Chapters 23 and 24. If not, turn to page 838, follow the instructions for preparing the application server, database, and Dreamweaver for this project. Then turn to page 902 and build the product catalog pages.

Adding an Insert Product Page

Start by opening a page you already created:

1. **Open the file named *add.php* in the *admin* folder of the local site you defined in Chapter 23.**

   This page contains three Spry tabbed panels like the ones you learned about on page 520. Instead of having several web pages, each dedicated to inserting one record into one database table, you can collect all the insert forms on a single page. Clicking a tab opens the tabbed panel with the appropriate insert form.

   You'll also notice that the CosmoFarmer web designer stored this page inside a folder named *admin*. You don't want site visitors to be able to see the pages that add and edit the store's products; you wouldn't want just anyone adding products—"The Electric Whoopee Cushion, by Mr. Hacker," for example—to the store. Accordingly, keep these pages in a folder reserved for site administrators. (In the next chapter, you'll learn how to password-protect these pages.)

   Each new product requires an ID number that identifies the product's manufacturer. The database for CosmoFarmer's products actually contains several tables: Products, Vendors, and Category. Information about each vendor (name and contact info) is in the Vendors table, while information on each product (price, description, and so on) is in the Products table. A third table contains a list of product categories, which you used in the last tutorial to create the category navigation bar.

   To keep the Vendors and Products tables connected, so you know which vendor manufactures which product, the Products table includes a field containing the vendor's ID number. Whenever you add an item to the Products table, then, you also need to insert the vendor's ID number. One way to do so would be to have a CosmoFarmer employee type the vendor *number* each time she adds a product to the page. But that approach is prone to error, since the employee needs to remember which number belongs to which vendor: "Is Gap Plants vendor 2 or 3?" A better method is to provide a pull-down menu that lists the name of each vendor, but which submits the vendor's ID number when you add the product to the database. To make this kind of dynamic menu, start by creating a recordset.

2. **Make sure the Bindings Panel is open (Window→Bindings). In the Bindings Panel, click the + button, and then select Recordset.**

   Or use any of the methods described on "Creating Recordsets" to add a new recordset; for example, choose Insert→Data Objects→Recordsets; click the + button in the Server Behaviors panel, and then choose Recordset (Query); or use the Recordset button on the Insert panel's Data category. Either way, the Recordset window opens. Make sure you use the Simple recordset option (see Figure 25-15). Next, you'll define this recordset's properties.

3. **In the Name box, type *rsVendors*. From the Connection menu, select "connCosmo". From the Table menu, select "vendors".**

   These three steps set up the name, database, and table required for the recordset. For a recap on creating recordsets, turn to page 858.

4. **Click the Selected radio button; from the Columns list, select "vendorID" and "vendorName".**

   You can do this by holding down the Ctrl (⌘) key while you click the name of each column. Finally, pick an order to sort the list of vendors.

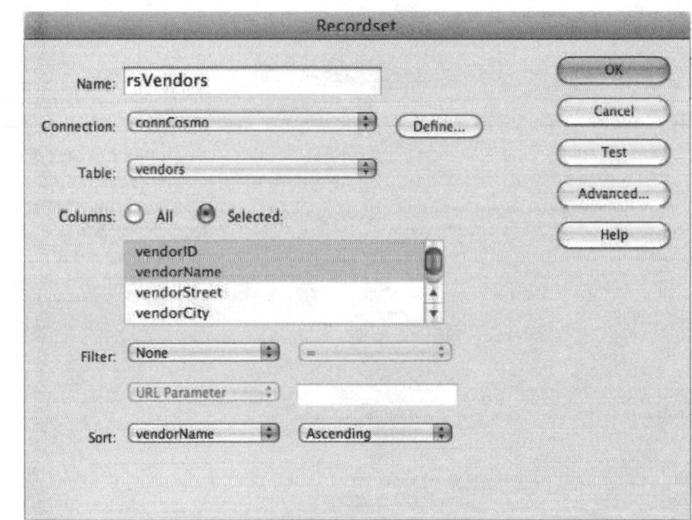

Figure 25-14: *When you create this recordset, make sure you use the window's Simple options. If you see a button labeled Advanced, you're in the right place. (If that button's missing, click the Simple button to access the basic recordset options.)*

5. **From the Sort menu, choose "vendorName". Make sure you have Ascending selected in the Order menu.**

   The Recordset window should now look like Figure 25-14.

6. **Click OK to close the window and insert the recordset in the page.**

   You just created a recordset that retrieves a complete list of vendor names and ID numbers in alphabetical order.

   Each product also belongs to a particular category. In the Products table in the database, a number represents the category, but the Categories table stores the category names. This is the same way the vendors' data works, so create a dynamic menu to insert the proper category name.

7. **Add another recordset to the page by following steps 2–6: Name the recordset rsCategories, select the "category" table, choose the All columns radio button, and then sort by "categoryName".**

   You just added a second recordset to this page. Now you're ready to add a form for inserting a new record. The page contains three Spry tabbed panels. You'll add a form for inserting new products into the database via the tab that's visible when you open the page—the Add Product tab.

8. **Click the empty area of the gray box directly below the Add Product tab. Choose Insert→Data Objects→Insert Record→Record Insertion Form Wizard.**

   You can also get to the Record Insertion Form Wizard from the Data category of the Insert panel (see Figure 24-3). The Record Insertion Form window opens (Figure 25-15). Next, you'll tell Dreamweaver which database to connect to, and which table will receive data from the form.

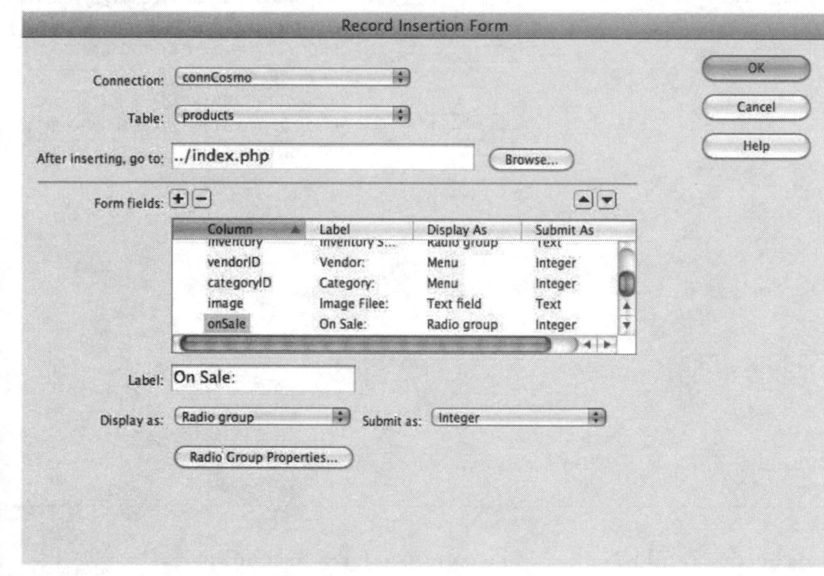

Figure 25-15: *While you can manually create a form and program it to insert a new record in a database, Dreamweaver's Record Insertion Form Wizard makes the task a whole lot easier.*

9. **From the Connection menu, choose "connCosmo." From the Table menu, choose "products".**

   You can insert data into only one table at a time. In this case, you select the Products table because it holds all the information for each item in the store. After you add information to the database, Dreamweaver redirects the staffer to another page. You'll set this up next.

10. **Click the Browse button. In the site's root folder, select the file *index.php*.**

    After you add a new product to the database, your staff is taken to the Products page (the one you created in the previous chapter). Since the newly added product is part of the database, browsing the products catalog reveals the newly added item.

Note: You could also choose *add.php* for Step 10 if you wanted to quickly add multiple product records. Then, after a staffer added one product to the database, he'd return to the product insertion form again, ready to input the next product.

---

11. **In the "Form fields" list, select "productID." Click the Remove (minus sign [–]) button to remove this field.**

    In some cases, the database itself fills in certain fields. For instance, every product in the database has its own unique ID—the table's primary key, which the database generates. When you add a new record, the database creates a new, unique number and stores it in the "productID" column. Since you don't want anyone entering the wrong information here, you should remove it from the form Dreamweaver is about to create.

12. **Select the "productName" column. In the Label field, change the label to "Product Name:".**

    The label you type here doesn't affect your database in any way. It's just the text a staffer sees next to the form field. (You'll do the same thing with each field, to make the labels reader-friendly.)

    You don't need to change any of the other "Form fields" options, such as "Display as" or "Submit as". You'll often change the "Display as" pop-up menu, which changes the type of form element—like a checkbox or menu—Dreamweaver displays (you'll see this in the next step). However, you should never change the "Submit as" pop-up menu, which determines how Dreamweaver submits the data to the database. Dreamweaver figures this out correctly based on the design of your database.

13. **Select the "description" column. From the "Display as" menu, choose "Text area".**

    The label for this column is fine, but since a description may be anywhere from several sentences to several paragraphs long, it's a good idea to provide a large text box (the "Text box" option allows just one line of text). See page 464 for more on multi-line text boxes.

14. **Select the "inventory" column, and then, in the Label field, change the label to "Inventory Status:".**

    The database tracks a product's inventory status whether the product is in the warehouse or on back order with the manufacturer. You could let a store administrator type in the correct status, but that would take time, and besides, he might make a mistake. (It wouldn't do for shoppers to see that the "Kudzu seeds" are on "Gack Order.") So you'll simplify the process by adding radio buttons.

15. **From the "Display as" menu, choose Radio Group, and then click the Radio Group Properties button.**

    The Radio Group Properties window appears (Figure 25-16). Add the radio buttons you want to appear on the form. Remember, the value of each button must match the data stored in the database (see page 941).

16. **In the Label field, replace "button1" with "In stock". Type *in stock* in the Value field.**

    Make sure you enter the value in all lowercase (that's how it appears in the database's inventory field). The label is what appears on the page, while the value is the information that gets stored in the database. You need to add one more button.

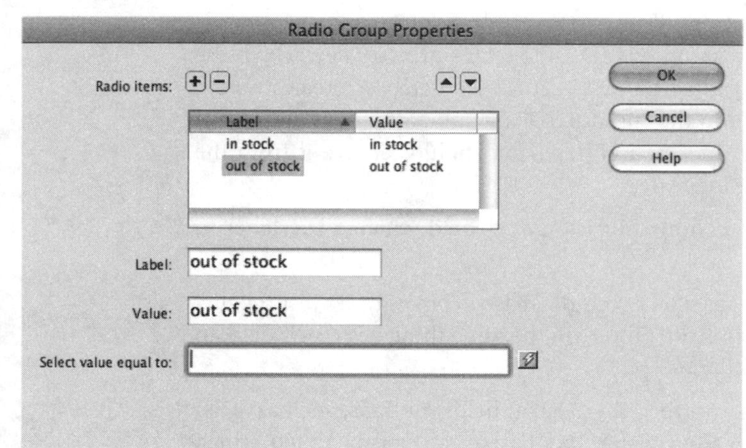

***Figure 25-16:** Use the Radio Group Properties window to add radio buttons to a form. Radio buttons make data entry faster and less error-prone.*

17. **Click the + button to add another radio button; repeat step 16, but type *Out of stock* and *out of stock* for the label and value of the second button.**

    The window should look like Figure 25-16.

18. **Click OK to close the Radio Group Properties window.**

    Again, in an effort to speed up data entry and make sure employees fill out the form correctly, make the next two fields pull-down menus. First, create a dynamic menu to display the list of vendors as follows.

19. **Select the "vendorID" column, and then change its label to "Vendor:".**

    This column stores only a number; Dreamweaver stores the vendor's name and contact information in a different table. To make entering this information easier, create a dynamic menu that lists all the vendors' names. When somebody chooses a name from the menu, Dreamweaver submits the appropriate *vendorID* number to the database.

20. **From the "Display as" menu, choose Menu. Then click the Menu Properties button.**

    The Menu Properties window opens (see Figure 25-17). Use this window to build the menu.

21. **Click the "From database" radio button. Make sure you have "rsVendors" selected in the Recordset menu.**

    You're telling Dreamweaver that the items it lists in the menu actually come from a database query. In fact, they come from the recordset you created at the beginning of this tutorial—"rsVendors".

22. **From the "Get labels from" menu, choose "vendorName". Then, from the "Get values from" menu, choose "vendorID".**

    The labels—the text that appears in the menu—are the names of each vendor. The value the web browser submits with the form, meanwhile, is the vendor's ID number.

    You can skip the "Select value equal to" field. It's useful if you want a particular value preselected when the form loads, which is usually the case when you *update* a record, since you need to display the current information in order to update it.

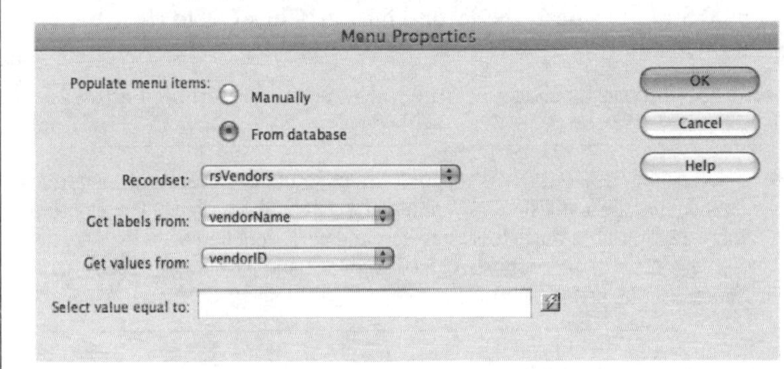

Figure 25-17: *Dreamweaver can create dynamic pull-down menus (also known as pop-up menus) that get their labels and values from a database.*

23. **Click OK to close the window.**

    The product category is another instance where a pull-down menu makes sense. You'll follow the same procedure as above to add a pop-up menu listing the names of all the categories available at the store.

24. **Select the "categoryID" column, and then change its label to "Category:".**

    The next few steps should feel familiar.

25. **Repeat steps 20-23; use the "rsCategories" recordset, retrieve the label from the "categoryName" field, and set the value to "categoryID".**

    In the next field, you change the label and manually enter a default value.

26. **Select the "image" column, and then change its label to "Image File:".**

    Because some products have no image, change the default value to point to a graphic you already created, one you use when a product has no graphic.

27. **In the "Default value" box, type *none.gif*.**

    Finally, set up the form element that lets you indicate products when they go on sale.

28. **Select the "onSale" category, and then change the label to *On Sale:*.**

    Either the product is on sale or it isn't. Radio buttons work well for this kind of yes or no option.

29. **From the "Display as" menu, choose Radio Group, and then click the Radio Group Properties button.**

    Numbers in the database represent a product's sale status: If the onSale field has a value of 1, the product is on sale; if the value is 0, the product isn't on sale. Because 1 and 0 might not make sense to anyone using the page to add a product to the database, you'll use plain language in the labels.

30. **In the Label field, replace "button1" with *Yes*. Type *1* in the Value field as well.**

    Just one more button to add.

31. **Click the + button to add another radio button; repeat step 30, but type *No* for the label and *0* for the value of the second button. Click OK to close the radio button window.**

    At this point, the Record Insertion Form window should resemble Figure 25-16.

Note: Dreamweaver doesn't provide any way to return to the Insert Record Form Wizard. If you accidentally close the window and insert the form before you finish all the steps in this section of the tutorial, you have to finish the form manually. Unless you're really sure how to do that, your best bet is to delete the form from the page, remove all server behaviors except for "rsVendors" and "rsCategories", and start at step 8 on page 952. Practice makes perfect, right?

---

32. **Click OK again to insert the form.**

    Dreamweaver adds a table, a form, and all the programming code necessary to add a new product to the database. The form has a blue background—one of Dreamweaver's signals that this form is special—indicating that this form uses one of Dreamweaver's server behaviors (see Figure 25-21 for information on how to hide or change this color).

33. **Choose File→Save.**

    You're nearly finished. You just have to finish up the design and take it for a test drive.

Finishing the Insert Form

To make your form ready for prime time, spruce up its appearance and test it:

1. **Select the table containing the form fields.**

   The fastest method is to click anywhere inside the table and then, in the Tag selector, click the <table> tag (the one farthest to the right in the Tag selector).

2. **In the Property inspector, choose Default from the Align pop-up menu.**

   The Default option aligns the table to the left without adding bandwidth-hogging HTML code. The table also has a little extra space around and inside each cell. You'll remove that next.

3. **With the table still selected, type *0* in the Property inspector's CellPad, CellSpace, and Border boxes.**

   You can repeat this step with the tables used for the two sets of radio buttons. In addition, if you don't like the way the buttons appear one on top of the other, you can move them. At this point, the labels, form fields, and tables in the form are fully editable. You could, for example, remove the labels and radio buttons from the table, place them side by side, and delete the small table.

   Now you'll apply a style to the table to improve its appearance.

4. **In the Property inspector, choose "insertForm" from the Class menu.**

   This applies a class to the table. A matching CSS class style in the site's style sheet contains the formatting information to make the table and the text inside it better match the site's style.

5. **Select each of the table cells in the left-hand column, and then, in the Property inspector, click the Header box.**

   You can select the cells by clicking the top cell, and then dragging down until you select all the cells in the left column; Ctrl-clicking (⌘-clicking) each cell works as well.

   The finished page should resemble Figure 25-18. Now you're ready to take the page for a spin.

6. **Press F12 (Control-F12) to preview the page in a browser. Type information into each of the fields, and then click the "Insert record" button.**

   If you filled out all the fields correctly, you should see the product page you built in the last chapter. Click the category name of the new product you just added, or navigate through the product pages until you find the newly added item.

You can enhance this page many ways. For example, you can make sure that no one at CosmoFarmer accidentally inserts a new product without a price, a description, or any of the other required pieces of information; just add Dreamweaver's Spry Validation tools discussed on page 478. In addition, you could use the Insert Record Form Wizard to add insert forms in the Add Category and Add Vendors tabbed panels. (See page 520 for information on how to work with Spry tabbed Panels.)

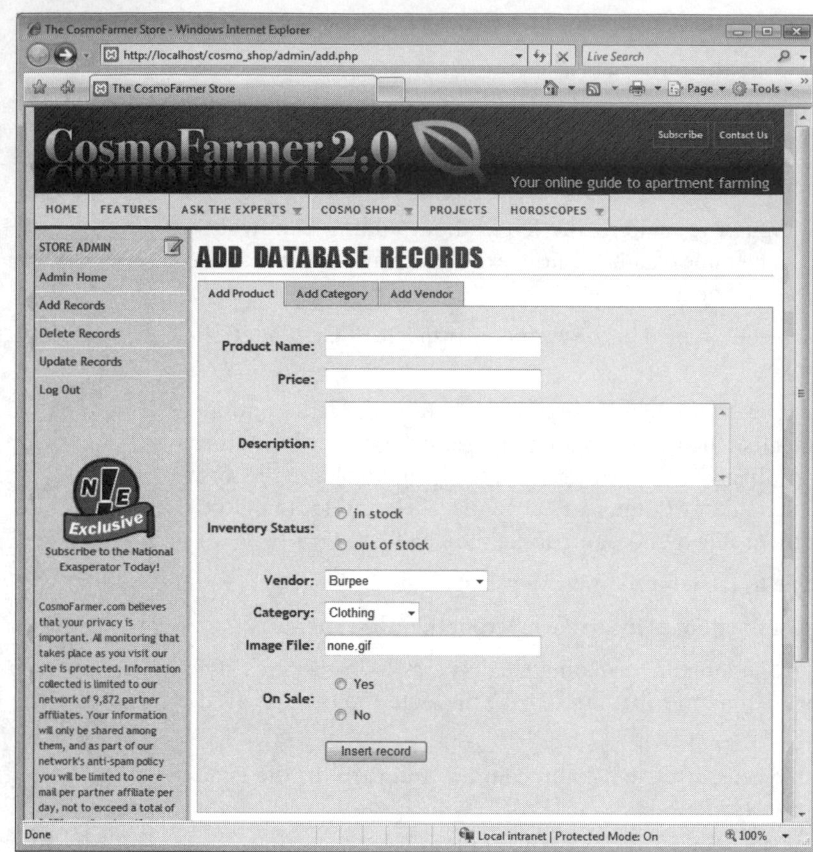

Figure 25-18: *No database-driven site would be complete without a way to add new records to the database. Use forms like this one to collect newsletter sign-up information, order and payment details, or to just create an online guest book.*

Building a Page to Edit Database Records

If employees at CosmoFarmer enter the wrong information for a particular product and have no way to correct it, they could be in a lot of trouble. After all, they'd be losing money hand over fist if the site were selling those $598 CAT Indoor Lawn Tractors for $5.98. That said, here's how to add an update-record page to the site.

Linking to the update page

An update page is very much like an insert-record page. The only difference is that the page first retrieves information about a single product from the database, and then fills out each form field with the information for that product. First, you have to tell the update page which product it's supposed to update. To do so, you must add a link to the product-details page you built in the last chapter.

1. **In the local site's root folder, open the file named *product.php*.**

   This page lists details for a particular product. As you may recall from last chapter, you access this page itself from the *index.php* page, which displays a list of all products in the database. By clicking the name of a product on that page, the *product.php* page retrieves and displays information on just that product.

   Now you need to create a link on this page that, when you click it, takes a store employee to an update page for the product.

2. **Click to the right of the Inventory Status line, and then hit Enter (Return) to create a new, blank paragraph. Type *Edit This Information*. Select the text you just typed, and then, next to the Link field in the Property inspector, click the "Browse for File" button (the little folder icon).**

   The standard Open File dialog box appears. (If you installed the extension described on page 898, you could also use the Go To Detail Page server behavior.)

3. **In the *admin* folder, navigate to and select the file *edit.php*, but don't close the window yet.**

   You need to add some additional information, which identifies the product that needs updating, to the end of the URL.

4. **Click the Parameters button to open the Parameters window. Click the name column, and then type *productID*.**

   The Parameters button lets you add a URL parameter to the end of a link, so you can pass information to another page. In this case, you want to pass a piece of dynamic data—the product ID number for the item currently displayed on the Product Details page.

5. **Click in the Value column. Click the dynamic data button that appears to the right of the column (the lightning bolt).**

   The Dynamic Data window opens. Here you can select data you already added to the Bindings panel, such as columns from a recordset.

6. **From the "rsDetails" recordset, select "productID," and then click OK.**

   (You may need to click the + button to the left of the word Recordset to see this option.) The link is nearly complete.

7. **Click OK to close the Parameters window. Click OK (or Choose on a Mac) once again to close the Select File window and apply the link.**

   When you're all done, the Property inspector's link box should look like this:

   ```
   admin/edit.php?productID=<?php echo $row_rsDetails['productID']; ?>
   ```

8. **Choose File→Save.**

Note: You probably wouldn't want a link like this to appear to the average visitor to your site. After all, customers shouldn't change information about the products you sell. In the next chapter, on page 1002, you'll learn how to hide this link from unauthorized eyes.

Creating the update page

Now that the initial legwork is out of the way, you're ready to build the actual Record Update Form. To start, you add a filtered recordset to retrieve information for the product to be updated:

1. **In the *admin* folder, open the file *edit.php*.**
2. **Add a recordset using any of the methods described on page 858. For example, choose Insert→Data Objects→Recordset.**

   The Recordset window opens. Make sure the Simple (as opposed to the Advanced) options are displayed, as shown in Figure 25-19.

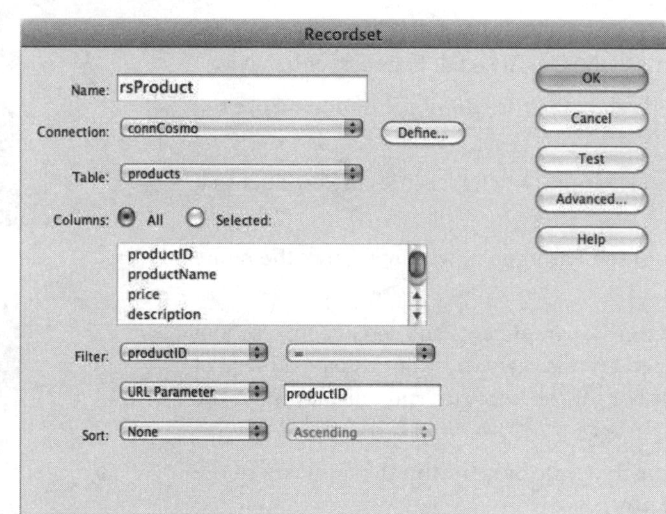

Figure 25-19: *When you filter on a table's primary key ("productID" in this case) using the = operator, the recordset never retrieves more than one record.*

3. **In the Name field, type rsProduct; from the Connection menu, choose "connCosmo", and from the Tables menu, select "products". Leave the All button selected.**

   Next, add a filter to the recordset to ensure that the recordset retrieves only a single record—for the product you want to update.

4. **From the Filter menu, select "productID". From the Comparison menu, make sure "=" is selected. From the Source menu, choose "URL Parameter". Finally, make sure the last field in the Filter area of the window says "productID".**

   After you select "productID", Dreamweaver most likely fills in the other three options for you. When you create a filtered recordset, Dreamweaver assumes you'll use a URL parameter with the same name as the selected field. The Recordset window should now look like Figure 25-19. In essence, it instructs the recordset to retrieve only the record whose productID matches the number passed in the URL parameter named "productID" (that's the name you supplied as part of the link in step 4 on "Creating the update page").

5. **Click OK to close the window and add the recordset to the page.**

   Next, you'll create two more recordsets—a listing of all your vendors and a listing of product categories. You'll use them to create dynamic menus, just as you did on the insert form.

6. **Follow steps 2-7 from the "Adding an Insert Product Page" part of this tutorial (see page 950) to create new "rsVendors" and "rsCategories" recordsets.**

   (You can also copy those recordsets from the insert product page as described on page 876.) The hard part's behind you. You can now use Dreamweaver's Update Record Form tool to finish the page.

7. **Click directly underneath the green line of the Edit Record headline. Choose Insert→Data Objects→Update Record→Record Update Form Wizard.**

   The Record Update Form window opens (see Figure 25-21). Next, you'll specify the recordset and fields the form should update.

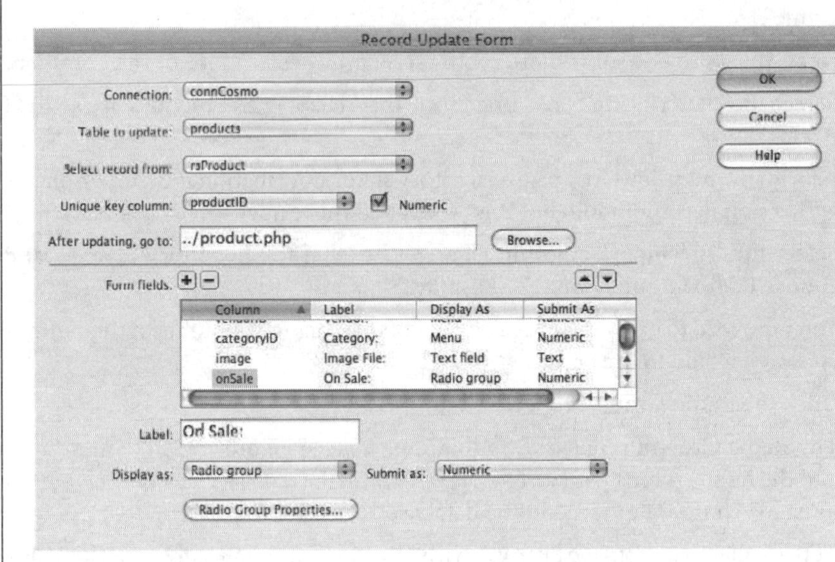

***Figure 25-20:** Dreamweaver's Record Update Form Wizard makes quick work of creating pages that update records in a database.*

8. **From the Connection menu, select "connCosmo". Make these selections for the next three menus: "products" in the "Table to update" menu, "rsProduct" in the "Select record from" menu, and "productID" in the "Unique key column".**

   Next, you need to specify which page appears after someone updates a record. Since the update page lets you edit a single product, it makes sense that after you submit changes, you should see the newly updated information on that product's detail page.

Note: As with the Insert Record Form Wizard, once you close the Update Record Form Wizard window, there's no way to return to it (see the note on page 956).

9. **Click the Browse button. In the Select File window, navigate to and select the file *product.php*. Click OK to choose the file.**

   Now you must specify which fields appear in the form. You also need to change which type of form element they should use, and edit their labels. This process is similar to the Insert Record form; it's summarized in the following steps.

10. **In the "Form field" list, select "productID"; click the Remove (minus sign [–]) button to remove this field from the list.**

    Since "productID" is a primary key the database generates, no one should be allowed to change it. Next, you'll change the text label that appears next to a couple of the fields.

11. **Select the "productName" form field, and then change its label to "Product Name".**

    Next, you'll provide some more room for lengthy descriptions of each product.

12. **Select the "description" column. From the "Display as" menu, choose Text Area.**

    As with the insert product page, inventory status information is better displayed with a simple pair of radio buttons. You'll add those now.

13. **Select the "inventory" column. Change the label to "Inventory Status:" and choose Radio Group from the "Display as" menu,.**

    You now need to give Dreamweaver a bit of information about the radio buttons you want to add to the page.

14. **Click the Radio Group Properties button.**

    The Radio Group Properties window appears (see Figure 25-16). You need to add the radio buttons you want to appear on the form. The value of each button must match the data stored in the database.

15. **In the Label field, replace button1 with "In stock". Type *in stock* into the Value field, too.**

    The pages displays the label on the page but uses the value as the information that is stored in the database. You need to add one more button.

16. **Click the + button to add another radio button; repeat step 15, but type *Out of stock* for the label and *out of stock* for the value of the second button.**

    The window should look like Figure 25-16, except that the "Select value equal to" box is filled with the programming code necessary to select the correct button. Since this is an update form, one of the buttons should *already* be selected when the page loads—information stored in the recordset determines which button it is.

17. **Click OK to close the Radio Group Properties window.**

    Again, in an effort to speed up data entry and make sure your employees fill out the form correctly, you'll create pull-down menus for the next two fields. First, you'll create a dynamic menu to display the list of vendors.

18. **Select the "vendorID" column, and then change the label to "Vendor:". From the "Display as" menu, choose Menu; click the Menu Properties button.**

    The Menu Properties window opens (see Figure 25-18).

19. **Click the "From database" radio button, make sure "rsVendors" is selected in the Recordset menu, and then, from the "Get labels from" menu, choose "vendorName". Now, from the "Get values from" menu, choose "vendorID".**

    Leave the "Select value equal to" field as is. Dreamweaver automatically selects the appropriate choice, based on which vendor manufactures the product.

20. **Click OK to close the Menu Properties window.**

    You need to repeat the process for the product categories menu.

21. **Select the "categoryID" column, and then change the label to "Category:". Choose Menu from the "Display as" menu; click the Menu Properties button.**

    The Menu Properties window opens.

22. **Click the "From database" radio button, make sure "rsCategories" is selected in the Recordset menu, and then choose "categoryName" from the "Get labels from" menu. Now, from the "Get values from" menu, choose "categoryID". Click OK to close the Menu Properties window.**

    As with the previous menu, Dreamweaver automatically adds the correct code for the product you want to edit when this update page loads.

23. **Select the "image" form field, and then change its label to "Image File:".**

    Finally, you'll provide a way to indicate whether a product is on sale.

24. **Select the "onSale" category, and then change the label to "On Sale:".**

    Either the product is on sale or it isn't. You can best represent this kind of yes or no option by radio buttons.

25. **From the "Display as" menu, choose Radio Group, and click the Radio Group Properties button.**

    Numbers in the database represent the sale status of a product: if the "onSale" field has a value of 1, the product is on sale; if the value is 0, the product isn't on sale. Because 1 and 0 might not make sense to anyone using this page, use plain language in the labels.

26. **In the Label field, replace button1 with *Yes*. Type *1* in the Value field as well.**

    Just one more button to add.

27. **Click the + button to add another radio button; repeat the previous step, but type *No* for the label and *0* for the value of the second button. Click OK to close the radio button window.**

    At this point, the Record Update Form window should resemble Figure 25-20.

28. **Click OK to close the Record Update Form window.**

    Dreamweaver inserts a table, form, form fields, and programming code to the update page. All that's left are some cosmetic touches.

29. **Repeat steps 1–5 from the "Finishing the Insert Form" part of this tutorial (page 957).**

    Doing so properly formats the form. Your finished page should resemble Figure 25-21.

30. **Save this page and close it.**

    To get a feel for what you've done, it's time to test your application.

31. **In the local root folder (the *cosmo_shop* folder), open the *index.php* page. Press F12 (Option-F12) to preview it in a browser.**

    The page lists the products in the database. Take a close look at one product.

32. **Click the name of any product in the list.**

    A details page for that product appears.

33. **Click the Edit This Information link near the bottom.**

    The Update Product page appears, with the form already completed.

34. **Change some of the information on the form, and then click the "Update record" button.**

    Voilà! You're taken back to the details page for this product listing, which proudly displays the freshly edited content.

Creating and Linking to the Delete Page

Obviously, if a vendor stops manufacturing a product, or the staff at CosmoFarmer decides to discontinue an item, you need a way to remove a product listing from the database.

Adding a link on the details page

To begin, you must provide a link to delete the product. A good place for this would be on the details page of each product. Since you already added an Edit This Information link to this page, you must now add a Delete This Product link:

1. **Open the file *product.php*.**

    Add a link that leads to a delete page.

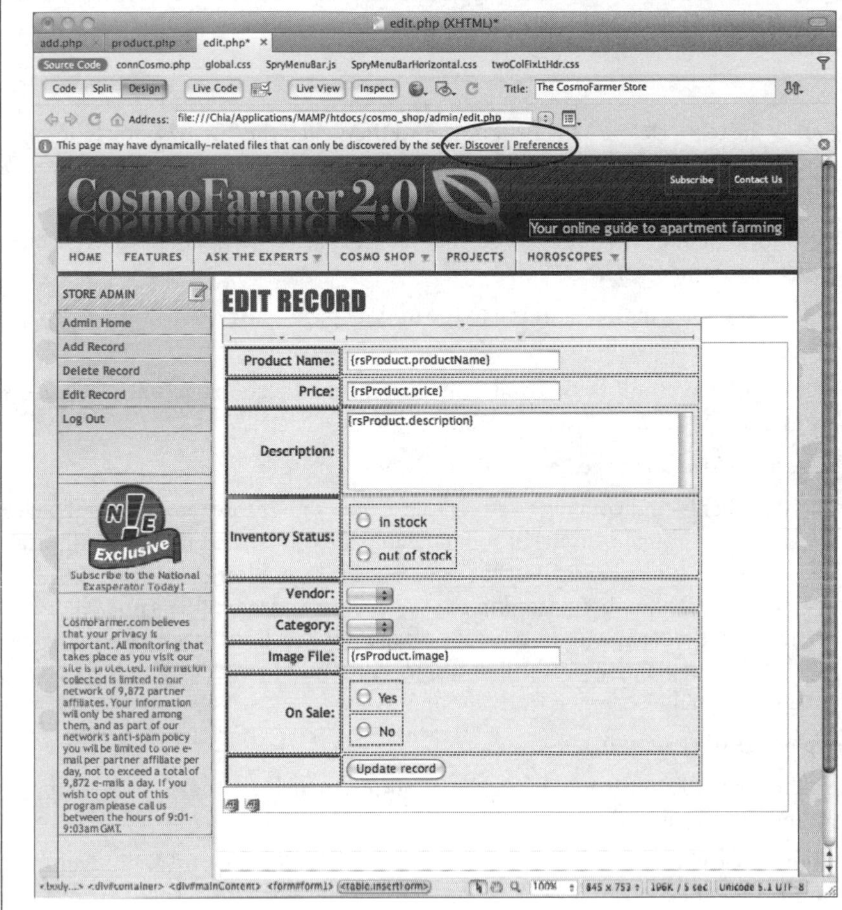

***Figure 25-21:** When you work in Design view, Dreamweaver highlights dynamic areas of the page—like this update form—in light blue. If you'd like to hide this coloring, open the Preferences window (Edit→Preferences [Dreamweaver→Preferences]), select the Highlighting category, and then turn off the two Live Data checkboxes. As mentioned on page 905, dynamic files have a special toolbar for finding dynamically related files (files added to a page using PHP). You can "discover" those types of file by clicking the Discover link (circled)—this feature, new in Dreamweaver CS5, is intended for big web applications like the WordPress blogging system, or Drupal content management system. It won't have any effect for the basic types of dynamic pages you're learning to create here. But, if you click the Discover link, that toolbar will go away. Clicking the Preferences link will let you turn this bar off permanently.*

2. **Near the bottom of the page, click to the right of the text you added earlier: Edit This Information. Press the space bar, followed by the | character and another space; type *Delete This Product*.**

   Now you'll link this phrase to the delete page.

Note: It's easy to accidentally click into the "Edit This Information" link. Doing so will make any text you type a part of that link. If that happens, just delete the new text you typed, click the <a> in the Tag selector at the bottom of the document window, and then press the right arrow key. This moves the insertion point to the right of the link.

---

3. **Select the text "Delete This Product", and then click the "Browse for File" button (the little folder icon) in the Property inspector. Navigate to the *admin* folder, and select the file *delete.php*, but don't close the window yet.**

   You need to add the information that lets the delete page form know which product it should delete.

4. **Follow steps 4-7 in the "Linking to the update page" part of this tutorial (page 959).**

   Doing so creates a link that not only goes to the delete page, but also passes along the ID number of the product you want to delete.

5. **Save and close this page.**

   You'll probably find yourself needing to use the same recordset on several pages on a site. For example, on the product detail page you created in the last tutorial, you created a filtered recordset that retrieved information on a single product (based on an ID number passed in the URL). You recreated that same recordset on the update record page you created on page 960. You'll also need it for the delete page (to select a single product to delete). Instead of recreating that recordset yet again, you'll just copy it from another page.

6. **Open the file *edit.php*.**

   You'll copy the recordset from the Bindings panel, so make sure it's open (Window→Bindings).

7. **Right-click (Control-click) on the "rsProduct" recordset, and then, from the pop-up menu, choose Copy.**

   You can also select the recordset in the Bindings panel, click the shortcut menu that appears in the panel's top-right corner, and then select Copy. Either way, you copy the programming code necessary for the delete page.

Creating the delete page

You just created a link to the delete page; now you need to make the delete page do its stuff:

1. **Open the file *delete.php*.**

   This is where you'll paste the recordset you copied a moment ago.

2. **Make sure the Bindings panel is open. Right-click (Control-click) in the empty area of the panel; from the shortcut menu, choose Paste.**

   Dreamweaver pastes all the programming code to create a recordset. This method is a fast way to reuse a recordset.

3. **In the Bindings panel, expand the recordset listing by clicking the small + button (arrow on Macs) to the left of the recordset.**

   Don't click the *large* + button, which lets you add additional recordsets. You just want to see an expanded listing of recordset columns so you can add some dynamic data to the page.

4. **Drag the "productName" column from the Bindings panel and drop it onto the document window, just to the right of the text "Record to delete".**

   This action inserts dynamic data into the page. When this page appears in a web browser, the name of a product appears in bold type.

5. **Click the empty space just below the name of the product. Choose Insert→Form→Form.**

   A red dotted line—the boundaries of the form—appears on the page. You need to set the form's *action* property (a URL to the page that collects the form information).

6. **In the Property inspector, click the Action box, and then type delete.php.**

   Now when you submit this form, its contents will be sent…to itself! This is a common maneuver with dynamic pages, which often do double duty depending on how you access them. In this case, when you submit the form, the programming code (which you'll add in a minute) receives the request to delete a particular product. Instead of displaying the page and form again, it merely deletes the record from the database, and then redirects the browser to a different page (see page 946 for more detail on how this works).

7. **Click in the empty space between the form's red dotted boundaries. Choose Insert→Form→Button. (If the "Input Tag Accessibility Attributes" window appears, click Cancel to close it.)**

   The button's label currently says Submit, but a more descriptive term, like Delete, would be better.

8. **In the Property Inspector, change the Value box to read *Delete*.**

   This button, when clicked, will remove one product from the database. However, you need to identify the product as well. A hidden form field containing the product's ID number will do the trick.

9. **In the document window, click to the right of the button you just added, and then choose Insert→Form→Hidden Field.**

   When you view the web page, you don't see a hidden field, but it provides useful information when you submit the form. In this case, it needs to supply the product ID.

10. **With the hidden field selected, change its name in the Property inspector from *hiddenField* to *productID*.**

    This step and the next are similar to adding a parameter to the end of a URL (for example, to link from a list of records to a detail page for a single record).

The only difference is that instead of placing the product's ID number in a URL, it's now embedded within a form. Now you need to add the product ID that's retrieved from the database.

11. **In the Property inspector, click the lightning bolt to the right of the value box.**

    The Dynamic Data window opens, displaying the rsProduct recordset.

12. **From the list of fields, select "productID", and then click OK to close the Dynamic Data window.**

    Now when someone views this page, the doomed product's ID number is stored in this hidden field.

13. **Open the Server Behaviors panel (Window→Server Behaviors). Click the + button, and then select Delete Record.**

    The Delete Record window appears (see Figure 25-22).

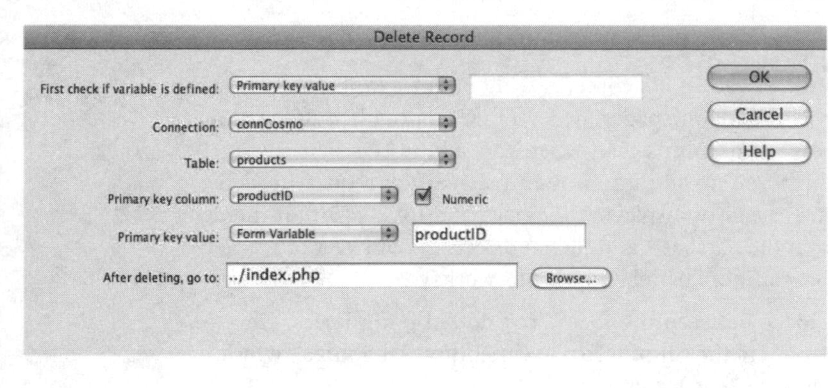

***Figure 25-22:** The Delete Record behavior adds all the necessary programming code to remove a record from the database. All you need to make it work is a recordset that retrieves a single record–and a form with a Delete button and a hidden field containing the record's primary key value.*

14. **From the first menu, select Primary Key Value.**

    This step tells the server behavior that it shouldn't delete the record until it's given a primary key value (you define when this happens in steps 17 and 18 below).

15. **From the Connection pop-up menu, choose "connCosmo".**

    Now tell Dreamweaver which table the record belongs to.

16. **From the Table menu, choose "products".**

    This menu indicates the table containing the record you want to delete. You next have to specify the primary key (see page 846) for the record.

17. **From the "Primary Key Column" menu, select "productID," and make sure the Numeric box is checked.**

    Now you need to let the server behavior know where the primary key value will come from. In this case, the ID number for the product you want to delete is embedded in a hidden form field named "productID".

18. **From the Primary Key Value field, choose Form Variable, and make sure "productID" appears in the box to the right.**

    To finish filling out this window, you'll just tell Dreamweaver which page should appear after someone deletes the record.

Note: It's important to choose Form Variable in step 18. Dreamweaver starts with the option "URL variable" selected. If you don't change this option, as soon as this page encounters a URL variable with the product ID number, it will delete that record. In other words, as soon as you get to this page (with the productID passed in the URL), Dreamweaver deletes the product and the innocent CosmoFarmer administrator will never have a chance to confirm the deletion.

---

19. **In the Property inspector, click the "Browse for File" button. Navigate to the root folder (*cosmo_shop*) and select the file *index.php*.**

    The Delete Record window should now look like Figure 25-22.

20. **Click OK (Choose on a Mac).**

    Dreamweaver adds the Delete Record server behavior to the page. You've done it! Now you need to test it out.

21. **Save and close this page. Open the *index.php* page. Press the F12 key (Option-F12) to preview it in a browser.**

    The page lists the products in the database. Take a closer look now at a specific item.

22. **Click the name of any product in the list.**

    A details page for that product appears.

23. **Click the Delete This Product link near the bottom.**

    The Delete Record page appears (see Figure 25-23). Notice that both the product name and a Delete button appear.

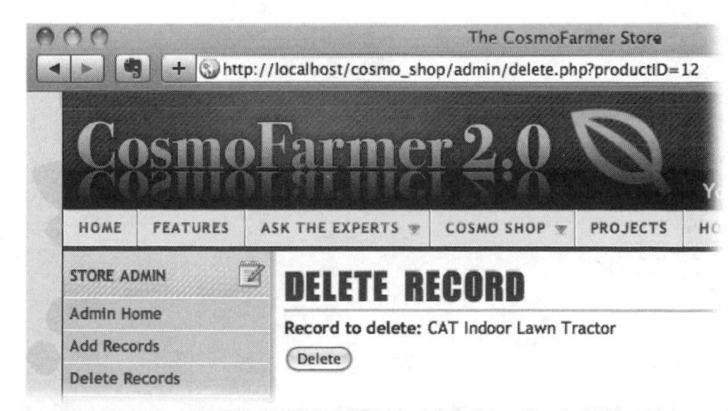

Figure 25-23: *When you first access this page (from a link on a product details page), it displays the confirmation shown here. But when you click the Delete button, the page reloads and sends a Delete command to the database.*

24. **Click the Delete button to remove the item.**

    Don't worry, you can always insert more products later! In any case, you'll note that that the products page no longer lists the product.

Of course, in the real world, you wouldn't want just anybody deleting, adding, or editing products on an e-commerce site. So in the next chapter, you'll learn how to keep prying eyes and mischievous fingers away from your coveted insert, update, and delete pages.

CHAPTER 26

Advanced Dynamic Site Features

Dreamweaver's basic database capabilities are impressive. But there may come a time when you need to dig deeper into the program to build successful web applications. Dreamweaver's advanced features let you, the mere mortal, do things that the pros do every day, like password-protect pages; display (or hide) content based on database results; and access information from forms, cookies, and URLs.

Password-Protecting Web Pages

Although Dreamweaver lets you create web pages that let others add, edit, and delete records from a database, your e-business wouldn't last very long if just *anyone* could remove orders from your online ordering system or view credit card information stored in your customers' records. And certainly your company's executives wouldn't be happy if someone got into the staff directory database and changed the boss's title to Chief Bozo. For these and other reasons, Dreamweaver provides a simple set of tools to lock your pages from prying eyes.

The User Authentication server behaviors can password-protect any page on your site. With this feature, you can limit areas of your site to registered users only, let customers access and update their contact information, create maintenance pages accessible only to administrators, or personalize pages with customized messages ("Welcome back, Dave").

To password-protect pages on your site, you need to get several elements in order:

- A database table containing the authorized users' login information.
- A registration form for adding new users to the system. (This is an optional step, but it's frequently useful when you want to automate the process of adding user login information to the database.)
- A login form.
- One or more pages you need to password-protect.

The Users Table

To password protect your web pages, your database must hold several pieces of information about the people who can access those secret pages. For example, each visitor must have a user name and password to log into your site. If the name and password match a record in the database, then Open Sesame: He's logged into the site and can access password-protected pages.

You might also want to include a field in the record that assigns an *access level* to each person. This way, your site can have multiple sections, accessible by different groups of people. Dreamweaver provides tools to do this, too.

For example, if your site has a members-only section that publishes special content to registered visitors, you could assign the access level "member" to people who register, and let them see these pages. However, you want only your site's administrators and staff to be able to update a product database or retrieve sales records, so you give these people "administrator" access.

At a minimum, then, your database needs a users table with three fields (username, password, and access level). You can either use a standalone table or incorporate this information into another table. For example, if you require people to provide their names, street addresses, email addresses, and so on when they register, you could include these three login fields in this table. If you have an e-commerce system, you could store login information in the table holding customer information.

Tip: Most database systems let you assign a default value to a column. That way, when someone creates a new record and supplies no information for a column, the application enters the default value instead.

For starters, it's a good idea to assign a default value for the access-level field. You can set your database to assign the lowest access level—"guest," say—whenever someone creates a new record. By doing this, if you use a web form to collect information from a new member to create a new record, you can omit a form field for assigning an access level. This method is a good security precaution, as adept (and malicious) web surfers could submit a fake form that grants a high access level, potentially giving them entrée into sensitive areas of your site.

Creating a Registration Form

Once you add a users table to your database, you need a way to add new members. If you plan to use password protection on pages only your site's staff should access, you probably *shouldn't* create a web form to add new administrative members. You'd run the risk of someone stumbling on the form and adding herself to the list of administrators. In such cases, you're better off adding the proper login records in the database system itself—using phpMyAdmin, or MySQL Monitor, for example.

Note: If you do create a form to add new members with high access levels, password-protect this form! Otherwise, anyone who inadvertently discovers it could add new administrative members–and from there, Pandora's box would be open.

On the other hand, if you want to let *lots* of people sign up as members of your site, you might want to add a registration form that *automatically* adds them to the list of the site's members. This would free you from the headache of manually assigning user names and passwords for everyone who wants to become a member.

If the site already includes a form to collect visitor information, you can simply add the proper user fields to this form. Say your site includes a "Sign up for our email newsletter" page that collects a visitor's name, email address, and other contact information. You could add a field called *username* and another called *password.*

Note: Organizations often use an email address as a person's user name for password-protected pages. If you're already collecting an email address, you can exclude the user name field from the form.

When the visitor submits the form, the web application adds all these fields to the database. (To add records to a database using a web form, see page 923.) While the process of creating a new member for password-protected pages is basically the same as that for adding a new record to a database, you do need to make sure that every visitor has a unique user name; if more than one person has the same name, then you can't distinguish between them.

Fortunately, Dreamweaver's Check New Username server behavior ensures that each user name a visitor submits is unique. If the name already exists, the server doesn't add the new record to the database, and it redirects the visitor to another page. To apply this server behavior, follow these steps:

1. **Add an insert-record form to a dynamic page.**

   The form should include fields for a user name and password. You might also add a field for an access level, if that's how you've structured your site. However, for a form that's accessible to the public, it's best to have the database set a default value for this; see the tip on page 972. (You'll need to use Dreamweaver's Insert Record server behavior. Creating insert-record forms is described on page 923.)

2. **Make sure the Server Behaviors panel is open (Window→Server Behaviors). Click the Add (+) button and, from the pop-up menu, choose User Authentication→Check New Username.**

   In the Insert panel's Data category, you can also use the User Authentication menu (see Figure 26-1). Either way, the Check New Username window appears (see Figure 26-2).

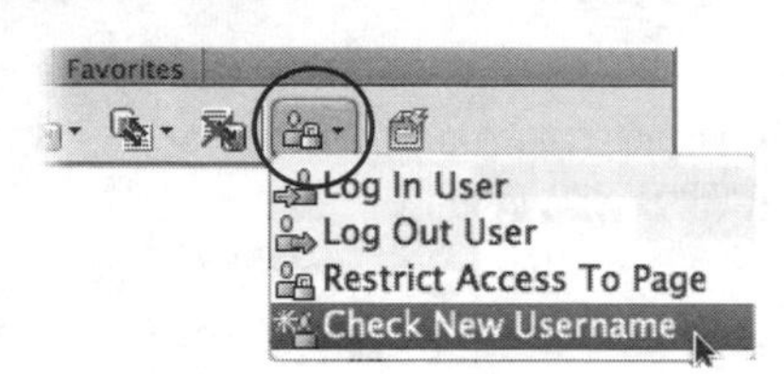

Figure 26-1:
Dreamweaver provides access to all user-authentication server behaviors from the Insert panel's Data category. (Here, the Insert panel appears in one of its many guises: Classic view, as described on page 23.)

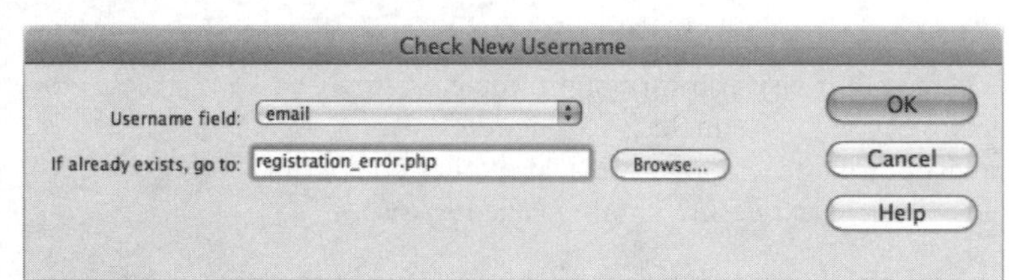

Figure 26-2:
When you add a new person to your database, the Check New Username server behavior lets you verify that no one else uses the user name.

3. **Select the name of the form field that captures the user name.**

   Note that this is the name of the form field *on the web page*—not the name of the column in the *database*. Dreamweaver already knows which form field applies to which database column—the Insert Record server behavior takes care of that.

4. **Click Browse, and then select a web page.**

   Here, choose the page that a visitor sees if someone else already uses the user name she typed in. This page (which you should create before applying this behavior) should include a note to your visitor, spelling out the problem (the user name is already in use and therefore unavailable). To make reentering information easier for your guest, you should include the insert form on this page as well, or provide a link back to the registration form page.

5. **Click OK to close the window and add the server behavior to the page.**

   Now when someone fills out the registration form, this behavior kicks in and makes sure that no one else has the same user name.

Note: Registering a new member doesn't automatically log him into the site. He still needs to go to a login page (described next).

After inserting the server behavior, Dreamweaver lists it in the Server Behaviors panel. If you wish to change any of its properties, double-click Check New Username to reopen the Check New Username window (Figure 26-2). To delete the behavior, select it, and then click the Remove (minus sign [–]) button.

Creating the Login Page

To access a password-protected page, your visitor must first log into the site using a web form. You need just two fields on this simple form—a user name field and a password field—and a Submit button.

When someone attempts to log in, the values she types into the form are compared with the user name and password columns in the database. If there's a match, Dreamweaver transports her to another page—often the main page of a password-protected area of the site. If there's no matching record, Dreamweaver carts the visitor away to a page of your creation—an "Access Denied!" page or maybe just the original login page.

To create a login page:

1. **Add a web form to a dynamic web page.**

   If your site includes password-protected pages aimed at a general audience, you can put this form on your home page. Or you could create a dedicated login page (remembering to provide links to this page throughout your site). However, if you're creating a login page for administrators, you might want to put the login form out of the way, so that the average visitor doesn't notice it.

   Either way, the form should contain only a user name field, a password field, and a single Submit button. Naming the fields "username" and "password" (rather than keeping Dreamweaver's factory-set field names) helps with step 3.

2. **Open the Server Behaviors panel (Window→Server Behaviors). Click the + button, and then choose User Authentication→Log In User.**

   You can also use the Insert panel's Data category (see Figure 26-1) or choose Insert→Data Objects→User Authentication→Log In User to open the Log In User window (see Figure 26-3).

3. **From the first three menus, select the names of the login form, the form field that collects the user name, and the password field, respectively.**

   You're telling Dreamweaver which form (if the page has more than one) and which fields to use for comparison to the users table in the database.

Tip: Dreamweaver automatically makes these first three menu selections for you if the following things are in place: You've got just one form on the page; the first field on that form is the user name field; and the second field is the password field.

4. **From the "Validate using connection" menu, choose the name of the database connection.**

   This connection should communicate with the database that contains the user login table.

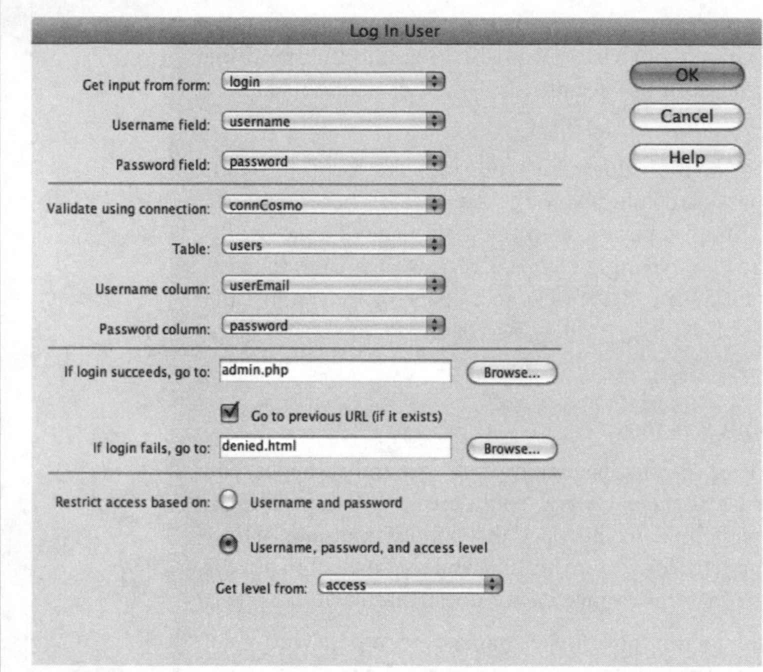

Figure 26-3: *Dreamweaver's Log In User server behavior lets visitors log into your site so they can visit password-protected pages. You have quite a few items to fill out here, but they're all straightforward. The last option lets you use access levels to limit pages of the site to particular groups of visitors—administrators, for example.*

5. **From the Table menu, choose the name of the users' table.**

   This is the table described on page 972, which includes the user name, password, and access level for anyone attempting to log in.

6. **From the "Username column" menu, select the database column that stores names. From the "Password column" menu, choose the database column for passwords.**

   The User Authentication server behavior searches these two columns for a match to the values your visitor types into the form.

7. **To the right of the "If login succeeds" field, click the Browse button; navigate to and select a page from your site.**

   Most of the time, this is the main page for a password-protected area of the site. If the site contains a members-only section, then, after logging in, the visitor arrives at the Members page. If you're adding features for administering the site—adding, deleting, and editing database info, for example—then create a main Administrators page with links to the database administration pages.

8. **Turn on the "Go to previous URL" checkbox.**

   This option is a little confusing, but very convenient. Imagine a visitor stumbling across a password-protected page (you'll learn how to protect pages in the next section). She simply comes across a link to a password-protected page, and clicks it. Of course, since she hasn't logged in, she's denied access to the page and sent to another page. At this point, you're probably redirecting her to the login page, so she can log in and continue clicking her way through your site.

   That's where this feature comes in handy. By turning on this box, you permit your visitor to log in, and then the login form takes her *back* to the page she couldn't get past at the outset. In other words, the visitor tries to access a password-protected page (*any* password-protected page in the site); she's not logged in, so the password-protected page sends her to the login page. After she successfully logs in, the login page takes her directly to the page she first tried to access (*not* the page you specified in step 7). This is very convenient for visitors who bookmark password-protected pages in your site, since it saves them the hassle of having to log in and then navigate to the page they wanted in the first place!

9. **To the right of the "If login fails" field, click Browse; navigate to and select a page from your site.**

   This page, which you need to create in advance, should explain that the user name and password were not correct. Since the visitor may have just made a mistake, it's polite to either include another login form on this page or a link back to the login page.

10. **If the database includes a column that stores access levels, select the "Username, password, and access level" radio button.**

    This option not only lets folks log into the site, but also tracks their access levels. In this way, you can limit areas of your site to people with the proper access level—administrators, for example.

11. **From the "Get level from" pop-up menu, select the name of the database column that contains visitors' access levels.**

    Dreamweaver lists all the columns in the table you selected in step 5. If the table doesn't have a column for this information, then go to your database application and add it, or deselect the Access Level radio button. (Even if you don't currently have plans to offer different levels of access, it's a good idea to keep this option in mind. In the future, you may very well want to add special pages for administrators or Super Premium Members. Without an access level, anyone who has a user name and password can visit all your pages.)

12. **Click OK to close the window and apply the behavior to the page.**

    You can edit or delete this behavior by double-clicking its name in the Server Behaviors panel.

The Log Out User Behavior

Dreamweaver's Log Out User server behavior lets someone log out by clicking a link. Thereafter, her browser can't load any password-protected pages in the site until she logs back in.

POWER USERS' CLINIC

Logging In: Behind the Scenes

The Log In User server behavior checks to see if the user name and password submitted in a form matches a user name and password in the database. If it does, the behavior generates two session variables (see page 986): MM_Username and MM_UserGroup. The first one (MM_Username) stores the user name of the logged-in visitor; the second (MM_UserGroup) stores the visitor's access level. (The MM stands for Macromedia, the name of the company that owned Dreamweaver before Adobe.) The variables follow visitors from page to page of the site, until they log out, close their browser, or don't do anything on the website for at least 20 minutes.

The password-protection scripts use these session variables to allow or deny access to a page. But you can take advantage of them in other ways. You can add MM_Username to the Bindings panel (see page 986), for example, and then add it to your pages, like other dynamic data, to customize pages: "Welcome back, *Kotter176@aol.com*."

Furthermore, since each user name is unique—just like a primary key—you can use the session variable to filter records in a recordset (see page 861). You could use this technique, for instance, when a logged-in visitor wishes to see all his contact information. Create a recordset that filters the user table by the session variable.

You can also use the MM_UserGroup variable to control the display of certain areas of a page. For example, while regular members of your site might see a simple listing of products on a dynamic catalog page, administrators might see additional items like "Edit this product" and "Delete this product" buttons. The tutorial at the end of this chapter has an example of this scheme in action (see page 1002).

This setup is useful when a visitor shares her computer with others, maybe at the library or at school, because it provides a sense of security. (It's not absolutely necessary, though; her computer destroys the cookie that identifies the session variable that keeps track of her login status as soon as she closes her browser. Furthermore, if a certain amount of time passes without any activity—usually 20 minutes—the web server automatically destroys the session variable, effectively logging out the visitor. Again, though, a logout link can be reassuring to your audience.)

To add a Log Out server behavior:

1. **Open a dynamic page.**

   Note that since this adds programming code to the page, it works only on dynamic pages. You can't add a logout link to a static HTML page. So if you want to provide this option on all your site's pages, you have to save each page in your site as a dynamic page.

2. **Click the page where you'd like to add a logout link.**

   The logout link is just a regular link, so you can place it anywhere that makes sense, such as an option in the navigation bar or a link in the page's footer. In addition, you can select text or an image that's already on the page to turn it into a logout link.

3. **Open the Server Behaviors panel (Window→Server Behaviors). Click the + button and, from the pop-up menu, choose User Authentication→Log Out User.**

   Alternatively, you can use the Insert panel's Data category (see Figure 26-1) or choose Insert→Data Objects→User Authentication→Log Out User. In any case, the Log Out User window appears (see Figure 26-4).

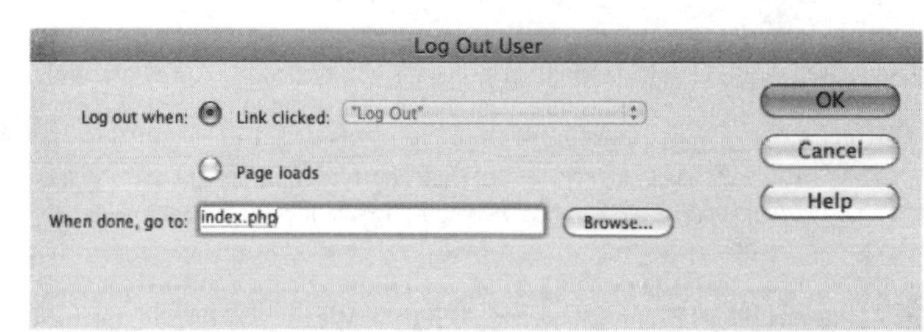

Figure 26-4:
To add a logout function to text or an image already on a page, simply select it and then apply the Log Out User server behavior.

4. **Select one of the two radio buttons.**

   You can log out a visitor two ways: when a page loads or when he clicks a link. Use the first method when you want to automatically log someone out when he reaches a specific page. For example, say you create an online testing application where students sit at a computer and answer page after page of questions. When students reach the last page of the quiz—maybe a page summarizing their results—you could automatically log them out. The next student sitting down at the same computer would have to log in, preventing the testing application from thinking the new test taker is the same person as the previous student.

   The second method lets visitors log themselves out by clicking a link, so the menu starts out reading, "Create new link: 'Log out'", which adds a new link with the words "Log out" to the page. After adding the behavior, you can then edit the page and change *Log out* to any text you like, or even add a graphic button to the link.

Tip: You can also first add some text like "Quit system", select it, and then apply the Log Out User server behavior. Dreamweaver automatically uses that text when it creates the link instead of its standard "Log Out" text.

5. **Click Browse; navigate to and select a page from your site.**

   Good choices for this page are the login page—so the next visitor can log in—or the home page.

6. **Click OK.**

   You just applied the link and server behavior.

Protecting Individual Pages

To password-protect a web page, apply the "Restrict Access to Page" server behavior. You have to do this for each page you want to protect, and you can apply it only to dynamic web pages. In other words, you can't password-protect regular HTML files, text files, graphics, or any other file that your application server doesn't process.

Note: Although some web servers let you password-protect an entire folder's worth of files, Dreamweaver doesn't give you any tools to do so. (If your site runs on an Apache server, however, you can use *.htaccess* files to password-protect an entire folder. You'll find a quick tutorial at *www.sitedeveloper.ws/tutorials/htaccess.htm*, and a free online tool to create these files at *www.webmaster-toolkit.com/htaccess-generator.shtml*. Visit *http://httpd.apache.org/docs/2.2/howto/htaccess.html* for more information.)

The "Restrict Access to Page" behavior works like this: When someone tries to load a password-protected page, programming code in the page determines whether he's already logged in. If the page also requires a particular access level—administrators only, for instance—it checks to see whether the visitor has the proper clearance as well; if so, the browser displays the page. If the visitor isn't logged in, however, or doesn't have proper access, the password-protected page redirects him to another page—like an "Access Denied" page or back to the login page.

To apply this server behavior, follow these steps:

1. **Open the dynamic page you wish to protect.**

   You can only protect a dynamic page—for example, a page ending in .php.

2. **Open the Server Behaviors panel (Window→Server Behaviors). Click the + button, and then choose User Authentication→"Restrict Access to Page".**

   The "Restrict Access to Page" window appears (see Figure 26-5).

3. **Turn on one of the two radio buttons.**

   If you want to allow access to anyone in the users table, select the "Username and password" button. However, if you want to limit the page to visitors with a particular access level, turn on the second button.

   The first time you use this behavior, you have to define the different access levels, so click Define. You must type in each access level exactly as it appears in the database—*admin*, *member*, and *guest*, for example. Capitalization counts.

You need to define the levels only once. Dreamweaver remembers the settings for other dynamic pages in the same site.

4. **In the "If access denied, go to" box, click Browse; navigate to and select the page people see if they aren't logged in.**

   It's often a good idea to redirect unregistered visitors to the login page. That way, if they're legitimate customers, they can simply log in and return to the page. (Dreamweaver can help with this. See step 8 on page 977.)

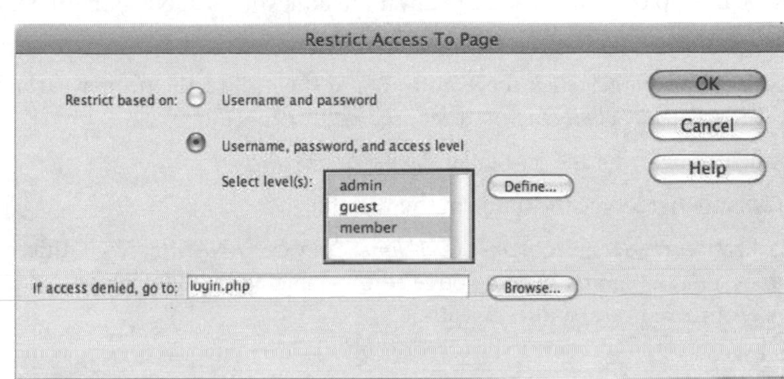

Figure 26-5: *If you want to give access to more than one group, Ctrl-click (⌘-click) more than one level in the Select Levels list to highlight the groups simultaneously.*

5. **Click OK to apply the link and server behavior.**

As with other server behaviors, Dreamweaver lists the "Restrict Access to Page" behavior in the Server Behaviors panel after you apply it. To change any of its properties, double-click its name. To delete the behavior, select it, and then click the minus (–) button.

Additional Data Sources

So far, you've used Dreamweaver's dynamic page-building features to retrieve information from databases to build catalog pages, product detail pages, and other database-dependent pages. But occasionally you want to collect data from other sources and add it to your page. For example, when someone logs into a site (see page 975), her user name travels along with her from page to page in what's called a *session variable*. Using the Bindings panel, you can capture this name and use it on a web page.

Similarly, you can create *cookies* to store small pieces of information on a person's computer—such as a counter that tracks how many times a visitor's been to your site—and use Dreamweaver's Bindings panel to add that information to a web page.

The Bindings panel lets you access these sources of data, as well as information submitted from form fields and embedded in URLs. You can add any number of other data sources to the Bindings panel (see Figure 26-6), and then add those data sources to your web page.

Adding a source to a page automatically inserts the programming code needed to retrieve the information from the data source. It's important to make clear that you aren't *creating* these various data sources—such as cookies, URL variables, or session variables—when you add them to the Bindings panel. Dreamweaver just provides an easy way to retrieve the value of already created variables. For example, adding a cookie variable to the Bindings panel doesn't actually create the cookie on a visitor's system, it just adds the programming necessary to use the cookie's contents on a page. (For information on creating cookies, see page 987.)

Regardless of the type of dynamic data you want to add, you go about gathering that data the same way.

1. **In the Bindings panel, click the + button, and then select the proper variable type: *URL*, *Form*, *Cookie*, or whatever (see Figure 26-7).**

   A window appears for the particular data source.

2. **In the Name field, type the name of the variable.**

   Capitalization matters; *username, UserName*, and *USERNAME* are all different variables. Find a naming system you're comfortable with (all lowercase, all uppercase, or mixed case) and stick with it.

3. **Click OK.**

   Dreamweaver adds the variable to the Bindings panel.

Tip: You can drag data sources listed in the Bindings panel into Code view, as well. Once you sharpen your programming chops, this trick lets you quickly add data to your own server-side programs.

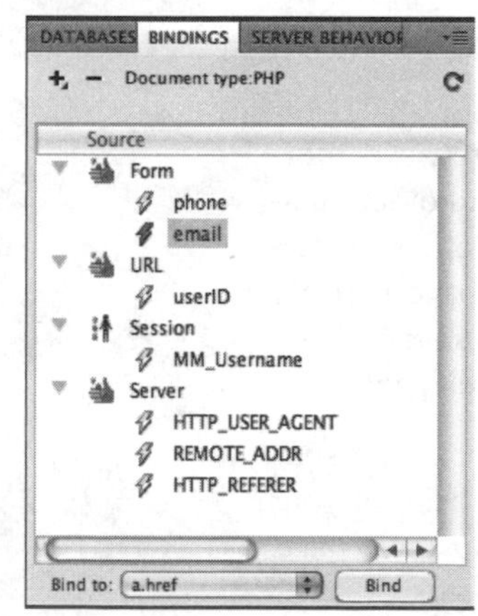

Figure 26-6:
Once you add a data source to the Bindings panel, you can add the data it contains to your page, just as you would with dynamic data from a recordset (see page 877). For example, you can drag the source from the Bindings panel and drop it onto a page, or click somewhere on a page, select the item in the Bindings panel, and then click the panel's Insert button. The result? Dreamweaver adds the programming code that accesses the value stored in that data source.

URL Variables

Some URLs include information tagged onto the end of the name of a web page, like this: *www.cosmofarmer.com/product.php?productID=10&action=delete*. The information following the *?* is known as a *query string*, and it provides additional information to a dynamic page.

Figure 26-7: *Recordsets aren't the only type of data you can add to the Bindings panel. You can add the names of cookies, session variables, form fields, and other data sources and then drag them onto a page. The Spry Data Set option is one of the Spry data tools discussed on page 544.*

In most cases, this information comes in the form of one or more name/value pairs, which Dreamweaver refers to as *URL variables*. The example above has two URL variables: The first is *productID*, and its value is *10*; the second is *action*, and its value is *delete*. Web developers often use URL variables to transfer specific information for use in a recordset. You did this in the tutorial in Chapter 24: You used a URL to pass the number of a product to the product details page, which used that number to retrieve details on the product.

You can also add a URL variable to the Bindings panel, and then include it in a web page or use it anywhere you'd use a dynamic data source. For example, you can use it as a parameter that you add to the end of a link to hand off information to another page.

Keep in mind that a page that links *to* the page using the URL variable must include the proper query string in the link. For example, if you add a URL variable named "username" to the page *crop_circles.html*, the page uses the query string to personalize the page: "Welcome, [username]". For this to work, you need to link to the *crop_circles.html* page with the query string attached to the URL, like this: *crop_circles.html?username=bob*. You can add a URL variable to a link using the methods described on page 867.

Tip: Don't use this method to access private or sensitive data. For example, suppose you use a URL variable as a way to access a customer's personal data, like this: *customer_data. asp?customerID=78*. A nefarious visitor could copy the URL into a new browser window, replace the number in the URL to, say, 79, and view all the personal data for customer number 79.

Form Variables

You can also add information from *forms* to the Bindings panel, and use them on your page. If you add a form on one page, you can submit that information to another page (the page specified in the form's *Action* property, as described on page 457). In other words, the receiving page can display the information on the page *or* use it in some other fashion—such as inserting it into a database, or creating a cookie or session variable.

If you're mainly using forms in conjunction with Dreamweaver's Insert Record and Update Record server behaviors, you won't generally take advantage of form variables. Those two behaviors work by collecting data from a form, adding or updating a database record, and then redirecting the web browser to another page. The page the visitor finally sees never has access to the form information, so you can't add any form variables to that page.

However, adding a form variable to the Bindings panel can come in handy when you want to create a search page. For example, suppose you create a page that lets guests search a database. The search form lets the visitor type in a name—of an author or musician, for instance. You then create a search *results* page that scours the database for records that match the search term. On that page, along with the database results, you could add text like "Search Results for: [search_term]", where *search_term* is the word the visitor typed into the form. Just add the form variable to the Bindings panel, and drag it to the spot in the search page where you want it to appear.

Note: If you use the *GET* method to submit a form, the web browser includes the names and values of each field in the URL. In this case, the application server considers the values as URL variables, so if you wish to add any of these fields to the Bindings panel, use the URL variable method instead. (For the difference between *GET* and *POST*, see page 458.)

Cookies

Normally, a web server doesn't remember if you previously visited or requested a page from it. This can be a problem.

Suppose, for example, that a site has a particularly long and annoying Flash movie that welcomes visitors with an ear-pounding, head-throbbing multimedia display. Even if the designer was kind enough to include a "Skip this nauseating display" button, the web server doesn't remember that you clicked it the *last* time you were there.

To overcome this limitation, most web browsers can store *cookies*—small text files with specific information—that web servers create and read. In the example above, the web server could drop a cookie onto your computer when you click the "Skip intro" button. The next time you visit the site, the server reads the cookie and ushers you past the Flash movie and directly to the home page.

You can use cookies to store information on visitors' computers, too. They're a great way to store customer ID numbers, the number of visits to a particular page, and other bits of identifying information.

Cookies play by a few rules:

- A browser stores a single cookie on just one computer at a time. If you log onto a site that adds a cookie to your computer, and then log on again later from the public library, that computer doesn't have access to the cookie. In fact, if you use a different web browser on the *same computer*, the web server can't read the original cookie from the other browser. (A variation: In some corporations, a web browser stores cookies on a network server. A particular browser—Internet Explorer, for example—*can* access this kind of cookie, even from different computers on the network.)
- Only the domain that created the cookie can read it. *You* can't create dynamic pages that read a cookie set by Amazon.com, for example. Fortunately, that means other websites can't read the cookies you set on your visitors' computers, either.
- Web browsers limit the size of a cookie to 4 KB, and allow only a limited number of total cookies (usually 300) per computer so that hard drives don't crumble under their weight.

You can add a cookie to the Bindings panel using the method described on page 981. Unfortunately, Dreamweaver doesn't give you the tools to create a cookie (you can submit feature requests for the next version of Dreamweaver to Adobe at *www.adobe.com/cfusion/mmform/index.cfm?name=wishform*). Several third-party developers have risen to the occasion, however:

- **PHP developers.** Dreamweaver extension developer Felice Di Stefano has a free cookie extension for the PHP server model. It includes server behaviors that add and delete cookies from a PHP page. In addition, it can set a cookie to the value of a form field, or redirect a visitor to another page if a specific cookie doesn't exist, or if it matches a particular value. You can find it at *www.felixonc.it.*
- **JavaScript cookies.** You can also use JavaScript to set cookies. This technique works with any type of page—even non-dynamic pages. The only catch is that the visitor's browser must both understand JavaScript and have JavaScript enabled (most do). Dreamweaver comes with two Snippets that set and read cookies using JavaScript. They're in the Snippets panel's JavaScript folder, in the cookies subfolder. See Chapter 19 to learn about Snippets. For the king of JavaScript cookie creators, check out WebAssist's Cookies Toolkit at *www.webassist.com/dreamweaver-extensions/cookies-toolkit/?PID=109* (this is a commercial product that runs around $50 and also includes tools that add cookies using server-side tools for PHP).

Session Variables

Web servers don't know or care whether the person requesting your company's home page just placed a $10 million order or is a first-time visitor. Of course, *you* probably care, and so do most web applications, which need to follow visitors as they travel through a site. For example, in a typical e-commerce site, people use a "shopping cart" to store items they're interested in. For this to work, however, you need to track each shopper's movement from page to page.

To make this possible, most web servers recognize what they call *session variables*. Web developers create session variables (or, more accurately, dynamic web pages create the variable) and it follows your visitor from page to page. This type of variable lasts, logically enough, for a single *session*: If a visitor closes his browser, the session ends and the variable disappears. Most web servers also limit how long a variable sticks around—usually 20 minutes. In other words, if a visitor doesn't interact with the site (click a page, or item) for 20 minutes, the server assumes he's no longer around, and destroys the session variable.

Note: Session variables take up resources on the web server. That's why the server gets rid of them as soon as it can. Creating lots of session variables for a busy site can slow down the server.

When it creates a session variable, the web server sends a cookie to the visitor's machine. The cookie contains a unique number (not the actual data contained in the variable), which the server uses to keep track of each visitor. When that person requests a page, the server reads the cookie with the unique ID. It can then retrieve session variables for that individual, which you can use in your own programs. That's why session variables don't work if a visitor's web browser doesn't accept cookies. (PHP, however, has a built-in way to maintain session information even when a guest has cookies turned off.)

Note: Dreamweaver itself creates session variables when you use the User Authentication server behaviors. See the box on page 978 for a discussion of these variables, and how you can use them.

You may wonder how cookies and session variables differ, and when you want to use one over the other. Cookies can last *between* visits. If you want access to a piece of information when a visitor comes back tomorrow, or next week, or next month, use a cookie. For example, use a cookie to remember a selection someone made from a previous visit, such as "Skip this crazy Flash Intro."

Session variables, on the other hand, provide better security. The information stored in a session variable *stays protected on a web server*, while cookies exist as text files on a visitor's computer that anyone with access to the computer can open and read. Accordingly, if you need to keep track of a confidential piece of information (someone's bank account password, for example), use a session variable.

You can add a session variable to the Bindings panel using the method described on page 981.

POWER USERS' CLINIC

Adding and Deleting Cookies Using PHP

Dreamweaver doesn't give you a tool to add the scripts necessary to create and delete cookies with PHP pages, but it isn't difficult to add the code yourself. (Dreamweaver can easily retrieve cookie information, as described on page 984.)

First, decide which page should add the cookie. The script runs when a visitor's browser *requests* the page, sending the cookie to the browser before it sends the page content. Thus, you could add this script at the beginning of a page that receives and processes form information. For example, if someone registers at your site, your script can store the name he enters in the registration form as a cookie on his computer. When he returns to the site, the home page reads the cookie and displays a message like "Welcome back, Bob."

To add a cookie to a page, switch into Code view (page 415) and put the following code (all on one line) above the <!DOCTYPE> declaration in the HTML code of the page.

```
<?php setcookie("name_of_cookie", "value_
of_cookie", time()+2419200); ?>
```

Remember to include the opening "<?php" and closing "?>", which tell the application server that everything in between is programming code and not HTML. Replace *name_of_cookie* with whatever name you wish to give the cookie: *username*, for example. Also replace *value_of_cookie* with whatever you want to store in the cookie. In many cases, this is a dynamic value—information from a recordset, a URL variable, or a form variable, for example. Using the steps described on page 981, add the appropriate dynamic data to the Bindings panel, and then drag it into the code, replacing the text (including the quote marks) "value of cookie".

Finally, you can set the amount of time the cookie stays on your visitor's computer. That's the *time()+2419200* in the code above. Essentially you're saying that the cookie should stick around for a certain number of seconds (*2419200*) after the current moment (*time()*). In this case, *2419200* is 30 days, about a month. If you want the cookie to stick around for an hour. use 3600; for 1 day, use 86400.

PHP is a little persnickety about where you place this code: It has to come before all the code in the page, with the exception of other PHP code. If there's even just a single blank line (not within the <?php ?> tags), you end up with the much-dreaded "Headers already sent" error. (You can get around this error by using two PHP functions named ob_start and ob_flush…if you're game for the technical details of this technique read more at *www.php.net/manual/en/function.ob-start.php* and *www.php.net/manual/en/function.ob-flush.php*.)

You can, however, place the code *after* other PHP code at the beginning of the file. For example, if you want to set the value of a cookie using information retrieved from a recordset, you need to place the cookie code *after* the recordset code.

You may also want to delete a cookie at some point. For example, on an e-commerce site, you can use a cookie to store items a visitor adds to her shopping cart. When she wants to empty her cart—after she buys everything in it, for example—you could simply delete the cookie. Just assign no value and a time in the past (no kidding) to the cookie you want to delete, like this:

```
<?php setcookie('name_of_cookie', '',
time()-3600); ?>
```

Again, make sure you type the above code on a single line in the Code view of your page.

Unfortunately, as with cookies, Dreamweaver doesn't provide any tools to create or destroy session variables. To find third-party extensions that work with session variables, try the Adobe Exchange (*http://www.adobe.com/exchange*). Click the Dreamweaver link, and search using the term *session*.

Note: Felice Di Stefano has developed a free session extension for the PHP server model. It includes server behaviors that add and delete session variables from a PHP page. You can find it at *www.felixone.it*.

Server Variables

Web servers collect and produce lots of information, much of which they hide from the everyday web surfer (and even the everyday webmaster). Some of that information is obscure, but some can come in handy. For example, you can find out which web browser a visitor uses, the IP address of the visitor's computer on the Internet, and what page the visitor was on before arriving at the current page. While the exact list of server variables differs by server, here are some useful ones that work on many web servers:

- **HTTP_USER_AGENT.** This gives you information about your visitor's browser. Unfortunately, it doesn't come in a neat little description like *Firefox 2 for Windows*. Instead, browser info is usually rather long-winded, like: *Mozilla/5.0 (Windows; U; Windows NT 6.0; en-US; rv:1.8.1.2) Gecko/20070219 Firefox/2.0.0.2*. To decipher this confusing jumble of information, visit *http://www.user-agents.org*.
- **REMOTE_ADDR.** This gives you the IP address of the computer requesting your web page. It looks something like 65.57.83.12. Depending on your visitor's setup, this could be the exact address of the computer. (Big Brother, where art thou?)

  Knowing a visitor's IP address has its uses. If someone frequently causes problems on your site—posts phony information to registration forms, say, or submits offensive messages to a message board—you can prevent submissions to your database from that IP address. (However, since many users' IP addresses frequently change, this solution isn't foolproof.)
- **HTTP_REFERER.** This is the URL of the page your visitor came from to get to the current page. For example, say she clicks a link on page A to get to page B. Page B's HTTP_REFERER server variable would be A.

  You can use this knowledge to create the ultimate Back button. Simply add the HTTP_REFERER server variable to the Bindings panel. Then add a link to whatever you want to use as a Back button—graphic or text—and use the server variable as the address. When visitors click this link, it takes them back to whichever page brought them there in the first place.

For a list of server variables you can use with the Apache server (the server most commonly used with PHP), visit *www.php.net/reserved.variables*. For a list of server variables that Microsoft's IIS web server supports, visit the Microsoft Developer's Network site at *http://msdn.microsoft.com/en-us/library/ms524602.aspx*.

Advanced Server Behaviors

In addition to the server behaviors described above, two other sets of behaviors come in handy on dynamic web pages.

POWER USERS' CLINIC

Adding and Deleting Session Variables Using PHP Pages

Dreamweaver doesn't provide a simple wizard to add the code necessary to create and delete session variables with PHP pages, it isn't difficult to add it yourself. (Dreamweaver does, however, make quick work of *retrieving* session variables; see page 986.)

The procedure is much like the one you use to add cookies (see the box on page 987)—for example, here, too, the script runs when a visitor requests the page. When someone registers at your site, therefore, you can store the email addresses they enter in the registration form as a session variable.

To add a session variable, you must do two things. First, in Code view (page 415), add this code (on a single line) near the top of the page:

```
<?php if (!isset($_SESSION)) session_
start(); ?>
```

This alerts PHP that you want to use session variables on this page (if you omit this line, you can't set or read session variables). Just as when you set a cookie, you can't have any HTML or even empty space before this line or you get a "Headers already sent" error. Next, you set the session variable.

```
<?php $_SESSION['name_of_
variable']='value_of_variable'; ?>
```

Replace *name of variable* with whatever name you wish to give the variable: *email*, for example. Also replace *value of variable* with whatever you want the variable to store. In many cases, this value will be a dynamic value, like information from a recordset, a URL, or a form. Using the steps described on page 981, add the appropriate dynamic data to the Bindings panel, and then drag it into the spot in the code just after the = sign (in this case, omit the set of quote marks:" "). As with cookies, *where* you place the session-creating code determines *when* it kicks in. So if you want to set a session with a value from a recordset, put the session code after the code that creates the recordset.

You may also want to delete a session variable to conserve server resources. (Dreamweaver's Log Out User server behavior uses this technique to log out visitors.) To delete a server variable, add this code to the beginning of a page:

```
<?php unset($_SESSION['name_of_vari-
able']); ?>
```

To delete all session variables for a particular individual in one fell swoop, use this code:

```
<?php
if (isset($_SESSION)) {
  session_destroy();
}
?>
```

Note: You can download many more third-party server behaviors from the Adobe Exchange. In the Server Behaviors panel, click the + button, and then choose Get More Server Behaviors. Dreamweaver launches your browser and connects you to the Dreamweaver Exchange site.

Not all extensions listed here work with Dreamweaver CS5. On the other hand, many of the server behaviors for Dreamweaver 8 also work with Dreamweaver CS5.

Recordset Paging

This set of four behaviors lets you add links to jump to different records in a recordset (straight to the last record, for example). In fact, Dreamweaver uses these same behaviors as part of its Recordset Navigation Bar object (page 887). You use these to move through a long list of records, like a complete list of products in a database.

To begin, add a recordset to a page. It should contain multiple records, since jumping to the *next* record when there's only one doesn't make much sense. The page could also contain a repeating region, so that several records appear at once.

You can add the recordset-paging server behaviors from the Server Behaviors panel or from the recordset-paging menu in the Insert bar's Data category (circled in Figure 26-8):

- **Move to First Page.** Adds a link that jumps to the first record in a recordset.
- **Move to Previous Page.** Adds a link that jumps to the record just before the current record. If you use a Repeating Region, then it jumps to the previous *set* of records. For example, say you create a Repeating Region that displays five records at a time. If the page currently displays records 6-10, clicking a link with this server behavior applied causes records 1-5 to appear.
- **Move to Next Page.** Adds a link that jumps to the next record or set of records in the recordset.
- **Move to Last Page.** Adds a link that goes to the last record or set of records in the recordset.

Using any of these four behaviors involves the same steps:

1. **Create a recordset, and then add dynamic content to the page.**

   For example, you could create a list of all the products your company sells. The recordset should contain at least enough records to span several pages. (You wouldn't use any of these behaviors if you displayed *all* the records on a single page.)

2. **Click the spot on the page where you wish to insert the link.**

   You can also select an item on the page—text or a graphic—that you want to turn into a link.

3. **From the Server Behaviors panel, click the + button. Select Recordset Paging, and then choose a behavior from the submenu.**

   The window for the particular server behavior appears (see Figure 26-9).

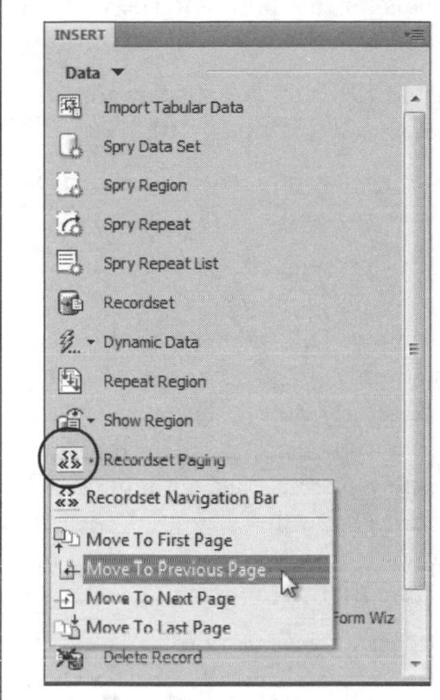

Figure 26-8:
You can create your own recordset navigation controls using the recordset-paging server behaviors.

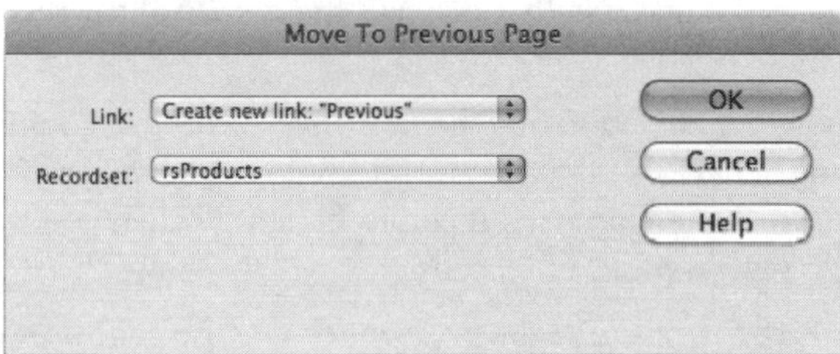

Figure 26-9:
Recordset-paging behaviors—like the "Move to Previous Page" behavior—can add a new link to preset text (for example, "Previous"), or add a link to text or an image you select on the page. You can also use the menu to select any link already on the page. That's usually not a good idea, however, since Dreamweaver erases the link you previously applied.

4. **From the Recordset menu, choose a recordset.**

   This is the recordset the behavior will move through.

5. **Click OK.**

   Dreamweaver adds the server behavior to the page, and adds its name to the Server Behaviors panel.

Show Region Server Behaviors

At times, you'll want to display different information on a page based on the results of a recordset. For example, if a visitor searches your site's product database for a product you don't sell, the search results page should say something like, "Sorry, we don't carry alligator skin bicycle seats." But if someone searches for a product you *do* sell, the page should present the relevant details for that product. The web page displays different text depending on whether the searched item was in the recordset.

Dreamweaver provides three sets of server behaviors that let you display any selection of HTML based on the results of a recordset search (Figure 26-10):

- **Show If Recordset Empty.** If the recordset retrieves no records, this behavior makes the selected HTML appear in the browser window.

  This behavior comes in handy for a search results page. Apply it to some text like "We're sorry, your search retrieved no results", and you've got yourself a friendly solution for searches that turn up empty. This behavior is also handy for pages that display detailed information about a single record, such as a detail page (page 892) or an update record page (page 931). Both of these pages retrieve data from a database, and you usually call them by using a URL variable like *product_details.php?productID=14*. If someone visits this page without the URL variable in place (if she goes to *product_details.php* in this example), she'll end up with a blank page. Use the Show If Recordset Empty behavior to list a message like "No product specified. Click here for a list of products."

- **Show If Recordset Not Empty.** If the recordset retrieves *any* records, this behavior displays the HTML you specify: a list of search results or details on a specific database record, for example. You'll often use this server behavior along with the Show If Recordset Empty server behavior. In this case, select the stuff you want to appear when a database query returns a record: As in the previous examples, select all the HTML and code that displays the details of the record, or the record update form.

- **Show If First Page.** This server behavior, like the next three, works in conjunction with recordset-paging behaviors. It makes the selected HTML appear when a page displays the *first* record of a recordset. It comes in handy when you want to let people step through several pages of records.

- **Show If Not First Page.** Is the opposite of the previous one. If the page *does not* contain the first record in a recordset, then the selected HTML appears.

  Dreamweaver uses this behavior in its Recordset Navigation Bar (see page 887). There, if a page displays anything *except* the first set of records in a recordset, the First Item and Previous Page links appear. If the page *does* display the first item in a recordset, the application server hides those links. (After all, you can't very well view a previous page if you're on page 1.)

- **Show If Last Page.** Functions just like the Show If First Page behavior, but for the last record in a recordset.

- **Show If Not Last Page.** Functions just like the Show If Not First Page behavior, but for the last record in a recordset. Dreamweaver uses this behavior to hide or show the Next Page and Last Item links in the Recordset Navigation Bar on the last page of records (page 887).

You can use these behaviors to show any selected object on a page—a paragraph of text, an image, a table, and so on. Your page can contain any combination of these behaviors, and you can use any behavior two or more times to display multiple objects on a page. For example, maybe you want two elements to appear after a successful search, a graphic in the page's sidebar and a message in the main area of the page. You'd apply the Show If Recordset Not Empty server behavior twice; once for each piece of HTML (the graphic and the message).

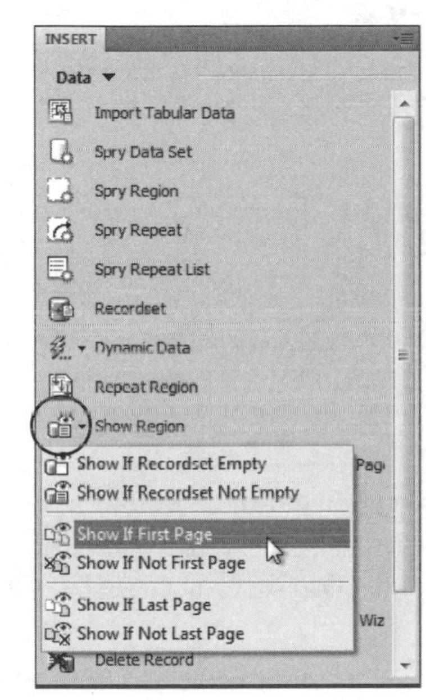

Figure 26-10:
You can find the Show Region server behaviors in the Insert panel's Data category (shown here), the Insert→Data Objects→Show Region menu, and the Server Behaviors panel.

You often use Show Region behaviors in pairs. For example, a search results page should include both the Show If Recordset Empty behavior (to display a "no results" message), and a Show If Recordset Not Empty behavior (to display the results of a successful search).

To apply any of these behaviors:

1. **Create a dynamic page containing a recordset.**

   This page could be a search results page or a master page that lists many records from the database.

2. **Select the HTML you want to display based on a recordset outcome.**

   For example, when you apply a Show If Recordset Is Empty server behavior to a search results page, select the message that should appear if the search returns no results.

3. **Open the Server Behaviors panel (Window→Server Behaviors). Click the + button, select Show Region, and, from the submenu, choose one of the six behaviors listed above.**

   A window like the one in Figure 26-11 appears. While the title of the window varies depending on the behavior you select, each of the six behaviors has just this one option.

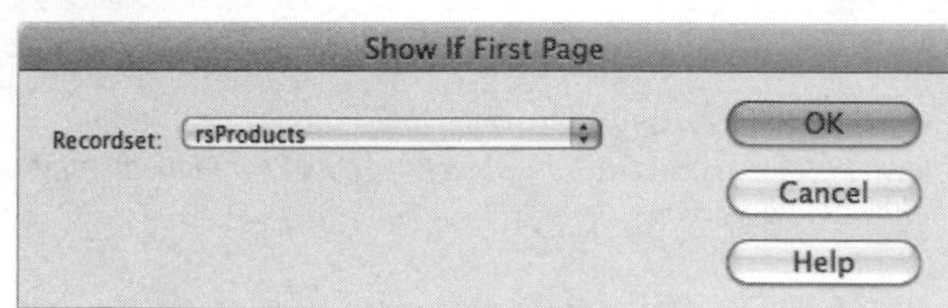

Figure 26-11:
Regardless of which of the Show Region server behaviors you apply, you can choose only one option: the recordset whose results control the display of the region.

Note: The last four behaviors–Show If First Page, Show If Not First Page, Show If Last Page, and Show If Not Last Page–work only on pages where you've also applied one of the recordset-paging server behaviors (discussed on page 990).

---

4. **Select the name of the recordset from the menu, and then click OK.**

   The recordset you select should be the one whose results you're interested in. For example, on a search results page, select the recordset you created to perform the search.

After you apply a behavior to a selection of HTML, a gray line appears around the selection, and a gray tab appears bearing the words "Show If". That area appears if the given recordset condition is met (for example, if the page is displaying the last record of the recordset).

To remove a Show Region server behavior, in the Server Behaviors panel, select its name and click the minus (–) button (or press the Delete key). Doing so removes the gray tab and outline. Now the affected HTML appears regardless of the recordset results.

Note: An extension called PHP Show If Recordset Field Condition Is True (available for free from *http://www.brettbrewer.com/component/option,com_vfm/Itemid,41/do,view/file,PHP_SIRFCIT.mxp/*) lets you display part of a page when a field from a recordset matches a certain condition. Suppose, for example, that you have a products database with a field that records whether a particular item is for sale. If the item is indeed for sale, you can use this behavior to display a large "For Sale" graphic on the product's detail page.

Tutorial: Authentication

In the tutorial at the end of Chapter 25, you created web pages that could add, delete, and update records in the *CosmoFarmer* database. But you don't want to allow just anyone to access those pages, let alone delete products from the site. So in this tutorial, you'll learn how to password-protect these sensitive, mission-critical web pages.

The following steps assume you've worked through the tutorial in Chapter 25, and you have all the completed files ready to go. You'll build on them in the following steps.

Building a Login Page

The first step is to create a login page—a simple form with fields for a user name and password. After a successful login from this page, an administrator can access the administration pages:

1. **In the site's *admin* folder, open the file *login.php*.**

   This page contains the form for typing in an administrator's user name and password. You'll add the form next.

2. **Click in the empty space directly below the headline "Administrator Login". Choose Insert→Form→Form.**

   Dreamweaver adds a red dashed line to the page, indicating the beginning and ending <form> tags.

3. **In the Property inspector, type *login* for the Form ID.**

   While this step isn't required, it's good to get into the habit of assigning your forms descriptive names. Next, you'll add a box for a user name.

Note: The next steps assume you have the Form Accessibility feature turned on (see page 461). To make sure this is in fact the case, open the Preferences window by choosing Edit→Preferences (Dreamweaver→Preferences), select the Accessibility category, and make sure the Form Objects checkbox is turned on.

4. **Choose Insert→Form→Text Field.**

   The Input Tag Accessibility Attributes window appears (Figure 26-12). You'll add a label that'll appear next to the form field on the page.

Note: You can also use the Insert panel's Forms category to add forms and form objects to your page, as described on page 459.

5. **In the ID box, type *username*; in the Label box, type *User Name:*; select the "Attach label tag using 'for' attribute" and "Before form item" buttons, and then click OK.**

   Dreamweaver inserts a text field with a descriptive label.

6. **In the Property inspector, from the Format menu, choose Paragraph.**

   This step wraps a paragraph tag around the label and form field. You now need to add a password field.

7. **Click to the right of the form field you just inserted, and then press the Enter (Return) key to add a new paragraph.**

   The routine for adding the next field is the same.

8. **Choose Insert→Form→Text Field. In the window that appears, in the ID box, type *password*; in the label box, type *Password:*; and then click OK.**

   This step inserts another form field and label.

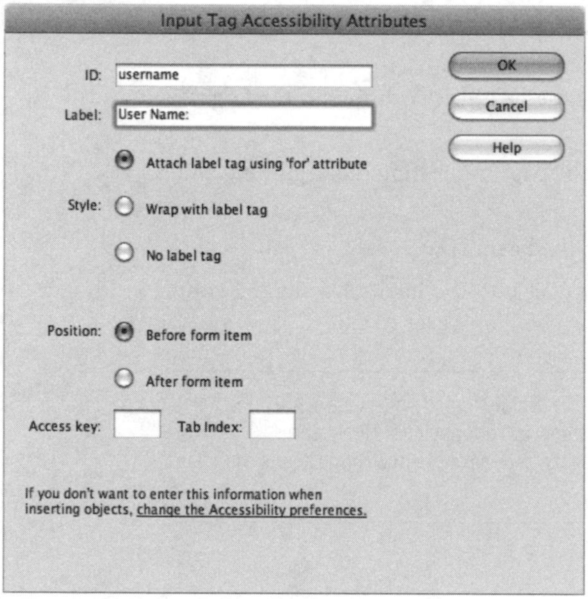

Figure 26-12:
Dreamweaver's Accessibility features let you add helpful controls–including a descriptive label–to form elements. Setting the ID adds an ID property to the field (see step 3 on page 461), which is useful for adding CSS or using JavaScript to control the field. In addition, Dreamweaver uses the ID you supply for the field's name.

9. **Select the new form field and, in the Property inspector, turn on the Password radio button.**

   By turning this form element into a password field, anything your visitors type in the field is displayed like this **** or this ••••, hiding the secret password from nosy passersby watching over their shoulders.

   To complete the form, you'll add a Submit button.

10. **In the document window, click to the right of the password field, and then press the Enter (Return) key. Choose Insert→Form→Button.**

    The Accessibility window appears yet again. In this case, however, you don't need to add a label, since text appears directly on the button.

11. **Click Cancel to close the Accessibility window and insert a Submit button. Select the new button and, in the Property inspector, change its value to "Login".**

    The form is complete. Now it's time to let Dreamweaver do its magic.

12. **Choose Window→Server Behaviors to open the Server Behaviors window.**

    Alternatively, you can use the keyboard shortcut Ctrl+F9 (⌘-F9).

13. **Click the + button, and then choose User Authentication→Log In User.**

    The Log In User window appears (see Figure 26-13). The first three items should already be filled out: the name of the form, the name of the user name field, and the name of the password field. If you had more than one form on the page, or additional fields inside the one form, you'd have to tell Dreamweaver which form and which fields to use to collect the login information.

14. **From the "Validate using connection" pop-up menu, select "connCosmo".**

    This step indicates which database contains the login information. You also need to specify which table and columns contain the user name and password.

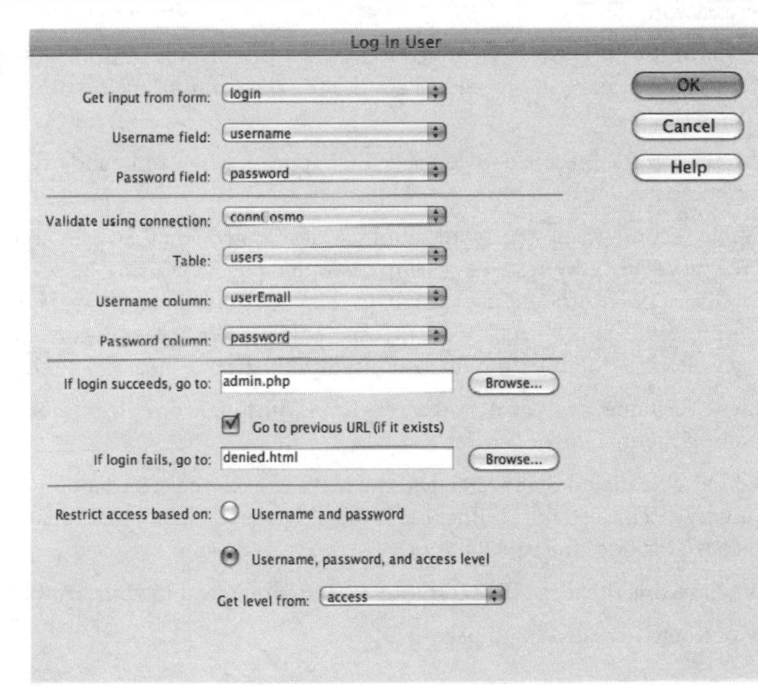

Figure 26-13: *Before visitors can access password-protected pages, they first need to log into the site. Dreamweaver's Log In User server behavior makes adding this feature a snap.*

15. **From the Table menu, select "users". From the "Username column" pop-up menu, choose "userEmail". From the "Password column" pop-up menu, choose "password".**

    You just established the basic logic of the login behavior: the programming in the web page compares whatever a visitor types into the two form fields with data stored in the *CosmoFarmer* database, inside the Users table.

    Next, you need to specify what happens when there's a match—when your visitor types in a valid user name and password—and what happens when he types in an invalid user name or password.

16. **To the right of the "If login succeeds, go to" field, click the Browse button. In the Select File window, navigate to and select the file *admin.php* inside the *admin* folder. Click OK.**

    You just chose the page that appears if your guest logs in successfully; her browser displays an administration page. In the next step, you'll provide a little help for visitors who have yet to log in, and who get bumped from a password-protected page to the login page. You can instruct the login page to send the visitor back to their original destination—the password-protected page—*after* they successfully log in.

17. **Check the "Go to previous URL" box.**

    Now you need to pick a page to send the visitor if he types in an invalid user name or password.

18. **To the right of the "If login fails, go to" field, click the Browse button. In the Select File window, navigate to and select the file *denied.html* inside the *admin* folder. Click OK.**

    This, of course, is the "access denied" page that appears when somebody types in an invalid user name or password.

    Because this section of the site is for administrators only, you'll add an additional layer of security by restricting administrative pages by using an access level as well as a password and user name. In this way, you can also have other password-protected pages—such as a special "paid subscribers" section—for registered visitors, without letting them access administrative areas of the site.

19. **Select the "Username, password, and access level" button. From the "Get level from" pop-up menu, choose "access".**

    The database table includes a special field that defines each registered members' access privileges. For example, in the *users* table's Access field, each administrator record also includes the value *admin*.

20. **Click OK. Save this file. Press F12 (Option-F12) to preview it in your browser.**

    Try out your newly created login page.

21. **In your browser, type anything you want in the two fields; click Login.**

    Unless you just made an incredible guess, you just typed in a user name and password that doesn't exist in the database. If the technology gods are smiling, an "Access Denied" page appears.

    Now try it again.

22. **Click the "Click here to try to login again" link to return to the login page. In the Username field, type *dibble@cosmofarmer.com*; in the Password field, type *sesame*; then submit the form.**

    This time, you're in; the browser takes you to the main administration page. Here, you can jump to the pages you created earlier to add, update, and delete products.

Tip (Important!): *sesame* is an awful password. Don't ever use it, or any word you can find in a dictionary. The reason? Web vandals often launch so-called "Dictionary attacks," in which they try to log into other peoples' accounts by submitting terms pulled from a dictionary looking for a password that matches.

The login script works just fine—you end up at the right page when you type in a valid user name and password. However, you haven't protected any of these pages yet. You can go directly to them by typing in their URL, even if you haven't logged in. In the next part of this tutorial, you'll lock down each *admin* page so only logged-in administrators can access them.

Password-Protecting the Administration Pages

Dreamweaver's password-protection features require you to add a server behavior to each page you want to protect:

1. **In the *admin* folder, open the file *admin.php*.**

   This page is the main jumping-off point for adding, deleting, and updating products. You only want administrators to access it, so add password protection to it.

2. **Open the Server Behaviors window (Window→Server Behaviors). Click the + button, and then choose User Authentication→Restrict Access To Page.**

   (Alternatively, in the Insert panel, you can use the User Authentication menu, as pictured in Figure 26-1.)

   The Restrict Access To Page window appears (see Figure 26-14). Since you want to limit access to administrators only, make sure you restrict the page to those with the proper access level.

3. **Select the "Username, password, and access level" radio button.**

   You want to specify which type of user has access to this page, but first you must tell Dreamweaver what the different levels *are*.

4. **Click Define to open the Define Access Levels window. In the Name field, type *admin*. Next, click OK to close the window.**

   In the "Select level(s)" box, the word "admin" appears. If you had other areas of the site with different access privileges, such as an area that only paying subscribers could access, add those levels by repeating this step.

5. **Click Browse; in the admin folder, select the *login.php* file, and then click OK. Click OK again to close the Restrict Access To Page window.**

   To finish this page, you'll add a "Log out" link.

6. **Select Log Out (in the page's left navigation bar, the last link).**

   Turn this text into a "Log out" link.

7. **On the Server Behaviors panel, click the + button, and then select User Authentication→Log Out User.**

   Again, this option is also available from the Insert bar, as pictured in Figure 26-1. In any case, the Log Out User window appears (see Figure 26-15). You should see the first radio button selected. The text "Log Out" appears in the menu.

   These are the proper settings; you're simply adding the logout script to the words you selected on the page.

   Next, tell Dreamweaver which page to go to after you log out.

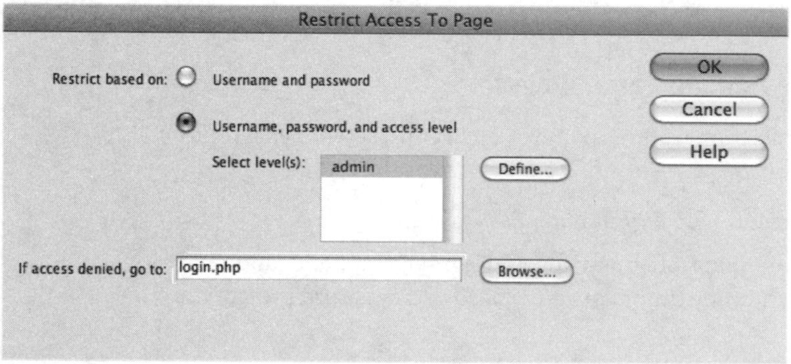

Figure 26-14: *You can reserve administrative pages for those with the access level "admin," while you can give regular subscribers access to pages intended for them.*

8. **Click the Browse button; navigate to the root folder for the site and select the file *index.php*, and then click OK.**

   When people log out, they simply end up at the main products page. Since they're no longer logged in as administrators, they can't access any of the administrative pages without logging back in. The Log Out User window should now look like Figure 26-15.

9. **Click OK to close the Log Out User window.**

   Now it's time to test the result.

10. **Choose File→Save; press F12 (Option-F12) to preview the page in your browser.**

    One of two things happens: you either end up on the Login page, or you see the CosmoFarmer administration page.

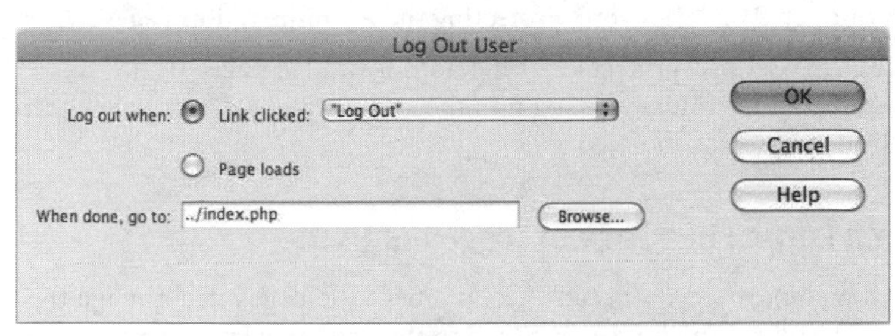

Figure 26-15: *This server behavior lets you offer visitors the polite option of logging out from your site. It destroys the session variables that track a visitor's login status.*

If you quit your web browser after the previous section of this tutorial, or never logged in to begin with, then the Restrict Access To Page server behavior is working: It doesn't recognize you as a registered administrator, denies you access to this page, and sends you to the login page. In the Username field, type *dibble@cosmofarmer.com*; in the Password field, type *sesame*; and then submit the form. You're now logged in, and taken to the *admin* page.

However, if you logged in following the instructions from the previous section in this tutorial, and you haven't quit your web browser in the meantime, you're still logged in. In this case, the Restrict Access To Page server behavior is again doing its job. You're allowed onto this *admin* page, because you *are* a registered administrator.

11. **In the left navigation bar, click the Log Out link.**

    The site logs you out, and takes you to the main products page. To make sure you really are logged out, you'll open the administration page again.

12. **Return to Dreamweaver and the *admin.php* page. Press F12 (Option-F12) to preview the page again.**

    You're immediately redirected to the Login page. You're not logged in, so you can't see the administration page. Hooray! The page is successfully protected from snoops.

Note: Some browsers "cache," or store, the previously viewed administration page, so you might not actually see the Access Denied page. In this case, reload the page by clicking your browser's refresh button.

Of course, everyone can still call up the most vulnerable pages (the update-, delete-, and add-product pages). You need to lock them down as well.

13. **Open the *add.php* page, and then repeat steps 2 through 5 on page 975.**

    Repeat this step for all other dynamic pages (*delete.php* and *edit.php*) in the *admin* folder, with the exception of *login.php*. (After all, *that page* should be visible to those who haven't yet logged in.)

    If you want, you can also add a Log Out link to each of the pages by repeating steps 6 through 9 on "Password-Protecting the Administration Pages".

    Now you've password-protected all the administrative pages in the site. Only authorized administrators who log into the site can add, edit, or delete records from the database.

Displaying a Portion of a Page to Logged-In Users

Even though unauthorized users can't access any of the pages that change the database, they *can* still see the links you added to the Product Details page in the last chapter—"Edit this Information" and "Delete this Product". Nothing particularly earth-shattering happens if they click these links—unauthorized users just end up at the login page—but even that's not very elegant. Wouldn't it be tidier if those links didn't even *show up*, except to people logged in as administrators?

You set that up this way:

1. **Open the *product.php* page from the root directory.**

   You'll do a little painless programming in Code view at this point.

2. **In the document window, click inside the text "Edit this Information"; in the Tag selector, click the <p>.**

   You just selected the paragraph containing the two links. This paragraph should appear only to administrators.

3. **Choose View→Code.**

   You can also click the Code button in the document window's top left. Either way, the document window switches into Code view (see Figure 26-16). If your monitor's big enough, you can use Split view instead (View→Split Code) so you can see Code and Design view side by side (see page 415 for more on Split view).

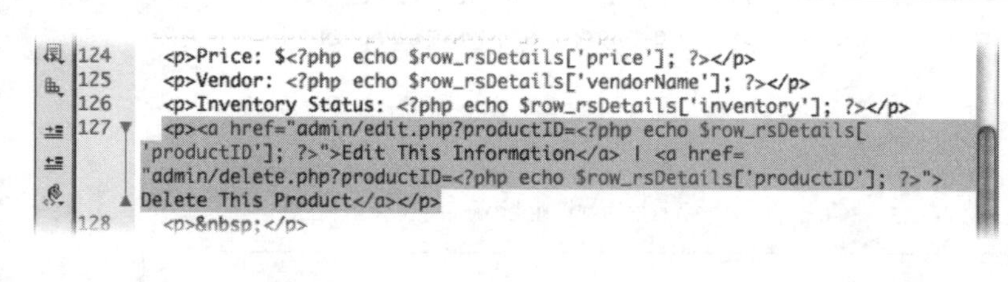

Figure 26-16: *When you enter Code view, Dreamweaver highlights the code for whatever you selected in Design view. The HTML outlined here includes the Edit and Delete product links you want to hide from unregistered visitors.*

4. **Click at the beginning of the selection, just before the opening <p>.**

   The insertion point is now at the start of the paragraph. You'll add some programming code here.

5. **On a single line, type *<?php if (isset($_SESSION['MM_UserGroup']) && $_SESSION['MM_UserGroup']=='admin') { ?>*.**

   The opening *<?php* tells the application server that some PHP code is coming. In other words, this code isn't HTML—it's a program that the application server needs to run. The IF part of this code is part of a *conditional statement*. In this case, it means, "*If* this person is logged in with an access level of 'admin', *then* the paragraph will appear on the page."

   To determine if the visitor is logged in with the proper access level, the code sneaks a peek at a session variable called MM_UserGroup. As mentioned on page 978, when someone logs into your site, the server behavior creates a session variable called MM_UserGroup. This variable follows the visitor around the site, and contains a word indicating his access level. The programming you just added first checks to see if the session variable exists (that's the *isset* weirdness), and then verifies that the session variable is *admin*, which indicates that the visitor is logged in as an administrator. If all of that is true, the paragraph letting the visitor access the edit and delete links appears.

6. **Click to the right of the closing </p> tag (just after "Delete this product"), and then type *<?php } ?>*.**

   This code concludes the conditional statement. In other words, all the HTML between the first line of code you added in the previous step and this final *<?php } ?>* appears *only* if the user is logged in as an administrator.

   The code should now look like Figure 26-17. You need to do one last thing on this page.

```
<?php if (isset($_SESSION['MM_UserGroup']) && $_SESSION['MM_UserGroup']
=='admin' ) { ?>
<p><a href="admin/edit.php?productID=<?php echo $row_rsDetails[
'productID']; ?>">Edit This Information</a> | <a href=
"admin/delete.php?productID=<?php echo $row_rsDetails['productID']; ?>">
Delete This Product</a></p>
<?php } ?>
```

***Figure 26-17:** Here's the finished version of the code that hides the "Delete this Product" paragraph from unregistered users.*

7. **Stay in Code view, and scroll to the top of the page. Place your cursor after the very beginning of the file, before the very first line, which begins with "<?php".**

   Now, you'll add a little code that lets the page access the session variables.

8. **Type *<?php session_start(); ?>*, and then press Enter or Return to move the code after this onto its own line. The first two lines in Code view should now look like this:**

```
<?php session_start(); ?>
<?php require_once('Connections/connCosmo.php'); ?>
```

The code you just added makes PHP turn on its magical session-handling powers. Now this page can "see" the current visitor's session variables—such as whether she's logged in, and if she's an *admin* user.

9. **Choose File→Save; press F12 (Option-F12) to preview the page.**

Since you logged out earlier, the links should now be invisible. To see them, you must log in, and then return to the product details page.

10. **Go back to Dreamweaver, and then open the *login.php* page. Press F12 (Option-F12) to preview the page. In the Username field, type *dibble@cosmofarmer.com*. In the Password field, type *sesame*. Click Submit.**

Now you're logged in, and the login page should send you to the main administration page. If you return to a product details page, the links miraculously return.

11. **In the top navigation bar on the page, click the Cosmo Shop button to go to the product listings page. Click the name of any product to see its details.**

Voilà! The links are back. You can freely edit or delete any product in the database. If you return to the administration page and click the Log Out button, you don't see these links until you log back in.

You could also use this trick to add "Log out" links to every page on the site, but make them visible only if the visitor is logged in. With no programming experience, you can use Dreamweaver's server behaviors (and perhaps bring in server behaviors from extension developers) to build sophisticated database-driven websites.

Now go forth and electrify your sites!

Tip: To get a full description of every Dreamweaver menu in a handy, printable PDF, go to this book's Missing CD page (*www.missingmanuals.com/cds*) and download Appendix B, "Menu by Menu Commands."

CHAPTER

27

Server-Side XML and XSLT

XML is everywhere. You find it in countless files on your computer, for everything from tracking information in your iTunes music library to providing the structure and options for Dreamweaver's menus. Webmasters use XML to broadcast news feeds and provide product, pricing, and availability information from sites like Amazon.com and eBay by using a technology known as *web services*. As you learned in Chapter 13, Dreamweaver lets you use XML, too, and probably the best use of Dreamweaver's XML tool is to add news, blog posts, and other information broadcast from *other* websites to your own.

So what exactly is XML? XML, or Extensible Markup Language, is a tag-based language somewhat like HTML. You tag the various parts of a document—headlines, text, names, dates, and so on—in a clear, easy-to-understand way that different computers, operating systems, and programs can understand. Using this common data language, they can quickly and easily exchange information.

As you learned in Chapter 13, Dreamweaver's Spry XML Data Set tools let you work with XML on the "client side" of things—that is, where the processing takes place on your or your visitor's computer. Here's how Dreamweaver's Spry Data Set works: When someone visits your XML-powered site, his browser downloads a page embedded with some Spry JavaScript programming and an XML file. Thanks to some fancy JavaScript magic, your visitor can interact with that XML data, giving him a richer browsing experience. For example, if your site includes a table of the top 100 baseball players of all time, with columns for their names, batting averages, ages, leagues, and so on, your visitor can sort these statistics simply by clicking a column's header (see page 544 for more about this trick).

Note: For a detailed introduction to XML, flip back to page 548.

The tradeoff with XML's client-side approach is that it forces your visitor's browser to download the XML file. If the file is large, this can take a fair amount of time, since the browser downloads the whole enchilada (even the stuff you never intend to display). In addition, a Spry Data Set can only use an XML file stored on the same server as your web page. In other words, you can't access the RSS feed (an XML format for broadcasting news, blog posts, and other information) of CNN.com or your favorite blogger because the XML file that powers those feature sits on someone else's server.

Fortunately, you can use Dreamweaver's *server*-side XML and XSLT tools to overcome these limitations. The program's XSLT server behavior produces regular HTML out of XML and XSLT style sheets. (Hang in there: more in a moment on what XSLT is all about.) And, fortunately, since Dreamweaver handles all the complex programming required to make this happen, you don't have a task any more challenging than building a dynamic web page.

Understanding the Technologies

Although XML is like HTML in many ways, it doesn't have any inherent formatting capabilities. Unlike HTML, where a browser that encounters an <h1> tag displays bolder and bigger text, browsers can't format XML tags. They need an intermediary that can read and translate XML tags and tell the browser how to format and structure the resulting page. Enter XSLT and XPath. They're two complementary (and very complex) languages that let you define how browsers display XML tags. Fortunately, even though these languages are hard to master, Dreamweaver takes care of the entire process. All you need to know is how to use Dreamweaver's Design view to create web pages chock-full of information from an XML file.

XPath identifies the tags and discrete sections of an XML file (see Figure 13-17). In other words, it's like a blueprint for an XML file—it identifies its component parts.

XSLT is the magic dust that transforms an XML document into an HTML document. It's a translator par excellence. In fact, XSLT can take a single XML file and create a document that displays properly on all kinds of products—web browsers, smart phones, printers, and so on. XSLT stands for Extensible Style Language Transformations, which is really just a geeky name for a programming language that converts XML tags—<event>Halloween Social</event>, for example—into something else, like the code a browser understands—<h1>Halloween Social</h1>. In a nutshell, that's what Dreamweaver's XML tools do: They use XSLT to transform XML into HTML.

Note: Because XSLT formats XML, much like Cascading Style Sheets format HTML, you'll often see an XSLT file referred to as an *XSLT style sheet*.

Think of it this way: XPath identifies the XML tags that XSLT transforms into HTML tags. XSLT does the actual conversion to HTML, but XPath identifies the tags that XSLT needs to convert. They work hand in hand to get the job done. And, fortunately, that's all you need to know. In fact, it's more than you need to know to use Dreamweaver to turn XML files into great-looking web pages.

Creating Dynamic Pages with XSLT and XML

Dreamweaver's XSLT server behavior processes all those "X" files and produces nothing but clean HTML for your visitors. To take advantage of this tool, you need to set up an application server as described in Chapter 23, so that you can run ASP, PHP, or ColdFusion pages.

Next, you need to either have an XML file in your site, or know the URL of an XML file out on the Web that you'd like to use—for example, *http://feeds.feedburner.com/oreilly/news*. One option is to create an entire XSLT page that includes the HTML that formats the page and the XML information you want to display. But this is generally an inefficient technique, since the server has to devote time and cycles to process the entire file (plain old HTML and all), and you can't take advantage of Dreamweaver templates to enforce the look of your site.

Note for PHP Users: For server-side XSLT to work, you need to use a version of PHP that supports XSLT. PHP 5 has this capability built in, but PHP 4 requires extra work to get this going. Fortunately, most web hosting companies offer PHP 5. So before moving ahead with your XML-fueled dynamic-page-creation efforts, call or email your hosting company to see if their PHP installation supports XSLT.

A better way to take advantage of Dreamweaver's XML support is to display XML information in one of your site's dynamic pages. To do that, you create what's called an *XSLT fragment*, and you add a "chunk" of formatted XML to just one part of your dynamic page. For example, say you want to display the top 10 headlines from CNN.com's RSS feed on your home page. Using Dreamweaver, you can transform the newsfeed from its native XML format into HTML. Of course, that won't be the only thing you want on your home page. Most of the page will consist of information related to your site. So in this case, you only want to dedicate a fragment of your page—like a sidebar on the right-hand edge—to these headlines.

Note: RSS and Atom (a competing standard) are simply two different XML-based formats that use tags to identify the elements that make up newsfeed–like an author's name, an article title, or a brief description of the article–and provide a link to the complete article. Webmasters on news sites and blogs commonly use these formats to syndicate their stories–to send readers regularly updated summaries and links. RSS stands for "Rich Site Summary" or "Really Simple Syndication" (depending on whom you ask). Atom is a more complex standard that pretty much does the same thing. For more information on RSS, see *www.w3schools.com/rss/*, and for Atom, see *www.atomenabled.org/developers/syndication/*.

The process of creating and inserting an XSLT fragment into a page is simple: create the fragment, add and format the XML information, open a dynamic page, and insert the XSLT fragment into it. When your visitors view the dynamic page, the application server processes the XSLT fragment (which, in turn, translates the XML to HTML) and adds its contents to your page.

Here's how to create and use an XSLT fragment:

1. **Choose File→New.**

   The New Document window appears.

2. **Click the Blank Page button on the left side of the window. From the Blank Page list, select XSLT (Fragment), and then click the Create button.**

   The Locate XML Source window appears (Figure 27-1). Because XSLT formats XML files, you need to tell Dreamweaver where to find the XML file to act upon. You have two choices when you work with server-side XSLT: a local file or a web-based file (one where you type in the URL of an XML file).

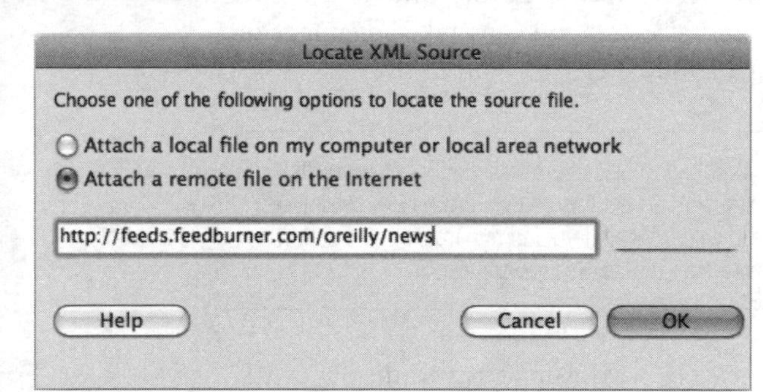

Figure 27-1: *You can use either an XML file on your own site, or type in the absolute URL of an XML file on the Web, such as the location of an RSS feed from a blog or news website.*

3. **Select either "Attach a local file..." or "Attach a remote file on the Internet".**

   If the XML file is on your site, choose the first option. Select the second option if the XML file is on another site.

4. **If you're using an XML file on your site, click the Browse button to locate the file. Otherwise, type an absolute URL—*http://www.the_site.com/xml_file.xml*, for example—into the box. Click OK.**

   If you're pointing to a file on the Internet, you *must* use a full, absolute URL including the *http://* part (Dreamweaver helps you out by adding *http://* to the box when you select the "Attach a remote file" button).

   Dreamweaver finds the file in your local site (or looks for it on the Internet), reads its contents, and displays the file's tags and properties in Dreamweaver's Bindings panel. At this point, jump to page 1011 to learn how to add XML data to the page.

Although Dreamweaver claims that it's "attaching" the XML file to the XSLT document, it's really just adding a comment tag to the XSLT file, like this: <!--DWXML-Source="news.xml" -->. This helps Dreamweaver know which XML file to use with the XSLT document you're creating—so don't delete it. Technically, you actually attach an XSL file to an XML file to make this whole process work (as described below).

Note: If you want to try this out for fun, you can load an XML file from O'Reilly's website: *http://feeds.feedburner.com/oreilly/news*.

---

5. **Save the new XSLT style sheet fragment to your site folder.**

   Name the file and make sure you use the extension .xsl. In addition, make sure you save the file in the same folder as the dynamic page that will hold the XSLT style sheet fragment. Otherwise, if the style sheet contains links, graphics, and other linked elements, they may not show up when visitors view the XML file.

Tip: One way to get around having to store everything in the same folder is to use root-relative or absolute URLs (see page 159) for links, and to add graphics and external CSS files to your XSLT style sheet. Of course, doing this is probably more work than simply saving the XSL file in the same folder as your dynamic web page.

---

6. **Add XML elements to the XSLT style sheet as described on page 1011.**

   You can also add regular web page content—images, tables, CSS styles, and so on—to the page, and format the XML just as you would text on any other dynamically generated page. Remember, this file will be just one part of your overall web page—for example, a sidebar with the latest news from CNN.com. Once you finish designing the XSLT fragment, add it to your dynamic web page.

Note: Because the XSLT fragment will be part of a larger web page, you won't be able to see the effects of that page's CSS styles as you format your XML data. Fortunately, if you use external CSS style sheets, you can use Dreamweaver's Design-Time Stylesheets feature to temporarily attach, preview, and use the same CSS styles you use on your final web page. See page 326 for instructions.

---

7. **Open the dynamic page that you want to add the XSLT fragment to.**

   This must be a dynamic page using the same server model as your site—for example PHP, ASP, or ColdFusion. Because the XML transformation magic occurs via programming that Dreamweaver inserts in the page, you can't add an XSLT fragment to a regular web page (an .html file).

8. **Click where you wish to insert the XSLT fragment.**

   The spot you pick could be inside a table cell or within another layout region—such as a sidebar—on the page. Dreamweaver adds the XSLT fragment to this spot, in the same way it adds a Library item (see page 736)—that is, as a chunk of HTML inside your page.

9. **Make sure the Server Behaviors panel is open (Window→Server Behaviors), click the + button, and then select XSL Transformation.**

   The XSL Transformation window appears (see Figure 27-3).

10. **Click the top Browse button to open the Select XSLT File window. Navigate to and select the XSL file you created earlier; click OK (Choose on the Mac) to choose the file, and then close the Select XSLT File window.**

    This tells Dreamweaver which XSL fragment to embed in your page. In addition, Dreamweaver should automatically fill out the path to the XML file (it reads the comment inserted in the XSLT file identifying which XML file to use—see the Note below). If the XML file path doesn't appear, click the Browse button next to the XML file box and select the proper XML file yourself. If you're using an XML from the Web, you'll see the URL for that file, and the Browse button will disappear.

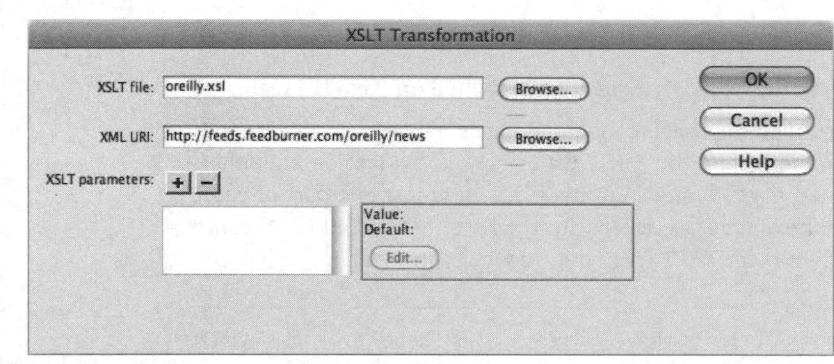

***Figure 27-2:** The XSL Transformation window lets you attach an XSLT style sheet to a dynamic page. You can also send special information–XSLT parameters–to the style sheet to format the page's display (this process is described on page 1024).*

    The "XSLT parameters" option lets you pass information to the XSL file that can alter what the XML file displays. You'll learn about this advanced feature on page 1024.

11. **Click the OK button to close the window and insert the fragment.**

    Dreamweaver displays the XSLT fragment in your web page. If you set up a testing server (see page 836), you can preview the effect by pressing F12 (Option-F12).

You can't directly edit the XSLT fragment inside your dynamic page. Dreamweaver treats it like a single, self-contained element. To change it—add graphics, change links, or reformat the XML, for example—you have to open the XSL file and make changes directly to it.

Note: Dreamweaver adds additional folders and files to your site when you use the XSLT server behavior. They contain the code necessary to successfully embed XML data into a web page. This means that when you move everything to your web server—the dynamic page, the XSLT fragment file, and the XML file—you need to upload these files, too. Dreamweaver stores them in a folder named *includes* in your site's local root folder, so upload this folder along with your other site files. (See Chapter 18 for instructions on using Dreamweaver's FTP tool.)

Inserting and Formatting XML

Now you know the basics of creating and using XSLT style sheets. But how do you actually add and format XML data? Dreamweaver makes it easy. If you've used the program's database tools, you already know how to do it: just use the Bindings panel. Once you create an XSL file and attach the XML file to it, Dreamweaver reads all the tags in the XML file and adds them to the Bindings panel (see Figure 27-5).

You can drag any element in the Bindings panel into your XSLT style sheet page, just as you'd drag information from a database recordset. That means you can place XML information in a table cell, a footer, or a banner—anywhere you can place regular HTML elements on a page.

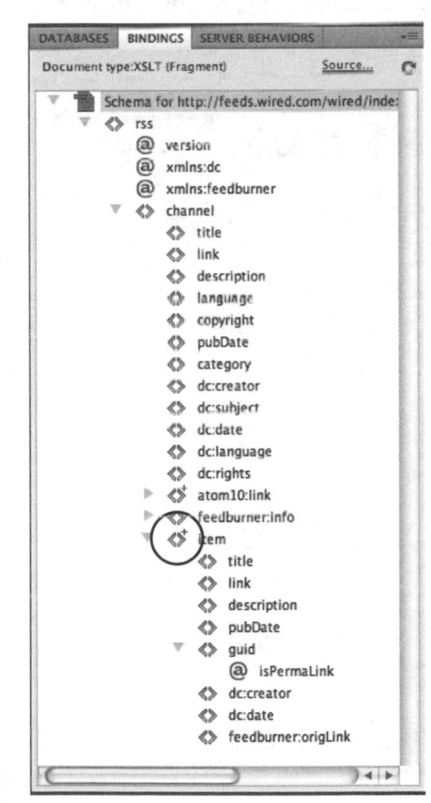

Figure 27-3: *When you use Dreamweaver's XSLT tools, the Bindings panel lists all the tags and properties in the XML file you format. Dreamweaver includes a few visual clues about the XML file: < > represents an XML tag and is the most common icon you'll encounter; the @ sign represents a tag property (also called an attribute; for example, in the tag <rss version="2.0">, "version" is an attribute); and next to some tags, you'll see a small + sign (circled in this image) or a ?. The + indicates that the tag is repeated multiple times; for example, an RSS feed usually has multiple news items, so in the feed's XML file each news item will have its own tag. The ? (not shown here) means the tag is optional, and it appears next to tags inside of other repeated tags (the ones with the +).*

You should keep a couple things in mind when you insert XML:

- You insert only the *contents* of the XML tags and properties, not the tags or property names themselves. For example, in Figure 27-5, dragging the <title> tag that appears inside the <channel> tag onto a document just prints the text inside this tag, not the tag itself. This is a good thing: You don't usually want to print the tags; otherwise, a title would look like this: "<title>An Important Story</title>". Instead, you just want to display: *An Important Story.*
- Dragging a tag that includes *other* tags often results in a hard-to-read mess. That's because Dreamweaver includes text from each of the nested tags as well. For example, dragging the root element—"rss"—from the Bindings panel pictured in Figure 27-5 adds the simple label {rss} to the page in Dreamweaver's Design view. But when you look at the page in a Web browser, you see one long paragraph of text from all the tags—the channel, the title, the description, and so on, as well as each of the repeated "item" tags as pictured in Figure 27-7. Dreamweaver treats this as a single big blob. To get around this, drag tags that don't include other nested tags. (Nested tags are called *child* tags.) For example, in Figure 27-5, the "title" tag that appears directly inside the "channel" tag doesn't have any tags inside it. Likewise, a repeating tag—<item>, for example—includes tags that don't have any children: "title," "link," "description," and "pubDate." These are all good candidates for adding to a document.

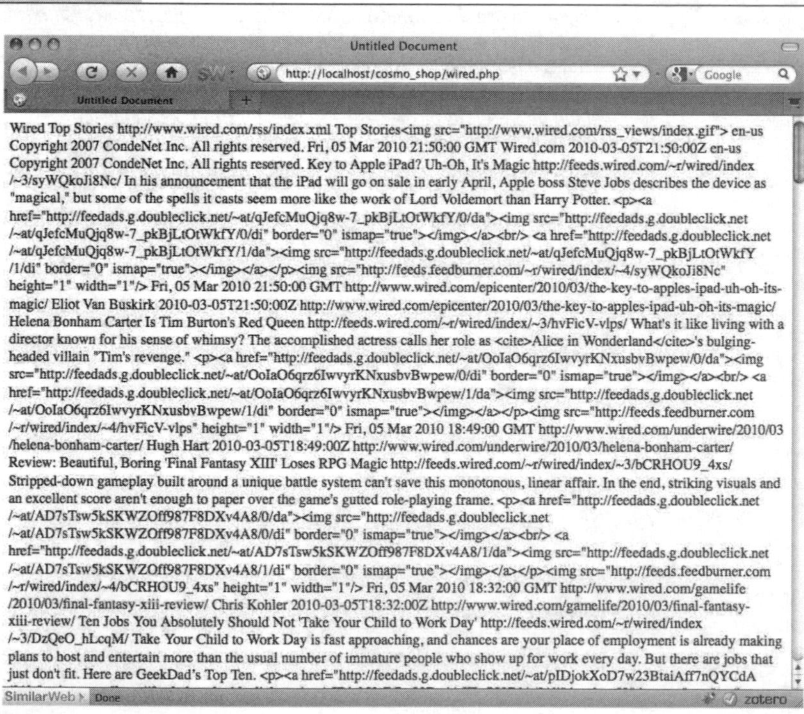

Figure 27-4: *If you use an XML tag that's too high up on the food chain–that is, one that has other tags nested inside of it–you can end up with a large chunk of hard-to-read text.*

You can also insert XML into an XSLT fragment by choosing Insert→XSLT Objects→Dynamic Text or by clicking the Dynamic Text button on the Insert panel's XSLT category (see Figure 27-9). Either method opens the XPath Expression Builder window (Figure 27-11). An XPath Expression is just a way of identifying a particular element—called a *node*—inside an XML file (see Figure 13-17).

To add dynamic text, select the XML tag or property you wish to insert. In the Expression box in the bottom half of the window, you'll see the XPath code required to locate your selection. For example, in Figure 27-11, the expression is *rss/channel/item/title/*. This is shorthand for "Find the title tag, which is inside the item tag, which is inside the channel tag, which is located inside the rss tag." In other words, this expression lists the order in which the tags are nested (in this sense, it's very much like the document window's Tag selector [see page 23]).

Dreamweaver also lets you apply some formatting options to the selected text using the Format menu. Almost all the options have to do with formatting numbers, so if you're inserting content from a tag that's actually a numeric value, these formatting controls can come in handy. For example, say you add a tag that indicates a price: <price>3.25</price>. Selecting any of the currency options adds a dollar sign in front of the number when a browser displays the page. If you're dealing with big sums of money—<price id="Federal Bailout">84317589585</price>—then the "Currency group to 3 digits, 2 decimal places" is a good option. That way, the number displays something like this: $84,317,589,585.00. Again, all but two of the options here format numbers, and the two that format text aren't very useful.

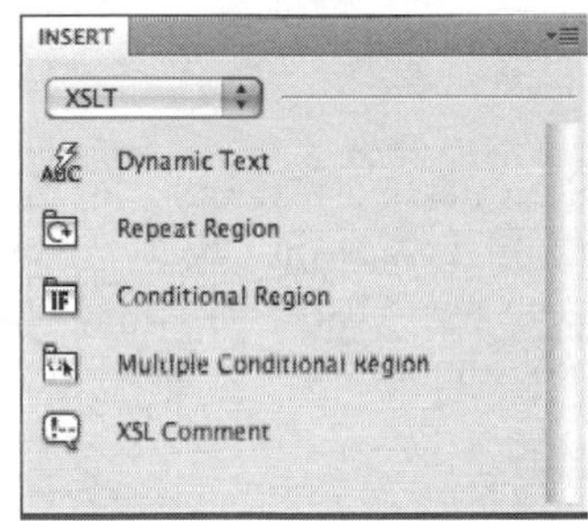

Figure 27-5:
The Insert panel's XSLT category includes five buttons so you can add XSLT objects. The XSL Comment object just inserts an XSL comment–which is just like an HTML comment (see "Coding Toolbar")–so you probably won't use it much, if ever.

After you select a tag and set a formatting option (if desired), click OK to insert the dynamic text. Dreamweaver adds a placeholder to the page, with a blue background and the XPath expression displayed inside curly brackets, like this: *{rss/channel/item/title}*.

Note: You can summon the XPath Expression Builder window again by double-clicking any dynamic XML text placeholder on the page.

Click an XML text placeholder to select it. You can then apply a CSS style to it, format it as a header or paragraph, or drag it to another spot on the page, just as you would any other HTML element.

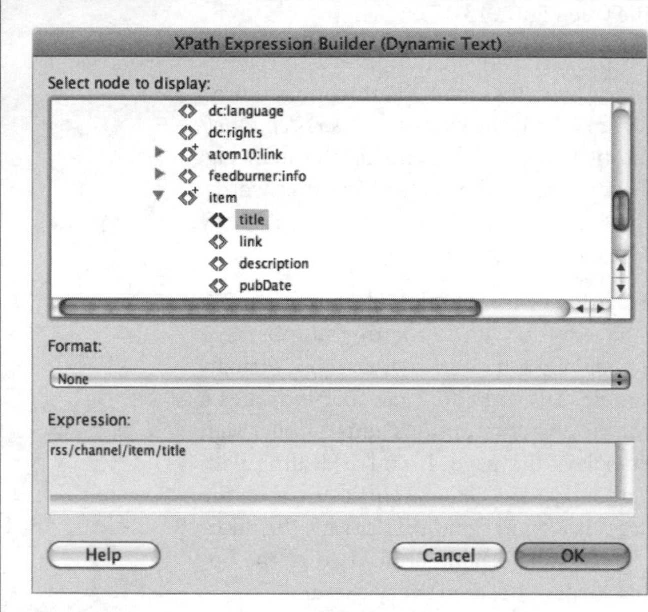

Figure 27-6: *Use the Format drop-down menu to apply a format to XML data. Unfortunately, the formats almost all apply to numbers—adding a $ sign to currency data, for example—so they won't do anything for text-only XML data.*

Inserting a Repeat Region

An XML file frequently uses the same tag multiple times. For example, an XML file that lists employee names and phone numbers might use the tag <employee id=XXXX> to begin each listing. You have to repeat this tag to list every employee in the company. The XML for two employees might look something like this:

```
<companyInfo>
<company>
<name>Big Co.</name>
<phone>555-3333</phone>
</company>
<employeeList>
<employee id="485734">
<name>Mark</name>
<phone>555-3333 x405</phone>
</employee>
<employee id="38753">
<name>Jane</name>
<phone>555-3333 x406</phone>
</employee>
</employeeList>
</companyInfo>
```

If you added the <name> tag inside the first <employee> tag to an XSLT style sheet, attached that XSL file to a dynamic page, and then previewed it in a browser, you'd see just a single name: the first employee named in the XML file. But, just as with recordsets, you usually want to display multiple XML records. In this case, you want to include the name and contact info of every employee. The answer is Dreamweaver's XSLT Repeat Region object. To use it:

1. **Insert elements that appear within a tag you want to repeat multiple times. (Use any of the methods described on page 1011.)**

   The Bindings panel lets you know if you repeat an XML tag multiple times: look for a tiny + symbol floating just above the right side of the <> icon in the panel (see Figure 27-5).

   So, in the employee list example above, you wouldn't insert the <name> tag that appears inside the <company> tag, since it appears only once in the file (to identify the name of the company). You would, however, insert the <name> tag (and the <phone> tag) inside the <employee> tag, since they both appear repeatedly in the employee list (twice in the truncated example above). Because the <name> and <phone> tags appear within the <employee> tag, they're called "children" of that tag.

Note: This example points out a sometimes confusing aspect of XML: Tags with the same name may appear as children within different kinds of tags. The <name> tag in the above example, for instance, appears both within the <company> and <employee> tags, but obviously refers to two different things—the name of a business and the name of a person.

   Articles in a web news feed are another case. Here, you want to list several headlines at a time. The RSS standard (see the note on page 1007) requires that you surround each news item delivered in an RSS XML document with an <item> tag that has the following children: <title>, <link>, and <description>. Therefore, for an RSS feed, the elements you want to add to the page (and repeat once for each news item) are <title>, <link>, and <description>.

2. **Select (by dragging, for example) the XML placeholders and any other content you want to repeat once for each instance in the XML file.**

   At the very least, this includes the XML placeholders you inserted in step 1, but may also include other HTML elements, such as a graphic repeated once for each item or a <div> tag that contains the XML data you're repeating. You can select only elements that are together: You can't, for instance, select an XML element at the top of the page and another at the bottom of the page, and use the same Repeat Region object.

Note: You can, however, include multiple repeat regions on a page, so you could repeat the same XML data in several locations on a page by adding multiple Repeat Region objects.

---

3. **Choose Insert→XSLT Objects→Repeat Region, or click the Repeat Region button on the XSLT category of the Insert Panel (see Figure 27-9).**

   The XPath Expression Builder window appears (see Figure 27-7). This window is similar to the one you see when you insert dynamic text (Figure 27-11). However, instead of a format menu, it includes a "Build Filter" option.

4. **Select the repeating tag.**

   This tag will always have a + to the right of its <> icon, and is usually the parent tag of the tags you inserted in step 1. So, in the employee list example above, you would select the <employee> tag; in the case of an RSS feed, you'd select the <item> tag.

5. **Build a filter to limit the information the XML file retrieves.**

   An XSLT filter works similarly to filters on recordsets (see page 861). It's a way to select only certain information from an XML file. For example, you might want to select only employees whose last name is Smith, or product tags that have only an <instock> XML tag containing the word "true." You'll learn about filters next.

6. **Click OK to insert the repeat region.**

   Dreamweaver adds a gray border around repeating elements and adds a gray tab labeled "xsl: for-each". (If you don't see these, make sure you turn on invisible elements: View→Visual Aids→Invisible Elements.)

You can see the effect by pressing F12 (Option-F12): Dreamweaver translates all that XSLT gobbledygook into a temporary HTML file. But to see the final presentation, you need to attach the XSLT style sheet to a dynamic page (steps 8–11 on page 1010) and preview it in a browser.

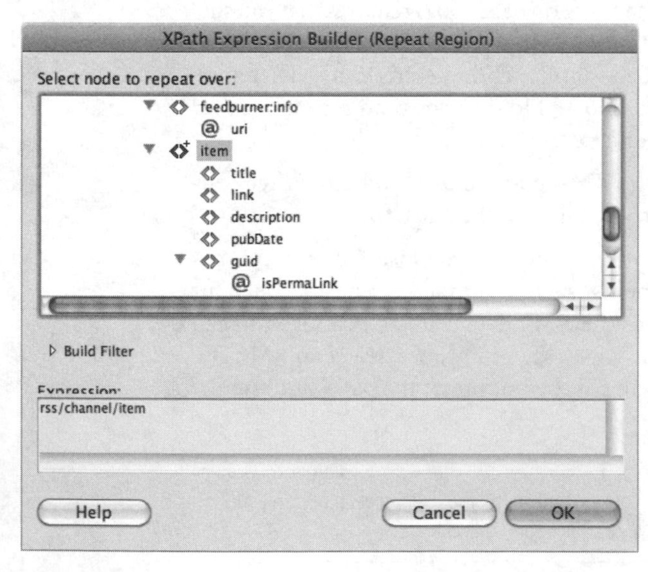

Figure 27-7: *Display repeating XML data using the XPath Expression Builder.*

If you want to edit the repeat region, click the gray tab to select it and, in the Property inspector, click the lightning-bolt icon to open the Repeat Region window again (Figure 27-7).

To remove a repeat region, right-click (Control-click) on the gray "xsl: for-each" tab and select "Remove Tag: <xsl:for-each>". You can also click anywhere inside the repeat region, right-click (Control-click) on "xsl: for-each" in the Tag selector (see page 23), and then choose Remove Tag. Don't try to remove the tag by hand in Code view: You have to change the code that specifies the tags inside the region, and Dreamweaver does this automatically and accurately.

Building a repeat-region filter

If the XML file you're using has lots and lots of repeating items, or you just want to hone in on a single item, you can build an XSLT filter that lets you search and select XML elements that match certain criteria. Say you want to display only employee tags with a "department" property whose value is "marketing." Fortunately, Dreamweaver lets you create very complex filters. In a nutshell, to filter a repeat region:

1. **Follow steps 1–4 on page 1015 to insert a repeat region.**
2. **In the "XPath Expression Builder (Repeat Region)" window, click Build Filter to display the filter tools (see Figure 27-15), and then click the + button to add a filter.**

   You build a filter by first selecting a tag that contains the information you wish to compare to a certain value.
3. **Click in the Filter By column and, from the pop-up menu, select a tag.**

   This menu lists the repeating tag, its parent tag, its parent's parent tag, and so on, up the food chain, until it reaches the top (root) element. For now, just leave it as the repeating tag you selected in step 4 on page 1016 (finish reading these steps and then read the following note to understand why this is the case).

Note (hold onto your thinking caps): A filter lets you select criteria that each repeated region is tested against. If it passes the test, the page displays the XML data. For example, the "id" property of the <employee> tag will vary with each employee listing. In a repeated region, the only elements that change are either a property of the repeated tag or the contents of other tags inside the repeated tag. That's why you should always select the repeated tag from the Filter By menu; the parent (and grandparent, and so on) of the repeated tag doesn't change with each region that repeats. If the parent has a property named "version," that property value will be the same whenever the page applies the filter to a repeat region. In other words, the filter will either always be true or never be true, and you'll either get all of the XML data or none of it from the repeated tags. Dreamweaver includes a more flexible tool to display or hide information based on some "test" or condition: conditional regions (see page 1019).

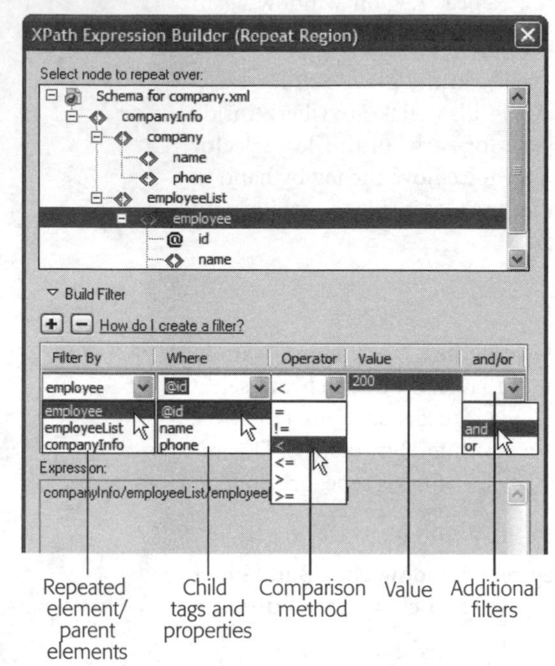

Figure 27-8:
Limit the XML data displayed by creating a filter that includes only XML tags that match certain criteria. Here's an example using the employee list XML code described in "Inserting a Repeat Region" on page 1014.

4. **Click in the Where column, and select an option from the pop-up menu.**

   This menu lists any properties of the repeated tag, and all the repeated tag's child tags. In the employee list code (page 1014), for example, each <employee> tag has a property named "id" and child tags called <name> and <phone>. So you see these options listed in the "Where" menu. Tag properties begin with an @ symbol, so in this example, Dreamweaver lists the "id" property as "@id" in the menu (see Figure 27-15).

   To continue with the employee list example, if you want to display only employees whose employee IDs are below a certain number (perhaps to list the company's first 200 employees), and then choose "@id" from the menu.

Note to Power Users: If you're up on your XPath expressions (and who isn't?), you can actually click in the Where column and type your own path to identify tags and properties located deeper in the tag structure.

---

5. **Select a comparison method from the Operator menu.**

   Your options are = (equal to), != (not equal to), < (less than), <= (less than or equal to), > (greater than), and >= (greater than or equal to). If the property or tag you selected in step 4 contains a number, you can use any of these *comparison operators*. So if you want to find employees whose IDs are below 200, then select <.

   For properties and tags that contain text (<department>marketing</department>, for example) stick to either the = or != options. That way, a repeat region shows only employees who are either in the "marketing" department (use the = sign) or not in it (use the != operator).

6. **Type a comparison value in the Value box.**

   The value is what you test against. If you're looking for employee IDs below 200, type *200*; for <department> tags that contain the word "marketing" type *marketing*.

7. **If you want to add more filters, select either "and" or "or" from the "and/or" menu, click the + button to add another filter, and then repeat steps 4–7.**

   This lets you add additional conditions that the information must meet for the page to display it. Say you want to display employees who are both in the marketing department *and* are one of the first 200 employees. In that case, select the "and" option and add another filter. Or suppose you want to display a list of employees who are *either* in the marketing department *or* the finance department: Select "or" and add a filter where the <department> tag is equal to "finance".

   The ability to add multiple filters lets you build complex filters that either let you narrow the number of regions the page repeats (by adding more and more *and* options) or that include more and more data from the XML file (by using additional *or* filters).

8. **After you add one or more filters, click the Close button to create a filtered repeat region.**

   Dreamweaver inserts the repeat region into the XSLT style sheet. You can edit or remove this region as described on page 1017.

Inserting a Conditional Region

At times, you may want to display XML only if certain conditions are met. As discussed in the previous section, the "Filter" feature of the Repeat Region tool offers some help, since it can display select XML data when a tag's property or contents passes a particular test: an *id* property that's less than 200, for example. But there are other occasions when the filter doesn't help. Say you want to display only the last item in a repeat region; it isn't wrapped in a tag or property, so a filter won't work.

Note to Power Users: If you use Dreamweaver templates, this problem may sound familiar. It's the same concept as a template optional region (see page 767).

Or maybe you want to display a graphic or another part of a page only when a certain XML property appears. Suppose an XML document listing products has a tag like this: <product stock="in">. The product tag's "stock" property indicates whether a product is available (in which case its value is "in") or when it's not ("out"). In such cases, you can use a conditional region to display an "out of stock" button next to each unavailable product.

To use a conditional region:

1. **Select a section of the XSL file you want to display if a condition is true.**

   A simple example is an "out of stock" or "on sale" graphic. But you could also select XML data placeholders: Maybe you want to display just the first five items inside a repeat region. In this case, select all the XML placeholders inside the repeat region (you need to add the repeat region first).

Note: Many web designers find it useful to place conditional regions inside repeat regions, since this lets them fine-tune the display of information on a per-item basis. For example, in a repeating list of products, you can display an "on sale" graphic only when those products are actually on sale.

2. **Choose Insert→XSLT Objects→Conditional Region or click the Conditional Region button in the XSLT category of the Insert panel (see Figure 27-9).**

   The Conditional Region window opens (see Figure 27-17).

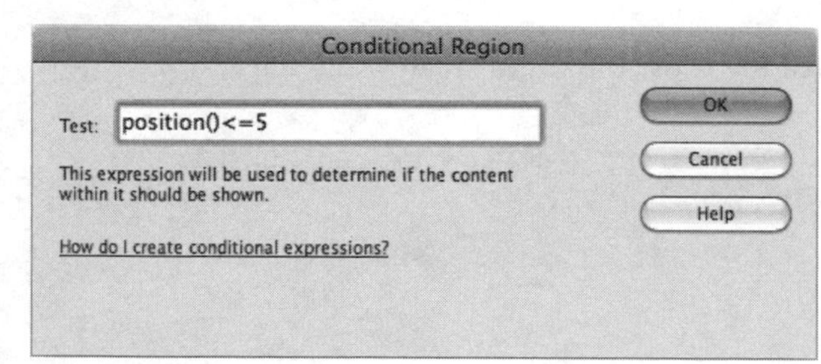

Figure 27-9: *The Conditional Region window lets you show or hide content based on certain conditions in the XML or XSL files.*

3. **Type a test condition in the Test box.**

   "But what am I supposed to type?" you ask. This is the tricky part, since Dreamweaver doesn't really give you much help. Your test condition can actually be a number of different things, many of which can be quite complex. Here are a few examples:

- **An XPath expression followed by some kind of comparison.** For example, say you're working with the XML document on page 1014. You create a repeat region listing all your company's employees, and you want an "employee of the month" graphic to appear in the listing, but only next to the employee whose ID is, say, 38753. To make that happen, the condition you'd type would be *@id=38753*. *@id* refers to the "id" property (you use @ before a property name) of the repeated tag (<employee>, in this example.) Likewise, if you want to highlight all employees named Jane (that is, the text inside the <name> tag is *Jane*), the condition would be *name='Jane'*. (Note that whenever you test whether a tag has text inside it—as opposed to just numbers—you must place single quotes around the word, like this: *'Jane'*.)
- **The position of an item in a repeated region.** When you apply conditions to content in a repeat region, you can access an item's position using *position()*. So if you want to have the selected page elements inside a repeat region appear only when Dreamweaver displays the first item, you could type in *position()=first()*; for the last item, you'd use *position()=last()*. And if you want to limit the repeat region to just 5 items (if you want to show only the first 5 headlines from a newsfeed, say), you could use this expression: *position()<=5*.
- **An XPath expression to determine if a tag or property exists.** You can also just enter an XPath expression for a particular *node* in the XML document. If the node exists, Dreamweaver displays the selected element; otherwise, it hides it. For example, say you have a repeat region that contains some optional tags. Again, using the employee list example, imagine that some employees have their own offices. For those employees, you might add an XML tag called <office> that includes the office number, like so: <office>Room 222</office>. You'd like to include the text "Office:" followed by the actual office number in your final web page. However, if someone doesn't have an office (meaning that her entry in the XML file has no <office> tag), you don't want the word "Office:" to appear. To make that happen with a conditional region, type *Office*: somewhere inside the repeat region (perhaps on a line below the employee phone number); next, drag the <office> tag from the Bindings panel to the page, and then select both the text and the XML placeholder. Finally, add a conditional region as described on page 1019 and simply type *office* as the condition. Now "Office:" and the office number appear only for <employee> tags that have an <office> tag inside them.
- **Tag or property values that begin with one or more particular characters.** Say you want to display only those employees whose names begin with 'M'. You can do this easily with the *starts-with()* function. In the Conditional Region box, you'd type *starts-with(name, 'M')*. Translated from XSLT-speak, this means any <name> tag whose contents start with the letter M will appear on the final web page; so <name>Mark</name> and <name>Mary</name> would match, but <name>Andrea</name> wouldn't.

4. **Click OK to insert the conditional region.**

   Dreamweaver adds a gray border around the page elements you selected in step 1 and adds a gray tab labeled "xsl:if" to indicate the conditional region. (If you don't see these, make sure you have invisible elements turned on by choosing View→Visual Aids→Invisible Elements.)

You can still change the page elements inside the conditional region's gray border: You can edit, add, or remove text, images, and XML placeholders. If you want to edit the conditional test, click the gray "xsl:if" tab to select the region, and then change the test listed in the Property inspector.

To remove a conditional region, right-click (Control-click) the gray "xsl:if" tab, and then select "Remove Tag <xsl:if>". You can also click anywhere inside the conditional region, right-click "xsl:if" in the Tag selector, and then choose "Remove Tag".

Using Multiple Conditional Regions

A conditional region is pretty straightforward: It either shows or hides part of a page based on the results of a simple test. But what if you want to display one thing if the condition is true, but show something else if the condition is false? Say you have two graphics called "In Stock" and "Out of Stock" that need to appear next to each product name in a repeat region. You can use two conditional regions: the first to display the "In Stock" image if the product tag's stock property is set to "in" (<product stock="in">) and another to display "Out of Stock" for out-of-stock products (<product stock="out").

Note: If you've ever done any computer programming, you'll recognize the upcoming maneuver as a variation on the venerable "if-then-else" statement.

But using conditional regions that way requires far too much work on your part. Fortunately, Dreamweaver's Multiple Conditional Region tool makes it easy to deal with these "either/or" situations. Here's how to use it:

1. **Select the part of the page you want to display if a condition is true.**

   This could be a graphical button with the text "In Stock" printed across it. This step is the same as a conditional region described on "Inserting a Conditional Region" previously. In fact, most of the steps are the same.

2. **Choose Insert→XSLT Objects→Multiple Conditional Region or click the Multiple Conditional Region button in the XSLT category of the Insert panel (see Figure 27-9).**

   The Multiple Conditional Region window opens. Except for its title, this window is identical to the Conditional Region window (see Figure 27-17).

3. **Type a test condition in the Test box.**

   For instance, if you use *@stock="in"*, the region displays if the value of the repeating tag's *stock* property is "in." For more examples, see page 1021.

4. **Click OK.**

   Dreamweaver inserts three pieces of XSL code, each marked with their own gray tab: "XSL:choose", "XSL:when", and "XSL:otherwise". The "XSL:when" section contains the actual condition or test you set in step 3 and the content you selected in step 1.

   The "XSL:otherwise" section is the part of the page that displays if the test *isn't* true. Dreamweaver adds "Contents goes here" to that area.

5. **Select and delete "Content goes here" and then add the page elements you want to display if the test from step 3 isn't true.**

   This is the alternative to the content selected in step 1—for example, an "Out of Stock" icon.

You can edit the contents of either the "XSL:when" or "XSL:otherwise" sections. To edit the test, either click the gray "XSL:when" tab or click anywhere inside the "XSL:when" section and use the Tag selector to choose the <xsl:when> tag. The Property inspector displays the test condition; edit it, and then press Enter or Return.

Removing a multiple conditional region is a bit trickier. You can't just right-click (Control-click) the gray "XSL:choose" tab and then select "Remove Tag <xsl: choose>" to remove all of the multiple conditional region code. You must remove each of the three sections separately. To do that, follow the same process you followed to remove a conditional tag, as described on page 1022.

Advanced XSLT Tricks

XSLT is a complex language with lots of bells and whistles—and just as many pitfalls. It's all too easy to head ambitiously into Code view and, with just a few keystrokes, completely break your XSLT style sheet. But since Dreamweaver's XSLT tools take you only so far, you'll undoubtedly find yourself wanting to dip into the code. Here are a couple of examples to help your explorations go a little more smoothly.

Sorting Data in a Repeat Region

The Repeat Region feature normally works by spitting out data it retrieves from an XML document in the order it appears in the XML file. In the case of an RSS feed, that's usually OK, since RSS feed usually sort items in chronological order, with the most recent feed first. But what if you want information sorted another way, or you have an XML file with other kinds of data, like the employee listing on page 1014? In that example, you might want employees listed in alphabetical order. Dreamweaver doesn't have a tool that lets you do this. Fortunately, adding the code yourself is pretty easy:

1. **Click inside a repeat region and then click the "Code" or "Split" button in the document window's toolbar.**

   Alternatively, you can choose View→Code or View→"Code and Design". Doing so drops you into the scary world of XSLT code.

2. **Locate the beginning of the repeat region.**

   You're looking for something like this: *<xsl:for-each select="company-Info/employeeList/employee">*, where the stuff in quotes after "select" is the XPath expression pointing to the repeating tag. You need to add your new code directly after this tag.

3. **Click immediately after the closing bracket (>), hit Enter, and then type** *<xsl:sort select="xml_tag_to_sort_on" data-type="text" order="ascending" />*.

   Replace *xml_tag_to_sort_on* with the XML tag inside the repeat region you want to use as the basis for the sort. For example, pick a tag used for a name or a price.

Note: Don't forget the forward slash at the end of the sort tag: />. The tag you're adding is an *empty tag* (meaning there's no accompanying closing tag). In XML, you have to write these types of tags as "self closed," using the forward slash (see page 548 for details).

You can use either "text" or "number" as the value for *data-type*. Pick the one that matches the type of data in the XML tag you're using as the sort key—"text" if you're sorting names and "number" if you're sorting prices.

Depending on how you want to sort the data—smallest number to largest, or largest to smallest—type either *ascending* or *descending*, respectively, for the *order* property. "Ascending" gets you smallest number to largest, or A–Z; "descending" results in largest number to smallest, or Z–A.

Using XSLT Parameters

The Repeat Region's filter feature is very useful. With it, you can winnow down a mass of XML data to a smaller collection of useful facts. But what if you want the data retrieved from the XML file to *change* based on information from a database or information that a visitor submits? Say you've already created an employee list page, and now you want to create separate pages for each employee (kind of like the master-detail pages described on page 892). You could create an XSLT style sheet for each employee, thereby filtering the XML file based on the employee's ID number. But creating one page for each employee is a lot of work. A better approach is to use an *XSLT parameter*.

XSLT parameters give you a way to pass information from an outside source to the XSLT style sheet, and the parameters can affect how the XSLT style sheet processes and displays the XML file. You've already encountered one way to pass a parameter to an XSLT style sheet—the XSL Transformation server behavior (see Figure 27-3). You can use the server behavior to pass either a value you manually enter, a dynamic value pulled from a database, or any of the other sources of data accessible in dynamic web pages (see page 981). By doing this, you can present a separate page for each employee simply by passing the employee's ID number to the XSLT style sheet (instead of manually creating separate XSLT files for each employee).

For this maneuver to work, you need to string together several concepts involving both dynamic pages and XSLT files that you learned about earlier in this book. Here's an example of how to use XSLT parameters to dynamically filter XML data:

1. **Create an XSLT fragment as described on page 1007.**

   You'll eventually include this fragment on a dynamic page (PHP, ASP, or ColdFusion) to display the final, filtered data.

2. **Follow steps 1–5 on page 1015 to insert a repeat region and create a filter.**

   With this technique, all the steps in creating a filter are the same as those on page 1017, except for entering the value in the Value box, as explained in the next step.

3. **In the filter's Value box type *$your_param* (see Figure 27-19).**

   Change *your_param* to a name you'd like to use for the parameter. For example, if you want to filter for an ID that matches a particular value, then you'd type *$id*. You must include the $ sign, but you can come up with whatever name you like. It helps if it's descriptive, like *$id, $name*, or *$price*. It also has to follow a few rules: use only numbers and letters, always start the name with a letter (not a number), don't use spaces, and stay away from punctuation marks, except for hyphens and underscores.

   Unlike a static value that you type into the Value box, like *38, Dave*, or *marketing*, a parameter can be different each time the XSLT style sheet does its magic. But to get it to work, you need to dip (just a bit) into Code view.

4. **Click the Code or Split button to view the XSLT code. Locate the line *<xsl:template match="/">*, and then click just before the opening bracket (<).**

   In XSLT, you first need to tell the style sheet that you'll be using a parameter.

5. **Type *<xsl:param name="your_param"/>*.**

   Replace "*your_param*" with the text you typed in step 3. Note that you leave off the $ sign. Also, make sure you include the forward slash before the final bracket, like this: />.

   You're done with the XSLT style sheet. It's all primed to have dynamic data sent to it. The next steps involve adding the XSLT fragment to a dynamic page.

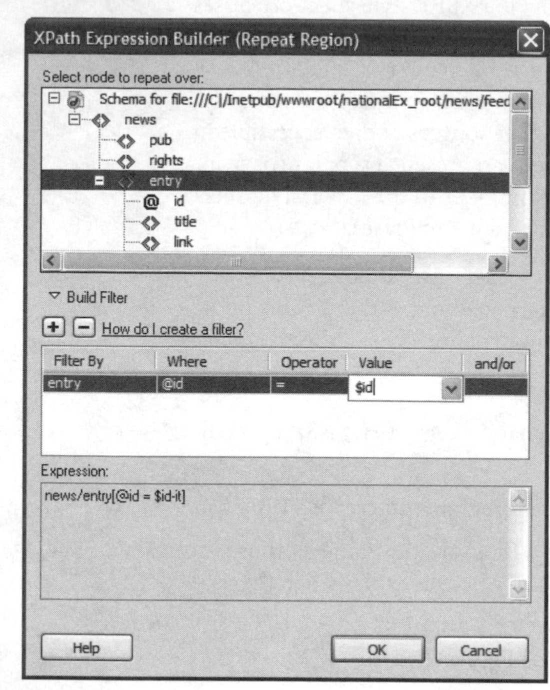

Figure 27-10:
You can use an XSLT parameter as a filter value. The parameter always begins with the $ sign and lets you dynamically filter the contents of an XML file.

6. **Repeat steps 8–10 on page 1010.**

   This step is the same process as adding any XSLT fragment to a dynamic page—that is, using the XSL Transformation server behavior.

   In the next step, you add the XSLT parameter.

7. **In the XSL Transformation window, click the + button next to the label XSLT Parameters (see Figure 27-3).**

   The Add Parameter window opens (Figure 27-21).

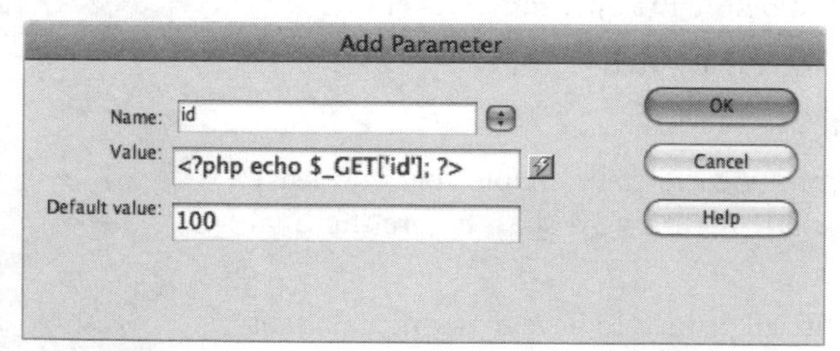

Figure 27-11:
While inserting the XSLT server behavior, you can add one or more parameters that let you pass information to the XSLT fragment. That way, you can control which data from the XML file Dreamweaver displays on the web page.

8. **In the Name box, type the name you used in steps 3 and 5 above (don't include the $ sign).**

   The value you enter here defines the name of the parameter that the dynamic page will pass off to the XSLT style sheet. Next (and this is the magic part), you'll add the value.

9. **Click the lightning-bolt icon to the right of the Value box to open the Dynamic Data window.**

   This is the same Dynamic Data window you encountered with dynamic pages (see Figure 25-7). Don't get it confused with the XSLT Dynamic Text box (Figure 27-11). Here, "dynamic" refers to any of the many sources of dynamic information you used to create database-driven pages—recordsets, URL variables, form variables, cookies, session variables, and so on. (For a recap on creating recordsets, see page 858; the other types of dynamic data can be added to the Dynamic Data window as described on page 981.)

10. **Select a source from the Field list and then click OK.**

    What you select here is the crucial part of the puzzle. You're telling the dynamic page where to get the information that will be passed off to the XSLT style sheet. To use the employee list example again, you would need to identify where the ID number used to select just a single employee comes from. Here are a few examples:

    - **Recordsets.** You could use the value from a field in a recordset. For this to work, you first need to add a recordset (page 858) to the dynamic page.
    - **Form fields.** One way to pass a value to a page is via a form. For example, you could add a form to a separate web page. The form submits data to this dynamic page (the one with the XSL Transformation) and includes a form pull-down menu that lists every employee's name (and includes the employee ID in the menu's value column—see page 470 for more on form menus). When a visitor selects a name from the list, the employee ID is submitted to the dynamic page, which turns it into an XLST parameter and hands it off to the XSLT style sheet for use in the repeat region filter. (Turn to page 984 to see how to add a form field name to the dynamic data window.)
    - **URL variables.** You can apply the same idea to URL variables, but instead of getting the employee ID from a menu, you attach it to a link to the dynamic page. For example, you might use a URL variable that looks something like this: *employee.php?id=15*. (Turn to page 983 to see how to add a URL variable to the Dynamic Data window.)

    These are just a few examples. As noted earlier, you can use dynamic data from any dynamic source: cookies, session variables, and so on.

11. **Type a value in the "Default value" box.**

    This is the value the dynamic page will use if the source you picked in step 10 doesn't come through—for example, if the dynamic page is accessed without adding a URL variable (in which case you'd be passing just *employee.php*, instead of *employee.php?id=15*). Entering a default value will ensure that the XSLT style sheet has some value to work with. If, as in this example, you're using this technique to dynamically control XML filtering, the default value should match at least one record in the XML file.

12. **Click OK to close the Add Parameter box, and then click OK once again to close the XSL Transformation window.**

    Dreamweaver adds the new server behavior and the new parameter to your page.

Note: If you want to remove or change the XSLT parameter, just reopen the XSL Transformation window by double-clicking its name in the Server Behaviors panel.

---

13. **Provide a way to pass the dynamic data to the page.**

    For example, if you selected a URL variable as the data source for step 10, you would add links to other pages on your site that would point to the page with the XSL Transformation—*products.php?sku=10294* or *employee.php?id=15*, for example.

Hopefully, by this point, your brain hasn't completely melted. As you can see, XML, XSLT, and all of the other X's can be pretty X-hausting.

APPENDIX

A

Getting Help

Hard as it may be to believe, even a book as voluminous and detailed as this one may not answer all your questions about Dreamweaver. Fortunately, a wide range of other resources awaits you when a particular feature doesn't work.

Getting Help from Dreamweaver

There's plenty of assistance built right into the program, from beginner tutorials to the Adobe Help system. You can also access Dreamweaver's electronic help system and online support center from the Help menu. You'll find details below.

Detailed Assistance

In Dreamweaver CS5, Adobe has changed their help system (again!). You can now tap into an Adobe Help program that contains Using Dreamweaver CS5 documentation. But it also lets you access online help from Adobe.com (*www.adobe.com*), as well as from select resources on the Web. The Help program is basically just a modified web browser that searches online documentation. Choose Help→Dreamweaver Help (or press the F1 key) to launch the Help program and view the *Using Dreamweaver CS5* documents. It includes a list of categories such as "Creating Pages with CSS" and "Previewing pages" where you can get more detailed information on various aspects of the program.

Note: If you prefer your documentation printed, you can download a PDF of the entire Dreamweaver manual. Choose Help→Dreamweaver Help (or press the F1 key) to access the online help documents. There, you'll find a link labeled View Help PDF that downloads a hefty Adobe Acrobat file containing Dreamweaver CS5 documentation.

Adobe has a more interactive version of their online help system called Community Help. It's kind of like a Google for Dreamweaver. When you search for a Dreamweaver-related topic—templates, for example—you get a list of pages that have something to do with Dreamweaver templates. However, rather than search the entire Web, including Joe's "I just learned Dreamweaver two seconds ago and now I'm an expert" blog, Community Help searches only selected websites. Adobe has determined which sites actually have good and accurate information on Dreamweaver—this includes not only Adobe's website, but other useful sites, such as *CreativePro (www.creativepro.com)* and CommunityMX (*www.communitymx.com*).

You can even search the help system (including Community Help) from within Dreamweaver. The Application toolbar includes a simple search box (see Figure A-1). Type a term in the box and click the magnifying glass icon to launch a browser and retrieve a list of results that match your search term. Of course, as with all things free on the Internet, you may or may not find an exact answer to your question.

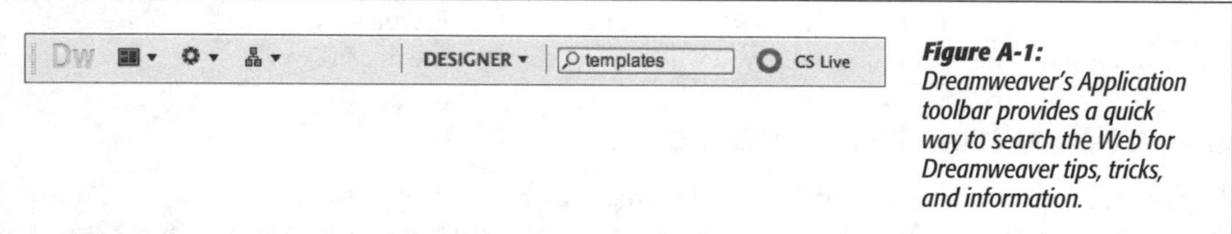

Figure A-1: *Dreamweaver's Application toolbar provides a quick way to search the Web for Dreamweaver tips, tricks, and information.*

The Help menu provides other useful jumping-off points for exploring topics like the Spry Framework, ColdFusion, and a few other commercial Adobe services ("Hi, Dreamweaver engineers. This is marketing, do you mind if we add a couple of links to your Help menu?"). If you're interested in refreshing your knowledge of HTML, Dreamweaver's Reference window (select Help→Reference, or press Shift-F1) provides in-depth information on HTML. However, skip the CSS, JavaScript, JSP, and other guides in the Reference material—it's outdated.

Getting Help from Adobe

You can also get more up-to-date and personalized support from Adobe, ranging from technical notes available on Adobe's site to pay-as-you-ask support plans.

AdobeeWebsite

www.adobe.com/support/dreamweaver/

The Dreamweaver support page (also available from Help→Dreamweaver Support Center, which launches the Adobe Help program as well) is command central for finding help from Adobe. Here you can search the vast database of technical notes (short articles on specific problems) that just may hold the answer you seek, and you can find basic tutorials on getting started with Dreamweaver, see a list of top issues (and their answers), as well as a list of the most recent technical notes.

You can click the Customer Service link (in the right-hand navigation bar) to go to a page listing common setup problems and their solutions, or click the Contact Customer Support link in the right-hand navigation bar to go to a page with various options for help: You can use Live Chat if you're having problems activating your copy of Dreamweaver, or to call for help with installation, or for Technical Support.

Paid Support

www.adobe.com/support/programs/creativesuite

If you have deep pockets, you can also tap into three levels of personalized, fee-based support, ranging from $29 for a single incident to the whole-hog luxury of the Gold Support program (for pricing on this option, Adobe tells you to "contact your Adobe reseller"—watch out!). For more information on these programs, go to the Web address above. Each program has its own phone number, so determine the type of support (from Bronze to Gold) you need. If you have just a single nagging question, the single-incident help program gets you an Adobe technician who will work with you to resolve the issue. But at $29, make sure you've first tried to answer the question yourself by using one of the free resources listed in this appendix. Customers in the U.S. and Canada should call 1-866-MYADOBE for this service.

The Forums

Adobe provides online forums you check out with a browser. To get to either of these, choose Help→Adobe Online Forums. The forums are a terrific source of information, offering almost real-time answers on Dreamweaver and related web-design techniques. Adobe sponsors several forums and newsgroups. Of most interest to average Dreamweaver users are the FAQ forum (answers to the most frequently asked questions), the General Discussion forum (answers to basic questions), and the Application Development forum, where people discuss Dreamweaver's dynamic web page features. If you're struggling with Dreamweaver's Spry tools, the Spry forum is a good place to seek help. Odds are one of the many knowledgeable experts who always seem to be hanging around will come back with an answer, sometimes within minutes.

You can access Dreamweaver's forums from this page: *http://forums.adobe.com/community/dreamweaver*.

Index

Symbols

A

F

G

H

J

K

L

M

N

O

P

Q

R

S

T

X

Z

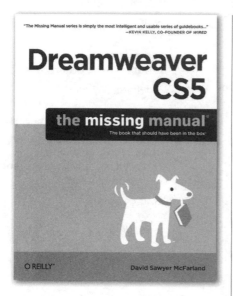